CIVILIZATION PAST AND PRESENT

A survey of the history of man—his political, economic, social; religious, intellectual, and artistic activities—from the earliest times to the present, in Europe, in Asia, in Africa, and in the Americas.

VOLUME TWO   1650-1966

1 Pablo Picasso: "Les Demoiselles d'Avignon" (1907). One of the hallmarks of the modern age has been sudden, violent, and often revolutionary change. The upheavals which have occurred in the political, economic, and social spheres during the last few centuries have been reflected in the arts by a ceaseless turnover of styles. The postimpressionist rebels of the late 19th century—Cezanne, Van Gogh, Gauguin—veered away from the nature-based realism which had dominated painting since the Renaissance. The traditional manner was even more completely shattered by the cubists during the first decade of the 20th century. In this canvas, one of the important works of modern painting, Pablo Picasso has treated the nude figure far more as a study in abstracted form and less as a vehicle of literary sentiment. Volume and space now become virtually one continuum, with concave and convex forms moving through the picture. The two heads on the right, which closely resemble African tribal sculpture, bear witness that modern art has gained as much inspiration from exotic sources outside the mainstream of classical European culture as from time-honored sources within it.

civilization

PAST AND PRESENT · VOLUME TWO · FIFTH EDITION

T. WALTER WALLBANK
Professor of History, University of Southern California

ALASTAIR M. TAYLOR
Professor of Political Studies and Geography, Queen's University

GEORGE BARR CARSON, JR.
Chairman, Department of History, Oregon State University

Critical Readers

Professor W. C. Gabel, Boston University
Professor James E. Gillespie, Emeritus, Pennsylvania State University
Professor L. Carrington Goodrich, Emeritus, Columbia University
Professor Harold J. Grimm, Ohio State University
Professor Alfred Guillaume, University of London
Professor H. W. Janson, New York University

Professor Arden S. King, Tulane University
Professor Hans Kohn, Emeritus, The City College of New York
Professor T. F. Mayer-Oakes, Wayne State University
Professor Franklin C. Palm, Emeritus, University of California
Professor Stuart Piggott, University of Edinburgh
Sir Maurice Powicke, Emeritus, Oxford University
Professor C. A. Robinson, Jr., Brown University
Professor Franz Schulze, Lake Forest College

SCOTT, FORESMAN AND COMPANY

Library of Congress Card Number 65-11902
Copyright © 1960, 1965 by Scott, Foresman and Company, Glenview, Illinois 60025
All Rights Reserved. Printed in the United States of America.
Regional offices of Scott, Foresman and Company are located in
Atlanta, Dallas, Glenview, Palo Alto, and Oakland, N.J.

PREFACE

When it was originally published in 1942, *Civilization Past and Present* was the first text to recognize and meet the need for a basic college history survey that would deal not just with political history but with all facets—economic, artistic, intellectual, and political—of world culture, and that would treat the history of man not as a European experience nor as a western experience, but as a global experience through which all the great culture systems have interacted to produce the present-day world.

From the Preface to Volume 1, fourth edition.

Almost a quarter of a century's continuous classroom use has validated the basic concepts utilized by the authors in planning the first edition of *Civilization Past and Present*. The original objectives of *Civilization Past and Present* have guided this revision of the text and underscore the authors' belief that a history text purporting to relate the significant events of the past three hundred years must include a balanced coverage of all the areas of the world. Of the many components of world history, one that is constant is the interaction among the members of mankind. In the present-day world, due to the tremendous speed of communication and transportation, interaction occurs much more rapidly than ever before. At one time a young American's world was confined to a relatively small area. Not so today. Now his world reaches out and includes Nasser's Pan-Arabism, South Vietnam, Kashmir, the political demise of N. S. Khrushchev, the roles of the U.S.S.R. and Communist China in Cuba, Sukarno's "confrontation" of Malaysia, and the whole gamut of problems relating to underdeveloped countries. These and many other challenges are part and parcel of the enlarged "American scene." For American citizens to ignore or even to minimize the importance of these challenges is to complicate, perhaps endanger, America's role as a great world power. And these challenges that now so affect the Western world can be understood only in terms of their historical roots and traditions.

The study of the background of these challenges requires a large body of material, and limited time is a vexing and perennial problem for the instructor who strives to cover the history of civilization in two semesters. Yet in order to permit the greatest latitude for the personal interest and emphasis of the instructor, all areas and eras should be included in a text of world history. The organization of this volume allows for individual selectivity. The nonwestern chapters are arranged so that they can be taught in whole or in part, assigned as outside reading, or excluded without detracting from the western narrative. Some of the other chapters also can be assigned for outside reading, thereby allowing for more intensive presentation of others in the classroom.

While the basic organization of the fourth edition has been largely retained in Volume II, there have been numerous shifts and revisions. Part 1, which includes the seventeenth- and eighteenth-century material, has been revised and reorganized. Chapter 1 has been largely rewritten, employing as a central theme the concept of the European search for order. This idea is also used as a unifying concept in all the chapters in Part 1. Chapter 4 has been extensively revised and is limited chiefly to a broad discussion of the French Revolution and the Congress of Vienna. There have been revision and reorganization of nineteenth-century history, both political and cultural. The section on the results of the French Revolution has been modified to highlight the twin legacies of the Revolution and of Napoleon. There is special emphasis on the unification of Germany and Italy and on the Near Eastern question—with a case study of Balkan nationalism, Bulgaria. In new Chapter 6, the separate strands of the Industrial Revolution have been drawn together; some of the material has been rewritten and reorganized; some topics have been expanded—for example, the interpretations of the Industrial Revolution and the ways in which various industrial factors influenced each other. In Chapter 18, world events have been brought up to date. A new feature in this post-1945 treatment is the expansion of the topic dealing with the emergence of the non-aligned Afro-Asian nations. The authors, when considering the complexity and vast quantity of material on the cultural and scientific facets of the contemporary world, decided to close the book with an epilogue that focuses attention on some of the basic issues and problems that confront mankind in the 1960's.

New, full-color art illustrations are included in this edition, and, in the six-color reference map section, the contemporary maps have been brought up to date and a new, present-day map of Africa has been added.

T. Walter Wallbank, Professor of History
University of Southern California

Alastair M. Taylor, Professor of Political Studies and Geography
Queen's University, Canada

George Barr Carson, Jr., Chairman, Department of History
Oregon State University

Contents

VOLUME TWO

PART 1 CHARTING THE PRESENT 1

1 THE NEW ORDER   Science, Thought, and Absolute Monarchy: 1650-1715. 7
Science Fulfills its Promise 8
The Crisis in the European Conscience 15
Order in the State: Louis XIV, the Epitome of Absolutism 19

2 THE COMPETITIVE STATE SYSTEM   Absolutism and the Politics of Power: 1650-1775 27
Evolution of Constitutional Monarchy in England 28
The Rise of Russia 38
The Emergence of Prussia 42
Dynastic War and the Duel for World Empire 46

3 NEW FORCES AND THE OLD REGIME   Economic and Intellectual Assaults
on Absolutism: 1690-1778. 57
The Impact on Europe of Overseas Expansion 58
Developments in Agriculture 64
Capitalism, Business, and Laissez Faire 66
The Enlightenment 73
The Rule of Order in the Arts 82
Absolutism in Maturity and Decay 85

4 THE RIGHTS OF MAN   The French Revolution and the Western World: 1778-1815. 89
France's Moderate Revolution 90
The Jacobin Republic 97
The Napoleonic Period 102
Reaction at Vienna 110
Suggestions for Reading 118
Chronological Table 120
FRONTIER   "The New Image of Sir Isaac Newton" by Henry Guerlac. 122

PART 2 FROM METTERNICH TO BISMARCK 125

5 ROMANTICS AND REBELS   Literature and the Fine Arts, Thought and Social Evolution: 1815-1850............127
        The Revolt Against Reason.................128
        The Idea of Progress.....................130
        The Triumph of Romanticism...............132
        Romantic Nationalism and Liberalism......141
        The Dignity of Man.......................145

6 INDUSTRIAL REVOLUTION   People and Machines, Laissez-faire
                           Capitalism, and Socialism: 1750-1850...........149
        The Onset of Industrialism...............150
        The Rise of the Age of Iron and Steel....159
        The Consequences of Industrialism........164
        The Middle Class Triumphant..............168
        Stirrings of Reform......................172
        The Challenge of Socialism...............177

7 TO THE BARRICADES!   Reaction and Revolution: 1815-1850.........185
        The Congress System......................186
        France, England, and the Revolutions of 1830....195
        Revolution Renewed in Western Europe.....203
        Central Europe: the Rise of the Nationalistic Spirit....210
        Revolutions that Misfired................212
        The Revolutionary Era in Retrospect......217

8 NATIONALISM AND THE MAKING OF NATIONS   The Politics of
                                           Power: 1850-1870..........221
        Nation-making in Italy...................222
        The Triumph of Blood and Iron in Germany....226
        Downfall of the Second French Empire.....229
        Formation of the Dual Monarchy...........232
        Storm over the Balkans...................234
        Suggestions for Reading..................244
        Chronological Table......................246
        FRONTIER   "The Meaning and Development of Nationalism" by Hans Kohn.................248

PART 3 THE WEST DOMINANT....................251

9 NEW EUROPES OVERSEAS   The British Dominions and Latin America: 1650-1914.................253
        The Making of New Nations: British Dominions................254

   The Making of New Nations: Latin America.................................262
   Common Denominators.................................274

10 THE WHITE MAN'S BURDEN European Imperialism: 1650-1914.................279
   The Dynamics of Imperialism.................................280
   British Rule in India.................................285
   Manchu China and the West.................................288
   Japan in Transition.................................293
   Imperialism in Southeast Asia and Oceania.................................297
   Britain and Russia in Asia.................................302
   The Great African Colony Hunt.................................304
   Imperialism: The Balance Sheet.................................311
   Suggestions for Reading.................................314
   Chronological Table.................................316
   FRONTIER "The Rediscovery of Africa" by T. Walter Wallbank.................................318

PART 4 REALISM AND REALPOLITIK.................................321

11 "SURVIVAL OF THE FITTEST" Science and Thought, Literature and the Fine Arts: 1850-1914.......323
   Darwin, Einstein, and Freud.................................324
   The Cult of Science.................................335
   Changing Social and Esthetic Standards.................................340
   From Realism to Expressionism.................................345
   The "Gilded Age".................................354

12 PARLIAMENTS AND POLITICAL REFORMS Constitutional Government and Social Justice:
        1871-1914.................................359
   Toward Democratization of British Life.................................360
   France: Painful Path to Democracy.................................369
   Germany: An Absolutism under Constitutional Forms.................................372
   Russia under Unenlightened Despotism.................................378
   Austria-Hungary and the Ottoman Empire.................................387
   Democratic Struggles in Other European Lands.................................391

13 PROMISE AND PERIL The Second Industrial Revolution and Power Politics in Europe: 1871-1914.........395
   The Second Industrial Revolution.................................396
   Forces of Compromise and Revolution.................................403
   Forces for Peace and Brotherhood.................................407
   Forces of War and Hate.................................410
   "The Lamps Are Going Out".................................414
   Suggestions for Reading.................................424
   Chronological Table.................................426
   FRONTIER "Marxist Socialism and the Web of Utopia: Science and Myth in the
      Making of an Ideology" by A. William Salomone.................................428

PART 5 THE WORLD ADRIFT...431

14 A WORLD FIT FOR HEROES   World War I and the Aftermath: 1914-1929.....................433
     No Man's Land..434
     The United States and Victory..440
     The Peace Settlement...444
     Bitter Fruits of Victory...451
     Burying the Hatchet..454

15 OPPOSING WAYS OF LIFE   The Political Scene: 1918-1930.............................461
     Dictatorship of the Proletariat in Russia..462
     Rise of Fascism in Italy...470
     Weimar Democracy: The Republic That Failed.......................................473
     Democracy in the Wasteland...475

16 AFRICA AND ASIA ASTIR   Africa, the Middle East, and India (1914-1939);
                           China and Japan (1914-1930)...............................487
     New Forces in Africa...488
     Tensions in the Arab World...492
     India Seeks to Rule Itself...500
     Nationalism in Southeast Asia and Oceania..503
     China Tries to Change..506
     Japan Becomes a World Power..509

17 THE TRAGIC DECADE AND GLOBAL CONFLICT   Depression and World
                                           War II: 1930-1945.........................513
     Depression Threatens Democracy and Breeds Totalitarianism........................515
     Aggression and Appeasement...526
     The World Divided..534
     Suggestions for Reading..550
     Chronological Table..552
     FRONTIER   "The Grapes of Wrath—An Analysis" by Russel B. Nye....................554

PART 6 THE CHANGING WORLD...557

18 THE COLD WAR AND COMPETITIVE COEXISTENCE   The World Scene
                                              Since 1945.............................563
     The Cold War...564
     The Free World...571
     The Communist World..575

The Non-Aligned Afro-Asian World..578

The World Today and Tomorrow..590

EPILOGUE Some Basic Issues and Challenges of the Contemporary World............597

Man and Nature..598

Man and His Fellow Man..602

Man Himself..606

Suggestions for Reading..608

Chronological Table..610

List of Readings 612

Footnotes..617

List of Illustrations..626

List of Maps..631

Index..632

Reference Maps..647

PART 1

Charting the Present

CHAPTER 1 THE NEW ORDER

CHAPTER 2 THE COMPETITIVE STATE SYSTEM

CHAPTER 3 NEW FORCES AND THE OLD REGIME

CHAPTER 4 THE RIGHTS OF MAN

The story of Europe and the New World in the period from 1650 to 1815 forms one of the most complex chapters in world history. Following the challenge to the ideas and institutions of the Middle Ages posed by the Renaissance, the Reformation, and the great religious wars, the search for principles of order became a consistent theme in the writings of scientists as well as in literature and the fine arts. This search for order also played an important role in the ambitious domestic and foreign ventures of autocratic rulers.

A succession of fresh concepts about the universe (in the seventeenth century), about society (in the eighteenth century) and about man (in the nineteenth century) called into question and in some cases overthrew long-established beliefs and institutions. The first major advance was the development in the seventeenth century of the scientific method, which relied upon deductive reasoning. Other new ideas, many stemming from the spread of the scientific method, began to develop in the areas we call the social and natural sciences.

In politics the late seventeenth century witnessed the high-water mark of absolutism under Louis XIV of France. But new liberal concepts rose rapidly to challenge royal prerogatives everywhere. The eighteenth century was the period of revolutions that established the precedents and voiced the ideology that were to become the inspiration for the whole liberal-democratic movement of modern times.

These political advances were accompanied, and indeed only made possible, by comparably important progress in thought. Outmoded ideas in economics and politics were attacked. So pervasive were the transformations in thought that they constituted an intellectual revolution known as the Enlightenment. Under the spell of the remarkable achievements of science—capped by the work of Newton—thinkers, writers, artists, and members of polite society sought to express a truly scientific, or at least rational, point of view. For many intellectuals, religion lost its emotional fervor and became a philosophical creed. Literature, in this Age of Reason, was guided by the mind rather than by the heart. Most painting and architecture was restrained and balanced in both form and spirit. In Paris, where the cult of reason reached its height, the salon was the temple of cultivated society. Here Europe's cosmopolitan intellectuals gathered to exchange views on all aspects of life; the result was witty, well-informed, and often brilliant conversation. The liberal tenets of the Enlightenment touched even the autocrats of the Continent; in Prussia, Austria, and Russia, benevolent despots made at least superficial attempts at reform.

While European politics, thought, and art pulsated with energy, commercial and economic life was equally dynamic. Overseas expansion stimulated trade, increased wealth, and introduced to home markets an abundance of products previously scarce or unknown. With the boom in trade came a demand for more rapid processing of raw materials and for greater quantities of manufactured goods. New inventions paved the way for the mechanization of the textile industry and the use of the steam engine in manufacturing. Industrial capitalism replaced commercial capitalism, and the doctrine of laissez faire began to supplant the theory of government-sponsored mercantilism. Most important, the middle class—chief beneficiary of the new wealth —grew in numbers, ambition, and influence. Many of the political movements of the eighteenth century were triggered by bourgeois aspirations.

The present owes much to the period from 1650 to 1815. That period provided us with the heart of our liberal political beliefs; it contributed the revolutionary idea of free business enterprise; it launched mechanized industry; and it encouraged religious tolerance and freedom of inquiry. Above all, it made man the focus of attention—his happiness, his freedom, his potentialities. All these developments made this period and its Age of Reason a time of hope for the future of mankind.

There was, however, a disquieting feature. The liberalism and rationalism we have discussed operated *within* but not *between* states. Humanitarianism did not touch international affairs. These were dominated by the competitive state system, in which each nation was a law unto itself and any weak neighbor was a potential victim. In this state of international anarchy, the nations of Europe evolved the balance of power to check the grandiose ambitions of national rulers whose only law was force, and to achieve some order in the relations between rival states. Thus, a coalition of rival powers thwarted the plans of Louis xiv, of the French revolutionary leaders, and finally of the brilliant and unscrupulous Napoleon, who sought to control all of Europe under the pretext of spreading the ideals of equality and liberty to suppressed peoples. The discrepancy between benevolence and liberalism, on the one hand, and force and autocracy, on the other, was to become increasingly a paradox of modern civilization.

2 (left) **Joseph Wright of Derby: "The Orrery"** (c. 1768). Science and the tools of science made a strong impact on European man during the Renaissance, and the 18th century witnessed an ever widening development of them. Joseph Wright of Derby, an English artist active during the early phase of the English Industrial Revolution, here depicts both the orrery (a complicated mechanical model of the solar system) and the fascination with which adults and children alike studied it. Wright appears to have painted the machine with the same meticulous concern for accuracy that must have gone into its construction. **3** (below) **Two Freemasons Contemplating a Globe** (1744). Similarly engrossed in a mechanical model of a sphere—this one of the earth—are the two diminutive figures in this German Meissen porcelain. They represent Freemasons, and the globe they observe so intently symbolizes the underlying world community of all faiths. The Freemason movement, vigorous in 18th-century Europe, was symptomatic of the increased religious tolerance and freedom of thought of the period. Porcelain was first employed in Europe during the 18th century; until then the secret of its manufacture was known only in the Far East.

4 Philippe de Champaigne: "Triple Portrait of Richelieu" (1635-1640). The rise of France to power in Europe was accompanied by the rise of French painting to a position of world leadership. The rulers of Bourbon France regarded art as a means of glorifying the monarchy, and they patronized artists liberally. French art of the 16th century still retained many medieval traits, but during the following century some of the noteworthy artistic qualities uniquely associated with French painting took form: clarity of drawing, sureness and subtlety of color, and measured emotional tone. Champaigne's triple portrait is a documentation of these characteristics. Handled with keen precision and coloristic finesse, the painting conveys the cool intellect, the poised manner, and the iron will of its subject, Richelieu, the brilliant and unscrupulous adviser to Louis XIII. It is, moreover, a typical example of both the naturalistic realism of French 17th-century painting and the gravity of Champaigne's own personal style.

5 (above) **Antoine Watteau: "The Music Party"** (early 18th century). Dulcet scenes of elegant society in parks and tranquil landscapes—the *fetes galantes*—are characteristic of the work of Watteau, the foremost master of French rococo painting. The fetes, a delicate blending of fantasy with acute observation of nature, bespeak the grace, the ease, the luxuriousness, and the gentle artificiality of 18th-century French court life. Watteau's painting is based largely on the style of the great Flemish painter, Peter Paul Rubens. The richness and sensuality of Watteau's work signal the end of the stringent dictatorial powers which the French Academy had previously wielded over French art. **6 Antoine Gros: "Napoleon at Arcola"** (1796). Napoleon Bonaparte was celebrated more eloquently by Gros than by any other painter save perhaps for J. L. David. In fact, the unmistakable romantic character of Gros' work provided the Bonaparte myth with a special magic which the more renowned David, because of the brittle coldness of his style, could not capture.

7 Palace of Versailles, Hall of Mirrors (c. 1680). The Age of Absolutism is exemplified best by the reign of Louis XIV and is symbolized most impressively by the magnificent palace and gardens at Versailles, where the "Sun King" kept his court. This immense enterprise was designed to give appropriate physical form to the majesty which Louis pictured in himself. His effort to project greatness was typical of the baroque period. Literally hundreds of architects, landscape designers, and decorators were hired to plan the buildings and the grounds. No part of Versailles is more powerful in its impact than the Hall of Mirrors, pictured here, which occupies nearly the whole center block of the palace.

CHAPTER 1

The New Order

SCIENCE, THOUGHT AND ABSOLUTE MONARCHY:

1650-1715

Introduction. The first phase of the transition from medieval to modern times in the western world ended about 1650. By this time the Renaissance with its emphasis on humanism and individualism had permanently established secularism in western life. The Protestant Reformation had permanently disrupted the universal medieval Church; it established individualism in the religious sphere by challenging the necessity for any intermediary between man and God in the achievement of salvation.

In 1648 the last of the great civil and international religious wars dragged to a close in the Peace of Westphalia. More than a century of strife had not achieved religious toleration as we know it; everywhere people seeking such toleration were compelled to accept some compromises to restore order. With the notable exception of

France, where Protestants enjoyed a limited right of public worship in restricted parts of a Catholic state (a right that was rescinded in 1685), official toleration of religious differences *within* states still did not prevail. But after the Peace of Westphalia, in practice the states of the Christian world tolerated the existence of religious differences *between* states. Tacitly, the members of the European state system had recognized that states could not impose ideas about the worship of God upon other states by force. At the height of the religious wars, Catholics and Protestants had each been certain that God would aid them in destroying the other, since neither believed the world could endure with both. The idea of religious coexistence was painfully but, by 1650, finally accepted at the international level.

Another phase of the transition from medieval

to modern times came in the period following 1650. The challenge to the Church's claim to control over achievement of the next life also weakened the Church's claim to authority concerning knowledge of the material universe. Instead of appealing to theology in order to justify the irrationalities of the existing conceptions of the universe, Copernicus, Brahe, Kepler, Galileo, Bacon, and Descartes sought to explain a rational universe by observation and mathematical deduction. By so doing, they were developing new principles of order to replace the old cosmology. The scientifically-oriented intellectuals of the time did not think God was irrational, but it required at least the genius of a Milton to attempt to justify the ways of God to man. The ways of God were hard to understand, and differences of interpretation often led to bloodshed. By contrast the ways of mathematics were clear, regardless of creed.

So important were the changes in the period following 1650 that the intellectual movement they comprised is identified as the Enlightenment and the time span in which they occurred is known as the Age of Reason. In the broadest sense, the Age of Reason extended from 1650 to 1815. The prime instrument of thinkers in the Age of Reason was the scientific method as elaborated by Descartes. This method used mathematics and deductive reasoning in the new language of science. No longer was reason to serve faith, mind to obey authority, and man to spend his life in preparation for the next world. The great age of science initiated by the publication in 1543 of Copernicus' heliocentric theory reached its climax in 1687 with Newton's explanation of the law of gravitation. The further achievement of the Enlightenment was not in discovering additional scientific laws but rather in translating the advances of science into a new philosophy and world view. In the rational universe constructed by the thinkers of the scientific revolution, God was no longer a *necessary* explanation of observed phenomena. Reason became the first law of the natural world. With the law of reason the universe and the place of the earth in it could be explained. With the law of reason Locke could explain the nature of society and man's place in it. Indeed, the Deists tried to explain the nature of God by means of the same law.

While the giants of the scientific revolution were working out the intellectual principles of the Age of Reason, the royal architects of the national state system reached the height of their power. During the age of absolute monarchy the king was in theory and in fact an autocrat responsible to God alone. The outstanding example of the absolute monarch was Louis XIV of France, known as the Grand Monarch, who believed as he once exclaimed to his fawning courtiers, "L'Etat, c'est moi" ("I am the State"). Absolute monarchs provided the strong governments needed to achieve civil order in the major states of the western world after a long period of internal strife.

SCIENCE FULFILLS ITS

PROMISE

Factors in the advance of science. By the midpoint of the seventeenth century, it was becoming apparent that respect for science and scientific attitudes was to be the keynote of the European culture of the next era. In the last half of the seventeenth century, science was stimulated by the popularization of a more effective scientific method as well as by the support of new scientific societies, the improvement of mathematics, and the development of better scientific instruments.

The universality of the European world in the Middle Ages, represented by the concept of the Empire and that of the universal Christian church, had yielded to the national feeling inspired in part by the rise of national monarchies and by the Protestant Reformation. But the idea of universality persisted in the realm of science, where ideas were the heritage of all men and where national boundaries were unknown.

Much of the rapid progress of modern science has been due to scientists' command of instruments of precision and to the fact that they make public the steps they take to reach their conclusions. The work of the Renaissance humanists and the discovery of printing put the scientific speculations of the ancients more fully at the disposal of investigators; and the academies for the advancement of knowledge formed by the learned men of the seventeenth century played an important role in continuing the dissemination of scientific experiment and theory. The first, the Academy of Experiments, was founded in 1657 at Florence, the birthplace of Galileo. In 1662 the Royal Society for Improving Natural Knowledge, the oldest and most illustrious of British scientific organizations, received its charter from Charles II. Four years later the French Academy of Science was established in Paris. These societies concentrated upon the promotion of experimentation and the collection of scientific data.

Just as the academies for the advancement of knowledge were important, so the universities were fundamental in the pooling of experiments and of new scientific knowledge. For example, the Englishman Harvey was studying medicine in Padua when the Florentine Galileo was conducting his informal academy there. Because of the ready availability of information about Galileo's physics and Vesalius' anatomy, Harvey was able to work out his theory of the circulation of the blood.

Galileo was a citizen of one of the hundreds of minute political entities which harked back to feudal decentralization in politics. Yet he, as much as Harvey or any scientist, drew upon the work of others in many parts of Europe and enjoyed an international reputation. Intellectually speaking, Galileo was a citizen of the universe of science, as were the other leading contributors to the scientific revolution.

The greatest mathematical achievement of the seventeenth century was infinitesimal, or fluxional, calculus, worked out independently by Isaac Newton (1642-1727) and by a German philosopher of remarkable versatility, Gottfried Leibnitz (1646-1716). This new calculus enabled mathematicians to consider quantitatively such problems as the movement of heat and the motion of stars, to compute quickly the content of circles, and to calculate stresses. In addition, the eighteenth century contributed the centigrade and the Fahrenheit thermometers, the chronometer,

Sir Isaac Newton: English scientist extraordinary.

the sextant, and the anemometer, a device for measuring the force of wind.

Newton and the law of gravitation. Great as the contributions of Brahe, Kepler, and Galileo had been to astronomy, their individual discoveries had yet to be united into one all-embracing principle or law which would explain the motion of all bodies in the planetary system and present the universe as one great unity operating according to unalterable principles. This goal was realized by Isaac Newton, the most illustrious scientist in the Age of Reason. The poet Alexander Pope wrote of him:

Nature and Nature's laws lay hid in night:
God said, Let Newton be! and all was light.[1]

Newton was born the same year Galileo died and nearly a century after the death of Copernicus. Newton's parents were small farmers, but by obtaining a scholarship he was able to attend Cambridge University, where his mathematical skill astounded his professors. He quickly mastered Euclidean geometry and the works of Descartes and

Kepler. At the age of only twenty-four he had made all his important discoveries: (1) the law of gravitation; (2) the principles of calculus; and (3) the compound nature of light.

The notion of gravitation occurred to him in 1666. In the words of one of his companions:

. . . [Newton's discovery] was occasion'd by the fall of an apple, as he sat in contemplative mood. Why should that apple always descend perpendicularly to the ground, thought he to himself. Why should it not go sideways or upwards, but constantly to the earth's center? Assuredly, the reason is, that the earth draws it. There must be a drawing power in matter: and the sum of the drawing power must be in the earth's center, not in any side of the earth. Therefore does this apple fall perpendicularly, or towards the center. If matter thus draws matter, it must be in proportion of its quantity. Therefore the apple draws the earth, as well as the earth draws the apple. That there is a power, like that we here call gravity, which extends itself thro the universe.[2]

At twenty-seven the youthful genius was given a professorship in mathematics at Cambridge University. Even though he had already discovered the principle of gravitation, he was not able to prove it mathematically until 1685. Two years later his momentous work was published in Latin under the title *Philosophiae Naturalis Principia Mathematica (Mathematical Principles of Natural Philosophy)*. By this work the numerous contributions of previous astronomers were synthesized in a master principle for the universe, the law of gravitation, which was expressed in a concise mathematical formula:

Every particle in the universe attracts every other particle with a force varying inversely as the square of the distance between them and directly proportional to the product of their masses.[3]

The publication of the *Principia* climaxed the near century and a half in which scientists had struggled against static tradition and intolerant authority.

Newton refined the methods appropriate to scientific procedure by effecting a reconciliation of the rationalism of Descartes and the new experimental techniques. Stressing doubt and skepticism and advocating a logical and mathematical analysis of problems, Descartes made substantial contributions to modern scientific method, but he also overemphasized the efficacy of intuition and deduction and undervalued observation and experimentation. While Newton made use of the positive aspects of Cartesian thought, he relied primarily upon experience and investigation. Newton thereby developed a fundamental principle from the facts Cartesian thought supplied and then offered similar evidence to prove that the consequences to be logically expected did, in fact, occur.

Within his own lifetime Newton was showered with honors; he was knighted and became president of the Royal Society but remained unspoiled by the acclaim. Speaking of Descartes, Newton observed:

If I have seen farther . . . it is by standing on the shoulders of giants.[4]

Laplace and the nebular hypothesis. The achievements of Newton initiated a rapid development in the field of astronomy. In 1682, using Newton's formulas, his friend Edmund Halley (1656-1742) calculated the orbit of the comet since known as Halley's Comet, and correctly predicted its return in seventy-seven years. Newton's *Principia* was widely read, and many books intended to popularize his theories appeared throughout Europe.

The data and arguments found in Newton's masterwork were expanded and enriched in the works of the brilliant French astronomer and mathematician Pierre Laplace (1749-1827), who has been called "the Newton of France." A professor of mathematics while still in his teens, Laplace is best known for his nebular hypothesis, which maintained that our sun was originally a gaseous mass, or nebula, and the planets of the solar system condensed out of the rings of matter thrown off by this nebula as it rotated and contracted. Until recently, the nebular hypothesis was accepted by many scientists as a satisfactory scientific explanation of the origin of the planetary system.

Boyle, father of modern chemistry. In addition to the progress made in mathematics and astronomy by the end of the seventeenth century, discoveries were being made in new fields of inquiry which were destined to change the lives of much of the earth's population.

The science of chemistry suffered from arrested development in the sixteenth and early seventeenth centuries as men followed the will-o'-the-wisps of alchemy and magic. Then appeared the son of an Irish nobleman, Robert Boyle (1627-1691), who is considered the father of modern chemistry. Boyle was the first to emphasize the difference between a compound (whose constituent parts have been unified by chemical action and cannot be dissociated without chemical changes) and a mixture (in which various ingredients are merely brought together by mechanical means). In 1660 he formulated the law that "the volume of a gas, if the temperature remains constant, decreases in proportion to the pressure" (Boyle's law). An inveterate, wide-ranging experimenter, Boyle investigated fire, respiration, fermentation, evaporation, and the rusting of metals. In his influential book *The Sceptical Chemist* (1661), he struck out against alchemy and urged the use of inductive inquiry in chemistry.

Priestley, the chemist-preacher. Joseph Priestley (1733-1804), an English chemist-preacher, divided his loyalty between his congregation and his crucible. A fearless reformer and liberal, Priestley belonged to a distinguished group of intellectuals who composed the Lunar Society. (Two of the other "Lunatics," as they called themselves, were James Watt, inventor of the steam engine [see p. 156], and Erasmus Darwin, grandfather of the scientist who announced the theory of evolution.) In 1791 a mob angered by Priestley's sympathetic attitude toward the French Revolution attacked his house and destroyed his laboratory. Three years later he emigrated to Pennsylvania.

In the course of his experiments, Priestley isolated ammonia, the gas which in modern times plays an important role in the refrigeration process, and in 1774 he discovered the gas later named oxygen. His last important experiment in 1799 was the production of carbon monoxide gas. Much of the gas used in our homes for cooking and heating purposes is made by the method first devised by Priestley.

Lavoisier and the downfall of the phlogiston theory. Through Boyle and Priestley, chemistry had come a long way from medieval alchemy, but it would not become an exact science until the phlogiston theory of combustion could be disproved. The German physician and chemist Georg Ernst Stahl (1660-1734) contended that in all inflammable things there existed a combustible substance called *phlogiston* (from the Greek "to set on fire") which was "a principle of fire, but not fire itself."

Destruction of the phlogiston theory was the remarkable achievement of the French scientist Antoine Lavoisier (1743-1794). Supporters of Stahl's theory maintained that phlogiston was removed during combustion. By using chemists' scales in his experiment, Lavoisier proved that nothing was given off, that, on the contrary, something was added. He carefully weighed certain metals and then burned them. Placed upon the balance after combustion, the metals were found to be heavier than before being burned. A fresh supply of the same metals then was burned in a sealed vessel, and it was found that the total weight in the sealed vessel—that is, of the air and the metals both before and after combustion—was the same. From these facts Lavoisier reasoned that burning is a process in which the "dephlogisticated air" (oxygen) discovered by Priestley is taken from ordinary air and unites with the substance consumed. By decomposing the red powder he had obtained by burning mercury, Lavoisier conclusively proved his thesis; the loss of weight of the powder was exactly equivalent to the weight of the dephlogisticated air given off. To the element so essential in combustion Lavoisier gave a new name—*oxygen*. Lavoisier announced his findings in 1777 and published his results a few years later. In the face of such incontro-

David: Portrait of Antoine Lavoisier and his wife

vertible facts, the phlogistonists laid down their arms.

In his experiments on combustion, Lavoisier also discovered the law of the conservation of matter—that matter cannot be created or destroyed. In his own words:

We may lay it down as an incontestable axiom, that, in all the operations of art and nature, nothing is created; an equal quantity of matter exists both before and after the experiment; the quality and quantity of the elements remain precisely the same; and nothing takes place beyond changes and modifications in the combination of these elements.[5]

With the knowledge that weight was a constant and that the scientist aided by his balance could accurately determine by weight the substances in any compound, measurements in chemistry could be made with the precision required of an exact science. Thus new principles of universal order in matter were introduced that still distinguish the modern science of chemistry from its medieval predecessor, alchemy.

Lavoisier was a man of unusual ability. At nineteen he was recognized as an authority on illumination; at twenty-five he was admitted to the Academy of Science; in 1775

the government appointed him head of the state powder works. Unfortunately for science, his career was cut short by the French Revolution. Because he was wealthy and was connected with the despised government of Louis XVI, he was, in the eyes of the revolutionists, no friend of the people. Falsely accused by the Revolutionary Tribunal, he died a victim to *la guillotine.*

The beginnings of electricity. An event that has influenced our lives tremendously in the twentieth century was the discovery of electricity, the efficient producer of light, heat, and power and the most important element in our systems of communication—telegraph, telephone, radio, and television.

Only three hundred years ago practically nothing was known of electricity and its seemingly magical potentialities. First to use the term *electricity,* which he derived from the Greek word for amber (*elektron*), was the sixteenth-century scientist William Gilbert (see Chapter 20, Volume I). Usually credited with the founding of the modern science of electricity, Gilbert in his work *De Magnete* (1600) described the attraction between magnets as well as the forces which are created when bodies such as amber are rubbed.

The next important step in the history of electricity was the creation of a crude machine to produce it. A device consisting of a globe of sulfur set in a glass sphere mounted on a revolving axis was invented in 1660. When rubbed by a cloth, it produced both sound and light. With this device, an electric current could be sent from one end of a thread to the other—the first hint of possibilities for the transmission of electricity.

The discovery in 1745 of the Leyden Jar at the University of Leyden in the Netherlands made possible the accumulation in a glass phial of the electricity produced by the primitive friction machines then in use. To display this new marvel of magic, showmen toured Europe, providing popular entertainment by jolting pompous townsfolk and clergymen into involuntary action during demonstrations of the Leyden Jar.

An illustration from Diderot's *Encyclopédie* shows the apparatus used for Volta's experiment in generating electricity. Notice how the copper plate (A) of one tumbler and the zinc plate (Z) of the next are connected.

Franklin's daring kite experiment. The next important advance in electricity is credited to Benjamin Franklin (1706-1790), who was America's first great name in science as well as an author, diplomat, and statesman. Believing that lightning was identical with the static electricity in the Leyden Jar, Franklin in June 1752 carried out his famous kite experiment. To find out if lightning, like electricity, was attracted by a sharp point, he flew a kite made of wood and silk with a wire point on the tip during a thunderstorm, holding the kite string with a key tied to it. He soon felt the tingle of electricity in the key, through which electricity was freely conducted as the rain soaked the string.

Franklin's experiment provided a rational explanation for what had been an awe-inspiring and terrifying phenomenon for thousands of years. The experiment led to the invention of the lightning rod, which soon became standard equipment on all important buildings. Franklin received universal acclaim and was made a fellow of the Royal Society.

Alessandro Volta. The next great name in electricity is that of Alessandro Volta (1745-1827), an Italian physicist. In 1800 Volta, a university professor, found a new way of generating electricity; he was able to make it flow continuously instead of discharging itself in one spark as was the case with the Leyden Jar. Volta's apparatus consisted of a set of glass tumblers containing water and a little sulfuric acid. In each solution two plates, one copper and one zinc, were immersed. The copper plate of one glass was wired to the zinc of the next, leaving the zinc and copper plates in the first glass uncon-

nected with each other. Electricity flowed through the connecting wires; the free copper plate carried a positive charge and the free zinc plate, a negative charge. Thus Volta's machine—the direct ancestor of modern electric cells and batteries—produced electricity simply but effectively.

Volta became famous overnight; he was requested to lecture before Napoleon, who awarded him a gold medal and a substantial pension. Volta's name has been immortalized in the term used for a unit of electrical measurement, the volt.

Hutton and the overthrow of the catastrophic theory. Another science which developed remarkably in the eighteenth century was geology. Thinkers in ancient Greece had made intensive observations of rocks, fossils, and erosion; and in the Renaissance a theory was advanced that stratified rocks represented the floors of ancient oceans. But after this encouraging beginning little progress was made until late in the eighteenth century.

The most important figure in the field of geology was a Scottish gentleman farmer, James Hutton (1726-1797). As he studied soils, he grew interested in the earth's surface —seemingly a jumble of complex, diverse, and unrelated features. *Theory of the Earth,* his two-volume work published in 1795, completely overthrew the catastrophic theory then current, which taught that the earth's surface was the result of sudden, catastrophic action. In brief, Hutton maintained that behind all the various formations of the earth's surface two fundamental processes are at work in a constant and relatively imperceptible manner. The two processes are disin-

In this eighteenth-century cartoon, a French doctor on his way to visit a patient is preceded by an assistant carrying a gigantic inoculator.

tegration, or decay, and reconstruction, or repair. Through the action of water and wind and chemical decomposition, the former continually wears away the earth's surface. The process of reconstruction takes place as the material, carried off and deposited on ocean, lake, and valley floors, constantly forms new strata.

By emphasizing that the best way to understand what has happened in the past is to observe what is taking place in the present, Hutton helped change the conception of the earth as a static thing. And, in addition, by stressing the immensity of geological time, he gave the world an entirely new time perspective.

Advances in botany and zoology: Linnaeus and Buffon. Stephen Hales (1677-1761), an Englishman, did notable early work in botany. The old idea of plant nutrition was that vegetation absorbed food from the ground in a ready-made form. In *Vegetable Statick* (1727), Hales showed that plants obtain food from the air and that leaves play an important role in the process.

Explorations and scientific investigations in the seventeenth and eighteenth centuries brought to light a vast body of new information on plant and animal life which had to be classified. But it was essential that classification be placed on a scientific basis. The old method, which had designated all living things as fish, birds, beasts, trees, herbs, or shrubs, was inadequate to cope with the wealth of new data. In 1735 appeared *Systema Naturae* by the Swedish naturalist Carolus Linnaeus (1707-1778). In this volume and his subsequent revised editions of it, he worked out a logical system of plant classification, dividing the plant kingdom into classes, orders, genera, and species. Although his system of classification has been amended in modern times, many of the scientific names he used are still employed.

The conception of ordering and classifying knowledge had been advanced by Sir Francis Bacon at the beginning of the seventeenth century; scientists like Linnaeus showed how accumulated knowledge could be understood and put to use. The mere collecting of information was incomplete as an addition to knowledge until the principles of order by which it should be classified were developed.

In the field of zoology, the French scientist Georges Buffon (1707-1788) performed the same function Linnaeus had performed in botany. As keeper of the Royal Museum and Botanical and Zoological Gardens at Paris, Buffon had an excellent opportunity to collect information. In 1784 there appeared the first volume of his monumental work, *Natural History of Animals,* which ran to more than forty volumes in all. Buffon's works and the *Systema Naturae* of Linnaeus became very popular and stimulated the collection of both plant and animal specimens.

Achievements in medicine. Apart from the founding of new branches of science, such as chemistry and geology, the eighteenth century also witnessed important advances in medicine. The most noteworthy was the introduction of inoculation. Smallpox was then a fatal and widespread disease, and inoculation was used to cause a mild case and thereby produce future immunity. Knowledge of this practice first came to England from Constantinople when a Greek physician sent an account to the Royal Society in London. The wife of the British ambassador to Turkey also gave a graphic description of inoculation in one of her letters:

The smallpox, so fatal and general amongst us, is here entirely harmless, by the invention of *ingrafting,* which is the term they give it. There is a set of old women who make it their business to perform the operation every autumn. . . . People send to one another to know if any of their family has a mind to have smallpox; they make parties for this purpose, and when they are met . . . the old woman comes with a nutshell full of the matter of the best sort of smallpox, and asks what vein you please to have opened. She immediately rips open that you offer her with a large needle . . . and puts into the vein as much matter as can lie upon the head of her needle. . . . The children or young patients play together all the rest of the day, and are in perfect health to the eighth [day]. Then the fever begins to seize them, and they keep their beds two days, very seldom three. They have very rarely above twenty or thirty [spots] in their faces, which never mark.[6]

The Greek physician's account was published by the Royal Society in 1714. In spite of opposition to the practice, the technique gradually came to be employed in England and the rest of Europe. In an effort to erase the fear and superstition surrounding this technique, Catherine the Great of Russia was the first in her land to submit to inoculation.

In about 1798 the less dangerous method of vaccination was introduced by Edward Jenner (1749-1823). Observing that dairymaids who had had cowpox did not catch smallpox, this English physician came to the conclusion that exposure to the former, relatively mild disease produced immunity to the latter, very serious one. To test his hypothesis, he inoculated a boy with the vaccine of cowpox and later found that he was immune to smallpox. By similar case studies Jenner proved the value of his method.

A great step forward in the advance of medical diagnosis was the invention of the stethoscope, a brain child of a French physician, René Laënnec (1781-1826). He devised a wooden stethoscope which consisted of a tube with a bell-shaped opening through which the sounds of the heart and respiratory organs could be heard. This instrument was later replaced by a more pliable rubber stethoscope, similar to the one used today. Still another advance was the study of

blood pressure, one of the most important means of discovering disease. This technique was developed by Stephen Hales, the botanist, who in 1710 made his first measurements by attaching a tube to a horse's artery and observing how high the blood rose in the tube. Although his method was crude, it led to the making of modern-day apparatus.

THE CRISIS IN THE

EUROPEAN CONSCIENCE

The spiritual crisis. In the latter part of the seventeenth century, much of western Europe was undergoing a revolution—not in the realm of politics but in the minds of men. Despite the pervasive influence of the Renaissance, in the first half of the century science still was the servant of theology, faith was more important than reason, curiosity was still controlled by authority, and the laws of the Church and God were the bases of society. Then came the impact of the scientific revolution, with Newton's discoveries as its crowning achievements.

A new concept of a universe without supernatural or miraculous forces came into being. This universe could be understood; it was a smooth-running machine with all parts fitting into a harmonious whole. Scientists now were inclined to regard God not as a personal Deity but as the embodiment of scientific natural law—operating the universe and holding the stars in their courses. One scientist explained the mechanistic view in the following way:

God, indeed, gave motion to matter . . . he so guided the motions of the various parts of it as to contrive them into the world he designed to compose; and established those rules of motion, and that order amongst things corporeal, which we call the laws of nature. Thus, the universe being once fram'd by God, and the laws of motion settled, and all upheld by his perpetual concourse, and general providence; the [mechanical] philosophy teaches, that the phenomena of the world, are physically produced by the mechanical properties of the parts of matter, and that they operate upon one another according to mechanical laws.[7]

By contrast with the harmony and reasonableness of the natural world revealed by the scientists, society and its institutions seemed to be more and more archaic, and the world of man seemed to be governed by intolerance, prejudice, strife, and unreasoning authority. However, the teachings of science convinced many men that their world of religion, law, and government could also be brought under control of reason.

Early in the eighteenth century a number of thinkers attacked the "unscientific" nature of old beliefs. At the same time, problems arose. How could one remain a Christian while repudiating supernaturalism? What was to become of faith if one followed the Cartesian method? What was to become of the traditional concept of a personal and unknowable God if the Deity were reduced to impersonal and measurable natural law?

The problem of how to reconcile old faiths with new truths had become, in the words of a noted French scholar, the "crisis in the European conscience." Scholars and thinkers, therefore, set about seeing what could be reconciled between the old and new, what faiths if any might be left intact, and what should be completely discarded.

The dualism of Descartes. We must now return briefly to Descartes, for in addition to his many other endeavors this pioneer thinker sought to reconcile medieval religious faith with a mechanistic world in which supernatural phenomena are impossible and in which everything must be explained rationally. Descartes' proof of the existence of God was based on his assertion that, as existence must be an attribute of perfection and as the Deity must by definition be the all-perfect Being, a God must perforce exist.

Descartes next proceeded to prove the existence of material things, not by what his senses told him of them, but only by the "primary" mathematical qualities of objects which for him were "real." He divided ultimate reality into two substances: mind and matter. He argued that there is no connection between the two realms except by God's intervention. The first is the realm of faith and theology, impenetrable and unknowable to science; the second is that of reason and the laws of nature, subject to the understandable processes of science. Man is a compound of mind and spirit plus a body composed of matter. Thus Descartes, a loyal Catholic, sought to reconcile the old and the new by his system of philosophical dualism.

Spinoza and pantheism. Deeply influenced by the mathematical method of Descartes was Baruch Spinoza (1632-1677), another thinker who sought to reconcile spirit and matter. Born in Holland of well-to-do Jewish refugees who had fled from the Inquisition in Portugal, Spinoza as a youth renounced Judaism and was promptly denounced by the Jewish elders. Although he earned only a meager living by grinding lenses, his poverty did not prevent him from continuing his studies in religion and philosophy. His writings were so important that he was offered the professorship of philosophy at the University of Heidelberg on the condition that he tone down some of his rather radical ideas. Spinoza refused this offer; to him independence of thought was vital. In 1677 he died, impoverished and persecuted.

Following the methods of Descartes, Spinoza strove to build a mathematical philosophy; his *Ethics* (1663) is filled with geometric axioms, postulates, and theories. But Descartes' dualistic system was rejected by Spinoza, to whom mind and matter were manifestations of one substance—nature, or God. In other words, the universe and God are one. While Spinoza was alive, both Jews and Christians persecuted him, but his true spirituality later became better understood. He has been called "the God-intoxicated man."

Leibnitz and atomicity. Differing from both Descartes and Spinoza on the nature of ultimate reality, the versatile German philosopher and mathematician Leibnitz believed that there was not one universal substance, as Spinoza thought, nor two, basic to Descartes' system of dualism, but rather an infinite number. According to Leibnitz, the countless monads which made up the universe were immaterial (consisting only of thought or force) and indestructible. They were the "real atoms of nature," each different and independent of the other. Each human being was a group of these monads with a dominant monad called the "soul." Furthermore, the monads were arranged in an ascending hierarchy in which the greatest of all monads was God, who had arranged everything into "the best of all possible worlds."

While many of Leibnitz' contemporaries found his reasoning about the existence of evil in the "best of all possible worlds" less than satisfactory—an opinion shared by most present-day students of philosophy—the body of works produced by this German philosopher put forth a wealth of important ideas. To a striking degree Leibnitz anticipated the twentieth century's scientific concept of atomic structure and the idea that energy is the ultimate form of matter.

Locke and empiricism. In the main, the Continental philosophers were rationalists who believed that knowledge is gained through reasoning. By contrast, English thinkers tended to believe that knowledge came only from sensory experience, a school of thought known as empiricism. Its founder, John Locke, the author of "Of Civil Government" (see p. 80), felt that there was too much abstruse and flighty thought in Europe and sought to work out a reasonable and simple philosophy so that there could be agreement on definitions and concepts.

In 1690 Locke published *An Essay Concerning Human Understanding*, which sought to analyze the human mind. According to him, the mind at birth is like a tabula rasa (a blank tablet) and the experience gained through the senses is recorded on this tablet. In Locke's own words:

Let us then suppose the mind to be . . . white paper, void of all characters, without any ideas; how comes it to be furnished? Whence comes it by that vast store, which the busy and boundless fancy of man has painted on it with an almost endless variety? Whence has it all the materials of reason and knowledge? To this I answer, in one word, From experience: in that all our knowledge is founded, and from that it ultimately derives itself.[8]

Unlike the rationalists on the Continent, Locke maintained that, of itself, the mind has no innate power to grasp reality. In acquiring knowledge, the mind is not, however, completely passive. Locke believed that reflection also played a role. By the process of association, the new and the old react on one another to form a new idea.

Locke's empiricism was of fundamental importance in the cultural development of modern Europe. A true son of the Age of Reason, Locke believed that investigation of such basic philosophical questions as the existence of God and the fundamentals of morality would lead men to a state of universal reasonableness and thereby free them from the necessity of relying blindly on authority. He was sincerely convinced that he was "not pulling up the foundations of knowledge" but instead "laying those foundations surer."

Locke was the first to apply the scientific principles of observation and experiment to the study of human nature. As we know, he conceived of the mind at birth as a blank tablet. The adult mind was formed by experience coming through sensation and refined and tempered by reflection, memory, and judgment. These ideas were basic to the development of the discipline of psychology, with its emphasis on the importance of environmental forces.

Deism: a solution to the spiritual crisis. By the end of the first quarter of the eighteenth century, the crisis in the European conscience had eased. After this time most intellectuals pegged their faith to the new science of Newton and the philosophy of Locke. This is not to say that religion was repudiated. Rather, the necessary reëvaluation and synthesis of science and religion had been made. Both Locke and Newton included God in their scheme of things, the latter declaring that:

This most beautiful system of the sun, planets, and comets, could only proceed from the counsel of an intelligent and powerful Being. . . . He endures forever, and is everywhere present; and by existing always and everywhere, he constitutes duration and space.[9]

Non est potestas Super Terram quæ Comparetur ei Iob. 41. 24.

This enormous monarch, his body made up of the tiny figures of his subjects, symbolizes an all-powerful government to which the people have surrendered their rights. The illustration appeared in the 1651 edition of Hobbes' *Leviathan*.

Upon this rationalistic, scientific basis the thinkers of the eighteenth century built their religion. Known as Deism, it stripped Christianity of most of its traditional dogmas, had no use for denominational squabbles, and endeavored to make religion accord with reason. God—thought of as an impersonal force—became in their eyes the First Cause, the custodian of the world machine, the master "clockwinder" of the universe. God had been necessary to create the universe, but once the universe had been set in motion, its immutable laws could not be altered. Alexander Pope in his *Essay on Man* describes the Creator as one:

Who sees with equal eye, as God of all,
A hero perish, or a sparrow fall,
Atoms or systems to destruction hurled,
And now a bubble burst, and now a world.[10]

It was regarded as useless to invoke the intercession of God to bring about a deviation from the laws of nature. Men must rely upon reason, not miracles, to solve the problems of society.

The Deistic concept of a "natural" religion included only a few basic beliefs: the existence of God as master of the universe, the necessity of worshiping God, the atonement by man for his sins, the doctrine of immortality, and the view that the aim of religion is virtue, or sensible living. All religions were to be based on these simple and rational essentials; anything additional was extraneous and not worth squabbling about. Deists maintained that if all creeds would give up or at least minimize their "extraneous" dogmas, religious intolerance and bigotry would cease. The God of Deism was universal and acceptable to all. It mattered little what He was called. In the words of Pope:

Father of all! in every age,
In every clime adored,
By saint, by savage, and by sage,
Jehovah, Jove, or Lord![11]

ORDER IN THE STATE:

LOUIS XIV,

THE EPITOME OF ABSOLUTISM

Centralized territorial monarchy. The search for new principles of order in the universe, as reflected in the scientific revolution and culminating in Deism, was paralleled by the establishment of new principles of order in European politics. One of the most far-reaching changes in the political scene during the seventeenth century was the consolidation of the national state as we know it today. While in England the authority of the crown was tempered by parliamentary oligarchy, on the Continent the idea of the king who ruled by divine right flourished. The absolute monarchy of the seventeenth and eighteenth centuries was a political reaction against the decentralization of the Middle Ages. Nevertheless, many of the characteristics of feudal political behavior, transferred to larger scale, and many important social and economic traits of the feudal period survived in the new national state.

Some of the characteristics which we ascribe to modern nations are more intelligible when we remember that the personification we unconsciously apply to the state had a real basis in the seventeenth and eighteenth centuries. Take, for example, the modern phrase "France's honor." At the beginning of the seventeenth century national honor had a personal meaning, for France's honor was the honor of its king Henry IV. The kingdom of France under God was Henry IV's personal estate or fief. The medieval conception of the king as the first among equals was disappearing as the result of the persistent aggrandizement of the royal domain by marriage, inheritance, escheat, or outright

aggression against other great feudal magnates. The territorial build-up of the great states of continental Europe was accomplished by expanding personal estates. They were not fully nations in the modern sense until the great French Revolution injected the idea of fraternity and changed men's thinking about themselves as units in the state. Men became citizens with rights and privileges rather than simply subjects owing unquestioning allegiance to the state.

The consolidation of royal power in the centralized territorial state of the seventeenth and eighteenth centuries did not mean the end of the almost incessant warfare of feudal society. The anarchy that had existed within the state became anarchy between states. The dynasties which ruled the great European states had family pride and family honor as might be expected, since they were feudal families with vastly improved resources for waging war. Although commercial factors had a rapidly rising importance, it is none the less true that the most fruitful cause of wars in the period of the absolute monarchy was dynastic rivalry. Dominated by feudal trends of political thinking, kings worked for personal and dynastic aggrandizement like any feudal lord. The evil effects of this policy during the period of the absolute monarchy are only now becoming fully apparent. So thoroughly were the attributes of the feudal lord associated with the dynastic states of the seventeenth and eighteenth centuries that when the dynasties disappeared and only the nation remained, men still attributed to the nation the personal characteristics of the feudal lords by whom they had been governed.

Architecture of absolutism. Political absolutism was not an innovation of the seventeenth century. The ideas inherent in the theory of the divine right of kings can be traced back to the pharaohs of ancient Egypt, Alexander the Great, and the Roman Caesars. Nevertheless, in the seventeenth century absolutism attained its most exaggerated form and its most refined philosophical expression. It was a logical response to the disorder, sometimes amounting almost to social anarchy, of the sixteenth and early seventeenth century. The fratricidal religious conflicts within states, the efforts of surviving feudal magnates to preserve their power and independence of each other and of the king by private war, the great destruction of property and disruption of trade that imperiled the livelihood of the bourgeoisie, these were evils that could be ended only by equal subjection of all classes to a superior force. In most of Continental Europe the absolute monarch was the superior force that established order by subordinating all classes equally to the state, including the clergy. The bourgeoisie in particular was willing to ally with the crown in the interest of security for life and property, even at the price of absolutism.

Under the system of absolutism the king's power touched every aspect of his subjects' existence. He was the supreme and only lawgiver—the fountain of justice. As head of the church he decided what religion his subjects were to follow and persecuted those who dissented. The worship of God was a matter of state, not the preserve of the individual conscience. The king regulated every phase of economic life, from the establishment of new industries to working conditions and standards of quality. In addition, he was the arbiter of manners and fashion, the patron of arts and letters, and the personification of national glory. A vast and obedient bureaucracy and a powerful royal army enforced his will.

Though such a system of all-pervasive absolutism is abhorrent to us today, in the seventeenth century it was generally unquestioned and often very popular. A powerful king stood for order, efficiency, security, and prosperity—values willingly exchanged for the uncertainties of upheaval and bloodshed such as had been experienced during the turmoil of the Middle Ages and the Religious Wars. Furthermore, the tradition of obedience to authority was still strong, as it had been in medieval times. The individualism and liberty born of the Renaissance were not to mature until a later day.

The new absolute state was explained and rationalized by a school of political theorists, chief of whom was Jacques Bossuet (1627-1704). The most prominent French churchman of his times, he was entrusted with the education of Louis XIV's son and was finally elevated to the position of bishop. By utilizing the doctrine of the divine right of kings, Bossuet composed a brilliant justification of absolute monarchy with religion as the base:

It appears . . . that the person of the king is sacred, and that to attack him in any way is sacrilege . . . the royal throne is not the throne of a man, but the throne of God himself. . . . Kings should be guarded as holy things, and whosoever neglects to protect them is worthy of death. . . . The royal power is absolute . . . [and] the prince need render account of his acts to no one. . . . Where the word of a king is, there is power. . . . Without this absolute authority the king could neither do good nor repress evil.[12]

However, Bossuet did not envisage a monarch ruling by divine right as exercising capricious power:

. . . although their power comes from on high . . . [such sovereigns] should not regard themselves as masters of that power to use it at their pleasure . . . they must employ it with fear and self-restraint, as a thing coming from God and of which God will demand an account.[13]

Unfortunately, the majority of monarchs stressed only the divine prerogatives and ignored the responsibilities of exalted office.

Inheritance of Louis XIV. The best example of political absolutism is offered by France in the days of Louis XIV, who reigned from 1643 to 1715. This proud Bourbon monarch inherited a realm which had been made powerful during the preceding fifty years. The previous century, the sixteenth, had been a sorry period in France's history. Wars with the other great states as well as civil war at home had weakened the country. The accession of Henry IV in 1589, however, soon brought peace and better times. The foundations of the great nation which was to enjoy economic, military, and intellectual leadership in the seventeenth century were laid during his reign. With his gay manner and warm heart, Henry IV endeared himself to his people. Although his favorite pastime was the pursuit of women, his amours did not deter him from making France strong and prosperous. By 1610, when Henry was assassinated by a religious fanatic, disorder had disappeared, and the French economy was vigorous and flourishing.

Richelieu: a Machiavellian behind the throne. The death of Henry left Louis XIII, a boy of nine, on the throne with an incompetent queen mother as regent. Fourteen years passed, and Henry IV's achievements were slowly undermined until in 1624 Cardinal Richelieu, the clever protégé of the queen mother, became the real power behind the throne. For eighteen years the biography of Richelieu was the real history of France. As chief adviser to Louis XIII the "grim cardinal" set about restoring and furthering the accomplishments of his royal master's father. His basic objective was to exalt the power of the monarchy and to make Louis' authority unchallengeable. Richelieu himself loved power; while he made his royal master the first man in Europe, he made the king the second man in France.

Under Richelieu's direction, the structure of absolutism quickly took shape. Castles of the nobility were torn down, the nobles' power as governors in the local districts was eliminated, officials of the central government called *intendants* were given the actual authority in each locality, and the Estates-General—a body that might have challenged the power of the king—was ignored. In foreign affairs Richelieu was equally decisive and crafty. As we have already noted in Chapter 17, Volume I, his intervention in the Thirty Years' War struck a staggering blow against the Hapsburgs and helped to make France the greatest power in Europe.

Richelieu was Machiavelli's "prince" in action. Though handicapped by a frail body and wasted by disease, he possessed inflexible determination and an iron will. His harsh campaign against the unruly nobles made him a hated figure among the aristoc-

Rigaud: Portrait of Louis XIV

racy. Against these opponents he knew no mercy; in all dealings with them he met deceit with deceit and opposition with relentless vengeance. An authority on this period points out that, due to the high death rate among the cardinal's enemies, France under Richelieu had little internal history.

Cardinal Mazarin: Richelieu's protégé. After the deaths of Richelieu in 1642 and Louis XIII in 1643, the throne of France was again occupied by a child, Louis XIV, who was less than five years old. Richelieu had anticipated this emergency, however, by grooming a promising young Italian, Cardinal Mazarin, to be adviser to the regent. Mazarin governed France with a firm and efficient hand during the minority of the king, although the royal authority was seriously challenged by civil outbreak. For six years (1648-1653), France was convulsed by disorder, but Mazarin eventually triumphed over the forces of disunity. This civil war—a reaction against the excesses of the now powerful royal administration—had no effect in tempering absolutism. In fact, the violence of the struggle served to convince many Frenchmen that the only alternative to royal absolutism was anarchy.

Following the death of Mazarin in 1661, Louis XIV, then twenty-three years old, took over the personal management of state affairs. He found his people obedient and docile; Henry IV, Richelieu, and Mazarin had done their work efficiently.

Louis XIV: the Sun King. Believing implicitly in the divine right of kings, Louis chose the sun as the symbol of his power. His courtiers dubbed him *Le Roi Soleil* (the Sun King), and he was also known throughout Europe as the Grand Monarch.

A burning ambition to make his reign glorious possessed him, and he frequently defended his pretensions in haughty style:

All power, all authority, resides in the hands of the king, and there can be no other in his kingdom than that which he establishes. The nation does not form a body in France. It resides entire in the person of the king.[14]

In personal appearance Louis XIV was well qualified to play the role of absolute king. He was regal and dignified, whether in his dressing gown or in the most magnificent robes of state. Of much more than average intelligence, the young king worked assiduously at what he described as "the business of being king." His duties in the council chamber and the perusal of the many documents which accumulated on his desk took from six to eight hours a day, and he was also required to attend numerous court ceremonies and palace fetes.

Versailles: symbol of royal elegance. The palace of the Louvre in Paris had been good enough for his predecessors, but Louis wanted a more magnificent symbol for his greatness. On barren marsh land a few miles from Paris, Louis ordered the construction of the palace of Versailles. Begun in 1669, the project employed as many as thirty thousand men at one time; the total cost of construction probably exceeded one hundred million dollars. The marsh land was transformed into a beautiful park surrounding the palace whose façade was more than a quar-

ter mile in length. Versailles had many great rooms richly decorated with gilding, carvings, tapestries, and statues. The most famous were the Salon of Apollo, with a solid silver throne, and the grand Hall of Mirrors. The symmetry in the design of formal gardens and surroundings for the palace reflects the orderliness that Louis XIV, throughout his long reign, tried to impose on the society of his age. (See illustration, page 83.)

Today, the palace of Versailles is merely a historical monument, a symbol of royal elegance and glittering court life that has no place in our modern world. But two hundred years ago it was the most fashionable spot in Europe. Here during the day the French nobles promenaded with their king among the groves, terraces, and fountains of the park or hunted and hawked in the nearby woods and meadows. At night lords and ladies in powdered wigs, silks, and laces attended balls, masquerades, and concerts. If the weather was favorable, aquatic carnivals were held on the grand canal in the park.

Just as science followed the rule of law, so life and manners conformed to rules of etiquette. Studied elegance, formal manners, extravagant expressions of courtesy, witty but superficial conversation all too often constituted the base of polite society, and manners were more important than morals. The aristocratic life of elegance, leisure, and polished deportment is well symbolized by the graceful minuet—a dance which "was a school for chivalry, courtesy and ceremony; the hundred slow graceful movements and curtseys, the pauses which had to be filled by neatly turned compliments, the beauty and bravery of attire—all were eloquent of graces and outward refinements which we cannot boast now."[15]

Palace etiquette was carried to ridiculous extremes; the "cult of majesty" resulted in the king's being treated practically as a god. Louis was surrounded by fawning sycophants and servile courtiers, and his every action was made a regal ceremony based on the strictest precedent. For example, a nobleman of designated rank was required to dry the king after his bath, and only a very illustrious noble could hand the king the royal shirt or breeches during the public ceremony of dressing.

The fashions, speech, and manners of the French courtiers set the standards of aristocratic behavior on the Continent. The splendor and formality of Versailles were envied, copied, but never matched by the other reigning monarchs of Europe.

Louis' absolutism: the positive aspects. During the late seventeenth century, France was the premier nation of Europe. In nearly every phase of government—in diplomatic practice, the functioning of the central government, the organization of the military services—the absolute state of Louis XIV was the model.

Louis increased the powers of the *intendants* instituted by Richelieu; reorganized the army, drawing it more closely under state control; and instituted a wide variety of economic reforms to increase revenue and strengthen the French economy. To carry out his economic policies, Louis was fortunate in possessing as his finance minister the able Jean Baptiste Colbert (1619-1683). Under Colbert's guidance new industries were encouraged, while imports from other countries were excluded by high tariff barriers. The removal of many provincial customs duties within France enabled internal trade to move more freely than ever before; agriculture was improved; colonies were founded; and the navy was strengthened to protect the colonies and the trade routes. Underlying this colonial exploitation was the philosophy of mercantilism, expressed in the doctrine of the "limited market." European statesmen believed that the world's commercial wealth was a fixed quantity and that if one nation extended its trade, others must necessarily lose theirs. Business practices and standards of quality and workmanship were minutely regulated. With its centralization of government control over all economic life, mercantilism was a reflection of the spirit of absolutism. This systematic embodiment of mercantilist doctrines came to be known as Colbertism, and Colbert's ideas influenced would-be despots all over Europe. Not the least recommendation for his system was the fact that it enabled a surplus of money to be accumulated in the royal treasury.

Louis' absolutism: the negative aspects. The positive side of Louis' reign—his own untiring administrative zeal and the financial genius of Colbert—was counterbalanced by other less fortunate manifestations of Louis' thirst for power and glory. One extremely unwise act was the revocation of Henry IV's Edict of Nantes. Since the publication of the Edict in 1598, the Huguenots, a Protestant minority within a Catholic state, had enjoyed a certain measure of religious freedom and independence. To an absolute monarch like Louis, complete uniformity within his state was a cherished ideal, and legal toleration of religious nonconformity was a serious flaw in the system of absolutism. Therefore, in 1685 Louis revoked the Edict and caused thousands of industrious Huguenots to flee to other lands, taking with them skills and knowledge which were to enrich the enemies of France. Another negative aspect of his reign was the excessive cost of his mammoth palace of Versailles. More regrettable, perhaps, was the fact that the pomp and pageantry of Versailles isolated Louis XIV from his people. He moved in a world of glitter and luxury, far from the sordid realities of the world known to his subjects.

Finally, and most important of all, Louis squandered the abundant resources of his realm in his passion for military conquest. His war minister, François Michel le Tellier, Marquis de Louvois (1641-1691), took full advantage of improvement in military techniques—as well as the regular revenues collected through Colbert's efforts—to train and equip an excellent standing army. The unreliable feudal levy was a thing of the past; war became a business, an all-important function of the state that required efficiency, organization, and discipline. Important changes were made in tactics and weapons: the improvement of firearms and the introduction of the bayonet eliminated the pike as the main infantry weapon; artillery and fortification methods were improved and so, in turn, were siege methods for the reduction of fortresses. Indeed, the tactics devised by Louis' military engineer, Sebastian Le Prestre de Vauban (1633-1707), for siege warfare established the principles that governed that science until the twentieth century. The capture of Yorktown in 1781 by the American and French armies and the French fleet, directed by French engineers, is a textbook case in Vauban's methods. Vauban's system of attack was so effective that, copied by France's enemies, even fortifications constructed by Vauban himself could not be successfully defended against it.

Emboldened by the knowledge that France possessed the strongest army in existence and the most capable generals of the age, Louis embarked on a series of wars to attain for France her "natural boundaries" by extending French territory northward at the expense of the Spanish Netherlands and eastward to the banks of the Rhine. Although a potential danger did exist because of the absence in these areas of such excellent geographical barriers as France possessed on the Alpine and Pyrenean frontiers, Louis' chief motive was not security for France but prestige for the monarchy.

Louis XIV acted upon the maxim "he who gains nothing, loses." We shall discuss his many wars in the next chapter, but we should note that they were an integral part of his conception of absolute monarchy. The Sun King recognized no authority over himself but God; when Louis XIV wanted something he took it, whether it was a woman or a province, and the only check upon him, in the last analysis, was superior force.

The balance sheet. Louis XIV did in his lifetime restore order in his kingdom. Heresy, for practical purposes, ceased to be a problem. The extreme Declaration of the Gallican Clergy (1682), which declared the king in effect head of the Church in France, was compromised by Louis XIV's later agreements with the papacy; but practical control remained in the hands of the monarch. By being compelled to live in idleness at Versailles, the nobility were subordinated and cut off from the land, the base of their strength. The bourgeoisie, on the other hand, profited by domestic peace. The French reputation for military prowess remained great. But the order and uniformity in the political and social life of France that seemed to mark the last years of Louis XIV's reign were, in many respects, the symptoms of a static governmental system. As we shall see in Chapter 3, the continued vitality of the new intellectual order and the emphasis on reason eventually led to a successful assault on absolute monarchy, secure though it seemed when Louis XIV died in 1715.

French drama. The veneration for order and restraint that characterized France under the absolutism of Louis XIV was reflected as well in the national drama. This, the neoclassical period in France, began about the middle of the seventeenth century and is comparable in importance to the Elizabethan Age in England. Emphasis was placed on the rules of classical tragedy as first outlined by Aristotle. French dramatists followed Aristotle's strictures, which had been expanded and redefined in the Renaissance as the three unities: unity of action (a single plot line shorn of irrelevant subplots), unity of time (confinement of a play's action to a single day), and unity of place (restriction of setting to one locale).

The works of the two greatest writers of tragedy—Pierre Corneille (1606-1684) and Jean Racine (1639-1699)—are important not so much for their scrupulous adherence to rigid conventions as for their psychological insights, concentrated emotional impact, and beauty of language. For plots, Racine and Corneille relied on tales from Greek and Roman mythology or events of antiquity; for heroes and heroines they drew idealized characterizations of the courtiers of their own day.

The wittiest comedies of the period were those of Molière (1622-1673). As a true voice of the Age of Reason, he believed that moderation and good sense were the keynotes of life and that any deviation from reasonable behavior was fair game for comedy. With rapier-like wit, he spoofed the pretensions of learned females and the

An eighteenth-century painting of a French salon shows a group of people gathered to read the works of Molière.

aspirations of the social-climbing bourgeoisie, reserving some of his choicest barbs for the medical profession. But like all the greatest writers of comedy, Molière created characters that were universal figures as well as individuals of his own time.

SUMMARY

The manifold activities of the sixteenth century, which extended the interests of Europeans into every field of thought and action, carried over into the seventeenth. They were most spectacular in the field of science, and nowhere was the international character of human society more evident than in the interchange of ideas among the great minds of that age. That the major scientific works of the seventeenth century were written in Latin is evidence that the world of learning preserved the intellectual universality of preceding centuries in a way the nation states did not. Copernicus, Bacon, Descartes, and Newton published their major works in Latin because they wanted to be read by other learned men, and they were.

The enormous progress of scientific knowledge in succeeding centuries occurred in large measure because all scientists had confidence in human reason and rational investigation and could therefore use each other's work to expand their own horizons. The promise of science initiated by Copernicus was fulfilled in Newton's brilliant postulation of the law of gravitation.

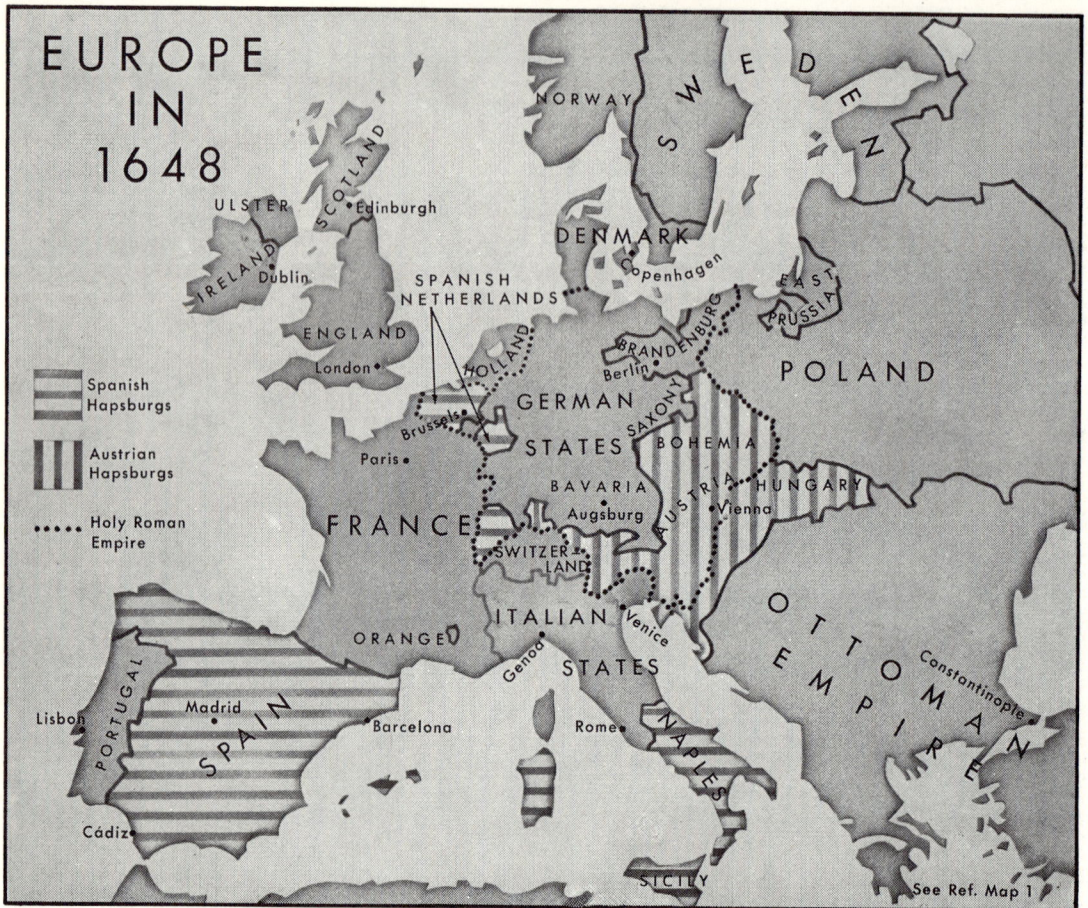

EUROPE IN 1648

Spanish Hapsburgs

Austrian Hapsburgs

..... Holy Roman Empire

See Ref. Map 1

The impact of the rapidly developing scientific method had a profound effect upon the world of ideas. When a scientist with international renown, like Galileo, publicly supported a new conception in which the earth's inhabitants were not the center of the universe, church leaders saw a mortal threat to the church's position as the leading institution of human society. The church's great powers of censorship were directed toward the suppression of many new scientific ideas and Galileo was persecuted. The European state system supported the church in this endeavor, for the two were mutually dependent, and any weakening of one would ultimately weaken the other. To many intellectuals, however, little seemed left of faith and traditional Christianity; and as men ceased to believe in miracles and denominational theology, what has been termed the "crisis in the European conscience" arose. Some met the crisis by turning to a new form of rational, scientific religion in which faith became a matter of logic and intellect.

Although national boundaries raised no barriers to intellectual exchanges in the seventeenth century, the growth of strong monarchies produced political problems. The absolutism of the French monarchy under the arrogant and ambitious Louis XIV made him both the envy and the model of other rulers. In the latter half of the century *Le Roi Soleil's* reputation and power were at their zenith. Consciously at times, unwittingly at others, he set the pace for Europe in all fields from fashion to war. As a symbol of national greatness he had no peers in his lifetime, and aspects of his policies and those of his ministers' dominated the century after his death.

CHAPTER 2

The Competitive State System

ABSOLUTISM AND THE POLITICS OF POWER: 1650-1775

Introduction. The century following the Peace of Westphalia (1648) was a vitally important period in European politics. Basic political philosophies that have influenced the actions of governments and peoples down to our own day were being formulated and put into operation. The allegiances and rivalries and the boundaries and battlefields of nineteenth-century Europe were foreshadowed by the stirring events of these times. In the weighing scales of power and military might, the modern hierarchy of nations was being established. Some of the old political structures were decaying: the Holy Roman Empire, Poland, and the empire of the Ottoman Turks. Such once powerful nations as Spain, Holland, and Sweden had passed their golden ages and were slipping into a tranquil state of ineffectuality in the realm of international affairs. In contrast, France and Britain were dynamic and aggressive; Prussia and Russia had achieved stability and gained vigor and were advancing rapidly into the category of first-class powers.

The advance and decline of nations would in itself have made the century after 1648 one of flux and movement in international affairs. But what might be called the natural rise and fall of nations was accelerated by the deliberate policies of strong powers operating in the political climate termed the competitive state system. The competitive nature of the state system of modern Europe distinguishes it from all previous and non-European civilizations of the world. Its essence has been said to lie "in the coexistence of independent and co-ordinate states, whose expansionist drive provoked incessant military conflicts and periodical reshufflings of the territorial and political map. . . ."[1]

In the perpetual competition between nations, the decisive weapon was force. No one nation, however, was allowed to become too strong; competitive states manipulated the balance of power to prevent the rise of an all-powerful nation. The grandiose ambitions of Louis XIV to promote French supremacy touched off a series of wars beginning in 1667 and ending in 1713, but France enjoyed only limited success because Louis was opposed by a series of alliances. Thus his plans were thwarted, and international equilibrium—the balance of power—was maintained.

Preserving equilibrium in the competitive state system during the eighteenth century required more wars between aggressive dynastic rulers. France remained the pre-eminent military power on the Continent, but Great Britain, which had led the triumphant coalition against France at the end of Louis XIV's reign, became the greatest naval and commercial power in the world. English success also marked the triumph of a system of government which differed from the pattern of absolutism on the Continent. This new political form, Aristocratic Liberalism, has been defined as "government in accordance with the agreed decisions of bodies which were drawn from a limited class but acted after free discussion and with some degree of tolerance and of consideration for the governed."[2] Its origins went back to the rise of lawmaking bodies in medieval times, but Aristocratic Liberalism was an important step toward modern democratic parliamentary government.

EVOLUTION OF

CONSTITUTIONAL

MONARCHY IN ENGLAND

Background for the English civil wars. The revolution in England that produced Aristocratic Liberalism in the eighteenth century grew out of English experience with divine right monarchy in the seventeenth century. The English civil wars (1642-1660), like most of the seventeenth-century conflicts on the Continent, were a complex blend of politics and religion. But unlike the Thirty Years' War, for example, the English struggle was a domestic duel between groups fundamentally opposed in viewpoint—traditionalists who upheld the power of the monarchy and those who favored a government more representative of the people. The religious implications of the English civil wars were important, but they have been overshadowed by the constitutional results stemming from the struggle. The outcome had a strong influence on the development of constitutional governments and the growth of democracy in modern times.

For hundreds of years English institutions had been developing slowly in the direction of constitutional, representative government. During the Wars of the Roses, after the conclusion of the 100 Years' War, constitutional progress was almost submerged in feudal disorder. Then, largely with the co-operation of Parliament and the approval of the English people, Tudor monarchs had restored law and order to England, broken with the Church of Rome, and ruled with a strong hand. No consistent breach of opinion developed between the crown on the one hand and Parliament and the people on the other to raise constitutional issues or to challenge the royal power so skillfully wielded by the Tudors.

If the spirit of liberty and the growth of constitutional government had been placed temporarily in cold storage, it had not been frozen. During most of Elizabeth's reign, the House of Commons was content to improve its procedures and gain parliamentary experience. Following the defeat of the Armada, however, the spirit of liberty began to reassert itself. On questions of taxation Parliament became increasingly independent. While this body usually enacted into law the measures laid before it by the queen's advisers, an unpopular measure would occasionally be rejected.

James I and Parliament. Elizabeth's successor was James Stuart, king of Scotland

and the son of Mary Stuart. Scotland and England, though still separate states, thus acquired a king in common. As James I of England, he reigned from 1603 to 1625.

A scholarly man, James appointed a commission to make a new English translation of the Bible. Published in 1611, the King James Version was a masterpiece of English prose. But notwithstanding his erudition and his sincere desire for peace, the new king was totally unfitted for his position. He lacked common sense and tact; small wonder that he was dubbed "the wisest fool in Christendom."

His most unpolitic move was advocating the divine right of kings. In the address to his first Parliament, he expressed his ideas of the monarch's power:

The state of monarchy is the supremest thing upon earth, for kings are not only God's lieutenants upon earth and sit upon God's throne, but even by God himself they are called gods. . . . That as to dispute what God may do is blasphemy, . . . so is it sedition in subjects to dispute what a king may do in the height of his power . . . I will not be content that my power be disputed upon. . . .[3]

Disregarding the temper of his new subjects, James made it plain that he meant to be an absolute monarch.

The religious issue. The constitutional issue of king against Parliament was complicated by religious issues. After the break with the Roman Church precipitated by Henry VIII's divorce, the independent Anglican Church had retained many aspects of Roman Catholic theology and ceremony. But during Elizabeth's reign a noticeable trend toward Protestant doctrine and ceremony developed. By the time James came to the throne, some Englishmen were content with the Anglican Church as it then was. Others hoped to reintroduce much of the ritual and some of the tenets of Roman Catholicism, although they had no desire to return to papal control. Still others took an extreme Protestant position.

The extreme Protestants were called Puritans because they wished to "purify" the Anglican Church still further, simplify the ritual, and lessen the authority of the bishops chosen by the king. The Puritans were mostly members of the urban middle class. Engaged in trade and commerce, they resented James' arbitrary and illegal taxation and wanted to secure laws for the protection and expansion of English commercial interest. Puritan lawyers supplied historical precedents as ammunition against the growing absolutism of the throne.

James' stand on religion further alienated the Puritans because he opposed their desire for more Protantism in the Anglican Church. Also, many Englishmen considered him overfriendly with Catholic sovereigns abroad, inclined to favor and protect English Catholics, and too much under the thumb of ambassadors from Catholic courts.

James' policy and its effects. James' arbitrary taxation, his obvious sympathy with the pro-Catholic or High Church movement, and his insistence upon royal prerogatives were the first steps leading to civil war. After quarreling with James over taxation and church matters, the House of Commons drew up an *Apology*, which was a statement of its parliamentary rights. The members claimed the right "that in parliament they may speak freely their consciences without check and controlment."[4] In retaliation, James dissolved Parliament and from 1611 to 1621 ruled the country without it.

In the latter part of his reign the Thirty Years' War raged on the Continent. The Puritans were sympathetic to the German Protestants and quite willing to enter the struggle. James, however, was not only pacifistic but pro-Spanish as well. Thus his foreign policy infuriated the Puritans, to whom Catholic Spain was anathema.

Charles I and Parliament. At the death of James I in 1625, his son Charles I inherited the English throne along with a host of problems similar to those which had beset his father. James' mistakes were repeated by Charles, and to an even greater degree. Like father, the son espoused the divine right of kings, was contemptuous of the rights of Parliament, and supported the pro-Catholic or High Church faction.

Insisting on absolute royal power, Charles opened his reign with stormy debates with Parliament; but in return for revenue from Parliament, he agreed in 1628 to the famous Petition of Rights—a parliamentary declaration that ranks with Magna Carta as one of the great documents in the development of representative government. The most important provisions denied the monarch the right to tax without parliamentary consent or to imprison a freeman without just cause.

Little immediate good came of the Petition of Rights, for Charles broke its provisions and from 1629 to 1640 ruled England without calling Parliament. During this period he resorted to methods of taxation which the supporters of Parliament considered illegal. Royal taxes fell heavily upon the shoulders of the prosperous Puritan merchants and shopkeepers. In addition, Charles punished those who refused to conform to his own religious beliefs, including several Puritan leaders in the House of Commons.

Cavaliers vs. Roundheads. When Charles attempted to force his brand of High Church Anglican religion on the Presbyterian subjects of his Scottish kingdom, they promptly took up arms against their king. Faced by a hostile army and without sufficient funds to put an army of his own into the field, Charles was forced to convene Parliament.

When Parliament refused to vote any money until Charles had redressed certain grievances, Charles promptly dissolved it. But riots in England and a Scottish invasion compelled him to recall Parliament. Sensing the weakness in the king's position, Parliament immediately set to work to make its powers at least coequal with his. This session became known as the "Long Parliament" because it lasted nearly twenty years.

As the tension between the crown and Parliament increased, two bitterly antagonistic parties quickly developed: the Royalist party and the Parliamentary party.

Composed largely of the middle class and the Puritans, the members of the Parliamentary party were dubbed "Roundheads" because they wore their hair cropped short while the opposing faction wore full wigs.

The Puritans in turn were divided between Independents and Presbyterians, who differed over questions of church government but agreed in holding generally to a Calvinistic system of religion and in demanding further reductions in the political and religious prerogatives of the monarch.

The Royalist party, the "Cavaliers," was supported mainly by the landowning class, who opposed extreme Protestantism. While agreeing with the Puritans in opposing royal despotism, the Royalists were unwilling to see the monarchy stripped of all its powers. In this party there were also a substantial number of clergy and laymen who, like their monarch, not only opposed Puritanism but seemed to be pro-Catholic; they were ready to return the Anglican Church to the fold of Rome.

In the struggle which followed, there was no clear-cut geographical division of parties in England—every shire had the two contending groups. The English civil war was "a war not of classes or of districts, but of ideas. . . . The French Revolution was a war of two societies; the American Civil War was a war of two regions; but the Great Rebellion [the English civil war] was a war of two parties."[5]

Typical of the confused thinking that persisted is this statement by a Cavalier noble:

I heartily wish the King would yield to the Parliament's terms. But I have eaten his bread and served him well nigh thirty years, and I will not do so base a thing as to forsake him. I chose rather to lose my life . . . to preserve and defend those things which are against my conscience to preserve and defend.[6]

Civil war. Civil war erupted in 1642; within four years, by virtue of control of the sea, greater economic resources, superior generalship, and an alliance with the Scots, the Roundheads defeated the king's armies.

A major factor in the triumph of the Roundheads was their remarkable military leader, Oliver Cromwell. A country gentleman and a prosperous farmer, this doughty warrior had noted how poorly the Parliamentary forces fared at the outbreak of the conflict. He referred to them as mostly "old

This satiric Dutch print depicts Oliver Cromwell dissolving the Long Parliament.

decayed serving-men and tapsters." A military genius of the first order, Cromwell trained new troops, instilled into his men a sense of discipline and religious mission, and sent them into battle singing hymns. His God-fearing, irresistible force became known as Cromwell's Ironsides.

At the end of 1646 the forces opposed to the king had achieved complete victory, and he had surrendered himself into their hands. For the next two years the monarch tried to play off his enemies against each other. Charles had ample opportunity, for the victorious coalition of the English Parliament, its army, and the Scots did not know exactly what to do with victory.

The Presbyterian faction which controlled Parliament wanted to impose its own brand of religion on the nation and was prepared to persecute other Protestant sects. Furthermore, the Presbyterians were willing to deal with the king so long as he reigned as a constitutional monarch and recognized Presbyterianism. Having no use for the army, they even tried to disband it. The army was made up mainly of the Independents who wished no monarchy, wanted no state church, and were anxious to punish Charles.

Charles managed to escape from custody and made a treaty with the Scots, by which Presbyterianism would be established in England with the aid of the Scots, the army would be disbanded, and the king's royal powers and prerogatives restored. If the king did not get his way, the Scots promised to invade England. The upshot was fierce resentment in England against the king, and for a brief period army and Parliament joined ranks as the Scottish army crossed the border. But the second civil war was over almost before it started. Cromwell and his army were supreme; they scattered all opposition and then moved against Parliament. All Presbyterian members were excluded in "Pride's Purge." The remaining members, favorable to the army and the Independents, now composed what was known as the "Rump Parliament." The second casualty was King Charles, who was tried, sentenced to death, and in 1649 met his fate.

The Protectorate and Cromwell. Abolishing the House of Lords and declaring the office of king unnecessary, the House of Commons proclaimed England a commonwealth. But in 1653 the Puritan army, still distrusting Parliament, overthrew the Commonwealth and set up a new form of government, the Protectorate, in which Oliver Cromwell held the office of Lord Protector, assisted by a council and Parliament. The structure and operation of the government was based on a written constitution called The Instrument of Government. This document, one of the earliest constitutions of modern times, was to become influential in the later European constitutional movement.

Now virtual dictator of England, Cromwell endeavored to achieve a religious settlement for the nation. Amid the rivalries between Independents, Presbyterians, Royalists, Scots, and others, he had been forced to assume the role of dictator, but at heart Cromwell was a moderate, believing in religious toleration and constitutional government. Yet he was forced to rule by the weapon of the army. As Lord Protector he tried to introduce a religious system based on toleration and to bind up the wounds of the nation.

It was impossible, however, to reconcile the Independents, the Presbyterians, the High Church party, and other religious factions. The last three years of Cromwell's life were filled with disappointment and trouble. Although he did not favor it, his more extreme Puritan colleagues muzzled the press and foisted on a pleasure-loving folk hateful prohibitions which closed the theaters and stamped out wholesome as well as unwholesome popular amusements.

The Restoration. Cromwell died in 1658 amid rising discontent with his rule. One contemporary observer claimed:

. . . it was the joyfulest funeral I ever saw, for there were none that cried but dogs . . .[7]

Seemingly, Cromwell's work had been a failure; yet his firm opposition to royal despotism and his advocacy of religious toleration were priceless legacies from the kingless decade. The civil wars and the Puritan commonwealth had also generated a substantial body of liberal and democratic thought. The magniloquent Puritan poet John Milton espoused political freedom in opposition to tyranny. Arguing that men are born free, that kings are elected deputies without power except that given by their subjects, Milton maintained that a republic is "held by wisest men of all ages the noblest, the manliest, the equallest, the justest government . . . ."[8] A group known as the Levellers—made up of small merchants, farmers, and artisans, many of whom were in Cromwell's army—contended that:

The poorest he that is in England hath a life to live as the greatest he. And therefore . . . it's clear that every man that is to live under a Government ought first by his own consent to put himself under that Government."[9]

Another group, known as the Diggers, stressed the importance of a social revolution. They even went so far as to deplore the existence of private property and unequal wealth. Such groups as the Levellers and Diggers eventually died out, but the slow ferment of their ideas influenced English political life.

Ironically enough, the Puritans—champions of liberty against the Stuarts—ruled England in more autocratic fashion than had Charles I. Oliver Cromwell was succeeded as Lord Protector by his son, who found it difficult to carry on his father's work and resigned in less than a year. Many Englishmen believed that the revolution had fostered dubious political measures and had destroyed too many traditions which were part of English life. In their opinion the return of a monarch would benefit the country. But they would not welcome another James I or Charles I.

Restoration of Charles II. When, in 1660, the exiled Charles Stuart, son of the late king, returned to England as Charles II, it was evident civil war and revolution had not been in vain. Charles was restored to the throne with the explicit understanding that he should rule through Parliament. Thus the English monarchy was made responsible to a representative body, in sharp contrast to the pattern of absolutism on the Continent.

To his subjects, Charles exposed an infectious smile and a debonair attitude welcomed by a people repressed by the blue laws of the Puritan regime. At first Charles gave the impression of being little more than a royal playboy; he was dubbed as a ruler who "never said a foolish thing or did a wise one." But his manner masked his designs to make the royal power supreme and to foster Catholicism in England and ultimately bring England into the papal fold. While believing in divine right like his father, the new king was much more adroit in statesmanship. He wished to avoid the life of an exile, which he had experienced during the civil wars.

Although the Restoration had ended the Puritan Commonwealth and brought back the Stuarts, the apparatus of government had changed in certain fundamental respects. The monarchy no longer possessed arbitrary courts or the power to make laws by royal proclamation, and taxes could not be levied without the consent of Parliament. Charles II could not be so absolute as his father had been—at least in theory. In short, power was now shared between the crown and Parliament. As long as they cooperated with each other, the workings of government could be efficient and satisfactory to both.

However, the king still wielded considerable power. He could veto laws; he commanded the militia; and unless he committed a breach of law serious enough to warrant his deposition, Parliament had no weapon other than its control of the national pocketbook to compel him to do its will.

Behind the backs of his anti-French subjects, the king in 1670 negotiated a secret treaty with Louis XIV of France—the Treaty of Dover. In return for an annual subsidy from the French government which made him financially independent of Parliament, Charles agreed to become a Catholic, make England a Catholic nation, and support Louis in his wars against Holland. This agreement was one of the most scandalous actions ever committed by an English monarch. After Charles had collected a sub-

Portrait of Charles II

stantial sum from Louis (see p. 47), he had the effrontery to persuade Parliament to grant him money for waging war against the French king, his secret ally. No ruler has ever been able to give a better performance of running with the hare and hunting with the hounds and making everyone like it.

To partially carry out his shady bargain with Louis, Charles in 1672 suspended by royal command the operation of laws directed against English Catholics. As the English had come to associate Catholicism with the menace of strong foreign foes and with despotic government, a political crisis resulted. One year later Parliament passed the Test Act, which excluded all Catholics from public office and attempted unsuccessfully to exclude James, a stanch Catholic, from succeeding to the throne upon the death of his brother Charles.

Monarch vs. Parliament. Two significant consequences of the controversy between Charles and Parliament were notable. The first was the gradual rise of political parties as we define these groups today. To thwart Charles' pro-Catholic tendencies, members of the House of Commons formed the Green Ribbon Club with headquarters at a London tavern. In time the club became the Whig party, which stood for the supremacy of Parliament, Protestantism, and the interests of the business classes. The Whig motto was "life, liberty, and property." In opposition, the Tory party, supported by the landed gentry, was organized. The members of this group championed "the king, the church, and the land." Although factional rivalries have existed in all times and in many places, England is considered the home of modern political parties. Whig and Tory organization and tactics have been imitated in free countries the world over.

The second important consequence of the conflict between king and Parliament was the passage of the Habeas Corpus Act in 1679. This law was another step as important in the reformation of the English legal system as the abolition of the secret and oppressive Court of the Star Chamber thirty-five years before. Anyone believing himself unjustly imprisoned could obtain a writ of *habeas corpus,* which compelled the government to explain why he had lost his liberty. Later this safeguard against arbitrary imprisonment became part of the Constitution of the United States.

James II antagonizes Parliament. In the latter part of his reign, Charles managed to outmaneuver Parliament and to set up, in effect, a royal despotism. When Charles II died in 1685 and his brother James ascended the throne, the cause of popular liberty seemed in danger of extinction.

James II was "as tactless as the first, without the latter's erudition; as stubborn as his father, the first Charles, with none of his more attractive qualities; while in politics he was a fool as compared with his older brother."[10] At the outset of his reign, James II tried to force Parliament to repeal the Test and Habeas Corpus acts. By royal order in 1687 he suspended all laws against Catholics; he intimidated the courts and attempted to appoint Catholics to office.

In the face of such unpopular actions the English set aside all factional rivalries and determined to remove James from the throne. An invitation from both Whigs and Tories was extended to William of Orange, ruler of the Dutch, to assume the English crown. This choice was dictated by two factors: William was considered the champion of Protestantism in Europe, and he was the husband of Mary, the older daughter of James II and the Protestant next in line to the throne. In November 1688, William set sail for England and landed without opposition. The discouraged James, forsaken by his army, escaped to France, and in December 1688 William entered London.

The Bill of Rights. Parliament offered the crown to William and Mary as joint sovereigns—an offer contingent on their acceptance of a declaration of rights, later enacted as the Bill of Rights. Rivaling the Magna Carta in importance, this declaration provided (1) the king was not to suspend the operation of laws; (2) no money was to be levied without consent of Parliament; (3) freedom of speech in Parliament was to be assured; (4) subjects were to have the right of petition and were also to be free of excessive fines, bail, and cruel punishment; (5) the king was to be a Protestant; and (6) sessions of Parliament were to be held frequently. These provisions have exercised a tremendous influence on the development of constitutional government. Many clauses of the Bill of Rights were embodied in the new state constitutions in America after 1776; and the first ten amendments to the Constitution of the United States, as well as the French Declaration of the Rights of Man (1789) show their debt to the English declaration of 1688.

Results of the Glorious Revolution. The events which placed William and Mary on the English throne are referred to by Englishmen as the Glorious, or Bloodless, Revolution. Without bloodshed Parliament had deposed the old line of kings and laid down the conditions under which future English sovereigns were to rule. In England, the theory of divine right was discredited; Par-

King William III sealed the success of the Glorious Revolution by defeating James II at the battle of Boyne in July 1690.

liament was now the dominant agency in government.

In foreign affairs the events of 1688 resulted in a switch from the pro-French policy of Charles II and James II. Acting as the champion of Protestantism on the Continent, William used England's resources to check the designs of Louis XIV. In addition, Parliament was more willing to vote money for foreign wars since it now had a strong voice in the conduct and planning of foreign policy. Thus the use of English power in international affairs increased.

The Glorious Revolution was consolidated by other actions supplementing the Bill of Rights. By the Toleration Act of 1689, Protestants outside the established Church of England were given the right of public worship, though full political privileges were not secured by them until early in the nineteenth century. In 1693 Parliament refused to pass the customary licensing act which former governments had used to muzzle the press. Given freedom of expression, the press thus became an increasingly important aid to representative government. Other acts following the Bill of Rights made judges irremovable and led to a more independent judiciary; large standing armies, the bugaboo of

liberty, were not to be maintained in peacetime without the consent of Parliament.

Significant as they were, the achievements of the Glorious Revolution were limited in scope. In essence the revolution was political; it did nothing to eliminate many social and economic abuses existing in England. The Bill of Rights, the Toleration Act, and subsequent legislation guaranteed certain fundamental rights to the common people, but the nation was now governed by a small, wealthy minority of merchants and gentry. However, the development of such concepts as popular sovereignty and the right of revolution which were established in England by the Glorious Revolution were later to have a profound influence on the world's governments and peoples.

Genesis of the cabinet. At the time of the Glorious Revolution, cabinet government was unknown. The power of the British monarch was limited; he could not maintain a standing army without Parliament's consent nor did he possess any lawmaking powers. Thus, in the last analysis, Parliament was supreme; but this supremacy could only be exercised in case of dire necessity by the impeachment of the king's ministers or the removal of the king himself.

First to reign in conjunction with Parliament after the Glorious Revolution was William III (1689-1702). William chose his own ministers, controlled their policies, and did not concern himself with Parliament's approval of this state of affairs. Because Parliament and the king agreed on fundamentals, however, a clash did not arise. Politics in England were now controlled by an oligarchy of great landed nobles and country squires plus wealthy commercial and banking families often related to the nobility. The loyalties of these groups were divided between two parties: the Tories and the Whigs. Although the parties quarreled about particular issues, they usually agreed on broad political principles.

During William's reign the King's Council, a body made up of the great officers of state, tended increasingly to direct the affairs of state. This body, in origin a permanent committee of the ancient *curia regis*, was to become the cabinet. The king tried to select his ministers from both the Whig and Tory parties, but he soon discovered that this situation involved a great deal of wrangling between the House of Commons and himself. Only when all the ministers in the Council were of the same party as the majority in Commons did the government function smoothly. For the time being, however, decisions were still frequently made by the monarch, who usually attended Council meetings. By 1714, at the end of the reign of William's successor, Queen Anne, the cabinet—as it was now known—was a distinct policy-making body.

George I and George II. With the accession in 1714 of the Hanoverian dynasty from the German state of Hanover, the creative period of cabinet government began. When the first Hanoverian, George I, came to the English throne, he was over fifty years old and was thoroughly German in speech, habits, and interests. He so remained and could never converse with his English chief minister in anything more convenient than poor Latin. His only interest in England was that its resources strengthened his hand in the game of petty politics among the small German states surrounding Hanover.

Under the leadership of Robert Walpole, the cabinet met with the prime minister instead of with the king, as had previously been the rule. Here, Walpole presides at a cabinet meeting.

Not only was George a foreigner; he was also unfit for kingship anywhere. Lord Chesterfield has given us a most unflattering portrait:

George the First was an honest, dull, German gentleman, as unfit as unwilling to act the part of king. . . . Lazy and inactive, even in his pleasures, which were . . . lowly sensual, he was coolly intrepid and indolently benevolent. . . . Even his mistress . . . with whom he passed most of his time, and who had all influence over him, was very little above an idiot.[11]

More English than his father but not much of an improvement as king was George II, whose only claim to fame was that he was the last English monarch to lead his troops on the field of battle. Fortunately for English constitutional development, George's queen was a devoted friend of the prime minister, and through her influence the king was easily managed.

Walpole: first prime minister. The outstanding statesman during the reign of the two Georges was Robert Walpole, who served from 1721 to 1742 as leader of the Whig Party and the House of Commons and real head of the government. In effect, he was the first prime minister.

Walpole established the principle that the entire cabinet had to act as the single administrative instrument of the House majority and that cabinet unanimity was a necessity. If any member refused to support the official policy, he had to resign.

A remarkably successful politician, Walpole managed the House adroitly, maintaining his majority by bribery and passing out lucrative favors. Advocating a program of peace and prosperity, he concentrated on sound economic policy. He cleared away the mess left by the collapse of the South Sea Bubble, encouraged the building of a large merchant marine, and tried to organize the levying of customs into a sound system.

Ironically, Walpole the pacifist went down to political defeat through the fortunes of war. He was pushed reluctantly into the War of Jenkins' Ear and, when the war went badly, he lost his majority in the Commons and resigned. This act confirmed the principle that the executive branch of government —in theory the king but in practice the prime minister—must resign when its policies are no longer supported in the Commons.

After the fall of Robert Walpole, the next dominating figure in British politics was William Pitt the Elder (1708-1778), the master of global war who directed the British war effort in the Seven Years' War. After a brief absence from public life, Pitt again became head of the government in 1766. He was an archfoe of corruption and was determined to cleanse British politics. Unfortunately, his health steadily declined, and his prestige and influence were cleverly reduced by a new power in politics. This was, surprisingly, the king!

Pretensions of George III. George III, who had come to the throne in 1760 as a mere youth of twenty-two, had very definite ideas of his role in government. Unlike his two predecessors, he had no use for his ancestral home of Hanover; he was an Englishman through and through. George III was determined to restore to the crown the power and stature lost since the days of William III. In short, his object was to destroy the cabinet system. This is not to say that he aspired to be a tyrant or to rule as a divine-right monarch. Rather, he wished to rule as a "Patriot King," above political parties and, of course, in accordance with his own ideas.

William Pitt believed he could protect liberty's cause at home and in the colonies, checking the king and his cohorts when necessary. But two years after he became prime minister in 1766, the aging statesman suffered a physical and mental collapse and the way was clear for the personal rule of George III. It took George only a few years to destroy the power of the Whigs and to secure control of Parliament. By 1770 all effective opposition to the king had been swept away, for George had filled the Commons with supporters known as the "King's Friends," bought by royal favors and pensions. The Tory party, dominated by the sycophants of the king, now had a commanding majority; the Whigs were an impotent opposition. Lord North, the unquestioning servant of the king, was prime minister, and for twelve fateful years, from 1770 to 1782, George III had his own way. In this period the successful war for independence of Great Britain's thirteen North American colonies took place.

Restoration of cabinet government. The American Revolution had profound consequences in Britain. The disaster to British arms in America dealt the king's policies and methods a crushing blow. In a sense, by gaining their liberty, the Americans helped the Britons to gain theirs. In 1780 a majority in the House of Commons voted the resolution "that the influence of the crown has increased, is increasing, and ought to be diminished."[12] By 1782 George III had to dismiss Lord North and employ ministers who were willing to make concessions to public opinion.

With the king in disrepute, the Whigs came back into power, but internal feuds and jealousies limited their term of leadership to a scant three months. At this critical juncture, George III called the son of the great war leader William Pitt to be prime minister. Only twenty-four, the new leader was greeted by his rivals with jibes and epithets. His cabinet was dubbed "a set of children playing at ministers." Undoubtedly

King George III of England

the king expected to control the youthful statesman, but he more than met his match. Appointed prime minister in 1788, the younger Pitt won a resounding victory in an election held the next year. A new Tory party, reinvigorated by his leadership, took firm control of the affairs of state and succeeded in keeping the Whigs out of office for over fifty years.

Pitt quickly gathered the reins of government into his capable hands. The king was no longer consulted on the day-to-day details of government and only occasionally tried to intervene. His increasing mental instability and final insanity definitely removed royal influence from governmental affairs. The prime minister and his cabinet colleagues now assumed control.

From the Glorious Revolution until another great peaceful revolution in 1832, England was the perfect example of Aristocratic Liberalism. Ingrained in this English system was a habit of political thought that gave room for reform to take place very gradually, until ultimately the narrow oligarchical

liberalism of the late seventeenth century broadened into the full democracy of the late nineteenth century.

THE RISE OF RUSSIA

Russia: "the last born child of European civilization." Because of its lack of good seaports and the wretched condition of its overland routes, Russia had been for centuries a backward, isolated land. Untouched by the Renaissance and the Reformation, Russia was a world apart from western Europe at the beginning of the seventeenth century.

Ivan the Great and Ivan the Terrible had established Russia as a potentially great power at the end of the Middle Ages (see Chapters 14 and 17, Volume I). The overlordship of the alien Tatar invaders had been overthrown, the government centralized, and expansion initiated northwest to the Baltic, east toward the far Pacific, and south toward the Black Sea. In fact, the story of modern Russia is largely concerned with this epoch of expansion as the Russian people spread out over the vast areas of steppe, tundra, and desert. After the death of Ivan the Terrible in 1584, progress was interrupted. Finally, in 1613, the period of confusion and civil war known as the Time of Trouble ended when representatives of fifty cities met in a national assembly and elected Michael Romanov to the throne. The Romanovs continued to rule until 1917.

Peter the Great and his objectives for Russia. One of the greatest figures in Russian history became tsar in 1682 and soon showed himself to be master of his unruly state. Peter had grown up without benefit of discipline or formal education, and all his life he remained a cruel vulgar barbarian.

Peter's attributes included an excellent mind and such great stores of energy that his contemporaries contended that "he works harder than any *muzhik* [peasant]." A modern historian has added that Peter "was like a moving thunderbolt."[13] Having a sound appreciation of what was essential for Russian progress, Peter pursued three basic policies during his long reign: (1) to Europeanize his people, (2) to obtain an outlet, "a window on the sea," and (3) to make the power of the tsar absolute.

Peter's Grand Embassy. Peter first turned his attention to the Turks, who blocked Russia's way to the Black Sea. In 1695 and 1696, expeditions were sent against Azov, the Turkish fortress commanding the entrance to the Black Sea. After Azov was captured, Peter organized a Grand Embassy to visit the capitals of western Europe. The object of his mission was twofold: to secure allies for an all-out attack against the Turks and to observe the most advanced European methods of government, education, trade, and industry. Traveling as plain Peter Mikhailov, Tsar Peter left Russia with the members of the mission in 1697 and visited the bustling states along the Baltic and North Sea coasts. He toured factories, medical centers, picture galleries, and business offices and astonished the rulers of western Europe by his curiosity as well as by his carousing and pranks. In Holland, Peter worked as a common ship carpenter in order to learn Dutch methods of shipbuilding at first hand. When the Russian mission visited England, Peter interested himself particularly in English shipbuilding and observed the British fleet on maneuvers. Peter and his boisterous companions left in a shambles an admiral s home which had been put at their disposal.

On his return to Russia, Peter learned that his palace guards had revolted. He hurried back to Moscow and crushed the rebellion with savage cruelty. In little more than a month, one thousand of his subjects were put to death. Peter himself took a leading part in the decapitations.

Although Peter learned a great deal from his European trip, he failed to create an aggressive alliance against the Turks. The ambitions of Austria against the Ottoman empire coincided with Peter's, but Austria had just thrust the Turks out of Hungary and had no desire to resume fighting. Peter had to rest content with the possession of the Black Sea port, Azov, and direct his energies elsewhere.

The Great Northern War. In 1700 the Swedish empire controlled most of the Baltic shores. Peter's ambitions for a "window on the sea" led him in 1699 to make a secret alliance with Poland and Denmark against Sweden. Peter hoped to take advantage of the youth and inexperience of Charles XII of Sweden, a young king of eighteen. Without waiting to be attacked, however, the youthful Charles began the Great Northern War with an invasion of Denmark and astounded the allies by quickly bringing the Danes to their knees. Led by its youthful sovereign, dubbed the Swedish Meteor, the Swedish army next landed at the other end of the Baltic and crushed Peter's army at Narva. Instead of delivering a decisive blow to Russia, Charles turned to Poland and wasted Swedish military strength in six years of campaigning there.

Undismayed by his early defeats, Peter the Great wrote in his *Journal* after Narva: "I know very well that the Swedes will have the advantage of us for a considerable time; but they will teach us at length to beat them." So confident was Peter of ultimate success that in 1703 he laid the foundations of St. Petersburg, his new Russian capital, on a Baltic shore captured from Sweden.

In 1708 Charles XII finally invaded Russia and pushed toward Moscow. Peter used the same tactics that were to be employed later with such devastating effect against Napoleon when he invaded the country of the tsars. Refusing to engage in a decisive battle, Peter allowed the rigors of winter to weaken his antagonist. By 1709 Charles' army had dwindled to a small force of men. Against his officers' advice, the Swedish king met a superior Russian force at Poltava, and his army was annihilated. Following the victory, Peter declared: "Now by God's help are the foundations of St. Petersburg securely laid for all time." He then entertained some captured Swedish officers, whom he greeted with the toast: "I drink to my teachers in the art of war."

For the next few years Charles of Sweden continued to harass the tsar by inducing the

A contemporary woodcut by a Russian artist lampoons the cutting off of beards in Russia following Peter the Great's decree.

Turkish sultan to declare war on Russia. Although Turkish victories forced Peter to surrender Azov, Sweden was increasingly hard pressed by enemies, which now included Denmark, Poland, Prussia, Saxony, and Hanover, as well as Russia. In 1718 the Swedish king was killed, but the Great Northern War continued until 1721, when Sweden sued for peace with the last of its enemies, Russia. The conclusion of the Great Northern War marked the end of Sweden as a first-class power and cost it nearly all of its empire along the Baltic coast. By the peace settlement, Russia obtained an important strip of coastline bordering the Gulf of Finland. Thus Peter secured one of his fundamental objectives—access to the sea. At tremendous cost in treasure and human life, St. Petersburg was built as a "window" on the Baltic. By the end of the eighteenth century, it was an imposing imperial capital of palaces, churches, parks, and statues.

Attempts to westernize Russia. After his gay but profitable mission in Europe, Peter resolved to change the age-old customs of his people in spite of their own opinions and desires. He instructed his male subjects to cut off their long beards, encouraged the adoption of European breeches for male attire instead of the flowing oriental robes which many men wore, and attempted to end the seclusion of women. Crude as he was in many ways, Peter endeavored to introduce the manners of polite European society into his country. Whereas former tsars had punished men for smoking by cutting off the noses of offenders, Peter encouraged the use of tobacco and invited husbands and wives among his nobility to social evenings where they were to engage in conversation and dancing. The "Assemblies," as they were called, were not successful; the sexes refused to mix, and frequently the men were carried home drunk.

Responsible for the revision and simplification of the old Russian alphabet, Peter also established printing presses, promoted the study of foreign languages, sent many young men to western Europe to study, and started new schools for advanced training in engineering, navigation, and accounting. In the economic field he was a stanch mercantilist who sought to make his country as nearly self-sufficient as possible. He has been called "the father of Russian industry," although, in fact, previous rulers also had taken active measures to stimulate industry. Agriculture was improved by the introduction of better tools, selected seeds, and new breeds of cattle.

Absolutism of Peter the Great. Peter the Great accelerated the molding of Russia into an absolutist state. All vestiges of local self-government were removed; and the central government was kept completely subordinate to the will of the tsar. The status of a noble was made to depend more upon service to the state and the tsar and less upon inherited family rank and position. The gentry were compelled to prepare their sons for governmental service by giving them a good education, and thus a powerful hierarchy of officials recruited from the aristocratic families served the government of the tsar.

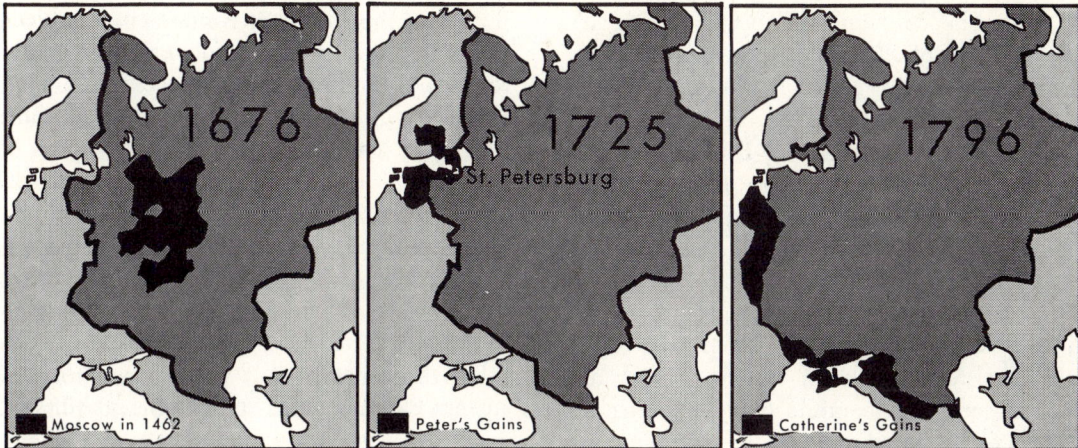

The Church was made a tool of the state. No successor was appointed for the patriarch who died in 1700. Later, the office of patriarch was abolished and a Holy Synod of bishops set up to govern the Church. The new body was dominated by a layman member called the procurator, who represented the tsar. For the next two hundred years the Church served as one of the most powerful agents and supporters of Russian absolutism.

Peter's achievement. It is difficult to assess the permanent effects of Peter the Great on Russian history. His many brutalities left an ugly stain on the record of his reign. A climax was reached when Peter executed his own son. Describing the terror which gripped St. Petersburg, a contemporary observed:

There have been so many accusations in the town, that it seems like a place of disaster; we all live in a sort of public infection, everyone is either an accuser or an accused person.[14]

This quotation has a curiously modern ring as though it might have been written about Soviet Russia during the purge of political leaders in the 1930's.

Some of Peter's reforms, such as the establishment of new industries, failed shortly after his death. In addition, his attempts to Europeanize his people were telescoped into a period so brief that they could not have many lasting effects, and his aggressive program of westernization provoked much hostility and reaction even during his reign. Peter's new ideas and policies did nothing to alleviate the arduous lot of the Russian peasants. However, Peter did achieve two of his objectives. He made Russia a great military power by eliminating Sweden as the dominant force in the Baltic, and he strengthened the autocratic tradition of Ivan the Great and Ivan the Terrible so that in Peter's reign absolutism became firmly established in Russia. Worn out from his exertions in politics and his excesses in drinking and brawling, Peter died in 1725 at the early age of fifty-three.

Catherine the Great. Catherine, also called the Great, was a German princess who married the Russian heir to the crown. Finding him half insane—"a moronic booby"—Catherine tacitly consented to his murder shortly after he had ascended the throne as Peter III. It was announced that he died of "apoplexy," and in 1762 she became tsarina. This brilliant and unscrupulous monarch waged war successfully against the Ottoman empire and made Russia the primary power on the Black Sea. By plotting with the ruling monarchs of Austria and Prussia, she secured three successive slices of Polish territory and pushed the Russian frontier westward.

Catherine served both her own interests and those of the Russian state with craft, shrewd diplomacy, and utter lack of conscience. She imitated the best features of the culture of Versailles and equaled its vices. In her own private life, she was frankly immoral, and stories of her misconduct were common all over Europe. Just as the mistresses of Louis xiv graced the French court, so the male favorites of Catherine were openly paraded in her palaces.

The Ideological Schism. In this period of Russian history, a conflict emerged which, from Peter's reign down to the present time, has persistently colored much of Russian thought and has complicated the plans of statesmen: What should the Russian destiny be? To be western, remain eastern, or develop a blend of both cultures? Peter did not answer this question, for although he introduced western science and technology, he strengthened the old despotic spirit of Russia, often brutal and primitive. The split between western and eastern tendencies—called the Ideological Schism—has still not been reconciled in the minds of twentieth-century Russians.

THE EMERGENCE OF PRUSSIA

Ingredients of the Prussian state. If the rise of Russia was remarkable, the development of Prussia was even more amazing. History has scarcely a parallel example of the manner in which one royal house, the Hohenzollern, expanded its territory and exalted its power by fair means or foul.

The history of the making of the Prussian state concerns largely the uniting of three small, separated territories: the electorate of Brandenburg, the duchy of East Prussia, and the Cleves-Mark lands on the lower Rhine.

With its efficient governmental institutions, its system of paternal despotism, and its smooth-working bureaucracy, Brandenburg was the nucleus of the Prussian state. East Prussia, the land of the Teutonic Knights, provided a landed nobility, the Junkers, well-trained in the arts of war. The Cleves-Mark territories were relatively unimportant until the Industrial Revolution of the early nineteenth century made the Ruhr valley a great industrial center.

Rise of the House of Hohenzollern. In the eleventh century the Hohenzollerns were relatively unimportant nobles occupying a castle on the heights of Zollern in south Germany. Shortly after 1400 the House of Hohenzollern made an important advance up the ladder of success. One of its members, Frederick Hohenzollern, supported the German emperor Sigismund in a war against the Turks and helped crush a rebellion against his lord; for his reward he was made ruler—the elector—of a sizable territory in eastern Germany, the Mark of Brandenburg.

During the Protestant Revolt of the sixteenth century, the Hohenzollern elector of Brandenburg adopted Lutheranism. As a result his house gained wealth by seizing lands and properties of the old Church. The elector also increased his authority by becoming the head of the new church in Brandenburg. He was very careful, however, not to become involved in the Religious Wars and waste his resources.

In the first decades of the seventeenth century, the Hohenzollerns made further gains in territory, the most important being the acquisition of East Prussia from the Teutonic Knights. In the thirteenth century, the Knights had shifted from their original purpose of crusading in the Holy Land and had conquered the southern shore of the Baltic from the Vistula to the Gulf of Finland. For about two hundred years they enjoyed power and prosperity, but in the fifteenth century they were crushed by Poland. In 1466 they ceded West Prussia to the conqueror and kept East Prussia as a fief of the Polish king. Searching for a strong leader, the Knights turned to the House of Hohenzollern and in 1511 elected Albert Hohenzollern as their grand master. Later the order of Teutonic Knights was dissolved, and Albert became the hereditary duke of Prussia, still, however, a vassal of the king of Poland. In 1618, when the duke of Prussia died without immediate heirs, the duchy passed to the elector of Brandenburg.

Just four years before this windfall, the elector had secured the lands of Cleves, Mark, and Ravensberg on the lower Rhine.

Thus by the early seventeenth century, the Hohenzollerns held territory as far east as the Niemen River and as far west as the Rhine, with Brandenburg located in the center. The policy of future electors was to bridge the gap between their detached lands and to forge a united state.

Frederick William, the Great Elector. The Thirty Years' War affected the fortunes of most German states and threatened the Hohenzollerns with ruin. Brandenburg remained neutral in the first stages of the war, but when Gustavus Adolphus of Sweden intervened, he forced the elector to join the Protestant side. After Gustavus' death the elector sued for peace, but peace did not improve Brandenburg's precarious position. Ignoring the elector's withdrawal from the hostilities, the Swedes stationed troops in Brandenburg while Poland took over most of East Prussia.

It was Frederick William, reigning from 1640 to 1688 and known as the Great Elector, who remedied this situation. Educated in Holland, he was impressed by the efficiency and industry of the Dutch. After his return to Berlin in 1640, he straightway made a truce with the Swedes, settled matters to his satisfaction with the Poles in East Prussia, and added to his prestige by marrying the daughter of the chief executive of Holland. By securing the diplomatic support of Holland and France and by building up a strong army, he made his position so strong that in 1648, when the Thirty Years' War ended in the Peace of Westphalia, Brandenburg was considered the most important Protestant state in Germany.

In 1655 war broke out between Sweden and Poland. In this conflict Frederick William had three choices: to remain neutral, to become the ally of Sweden, or to ally himself with the Poles. He did not adopt any one of these courses consistently but followed all three, one after the other. First he remained neutral. Then in 1656 he joined the Swedes. (This was the first time that troops from all the scattered parts of the Hohenzollern realm fought together as a single army.) After Poland had been weakened considerably, Frederick William deserted the Swedes and joined forces with the Poles on condition that Poland's overlordship over East Prussia would be terminated. The war ended in 1660, and one of the provisions of the peace settlement acknowledged the Great Elector's full sovereignty over East Prussia.

Frederick William also accomplished much in fields other than politics. Immigrants were brought into the country—particularly Dutch farmers, who were models of diligence and economy with their knowledge of land drainage, their spick-and-span dairy farms, and their productive potato fields. After Louis XIV revoked the Edict of Nantes, many Huguenots also emigrated to Brandenburg.

The Great Elector's interest in sea power and commercial development led to the establishment of a board of trade and an admiralty. He also chartered the Brandenburg African Trading Company and founded a fort called Great Fredericksburg on the west African coast. After his death, however, interest in colonial projects declined and was not revived until the middle of the nineteenth century.

Frederick, "King in Prussia." The Great Elector's successor, another Frederick, who reigned from 1688 to 1713, succeeded in changing his title from elector to king. As the vassal of the Holy Roman emperor, Frederick required the emperor's permission before making any change in title. When the War of the Spanish Succession began, the emperor needed both men and money, and Frederick saw his opportunity. In return for royal rank, he promised to cancel an old debt owed him by the emperor and to furnish him ten thousand soldiers. The offer accepted, a message was addressed to Frederick:

Most Serene Elector, and *soon, soon*, to be Most Mighty King.[15]

The exact wording of Frederick's new title was a ticklish problem. The title "King of Brandenburg" would involve difficulties of precedence and status with other states

1415

1624

1740

1797

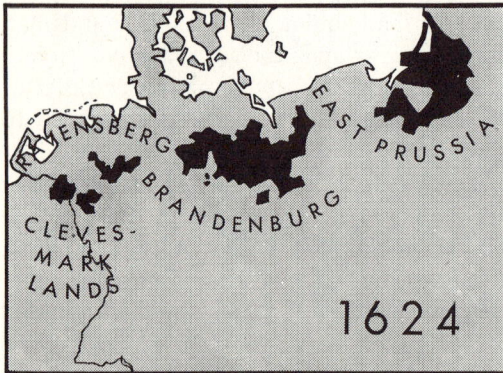

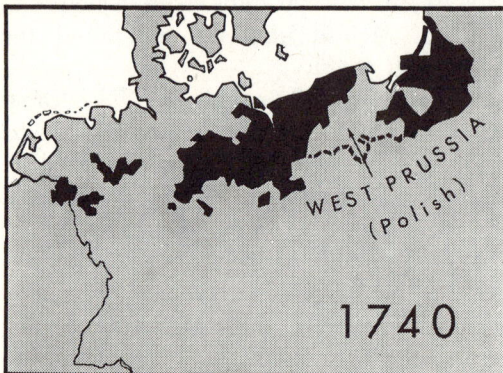

in the empire. Frederick's German neighbors would hardly recognize him as "His Majesty." "King of Prussia" would not do either, because Poland was sovereign over part of this territory—West Prussia. It was agreed, therefore, that the title should be "King in Prussia."

The coronation was celebrated in Königsberg, the capital of East Prussia, where, with much pomp and great rejoicing, Frederick was acclaimed King Frederick I in 1701. The next important acknowledgment of the House of Hohenzollern's rise to a position of leadership in Europe came when the European powers recognized the new title of the Prussian king in the Treaty of Utrecht (1713).

Prussia, a military state. By the opening of the eighteenth century, Brandenburg (or Prussia, as the combined lands of the Hohenzollerns now came to be called) had almost reached a position where it could embark on more ambitious and aggressive programs of expansion. The discipline and strength of another sovereign was necessary, however, before this new phase in Prussian history could begin.

It was King Frederick I's successor, Frederick William I, who marshaled the resources of his state to create a superb fighting machine during his reign (1713-1740). As his contemporaries put it:

Prussia is not a State which possesses an army, but an army which possesses a State.[16]

Firmly believing that the destiny of Prussia lay with its army, the king scoffed at his advisers who felt that prestige and territory could be secured for Prussia by diplomacy. In 1713 the Prussian army stood at 38,000 men; at the end of the reign of Frederick William I in 1740, its strength was 83,000— already in size the fourth army in Europe and without a doubt the most efficient.

King Frederick William was more than just a confirmed militarist. He created an all-powerful and efficient central government, a trained and obedient civil service, and a docile citizenry, who were told by their crusty king: "No reasoning, obey orders." Woe to any subject who was thought to be lazy or frivolous! Frederick William's jaunts around Berlin were dubbed *tours de baton* because he would stop to cane anyone he caught frittering away his time.

No one in his realm worked harder than the king, who toiled from early morning to late evening as the servant of the state and who directed every minute detail of administration. For example, when the supreme government board (the General Directory) was established, Frederick William drew up exact, detailed directions. It was provided that the board should meet in the summer at seven in the morning, in the winter at eight. No member was to leave the board until all work was done, and only if the session lasted until 2 P.M. were the members to be given "four good dishes" of food. Only half of the members could eat at one time; the others had to remain at work.

Thus the army and the bureaucracy (the civil service) formed the two main pillars of the Prussian state—a condition which remained true down to modern times. The bulk of political functions in Prussia were carried out by well-trained, efficient civil servants dedicated to the state.

Training of Prince Frederick. The frugal, stern, and militaristic Frederick William demanded implicit obedience from his own children as well as from his subjects. With high hopes for his eldest son, Frederick, the king carefully regulated all of the prince's activities—his political, religious, and social training, his dress, and his personal habits.

A sensitive youth, the young Prince Frederick had little of his father's enthusiasm for things military and intensely disliked the king's barracks-like discipline. To his father, Prince Frederick was "a piper and poetaster" because he spent too much time with music and poetry. Rebelling against the Spartan training, which included frequent canings, Prince Frederick ran away with two young friends. Upon their capture, one of his accomplices, his closest friend, was beheaded before Frederick's eyes, and the young prince was then subjected to years of the severest discipline.

Frederick the Great of Prussia

Later, Frederick adopted his father's point of view and became thoroughly militaristic and cynical. King Frederick William was delighted and in the last years of his reign permitted his son to live on a pleasant estate near Berlin. There the prince wrote for his own amusement, read omnivorously, corresponded with intellectuals all over Europe, and played his flute.

Prussia becomes a European power. Frederick William I has well been dubbed "the Potsdam Führer," for it was through this ruler, with his maxims of "order, discipline, and work" and "Salvation belongs to the Lord, everything else is my business," that Germany developed its tradition of subordination to the state and blind confidence in the military point of view.

As the old king neared his last days he is supposed to have said: "O my God, I die content, since I have so worthy a son and successor." Frederick William was correct; his son was eventually to become the greatest soldier of his day and a master of Machiavellian diplomacy. Prince Frederick, who became King Frederick II in 1740 and was known later as Frederick the Great, brought Prussia fully into the arena of European politics (see p. 51). He also continued his father's work of building a powerful Prussian state at home. The remarkable rise of Prussia is illustrated by the chart below:

THE RISE OF PRUSSIA

	1648	1740	1786
Population	750,000	2,500,000	5,000,000
Army	8,000	83,000	200,000
Annual revenue in thaler	?	7,000,000	19,000,000
Stored treasure in thaler	0	8,000,000	51,000,000

Adapted from S. B. Fay, *The Rise of Brandenburg-Prussia to 1786* (New York: Henry Holt and Co., Inc., 1937), p. 141.

DYNASTIC WAR AND THE

DUEL FOR WORLD EMPIRE

Dynamics of the competitive state system. Although the immediate cause and the early stage of the Thirty Years' War, ended by the Peace of Westphalia (1648), had a religious emphasis, the conflict had other complications. In part it was a civil war in the Germanies to prevent the extension of imperial control by the Hapsburg emperors at the expense of the independent rights of the other German states, large and small. Spain became involved because its Hapsburg rulers were bound by family ties to the interests of their Austrian cousins. The ties were stronger because, since the English defeat of Spain on the seas, the principal supply route over which reinforcements were sent to Spanish forces in the Netherlands was by way of northern Italy, Austria, and the Rhine Valley. Ultimately Spanish control of the Netherlands helped provoke open French intervention. The Dutch, in their war for independence, fought against Spain not only to free themselves from political and religious tyranny but also to promote their commerce

and develop their colonies. Richelieu, whose aim was to establish French hegemony in Europe, brought France into the war on the side of the German Protestants in their successful struggle against the Catholic Hapsburgs of Austria and Spain, though he was a cardinal of the Roman Catholic Church. The last phase of the war was an open dynastic struggle between the Bourbons and the Hapsburgs.

More significant than the specific results of the Thirty Years' War was the implacable fact that the dynastic national state had emerged to stay. A political entity completely independent and a law unto itself, the dynamic and expansive national state was ready to spring upon any weaker rival. Aggressive monarchs usually justified their actions by claiming that they were protecting their subjects and ensuring the general welfare. But in reality the strife of states and kings stemmed from the greed for power, riches, and glory.

Pattern of strong and weak nations. The dynamic and aggressive powers of Europe were France, England, Russia, and Prussia. Others were stagnant, on the verge of decline, or had fallen far below their former powerful role. Sweden controlled the Baltic and substantial portions of the north German coast in the latter part of the seventeenth century. This nation's endeavors to maintain its empire were bound to fail because it did not possess either the population or the economic resources sufficient to support its conquests. Holland was in a similar position. Following the Dutch victory over Spain in the mid-seventeenth century and the acquisition of the East Indies, this tiny land with its flourishing commerce had become a major power in world affairs. But it would soon lose commercial and naval leadership to England. Spain, which had been the greatest power in the western world during the sixteenth century, was far along in its decline.

In the heart of Europe lay two great states which were lapsing into impotence. One was the Ottoman empire; its vast domains began just short of Vienna and extended all through the Balkan Peninsula and along the north shore of the Black Sea, as well as through western Asia and along the northern coast of Africa. Europeans no longer dreaded the redoubtable Turk; the empire of the Ottomans would soon find itself caught in a net of intrigue woven by Russia and Austria. North of the Balkans was Poland, protected by no natural boundaries, its resources neglected, and its government ineffectual. In the latter part of the eighteenth century, Poland would become the most notable victim of aggression by more powerful states.

A third region which was tempting to an aggressor was the Holy Roman Empire, a loose, polyglot collection of over two hundred states, which (before the Thirty Years' War) had been nominally under the control of the Austrian Hapsburgs. The Hapsburgs' hopes of integrating their empire had been shattered by the long struggle. In the Germanies, a multiplicity of small states existed. All were free agents owing allegiance to no one. Within this broken hulk of an empire, there was no imperial army and no central revenue or treasury; and the Diet, or imperial assembly, had no effective authority. Austria, itself a peculiar combination of lands under direct Hapsburg rule, was sometimes weak and vulnerable but more often showed itself to be strong and capable of holding its own in the competitive state system. Austria continued to dominate large areas of Italy, a land fragmented into petty city-states whose people did not yet possess any feelings of national unity.

France threatens the balance of power. Certainly the foremost example of aggrandizement by dynastic states was the policy of Louis XIV in France during the latter half of the seventeenth century. Emboldened by the knowledge that France possessed the strongest army in existence and the most capable generals of the age, Louis embarked on a series of wars to attain for France its "natural boundaries" by extending French territory northward at the expense of the Spanish Netherlands and eastward to the banks of the Rhine. Although a potential danger did exist because of the absence in these areas of such excellent geographical

barriers as France possessed on the Alpine and Pyrenean frontiers, Louis' chief motive was not security for France but prestige for the monarchy.

In 1667, French armies marched into the Spanish Netherlands (modern-day Belgium), and Louis prepared to annex this region to France. The Dutch, alarmed by Louis' easy conquest at their very doorstep, formed a coalition of European powers, and Louis was forced to abandon his plans temporarily. Irritated at the interference with his designs, Louis bought off the allies of the Dutch—England and Sweden—with French gold and in 1672 declared war on Holland. The Dutch, attacked by France and plagued by internal disorders, were in desperate straits. Then William of Orange (great-grandson of William the Silent who had led the revolt against Spanish tyranny in the previous century) rallied the Dutch forces, gained some allies, and by 1678 halted Louis short of a major victory.

Despite the heavy cost of the conflicts, Louis precipitated another war by seizing some German border districts along the Rhine in 1686. Fearful of Louis' ambitions, the Hapsburgs formed the League of Augsburg to stop him. William of Orange, who with his English wife Mary had replaced James II on the throne of England in 1688, became the vigorous leader of this coalition. With the support of his newly acquired subjects and the resources of England at his command, William transformed the League of Augsburg into a Grand Alliance against Louis. For eight years the allies—England, Austria, Holland, Sweden, Savoy, and a few German states—struggled against the almost invincible armies of the Grand Monarch. Warfare exhausted both France and the members of the league. Finally, in 1697, the Treaty of Ryswick was signed. Louis retained a few small additions of territory, but the peace marked a serious check to his ambitions. Louis' gains had been costly, and he had not succeeded in upsetting the balance of power in Europe.

War of the Spanish Succession. The death of the childless king of Spain left the Spanish throne open to the conflicting claims of distantly related princes of both Hapsburg Austria and Bourbon France. Although Spain was no longer a first-class power, it controlled the Spanish Netherlands, the kingdom of Naples and Sicily, the duchy of Milan, Sardinia, and considerable territory in the New World. In his will the dying king left this great prize to Louis XIV's grandson, Philip. All Europe realized that, with his grandson as king of Spain, Louis would have an empire stretching from Holland to Sicily, rivaling in its extent and power the possessions of Charles V in the sixteenth century. Louis defied the Austrian claim and European sentiment by accepting the Spanish throne for Philip and aroused apprehension in England and Holland by a series of hostile acts which threatened their governments and merchant classes. He seized a string of fortresses along the border of the Spanish Netherlands; he challenged William of Orange's right to the English throne by recognizing the claim of the deposed Stuarts; and, finally, he secured special privileges for French merchants in Spain's American colonies.

In answer to what was to be Louis' last menacing move to dominate Europe, England organized another alliance against him. From 1702 to 1713 French armies fought the combined forces of this coalition in Spain, Italy, France, Germany, and the Low Countries. The allies were blessed with a remarkable English commander, John Churchill, who became titled as the duke of Marlborough and is also remembered today as an ancestor of the redoubtable Winston Churchill. Churchill's most famous triumph was the battle of Blenheim (1704), considered by many authorities a victory as great as that won by England earlier at Agincourt and later at Waterloo.

Treaty of Utrecht. In 1713 the War of the Spanish Succession ended with the forces of France considerably weakened and the Grand Alliance split by petty rivalries. Comparable in importance to the Peace of Westphalia which had ended the Thirty Years' War was the series of treaties signed at Utrecht between France and the members of the alliance. No one nation was excessively weakened, no single power was made too strong, and, as a result of this peace settlement, a fairly satisfactory balance of power was maintained on the Continent for nearly thirty years without any major conflicts. The most important terms of this settlement were as follows:

(1) Louis' grandson, Philip V, was permitted to remain king of Spain so long as the thrones of France and Spain were not united.

(2) France was allowed to retain most of the modest territorial gains made along its boundaries in Louis' war, thus giving the French nation frontiers more easily defensible than those existing before.

(3) The Spanish empire was divided: Spain and Spanish America were retained by Philip V, while Austria obtained Naples, Milan, Sardinia, and the Spanish Netherlands.

(4) England gained important colonies from France and Spain—Nova Scotia, Newfoundland, and the Hudson Bay territory—and valuable Mediterranean naval bases in the Balearic Islands and at Gibraltar.

(5) The Dutch regained the fortresses guarding their southern frontier as protection against further aggression from France.

(6) The duke of Savoy, an Italian ruler, was given the title of king, and Sicily was added to his possessions.

(7) The Hohenzollern elector of Brandenburg was recognized as "King in Prussia" as a reward for his support of the alliance against France.

The significance of several provisions in this peace should be noted. The accession of the Bourbons to the throne of Spain after almost two centuries of Hapsburg rule marked the end of an era. The long-standing French-Spanish rivalry was now replaced by a strong French-Spanish family alliance as Bourbons occupied the two thrones. The English acquisition of important colonies and naval bases marked an important stage in the rise of Great Britain to world power. The treaty also gave recognition to two aggressive ruling families, the House of Savoy and the House of Hohenzollern. In the nineteenth century, as discussed in later chapters, the House of Savoy succeeded in unifying Italy, and the Hohenzollerns did the same for Germany.

Consequences of Louis' wars. Shortly after the end of the war in 1715, Louis XIV died, leaving behind him a kingdom demoralized and bled white by costly wars. In spite of this defeat, France continued through the eighteenth century to be a first-class power, and French culture was universally admired and imitated. But in retrospect we can see that Louis' reign did much to discredit the system of absolutism.

Leaving behind a record of misery and discontent, Louis paved the way for the French Revolution and the bloody downfall of his dynasty. In his own day, however, so great was his prestige and glory and so strong was the tradition of absolutism in Europe that for a century and more the Continental monarchs continued to applaud his achievements and to imitate them, often with great success.

During the numerous wars which agitated Europe from 1667 to 1713, there evolved what was to become the guiding principle of international diplomacy in modern times— the concept of the balance of power, the beginnings of which we noted in an earlier period (see Chapter 17, Volume I). To prevent France from dominating Europe, coalition after coalition was formed to resist the aggressions of Louis XIV. Relations among European nations fell into a definite pattern: the various powers refused to permit any single state or combination of nations to exercise too much power. Because of its geographical isolation from the Continent, England became the balance wheel in the maintenance of this delicate equipoise, throwing support from one side to the other in order to maintain the balance of power on the Continent.

Another important development was that wars were becoming world wide in scope. In the War of the Spanish Succession the struggle was carried on by fleets in the Mediterranean and Atlantic and by armies in Europe and far-off colonial America. Although warfare became less localized, it was still largely confined to the soldiery and did not involve the total population of a state as it was to do in more recent times, beginning with the wars accompanying the French Revolution.

European rivalries in the colonial world. The competition among national states was intensified by bitter rivalries in the acquisition and exploitation of colonial possessions. As the eighteenth century advanced, the colonial issue bulked large in the minds of European statesmen, who realized that the modern stakes of diplomacy were commerce, raw materials, and territory overseas. Strong rulers also encouraged the improvement of military techniques and the development of powerful armies and navies to make war in both the Old and New Worlds. These factors sharply accentuated the strengths and weaknesses of various European states; they explain clearly why certain nations made rapid strides in the international arena of power politics while those lacking in bold foresight, firm leadership, and a vital economy slowly declined.

Beginning with the first decades of the seventeenth century, European colonial activity increased at a rapid pace. The Spanish and Portuguese monopoly was shattered as the Dutch, English, and French intruded. In North America the Dutch had a toe hold along the Hudson River, and the French, having settled on the banks of the St. Lawrence at Quebec and Montreal, were beginning to push south down the Mississippi Valley toward the Gulf of Mexico. Along the Atlantic seaboard a group of English colonies had been established—ultimately to number thirteen. In the West Indies the newcomers were settling the small islands ignored by Spain. And French, Dutch, and English trading and colonial activity also flourished in other parts of the world: western Africa, India, and the East Indies.

Colonial possessions proved to be bonanzas; an increasing volume of raw materials crossed the seas to enrich the mother countries in western Europe. Neither monarchs nor the newly prosperous merchant classes could ignore problems relating to the control and supply of such products as spices, coffee, slaves, cotton, silks, tobacco, tea, furs, hardwoods, gold, and silver. Therefore, the power struggles waged in Europe tended increasingly to involve rich areas overseas.

Although historians may denounce the monarchs and governments of this period for their brutality, immorality, and complete lack of scruples in foreign affairs, military affairs cannot be ignored in an account of civilization. Some writers have pointed out that in early modern times war was basic to civilization and that military organization was a barometer of social and cultural progress. In explanation, they maintain that the discipline, organization, and administration essential for an efficient military machine influenced all aspects of the state, particularly the domain of public finance and the fields of technology and science. Reasoning thus, it is claimed that "despite the appalling waste of energy and human lives caused by incessant wars, this competitive state system exercised a dynamic function. It communicated a stimulus to intensive economic enterprise and forced upon statesmen an ever greater rationalization and modernization of their political and military mechanisms. The spirit of enterprise which lay at the root of early modern capitalism had its counterpart in the enterprise and competition of the statesmen of this epoch of state-building."[17]

Anglo-French rivalry in the colonial world. From the middle of the seventeenth century on, western Europe advanced economically at an impressive rate. Capital was accumulated, manufacturing was improved, and the standard of living advanced.

The key factor in economic progress was the existence of profitable colonies. In the eighteenth century, more than half of Britain's trade was with non-European areas. French trade from 1700 to 1760, most of it with its colonies, increased more than 500 per cent. All types of goods heretofore scarce or relatively unknown flowed across the seas to add to the comfort and enjoyment of the Old World (see Chapter 3).

Before 1700, France and Britain had begun a long duel on a world-wide stage for colonial possessions in North America, the West Indies, and India. As early as the 1680's, the British colonies along the Atlantic seaboard had a total population of about 300,000. There were also English settlements in Newfoundland and on Hudson Bay. The French colonies in the New World were spread over a wider area but were more sparsely settled than the English holdings. From Quebec and Montreal on the St. Lawrence River, intrepid French trappers and missionaries made their way to the Great Lakes and south to the Ohio Valley. LaSalle laid claim in 1682 to the entire Mississippi Valley region. French and British planters in the West Indies shared the lucrative returns of the sugar trade; the English controlled Jamaica, Barbados, and the Bahamas, and the French controlled the two rich possessions of Martinique and Guadeloupe. Both France and Great Britain held a string of trading posts on the west coast of Africa—the English at the mouth of the Gambia River and along the Gold Coast, the French at the mouth of the Senegal and on the island of Goree.

As the eighteenth century opened, India was on the threshold of momentous events. The once dynamic Mogul dynasty was fast weakening, and it was logical that enterprising western nations should attempt to fill this power vacuum. The two European nations with important interests in India were France and Britain; both were represented by successful trading companies. The English were gradually building their strength around three posts—Calcutta, Madras, and Bombay. Chandernagor and Pondichéry were the important French posts.

As the eighteenth century progressed, the colonial rivalry between France and Britain would become increasingly intense. In line with the philosophy of mercantilism, one London merchant expressed the clash of economic interests in this fashion: "Our trade will improve by the total extinction of theirs."[18] Conscious of the intensity of this struggle, a Frenchman observed:

The English will rule the seas through their fleets and the land through their wealth, and America will furnish them with the means of dictating to Europe. . . . France alone is in a position to prevent this catastrophe, and France must do so for her own sake and that of all Europe.[19]

Since the days of Louis XIV, England had been pitted against France in the various wars which have already been discussed in this and the preceding chapters. One of England's motives was to preserve the balance of power in Europe. As the issue of colonies became more important, England came to realize that it could best checkmate French ambitions in Europe by destroying French commerce and sea power in North America and India. Thus, in the wars from 1688 to 1750, the English perfected a policy which made best use of their various resources toward this end. This was the practice of obtaining and subsidizing allies to keep the French occupied in Europe while at the same time the bulk of British troops, especially naval forces, concentrated on the task of conquering the colonies and destroying the commerce of the French overseas, where distance served to neutralize France's advantages as a land power. The French, on the other hand, divided their energies by trying to play the game of power politics in Europe and at the same time endeavoring to compete with England over colonies. The result was to spell failure for France in both policies.

War of Jenkins' Ear. In 1738 Robert Jenkins, a British sea captain, appeared before the House of Commons to exhibit a withered ear carried in a box. He claimed that his ear had been cut off by bloodthirsty Spanish officials in the West Indies during the quarrel between Britain and Spain over trading rights there.

This dramatic revelation set off a wave of emotionalism in England. The prime minister, Sir Robert Walpole, was aware of the strong ties between Spain and England's arch-rival, France. Although he feared the outbreak of a full-scale world conflict, in 1739 he reluctantly agreed to a declaration

In this contemporary English print, Captain Jenkins shows his ear to an uninterested Sir Robert Walpole, seated at the left. At the far right, a merchant who has brought a complaint against Spanish depredations is pushed out the door, while the gentleman in the center, a French mediator sent to bring about an agreement over trading rights, is given close attention.

of war against Spain—the War of Jenkins' Ear. In reference to the English people, he observed coolly: "They are ringing their bells now; they will be wringing their hand[s] soon." And true to Walpole's words, the minor Anglo-Spanish skirmish fought in the West Indies merged into a bloody drama of much greater scope. By 1742 hostilities had died down between Spain and England, but both became participants in a struggle that began in central Europe and later spread to North America and to India.

War of the Austrian Succession. It was the Austrian emperor who set the stage for a struggle on the Continent. Foreseeing the difficulties his young daughter, Maria Theresa, would have coping with greedy neighboring monarchs, he had drawn up in 1713 a document called the Pragmatic Sanction. The rulers who signed this document, including Frederick the Great's father, agreed to respect the territorial boundaries of Austria upon Maria Theresa's accession to the throne; but when the emperor died in October 1740, Frederick the Great, who had become king in Prussia in May of that year, had no intention of honoring the Pragmatic Sanction. He trumped up spurious claims on Maria Theresa's rich province of Silesia. On examining the document containing his demands, Frederick exclaimed to his advisers:

Bravo! This is the work of an excellent charlatan. If there is anything to be gained by honesty, then we shall be honest; if we must dupe, then let us be scoundrels.[20]

In December 1740, he invaded Silesia, and the War of the Austrian Succession began. Riding at the head of his well-trained troops, Frederick defeated the Austrians easily and occupied Silesia. France, Spain, Bavaria, and Saxony then threw in their lot with Frederick to obtain a share of the loot. But having secured Silesia, Frederick had no desire to continue fighting so that his allies also could filch territory from Austria. And so, in 1741, he withdrew from the conflict.

At first, England remained aloof, content to send subsidies to the hapless Maria Theresa. But in 1742 England entered the fray allied with Austria, Holland, and Hanover against the Franco-Spanish coalition. Meanwhile, Frederick the Great had reëntered the war, and in 1745 his army roundly defeated the Austrians. Prussia and Austria then withdrew from the conflict, but fighting continued and the war broadened into a world-wide conflict involving the European colonial possessions. Thus it was, as the famous English historian Macaulay observed, "Because a monarch robbed a neighbor he had promised to defend, red men scalped each other by the Great Lakes of America, while black men fought on the [Indian] coast of Coromandel."[21]

The French triumphed in India, seizing the British outpost of Madras, but the British took the offensive in North America by capturing the French fortress of Louisburg, a stronghold guarding the entrance to the Gulf of St. Lawrence. On the seas, the British fleet successfully held off the French.

The war dragged on until 1748, when a general peace was signed at Aix-la-Chapelle. Louisburg was returned to the French and Madras to the English, and Frederick was confirmed in his possession of Silesia. The Peace of Aix-la-Chapelle—called "the peace without victory"—settled nothing. In derision, the French coined a proverb: *Bête comme la paix*—"As stupid as the peace."

The rivalries which had ignited the conflagration continued to smolder, and in less than a decade they were to blaze forth in another major war. Maria Theresa dreamed of the day she might be avenged on Frederick; in North America French and English colonists continually clashed; in India rival trading companies schemed for power; and in London and Paris statesmen and influential businessmen both foresaw that a showdown between France and Great Britain was inevitable.

The Diplomatic Revolution. The duel for world empire between England and France reached a decisive stage in the Seven Years' War (1756-1763), known in American history as the French and Indian War. The war was preceded in North America and India by preliminary skirmishes, while England and France were still ostensibly at peace, and in Europe by a very significant regrouping of alliances in which two sets of traditional enemies became allies.

Thirsting for revenge against Frederick the Great, Maria Theresa turned to her country's hereditary enemy, France, and suggested to Louis xv that an alliance be formed against Frederick. As an inducement, France was to receive Frederick's Rhenish provinces. At first the French king refused, but the suave Austrian diplomat Kaunitz enlisted the support of Madame de Pompadour, born Jeanne Antoinette Poisson, who was Louis' chief mistress and was reputed to be the daughter of a fishwife. Madame de Pompadour had been infuriated by Frederick's frequent allusions to her as "Mademoiselle Poisson" ("Miss Fish") and by the scandalous verses he wrote about her. But although her influence at the French court was important, undoubtedly the determining factor in Louis' decision to accept the Austrian offer was his realization that England, not Austria, had by now become France's most dangerous rival. In the spring of 1756, Louis signed a pact whereby France joined Russia, Sweden, and various states in the Germanies as allies of Austria.

To check French ambitions on the Continent, England in the meantime had made

Three successive stages in the taking of Quebec are shown in this old print. At the right is the blockading fleet; in the center, British soldiers capture the heights; and at the left, the battle rages on the Plains of Abraham.

an alliance with its recent foe, Prussia. So thoroughly had the traditional alignment of powers been reversed that this new grouping of nations—Austria and France vs. England and Prussia—is referred to as the Diplomatic Revolution of the eighteenth century.

Frederick opens the Seven Years' War. Frederick the Great applied the match to the international powder keg in 1756, making the droll observation:

If Austria is pregnant with war, I shall offer the service of the midwife.[22]

Quickly attacking the coalition, he aimed heavy blows at Austria before France and Russia could threaten him. Despite successes, he met powerful resistance, and Prussia was attacked on all sides. With brilliant strategy, Frederick marched and wheeled his forces, winning astonishing victories over the invaders of his realm. Frederick's allies, England and Hanover, won no spectacular victories but managed to divert the French armies from attacking Frederick in full force.

William Pitt's "system." In the colonial phase of the Seven Years' War, Great Britain at first suffered severe defeats. Minorca, an important Mediterranean island base, was captured by the French, and in North America the brilliant French commander Montcalm repeatedly trounced the English.

During this period, England suffered from ineffective leadership. The fussy and pompous duke of Newcastle, of whom it was said "[he] lost an hour in the morning and spent the rest of the day in running after it," was prime minister. But the crisis ended when a remarkable statesman, William Pitt, took charge of the war effort as secretary of state in Newcastle's cabinet.

Pitt had supreme confidence in his own abilities, once saying: "I am confident that I can save the country and that no one else can." He developed a shrewd global strategy of war, known as his "system," which consisted of (1) providing large subsidies of money to Prussia; (2) destroying French sea power and thus preventing men and supplies from reaching the French possessions overseas; and (3) dispatching well-equipped English forces to the colonies to conquer the isolated French armies.

After this "system" was inaugurated, English victories fairly rained. An Englishman of the day noted: "We are forced to ask every morning what victory there has been, for fear of missing one." In 1759 one French fort after another fell in North America: Duquesne, Louisburg, Niagara, and Ticonderoga; and in September the defeat of France in North America was sealed when General Wolfe vanquished Montcalm's forces and captured Quebec. In India there was a similar chronicle of victories. French trading posts fell to the British as the fleet prevented the arrival of fresh troops and supplies from France.

The most decisive English victory resulted from the infamous incident concerning the Black Hole of Calcutta. The native ruler of Bengal, allied with the French, captured Calcutta and cruelly forced 146 English captives into a small dungeon, where during the night all but twenty-three died of suffocation and thirst. British forces commanded by Robert Clive avenged this act by defeating the ruler of Bengal in the decisive battle of Plassey (1757). Clive's victory laid the foundation for nearly two hundred years of British rule in India. The rich province of Bengal continued to be governed by the native ruler, but this official was now a puppet in the hands of the English. The Company was the de facto ruler.

Notwithstanding the crushing defeats inflicted by the English upon France, Spain foolishly declared war on Great Britain in 1761. With little difficulty British naval forces captured Havana and Manila from Spain. In these final phases of the Seven Years' War, Pitt was no longer in command, but his spirit inspired the English to further victories.

Survival of Prussia. The victories won by Great Britain contrasted markedly with the ordeals suffered by Prussia. In spite of Fred-

erick's tactical victories, Prussia lacked the necessary man power to defeat the combined forces of Austria, France, and Russia. His country attacked on all sides, Frederick compared himself to a man assaulted by flies:

When one flies off my cheek, another comes and sits on my nose, and scarcely has it been brushed off than another flies up and sits on my forehead on my eyes and everywhere else.[23]

Frederick's fortunes took a turn for the better in 1762. The pro-French Russian empress, Elizabeth, died and was succeeded by Peter III, a great admirer of Prussia and of Frederick. Although Russian armies were at the gates of Berlin, Peter withdrew from the war, refused indemnity, and made an alliance with Frederick, thus accomplishing one of the few significant actions in his very short reign. Hostilities on the Continent ceased one year later. The peace settlement between Prussia and Austria reëstablished the prewar boundaries and confirmed Prussia's hold on Silesia.

Treaty of Paris. In 1763 peace was also concluded between Great Britain, France, and Spain by the Treaty of Paris. This document provided for French cession to England of Canada and all the territory east of the Mississippi River. Spain ceded Florida to England and, as compensation, received from France the Louisiana territory including New Orleans. France also gave several West Indian islands and posts in west Africa to England. In India, France received its small trading posts back, but the treaty specified that the posts were to remain unfortified. Martinique and other rich islands in the West Indies were returned to France, and Spain recovered Havana and Manila. Thus British demands were moderate.

By the Treaty of Paris, Great Britain became the greatest colonial, commercial, and naval power in the world. That a country of 6,500,000 should triumph over a nation such as France, with a population of 23,000,000, was remarkable. As one Englishman wrote:

I shall burn my Greek and Latin books. They are the histories of little people. We subdue the globe in three campaigns, and a globe as big again as it was in their days.[24]

To unify his state, Frederick the Great wished to seize from Poland the territory of West Prussia, which separated his own region of East Prussia from the bulk of his kingdom. In order to maintain the balance of power in Europe, Frederick suggested to Russia and Austria that they join him in a "collective partition" of Poland. Austria abstained in the second partition. After 1795, Poland no longer existed as an independent state and was not to exist as such again until after World War I.

The British victory over France in the Seven Years' War had within it the seeds of later humiliation. With French rule eliminated in North America and the need for England's protection there decreased, the colonists along the Atlantic seaboard agitated for a revision of stringent British political and economic controls and, in 1776, rose up against their mother country in open rebellion. Partly because of its defeat in 1763, France intervened in the American Revolution but in helping to defeat Britain brought financial hardship and disaster to itself: the success of the American Revolution inspired the French people in their opposition to tyrannical rule. Only a few years separated the surrender at Yorktown from the fall of the Bastille.

Partition of Poland. The eighteenth century offers many illustrations of the callous and cold-blooded manner in which wars were precipitated, promises broken, and allies deserted. Yet today, in an age accustomed to accepting the right of national self-determination, the most shocking example of completely unprincipled statecraft was the ruthless partition of Poland by Prussia, Russia, and Austria.

Without natural barriers to mark its boundaries or to aid in its defense, Poland was a handicapped nation. In addition, it was dominated by a corrupt nobility whose bitter quarrels rendered the central government almost powerless. The monarchy was elective, and as the Poles usually could not agree on the choice of a king from among their own factions, only two native-born Poles had been elected to the throne in two hundred years. The Central Diet was completely impotent; by the Liberum Veto, any single member could force the dissolution of this body. Such action was called "exploding the Diet," and from the midpoint of the seventeenth century to the middle of the eighteenth, forty-eight of fifty-five Diets were "exploded." This was not government but anarchy in political dress!

With the aid of her army, Catherine the Great of Russia forced the Poles in 1763 to accept one of her discarded lovers as king. Russia did not gobble up Poland, however, because Catherine feared the jealousies of both Prussia and Austria. Also, with the termination of the Seven Years' War, she did not want to upset the delicate balance of power in eastern Europe.

After the peace settlement between Austria and Prussia in 1763, Frederick turned his attention to the problem of unifying his state. The province of East Prussia was separated from the main block of his kingdom by West Prussia, held by Poland. This narrow, strategic region gave Poland access to the Baltic Sea but blocked the unification of Prussia. (The Polish Corridor has figured importantly in our own times; claiming his right to this land, Hitler in 1939 ordered German troops into Poland.)

How was Frederick to unify his state without upsetting the balance of power? The Prussian king stepped forward with his magic diplomatic wand to save the peace and yet, at the same time, to increase the holdings of the other interested parties—Russia and Austria. He persuaded Catherine to accept the principle of "collective partition." Maria Theresa, it is said, declared Frederick's proposal immoral, but, realizing that her abstention would allow Prussia and Russia to annex all of Poland, she reluctantly joined in the territorial surgery. In 1772 Prussia, Austria, and Russia obtained their first helping of Poland, and the cynical Frederick, hearing that Maria Theresa deplored this action, wryly commented, "She wept, but she kept on taking." Thus Frederick acquired West Prussia and made East Prussia a contiguous part of his realm.

In 1793 and again in 1795, Polish territory was annexed, Austria abstaining in the second operation. By the third partition, Poland ceased to exist as an independent state. But, although dismembered and under the alien rule of three different governments, Poland still continued to live in the hearts of the Poles, who hoped for the resurrection of their nation. Their faith was not rewarded until after the World War of 1914 to 1918 (see Chapter 14).

SUMMARY

The concentration of power in the hands of absolutist kings resulted in a succession of wars that convulsed Europe during this period: the War of the Spanish Succession, the Great Northern War, the War of the Austrian Succession, and the Seven Years' War. Declining states, such as Turkey, and temporarily weakened states, such as Austria at the accession of Maria Theresa, were susceptible to the designs of their dynamic, aggressive neighbors. In Poland's case, Prussia, Russia, and Austria joined in territorial banditry or, as it is more politely described, the "collective partition" of this doomed land.

By 1700, commercial and colonial rivalry added to the intense competitive spirit existing in Europe and culminated in the world-wide duel for empire between France and Great Britain. Great Britain, as the leader of various coalitions and the self-appointed caretaker of the Continental balance of power, emerged victorious over France and the monarchical despotism it symbolized. In England the successful Glorious Revolution heralded the triumph of Aristocratic Liberalism—the rule of Parliament and of law. The most wealthy and influential elements in society controlled the government, and their support made for a stronger and more united government than that operating from Versailles. The English government thus proved fit to achieve victory in foreign diplomacy and warfare.

The interplay of international rivalries during the last half of the seventeenth century and the first three quarters of the eighteenth century had many significant and interesting implications for modern times. In this period it was determined that North America would be mainly Anglo-Saxon in culture; British rule was firmly established in India; and Britain's sea power gained the world-wide supremacy it was to hold well into the twentieth century. This period also saw the rise of the Prussian type of absolutism—the militaristic state—and the birth of the Russian policy of securing access to the Baltic and Mediterranean seas.

CHAPTER 3

New Forces and the Old Regime

Introduction. The beginnings of the transformation of Europe from a medieval to a modern pattern of life can be traced back to the Renaissance and indeed to the twelfth century. Dynamic forces of change became ever stronger until, in the closing years of the seventeenth century, they were assailing the very foundations of the Old Regime.

There was much to challenge and attack in this outmoded system. In France, particularly, the Old Regime was characterized by an aristocracy that was both arrogant and parasitic and by a Church that controlled one fifth of all land but was exempt from taxation. There was a jumble of law codes, a lack of uniformity in standards of weights and measures, and conflicts in the jurisdiction of customs areas. Justice was uncertain and capricious, and the royal government was highly centralized, overworked, arbitrary, and often corrupt. Elsewhere also, Continental Europe was plagued by a parasitic nobility which exacted onerous personal services and heavy financial dues from the peasants. And now that the political power of the nobility had been broken by the king, in most of Europe the monarchs were absolute rulers presiding over despotic and inefficient governments. All this added up to a society in which only one per cent of the population enjoyed privilege, exercised authority, and escaped taxation without making any corresponding contributions to the welfare of the state.

From 1650 to the closing decades of the eighteenth century, new social, economic, and intellectual forces were unleashed—forces that were to weaken the Old Regime and its main buttress, monarchical absolutism. At the core of these forces was European expansion overseas. The increasing importance of colonial trade and the flood of exciting information from the new worlds not only stimulated warfare and commercial rivalries between European powers but also brought revolutionary changes to the social and economic life of these nations. The trade in new foods and beverages and welcome luxuries increased wealth, promoted the rise of the middle class, and encouraged a new system of doing business—capitalism. Accompanying the stimulus of overseas trade and the new wealth it created was a growth of population.

The deep and widespread changes in the socio-economic structure of western Europe were reflected in ideological attacks on the existing order. As spokesmen of the bourgeoisie, the physiocrats attacked the old restraints and repressive rules of mercantilism; and a brilliant coterie of intellectuals, the *philosophes*, made bitter attacks upon absolutism for its intolerance, superstition, and capricious despotism. The most influential figures were a trio of Frenchmen: Voltaire, Montesquieu, and Rousseau. Some monarchs heard the voice of reform and tried to be benevolent despots. But their efforts were half-hearted or doomed to failure, and the gnawing evils of the Old Regime remained.

THE IMPACT ON EUROPE

OF OVERSEAS EXPANSION

New wealth transforms Europe. One of the most potent forces molding modern world history was the thrust of European political power, commerce, and culture over the globe in the eighteenth century. The drive outward from Europe was manifested by two important movements—colonization and imperialism. The migration of vast numbers of people from the European homeland to sparsely inhabited areas in the Americas, South Africa, and the Pacific created new Europes that were colonial projections of western culture.

The second movement, European Imperialism, established rigid and powerful controls over millions of native peoples in Africa, India, and south Asia. In chapters 9 and 10 we shall study these two movements; in this chapter, the "inward" consequences of expansion—the effects of this powerful drive upon European customs and institutions—will be discussed.

After 1700, as France, England, and other European countries accumulated wealth at a rate theretofore unprecedented, the wide imbalance of wealth between non-European lands that today are termed the "underdeveloped nations" and the prosperous states of western Europe became evident. In England the total national wealth increased from £17,000,000 to £88,000,000 between 1600 and 1688; and the rate of increase accelerated after the end of the century. Within the first half of the eighteenth century, England's exports tripled in value. French foreign trade, second only to England's, increased four times from 1715, the end of the reign of Louis XIV, to 1789.

One of the most important factors stimulating business and the accumulation of wealth was the influx of a huge amount of bullion into Europe from the New World. It is estimated that from 1781 to 1800, the world's production of gold and silver was just under the value of one billion dollars. Business boomed in this expanding European economy.

Mercantilism: partner to absolutism. In several European states, the growth of the national state system had brought political unification. The means used to bring about a strong, self-sufficient economy as a natural partner to strong central government was termed mercantilism. The aims of mercantilism and absolutism coincided; the control of a nation's economic life by a centralized government strengthened both the economy and the political structure of the state at the expense of rival national powers.

Because gold and silver were believed to be indispensable to a nation's wealth, mercantilists stressed the importance of accumulating precious metals. Colbert, the minister of finance under Louis XIV, once stated:

It is only the abundance of money in a state that determines its greatness and power.[1]

But as we noted in the case of Spain (see Chapter 19, Volume I), this viewpoint was fallacious. Money does not necessarily spell wealth; money itself is only a measure of value and a means of exchanging real wealth. For coinage and the payment of armies and navies, however, gold and silver were necessary. Many Europeans believed that "money is the sinews of war."

A second tenet of mercantilism was that a nation should maintain the most favorable balance of trade possible: it should export more than it imported so that foreign nations would have to pay the difference in precious metals. Only raw materials which could not be obtained at home were to be imported; after these materials had been manufactured into finished articles, they were then to be exported. Government subsidies and bounties were rewards given for increased home production of manufactured goods.

Mercantilists believed that when raw materials were native, the profit to the home country was 100 per cent. Therefore, if a country could not supply its own materials, it should acquire colonies from which they could be procured. Furthermore, colonies constituted not only sources of supply for raw materials but also markets for finished products. Because the mother country did not want competition for its infant industries, colonies were prevented from engaging in manufacturing. In addition, the colonies were prohibited from trading with foreign powers. In the sixteenth century, Spain and Portugal attempted to prevent interchange between their empires and alien merchants and colonists. England forbade the export of raw wool so that its cloth industry might be nurtured at home.

Seeking to increase the revenues of his royal master, Jean Baptiste Colbert developed an economic system that affected all France and influenced other European nations as well.

In the seventeenth century, Colbert in France developed an extensive system of rigid state controls over the quantity and quality of merchandise, a policy known as Colbertism. Other nations also embraced mercantilistic ideas; in Prussia mercantilism, called Cameralism, was designed to strengthen state control of domestic industry and trade. The emigration of skilled artisans was forbidden, the quality of goods was prescribed to the minutest detail, and the use of foreign commodities was prohibited.

Mercantilism reached its zenith in the eighteenth century and then declined, but mercantilistic policies were not abandoned in all countries at the same time. The most important commercial powers—England, France, and Holland—had been among the first to embrace mercantilism, and they were the first to discard it. The more backward economic powers such as Prussia, Russia, and the Scandinavian countries still favored mercantilism long after other nations had turned to newer doctrines.

Rivalries in colonial expansion. As overseas colonial trade became more and more lucrative, different European nations became commercial leaders only to be pushed aside by aggressive rivals. Thus in the sixteenth century the Italian trading cities were elbowed from commercial leadership by Portugal, which, in turn, was superseded by Spain. In the early decades of the seventeenth century, Holland forged ahead of all competitors, making itself the trading and financial center of Europe. Nevertheless, Holland, like Portugal, was a small nation, and it was inevitable that larger states would wrest away its commercial leadership. Rivalry between England and Holland during the latter half of the seventeenth century resulted in wars which seriously weakened Dutch sea power and brought about the crash of the East India Company and the Bank of Amsterdam.

With a population of about fifteen million in the seventeenth century, France was the premier nation of Europe. Its abundant economic resources were assiduously cultivated by Colbert, who sponsored French colonization, expanded colonial trade, and encouraged manufacturing in France. But although his aggressive mercantilist policies appeared to work well at first, gradually the merits of his program were offset by evils inherent in the system. Many industries, such as textiles, porcelains, and tapestries, were subsidized by the government, but the numerous official decrees controlling them were more of a handicap than an aid to economic development. Furthermore, the extravagant court life at Versailles created a market for luxury commodities limited to the upper classes, while the needs and desires of the common people were ignored.

After the death of Colbert in 1683, his mercantilistic system began to develop creaks and strains. Lacking Colbert's guiding genius, his followers added all kinds of minute and irksome regulations. The system's weaknesses also became apparent when, in retaliation for Colbert's restrictions against foreign imports, other nations refused to purchase French farm products and wines. Furthermore, the big governmental monopolies were increasingly unpopular with businessmen, who demanded the removal of governmental regulations and of controls by the old medieval guilds.

In addition, it has been estimated that between 1685 and 1715 France lost a million subjects through warfare, the surrender of colonies, and the drain of emigration. The revocation of the Edict of Nantes in 1685 resulted in the flight from France of a large group of industrious, middle-class Huguenots, who took their capital and skills to neighboring countries. And the rivalry between France and England during the Seven Years' War culminated in English victory and French disaster. Thus France, still feared, envied, and flattered by other European states, lost to England the commercial supremacy which it might have had. It is to England, then, that we must turn to witness the changes most symptomatic of the times.

Rise of England's sun. Although England was inferior to France in area, fertility of soil, and population, this island kingdom had many factors in its favor which more than compensated for its disadvantages. Geographical isolation discouraged military conquest from the Continent—the last invasion by a foreign power had taken place in 1066 —and the English economy had not been shaken by foreign assaults on the homeland or undermined by the cost of maintaining large standing armies. After the union of England and Scotland in 1707, internal trade flourished in the largest customs-free area in western Europe. The aristocracy and middle class which controlled Parliament also controlled the principal trading and banking companies so that the growth of new enterprises was more peaceful and steady than anywhere else in Europe. The gradual control of the seas, the establishment of trading posts in exotic lands, and the shrewd policy of taking overseas territory as its booty from successful European wars enabled England to gain commercial benefits and to build the world's largest empire.

In 1651 Oliver Cromwell had passed the famous Navigation Act, a statute reënacted by later governments. By the Navigation Act all goods imported into England from Africa, America, or Asia had to be shipped in vessels belonging to English owners, built in England, and manned by English sailors. All goods exported from England to these areas came under the same injunctions. By maintaining a favorable balance of trade, this vigorous island kingdom in 1750 had already outstripped its European rivals in commerce and had laid the foundations for its economic domination of the world in the nineteenth century.

England's supremacy in the textile market was no small factor in accounting for its overall growth. Daniel Defoe, the author of *Robinson Crusoe*, maintained that the woolen industry in England was "the richest and most valuable manufacture in the world,"[2] of greater value to England than the rich mines of Peru and Mexico were to Spain.

New foods and beverages. While colonial expansion and the introduction of new products transformed life and manners in countless ways throughout western Europe, our discussion will primarily concern England, the greatest trading nation of its day. Before the seventeenth century, diet was substantial enough for most Englishmen but lacked variety; staples included beef, fowl, bread, ale, and beer. As overseas trade boomed, the variety of available foods and beverages increased rapidly. The potato was one of the most important new items of diet. Considered at first a luxury and a curiosity, it gradually became available for both rich and poor alike. Fish had always been basic to the English diet, but now enormous supplies came from New England and the Grand Banks of Newfoundland. Englishmen soon began to regard the famous "kipper" or "bloater" as one of the mainstays of their breakfasts. During this time, rice pudding, sago, and tapioca were also introduced.

The tomato, or "love apple," was first presented to the English people as a decorative garden plant rather than an edible fruit. Only after 1800 did its edibility become appreciated. A contemporary writer observed:

. . . that this fruit has long been used by the wealthy . . . in this country; and within these last few years it has come into great use with all our best cooks, as it possesses in itself an agree-

Chinensis cum olla cui incoquuntur folia The

The Chinensis cum stirpe

An illustration like this one, showing a Chinese tea drinker and the cultivation of the shrub from which tea is obtained, made Europeans aware of the far-flung sources of the products they were beginning to use regularly in their daily lives.

able acid, a very unusual quality in ripe vegetables, and which makes it quite distinct from all garden vegetables that are used for culinary purposes in this country. . . . Love-apples are now to be seen in great abundance at all our vegetable markets. . . .[3]

Other welcome additions to the national diet were peanuts, asparagus, spinach, watermelon, and rhubarb. Oranges and lemons from the Orient graced dining tables, as did dates and figs from the Near East and North Africa. The pineapple was regarded as a very rare and exotic fruit. Its initial appearance at the English royal court has been recorded in a tract published in 1684:

When some of them, by great care, and the favour of a speedy voyage, were brought into England (for very rarely can they be preserved so long) and presented to King James, he was so ravisht with its [sic] charming deliciousness, that he said: It is not fit to be tasted by a Subject, but only proper to Regale the Gusto of Princes inured to the highest delicacies.[4]

Sugar enriched and sweetened the daily diet. At first its cost was too high for the masses, but by the eighteenth century the price dropped to about twenty-five cents a pound and it was considered a necessity even by the poor.

From distant lands came the new beverages: chocolate, tea, and coffee. Chocolate, or cocoa, once the sacred drink of the Aztecs, was introduced to Europe by Spanish voyagers. Tea, now so inseparable a part of English life, was introduced into Europe by the Dutch in the seventeenth century; and tea merchants claimed that it could cure giddiness and headaches, banish bad dreams, and strengthen the stomach and liver. By 1800 tea had become universally popular in England. Coffee, first brought to Europe from Arabia, was responsible for a famous English institution, the coffee house, which was most popular in the first decade of the eighteenth century. Made from West Indian molasses, Jamaican rum was considered more healthful than brandy.

Changes in customs and manners. In this age when so many tempting products were crowding in from all over the world, there were many cases of extravagance and vulgar display. Young fops would spend as much as five hundred guineas for a single suit, and the rich employees of the East India Company, called nabobs, returned from India to scandalize established society by their gross appetites and execrable tastes. They built great country mansions and filled them with bric-a-brac, furniture, and pictures.

But the greater comfort and luxury available resulted also in a refinement of English life; manners were improved and life became more gracious. In the sixteenth century it had been necessary for books of etiquette to caution against picking teeth with a knife or throwing bones on the floor. The refining influence of an attractive, clean, and well-set table worked wonders. Doilies, napkins, and tablecloths could now be made of reasonably cheap and easily laundered materials. Meals were served on dainty chinaware from the Orient, and the great quantities of silver from the Americas made it possible to manufacture graceful eating utensils which had not been available before. Eating became an art as well as a necessity. Books on etiquette told people how to cope gracefully with the new tableware and recommended the cultivation of wit and pleasant conversation at dinner or afternoon tea.

A torrent of new or formerly very rare products—muslins, calicoes, silks, cottons, ivory, ostrich feathers, fans, furs, precious stones, cosmetics, and perfumes—came to be used for personal adornment, especially by the women. Joseph Addison, the essayist, expressed a typically male point of view on this matter:

I consider woman as a beautiful and romantic animal that may be adorned with furs and feathers, pearls and diamonds, ores and silks. The lynx shall cast its skin at her feet, to make her a tippet; the peacock, parrot and swan shall pay contribution to her muff; the sea shall be searched for shells and the rocks for gems; and every part of nature furnish out its share towards the embellishment of a creature that is the most consummate work of it.[5]

Highborn ladies decked themselves out in imported brocades, parasols, mirrors, fans, and much gold and silver lace. Bewigged nobles and wealthy merchants were resplendent in white silk coats, knee breeches, silk stockings, ruffles, and gold-braided hats.

More widely shared benefits followed the popularization and cheapening of the price of various cloths, especially cotton. Ordinary people could dress better, and the economy of the new materials tended to narrow class distinctions in dress. For the first time handkerchiefs and underclothing became common, and people changed their clothing more frequently.

Among the well-to-do, overseas influences were quite marked in interior decoration.

Opportunities for spending money multiplied in the eighteenth century. In this scene from "The Rake's Progress," a series created by William Hogarth, the hero is besieged by a dancing master, an architect, a fencing master, a jockey, a professional bodyguard, and a variety of other artists and tradesmen, all seeking to relieve him of a share of his wealth.

Carpets and rugs from India and Persia were much sought after, and a wide variety of imported chintzes, ginghams, and cretonnes were used for upholstery and drapery fabrics. There was also a passion for things Chinese and Japanese. Huge cabinets housed collections of chinaware; and elaborately decorated screens, lacquer-covered trays, and gilded tables and cabinets were designed in the oriental style. This style is still known as Chinese Chippendale, so called after its chief exponent, an English cabinet maker named Thomas Chippendale.

The use of one commodity—tobacco—spread rapidly among rich and poor alike. It was used mainly in the form of snuff or for smoking in pipes. Upon its introduction to England, the medicinal qualities of tobacco were strongly recommended; even schoolchildren were forced to smoke during the Great Plague in London. For nearly a century tobacco was widely employed by pharmacists for such weird-sounding concoctions as "tobacco wine" and "tobacco gruel." Seventeenth-century claims for tobacco were as extravagant as some that we hear today:

Divine Tobacco! which gives Ease
To all our Pains and Miseries;
Composes Thought, makes Minds sedate,
Adds Gravity to Church and State . . .[6]

Coiffure nouvelle dilte le Caprice des jolies femmes

Coiffures reached an extreme of artificial elegance in eight-eenth-century France. Worn at the royal court, such head-dresses called attention to the fact that their wearers were well supplied with money, servants, and total idleness.

Cultural impacts. Overseas expansion not only increased Europe's well-being and grad-ually changed social customs and ways of life but also modified the intellectual climate of the times. A variety of novel and exciting facts about strange peoples and customs, un-known plants and flowers, and precious min-erals poured into Europe and piqued the curiosity of artists, philosophers, and the man in the street. Although much of this information was highly colored or completely false, it stimulated new scientific discoveries. The literature of travel was abundant; tales such as Daniel Defoe's *Robinson Crusoe* be-guiled a wide audience, and numerous ex-plorers wrote diaries and journals which were eagerly snapped up by a fascinated reading public.

The impact of European expansion over-seas also created what might be called the comparative approach in political science. European political thinkers began to com-pare and evaluate their own governments and societies with those reported by voyag-ers and envoys to exotic courts. While the comparisons were not always accurate, they eventually led to widespread criticism of European institutions, especially in France.

DEVELOPMENTS IN AGRICULTURE

Innovations in agriculture. The condition of agriculture was a basic socioeconomic factor in the life of the period, for agricul-ture provided the majority of Europeans with their livelihood. The rapid increase in population during the latter half of the eighteenth century, coupled with a succes-sion of poor harvests, shot food prices sky-high. The result led a contemporary Eng-lishman to remark that prosperity had transformed the farmer into a person with:

. . . [a] fox-hunting horse, polished boots, a spanking trot to market, a "Get out of the way or by God I'll ride over you" to every poor devil on the road, wine at his dinner, a servant (sometimes in livery) to wait at his table, a painted lady for a wife, sons aping the young squires and lords, and a house crammed up with sofas, pianos, and all sort of fooleries.[7]

In England a combination of political, so-cial, and economic factors wrought signifi-cant changes on the agrarian scene. The profit-making potentialities in farming at-tracted enterprising, middle-class tradesmen, who bought up large tracts of land. Because the possession of land had always been the mark of nobility, the *nouveau riche* consoli-dated their position in polite society by ac-quiring estates and marrying into the landed gentry. The alliance between land and trade created a powerful new group in Parliament —a class which promoted legislation favor-able to its own needs and desires, often at the expense of the national good. But the satisfaction of the profit motive had a bene-ficial effect upon agriculture. Discontented with primitive farming techniques, the new commercial landowners applied efficient business methods to the management of their estates. They encouraged the use of new tools and crops and were sympathetic to new ideas in stock breeding and soil development.

A pioneer agronomist was Jethro Tull (1674-1741), who advocated careful plowing of the land, planting seeds in neat rows by the use of a drill he invented, and keeping the plants well cultivated as they grew to maturity. These directions for planting and cultivating appeared in his work, *The Horse-Hoeing Husbandry* (1733), still considered a valuable source book for proponents of scientific agriculture. By mixing clay and lime into the soil, Viscount Charles Townshend (1674-1738) restored the fertility of land that had once been worthless swamp and sand. He also suggested crop rotation as a method of soil restoration superior to the wasteful custom of allowing good farm land to lie fallow. So enthusiastic was he over turnips, his pet crop for livestock feed, that he was nicknamed "Turnip Townshend."

Robert Bakewell (1725-1795) was responsible for attacking the problem of livestock breeding. Haphazard breeding had resulted in sheep weighing only from twenty-five to forty pounds and cattle of about four hundred pounds. Through the select breeding of choice animals, Bakewell raised larger livestock, improved the quality of the meat, and increased the quantity of milk available from his dairy cattle. His methods were so enthusiastically adopted by other farmers that by 1800 the average sheep weighed eighty pounds and the average beef, eight hundred pounds.

The most ardent publicist of his countrymen's achievements was Arthur Young (1741-1820), who lectured throughout Europe and edited a farm journal. Translated into many foreign languages, his writings popularized the advantages to be gained from well-equipped farms and economical agricultural techniques and did much to free English agriculture from the inefficient, unproductive farming techniques of the past.

While the tempo of agricultural reform was much faster and more general in England than on the Continent, there was evidence of some progress in farming methods there also. In the western portion of the Continent, serfdom was disappearing, although vexatious dues remained to infuriate the peasantry. Here and there, especially in Holland, the Rhine Valley, the environs of Paris, and northern Italy, there was experimentation with crop rotation and fertilization, better use of grasses, such as clover, and utilization of root crops, such as turnips. In fact, the great advances made in English agriculture owed much to Continental techniques and improved seeds, but these achievements were applied much more systematically, more thoroughly, and more enthusiastically in England.

Changes on the agrarian scene. The practice of enclosing open lands, a development which had begun in England during Tudor times, was accelerated by the changes in farming methods. Aided by special acts of Parliament, members of the new commercial landowning class seized the opportunity to enclose the common lands, where for hundreds of years English villagers had grazed their cattle, and to purchase and fence in the small farms owned and operated by the sturdy, independent yeoman class. These portions of land were consolidated into holdings which were, in effect, large-scale business enterprises requiring substantial amounts of capital for operation and upkeep. The demand for wool in the textile industry resulted also in the enclosure of large tracts of arable land for sheep raising.

The controversy over the enclosure movement reached its climax between 1750 and 1810. Arthur Young and the advocates of enclosure justified amalgamation of small agricultural holdings by claiming that new methods of stock breeding and crop rotation could not be practiced on unfenced land. From an economic standpoint, enclosure was inevitable, and some historians believe that the enclosure movement resulted ultimately in a more careful use of a greater amount of land than had been available before. Like

Even before the eighteenth century attempts were being made to improve the state of agriculture in England. Here is the frontispiece from a manual of husbandry printed in 1685.

most drastic economic changes, however, the enclosure movement spelled misery and dislocation to thousands of country folk. Below is a petition against enclosure:

A ruinous effect of this enclosure will be the almost total depopulation of the . . . [towns] now filled with bold and hardy husbandmen, from among whom . . . the nation has hitherto derived its greatest strength and glory, in the supply of its fleets and armies; and driving them, from necessity and want of employ, in vast crowds, into manufacturing towns, where the very nature of their employment, over the loom or the forge, soon may waste their strength, and consequently debilitate their posterity, and by imperceptible degrees obliterate the great principle of obedience to the Laws of God and their country, which forms the character of the simple and artless villagers . . . on which so much depends the good order and government of the State.[8]

The saga of the yeomen's misfortunes did not end with their departure from the villages; its finale took place in the cities. When the story of industrialism is taken up in Chapter 6, we will view the bleak and harsh environment of displaced rural people as they labored long and hard in grimy factories and lived as best they could in ugly, disease-ridden slums.

CAPITALISM, BUSINESS, LAISSEZ FAIRE

Growth and development of capitalism. Although their roots can be found in Greek and Roman times, modern capitalistic practices did not come into being until the seventeenth century. Some economists who stress the role played by the joint-stock companies of the seventeenth and eighteenth centuries in the growth of capitalism define capitalism as the presence of capital in the form of negotiable stock, viewed as an investment to yield interest. Although the term defies simple definition, a more comprehensive explanation of capitalism would include other important factors. Capitalism may be said to be an economic system characterized by private ownership of property, the presence of large amounts of capital (money, land, raw materials, equipment), and the existence of specialized business techniques such as banking, credit, and insurance. But whatever the definition, it can safely be said that the driving force behind capitalism is the securing of profits. Under the conditions of perfect competition, capitalism secures the most economical use of resources.

What were the conditions favorable to the growth and development of capitalism in eighteenth-century Europe? Governmental interference with the economy declined, and states began to allow businessmen a wide measure of freedom in conducting their affairs. As joint-stock companies and large-scale enterprises were created and grew, great amounts of capital or liquid wealth were amassed. Business operations were facilitated by the establishment and growth of banks, insurance companies, and stock and commodity exchanges. As the business classes grew in political power, they gradually assumed equality of status with other leading groups in society. Significantly, business was motivated by the acquisitive spirit; the individualistic drive of the entrepreneurs was based upon the urge to make profits and accumulate wealth and the desire for power and acclaim—motives which offer a marked contrast to the self-abnegation and other-worldliness of the Middle Ages. Whatever the motive of either age, the lot of the common man left much to be desired.

Three phases of capitalism. Much of the history of the 200 years between the mid-point of the eighteenth century and the present day is concerned with the virtues and sins of capitalism, its philosophical defense and condemnation, and its development (as in the United States) or rejection (as in the case of the Soviet Union). Its history can be traced in three distinct stages.

The first stage—commercial capitalism—is associated with geographical discoveries, colonization, and the astounding increase in overseas trade (see Chapter 19, Volume I). At this time early capitalists, protected by governmental controls, subsidies, and monopolies, made profits from the transportation of goods. Beginning about 1750, the second phase—industrial capitalism—was made possible by the adoption of new energy sources and machines to manufacturing, the development of the factory system, and the rapid growth of wealth. The essence of industrial capitalism was profit making from the manufacturing process itself. In the mid-nineteenth century, this phase reached its zenith with large factories, efficient machines, and the concentration of capital in the hands of the middle class. In the last decades of the nineteenth century, when the ultimate control and direction of industry came into the hands of financiers, industrial capitalism gave way to financial capitalism. The establishment of mammoth industrial concerns or empires and the ownership and management of their assets by men completely divorced from production were the dominant features of this third phase.

The machinery of business. During the latter half of the seventeenth century and throughout the eighteenth, improvements in the machinery of business kept pace with the growth of business ventures and extended capitalistic practices into new areas of a nation's economy. The Bank of Eng-

The famous insurance association known as Lloyd's of London took its name from Lloyd's coffee house, where the insurance underwriters used to meet with merchants and shipowners. This scene at Lloyd's dates from the early nineteenth century.

land (the "Old Lady of Threadneedle Street") was established by an act of Parliament in 1694. This famous institution did not compete with private companies for the accounts of the general public but became the bankers' bank and a semiofficial institution which marketed the government's securities and administered the currency.

In Chapter 19, Volume I, the origins of modern insurance companies in the commercial centers of the Mediterranean were discussed. Specializing in certain types of risks, insurance companies continued to grow; the first exclusively marine insurance company was set up in Paris in 1668. The most famous of all marine insurance groups, Lloyd's of London, came into being about twenty years later. Lloyd's was not a stock company but an association of shipowners, merchants, and underwriters who first met together in a London coffee house owned by Edward Lloyd. Since its modest beginnings, Lloyd's has grown steadily and branched out into other forms of insurance. Today it is the world authority on matters of ship classification and it publishes *Lloyd's List*, a daily paper which indicates the whereabouts of all registered vessels. When a ship is officially missing or destroyed, a bell is rung on the premises.

After the disastrous London Fire of 1666, fire insurance companies were started, and in the same period companies specializing in

The "Mississippi Bubble" was inflated by a Scotsman named John Law, whose grandiose economic schemes included the promotion of colonization in the Mississippi valley. Thousands of Frenchmen emigrated, only to have their settlements cut off from financial

life insurance were also formed. In 1684 the Friendly Society was organized. This society was the first mutual company—an association in which policyholders receive a share of the company profits.

Toward the end of the seventeenth century, the creation of joint-stock companies that issued shares easily transferable from one person to another led to the establishment of a stock exchange which existed independently of the older commodity exchange, the Bourse. The rapid increase of trade brought about an avalanche of speculation in the shares of stock issued by joint-stock companies such as those promoted by the governments of France, Holland, and England. To compete with the powerful

Dutch and English East India companies, Colbert in 1664 established the French East and West India companies. He also established the Levant Company in 1670 to trade with the Near East and the Senegal Company in 1673 for African commerce. England organized the Hudson's Bay Company in 1670 and the Royal African Company two years later.

Speculation and business bubbles. One authority comments on the fantastic nature of some of the wildcat schemes "which promised to earn great dividends by trading in human hair, making square cannon balls, getting butter from beech trees, marketing an air pump for the brain, perfecting a wheel for perpetual motion, searching for rich

VEUE
DU CAMP
DE
LA CONCESSION
DE
MONSEIGNEUR
LAW.
AU NOUVEAU
BILOXY. COSTE
DE LA
LOUISIANNE

support when the "Bubble" burst. Here is Biloxi in 1720, a wilderness village of tents and huts. Surviving the collapse of Law's plans, it served for a time as capital of Louisiana.

wrecks off the Irish coast, or importing jackasses from Spain."[9] The two most notorious speculative companies were the South Sea Company in England and the Mississippi Company in France.

The financiers of the South Sea Company assumed the British national debt of about £9,000,000 in return for a 6 per cent annual interest payment and a monopoly of British trade with South America and the islands in the South Seas. The price of company stock rose, encouraging the creation of other similar ventures. However, the time came when the price of the South Sea Company stock no longer reflected its true value; it had risen far beyond the value of its earnings in trade. In 1720, when banks could not

collect money for loans made on the inflated stock, this huge speculative bubble burst.

The Mississippi Company had a similar history. Formed to promote French holdings in the Mississippi valley, the company controlled virtually all French colonial trade and in addition directed the administration of the royal bank. But the lack of valuable assets in the sparsely populated Mississippi valley region, coupled with the orgy of speculation which resulted from this scheme, brought the company to ruin in 1720.

In England the South Sea Company was investigated and reorganized through the efforts of Robert Walpole, chancellor of the exchequer; but in France the failure of the Mississippi valley stock scheme demoralized many citizens and helped to discredit the Old Regime. Such disastrous financial crashes slowed the growth of banking and credit organizations, for the public was justifiably suspicious of all business promotions for many decades afterwards. But the wild mania for speculation and quick profits revealed previously untapped sources of wealth available for investment and gave a stimulus to new techniques for extending credit.

England's merchant princes. The emergence of the businessman, who worked for profits in commerce, manufacturing, banking, or the new agriculture, was one of the most significant developments in the eighteenth century. The power of this middle-class group was not only to alter European class structure radically and to sweep aside monarchical despotism but was indeed to influence the course of history throughout the world.

In England hundreds of merchant and industrial princes rose from lowly circumstances to great wealth. Birmingham, a thriving manufacturing center by the end of the eighteenth century, numbered among its businessmen three worth £100,000; seven, £50,000; eight, £30,000; and seventeen, £20,000. Another 174 were worth between £10,000 and £5,000. Of these 209 businessmen, 103 began at the bottom of the economic ladder with only the assets of initiative, shrewdness, and ambition. Originally a porter and ship's carpenter, William Miles of Bristol invested in the Jamaican sugar trade, soon amassed a fortune, and ended by controlling the largest sugar-refining business in his native city. In like fashion, many self-made men founded important families, such as the Pitts, Peels, Wedgwoods, and Wilkinsons.

John Wilkinson (1728-1808) was typical of the energetic and successful middle-class man. His father had been a day laborer, but as a producer of cannon and shells for the British government, the son became one of the wealthiest ironmasters of his day. He pioneered the use of coal instead of charcoal for smelting iron and improved Watt's steam engine by designing a new cylinder for it on a boring machine of his own making. Because he had unbounded faith in iron, he was called "iron mad"; but in spite of his detractors, he built the first iron bridge in the world, lived to see the first iron ship afloat, and was appropriately buried in an iron coffin.

Considerable prejudice existed among the English nobility against these business "upstarts," who were rapidly gaining political power, but there was not the same degree of antagonism between business and the aristocracy as existed in France. English aristocrats had no qualms about making money in business, and the younger sons of noble families frequently went into trade or married the daughters of wealthy middle-class entrepreneurs and joined the family business. Wealthy English merchant princes improved their family pedigrees, and landed aristocrats exploited their noble lineage to replenish or regain their fortunes.

There were still signs of friction, however. A contemporary champion of the new industrial leaders praised the middle class and criticized the nobility in the following lines:

Such are England's true patriots, her prop and
    her pride;
They draw wealth from each state, while its
    wants are supply'd;
To mankind all at large they are factors and
    friends,
And their praise with their wares reach the
    world's farthest ends. . . .
Is it then, ye vain lordlings! ye treat us with
    scorn,
Because titles and birth your own fortunes adorn?
What worth to yourselves from high birth can
    accrue?
Are your ancestors' glories entailed upon you?
And is your lazy pomp of much use to a nation?
Are not parks and wide lawns a refined devastation? . . .
Their blood in pure currents thro' ages conveyed
It were impious to taint with the contact of
    trade.[11]

A discontented bourgeoisie in France. By the eighteenth century, in France as in England, the middle class had become the dynamic element in society, providing the captains of business and industry. Embracing education and culture with enthusiasm, they were, for the most part, a cultivated, intellectual group. They attended salons and eagerly accepted the reformist ideas of the *philosophes.*

In his *Memoirs,* a nobleman of the times described the growing prominence of the bourgeoisie:

. . . [The bourgeoisie] had gathered all the re-spect, the wealth, and the real power which the clergy and nobility had lost . . . immense riches which had flowed into the country [from col-onies] had fallen only into the hands of the middle classes, since the prejudices of the nobles excluded them all from trading, and prevented them from engaging in any of the mechanical or liberal arts . . . Nearly all small towns had become more or less commercial, and were in-habited by small *bourgeois,* who were richer and more industrious than the nobility. These [the middle class] had received an education which was more essential to them than to the gentry, of whom many obtained the highest posts in the State without any merit or ability on their part, while the majority were destined to fritter away their existence in the lower commissioned ranks of the Army. In Paris . . . the *bourgeoisie* was far superior in wealth, ability, and personal merit.[11]

Unlike their prototypes across the Chan-nel, the French middle class had wealth with-out responsibility, intelligence without au-thority, and ability without recognition. Important government posts were denied them because the courtiers at Versailles dis-pensed the offices of state according to birth and not by reason of merit. Although much better educated and more refined than many members of the aristocracy, the bourgeoisie were often snubbed by them. Successful en-terprises supported the bulk of governmental tax revenues and the extravagances of the royal court, yet the bourgeoisie had no power to censure an inefficient, despotic govern-ment.

Perhaps the most important factor in mid-dle-class discontent was the government-sponsored system of mercantilism, by which such outworn relics of the Middle Ages as the guilds were coddled. The bourgeoisie were determined to sweep away these anachronisms, which controlled prices un-fairly and throttled the spirit of competition. In fact, nearly all aspects of industrial capi-talism were antithetic to mercantilism. As early as the 1620's, English economists had

Social stratification under the Old Regime in France is bitterly satirized in this cartoon, which shows the First Estate and the Second Estate—the clergy and the nobility—riding on the back of the Third Estate, represented here by an aged, toil-worn peasant.

advocated the importance of mutual trade between nations rather than the hoarding of gold and silver by any one nation. To weaken the traditional mercantilistic system, the middle class whole-heartedly supported an influential group of economic thinkers who took up their pens to champion capitalism.

The physiocrats and *laissez faire.* Led by their founder, François Quesnay (1694-1774), the physician of Louis xv and Madame Pompadour, the physiocrats based their sys-tem of economics on the concept of natural law. To the physiocrats, money circulated under the influence of natural forces much as the blood does in the human body, and natural laws controlled prices, regulated the flow of trade, and resulted in national prosperity or poverty. They believed in a "free market," the concept which implies that natural forces of supply and demand should be allowed to regulate the conduct of business. Deploring tariffs or restrictions on commerce, they believed that the government should adopt the policy of laissez faire (letting business alone).

Quesnay argued that the true wealth of a nation could be measured not by quantities of gold and silver but by the value of its products. Industry and commerce could not add to the wealth of the nation but could aid in stabilizing prices so that a fair return for agricultural products was possible. Although it appeared that the physiocrats were minimizing the importance of industry, their argument that the only source of wealth was agriculture was not without comfort to the bourgeoisie. Because only the land produced wealth, to tax anything but land was futile—an argument that appealed to the middle classes.

Apart from their specific doctrinal proposals, the physiocratic principles were important because they stemmed from the same philosophic assumption held by the freedom-loving *philosophes* that all human activity—social, political, and economic—was subject to natural laws similar to those governing the physical universe. Unhappiness, misery, and injustice were the result of unnatural laws and restrictions. Thus all arbitrary acts of government based on absolutism had to be uprooted.

One of the best known physiocrats was Pierre Du Pont de Nemours (1739-1817), from whose work *Physiocracy, or the Natural Constitution of That Form of Government Most Advantageous to the Human Race* (1767), the name for this group of thinkers was derived. The descendants of Du Pont de Nemours founded the famous E. I. Du Pont de Nemours Company in the United States.

Adam Smith and the *Wealth of Nations*.
Probably the most influential advocate of laissez-faire economics was a Scottish professor, Adam Smith (1723-1790). Educated at the universities of Glasgow and Oxford, Smith returned to his native Scotland to teach logic and moral philosophy at his alma mater. In 1776 his most famous book, *An Inquiry into the Nature and Causes of the Wealth of Nations*, was published.

Smith was indebted to the physiocrats for his views of personal liberty, natural law, and the position of the state as a regulatory medium, but he differed with them regarding the importance of agriculture in national economy. To him, the labor of a nation is the source from which all the necessities and luxuries of life derive. He also advanced the theory that rapid production depends largely on division of labor, and he believed that each individual in society should perform the work for which he is best fitted. By a wise division of labor, each member of society will perform quickly and efficiently the tasks for which he has an aptitude and will have a large field in which to exchange the results of his own labor for commodities produced by the labor of others.

Smith maintained that every individual is motivated by prudent self-interest:

It is not from the benevolence of the butcher, the brewer, or the baker, that we expect our dinner, but from their regard to their own interest. We address ourselves, not to their humanity but to their self-love, and never talk to them of our own necessities but of their advantages. . . . Every individual is continually exerting himself to find out the most advantageous employment for whatever capital he can command. It is his own advantage, indeed, and not that of society, which he has in view.[12]

The philosophy of *Wealth of Nations* can be summed up in the phrase *laissez faire*. Smith felt that a government should avoid placing any restriction on private trade or industry. He looked on all fixing of wages, trade unions which limit apprenticeship, tariffs, and governmental interference as injurious to trade, and he scoffed at the mercantilists' view that the wealth of a nation depends on the achieving of a surplus of exports, the amassing of bullion, and the crippling of neighboring countries. Trade works for the benefit of all nations the world over:

The wealth of a neighboring nation . . . though dangerous in war and politics, is certainly advantageous in trade. In a state of hostility it may enable our enemies to maintain fleets and armies superior to our own; but in a state of peace and commerce it must likewise enable them to exchange with us to a greater value, and to afford a better market, either for the immediate produce of our own industry, or for whatever is purchased with that produce. . . . The modern maxims of foreign commerce, by aiming at the impoverishment of all our neighbors so far as they are capable of producing their intended effect, tend to render that very commerce insignificant and contemptible.[13]

Smith was pointing up the truth that a country cannot thrive and its trade flourish if its neighbors are not prosperous. This fact was pointedly illustrated after World War II when the United States expended billions of dollars in helping to put not only its recent allies but also its former foes on their feet.

THE ENLIGHTENMENT

The philosophes, critics of society. In the mid-seventeenth century, France had been the intellectual center of Europe. But by the end of the century the reputation of Newton and the success of an advanced governmental system had made England the exponent of new systems of politics and science. However, due largely to two famous French thinkers, Voltaire and Montesquieu, English thought was transmitted to the Continent in the first half of the eighteenth century, and soon France again enjoyed intellectual supremacy in Europe. By 1750 France was so decidedly the leader in culture, language, ideals, and manners that it has been said "an opinion launched in Paris was like a battering ram launched by thirty millions of men."[14] Here a group of thinkers and writers known as the *philosophes* brought the Age of Reason to its climax.

The term *philosophes* cannot be translated as "philosophers," because the thinkers to whom it referred—eloquent and devastating critics of the Old Regime—were not philosophers in any strict sense, but rather students of society who analyzed its evils and advocated reforms. They were, above all, apostles of an eighteenth-century intellectual movement identified as the Enlightenment. The spirit and purpose of the Enlightenment were eloquently expressed by the *philosophe* Baron d'Holbach (1723-1789):

Let us then endeavor to disperse those clouds of ignorance, those mists of darkness, which impede Man on his journey, which block his progress, which prevent his marching through life with a firm and steady step. Let us try to inspire him . . . with respect for his own reason—with an inextinguishable love of truth . . . so that he may learn to know himself . . . and no longer be duped by an imagination that has been led astray by authority—so that he may renounce the prejudices of his childhood—so that he may learn to base his morals on his own nature, on his own wants, on the real advantage of society . . . so that he may learn to pursue his true happiness, by promoting that of others . . . in short, so that he may become a virtuous and rational being, who cannot fail to become happy.[15]

The thinkers of the Age of Reason believed in happiness and fulfillment in this world; they regarded mind rather than faith as the best source of guidance and were suspicious of emotion, myth, and supernaturalism. The chief support of the cult of reason was science, with its new laws and methods. The supreme achievement of the Enlightenment, however, was not in discovering additional scientific laws but rather in translating the advances of science into a new philosophy and world view. Exaltation of science, faith in reason, and belief in humanitarianism led writers and thinkers of the Enlightenment to reevaluate all aspects of society. They were positive that reason could solve all human problems. All thought was colored by a belief in mankind's ability to improve itself.

The Old Regime in France. In the eighteenth century, French monarchs failed to achieve an effective, advantageous foreign policy or to establish a sound and efficient internal government. The century had opened with the costly wars of Louis xiv; and Louis xv, who reigned from 1715 to 1774, was indifferent to matters of state. Preoccupied with his mistresses, Madame de Pompadour and Madame Du Barry, Louis did not provide strong, able leadership for his country, the premier nation of Europe. The next monarch, Louis xvi, was well meaning, but ill-educated, indolent, and shy. Shirking matters of state, Louis spent his happiest hours in a workshop tinkering with locks. Louis married Marie Antoinette, who lacked the vision and strength of character of her mother, Maria Theresa of Austria.

France suffered greatly from the indifference and incompetence of its rulers, especially since governmental administration was centralized in the hands of the king. Because few vestiges of self-government remained in the local districts, the governmental bureaus in Paris were cluttered with a mass of trivial and inconsequential reports and requests from the provinces. Many of these provinces had retained their own local customs and administrative machinery from medieval times, and, consequently, there was an alarming lack of uniformity in legal codes, tariff boundaries, weights and measures, and taxation throughout the realm, which added to the confusion and inefficiency of government. There was no body comparable to the English Parliament for registering public opinion and shaping governmental policy. The Estates-General had not been called into session since 1614.

Discrimination and injustice prevailed in the social structure. Under the Old Regime, birth, not intelligence or achievement, assured success and social position. Of France's total population of 25,000,000 people, only 200,000 belonged to the privileged classes—the clergy and the nobility. These two groups controlled nearly half of the nation's land, monopolized the best positions in the Church, army, and government, and evaded much of the taxation. The peasants—80 per cent of the population—were saddled with intolerable burdens. The *taille,* a land tax; the tithe, levied by the Church; the *gabelle,* a tax on salt; and various other taxes took nearly half of a peasant's income. In addition, while the practice of serfdom had practically disappeared, peasants suffered from many vestiges of medieval social discrimination. Fishing, hunting, and keeping pigeons were activities reserved exclusively for the nobility. Although wild game might destroy crops, peasants were forbidden to molest the deer and rabbits. Grain fields were often trampled underfoot by hunting parties of nobles, and swarms of pigeons gobbled up newly planted seed. Many nobles were absentee landlords who squandered the hard-earned peasants' dues in ostentatious expenditures at Versailles.

Philosophes urge political reforms. Working with the physiocrats as they sought to remove outworn economic abuses, the *philosophes* carried on an offensive against tyranny, misgovernment, and unjust laws. The reform movements of the physiocrats and the *philosophes* were inseparably connected, for only by obtaining efficient and rational government could the instrument be secured to carry through essential economic reforms. The *philosophes* were one in militantly advocating the end of arbitrary government and the adoption of such rights as civil liberty, trial by jury, and freedom of expression—freedoms which they construed as implicit in natural law. By expressing the belief that laws and institutions could be based on a natural law as immutable as Newton's laws of physics, they helped to undermine the edifice of absolutism.

Because these impudent critics were subject to strict laws of censorship at home, they frequently had their works published in states enjoying more liberal regimes, such as Holland. Or, as often happened, the French censors, themselves seduced by the arguments of the *philosophes*, closed their eyes to the inflammatory passages. Thus "in France . . . despotism [was] tempered by epigram."[16] Foremost among these *philosophes* were Voltaire, Montesquieu, Diderot, and Rousseau.

Voltaire, prince of the philosophes. Voltaire (1694-1778), more than any other thinker, personified the skepticism of the eighteenth century toward traditional religion and the evils of the time. Christened François Marie Arouet, he came from a middle-class Parisian family and attended a Jesuit secondary school, one of the best in France. After completing his formal schooling, this "crasher of noble gates" gave up his family name, assuming the more aristocratic "Monsieur de Voltaire." A member of a club of young intellectuals who scoffed at the illogical customs of their time, the young Voltaire was clever, witty, and inordinately vain. Above all he enjoyed exercising a caustic pen; when the crown in the name of economy disposed of half the horses in the royal stables, Voltaire observed that it would be much more logical to get rid of the asses that made up much of the royal court. By criticizing the stupidities of high officials and members of the nobility, he soon ran afoul of the law, twice was imprisoned in the Bastille, on one occasion received a cruel beating at the hands of the servants of a nobleman he had ridiculed, and finally was banished to England for three years. There Voltaire met English intelligentsia, wrote, and gathered ammunition for a relentless attack on the abuses of his day.

Upon his return to France, Voltaire again championed tolerance, popularized the science of Newton, fought for personal liberty and freedom of the press, and acted as an influential propagandist for Deism. Amid his books, manuscripts, and laboratory equipment (like all eighteenth-century thinkers Voltaire liked to think himself a scientist), he turned out a prodigious number of works: histories, plays, pamphlets, essays, and novels. In his correspondence—estimated at ten thousand letters—he wittily spread the gospel of rationalism and scathingly attacked the abuses of the Old Regime. For three years Voltaire stayed at the court of Frederick the Great in Berlin, but the "statesman who wanted to be a poet" and the "poet who wanted to be a statesman" got on each other's nerves. After a violent quarrel with his royal patron, Voltaire wandered over Europe for two years, finally settling down near Geneva.

Voltaire achieved his greatest fame as the most relentless critic of the established churches, Protestant and Catholic alike. He was sickened by the intolerance of organized Christianity and disgusted by the petty squabbles which seemed to monopolize the time of many priests and clergymen. Yet in spite of his vituperation against Christianity, Voltaire did not wish to wreck religion. He once said that if a God did not exist, it would be necessary to invent one.

Voltaire's short fictional satire *Candide* (1759) was a biting attack on the easy optimism of Leibnitz and his view that this world is "the best of all possible worlds." As

Houdon: Portrait of Voltaire

his hero, Voltaire used a naïve young man, Candide, who learns after many hair-raising and comic adventures that the "best of all possible worlds" is rent by earthquakes, famines, plagues, greed, war, and injustice. Here is a fictional battle observed by Candide:

Nothing could be smarter, more splendid, more brilliant, better drawn up than the two armies. Trumpets, fifes, hautboys, drums, cannons, formed a harmony such as has never been heard even in hell. The cannons first of all laid flat about six thousand men on each side; then the musketry removed from the best of worlds some nine or ten thousands blackguards who infested its surface. The bayonet also was the sufficient reason for the death of some thousands of men. The whole might amount to thirty thousand souls. Candide, who trembled like a philosopher, hid himself as well as he could during this heroic butchery. At last, while the two Kings each commanded a Te Deum in his camp, Candide decided to go elsewhere to reason about effects and causes. He clambered over heaps of dead and dying men and reached a neighboring village, which was in ashes; it was an Abare village which the Bulgarians had burned in accordance with international law. Here, old men dazed with blows watched the dying agonies of their murdered wives who clutched their children to their bleeding breasts; there, disemboweled girls who had been made to satisfy the natural appetites of heroes gasped their last sighs; others, half-burned, begged to be put to death. Brains were scattered on the ground among dismembered arms and legs. Candide fled to another village as fast as he could; it belonged to the Bulgarians, and Abarian heroes had treated it in the same way. Candide, stumbling over quivering limbs or across ruins, at last escaped from the theater of war. . . .[17]

The story ends with Candide advising his former tutor, Dr. Pangloss, that we must "cultivate our garden" (instead of concerning ourselves with unanswerable philosophical questions)—a succinct expression of Voltaire's common-sense approach to life.

Voltaire did not have a systematic philosophy of politics. Scattered here and there in the ninety-three volumes he wrote are his diatribes, reflections, and recommendations on all things governmental. Basic to his views was the idea that the state did not exist for the ambition and glory of its ruler but as an instrument by which the needs of its subjects could be met. Only by guaranteeing to all men such basic rights as liberty of conscience, freedom of speech, and freedom from arbitrary arrest and imprisonment could the state fulfill its true function.

Voltaire thought the ideal form of government to be a representative democracy with a carefully limited group of intelligent voters. In England he found a system which he praised eloquently:

It has not been without some difficulty that liberty has been established in England . . . nevertheless, the English do not think they have purchased their laws at too high a price. Other nations have shed as much blood; but then the blood they spilled in defense of their liberty served only to enslave them the more. . . . The House of Commons daily becomes more powerful. . . . Here is no such thing as the distinction of high, middle, and low justice in France . . . [a] nobleman . . . pays his share of the taxes as others do, all of which are regulated by the House of Commons. . . .[18]

In viewing the governments in existence, however, Voltaire thought the most preferable to be government by a wise, paternal, just, and all-powerful king—a benevolent despot. An enlightened monarch would respect the basic natural rights of his people and use his extensive powers to carry out desirable reforms.

Montesquieu and the Persian Letters. Montesquieu (1689-1755), a French nobleman, was born just a century before the outbreak of the French Revolution and was destined to become the most systematic and comprehensive student of government during the first half of the eighteenth century. Although a judicial official and a member of the privileged class, he dominated the course of criticism directed against absolute monarchy.

Following his scholarly inclinations, Montesquieu read the many travel books dealing with European exploration and contact with the New World. These works about previously unknown or little-known societies gave him the opportunity to compare European institutions with those existing elsewhere. His famous Persian Letters (1721) purported to be the correspondence of two rich and noble oriental gentlemen writing their friends in the East while traveling about France. The pretense of authenticity was only a thin disguise; Montesquieu wanted his readers to see through this trickery and realize that he, with tongue in cheek, had written a devastating satire on religion and government in France. The sophisticated bourgeoisie were delighted as they read such comments as:

It is by sitting on chairs that nobility is acquired. A great noble is a man who sees the King, speaks to his ministers, and who possesses ancestors, debts, and pensions.[19]

Montesquieu called the pope "an old idol"; and he slyly poked fun at Louis xv, who had a minister only eighteen years old but a mistress of eighty and who was as fearful of having a really great general at the head of his own troops as at the head of the enemy's forces. Montesquieu also attacked the evil of religious wars, the practice of dueling, the king's debasing of the currency, and the belief that there was only one true religion.

The Spirit of Laws. The next important work from Montesquieu was *The Spirit of Laws* (1748), a massive study of the salient features of numerous governments known to have actually existed. Widely discussed in the French salons, it later became the political bible of important statesmen in England and colonial America. Unlike the English philosopher Locke and many of the *philosophes*, Montesquieu did not use the intuitive approach in his writings. He did not seek to discover certain universal principles or natural laws and then proceed to describe a perfect society based on nature; his interest lay not in generalizations but in facts. His method was to describe and analyze governments and then to show how they reflected the environment in which they functioned.

In *The Spirit of Laws,* Montesquieu concluded that all governments conformed to certain specific factors of geography, economics, and race, which varied from country to country. Since the value of any governmental system depended on its relation to these specific factors, no one form of government could be better than another, nor could there be a "best" form of government.

Montesquieu was a relentless critic of tyranny and a champion of liberty. Although he did not endorse any one form of government, he admired the limited parliamentary monarchy of England. In the separation of executive, legislative, and judicial powers, he found the bulwark of liberty. In the words of Montesquieu:

When the legislative and executive powers are united in the same person, or in the same body of magistrates, there can be no liberty, because apprehensions may arise lest the same monarch or senate should enact tyrannical laws, and then execute them in a tyrannical manner. Again, there is no liberty if the judiciary power be not separated from the legislative and executive. Were it joined with the legislative, the life and liberty of the subject could be exposed to arbitrary control; for the judge would be then the legislator. Were it joined to the executive power, the judge might behave with violence and oppression.[20]

Astute as he was in his judgments, Montesquieu misinterpreted the operation of the unwritten English constitution, for the English government was moving toward unity of powers. However, this concept of separation of powers greatly influenced the planners of the American Constitution.

Diderot and the Encyclopédie. Voltaire had many disciples and imitators, but his only rival in spreading the gospel of rationalism and Deism was a set of books—the famous French *Encyclopédie,* edited by Denis Diderot (1713-1784). Diderot wanted the *Encyclopédie* to serve not only as a repository of knowledge but also as a weapon against traditional abuses and authority.

Published between 1751 and 1772, the *Encyclopédie* became the great medium for spreading the new ideas of the Enlightenment and constituted the chief monument of the *philosophes.* Its seventeen volumes contained articles whose authors—tradesmen as well as scientists and philosophers—declared the supremacy of the new science, championed tolerance, denounced superstition, and criticized in a moderate tone unfair taxation, the slave trade, and the cruelty of the existing criminal code. Article after article underlined the political backwardness of France, where the king was absolute ruler, where clergy and nobles were practically exempt from taxation, and where the administrative system prevented the fruits of the Enlightenment from coming to full development.

Birth of the social sciences. One of the great achievements of the eighteenth century was the application of the methods of science to the better understanding of man. The *philosophes* believed that by such application the laws governing society could be discovered. As one of them observed:

In one of his illustrations for *The Rake's Progress*, William Hogarth depicts the dreadful conditions existing in a madhouse.

I believe that morals should be treated like all other sciences, and that one should arrive at a moral principle as one proceeds with an experiment in physics.[21]

Pervading the thought of the Enlightenment was a deep concern for the welfare of mankind—a desire to reduce its errors, add to its happiness, and ennoble its future. This interest in humanity and its problems led to important innovations in the writing of history and the creation of those studies known today as the social sciences—political science or government, economics, anthropology, and psychology. In addition, important advances were made in criminology, education, and humanitarianism.

One of the most potent forces fashioned by the eighteenth century was a desire to help the unfortunate. This humanitarianism did much to focus attention on the need for a science of man. Study of social problems indicated that there were many social evils which cried aloud for rectification: Negro slavery was legal, administration of justice was barbarous, the insane were treated like animals, the poor laws were inadequate, and religious intolerance persisted in many lands. There had been much improvement in the preceding five hundred years, but Europeans were now more than ever aware of the need for widespread reform. The intellectual protest against intolerance and cruelty was a by-product of the desire of enlightened intellectuals to create a body of scientific studies about man to the end that his lot might be made happier. This was part of the growing concern with a pleasant existence on this earth.

In the field of sociology, Cesare Bonesana Beccaria (1738-1794), an Italian nobleman interested in social reform, published his *Essay on Crimes and Punishments* (1764). With its insistence that prison terms should be deterrents to crime rather than punishments for crime, this work established the science of criminology. Beccaria's ideas soon were widely recognized, and in many countries new criminal codes were based on his principles. Torture in obtaining evidence and such punishments as whipping, branding, and the slitting of ears were gradually eliminated from most codes.

John Howard (1726-1790), the outstanding prison reformer of eighteenth-century England, was the son of a wealthy merchant; he spent his days in reading and study and in building model cottages and erecting schools for the common people. On an inspection tour of his home district, he was astonished to find that the jailers did not receive a regular salary but had to collect their remuneration in fees from their unwilling boarders. In some cases persons who had been acquitted by a jury had not been released from prison because they had no funds to pay for their "board." In 1774 Howard gave evidence before a committee of the House of Commons which resulted in an act providing pay for jailers, and in 1777 appeared his important work, *The States of the Prisons in England and Wales*. This study stressed the need for efficient prison administration and maintained that the chief aim of imprisonment should be reformation of the criminal.

Natural law and natural rights. Although Montesquieu is credited with producing the first systematic study of political systems, others among the *philosophes* emphasized the doctrine of natural rights in developing the science of government. We have seen how Bishop Bossuet, in the seventeenth century, had justified absolute monarchy by the doctrine of divine right (Chapter 1). The rationalism of the *philosophes* rejected religious authority, but absolute monarchy also had powerful support from political theorists who used only secular arguments.

In the long run, it was Thomas Hobbes (1588-1679) who composed the most penetrating and influential justification of absolutism. To this English thinker and student of new scientific thought, absolutism was not to be defended by resort to legal theory or to religion. In the *Leviathan* (1651), Hobbes drew upon science and its servant, psychology. From the horrors of the English civil wars, the excesses of civil strife in France, and the barbarisms committed during the Thirty Years' War, Hobbes discovered what he believed to be the essential nature of man when not restrained by law. A pessimistic, cynical observer of human conduct, Hobbes saw man "as a wolf to his fellow man" and mankind, uncontrolled by authority, as essentially selfish and cruel. Without law and absolute authority, mankind lived under the adverse conditions of the state of nature, in which:

> . . . there is no place for industry . . . no culture of the earth . . . no arts; no letters; no society; and which is worst of all, continual fear, and danger of violent death; and the life of man, solitary, poor, nasty, brutish, and short.[22]

There being no future for mankind in the state of nature, absolute authority was essential. To create a workable society, people had surrendered all their rights and powers to a sovereign government, an action which bound them to an irrevocable contract. While Hobbes undoubtedly was influenced by travelers' accounts of the brutality of savage groups encountered in exotic lands, he did not actually believe that there had once existed a "state of nature" and that at some specific date in world history, mankind had decided to create, by contract, a despotic, all-powerful government. Rather, his explanation of this procedure was, to him, a rational explanation of what might have happened. If not demonstrable by resort to experience, his argument was natural in terms of rational thought.

Hobbes' Leviathan, the sovereign state, could be any one of a number of forms of government. But, to Hobbes, monarchy was the most effective and desirable. In Hobbes'

John Locke: challenger of absolutism

theory, the monarch was supreme and immune to criticism. Only thus could peace and security be maintained. There was no right of revolution, even against tyranny.

Locke's doctrine of popular sovereignty. By the end of the seventeenth century, however, after the Glorious Revolution, another great English political theorist stepped forth to justify the toppling of James II from the throne. John Locke (1632-1704) was one of the most eminent men of his day; he was an Oxford graduate, a doctor of medicine, a member of the Royal Society, a political scientist, and a famous philosopher. In his "Of Civil Government," the second essay in *Two Treatises of Government,* published in 1690, Locke gave his answer to absolutism by expounding the following ideas:

(1) Before government was established, all men, living in a state of nature, possessed certain natural rights. Inherent in the very order of nature, these natural rights consisted principally of the rights to life, liberty, and property. The concept that men possess

certain natural, inalienable, and sacred rights did not originate with Locke but can be traced back as far as Aristotle and Roman law. In the English civil war of the seventeenth century, however, the idea of natural rights received its first effective impetus.

(2) Locke took a much more hopeful and optimistic view of human nature than did Hobbes. Men living in the state of nature were reasonable and moral, one to the other, and were not bent on mutual destruction as Hobbes supposed. But while life in the state of nature was not frighteningly ruthless, it was unsatisfactory because society was handicapped in many ways by the absence of government. There was no superior agency to enforce the law of nature, which is a body of rules governing men's conduct in such a way as to ensure the equality of all men and every man's enjoyment of his natural rights. The determinant of natural law is reason, but since men in a state of nature arrived at different interpretations of natural law, uncertainty and conflict often resulted.

(3) Therefore, government is necessary to maintain natural law and guarantee the enjoyment of man's natural rights. By common consent, an agreement, or compact, is entered into by which a sovereign is set up with power to govern and enforce the laws of nature.

(4) Through this contract the people give up some of their rights to the government, but their basic natural rights are in no way surrendered.

(5) The social contract, which does away with the chaotic state of nature and establishes an organized society with a government, is bilateral, or binding upon both parties. The government, for its part, can demand the obedience of the people, but the people may also expect that the government will keep its part of the contract by not in any way abridging the natural rights of the people. If these rights are violated, if the government rules unwisely and tyrannically, the people have a perfect right to overthrow their rulers. In short, the people are the real rulers, the custodians of popular sovereignty.

It was the great achievement of Locke to give, for the first time, a clear and comprehensive exposition of what we call the doctrine of popular sovereignty, which gives the people the right of revolution. Thus, unlike Hobbes, Locke used the social contract theory to challenge rather than to support absolutism.

Rousseau and the Social Contract. Jean Jacques Rousseau (1712-1778) was one of the most strange and enigmatic yet significant persons of his time. One of his contemporaries wrote of him:

Jean Jacques is a madman who is very clever, and who is only clever when he is in a fever; it is best therefore neither to cure nor to insult him.[23]

Although believing in the general objectives of the *philosophes,* Rousseau, unlike Voltaire, distrusted reason and science. He gloried in impulses and intuitions, trusting emotions rather than thoughts, the heart rather than the mind. A bundle of contradictions, his words have been cited to justify the arguments of such divergent political philosophies as democracy and totalitarianism.

His first essay, *Discourse on the Arts and Sciences,* was a flaming indictment of civilization. According to Rousseau, only the simple life, the back-to-nature existence, could save mankind from the corrupting influences of civilization. His key idea was that man is naturally good and that civilized society with its rules, conventions, injustices, and artificialities destroys the pristine virtues of natural man and makes him wicked.

The same thesis appeared in his second essay, *Discourse on the Origin of Inequality Among Men* (1754), which attacked governments for protecting private property. Rousseau believed private property to be a great evil and the measure of inequality among men. His early hand-to-mouth existence and the rebuffs and ridicule he suffered from polite society contributed to his hatred of the Old Regime and the status quo. He was also influenced by a concept which, during this period, was gaining currency from the idealized accounts by European travelers of unspoiled native peoples—the ideal of the "noble savage" who lived:

. . . without faith . . . law . . . [with] neither king, nor judge, nor priest . . . nor taxes, nor prisons.[24]

It was not surprising, then, that Rousseau's *Discourse* excoriated the society that had refused to open its doors to him, urged the overthrow of artificial modes of life, and encouraged men to listen to their hearts and to the voice of nature rather than to their minds and the postulates of formal philosophy.

This message hit the salons of Europe like a bolt of lightning. To the aristocrats and idle rich who found life boring, it was a novel idea and an attractive one. To live the simple life became fashionable. Sentiment became popular, tears respectable. The queen of France fancied herself a milkmaid and acted out this role in the village built especially for her at Versailles.

Social Contract. Rousseau's most important work and indeed one of the most influential books on political theory of modern times was his *Social Contract* (1762), which opens with the stirring statement: "Man is born free, but is everywhere in chains."

In this work, Rousseau endeavored to construct a theory of government based on the consent of the governed while reconciling the conflicting demands of individual liberty and social organization. Using Locke's basic assumptions of the social contract and natural law, Rousseau expounded the doctrine of popular sovereignty, the supremacy of the common people, and their right of revolution:

. . . the depositories of the executive power are not the people's masters, but its officers . . . it can set them up and pull them down when it likes . . . for them there is no question of contract, but of obedience . . . in taking charge of the functions the State imposes on them they are doing no more than fulfilling their duty as citizens. . . .[25]

But Rousseau's solution for reconciling the natural freedom of the individual with membership in a social group ruled by law is replete with contradictions and bad logic. In Rousseau's ideal society, an individual can surrender all his natural rights—as envisaged by Locke—to the group and yet retain his freedom. This happy situation is secured by each individual's voluntarily forming part of what is called "the General Will." Because he forms part of this whole, he continues to remain free. It is then argued that the majority, which always knows what is best for the group, is the custodian of the General Will. In fact, the majority is a better judge than the individual of what is best for him, and thus the individual must obey its commands. "In his attempt to solve the problem of political obligation, to reconcile liberty and authority, Rousseau has come full circle. Starting with complete individualism, he ends in complete collectivism, with the individual submerged in the state and having to it a duty of unquestioning obedience, without benefit of constitutional protection.[26]

In advancing the cause of democracy and in exposing the evils of a morally bankrupt absolute monarchy, Rousseau spread a hatred of oppression and was hailed as the champion of the masses. His writings fanned the flames of discontent and revolt —a revolt that was to crumble the Bastille and drag the nobility to the guillotine. There is wit in the observation that the hides of the aristocrats were used to bind the second edition of the *Social Contract*. But it is also true that Rousseau's doctrine of the General Will came to be used later by ambitious despots. Claiming that he alone knew what constituted the General Will, a shrewd leader could justify his seizure of power. It is one of history's ironies that the *Social Contract*, written to justify popular revolution, was used later on to justify totalitarianism.

Effects of the philosophes. The reforming rationalism of the *philosophes* spread to many of the royal courts of Europe, but, ironically enough, the influence of these thinkers did not measurably affect the operation of their own government. France remained a hotbed of criticism against the Old Regime, with no important reforms inaugurated by the rulers.

The most prominent French political thinkers represented three viewpoints concerning what constituted the best form of government. Voltaire placed his faith in benevolent despotism, Montesquieu favored the English parliamentary system, and Rousseau proclaimed democracy, the rule of the majority. Other *philosophes*—Diderot, Holbach, Condorcet—energetically attacked the Old Regime and, while not advocating any specific form of government, leaned toward benevolent despotism. What mattered most, however, was that government should be run according to the laws of reason and that reforms should be enacted to eliminate specific evils. As Pope, poetic exponent of the Age of Reason, wrote:

For forms of government, let fools contest;
Whate'er is best administer'd is best.[27]

Traditionalists in their approach to reform, the *philosophes* did not advocate violent revolution. They believed that good government, whatever the form, should be in the hands of the well-to-do and the educated.

The extent to which the ideas of the *philosophes* caused the French Revolution has long been a subject of heated controversy. As we shall see in the next chapter, the selfishness of the nobles, extravagances of the government, and impending national bankruptcy finally brought on the crisis precipitating revolution. But in the background were the *philosophes* and their ideas. By criticizing the evils of the times, stimulating discontent—especially among the bourgeoisie —and offering a logical picture of what a well-ordered society might be, the *philosophes* created a widespread atmosphere of grievance and supplied political philosophies and panaceas for the future.

THE RULE OF ORDER
IN THE ARTS

Classicism and the arts. The several quotations from Pope (see pages 9, 19, 82) call attention through his rhythmic couplets to one of the outstanding aspects of the arts in the period when the aristocracy of Europe

At the right is St. Paul's Cathedral in London, designed by Sir Christopher Wren; above is an aerial view of the magnificent palace and park of Louis XIV, bordered by the town of Versailles. In the days of the Bourbon monarchs, "Versailles was like a vast and gorgeous theatre, where all were actors and spectators at once; and all played their parts to perfection. Here swarmed by thousands this silken nobility, whose ancestors rode cased in iron. Pageant followed pageant. A picture of the time preserves for us an evening in the great hall of the Château, where the King, with piles of louis d'or before him, sits at a large oval green table, throwing the dice, among princes and princesses, dukes, and duchesses, ambassadors, marshals of France, and a vast throng of courtiers, like an animated bed of tulips; for men and women alike wear bright and varied colors. Above are the frescoes of Le Brun; around are walls of sculptured and inlaid marbles, with mirrors that reflect the restless splendors of the scene and the blaze of chandeliers, sparkling with crystal pendants. Pomp, magnificence, profusion, were a business and a duty at the Court. Versailles was a gulf into which the labor of France poured its earnings; and it was never full."[*]

[*]Francis Parkman, *Montcalm and Wolfe*.

was in its heyday and reason was king. The respect for forms and conventions, for elegance and wit was a mark of the fashionable world of the aristocracy and was equally reflected in the literary and fine arts. Inspired in part by the order and symmetry of the world as revealed by science, the creative artists of the eighteenth century prided themselves on their rationalism, sophistication, balance, and self-control. Furthermore, the Enlightenment was a continuation of Renaissance humanism and its revival of antiquity, coupled with the new scientific outlook. In literature and the arts there had to be respect for definite rules and conventions. The men of the time felt spiritually akin to Rome's Augustan Age and strove to exhibit the same stability, refined polish, and control over unrestrained emotion. In consequence, every work of art tended to have a cold, rational aspect, whether it was a philosophical poem by Pope or a dainty symphony by Haydn. Inspiration sprang from the intellect, not the heart; from reason, not emotion.

Generally speaking, classical forms were slavishly imitated; style of expression was considered so all-important that many writers were satisfied to express old ideas so long as they were elegantly phrased. Poets and playwrights imitated various literary giants of antiquity; orators such as Burke used Demosthenes as a model; and letter writers like Lord Chesterfield turned to the epistles of Cicero for inspiration.

Alexander Pope. The foremost exponent of the classical spirit in the Age of Reason was the English poet Alexander Pope (1688-1744). An imitator of the classical satirists Horace and Juvenal, Pope exposed the frailties and vices of his contemporaries in rhyming couplets. These lines were aimed at certain noted critics and scholars of his day:

Pains, reading, study, are their just pretense,
And all they want is spirit, taste, and sense.
Commas and points they set exactly right,
And 'twere a sin to rob them of their mite.
Yet ne'er one sprig of laurel graced these ribalds,
From slashing Bentley down to piddling Tibalds:
Each wight, who reads not, and but scans and
    spells,

Each word-catcher, that lives on syllables,
E'en such small critics some regard may claim,
Preserved in Milton's or in Shakespeare's name.[28]

A Roman Catholic and the son of a retired linen merchant, Pope was at first excluded from elevated English society. To the handicaps of a suspect religion and low social status was added the fact that he was a cripple. But by the sheer force of his intellect and poetical genius, Pope made a brilliant literary success and became England's foremost Neoclassical poet. Perhaps his most famous poem is *An Essay on Man* (1733), in which he reduced to a series of epigrams the philosophy of his day as expressed by Hobbes, Locke, and Newton. Reflecting the strong note of optimism so characteristic of the Enlightenment, Pope accepted the cosmos thus:

Of systems possible it is confessed
That wisdom infinite must form the best. . . .
All are but parts of one stupendous whole,
Whose body nature is, and God the soul. . . .
All nature is but art, unknown to thee;
All chance, direction, which thou canst not see.
All discord, harmony not understood;
All partial evil, universal good;
And, spite of pride, in erring reason's *spite,*
One truth is clear: *Whatever is, is right.*[29]

Baroque architecture. In Volume I, we followed the modifications of Renaissance architecture as it became more highly decorated. Called Baroque, this art form became increasingly grandiose and extravagant. In its first phase in southern Europe, Baroque was used in church architecture. Baroque style was later employed by rulers in buildings designed to serve as symbols of their power and magnificence. Versailles is an example of this.

Rococo style. Developing within the Baroque period was an extravagant, Italianate style of architecture and interior decoration —the Rococo. It was more intimate, "private," and sophisticated than the Baroque and could be used in small country or town houses.

The Neoclassical style in architecture. In the eighteenth century a reaction set in against the Baroque and Rococo styles, manifesting itself in a return to the intrinsic dignity and restraint of Greek and Roman art forms. In England this return to a classical style appeared earlier than on the Continent and produced memorable results.

The architect Sir Christopher Wren (1632-1723) is famous for the churches in London which he was commissioned to rebuild after the fire of 1666; the largest was St. Paul's Cathedral, whose dome still dominates the city. Wren's smaller churches had to be sandwiched in among the shops of the congested city, and in order to make them stand out against the skyline, Wren used spires, although the spire was a form carried over from the Gothic period.

As in literature, the trend in England's architecture reflected the eighteenth century's growing preference for the cold logic of scientific reason rather than the exuberant emotion reflected in Baroque. The Neoclassical architectural style emphasized close imitation of classical models rather than the free adaptation of the Baroque. The great country houses of the English nobility exhibited a purity of design and a dignified exterior which often included a portico with Corinthian columns.

This classical revival was seen in other parts of Europe as well. In France, the Place de la Concorde was laid out in restrained classical style, and the Petit Trianon at Versailles—built as a residence for Madame Pompadour—was a return to greater simplicity in architecture. The Church of St. Genevieve in Paris imitated the portico and dome of the Pantheon in Rome. Germany also reflected the new trend: the Royal Opera House in Berlin was built with a Corinthian portico, and the Brandenburg Gate in that city is an imitation of an Athenian model.

Developments in music. The Age of Reason broke with the past in music as it had in science and philosophy. With the development of opera and the increasing popularity of other forms of secular music, no longer was music the exclusive servant of the Church. Religious music did not cease to be important, however. The German-born, naturalized Englishman Frederick Handel (1685-1759) achieved his greatest success with the oratorio *Messiah* (1742). Deeply religious works were among the greatest compositions of the prolific German organ master and choir director Johann Sebastian Bach (1685-1750).

New musical forms reflected new trends in instrumental music. As symphonies, sonatas, concertos, and chamber music appeared, music became more than the mere accompaniment to religious services, operatic performances, or ballroom dances. The chamber music played in courts and salons was written for woodwinds and brasses as well as strings. Thus the modern orchestra developed along with the symphonic form.

About 1760 Italy ceased to dominate in music, and a new capital arose at Vienna. The supremacy of this city began with Franz Joseph Haydn (1732-1809), who gained the admiration of all Europe with his compositions, including operettas, chamber pieces, and over one hundred symphonies. Haydn encouraged a struggling young fellow Austrian and former child prodigy, Wolfgang Mozart (1756-1791), whose opera *The Marriage of Figaro* (1786) became a model for all subsequent comic operas. Mozart wrote forty-nine symphonies and numerous other works, climaxing his career with the operas *Don Giovanni* (1787) and *The Magic Flute*.

The music typical of the Age of Reason is termed classical because it reflects the same formalism and close adherence to established musical canons as is exhibited in the literature and art of the period. Brilliant as were the contributions of Bach, Handel, Haydn, and Mozart, the ordinary music of the period tended to be monotonous.

ABSOLUTISM IN MATURITY AND DECAY

Faith in benevolent despotism. The majority of the *philosophes* believed that the most logical way to attain desirable reforms was through the rule of a benevolent despot: secure a well-meaning, intelligent monarch imbued with the philosophy of the Enlightenment and all would be well. In a sense, this theory of government was akin to the Platonic ideal of a society where philosophers would be kings.

A few eighteenth-century monarchs were progressive, sincerely believing in the ideas of the *philosophes*. In this, the "monarch's age of repentance," major figures who were touched by the Enlightenment and became (or seemed to become) benevolent despots were Frederick the Great of Prussia, Catherine the Great of Russia, and the Austrian emperor Joseph II. Lesser rulers included Leopold of Tuscany, Charles III of Spain, and Gustavus III of Sweden. In the royal courts of these monarchs, the works of the *philosophes* were read avidly; the rulers corresponded with the French thinkers and played host to *philosophes* such as Diderot.

Frederick, a model ruler. In Chapter 2 we met Frederick as an unscrupulous aggressor and a mighty warrior. The first half of his reign was almost wholly warlike; the last half, almost wholly peaceful.

It was during the latter period that Frederick became the *beau ideal* of benevolent despots. His writings were sought by monarchs who wished to rule according to the laws of reason. Dedicated to the improvement of the Prussian state, Frederick expressed his concept of the benevolent monarch's role thus:

Princes and monarchs . . . are not invested with supreme authority that they may, with impunity, riot in debauchery and voluptuousness . . . the sovereign represents the State; he and his people form but one body, which can only be happy as far as united by concord. The prince is to the nation he governs what the head is to the man; it is his duty to see, think, and act for the whole community. . . . The monarch is only the first servant of the State, who is obliged to act with probity and prudence, and to remain as totally disinterested as if he were each moment liable to render an account of his administration to his fellow-citizens. . . . As the sovereign is properly the head of a family of citizens, the father of his people, he ought on all occasions to be the last refuge of the unfortunate.[30]

"Old Fritz," as his subjects affectionately called him, traveled a great deal about his kingdom, studying its problems and hearing complaints from his people. No aspect of government escaped his attention. His reforms included the abolishment of torture, the reorganization of the civil service, and the recognition of equality of status for his Catholic subjects. In the area of economics, he encouraged immigration to his country, promoted the conservation of Prussia's natural resources, and established textile and silk factories. Until he died in 1786 at the age of seventy-four, Frederick worked diligently at the occupation of kingship, aware that he had made Prussia a great European power.

Enlightened despotism in Russia. Like her contemporary, Frederick the Great, Catherine of Russia was a shrewd, ruthless double-dealer in foreign affairs. As we have already seen, she joined Prussia and Austria in the callous annihilation of Poland. But in the early part of her reign, she prided herself upon being a patron of learning and the arts, a friend to the *philosophes,* and an exponent of the Enlightenment in government.

Catherine worked diligently to improve Russian law and its administration, the best evidence being the *Instructions* she prepared for a commission which had been organized to draft a new code of laws. In this document, Catherine indicated that, although the supreme ruler, the monarch, was the sole judge of what was right or wrong, nothing cruel or unjust should be done to a king's subjects. By "equality" she meant that all people were subject to the same laws of the realm; by freedom, "the right to do everything that the laws allow."

European reformers and philosophers applauded her writings and her publicly announced policy of reform. To them she was the "star of the north." But as we shall see, "The Enlightenment was a fashion in Russia, never a fact."[31]

Joseph II of Austria. The most sincere of the benevolent despots was Joseph II, the Hapsburg scion and son of Maria Theresa. During his reign he had two basic problems: the consolidation of the Austrian empire and the initiation of reform movements in which he strongly believed.

As the governments of Bohemia and Hungary—heretofore almost autonomous kingdoms—were linked closely with Austria's, the imperial power of Vienna became more authoritative than it had been in the early part of the century. Local governing bodies lost their powers, and the tax collection system was made efficient. While the presence of a variety of minority groups prevented Joseph from combining his holdings into a tightly knit national state, enough unity was achieved to maintain the Hapsburg empire intact until the end of World War I.

Joseph's reforms included the establishment of an equitable basis for taxation and the improvement of education. His abolition of serfdom was the most revolutionary decree of this period, but his most lasting reform was the creation of a national court system. Joseph was truly the philosopher king in action.

Failure of benevolent despotism. Benevolent despotism was incapable of rooting out the deep-seated evils of the Old Regime. No matter how sincere and devoted to reform, an enlightened ruler such as Joseph of Austria could not achieve success against the selfishness of his nobility and the ignorance of his peasantry. Many of Joseph's reforms appeared premature, and he was considered too hasty in adopting new measures. Frederick the Great observed that "Joseph always wishes to take the second step before he has taken the first." In his last years Joseph wrote mournfully:

The work piles up daily and nothing is done. I labor unceasingly all morning, and until five and six in the afternoon, with fifteen minutes out while I eat a solitary lunch, but there is no result. The petty objections, the intrigues, of which I have been so long the victim, hinder and delay me, and with the delay everything is going to the devil.[32]

He died in 1790, a broken-hearted man.

In a number of cases enlightened absolutism was nothing but a facade, a mere playing at reform because it was fashionable. With the passage of years, Catherine the Great's views of Enlightenment changed considerably. By the end of her reign, she no longer quoted her "dear *philosophes*" or pro-

Her professed interest in the Enlightenment did not prevent Catherine of Russia from strengthening serfdom as a basic institution in Russia's social and economic structure.

claimed their ideas. She had repressed a widespread revolution in her land with savage cruelty, and the French Revolution had elicited this comment from her:

. . . [It was an] irreligious, immoral, anarchical, abominable, and diabolical plague, the enemy of God and of the Thrones.[33]

Even half-hearted benevolent despotism was better than no benevolence at all, however. And if we separate the domestic policies of Frederick the Great from his foreign ambitions, there is much to praise in his reign. But the evils inherent in an all-powerful monarchy tainted the system of benevolent despotism. In dominating his people, Frederick neglected to educate them to political realities. The British ambassador in Berlin wrote:

The Prussian Monarchy reminds me of a vast prison in the centre of which appears the great keeper, occupied in the care of his captives.[34]

When Frederick died, there was no one trained to take his place. Prussia nearly melted away in the fires of the Napoleonic Wars, lacking the steel-like qualities of leadership provided by "Old Fritz."

SUMMARY

There is much to be said for the interpretation of history which places more emphasis upon the force of ideas and the often imperceptible influence of pervasive social and economic forces than on stirring speeches in legislative halls and victories won on battlefields. In the eighteenth century the new wealth, the rising ambitions of the bourgeoisie, the gradual transformation of business methods, and a mounting skepticism and curiosity sounded the passing of the Old Regime. Europe was ready for change.

The most obvious transformation was brought about by the effects of colonial expansion, new products, increasing population, and developments in industry and agriculture. But our discussion has also dealt with the changes in the realm of thought. The chief protagonists in this field were the champions of the middle class, who demanded reform in both politics and economics. In both these fields the keynote was freedom for the individual. But to the *philosophes* it was mainly freedom and opportunity for a very special kind of individual— the well-educated, intelligent, and preferably well-to-do. Voltaire was the most tireless propagandist, asking for basic rights for all. He believed, however, that the blessings of an enlightened society could best be secured by the rule of benevolent despots. On the other hand, Montesquieu, the first systematic modern student of the art of government and of political science, saw the English parliamentary system as the means to good government. Rousseau sought the same ends but used entirely different means. He cast aside reason, had no use for books, and disdained civilization. Writing a flaming justification of revolution and democracy, he unwittingly provided ammunition by his confused and tortuous logic for the arguments of later dictators.

The *philosophes* created an enlightened climate of opinion and a widespread tendency toward reform in western Europe. Their ideas crossed the Atlantic and profoundly influenced public opinion in the Americas. In Europe many monarchs thought it stylish to follow the writings and teachings of men like Voltaire and Montesquieu, but these benevolent despots failed to ward off the ultimate downfall of the Old Regime because their reforms were not sufficiently comprehensive and thorough. They proposed or practiced reform, but only on the epidermis of the status quo. Drastic internal surgery was needed. In countries such as Prussia and Austria, benevolent despotism had some limited successes, but in France, hotbed of reformist philosophy, the kings refused to be enlightened. The French monarchs presided in an incredibly short-sighted fashion over a regime that was locked in stagnation and paralysis. The result could only be a violent upheaval, and the account of this cataclysm will form one of the themes of our next chapter, "The Rights of Man."

CHAPTER 4

The Rights of Man

REVOLUTION IN THE WESTERN WORLD: 1778-1815

Introduction. The period from 1778 to 1815 is a watershed in western political history. Before this period little is heard of the rights of the people; after it, democracy is in the ascendancy. Even stronger voices speak forth for the rights of citizens, for bills of rights and constitutions—political concepts which have had an immeasurable influence on the course of western civilization. In this chapter we shall trace the course of the momentous political changes in France and their impact on Europe during the last quarter of the eighteenth century and the early years of the nineteenth.

While financial disaster was the immediate cause of the French Revolution, the revolt of the thirteen British colonies in America exercised a potent influence upon the course of revolution in France. In defiance of authority the French overthrew an ineffectual king and created a new republic in the suffering and bloodshed of revolution. The rise of republican France was a challenge to despotic regimes throughout Europe, and the result was intermittent warfare on the Continent from 1792 to 1815. In the midst of this troubled era, Napoleon came to power. Turning the newborn republic into a tool for conquest, the Little Corporal threatened all Europe until defeat at Waterloo crushed his dreams of empire.

Not since the fall of Rome had there been so much turbulence and war in Europe as in the period from 1792 to 1815. The sound of marching armies was heard from Moscow to Madrid, and the crash of naval guns echoed over the seas from the Indian Ocean to the Caribbean. Following the victory of the allies at Waterloo, Napoleon was hustled off to oblivion on St. Helena, and the statesmen of the great powers found themselves confronted with the task of building a new Europe out of the one which Napoleon constructed.

The leaders who had humbled Napoleon set out to meet these needs—as they interpreted them—at the Congress of Vienna. Their solutions were conservative. Sincerely believing that the explosive forces of nationalism and democracy liberated by the French Revolution had been primarily responsible for more than two decades of destruction and suffering, they were determined to return as much as possible to the "good old days"

before the Revolution. With this end in mind, they deliberately sought to extirpate the revolutionary ideas and attitudes that had been released by French republicanism; they restored the old royal lines and endeavored to create among the nations of Europe a harmony and stability which would make a recurrence of revolutionary violence impossible. After this conservative peace had been established, international machinery known as the Congress System was devised to defend the political arrangements of 1815 and to crush any attempts to upset them.

FRANCE'S MODERATE REVOLUTION

The American Revolution and France. In 1776 the thirteen American colonies officially declared their independence from England. Due to the determination of some of the colonists and their leaders, vital aid from France, and the disarray of England's armed forces, the rebellion succeeded. Peace and liberty were achieved by the Treaty of Paris (1783).

The impact of the American Revolution in France was deep and widespread. Some even maintain the French Revolution might not have occurred without it, for the Americans showed that an antiquated government could be removed. Louis XVI and the French aristocrats who sympathized with the colonial rebellion failed to realize the danger of the example the New World set for the Old.

The financial crisis. Whatever its effect on the climate of opinion in France, the most immediate influence of the American Revolution upon France was an acceleration toward bankruptcy. Participation in the American Revolution had cost France almost $400 million. The credit of the government became so poor that it had to pay an interest rate of 20 per cent on its loans, whereas England paid only 4 per cent. By 1789 the government was faced with an annual deficit of $27 million, and interest payments

on the national debt took half of the total national revenues.

Although he usually paid small heed to problems of government, even Louis XVI appreciated the danger of bankruptcy. But despite attempts by him and his advisers to put French finances in order, no solution was found, and the crisis deepened. In desperation Louis convened the Estates-General, which had been inactive since 1614. This body was composed of representatives of the First Estate (the clergy), the Second Estate (the nobility), and the Third Estate (the middle class and the peasants). As a gesture to the bourgeoisie, the Third Estate was granted twice the number of representatives allowed each of the other two estates. But the middle class, having long waited to make its voice heard, was not satisfied with this concession. Although the king did not realize it, his decision to call the Estates-General initiated the French Revolution.

The National Assembly. The calling of the Estates-General in 1789 precipitated a demand for reform all over France. For the guidance of the delegates to the assembly, *cahiers* (notebooks) of grievances were prepared by the people. The *cahiers* included demands for personal liberty, a national legislature to make the laws, a jury system, freedom of the press, and abolition of unfair taxation. Thus the *cahiers* presented a program of wide social and economic reform; but in tone they were moderate and expressed no disloyalty against the monarchy.

On May 5 the Estates-General was formally convened. The delegates of the Third Estate consisted of some six hundred deputies; half were lawyers, the remainder merchants, bankers, governmental officials, and farmers. According to custom the three estates were expected to vote by orders—that is, by estates rather than as individuals. This would mean that any schemes of reform formulated by the Third Estate could always be defeated by a two-to-one vote at the hands of the clergy and nobility.

After six weeks of wrangling on the question of whether voting should be by order or by head, the Third Estate, joined by a few members of the two other orders, declared itself a National Constituent Assembly competent to pass laws for France. A few days later its members were barred from their meeting place by order of the king. Thereupon, they assembled at a nearby indoor tennis court and solemnly took the Tennis Court Oath, declaring that they would not disband until a constitution had been drawn up. Three days later the king appeared, demanding that the members of each estate meet separately. Following Louis' departure, a royal official sent to order the Assembly to disband was told by the defiant leader Mirabeau, "Sir, go tell your master that nothing but bayonets will drive us out of here." Louis weakly yielded, and the Third Estate, now continually augmented by members of the other orders proceeded with its role as the National Constituent Assembly.

Collapse of absolutism. All over France millions of eyes were watching the events at Versailles. Peasants and city workers grew bold at the capitulation of the king, and in July 1789, disorders and riots broke out throughout the land. In the cities, houses of the nobility were sacked; in the country, peasants demolished the castles of their lords. Everywhere, it was manifest that royal government in France was collapsing. Paris seethed with radical and revolutionary opinion: pamphlets exhorted the people to revolt, and radical political organizations fanned the flames of discontent.

Following a rumor that the king was concentrating troops at Versailles as a means of browbeating the Assembly, a Parisian mob attacked the Bastille, a grim fortress which was the hated symbol of the Old Regime. Although on that fateful day of July 14, 1789, the Bastille contained only seven prisoners (four counterfeiters, one habitual drunkard, and two lunatics), the fortress was stormed and its defenders slain. On hearing this, King Louis is said to have remarked to the messenger, "This is a revolt." "No, Sire," was the reply, "it is a revolution."

In October came another disquieting instance of mob violence. Suffering from lack of food and aroused at the news that the king was unwilling to cooperate with the Assembly, a Parisian mob marched on Versailles and encamped near the palace. The mob demanded that the royal family return to Paris. The next day a procession of more than thirty thousand people marched back to Paris with the royal coach, shouting as they went: "We have the baker and the baker's wife and the little cook-boy; now we shall have bread."

Renunciation of the Old Regime. The National Constituent Assembly, which accompanied the king to Paris, was in session from June 1789 until October 1791. During this period the Assembly passed more than two thousand laws and effected a peaceful and moderate revolution. Speaking of its accomplishments, one historian has written: "No other body of legislators has ever demolished so much in the same brief period."[1]

One of the most important and dramatic acts of the Assembly took place in the critical days of August 1789. The Bastille had just fallen, and peasants all over France, determined to destroy the manor rolls which authorized the levying of dues and feudal obligations, fell upon their hated oppressors. If a lord resisted, he might be mobbed or killed and his chateau destroyed. This was the time of the "Great Fear": reports that royalist troops were about to massacre the peasants and rumors that great bands of brigands were pillaging the countryside spread panic through the provinces.

The Paris mob launches its successful assault on the Bastille.

As the frightening news reached Paris, the deputies in the Assembly realized that immediate action had to be taken. During the night of August 4, deputy after deputy arose to renounce his feudal dues and privileges. By these proclamations, known as the August Decrees, serfdom was abolished, the old game laws were repealed, the courts of the manor were swept away, and the tithes and all other fees of the Church were ended. It was declared that from that time on taxes were to be collected from all citizens irrespective of rank, the sale of judicial and municipal offices was to cease, justice was to be freely dispensed, and all citizens, regardless of birth, were eligible for any office.

Thus the lawmakers of the Assembly demolished the feudal system; there were no more serfs, no more privileges for the clergy and nobles, and no more titles. All men were now equal before the law. During the long night, the Old Regime came to an end, and with the dawn a new France was born.

The Declaration of the Rights of Man. Those who saw the salvation of France in the workings of the Assembly now eagerly awaited the new constitution it was pledged to draft. Before drawing up the new scheme of government, the deputies produced a document which summarized the principles upon which the new regime should be based—

the Declaration of the Rights of Man. The philosophy underlying this document came largely from the *philosophes* and from the American and the English Bills of Rights. Thomas Jefferson, then American minister to France, was frequently called upon to give his advice on the Declaration.

When completed, the Declaration of the Rights of Man contained seventeen provisions. Among the most important were:

1. Men are born and will remain free and endowed with equal rights. Social distinctions can be based only upon usefulness to the common weal.
2. The end and purpose of all political groups is the preservation of the natural and inalienable rights of Man. These rights are Liberty, the Possession of Property, Safety, and Resistance to Oppression. . . .
4. Liberty consists in being able to do anything which is not harmful to another or to others; therefore, the exercise of the natural rights of each individual has only such limits as will assure to other members of society the enjoyment of the same rights. These limits can be determined only by the Law. . . .
6. The Law is the expression of the will of the people. All citizens have the right and the duty to concur in the formation of the Law, either in person or through their representatives. Whether it punishes or whether it protects, the Law must be the same for all. . . .
9. Every individual being presumed innocent until he has been proved guilty, if it is considered necessary to arrest him, the Law must repress with severity any force which is not required to secure his person.
10. None is to be persecuted for his opinions, even his religious beliefs, provided that his expression of them does not interfere with the order established by the Law.
11. Free communication of thought and opinion is one of the most precious rights of Man; therefore, every citizen can speak, write, or publish freely, except that he will be required to answer for the abuse of such freedom in cases determined by the Law. . . .
17. The possession of property being an inviolable and sacred right, none can be deprived of it, unless public necessity, legally proved, clearly requires the deprivation, and then only on the necessary condition of a previously established just reparation.[2]

The Declaration of the Rights of Man was of historic importance because it was a summation of the spirit of constitutional government and political liberalism underlying the Glorious Revolution in England and the revolt of the Thirteen Colonies in America. This French pronouncement appealed immediately to reform groups in various European nations, and during the nineteenth century it inspired many oppressed peoples to throw off the yoke of their tyrannical rulers. But the Declaration was not a claim for the "pure" democracy and mass rule advocated by Rousseau; it expressed the middle-class belief in natural law and the right of the wealthy and intelligent to rule.

The new constitution. By September 1791 the National Constituent Assembly had formulated a new plan of government which, in effect, made Louis xvi a constitutional monarch. The chief organ of national government under the new constitution was the Legislative Assembly. This elective body alone had the power to initiate and pass laws, and its consent was required for declarations of war and for the acceptance of peace treaties.

The king still enjoyed important powers, but these were subject to check by the Assembly. Louis xvi was given only a suspensive veto over legislation, a device which could retard action by the Assembly but could not block its will indefinitely. In the event that three sessions of the Assembly passed a bill, it was to become law without the king's signature. The monarch could not squander public revenues to satisfy his own whims and fancies. All expenses for his family and the court had to be met from a generous annual grant called the civil list. No longer could the king use the formula of Louis xiv, *L'état, c'est moi;* the monarch was now "Louis by the grace of God and the Constitution, King of the State."

Despite the rights guaranteed in the Declaration of the Rights of Man, the suffrage was not given to all adults. Frenchmen were divided into two classes on the basis of wealth. "Active," or tax-paying, citizens could vote; "passive" citizens were barred from the polls. The voice of the people was further weakened by having the active citizens elect so-called electors, who in turn elected the deputies to the national Legislative Assembly. Because electors had to meet certain property qualifications and deputies had to fulfill still more stringent conditions, not more than 50,000 of a total of 26,000,000 people could serve as electors and fewer still could serve as deputies. Thus, the most striking feature of the French constitution of 1791 was its reflection of the interests of the influential bourgeoisie.

Reforms of the Assembly. The Constituent Assembly achieved many long-overdue reforms. The old chaotic units of local government were abolished and replaced by eighty-three departments. Justice was also materially improved and made available to the masses. Other reforms ended the numerous medieval restrictions on trade and the conduct of business. Every effort was made to encourage individual enterprise. Thus, men were to enjoy freedom not only in politics but also in business.

The status of the Church was substantially changed. Its lands were taken by the government and used as collateral for paper money called *assignats.* By the Civil Constitution of the Clergy, the Church was secularized. Its officials were subject to governmental regulation and were elected by the people and paid by the state. The pope no longer had any authority in France.

The Revolution believed to be over. When the new government, the Legislative Assembly, met in October 1791, the majority of people in France believed the Revolution was over. The new scheme of government was a marked improvement over the system of privilege, incompetence, and confusion presided over by Louis xvi and the privileged classes before 1789. There was no reason why, given a reasonable opportunity, the Legislative Assembly should not have assured France stable and progressive government.

This phase has been called France's First, or Bourgeois, Revolution. In essence the country was now under a limited monarchy. After relatively little violence, the upper middle class was in control. The objectives of those in charge of the government were to "stabilize" the Revolution, to block further change, and to hang onto their wealth.

But the peasants were discontented, and the city workers were especially disgruntled. The cost of living was going up, and unemployment had been spreading. Therefore, the poor—both rural and urban—wanted more radical reforms; they wanted a complete socio-economic revolution at the expense of all the well-to-do, whether members of the aristocracy or of the middle class.

Opposition to the new government. By the first clause of the August Decrees, the Constituent Assembly had declared the feudal system completely abolished. Most peasants thought that all their old payments had been wiped out. When it came to formulating their decrees into laws, however, the nobles were not quite so generous as their lofty and eloquent statements on the night of August 4 seemed to imply. The Assembly ruled that many privileges, such as possession of serfs, personal corvées, and hunting and fishing rights, were to be abolished without compensation. On the other hand, land rents and dues that had been commuted into money payments were regarded as property rights of the nobles to be purchased by the peasants. To free himself from these payments, a peasant would have to possess a sum of money equal to at least twenty years of dues.

Some peasants were able to buy out their landlords, but the majority neither bought off their lords nor continued to pay the dues. Hatred against the men of wealth and property and their agents in the Assembly grew. (Between 1792 and 1793, when champions of the poorer classes were much more influential in the government, feudal dues were finally abolished without any compensation.)

Instead of accepting the moderate changes brought about between 1789 and 1791 and thus helping to consolidate and strengthen the moderate revolution, Louis XVI did his best to weaken the new regime. The king apparently did not understand that if the Legislative Assembly failed, the Revolution would take a radical turn and the monarchy would be swept away. With his family, the king melodramatically tried to escape out of the country. Crudely disguised, he and his party were apprehended while en route to the border and forced to return to Paris amid mounting antiroyalist sentiments. In addition, many people suspected that the king was in league with the enemies of France.

The Civil Constitution of the Clergy had been condemned by Pope Pius VI, and consequently many of the clergy refused to take the oath of fidelity to the constitution. These nonjuring priests, as they were called, told the people that sacraments administered by priests who had accepted the Civil Constitution of the Clergy were null and void. In the country districts the peasants supported their nonjuring priests, and serious disorders broke out. Thus, from the outset, the Legislative Assembly was faced with the enmity and opposition of a determined Catholic group.

The common people of the cities—artisans and workers—opposed the Legislative Assembly as the creature of the selfish middle class. By their control of the Assembly, the businessmen and large landowners had denied the masses the right to participate in the government, despite the noble-sounding Declaration of the Rights of Man. Largely illiterate and motivated by emotion, these urban workers could be stirred up to wild passions of frenzy by eloquent leaders, and as time passed, they became increasingly dangerous.

Factions in the Assembly. The division of opinion in the country at large was mirrored by factionalism in the Assembly itself. About one third of the deputies were conservatives; they made up the party of the Right, which supported the king and was satisfied with the achievements of the moderate revolution. Seated in the middle of the Assembly was the party of the Center, made up of representatives who had no particular program or principles. Next to the apathetic Center were the deputies of the Left, dynamic and aggressive young radicals who distrusted the king, were dissatisfied with the constitution of 1791, and wished the Revolution to continue. From the very start, the enemies of the constitution assumed the leadership of the Legislative Assembly and worked for its downfall.

Leaders of the Jacobin movement. The enthusiastic radicals who were determined to advance the Revolution formed various clubs in Paris that were centers of agitation and revolutionary propaganda. The most important of these organizations met in the convent of the Jacobin Friars and took the name "Society of the Friends of the Constitution Meeting at the Jacobins in Paris." Their program was the overthrow of monarchy and greater justice and opportunity for the masses. Soon, Jacobin Clubs sprang up all over France.

Most prominent in Jacobin circles were Jean Paul Marat (1743-1793), Georges Jacques Danton (1759-1794), and Maximilien Robespierre (1758-1794). Swiss by birth, Marat had gained recognition in Paris as a physician and student of science, but when the stirring days of 1789 came, he was bedridden with an incurable disease and suffering from a life without purpose or hope. The Revolution galvanized him into action. He became the champion of the masses and the propagandist of proletarian rights. To carry on his ideas, he founded the newspaper *L'Ami du Peuple* (*Friend of the People*). Notwithstanding continual physical discomfort from his afflictions, Marat carried on his propaganda against social injustice until 1793, when he was struck down by an assassin's dagger.

Robespierre, a lawyer by training, had been a criminal judge but had resigned because he was squeamish about inflicting the death penalty. Deeply influenced by the works of Rousseau, Robespierre became a fanatical reformer, a crusader who quietly bided his time until he possessed the necessary power to establish his republic based on virtue and justice. At first many of Robespierre's friends refused to take him seriously, but one of his colleagues sized him up correctly when he said, "He will go far because he believes everything he says."

The greatest orator among the Jacobins was Danton. Equipped with a "voice of thunder," he was referred to admiringly by his colleagues as "Atlas," "Hercules," or "Cyclops." Unlike the theorist Robespierre, Danton was a practical politician. Believing in a radical program that sought the end of the conservative Assembly, he had little use for utopias.

Stabbed by Charlotte Corday, the Jacobin leader Marat lies dead in his bath in this famous painting by David.

The Jacobin Clubs found their strongest support in the cities. As followers were recruited throughout France and sent to the capital, the Jacobin leaders secured a potential army. Known as "federates," these forces were available to carry out the program of radical leaders such as Danton and Robespierre.

Opposition to the Assembly outside France. As strenuously opposed to the Assembly as the Jacobins but for a different reason were the émigré nobles. To the Jacobins the constitution of 1791 had not gone far enough; to the émigrés it had gone too far.

Members of the nobility who had fled the country and taken refuge mostly in various states along the Rhine, the émigrés were enemies of the Assembly because it represented the Revolution that had wiped out their ancient privileges. These exiled nobles passed the time plotting against the government of France.

The émigrés found receptive ears for their conspiracies and machinations. Many German bishops and princes who possessed lands in French Alsace were indignant over the abolition of feudal dues and services. Furthermore, many German nobles feared that the freeing of the serfs in France would lead to insurrections on their own estates.

Although they were uneasy about the trend of events in France, the rulers of the large European states adopted a "wait-and-see" policy, hoping that factionalism in France would weaken the nation and perhaps reduce it to a state of impotency like that suffered by unhappy Poland. Leopold II of Austria, brother of the French queen, was concerned over her safety and, with the king of Prussia, issued the Declaration of Pillnitz (August 1791), which declared that the restoration of order and of the power of the French monarchy was of "common interest to all sovereigns of Europe."

France vs. Austria and Prussia. Opposed from without and weakened from within, the moderate constitutional monarchy was doomed to failure. The shock of foreign war precipitated its downfall.

Nearly all the factions in France favored war—each for a different reason. The king and his supporters, as well as the émigré nobles, favored war because they believed the government would be defeated, discredited, and then overthrown. The victorious armies of the Old Regime could then proceed to undo the work of the Revolution in France, and Louis and his nobles would again be masters of the state. The radicals, especially a faction called the Girondists, who at first formed part of the Jacobin organization, were eager to involve France in a conflict because, in their opinion, war would discredit the monarchy and give them a chance to rise to power and establish a republic. According to the Girondists, with the advent of war:

We shall see discipline re-established under the breath of battle: hidden treason will be forced to cast away its mask![3]

Egged on by the Girondists, France declared war on Austria in April 1792. Prussia shortly afterwards entered the conflict as an ally of Austria.

The French went into the conflict in a light-hearted mood. Few Parisians in 1792 had any idea that the war against Austria and Prussia was the beginning of a series of wars that would keep armies marching and the Continent in turmoil for more than twenty years. Yet, while eager for war, the French were utterly unprepared for it. At the first encounter with the enemy, the French forces fled in confusion. An Austrian army was soon in a position to march on Paris. Fortunately for the government there, this opportunity was not seized, for both the Austrian and Prussian governments were preoccupied with the second partition of Poland (see pp. 55-56). By the summer of 1792, however, the Prussian and Austrian armies began to roll again, and fortress after fortress fell to the invaders.

The Brunswick Manifesto. By the middle of July, the French situation was critical, and the government of the Legislative Assembly was in grave straits. On July 27 the duke of Brunswick, commander of the allied forces invading France, issued a manifesto designed to cow the French revolutionaries and to strengthen the king's position. The actual result of the manifesto, however, was to bolster the position of the most radical groups, discredit the king completely, and end the monarchy in France.

The duke declared his object to be:

. . . to put an end to the anarchy in the interior of France, to check the attacks upon the throne and the altar, to reëstablish the legal power, to restore to the king the security and liberty of which he is now deprived and to place him in a position to exercise once more the legitimate authority which belongs to him.[4]

He announced furthermore that captured French soldiers would be punished as rebels to their king and that if the royal family was harmed, the Austro-Prussian forces would destroy Paris. In the minds of many Frenchmen—especially the masses in Paris and their Jacobin leaders—the manifesto was proof positive that the king was in league with the foreign invaders.

Insurrection in Paris. The reply to the manifesto was the insurrection of the ninth and tenth of August. The revolt was mainly the work of the extreme radicals together with the city proletariat and the federates from the provinces. The municipal government of Paris was seized, and rebel leaders set up an insurrectionary commune.

A large mob converged upon the king's palace in Paris, the Tuileries. Louis was persuaded to take his family for protection to the Legislative Assembly, which was meeting in the riding school not far away. Meanwhile, the mob stormed the palace and massacred large numbers of the king's loyal Swiss guards.

During the insurrection the Assembly was in session, but most of the deputies of the Right stayed away, fearing the mob. It was easy, therefore, for the deputies who were present, mainly the representatives of the Left, to vote to suspend the monarchy, place the country under a provisional government, and call elections for a National Convention to change the constitution. As head of the provisional government, Danton became dictator of France. At the same time, much power was wielded by the Commune of Paris, representing the lower classes of the city.

The September massacres. On September 2, news reached Paris that the fortress of Verdun had fallen to the invaders. As reinforcements were sent off to the front, the Commune of Paris took good care that no traitors were left behind at home. Many citizens believed that counterrevolutionists, in league with the Austrians, would try to seize power. On September 1, a pamphlet had been distributed all over Paris entitled: "The Great Treason of Louis Capet [Louis XVI]. Discovery of a plot for assassinating all good citizens during the night between the 2nd and 3rd of this month. . . ."

The response was the massacre of royalists in Paris. All suspected of sympathy for the monarchy were butchered. The prisons were emptied of nonjuring priests and suspected nobles, who were then executed without trial. The object of this terrorism was to intimidate the opponents of the Revolution at home so that the government could muster all its strength to hurl back the foreign invader. During the five days from September 2 to September 7, nearly two thousand suspected royalists were killed.

Inauguration of the Republic. Following the suspension of the monarchy, the Assembly proceeded to abolish the classification of Frenchmen as active and passive citizens. All males twenty-one years of age and over were given the vote and were eligible to elect representatives to the new National Convention. The elections were duly held, and the limited monarchy with its agent, the Legislative Assembly, came to an end on September 20, 1792, when the National Convention held its first meeting.

The following day the members voted royalty abolished in France and proclaimed September 22, 1792 as beginning Year I of the Republic. France was now a republic, the former king Louis XVI a prisoner in fear for his life, and the first phase of the French Revolution—that of moderate reform—a failure.

THE JACOBIN REPUBLIC

Problems facing the Convention. The National Convention remained in session three years. At the outset it was faced with serious problems: (1) foreign armies had to be defeated and driven out of France; (2) an all-important decision had to be made as to what should be done with the king; (3) revolts breaking out all over the country had to be suppressed; (4) a new constitution based on a republican form of government had to be framed; and (5) the social and economic reforms initiated between 1789 and 1791 by the Constituent Assembly had to be completed and put into action.

On the same day that the National Convention first met, news was received that the enemy had been checked at Valmy. This victory was a crucial turning point. Had the French been defeated, more than twenty years of wars and conquest that were to carry French armies and revolutionary ideas all over Europe would have been nipped in the bud.

Danton proceeded with alacrity and enthusiasm to increase the armed forces and give them new life and spirit. During the

The head of Louis XVI is displayed to the mob after his execution by guillotine on January 21, 1793.

autumn of 1792, the tide of foreign invasion receded, and French armies began to take the offensive. The Rhine was crossed, Savoy and Nice occupied, and the Austrian Netherlands (Belgium) conquered.

Trial and execution of Louis XVI. The fate of Louis XVI was soon settled. His trial began in December 1792, and the final vote was taken in the National Convention on January 14. The death of the king was made more or less certain when secret documents showing that Louis had carried on treasonable correspondence with the émigrés were found in a hidden compartment discovered in the Tuileries.

Now more moderate in their opinions and split from the Jacobins, the Girondists wished to postpone the king's trial until after the war. But the Jacobins were intent on his death, insisting upon his execution because he had committed treason and because by this act they hoped to forestall any future royalist plots involving the restoration of the

monarchy. A follower of Robespierre echoed Jacobin sentiments when he declared:

The death of the tyrant is necessary to reassure those who fear that one day they will be punished for their daring, and also to terrify those who have not yet renounced the monarchy. A people cannot found liberty when it respects the memory of its chains.[5]

The execution of Louis XVI was carried out on January 21, 1793. On the scaffold the king acted with quiet dignity and splendid fortitude. A French historian has declared: "he was greater on [the scaffold] . . . than ever he had been on his throne."[6]

Louis XVI can be neither praised nor blamed for his actions during the decisive years from 1789 to 1792. He was part of a social system and a symbol of a political philosophy which had been accepted in France, and indeed in all of Europe, for centuries. He had been trained and conditioned to his role of absolute monarch. To expect him to have the vision and foresight to accept the new order would have been to expect too much of him. Louis played the game as he thought it should be played, not understanding that the rules had been changed.

European opinion turns against the Revolution. During the first year of the French Revolution, a strong body of European opinion had acclaimed the reforms of the Constituent Assembly. Liberals cheered the news of the fall of the Bastille. Living in France at the time, the English poet William Wordsworth described his feelings during the early days of the French Revolution in these stirring lines:

Bliss was it in that dawn to be alive,
But to be young was very heaven![7]

But there had also been voices raised in warning against the Revolution in France. The influential English statesman Edmund Burke published in 1790 his *Reflections on the Revolution in France.* Burke was an eloquent defender of conservatism, as opposed to reaction and radicalism. In this powerful and widely read treatise, he likened the Revolution to:

. . . a strange chaos of levity and ferocity, and of all sorts of crimes jumbled together with all sorts of follies.[8]

To him, the rule of the mob was as terrifying and as unjust as the rule of a capricious absolute monarch; stability, gradual change, and respect for the old as well as receptivity for the new were the basis of the good society.

Is it in destroying and pulling down that skill is displayed? . . . The shallowest understanding, the rudest hand, is more than equal to that task. Rage and frenzy will pull down more in half an hour than prudence, deliberation, and foresight can build up in a hundred years. . . . At once to preserve and to reform is quite another thing. . . . People will not look forward to posterity, who never look backward to their ancestors. . . . Thus, by preserving the method of nature in the conduct of the State, in what we improve, we are never wholly new; in what we retain, we are never wholly obsolete. . . . A disposition to preserve, and an ability to improve, taken together, would be my standard of a statesman.[9]

While the Legislative Assembly was in power and Louis XVI was on the throne, many observers thought Burke's arguments exaggerated; but the fall of the monarchy, the September massacres, and the execution of Louis began to make most Englishmen of the upper class and many Continental aristocrats believe that Burke was right.

French territorial aggression. In the fall of 1792, French armies gained notable successes, and these victories stirred the military spirit of the French people. The earlier ideals of the Revolution—of brotherhood and peace—were replaced by nationalistic territorial ambitions. The French revolutionary leaders began to realize that in the name of liberty their armies could overthrow tyrannical kings and at the same time extend the national frontiers of France. They announced that the Alps and the Rhine had been the old frontiers of France and that they were resolved to reunite them to the fatherland.

In November 1792 the Convention declared that "France will grant fraternity and assistance to all peoples who shall desire to recover their liberty." This announcement was equivalent to a French declaration of war against all the monarchical governments of Europe. Again in December the Convention stated that "it considered itself called to give liberty to the human race and to overthrow all thrones" and declared war on tyrants. At the same time it was announced that in all countries conquered by the French, the inhabitants had to accept all the principles of the French Revolution; property belonging to the nobility and to the Church was to be seized and used as security for the issuance of French currency—the *assignats.*

England as the leading anti-French power. In the face of French aggression, which threatened the balance of power in Europe, England, Spain, Holland, and Sardinia joined Prussia and Austria in the First Coalition to wage war on the French Republic. Of all the allies arrayed against France, England was to be the most implacable foe. From 1793 to 1815, England and France were at war almost continuously.

The prime minister in England at this time was William Pitt the Younger. A liberal and a reformer at the beginning of his career, Pitt wanted no war with France and considered Burke's dire warnings about the Revolution exaggerated. By the end of 1792, however, Pitt had changed his opinions; he now believed that war with France was inevitable. As French armies occupied the Austrian Netherlands and threatened Holland, England prepared for war.

Pressures inside and outside France. In the spring of 1793 the armies of the First Coalition began to converge on France. The Revolution was in peril. And in addition to this outside menace, France was rent by internal strife. Two factions in the National Convention fought for control: the Girondists and the Jacobins. Representing the bourgeoisie, the Girondists were moderates who feared the city mob and radical reforms; to them the Revolution had gone far enough. By contrast, the Jacobins were tough realists who sided with the masses, welcomed more bloodletting, and were determined to advance the Revolution. Finally, the Jacobins managed to oust their rivals from the Convention and place them under arrest. Some of the Girondists, however, escaped to the country, where they organized a rebellion against the tyranny of the radicals in Paris. At the same time royalist Catholics rose again in rebellion. These disorders weakened the economy of the country, and bread riots broke out in Paris.

The Reign of Terror. To meet the challenge of rebellion, the government of the National Convention entrusted its power to the Committee of Public Safety. Also created were two subsidiary bodies: the Committee of General Security and the Revolutionary Tribunal. The task of the former was to ferret out traitors; the latter body judged and executed them at the hands of "Madame Guillotine." The Convention passed a decree making liable to arrest every person of noble birth, anyone who had any contact with an émigré, and anyone who could not produce a certificate of citizenship.

The establishment of the Committee of Public Safety and its allied agencies inaugurated what is known as the Reign of Terror. Thousands of suspected royalists were ar-

rested and thrown into prison. After a summary trial, many of them were thrown into carts—the tumbrels—and taken to the public square to be guillotined. Perhaps as many as five thousand persons were executed in Paris; in the provinces, the number was probably twenty thousand. Terrible as the Terror was, many believed it to be the only way of obtaining unanimity in France at a time when the armed might of the First Coalition threatened the existence of the government. As one of the Jacobins put it:

What constitutes the Republic is the complete destruction of everything that is opposed to it.[10]

The French war effort. With subversive activity crushed on the home front, the leaders of the Republic turned their attention to the danger of foreign armies. To meet its enemies, France forged a new weapon, the "nation in arms." Compulsory military service was introduced. In February 1793 the Convention passed a decree calling 300,000 men to the colors and making liable for military service all men between eighteen and forty. Military seniority was discarded, and brilliant young generals were given the highest commands. Results were demanded from these officers; it was victory or the guillotine.

In August 1793 the Convention decreed a general mobilization of the country. Scientists were enlisted to help the war effort, and workmen were conscripted and shifted from nonessential to war work. In Paris alone, 258 forges were set up out in the open to make 1000 gun barrels a day. Business was organized to produce vast quantities of medicines, shoes, and uniforms.

During 1794 and 1795 the new French armies carried out a series of great campaigns. The citizen armies of the Republic were motivated by a spirit not found in the professional and mercenary armies of their opponents. The French citizen-soldier believed he was fighting for his own liberty and for the right to enjoy the fruits of the Revolution.

By 1795 the First Coalition had almost been dissolved. Charles IV of Spain had to humble himself and make an alliance with the Republic that had executed his royal cousin. By the Treaty of Basel (1795), Frederick William II of Prussia gave France a free hand on the left bank of the Rhine. The stadholder of Holland was deposed and his country changed into the Batavian Republic, allied with France. Belgium was annexed outright, and French troops controlled all the territory up to the Rhine. In three years the Republic had gained "natural frontiers" that had been the objective of French monarchs for centuries. By 1795 only England, Austria, and Sardinia remained at war with France.

Social changes under the Jacobin Republic. The period of the Jacobin Republic was an exciting time for the French people. The days of the Old Regime seemed completely dead; a new society was being born. In a dozen and one ways the life of the people was transformed and modified.

A strong anti-Christian movement was initiated. Churches were closed and religious images destroyed. In the Festival of Reason, held in Paris in November 1793, the anti-Christian movement reached a climax. Deputies wearing red liberty caps marched to the Cathedral of Notre Dame to consecrate the church to the worship of reason and to enthrone an actress as the Goddess of Reason.

The cult of reason went too far for Robespierre, who substituted in its place a new religion based upon belief in a Supreme Being and in immortality of the soul. The new religion provided for a number of festivals honoring the Supreme Being, Life and Liberty, the Human Race, and other idealistic concepts. One of the festivals was titled *A la Maternité,* a forerunner of Mother's Day in the United States.

While experiments were being made with a republican religion, everything that smacked of royalty and privilege was discarded. Knee breeches, a symbol of the aristocracy, were declared unpatriotic. In their place were substituted long trousers, the *sans culottes* (literally, "without short breeches"), which "made all legs equal by concealment." Titles were discarded; the proper form of address became "citizen" and "citizeness."

An image of Freedom is drawn through the streets of Paris in one of the great festivals held in revolutionary France.

Both men and women gave up aristocratic wigs and powdered hair, and men adopted mustaches as a symbol of virility and patriotism. It was unpatriotic to wear jewelry, although women could wear brooches representing the head of Marat, the Revolution, or the fall of the Bastille. There was much revolutionary bric-a-brac. Homes contained busts of revolutionary heroes, stones from the Bastille as paperweights, and miniature toy guillotines as children's toys. Since kings and queens were out of fashion, new packs of cards were designed featuring liberty, equality, and so on.

Names had to be changed. Streets formerly named for kings or nobles now bore names commemorating revolutionary events or heroes. And men changed their names, especially if their Christian name was Louis. Even the name of the queen bee was changed to "laying bee."

The Terror continues. While the French armies rolled back the armies of the Coalition, the Reign of Terror reached its height. In the autumn of 1793, the Girondists who had been expelled from the National Convention were executed, and the guillotine also claimed as its victim the queen, Marie Antoinette. By controlling the all-powerful Committee of Public Safety, Robespierre was now the dominant force in the government.

By the spring of 1794, victory had been secured by the French armies, and practically all the revolts and plots within the country had been stamped out. There was no longer any justification for continuance of the Terror. But the fanatical Robespierre and his cohorts continued the policy of terrorism in order to cleanse the Republic of weak and lukewarm republicans. To Robespierre, a republic of virtue had to be achieved, in which there would be no excesses of wealth, where every citizen would serve the public good, and where justice and love would prevail. To attain this utopian Jacobin commonwealth, Robespierre believed that "the people's prejudices must be destroyed . . . its habits altered, its vices eradicated, and its desires purified."[11]

While Robespierre professed to love humanity, he had no compunctions about destroying those who opposed him; he had long lost the squeamishness which had once forced him to give up a judgeship because he could not bear to sentence the condemned to death! While a bewildered Paris looked on, many courageous leaders of the Revolution who dared to disagree with his fanatical views were executed. The great orator Danton was executed because he wished to end the policy of terror.

Disgusted at the unnecessary bloodshed instigated by Robespierre, the members of the Convention finally threw over his leadership, arrested him, and sent him to the guillotine, where so many of his innocent victims had already met an unjust fate. As Robespierre and twenty-one of his colleagues were taken by the tumbrels through the streets of Paris to the place of execution, the "mob applauded: it was in the highest spirits. The sky had cleared after the storm; there was a sort of intoxication in the air. The populace felt the era of the hecatombs was almost over, already a storm of wild delight was brewing. But there were women in the crowd, widows and mothers in mourning, who called down curses on the tyrant."[12]

Reaction against the Terror. After the execution of Robespierre, Frenchmen hoped that the long period of excesses was over and that the nation could bind up its wounds and settle down to a period of tranquillity and repose.

Thousands of suspects were freed, the laws of Robespierre were replaced, the Paris Commune was dissolved, and the extraordi-nary powers of the Committee of Public Safety and the Revolutionary Tribunal were swept away. In Paris, gangs of young men attacked Jacobins, and in the provinces there was a veritable "White Terror" against the radicals. The Jacobin Clubs were closed and the Catholic churches were reopened.

Conservatism was now the order of the day. It was not that the people wanted to go back to the old days. They passionately wanted to see the gains of the Revolution safeguarded and perpetuated, but they were tired of extremists and fanatics.

THE NAPOLEONIC PERIOD

The Directory. The energies of the Convention during the Reign of Terror had not been spent wholly in hounding suspects. Important reforms were achieved: the plan for a national system of education, abolition of Negro slavery in French colonies, final eradication of feudal dues without compensation, and the establishment of a metric system of weights and measures. In addition, the National Convention drafted a new system of government, the Directory, which was composed of two legislative chambers and an executive body of five members called directors.

Assuming power in 1795, the Directory soon proved to be an incompetent and even venal government. The directors were mediocre politicians who engaged in an orgy of graft. It was said of one director that:

He would throw the Republic out of [the] window to-morrow if it did not pay for his dogs, his horses, his mistresses, his table, and his cards![13]

Although the middle class profited under this bourgeois government, the poor lacked employment and the necessities of life.

Determined to smash the remnants of the First Coalition, the Directory commissioned three armies to invade Austrian territory. Two of these forces failed, but the one led by an obscure young general named Napoleon Bonaparte crossed the Alps in 1796 and crushed the Sardinians and the Austrians. With a French army at the gates of Vienna, the Austrians were forced to accept the

Treaty of Campo Formio (1797). Only Great Britain, protected by its fleet, remained at war with France.

Napoleon rises to power. Following his triumph over Austria, Napoleon obtained the consent of the Directory to invade Egypt in order to menace English interests in India. He is reputed to have said, "This little Europe does not supply enough glory for me." Evading the English fleet, Napoleon and his army landed in Egypt and were at first victorious. Efforts to crush Turkish forces were not successful, however, and in the meantime the English Admiral Nelson in 1798 destroyed Napoleon's Mediterranean fleet in the battle of the Nile. Aware that the Directory was becoming more and more incapable of coping with the problems of France, Napoleon deserted his army and returned to France. Making no reference to his defeats, the young general thrilled the French with the glories of his Egyptian campaign.

In 1799 France was again in a state of crisis. A newly formed Second Coalition threatened to invade the country, and the economy showed signs of collapse. Faced with financial ruin and invasion, the French turned to the one man they believed could save the day—Napoleon, the Little Corporal who spoke of himself as the "man of destiny." Sensing the mood of the nation, Napoleon in 1799 swept the effete Directory from power and established a new government called the Consulate—ostensibly a republic but with nearly all power centralized in the first consul, Napoleon.

Napoleon's genius for leadership. What manner of man was this "savior" of France? Born in Corsica in 1769, the young Napoleon was a member of the Corsican lower nobility of Italian origin. Educated in a French military school, he was described by one of his teachers as:

. . . taciturn, preferring solitude, capricious, haughty, and inordinately self-centered, [and with ambitions] that stop at nothing.[14]

After graduation, Napoleon returned to Corsica several times to carry on intrigues for its independence from France, but nothing

David's sketch of the fanatical revolutionary leader Robespierre on the day of his execution in 1794.

came of these efforts. When the French Revolution broke out, he joined the French army. Within a short time his abilities were recognized; his marriage in 1796 to the widow Josephine de Beauharnais, who was influential with the directors, gained him his first big chance—command of the army of Italy.

Intelligent, ambitious, and unscrupulous, Napoleon believed he was destined to play a great part in Europe's affairs. He once remarked: "I am no ordinary man, and the laws of propriety and morals are not applicable to me." He had a great reservoir of energy which enabled him to be in the saddle all day and to pore over his maps most of the night. For fifteen years the Little Corporal amazed and confounded his opponents by his brilliant tactics and strategy and by the *élan* he inspired in his troops.

After becoming first consul, Napoleon quickly scattered the forces of the Second Coalition. The Austrian forces were vanquished, and the Austrian government was compelled to sign the Treaty of Lunéville (1801). Although Great Britain was not defeated, in 1802 a temporary peace between France and England was arranged.

Napoleon's domestic reforms. The first consul then turned his attention to domestic reforms. The system of local government was reorganized to provide a completely centralized governmental structure. Prefects appointed by the central government were given almost complete charge of local affairs, an arrangement which made for efficiency at the expense of liberty. Next, Napoleon grappled with the financial problem. Graft and inequality in tax collection were ended, economies in public expenditures were effected, and, most important, the Bank of France was established. In the field of public finance, this institution was Napoleon's greatest contribution. It still exists today as a model of banking stability.

In their enthusiastic attacks on the clergy, the French revolutionaries had not been content to reform the Church but had become so antireligious that they threatened the very existence of Christianity in France. While irreligious himself, Napoleon as a shrewd statesman realized that the people demanded the reëstablishment of the Church. In the Concordat (1801), an agreement with the pope was reached in which Napoleon declared that the French government would pay the salaries of the clergy. The Catholic Church was now restored in France, but without much of its former power.

Before 1800 scarcely 25,000 children in France were attending elementary school. To remedy this situation, Napoleon created a system of public education which provided an educational pyramid of public elementary schools, secondary institutions (*lycées*), special schools for technical training, and the University of France. The latter was not a teaching body but an administrative one; its function was to regulate and control the entire educational system.

Napoleon believed in rewarding ability and in opening the way for talent. In 1802 he created the order of the Legion of Honor to honor citizens who made outstanding contributions to society. Napoleon told his advisers:

. . . men are led by toys . . . I don't think that the French love liberty and equality: the French are not at all changed by ten years of Revolution: they are what the Gauls were, fierce and

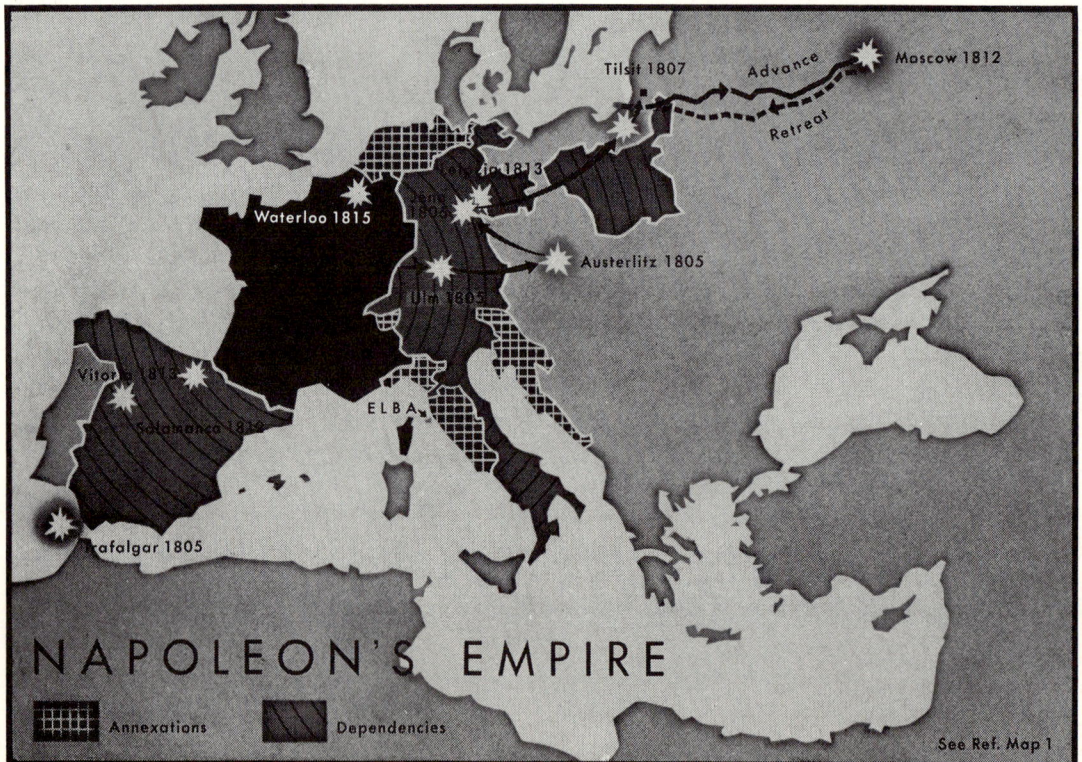

Tilsit 1807   Advance   Moscow 1812
Retreat

Waterloo 1815   Leipzig 1813   Jena 1806
Austerlitz 1805
Ulm 1805

Vitoria 1813
Salamanca 1812
ELBA

Trafalgar 1805

NAPOLEON'S EMPIRE

Annexations   Dependencies

See Ref. Map 1

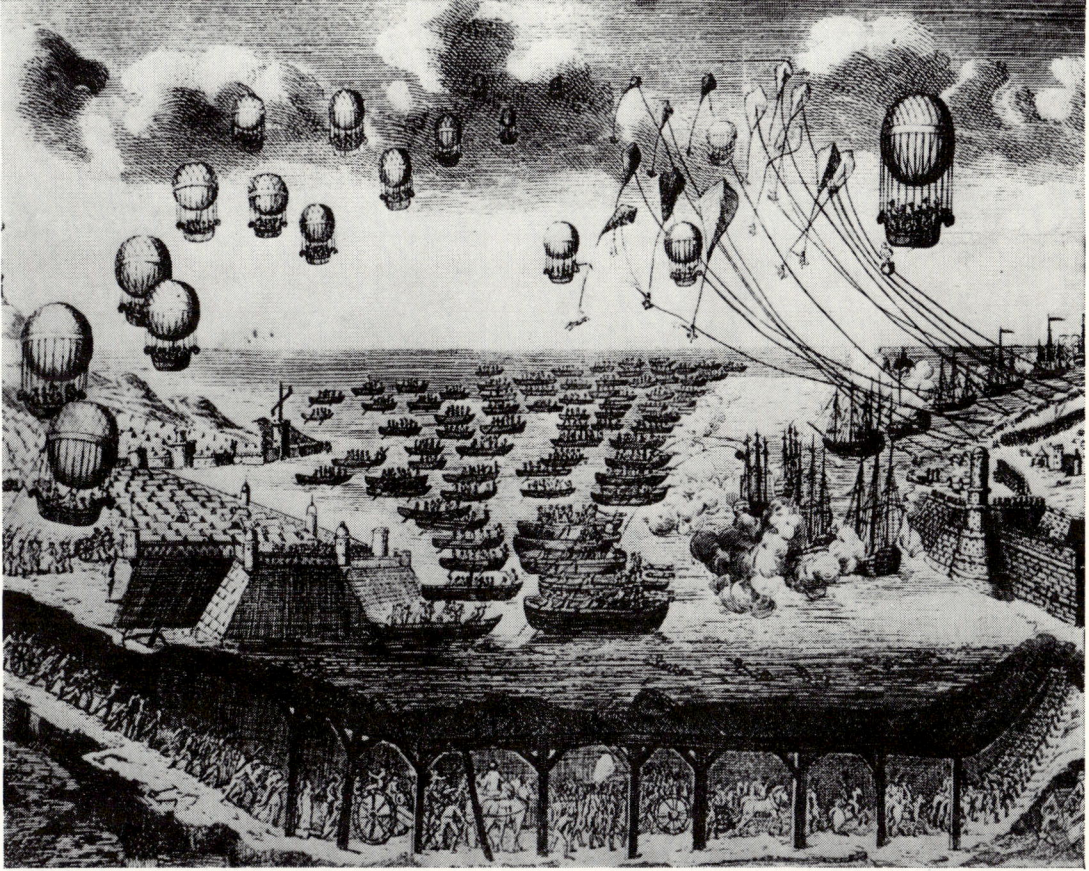

In this satirical version of Napoleon's plans for invading England, a contemporary artist shows balloons and monster kites floating over the English Channel, an invasion fleet crossing on the surface, and an army marching through a tunnel.

fickle. They have one feeling—honour. We must nourish that feeling: they must have distinctions.[15]

Most famous of Napoleon's accomplishments was his codification of the French law, which brought legal order out of chaos. Completed in 1804, the great Civil Code was written with precision and clarity; it guaranteed many achievements of the French Revolution, such as religious toleration and the abolition of serfdom. A code of civil procedure and a criminal code were also produced. These codes have exerted a marked influence upon the codes of other countries. Years later, the exiled Napoleon said:

My true glory is not that I have gained forty battles. Waterloo will efface the memory of those victories. But that which nothing can efface, which will live forever, is my Civil Code.[16]

When Napoleon declared himself emperor in 1804, a grateful and contented people approved his action. The Republic was now no more.

Napoleon at the height of his power. Just before Napoleon assumed the crown of emperor, war between Great Britain and France broke out once more. Napoleon welcomed war. His meteoric rise from a nonentity to the first citizen of France had not satisfied his lust for glory. During 1803 and 1804 he directed extensive preparations for an invasion of England, but the inability of Napoleon's naval forces to gain control of the approaches to England and the formation of the Third Coalition (composed of Great Britain, Russia, Austria, and Sweden) compelled him to forgo his cherished plan. Then, in 1805, he suddenly marched eastward

Spanish patriots are shot down by the French invaders in a drawing from the series "The Disasters of War" by Goya.

against his Continental enemies and, in victory after victory, effectively destroyed the armies of the Third Coalition.

Meanwhile, Napoleon's hopes of securing control of the seas and invading or at least starving out Britain were ended rudely in the smoke of Trafalgar (October 1805). In this decisive naval battle, Lord Nelson defeated the combined French and Spanish fleets. Undaunted, Napoleon marched on to defeat Prussia decisively in 1806 and to organize into a French dependency the territory seized by Prussia in the partitions of Poland. In 1807, at Tilsit, the Russian emperor agreed to assist France in disposing of the emperor's stubborn antagonist—England.

By 1808 Napoleon ruled over a France which extended from the North Sea to the Pyrenees and included much of Italy. Several of his relatives had been placed on the thrones of nearby countries. Prussia and Austria were impotent before French power, and Russia appeared to be only a Napoleonic satellite.

Napoleon was now at the height of his great powers. Few men in history have possessed his gifts and achieved such amazing results. He was the dynamo and the brain of his empire: "He controlled every wheel and spring, large or small, of his vast machinery of government. It was, as it were, his plaything. He was his own War Office, his own Foreign Office, his own Admiralty, his own Ministry of every kind. . . . His financial management, by which he sustained a vast empire with power and splendour, but with

The women of Spain fight Napoleon's soldiers in Goya's drawing "And they are like wild beasts."

rigid economy and without a debt, is a marvel and a mystery. In all the offices of state he knew everything, guided everything, inspired everything."[17] But, as we shall shortly see, the load was too much for one man. This is the supreme defect of dictatorship—power is not shared. The powers of Napoleon began to decline while his problems continued to increase.

Importance of British sea power. By 1808 it was apparent that the Napoleonic empire could not survive unless it defeated England. Lord Nelson's victory at Trafalgar had confirmed Great Britain's supremacy on the seas. Safe behind warships, English factories turned out more and more war goods. British commerce and wealth increased, while French trade declined. Napoleon sought to crush England's economy by prohibiting the entry of British vessels into countries under his control, a policy known as the Continental System. But Great Britain imposed a counterblockade. Fundamentally, the war was now a struggle between the sea power and industrial superiority of England and French military power on the continent of Europe.

Thus British sea power was the all-important obstacle standing in the way of Napoleon's mastery of Europe. "The world has never seen a more impressive demonstration of the influence of sea power upon its history. . . . Those far distant, storm-beaten ships, upon which the Grand Army never looked, stood between it and the dominion of the world."[18]

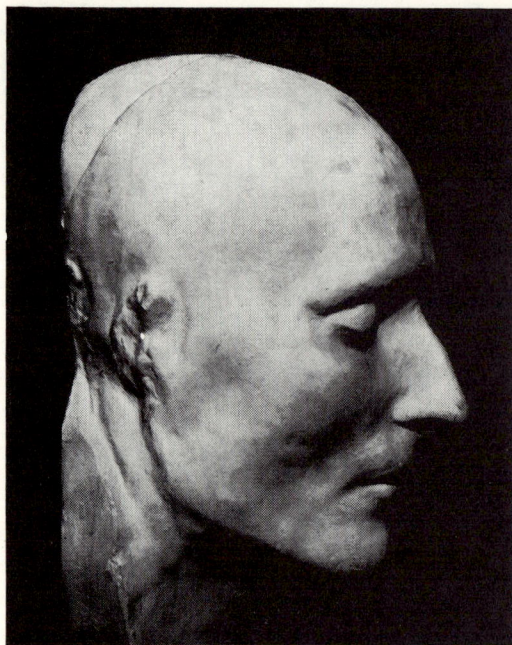

The death mask of Napoleon Bonaparte

Reaction against French imperialism. Ostensibly "liberators" of subject people in Europe, the armies of Napoleon disseminated the French revolutionary ideals of liberty, equality, and fraternity. But as Napoleon became more and more imperialistic, the people he had "emancipated" realized that they had merely exchanged one despotism for another. In posing as the champion of the Revolution, Napoleon had sown the seeds of nationalism and liberty which were to prove his undoing.

The occupation of Portugal (1807) and Spain (1808) are cases in point. In both nations, uprisings soon broke out. And, as we shall see later in this chapter, Napoleon's intervention in the Iberian peninsula triggered a revolutionary movement in the Latin-American colonies.

All over Germany, a wave of nationalism stirred the people to prepare for a war of liberation. Prussia in particular underwent a regeneration. The Emancipation Edict of 1807, known as "the Prussian Magna Carta," ended serfdom, abolished caste barriers to vocations, and gave farmers a clear title to their land. The people now had something to fight for! Although Napoleon had limited the Prussian army to 42,000 men, the Prussians undermined this provision by a subtle subterfuge: as soon as one army was trained, it was placed on reserve and a new army was called up for training. In this way, Prussia managed to prepare a potential army of 270,000 men. The Prussian intellectuals used education as a means of nationalistic propaganda. Founded in 1810, the University of Berlin became a center of strong nationalistic movements.

Invasion and retreat in Russia. Napoleon made his first major misstep when, after a quarrel with Alexander I of Russia, he launched an invasion of the tsar's realm in 1812. The campaign was a catastrophe. Although Napoleon's Grand Army of 600,000 fought its way to Moscow, the enemy forces remained intact, and the Russians' scorched-earth strategy prevented the invaders from living off the country. While the French occupied Moscow, fires broke out and destroyed three fourths of the city; this disaster was compounded by the outbreak of pestilence. After spending thirty-three days in the empty shell of Moscow, Napoleon gave the order to retreat.

As the Grand Army marched west along the frozen Russian roads, it rapidly disintegrated. Guerrilla forces, mainly Cossacks, hovered about the retreating columns, continually pouncing on stragglers. In the bitterly cold weather, campfires were inadequate, shoes soon wore out, and thousands died in the snow. Pneumonia and typhus also took their grisly toll. Out of the more than half a million men who had crossed the Russian frontiers in June, a tattered fragment of barely 20,000 troops was able to make a wintry escape from Russia to Germany. Over a century later, another would-be world conqueror—Adolf Hitler—made the same mistake as Napoleon. History, on occasion, does repeat itself.

Downfall of Napoleon. The nations of Europe now struck relentlessly at the tottering French empire. Commanded by the duke of Wellington, "The Iron Duke," English troops cleared French armies out of Spain, and in 1813 at Leipzig the allies inflicted a disastrous defeat upon Napoleon in the Battle of the Nations. Napoleon, however, remained confident of ultimate triumph, spurning a peace offer made by Metternich, the Austrian statesman, in these words:

What is it you wish of me? That I should dishonour myself? Never. I shall know how to die, but never to yield an inch of territory. Your sovereigns, who were born on the throne, may get beaten twenty times, and yet return to their capitals. I cannot. For I rose to power through the camp.[19]

After Leipzig the empire of Napoleon tumbled like a house of cards. In March 1814, allied forces entered Paris. Two weeks later the French emperor abdicated his throne, receiving in return sovereignty over Elba, a little island not far from the Italian coast. Nearly one year later, in February 1815, Napoleon eluded the British fleet, landed in France, and after a tumultuous welcome entered Paris and raised another army. In haste, an allied army under Wellington marched toward France.

At Waterloo, Napoleon took the field for the last time and met his match. The French army was defeated decisively by the combined forces of Britain and Prussia. Following this reversal, Napoleon sought refuge on board a British warship. Taking no chances, the allies shipped the former emperor to the island of St. Helena, about twelve hundred miles off the west coast of Africa. Here, in 1821, he died, a victim of cancer.

Why did the French empire, which appeared invincible under Napoleon, collapse? When Napoleon's physical vigor and mental brilliance began to flag after the destruction of the Third Coalition, his empire—the creation of one man's military and administrative genius—began to fall apart. A tired man, Napoleon fast became corpulent and lethargic. And if the emperor was tired, the French people were also suffering from war weariness. In addition, the resurgence of nationalism in Europe was bound to destroy any dictator who first stimulated it by prating about liberty, equality, and fraternity and then enslaved those he had "liberated."

Students of warfare point out that the defeat of Napoleon is explained chiefly by the relative importance in that day of sea power on the one hand and land power on the other. These students of military history maintain that British command of the sea finally led to the Napoleonic collapse. Finally, there are those who see Napoleon's greatest blunder in his invasion of Russia, which boomeranged and ended with the disastrous retreat from Moscow.

Accomplishments of Napoleon. Napoleon's rise to power is one of the most remarkable stories in all history. H. G. Wells, likening him to "a cockerel on a dung-hill," said: "The figure he makes in history is one of almost incredible self-conceit, of vanity, greed and cunning, of callous contempt and disregard of all who trusted him, and of a grandiose aping of Caesar, Alexander, and Charlemagne which would be purely comic if it were not caked over with human blood."[20]

But Napoleon's significance in history cannot be dismissed with only a negative verdict. It is true that his wars killed perhaps as many as six million people, but his interference throughout Europe kindled nationalism in many areas. For example, he made possible the first step toward the national unification of Germany. Throughout the Middle Ages, the multiplicity of German states had been a barrier to national unity. To create a defensive barrier on France's eastern frontier, Napoleon wiped out more than one hundred petty German states and merged them with large states. Another important obstacle to unification was removed in 1806 when he did away with the Holy Roman Empire.

The legacy of the French Revolution. Napoleon is especially important because he preserved and disseminated many aims of the French Revolution. French Revolutionary and Napoleonic developments, although arising inside France, affected all Europe. Of prime importance, certainly, was the triumph of the bourgeois class and its enshrinement in the government.

Accompanying the triumph of the bourgeoisie was the new predominance of the bourgeois conception of legal equality and the sanctity of property, especially as reflected in the famous Napoleonic code. The code was completed and published in parts. The Civil Code (1804) dealt with relations between individuals and between individuals and the state in matters of property and political behavior. The Code of Civil Procedure (1807) dealt with the behavior of the courts in civil cases, and the Commercial Code (1807) was an expansion of the Civil Code pertaining to matters of business. The Code of Criminal Instruction (1808) dealt with the relationship of the courts to individuals in criminal cases. The Penal Code (1810) dealt with the punishment for criminal violations.

As a result of the Napoleonic code, all unwritten feudal vestiges were abolished. The relation of individuals to each other, to landlords, to tax collectors—areas of abuses under the Old Regime—were fixed by written code, under which all French citizens had the same rights. The chief victories of the French Revolution thus were in French life.

In regard to family, labor, and the position of women, however, the Napoleonic code was reactionary. The father was legally head of the family, and the wife could not enter contracts without the husband's consent. Only a portion of the property could be disposed of freely; the rest was restricted to ensure the heritable rights of the children. The inheritance provisions of the codes had a conservative influence on peasant proprietorship and provided an important element of stability and conservatism in nineteenth-century France. The Napoleonic code also prohibited both employer and labor combinations, thereby retarding trade union activity for decades. The disadvantages as well as the advantages of the Napoleonic code (undeniably the greatest single achievement of the Revolutionary period) spread with it through Europe.

Another legacy of the French Revolution with far-reaching results was the use of violence to achieve both the sovereignty of the individual (political liberty and equality) and the sovereignty of the nation (self-determination). Violence within Revolutionary France was followed by nearly two decades of unparalleled French aggression; the Napoleonic period witnessed the spread of the concept of total war and with it the idea of making war profitable. The levee en masse involved the whole population in wars for the first time, and the nation in arms became the highest expression of the Revolutionary slogan of "fraternity"—an ideal of the brotherhood of man which stopped at national boundaries. To a considerable degree Napoleon, in a still strongly agrarian and mercantile Europe, made war profitable for France by collecting indemnities from the losers. But the idea of total war, and making the losers pay, would prove almost as ruinous to the victors as to the vanquished by 1900 when economic interdependence would have developed in most of Europe.

The most significant heritage of the French Revolution was the achievement of political reform, which resulted in personal liberty and more democratic government. At the same time, the French Revolution at least set in motion the wheels of social reform for which, because of the Industrial Revolution, there would soon be new and pressing need. However, the French Revolution passed on an ominous lesson for the future: the model of achieving political liberty by violence.

REACTION AT VIENNA

The Congress of Vienna. In September 1814, during Napoleon's exile on Elba, a brilliant gathering of diplomats and rulers assembled at Vienna to remake the map of Europe. Representatives from every state in Europe except Turkey were in attendance. The Austrian government acted as a lavish host to the treaty makers, sponsoring a round of festivals, hunts, balls, and musicales. Beethoven conducted the premiere of his *Seventh Symphony*. For ten months kings, princes, and diplomats, with their ladies, dined, danced, and worked—not too industriously—at remaking the Continent.

In this atmosphere of high society and what frequently turned out to be low diplomacy, intrigue and espionage flourished. Although there were a few formal meetings of the more important representatives, the Congress as such never met. Generally speaking, the new map of Europe was made in small, secret conferences held amidst the pomp of balls, masques, and pageants: "At a ball, kingdoms were enlarged or sliced up —at a dinner an indemnity granted—a constitution sketched while hunting; occasionally a *bon mot,* or a witty idea, brought an agreement where conferences and notes failed."[21]

The chief actors. The leading delegates at the conference were Tsar Alexander I of Russia (1777-1825), Lord Castlereagh of Great Britain (1769-1822), Talleyrand of France (1754-1838), and Prince von Metternich (1773-1859), the spokesman for Austria and the official host of the conclave. These diplomats arrived in Vienna with different objectives and ambitions. The tsar was the leader of the mightiest land power in Europe. For the first but not the last time, his nation had effectively intervened in the destinies of the Continent. But Alexander was a badly confused mixture of liberalism, religious mysticism, and personal ambition. By contrast, the English delegate, Castlereagh, was sound and moderate in his views. His program was to prevent the return of any military dictator who might threaten Europe, to establish a new balance of power whereby all the great nations of Europe would have a voice in the destinies of the Continent without any one being too powerful, and to offer defeated France such a peace as would not humiliate the nation and cause it to embark on a war of revenge. It was not Castlereagh's aim to acquire large indemnities and annexations for Britain, "not to collect trophies, but to bring back the world to peaceful habits."[22]

Talleyrand, the spokesman for France, almost single-handedly secured for his defeated country an important voice at the Congress; he was one of the most astute and unscrupulous diplomats of his day. His suppleness and dexterity had enabled him to survive successfully the many phases of the French Revolution, and after the advent of Napoleon in 1799, he was foreign minister until 1807. While completely ruthless in his methods, Talleyrand, like Bismarck a generation later, was essentially moderate in his ends. He had disapproved of Napoleon's foreign policies, realizing that flouting the freedom and pride of all Europe's peoples could mean in the end only disaster for France. Characteristically, Talleyrand had prepared to desert Napoleon, thereby earning the emperor's bitter wrath:

You are a coward, a traitor, a thief. You do not even believe in God. You have betrayed and deceived everybody. You would sell even your own father.[23]

Yet Talleyrand may have acted in what he thought were the best interests of France. He undoubtedly loved his country, though he probably loved himself even more; he did well in making these loyalties so often coincide.

The "prince of diplomats," the most important figure at the Congress, was Metternich. Born of a noble Rhineland family, he associated from early youth with the most elegant society; and though his family's estates were lost when the armies of revolutionary France invaded the Rhineland, he managed to marry the richest and most eligible heiress in Austria. In 1801 he began his brilliant diplomatic career in earnest. It was to continue until he was forced to flee Austria during the revolution of 1848.

During the Napoleonic period Metternich had become an inflexible opponent of the French emperor. After Waterloo, he resolved that there should be no return of the revolutionary ideas circulated by France between 1792 and 1815. Referring to the French Revolution, Metternich declared it was:

. . . the disease which must be cured, the volcano which must be extinguished, the gangrene which must be burned out with the hot iron, the hydra with jaws open to swallow up the social order.[24]

Most of the rulers attending the Congress agreed with these sentiments. The king of Prussia declared:

Although history was made at the Congress of Vienna under the leadership of the determined Metternich (left) and other sober statesmen, there was opportunity for entertainment and relaxation. The illustration above shows a horse show staged to amuse the distinguished guests, and the following quotation from the memoirs of Prince de Ligny further reveals the lighter side of the great international conference: "The day after my arrival [at Vienna] I went to pay my respects to the prince, who readily agreed to be my guide and instructor whenever circumstances threw me in his way. 'You have come,' he said, 'just at the right moment. If you like fetes and balls you will have enough of them; the Congress ne marche pas, il danse.' [The Congress dances, but does not advance.] There is, literally, a royal mob here. Everybody is crying out: 'Peace! justice! balance of power! indemnity!' As for me, I am a looker-on. All the indemnity I shall ask for is a new hat; I have worn mine out in taking it off to sovereigns whom I meet at the corner of every street.

"At nine O'clock we reached the Burg, the Imperial palace where the Ridottos [music and dancing] were held. The ballroom, which was brilliantly lighted, is surrounded by a gallery leading to the supper-rooms. In it were seated groups of elegant women; some in dominoes [masquerade dress], some in fancy costumes; bands of music, stationed in different parts of the hall, played waltzes and polonaises alternately ... Impossible to imagine anything more remarkable than this assemblage, masked and unmasked, amid which the rulers of mankind were walking about and mingling with the crowd without the slightest distinction."

The whole world is mad and wants new constitutions.[25]

At the conference Metternich exercised a kind of moral dictatorship. Witty, egotistical, and astute, he flirted elegantly with the ladies and influenced his fellow diplomats with his eloquent speech and his iron opposition to all revolutionary principles. His leadership initiated the reactionary era which we now call the Age of Metternich and which was to last until the middle of the nineteenth century.

The task confronting the Congress. The task confronting the diplomats at the Congress of Vienna was threefold: What was to be done with France? How should the old governments and political boundaries so ruthlessly abolished by Napoleon be reconstituted? And, finally, how should the Congress deal with the radical ideas developed and spread abroad by revolutionary France?

Many Europeans, especially those of the middle class, hoped that the peace settlement would be guided by two principles that had grown rapidly during the stormy days from 1789 to 1815. These were nationalism on the one hand, and on the other democracy and political liberalism. The first principle promised all peoples the right to rule themselves, free of the control of foreigners. Both democrats and liberals opposed despotic government, but while democrats believed in the right of all citizens to participate in government, bourgeois liberals believed in control by the well-to-do.

Unfortunately, the Congress of Vienna was in no mood to respect the aspirations of the people. Much of the subsequent discontent and turmoil in nineteenth-century Europe resulted from the reactionary efforts of the Congress to restore as much of the Old Regime as could conveniently be retrieved.

Treatment of France. Regarding the future of France, the Congress proved to be sensible and moderate. The Treaty of Paris, signed by French representatives in May 1814, had given France about the same boundaries it possessed in 1792, and no indemnity was required. Following this treaty, however, Napoleon escaped from the island of Elba, where he had been exiled, and during his so-called "Hundred Days" of freedom again led French armies against the allies, while the diplomats at Vienna awaited events with much trepidation. After Waterloo and the banishment of Napoleon to St. Helena, a second and more severe treaty was imposed upon France. This second treaty of November 1815 somewhat diminished French territory, but even with this reduction France's frontiers were larger than they had been in 1789. A war indemnity was imposed, and a number of strategic fortresses were to be occupied by allied troops for a maximum period of five years.

Geographic and political realignment. In the reëstablishment of the European political order, four principles were followed: (1) legitimacy, (2) encirclement of France, (3) compensations, and (4) balance of power. It was agreed that, wherever possible, the legitimate rulers who were in power before their deposition by Napoleon should have their thrones restored to them. Following this principle, all the rulers who had been established by Napoleon were removed. (The one exception was Bernadotte, one of Napoleon's marshals and founder of the present dynasty of Sweden.) In the person of Louis XVIII, the Bourbon House was restored in France, and other Bourbon rulers were returned to their thrones in Spain and in the kingdom of Naples. The House of Savoy reigned again in Sardinia-Piedmont,* and the House of Orange was restored in Holland.

In the reconstruction of the political boundaries of Europe, the keynote again was the restoration of the past. France, as we have seen, was reduced to substantially its former size; Spain, Holland, and other former Napoleonic possessions were restored to independence. Switzerland was given back three small cantons which had been in-

*Sardinia-Piedmont is often referred to as either Sardinia or Piedmont (the Continental portion of the kingdom). In the text hereafter, unless otherwise noted, *Sardinia* will be used to indicate Sardinia-Piedmont.

In a contemporary French cartoon satirizing the Congress of Vienna, political "balance" is achieved by matching the weight of subject peoples with the weight of British gold.

Territorial adjustments are represented by bales and baskets full of people; while the Continental statesmen divide the booty, the Duke of Wellington adds money to the scale.

corporated into France, and in addition Swiss neutrality was guaranteed by the European powers. The map of Europe looked much as it had before the French Revolution (see Reference Map 1).

However, the pre-Napoleonic boundaries were not everywhere restored. The Holy Roman Empire remained dissolved; in place of the hundreds of states existing in prerevolutionary times, the thirty-eight set up by Napoleon were retained and organized into a German Confederation dominated by Austria.

Certain features of the map of Europe were modified in accordance with the principle of encirclement. The allied statesmen were resolved that a protective belt should be fashioned to surround France, hem it in, and prevent any future French aggression. The Austrian Netherlands (Belgium) was turned over to Holland, making this country a stronger barrier on France's north; Savoy, belonging to the kingdom of Sardinia, was enlarged in order to block any French invasion of Italy; and Prussia was given extensive territory along the Rhine.

The granting of compensations to states surrendering territory was another principle modifying the map of Europe. For example, Austria was compensated for giving up the Austrian Netherlands by being given Lombardy and Venetia (Venice and the surrounding area) in northern Italy and part of the Adriatic coast as well. In such fashion the diplomats at Vienna portioned out the spoils so that no important power was slighted. When Sweden agreed to allow Finland to be retained by Russia, Sweden's compensation was the acquisition of Norway. England's share was the retention of colonies and naval bases it had captured in the wars, notably the Dutch colonies of Ceylon and South Africa.

While the most urgent problem was how to guard against any future French aggression, the diplomats also had to create a new balance of power among the nations. Among the Big Four there existed deep jealousies. Prussia coveted all of Saxony, while Austria feared growing Prussia. Russia wanted to expand by securing all Poland. And Britain believed that an enlarged Russian state would menace the balance of power and—indirectly—British security.

While the victors haggled, Talleyrand wormed his way into the good graces of Britain and Austria. A secret treaty was arranged, pledging the three countries to use force if necessary to restrain Prussia and Russia. Confronted by this threat, Russia and Prussia reduced their claims for more Polish and Saxon territory. The power struggle at Vienna demonstrated that peace making is often as dangerous as war making; this same lesson of history later was to be illustrated at the Paris Peace Conference after World War I and even more so in the Cold War between the victors of World War II.

Quadruple and Holy Alliances. So much for the territorial changes made in 1815. The most vital problem facing the Congress, however, was not how to allocate land but how to check the growth of revolutionary ideas, particularly the ideas of popular sovereignty and constitutional government. Under the leadership of Metternich, every effort was made to reëstablish the supremacy of autocracy and benevolent despotism.

On November 20, 1815, as a result of Metternich's influence, Austria, Prussia, Russia, and England signed the Quadruple Alliance. The object of this document was stated to be the maintenance of "tranquillity" in Europe, and for this purpose the members were to meet from time to time to agree on the proper measures to be taken. In 1818 France was admitted to the compact, making it a Quintuple Alliance.

Such an alliance system, providing for collective security against any renewal of French aggression and for consultation on common problems, was both logical and desirable. Unfortunately it became apparent soon after 1815 that the real purpose of the alliance was to crush relentlessly any growth of political liberalism. After 1820 the Congress System became in effect a trade union of kings for suppressing the liberties of peoples.

The Holy Alliance, another famous league formed at Vienna, was proposed by the visionary Alexander I of Russia and was joined by most of the powers attending the Congress. They agreed that they would base their policies on those of that "holy religion, namely, the precepts of justice, Christian charity, and peace." No one was quite sure just what Alexander meant by this pact, and there was much joking by the diplomats at his expense. Castlereagh described the Holy Alliance as "a piece of sublime mysticism and nonsense." The opponents of reaction at this time confused the Holy Alliance with the Quadruple Alliance and regarded the former as the instrument which was responsible for the reaction and repression following the Congress. Actually these unfortunate policies were the consequence of Metternich's Quadruple Alliance.

Nationalist sentiment disregarded. The arrangements made at the Congress of Vienna shaped the course of political events in Europe during most of the nineteenth century, just as the provisions of the Treaty of Versailles influenced postwar developments in Europe after 1919. The most serious mistake in the territorial settlements made at Vienna was the disregard of the principle of nationalism. During the great wars against Napoleon, there had arisen in Europe, especially in Italy and Germany, a new kind of patriot and nationalist who dreamed of belonging to a strong and united nation. But the nationalist aspirations of these patriots were disregarded. Austria, for example, did not want a united Italy. An Italy split up into petty states, some of which had Hapsburg rulers, was, in Metternich's disdainful phrase, only a "geographical expression," not a nation, and was so treated. These con-

led to armed conflict which ultimately brought unification of Germany under Prussian auspices. The principle of nationalism was again violated when Norway was arbitrarily given to Sweden and the Belgians were turned over to the Dutch. Poles and Finns also simply exchanged masters. These peoples were not content to be placed under alien governments, and during the nineteenth century they continued the struggle to secure national sovereignty and a greater share of personal liberty.

By their Quadruple Alliance the diplomats of Vienna also created and set in motion the Congress System (see p. 180)—machinery designed to stifle and discourage the development of democracy. This policy, coupled with the violations of nationalism, was to result in three important series of revolutions engulfing Europe—in 1820-1821, 1830-1831, and 1848.

Tsar Alexander I (pictured above) went to the Congress of Vienna intent upon obtaining all of Poland but, due in large part to Castlereagh, was obliged to settle for control over Warsaw and the central portion of the Polish state.

It is quite plain that the Congress of Vienna failed in many ways to live up to its opportunities. Its denial of nationalist aspirations and its chronic suspicion of political liberalism led to popular unrest and revolution. But in view of the subsequent failures of the peacemakers after 1919 and 1945, it would be unfair to pass too harsh a judgment on those of 1815. The problems of peace making after the First and Second World Wars showed that an ideal peace arrangement is practically impossible to attain, for statesmen are bound by war promises, influenced by the passions and enthusiasms of the time, and unaided by the perspective which makes the errors of one generation so clear to the next. Perhaps the following is a reasonable evaluation of the accomplishments of the diplomats of 1815: "It has been customary to denounce the peacemakers of Vienna as reactionary and illiberal in the extreme. It is indeed true that they represented the old regime and were, to a large extent, untouched by the new ideas. But they represented the best and not the worst of the old regime, and their settlement averted any major war in Europe for forty years"[26]

ditions led to the development of a vigorous nationalist movement in Italy, which triumphed in 1860.

Nationalist aspirations were also frustrated in Germany, where a weak and loosely organized German Confederation of thirty-eight states was established, with Austria at its head. This was largely Austria's doing again, for Austria saw in a united Germany a threat to Austrian dominance in central Europe. Later in the century, this situation

Overconfident because of victories in France against the Allies early in 1814, Napoleon turned down a peace settlement providing France with her 1792 boundaries. Subsequent defeats forced Napoleon to abdicate in April of the same year.

SUMMARY

Some historians have asserted that the upheaval in France could not have taken place without the successful revolution in the Thirteen Colonies. The American Revolution gave France leaders experienced in diplomacy and war, a revolutionary credo, and the example of a functioning and stable system of free government. But the excesses of the Jacobin Republic led to a revulsion in public opinion and to the meteoric career of Napoleon Bonaparte. Perhaps no better evaluation of Napoleon has ever been given than De Tocqueville's: "He was as great as a man can be without virtue."[27] Motivated primarily by personal ambition, Napoleon was the unwitting instrument for the spread of French revolutionary ideals throughout Europe.

The congress of European powers assembled at Vienna to remake the map of Europe after Napoleon's final defeat reflected a strong conservative reaction to the French revolutionary ideals. Prince Metternich, the Austrian delegate and a dominant personage in the congress, had watched the French Revolution with disgust. To him its boasted liberties were anathema, and as the architect of a restored Europe Metternich attempted to ensure Europe not only against a recrudescence of French imperialism but against the subversion of legitimate governments by revolutionary political and social principles.

The French Revolution from 1789 to 1815 was more radical and more influential than the English and American revolutions that preceded it although, paradoxically, certain basic ideals of the Revolution, such as constitutional government, were not fully realized in France until later. More so than the English and the American revolutions, the French Revolution was social as well as political; intellectual, economic, and religious freedoms were all given strong emphasis. Much of the history of the nineteenth century is concerned with the strivings and amplification of democracy, intellectual and religious freedom, and laissez faire.

SUGGESTIONS FOR READING

POLITICS AND ECONOMICS

Trevelyan, G. M., *The English Revolution, 1688-1689,* Holt, 1939. A lucid, well-balanced evaluation of the Glorious Revolution by one of the greatest English historians.

Lindsay, J. O., ed., *The Old Regime, 1713-1763,* Cambridge, 1957. This work, Volume VII of *The New Cambridge Modern History,* surveys the political, military, and diplomatic aspects of European expansion. Penetrating analyses of seventeenth-century political developments will be found in both D. Ogg, *Europe in the Seventeenth Century,* Macmillan, 1952; and C. J. Friedrich and C. Blitzer, *The Age of Power,* Cornell,* 1957. A broader view of the period with an emphasis upon leading historical figures is offered by B. Willey, *The Seventeenth Century Background,* Anchor,* 1953.

A brilliant study of French society before 1789, first published over a century ago, is Alexis de Tocqueville, *The Old Regime and the French Revolution,* Anchor,* 1955. See also W. H. Lewis, *The Splendid Century,* Anchor,* 1957; A. L. Guérard, *The Life and Death of an Ideal,* Braziller, 1956; A. Cobban, *A History of Modern France,* I, Penguin,* 1957.

The duel for empire between France and England is described vividly in W. L. Dorn, *Competition for Empire, 1740-1763,* Harper, 1940. G. M. Wrong, noted Canadian historian, analyzes the causes of the loss of the French empire in *The Rise and Fall of New France,* 2 vols., Macmillan, 1928.

Palmer, R. R., *The Challenge,* Vol. I of *The Age of the Democratic Revolution: A Political History of Europe and America, 1760-1800,* Princeton, 1959. A valuable synthesis, showing that all the major revolutions of this period resulted from similar ideas and needs.

Gipson, L. G., *The Coming of the Revolution, 1763-1775,* Harper, 1954. A work of superior insight which shows how political and commercial relations between England and the American colonies became increasingly strained before the outbreak of the American Revolution. See also J. C. Wahlke, ed., *The Causes of the American Revolution,* Heath,* 1950, for differing analyses of the Revolution by an able group of scholars.

Lefebvre, G., *The Coming of the French Revolution, 1789,* Vintage,* 1957. A penetrating interpretation by a famous French historian.

Gershoy, L., *The Era of the French Revolution, 1789-1799: Ten Years That Shook the World,* Anvil,* 1957. A brief but scholarly study of the Revolution.

Acton, Lord J. E. E. D., *Lectures on the French Revolution,* Noonday,* 1959. The author contends that the tragedies of the Revolution were largely due to a failure to reach an agreement with the Church.

*Indicates an inexpensive paperbound edition.

Brunn, G., *Europe and the French Imperium: 1799-1814,* Harper, 1938. An analysis of the Napoleonic empire: how it functioned and what it meant to Europe. Also recommended is F. M. H. Markham, *Napoleon and the Awakening of Europe,* Macmillan, 1954.

Madariaga, Salvador de, *The Fall of the Spanish American Empire,* Macmillan, 1948. Examines the reasons for the disintegration of Spanish power in America and analyzes the influences in Latin America of the *philosophes* and the French Revolution. See also A. P. Whitaker, ed., *Latin America and the Enlightenment,* Appleton-Century, 1942; and V. A. Belaunde, *Bolivar and the Political Thought of the Spanish American Revolution,* Johns Hopkins, 1938.

Mahan, A., *The Influence of Sea Power on History, 1660-1783,* Hill and Wang,* 1957. A stimulating and controversial study.

For further information about economics in the period discussed in Chapters 1-4, see the pertinent chapters in H. Heaton, *Economic History of Europe,* rev. ed., Harper, 1948. Also recommended are E. F. Heckscher, *Mercantilism,* 2 vols. (rev. ed. by E. F. Söderlund), Macmillan, 1956; C. W. Cole, *Colbert and a Century of French Mercantilism,* 2 vols., Columbia, 1939; T. Ashton, *The Industrial Revolution: 1760-1830,* Oxford, 1948; M. D. George, *England in Transition: Life and Work in the Eighteenth Century,* Routledge, 1931.

Diderot, D., *A Diderot Pictorial Encyclopedia of Trades and Industry,* 2 vols. (ed. by C. C. Gillispie), Dover, 1959. This selection of 485 plates from the *Encyclopédie* provides a fascinating introduction to the trades, crafts, machinery, and industries of the eighteenth century.

THOUGHT AND ART

Snyder, L. L., *The Age of Reason,* Anvil,* 1955. A useful résumé of the forces and trends characteristic of the Enlightenment. See also F. E. Manuel, *The Age of Reason,* Cornell,* 1951.

Hazard, P., *The European Mind; The Critical Years (1680-1715),* Yale, 1953. A critical evaluation of the intellectual currents of this seminal period. Economic and political aspects as well as intellectual trends are covered in F. L. Nussbaum, *The Triumph of Science and Reason, 1660-1685,* Harper, 1953. See also A. Wolf, *A History of Science, Technology, and Philosophy in the Sixteenth and Seventeenth Centuries,* 2 vols., Torchbooks,* 1959.

Turberville, A. S., *English Men and Manners in the Eighteenth Century; An Illustrated Narrative,* Galaxy,* 1957. Colorful vignettes of life in a society which was being affected profoundly by the geographical revolution.

Fosca, F., *The Eighteenth Century: From Watteau to Tiepolo,* Skira, 1953. Superbly illustrated review of trends in art. See also A. Schonberger and H. Soehner, *The Rococo Age: Art and Civilization of the 18th Century,* McGraw-Hill, 1960.

Faniel, S., ed., *French Art of the Eighteenth Century,* Simon and Schuster, 1957. Over 600 illustrations, representing every facet of the major and minor arts of the period in France.

Of particular interest to the art history student are Francisco de Goya, **Complete Etchings,** Crown, 1958, with a foreword by Aldous Huxley; and W. Hogarth, *Marriage à la Mode, and Other Engravings,* Lear, 1947, which includes the sermonizing texts originally accompanying each plate.

BIOGRAPHY

Klyuchevsky, V., **Peter the Great,** St. Martin's, 1958. A vivid account of the life of the ruler who placed his stamp on Russian social, economic, and intellectual history. Another of Russia's most celebrated rulers is depicted superbly in G. S. Thomson, *Catherine the Great and the Expansion of Russia,* Macmillan, 1950.

Ergang, R., *The Potsdam Führer, Frederick William I,* Columbia, 1941. A graphic portrayal of life at the court of a re- markable autocrat. His son's career is painted with bold strokes in G. P. Gooch, *Frederick the Great: the Ruler, the Writer, the Man,* Knopf, 1947.

Told with style and wit are the life stories of two royal mis- tresses and an ill-starred queen: J. H. Wilson, *Nell Gwyn, Royal Mistress,* Farrar, Straus, 1952; N. Mitford, *Madame de Pompadour,* Random House, 1954; A Castelot, *Queen of France; A Biography of Marie Antoinette,* Harper, 1957.

Palmer, R. R., *Twelve Who Ruled: The Year of the Terror in the French Revolution,* rev. ed., Princeton, 1958. A vivid portrait of the men who tried to save the Republic by the guillotine until they themselves became trapped by the situa- tion they had created.

Kircheisen, F., **Napoleon,** Harcourt, 1932. The stirring story of the Little Corporal, from Corsica to St. Helena.

These biographies of the Liberators are highly recommended: G. Masur, **Simón Bolívar,** Univ. of New Mexico, 1948; Salva- dor de Madariaga, **Bolívar,** Pellegrini, 1952; R. Rojas, **San Martin: Knight of the Andes,** Doubleday, 1945.

Andrade, E. N., **Sir Isaac Newton,** Anchor,* 1958. Explained and fitted into the mainstream of science are the discoveries of the "prince of seventeenth-century scientists."

Krutch, J. W., **Samuel Johnson,** Holt, 1944. An absorbing life story and a colorful picture of Johnson's London. See also C. Abernethy, *Mr. Pepys of Seething Lane; A Narrative,* McGraw-Hill, 1957; and P. C. Quennell, *Hogarth's Progress,* Viking, 1955.

Green, F. C., *Jean-Jacques Rousseau; A Critical Study of His Life and Writings,* Cambridge, 1955. The best biography available of the man whose ideas helped shape political, religious, and educational developments of the modern world.

Turner, W. J., *Mozart: The Man and His Works,* Anchor,* 1954. A vivid study, showing the charm and pathos of this great artist's life.

SOURCE MATERIALS

Burke, E., *Reflections on the French Revolution,* Gateway,* 1955. One of the most influential studies of political philoso- phy produced in the eighteenth century, written in vibrant prose.

Stewart, J. H., *A Documentary Survey of the French Revolu- tion,* Macmillan, 1951. The chief phases of the Revolution as revealed in documentary evidence.

The American Revolution described by the men who fought in it: H. S. Commager and R. B. Morris, eds., **The Spirit of 'Seventy Six,** 2 vols., Bobbs-Merrill, 1958; G. F. Scheer and H. F. Rankin, **Rebels and Redcoats,** Mentor,* 1959; H. T. Wade and R. A. Lively, **This Glorious Cause,** Princeton, 1958.

Ségur, Philippe, Comte de, **Napoleon's Russian Campaign,** Houghton, 1958. A first-hand narrative of the disastrous Rus- sian campaign by Napoleon's aide-de-camp. See also the memoirs of A. A. de Caulaincourt, *With Napoleon in Russia,* abr. ed., Universal,* 1959.

Convenient, well-selected excerpts from the writings of the seventeenth- and eighteenth-century philosophers will be found in S. Hampshire, ed., *The Age of Reason: The Seventeenth Century Philosophers,* Mentor,* 1956; and Sir Isaiah Berlin, ed., *The Age of Enlightenment: The Eighteenth Century Philosophers,* Mentor,* 1956.

Recommended editions of famous works of the Enlightenment include J. Locke, *Of Civil Government, 2nd Essay,* Gate- way,* 1955; Montesquieu, *The Spirit of the Laws,* Hafner, 1949; J. J. Rousseau, *The Social Contract,* Gateway,* 1954; A. Smith, *The Wealth of Nations,* Gateway,* 1953.

Voltaire, F. M. A., *The Portable Voltaire* (ed. by B. R. Redman), Viking,* 1949. An excellent introduction to the ebul- lient *philosophe.*

Spinoza, B., *Selections* (ed. by J. D. Wild), Scribner's,* 1958; R. Descartes, *Selections* (ed. by R. M. Eaton), Scribner's,* 1959; and I. Kant, *Selections* (ed. by T. M. Greene), Scrib- ner's,* 1957, contain well-chosen representative writings that reveal the heart of the works of these philosophers.

FICTION

Fielding, H., *The History of Tom Jones, A Foundling,* Modern Library,* 1950. A brilliant, robust novel of eighteenth-century England.

Shepard, O. and W., *Jenkins' Ear; A Narrative Attributed to Horace Walpole, Esq.,* Macmillan, 1951. An intriguing novel in which the War of Jenkins' Ear is revealed as a plot by the Whigs against Prime Minister Robert Walpole. Another histor- ical fantasy is N. E. Wyckoff, *The Braintree Mission,* Mac- millan, 1957, which posits what might have happened if George III's government had been more reasonable and John Adams had become a peer in the House of Lords.

Available in many editions are the justly famous historical novels written in the nineteenth century: A. Dumas, *The Three Musketeers* and *Twenty Years After* (daring adventures in the France of the Old Regime); C. Dickens, *A Tale of Two Cities* (London and Paris during the Terror); L. Tolstoy, *War and Peace* (Napoleon's invasion of Russia).

Forester, C. S., **Lord Hornblower,** Grosset, 1947. Thrilling adventures on the high seas during the Napoleonic Wars.

POLITICS

Richelieu, adviser to Louis XIII and real authority behind the French throne, exalts power of the monarchy 1624-1642
Frederick William, the Great Elector, makes Brandenburg the most important Protestant state in Germany 1640-1688
Mazarin governs France during minority of Louis XIV 1643-1661; triumphs over enemies during civil war 1648-1653
Peace of Westphalia ends Thirty Years' War; France emerges as greatest military power on the Continent 1648

1650

Restoration of Stuart kings in England—controversy between Charles II and Parliament 1660-1685; Charles II negotiates secret Treaty of Dover with Louis XIV 1670; Whig and Tory parties organized; Habeas Corpus Act passed 1679
Louis XIV takes over personal management of French state; becomes **epitome of absolutism** 1661-1715

Louis XIV invades Spanish Netherlands, Holland, German border districts 1667-1686; opposed by Grand Alliance 1689-1697
Peter the Great, absolutist tsar, captures Azov on Black Sea, tours Europe, attempts to westernize Russia 1682-1725
James II of England attempts to impose absolute rule 1685-1688
Louis XIV revokes Edict of Nantes 1685

Glorious Revolution—Whigs and Tories invite William of Orange to rule England; Bill of Rights passed; Parliament dominant agency in government 1688

Treaty of Ryswick—Grand Alliance checks ambitions of Louis XIV 1697
1700 Great Northern War—Charles XII of Sweden defeated by Peter the Great and allies; Russia gains outlet on Baltic 1700-1721
War of the Spanish Succession—English and allies renew struggle against French 1702; great victory by allies at battle of Blenheim 1704; Treaty of Utrecht ends war 1713
Frederick William I of Prussia creates all-powerful central government; builds up army 1713-1740
George I initiates Hanoverian dynasty in England; beginning of creative cabinet government 1714

Speculative bubbles of South Sea Company and Mississippi Company burst 1720
Robert Walpole becomes first prime minister of England 1721-1742

War of Jenkins' Ear 1739-1742
Frederick II, the Great, makes Prussia important power in European politics 1740-1786
War of the Austrian Succession—Frederick the Great invades Silesia; France and England struggle in first stage of duel for world empire 1740-1748

1750

Seven Years' War—Diplomatic Revolution aligns Austria and France against England and Prussia; struggle on Continent and in colonies; William Pitt's system brings English victories, such as battle of Plassey (1757), battle of Quebec (1759); Treaty of Paris makes Britain greatest colonial, commercial, naval power in world 1756-1763

Catherine the Great makes Russia primary power on Black Sea 1762-1796
George III (1760-1820) of England opposes reform, secures control of Parliament 1770-1782
Poland partitioned in three stages among Russia, Prussia, Austria 1772-1795
American Revolution 1775-1783

American Articles of Confederation 1781
Pitt the Younger becomes prime minister, makes reforms in government, restores cabinet government 1783

American Constitution adopted 1789
French Revolution, first phase—storming of Bastille; National Constituent Assembly draws up Declaration of the Rights of Man, sets up new constitution and government (Legislative Assembly) 1789-1791
French Revolution, second phase—radical insurrection in Paris; National Convention proclaims the Republic; France repels invasion by Austria and Prussia 1792
Louis XVI executed; Reign of Terror under Robespierre; compulsory military service introduced; Robespierre executed; Directory assumes power, smashes First Coalition, except for England 1793-1797

Napoleon establishes Consulate, scatters Second Coalition 1799-1802; Napoleon climaxes reforms with Civil Code, proclaims himself emperor 1804; Napoleon destroys armies of Third Coalition, is defeated by British at Trafalgar, defeats Prussia 1805-1806;
1800 Napoleon's invasion of Russia fails 1812
War of 1812—United States vs. England 1812-1814
English and allies defeat Napoleon at Leipzig; Napoleon abdicates throne, goes to Elba 1813-1814
Napoleon escapes prison, is defeated at Waterloo and exiled to St. Helena 1815

SCIENCE AND TECHNOLOGY, THOUGHT AND ART

Neoclassical dramatists in France—Corneille, Racine, Molière
Defenders of absolutism—Hobbes (author of *Leviathan*, 1651) and Bossuet
Boyle's law is formulated 1660

1650

Spinoza expresses his pantheistic philosophy; publishes *Ethics* (1663)

Leibnitz formulates theory of atomism c. 1685

Newton expounds gravitation theory in **Principia Mathematica** 1687

Locke advances doctrine of popular sovereignty as argument against absolutism in "Of Civil Government" 1690; expresses philosophy of empiricism in *An Essay Concerning Human Understanding* 1690

1700

Rococo painting exemplified by Watteau; English portrait painting by Reynolds, Gainsborough
Novel appears—Defoe's *Robinson Crusoe* (1719); Swift's *Gulliver's Travels* (1726); Richardson's *Pamela* (1740-1741); Fielding's *Joseph Andrews* (1742) and *Tom Jones* (1749)
Philosophe Montesquieu satirizes absolutism in *Persian Letters* 1721; analyzes governments in *The Spirit of Laws* 1748
Pope, foremost Neoclassical English poet, publishes *The Essay on Man* 1733
Hogarth's "The Rake's Progress" 1735
Linnaeus' *Systema Naturae* 1735; Buffon's *Natural History of Animals* 1749-1804
Intellectuals adopt new belief, Deism, which regards God as the "clock-winder" of universe; Pietism develops to restore emotion and faith to religion; Wesley brothers found Methodist movement in England 1738; Quietism is crushed in Catholic countries
Inventions revolutionize textile industry—flying shuttle 1738; spinning jenny 1764; water frame 1769; spinning mule 1779; power loom 1785; cotton gin 1792

Discoveries in electricity—Leyden Jar 1745; Franklin's experiment with kite 1752
Formalism in music—Handel, Bach, Mozart, Haydn
Reaction on the Continent against Baroque and Rococo styles of architecture is manifested in Neoclassical style c. 1750
Industrial capitalism—second phase in growth of capitalism c. 1750-1870
Encyclopédie, edited by Diderot, spreads doctrines of rationalism and Deism 1751-1772
Johnson's *A Dictionary of the English Language* 1755; Boswell's *The Life of Samuel Johnson, LL.D.* 1791

1750

Voltaire—prince of French philosophes, critic of his times—publishes *Candide* 1759
Modern canal building in England begins 1759; macadam roads invented 1815
Quesnay and other physiocrats advocate policy of laissez faire
Rousseau spreads hatred of oppression, expounds doctrine of popular sovereignty in *Social Contract* 1762; emphasizes self-expression in education in *Émile* 1762

Priestley isolates ammonia; discovers oxygen 1774; produces carbon monoxide gas 1799

Adam Smith's Wealth of Nations defends laissez-faire economics 1776
Gibbon's *Decline and Fall of the Roman Empire* 1776-1787
Lavoisier announces the law of the conservation of matter and his combustion theory 1777
Kant's *Critique of Pure Reason* 1781

Henry Cort's puddling process climaxes new methods of refining iron 1784; Watt's steam engine is used in industry 1785

Hutton's *Theory of the Earth*, pioneer work in geology 1795
Laplace sets forth nebular hypothesis in astronomy 1796
Jenner develops safe vaccination against smallpox c. 1798

Volta discovers method for generating continuous flow of electricity 1800
Goya's "The Disasters of War" 1810

1800

Frontier

THE NEW IMAGE OF SIR ISAAC NEWTON   by Henry Guerlac

Distinguished historian of science and Professor of the History of Science at Cornell University, Dr. Henry Guerlac is a member of the Académie Internationale d'Histoire des Sciences and a fellow of the Royal Society of Arts (London) and of the American Academy of Arts and Sciences. From 1953 to 1955, Dr. Guerlac was associated with the Institute for Advanced Study at Princeton, and since 1957 he has been president of the History of Science Society.

One of the newest and least explored branches of historical inquiry is the history of science. As a serious scholarly discipline, this field first came into being early in this century, in response to the rapid growth of modern science with its manifold effects on our daily lives, and stimulated by the crisis in theoretical science, especially physics. Between 1890 and 1914 a host of new discoveries exposed the inadequacy of classical physics and led to the revolutionary formulations of Max Planck and Albert Einstein (see p. 332). This prompted a reëxamination of the basic assumptions of science and a serious inquiry into its history. At the hands of certain scientists and philosophers, historical investigations came to play a significant part in this reassessment, and men were led back to the time of Sir Isaac Newton and to still more remote periods of scientific thought. Pioneer historians of science—chief among them George Sarton (1884-1956)—began to supply those aids to research which all fields of scholarship require: bibliographical tools, carefully edited texts of scientific classics, and a journal in which specialized studies could be published. Sarton's *Isis*, the oldest and most successful of the journals, was founded in 1913 and is still flourishing. It was not long before chairs and even departments of the history of science were established in European and American universities; and soon national and international societies were formed to bring together interested scholars.

Much of great interest has been uncovered by historians of science in the past fifty years, enough at least to show how little had actually been known about the past of science and how much there still remains to uncover. Perhaps the most important revelation concerns the nature of science itself and the proper spirit in which to study it historically. It is no longer believed that scientists merely discover facts that are simply waiting to be turned up by a patient observation of nature and the application of that mysterious and infallible tool "the scientific method." Instead, at least on the highest level, scientific discovery is seen as the organization and interpretation of experience, a form of intellectual creation, not unlike that of the poet or the artist, though subject to rather more stringent rules of the game. Historians must therefore be alert to all the varied forces that may affect the development and elaboration of scientific ideas and theories: the character and personality of the scientist; his education, philosophy, and religious views; and the intellectual climate and material conditions of his time. A brief account of our new image of one of the greatest scientists, Sir Isaac Newton (1642-1727), may serve to illustrate this approach.

The somewhat idealized image of Newton, both the man and the scientist, has not survived the close scrutiny to which the facts of his career have been subjected. His scientific stature is undimmed; but his odd personality, the degree of his uniqueness and originality, and the later influence of his remarkable achievement have all been reappraised. The reassessment has not been an easy task. The essential primary sources—Newton's published writings and his letters and private papers—have not been brought together in a carefully edited modern edition. Even now there are no critically edited modern editions of his two greatest works, the *Opticks* and the *Mathematical Principles of Natural Philosophy*, usually called (from its original Latin title) simply the *Principia*. Nor, until recently, have scholars had access to the surviving manuscripts of his letters and private papers.[1]

Among Newton's papers, perhaps the most important discovery has been a series of notebooks which Newton kept as a student at Cambridge. One of these notebooks contains the earliest record of his experiments on color and hints of his debt to such earlier scientists as René Descartes and Robert Boyle. What has been learned about Newton's interest in chemistry, which in his day was scarcely distinguishable from alchemy, the pseudoscience of gold-making, may prove to be even more striking. Earlier scholars knew very little and cared less about this "disreputable" side of Newton. But the testimony of his library and of the many alchemical manuscripts in his handwriting has put the question of Newton's devotion to alchemy beyond dispute. One Newton scholar, the eminent economist Lord Keynes, stressed what seemed to him evidence of Newton's credulous and mystical inclinations; Keynes even described Newton as "the last of the magicians." Other scholars disagree. They see Newton as primarily and legitimately interested in the grains of scientific truth hidden in the alchemical chaff; they point to the surprising knowledge of chemistry displayed in some of his published writings—notably the *Opticks* —and to the profound influence his outline of chemical theory exerted in the century after his death. Undoubtedly, more light will be shed on this vexed question by the further study of Newton's early notebooks.

It has been, however, the detailed study of the *Principia* in all its aspects which has done most to increase understanding of Newton's mind and thought. More has been learned of the debt he owed his predecessors for his mathematical techniques and even for his fundamental principle of universal gravitation. The mystery of the twenty-year delay between the time Newton hit upon the fundamental answer to his problem and the time he set himself to work it out in detail in the *Principia* has apparently been solved. From the very substantial changes Newton made in his famous work as it passed through three editions during his lifetime,[2] scholars have learned how his views changed and how he responded to the criticism leveled against his novel ideas and his radically different way of studying nature.

Such detailed historical study, and such minute detective work, is amply justified by the importance of Newton's epoch-making work. In the *Principia* he demonstrated beyond a doubt that earthbound bodies and the planets all follow the same fundamental laws of nature: his three laws of motion and the very important auxiliary principle or law of universal gravitation. By applying these mathematical laws to the heavenly bodies, Newton showed that the planets must follow the rules by which Kepler, earlier in the seventeenth century, had neatly summed up their behavior. Moreover, Newton could not only describe and predict the planetary motions; he could explain them—at least in the sense that he showed Kepler's "laws" to be consequences of his own more fundamental laws governing the behavior of all matter. From long

experience in observing the heavens, astronomers had succeeded in making fairly accurate predictions of the future positions of the planets—but they rarely sought or cared much about any underlying physical explanation. Newton was the first who could do both successfully, who could use his results both to predict and to explain. More than that, his theory led to *predictive discovery;* that is to say, it led him and his followers to observe phenomena which had not been dreamed of or seen before, such as the flattened shape of the earth or the closed elliptical paths of comets. The most dramatic predictive achievement came long after the publication of the *Principia* and after many refinements had been added to Newton's theory by others: this was the discovery of the new planet Neptune (1846), which was observed when astronomers turned their telescopes to a point in the skies where a Newtonian calculation had told them to look.

For a long time, students of Newton's work were content to study his scientific achievement and to show how it influenced the thought of later scientists and philosophers. But it was well known that the laws of nature Newton enunciated, and which led to such remarkable conclusions, reposed on his belief that there must be a single, absolute, and unvarying flow of time and a single, absolute frame of space in which the planets carried out their motions.

Men were slow to realize that for Newton these were philosophical notions, perhaps scientifically unjustified, not scientific notions in the ordinary sense. And they were slower still to realize that these assumptions were related closely in Newton's mind to his religious ideas (as was also, for example, Newton's firm belief that the universe was the result of a creation, not of a cosmic process of evolution). As a result of the "Second Revolution in Physics" (about 1900), it was demonstrated that the old notion of an absolute time and absolute space was a mirage, or at least an unjustifiable extension of everyday experience. Yet many students of Newton's work continued to stress the empirical and experimental side of his achievement and only belatedly realized how abstract his work was, how essentially complex and subtle was his thought, and to what extent philosophical ideas undoubtedly entered into his theories. But after the investigations of men like E. A. Burtt and Alexandre Koyré it is no longer possible to believe that Newton's thought was shaped only by technical considerations.

Like his contemporary Leibnitz, indeed like all his contemporaries, Newton was deeply concerned with religion, though his views were some-what unorthodox. He spent long hours in the study of Biblical chronology and of the prophetic and apocalyptic books of the Bible. This aspect of his career was glossed over by nineteenth-century writers or treated as the aberration of a fine scientific mind weakened by the severe nervous breakdown he is known to have suffered. Yet, in his own day and after his death, his views on these matters were widely respected.

But was this religious interest a significant factor in shaping Newton's scientific thought? The question is still being debated. Certain passages which Newton added to the second edition of his *Principia* (e.g., the famous *scholium,* or explanatory section on God) would appear to be convincing evidence that this was the case. That he believed in religious implications of his scientific discoveries is clear from the famous letters which he wrote to the clergyman Richard Bentley and the series of letters exchanged between Leibnitz and Samuel Clarke, a disciple of Newton, in the years 1715 and 1716.

But did this religious side of Newton's character influence the actual composition of the *Principia?* Newton practically said as much when he wrote to Bentley in 1692 that when he was preparing the *Principia* he "had an eye upon such principles as might work with considering men, for the belief in the Deity." One answer has been supplied by the leading Newton scholar, Professor Koyré, in *From the Closed World to the Infinite Universe* (1957). Koyré has argued persuasively that the speculations of Henry More, a religious philosopher who belonged to the group of so-called Cambridge Platonists, helped to convince Newton that space and time are absolute and are manifestations or expressions of the Godhead.

Although the emphasis on the philosophic and religious background of Newton's *Principia* has enriched our understanding, this sort of interpretation can be carried too far. Newton, at least when he was at work on the *Opticks* and the *Principia,* was first and foremost a scientist and mathematician. It is possible (as one recent critic of Koyré's work has suggested) that Newton had little concern with these religious matters when he was actually engaged in his scientific work and that it was only later in life that he gave a theological interpretation to his writings. Be that as it may, Newton's prime importance lies in the tools of investigation which he perfected and in the method of inquiry he employed, for these have proved more enduring and fruitful than the substantive findings themselves.

This case history can serve as an illustration of the dialectic which marks all progress in historical study. Perhaps overstatement and overemphasis are sometimes needed to shake man free from prejudices and earlier entanglements. In turn, this overemphasis later demands correction. Our historical knowledge seems to advance not in a straight line but in a wave motion, moving sometimes far to one side and then to the other as it progresses. In the history of science we are still far from the middle line. Clearly, there is much work and much thinking to be done in this still fertile field of inquiry.

1 At his death in 1727, Newton bequeathed his private papers to his niece. From her they passed to the family of the Earls of Portsmouth, where they remained until 1872, when the strictly scientific papers were given to the library of Newton's old university, Cambridge. In 1936 the family put up the balance of the papers at the auction block. Shocked by the threatened dispersal of this valuable material, Keynes purchased the greater part of it and tried to recover the papers that had been bought by others. The collection he formed, now at King's College, supplements the older mass of materials in the Cambridge University library. A substantial part of Newton's own library, miraculously tracked down and given to Cambridge, is now housed in Trinity College, where Newton once lived and worked. These materials are now being carefully studied, and, in addition, efforts are being made to locate other Newton papers and letters that have found their way into other private or public collections. The letters are being published under the auspices of the Royal Society of London; see H. W. Turnbull, ed., *The Correspondence of Isaac Newton* (3 vols.; New York, 1959-1961).

2 Professor Alexandre Koyré and Professor I. B. Cohen are jointly preparing a variorum edition of the **Principia,** a critical modern edition in which the changes introduced by Newton in the different editions are to be precisely noted and their significance explained.

SUGGESTED READINGS

Louis Trenchard More, **Isaac Newton, A Biography** (New York and London, 1934); G. N. Clark, **Science and Social Welfare in the Age of Newton** (Oxford, 1937); J. W. N. Sullivan, **Isaac Newton, 1642-1727** (New York, 1938); E. N. da C. Andrade, **Sir Isaac Newton** (Garden City, N.Y., 1948), a Doubleday Anchor Book; H. S. Thayer, ed., **Newton's Philosophy of Nature: Selections from His Writings** (New York, 1953); E. A. Burtt, **The Metaphysical Foundations of Modern Science,** rev. ed. (New York, 1932), reprinted as Doubleday Anchor Book (Garden City, N.Y., 1954); I. Bernard Cohen, ed., **Isaac Newton's Papers and Letters on Natural Philosophy** (Cambridge, Mass., 1958); H. G. Alexander, ed., **The Leibniz-Clarke Correspondence, with Extracts from Newton's** Principia **and Opticks** (Manchester, 1956); Alexandre Koyré, **From the Closed World to the Infinite Universe** (Baltimore, 1957).

PART 2 From Metternich to Bismarck

CHAPTER 5 ROMANTICS AND REBELS

CHAPTER 6 INDUSTRIAL REVOLUTION

CHAPTER 7 TO THE BARRICADES!

CHAPTER 8 NATIONALISM AND THE MAKING OF NATIONS

Certain key trends dominated the internal affairs of Europe from the battle of Waterloo to the unification of Germany in 1870. The first—reaction and conservatism—developed in opposition to the radical ideas circulated by France between 1792 and 1815. Controlled by Metternich, the Congress of Vienna ignored the nationalist and liberal sentiments of the people and attempted to restore autocracy and privilege. But though its goals were reactionary, in one respect the Congress System was a step forward—it represented the first serious attempt to solve problems by international cooperation.

New patterns of thought quickly challenged the conservative ideology, however. Nationalism remained a powerful force among the masses of Europe, and political and economic liberalism—the creed of the growing middle class—constituted another potent weapon directed against the fortress of reaction. The bourgeoisie sought to secure a limited extension of the franchise, establish parliaments and constitutions, and bring about moderate reforms. But the fruits of bourgeois liberalism were, in the main, only for the rich and powerful members of the middle class; little thought was given to the workers, who remained without political power and social advantages. In the economic realm, liberalism supported the businessman's philosophy of laissez faire, which strenuously opposed any regulation of business by the state. Both nationalism and middle-class liberalism found strength in the romantic movement of the first half of the nineteenth century. As rationalism furnished the weapons for attacks against political and economic evils in the eighteenth century, so romanticism supplied the emotional fervor behind the drive for liberty in the first decades of the century that followed.

In the revolts which broke out in Europe between 1820 and 1848, middle-class entrepreneurs and factory workers united to overthrow arbitrary rule by despots and enact constitutions. But the rash of revolutions occurring in 1848 brought the complication of a new ideological pattern—that of socialism. The cooperation between workers and bourgeoisie broke down, and the deep-seated antagonism and suspicion between the two classes were revealed. Champions of the masses, such as Marx, now demanded the supremacy of the workers. The modern class struggle had begun.

Together with diverse national rivalries and the half-baked utopian programs of starry-eyed reformers, this rapidly mounting antagonism between the business classes and the new city proletariat resulted in the failure of the revolutions of 1848. The ardent hopes for political advancement were cruelly dashed in France, Italy, Prussia, and the Austrian empire. The price paid for such failures was high. After 1870 ruthless realism rather than romantic idealism appealed to leaders as the path to success; and while much that was out of date was removed by 1870, the legacy of the class struggle remained—the issue between socialism and moderate reform continued to plague the statesmen of the western world.

In the interplay among bourgeois liberalism, socialism, and nationalism, technology and science performed important roles, and it was amid these forces that the First Industrial Revolution emerged. Influenced by all of them, it was perhaps the most potent factor shaping nineteenth-century civilization. Its machines and factories produced complex urban life, an all-powerful business class, and a constantly growing mass of discontented industrial workers. The clash of interests between business and labor—a product of the machine—becomes one of the major themes of modern history. Taking to the sea lanes, men distributed the products of the Industrial Revolution—also the methods and the outlook of the middle-class businessmen who produced them—to all the continents of the world. The impact of western industrial civilization on the ancient cultures of Asia in particular was to have far-reaching effects; the idea of progress and all it implied accompanied the traders and their wares, planting the seeds of political and social revolution that were an inseparable concomitant in nineteenth-century European culture.

CHAPTER 5

Romantics and Rebels

Introduction. After World War I, it became fashionable to ridicule the Victorian era, particularly the artistic tastes, the moral code, and the middle-class complacency of the Victorians. But since World War II, attitudes toward the nineteenth century have undergone a noticeable change; today many people look back upon those times with nostalgia and envy. When compared with today's world of confusion and stress, the Victorian era seems a time of serene confidence. "This unquestioning sense that life has momentous meaning . . . gives to . . . the last century a quality which inevitably overawes the present generation —a generation which has so largely lost its sense of direction and of any distinct moral summons, and yet is anxious to recover both."[1]

The purpose of this chapter is neither to ridicule the nineteenth century nor to exaggerate its vir-
tues, but to present a balanced evaluation of its thought, science, and arts, both as significant phenomena in their own right and as factors influencing the major political and economic movements of the age. We shall concentrate on certain key trends—romanticism, nationalism, liberalism, and realism—and illustrate their significance for yesterday and today with examples from nineteenth-century literature and art. Of course, no historical movement or ideational trend is a simple, clear-cut phenomenon. New movements grow from old ones—sometimes to reaffirm former values, more often to react against them. Between 1815 and 1870, certain trends of thought became dominant, creating an intellectual environment different from that of the previous century.

Among those trends was a widespread faith in the idea of progress—the perfectibility of man and his society—and the artistic and intellectual movement known as romanticism. Even as the martial strains of the "Marseillaise" had carried the revolutionaries of France to triumph, so new "marching songs" in the form of poems, symphonies, and paintings accompanied the advance of the new era. European poets, composers, and painters of the romantic school sought new techniques of expression, along with new subject matter, new harmonies, and new color patterns. Spurred on by their enthusiastic faith in man, the romanticists rebelled against political oppression, social injustice, and the classical, intellectual, and esthetic standards of the previous century.

Between 1815 and 1870, society was also shaped by another major force—industrialism. Steam engines, railways, and industrial towns with their smoke-belching factory chimneys were·altering the landscape of western Europe. The new dynamism of industrialism propelled to the top of the social heap the owners of those chimneys— the capitalistic owners of the means of production —the bourgeoisie, or middle class. The triumph of the middle class had two important aspects: in the political sphere, the middle class obtained the right to vote (which most workers did not enjoy during this period) and became a dominant voice in government; in the economic sphere, the bourgeoisie profited from the doctrine of laissez faire —that is, unrestricted competition and governmental noninterference with business enterprise— and piled up increasing wealth. Having achieved both power and prosperity, the new capitalists stoutly resisted demands for drastic social change, but, as children of their times, the more enlightened and humanitarian among them supported programs of gradual reform and supported the philosophy summed up in the term *liberalism*.

Nineteenth-century liberalism, which was to survive along with bourgeois dominance of politics and economics until well after 1870, achieved numerous democratic and humanitarian goals. Yet from other quarters, angry voices cried out against industrial ugliness and blight and against the poverty and social injustice which resulted from unbridled competition. These critics of the status quo attacked bourgeois complacency and the laissez-faire liberalism which found such favor with the middle class. Their voices were to become increasingly strong as the century progressed.

THE REVOLT AGAINST REASON

Reaction against Deism. The Scientific Revolution, the development of Deism, the rationalist attack on supernatural elements in traditional religions, and the increasingly atheistic and materialist philosophy of Diderot and the last generation of *philosophes* inevitably produced a reaction. True, Deism produced more tolerant, enlightened clergymen and encouraged moderation and good sense. But in so far as Deism taught people what not to believe without offering anything to replace the familiar pattern of ritual worship, Deism was negative, tending to destroy reverence for the Church and thereby encourage indifference to religion generally. The appeal of Deism was mainly limited to the educated upper classes; the common people derived little satisfaction and solace from its cold rationalism.

Pietism. In the middle of the eighteenth century there had developed a new religious movement, known as Pietism, to restore faith, emotion, and the spirit as the mainsprings of worship. Pietism was foreshadowed by the teachings of George Fox (1624-1691), the founder of the religious sect called the Quakers, or the Society of Friends. Fox believed that the external aspects of Christianity—dogma, organization, and ritual—were unimportant compared to the spiritual experience of the individual (the "inner light"). The Quakers criticized religious intolerance severely and condemned warfare.

The surge of Pietism got under way in England in 1738, when the brothers John and Charles Wesley began to preach to the people in a new way, discarding the formalism of the established church for a glowing emotionalism. Instead of stilted sermons, the Wesleys offered extemporaneous appeals charged with religious fervor. *Methodist*— at first a term of derision—came to be the respected and official name of the movement.

After John Wesley's death in 1791, the Methodists officially broke away from the Anglican Church, and the new denomination became one of the most important religious forces in England's national life.

On the European continent, a German Lutheran named Philipp Spener (1635-1705), who stressed what he called "the religion of the heart" rather than that of unimportant externals, influenced the philosophers Leibnitz and Kant. Another European Pietist was Emanuel Swedenborg (1688-1772), the brilliant son of a Swedish professor of theology. After an intense religious experience in 1745, Swedenborg devoted himself to writing religious works tinged with a strong mystical spirit. After his death his followers established the Church of the New Jerusalem, which has retained its mystical, Pietistic character to the present day. In some Catholic countries Quietism, a religious movement similar to Pietism, was quickly crushed by the alliance of Church and state.

Kant and the *Critique of Pure Reason*. The German philosopher Immanuel Kant (1724-1804) was a symbol of the revival of the heart and of faith. In him were combined the rationalism of science, the humanitarian's concern for mankind, and the deep faith of Pietism. He tried to reconcile these elements in his philosophy.

Kant enjoyed a serene and contemplative life as professor of philosophy at the University of Königsberg, never venturing more than forty miles from home in all his eighty years. Kindly, high-minded, and above all methodical, this quiet dreamer was thoroughly aroused by the exaggerated skepticism and materialism of the age. He determined to shift philosophy back to a more sensible position without giving up too much of its "rational" basis. Kant's answer, contained in the *Critique of Pure Reason* (1781), marked the end of eighteenth-century natural philosophy and ushered in philosophical idealism, so important in the first part of the nineteenth century.

While agreeing with Locke on the importance of the senses in acquiring knowledge, Kant believed that all sensations must be

An old print shows John Wesley, the founder of the Methodist movement, calmly preaching to a hostile mob.

sifted and interpreted through patterns of the mind which are the product of reason. To resolve the conflict between mind and matter, Kant resorted to dualism. Beyond the realm of physical nature to which the laws of science can be applied lies the world of "things-in-themselves," which science can never penetrate and which is the proper domain of philosophical inquiry. Kant agreed with his contemporaries that the existence of God could not be demonstrated scientifically but declared that man's moral sense compels him to believe in the immortality of the soul and in the presence of God.

Thus Kant put as the basis of religious faith not reason, which is subject to experience, but an absolute, innate moral sense, a conscience which is independent of experience yet able to distinguish between right and wrong. On this basis, Kant believed that free will and the existence of God could be proven. Reason cannot prove that there is a just God behind the world as it is, but our moral sense demands such a belief. Thus there are truths of the heart above and beyond those of the head.

Condorcet, French mathematician, politician, and philosopher

New religious attitudes. As part of the adjustment being made in European life and thought as medieval ideas and institutions gave way to those of the modern age, the religious life of Europe had been beset by almost continuous strife and uncertainty for three hundred years. But by the year 1800 a more balanced Christianity was emerging from the suffering brought about by the Religious Wars, the excesses of the controversy between science and religion, and the repercussions of Deism and Pietism. Undue belief in the helplessness of man and the depravity of human nature was superseded by recognition of man's mental and moral dignity. Intolerance and undue emphasis upon dogma and form were giving way to the practical application of Christ's teachings and to tolerance toward atheists and such minorities as Jews and Quakers. Another healthy sign was the slow but sure dying out of witch hunting. As reason rebelled against blind faith, some misguided churchmen tried to retain power by playing upon the superstitious credulity of the people. But the Enlightenment overcame the worst excesses of superstition.

THE IDEA OF PROGRESS

Condorcet and the perfectibility of man. The fact that Kant and early romanticists found other values they cherished above reason did not mean that nineteenth-century romanticism and liberalism had abandoned all the ideals that the eighteenth-century rationalists had developed. One of the most important legacies of the Enlightenment was a new idea about change in man, in his institutions, and in his society.

During the period of the Enlightenment, reformers—English, French, and German—had spent much of their time trying to show that certain natural rights were the heritage of all men. Whether enacted into statutory law or not, these natural rights were supported by a higher law, which could be invoked to defend the individual against oppression. In his *Sketch for a Historical Picture of the Progress of the Human Mind*, the Marquis de Condorcet (1743-1794), French mathematician, philosopher, and politician, analyzed the main causes of the difference between rights in law and rights in fact and suggested methods that would eliminate them.

Condorcet was first known as a mathematician; his work on the theory of probability was a valuable contribution to mathematics (1785). During the early years of the French Revolution, he was a member of the Legislative Assembly, where, among other actions, he advocated reform of the educational system and was among the first to recommend a republic. His vote against the death penalty for Louis XVI made him unpopular, and in 1793 his opposition to the arrest of the Girondists (discussed in Chapter 4) resulted in his condemnation and outlawry. In fear for his life, he went into hiding for several months, but eventually he was seized, whereupon he took poison and died in prison soon after. While in hiding, he wrote his best-known work, *Progress of the Human Mind*, which was published after his death.

The book is a testament to Condorcet's faith in the continuous progress of the human race to an ultimate perfection. The belief in the illimitable perfectibility of man and his institutions provided a background for the notable confidence and optimism of nineteenth-century scientists, philosophers, and reformers. Because Condorcet stated clearly and forcefully some of the major concepts of the eighteenth-century philosophers, a fairly detailed consideration of his ideas will follow.

Condorcet traced the evolution of man through nine stages, emphasizing the most important cultural developments in each. He represented man as starting from the lowest stage of barbarism, with his bodily organization his only superiority over the other animals, and as advancing almost uninterruptedly on the way to enlightenment, virtue, and happiness.

According to Condorcet, the ninth stage began with the intellectual revolution in the seventeenth century and ended with the political and moral revolution of 1789. He attributed much of the progress of mankind to the seventeenth-century scientific revolution. He recognized the interdependence of all the sciences in the progress that had been made and realized that the universal language of mathematics ignored national boundary lines—or any boundaries but those of reason. Progress in the physical sciences was not restricted by self-interest, birth, profession, or position in society. The liberty and equality that prevailed in the relations between physical scientists should be the model for all fields of knowledge. As education spread knowledge, men would be able to discover the general laws that govern the universe. Condorcet assumed the same predictability of phenomena in social as in physical science once the general laws became known—an idea restated and forcefully developed later in the work of Karl Marx. Condorcet believed that the ninth stage was made illustrious by such thinkers as Newton, Locke, and Rousseau in their studies of the physical universe, of human nature, and of society respectively. Most im-

portant, he was convinced that in this stage man had achieved the supremacy of individual reason and stood on the threshold of further progress that almost defied the imagination.

After tracing man's progress to the 1790's, Condorcet presented his view of the future. He maintained that the general laws governing the past justified general inferences as to what lay ahead. The fundamental basis for hope was the improvement in man's environment—and even in man himself—made possible by knowledge of the general laws of society. He summarized future hope under three heads: the abolition of inequality between nations, the progress of equality within nations, and the true perfection of mankind. Condorcet believed that the equality toward which nations and individuals were directed was not absolute equality but, rather, equality of freedom and of rights. Both nations and men were equal if they were equally free, and they were all moving toward equality because they all tended toward freedom.

Condorcet recognized that progress was tempered both by the constitution of man and the state of his surroundings. But he insisted man's movement toward perfectibility was constant, because even these conditions were susceptible to endless progress; he declared that the human mind could assign no fixed limits to its own advancement in knowledge and virtue or even to the length of bodily life. (Because of this theory, Condorcet attached great importance to popular education, to which he looked for all sure progress.) Progress was inevitable—the whole history of mankind was a witness to the fact—and government's relationship to it could be either peaceable or violent, depending upon its wisdom or its resistance.

Consideration of change and progress. Many eighteenth-century reformers agreed that since change was inevitable, good government institutions must make provision for change. Constitutional reform, therefore, both in the internal affairs of states and in the mechanism for relations between states, was essential. At a fearful rate in Condorcet's own day, the leaders in the French Revolution were trying to make changes—many of them long overdue—through a period of constitutional experimentation that was hardly peaceable. The rash of constitution making in the first half of the nineteenth century and the efforts through the Congress System to regulate changes in international status represent efforts to provide for peaceable rather than violent change (see Chapter 7).

To be sure, change alone is not progress; any but a superficial acceptance of the idea of progress requires an answer to the question "Progress toward what?" Nineteenth-century philosophers generally took progress for granted as "a good thing" in the abstract and without concrete definition. But in practice progress was directed toward the achievement of the fullest liberty of the human reason, the fullest equality of all men in the search for knowledge. To Condorcet, one of the important goals of progress was to remedy the difference between rights in law and rights in fact. He saw the main causes of the difference as three: inequality in wealth, inequality in status (some had hereditary property and income, whereas others had to work to survive), and inequality in education. Condorcet believed these inequalities would be removed eventually by the progressive improvement of social organization.

Both the utopian and the scientific socialists of the nineteenth century were concerned with solving these problems of inequality—as were various others who were not socialists, for example, the Earl of Shaftesbury in England (see page 173). Most reformers of the nineteenth century took progress for granted as "a good thing" in the abstract and without concrete definition. But some believed that progress should be directed toward the achievement of the fullest equality of human reason, the fullest equality of all men in the search for knowledge.

The hopes pinned on the achievement of liberty and equality in all their ramifications may seem naïve to people of the twentieth century who are accustomed to a considerable degree of both but who find that nations have still not learned how to make peaceable changes in many instances when dealing with problems of inequality. Many of today's problems are created by the presence of vast multitudes of the world's population who still lack liberty and equality as the eighteenth-century rationalist Condorcet had conceived them.

THE TRIUMPH

OF ROMANTICISM

Romanticism defined. In contrast to the rationalism of the eighteenth century, with its exaltation of classical rules of self-restraint and artistic self-discipline, the romanticism which flowered early in the nineteenth century was characterized by strong elements of individualism, idealism, and revolt against all rules and accepted authority. Of course, the eighteenth century did not lack individuals possessing idealistic and even revolutionary philosophies—we need only recall Voltaire, Locke, and Jefferson—but such thinkers of the age relied on the power of reason to analyze and solve the problems of their time. Reason proved an excellent catalyst, but it was evident that it was no magic elixir.

With their dreams of a more rationally organized society that would raise the status and dignity of men everywhere, the leaders of the Enlightenment unleashed powerful human emotions. As we saw in the discussion of the French Revolution in Chapter 4, the revolutionary tide often swept the programs of reasonable reform far beyond the point called for by the rationalists—and sometimes drowned the reforms completely. The appeal to reason, it appeared, was insufficient to create a new society or to defend an old one. Disillusioned with the supposed rationality of man, the romanticists exalted instinct and emotion.

To the classicist, man is a rational, finite being—an integral member of a society which itself is governed in accordance with law and well-defined rules of conduct. Within this well-ordered social structure, man finds fulfillment, even as, in his intellectual and artistic expression, he emphasizes form and order and harmony. To the romanticist, on the other hand, man is a creature of feeling no less than of thought. He seeks ever after the infinite because he is not simply a cog in a finite human society but instead an irreplaceable part of nature and the whole creative process. The romanticist argues that society's laws and rules of conduct serve only to confine the natural soaring instincts of man. To the classicist's insistence upon the overruling claims of society, the romanticist opposes the right of self-determination, whether of the individual or of any group of like-minded individuals—for example, a nation. Where the classicist's esthetic ideal is manifested in elegance, symmetry, and order, the romanticist is charmed by the "natural," the wild, and the unruly. The classicist finds beauty in logic and in acceptance of what exists; the romanticist makes it synonymous with feeling and with longing after the ultimate. "Classicism is symbolized in the static perfection of the Greek temple, with its joy in the finite work of man. Romanticism soars restlessly into the unknown with the Gothic cathedral."[2] As we shall see in this chapter, the romanticists' concern with the Gothic was not accidental.

The "preromantics": Rousseau, Schiller, Goethe. While the Age of Reason typically produced works that were coldly elegant and structurally harmonious, the eighteenth century was not without vigorous rebels who challenged the literary conventions and the philosophical assumptions of the Enlightenment. Jean Jacques Rousseau, whose *Social Contract* (1762) has been termed the bible of the French Revolution, was a romanticist who believed that the human heart is the infallible source of wisdom, that we should trust in our instincts, that man is capable of constant improvement, and that in nature men find their truest happiness. Rousseau helped popularize the cult of the "noble savage" and urged mankind to return to a more "natural" form of society by abandoning artificial conventions and institutions. He proved a most potent influence

both to the political rebels of his own century and to the romanticists of the next.

In the latter part of the eighteenth century, Germany witnessed a dynamic cultural revival; the long pent-up nationalistic emotions of the Germans found an outlet in the development of a distinctive national literature. Among the greatest of German writers was Johann Christoph Friedrich von Schiller (1759-1805), an outspoken critic of tyranny who expressed his passionate belief in liberty in all his writings. Although he wrote several histories, philosophical studies, and many poems, Schiller gained his greatest fame as a dramatist. His most famous drama, *Wilhelm Tell* (1804), deals with the struggle of the Swiss for their national independence and makes an impassioned attack on tyranny.

The works of Schiller's friend Johann Wolfgang von Goethe (1749-1832) offer the finest example of the transition from eight-

Depicting the despair of the rejected young lover, this illustration from an early edition of *The Sorrows of Young Werther* captures the exaggerated emotionalism of Goethe's work.

eenth-century classicism to nineteenth-century romanticism. In 1773 Goethe published a drama about medieval chivalry which was perhaps most notable for its use of a German character as the central figure. The following year he published *The Sorrows of Young Werther*—an extravagantly sentimental tale of a youth, disappointed in love, who kills himself with the pistol of his successful rival. Written as a result of Goethe's own experiences, which had led him to contemplate suicide, the novel had an enormous success all over Europe. *The Sorrows of Young Werther* delighted a public weary of classicism's repression of human emotions and eager to shed tears over the death of a lovesick hero.

At Weimar, which he made the intellectual center of Germany, Goethe turned out lyric poems, novels, and plays. By far the greatest of his works is *Faust* (Part I published in 1808, Part II in 1832). Based on an old German legend, this verse drama relates the story of an aging scholar, Faust, who makes a pact with the devil, Mephistopheles. In return for twenty-four years of youth and pleasure, Faust gives his soul to the archfiend. In Goethe's adaption, the legend becomes the vehicle for a magnificent philosophical discussion of the trials and triumphs of the human soul. Faust is saved—but only because he ultimately rejects self-gratification and accepts service to his fellow man. This theme is in harmony with the tenets of romanticism. Goethe demands, on the one hand, a full realization of the individual personality through a multitude of experiences—intellectual, sensual, and spiritual alike—even at the risk of salvation. On the other hand, he seeks an integration of the now-developed personality with the collective good of the nation or society to which the individual must dedicate his gifts.

Love of nature — transcendentalism in Wordsworth. In the early nineteenth century, romanticism assumed many different aspects. Most important, all these aspects were products of a state of mind in rebellion against accepted values. Let us now look at some of the forms which this revolt took among writers.

In 1798 two young English poets, William Wordsworth (1770-1850) and Samuel Taylor Coleridge (1772-1834), who were in rebellion against the standards and artificiality of contemporary English poetry, published a revolutionary volume of verse called *Lyrical Ballads*. In the preface of this work, Wordsworth defined poetry as "the spontaneous overflow of powerful feelings recollected in tranquility"—a concept which was at once romantic and very much at odds with the views of the previous century. To give expression to "the great and universal passions of men . . . and the entire world of nature," Wordsworth rejected the high-flown and mythology-laden diction in which the classicists delighted, employing instead a simple vocabulary or, to quote his own words, the "very language of men."[3]

In his works, Wordsworth emphasized the world of nature and man's relationship to it. He believed that by contemplating nature in all its aspects and moods, it was possible to grasp reality intuitively—a view associated with the philosophy known as transcendentalism, which developed out of the work of Kant and his followers and later won many adherents in America, including Emerson and other New England intellectuals. Here is a passage which displays Wordsworth's deep-rooted transcendentalist beliefs:

. . . For I have learned
To look on nature, not as in the hour
Of thoughtless youth; but hearing oftentimes
The still, sad music of humanity
. . . And I have felt
A presence that disturbs me with the joy
Of elevated thoughts; a sense sublime
Of something far more deeply interfused . . .
A motion and a spirit, that impels
All thinking things, all objects of all thought,
And rolls through all things.[4]

The romanticist as a social rebel: Byron, Shelley, Heine. The work of the handsome, impulsive, and emotionally unstable George Gordon, Lord Byron (1788-1824), expresses the romanticist's rebellion against the constraints of society. The following lines are quoted from his masterpiece, *Don Juan* (1818-1824):

8 Joseph Mallord William Turner: "Dutch Fishing Boats" (1837-1838). The role played by landscape painting was germinal to the development of art in the 19th century. In the work of some artists, like the Englishman John Constable, landscape painting was an instrument for the direct and analytical observation of nature, in the best materialist tradition and scientific spirit of the time. However, in the hands of another Englishman, J. M. W. Turner, landscape painting became a means of expressing all the passions and restless energy of romanticism, a movement no less typical of the early 19th century. Turner usually made preliminary watercolor studies of his subjects. But in the execution of the finished works in oil he permitted his imagination to soar. Here, by means of bold brushwork and a brilliant treatment of light (both devices anticipating the impressionists), and by enlivening the composition with a curvilinear movement in the water and sky, Turner has given grandeur both to nature and to the men who struggle against her.

9 Eugene Delacroix: "Combat Between the Giaour and the Pasha" (1827). Romanticism, which was in significant part a reaction against the stultifying effects of a burgeoning industrialism in Europe, often led to a nostalgic yearning for past ages and faraway lands. The art of the leading French romantic painter, Delacroix, frequently features Arabian subjects, such as the gallant horsemen pictured here. The violent temper of this narrative work was particularly satisfying to the ardent romantic spirit. Delacroix's scintillating color and agitated compositional rhythms are similarly effective in evoking a strong emotional reaction in the viewer.

10 (above) **Edouard Manet: "Execution of Maximilian"** (1867). Manet is a central symbolic figure in the conflict between artist and public which erupted in the middle of the 19th century. With the industrial and political revolutions of the 18th century, the long-standing art patronage of the aristocracy and the church largely came to an end. In consequence, progressive 19th-century artists concerned themselves more with the qualities of pure form in painting than with literal subject matter, narrative, and "message." The neutral, dispassionate attitudes of the soldiers and the un-idealized treatment of the Austrian archduke Maximilian very likely reflect Manet's lack of deep involvement in the significance of the story. 11 (right) **Jean Auguste Dominique Ingres: "Mme. Moitessier"** (1851). As Delacroix was the standard-bearer of the Romantics, Ingres was the leader of 19th-century Neoclassicism. The two schools represented opposite stylistic poles in the art of the time. Delacroix depended on color to induce strong feeling, while Ingres sought to create a cooler, more sober kind of response. Firm hard drawing, clear contours, and modeling in light and dark were the instruments of the Neoclassicists.

12 Houses of Parliament, London (1840-1860). Much of 19th century architecture combined a revival of styleistic elements from past cultures with a spirit of nationalism. Countries resurrected styles which they associated with their national glory. The new houses of Parliament, which replaced those destroyed by a fire in 1834, were designed by Sir Charles Barry and hark back to the medieval English Perpendicular mode.

Well—well; the world must turn upon its axis,
And all mankind turn with it, heads or tails,
And live and die, make love and pay our taxes,
And as the veering wind shifts, shift our sails;
The king commands us, and the doctor quacks us,
The priest instructs, and so our life exhales,
A little breath, love, wine, ambition, fame,
Fighting, devotion, dust—perhaps a name.[5]

When the Greeks revolted against the Turks in 1823 (see p. 194), Byron—a rebel to the end—joined the cause of independence and died of fever in Greece.

Percy Bysshe Shelley (1792-1822) showed his rebellious tendencies at an early age when he was expelled from Oxford for writing a pamphlet advocating atheism; later he was condemned by his contemporaries for his unorthodox personal life. Shelley wrote passionately on liberty and believed that human perfectibility was possible only through complete freedom of thought and action. In *Prometheus Unbound* (1818-1819), he pictured his ideal of humanity in a new world of perfect freedom and equality:

The loathsome mask has fallen, the man remains
Sceptreless, free, uncircumscribed, but man . . .
Exempt from awe, worship, degree, the king
Over himself; just, gentle, wise.[6]

The German poet Heinrich Heine (1797-1856) was, like Byron, a trenchant satirist of contemporary society and, like Shelley, a splendid lyricist. Today Heine is best remembered for his *lieder,* or songs, many of which were set to music by Schubert and Mendelssohn.

Keats and the cult of beauty. A contemporary of Shelley and Byron was John Keats (1795-1821), whose works are notable for their melodic beauty and sensuous imagery.

Keats was not a social thinker; unlike his compatriots Byron and Shelley he was not interested in revolution or reform. Of prime importance to him was the worship of beauty—it was the motive and message of his poetry. As expressed in *Endymion* (1817):

A thing of beauty is a joy forever:
Its loveliness increases; it will never
Pass into nothingness; but still will keep
A bower quiet for us, and a sleep
Full of sweet dreams, and health, and quiet
  breathing.[7]

And in the *Ode on a Grecian Urn* (1820), Keats concludes the poem with these lines:

"Beauty is truth, truth beauty,"—that is all
Ye know on earth, and all ye need to know.[8]

This sketch of Lord Byron was made a year before his death.

The Gothic style in architecture which was revived in the early decades of the nineteenth century had been fashionable in England even during the preceding century, when Neoclassicism was the vogue in the fine arts. Horace Walpole, the son of the famous prime minister Robert Walpole, built for himself in about 1750 what he termed "a little Gothic castle" at Strawberry Hill near London. At the left is shown the gallery of Walpole's villa. A worthy example of the Neoclassical style, typical of eighteenth-century taste in architecture, is the Church of the Madeleine (below) in Paris. Construction was begun in 1764, but progress was delayed by the French Revolution. The building was recommissioned by Napoleon as a Temple of Glory, became a church once more after the Bourbon restoration, and was finally completed in 1842. Modeled after a temple of the Roman Corinthian order, the church has columns sixty-three feet tall, a height which surpasses that of the temples of antiquity. The structure has no windows in the walls; light is furnished by rounded windows in the roof.

The Royal Pavilion at Brighton (above) typifies the romanticists'
taste for the exotic. Built early in the nineteenth century by the
prince of Wales, the many-domed structure led one wit of the
day to remark, "St. Paul's [Cathedral in London] has come to
Brighton and pupped." In dramatic contrast to the whimsical
extravagance of the Royal Pavilion is the elegant simplicity of
the rotunda and library pictured at the right. Classical Ionic
columns, an interior frieze, and graceful furnishings mark the
Regency style (1811-1830).

In Gustave Doré's illustration for Coleridge's poem, the Ancient Mariner is shown bearing the terrible burden of the albatross. Dying of thirst on their becalmed ship, the Mariner's companions hung the body around his neck as a curse for killing the bird of good luck.

Thus Keats exemplifies an important aspect of the romantic movement—estheticism, or the acceptance of artistic beauty and taste as a fundamental standard, superior to ethical and other standards.

The exotic and nonrational: Coleridge. The coauthor of the *Lyrical Ballads,* who stated that his endeavors were "directed to persons and characters supernatural or at least romantic,"[9] emphasized still another important aspect of romanticism—exoticism. Especially vivid is his description of the imaginary Xanadu in his poem *Kubla Khan* (1798):

> In Xanadu did Kubla Khan
> A stately pleasure-dome decree:
> Where Alph, the sacred river, ran
> Through caverns measureless to man
>   Down to a sunless sea.
> So twice five miles of fertile ground
> With walls and towers were girdled round:

And here were gardens bright with sinuous rills,
Where blossomed many an incense-bearing tree;
And here were forests ancient as the hills,
Enfolding sunny spots of greenery.
But oh! that deep romantic chasm which slanted
Down the green hill athwart a cedarn cover!
A savage place! as holy and enchanted
As e'er beneath a waning moon was haunted
By woman wailing for her demon-lover![10]

In other works, particularly *The Rime of the Ancient Mariner* (1797), Coleridge voiced his dissatisfaction with an approach to man and his problems that was incapable of expressing adequately the nonrational and even irrational elements in human experience. These elements, whose importance was later demonstrated by the researches of Freud and other psychologists (see Chapter 11), are often described in literature in terms of fantasy, symbolism, dream states, and the supernatural. For example, the albatross hung about the neck of Coleridge's ancient mariner is interpreted by some literary critics and psychologists as symbolic of a sense of guilt.

The medieval revival: Scott and Hugo. Romantics were intrigued with the somewhat irrational processes of history. For Thomas Jefferson, a nonromantic, eighteenth-century figure, history provided only examples of the past errors and crimes of humanity. For romantics like Sir Walter Scott (1771-1832) and Victor Hugo (1802-1885), the past provided colorful and exciting examples of men who lived stirring, passionate lives.

The fascination of the past for romanticists is evident in the romantic treatment of the Middle Ages. In his Waverley novels, the first of which appeared in 1814, and in his collection of Scottish border ballads, his long narrative poems, and his famous adventure story of medieval chivalry, *Ivanhoe* (1819), Scott stirred the imagination of his contemporaries by his vivid re-creation of medieval life. His strong antiquarian interests were characteristic of the nineteenth century, a period of considerable scholarly examination of the Middle Ages (see p. 143). As Scott glorified the formative period of the Scottish state and at the same time adroitly paid heed to the sensibilities of his large English reading public by extolling the chivalric exploits of medieval England, Victor Hugo performed much the same function by re-creating the national past in France.

Romanticism in American literature. Examples of romantic literature from British and Continental sources can be paralleled by examples from American literature, for it was not long before romanticism crossed the Atlantic and became the chief form of literary expression among important American writers. Washington Irving (1783-1859) adapted romantic German legends to an American locale in "The Legend of Sleepy Hollow" and "Rip Van Winkle." James Fenimore Cooper (1789-1851), sometimes called the "American Scott," wrote a series of popular novels, the *Leatherstocking Tales,* in which colonial life was treated in a highly romantic vein. Edgar Allan Poe (1809-1849), Nathaniel Hawthorne (1804-1864), and Herman Melville (1819-1891) exemplified in widely varying ways romanticism's penchant for the bizarre and supernatural; William Cullen Bryant (1794-1878) wrote nature poetry that, in approach, was reminiscent of Wordsworth's; Ralph Waldo Emerson (1803-1882) and Henry David Thoreau (1817-1862) voiced the transcendental philosophy in their works; and Walt Whitman (1819-1892) brought a romanticist's vision to his declamatory free-verse poems about the American scene and his gospel of political and social democracy.

Revolt against classical painting. At the beginning of the nineteenth century, the classical style dominated painting. For example, the leading French painter Jacques Louis David (1748-1825) portrayed the heroes of the Revolution in classical poses.

Romanticist painters rebelled against classical models and the emphasis upon precise draftsmanship because they felt that color was more important than drawing and that subject matter should give unhampered scope to the imagination and emotions. Old legends and exotic and picturesque scenes, such as were to be found in North Africa and the Near East, became popular. One of the first major rebels was Eugène

Delacroix (1798?-1863), a French artist whose flamboyant canvases convey the heightened emotional approach of the romanticists (see Color Plate 9). His "Massacre of Chios" (1824), painted under the direct impact of the news of the slaying of Christians on the island of Chios by the Turks, was unjustly dubbed the "Massacre of Painting" by conservative critics.

The effects of the cult of nature were no less marked upon romantic painting than upon poetry. Artists were inspired to look at nature with a fresh appreciation. The English painter John Constable (1776-1837) was in some respects the creator of the modern school of landscape painting. He considered it essential that a sketch be made directly from nature and at a single sitting. In the eyes of his contemporaries, his choice of colors was revolutionary, for he used greens freely in his landscapes, an innovation considered audacious by men who had stressed the necessity of painting nature in browns. It is said that when a friend remonstrated with him for not giving his foreground the requisite mellow brown of an old violin, Constable placed a violin before him on the grass to demonstrate the difference between the fresh green of nature and the brown tones demanded by artistic convention.

Another English landscape painter whose originality created a profound stir was J. M. W. Turner (1775-1851). Gifted with a vivid sense of color and a powerful imagination, Turner was particularly adept in creating atmospheric effects (see Color Plate 8). He used a color technique similar to that employed later in the century with dazzling success by the French Impressionists.

Romanticism in architecture: the Gothic revival. Until about 1830, architecture in Europe and America was based largely on classical models. Roman triumphal arches were emulated in the huge Arc de Triomphe, commemorating revolutionary and Napoleonic victories; and the Church of the Madeleine in Paris was built in imitation of a temple of antiquity. In the United States, the national Capitol and various statehouses were designed in the spirit of Greece and Rome.

In England, however, the Gothic style had never died out. Christopher Wren, a renowned English architect, had employed Gothic forms in some of his churches in London; and in 1750 the writer Horace Walpole had built at Strawberry Hill near London a country house in the Gothic style which influenced architects throughout Europe. But the great period of the Gothic revival, in which towers and pointed arches became the chief characteristics of architectural design, occurred after 1830 (see Color Plate 12). The revival was stimulated in England by the romances of Sir Walter Scott, whose own residence at Abbotsford was designed along Scottish baronial lines, while in France the movement gained impetus from the publication of Hugo's melodramatic novel of fifteenth-century life, *Notre Dame de Paris* (1831).

Romanticism in music. The eighteenth century possessed a style of music in accord with its social patterns. In the age of the minuet and the sonata, orchestras were small and were composed chiefly of stringed instruments. The nineteenth century brought a radical change; the regularity of the minuet, the precision of the sonata, and the limitations of the small chamber orchestra were not adequate to express the powerful forces of romanticism.

The genius who broke the classical mold and revitalized music was the German composer Ludwig van Beethoven (1770-1827), a titan who acted as a bridge between classicism and romanticism. Accustomed as we are today to the dynamics of his music, it may seem strange to learn that Beethoven's compositions were castigated by at least one critic of his own day as the "obstreperous roaring of modern frenzy!" A lover of nature and a passionate champion of freedom and the rights of man, Beethoven unleashed emotional forces never before heard in music. While retaining the classicist's sense of proportion in the structure of his works, he added flexibility to music forms by developing new harmonies and enlarged the scope of the orchestra to handle them. In short, Beethoven succeeded in freeing music from arid formalism.

The momentum of the forces which Beethoven set in motion carried through the entire century. Johannes Brahms (1833-1897) is generally regarded as the greatest symphonic composer of the second half of the century, but the age is studded with names of great composers: from Germany, in addition to Brahms, came Schubert, Schumann, Mendelssohn, Weber, and Wagner; from France, Berlioz and Franck; from Italy, Rossini and Verdi; from Poland, Chopin; from Hungary, Liszt; from Russia, Glinka, Rimski-Korsakov, Mussorgsky, and Tschaikovsky. This was an age marked by an outpouring of romantic symphonies, symphonic overtures, and concertos, all of which exploited the new and varied effects made possible by an orchestra which had been greatly expanded. And a fresh impetus was given to the composition of the solo song, known in Germany as the *lied*. Songs and operatic arias made use of romantic subject matter infused with sentiment—and, not infrequently, sentimentalism. The emotional content was heightened also by warm romantic melody and the development of new chords and harmonic variations. Romantic interest in the traditional elements of national culture came to the fore as composers turned for inspiration to their native folk music and dances.

Closely influenced by nationalism and romanticism, opera developed along separate lines in the various nations of Europe. Karl Maria von Weber (1786-1826), who had lived during Napoleon's occupation of the German states and had as a consequence acquired strong patriotic sentiments, composed *Der Freischütz* (1821), an opera completely German in language and character. Achieving immediate success, it laid the foundations for a national opera, which was to culminate later in the century in the fervid Germanic works of Richard Wagner (1813-1883), in which plot, poetry, stagecraft, and music were so integrated as to create a dramatic unity. For his plots, Wagner used German folklore and the old Teutonic myths, infusing them with typically romantic characteristics such as emphasis on the supernatural and the mystic.

Italian opera was stimulated by Gioachino Rossini (1792-1868), whose best-known work is the gay and tuneful comic opera, *The Barber of Seville* (1816). The greatest Italian composer of the century was Giuseppe Verdi (1813-1901). With *Aïda* (1871-1872), a highly colorful pageant and romantic tragedy set in ancient Egypt, Verdi's popularity reached its zenith.

As a result of the great changes in political and economic conditions, the position of music in society was radically altered. No longer was music exclusive and aristocratic as it had been in the eighteenth century. Music was now supported chiefly by the middle classes and maintained by their thriving commercial prosperity. Public concerts, symphony orchestras, quartet societies, piano and song recitals, music festivals, public opera houses—all were attainments of the nineteenth century which had had only faint beginnings up to 1800. Gifted artists interpreted musical works with suggestive power unknown to former ages—the pianists Chopin, Mendelssohn, and Liszt, the violinist Paganini; the conductors Weber, Wagner, and Berlioz; in addition to scores of *lieder* and opera singers.

An important outgrowth of the romantic movement was the discovery and interpretation of lost or forgotten works of art. The beginning of the great Bach revival in Germany stemmed from Mendelssohn's first public performance in Berlin in 1829 of Bach's *St. Matthew Passion*. Musicology, the science of musical research, owes much to the musicians and composers of the romantic age.

ROMANTIC NATIONALISM

AND LIBERALISM

Nationalism, ally of romanticism. In glorifying the uniqueness of the individual and his rights, romanticism exhibited a close affinity with another powerful emotional force of this period—nationalism. With its emphasis upon the uniqueness of particular groups, nationalism was a potent historical catalyst among the peoples of nineteenth-century Europe.

Nationalism can perhaps be described as a state of mind which inspires supreme loyalty toward one's own country. Nationalistic feelings, reinforced by ties such as a common language, history, and cultural traditions, set the members of one nation apart from those of another. And, at the same time, nationalism generates feelings of superiority; members of one group place a higher value on their particular institutions and attitudes than on those of any other people.

In the nineteenth century the feelings of nationalism came more and more to imply the willingness of an individual to live and die for his country. His loyalty to the state transcended all other loyalties. Unhappily, too, extreme nationalism implied that a state could do no wrong and that self-interest was the only test for its behavior. Here again we see the close affinity between romanticism and nationalism—the former advocating unrestricted self-expression for an individual, the latter demanding unrestricted self-determination for a group (see Frontier essay, pp. 248-250).

The growth of national states, which began toward the end of the Middle Ages, fostered a love of country among the common people. And in the period of the French Revolution, an entire people for the first time rose *en masse* to repel invaders who sought to nullify the gains achieved by the revolutionaries. If the shock of invasion and the prospect of alien armies destroying newly won rights gave Frenchmen a sense of unity, so opposition to the later imperialistic designs of Napoleon created among the peoples of the alliance which finally defeated him a sense of common purpose and achievement. Moreover, the Napoleonic Wars sparked a greater love of country throughout Europe as a result of the perils of invasion and occupation which were finally surmounted.

Romantic nationalism in literature. This strongly felt emotion is well exemplified in a sonnet Wordsworth composed upon his return in 1802 from the Continent to England:

Here, on our native soil, we breathe once more.
The cock that crows, the smoke that curls, that
    sound

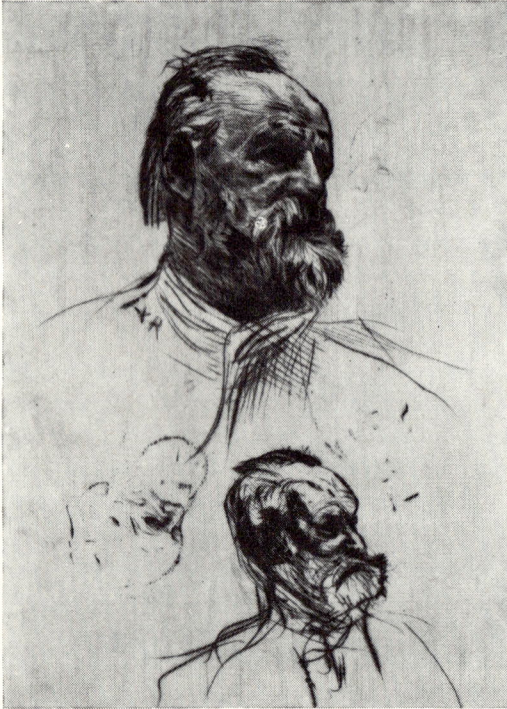

Auguste Rodin: "Sketch of Victor Hugo"

France, Victor Hugo expressed hostility toward tyranny at home and abroad and espoused the aspirations of the common man. Like Byron and Delacroix, Hugo was a stanch supporter of the struggle for Greek independence. Here he explains and justifies the origin of revolutions:

For revolutions, which revenge fulfil,
Eternal good produce from fleeting ill.
These revolutions are the evidence
Of horrors through long years become intense.
When sufferance has attained lugubrious size . . .
When ignorance does e'en the future blind,
And being able naught to seize or find,
Hope is no more but a small part of man;
When by all plagues consumed, and gaunt
    and wan;
When everywhere are wars and enmities,—
Then suddenly one day uprise, uprise,
The plainings by the wretched spectre made:
Grief, the fell giant, vast, unmeasured shade,
Starts forth. A cry from height to height is flashed.
The social worlds are 'gainst each other dashed.
All the dread hulks of pariah arise;
Whips, fetters, swords, affront the ears, the eyes;
Murder, sobs, hunger, howlings of abuse,—
Noises of all past in hell let loose. . . .
                    the tocsin fell
Shakes with its rope and hoarse sepulchral knell
The church, the palace; so to ruin bring
Luther the Pope, and Mirabeau the king.
The whole is said: thus old worlds crumbled are.
The time is come! Floods roll unheard afar,
And across rumours, corpses, mourning, foam,
And mountain-tops, which sunken rocks become,
The ages in despair before them drive
These revolutions,—tides that whelm and rive,
Oceans which human tears create, expand.[12]

Of bells: those boys who in yon meadow-ground
In white-sleeved shirts are playing; and the roar
Of the waves breaking on the chalky shore;—
All, all are English. Oft have I looked round
With joy in Kent's green vales; but never found
Myself so satisfied in heart before.
Europe is yet in bonds; but let that pass
Thought for another moment. Thou art free,
My Country! and 'tis joy enough and pride
For one hour's perfect bliss, to tread the grass
Of England once again. . . .[11]

The excesses of the French Revolution and Napoleon's perversion of its principles alienated many of the romanticists. But the pendulum swung back again as a result of the system of political reaction set up in 1815 by the Congress of Vienna (see Chapter 4). There the Old Regime mustered the forces of the restored monarchies, the large landowners, and the conservative elements in the Church to repress nationalist movements and efforts to bring about political and social reform.

In the years that followed, some of the leading romanticists were again the vocal champions of nationalism and revolution. In

In Russia, where nationalism had been greatly stimulated by the people's heroic resistance to the Napoleonic invasion in 1812, still other romantic rebels were attracting the sympathetic response of the reading public (and also the hostile attention of the tsar's secret police). Greatest of the romanticist poets was Alexander Pushkin (1799-1837), whose unrestrained personal life and literary lyricism justify his being called the "Byron of Russia." His subject matter was largely derived from Russian tales and folklore, and his dramas and his verse-novel *Eugene Onegin* (1831) have a strong nationalistic appeal. Like Byron, Pushkin denounced tyranny and the reactionary movement which had set in after the Napoleonic Wars. As he wrote to an old classmate:

While freedom kindles us, my friend,
While honor calls us and we hear it,
Come: to our country let us tend
The noble promptings of the spirit.
Comrade, believe: joy's star will leap
Upon our sight—a radiant token;
Russia will rouse from her long sleep;
And where autocracy lies, broken,
Our name shall yet be graven deep.[13]

One aspect of romantic nationalism was a new-found interest in philology and folk literature. In Britain, for example, Scott published collections of medieval English and Scottish ballads, while German scholars collected medieval folk tales and *minnelieder*. Jacob and William Grimm issued their *Fairy Tales* (1812-1815), which had originated as German folk legends, and compiled a dictionary that ranked as an authoritative work on German philology. Such works found the most significant characteristics of national culture in the intuitions of the common folk. German linguists also studied the origins of the Indo-European language family.

Romantic nationalism in jurisprudence, philosophy, and history. In Germany, the so-called historical school of jurisprudence stressed traditional aspects in law as the only valid basis for legal institutions. For the members of this group, the idea that men could establish legitimate and lasting governments or create an ideal new social order by means of codes and paper constitutions was ridiculous. They saw law as the result of a slow evolution, a process of trial and error that over the ages summed up the intuitive wisdom of the nation. Each nation having had a different historical evolution, it followed that each nation must have its own distinctive system of law. This movement was romantic in that it exalted the legal intuitions of the people (*Volk*) over the rationalistic schemes of reformers. It was national in that it represented a rejection of the efforts of pro-French elements to impose a French-style law code in Germany.

Meantime, the glorification of the state became characteristic of various German thinkers, especially Georg Wilhelm Friedrich Hegel (1770-1831), perhaps the most influential philosopher of the time. To Hegel, history was a process of evolution in which the supremacy of primitive instincts gave way to the reign of clear reason and freedom —the "World Spirit"—as manifested in the state. Hegel believed that the Prussia of his day offered the best example of the state as a spiritual organism, because in Prussia the individual was given the greatest "freedom"—which to Hegel meant only the right to obey the laws of the governing group. Hegel did not believe in parliamentary democracy but rather in rule by a carefully trained, responsible bureaucracy.

With their mystical concepts of the state and their belief in the historic role and special virtues of the German people, Hegel and other German thinkers did much to lay the metaphysical foundations for that irrational ideology of our own century, Nazism. Hegel's teachings contributed to the growth of ideas which are at the core of virulent nationalism: the exaltation of the state at the expense of individual interests and morality, the praise of war and the superman, and the concept of a nation endowed with a divine mission.

The exaltation of the traditional and the evolutionary over abstract and rationalistic schemes as the only true source of stable institutions also stimulated historical research and the writing of national histories. A new interest was taken in the contents of the national archives in Paris, London, and other capitals; and scholars hastened to edit and make use of the invaluable source materials stored there. The period produced a number of outstanding national historians. In France, Jules Michelet (1798-1874) wrote a nineteen-volume *History of France* that was marked by liberalism and romantic nationalism and stressed the role of the common people. Across the Atlantic, George Bancroft (1800-1891) produced a United States history described as "explaining the wonder-working providence of God in the United States."[14] In England, too, it was a splendid era for historians, of whom the most brilliant was Thomas Babington Macaulay (1800-1859). His famous *History of England*, a notable example of literary as well as historical crafts-manship which is still widely read, reflected the liberalism of the majority of the middle class. However, its general attitude, reflect-ing the author's conviction that his age rep-resented the best of all possible worlds, con-flicted with that expressed in the works of that romantically indignant critic of contem-porary society, Thomas Carlyle.

Some historians attempted to be fair and scholarly; others were less concerned with writing objective accounts than with roman-ticizing the past in order to glorify a particu-lar people or national state to the detriment of others.

Liberalism: its meaning and impact. To this point, we have been dealing with two major trends in the intellectual history of the nineteenth century—romanticism and na-tionalism. Both were strongly charged with idealism, both made a great impact in the first half of the century, and both cut across class distinctions. Among the romanticists, for example, we find an aristocrat (Byron) and the son of a London livery stable keeper (Keats). Similarly, nationalism in its ro-mantic aspects and ideals drew recruits from all segments of society.

We now come to a third major ideational concept—liberalism—which reached the fore-front in the 1830's. Unlike romanticism and nationalism, nineteenth-century liberalism was associated almost exclusively with the middle class. Let us see why.

Like romanticism, liberalism vigorously af-firmed the dignity of man and the "pursuit of happiness" as his inherent right. Like the philosophy behind the American and French revolutions, the liberal philosophy was an outgrowth of the philosophy of the Enlight-enment. But where romanticism accepted revolution as a justifiable means to give ex-pression to the "rights of man," liberalism stood for gradual reform through parliamen-tary institutions. And where both the ration-alists and the romanticists tended to speak of man in the abstract—that is, "Man"—and to conceive of him as a philosophical ideal in opposition to, say, the "state" or the "king," nineteenth-century liberals thought in terms of individual men who shared cer-tain basic rights in common, who worked together to obtain parliamentary majorities and political power, and who made use of that power to ensure that each of them would be given a maximum of freedom from state or external authority. Liberalism, then, was the creed of individualism, the right of a person to be left alone as much as possible.

In the economic sphere, liberalism was expressed in the doctrine of laissez faire—competition among individuals with a mini-mum of governmental interference or regu-lation. Nineteenth-century liberals believed that society benefited most from competition, which brought the more ambitious, intelli-gent, and efficient individuals the greater rewards. Although governments were re-sponsible for the protection of life and prop-erty, the hands of government should be kept off business; the best interests of society would be served by permitting the natural "laws" of supply and demand to operate un-impeded.

It is readily apparent why liberalism was primarily a philosophy of the middle class. The bourgeoisie were the chief owners of the new factories, railroads, and mines through which the Industrial Revolution had been transforming the economy of western Europe. In the new industrial societies, mid-dle-class entrepreneurs had everything to lose from revolution and everything to gain from governmental protection of property rights. To win such protection, however, they had to obtain a dominant voice in govern-ment. As government immediately after the Napoleonic Wars was largely controlled by the nobility and landed classes, this meant in turn that the middle class had to secure a limited extension of the suffrage—an exten-sion that would give them the vote without granting voting privileges to the working classes. Thus the members of the middle class demanded political power commen-surate with their steadily increasing econom-ic strength. In England this goal was at-tained in 1832; with the passage of the Eng-lish Reform Bill, we find the middle class in Britain taking over the driver's seat.

As the century progressed, the liberal doc-trines of the middle class were increasingly challenged by a new social philosophy—socialism. In Chapter 6 we shall discuss the early socialists, Saint-Simon in France and Robert Owen in England, and early nineteenth-century socialism, which was of a romantic or utopian nature. We shall also contrast the romantic form of socialism with the so-called scientific brand, based on class division and violence and first proclaimed in the *Communist Manifesto* (1848) of Karl Marx and Friedrich Engels.

We might pause here to note the change that has taken place regarding the meaning of "liberalism." Today it still stands for reform, in contrast to conservatism with its defense of the status quo or to radicalism with its demands for immediate, drastic change. But in the economic sphere especially, liberalism has undergone a profound modification. Unlike his nineteenth-century predecessor, the twentieth-century liberal believes that the state should take an active role in minimizing the extremes of wealth, in balancing the great power enjoyed by big business and big organized labor, in conserving natural resources, in providing social security, and in actively opposing racial discrimination.

THE DIGNITY OF MAN

Humanitarianism. Among the many ideas promoted by the *philosophes* was humanitarianism. Their protests against barbarous punishments helped inspire an interest in penal reform; their ideal of liberty sometimes worked momentous changes even at considerable economic cost. Perhaps the most clear-cut example of the success of humanitarian and religious principles prevailing over pecuniary interest was the movement to end the slave trade. Begun in England in the late eighteenth century, the campaign to end the slave trade scored notable achievements in the first half of the nineteenth century and was followed by major efforts to abolish slavery altogether.

Respect for the dignity of man was incompatible with slavery, and even Montesquieu, who recognized the historical fact of societies based on slavery, could not bring him-

William Wilberforce, British statesman and humanitarian

self to condone it. Even the most benevolent treatment of the slave did not justify traffic in human flesh, and the African slave trade was anything but humane.

Actions taken against slave trade. The first important modern agitation against the slave trade was among English Quakers, but many others soon took up the crusade. William Wilberforce (1759-1833), who had been something of an idler at Cambridge and in his early parliamentary years, was converted to evangelical Christianity in 1784 and soon after undertook to champion in Parliament the abolition of the slave trade. William Pitt, the Younger, a friend of Wilberforce since his Cambridge days, encouraged the latter's active leadership in the efforts to end the slave trade. Beginning in 1789, Wilberforce continued to introduce motions in the House of Commons to end this traffic, until in 1807 the slave trade in British territories was legally abolished.

In view of Britain's naval and maritime supremacy during the Napoleonic period and after, English abolition of the slave trade was of major importance, but it was

The crowded deck of the "Wildfire" was typical of slave ships.

paralleled by actions in other countries. The United States prohibited the importation of slaves after 1807, but as early as 1794, Americans were prohibited from participating in slave trade with foreign countries. Napoleon formally abolished the French slave trade during his short return to power in 1815, but this prohibition was not confirmed by the restored monarchy until 1818. Denmark abolished its slave trade in 1792, Sweden in 1813, Holland in 1814, Portugal by stages between 1815 and 1836, and Spain in 1820.

In spite of the actions taken by the various nations in abolishing the slave trade, Great Britain was the only nation that established a permanent naval patrol in West African waters to combat the then illegal slave trade. In the 1840's about twenty British ships were engaged in this work.

Abolition of slavery. The unspeakable conditions under which slaves were transported—often the death rate was 15 per cent or more—and the problem of policing the ban on the slave trade, encouraged the next step, the abolition of slavery itself. Partial measures, designed to improve the treatment of slaves, proved ineffective. When it be-

came plain that slave owners would not move toward eventual liberation of the slaves, the English Parliament abolished slavery in 1833 and voted a substantial compensation to the former slave owners. This example of humanitarian reform, peaceably accomplished, was only gradually and partially followed by other nations. Some of the Spanish-American countries provided for gradual emancipation at the time of their own independence movements (Argentina in 1813, Colombia in 1821, Mexico in 1829), but France did not abolish slavery until 1848, and the Netherlands did not until 1863. It was not until the tragedy of a great civil war that slaves were emancipated in the United States. Slavery was finally forbidden in Brazil in 1871 (though the existing slaves were not freed) and in Portuguese colonies in 1878.

Since most of the nineteenth century was required to bring about the elimination of slavery in the overseas territories of European states and in America, the record is a somber one. But the inspiration for the ultimately successful movement to abolish both the slave trade and slavery was undoubtedly religious and humanitarian in the best sense. Abolition was a battle against some of the profoundly held convictions of contemporary civilized society—the sanctity of property right, laissez-faire policy in government, and belief in the natural inferiority of backward peoples. The appeal of the movement was moral, based on the dignity of man rather than on any demonstrable self-interest for individuals or society.

Civil liberty. The long agitation for the abolition of the slave trade and slavery was one practical aspect of the nineteenth-century interest in liberty as an ideal. The culminating positive statement of the nature of liberty as the nineteenth-century liberals—heirs of the Enlightenment, the French Revolution, and romanticism—saw it, was John Stuart Mill's essay *On Liberty*, published in 1859. Essentially, Mill defined his problem as an inquiry into "the nature and limits of the power which can be legitimately exercised by society over the individual." The one simple principle Mill applied in answering the question was self-protection; that is, the individual may only be constrained not to do what harms others.

Phrased so succinctly, the problem of liberty might appear merely a question of having government keep out of the affairs of individuals or having government controlled by the people. Mill's discussion is not so simple. He thought that in order to protect individual liberty it was as necessary to place limitations on the power of government when the people ruled as when an autocrat ruled. Without such limitations, the individual would fall under the tyranny of the majority; such tyranny must be curbed if one part of the people were not to oppress the other part. Social tyranny, Mill believed, was as dangerous as political tyranny, because the individual was made to conform to whatever model the society of the moment accepted. Society and individuals alike, according to Mill, are naturally intolerant of opposition on questions of deep concern. The only practical—not legal or ethical—basis for religious toleration, for example, is a degree of religious indifference sufficient to avoid cutting throats over conformity. Mill was concerned with protecting the sovereignty of the individual over himself; and since he believed that the individuals should have full liberty to think, speak, act, or otherwise enjoy the fullest realization of his own gifts, the rightful limits society might impose were necessarily very narrow indeed.

Society's duties and limitations: Mill. The theory that the basis of society implies some form of contract was not accepted by Mill, nor, consequently, any self-imposed restraint on individual sovereignty. Society, in protecting the rights of others from injury by an individual, did not acquire any right to protect the individual against himself. Morally it was the duty of society to reason with any individual who wanted to harm himself, and to persuade him not to do so, if possible. But, according to Mill, society should not actually offer physical restraint if the person's proposed action would hurt only himself. Even if individual behavior were re-

pulsive to others, society could punish only by the condemnation of public opinion, so long as the constituted rights of other individuals were not violated. Since society had had the opportunity to educate the individual, and since majority opinion on individual conduct simply reflected the preferences of the individuals in the majority, personal behavior that violated no rights of others was no cause for society's interference.

The untrammeled sovereignty of the individual in matters of his own interest is, of course, a bulwark of civil liberty. Rousseau had written, at the beginning of his *Social Contract*, "Man is born free, and everywhere he is in chains." To the great nineteenth-century liberals, nothing could make such a situation legitimate. The necessity to protect the individual not merely against one form but against all forms of tyranny by his fellow man—political, social, religious, economic, or the tyranny of custom—was a logical culmination of the movement for liberty.

Mill allowed one further rightful intervention by society upon the sovereignty of the individual: society could require the individual to take his share "of the labours and sacrifices incurred for defending the society or its members from injury and molestation." In an age of nationalism this right of the society over the individual became a very great restraint. For the idea of the untrammeled sovereignty of the individual was transferred to the nation-state, and the individual nation assumed the same liberty as regards its own interests that Mill recognized in the individual. In extreme forms of the national state, individual interest is ultimately subordinated to national interest. Unfortunately the nation state has been slower to recognize an inseparable part of Mill's treatment of liberty—that society may impose limits to sovereignty in order that the individual (state) not injure the interests of others.

SUMMARY

In this chapter, we have presented a cross section of the forces which dominated the period between 1815 and 1870—romanticism, nationalism, and liberalism. The romanticists were in revolt against what they felt to be the one-sided rationalistic emphasis of the eighteenth-century *philosophes* and the efforts of the French revolutionists to "rationalize" society. In place of reason, the romanticists worshiped intuition, emotion, the picturesque, the Gothic, and the grotesque. Some romanticists sought fulfillment in nature, some in flights of fancy to faraway places, others in pursuing the ideal of beauty or of human betterment, still others in conjuring up the supernatural or in plumbing the irrational levels of man's own consciousness. Whatever they did, the romanticists worked with a concentrated tension—and the result was one of the most fruitful epochs in literature and the arts, as underscored by the work of such men as Wordsworth and Keats, Delacroix and Constable, Beethoven and Chopin.

Closely allied to romanticism was another powerful emotional force of the period, nationalism. This force caught up idealists in all nations and was in turn given eloquent expression by such romantic poets as Byron on behalf of Greece, Pushkin in Russia, and Victor Hugo in France. Nationalism developed with romantic fervor only to crash in vain against the barricades of entrenched authority in 1848, after which it was destined to assume new, and even menacing, forms of expression.

Allied in turn to nationalism was nineteenth-century liberalism, which, with its emphasis upon basic rights for the individual in both the political and economic spheres, became the social philosophy of the triumphant middle class. In effect, political liberalism stood for the rule of law and evolutionary change rather than revolutionary change, while laissez faire, its counterpart in the economic world, called for competition among individuals with the government maintaining a hands-off attitude. Middle-class liberalism reached its heyday at this time, on the crest of an industrial expansion which in turn was controlled by the triumphant bourgeoisie. But this rapid techno-logical transformation of Europe was being bought at a heavy price. Social critics decried the fast destruction of the countryside and viewed with apprehension the growing acceptance of unbridled competition and materialistic values.

The period from 1815 to 1870 was inevitably marked by striking changes in outward appearance as well. The stagecoach gave way to the steam locomotive, horses increasingly to "horsepower." In the next chapter we shall discuss the technological revolution that was taking place, the enormously increased population to which that revolution, along with improved public health and higher living standards, led, and the social and economic consequences of the revolution.

The fruitful work in the literary and fine arts that resulted from the romantics' explosive energy in exploring the fullest possible realization of individual genius had its counterpart in the increasing recognition of the dignity of man even among the lowliest. The slave trade was abolished in the leading countries, and Great Britain established a naval patrol along Africa's west coast in an attempt to combat the slave trade. The movement for the abolition of slavery made progress. A more humane treatment of the criminal and the insane also appeared. The most brutal physical punishments were eliminated, and the excessive use of capital punishment for trivial offenses was done away with. In England the system of transportation, that is, the shipping of convicts to Australia for settlement, continued until about 1839; France followed a policy of deporting some criminals to colonial territory through the century.

Yet despite its anguished moments, this was a forward-looking, dynamic period, still sustained by a deep-rooted belief in the perfectibility of society. Thus the bourgeoisie of the mid-century could agree with Robert Browning when he had one of his poetic characters declare:

God's in his heaven—
All's right with the world![15]

CHAPTER 6

Industrial Revolution

Introduction. During the decades after Waterloo, strong political currents of nationalism, democracy, and middle-class liberalism threatened to undermine the work of the conservative statesmen who had attended the Congress of Vienna in 1815, but these forces did not substantially alter the European political system until the unifications of Germany and Italy (1859-1871). At the same time, however, many basic changes occurred in other fields. Momentous events were taking place in industry, economic thought, and the alignment of classes.

The technological transformation that took place in industry during the late eighteenth century and the early part of the nineteenth, coupled with new agricultural patterns and with the introduction of the factory system, marks the first great period of the Industrial Revolution. Its stage was primarily western Europe, and its most rapid and extensive growth occurred in England. In this chapter we shall see how the new industrialism brought about the rise of large manufacturing cities, the growth of a small, extremely wealthy class of industrial proprietors, and the development of an ever-increasing class of discontented, often miserable industrial workers.

By 1870 the sleepy rural life of early nineteenth-century western Europe had been radically altered by the growth of a dynamic urban economy. Quiet villages, town criers, sailing vessels, and hand looms had been superseded by factory towns, cheap newspapers, railroads and steamships, and machines for mass production. New class divisions were crystallizing, each with its own program and philosophy. The new class of industrial entrepreneurs championed laissez-faire economics, individual enterprise, private ownership of capital, and the unimpeded operation of the laws of supply and demand. On the other hand, some of the workers, particularly on the Continent, found a new philosophy and a bold program of action in socialist doctrines, the most extreme of which was that developed by the German theorist Karl Marx. For good or evil, much of the history of the western world after 1848, the year the *Communist Manifesto* was published, concerns the duel between capitalism and communism. Today this struggle continues on a lethal international scale.

THE ONSET OF

INDUSTRIALISM

Interpretations of the Industrial Revolution. The growth of population before the eighteenth century was relatively slow; in spite of the new wealth and activities occasioned by European expansion overseas and vigorous commercial rivalries among national states, agriculture remained the dominant occupation. The village rather than the town was the basic social unit, and most people lived an isolated existence, for transportation was slow, costly, and uncertain. In manufacturing, little machinery or power other than human muscles was utilized. Altogether then, the early 1700's can be pictured accurately as a slowly changing period.

With the advent of industrialism, the picture was modified drastically. The nineteenth-century French economist Jérome Adolphe Blanqui was the first to call this crucial transformation the Industrial Revolution, but the first historian to give wide currency to the epithet was Arnold Toynbee (1852-1883) of Oxford, the uncle of the famous contemporary British historian Arnold J. Toynbee. In a series of lectures published posthumously in 1884—*Lectures on the Industrial Revolution of the 18th Century in England*—Toynbee pointed out that: (1) the essence of the Industrial Revolution was the substitution of competition for the medieval regulations which had previously controlled the production and distribution of wealth; (2) population growth between 1760 and 1830 was much more rapid than before; (3) agricultural population declined relative to the total population in Great Britain in the same years; (4) an agrarian revolution in Great Britain was accomplished between 1750 and 1810 through the enclosure movement, drastically reducing the number of farmers and of small farm proprietors; (5) the factory system was substituted for the domestic system. Toynbee concentrated his attention upon Great Britain between 1760 and 1830, and upon the inventions and new techniques introduced during those years, as well as on the ideas of Adam Smith, Thomas Malthus, David Ricardo, and John Stuart Mill. He also emphasized heavily the evil effects upon the agricultural yeoman class and the development of a factory workman class under appalling urban conditions.

This traditional interpretation has been criticized in the past twenty-five years by various economic historians who assert that the change was less a revolution than a simple speeding up of evolution. They point out that some of the critical inventions were made in principle before 1760, and that some of those made during Toynbee's chosen period were not properly or extensively utilized until long after 1830—the Jacquard loom in France, for example. Some economic historians criticize especially the black picture of the evil effects of the Industrial Revolution on the common people. Such historians maintain that the condition of agricultural labor in the eighteenth century was fully as bad as the condition of factory labor in the nineteenth. Indeed the Industrial Revolution was a boon, critics of the classical account insist, since the worker in a manufacturing society was enabled to earn his living without owning either the means of production or the tools necessary to his work—a marked contrast to most people in an agrarian society.

With the spread of industrialization to the Continent, the iron and coal of the Saar region became increasingly important.

Above is a metal foundry in the factory district of the Saar as it was portrayed about one hundred years ago.

While the modification of the "revolutionary" thesis by the "evolutionary" thesis has added greatly to our understanding of industrialization, the term *Industrial Revolution* still seems a valid one to employ in discussing this movement. Certainly modern study has provided valuable correction and extension of the statistical series on population growth, wage levels, and purchasing power available to Toynbee. But the student who charts the dates for patenting or employing the inventions or techniques in manufacturing and transportation, which transformed the western world and made possible the nineteenth-century age of iron and steel, will find the great majority of these developments fall in a relatively short span of years, as in the case of Great Britain. Although Great Britain was the acknowledged leader, major contributions came from other countries, including the United States.

During the last decades before the French Revolution of 1789, the royal government in France was attempting to break down the traditional stagnation in the textile industry, where much of the early Industrial Revolution in Great Britain took place. And however true it may be that the factory system enabled any person to earn a livelihood without owning even the most rudimentary tools of a trade, the evil political and social consequences of early industrialization and the abuses of the factory system cannot be wished away.

The Industrial Revolution cannot properly be narrowed to any single aspect of the thoroughgoing reorganization of society that took place in the nineteenth century. The agrarian revolution—meaning enclosure—that Toynbee insisted accompanied the Industrial Revolution, the extensive introduction of scientific in place of unscientific culture, and the expanded use of non-human power, was as essential—if not as spectacular—as the machines and the factory system.

The domestic system. In the Middle Ages, manufacturing had been carried on under the guild system. The impetus of commercial expansion caused an important change in the organization of industry. The domestic, or putting-out, system evolved and reached its widest application among the textile industries in England. Although the system had first appeared in Italy as early as the thirteenth century, it did not become common in England until the sixteenth. It operated in this fashion: a merchant capitalist, or entrepreneur, would buy raw materials, assign them to artisans to be worked on in their own homes, take the finished product, and sell it to his customers. Thus, between producer and customer, a middleman intervened—an entrepreneur who accumulated capital by selling his goods at a profit. Because work was no longer planned and conducted by master and apprentice under one roof, this system widened the gulf between employer and employee. Sometimes the worker owned his own tools and furnished raw materials, but most craftsmen became more dependent upon the entrepreneur as the domestic system became more widely adopted.

The domestic system had both advantages and disadvantages. The accumulation of capital in the hands of the merchants made possible the purchase of raw materials in greater bulk and allowed for marketing of finished products on a larger scale than had been possible under the guild system. The domestic system also contributed to an increased specialization of skills within an efficient system of overall production; a merchant could have his raw wool sent to spinners, then to weavers, and finally to dyers. From the workers' point of view, it was now possible for agricultural tenants to augment the bare subsistence they eked from the soil by working at home.

But many abuses existed: child labor, low wages, long hours of work, and various occupational diseases. The employer found it difficult to supervise his scattered workmen, who sometimes failed to complete their work or substituted inferior substances for the raw material he had sent them, selling the stolen material to unscrupulous brokers. More important, time and money were wasted by delivering material to the workmen and then collecting the finished product.

With all its faults, the domestic system persisted for two hundred years in England, although central shops began to appear before the beginning of the factory system proper. While the domestic system was established in a few localities on the Continent, the guild system remained strong. Guilds were an indispensable part of the prevailing system of mercantilism in a society where change was unwelcome. Any merchant who defied guild regulations by setting up a domestic system of production was severely punished by the law.

Mechanization of the textile industry. Prior to the 1700's, mechanized industry was almost unknown because the machinery of the period was crude and imperfect, power facilities were inadequate, and governments restricted the use of new mechanisms to protect vested interests such as those which enjoyed various kinds of monopolies and especially those which had substantial capital invested in the old crude manufacturing devices. But the eighteenth century produced a series of inventions which were to have tremendous significance for manufacturing, particularly in England. These inventions were of two sorts—machines which increased industrial output far beyond that which had been possible when products were handmade, and machines which harnessed new power sources, thereby increasing output even further.

The textile industry was the first to be revolutionized by machines. In 1738 John Kay (1704-1764) invented the flying shuttle —a device which permitted one person instead of two to weave wide bolts of cloth. But Kay's invention permitted cloth to be woven much faster than thread could be supplied; one weaver required ten spinners to produce sufficient yarn for him. With the

A mid-nineteenth century English periodical shows a military tailor and his family employed under the domestic system.

invention of the spinning jenny in 1764 by James Hargreaves (d. 1778), the production of spinners equaled that of weavers, and a significant gain in time and labor was effected. The spinning jenny, named in honor of Hargreaves's wife, made it possible for one workman to spin eight, then sixteen, and finally as many as eighty threads at once.

Although the spinning jenny was inexpensive and easy to operate, it had one serious defect. The spun yarn was so coarse and loose that flax had to be mixed with the cotton to produce a suitable fabric. In 1769 a former hair dyer and wig maker named Richard Arkwright (1732-1792) patented his water frame. Powered by water, this machine for spinning thread made it possible to employ pure cotton, thus replacing the half-cotton, half-linen yarn. Ten years later Samuel Crompton (1753-1827), a spinner, combined the spinning jenny and water frame into the spinning mule—so called because of its hybrid origin. This machine could be powered as the water frame had been but was lighter and easier to operate.

More important, the thread which it spun was so strong and fine that muslins, cambrics, and other sheer materials could now be woven.

The spinning process had been so improved that the weaving process lagged behind it; the hand loom could no longer weave cloth as fast as the machine could spin yarn for it. Hand weaving was soon supplanted by the use of the power loom, patented in 1785 by Edmund Cartwright (1743-1823).

The suppliers of raw cotton had great difficulty in meeting the increasing demands for their crop because cotton seeds were separated from the fiber by hand and the most skillful worker could prepare not more than five or six pounds a day. In 1792 a young American, Eli Whitney (1765-1825), invented a cotton gin which enabled one worker to clean as much as a thousand pounds of cotton a day. The chart on the next page shows the amazing growth in the amount of cotton exported by the United States.

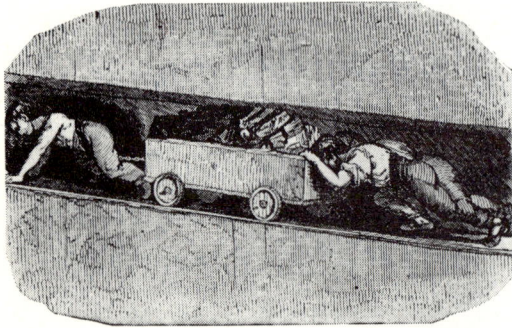

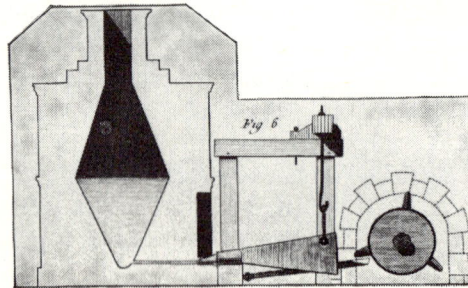

Three of the illustrations on the opposite page are from Diderot's famous *Encyclopedia*, which allotted considerable space to industry and technology. The tool makers in the shop scene at the top and the metalworkers at right center rely on their own power, transmitted through levers, wheels, and pulleys and supplemented by the strength of a blindfolded horse. At the bottom of the page is a cutaway diagram of an early blast furnace, its bellows operated by a giant cogwheel. In contrast to Diderot's spacious workshops is the dark, narrow tunnel at the far left, through which young boys pull and shove a heavy cart loaded with coal. At right is Hargreaves' revolutionary spinning jenny, and below textile workers operate the spinning mule, which was powered by water.

U.S. EXPORT OF COTTON

YEAR	AMOUNT IN LBS. (ALL FIGURES APPROXIMATE)
1793	500,000
1795	6,000,000
1801	20,000,000
1803	40,000,000
1810	90,000,000
1820	120,000,000
1832	300,000,000

Adapted from J. L. and Barbara Hammond, *The Rise of Modern Industry* (London: Methuen and Co., Ltd., 1927), p. 184. By permission of J. L. and B. Hammond and Methuen and Co., Ltd.

Small wonder that cotton was king in the South and that it rapidly became the staple crop of that area.

Steam power to run machines. With improvements in machinery came corresponding improvements in power. Early sources of power were horses, oxen, and water mills. Although a cheap source of energy, water was not always accessible to centers where raw materials or ready markets could be obtained, nor was it always available in sufficient quantity. The solution to the power problem, the harnessing of steam power, was not exclusively a discovery of the eighteenth century. In ancient times, Hero of Alexandria had developed a device similar to the steam-reaction turbine or the common lawn sprinkler of the present day. But this mechanism had been given only lowly employment—turning the spit in the kitchen. In 1705 an English engineer, Thomas Newcomen (1663-1729), devised an engine in which a piston was raised by injected steam, the steam condensed, and the piston returned to its original position as it cooled off. Used to pump water from coal mines, Newcomen's invention doubled the depth in the ground at which coal could be worked but consumed large quantities of coal, which the mines could supply cheaply but which factories could not.

The transformation of the atmosphere engine into the true steam engine was the achievement of James Watt (1736-1819). This Scottish genius was employed at the University of Glasgow as its mathematical instrument maker. One day when repairing the university's Newcomen engine, Watt was struck by the waste of steam resulting from the alternate heating and chilling of the cylinder. Four fifths of the steam used was lost in heating the cold cylinder; only one fifth served a useful purpose by acting on the piston. Using steam to force the piston back and forth inside a closed cylinder, Watt devised a separate condenser to control the supply of steam. The first steam engines were used for pumping; after 1785 they were employed in cotton manufacturing; and still later they were adapted to the needs of the steam locomotive and the steamship. It was a Watt engine that drove Robert Fulton's *Clermont* up the Hudson River in 1807 (see p. 162).

Improved methods for refining iron and mining coal. The rich iron deposits in northern England had never been fully exploited because of the primitive refining methods employed there. Vast quantities of timber were used to produce charcoal for smelting, and the demand for wood seriously menaced the forests of England and the Scandinavian countries. In 1709 Abraham Darby (1677-1717) introduced the use of coke for smelting, and John Smeaton (1724-1792) followed this innovation in 1760 with a cylinder blowing machine to force air on the coke. After 1788 Watt's steam engine was used to produce the blast of air necessary for the process.

Until 1784 iron was available only in an impure state—cast iron which would break rather than bend and which was too brittle to withstand hard strains and blows. In that year Henry Cort (1740-1800) invented a method of making iron malleable by burning the impurities out and leaving the iron clean and tough. The molten iron was then stirred with a long rod, a technique known as "puddling." Widespread adoption of this process enabled Great Britain to produce cheap wrought iron; the chart below shows the figures for the output of pig iron.

GROWTH OF IRON

INDUSTRY IN ENGLAND

YEAR	THOUSANDS OF TONS
1740	17
1788	68
1796	125
1806	258

Adapted from Clive Day, *Economic Development in Europe* (New York: The Macmillan Co., 1942), p. 134. By permission of The Macmillan Co.

Improvements in the coal-mining industry were slow. The steam engine made it possible for deep mine shafts to be sunk and for water to be pumped out of the shafts. But the deeper the shaft was sunk, the greater was the danger from suffocation through chokedamp and explosion from coal dust. Ventilation was improved by employing large fans and sinking a second shaft containing a fire, which made an upward draft and drew fresh air down the first shaft. But explosions were still a great hazard, for miners needed light to work by and the heat of the flame in their lamps ignited the gases present in the mine shafts and tunnels. In 1815 Humphry Davy (1778-1829) solved this problem by enclosing the flame of the miner's lamp with a wire gauze screen that was heat absorptive.

Despite such improvements and the invention of mechanical picks to hew coal, in many mines women and children were still employed to carry the coal in baskets up long flights of ladders to the earth's surface. This inhuman labor was later taken over by trucks which rolled along metal tracks.

Improvements in transportation. In the seventeenth century the highways of England were bumpy, rough trails in the summer and sticky, muddy bogs in the winter. Daniel Defoe described one highway as:

. . . not passable but just in the middle of summer, after the coal carriages have beaten the way, for the ground is a stiff clay, so after rain the water stands as in a dish, and the horses sink in it up to their bellies.[1]

In 1815 a Scotsman, John McAdam (1756-1836), constructed a road by a simple but revolutionary method: small stones in compact layers were placed directly on the earth roadbed. The passage of traffic packed the stones down so tightly that a strong and fairly smooth surface resulted. *Macadam*, the term given today to roads of this type, is derived from the name of the inventor. In the same period another Scotsman, Thomas Telford (1757-1834), built roads with a foundation of large stones, topped with a macadam surface. Telford's method is still employed for roads designed to bear heavy loads of traffic and in areas of flaky or spongy subsoil.

Stagecoaches reached new top speeds as their horses galloped over the improved roads. It had taken four and a half days to travel the 160 miles from London to Manchester in 1754; thirty-four years later the journey had been shortened to twenty-eight hours.

Modern canal building in England began in 1759 with the construction of a waterway from the duke of Bridgewater's colliery to Manchester, a distance of seven miles. As a result of this project, the price of coal in Manchester was halved and all England became "canal conscious." Seventy years later England had nearly four thousand miles of improved rivers and canals. Better roads and new canals made hauling of goods cheaper and easier. Many acres of new iron docks were constructed in London, making this port the largest in the world.

Retrospect on the advent of industrialism. During the 150 years from the middle of the seventeenth century to the beginning of the nineteenth, overseas trade was a powerful stimulant to industry. The growth of the European textile industry depended upon the dyestuffs, such as indigo and cochineal, which were imported from distant lands. The introduction of East Indian cottons created a

The Worsley-Manchester canal, built by James Brindley, helped to start England's canal boom. This illustration shows the canal entering an underground tunnel that led to a coal mine. The crane was used to hoist blocks of quarried stone onto the canal boats. Construction of the canal enabled the Duke of Bridgewater to transport his coal and stone to Manchester.

horseless carriages and submarines. There also appeared numerous trivial inventions—a mechanical turnip slicer, for one.

INVENTION IN ENGLAND

YEAR	NO. OF PATENTS
1660-1669	31
1670-1679	51
1690-1699	102
1720-1729	89
1760-1769	205
1770-1779	294
1780-1789	477

Adapted from Witt Bowden, *Industrial Society in England Towards the End of the Eighteenth Century* (New York: The Macmillan Co., 1925), p. 12. By permission of The Macmillan Co.

huge demand for similar but cheaper goods. This need was met by new machines turning out products both superior to and less expensive than the imported fabrics. In addition, the constantly increasing volume of raw materials arriving from the new lands could not be processed by hand labor, and this phenomenon gave a further stimulus to invention.

The seventeenth century had been a great age in the advance of pure science, as typified by Sir Isaac Newton. In the following century, the man of science was overshadowed by the shrewd, practical inventor, particularly in England. There was a deluge of inventions and new gadgets. Various societies were founded with the express purpose of encouraging invention, and the English government joined these organizations in giving medals and money grants to successful inventors. (The figures in the chart on this page show the number of patents issued by the patent office in England.)

No wonder men took to the air in the first balloon in 1783 and others talked about

Almost constantly at war from 1740 to 1815, Britain had to make an all-out effort to escape conquest during the spectacular triumphs of Napoleon Bonaparte. From 1793 on, factories poured forth a stream of cannon, muskets, ammunition, and uniforms; shipyards hummed with activity; and the whole nation experienced a wartime inflation. At the same time, the domestic market expanded rapidly. In 1714 the population was about 5,500,000; a century later it was nearing 11,000,000. New mouths to feed and bodies to clothe created a rising demand for both food and manufactures.

The three basic factors of technological change in the first phase of industrialism were: (1) the introduction of new machinery in the textile industry, (2) the adoption of the steam engine in manufacturing, and (3) the use of the puddling process for manufacturing bar iron. In its first stages, industrialism—contrary to past beliefs—was not exclusively an English phenomenon. Continental powers were moving in the same direction at roughly the same speed. In France the rate of mechanization until 1785 matched that of England. Large textile factories were erected, and iron production improved in famous works such as the Creusot foundry in central France. In the closing decade of the century, however, English manufacturing began to run rapidly ahead of its Continental rivals. There was a large free-trade area in the British Isles, and by gaining command of the seas, Britain opened and controlled profitable markets for its goods. Furthermore, the British system of government was responsive to the needs of the middle class. And finally, more than in any other land, technicians in England poured forth a veritable flood of inventions.

Perhaps too much stress has been placed on textiles in this story of mechanization. Wool spinning by hand was carried on in some English homes as late as 1850. In 1800 there were only 320 Watt steam engines in use, and thirty years later one quarter of the power used by cotton mills still came from water mills. Apart from the textile plants and the foundries, most industries changed by evolution rather than revolution. But changes in technology were now at work that would transform the lives of England's people. The value of imports, mainly raw materials, tripled in both the 1780's and 1790's. In 1710 the export value of cotton manufactures was £5000; in 1780, £344,000; and in 1800, £5,406,000. Despite improvements in agriculture, Britain was compelled to import grains because of the rapid increase in population. The basic nature of Britain's national economy was crystallizing: a tremendous volume of raw materials and food imported, an even greater volume of manufactured goods exported.

THE RISE OF THE AGE OF

IRON AND STEEL

Heavy industry. The machines, the factories, the tools, and the products were the most impressive outward manifestations of the Industrial Revolution and the industrial society it produced. In the long run, however, the heavy-metal industries were basic. The age of iron and steel was built up by

the quantity production which developed, mainly in England, late in the eighteenth century and early in the nineteenth. Comparatively small quantities of cast iron had long been used for tools and hardware. Structural use of cast iron had been made in the 1770's, tremendously increasing the amount needed. This was followed by its use in canal boats in the 1790's and then, as a fireproofing measure, in mills shortly after the turn of the century. Simultaneously, arched bridges using cast-iron girders were being constructed, and by the end of the first quarter of the nineteenth century the practical limits of cast-iron structural development were approached.

During the middle third of the century wrought iron replaced cast iron, a development forced by the demands of shipbuilding and railroad construction, for which cast iron was unsatisfactory. The use of wrought iron meant not only economy of material but the doubling of its application. The growth and expansion of the iron industry in Great Britain was phenomenal, owing to huge home consumption and a large export market because of Britain's leadership in the building up of basic heavy industry. After the middle third of the century, when large-scale steel processes were invented, in many instances steel products replaced earlier products. Since Britain's resources were not so well adapted to steel production, leadership began to shift from Great Britain to Germany and the United States. The unification and expansion of Germany and the United States made competition possible; both nations had large-scale ore deposits which steel manufacturing processes demanded. Great Britain was forced to import supplementary ores from Sweden and Spain, and a gradual decline in British iron exports set in. Britain, however, retained in large measure the great world carrying trade which it had built.

The advent of railroads. Railroad and locomotive development provided impetus

As shown by this illustration of a train on the London and Greenwich Railroad line in 1833, the railroad cars were shaped like carriages. The train also transported privately owned carriages on flat cars.

for the inauguration of an age of iron and steel, and the story is now generally familiar. Increased demands for coal and the expansion of mines led to the necessity for devices capable of hauling large loads. This was met by rails, wagons to move on them, and finally machine power to pull them. The first successful commercial railroads were built to move coal from mines to ports. As early as 1801, Richard Trevithick had constructed a crude form of steam locomotive, but his contraption was not powerful enough to haul a load. Later, the forty miles of track between Stockton and Darlington in England served as a testing ground for the improved locomotive built in 1825 by George Stephenson, the brilliant son of a poor miner. With the locomotive noisily belching smoke, the train made its first run. An eyewitness described the event in this fashion:

A man on horseback rode in front of the train to drive off cows and careless farmers. . . . At times the horseman had to break into a gallop, so swift was the speed of the train.[2]

Five years later when Stephenson's *Rocket* attained the terrifying speed of thirty-six miles per hour, the railroad era was on its way.

The steam engine goes to sea. After the development of steam locomotive power came steamships of iron construction. Although others had used steam to propel boats earlier, the man who reaped the lion's share of glory for this feat was Robert Fulton (1765-1815) of the United States. Fulton used a Watt engine to drive his *Clermont* 150 miles up the Hudson River in 1807.

Causing great consternation, the trip was described by one skeptical observer as "the Devil on the way to Albany in a sawmill." About thirty years later Samuel Cunard initiated regular transatlantic passenger steamship service. This line still proudly bears the name of its Canadian founder.

The building of steamships necessitated the establishment of coaling stations; the location of coaling stations powerfully influenced steamship lines and trade. Britain attained preëminence in the coal-carrying trade, exporting coal and supplying the distant coaling stations; British ships on the return voyages brought the heavier foods and raw materials produced in the world's colonial areas.

Some of the important factors in the development of iron ship construction were a decline in the European supply of wood, the rising cost of ship construction, and the increased demand for carrying space. The construction of iron ships was accelerated by the availability of ore for ship building and the enlarged carrying capacity of such ships. Eventually the cost of building iron ships dropped below that of building wooden ships in the United States—to the detriment of American shipping.

Concentration of population and industry. The factory system was one of the major causes of social changes, but perhaps equally important were the modifications of the transportation system effected by railroads and steamships. The practical limit to the size of wooden ships was between four and five thousand tons. Iron ships could be built many times larger, and their size affected the distribution of shipping, bringing it more and more into ports suitable to large vessels. Great concentrations of population were difficult to maintain in the days before carriers such as the railroad and the steamship came into use, but with the new techniques in transportation the balance between urban and rural areas was upset. In the industrial society that supplanted the agrarian, fuel for the machines was more important, relatively, than food for men. Machines could be located near the sources of power, and food brought from distant areas to the men that worked the machines. Population became increasingly concentrated around the machines, destroying the rural village and market towns—which had existed because of the need for proximity to the food-producing areas—and building up that noteworthy feature of modern industrial society, the predominantly urban settlement.

Improvements in communication. Parallel with improvements in transportation went great advances in communication. The introduction of the penny post in 1840 in England made correspondence by mail substantially cheaper. Initially, there was much opposition to this move; even the postmaster general believed that:

. . . the Post Office buildings would collapse under the weight of letters likely to be put in them if postage became so cheap.[3]

Another revolutionary method of transmitting information appeared when Samuel Morse (1791-1872), an American artist and inventor, perfected the electric telegraph in 1844. Twenty-two years later Cyrus Field (1819-1892), another American inventor, laid the first successful Atlantic cable.

England, "workshop of the world." The sinews of Britain during the nineteenth century were its magnificent industrial system, which far surpassed that of any of its competitors until after 1870. With its head start in industrial development, Britain for a long

The "Great Eastern," a British iron steamship engaged by Cyrus Field, laid the first successful Atlantic cable in 1866.

time enjoyed a virtual monopoly in some manufacturing techniques. Between 1851 and 1870 its railroad mileage doubled, and a comparable increase was registered in shipbuilding, coal mining, textile production, and metal manufacturing. It was England's undisputed leadership in the First Industrial Revolution that explained the tremendous volume of the nation's exports, its accumulation of enormous capital, and its long-held position as the world's commercial center.

There were reasons for England's technological leadership. On this small island were rich deposits of coal and iron to supply the needs of industry. The wool of English sheep, unsurpassed in quality, provided the essential raw material for the nation's textile mills. Britain's stable government catered increasingly in the nineteenth century to the interests of the trading and industrial classes, and its unrivaled navy not only protected

In 1807, Fulton's *Clermont* made its first voyage up the Hudson River, traveling the 150 miles from New York to Albany in 32 hours.

the country from invasion but kept open the trade routes for the merchant fleet. There was also surplus capital, accumulated from trade with America and the Orient. Finally, England concentrated on staple goods, adaptable to mass production, whereas France, for example, specialized in luxury commodities demanding individual craftsmanship.

Even while England was enjoying its role as world leader of industry and trade, understudies were preparing to usurp the starring role. As envious businessmen in France, Germany, and other lands began to imitate British factory methods, the head start in technology which Britain had enjoyed was rapidly overcome. In some instances the Industrial Revolution was "smuggled" out of England. For example, Samuel Slater, an English mechanic, memorized the particulars of cotton-spinning machinery before migrating to New England, where he helped set up a textile mill in Providence, Rhode Island. William Cockerill, another English mechanic, established a large machine shop in Liège, Belgium, and his son John built a foundry nearby which, by 1840, had become the largest ironworks in the world.

Slow tempo of industrialization in France. In the eighteenth century it seemed likely that the rate of industrialization in France would equal that of England, but after

1785 England rapidly outstripped its Continental rivals. Although railroads, iron foundries, and steam-powered factories became increasingly common features of the French landscape in the nineteenth century, industrial progress in general was much slower than in England. The development of heavy industry lagged. There was a shortage of coal, and although the output of iron ore increased about 65 per cent between 1830 and 1865, the deposits of ore were not conveniently located. With the invention of the Jacquard loom (1804), on the other hand, French silk production came to exceed that of all the rest of Europe.

Unlike England, where a large proportion of the country people migrated into raw and overcrowded cities with the onset of industrialism, France did not become predominantly urban. The typical small farmer in France had no desire to exchange his good land for the dingy streets of a city. He had his few acres of fertile soil and his village cronies with whom he liked to sip his wine and smoke his pipe.

Genesis of German industry. The progress of industrialism in Germany was retarded by numerous obstacles, such as political disunity, antagonism and conflict of interests between nobles and merchants, and the backwardness of the peasantry. In 1803, 80 per cent of the population lived as farmers, and not until the first quarter of the nineteenth century did various medieval class distinctions disappear in most of the German states. As in France, the guild system discouraged competition and innovation in the country's economic life. In addition, there was a lack of foreign markets, insufficient capital, and much improverishment after the Napoleonic Wars.

The reverses suffered during the Napoleonic Wars, however, helped stimulate the economic unification of the German states—a decisive event in modern history. Under Prussia's leadership, a tariff union, the Zollverein, was formed with the motto "Freedom of trade through unity." By 1842 most of the German states belonged to the Zollverein. The wider trading advantages of the tariff union helped stimulate industry, and machines were imported from England to set up textile manufacturing plants. Railroad construction began in 1835. After 1850 improved methods in metallurgy were introduced, and in the next twenty years German furnaces increased output fourfold. Coal production likewise mounted rapidly.

During the twenty-two years that separated the revolutionary year 1848 from the outbreak of the Franco-Prussian War, modern capitalistic and industrial Germany was formed. The fabulous development of the Krupp works exemplified the fast growth of German industry. Inheriting a broken-down steel mill employing only four workers, Alfred Krupp (1812-1887) introduced a steam engine into his factory and gradually expanded his work force. From the invention and exploitation of a steel gun, cast-steel axles, and a breech-loading rifle, Krupp created a large-scale enterprise which by 1873 was employing sixteen thousand workers. The Krupp works was to become the symbol of German industrial efficiency and of Germany's successful application of technology to the weapons of war.

Industrialization in other nations. Another center for the growth of industry was diminutive Holland, a nation of thrifty and hardworking people. After 1830 Dutch industrialists made important progress in shipbuilding, diamond cutting, brewing, cigar making, and the production of fine porcelain. In the main, however, Dutch economic activity was in commerce. Tremendous quantities of raw materials such as spices, copra, tobacco, sugar, and indigo were exported from the Dutch East Indies to markets the world over.

By pirating British manufacturing techniques, Belgium also achieved rapid industrial growth. During the nineteenth century, in fact, Belgium produced more coal and iron than its much larger neighbor, France, and Belgian railroad construction boomed until this small nation boasted a greater railroad mileage per capita than any other country. Meanwhile, the Belgian factories and mills turned out quantities of lace, carpets, cutlery, and iron products.

A nineteenth-century illustration shows the famous Krupp works in Essen, Germany.

The Industrial Revolution in the United States began about 1789, when wars in Europe cut off imports. Factories and railroads had become important by the 1840's, and by 1860 American textile, iron, steel, and shoe industries were developing rapidly. At mid-century large-scale corporate enterprises had begun to replace small-scale businesses, and after 1861 the government was usually in the hands of legislators friendly to corporate enterprise, instead of under agrarian control as it had been in earlier decades. Protective tariffs were passed to assure American manufacturers a ready home market, and the power of the states to regulate business was restricted; thus the basis was laid for large-scale industrial development, already stimulated by military needs during the Civil War. By 1870 the nation was crisscrossed with railroads, the northeastern part of the country was heavily industrialized, and new factories and mills seemed to be springing up everywhere.

Outside the industrial pale. In Italy, economic growth was hindered by a lack of natural resources, the chronic poverty of its people, and the lack of national unity. Yet by 1870, when unification was completed, some gains had been registered. The forces that worked for Italian political unification had also encouraged economic development. Count Cavour, Sardinia's outstanding statesman and the architect of Italian unity, had promoted his country's first railroad, a steamship line, and various forms of manufacturing.

In the Iberian peninsula, in eastern Europe, the Balkans, and Russia, industry either hardly existed or grew very slowly. Spain was in the grip of a landed aristocracy, and its middle class was relatively unimportant. Portugal was backward and primitively agricultural. Eastern Europe and the Balkans were still dominated by feudal classes which maintained a static, medieval way of life. Nor was there significant economic improvement in Russia before 1890. Its first railroad tracks were laid in 1836, and from 1856 to 1878 some six hundred miles of railroad were built each year; but considering the tremendous size of the country, this was a drop in the bucket.

Before 1870 industrialism made little progress in South America, Africa, the Middle East, and Asia, although the British introduced railroads, modern plantations, the telegraph, and a few factories into India and Ceylon. Japan took no steps toward industrialization until a fundamental change was made in its government in 1867 (see p. 294), and China remained industrially dormant until the twentieth century.

CONSEQUENCES OF

INDUSTRIALISM

New markets for new goods. An important result of industrialism was the increase in productivity. The new machines poured forth textiles, sheet iron and rails, pottery, cutlery, and a host of other commodities. In some industries productivity increased a hundredfold and in others as much as a thousandfold. This amazing upsurge in manufactured commodities had an important effect upon the extent of the market. It soon became apparent that home markets could not absorb all the goods the factories could produce, and western European powers therefore began searching for trade outlets all over the world. International trade required a network of world transportation, a need which was met by the development of the railroad and steamship. The world was becoming an integrated economic unit connected by strands of international commerce.

Accompanying the mounting demand for overseas markets was the need for raw materials. These aims led to the European penetration of African and Asian lands. Isolated and primitive peoples were brought into touch with western culture by traders seeking markets and raw materials. And with these traders usually came officials and troops to take over territories as protectorates or colonies. Thus in the nineteenth century, and increasingly after 1871, the great industrial powers of Europe pursued a program of imperialism by which vast chunks of Asia and practically all of Africa came under European political and economic control.

Changing population trends. The best markets for the new products were still in Europe, where the industrial era was accompanied by a substantial and continuous increase in population. It has been estimated that Europe in 1800 had about 175,000,000 people, whereas by 1900 it had 400,000,000.

Up to early modern times, populations were checked by food scarcity, pestilence, and high infant mortality. Now the growing agricultural productiveness of European countries, achieved through intensive farming and the adoption of the techniques of scientific agriculture, supported larger populations. Because of the spread of transportation facilities, Europe was also able to import more food from other continents. Furthermore, a mounting birth rate was accompanied by a lowered death rate. A reduction in infant mortality was the reward of medical progress; in the eighteenth century it had been not uncommon for a mother who bore ten children to lose seven of them. By the latter part of the nineteenth century, medicine and public health were slowly but surely conquering the dreaded plagues—cholera, typhus, and smallpox.

An increasing majority of these people were city dwellers. Ever since the late Middle Ages, the city had been emerging as an important factor in Europe. Now the process was accelerated. First in England, then in Belgium, France, and Germany, and later in other parts of the world, old cities outgrew their boundaries, and many new ones were founded. In general, from 1750 down to the present, people have more and more tended to concentrate in cities, while population in the country has declined.

Aside from the country-to-city migrations, there were often regional shifts in population. For example, in England the industrial transformation brought a shift in population from the south to the north. No longer would the bulk of the English people live south of the river Thames. When coal and iron were discovered in the north, industrial centers such as Birmingham and Manchester were founded in the vicinity of these raw materials. On a wider scale, the opportunities in America attracted thousands of immigrants, who joined the country-by-country migration.

New social structure. Along with changing population statistics, the Industrial Revolution brought about a realignment of the social classes. Out of the factory system emerged two groups—the workers and the owners. The workers sold their labor to the factory owner in return for wages. The upper bourgeoisie was composed of that group which owned or controlled the means of production (principally factories and machines) and got profits, not wages, as a reward. Because they usually owned or controlled the capital that built the great factories, they are frequently referred to as capitalists.

Between these two classes existed the "not-so-rich" and the "not-so-poor"—the small shopkeepers, government officials, lawyers, doctors, independent farmers, and teachers. These are sometimes termed the *petite bourgeoisie* to distinguish them from the *haute bourgeoisie*—the wealthy industrialists and capitalists whom we have already mentioned. They played an important role in the formation of public opinion but not in the control of industry.

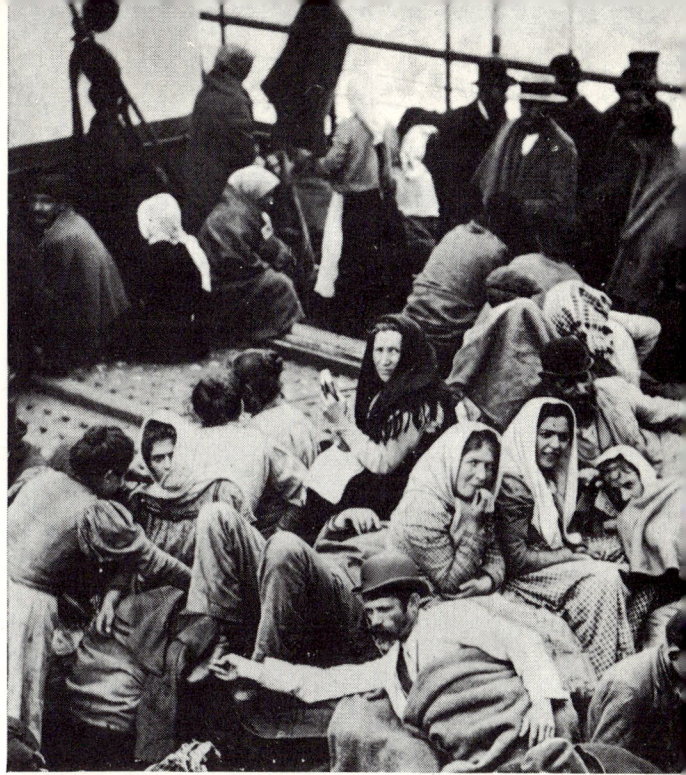

During the nineteenth century, hundreds of thousands of European immigrants voyaged to the United States, hoping to make their fortunes in a free, fast-developing country.

The factory, symbol of the new order. The most important symbol of the new industrial order was the factory, for here was the site of the machinery and power that made industrialism possible. The factory system did not replace the cottage or domestic system of home manufactures overnight; the two existed side by side for decades, with the former waging a winning fight. Let us trace the victory of the factory system in the English textile industry.

In former times the making of yarn and the weaving of cloth had been a small-scale hand enterprise well suited to the domestic system, but as soon as inventors had adapted the processes to factory production, the change began. Although at this stage a man might still install one of the new machines in his own home, when the transformation in power occurred and when machines capable of turning out huge quantities of goods were created, the ordinary worker could neither buy nor maintain the equipment.

Up to 1815 the hand-loom weaver did not suffer substantially, but after that he had to compete with a machine that could turn out more goods at a lower cost. To cut their costs, manufacturers installed more and more mechanical looms. In consequence, the hand weavers had to accept lower and lower wages to compete with the cheaper goods made by the power looms. Ultimately, they lost their hopeless battle and were forced to move to the communities where the new factories offered employment. What happened to the hand-loom weavers in England may be taken as an illustration of the fate of handworkers in general during the early era of the factory.

This displacement of human skills by machinery, known as technological unemployment, remained a constant source of fear as the Industrial Revolution spread. Even today, the twentieth-century advance in labor-saving machinery—automation—is causing serious concern to factory workers and their union leaders.

Wretched working conditions. The first factories thrown together during the extraordinary rise of such industrial centers as Manchester and Birmingham were lacking in the most elementary sanitary and safety facilities. The buildings were dingy, had low ceilings, and lacked proper ventilation or light. Because the new machines were not fenced off, horrible cases of mangling were a common occurrence among the factory workers. Furthermore, under English common law, any accident a worker might suffer was considered a result of his own negligence, for which the employer could not be held responsible. There was no system of workmen's compensation or health insurance; an injured worker was likely to be thrown out in the street destitute and his job given to one of the thousands who had flocked to the new cities in search of employment. A graphic picture of working conditions has been given us by the English novelist Charles Kingsley in his exposé of the tailoring industry. Describing a young apprentice's introduction to his workroom, he wrote:

I stumbled after Mr. Jones up a dark, narrow, iron staircase till we emerged through a trap-door into a garret at the top of the house. I recoiled with disgust at the scene before me; and here I was to work—perhaps through life! A low lean-to room, stifling me with the combined odours of human breath and perspiration, stale beer, the sweet sickly smell of gin, and the sour and hardly less disgusting one of new cloth. On the floor, thick with dust and dirt, scraps of stuff and ends of thread, sat some dozen haggard, untidy, shoeless men, with a mingled look of care and recklessness that made me shudder. The windows were tight closed to keep out the cold winter air; and the condensed breath ran in streams down the panes, chequering the dreary outlook of chimney-tops and smoke.[4]

Despite the innovation of "labor-saving" machinery, the worker was certainly not saved any labor. Each day the factory bell summoned him to long hours of monotonous drudgery. Women were forced by poverty to work until a day or two before delivery of their children and then to report back to work within another two or three days after the child was born. Lung trouble, rheumatism, and distortion of limbs commonly beset the workers as a result of the unhealthful factory conditions and the monotonous hours of toil.

Children were the most unfortunate victims of the factory system. The mills employed some youngsters only four or five years of age, and in the coal mines children were used to carry baskets of coal up ladders. An English girl, aged fourteen, told the following story to the Mines Commission of Investigation in 1842:

I have worked down in the pit five years. Father is working next pit. I have twelve brothers and sisters—all of them but one live at home. They weave, and wind, and hurry [drive, i.e., drive a coal wagon], and one is a counter, one of them can read, none of the rest can, or write. They never went to day-school, but three of them go to Sunday-School. I hurry for my brother John, and come down at seven o'clock about. I go up [from the mine] at six, sometimes even seven. I do not like working in pit, but I am obliged to get a living.[5]

Employers sometimes contracted with public officials for the assignment of pauper children to the factories, where, working ostensibly as apprentices, they were treated with incredible cruelty. The youngsters often worked in relays, so that the beds in which they slept never cooled as one batch followed another on the piles of vermin-ridden rags. A story published in the English radical magazine *The Lion* (1828) tells how eight pauper children were sent off to a factory where they were whipped to keep them working steadily. One of the boys was transferred to another factory where the children actually scrambled for slop in a trough and were frequently kicked and pinched by inhuman overseers. As a West Indian slavemaster summed up the whole treatment of working minors:

. . . I have always thought myself disgraced by being the owner of slaves, but we never in the West Indies thought it possible for any human being to be so cruel as to require a child of nine years old to work twelve and a half hours a day, and that, you acknowledge, is your regular practice.[6]

Children employed in the mills received almost no education, for schooling was neither compulsory nor free. The facilities for obtaining even the most rudimentary training were insufficient, and evening schools were of little benefit to children who had to toil twelve hours during the day. A Children's Employment Commission report showed the dismaying results: One boy of seventeen could not even tell what two plus two equaled; other boys had never even heard of London; several did not know who the queen was and were ignorant of such names as Nelson, Wellington, and Bonaparte, while one child had heard the name Jesus Christ but did not know who He was.

Ugly, disease-ridden slums. Contemporary accounts of the workers' quarters in the new industrial cities fill us with loathing and pity. In his novel *Hard Times*, Charles Dickens describes a typical English factory town of a century ago, as follows:

It was a town of red brick, or of brick that would have been red if the smoke and ashes had allowed it; but as matters stood it was a town of unnatural red and black, like the painted face of a savage. It was a town of machinery and tall chimneys, out of which interminable serpents of smoke trailed themselves for ever and ever, and never got uncoiled. It had a black canal in it, and a river that ran purple with ill-smelling dye, and vast piles of buildings full of windows where there was a rattling and a trembling all day long, and where the piston of the steam-engine worked monotonously up and down, like the head of an elephant in a state of melancholy madness. It contained several large streets all very like one another, and many small streets still more like one another, inhabited by people equally like one another, who all went in and out at the same hours, with the same sound upon the same pavements, to do the same work, and to whom every day was the same as yesterday and tomorrow, and every year the counterpart of the last and the next.[7]

This was Coketown, the drab center where self-made, rich, boasting, and calculating Joseph Bounderby was part owner of a textile mill that turned out "elegancies of life" for the fine lady who could scarcely bear to hear the place of their origin mentioned. If Coketown were worse, it could not produce goods; if it were better, profits would be less.

If we had visited a working-class district in Manchester early in the nineteenth century, we should have seen whole blocks of jerry-built homes, thrown together back to back by speculators so that the rear rooms had no windows. The houses faced on narrow, unpaved alleys or courts in which garbage and sewage were dumped. The living quarters for factory workers were chronically overcrowded and lacked adequate sanitary facilities. No wonder epidemics such as cholera were frequent. In 1842 a commission reported that the deaths caused by filth and lack of public sanitation outnumbered the loss in any wars that England had fought in modern times.

And what could the workers do with what little spare time they had? Outside their squalid hovels, the streets were filthy, and the air was polluted by stagnant drains. For recreation, both men and women frequented the public houses, the "pubs," where they spent their meager wages on gin, cheap whiskey, and beer. Drink was the path to forgetfulness.

In recent years there has been a closer scrutiny of the effects of the Industrial Revolution in the early nineteenth century.

Gustave Doré's nineteenth-century engraving depicts the filthy, overcrowded slums which housed the industrial workers of London.

Some historians believe there has been too much "[s]entimental unhistorical hysteria"[8] in assessing this period with its so-called seven deadly sins: unsanitary and dangerous factories, inhumanly long hours, child labor, the exploitation of women, low wages, slums, and intermittent unemployment. Perhaps it is true that bad living conditions for the mass of men were not completely new. Perhaps it is also true that the humanitarian conscience magnified the misery that industrialism brought in its train. But though some workers may have actually enjoyed better living standards than they had under the old domestic system, these lucky few did not begin to match the thousands of victims of the changing order. Until the advent of reform, the evils of industrialism far out-

weighed its blessings. Coketowns existed first in England; but with the spread of the Industrial Revolution to other lands, they began to blight the landscape of Belgium, France, Germany, the United States, and Russia.

THE MIDDLE CLASS

TRIUMPHANT

Bourgeois economic theory—laissez faire. The bourgeoisie achieved their success in the era of industrial capitalism, which superseded the predominantly commercial, or trading, phase of business (see Chapter 19, Vol. I). In industrial capitalism, profits were made primarily from investment in machinery and raw materials and utilization of other people's labor. Controlled and administered by factory owners, the new industrial capitalism soon resulted in important changes in business organization. The corporation became the characteristic form of business organization, largely replacing individual proprietorship and partnership, both of which proved inadequate to meet the needs of the factory system. The corporation, which could raise and utilize large sums of capital possessed many advantages over other forms of business organization.

With the triumph of the middle class in the nineteenth century, we find also the triumph of their economic philosophy—laissez faire. The textbook of this school of thought was Adam Smith's *Wealth of Nations* (see p. 71), which postulated that every man, laborer or owner, pursued his own best interest financially. Theoretically, the complete freedom of business to produce and sell its goods in the open market redounded for the public good in more and better products. Any government interference in business was felt to hinder the operation of economic "laws," which dictated free choice. The essence of laissez-faire liberalism was expressed by Lord Macaulay in the following words:

Our rulers will best promote the improvement of the nation by strictly confining themselves to their own legitimate duties, by leaving capital to find its most lucrative course, commodities their fair price, industry and intelligence their natural reward, idleness and folly their natural punishment, by maintaining peace, by defending property, by diminishing the price of law, and by observing strict economy in every department of the state. Let the government do this: the people will assuredly do the rest.[9]

The theory of laissez-faire economic liberalism held that it was impossible to correct the social evils of industrialism. Each man, enjoying free choice, could only improve his own circumstances by hard work, economy, and limiting the size of his family. The state could not do this for him. Economists such as Ricardo and Malthus offered so little hope for improvement of the economic status of the common people that economics came to be known as the "dismal science."

No chances were taken to see if labor unions could bring about better working conditions. Drastic laws, such as the Combination Acts of 1799-1800 in England, forbade unions on the grounds that they would restrain trade. Strikes were classed as conspiracies, and strikers were harshly punished. While emphasizing the necessity for "freedom," the proponents of laissez faire completely disregarded the individual worker's lack of bargaining power. Today we wonder what could be "free" in the bargaining of weakness with strength, of the unorganized worker with the gigantic corporation.

Malthus' theory of population. Among the gloomier prophets was Thomas Robert Malthus (1766-1834), an English clergyman whose fame rests on his *Essay on Population* (1798). This study asserts that:

. . . the power of population is indefinitely greater than the power in the earth to produce subsistence for man.[10]

In his own day Malthus could accurately point to a comparatively limited food supply and a population that was increasing by leaps and bounds. From this evidence, he deduced that the inevitable lot of the mass of mankind was misery, as the birth rate would always outrun the food supply.

Malthus' only solution to what he believed to be a permanent problem was the practice of self-restraint in reproduction. The postponing of early marriages seemed to Malthus an excellent means of preventing the working classes from having too many children in proportion to their income.

Ricardo's theory of wages. Using Malthus' line of reasoning in developing his own thesis, the English economist David Ricardo (1772-1823) advanced his "subsistence theory of wages." Ricardo maintained that labor has a natural price and also a market price. The natural price is that:

. . . which is necessary to enable the laborers . . . to subsist and to perpetuate their race without either increase or diminution.[11]

The market price depends on the law of supply and demand. When labor is scarce and in demand, it is well paid; when it is plentiful, it is poorly paid. In the first instance, the market price of labor exceeds the natural price; the result is prosperity for the laborer. In the second instance, the reverse is true.

Unfortunately, said Ricardo, labor tends to increase faster than available capital, so that wages fall to the natural price. Although varying circumstances might qualify the situation, Ricardo felt that he had stated an ironclad law which nothing could or should change.

Like all other contracts, wages should be left to the fair and free competition of the market, and should never be controlled by the interference of the legislature.[12]

Laissez-faire theory expanded and modified. Other writers who popularized laissez-faire doctrine (also known as "economic liberalism") were Jeremy Bentham, James Mill, and John Stuart Mill.

Jeremy Bentham (1748-1832), whose work spans the late eighteenth and early nineteenth centuries, was a wealthy British jurist who devised the doctrine of utilitarianism, or "philosophical radicalism," based on the two concepts of utility and happiness. He correlated these two terms by saying that each individual knows what is best for himself and that all human institutions should be measured according to the amount of happiness they give—Bentham's celebrated "pain and pleasure" principle.

He who adopts the *principle of utility*, esteems virtue to be a good only on account of the pleasures which result from it; he regards vice as an evil only because of the pains which it produces.
. . . As a general rule, the greatest possible latitude should be left to individuals, in all cases in which they can injure none but themselves, for they are the best judges of their own interest. If they deceive themselves, it is to be supposed that the moment they discover their error they will alter their conduct. The power of the law need interfere only to prevent them from injuring each other.[13]

Bentham believed strongly that the function of government should be the securing of as great a degree of individual freedom as possible, for freedom made for happiness. Utilitarianism has been defined as "The greatest happiness for the greatest number."

James Mill (1773-1836), a British philosopher and economist, was a stanch exponent of the ideas of both Ricardo and Bentham. To his mind the bourgeois merchants and factory owners should be allowed the maximum freedom to conduct their affairs. In the long run the self-interest of the manufacturers would coincide with that of the workers.

His eldest son, John Stuart Mill, was not so sure, however. Adam Smith had seen the cause of wealth in the unrestricted increase in productivity. Malthus found the cause of poverty in the unrestricted growth of population. Ricardo had tried to reconcile the paradox of increasing wealth accompanied by increasing poverty by studying the unrestricted distribution of wealth operating through the law of wages. Mill tackled the question of "how wealth *ought to be* distributed." While admitting that the maximum freedom should be permitted in the processes of production according to natural law, he insisted that the distribution of wealth depends on the laws and customs of society, and these can be changed by the will of men. The idea that all competition was good needed examination; competition in production increased the volume of goods, to the general advantage of society, but competition over the division of the products favored the strong against the weak, and civilized society might revert to the jungle. Mill's ideas gained influence only very slowly.

The middle class in politics. The middle class wanted no governmental interference in its affairs; but it cannot be said that the nineteeth-century businessman, therefore, was not interested in participating in politics. On the contrary, the middle class made a determined effort to secure control of the government. Such an ambition, as we have seen, was back of the great Reform Bill of 1832 in England and behind the movement to enlarge the suffrage in France in 1830 and 1848. As we noted in Chapter 5, middle-class political liberalism was not democratic or equalitarian. A voice in politics was to be

Shown above are four men whose writings greatly influenced the economic philosophy of the nineteenth century. David Ricardo (far left) and Thomas Malthus (center left) believed that economics operated according to natural laws and that the industrial class as a whole was doomed to misery. Jeremy Bentham (far right) felt that the main function of government should be the creation of individual freedom, for freedom led to happiness. John Stuart Mill (center right), on the other hand, thought that the state should impose some controls on businessmen for the sake of the workers; individual freedom, he felt, should be considered secondary to the interests of the people as a whole.

enjoyed only by those who had a substantial position in society.

In England "the Manchester School" was the name given to a group of politicians who strove in Parliament to defend and spread the tenets of economic liberalism. They advocated the repeal of various import duties on grain known as the Corn Laws, the adoption of free trade, and a foreign policy based on economic cooperation rather than international rivalry. During the middle years of the nineteenth century, the policies of these men won wide acceptance and made supreme the economic and political prestige of a middle class thoroughly devoted to laissez faire.

In England the middle class wished to remove the tariffs that still remained as a vestige of the mercantilistic system. These duties, mainly the Corn Laws, protected the Tory agricultural interests. Uninterested in profits for the landed gentry, the businessmen wanted cheap food for their workers. The Anti-Corn Law League, organized at Manchester in the heart of industrial England, put on a brilliant propaganda campaign and, partly as a result of crop failure and high food prices, succeeded in having the hated laws removed from the statute books in 1846.

In theory, at least, the middle class was interested in maintaining laissez faire in both the domestic and the international fields.

Technologically more advanced, England became for a time a free-trade country, an indication that it did not fear the competition of foreign products in its home market. However, in other countries the middle class wanted business freedom at home but government protection against foreign imports which might undersell the local goods. By sponsoring lopsided tariff laws, these businessmen hoped to discourage the cheaper English goods from competing with their own wares.

Theory and practice diverge. Summarizing the views of economic liberalism, we obtain the following middle-class political, economic, and social philosophy, which dominated not only England but eventually all the western world until the 1870's:

(1) Every man knows what is best for himself, and if every person is free to do those things for which he is best fitted, society will obtain the maximum contributions from its members.

(2) There should be as little regulation of business by government as possible. The economic structure should consist of freely competing units "held in equilibrium by force of competition, much as the material universe is held together by the attraction of gravitation."

(3) Society should not have to support economic parasites. If competition is allowed to work unimpeded, weak and inefficient

firms will be forced out of business. The force of competition will also remove the dishonest businessman who adulterates his products or cheats the public in other ways, because the consumer will buy only from the ethical businessman.

(4) If the forces of supply and demand are allowed to work at will, prices will tend to reach an equilibrium which will be fair both to the producer and to the consumer.

(5) Unimpeded self-interest will be the "dynamo of progress." Goods will become better, new commodities will be introduced, and important inventions will be perfected because there will be no limit to the rewards offered to the intelligent and to the persevering.

(6) There is an alliance between wealth and virtue. Freedom in the business world offers rewards commensurate with a person's ability, sacrifices, and application. Poverty is not the concern of the well-to-do, for it is mainly the consequence of improvidence, shiftlessness, immorality, and laziness.

(7) The government should be used only to protect the nation from foreign aggression, to protect foreign investments, to maintain peace and order at home, to enforce contracts, and above all to protect private property.

On paper, the laissez-faire philosophy of the middle class seemed logical and, indeed, a positive aid to social and economic progress. However, a wide gulf soon appeared between theory and practice. Because of monopolistic practices and secret collusion between competitors, the operation of competition did not always ensure fair prices. Nor did competition ensure the survival of honest and efficient businesses. Underhanded and unfair competition often wrecked the more ethical and scrupulous firms. Unable to obtain the necessary information, the public was not able to judge whether or not goods were adulterated or stock watered.

It also became increasingly difficult to reconcile the great wealth enjoyed by a few with the poverty borne by the many. In our discussion of the factory system, we saw the terrible living and working conditions of most of the people. Furthermore, legislation prevented them from achieving anything like an equal bargaining position with their economic masters. In time it became obvious even to the middle class that poverty was not necessarily a result of personal improvidence.

STIRRINGS OF REFORM

Beginnings of social protest. Gradually, the bourgeoisie were faced with a rising class consciousness among the mass of working people. In the opening decades of the nineteenth century there were numerous angry demonstrations by workers rebelling against their miserable lot. In 1819 in Manchester, for example, a mass meeting of common people, called to discuss their grievances, was forcibly dispersed by soldiers. In the melee a dozen people were killed and several hundred wounded. But protest was not restricted to the working class alone. Liberal-minded members of the middle class protested against the social ravages of burgeoning industrialism. Intellectuals in such countries as England, France, and Germany became appalled by the human misery that had come in the wake of the Industrial Revolution, and their sentiments did not long remain unexpressed. In England the writings of Dickens, Disraeli, Carlyle, and Ruskin attacked the ugliness, meanness, and misery of industrialism. In Disraeli's novel *Sybil* (1845), the author points out that Queen Victoria really rules over two nations:

. . . between whom there is no intercourse and no sympathy; who are as ignorant of each other's habits, thoughts, and feelings, as if they were dwellers in different zones, or inhabitants of different planets; who are formed by a different breeding, are fed by a different food, are ordered by different manners, and are not governed by the same laws . . . THE RICH AND THE POOR.[14]

Thomas Carlyle stormed against the worship of Mammon by the industrial capitalists, whom he dubbed the "Working Aristocracy":

The Working Aristocracy must strike into a new path; must understand that money alone is *not* the representative either of man's success in the world, or of man's duties to man; and reform their own selves from top to bottom, if they wish England reformed. England will not be habitable long, unreformed.[15]

Ruskin, too, despised the hectic pursuit of wealth under the competitive rules of laissez faire. In a famous passage he characterized the two classes in this fashion:

In a community regulated by laws of demand and supply, but protected from open violence, the persons who become rich are, generally speaking, industrious, resolute, proud, covetous, prompt, methodical, sensible, unimaginative, insensitive, and ignorant. The persons who remain poor are the entirely foolish, the entirely wise, the idle, the reckless, the humble, the thoughtful, the dull, the imaginative, the sensitive, the wellinformed, the improvident, the irregularly and impulsively wicked, the clumsy knave, the open thief, and the entirely merciful, just, and godly person.[16]

Similar criticisms were expressed in France by the celebrated authoress George Sand, who wrote sympathetically about French workers.

Sources of political pressure. What groups applied the political pressure necessary to pass reform bills? In England the landowning aristocracy were a powerful force in this camp. Resenting the rise of the *nouveau riche* mill owners in the cities, the nobles were willing to curb middle-class power by passing Factory Acts setting various restrictions on woman and child labor and excessively long working hours. As leader of the Tory landed gentry, Disraeli advocated a political alliance between the workers and the nobility to counteract the power of the bourgeoisie (see Chapter 12). Among the factory owners themselves, such men as Robert Owen (see p. 178) realized that altruism and profits made a good team. If the conditions of the workers were improved, their efficiency and productivity would likewise rise.

The men most responsible for the Factory Act of 1833 were Tory squires who had little use for democracy but possessed a humanitarian spirit and resented the callous indifference of the urban mill owners toward human rights. Among these Tories was Anthony Ashley Cooper, Earl of Shaftesbury (1801-1885), who contributed his religious zeal to the cause of social philanthropy and was the father of all nineteenth-century factory legislation. In teaching the governing classes of England to assume responsibility for the welfare of the people, he tried unsuccessfully to push through an act that would provide public schools for children of the poor. He also urged better public health facilities and improvement of the condition of agricultural laborers.

Early factory reforms. England, the birthplace of the new industrialism, led the way in enacting reform legislation that ameliorated the lot of the workers. As early as 1802 an act forbade the employment of children for more than twelve hours a day, exclusive of time for meals, and in some cases night work was prohibited. But because supervision was in the hands of local authorities, little benefit resulted. In 1819 another attempt was made to ease the plight of children under nine years of age and to limit to twelve hours a day the work of youngsters whose ages ranged from nine to sixteen. Again, unfortunately, no real provision was made for the enforcement of an anythingbut-radical reform.

Conditions in the factories remained so brutal, unhealthful, and inhuman that finally an aroused public demanded a complete investigation. Such appalling statistics were disclosed that the first effective Factory Act in British history was passed in 1833. This law forbade the employment in textile factories of children under nine, restricted the hours of labor for children between nine and thirteen to forty-eight a week and the hours of children between thirteen and eighteen to sixty-eight, and made it illegal for anyone under eighteen to work at night. Government inspectors were to help administer the act. This piece of legislation, which strikes us today as laughably inadequate, prompted such manufacturers as John Bright to exclaim that it was "most injurious and destructive to the best interests of the country" and violated "the liberty of the subject" and "freedom of contract"—as though

The sketch above, from an early edition of Charles Dickens' *Bleak House* (1852-1853), illustrates a passage in which the author satirized the aggressive, middle-class "do-gooders" whose willful and stern philanthropy was often worse than no philanthropy at all. The passage below describes the visit of the particularly aggressive Mrs. Pardiggle to the cottage of a poor bricklayer and his family and shows the antagonism which she created there:

"Mrs. Pardiggle, leading the way with a great show of moral determination, and talking with much volubility about the untidy habits of the people (though I doubted if the best of us could have been tidy in such a place), conducted us into a cottage ... the ground floor of which we nearly filled. Besides ourselves, there were in this damp offensive room—a woman with a black eye, nursing a poor gasping baby by the fire; a man, all stained with clay and mud, and looking very dissipated, lying at full length on the ground, smoking a pipe; a powerful young man, fastening a collar on a dog; and a bold girl, doing some kind of washing in very dirty water. They all looked up at us as we came in, and the woman seemed to turn her face towards the fire, as if to hide her bruised eye; nobody gave us any welcome.

'Well, my friends,' said Mrs. Pardiggle; but her voice had not a friendly sound, I thought; it was much too business-like and systematic. 'How do you do, all of you? I am here again. I told you, you couldn't tire me, you know. I am fond of hard work, and ... the harder you make mine, the better I like it.'

'Then make it easy for her!' growled the man on the floor.

'I wants it done, and over. I wants a end of these liberties took with my place.... Now you're a-going to poll-pry and question according to custom—I know what you're a-going to be up to. Well! You haven't got no occasion to be up to it. I'll save you the trouble. Is my daughter a-washin? Yes, she *is* a-washin. Look at the water. Smell it! That's wot we drinks. How do you like it, and what do you think of gin, instead! An't my place dirty? Yes, it is dirty—it's nat'rally dirty, and it's nat'rally onwholesome; and we've five dirty and onwholesome children, as is all dead infants, and so much the better for them, and for us besides. Have I read the little book wot you left? No, I an't read the little book wot you left. There an't nobody here as knows how to read it; and if there wos, it wouldn't be suitable to me. It's a book fit for a babby, and I'm not a babby.... How have I been conducting of myself? Why, I've been drunk for three days; and I'd a been drunk four, if I'd a had the money. Don't I never mean for to go to church? No, I don't never mean for to go to church. I shouldn't be expected there, if I did; the beadle's too gen-teel for me. And how did my wife get that black eye? Why, I giv' it her; and if she says I didn't, she's a Lie!'

He had pulled his pipe out of his mouth to say all this, and he now turned over on his other side, and smoked again. Mrs. Pardiggle, who had been regarding him through her spectacles with a forcible composure, calculated, I could not help thinking, to increase his antagonism, pulled out a good book as if it were a constable's staff, and took the whole family into custody. I mean into religious custody, of course; but she really did it, as

if she were an inexorable moral Policeman carrying them all off to a station-house."

A cartoon from an 1843 edition of *Punch* shows vividly the contrast between the aristocratic ease of the rich and the misery of the poor. In the satirical words of *Punch*, "It's gratifying to know that though there is much misery in the coalmines, where the 'labourers are obliged to go on all-fours like dogs,' there is a great deal of luxury which results from it. The public mind has been a good deal shocked by very offensive representations of certain underground operations, carried on by an inferior race of human beings, employed in working the mines, but *Punch*'s artist has endeavoured to do away with the disagreeable impression, by showing the very refined and elegant result that happily arises from the labours of these inferior creatures."

The lithograph by Daumier at the right, made in 1848, contrasts the gluttonous bourgeois in his frock coat and top hat with the earnest workingman in his shabby clothes. Daumier was a merciless critic of the bourgeois society of his native France. He once suffered a prison sentence for a vitriolic cartoon which showed members of the middle class directing the ragged, starving lower classes to feed incessantly a greedy giant, Louis Philippe. At the end of his career, Daumier had produced almost four thousand lithographs, considered masterpieces of the art. See also "The Legislative Belly" on page 206.

children of nine had freedom of contract in bargaining with mill owners.

Other reforms in England gradually whittled away at the old doctrine of laissez faire by broadening state regulation of economic enterprise. While conditions in the textile factories were improved by the 1833 Factory Act, those in the mines remained ghastly. Children of six and seven were employed underground twelve hours a day to open and shut ventilation doors and to be harnessed "like dogs to a go-cart" to haul coal wagons. In 1842 a law was passed forbidding the employment in the mines of women and of girls and boys under ten. In 1846 a law was enacted to limit the work of women and children in textile factories to ten hours a day, and in succeeding years other improvements were made in factory conditions. Inspection and enforcement of health and safety in factories and railways were required by law. As industrialization spread, other countries tended to pass regulatory legislation similar to that in England. In 1836 Massachusetts passed the first act regulating child labor in the United States.

Labor unions legalized. In the field of labor relations, measures were enacted giving workers freedom to organize trade unions. In 1824 the harsh Combination Acts were repealed in Britain, and from this time on workingmen had the legal right to organize and to bargain peacefully with employers, though legal restrictions continued to limit trade union activity. For a long time the authorities vigorously opposed strikes, thereby restricting the strength and effectiveness of the unions.

On the Continent, meantime, the workers who had failed to achieve substantially more political and economic rights in the revolutions of 1848 turned more and more to unions as a means of obtaining their demands for higher wages, shorter hours, and more healthful working conditions. In France in 1864 workers were allowed by law to combine for strikes. During the 1860's, trade unionism made progress in Germany, as it did in the United States, where the number of local unions multiplied almost fourfold between 1861 and 1865. In 1869 a powerful industrial union made its debut in America under the florid name "The Noble Order of the Knights of Labor."

Philanthropic movements. The nineteenth-century middle class—whether in England or elsewhere—was hardly consistent in its attitudes. On the one hand, the middle class espoused an economic doctrine which fostered ruthless competition and opposed giving either help or protection to the factory workers because this would interfere with laissez-faire "laws." On the other hand, middle-class humanitarian sympathies and the emphasis upon the rights and dignity of individual men (both stimulated, as we saw in Chapter 5, by the romantic movement) combined with the persistent influence of Christian doctrine to favor a humanistic rather than a mechanistic solution to social problems. In evaluating nineteenth-century attitudes, a social historian has stated: "As the Nineteenth Century grew older, humanity pervaded more and more all the dealings of life . . . The advance in humanity, far more than the boasted advance in machinery, was the thing of which the Nineteenth Century had best reason to be proud; for in the wrong hands machinery may destroy humanity."[17]

During the opening decades of the nineteenth century, individual efforts to improve social and economic conditions increased. Private individuals with large fortunes, and with equally large hearts, set to work to found hospitals, homes for orphans, schools, and other charitable agencies. In the United States, for example, George Peabody was an outstanding philanthropist. In 1862 he gave $700,000 to provide better housing for workers, and five years later he established a fund of $3,000,000 for advancing education in the American southern states. Other philanthropists in both England and America gave funds for mechanics' and apprentices' institutes, such as Cooper Union in New York, which sponsored free educational courses for workers and provided free access to books. Apprentices' and mercantile libraries in the United States laid the basis for the free public library movement, which began around 1850.

Governments also began to take an interest in the social welfare of their people. In France between 1850 and 1870 the government of Napoleon III enacted various laws for protecting and improving the lot of the common people. Savings banks were set up, as were orphan asylums, and the law permitting imprisonment for debt was repealed.

By the 1840's there had been substantial modification of the middle-class theory of laissez faire. The state was increasingly expanding its jurisdiction over industry, protecting workers in mines, factories, and on the railways. In addition, philanthropy by private individuals was doing much to make life easier and fuller for the masses. In spite of these reformist efforts, there was evidence of a growing rift between the bourgeoisie and the workers.

THE CHALLENGE OF SOCIALISM

The emergence of socialism. In all ages men have dreamed of ending misery and poverty by creating some form of model society. Plato in his *Republic* imagined just such an ideal state. During the Middle Ages, the Age of Faith, it was natural that men should envision their better world in the hereafter; but with the Renaissance came a growing interest in this world. Hopes of heaven were not enough for Renaissance worldlings or for their ideological successors, the eighteenth-century *philosophes,* who preached that intelligence applied to human problems could create a better and more harmonious society—a veritable heaven on earth.

With the advance of the factory system after 1815, enlightened men everywhere, in both the upper and lower ranks of society, criticized its evils and proposed reforms. Many of these critics were simply well meaning, liberal-minded humanitarians, but some, to be known later in the century as socialists or communists (the two terms were once used synonymously), were determined advocates of basic change in the existing political and economic systems. Attacking the nineteenth-century capitalistic system with its laissez-faire philosophy as both unplanned and unjust, they condemned the concentration of wealth and called for public or worker ownership of business. Above all, they insisted that harmony and cooperation—not ruthless competition—should control economic affairs. Generally convinced of the goodness of human nature, they dreamed of a happy future when:

. . . there will be no war, no crimes, no administration of justice, as it is called, no government. Besides there will be neither disease, anguish, melancholy, nor resentment. Every man will seek, with ineffable ardor, the good of all.[18]

This humanitarian idealism, a legacy of the Enlightenment, was typical of the small band of theorists who created the early socialist movement.

Utopian socialism: Saint-Simon, Fourier, Owen. The early socialists of the nineteenth

An illustration from the American magazine *Puck* praises the philanthropic efforts of the American industrialist Peter Cooper. In the background is Cooper Union, which the philanthropist established to provide free lectures, libraries, and art galleries for the workingmen.

century are known as the Utopians. (They were so called by Karl Marx later in the century, and the name has stuck.) The Utopian socialists were inspired largely by the ideas of the Enlightenment and the French Revolution, namely, the belief in the progress and perfectibility of man. The first prominent Utopian was a French nobleman, Claude Henri de Rouvroy, Count de Saint-Simon (1760-1825). Primarily a believer in the idea that human society must be scientifically organized and directed, this thinker had no use for what he considered to be the hit-or-miss system of laissez faire.

Although his views were misty and ill-formed, Saint-Simon influenced many prominent thinkers, notably the pioneer French sociologist Auguste Comte (see Ch. 11). In his last years Saint-Simon suffered much adversity and escaped starvation only through the help of a few loyal friends. But he continued to express his conviction that society should be planned. Defining a nation as "nothing but a great industrial society" and politics as "the science of production," Saint-Simon took as his motto, "Everything by industry; everything for industry." He believed that men should voluntarily accept the rule of a paternalistic despotism of scientists, technicians, and captains of industry who would "undertake the most rapid amelioration possible of the lot of the poorest and most numerous class."[19]

Francois Fourier (1772-1837), another French reformer, also believed that future society must be cooperative. He spent much time in working out an ideal plan for a communal living unit, which he termed the "phalanstery." Some eighteen hundred persons were to work and live together in an economic "phalanx" composed of agricultural laborers, mechanics, and artisans. Each person in this voluntary, cooperative group was to pursue that type of work which best suited his taste. Fourier believed that the phalanx would be very profitable, with profits running as high as 30 per cent of the investment. All such profits would be divided five-twelfths to labor, four-twelfths to capital, and three-twelfths to management. While the plan was endorsed by many prominent thinkers of the day, attempts to found cooperative Fourierist communities were unsuccessful. The famous Brook Farm colony in Massachusetts was one such short-lived experiment.

A more practical reformer and Utopian socialist was Robert Owen (1771-1858), a successful mill owner in Scotland. It was his cardinal belief that man was shaped by his environment. This optimistic view of human nature held that if men lived in the right surroundings, their moral and physical standards would be improved.

To prove his point, Owen transformed New Lanark, the site of his textile mills, into a model community. Here between 1815 and 1825 thousands of visitors saw neat rows of workers' homes, a garbage collection system, schools for workers' children, and clean factories where the laborers were treated kindly and where no children under eleven were employed. After having brought about factory reforms in Parliament, Owen migrated to the vicinity of Evansville, Indiana, where, in 1825, he founded a Utopian colony called New Harmony. This, however, lasted only a short time as a socialist community.

Partly because of the impracticality of such colonies as New Harmony, which were usually based upon the somewhat naïve notion that men naturally loved one another (or could be educated to love one another) and that men could live happily together in a communal society were it not that capitalist competition set man against man; partly because the Utopians made no practical, large-scale attempts to meet the problems of the depressed nineteenth-century industrial classes as a whole; and partly because ultimately Marxist socialism supplanted it— Utopian socialism failed.

Christian socialism. In addition to the Utopians, another school of nineteenth-century socialists arose that drew its inspiration directly from the teachings of Christianity. This group, the Christian socialists, aimed at showing that the doctrines of the Sermon on the Mount were socialistic in character.

In England, the Christian socialist leaders were drawn largely from the Methodists, the Unitarians, the Quakers, and the Broad

Church party of the Church of England. Generally credited as the founder of Christian socialism in England was the author and clergyman, Frederick Denison Maurice (1805-1872). A strong advocate of mass education, he established a college for women and another for workingmen. Another well-known Christian socialist was the famous novelist, reformer, and chaplain to Queen Victoria, Charles Kingsley (1819-1875), whose indictment of social evils appeared in his novels *Alton Locke, The Water Babies,* and *Yeast.*

The French socialist Louis Blanc, although himself not a member of the Christian socialist group, once summed up the ideas of this group in these words:

What is socialism?—It is the Gospel in action. How so?—Socialism has as its goal to realize among men the four fundamental maxims of the Gospel: Love one another; Do not unto others what you would not have that they should do unto you; The first amongst ye shall be the servant of the rest; Peace to all men of good will.[20]

Abhorring violence and drawing upon traditional ideas of a universal Christian community, the Christian socialists preached good will between all classes and favored experiments with socialist colonies. They stimulated interest in working-class reforms and attempted to instill into organized Christianity a realization of the social aspects of the teachings of Christ.

Anarchism. Another socialist school of thought that became known as anarchism was founded by the French theorist Pierre Proudhon (1809-1865), who wrote pamphlets urging the organization of society on a purely voluntary basis. The anarchists insisted that human nature is inherently good but is warped and depraved by authority. They repudiated all governmental compulsion, proposing instead free cooperation among the members of society. Proudhon's dictum, "Property is theft," was widely repeated by radicals everywhere.

In discussions on how to achieve their ends, the anarchists heard advocates of divergent tendencies—on the one hand, pacifists and humanitarian philosophers who were content to dream about a perfect society; on the other, devotees of violence. As you will read in later chapters, a member of the latter group was Michael Bakunin, an expatriate Russian revolutionary who insisted that God, the family, and the state must all be repudiated and that only when the world was without law could it be free.

Karl Marx and scientific socialism. Up to the middle of the century, socialism remained a minor factor in European thinking, as the principal goal of groups of ordinary people was the winning of political equality and universal suffrage. Economic questions remained secondary. Furthermore, the theoretical tendencies of early socialism were not very alarming to the wealthy and aristocratic classes.

This calm was shattered in 1848 when workers on the Continent began demanding the "right to work" during the revolutions of that year. Simultaneously, and almost unnoticed, there appeared early in 1848 a new form of socialism that advocated violence, preached warfare between the classes, and repudiated traditional religion and morality. The instigator of this rabid form of socialism was the German social philosopher Karl Marx.

Born in the Rhineland, at Trier (Treves), of German-Jewish parents who had been converted to Christianity, Karl Marx (1818-1883) obtained his doctor's degree after studying the philosophical ideas of Hegel. Failing to find a career in university teaching, he was forced to make a precarious living as a journalist. Following his marriage to Jenny von Westphalen, a girl of aristocratic family, he went to Paris where he became interested in socialistic ideas. It was in this city that he began his lifelong friendship and literary collaboration with Friedrich Engels (1820-1895), the son of a wealthy German factory owner. In 1845 Marx was expelled from France by the authorities, and with Engels he went to live in Brussels.

In January 1848 Marx and Engels published the famous *Communist Manifesto.* This stirring document contained practically all the elements of what came to be known as scientific socialism. It opened

While in London, Karl Marx once worked as a feature writer for Horace Greeley's New York *Tribune*, supplying the paper with five hundred articles. Dissatisfied with his payment of five dollars per article, Marx accused Greeley of the "lousiest petty-bourgeois cheating."

with an ominous declaration: "A spectre is haunting Europe—the spectre of Communism." The *Manifesto* called for an implacable struggle against the bourgeoisie, proclaimed the inevitable revolution and the triumph of the masses, and closed with a stern warning:

The Communists disdain to conceal their views and aims. They openly declare that their ends can be attained only by the forcible overthrow of all existing social conditions. Let the ruling classes tremble at a Communistic revolution. The proletarians have nothing to lose but their chains. They have a world to win. Working men of all countries, unite![21]

The revolutions of 1848 (not in the least influenced by Marx, an obscure figure at the time) were welcomed by Marx as the dawn of a new era, the birth of a new society. Going to Germany to assist in its arrival, he was forced to flee when the revolutionary movement collapsed. From that time until his death in 1883, he lived a life of penury in London, supported largely by contributions from friends, especially Engels. Nearly every day Marx would make his way to the British Museum, where he collected material

for his various books, especially *Das Kapital* (*Capital*).

Marxian dialectical materialism. No matter what one may think of Marxian socialism, no one can doubt that *Das Kapital* constitutes one of the most influential books of modern times. In the mid-twentieth century, nearly half of the world has been organized on the basis of its teachings. Of the three volumes of *Das Kapital* (1867-1894), the last two, compiled from his notes and teachings largely by Engels, came out after Marx's death. In *Das Kapital*, some of Marx's essential principles were borrowed—with changes—from Hegel's philosophy.

Hegel, a leading German philosopher of the early nineteenth century, felt that history is not just a matter of chance. It is dynamic and unfolds as the result of a definite plan or process of change. History is made up of a number of culture periods, each the expression of a dominant spirit or idea. After fulfilling its purpose, the period is confronted by another contradictory idea or set of values. In Hegelian phraseology, the traditional "thesis" is challenged by the new "antithesis." Out of this struggle there emerges a "synthesis" of old and new. Then the cycle starts all over again. Thus, to Hegel, history is a process of unfolding, determined by an absolute purpose or idea, which orthodox Hegelians called God; the machinery of change was called historical dialectic.

Adapting Hegel's ideas for his own purposes, Marx set down the basic theories of his socialist system:

(1) The materialistic conception of history: "economic determinism." Marx believed with Hegel that history was a series of periods. Unlike Hegel, however, Marx was a materialist. In Marx's theory each era was characterized by distinctive all-determining economic features rather than by a dominant pattern of ideas. Marx held that economic forces are elemental in dictating the course of history; all other supposed factors—patriotism, religion, art—are only "ideological veils." For Marx, all history could be explained in terms primarily of the social organization best adapted to the current

means of economic production. When the economic organization of any era changed, it took the whole social and ideological structure with it to a new phase of history.

(2) The dialectic. In addition to Hegel's unfolding process, Marx adopted the Hegelian concept of change—the dialectic—but the combatants became social classes, not ideas. Marx maintained that history was a series of clashes between the exploited and the exploiting group: slave against master in ancient Greece, plebeian against patrician in Rome, serf against lord in the Middle Ages. The bourgeoisie, who by means of the organization of trade and the Industrial Revolution had created a new urban and industrial society, were now opposed by the modern industrial proletariat. The bourgeoisie themselves had helped create the factory system of production—and with it their own nemesis, the proletariat. The latter class was destined to learn, through the mutual association and cooperation necessary in performing the tasks of modern factory production, how powerful it could be if united against the dwindling body of "exploiters," destined increasingly to be the objects of its hatred. Finally, realizing its true power and common interests, the proletariat would inevitably unite and overthrow its natural enemy, the bourgeoisie.

(3) The concept of "surplus value." Here Marx borrowed from the laissez-faire economists who held that economic value represented "congealed labor." Only human labor, Marx argued, can create new economic values. But under the capitalist system, the worker is not fully paid for all the values he creates. Suppose, for example, that a worker could produce in six hours the necessary economic values to supply his needs. However, the employer, as employers often did in the nineteenth century, keeps the worker producing goods for, say, twelve hours. The employer is in possession of a "surplus value" of six working hours, which he has "expropriated" from the worker. From this "stolen" surplus value the employer draws profits and capital. With the latter he buys necessary buildings and machinery; and from it also comes interest and rent, the

fruits of capital. Under capitalism, organized for the benefit of the dominant social class—the bourgeoisie—the workers are systematically robbed of the fruits of their toil and, because they must sell their labor for the best terms they can get, are paid only enough to keep them from starvation.

(4) Increased mass poverty. Under the capitalist system, Marx and Engels argued, it is inevitable that the proletariat will get progressively poorer and that they will become increasingly bitter at being exploited.

(5) Concentration of capital. As competition is a relentless rule of capitalism, the most ruthless of the bourgeoisie will destroy more and more of their competitors, forcing them into the ranks of the proletariat.

(6) Recurrent economic crisis. Because the masses cannot buy the goods they produce, economic crises, with overproduction and unemployment, will become the rule.

(7) The classless society. Finally comes the day when the proletariat rises up and takes over the means of production. When labor is driven to such a desperate plight, then, says the *Manifesto*, "The knell of capitalism is sounded. The expropriators are expropriated."[22] When the bourgeoisie are eliminated as the owners and controllers of all business, classes will cease to exist. In this apocalyptic new society, private property will be abolished, exploitation of one class by another will cease, class warfare will end, and the millennium, a virtual heaven on earth, will arrive. Out of the conflict between the masses and the bourgeoisie will appear the new synthesis, the classless society, the ultimate social organization of the modern industrialized era.

Furthermore, all this was inevitable; it was inherent, said Marx, in the social process. Some modern-day liberals might believe that social progress is principally achieved by peaceful means—through education and the free development of the individual. Marxists believe that progress comes inevitably through conflict and struggle.

Devoting most of his ammunition to attacking the obvious injustices of unreformed nineteenth-century industrial society, Marx paid comparatively little attention to the kind of society that would supersede the bourgeois state. He once remarked that he had no interest in "writing the kitchen recipes of the future." The final transition, he enigmatically indicated, would be the "dictatorship of the proletariat" (Lenin would elaborate later on this idea), after which the state would supposedly wither away, leaving a society in which there would be no coercion.

The First International. Marx did not live to see the gradual spread of his ideas and their later amazing expansion; but he did help to found an international organization of workers, called the First International. At the initial meeting in London in 1864, Marx was able to commit the organization to his program by forcing the secession of the moderate wing. Believing that the solidarity of proletarian class interests took precedence over loyalty to any country, Marx was eager to encourage proletarian internationalism; but the First International failed to make much headway. There were savage quarrels between the anarchist group led by Bakunin and the majority commanded by Marx. While Marx and his followers would utilize the state as the agency for initiating their classless society, the anarchists bitterly opposed this extension of state activity. Finally, in 1873, the First International closed up shop.

Weaknesses in Marxist doctrine. Shortly after the publication of *Das Kapital*, certain weaknesses and inconsistencies in its argument were perceived. In interpreting history, Marx sees at work in all ages his "dialectical materialism," the class struggle. Yet in some miraculous fashion this "dominant" feature of history is to disappear when the communist society is established.

Furthermore, there is something ironic in Marx's term *scientific socialism* (i.e., based upon supposed inevitable laws of social development "scientifically" observed and explained by Marx) "in contrast to the Utopian variety." With his talk of a final social stage in which there would be no coercion and no exploitation and with his vague notions about the organization of his ideal society, he really was akin to utopian dreamers of all ages. (See the Frontier essay on p. 428.)

Marxism attempted to explain all historical events as the consequence of a single cause. Most historians do not find the problem of historical causation so simple. Explaining all social and intellectual phenomena in terms of economics and class struggle, Marx's theory denied the importance of intellectual and idealistic influences, although Marxism itself as a body of ideas about history and social change became in time a great intellectual influence and historical force.

Marx's alter ego Engels once declared:

The final causes of all social changes and political revolutions are to be sought, not in men's brains, not in man's better insight into eternal truth and justice, but in changes in the modes of production and exchange. They are to be sought, not in the *philosophy* but in the *economics* of each particular epoch.[23]

And Marx himself once stated:

It is not the consciousness of men that determines their existence, but, on the contrary, their social existence determines their consciousness.[24]

If socialism is inevitable and not the product of human thought and willful human action, why is it necessary for Marxists to seek converts and to exert efforts to put their socialist program into effect? Why did Marx organize an international party to carry out his ideas? To some critics, it appeared that Marxists were rationalizing their own ruthless will to power and hatred of those in power by means of a dogma about their "inevitable" success. The true dynamics of Marxism appeared to be the hatred and envy of Marxists for those more fortunate than they.

Marxism in its orthodox form appeared to predict for the world an era of strife and catastrophe that would end only with the advent of an impossible utopia. "Progress" brought about through inevitable economic upheaval and class warfare did not appear to most moderate-minded men to be progress at all but the exaltation of irrational and violent factors in human development.

Another basic weakness in Marxian socialism was that Marx's materialism and atheism were unacceptable to supporters of all the world's major religions. For the traditional religious belief in a happy afterlife where all earthly injustices and evils would be corrected, Marx substituted the promise of a heaven here on earth, the hope of a worldly utopia. Supporters of Marxist dogmas were assured that it was in the "nature of the historical process" (an ideological substitute for Divine Providence) that this should be so. One had but a single choice: to get into step with the "inevitable" or be destroyed. True believers were convinced that they alone possessed the truth. For this reason Marxism itself has been termed a "surrogate religion"—a materialistic substitute for true religion.

As we shall see in Chapter 13, it became increasingly evident that many of the prophecies made in the *Communist Manifesto* were not to be borne out by events. Workers in most capitalist societies did not think of themselves as proletarians at all but as patriotic adherents of a national state, or as members of a trade or of a church or of any of the other diverse social groups into which men normally associate themselves. The "proletariat" was a myth, for the "proletarians" did not think of themselves as such.

While there was, of course, movement in all societies up and down the social scale, Marx's prediction that the mass of men under capitalism would become increasingly reduced to economic misery and near starvation did not come about. Instead, the miserable economic position of workers in many industrial countries in the nineteenth century improved as more efficient means of production made industrial products more readily available to all and reformist legislation and trade unions helped raise industrial wages and improve working conditions. An increasing number of industrial workers, indeed, enjoyed a "middle-class" standard of living and could not be convinced that they belonged to a society in which they were members of an exploited proletariat.

Nineteenth-century critics of Marxist dogmas saw in Marxism only the promise of a massive, despotic leviathan state that would control all and dictate to all. They pointed to Marx's claim that the heads of representative government in bourgeois states, even though democratically elected, were only an "executive committee" of capitalists, a government by and for capitalists. Marx did not place any real faith in traditional democratic techniques. Yet, some radicals who wished to attain socialism by democratic means accepted parts of the Marxist position. While these political leaders, known as Social Democrats, did enjoy some electoral success later on (see Chapter 12), the more dogmatic supporters of Marxist doctrines were to achieve power in the twentieth century—notably in Russia and China—only by force and the concerted efforts of a small elite of professional revolutionists. No majority vote ever sanctified their accession to power.

Another difficulty Marxists encountered was the patriotism of most European workers. Faced by a choice between supporting national interests, as in World War I, and supporting Marxist dogmas about the class nature of war under capitalism, most European workers chose to support their nations. Nationalism was a stronger influence than socialism.

Despite the erroneous impression that in 1848, with a mighty blast of the trumpet, Marx and Engels thundered forth their doctrines to the amazement of the entire world, Marxist ideas were slow to take hold. Their greatest period of acceptance came later in the nineteenth century and in the first half of the twentieth century. But after 1848 disgruntled workers had a program of action, a gospel of faith, that held out the assurance of a promised land of security and plenty. They had the flaming indictment of capitalism provided by the *Communist Manifesto*. Radical thinkers who were later to adopt scientific socialism as laid down in *Das Kapital* confidently expected the imminent triumph of proletarian revolution, much the same way as their ideological forefathers during the French Revolution had expected the imminent universal rule of rationality and virtue.

SUMMARY

Inventions, new industrial processes, the growth of populations, the spread of industrialism, the rise to dominance of the middle class, and the genesis of the class war in Marxian socialism—all the changes brought about during the First Industrial Revolution (1815-1870) added up to a radical transformation in the lives of men in the western world. Previously untapped sources of power were harnessed to operate railways and steamships. Efficient new machines gradually replaced hand methods of production. The nineteenth-century factory, with all its accompanying evils—the employment of young children, the lack of safety precautions, the hideous slums—turned out more and more goods. From its focal point in England, the Industrial Revolution spread to much of Europe and later circled the globe.

The first effects of the Industrial Revolution were abysmally cruel. The urban workers, the so-called proletariat, became industrial serfs at the mercy of the middle class. Man's inhumanity to man has seldom been so vividly illustrated. An unregulated, junglelike system of industry was sanctified and justified by bourgeois moralists and laissez-faire philosophers who held that all human ills were solely the fault of the individual, not of society.

Voices were soon raised against the exploitation of the many by the few. Middle-class intellectuals and humanitarians denounced the dismal social conditions which followed in the wake of the factories and demanded a more enlightened view of human welfare. Reform legislation corrected some of the worst abuses. In another vein, Utopian and Christian socialists proposed the complete reconstruction of society.

With the appearance of the *Communist Manifesto* in 1848, Karl Marx preached a hard and ruthless dogma. He felt that an unbridgeable chasm divided two warring classes—the bourgeoisie and the proletariat. The danger of a class war, however, was to be averted in most of the advanced industrial nations by social reforms and by improvement in the economic status of the masses. In tsarist Russia the misery of the masses appeared to support the contentions of *Das Kapital* and the *Communist Manifesto*. Under the leadership of Lenin and his followers, Marx's doctrine was to be elaborated upon and propagated in a fanatical form that would plague the twentieth century.

CHAPTER 7

To the Barricades!

REACTION AND REVOLUTION: 1815-1850

Introduction. When the Congress of Vienna completed the task of remaking the map of Europe in 1815, the triumph of conservatism seemed accomplished. The aggression of France was checked; Napoleon Bonaparte had been made the scapegoat for French Revolutionary imperialism; legitimate monarchs were reëstablished and encouraged to curb radicalism. But the edifice of reaction built at Vienna was not strong enough to withstand the forces directed against it. In the great revolutionary upheaval that originated in France and spread through much of Europe, such ideas as popular suffrage, intellectual and religious freedom, pride in nation, and equality for all under the law had been given wide currency, and though the upheaval was ended, both intellectuals and the underprivileged in many lands clung to these liberal concepts. In addition, the conquests of

territories and subjugation of peoples by Napoleon had actually strengthened the counter-spirit of nationalism. During the revolutionary and Napoleonic eras the spirit of nationalism had risen in Russia, Spain, Italy, the Germanies, and other lands violated by French imperialism. After 1815 those peoples who enjoyed national liberty were resolved to defend it, while those who were denied this privilege and lived under alien governments were increasingly determined to throw off the foreign yoke.

The bankers, merchants, and industrialists who rose to prominence with the expansion of manufacturing, as well as the new class of industrial workers, gained no satisfaction from the salvaging of aristocratic privilege at the Congress of Vienna. In time, captains of industry and factory employees would unite to topple despots and eject foreign governments. As we shall see, a flurry of revolts broke out in 1820 and 1821, another epidemic of revolutions challenged conservatism in 1830, and a climactic outbreak of rebellion and overthrow came in the historic year of 1848.

After 1815 the forces of nationalism, democracy, and middle-class ambition all found expression in the Romantic Movement. Reacting against the cold rationalism of the Age of Reason, which had seemed to reach its unhappy fruition in the bloody days of the Jacobin Republic and the military campaigns of Napoleon, men turned to romanticism for hope and promise. The romantics wrote enthusiastically of liberty, of nonconformity, of the virtue of nationhood or the sin of despotism, of the wonderful brotherhood of man. Leaders like Lamartine, Mazzini, and Kossuth minimized the many disagreeable difficulties standing in the way of the achievement of equality and liberty and naïvely placed their faith in fine-sounding constitutions and the "natural" goodness of man.

In the decades after 1815 much was done to alter the conservative arrangements made at the Congress of Vienna. Belgium, Greece, and Serbia were freed from alien rule, and in France and Britain government was made more responsible. But the failure of the revolutions of 1848 cruelly dashed the hopes of millions of liberty-loving Europeans. Romanticism had failed to face the prosaic facts of economics. And while the trend after 1848 was a transfer of political power from the landed gentry to the middle class, the result was a new antagonism between the workers and their employers, the new moneyed interests.

The middle class, representing the philosophy of liberalism, championed the rights only of the rich and the successful. The workers demanded democracy, universal suffrage, equal political rights for all. The violent contradiction between these two attitudes was ignored for a time, while working class and middle class united to seize political influence from the aristocracy and its instrument, irresponsible monarchy. But as the era of reaction following the Congress of Vienna faded, the course of several revolutions exposed the coalition as unnatural and unworkable. Much of the history of western Europe after 1850 will concern the new power struggle between capital and labor.

THE CONGRESS SYSTEM

The problem of change. Reactionary as the settlement made by the Congress of Vienna seemed, Metternich and the other conservative statesmen who were its architects actually introduced with it a principle of great potential significance. The so-called "Concert Europe," a system of diplomacy initiated by the Congress of Vienna, was a very primitive step toward the principle of international government.

Metternich recognized the connection between domestic affairs and international relations. As one of those responsible for the ultimate curbing of the French Revolution and overthrow of the French Empire, Metternich believed that any move anywhere toward liberalism or nationalism, which had proved such potent weapons in the French arsenal, might provoke new revolution, disturbing the peace and threatening his control. If revolution were to be prevented and the restored Old Regime maintained, the affairs of any European nation were the concern of all where questions of liberalism and nationalism were concerned.

Metternich's immediate purpose, of course, was to maintain the Vienna settlement. The Quadruple Alliance, signed by Austria, Prussia, Russia, and Great Britain in November 1815, was in effect a declaration of intent among the great powers to act in concert to support a new instrument of international law, the treaty created by the final session of the Congress of Vienna in June 1815. The concept of the concert of Europe persisted through a series of nineteenth-century congresses until the Congress of Berlin in 1878. The first congress after Vienna, held at Aix-la-Chapelle in 1818, actually registered changes: France was admitted to the circle of great powers on the basis of good behavior since Napoleon, and the Quadruple became the Quintuple Alliance; foreign occupation troops were withdrawn from France and the indemnity reduced. The Metternich principle that the maintenance of peace re-

In one of the many contemporary French cartoons satirizing the Congress of Vienna, Talleyrand (from left to right) stands by waiting to see how matters develop, Castlereagh hesitates, Metternich leads the "dancing," the king of Saxony clutches his crown in fear, and Genoa slavishly tries to enter into the spirit of the occasion.

quired maintenance of the *status quo* was reaffirmed, however.

Although the early congresses attempted to prevent changes in the *status quo* internally, in the long run the concert system became a means for attempting collective action on necessary changes among the European states. Prior to the nineteenth century, treaties had made no provision for change; the agency of change was the unilateral application of force, or war. At first under the congress system, force was used by and with the consent of the concert. Later, forceful change already initiated was registered and approved, or modified, by action of the concert. The concert of Europe did not solve the problem of international government to preserve order in the international community, but it implied the problem existed. The problem of international government has still not been solved in the twentieth century, and for much the same reason that Metternich's congress system broke down—the force of nationalism.

Nature of the nationalist movement. In 1815 the people of the western world turned eagerly to the pursuits of peace. For about a quarter of a century their lives had been disrupted by almost continuous war. Now the Congress of Vienna signaled the return of peace—though not, unfortunately, of tranquillity and prosperity. The return of economic stability was delayed by the destruction and dislocation of war and by the disturbing new industrialization. In addition to economic tensions, there was also deepseated political uneasiness as the spirit of Liberty, Equality, and Fraternity continued to influence the peoples of Europe. Almost immediately after the Congress of Vienna, various groups impelled by the force of nationalism began to work against the political arrangements made in 1815.

In this chapter we shall begin the story of the successes and the failures of nationalism in Europe after 1815. As we trace the development of European nationalism, it will become apparent that this movement assumed three forms. One involved the unification of separate states, inhabited by people of the same nationality, into a single large national state. The classic examples of this form of the nationalistic movement are the unification of Germany and Italy. The second form of nationalism was the striving of such subject nationalities as the Norwegians, Greeks, Irish, Serbs, Poles, and Czechs for independence from alien rule. When an independent nation desired to unite with itself people of the same nationality living under an alien government, this third aspect of nationalism was known as irredentism. Later in the century—after most of Italy had become united and independent—patriotic Italians regarded Venetia, populated by Italians but still under Austrian rule, as *Italia irredenta* (unredeemed Italy).

Pillars of the Old Regime. While not always attempting to bring back the most obvious evils of the Old Regime, European statesmen in the Age of Metternich did wish to restore much of the "good old days" as they existed before 1789. Working in their favor was the universal revulsion against bloodshed and turmoil. Many Europeans who enjoyed none of the privileges of the old order accepted its return as a price they were content to pay for peace.

In most of the nations the forces of conservatism were based on the restored monarchies, the Church, and the aristocracy. Despite the blows dealt to monarchism by the French Revolution, this system had behind it a strong tradition. The recent excesses of republicanism and Napoleonic ambition had given monarchy, as a concept of legitimately constituted authority, a new vigor which was to carry it down to the end of the nineteenth century almost unscathed. In addition to monarchy, the forces of conservative restoration could, in general, rely upon the Church. For many Europeans, the logical rationalism of the Enlightenment and its *philosophes* had proved inadequate in trying times of conflict. There was, in consequence, a revival of religious faith and a turning back to the Church, both in Protestant and Catholic circles. As Madame de Staël, one of the foremost intellectuals of the early nineteenth century, declared:

I do not know exactly what we must believe, but I believe that we must believe! The eighteenth century did nothing but deny. The human spirit lives by its beliefs. Acquire faith through Christianity, or through German Philosophy, or merely through enthusiasm, but believe in something.[1]

This religious revival, in natural opposition to the revolutionary denial of both divine and secular authority, threw support to authority in the form of the restored monarchs.

Behind kings and clerics were the large landowners, mainly from the old aristocracy. While industrialism was gaining rapidly in England and making inroads in Belgium and France, the bulk of wealth was still in land and the dominance of political power still in the hands of landowners. The great landowners were naturally inclined to support the post-1815 restoration.

Conservatism triumphant. These conditions help explain why the forces of nationalism, liberalism, and democracy were effectively stifled for some time after 1815. In Italy and Spain, restored rulers savagely repressed reform movements. Even though England was regarded as the most liberal regime in Europe, here also the ruling classes showed their fear and suspicion of new ideas and suggestions for reform. In France, where the restored monarch, realizing the impossibility of returning completely to conditions of 1789, granted the people a legislature and a charter of basic social and legal rights, the prevailing atmosphere was nevertheless quite conservative and the franchise was given only to the wealthiest citizens.

Under the strong hand of Europe's most influential statesman, Metternich, the Austrian empire can be regarded as the classical land of reaction after 1815. Practically the whole paraphernalia of the Old Regime was carried on into the nineteenth century. Everywhere there was surveillance and censorship. No printed matter could be imported without special permission. In the schools the study of history and government almost disappeared. The universities were singled out as dangerous sources of sedition; government spies attended lectures, and professors had to supply lists of the books they read. Students were closely observed by the government; they could not form societies or go to foreign countries to study, and they had to attend church and go to Confession. The great mass of people in the Austrian empire had no voice in government and no safeguard against government violation of their basic rights.

As in Austria, the rulers of most of the German states tried to go back to the *status*

Again in 1830 barricades appeared in Paris (below right) when the French revolted against the arbitrary acts of Charles X. Charles fled to England and for a short time gains were made under Louis Philippe. During the rash of revolutions in 1848 Louis Kossuth (above left) made a stirring speech before the Hungarian Diet in which he criticized the government and demanded reforms. This speech helped in-

spire the Viennese to rise in revolt (above right). After the March Laws made Hungary practically independent, it became clear that Kossuth was interested in the Magyarization of Hungary but not in the claims of other national groups there. In March 1848 rioting in Berlin (below left) led Frederick William to promise governmental reforms that he failed to carry out.

REVOLUTIONS 1820-1821

PORTUGAL
SPAIN
SARDINIA-PIEDMONT
NAPLES
GREECE

REVOLUTIONS 1830

BELGIUM   BRUNSWICK
HESSE-CASSEL   SAXONY   POLAND
FRANCE
PARMA
MODENA
PAPAL STATES

REVOLUTIONS 1848

PRUSSIA
SAXONY
HESSE-CASSEL   BOHEMIA
FRANCE   AUSTRIA
SARDINIA-PIEDMONT   LOMBARDY   HUNGARY
VENETIA
PAPAL STATES
NAPLES

common German nationality or flag. There were no central courts and no executive; there was only a legislature of dubious status. The Confederation consisted of a potpourri of free cities, electorates, margraviates, duchies, grand duchies, and five kingdoms—all of which were sovereign. The legislative body of the Confederation, the Diet, was in effect a meeting of ambassadors representing the states. And the Diet was devised to block change, for all important measures required a two-thirds vote.

As to conditions in the Balkans and eastern Europe, the nearer one approached Moscow and Constantinople, the farther away appeared the prospects of reform and good government. In the Balkans a decaying and vicious empire under the Turkish sultans oppressed and mistreated such subject peoples as the Greeks, Rumanians, and Bulgarians. In Russia, notwithstanding Tsar Alexander's flirtation with liberalism, the country was backward and the tsar's rule despotic. There was little industry, the volume of trade was small, and the middle class was almost nonexistent. In the social scale there were only two classes of people: rich, cultured nobles, living on large estates, and peasants, living in misery as serfs on their masters' lands.

It can be seen that after 1815 little opportunity was given for the growth of European nationalism and liberalism. Despite the most careful precautions, however, violent revolutions soon broke out against the reactionary regimes in Italy and Spain. It was to safeguard against the consequences of such uprisings that the Congress System, whose origins we have just examined, was devised.

Reaction and repression in Spain and Italy. In 1812, during the struggle against Napoleon, groups of Spanish liberals had convened a parliament that had adopted a democratic constitution, but it was ignored by the Bourbon monarch Ferdinand VII after his restoration to the throne in 1814. Cruel and utterly ruthless, Ferdinand has been described as "having the heart of a tiger and the head of a mule."

After 1814 all thought of reform in Spain was swept aside. The former privileges of

quo ante, before Napoleon had brought into their domains the disturbing notes of Liberty, Equality, and Fraternity. Nearly all the German states except Bavaria, Baden, and Württemberg were ruled by absolute governments. Many German liberals, imbued with nationalism, were indignant at the failure of the Congress of Vienna to unify the German states into a strong nation. Instead, the weak and ineffectual German Confederation was set up with no provision for a

the nobility and the Church were restored, the Inquisition was reinstated, and the Jesuits were given control of education. There was no parliamentary government; the country was run by the *camarilla*, a selfish inner clique around the king. The press was gagged, there was no free speech, and political offenders were imprisoned by the thousands. Furthermore, the majority of Spain's impoverished and ignorant inhabitants remained primitive in agriculture and backward in industry.

The more intelligent and liberal Spaniards were aroused by the pitiable conditions of their country, and in all the important towns revolutionary bodies called *juntas* were set up. Most dangerous to the reactionary monarchy was the rising discontent in the army, where bad food and lack of pay had brought many troops to the brink of mutiny.

In Italy conditions were, if anything, worse. The consequences of the French Revolution had been felt here more than in any other land outside of France, because Napoleon had destroyed so many of the institutions of the Old Regime. The old despotic states had for a time been replaced by French-inspired regimes; new systems of administration and law had been introduced; and the Inquisition and the last remaining vestiges of serfdom had been swept aside. All in all, the effect of the Napoleonic conquest had been to give the mass of the Italian people more liberty than they had ever known before and to bring a considerable measure of political unity to their native land.

After the Congress of Vienna, however, the country was again fragmented. Lombardy and Venetia, as we have seen, were turned over to Austria. The rest of the country was divided into minor states, most of which were under the thumb of the Austrian government. The state governments returned to their old inefficient ways. Taxes were high, favoritism and corruption flourished, and desperate men took the easy road of brigandage as a way out. Many patriotic Italians joined a secret revolutionary society, the *Carbonari* or "charcoal burners," who

had first organized in the mountain forests and soon spread throughout Italy and into France and Spain.

First attempts to overthrow the Vienna settlement: Spain and Italy. In 1820 a mutiny in the Spanish army was followed by a general uprising. In answer to the rebels' demand that the liberal constitution of 1812 be restored, Ferdinand VII glibly agreed. A liberal parliament was assembled, various reforms were carried out, and the king was kept a virtual prisoner.

The news of the successful Spanish revolt reached the kingdom of Naples and Sicily in Italy, where the people were living under the oppressive regime of their Bourbon king. Revolution broke out, and the king was forced to give his people a constitution patterned after the one drawn up in Spain in 1812. The king then swore to defend the constitution.

In addition to the revolt in Naples, an uprising took place in the kingdom of Sardinia, where revolutionists forced the abdication of the king. In Portugal, too, there was an uprising and a movement for constitutional government. At the same time, news arrived from the Balkans that the Greeks had risen against their Turkish overlords (see p. 194).

Congress of Troppau and Congress of Laibach. This startling news disturbed the conservative statesmen of Europe. Determined to stamp out rebellion and to support the 1815 settlement, Metternich set about organizing collective action for the suppression of the revolutions.

In 1820 the members of the Quintuple Alliance met in the Congress of Troppau to decide what should be done about the uprising in Naples. Representatives of Russia and Austria urged intervention. England opposed such action; Castlereagh, the English foreign secretary, insisted that the purpose of the alliance was to maintain the boundaries set up in 1815, not to interfere in the domestic affairs of states. But despite England's opposition and the lukewarm attitude of France, the three other powers (Prussia, Russia, and Austria) drew up the Protocol of Troppau, which stipulated:

States which have undergone a change of government due to revolution, the results of which threaten other states, *ipso facto* cease to be members of the European Alliance. . . . If, owing to such alterations, immediate danger threatens other states, the powers bind themselves, by peaceful means, or if need be by arms, to bring back the guilty State into the bosom of the Great Alliance.[2]

Having decided to intervene in the Neapolitan revolt, in 1821 the conservative powers met at Laibach (see Reference Map 1). At this conference England was represented only by observers. The Congress of Laibach invited the king of Naples to appear before it. Rightly suspecting their monarch of treacherous designs, his parliament was reluctant to see him go, but the king avowed, "I will do everything to leave my people in the possession of a wise and free constitution." Once among his reactionary friends, however, the king of Naples repudiated his promises, supported intervention, and welcomed the use of an Austrian army to place him back on the throne. The Austrian troops quickly scattered the rebel forces, and the king was restored to the throne of Naples. The restoration was a triumph for Metternich.

Congress of Verona: intervention in Spain. Meanwhile, liberal sentiment in England was growing stronger, and the government was drifting further away from its ultraconservative allies on the Continent. When another congress was convened in 1822 at Verona to consider intervention in Spain, the English foreign secretary Canning sent word to the conclave that:

. . . while England was no friend to revolution, she did emphatically insist on the right of nations to set up for themselves whatever form of government they thought best, and to be left free to manage their own affairs, so long as they left other nations to manage theirs.[3]

After this time the British refused to send any representatives to these gatherings.

The fact that the reactionaries in France had by now gained the upper hand, despite the moderate tendencies of King Louis XVIII, explains why the French government at the Congress of Verona volunteered to send an army into Spain to crush the reform movement. The French troops carried out their assignment, and a brutal reaction followed. Terrible punishments were meted out to the patriots who had forced the king to restore the constitution of 1812; all acts of the liberal Spanish parliament since the rebellion of 1820 were annulled; and *juntas* were set up to seek out and punish all liberals.

Weakening of the Congress System. Elated by its success in Italy and Spain, the conservative alliance sought to restore the authority of the Spanish king over his rebellious subjects in Latin America. First revolting against Napoleon's intervention, then against the reactionary Ferdinand, most of the American colonies had secured their independence by the early 1820's. In trying to intervene in this struggle on behalf of the Spanish king, the European Congress System met its first defeat. Great Britain, which enjoyed a flourishing trade with the new Latin-American states, displayed no enthusiasm for renewed Spanish control. As if the shadow of the British navy was not sufficiently daunting, President Monroe in 1823 warned the European powers that the United States would regard the proposed intervention as an unfriendly act.

For all practical purposes the experiment in suppressing revolution through international government was beginning to fail, although efforts continued until the breakdown of the system had become unmistakable. When Tsar Alexander attempted to convene the Congress powers in 1824 to discuss the problem of Greece and Turkey, Canning refused to send an English representative. Delegates of Russia, Prussia, Austria, and France met in St. Petersburg early the next year, but in May 1825 the meeting disbanded without registering any accomplishments. Austria, in particular, had refused to sanction a plan for using Russian troops against Turkey. Canning could well declare that from now on it was "Every nation for itself, and God for us all."[4] The Congress System was to receive a final shattering blow later in the decade when stra-

THE OTTOMAN EMPIRE 1815

(Map showing the Ottoman Empire in 1815, with labels including Montenegro, Bosnia, Serbia, Belgrade, Moldavia, Wallachia, Bucharest, Bulgaria, Albania, Greece, Athens, Constantinople, Black Sea, Armenia, Caspian Sea, Turkey, Syria, Bagdad, Mediterranean Sea, Jerusalem, Egypt, Cairo)

tegic and sentimental interests led some of the great powers to align themselves with the cause of revolution in Greece.

The Turks and their subject peoples. Let us turn our attention now to the Near East, soon to become a perennial trouble center threatening the peace of Europe and, in the twentieth century, the world.

Outside the family of European nations and not represented at the Congress of Vienna, the Ottoman empire of the Turks ruled over a medley of restless and miserable subject peoples. In 1815 the sultan in Constantinople was still the head of an empire which included the Balkan peninsula as well as much of North Africa and Asia Minor. The Christian subjects of the Turks were concentrated mainly in the Balkans.

The Balkan peninsula lies between Asia and Europe, roughly south of the Danube and Drava rivers. Rumania, which is north of this Danube-Drava boundary, is also usually included as part of the Balkans. Easily

accessible from both Europe and Asia, this area has long been an international crossroads and battleground. Mountains break the Balkans into many distinct and often almost inaccessible regions. The largest element in the area is Slavic, although some of its peoples, such as the Greeks, are a mixture of many racial strains. Scattered all over the Balkans in the nineteenth century were Jews and Armenians, who, with the Greeks, carried on most of the commerce of the region.

In the Balkans the Turks were a small minority lording it over their Christian subjects, who were known as *rayahs,* a word that means "herds" or "cattle." The *rayahs* were mistreated by the local officials, called *pashas,* who were quite capable of appropriating the daughters of *rayahs* for their harems. The *rayahs* were forced to pay a special tax and were forbidden to have firearms. Most galling was the "squeeze" put on every promising trade and business by dishonest officials.

THE TREATY OF ADRIANOPLE 1829

The Greek revolt of 1821. While these revolts early in the century had begun to shake Turkey's Balkan empire, it was the uprising of the Greeks in 1821 that attracted the attention of Europe in general and the Congress powers in particular. The French Revolution had stirred the nationalistic spirit of the Greeks, and patriots emerged to urge independence. In 1821 an uprising took place. Turkish officials in southern Greece were murdered, and in retaliation the sultan ordered the massacre of all Greeks in Constantinople—even the patriarch there was hanged. The fighting was carried on by both sides with extreme brutality. In 1822 the world was horrified by news of the Turkish massacre of the entire Greek population of the island of Chios.

Metternich wanted the revolt to burn itself out, but the Greek cause had many friends. Hellas had been the cradle of European freedom and civilization, and liberals and intellectuals everywhere demanded that Greece be liberated. Lord Byron wrote:

The isles of Greece! the isles of Greece!
Where burning Sappho loved and sung,
Where grew the arts of war and peace,
Where Delos rose and Phoebus sprung!
Eternal summer gilds them yet,
But all, except their sun, is set.[5]

Philhellenic societies were formed, and both supplies and volunteers were sent to aid the Greeks. The most famous of these volunteers, Byron, lost his life from fever while with the rebel army.

Meanwhile, the Turks turned for help to their powerful, semi-independent vassals in Egypt. Up to this point the Greeks had controlled the sea, but a strong Egyptian fleet managed to land a well-trained army in Greece, and by 1827 the country was reconquered.

Greek independence achieved. In Russia, in 1825, Nicholas I had ascended the throne. While detesting revolutions, the new tsar detested the Turks more, and from a national point of view it was good Russian policy to weaken Turkey in order to pave the way for Russian annexation of the Dardanelles. The

The Turks made no attempt to root out Christianity. Religious toleration was practiced, and in some cases the Turkish government supported the Church as a means of ruling the *rayahs*. As all Muhammadans were equal in status regardless of race or nationality, it was a temptation for the *rayahs* to accept Islam. Many did so, but most Christians remained true to their faith.

Revolt of Montenegrins and Serbs. The first Balkan people to obtain independence from Turkish rule were the Montenegrins, Serbians who lived in a particularly mountainous area near the Adriatic. In 1799, after a long, heroic struggle, these brave mountaineers had won a formal recognition of independence from the sultan.

In Serbia itself (an area north and east of Montenegro), another independence movement had begun in 1804 with a general uprising led by a patriot named George Petrovich, popularly known as "Black George," who secured Russian support. In 1826 Turkey was forced to place Serbia under Russian protection.

growing interest of Russia in the Greek question caused Great Britain much concern, for Britain was opposed to allowing Russia a free hand in the Balkans. The upshot was an agreement in 1827 between France, Britain, and Russia, whereby these powers pledged themselves to secure the independence of Greece. This was another serious blow to Metternich's Congress System.

The three powers sent a squadron of warships to Greek waters, and in the naval battle at Navarino the allied squadron totally destroyed the Egyptian fleet. Although an armistice was requested by the allies, a new war with Turkey now ensued. French troops drove the Turks out of Greece, and a Russian army crossed the Balkan peninsula. The sultan had no recourse but to make peace, which was arranged in 1829 by the Treaty of Adrianople, and thus Greek independence was recognized. The treaty also established Serbian autonomy, although the Serbs continued to pay tribute to the Turkish government.

Nationalism in the Balkans had registered important advances, but the victory was far from complete. Many Greeks still lived under Turkish rule, as in Crete; complete independence had still to be secured by Serbia and Rumania; and the restless Bulgarians still remained under the harsh Ottoman yoke. These national frustrations were eventually removed by diplomacy and war.

FRANCE, ENGLAND, AND

THE REVOLUTIONS OF 1830

Liberal institutions in France. The defection of Britain had heralded the demise of the Congress System, and by 1829, the year in which Greek independence was recognized, it was no longer an effective weapon of international conservatism. In 1830 additional sledge-hammer blows fell upon the machinery of coercion devised by Metternich and his backward-looking colleagues. The eruption began in France, the only great

power which at all approached England in liberal political institutions.

The restored Louis XVIII, brother of the unfortunate Louis XVI, who had fallen victim to the guillotine in 1793, had been willing to accept many of the reforms of the French Revolution. Accordingly, a charter had been given to France which established a form of constitutional monarchy. The king still had extensive powers: he could direct foreign affairs, appoint and dismiss all officials, and propose laws. In the bicameral legislature, patterned after the British Parliament, members of the upper house belonged by hereditary right, and those of the lower chamber were chosen by an electorate limited to the highest taxpayers; only one man in seventy could vote. Since members of the legislature were not paid, they were invariably drawn from the wealthier classes. The effect of these provisions was to limit representative government to deputies of the nobles and other wealthy landed proprietors. Although France in 1815 had a governmental system much more liberal than that presided over by Louis XVI, the country had a long way to go before it could claim to have democratic institutions.

Outside the realm of government proper, the charter granted the French people substantial social, religious, and legal rights. All citizens were now equal before the law. Freedom of speech and of religion were guaranteed, and arbitrary arrest was forbidden. The restored government of Louis XVIII accepted the abolition of feudalism and made no attempt to restore the properties confiscated from the Church and nobles during the Revolution. Napoleon's most significant measures, such as the Napoleonic Civil Code, the Concordat with the pope, the centralization of local government, and the administrative system, were also retained. So, too, was the state's tight control over education. State control over what was taught in Church-supported primary and secondary schools remained a source of bitter controversy throughout the nineteenth century and often became a determining factor in French politics.

The Parisian worker, shown here in a sketch published in 1830, exerted a powerful influence on French politics.

Divisions of political sentiment in France. Moderate though the restoration seemed, it had the backing of only a small party. Among the politically conscious in France, two antagonistic groups developed, neither of which supported the restoration settlement. On the one hand were the Ultras, opponents of the Revolution and supporters of strong monarchy and privilege, who thought the constitution too liberal and wanted to turn the clock back to the days of the Old Regime. At the core of the Ultra faction were the nobles, many just returned from exile, and the leaders of the Church, whose position in France had been seriously reduced by the Revolution.

At the other end of the political spectrum were the liberals and radicals (republicans) —the disenfranchised lower bourgeoisie, students and intellectuals, and laborers in the larger cities—who wanted the constitution made more democratic and the electorate broadened to include themselves. The truth was that the Revolution, though over, was still an issue; the government of France was to be balanced precariously between the opponents and adherents of the Revolution, or toppled over, until the ideals of the Revolution were finally fulfilled in the last decade of the century in a fully democratic republic.

France under Louis XVIII. In his nine years on the French throne, Louis XVIII managed with fair success to steer a middle course between the Ultras on the one hand and the liberal and radical reformers on the other. His aim was to "heal the wounds of the Revolution." In the sessions of the legislature, ultraroyalist and republican representatives engaged in bitter debates. Fully reported in the press, these harangues did much to educate the public concerning basic political principles as well as current issues.

During Louis' reign a characteristic feature of modern French politics emerged—the multiparty system. Whereas in England there were but two political parties, both recruited in the main from similar strata of society and sharing a common political tradition, in France numerous loosely organized factions appeared, and as time went on it became the practice for ministries to be formed of men from a coalition of parties in the legislature instead of from one majority party as in England. Thus the basis was laid for a pattern of government destined to be less stable than those of Britain and the United States. Majority government may be weakened by factional squabbles within the major parties, but coalition government, representing numerous minority parties, is far more likely to be accompanied by bewildering changes and upsets in administration, as witnessed by the Third and Fourth French Republics in our own time.

Charles X and reaction. Louis XVIII was succeeded on his death in 1824 by Charles X, and the political balance maintained precariously by Louis at once swung heavily to the Right. Like the late monarch, Charles

The barricades, symbol of revolution in France, are immortalized in Delacroix' dramatic painting of the July Revolution of 1830.

was a brother of the beheaded Louis XVI and had been an émigré during the Revolutionary era, but, unlike the late king, Charles accepted none of the facts of his age and had long been leader of the Ultras. Historians have little to say of this monarch except in denunciation. In a word, Charles X was the reincarnation of the reactionary aristocrat of the mid-eighteenth century. The "King of the Ultras" was a stanch exponent of divine right, did not believe in religious freedom, and possessed a fanatical urge to rule France arbitrarily; but, being a man of mediocre mind, he had neither the ability nor the determination to do so.

The July Revolution in Paris. Having become involved in a squabble with the legislature, which refused to support his attempt to force an ultraroyalist program on it in July 1830, Charles dissolved the legislature and issued a series of ordinances gagging the press and limiting the franchise. Galled by this violation of the constitution, Parisians arose in rebellion. The then narrow streets of Paris were quickly choked with overturned carts, boxes, tables, and paving stones. Behind these barricades crouched the armed revolutionaries, who returned the fire of the soldiers with good effect, while from the roofs of the houses their families showered tiles and rocks upon the royal forces. Again and again in nineteenth-century revolutions, patriots fighting from behind such barricades succeeded in toppling despotism.

After three days a new liberal faction took over the government, and Charles fled to

England. The new government was constituted by an agreement between the French republicans, led by the aging Marquis de Lafayette, and the liberal monarchist supporters of the Orleans branch of the Bourbon monarchy.

The bourgeois monarchy of Louis Philippe. The July Revolution gave France a new king, Louis Philippe (1830-1848), the duke of Orleans, and a new, definitely bourgeois outlook. Like William III of England in 1688, the new king accepted his crown from the people; he was "king of the barricades" and "king of the French," in contrast to Louis XVIII and Charles X, who had claimed to rule by divine sanction. Thus the principle of the sovereignty of the people supplanted the principle of divine right. In token of this, the revolutionary tricolor replaced the white flag of the Bourbons as the emblem of France. The form of government remained almost unaltered; the suffrage was extended to include the moderately wealthy bourgeoisie, but it did not yet include the lower middle class or the common people. The new regime was the first wholly middle-class government to be set up on the Continent.

The 1830 revolts elsewhere in Europe. Word of the July Revolution spread like the wind throughout western Europe, and patriots and liberals everywhere determined to strike for freedom against the Metternich system (see p. 210). In central Italy there were revolts against the reactionary regimes in the Papal States, Modena, and Parma. In the German Confederation, though Prussia and Austria were untouched, uprisings occurred in several states, forcing the ruler's abdication in two of them and in others the grant of more liberal constitutions.

Revival of Polish nationalism. During these 1830 revolutions, some of the most heroic and exciting events took place in Russian Poland, which since the Congress of Vienna had been ruled by the tsar as a semi-independent kingdom. After 1815 a remarkable national revival had stirred the Poles, who worked to restore the prosperity of their country and to make their city of Warsaw an imposing capital. A national bank was founded, and textile weavers from Saxony established the foundations of a flourishing textile industry. The University of Vilna became a center for the study and dissemination of Polish culture.

For a few years the Poles remained content with their rising prosperity and mounting national hopes; unfortunately, however, the Russian tsar, Alexander I, had begun to lose the tinge of liberalism he had exhibited at the Congress of Vienna and was now anxious to repress Poland's growing national spirit. As Lord Byron wrote, this autocrat:

. . . had no objection to true liberty,
Except that it would make the nations free.[6]

In 1824 the secret Polish student societies were betrayed, and stern repression followed. The following year the ultrareactionary Tsar Nicholas I came to the Russian throne. He opposed the nationalist sentiment in the Polish Diet, and unrest among liberals mounted rapidly. News of the July Revolution in France met with enthusiasm in Warsaw. In November 1830, Russian authority in Warsaw was overthrown by patriots who seized the treasury and arsenal and took control of the army. The Diet proclaimed Poland independent of Russia, with the right to select for itself the ruler of Poland.

Despite some brilliant victories, Polish resistance was effectively broken by Russian arms. By the summer of 1831 the Russian general could write to his master, the tsar: "Sire, Warsaw is at your feet." The revolt's chances of success had been lessened by the factions which developed around its own leaders, but it was crushed primarily by overwhelming Russian forces.

Under the shattering blows of defeat, Poland's liberties almost completely disappeared. The national Diet was abolished, and Poland sank to the status of an ordinary Russian province governed directly by Russian officials in St. Petersburg. Polish universities were closed. Thousands of patriots were deported to the Caucasus or Siberia, while others fled to western Europe or migrated to the United States. Notwithstanding its tragic defeat, however, Polish nation-

Breakup of the "marriage" of Belgium and Holland—a match arranged at the Congress of Vienna—is shown in this cartoon.

alism continued to live on. Many exiles made their way to Paris, where a hotel was purchased to house the headquarters of a Polish foreign office and court. Émigré scholars continued to create an important body of Polish literature.

In 1846 a brief but very bloody insurrection broke out, centering on the independent city of Cracow in the heart of Austrian Poland. Again, the uprising failed; but though their homeland was ruled by three powers —Russia, Austria, and Prussia—the Poles refused to give up their struggle for independence. Once again, in 1863, they made still another unsuccessful attempt to achieve their independence.

The Belgian revolution. In contrast to the disappointing outcome of the Polish revolution, the spirit of nationalism triumphed in Belgium. We recall that at the Congress of Vienna the Belgians had been united with Holland under the Dutch crown—a union which proved most unhappy. Wide differ-

ences in culture separated the two peoples. The Dutch were mainly Protestant, the Belgians Catholic; the Dutch were seafarers and traders, the Belgians farmers and industrial workers. The harsh and short-sighted policy of King William I of Holland toward his Belgian subjects caused deep resentment. Determined to make the Belgians into good Dutchmen, the king imposed on them Dutch laws, officials, and language.

When news of the July Revolution in Paris reached the Belgians, nationalistic feeling rose high in Brussels. An uprising began when excitable students attended an opera which glorified an Italian rebellion against foreign rule centuries earlier. The singing of the duet "O Sacred Love of the Fatherland" was the spark setting off demonstrations in the Belgian audience. Rioting broke out in the city, and a Dutch army sent to quell the disturbances was repulsed with heavy losses. The Belgians then announced their independence and drew up a liberal constitution.

The Dutch king immediately appealed to the conservative alliance for aid. The Belgian coup, he asserted, undid the territorial arrangements of the Congress of Vienna and ignored the legitimate rights of the Dutch House of Orange. Under other circumstances Metternich and the other supporters of the Congress System might have come to the assistance of the Dutch king. The Russian tsar, however, was busy "tranquilizing" the Poles, and Austria was occupied with revolutions in Italy. No help was forthcoming from France, for Louis Philippe's government, created in 1830 by revolution, was itself a repudiation of the principle of legitimacy laid down in 1815. England, whose political and commercial interests would generally be served by the independence of small states, saw no reason to oppose Belgian aspirations as long as the new state did not become a puppet of France.

Thus favored by fortune, with the support of France and England, a national assembly met in Brussels in 1831 and chose Prince Leopold of Saxe-Coburg-Gotha as king. When the Dutch monarch refused to accede, a French army forced his troops from Belgium while an English fleet blockaded the Dutch coast. Under such circumstances the king of Holland had no choice but to recognize the independence of the kingdom of Belgium. In 1839 the international status of the new state was settled. A treaty was drawn up in that year, signed by England, Austria, Prussia, Russia, France, and Belgium, which declared Belgium to be a "perpetually neutral state." (This was the treaty which Germany contemptuously dismissed as a "scrap of paper" when its troops invaded Belgium in World War I.) The signatory powers agreed to defend Belgium against aggression, and Belgium agreed not to become the ally of any nation and to defend itself in case of attack. After centuries of foreign rule —under the dukes of Burgundy, kings of Spain, rulers of Austria, and king of Holland —the Belgians secured their own government.

Depression and political reaction in England. The first decade after 1815 was a period of reaction in England as well as on the Continent. After a generation of almost continuous warfare, England in 1815 returned to the pleasant prospects of peace. The disturber of the peace in Europe, "Old Boney," had come to the end of his dazzling career at Waterloo, and never had English prestige been higher on the Continent.

For the masses of English people, however, victory over Napoleon did not bring contentment or plenty. After the government brought its huge war purchases to an end, the country became overstocked with goods, and factories soon closed down. Unemployment, further augmented by the demobilization of 300,000 soldiers, rose rapidly and resulted in widespread suffering. In a particularly sad state of distress and despair were the handloom weavers and other hand-skilled workers, who now began to feel the relentless squeeze of the machine. During the Napoleonic Wars, while prices were high, their products had been able to compete with machine-made goods, but the severe drop in prices after 1815 made it impossible for handworkers to make a living. In consequence they turned to wrecking factories and smashing machines. The gangs of masked workers who took part in this violence were called "Luddites" after a legendary leader known as "Ned Ludd."

Instead of sympathizing with the plight of the poor, unemployed, and even starving lower classes, England's aristocrats saw in their discontent only the evil Jacobin influence of the French Revolution. The Tory party, controlling the government, followed the doctrine of "peace, law, order, and discipline." In 1816 a mass meeting in London which passed a resolution calling attention to the intolerable economic condition of the people was forcibly dispersed. A serious epidemic of strikes broke out in the industrial areas. In 1819 a large meeting held in the city of Manchester to demand universal suffrage was dispersed by a cavalry charge with the loss of several lives. Terrified by what they believed to be the imminence of revolution, the ruling class enacted repressive legislation. Public meetings were restricted;

liberal newspapers were repressed; heavy fines were imposed on "seditious literature"; and in 1817 the Habeas Corpus Act was suspended.

The English monarchy had sunk to the lowest ebb in its history. In 1815 George III was seventy-seven years old and quite insane. The duties of kingship were administered by his son George, who was despised by most of his subjects. This ineffectual and immoral prince regent has been well described by an English historian as "always a liar, always selfish, bad in his private and public conduct, and without the least understanding of his age."[7]

In 1815 England was regarded by many European liberals of the middle class as the possessor of an ideal, time-tested form of government. But though England's political system was more advanced than most of those on the Continent, it left much to be desired. In the political union known as the United Kingdom of Great Britain and Ireland, for example, the Irish were a bitter, exploited national minority. (In Chapter 12 we shall see that the Irish problem was one of the most serious issues to face British statesmen in the nineteenth century.)

While England in 1815 can be said to have had a representative system of government, the British Parliament could not be regarded in any sense as expressing the will of the nation. Only 5 per cent of adult males could vote, and these were frequently under the control of men whom we would label today "political bosses." In religion there was toleration but no equality. The law divided the people into four groups: Anglicans, Nonconformists (such as Baptists, Quakers, and Methodists), Catholics, and Jews. Members of the Church of England—that is, the Anglicans—enjoyed many privileges denied to members of other religious sects. Catholics and Jews in particular suffered much discrimination.

Yet bad as conditions were in England, they were an improvement over those under which most of the people lived on the Continent. A visitor to the British Isles in 1811, for example, wrote:

. . . I should admit very readily that I have found the great mass of the people richer, happier, and more respectable than any other with which I am acquainted. I have seen prevailing among all ranks of people that emulation of industry and independence which characterise a state of advancing civilisation properly directed.[8]

The period of postwar reaction finally ended in the late 1820's with a series of well-considered, evolutionary (as opposed to revolutionary) reforms sponsored by the liberal branch of the Tory party under the leadership of Robert Peel and George Canning. These bills abolished capital punishment for over one hundred offences (a reform long demanded by Jeremy Bentham and other utilitarian philosophers and writers), created a modern police force for London, began the recognition of labor unions, repealed old laws which forbade non-Anglican Protestants to sit in Parliament, and by the Catholic Emancipation Bill gave equal rights to members of the Catholic faith. Then in 1832 came the great crisis in political reform and its successful resolution.

Reform movement in England. The July Revolution of 1830 in France contributed the impetus necessary for political reform in Great Britain. By this time not only was the British working class incensed against the system of privilege which ruled it, but British businessmen were determined to break the monopoly of the aristocracy in government. In this year the Duke of Wellington, now prime minister, made a fateful speech in which he declared that the constitution of the country was quite satisfactory for all its needs. This so aroused public opposition that the Iron Duke was forced to resign, and Lord Grey, the leader of the Whig party, became head of the government, thereby ending sixty years of almost continuous Tory rule, which had been dedicated to the maintenance of the status quo.

The new government under Grey immediately set about reforming Parliament. There was a crying need for such action. The House of Lords was dominated by the great nobles, while the House of Commons was heavily influenced by the landed gentry.

In a cartoonist's tribute to the Reform Bill of 1832, political corruption and the "rotten" boroughs are put through a grinder by Whig leaders and Britannia emerges triumphant.

Representation in the House of Commons had virtually no relation to the population; it has been estimated that 3 per cent of the population dictated the election of the members. Of 571 members of the Commons, 82 were elected by the counties controlled by the landed aristocracy, and the remaining 489 members came from incorporated towns, called boroughs. Many "pocket" boroughs were under the control of "borough mongers," political bosses who dictated the choice of the voters. In various depopulated "rotten" boroughs, members of Parliament were elected to represent areas which boasted only a handful of people or no longer contained any inhabitants. On the other hand, new and rapidly growing industrial towns, such as Manchester with 140,000 inhabitants and Birmingham with 100,000, had no representatives.

Reform Bill of 1832. Supported by members of the rising middle class, who were determined to break the aristocracy's political monopoly, and also by the workers, Grey's government introduced a bill to abolish the rotten boroughs, widen the franchise, and give representation to the new industrial towns. Defeated in the Commons at the outset, the bill was again introduced and passed, only to be defeated in the House of Lords. A revolution now seemed imminent.

After the bill had been introduced a third time but drastically changed by the upper house, the king, William IV, finally threatened to create enough new peers who would vote for the bill to pass the measure in the House of Lords. Confronted by this threat, the upper house passed the measure on July 7, 1832.

The measure as enacted did not represent a radical political change. It transferred the balance of power from the landed gentry to the upper middle class and emphasized the growing supremacy of the Commons over the Lords. The important fact is that, while the great Reform Bill did not represent an immediate substantial widening of the franchise (the working class was still disenfranchised), the bill indicated a new sensitivity to popular forces and thus constituted an initial step in breaching the wall of political privilege. The Reform Bill of 1832 did not introduce democracy into England, but it did make democracy ultimately possible. It foreshadowed future political reforms such as the second Reform Bill in 1867 and the third in 1884. The trend was thus begun which by 1900 was to make Great Britain the most democratic great power in western Europe.

The achievement of political democracy in England stands in sharp contrast to the same process in France. In the latter, there were wars and revolutions; in the former, the keynote was evolution and political gradualism. Great Britain has had an instinct for keeping intact its old political framework and adapting it to new uses with changing conditions. This explains why Great Britain has been able to keep its age-old monarchy and yet fit it into the structure of a modern political democracy.

Additional reforms. In the 1830's and 1840's, the humanitarian movement stimulated reform. Immediately following the first Reform Bill, several other notable reforms were enacted. Slavery was abolished in the British empire in 1833. The first important Factory Act (see Chapter 6) was passed in the same year, and in 1834 improvements were made in poor-law administration. In

1835 the Municipal Corporations Bill was enacted; up to this time the towns had frequently been governed by small, exclusive, aristocratic bodies that often filled their own pockets with taxes, but the new act instituted a uniform system of town government with popular election.

Tempers ran high both inside and outside Parliament. The historian Macaulay expressed the prevailing moderate view of preferring peaceful change to bloody revolution when he declared in the House of Commons:

Turn where we may, within, around, the voice of great events is proclaiming to us, "Reform, that you may preserve" . . . everything at home and abroad forebodes ruin to those who persist in a hopeless struggle against the spirit of the age. . . . Save the greatest, and fairest, and most highly civilized community that ever existed, from calamities which may in a few days sweep away all the rich heritage of so many ages of wisdom and glory. The danger is terrible. The time is short.[9]

The accession of the popular young Queen Victoria in 1837 was in itself a kind of reform. For more than fifty years, the fumbling and morally corrupt monarchy had been losing the respect and loyalty of the British people. Victoria did much to save the monarchy by making it an accurate mirror of middle-class convention and creed.

Breakdown of the Congress System. The liberal upsurge had won victories—by revolution in France, by an appeal to common sense in England. But in other areas—notably in Poland—the spirit of 1830 was unsuccessful. Liberalism also failed in central Italy, where the "white coats" of the Austrian army rooted out revolution and returned deposed rulers to their thrones. In the German Confederation, Metternich made a desperate attempt to stem the liberal tide and in 1832 persuaded the Diet to adopt his repressive Six Articles, somewhat reminiscent of the Carlsbad Decrees (see p. 210). Furthermore, in some of the German states where nominal political reforms had been achieved, the rulers managed to place in power conservative ministers who did their best to make the new reforms meaningless.

Despite these disappointments, the revolutionary surge—by its success in France, Greece, and Belgium and by the peaceful program of reform in Britain—had definitely obliterated the Congress System. By the early 1830's it was apparent that the conservative unity established in 1815 for the governance of Europe had broken up because of its failure to adapt itself to the growing forces of nationalism, middle-class liberalism, and industrialism.

During the 1830's and 1840's, the spirit of liberty and romantic nationalism continued to mount. The failure of some of the revolutions of 1830 had driven many of the young patriots underground or into exile, where the political air they breathed was filled with conspiracy, plots, and vague dreams of liberty. Many secret societies were formed following the example of those founded earlier to resist Napoleon. A book that was the bible of many young revolutionaries was written by a French radical, Buonarroti. His two-volume account of Babeuf's plot against the government of the Directory in France in 1796 was eagerly read by the radicals who likewise nourished plots against those in power.

REVOLUTION RENEWED IN WESTERN EUROPE

Growing spirit of discontent. In the wave of revolutions that swept western Europe in 1848, middle-class political liberalism, socialism, nationalism, and romanticism all exerted an important influence. As we shall see, the intellectuals and reformers who headed the uprisings tended to think of democracy and nationalism only in the abstract. They did not as a rule concern themselves with such problems as how liberty was to be shared once it was won. Were the workers to be given a voice proportionate to their numbers? Would the wealthier middle class agree to such an arrangement? And what exactly did nationalism mean? Did it guarantee self-determination for all national groups? If a country was made up of several nationalities, should one rule all or should each enjoy some kind of cultural autonomy? These were the practical issues that were to confront the reformers of 1848.

By the year 1848 a strong concentration of explosive discontent was shared by idealistic romantics, practical businessmen who sought the control of government, and city workers who desired a more equal distribution of the profits of industry. Particularly difficult was the plight of many peasants and workers in western Europe, as crops failed and an economic depression set in. There were food riots all over Europe in 1847. Political disturbances had also broken out in Austrian Poland in 1846 and in Switzerland in 1847. Although Austria suppressed its Polish rebels, Metternich's aid was insufficient to prevent a victory of the anticlerical, nationalist faction in Switzerland. A prophetic note for all Europe was sounded in the French legislature early in 1848, when Alexis de Tocqueville, who had written a famous book on democracy in America, warned his listeners:

We are sleeping on a volcano. . . . Do you not see that the earth trembles anew? A wind of revolution blows, the storm is on the horizon.[10]

France under Louis Philippe. The new social and economic forces of discontent were particularly strong in France. Since 1830 France had been ruled by the bourgeois monarch, Louis Philippe, who prided himself on being the representative of the business interests of his country. In his early years on the throne, the "king of the bourgeoisie" had made a point of walking about in the streets of Paris in a frock coat and top hat and carrying an umbrella like any solid middle-class citizen. For a time he had allowed ordinary citizens to flock through his palace, much as their American contemporaries poured through the White House during the presidency of Andrew Jackson.

Many achievements had been registered since 1830. The country was fairly prosperous, and the government, while not democratic, was moderate and sensible. Algeria, first invaded late in the reign of Charles x, had finally been pacified by the growing

French army, and French diplomacy had helped to establish an independent Belgium. At the same time, important gains had been made in railway construction and a good start secured in the direction of free elementary education.

On the debit side, it soon became apparent that the July monarchy had little concern with the lower classes. "Work, get rich, and then you can vote," was the government's advice. To Louis Philippe and his ministers prosperity, order, and, above all, international peace required the maintenance of the status quo. The king believed that peace was threatened by the demands of many liberals and republicans that France aid the nationalists of Poland, Switzerland, and Italy. "No reform!" became the platform of his reign.

Karl Marx, founder of modern socialism, attacked this bourgeois monarchy as:

. . . a stock company for the exploitation of France's national wealth, whose dividends were divided among ministers, Chambers, two hundred and forty thousand electors, and their following.[11]

Rise of proletarian and socialist opposition. What Louis Philippe failed to perceive was that new economic and social forces were at work which were bound to affect the political picture as well. The Industrial Revolution, entering France from England at an increasing tempo during his reign, was fattening the bourgeoisie whom he so sedulously represented, but it was also swelling the ranks of the politically conscious proletariat and creating those wretched conditions which gave rise to socialism with its aim of redesigning the whole economic and political system. Discontent grew rapidly among the working classes. In their city tenements and hovels, the proletariat brooded over their hatred and awaited an opportunity to settle accounts. This smoldering atmosphere was described by the German poet Heine, when he wrote about conditions in Paris in 1842:

Today when I visited some of the factories in the Faubourg Saint-Marceau and discussed there what kind of reading matter was being spread among the working men . . . I thought of Sancho's proverb, "Tell me what you have sown today and I will predict to you what you will reap tomorrow." For here in the workshops I found several new editions of speeches by old Robespierre, Marat's pamphlets at two sous a copy . . . and Buonarroti's *Baboeuf's Doctrine and Conspiracy*—all writings which smell of blood. The songs which I heard them singing seem to have been composed in hell and had a chorus of the wildest excitement. Really people in our gentle walk of life can have no idea of the demonic note which runs through these songs. One must hear them with one's own ears—for example, in those enormous workshops where metals are worked and where the half-naked, defiant figures keep time to their songs with the mighty blows which their great iron hammers strike upon the ringing anvil. . . . Sooner or later the harvest which will come from the sowing in France threatens to be a republican outbreak.[12]

Louis Blanc (1811-1882), a socialist theorist and journalist who had a large following among French workers, demanded state factories in which all the workers could obtain employment and where they would be allowed to divide among themselves the fruits of their labors. The discontented industrial workers concentrated in Paris and other growing factory towns added their demands for reform to the moderate requests of the lower bourgeoisie, who simply wanted the vote for themselves, and those of the intellectuals who were devoted to republican principles.

Another cause of the government's general unpopularity was the corruption that had pervaded the administration. Officials speculated with public funds, commissions in the army were sold, and a series of scandals in high society rocked the country. In addition, the reign of Louis Philippe was colorless and dull. So anxious was he to avoid issues that might threaten his position on the throne that scarcely a single event stands out to enliven his reign. Louis Philippe gave France a smug prosperity but little glory. The nation had little use for the pro-Austrian foreign policy of Louis' chief minister, François Guizot, who was excoriated as "a priest in Rome, an Austrian in Piedmont, a Russian at Cracow, and a Frenchman nowhere."[13]

Louis Philippe, "king of the bourgeoisie"

"Business before national honor" seemed to be the king's policy in foreign affairs. The people began to think back fondly to the immortal deeds of the great Napoleon and yearn for national glory once again.

The Revolution of 1848. In the face of rising opposition, the king turned to a policy of coercion, but this step antagonized the opposition instead of crushing it. In February 1848 a Paris insurrection once more turned into a political revolution. Again, as in 1830, mobs of excited citizens began to congregate and the barricade—the inevitable symbol of revolution—appeared. More than 1500 barricades were thrown up in Paris. "In small streets they seemed to rise almost every ten feet, while at important squares huge ones rose that were to become legends. Enthusiastic Paris citizens . . . went methodically to work with crowbars to dig up the foot-square paving stones. They politely stopped omni-

Stupidity and indifference characterize the paunchy, middle-class members of the French legislature in this scathing portrayal of the lawmakers in session under the July monarchy. It is the work of Honoré Daumier, a master of political and social satire.

buses, unhitched the horses, and turned the vehicles over to be weighted down with stones. They tore iron railings from houses, cut down four thousand trees along the boulevards and destroyed nearly as many lamp-posts, so that afterwards the streets looked as if they had been swept by a tornado. Between the barricades men crouched around huge fires casting lead balls. All over town, houses had been ransacked for arms, and chalked on doors one could read, 'Arms Given Up,'—some added, 'With Pleasure.' Through the incessant tocsin, the *Marseillaise* sounded everywhere . . ."[14] A provisional government proclaimed a republic, and Louis Philippe fled to England. Universal suffrage was immediately established, giving France suddenly a full political democracy.

The new regime, known as the Second Republic, was to have a brief and inglorious existence. Created somewhat unexpectedly,

without real preparation, it was hamstrung by complete inexperience in democracy among both its officials and the newly enfranchised common people. In addition, the reformers who had been united in their opposition to Louis Philippe broke into diverse factions after his removal. The republicans at once split into two groups—the moderates, of bourgeois stamp, who favored political democracy within the existing social order; and the socialists, supported by mobs of unemployed Paris workers, who wanted the revolution to be economic and social as well as political. A provisional government representing both groups was set up, with the moderates well in the majority and a moderate, the poet Alphonse de Lamartine (1790-1869), at its head. With his idealism, humanitarianism, and unrivaled eloquence, this poet-statesman was the heart and soul of the revolution. It had been he who had exactly expressed France's attitude when he had predicted the overthrow of Louis Philippe as the coming "revolution of contempt." But instead of solving France's problems, Lamartine and his colleagues talked and procrastinated. Above all, Lamartine and the men around him failed to heal the growing gulf between the moderate republicans and the radicals and champions of workers.

Within a few months the new regime came to grief over the issue of national workshops. As a concession to the workingman, whom the moderates sincerely wanted to help, so-called national workshops—actually a form of work relief similar to the American WPA of the 1930's—were established to create jobs for the unemployed. But their organization and operation were entrusted to men determined to discredit another national workshop scheme for socialistic enterprises advanced by Louis Blanc. As a result, such projects as carrying dirt from one end of a park to the other soon made the workshops a laughingstock.

In June the workshops were disbanded, whereupon another violent insurrection, known as the "June Days," broke out in the streets of the capital. The unemployed workers, unwilling to use the tricolor as their symbol, hoisted the red flag as the sign of revolution—the first time that the red flag appeared as the symbol of the proletariat. With the cry of "Bread or Lead," these Paris workers erected barricades and sought to overthrow the government. Not since the Reign of Terror had the capital witnessed such savage street fighting. The insurrection was crushed after much loss of life. It left among the working class a bitter hatred of the bourgeoisie and among the bourgeois element a deep and lasting fear of left-wing violence.

Louis Napoleon and the Second Empire. The bloody upheavals in Paris produced a wave of reaction throughout the country, especially among the conservative peasantry. Lamartine was now regarded as a back number. When the election for the presidency of the new republic was held, the victor was not one of the revolutionaries who had founded the new government but a hitherto obscure bearer of the magic name *Napoleon*—Louis Napoleon, nephew of Napoleon I.

Since 1830 the Napoleonic legend, the memory of France's days of glory, had slowly recaptured the imagination of the French people, who wearied of the do-nothing, bourgeois, laissez-faire character of the regime of Louis Philippe. The king had made some attempts to satisfy the French appetite for glory by rehabilitating the royal palace at Versailles and by ordering the return of Napoleon's ashes from St. Helena to Paris in 1840; but his action only served to increase French nostalgia for the days when France was the greatest power in Europe.

Under Louis Philippe, France had had two sets of pretenders to the throne, one led by the Bourbon duke of Bordeaux, in exile in Austria, the other led by the Napoleonic heir, Louis Napoleon. Following the death in 1832 of the emperor's only son, Louis had assumed the headship of the Napoleon clan. Early he became convinced of the magic of his name and the great destiny it was yet to play in the history of France. Up to 1848, however, his career had had something of the quality of a comic opera. In 1836 he appeared before the French garrison at Strasbourg, appealing to the soldiers to revolt against King Louis Philippe. He was captured but was subsequently released and allowed to sail to the United States. In 1840 he returned to the French coast from England with a small group of conspirators, hoping to emulate his late uncle's return from Elba. Prince Louis even brought along an eagle, the symbol of empire. The tame bird "was to hover above Napoleon's head, attracted by a piece of bacon concealed in the historical hat."[15]

Again Louis' efforts fizzled miserably, but at his trial he had an opportunity to address the nation:

For the first time in my life, I am at last able to make my voice heard in France and to speak freely to Frenchmen. . . . The cruel and undeserved proscription which for twenty-five years has dragged my life from the steps of a throne to the prison which I have just left has not been able to impair the courage of my heart. . . . I represent before you a principle, a cause, a defeat. The principle is the sovereignty of the people: the cause is that of the Empire: the defeat is Waterloo.[16]

Sentenced to life imprisonment, Louis Napoleon occupied his time writing tracts and articles. Radical journalists such as Louis Blanc and Pierre Proudhon and the woman novelist George Sand became interested in the prisoner and his apparent concern for the depressed industrial workers and unemployed. In 1846 he escaped from prison in the clothing of a carpenter and fled to England; two years later, with the overthrow of Louis Philippe, he returned to Paris. Free from any involvement in the events of June, when he had not even been in the country, he was able to obtain broad national support in his well-organized campaign for the presidency.

Louis Napoleon was elected president of the Second Republic by an overwhelming majority. He considered himself, not the legislature, as representing the national will—a version of popular sovereignty known as Caesarian democracy. In his mind burned the imperial traditions of his famous uncle. In December 1851, while serving as president, Louis Napoleon forcibly dissolved the government, which played into his hands by attempting to abolish universal suffrage. Imitating the methods of his illustrious uncle and anticipating the techniques of modern dictators, he then carried out a plebiscite which gave almost unanimous support to his action. Again, in 1852, Napoleon effected a sweeping change in the government by proclaiming himself emperor. The Second Republic was no more. France still did not seem to be ready for republican institutions.

The Chartist movement in England. In addition to the revolutions which the Paris uprising of 1848 helped spawn throughout much of Europe, there were repercussions of a lesser sort in some of the small countries and in Great Britain. Under duress, the sovereigns of both Holland and Denmark, for instance, granted their subjects new constitutions of a more liberal nature, and in Belgium the franchise qualifications were liber-

alized. Great Britain, on the other hand, rode out the storm of unrest in the late 1840's with relatively good temper among its people. It was the one great power in western Europe to pass through the period of violence in comparative calm.

In the early 1830's, a strong popular movement known as Chartism had developed in England. In 1838 its leaders published the People's Charter, containing six demands: universal suffrage, secret voting, no property qualifications for members of Parliament, payment of members so that poor men could seek election if they wished, annual elections to Parliament, and equal electoral districts. In 1839 the Chartists, widely supported by the workers and lower classes, presented their petition, with over a million signatures, to the House of Commons. Again, in 1842, a procession two miles long marched through the streets of London and presented a similar petition. In each case the government ignored the petition.

In 1848, following the news of the February Revolution in France, a Chartist convention met and prepared a third petition. This was to be presented to Parliament accompanied by a huge parade and demonstration. The alarmed British government mustered seventy thousand special constables and forbade the procession but allowed the Chartists to bring their petition to Parliament with a small escort. A few militant groups among the Chartists planned an armed insurrection in protest, but their plans were divulged by an informer and the ringleaders seized. The bulk of the English people, Chartists or otherwise, apparently preferred to avoid violence as an instrument of political and social reform.

The failure of the Chartist movement to explode into violence was an example of British devotion in the nineteenth century to gradualism and peaceful change. Although the movement was once more unsuccessful in 1848 and subsequently declined, partly because of financial scandals in its management, all but one of its demands—annual elections to Parliament—were enacted into law within the next century, forming the very foundations of modern British democracy.

Repeal of the Corn Laws. Another reason why the Chartist movement declined so quickly was a basic change in the government's economic policy, which now leaned more toward economic liberalism and helped stimulate the rapid growth of employment, wealth, and industry after 1850. The Corn Laws, protective duties on imported corn (i.e., grain) which had favored the hitherto dominant farming gentry, were dropped in favor of a policy of free trade. These laws had been designed to encourage exports and to protect the English landowners from foreign competition. By the middle of the nineteenth century, the population of England had increased to such an extent that English agriculture could no longer feed the country, and the price of bread rose alarmingly. The famine of 1845 in Ireland (see p. 365) dramatically spotlighted the seriousness of the situation. Repeal of the Corn Laws in 1846 made possible the import of low-priced wheat from abroad, cheaper food for the masses, and a more contented labor supply for the factory owners. At the same time, this victory of the freetraders reflected the growing political dominance of those members of the middle class who believed in laissez faire in England, feeling that tariffs restricted the free flow of goods. The long-range significance of the repeal was that it led to the relative decline of British agriculture in favor of industry. Thenceforth the British economy was increasingly geared to industry, and England became dependent on imports to feed its population.

The repeal of the Corn Laws was shortly followed by the abandonment of customs duties of every kind. The free trade advocated by the followers of Adam Smith was at last a reality; another victory for liberalism had been achieved. For half a century the policy was eminently successful, as the flourishing English industries needed no protection against outside competitors and the English economy throve on the stimulus of cheapened imports of raw materials and food.

A contemporary cartoon shows a demonstration of the kind that helped bring about repeal of the Corn Laws in 1846.

Pattern of reform in Britain. The gradual process of reform in other fields also helped to conciliate the workers. The Ten-Hour Law passed in 1846 was, as described in Chapter 6, an important piece of factory legislation, and the first Public Health Act of 1848 was a substantial stride forward in helping to alleviate unhealthy conditions such as filthy streets and wretched housing.

By midcentury, Britain was a wealthy nation taking pride in the stability of its political institutions. The pattern of restraint and of gradual social and political reforms, so characteristic of England's history for the next hundred years, had been firmly established. Britain would move forward by evolutionary rather than revolutionary reform.

There was, however, one conspicuous failure in the British picture—the failure to conciliate rising nationalism in Ireland and to remedy the wretched living conditions of the masses of Irish peasantry. In 1848 a group of Irish nationalists, belonging to a revolutionary group called Young Ireland, tried to stage a revolution. This move was ill planned and easily squelched, but Irish nationalism persevered and grew stronger (see Chapter 12).

CENTRAL EUROPE: THE RISE OF THE NATIONALISTIC SPIRIT

The Old Regime maintained in Austria. During the revolutions of 1820 and again in 1830, there had been sympathetic vibrations of unrest and minor insurrections in the German states and the Austrian empire. In the main, however, the political arrangements made at Vienna in 1815 were not seriously challenged. Under the strong hand of its chief minister, Metternich, Austria continued to be a bulwark of reaction in central Europe and throughout its sphere of influence among the multitude of states in Germany and Italy.

Nationalism menaced not only the Hapsburg domination of Germany and Italy but also the Austrian state itself, for the Austrian empire did not constitute a nation but rather a bewildering jumble of diverse nationalities. Austria proper, the seat of the governing house of the Hapsburgs, was German. To the east of Austria was the great plain of Hungary, the habitat of the Magyars, who were originally of Asiatic origin and spoke a language not related to most European tongues. All around the fringes of the Austrian and Hungarian center were primarily Slavic peoples: Czechs, Slovaks, and Poles to the north, Rumanians to the east, and Serbs, Croats, and Slovenes to the south. In addition, south of Austria were the large provinces of Lombardy and Venetia, purely Italian in population. In this polyglot Austrian empire the Germans were the ruling nationality. Although they comprised only about 20 per cent of the total population, they constituted

the bulk of the upper and middle classes, controlling the government, the Church, and the army. In appearance, then, Austria was German, but it was actually "a Slav edifice with a German façade." Only by excluding the ideas of nationalism and popular government could Metternich and Emperor Francis I hope to keep their ramshackle empire intact.

The Austrian middle class was very small, the great bulk of the inhabitants being poor peasants. There was no such thing as representative government. Local assemblies, called Diets, were endowed with little power and were representative only of the nobility. Although Hungary had developed the tradition of a strong Diet, its assembly was not even convened between 1812 and 1825.

The German nationalist youth movement. In the several dozen German states, both large and small, Austrian influence was paramount. Here again Metternich perceived that his most menacing danger was nationalism. For if the German people, now divided, should unite, the new nation might repudiate Austria's leadership both within Germany and in central Europe.

Notwithstanding the stern opposition of Metternich, supported by most of the German rulers, nationalism and political liberalism advanced in the German states after 1815. Much of the inspiration for this movement was derived from the romantic nationalism so strongly expressed by German professors, poets, and philosophers.

In 1817 a great student festival was held at Wartburg to arouse German patriotism. The festival was followed by some disturbances, including the murder of a spy in the secret service of the Russian tsar. The response of Metternich was immediate and harsh. He persuaded the German rulers, assembled at Carlsbad in 1819, to draw up a number of decrees which were later adopted by the Diet of the Confederation. The Carlsbad Decrees dissolved student associations, muzzled the press, and throttled the professors' freedom of speech.

Romantic nationalism in Austria's orbit. The long shadows of Byron and Scott reached out to touch impressionable young intellectuals living in the multinational domains and orbit of the Hapsburgs. Fed from France, Britain, and the Germanies, romantic nationalism produced poets and historians who sought to restore the memory of the subject peoples' past greatness, to collect ballads and folk literature, and to produce literary works in the various national languages instead of in French and German as was the general practice.

Magyar nationalism had been rising rapidly against the German dominance of Vienna. Its first great exponent was István Széchenyi (1791-1860), a wealthy aristocrat who sought to interest his countrymen in their historic past and to make Hungary great by developing its economic resources.

In the Hungarian Diet, Széchenyi was the first to use his native Magyar instead of the usual Latin. In 1825 he gave the equivalent of one year's income from his estates to found a society for studying Magyar. Like the English, whom he admired, he believed in practical and gradual reform. He sponsored such projects as the dredging of the Danube, the establishment of a national theater, and the scientific breeding of cattle.

The romantic movement was also influential in the development of the Slavic revival. Czechs, Poles, Croats, Serbs, and Bulgars began to take pride in their distinctive national cultures, to agitate for national independence where it was lacking, and to feel a sense of kinship and common destiny with all Slavic groups. In Bohemia, nationalist scholars studied the literature and customs of the Bohemian people, and newspapers in the Czech language were established.

Mazzini and the *Risorgimento*. In Italy after 1815, the Hapsburgs ruled over some unhappy provinces in the north and northeast and dominated the little independent states throughout the peninsula. It was perhaps natural that this frustrated land should produce the most famous exemplar of romantic nationalism, Giuseppe Mazzini (1805-1872), the son of a professor at the University of Genoa. Fired by the revolutionary zeal of romantic poets such as Byron, Mazzini in the 1820's joined a secret revolutionary organization known as the *Carbonari*. He has explained how the sight of revolutionaries fleeing south from Piedmont and seeking refuge in his native city of Genoa stirred his sympathy and created in his mind the first outlines of a program of action that was to dominate his whole life:

That day was the first in which a confused idea presented itself to my mind—I will not say of country or of liberty—but an idea that we Italians *could* and therefore *ought* to struggle for the liberty of our country . . . the idea of an existing wrong in my own country, against which it was a duty to struggle, and the thought that I too must bear my part in that struggle, flashed before my mind on that day for the first time, never again to leave me.[17]

In 1830, Mazzini was implicated in an unsuccessful revolution against the royal government of Sardinia and was imprisoned for six months. Following his release, he established a new patriotic society known as Young Italy. Appealing mainly to students and intellectuals, he urged them to work unceasingly and fearlessly for the creation of a united and independent Italy, a sovereign nation of free and equal men. Fleeing to England in 1837, this national patriot incessantly plotted and conspired against the despotic regimes in Italy. His teachings spread over the land and initiated a new phase of the Italian nationalist movement known as the *Risorgimento* (Resurgence).

Mazzini was intensely religious, and to him loyalty to the nation came midway between a man's loyalty to his family and that to his God. However, unlike leaders of nationalism later in the century, who arrogantly preached the superiority of their own people, Mazzini believed that the people of every nation should work for the benefit of their brothers throughout the world. We shall see shortly how, after kindling the spark of nationalism in Italy, Mazzini played a leading part in the Italian revolutionary movement of 1848. Regrettably, the realization of his main aim—unification—was achieved by other leaders who used cynical calculation and ruthless force.

Mazzini, Italian patriot and revolutionary

Conservatism maintained in Austria. Thus there were stirrings of liberalism and nationalism in the German states and in the medley of lands making up the Austrian empire. But until 1848 Austrian conservatism moved along its tranquil way with little difficulty, for the driver of the Austrian Hapsburg coach was still the imperturbable Metternich, champion of conservative institutions at the Congress of Vienna. In his defense it must be stated that Metternich, while having no use for popular assemblies and universal suffrage, had an equal dislike for inefficiency and made numerous attempts to persuade his royal masters to initiate reforms that would modernize the ramshackle system of administration. A major historian has written that "the chief blame for the stagnation and rigidity of the Austrian system lay not so much with Metternich, after whom popular tradition has named it, as with [Emperor] Francis [i], who neutralized his Minister's repeated attempts to repair the outworn machine of State."[18]

REVOLUTIONS THAT MISFIRED

Berlin follows the example of Paris. The echo of the Parisians' February revolt against Louis Philippe's bourgeois monarchy did not take long to reach discontented liberals and workingmen throughout Europe, leaving only Russia and Turkey untouched. At public assemblies convened in various cities just a few days after the flight of Louis Philippe, patriotic German liberals declared the unity of Germany and began to plan for a national assembly at Frankfurt to draft a German constitution.

Up to this point, Prussia had been the keystone of reaction and conservatism among the German states. In 1847, in his celebrated "Scrap of Paper Speech," King Frederick William iv had repudiated any idea of giving his people a constitution:

. . . neither now or ever will I allow a scribbled sheet of paper to intervene like a second Providence between our God in Heaven and this land of ours . . .[19]

Nevertheless, on March 15, 1848, his subjects finally gave vent to their long-repressed political aspirations in serious rioting in Berlin. As in Paris, barricades sprang up all over the city, and for several days bloody fighting went on between the people and the army. In this crisis the king lost his nerve, ordered his soldiers to leave Berlin, and proceeded to make peace with "his dear Berliners." The populace arranged to have a funeral service in the courtyard of the king's palace for the citizens killed during the rioting. Frederick William was forced to gaze upon the bodies of his slain subjects and to take off his hat as a token of respect for the martyrs! Humiliated and coerced, the sovereign promised a constitution, a parliament, and support for a united Germany. Following this remarkable popular victory, the governments in other German states fell to pieces. Their rulers agreed to establish constitutional governments and granted various privileges such as freedom of the press.

The Frankfurt Assembly. As the crowning symbol of the revolutionary fervor that was sweeping Europe in 1848, the Frankfurt Assembly opened its first session on May 18. Over five hundred members attended, coming from the various German states, from Austria proper, and even from Bohemia, which had a large German minority in its population. The guns boomed, the church bells pealed, and a vast crowd applauded as the newly inducted president of the Assembly announced:

We are to create a constitution for Germany, for the whole Empire.[20]

This objective posed two fundamental problems: Just what was meant by "Germany," and what manner of government should be devised for the new empire? In regard to the first problem, some believed that a united Germany should include all Germans in central Europe; such a state would include Austria proper (but not Hungary) and probably, because of its large and prosperous German minority, Bohemia. On the other hand, some representatives believed that Austria should not be included in the new Germany. The first faction wanted to offer the new imperial crown to the Hapsburg sovereign in Vienna, the second to the Hohenzollern king of Prussia.

The Frankfurt Assembly was an unusually distinguished body, mainly professional and middle class in its composition and point of view. As the various members surveyed the political scene in Europe in May 1848, to all appearances the revolutionary movement and the cause of freedom were universally successful. Commenting upon these days of optimism, a historian of the 1848 revolutions observes: "This was indeed the *Völkerfrühling*, the people's springtime, when it looked as if all the ills of mankind were going to be washed away in a torrent of beautiful words. Never before had people believed so implicitly in the magical power of resolutions and speeches."[21]

Failure of the Frankfurt Assembly and the "Humiliation of Olmütz." Perhaps the most tragic disappointment of 1848 was the fail-

A session of the do-nothing Frankfurt Assembly, which frustrated the hopes of German liberals, is shown in this woodcut.

ure of the Frankfurt Assembly and, with it, of the liberal cause in Prussia. From May to December 1848, a period in which the need for action was imperative, the Frankfurt Assembly spent its time eloquently debating academic topics. As a German historian put it: "The Frankfort parliament was too much of a university and too little of a political stock exchange."[22]

During the windy sessions of the Frankfurt Assembly, the liberal uprising gradually subsided as conservatives in the German states began to rally around their rulers to undo the work of the reformers. King Frederick William gradually regained his confidence; the army proved loyal; and the peasants apparently had little interest in political reform. By November 1848 the army was again in control of Berlin.

In December, even though the forces of reaction had definitely gained the ascendancy, the Assembly continued its work. It approved the Declaration of the Rights of the German People, a liberal and inspiring document which set forth the political and social ideals of the reformers. In April 1849 a constitution was approved for a united Germany, at the head of which was to be an emperor advised by a ministry. The legislature was to be elected by secret manhood suffrage. In this blueprint, Austria was excluded for the simple reason that it had refused to join the new union. The leadership of the new Germany was offered to King Frederick William IV of Prussia, who was not loath to accept an emperor's crown but found certain disagreeable features associated with acceptance. The king did not like accepting a crown from a popular assembly; he knew that if he did accept, there would probably be trouble with Austria; and it was also apparent that force would have to be used to compel some of the German states to enter the union. Therefore, when a deputation from the Frankfurt Assembly waited on the king and offered him the German crown, he refused to accept it, later declaring that he could not "pick up a crown from the gutter."

After the Prussian king's contemptuous refusal to head the proposed new German Reich, most of the members of the Frankfurt Assembly sadly returned to their homes. A few determined liberals, however, went to Stuttgart, where they promulgated their own constitution and called for the election of a new German parliament. The Prussian army was called in to disband this final remnant of the Frankfurt Assembly and also to quell riots in various parts of the Germanies. Thousands of prominent middle-class liberals fled Germany, many migrating to the United States.

In 1850, after the disbanding of the Frankfurt Assembly, the Prussian king issued his own constitution, a document that paid lip service to parliamentary government but kept all real power in the hands of the sovereign and the upper classes. Meanwhile, Prussia sponsored a confederation of north German states, without Austria and with Frederick William himself as head. This plan was not to the liking of either Austria or Russia, which feared the idea of a strong, Prussian-dominated Germany. A conference of the three interested powers followed at Olmütz in 1850. The Prussian king was persuaded to drop his plan, and it was agreed to restore the German Confederation as set up

at the Congress of Vienna in 1815. Austria was still the mistress of central Europe, and Prussian ambitions to secure the leadership of the German states had been checkmated. Austria's disregard for Prussian interests and the weakness of King Frederick William in defending them became known by anti-Austrian Germans as the "Humiliation of Olmütz."

Revolts in Hungary and Bohemia. A foretaste of the revolutionary explosion that was to throw the Hapsburg realm into chaos had come in 1846 when patriots in the independent city of Cracow in the Austrian portion of Poland rose against foreign domination of their land. This nationalist uprising was quelled with stern repression, and the Poles remained quiescent during the stirring days of 1848 when revolutions abounded in Europe. Meanwhile, however, another national challenge to Hapsburg rule was taking form.

In 1847 a majority of Hungarian liberal patriots were elected to the Hungarian Diet, and agreement was reached on a program of reform, the so-called Ten Points (later famous as the March Laws). This program called for responsible government, abolition of feudal dues, religious liberty, popular representation, and other reforms. It was at this juncture that Louis Kossuth (1802-1894) stepped forward to displace Széchenyi as Hungarian national leader. A great orator, more impetuous in his tactics and more uncompromising in his nationalism than the moderate patriot whom he now brushed aside, Kossuth had become the idol of Hungarian nationalists in the mid-1840's.

As a member of the Diet, on March 3, 1848, Kossuth gave a momentous speech on Austro-Hungarian relations. He electrified his listeners as he castigated the "stagnant bureaucratic system" and spoke of "the pestilential air blowing from the Vienna charnel house and its deadening effect upon all phases of Hungarian life." He demanded parliamentary government for the entire empire and an independent finance ministry for Hungary. Avidly read in Vienna, this speech inspired Austrian students and workers to rise in revolt, invade the palace, and fight furious street battles with the soldiery. As in the case of the Prussian revolt, the Austrian government was taken wholly by surprise. Metternich resigned and on March 13 secretly fled to England. A few days later the emperor promised a constitution and the abolition of censorship.

In the meantime, the Hungarian Diet passed its famous March Laws, which made the nation almost independent, tied to Austria only through a common sovereign. These laws gave Hungary popular government, with fundamental political rights guaranteed the people, and obliterated the remnants of feudalism and the special privileges of the nobility.

The same course of events took place in Slavic Bohemia, home of the Czechs, where the Austrian emperor was forced to promise a constituent assembly that would create a kingdom of Bohemia similar to that in Hungary. The revolutionary movement had reached an amazing pinnacle of success by May, but it began to falter the very next month. In Bohemia, German and Czech nationalists began to quarrel, and the upshot was that the Czechs revolted on June 12. Austrian forces bombarded and subdued Prague; thus ended all aspirations for an autonomous new kingdom of Bohemia.

Collapse of Hungarian independence. Austria's success in Bohemia gave the emperor's advisers a pattern to follow. The quarrel between German and Czech in Bohemia was being paralleled in Hungary, where, since the passage of the March Laws, the confident Magyars had been creating a new state. Budapest was declared the national capital, and the official language was changed from Latin to Magyar. At this point Kossuth, the head of the government, began to make it clear that he would not recognize the claims of any of the other national groups in Hungary. The program of Kossuth's government was evidently to be one of rigorous Magyarization. In protest against this Magyar nationalist policy, South Slavs under a capable Croatian leader named Jellachich attacked the Magyars, and a desperate civil war ensued. Vienna was not slow to take advantage of the situation, and Jellachich was named an imperial general.

In the meantime, liberal leaders in the Hapsburg capital began to realize that a policy of "divide and rule" was being cleverly utilized by the Hapsburgs. Once the Croats were victorious over the Magyars, there would be no compunction against using them to stifle liberalism in Vienna. A second uprising therefore took place in Vienna, forcing the emperor to flee; but the reactionary Austrian army commander, having accomplished his task in Prague, now came down from Bohemia and in October 1848 forced the surrender of the liberals in control of the Austrian capital.

The next step taken to counter the revolution was to induce the weak and incapable Emperor Ferdinand to abdicate in favor of his young nephew, Francis Joseph. After Ferdinand's abdication in December, the Austrian government proceeded to repeal its concessions to Hungary, arguing that the new emperor was not bound by the acts of his predecessor. Infuriated at this treachery, the Hungarians declared complete independence and proceeded to put up a desperate defense against the invading Austrian armies. Kossuth inspired his people to heroic efforts, and his leadership gave promise that Hungary might be saved. But in Russia, which was not affected by the revolutionary contagion, Tsar Nicholas determined to intervene in behalf of his fellow ruler in Austria. The intervention in Hungary of the tsar with 100,000 troops in the summer of 1849 ended any hope of victory, and in August all resistance ceased. The sequel to the tragic collapse of the Hungarian war of independence was stern repression, with many hangings and imprisonments. Kossuth escaped to England, made a tour of the United States before wildly sympathetic crowds, and lived the rest of his life in exile from his native land.

Revolution and reform in Italy. While barricades had been thrown up in Paris, Berlin, and Vienna, and the pillars of reaction and conservatism had been severely weakened in France, the Germanies, and the Austrian empire, the Italian peninsula likewise had seethed with revolt. An insurrection had taken place as early as January 1848, when the people of Sicily had revolted against the corrupt rule of the king of Naples and had forced him to promise a liberal constitution. In March the Venetian populace rose against their Austrian rulers and proclaimed a republic. Milan, the center of discontent against Austria in Lombardy, witnessed the "five glorious days," in which broken tiles, pieces of furniture, and blazing oil were hurled down upon the occupying Austrian soldiers. A few homemade cannon and an assortment of firearms wielded by an indomitable citizenry forced the Austrian army to withdraw to the safety of a ring of northern Italian fortresses known as the Quadrilateral. In this same March, the king of Sardinia, Charles Albert of the House of Savoy, voluntarily promulgated a new liberal constitution, the *Statuto,* which was to become the constitution of a united Italy and to remain so until the rise of Mussolini's Fascist dictatorship after World War I. Charles Albert also assumed the leadership in driving Austrian influence out of Italy, declaring *"Italia fara da sa"* ("Italy will do it herself"). Declaring war against Austria, Charles Albert sent his forces to the assistance of his countrymen in Lombardy and Venetia, and after hard fighting the Austrians were compelled to withdraw.

Other states such as Tuscany granted their people liberal constitutions, and absolute government in Italy almost disappeared. In the Papal States a program of reform had begun as early as 1846, when Pius IX had been elected pope. The new pontiff had immediately set out to rectify the arbitrary unpopular rule of his predecessor. A man of liberal sympathies in these first two years of his reign, he soon gained the admiration and support of his subjects by releasing many political prisoners and initiating moderate political reforms. Pius IX earned respect throughout western Europe—except in reactionary circles—and became known as the "Reforming Pope." In 1848 the Italian people expected much from this liberal in the Vatican. Many believed that he would declare war against Austria, thus leading a national crusade against Vienna.

Hapsburg control reëstablished in Italy. In spite of the liberal triumphs in Italy, the tide was to turn against the victors. While regaining their mastery of Hungary, the Hapsburgs also gradually began throttling the liberal national movement in Italy. In the early spring of 1848, faced with rebellion at home as well as the invasion of Lombardy by the armies of Charles Albert, the Austrian government had sought the mediation of England in seeking peace with Sardinia. The Austrian commander, however, pleaded with Vienna for time and gradually built up his arms. Unfortunately for the success of the Italian cause, Charles Albert frittered away his opportunity instead of immediately taking the offensive against the Austrian forces. The Italians, furthermore, suffered not only from bad generalship but also from disunity and jealousy among their leaders. The republicans in Venice and those led by Mazzini in Rome (to be discussed shortly) did not trust the king of Sardinia; they wanted a republican Italy, not a united Italian monarchy.

Thus while Charles Albert missed his chance for military victory and while disunity weakened the Italian cause, the Austrians strengthened their forces and in July 1848 defeated Charles Albert's army at the decisive battle of Custozza. The Sardinian troops were forced to evacuate Lombardy. A truce was arranged, and Charles Albert retired with the hope of building up his weakened forces. In May 1849, thinking his army had been satisfactorily rebuilt, the king reopened the war and invaded Lombardy, but the Sardinian troops were again outfought and their leaders outgeneraled. After being defeated at the battle of Novara, Charles Albert abdicated the throne of Sardinia in favor of his eldest son, who became Victor Emmanuel II. The crushed and disillusioned former monarch left his homeland for Portugal, where four months later he died.

Victorious over the House of Savoy, which had been the one champion of Italian liberty strong enough to constitute a serious threat, Austria quickly helped restore old rulers and systems of government throughout Italy as they had been before 1848. The grand duke of Tuscany, for example, was placed back on the throne, and the republic of Venice was starved out and in August 1849 forced to surrender. In Lombardy and Venetia the cruelties of the Austrian general Hayenau earned him the title of "General Hyena." In the south, the Sicilian liberal movement was crushed by the king of Naples, who abolished the new constitution. Suppression was particularly brutal in Naples, so much so that the English statesman Gladstone referred to the Neapolitan government as the "negation of God created into a system."

The final episode of the Italian revolutions was the rise and fall of the republic of Rome. In spite of the reformist character of the administration instituted by Pope Pius ix, it did not go far enough to suit extremists and nationalists in the Papal States, who wished to abolish clerical domination of the local government and join actively against Catholic Austria in the struggle for a united Italy. In November, having become virtually a prisoner of the revolutionary militia and having had his prime minister assassinated, the embittered pope was forced to flee from Rome. A republic was declared in his domains in February 1849. One of its leaders was Mazzini, who had returned from exile. The flight of the pope had brought a wave of indignation in conservative circles throughout Europe, and Louis Napoleon, president of the Second French Republic, gained the support of French Catholics and conservatives by sending an expeditionary force to Italy to crush the Roman republic.

Garibaldi, soldier of fortune. The last days of the Roman republic were made notable by the valor of the patriot and soldier of fortune, Giuseppe Garibaldi (1807-1882). Garibaldi had been implicated in the plots of Mazzini's Young Italy movement and in 1835 had fled to South America. The revolution of 1848 brought Garibaldi back to Italy. Becoming leader of the defenses of the Roman republic, he dealt the vastly more powerful French army heavy casualties. Finally in 1849 the walls of Rome were successfully stormed by the French, and the republic was no more. Both Mazzini and Garibaldi fled the city. Upon leaving, Garibaldi declaimed:

Let those who wish to continue the war against the stranger come with me. I offer neither pay, nor quarters, nor provisions; I offer hunger, thirst, forced marches, battles and death. Let him who loves his country in his heart and not with his lips only, follow me.[23]

Accompanied by a small remnant of his men, Garibaldi broke through the cordon around Rome and made his way to northern Italy. Harassed by enemy forces, the little band broke apart, and Garibaldi barely managed to cross into the sanctuary of Sardinia. From this friendly area he traveled to Gibraltar, hence to North Africa, and finally to New York, to return as a triumphant leader to his native land ten years later (see Chapter 8).

THE REVOLUTIONARY ERA IN RETROSPECT

Why democratic movements failed. The account of the rise and fall of the short-lived Roman republic ends the story of the widespread struggles for reform during 1847 and 1848. A Hapsburg emperor still sat on the throne in Vienna, supported by a more efficient system of autocracy consisting of "a standing army of soldiers, a sitting army of officials, a kneeling army of priests, and a creeping army of informers";[24] in France a Bonaparte ruled as hereditary emperor instead of elected president; and in the German states the Prussian king had successfully ridden out the revolutionary tempest and drafted his own constitution. Germany was still disunited; Austrian influence in Italy survived; subject nationalities in the Austrian empire, especially the Czechs and Hungarians, were forced back into their subordinate positions; and the promising gains toward constitutional government were largely nullified.

Looking back from the perspective of a little more than a hundred years, we can now see that the failure of the democratic movement in Europe in 1848 was one of the most decisive happenings in modern history; it helped shape the course not only of the nineteenth century but also that of the twentieth. What accounted for the failure? It is apparent that most armies, led by the aristocrats, were loyal to the existing regimes. Since another class, the peasants, had little interest in revolution once the old feudal obligations had been removed, the movement became primarily the product of the middle class and the large-city workers. In the case of Hungary, the intervention of Russia was decisive. These elements were all important in explaining the failure of 1848, but there were three additional factors of significance.

Excessive nationalism. The first of these factors was excessive nationalism. Metternich had prophesied the "war of all against all," and this had come to pass, especially in Hungary. It had been Mazzini's hope that men could be good Europeans as well as solid nationalists; but the events of 1848 showed that Europeans, whether democrats or reactionaries, were first and last Italians or Czechs or Germans, as the case might be. We have seen how Kossuth refused to recognize the same national rights for the Croats and Serbs that he demanded for his own Magyar people. Because of its narrow nationalism, the Frankfurt Assembly was quite happy over the failure of the Czech revolution; the members thought not as liberals but as Germans when nationalism and liberalism conflicted.

The problem posed to the men of 1848 was how to devise arrangements that would allow the various national groups to exercise political rights and enjoy cultural autonomy within some larger unit of cooperation. Little progress was made in this direction in the second half of the nineteenth century. In fact, some students of the 1848 revolutionary movement believe that much of the misery of Europe in the mid-twentieth century springs from this failure.

Impracticality of romantic idealism. Another element explaining the course of events in this study of revolution was the fact that romantic idealism—no matter how inspiring, logical, and just in itself—was shown to be ineffectual in the realm of practical affairs. The idealist, the pacifist, and the internationalist were completely discredited. After 1848, romanticism in politics was superseded by the doctrine of realism, which placed its faith in power and resorted to any means to gain its ends. As the next chapter will show, the rise of the new realism did not mean the total abandonment of the nationalist objectives of 1848. But these goals were to be attained by more ruthless and realistic means, as illustrated in the achievement of national unity for Germany and Italy.

Sharpening of class conflict. The most significant factor explaining the failure of the revolutions of 1848, however, was the emergence of class struggle as a factor in European politics. The events of this year made it quite plain that the middle class and the industrial workers had very different views on revolution and reform. The former wanted to transfer power from the aristocrats and upper bourgeoisie into their own hands; the latter wanted a social and economic change that would guarantee them a fair share in profits and in political control. In numerous instances a revolution was effected by a coalition between workers and bourgeoisie, but this cooperation soon broke down. The importance of the bloody June Days in Paris cannot be overestimated. The excesses of the proletarian Paris mob horrified both the intellectual and the bourgeois. By the end of 1848 it seemed that the observations of Marx and Engels in the Communist Manifesto issued on the eve of the revolutions of 1848 (see p. 180) might be justified—that perhaps there was an irreconcilable gulf between proletariat and bourgeoisie that was resolvable only by force. One consequence of 1848 was that, for many reformist members of the European middle class, violence of the French revolutionary type as a means of reform lost its allure. More faith was henceforth placed in English-style gradualism.

Achievements of the 1848 revolutions. In spite of the overall failure of the revolutions of 1848, there were important immediate gains. The feudal system was not restored in the Austrian empire, Sardinia maintained its liberal constitution, and all the German states—even Prussia—had parliaments, even if most of them were not of the democratic variety. In both Denmark and the Netherlands, the king was ruling by and with the consent of a legislature elected by the well-to-do classes. One nation, England, had liberalized its political and economic institutions through a process of gradual and peaceful reform. Even these limited successes offered fair indication that the nationalistic and democratic movements would continue to press forward in important areas, that the victory of absolutism and reaction would not be permanent. Within the next twenty years the political structure of Europe was to be turned topsy-turvy, as constitutional government and nationalism made significant gains.

Metternich's place in history. As one looks back on this turbulent revolutionary era with its clash of opposing ideas, two symbols stand out in bold relief—the barricades and Metternich. In recent years some historians have been more kind in evaluating the Austrian statesman than were his contemporaries. Appalled by the chaos and conflict of the twentieth century, which they attribute to breakneck change, the fanaticism of nationalism, and the frequently emotional basis of politics in twentieth-century mass democracy, these scholars see a praiseworthy stability in the conservative system championed by Metternich from 1815 to 1848. Yet a complete absence of change is no better than too much change. Metternich cannot be placed in the category of the world's greatest statesmen. His tragic weakness was that he failed to allow for any

growth or change in Europe's political institutions; he failed to understand that the art of real statesmanship must provide for the attempt to bring together, in reasonable equilibrium, the best of the old forces and the most promising of the new. As a British historian has observed: "He saw no mean between revolution and autocracy, and since revolution was odious, he set himself to repress that which is the soul of human life in society, the very spirit of liberty."[25]

SUMMARY

The principal theme of this chapter has been the political history of western Europe from 1815 to 1850 as expressed mainly in the development of nationalism and democracy. The narrative has concerned the plans and activities of such statesmen as Metternich, Castlereagh, Canning, and Talleyrand and the aspirations of such revolutionary leaders as Lamartine, Mazzini, Garibaldi, and Kossuth. This period witnessed such important events as the realization of Greek and Belgian independence, the passing of the Reform Bill of 1832 in England, the brief experiment with the Second Republic in France, and a rash of revolutions in Italy, the Austrian empire, and the Germanies in 1848.

Behind all these events were three movements or attitudes of mind—nationalism, democracy, and romanticism. Nationalism moved all national groups to struggle for independence and the freedom to direct their own affairs without interference. Democracy—government by the consent of the governed—was neither prevalent nor popular before 1850; affairs were in the hands of the middle class, which had no use for despotic kings but also had little sympathy for the rights of the poor. Still, democratic ideals were spreading. The intellectual and artistic movement known as romanticism glorified the rights of the individual and believed somewhat naïvely in the essential goodness of human nature. By reviving legends of long-dead heroes who fought for the freedom of the poor and oppressed, romantic authors frequently added strength both to nationalism and democracy.

The first great epidemic of revolutions after the Congress settlement occurred in the 1820's. The revolutions of 1830 definitely showed that the European pattern laid out in 1815 by ultraconservative statesmen could not be maintained. After the July Revolution in Paris, the creation of an independent Greece, and the establishment of a Belgian state separate from Holland, there was a comparative lull in politics while the basic forces of romantic nationalism and democracy carried on their work of influencing men's minds. By 1848 a new and prosperous middle class had arisen, together with a numerous body of intellectuals who had been strongly moved by the gospels of freedom and nationality. And in the cities, the Industrial Revolution was creating a growing mass of workers who resented their poverty and who also had dreams of their own.

In 1848 the great explosion came, leaving only Turkey and Russia untouched. France quickly got rid of Louis Philippe and proclaimed the Second Republic. In Italy governments toppled everywhere, and Charles Albert, king of Sardinia, made the cause of Italian freedom his own by declaring war on Austria. In the Austrian empire the Germans demanded and were promised a more liberal government, while elsewhere, as in Bohemia and Hungary, other nationalities insisted upon national autonomy as well as liberal parliamentary government. And in the Germanies, rulers were forced to make concessions in most of the states; the haughty Prussian king was cowed by the Berlin populace; and, most important for the future of Germans, a national assembly convened at Frankfurt to draft a new constitution for a united fatherland.

The revolutionary fervor of 1848 did not, however, fulfill its expectations. Perhaps never has such a widespread, popular, and seemingly successful movement collapsed so quickly. Civil war in Hungary, the rise of dictatorship in France, the regaining of royal prerogative in Prussia, military defeat for the national cause in Italy, and empty words at Frankfurt were the sequel. The explanation for this failure is complex, but three factors of special importance should be singled out. The first was the inexperience and lack of realism of popular leaders. There was too much discussion and too little practical planning. Secondly, the force of nationalism, so powerful an enemy of autocracy at the outset, soon showed itself to be a selfish and exclusive movement that set the various liberated nationalities to quarreling among themselves. Thirdly, the development of class consciousness put the middle class and the proletariat at odds.

Turning to the international scene, a significant phenomenon in European history between 1815 and 1848 was the experiment in intergovernmental consultation and cooperation which we have studied as the Congress System. Although the ends it sought were the prevention of change and the extinction of liberty and although its effectiveness was short-lived, yet the Congress System—the first serious attempt to solve problems by international cooperation—represented a positive step forward. It established a precedent for personal conferences between statesmen, and it initiated the habit of consultation on common problems.

CHAPTER 8

Nationalism and the Making of Nations

THE POLITICS OF POWER: 1850-1870

Introduction. From roughly 1850 to 1870 the spirit of nationalism was in the ascendant; not only in Europe but all over the world, existing national states sought to increase their power and prestige, new national states fought their way into existence, and national movements, surviving crushing setbacks, gathered strength for renewed revolts against foreign domination. The triumphs and failures of national movements in the non-European world will be discussed in Chapters 9 and 10. This chapter deals with the course of European politics and the significant changes in the power structure of Europe during this crucial twenty-year period.

Divided Italy, so long merely a "geographical expression," at last achieved national unification. Under Prussian rule, the German states were welded into an empire. France, stirred to nationalistic fervor by its memories of an earlier Napoleon, supported Napoleon III in his quest for new glories for the "mistress of Europe." Austria achieved an uneasy accord as the Germans of Vienna and the Magyars of Budapest joined forces to check the aspirations of other nationalities in the creaky Hapsburg empire.

This era of nation-making is important not only for what happened but also for the attitudes of those involved. Political objectives were neither confused with the romantic dreams of poets nor modeled on the utopias imagined by idealistic intellectuals. Instead, they were practical goals, ruthlessly pursued by practical men. The attitude of such statesmen as Bismarck and Cavour, who were instrumental in directing the course of European politics in the 1850's and 1860's, is well summed up in the observation of an English historian that "States are not created or destroyed, and frontiers redrawn or obliterated, by argument and majority votes; nations are freed, united or broken by blood and iron, and not by a generous application of liberty and tomato-sauce; violence is the instrument of national movements."[1]

Generally speaking, nationalism and nation-making in mid-nineteenth-century Europe was a bloody business. From 1815 to 1848 no single major conflict occurred. But from the midpoint of the century to the 1870's, six wars were fought—some of major proportions. Within this period, every major European power went to war at least once. These conflicts swept away the settlements created at Vienna in 1815. The smashing defeat of France in the Franco-Prussian War (1870-1871) marked the demise of the Second French Empire and heralded the rise of the new German empire to a position of supremacy on the Continent.

The creation of major nations by extraordinary unification movements as in Italy and Germany was paralleled by the formation of several smaller nations from the European part of Turkey. The Balkan subjects of the Ottoman empire were infected with the nineteenth-century fever of European nationalism. Yet, the efforts of the Balkan peoples to attain national self-determination were repeatedly frustrated by the major European powers, following their own imperial interests.

From the era of the French Revolutionary wars on, a prime objective of Russia's tsars was to partition the dominions of the Turks, seize Constantinople, and gain access to the eastern Mediterranean. This ambition was persistently blocked by British diplomacy and British arms. The conflict between the great powers—especially the rivalry between Russia and England—over the holdings of the decaying Ottoman empire came to be known as the Near Eastern Question. This international issue was complicated by continuing Balkan unrest under Ottoman rule. The Near Eastern Question has continued into the twentieth century, becoming critical once again in the years following World War II. The Russians, whether tsarists or Communists, have never abandoned their plans to one day gain control of the Turkish Straits and extend their rule to the shores of the Mediterranean Sea.

NATION-MAKING IN ITALY

Common denominators in Italian and German unification. The two most important achievements of nineteenth-century European nationalism were the unification of Italy and Germany. Let us now see how these achievements radically altered the European state system.

In the case of both Italy and Germany, there was a dynamic nucleus—Sardinia* in Italy and Prussia in Germany—around which a nation was built. Both Italy and Germany were led by master practitioners of the art of calculating diplomacy: Cavour and Bismarck. Both Italy and Germany had a common obstacle to national unity—Austria, since 1815 master of central Europe. In the case of Italian unification, however, a special complication was the existence of the Papal

* The kingdom of Sardinia included both the island of Sardinia and mainland territories, especially Piedmont. *Sardinia* is used, as in Chapter 7, to refer to the entire kingdom.

States ruled from Rome by the pope. The Italian nationalists were faced with the problem of stripping this great religious leader of his secular powers and absorbing his territories into a united Italy without incurring the wrath of the Catholic powers in Europe.

There were strong economic forces back of the *Risorgimento* in Italy, as there were behind German nationalism. It was said that Italy needed a thorough economic transformation: good communications (especially a network of railways), modern banks, the removal of local tariffs, a uniform currency, uniform weights and measures, and the encouragement of agriculture and industry.

Both the German and Italian unifications were ultimately achieved not by romantic poets or intellectuals but by the dispassionate calculations of practical statesmen who exercised the art of diplomacy divorced from ethical considerations. This kind of statecraft is known as *Realpolitik;* in Germany it became identified with the policy that Bismarck called "blood and iron."

Latent nationalism in Italy. In the early 1850's, Italy still remained what Metternich had contemptuously called it—"a geographical expression." The Young Italy movement of Mazzini and the first phase of the *Risorgimento* had failed. Except in Sardinia, where young King Victor Emmanuel II refused to abrogate the liberal constitution grudgingly granted by his late father, Charles Albert, there was reaction and repression.

This victory of autocracy, however, was more apparent than real. Mazzini's appeal for a free Italy had been addressed to:

. . . men speaking the same language, treading the same earth, cradled in their infancy with the same maternal songs, strengthened in their youth by the same sun, inspired by the same memories, the same sources of literary genius.[2]

This appeal had taken root and proceeded to grow quietly but rapidly in the decade following 1848.

Count Cavour. A new phase of the Italian *Risorgimento* began with the career of Count Camillo Benso di Cavour (1810-1861), one of the most important statesmen of the nineteenth century. Born of a noble family in Sardinia, Cavour was educated for a military career, but after traveling in Switzerland, France, and England, he became a thoroughgoing liberal and began to ponder on how best to free Italy from Austrian domination. He founded a newspaper, named it *Risorgimento,* and used it to spread his nationalist views.

In 1852 Cavour became prime minister of Sardinia. He carried through a series of important economic reforms in the kingdom but soon realized that Italian unity could not be gained by measures which tended to promote economic unity only—that in order to unify Italy, it would be necessary to resort to cannon and to fight Austria. He realized also that Sardinia could not fight Austria unaided; an ally was indispensable. To advertise his cause and "put Sardinia on the map," Cavour in 1855 astonished Europe by joining Great Britain and France in their fight against Russia in the Crimean War (see p. 237). Although this step at first appeared ridiculous, it enabled Cavour to make a

Two months before his death, Cavour saw his life's work culminate in the proclamation of Victor Emmanuel II as king of a united Italy.

speech calling attention to the grievances of Italy at the peace conference one year later.

The Austro-Italian War. Cavour's speech impressed Napoleon III, who was to become the ally Cavour was seeking. In 1858 the emperor of the French and Cavour held a secret meeting in France. It was agreed that if Cavour could trick Austria into war, France would come to Sardinia's assistance and help eject Austria from the Italian provinces of Lombardy and Venetia. Sardinia was then to rule over all of northern Italy. In return, France would receive from Sardinia two provinces—Nice and Savoy—which had been part of France during the Napoleonic period.

Napoleon III promised aid in the belief that a new northern Italian kingdom friendly to France would make his position stronger on the diplomatic checkerboard of Europe. And, as a Bonaparte, he was intrigued by the prospect of territorial gain and military glory.

Within a year Cavour had tricked Austria into war by blowing up into major proportions a minor crisis over the conscription of soldiers from Lombardy and Venetia for the Austrian army. He offered sanctuary to Italian deserters and began to mobilize the Sardinian army—moves which prompted Austria to attack. Two bloody battles were fought at Magenta and Solferino, and the Austrian troops were driven out of Lombardy by Sardinian and French soldiers. Again, the call for Italian unity was heard across the land. Revolutions broke out in Tuscany, Modena, Parma, and Romagna.

During the progress of the fighting, Napoleon III was acclaimed by Italians as their savior and liberator. But before the allied armies could invade Austrian-held Venetia, the French emperor—without consulting Cavour—made a separate peace with Austria. Too late, Napoleon III realized that he had started a movement destined to unite not only northern Italy but the whole peninsula, creating a strong rival on the borders of France. Another factor influencing Napo-

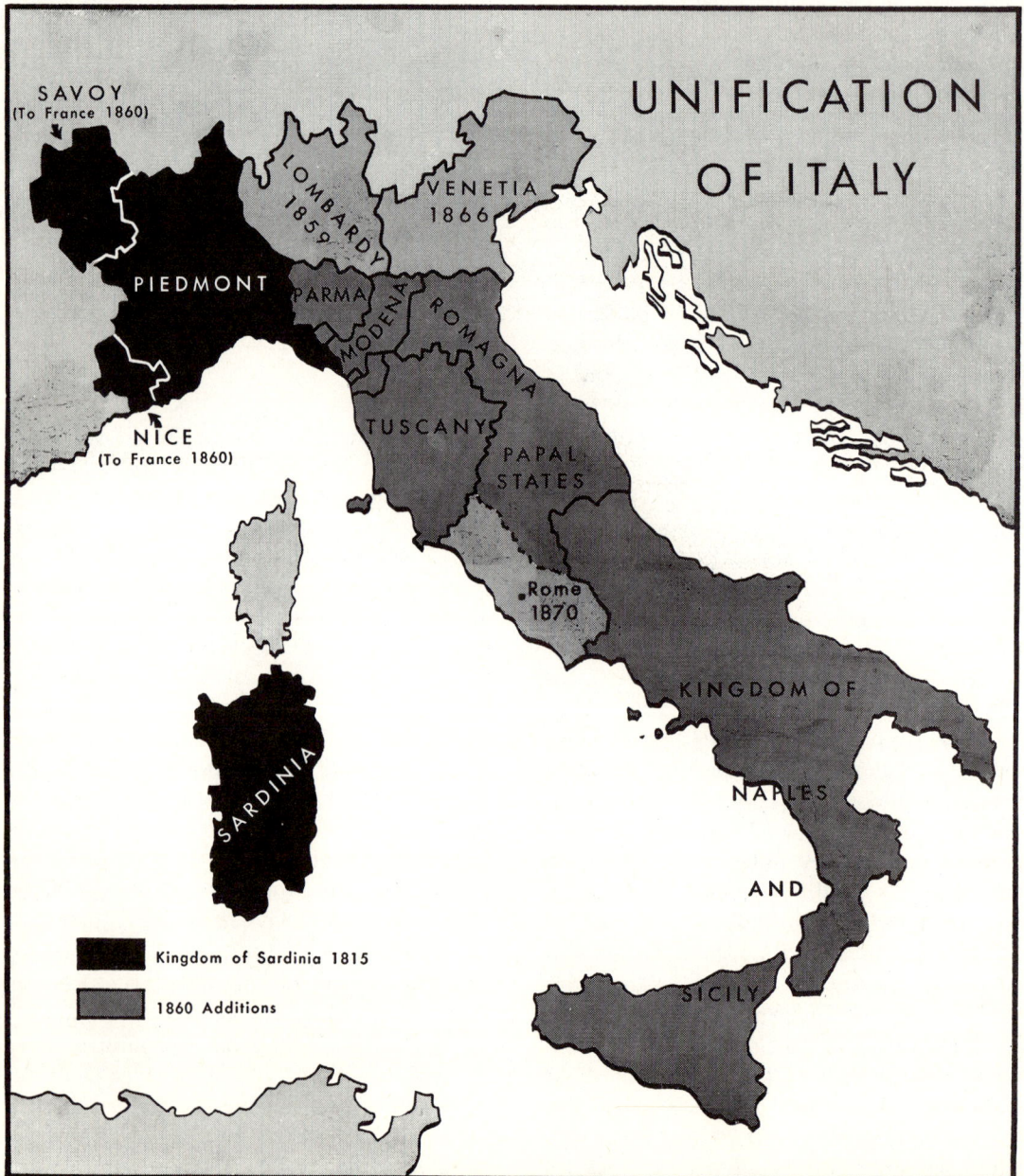

UNIFICATION OF ITALY

SAVOY
(To France 1860)

LOMBARDY 1859

VENETIA 1866

PIEDMONT

PARMA

MODENA

ROMAGNA

NICE
(To France 1860)

TUSCANY

PAPAL STATES

Rome 1870

SARDINIA

KINGDOM OF

NAPLES

AND

SICILY

Kingdom of Sardinia 1815

1860 Additions

leon's action was his fear of Prussian military moves on the Rhine frontier while he was occupied in Italy. He also suspected that Cavour had designs against the Papal States, a policy which would alienate the support of the French Catholics.

Although Cavour was furious, in 1859 he agreed to a peace settlement with Austria by which Lombardy was added to Sardinia, the exiled rulers of Parma, Modena, Tuscany, and Romagna were restored, and an Italian confederation was created in which Austria, as ruler of Venetia, was included. One year later, largely through the auspices of Great Britain, plebiscites were conducted in Italy. Tuscany, Modena, and Parma voted to join Sardinia. French expectations were satisfied when Nice and Savoy were ceded to France.

Garibaldi and his Red Shirts. The center of interest now shifted to southern Italy and to a new Italian leader. Giuseppe Garibaldi, the follower of Mazzini who had been forced into exile after taking part in the unsuccessful revolutionary movement of 1848, returned to Italy in 1854. Secretly subsidized by Cavour, Garibaldi recruited one thousand tough adventurers, his immortal Red Shirts, and in 1860 successfully invaded and conquered the island of Sicily, part of the reactionary, pro-Austrian kingdom of Naples and Sicily. Next he turned to the mainland and attacked the remaining forces of the king of Naples and Sicily. The Neapolitan troops were not loyal, and Garibaldi easily conquered the kingdom, entering Naples in triumph.

Garibaldi planned to set up a separate democratic government, which would have been a serious obstacle to the creation of a united Italy. Cavour therefore rushed troops to Naples, and Garibaldi surrendered his power to the king of Sardinia, Victor Emmanuel II. By November 1860, Sardinia had annexed the former kingdom of Naples and Sicily and all the papal lands except Rome and its surrounding territory, known as the Patrimony of St. Peter.

Garibaldi was a romantic nationalist and a daredevil adventurer, but he had little of the diplomat in him. Without realizing the political danger of his action, the conqueror

Although his dream of an Italian republic was not realized, Giuseppe Garibaldi has remained a national hero because of his fight for the unification of Italy.

of Naples resolved to attack the territories still under papal rule and bring the Eternal City itself into the united Italian kingdom. Such a move would certainly alienate Catholics all over the world and probably precipitate war with France, since Napoleon III had stationed troops at Rome to protect the pope. To avoid the danger, Sardinian troops in 1862 forcibly restrained the Garibaldian volunteers from attacking Rome. This action disgusted Garibaldi, who had little use for high diplomacy. Refusing all the financial rewards and honors proffered him by Victor Emmanuel, he sailed once more into exile, this time self-imposed, carrying "nothing but a sack of flour, a box of red herring, four crowns, a morsel of cheese, and a small crust of bread."[3]

Unity achieved. Italy's first parliament met at Turin in February 1861. A new nation of 22,000,000 citizens had been created, but the task had not yet been completed. Austria still controlled Venetia, while Rome and the Patrimony of St. Peter were still under papal control. Cavour, who died in 1861, did not live to see the full fruits of his works, but he realized that a united Italy was not far off. Although many have criticized his duplicity, he himself made no attempt to hide the true nature of his methods. He once said:

If we did for ourselves what we do for our country, what rascals we should be.[4]

Cavour was not the sole creator of the *Risorgimento,* but from the day he took charge, "everything changed. . . . Italian patriotism was disciplined . . . a new spirit animated it; dissension, disunion, vain dreaming, gave way to ordered, logical, and practical action."[5]

By acting as an ally of Prussia during the war between Prussia and Austria in 1866 (see p. 228), Italy obtained Venetia. And when the Franco-Prussian War broke out in 1870 and French troops were withdrawn from Rome, Italian troops took possession of the Eternal City and the last chapter in Italian unification was written.

THE TRIUMPH OF BLOOD

AND IRON IN GERMANY

Acceleration of German nationalism. Although the German revolution of 1848 and the Frankfurt Assembly failed to achieve their liberal-national purposes, the nationalist movement in Germany was far from dead. The unification movement was stimulated anew by the Austro-Italian War of 1859. A German patriotic society was formed for "achieving the unity of the fatherland and the development of its liberties."

The activities of a group of remarkable German historians also accelerated German nationalism. Such scholars as Heinrich von Treitschke saw in the Italian struggle a clear example to follow:

Whoever . . . has not lost his understanding of true human greatness, must gaze at this wonderful spectacle with utmost joy, how within fifty years a nation, sunk to the lowest moral depths, has raised itself to honorable unity and readiness

to self-sacrifice and, out of the mere geographical expression of Italy, has become a political reality.[6]

Treitschke eloquently advocated the union of all Germans under the leadership of Prussia:

There is only one salvation! One state, one monarchic Germany under the Hohenzollern dynasty.[7]

Prussia's growing strength. During the first half of the nineteenth century, Prussia deferred to Austrian leadership in central Europe; in 1848 it was still subordinate to Austria. Metternich's influence was strong, and the Hapsburgs, who held the glorious memory of the now-extinct Holy Roman Empire, still enjoyed a great deal of prestige. The will of the popularly elected German representatives of the Frankfurt Assembly to unite Germany had been blocked when King Frederick William IV of Prussia refused the crown of a new German empire for fear of the Hapsburgs. A later plan by the Prussian king himself to unite Germany had been thwarted by Austria and Russia. Prussia, however, had been transforming itself into a prosperous, well-administered state quite capable of taking care of the Austrian empire.

The same economic forces that had been operating in Italy had been working for national unity in Germany. By midcentury the Industrial Revolution had begun in earnest. Of special importance was the Zollverein, or customs union, established in 1834, which instituted free trade throughout Prussia and the territories of other member states. By 1842 most of the German states belonged to the Zollverein. This tariff union not only demonstrated that closer economic cooperation was good business for the various states but also strengthened the position of the middle-class leaders of the German nationalist movement. Most important, by increasing the economic ties between the German states, the Zollverein made easier their political unification under Prussia.

Although accounts of Germany's political unification are often limited to discussions of Bismarck's accomplishments in the 1860's and 1870's, Germany had already achieved considerable economic unity under Prussian leadership before Bismarck came to power in Prussia in 1862. (All of the members of the Zollverein except Luxemburg eventually became part of the German empire.) Austria, on the other hand, remained aloof from the Zollverein, not appreciating its political significance and its implied menace to Hapsburg dominance.

Prussian government and public administration were modern and efficient. Civil servants were well trained, honest, and highly devoted to the service of the state. The hierarchy of government bureaus and departments was logical and functional. By the middle of the century, the general citizenry of Prussia attended public schools far in advance of those found in any of the other great powers, including the United States; and Prussian higher education enjoyed an enviable reputation throughout Europe. Prussia by 1850 was rapidly building up the strength to compel central Europe to do its bidding, but it was twelve years before there appeared the man who was to formulate the necessary orders.

Bismarck and his policy of blood and iron.
The unification of Germany was achieved through the genius of a consummate statesman, Otto von Bismarck (1815-1898). The future German chancellor grew up a typical Prussian aristocrat, or Junker, an enemy to all liberal ideas and a fanatical supporter of the Prussian state and its king. As a university student, Bismarck made little impression on his professors but astonished his comrades by his beer-drinking capacity and gained renown as a duelist. A great bear of a man, he continued throughout his career to amaze others with his lusty appetites. He smoked Havana cigars constantly and once boasted he would consume five thousand bottles of champagne in his lifetime.

After his university days, Bismarck entered the Prussian civil service but found his post monotonous. Returning to his estate, he tried politics in 1847 and found this career to his liking. Soon he joined the diplomatic corps and carried out valuable missions in St. Petersburg and in Paris.

A skillful diplomat and a ruthless advocate of military might, Otto von Bismarck engineered the unification of the German state.

In 1862 Bismarck was called to be chancellor. His appointment coincided with a serious crisis: the king wished to strengthen the army, but the legislature would not approve the necessary appropriations. Following Bismarck's advice, the king successfully defied the parliament and levied the necessary taxes without its consent.

The Prussian constitutional crisis of 1862-1866 was one of the most fateful periods in German history. Bismarck's strength as Prussian chancellor was due to his strong monarchist position and, in turn, the complete support of the king. The Prussian Chamber of Deputies repeatedly refused to accept the government's budgets; the chamber was dissolved, but new elections resulted again in new chambers opposed to Bismarck's government. The government had the machinery for collecting taxes, and the chamber could not prevent it from unconstitutionally spending the money for the army.

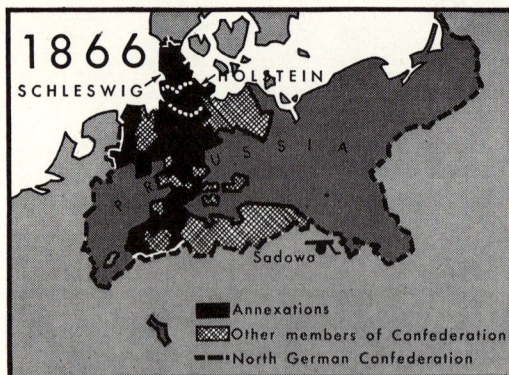

Formed after the Austro-Prussian War, the North German Confederation was dominated by Prussia and excluded Austria and four southern German states. Prussia's two new acquisitions were Schleswig, gained in the war with Denmark in 1864, and Holstein, ceded by Austria in 1866.

In the end the Chamber of Deputies withdrew its constitutional opposition to Bismarck's budgets in recognition of his spectacular foreign policy success, for the chancellor soon undertook the union of the German states under the leadership of Prussia. In spite of the strong nationalist movement, there were great difficulties in the way of his project. Among the various German kingdoms, a strong tradition of state rights existed. How could they be induced to give up their sovereignty? Was the Prussian army equal to the serious fighting that must come in the process of unification? Would the Prussian people be willing to fight against their blood brothers in Austria? Could France be weakened and its opposition to German unification be destroyed?

With meticulous care Bismarck prepared for the task of building a powerful new German empire. Not only was he a superb master of diplomatic intrigue, but he worshiped force. Boldly, he declared:

Germany does not look to Prussia's liberalism, but to her power. . . . The great questions of the day are not to be decided by speeches and majority resolutions—therein lay the weakness of 1848 and 1849—but by blood and iron![8]

Wars against Denmark and Austria. In 1864 Bismarck invited Austria to join Prussia in waging war on Denmark, the issue being the status of two duchies bordering on Prussia and Denmark—Schleswig and Holstein—which were claimed by both Denmark and the German Confederation. The Prussian army, aided by Austrian forces, easily smashed the Danish defenses; the administration of Holstein was awarded to Austria, while Schleswig came under Prussian rule.

Once Denmark had been defeated, Bismarck next proceeded to isolate Austria, for until Austria's influence was removed from the German Confederation, Prussia could never unify Germany. Sardinia was promised Venetia if it would assist Prussia when war came, and the French emperor was induced to be neutral by intimations of Prussian support should France seek to widen its frontiers.

Bismarck provoked war with Austria without difficulty. He expressed alarm over the way the Austrians were ruling Holstein and sent Prussian troops into the province. Hostilities broke out in 1866 and lasted only seven weeks. At the battle of Sadowa the Austrian army was defeated by superior Prussian forces, which had been made into the most efficient fighting machine in the world. To avoid humiliating Austria, Prussia offered a moderate peace settlement, ending the old German Confederation. In its place the North German Confederation was formed under Prussian domination, with Austria and four southern German states excluded. The province of Holstein was annexed by Prussia.

In four years Bismarck had succeeded in unifying all of northern Germany under Prussian leadership, thus ending centuries of Austrian predominance in German politics. Faced with this success, the Chamber of Deputies in 1866 legalized ex post facto Bismarck's unconstitutional actions. The Prussian tradition of executive independence from popular control remained a permanent feature of German constitutional organization.

Both Bismarck and Cavour faced formidable obstacles in achieving national unification; both exercised a decisive influence on the course of events through personal leader-

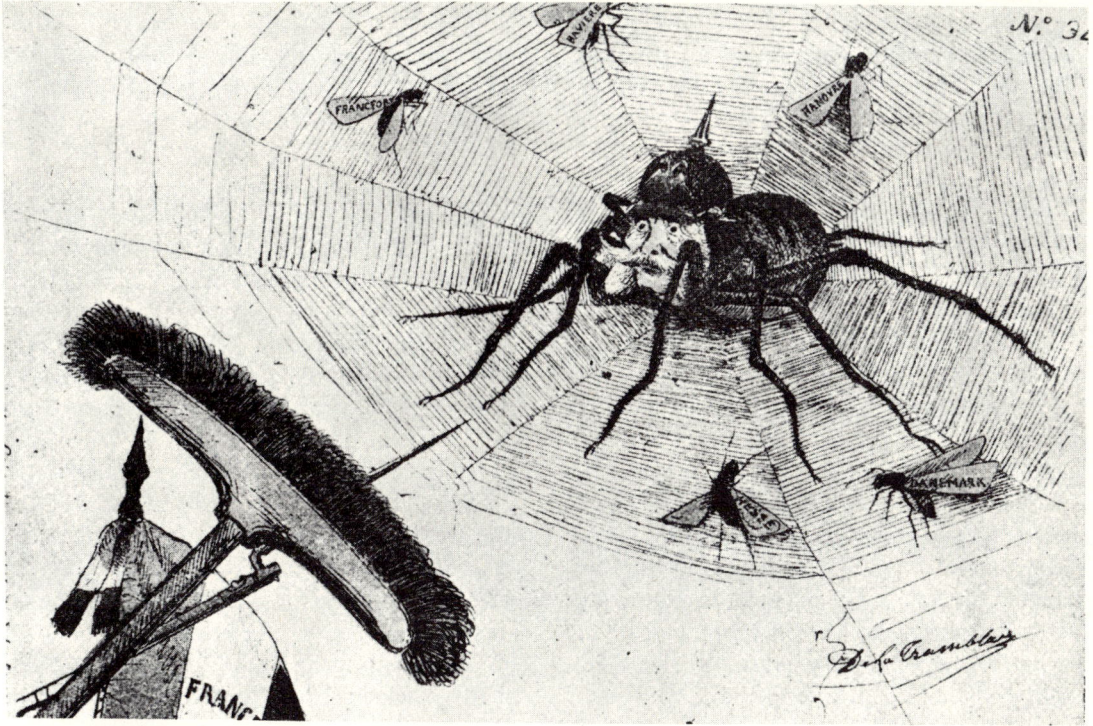

A French cartoon before the Franco-Prussian War shows France about to sweep away Bismarck's victim-laden web.

ship. Cavour had the advantage that much of the territory annexed to the kingdom of Sardinia was not under Italian rule. Liberation from foreign rule came simultaneously with unification, and Cavour, unlike Bismarck, for the most part had little domestic opposition with which to contend. Most of the German territories of Bismarck's North German Confederation had been independent; for them the price of unification was Prussianization.

DOWNFALL OF THE SECOND

FRENCH EMPIRE

Prosperity without liberty under Napoleon III. At this point in our narrative, it is essential to discuss the chief barrier between Bismarck and his twin objectives—a greater Germany and German mastery of western Europe. This obstacle was the Second French Empire of Napoleon III, which

since its establishment in 1852 had prospered in both domestic and foreign affairs. In fact, the successful outcome of two wars, the Crimean War and the Austrian-Italian War (p. 225) had made France by 1860 the mistress of Europe. Over a period of eighteen years, Napoleon III, the "emperor boss," gave his realm glory, prosperity, and, above all, order and discipline—nearly everything a great nation could desire, in fact, except liberty. Although the governmental structure retained the outward forms of a parliamentary regime, the suffrage was juggled to give the supporters of the emperor a safe majority in the legislature—which had little power anyway. An efficient secret police was established to hunt down "dangerous elements," the press was censored, and parliamentary debates were not allowed to receive any publicity.

But if the France of Napoleon III lacked liberty, it did enjoy prosperity. Scientific farming became more prevalent, and under the emperor's benevolent despotism, a national mortgage bank was set up to provide capital for peasants on the security of their land. Capital accumulated, large-scale industries and corporations developed, and in two decades production doubled. France sponsored the building of the famous Suez Canal (1869), railway mileage increased fivefold, and steamship lines prospered. An ambitious program of public works was undertaken. Paris was transformed by broad boulevards, sweeping vistas, and harmonious architecture. The Great Exhibition held at Paris in 1855 served as a symbol of French prosperity.

Successes and failures in foreign affairs. Called "Saint-Simon on horseback" after the French socialist who believed in a kind of planned economy benefiting all men, Napoleon III thought of himself as the first servant of the empire, devoted to the task of making the state prosperous and progressive. He once said:

The Napoleonic idea is not one of war, but a social, industrial, commercial, humanitarian idea.[9]

But though he was a man of peace, he was heir to the Napoleonic legend. He had no choice but to pursue a spirited role in international affairs.

For ten years the foreign policy of Napoleon III was remarkably successful. Allying France with England in the Crimean War, he gained the desired victory against Russia and appeared at the peace conference as the arbiter of Europe. In 1859 his support of Cavour in Italy against Austria earned him military glory and gained Nice and Savoy for France. Furthermore, during this period the empire expanded its colonial possessions, cooperated with England in a successful war against China, and intervened to safeguard the interests of Christians under Turkish rule in Syria.

Until 1861 Napoleon III could boast that France was mistress of Europe, but after this date the emperor seemed to lose his touch in foreign affairs. And he was beset by a series of internal problems. In the 1860's the morale and efficiency of the Second French Empire rapidly declined. The army

rested on old laurels; the imperial court and the bureaucracy were corrupt. In a bid for liberal support, Napoleon III allowed the debates of the legislature to be published once again and increased the financial powers of the legislature. Nevertheless, the people tired of his regime; they expected their sovereign to provide them with a continuous stream of triumphs.

In 1863, while the United States was distracted by civil war, Napoleon III embroiled France in the madcap scheme of placing Maximilian, a Hapsburg prince, on the Mexican throne. Some forty thousand troops were involved in this expensive adventure, which ended in the withdrawal of the French forces and the capture and execution of Maximilian by Mexican patriots (see Chapter 9). While discontent increased at home, Napoleon III in 1863 failed to intervene in Poland on the side of the patriotic rebels who had risen against Russian rule. Had he championed Polish nationalism, perhaps he could have rallied all parties in France to his support.

Again in 1865, Napoleon III in a fateful conference with Bismarck allowed himself to be completely hoodwinked. In return for vague promises, in which the German statesman mentioned securing for France "perhaps the Palatinate and the Rhine frontier, perhaps Luxemburg, perhaps part of Belgium or Switzerland,"[10] the French emperor pledged himself not to interfere in any Austro-Prussian war. After the conflict had been decided by the Prussian victory at Sadowa, Napoleon III reminded Bismarck of his promised reward. When the French ambassador pressed the matter, the Prussian chancellor is reported to have laughed in his face. Bismarck announced that he had no recollection of promises made to France. The ambassador thereupon specifically raised the possibility of French compensation at the expense of Belgium, and an agreement was drawn up in which Bismarck backed this claim in return for French recognition of the federal union of all German states. The chancellor next saw to it that the document was made public in England, the nation where it would do the most harm to the French empire. When it appeared in the London *Times,* the public was incensed at this threat to Belgian independence. British public opinion became openly hostile to Napoleon III, and Bismarck thus made certain that there would be no British support of France in case of war. At the same time, by supporting Russia during the Polish revolt in 1863 and by offering Austria a moderate peace in 1866, Bismarck successfully isolated these two states from France.

The Franco-Prussian War. Too late, Napoleon realized that a great rival power was in the making. No longer would it be possible for France to dominate Europe. "Revenge for Sadowa" became a common cry in France. The emperor himself did not work hard for peace, because he felt the French imperial house must have martial glory.

Bismarck also welcomed war. He was convinced that Napoleon's need to recoup his prestige would lead finally to his undoing. Referring to Napoleon III, Bismarck declared:

The adventurer on the throne . . . must always produce an effect. His safety depends on his personal prestige, and to enhance it sensations must follow each other in rapid succession. Napoleon III has recently lost more prestige than he can afford. To recover it he will start a dispute with us on some pretext or other. I do not believe he personally wishes war . . . but his insecurity will drive him on.[11]

So long as a powerful France existed, it would be a menace to the fulfillment of German unification. A conflict with France, Bismarck felt, would stimulate a common patriotism in the hearts of all Germans, irrespective of the state in which they lived.

The immediate cause of the war centered about the succession to the Spanish throne, left vacant after the exile of the Spanish queen. Anxious to avoid the extreme solutions proposed by equally fanatical royalists and republicans, the Spanish legislature sought stability by searching for a new king. The throne was offered to Leopold, a Hohenzollern prince. In the eyes of the French government, a Prussian on the throne of

Spain would be a most unwelcome extension of Prussian influence, which was appearing more and more formidable. Because of French protests, Prince Leopold withdrew his candidacy. Then the French government made a fatal mistake. The French ambassador was sent to Ems, where the Prussian king was visiting, to demand that William I promise that no Hohenzollern would ever sit on the Spanish throne. The king politely refused this unreasonable request and directed that a dispatch (the "Ems dispatch") be sent to Bismarck acquainting him with the results of the interview. Bismarck altered the dispatch slightly in order to give the impression that the French ambassador had insulted the Prussian king and that the ruler had thereupon retaliated and insulted the ambassador. When this version of the dispatch was published, both the French and the Prussian people were infuriated.

France declared war in July 1870, and amid wild enthusiasm and shouts of "On to Berlin," the French regiments marched to the front. But there was no comparison between the superbly trained Prussian hosts and the chaotically disorganized army of Napoleon III. The uncoordinated state of the French military machine was described by one of the generals:

In the supply depôts no camp-kettles, dishes or stoves; no canteens for the ambulances and no pack-saddles; in short no ambulances neither for divisions nor corps. Up to the 7th it was all but impossible to obtain a mule-litter for the wounded. That day thousands of wounded men were left in the hands of the enemy; no preparations had been made to get them away. . . . On the 6th an order was given to blow up a bridge, no powder could be found in the whole army corps, nor with the engineers, nor with the gunners![12]

The French suffered reverse after reverse. In September came the crowning disaster —the surrender at Sedan, where an entire French army and the emperor himself were forced to capitulate. Thus the glory of the Second French Empire and the power of its creator, Napoleon III, perished on the battlefield just as the empire of his uncle, Napoleon, had disintegrated before the unbending squares of British infantry at Waterloo.

News of this debacle swept the discredited Second Empire from power, and a republic was proclaimed in Paris. New leaders emerged to carry on resistance against the German forces, and Paris itself came under siege. The words of a young doctor, Georges Clemenceau, who had been appointed mayor of one of the city's twenty boroughs, symbolized the gallant spirit of the Parisians:

Citizens, must France destroy herself and disappear, or shall she resume her old place in the vanguard of nations? . . . The enemy is at the gates of the city. The day may not be far distant when our breasts will be the last rampart of the mother-country. Each of us knows his duty. We are children of the Revolution: let us seek inspiration in the example of our forefathers in 1792, and like them we shall conquer. Vive la France! Vive la République![13]

In casting off the decrepit spirit of Napoleon III's regime, France had rediscovered itself. But it was too late. After a siege of four months, Paris was forced to surrender. By the Treaty of Frankfurt, France lost Alsace and part of Lorraine to Prussia and was required to pay a huge indemnity. Men like Clemenceau never forgot this humiliation. History was to give France a chance to retaliate after World War I.

German and Italian unification completed. During the Franco-Prussian War the southern German states had joined the North German Confederation. Thus the common struggle against France removed the last obstacle to national unification. In January 1871, in the Hall of Mirrors at the palace of Versailles, King William of Prussia was proclaimed German emperor.

Bismarck's most important work was completed by 1871, although he remained chancellor of the German empire until 1890. To achieve his ends, he had used ruthless means. But perhaps, as in the case of Cavour, he felt that circumstances left him no alternative. It was a tragedy for the world that to Bismarck blood and iron seemed essential in forging a united Germany, for his

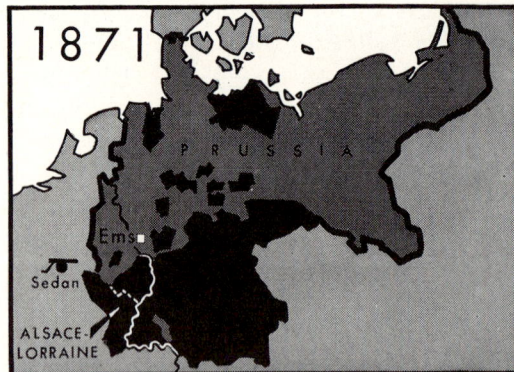

The unification of Germany was completed during the Franco-Prussian War, when the southern German states joined the North German Confederation. Alsace and part of Lorraine were acquired from France by the Treaty of Frankfurt.

successes strengthened the notion that war is a national business that can be made to pay big dividends. Furthermore, from the time that Bismarck defied the will of the Prussian parliament in 1862, there was no opportunity for German public opinion to unseat the executive or to control governmental policy. The German state was now thoroughly set in a pattern of despotic government even though it retained its constitutional forms. This situation continued until the end of the Hohenzollern dynasty in 1918.

As an important by-product of the Franco-Prussian War, the ambitions of Count Cavour were finally realized. Faced with defeat at the hands of the Germans, Napoleon III in 1870 withdrew his troops from Rome. An Italian army then occupied the Eternal City, and in 1871 Rome became the capital of Italy.

FORMATION OF THE DUAL

MONARCHY

Weakening of the Austrian empire. The military triumphs of Prussia had important repercussions in Austria. As we have already seen in Chapter 7, the collapse in 1848 of the liberal and nationalistic movements in eastern Europe had been followed by stern repression. As part of this reaction a

With Paris about to fall to the Prussian armies, King William of Prussia is proclaimed German emperor by his princes in the Hall of Mirrors of the palace of Versailles. Smiling with satisfaction, Bismarck stands foremost at the foot of the dais.

new constitution, promulgated in 1851, imposed an undisguised system of absolutism upon all peoples in the Austrian empire. Measures were taken to centralize governmental administration by concentrating authority in Vienna. An active policy of Germanization was carried out among the non-Teutonic peoples of the empire. In Hungary, for example, government posts were filled by Germans and Czechs; Hungarian was displaced by German as the official language; and the area was made a mere province of the Austrian empire.

The defeat inflicted upon Austrian armies in 1859 by French and Sardinian forces, however, doomed these reactionary measures. The old ways were thoroughly discredited, and in Vienna it was realized at last that if the Austrian empire was to survive, Hungarian nationalism would have to be appeased. But though willing to grant constitutional government to Hungary, German liberals and reformers in Austria had

no sympathy for the Hungarian desire for independence and wished to have a single parliament for the whole empire. As a result, in 1861, a year after local self-government had been restored in Hungary and German officials had been removed, a new imperial constitution was framed in which representatives were to be elected from the various provincial parliaments to a central, imperial Diet. The Hungarians would have nothing to do with these measures, and the country seemed on the verge of revolt.

Deák, leader of the Hungarians. At this point a new leader, Francis Deák (1803-1876), became the champion of Hungarian nationalism. Deák followed in the steps of Kossuth, the hero of 1848, but he was a wiser statesman—firm but moderate, courageous yet cautious. He had little use for revolutions and always expressed loyalty to the monarchy. A statement of the Hungarian Diet, drawn up by Deák, declared: "We do not wish to dissolve the union." The statement accepted the need for joint action by Austria and Hungary in "common affairs" but argued that "a forced unity will never make the Empire strong."[14]

Following Austria's disastrous defeat by Prussian arms at Sadowa in 1866, Deák was asked what Hungary demanded. In his famous reply the Austrians were told, "Hungary asks no more after Königgrätz [Sadowa] than she asked before it."[15] The Austrian emperor responded by offering to establish the Magyars as equal partners in ruling the empire. The offer was accepted, and in 1867 the constitution known as the *Ausgleich* (Compromise) was promulgated.

The Dual Monarchy established. The prime minister of Austria at the time has left an interesting account of his reasons for accepting the dual system:

So long as Austria was a purely despotic State, and the Emperor ruled over it as an absolute monarch . . . the governors were there [in the provinces] but to register the sovereign's Imperial will and to enforce it by arms if the necessity should arise. The revolutionary wave of 1848 . . . raised for the first time among the masses . . . objections and antipathies which generated the firm resolve in their minds to sweep the whole system away. . . . In the scheme which I have developed I have endeavored to give Hungary not a new position with regard to the Austrian empire, but to secure her in the one which she has occupied. The Emperor of Austria is King of Hungary; my idea was that he should revive in his person the Constitution of which he and his ancestors have been the heads. The leading principles of my plan are, not the creation of a new kingdom and a new Constitution, but the resuscitation of an old monarchy and an old Constitution; not the separation of one part of the empire from the other, but the drawing together of the two component parts by the recognition of their joint positions, the maintenance of their mutual obligations, their community in questions affecting the entire empire, and their proportional pecuniary responsibility for the liabilities of the whole State. It is no plan of separation that I have carried out; on the contrary, it is one of closer union, not by the creation of a new power, but by the recognition of an old one.[16]

Setting up a unique form of government, a Dual Monarchy known as Austria-Hungary, the *Ausgleich* made the Hapsburg sovereign king in Hungary and emperor in Austria. Each country had its own constitution, official language, flag, and parliament, but finance, defense, and foreign affairs were under ministers common to both countries. These common ministers were supervised by the "Delegations," which consisted of sixty members from the Austrian parliament and an equal number from the Hungarian legislature. The *Ausgleich* also provided for ten-year agreements on matters common to both countries, such as commerce, railways, and taxation.

While the Germans of Austria recognized the equality of the Magyars of Hungary, these two dominant nationalities made few concessions to the aspirations of their subject nationalities. In Chapter 12 we shall examine in more detail how this problem was handled in the empire. We shall also see how the restlessness of the subject peoples in Austria-Hungary became enmeshed with a Pan-Slav movement sponsored by Serbia and Russia—a movement which threatened the very existence of the Austrian empire. Nationalism was ultimately to prove the undoing of Austria-Hungary and to involve Europe in the First World War.

STORM OVER THE BALKANS

Balkan nationalities. While Germany and Italy were achieving national unity and preparing to join the ranks of the major European states that claimed great power status, nationalism was also stirring among the subject peoples in the Balkan territories of the Ottoman empire. During the nineteenth century, Serbs, Greeks, Rumanians, and Bulgarians all developed a sense of national feeling and the same intense desire for independent national statehood that characterized their more powerful neighbors.

One branch of the Serbs, inhabiting the almost inaccessible mountain fastnesses of the region known as Montenegro, had never been entirely subdued by the Turks. Of the main body of the Serbian population in the Balkans, those in the north had secured recognition (through revolt) as an autonomous principality shortly after the Napoleonic period. The southern part of the Greek peninsula became a fully independent kingdom by the early 1830's. In spite of these instances of autonomy and independence, many more people of the two nationalities—people who were Serbs or Greeks by language and religious or cultural tradition—remained fully under Turkish rule.

The Near Eastern Question. One of the ambitions of the autonomous Serbs, the independent Greeks, and the other Balkan peoples, once independent, was to expand until all their nationals were included in appropriate independent Balkan states. Since the nationalist aspirations of the Balkan peoples could be satisfied only at the expense of the Ottoman empire, however, Balkan independence movements were never permitted to take their own course; instead, they were always complicated by the intervention of the great powers. The problem of the Ottoman empire in Europe was the single most persistent source of great power rivalry in the nineteenth century, forming what was known as the Near Eastern Question.

The Near Eastern Question has been defined as "the problem of filling up the vacuum created by the gradual disappearance of the Turkish Empire from Europe."[17] To this definition might be added the persistent factor of Russian imperialist pressure to gain control of the Dardanelles and the Bosporus, the strategic straits connecting the Black Sea with the eastern Mediterranean. To obtain a natural, warm-weather outlet to the Mediterranean, Russia needed control of the Straits, of Constantinople which stood guard over them, and, for complete security, of the Balkans as well. The acquisition of Constantinople would also have meant the realization of an old dream for Russia, which considered itself the true heir of the Byzantine empire.

Britain, which consistently opposed Russian designs on the Near East, feared that if any great power should gain control in that area, the balance of power in Europe would be altered decisively. And, if Russia were to obtain the Straits, Russian naval power in the eastern Mediterranean would challenge Britain's communications with India. Although most Englishmen detested the corrupt rule of the sultans, during most of the nineteenth century the British government preferred to support a weak but independent Turkey.

Although the rivalry between Great Britain and Russia in the Near East was one of the most consistent factors in the Near Eastern Question, other great powers had strong interests in the Ottoman empire, too. France, as a Mediterranean power, had long been involved in the Levant trade. During the French Revolutionary period Napoleon himself had led French armies into the important Ottoman provinces of Egypt and Syria. French was the language of business and commerce in the nineteenth century throughout the eastern Mediterranean, and France was a traditional spokesman for Roman Catholic interests in the Holy Land. In the Balkan territories of the Ottoman empire Austrian interest was of major concern. The Hapsburgs were the traditional bulwark of Christian Europe against the Turkish menace; as Ottoman power waned Hapsburg aggrandizement steadily chipped away at the frontier regions. After Italian unification deprived the Austrian monarchy of its provinces in Italy, and the Prussian unification of Germany removed Austrian influence from the north German states, the Balkans offered the only remaining area for Austrian expansion. In the latter part of the nineteenth century the new kingdom of Italy, aspiring to the status of a major Mediterranean power, claimed a share of Ottoman territories both in the Balkans and in North Africa. Only Germany, of the greatest powers, claimed no direct stake in Ottoman affairs, but the close diplomatic alliance between the Austrian and German empires late in the nineteenth century eventually brought about significant German involvement in the Near Eastern Question.

In the nineteenth century this Near Eastern power struggle brought on three Russo-Turkish wars and two wars in which France, England, and Russia fought either with or against Turkey, in addition to numerous revolts by subject nationalities against the Ottoman hegemony. The same Near Eastern Question in the twentieth century led to three wars before 1914 and helped precipitate the catastrophe of the First World War. In Chapter 18 we shall see that the Near Eastern Question still endangers world peace.

Anglo-Russian rivalry in the Near East. Russian expansion at the expense of the Turks had begun during the reign of Catherine the Great. After six years of war, Turkey had been compelled to sign the Treaty of Kuchuk Kainarji (1774), which awarded Azov and the north coast of the Black Sea to Russia, granted the Russians free navigation for their merchant ships in Ottoman waters (including the Straits), and, lastly, recognized the tsar as the protector of all eastern Orthodox Christians in the Ottoman empire. On several occasions Russia was to use this final concession as an excuse to intervene in Turkish affairs.

From 1788 to 1791 Austria and Russia fought the Turks, securing some territorial gains. At this time, the famous British statesman William Pitt the Younger denounced Russia's ambition to dismember Turkey. Beginning also to fear Russian expansion, Austria returned to the Ottomans the territory won from them. Britain and Austria realized that Turkey was a danger to their national interests, not because Turkey was strong but because it was weak.

In the meantime Russia continued to take over former territories of the Ottoman empire, thereby expanding westward along the north shore of the Black Sea and south-eastward along its east shore, which extended into the Caucasus region. During the Greek revolt of 1821, British statesmen feared that this uprising would give Russia an excuse to attack Turkey and thus expand further in the name of Greek independence. The jealousies of the big powers finally led France, England, and Russia to act cooperatively in putting an end to the fighting between Greek and Turk. The result was Greek independence without an undue expansion of Russian influence in the Balkans.

The Ottoman empire seemed on the very point of extinction in 1831, when the sultan's nominal representative in Egypt, the Pasha Mohammed Ali, attacked his master. To prevent the establishment of a new and probably stronger government at the Straits, the tsar sent an army to protect the Ottoman capital, extracting in return the Treaty of Unkiar Skelessi. In essence, this document made Turkey a protectorate of Russia. The Straits were closed to all war vessels except those of the signatories, making the Black Sea a Russian lake.

Turkey, the "Sick Man of Europe." The Treaty of Unkiar Skelessi had marked the high point of Russian influence over the Ottoman empire. In the years that followed, the Russian success did not go unchallenged. Chagrined by this Russian coup, British statesmen determined to stop Russia. For twenty years the leading advocate of this policy was Lord Palmerston.

From the early 1830's the mistrust between Britain and Russia deepened. Not only did Tsar Nicholas I see in Britain the main obstacle to what he believed was his nation's rightful destiny, but as an autocrat he thoroughly feared and detested the liberal tendencies of English politics. English sentiment was reflected by the poet Tennyson, who referred to Tsar Nicholas I as the "icy Muscovite" and the "o'er-grown barbarian of the east."

Nor was it only Russia's expansion in the Balkans that gave Britain concern. Russian pressure in central Asia sparked British attempts to control Afghanistan and make it a friendly buffer state between the Russians and India (see p. 303).

Nicholas I, stern soldier and unbending autocrat, was determined to carry on his predecessor's policy of expansion at the expense of decrepit Turkey. While visiting England in 1844, the tsar referred to Turkey as "a dying man" and proposed that England join in a dissection of the Ottoman carcass. British statesmen had no wish to be a party to an agreement that would result in Russia's taking over Constantinople. With his usual brusque manner, Lord Palmerston declared:

All that we hear every day of the week about the decay of the Turkish Empire, and its being a dead body, or a sapless trunk, and so forth, is pure and unadulterated nonsense.[18]

In the early 1850's the tsar raised for the second time with Great Britain the possibility of dismembering Turkey. Nicholas I hinted at a peaceful settlement which would involve the granting of independence to all Balkan nationalities under Russian protection, the transfer of Constantinople and the Straits to Russia, and the acquisition of Egypt by Great Britain. The latter showed no interest in these suggestions.

British policy at Constantinople was to encourage internal efforts to reform the Ottoman empire. Nicholas I apparently believed that Turkey was incapable of reform. Furthermore, a reform sufficient to preserve Turkey from dissolution was alarming to Russia, since the preservation of the Ottoman empire meant the end of Russian expansion toward the Mediterranean. Although Russian troops withdrew from the Principalities in 1851 after the revolutionary tide of 1848 had receded, in 1852 a quarrel between Nicholas I and Napoleon III over the management and protection of the holy places in Palestine gave Russia a new excuse to intervene in the affairs of the Ottoman empire. Ostensibly motivated by religious sentiments, the tsar reconfirmed Russia's protectorate over all Greek Christians in the Ottoman empire. His primary interest, of course, was the traditional Russian goal—to secure control of Constantinople and to ensure an entrance from the Black Sea to the Mediterranean.

The Crimean War. When, in 1853, an Anglo-French fleet was sent to bolster Turkish resistance to Russian demands, Nicholas once more occupied the Danubian Principalities as a counter pressure. Out of this jockeying for power in the Ottoman empire grew a war which none of the great powers really wanted. Turkey actually declared war alone (1853), whereupon the Russians destroyed the Turkish Black Sea fleet in a naval engagement. To protect Turkey, the Anglo-French fleet entered the Black Sea and, when Russia ignored an ultimatum to quit the Principalities, Great Britain and France also declared war (1854). With singular ingratitude—Russian armies had saved Austria from losing Hungary as recently as 1849—

Austria agreed to remain neutral only on condition Russia should withdraw from the Danubian Principalities. As soon as the Russian troops moved out the Austrians moved in as guardians, while the principal military activities of the war concentrated around the great Russian fortress of Sevastopol in the Crimea.

The Crimean War is an excellent example of the way in which great power rivalry used the Ottoman and Balkan territories in complete disregard for either the interests or the wishes of the inhabitants. Napoleon III saw in a war with Russia an opportunity to enhance the reputation of his dynasty. Sardinia participated to gain a seat at the conference table with the great powers. Great Britain was opposed to Russian presence at the Straits, and Austria opposed the further extension of Russian control in the Balkans because it would collide sooner or later with Austrian ambitions in that region.

The French and the British were poorly prepared for their offensive campaign. The soldiers at the front had no heavy coats to protect them from the severe winter weather, the horses had no hay, and the wounded had no medicines. War correspondents of the London *Times* brought these deplorable conditions to the attention of the British public:

. . . incompetency, lethargy, aristocratic hauteur, official indifference, favour, routine, perverseness and stupidity reign, revel and riot before Sebastopol.[19]

In September 1855 the fortress of Sevastopol finally fell to the combined armies of Britain, France, and Sardinia. Thwarted in the attempt to carve up the "Sick Man of Europe," Russia sued for peace. The Treaty of Paris (1856) affirmed the integrity of the Ottoman empire. Specifically, it provided for the neutralization of the Black Sea (neither Russia nor Turkey was to maintain forts or naval depots on its shores), closed the Straits to foreign warships, and declared that no power had the right to interfere on behalf of Turkey's Christian subjects.

Another important provision related to Rumania. To reduce Russian influence in the

The world's first battlefront pictures were taken during the Crimean War by Englishman Roger Fenton, who made this glass plate photograph of British infantry encamped near Russian positions northeast of Sevastopol in the spring of 1855.

Balkans, the Congress of Paris ended the Russian protectorate over Rumania that had been established in 1829, placed the country under the protection of the great powers, and permitted Turkey to maintain its suzerainty.

Significance of the Crimean War. The Crimean War has been described as "a contest entered into without necessity, conducted without foresight, and deserving to be reckoned from its archaic arrangements and tragic mismanagement rather among mediaeval than modern campaigns."[20] Of the many bloody battles of the war, Balaklava is best remembered for the gallant but tacti-

cally absurd charge of the British Light Brigade, described in the famous poem by Lord Tennyson which bears the refrain: "Into the valley of death rode the six hundred." The chivalric gallantry of the Light Brigade has been taken as a symbol of an outmoded attitude toward the grim business of modern war.

No great leaders emerged during the war, which was badly handled by both the allies and Russia. Great Britain's military reputation suffered a severe blow, and the Crimean army scandal brought about the resignation of the British prime minister. The only great name to come out of the war was that of

Florence Nightingale, who directed attention to the medical needs of soldiers during wartime. Sent to the base hospitals, the "Lady with the Lamp" brought about a complete change in the treatment of the wounded. Under her efficient charge, medical facilities were improved so that the terrible mortality due to cholera, dysentery, and gangrene was materially reduced.

The Crimean War momentarily halted Russian advance into the Balkans. But it did little to assuage the bitter international rivalries in that area. Bitterly resentful of what was regarded as gross Austrian "ingratitude," Moscow gave up the idea of having Austria as an ally in the carving up of the Ottoman empire and decided instead that this objective now required the weakening of Austria:

The eastern question can be solved only in Austria, not in Turkey; the way to Constantinople lies through Vienna.[21]

Pan-Slavism, agent of Russian expansion. The antiwestern Slavophile movement, which lauded Russian institutions, took on a political complexion after the Crimean War. Known as Pan-Slavism, this movement championed Russia as the protector of its "little brother Slavs," with the duty of freeing them from the barbaric rule of the Turks. Moreover, exponents of Pan-Slavism preached that it was Russia's destiny to create and rule a great Slavic empire. This faith in Russia as a dominant force in world history was born of a desire for recognition as a nation and was intensified by the humiliation suffered in the Crimean War.

After 1856, Slavonic Benevolent Committees were set up in the Balkans to encourage education and cultural exchange. And in a Slav Congress convened in Moscow, the tsar addressed the delegates as "brother Slavs." In the 1860's and 1870's, Pan-Slavism carried the message of Slavic solidarity to the Balkans, encouraging revolt.

Nationalist aspirations in the Balkans. In the theocratic Ottoman empire nationality was a matter of religion. Muslims enjoyed full legal rights, and the law was adminis-

tered by Muhammedan authorities. The administration of Christian subjects was largely turned over to the Christian authorities, which in most of the Balkans meant the Greek Orthodox Church. The Greek patriarch and the most prosperous and influential Greeks of the Ottoman empire lived in a quarter in Constantinople called the Phanar; for this reason, they are known as phanariots. The important position of the Greeks in commerce and administration was a factor in the development of Greek nationalism. At the same time, Greeks occupying privileged positions in the Ottoman empire often restricted or oppressed the nationalist aspirations of non-Greeks and promoted the Greek language and culture at the expense of the native ones.

Of all the Balkan peoples, probably the most oppressed by both the Turks and the phanariots were the Bulgarians. The Greek clergy followed a policy of systematic Hellenization designed to obliterate Bulgarian culture. Greek was the official language; even when the Bulgarian language was written Greek characters were used; in fact, the name Bulgaria was almost unknown in Europe at the beginning of the nineteenth century. The name Rumelia appeared on maps for the provinces inhabited principally by Bulgarians. The Hellenization of educated Bulgarians was extensive, but the mass of the peasantry were illiterate, and through them the Bulgarian language survived.

In the middle of the nineteenth century a literary and cultural revival, the invariable prelude to nationalism, began. In 1835 a Bulgarian school was founded at Odessa in Russia; more such schools were established in the years that followed. A national Bulgarian periodical was started at Smyrna. Progress was slow. Before 1877 there was only one printing press in the region inhabited principally by Bulgarians. Little education was available outside of schools in which Greek was spoken or those abroad. Despite the limited education available, Bulgarians eventually learned that the principle of nationality could be applied to them as well as to the Greeks.

A decisive step in the growth of the Bulgarian nationalist movement was the creation in 1870, with the approval of Turkey, of a Bulgarian national church. The head of this new church, the exarch, was situated in Constantinople. Russia had pressured Turkey to make this move, in part to reduce Greek-Bulgarian antipathy within the Orthodox Church. The Greek patriarch responded by excommunicating the exarch, and a tremendous struggle for support began. Under theologically-oriented Turkish law religious groups were thought of as national groups. Followers of the Greek patriarch were considered Greeks; followers of the Bulgarian exarch were considered Bulgarians. A subsequent Turkish law in 1870 permitted any community by two-thirds vote to shift from the Greek church to the exarchate; the Bulgarian nationalist movement thereby received further impetus. Rivalry, however, was not over religious but national control, and the Bulgarian church archieved marked success at the expense of the Greek Church among the Slavic inhabitants in most of Macedonia and the southern Balkans.

The revolts of 1875. At this point the story of Bulgarian independence becomes entwined with events in the whole Balkan area and with the growing interests of the great powers in this troubled region. In 1875 peasants revolted in the Turkish-governed district of Bosnia, a Serbian province not included in the autonomous Serbian state. Turkish tax collectors were leaving the peasants with less than a third of their crops. The complexity of nationality problems in the Balkans is illustrated by the case of the Turkish province of Bosnia. Many of the Serbian nobility had become Muhammedans, and thus remained landowners, but the bulk of the Serb peasants were Orthodox or Roman Catholic. Serbian nationalism among the Serbs living in either Turkish or Austrian territory was strongly influenced by the existence of an independent Serbia. The Bosnian revolt was followed by a declaration of war by Serbia and Montenegro against Turkey.

At the same time, the Bulgarians broke into revolt, but the Turks crushed the rebels with extreme cruelty. The "Bulgarian Massacres" caused a gasp of horror among people all over the world. In one incident, over one thousand people, including children, were burnt alive in a church where they had sought sanctuary. An investigation by the British government disclosed that at least fifty-nine villages had been destroyed with a loss of life estimated at twelve thousand.

In Great Britain, particularly, public opinion was incensed. Gladstone, then in opposition, publicized the atrocities and criticized the government's support of Turkey. He demanded that action be taken against the Turks and that they abandon despoiled Bulgaria immediately:

Let the Turks now carry away their abuses in the only possible manner, namely by carrying off themselves. . . . This thorough riddance, this most blessed deliverance, is the only reparation we can make to the memory of those heaps and heaps of dead. . . .[22]

The Treaty of San Stefano and the Congress of Berlin. While public opinion was being aroused in Europe against the "unspeakable Turk," the Serbs and Montenegrins had been forced to sue for peace with Turkey because of Turkish military success. The Turkish government, aware from long experience of the menace of European intervention, promised new reforms and in 1876 proposed a liberal constitution. The Russian government, with long experience in the futility of expecting genuine Turkish reform, insisted upon European supervision of the implementation of the promised reforms. When the sultan demurred, the Russian tsar declared war.

The Russo-Turkish War (1877-1878) was hard fought. In one case a beleaguered Turkish army held off the Russians for five months before surrendering, and then only after Rumania had come to the aid of the Russian army. Serbia and Montenegro reëntered the war against Turkey. Faced with an imminent Russian attack on Constantinople, Turkey finally sued for peace. With the lesson of the Crimean War fresh in mind, Rus-

THE TREATY OF SAN STEFANO 1878

RUSSIA

RUMANIA (Independent)

SERBIA (Independent)

MONTENEGRO (Independence reaffirmed)

BULGARIA

TURKEY

THE CONGRESS OF BERLIN 1878

RUSSIA

(Occupied by Austria)

BOSNIA

HERZEGOVINA

SERBIA

RUMANIA

MONTENEGRO

BULGARIA (Independent Principality)

(Autonomous; occupied by Turkey)

(Returned to Turkey)

TURKEY

sia had tried to insure itself a free hand by agreeing to Austrian occupation of Bosnia and Herzegovina. But when Constantinople was endangered, Britain threatened to intervene and ordered a fleet into the Straits. On March 3, 1878 Russia and Turkey signed the Treaty of San Stefano.

The most significant aspect of the treaty was the creation of a large Bulgarian state. Most of the Balkan territory south of the Danube, extending from the Black Sea west to Montenegro and including part of the Aegean coast, was incorporated in it; the boundary line was drawn to include all territory claimed by the exarchate. With both a Black Sea and an Aegean coastline, Bulgaria would have provided a by-pass around Constantinople. Since the treaty also recognized the complete independence of Serbia and Rumania, the remaining Turkish territory in Europe would have been very limited indeed.

Great Britain once again assumed the role of defender of the territorial integrity of the Ottoman empire. Britain was alarmed over the prospect of much of the Balkans coming under the domination of Moscow. And Austria was determined that Turkey as a political entity must be preserved or, at the very least, that its territory be prevented from falling under Russian influence. The Austro-Hungarian position was explained by an Austrian statesman in this way:

Turkey possesses a utility almost providential for Austria-Hungary. For Turkey maintains the status quo of the small Balkan states and impedes their [nationalistic] aspirations. If it were not for Turkey, all these aspirations would fall down on our heads . . . if Bosnia-Herzegovina should go to Serbia or Montenegro, or if a new state should be formed there which we cannot prevent, then we should be ruined and should ourselves assume the role of the "Sick Man."[23]

Fearing an increase of Russian power in the Balkans, Great Britain and Austria forced a reconsideration of the Treaty of San Stefano at the Congress of Berlin later in the same year.

The Congress of Berlin was the last great nineteenth century gathering of European statesmen in the pattern inaugurated at the Congress of Vienna in 1814, a showcase for some of the most brilliant diplomats of the age. Prince Gorchakov of Russia and Count Andrassy of Austria-Hungary vied with each other at Berlin in the resplendence of their

A *Punch* cartoon of 1878 pictures Disraeli returning from the Congress of Berlin in a blaze of triumph with the Turk on his back

dress. But the most successful participants were unquestionably the English Conservative prime minister Lord Beaconsfield (Benjamin Disraeli) and the German Empire's Prince Bismarck; the former came in quest of British imperial interests and the latter served as a self-styled "honest broker" for the interests of the powers involved. Bismarck's skill was illustrated by an anecdote of the opening session. The diplomatic language of the nineteenth century was French, and Disraeli, formerly one of the House of Common's most celebrated orators, was determined to address the congress in that language. Unfortunately, Disraeli's French was atrocious, and the British delegation, fearing he would disgrace them, appealed to Bismarck. The chancellor simply remarked that he would be very disappointed not to hear so famous an orator speak in his native tongue. "Dizzy" was flattered and obliged gladly. Everyone was satisfied.

Although the liberal Gladstone had been shocked over the Bulgarian massacres, the imperial-minded Conservative prime minister Disraeli believed that such compassionate sentiments were diametrically opposed to British interests. Therefore, supported by Austria, he exerted pressure to force Russia to disgorge some of its gains. Russia was compelled to agree to a revision of Bulgaria's status, and the large Bulgarian state set up by the Treaty of San Stefano was divided into three parts. The northernmost part remained an independent principality paying tribute to Turkey; south of this region was an autonomous province to be occupied by Turkish troops; and the southernmost region was given back to Turkey to administer. By this settlement England and Austria sought to maintain Turkish power in the Balkans as a counterweight against growing Russian influence in the region.

Among the other provisions of the Berlin settlement was one relating to Bosnia, where the revolts of 1875 had started. This province and the province of Herzegovina were given to Austria "to occupy and administer." Thus Austria added to its polyglot empire two new territories, one of which was to be the scene of the incident which set off World War I. Serbian and Rumanian independence was recognized, and there was some changing of borders for Montenegro, Serbia, and Rumania. Greece received nothing; however, the destruction of Russia's proposed large Bulgaria was to Greek advantage. Russia, which fought the costly war, received some extension of frontiers on the eastern Black Sea border with Turkey. Britain was compensated by receiving Cyprus.

On his return from Berlin, Disraeli boasted that he had secured "peace with honor." Russian expansion had been checked—but at a high price. The Turks continued to oppress and even massacre the Christians left under their rule. Meanwhile the Russians made a mockery of Pan-Slavism by trying to control the policies of their "brother Slavs" just freed from the Turk, particularly in Bulgaria. Russian satellites, so much discussed following the creation of Soviet puppets in eastern Europe and the Balkans after World War II, are nothing new in history.

SUMMARY

From 1848 to the mid-1870's, nationalism was the arbiter of history. Its two most important successes were registered by the unification movements in Italy and Germany. Democracy, for the moment, was overshadowed by the momentous events of nation-making in these two additions to the powers of Europe.

While the force of nationalism was uniting important regions of central Europe, it was proving a fatal malady for the once formidable Ottoman empire in southeastern Europe. New nation states were gradually carved out of the Balkan territory of the "sick man of Europe." By 1878 the great powers had recognized the sovereignty of Montenegro, Serbia, Greece, Rumania, and Bulgaria.

The intermingling of peoples in the Balkans made national boundaries difficult to define; consequently, none of the new states included all of the territory inhabited by fellow nationals. Nationalism in southeastern Europe constituted a most dangerous divisive force for the Ottoman empire and increasingly for the Austro-Hungarian monarchy. The independence movements of the Balkan peoples invariably provoked intervention, because the balance among the great powers was jeopardized by the creation of any new spheres of influence or by outright annexation, particularly by Russia, of Turkish territory.

Russia was the most aggressive challenger, Great Britain the most ardent champion of the territorial integrity of the Ottoman empire. Russia fought three wars with Turkey, but only once, in the Crimean War, did the great powers fight each other over this area. The Treaty of San Stefano provided for a large extension of Russian power in the Balkans, which the powers insisted on decreasing at the Congress of Berlin. Although the Treaty of San Stefano was never implemented, it contained an essentially Slavic solution to the problem of Balkan organization, a problem still unsolved. Greek and Slavic culture clashed in the Balkans; the western powers supported Greece and the principle of dividing the Slavic groups, while Russia worked for their union. Bulgaria, which is still small, has never forgotten the vision of the large Bulgaria proposed by the Treaty of San Stefano.

The Balkan nationalist liberation movements were perverted by the rivalries of the great powers. To most of us—even though we have often seen the term abused in our own lifetimes—*liberation* suggests idealism and high purpose. But European diplomats and military leaders of this period had little interest in either high purpose or ideals. In his work *On War*, the Prussian general Karl von Clausewitz gives classic expression to the hard-boiled realism that motivated these men:

War is only a continuation of State policy by other means. . . . War is not merely a political act, but also a real political instrument, a continuation of political commerce. . . . Is not war merely another kind of writing and language for political thought? . . . War is nothing but a duel on an extensive scale. . . . Let us not hear of Generals who conquer without bloodshed. . . . The best strategy is always to be strong.[24]

SUGGESTIONS FOR READING

POLITICS AND ECONOMICS

Nicolson, H. G., *The Congress of Vienna; A Study in Allied Unity, 1812-1822,* Harcourt, 1946, is a careful analysis of an often misunderstood series of events. Also recommended for coverage of the same period are H. A. Kissinger, *A World Restored,* Houghton, 1957; F. B. Artz, *Reaction and Revolution, 1814-1832,* Harper, 1939; A. J. May, *The Age of Metternich, 1814-1848,* Holt,* 1933.

Lucas-Dubreton, J., *The Restoration and the July Monarchy,* Putnam, 1929. A comprehensive study of the post-Napoleonic period in France.

Postgate, R., *Story of a Year: 1848,* Oxford, 1956. With consummate skill, the author gives a play-by-play account of the events in the western world during this crucial year. A more thematic treatment is offered by P. Robertson, *Revolutions of 1848: A Social History,* Torchbooks,* 1960. See also G. Bruun, *Revolution and Reaction, 1848-1852: A Mid-Century Watershed,* Anvil,* 1958; and Sir L. B. Namier, *1848: The Revolution of The Intellectuals,* Oxford, 1946.

Binkley, R. C., *Realism and Nationalism, 1852-1871,* Harper, 1953. A scholarly survey of the period with excellent chapters on the wars of nationalism and on the new science.

Guedalla, P., *The Second Empire,* Putnam, 1922. Covering a longer span of time than is indicated by the title, this work begins with the birth of Napoleon III, follows his career as prince, president, and emperor, and includes as well a study of the empire period. Well documented with memoirs and contemporary opinions is J. M. Thompson, *Louis Napoleon and the Second Empire,* Noonday, 1955.

Trevelyan, G. M., *British History in the Nineteenth Century and After, 1782-1919,* Longmans, 1938. One of the best accounts of the period. An excellent, brief review is D. Thomson, *England in the Nineteenth Century,* Penguin,* 1952. Social, political, enonomic, and intellectual aspects of the period are smoothly integrated in both E. L. Woodward, *The Age of Reform, 1815-1870,* Oxford, 1938; and in G. M. Young, *Victorian England: Portrait of an Age,* Anchor,* 1954.

Tocqueville, Alexis de, *Journeys to England and Ireland* (ed. by J. P. Mayer), Yale, 1958. The first translation of this nineteenth-century historian's acute, prophetic impressions of Reform-Age England.

The political unification of Italy is the theme of the following useful introductory surveys: J. A. R. Marriott, *The Makers of Modern Italy; Napoleon—Mussolini,* Oxford, 1931; and A. J. B. Whyte, *The Evolution of Modern Italy, 1715-1920,* Macmillan, 1951.

Hamerow, T. A., *Restoration, Revolution, Reaction: Economics and Politics in Germany, 1815-1871,* Princeton, 1958. An excellent interpretation of how the advent of industrialism

*Indicates an inexpensive paperbound edition.

changed urban life and how political events were profoundly affected by the transition from economic agrarianism to capitalism.

Taylor, A. J. P., *The Hapsburg Monarchy, 1809-1918,* Macmillan, 1948. A concise, well-organized survey. See also R. A. Kann, *The Multinational Empire; Nationalism and National Reform in the Habsburg Monarchy,* 2 vols., Columbia, 1950, for a thorough discussion of the problems created by the numerous nationalities in the Hapsburg domain.

Highly recommended for a study of nationalism in the nineteenth century is H. Kohn, *Prophets and Peoples: Studies in Nineteenth Century Nationalism,* Macmillan, 1946. See also by the same author, *Nationalism: Its Meaning and History,* Anvil,* 1955. Mosse, W. E., *Alexander II and the Modernization of Russia,* Macmillan, 1958. A sound interpretation of a crucial era in Russian history and an expert analysis of the foreign policy of the period.

Woodham-Smith, C., *The Reason Why,* Everyman,* 1960. A polished, urbane account of the tragicomic Crimean War and a dual biography of the two men responsible for the ill-fated charge of the Light Brigade.

For a well-balanced review of the forces of industrialism on the Continent, see A. L. Dunham, *The Industrial Revolution in France, 1815-1848,* Exposition Press, 1955. The revolutionary tendencies that accompanied the rise of industrialism are well treated in J. J. Saunders, *The Age of Revolution; The Rise and Decline of Liberalism in Europe Since 1815,* Roy, 1949.

Hammond, J. L. and B., *The Bleak Age,* Longmans, 1934. A graphic study of the shocking social effects of the Industrial Revolution. A less alarming picture is painted by M. C. Buer, *Health, Wealth and Population in the Early Days of the Industrial Revolution,* Routledge, 1926.

Toynbee, A., *The Industrial Revolution,* Beacon,* 1956. First published in 1884, this work was one of the first attempts to evaluate the impact of industrialism.

THOUGHT AND ART

Two brilliant critical studies of the romantic movement are I. Babbitt, *Rousseau and Romanticism,* Meridian,* 1955; and G. Boas, *French Philosophies of the Romantic Period,* Johns Hopkins, 1925.

Goethe, J. W. von, *Great Writings of Goethe* (ed. by S. Spender), Mentor,* 1958. Selections from the poetry, letters, prose, and epigrams of one of the world's most creative minds.

Schilling, B. N., *Human Dignity and the Great Victorians,* Columbia, 1946. Reviews the attitudes of Carlyle, Ruskin, and other figures to the socio-economic problems of the day. Also recommended for incisive analyses of the intellectual climate are J. Barzun, *Darwin, Marx, Wagner; Critique of a Heri-*

tage, Anchor,* 1958; and J. S. Schapiro, *Liberalism,* Anvil,* 1953.

Heilbroner, R. L., *The Worldly Philosophers; The Lives, Times and Ideas of the Great Economic Thinkers,* Simon and Schuster,* 1955. Excellent chapters on Adam Smith, the Utopians, and Marx. The author disproves the maxim that economics is a "dismal science."

Marx, K., and F. Engels, *Basic Writings on Politics and Philosophy* (ed. by L. S. Feuer), Anchor,* 1959. A sizable selection from the writings of Marx and Engels, including the *Manifesto* in full. The material has been chosen to point up aspects of their thought that are having an impact on the world today, particularly in the underdeveloped nations. See also F. Hegel, *Selections* (ed. by J. Loewenberg), Scribner's,* 1958; and K. Marx, *Das Kapital* (abr. and ed. by S. Levitsky), Gateway,* 1960.

Aiken, H. D., ed., *The Age of Ideology; The 19th Century Philosophers,* Mentor,* 1956. Includes typical selections from the works of Kant, Hegel, Mill, and Kierkegaard among others.

Schwartz, G. L., and P. W. Bishop, eds., *The Development of Modern Science,* Vol. II of *Moments of Discovery,* Basic Books, 1958. Selections from the writings of the great scientists Darwin, Mendel, Pasteur, Koch, Dalton, and Faraday.

Raynal, M., *The Nineteenth Century; New Sources of Emotion from Goya to Gauguin,* Skira, 1951. A first-rate introduction to nineteenth-century painting.

For a better understanding of important developments in music's "golden century," see the following: M. Brion, *Schumann and the Romantic Age,* Macmillan, 1956; A. Einstein, *Music in the Romantic Era,* Norton, 1947; P. A. Scholes, *Romantic and Nationalist Schools of the Nineteenth Century,* Vol. II of *The Listener's History of Music,* 3rd ed., Oxford, 1943; H. C. Colles, *Ideals of the Nineteenth Century, the Twentieth Century,* Pt. III of *The Growth of Music* (rev. by E. Blom), Oxford, 1956.

BIOGRAPHY

Strachey, G. L., *Queen Victoria,* Harbrace Modern Classics, 1949. A classic of modern biography. Relations between the royal court and Victoria's prime ministers are set in sharp relief in A. Cecil, *Queen Victoria and Her Prime Ministers,* Oxford, 1953.

Valuable for the insights into life in Victorian England as well as into the lives of its leaders are Sir P. M. Magnus-Allcroft, *Gladstone: A Biography,* Dutton, 1954; J. L. Hammond and M. R. Foot, *Gladstone and Liberalism,* Macmillan, 1953; A. Maurois, *Disraeli, A Picture of the Victorian Age,* Modern Library, 1942.

Strachey, G. L., *Eminent Victorians,* Modern Library, 1933. In witty, polished phrases, the author debunks four idols of the Victorian era (Cardinal Manning, General "Chinese" Gordon, Thomas Arnold, Florence Nightingale). A more balanced estimate of the latter figure is C. Woodham-Smith, *Florence Nightingale,* Grosset, 1958.

The zealous, romantic Italian nationalist and his hard-grained, realistic successor are treated, respectively, in E. E. Y. Hales,

Mazzini and the Secret Societies, Kennedy, 1956; and in M. Paléologue, *Cavour,* Harper, 1927. The latter work is rather outspokenly laudatory.

Simpson, F. A., *The Rise of Louis Napoleon,* Longmans, 1925; and A. L. Guérard, *Napoleon III,* Knopf, 1955. Two comprehensive studies of Napoleon III, the first-mentioned focusing upon his early struggles. See also the works (previously cited) by P. Guedalla and J. M. Thompson.

The architect of the German state is presented in a vivid and objective manner in both I. F. D. Morrow, *Bismarck,* Macmillan, 1957; and in A. J. P. Taylor, *Bismarck: The Man and the Statesman,* Knopf, 1955.

Berlin, Sir Isaiah, *Karl Marx; His Life and Environment,* Galaxy,* 1959. By a distinguished British political theorist, this work is the best brief study of Marx and his ideas. Also stimulating is E. Wilson, *To the Finland Station: A Study in the Writing and Acting of History,* Anchor,* 1953, which includes vivid accounts of the careers of Marx and Engels.

Lippincott, B. E., *Victorian Critics of Democracy,* Univ. of Minn., 1938. Includes material on Ruskin, Arnold, and Carlyle. For individual biographies, see E. K. Brown, *Matthew Arnold: A Study of Conflict,* Univ. of Chicago, 1948; L. Trilling, *Matthew Arnold,* Meridian,* 1955; P. C. Quennell, *John Ruskin: The Portrait of a Prophet,* Viking, 1949; D. Gascoyne, *Thomas Carlyle,* British Book Centre,* n.d.

Well-organized and smoothly written biographies of three titans in the world of music are M. N. Scott, *Beethoven,* Farrar, Straus, 1949; E. Valentin, *Beethoven; A Pictorial Biography,* Viking, 1958; P. Latham, *Brahms,* Farrar, Straus, 1949; R. L. Jacobs, *Wagner,* Farrar, Straus, 1949.

FICTION

Stendhal (pseud. of Henri Beyle), *The Charterhouse of Parma,* Penguin,* 1958. A panorama of post-Napoleonic Italy and life at the reactionary court. The novel opens with a brilliant description of the battle of Waterloo.

Particularly noteworthy among Balzac's many novels for the incisive manner in which the effects of gross materialism on bourgeois society are depicted: *Père Goriot* and *Eugénie Grandet,* Modern Library, 1946; *Cousin Bette,* Modern Library, 1958.

Readers who may be put off by Dickens' triple-decker novels will find shorter works, such as *Oliver Twist* and *Hard Times* (both available in many editions), rewarding reading. The former paints a vivid picture of the degradation in London's underworld; the latter is a vigorous attack upon the Manchester school of economics.

Powerful novels by Émile Zola, the proponent of naturalism in fiction, are *Germinal,* Penguin,* 1956, which deals with a violent, tragic coal mine strike; and *The Downfall,* P. Smith, n. d., an exposé of the corruption and confusion among the French military leaders during the Franco-Prussian War.

Mann, T., *Buddenbrooks,* Pocketbooks,* n. d. A family chronicle which pictures with charm and fidelity the rigid upper middle-class society of northern Germany before 1870.

POLITICS

Congress of Vienna—Russia, Britain, France, Austria attempt to restore Old Regime; legitimate rulers restored; boundaries modified to hem in France; Quadruple (later Quintuple) Alliance formed; principle of nationalism disregarded 1814-1815
Louis XVIII of France establishes constitutional monarchy 1814-1824

1815 Reaction in England—political, religious inequality under Tories; reforms ease reaction c. 1815-1830

Carlsbad Decrees, sponsored by Metternich, temporarily discourage German nationalist youth movement 1819

Revolutions in Spain, Portugal, Naples, Sicily, Sardinia 1820
Congress System—Congress of Troppau, Congress of Laibach stifle Italian revolt 1820-1821; Congress of Verona stifles Spanish revolt 1822
Congress System declines—Britain refuses support in suppressing revolts 1820-1822; United States announces Monroe Doctrine 1823; Greeks rise against Turkish rule 1821-1827; France, Britain, Russia secure Greek independence, Serbian autonomy at Treaty of Adrianople 1829
Charles X, exponent of divine right, ascends French throne 1824; dissolves legislature, limits franchise 1830
Tsar Nicholas I crushes Decembrist Revolt 1825; Nicholas System in Russia, Poland; Nicholas makes limited reforms 1825-1855

1830 **Revolutions of 1830**—July Revolution in Paris deposes Charles X, enthrones Louis Philippe; Belgians throw off Dutch rule; revolts unsuccessful in central Italy, Poland; revolts temporarily successful in parts of German Confederation
Mazzini active leader in Italian *Risorgimento* 1830-1848
Whigs gain power, end reactionary Tory rule 1830; **first Reform Bill** extends vote to upper middle class 1832; act abolishing slavery, other reforms passed 1833-1835
Russia protects Constantinople against invasion by Egypt; Turkey falls under influence of Russia 1831

Zollverein, customs union, strengthens ties between German states 1834

Uprising in Austrian Poland fails 1846

Revolt of Irish nationalists is crushed by England 1848
Chartist movement for reform fails but lays foundations for future reforms in England 1848
Revolution of 1848 in France—Parisians end Louis Philippe's government, set up Second Republic with moderates in control; revolt of radical workers is crushed by bourgeoisie; Louis Napoleon becomes president 1848
Revolution of 1848 in Germany—Frederick William IV of Prussia grants parliament; other German rulers follow; Frankfurt Assembly fails to establish new union when Frederick William refuses leadership; German Confederation restored at Olmütz 1848-1850
Revolutions in Hungary, Bohemia, Vienna, Italy fail 1848-1849

1850 Reform movements in Russia—Herzen, Bakunin inspire intelligentsia; reformers divided into Westernizers and Slavophiles; Nihilism develops in 1860's

Louis Napoleon (Napoleon III) dissolves Second Republic, establishes Second Empire, proclaims himself emperor 1851-1852
Crimean War—Russia invades Turkey 1853; France, Britain, Sardinia invade Russian Crimea, defeat Russia at Sevastopol 1854-1855; Treaty of Paris affirms integrity of Ottoman empire, halts Russian advance into Balkans 1856

Unification of Italy under Cavour—Austro-Italian War leads to territorial gains for Sardinia, France 1859; Sardinia annexes Italian territory conquered by Garibaldi 1860; first Italian parliament meets 1861; Italy obtains Venetia 1866; Italy obtains Rome, *Risorgimento* ends 1870

Tsar Alexander II (1855-1881) abolishes serfdom 1861; reforms local government, courts, army c. 1864-1874
Polish insurrection is repressed by Alexander II 1863
Unification of Germany under Bismarck—Prussia defeats Austria and Denmark, gains Schleswig-Holstein, dominates new North German Confederation 1864-1866; Prussia wins Franco-Prussian War, gains Alsace-Lorraine at Treaty of Frankfurt 1870-1871; William of Prussia is proclaimed emperor of united Germany 1871
Ausgleich sets up Dual Monarchy of Austria-Hungary 1867
Gladstone, Disraeli alternate as English prime minister 1867-1880; **Reform Bill of 1867** extends vote to city workers; Gladstone's Glorious Ministry passes Education Act of 1870, reforms civil service and army, establishes secret ballot 1868-1874

1870 Second Empire in France swept from power during Franco-Prussian War; Third Republic proclaimed 1870
Turkey crushes Bosnian and Bulgarian revolts, defeats Serbia, Montenegro 1875; Russia defeats Turkey 1877-1878; Treaty of San Stefano gains independence for Serbia and Rumania, puts Bulgaria under Russian dominance 1878
Congress of Berlin—Britain and Austria return part of Bulgaria to Turkish domination, make part independent, part autonomous; award Bosnia, Herzegovina to Austria 1878

ECONOMICS AND SCIENCE

Laissez-faire theory popularized—Malthus advances theory of overpopulation; Ricardo develops subsistence theory of wages; Bentham devises doctrine of utilitarianism
Lamarck advances doctrine of inheritance of acquired characteristics 1801; Dalton formulates atomic theory c. 1808; Cuvier founds science of paleontology c. 1812
Fulton's steamship *Clermont* makes first voyage 1807

First Industrial Revolution—industrialization moves into high gear; industrial capitalism reaches zenith; technological leadership makes England "workshop of world"; Europe's population increases; country-to-city, regional shifts in population promote rise of large manufacturing cities; trade unionism grows 1815-1870
Utopian socialists Saint-Simon, Fourier, Owen formulate plans for scientifically planned, cooperative societies
Development of railroads—Stockton and Darlington, first railroad in world, is laid in England 1820's

Erie Canal 1825

Lyell's *Principles of Geology* 1830-1833

Faraday invents first electric dynamo 1831
English social, economic reforms—first effective Factory Act 1833; Ten-Hour Law 1846; first Public Health Act 1848
Communication—penny post introduced in England 1840; Morse perfects telegraph 1844
Repeal of Corn Laws reflects dominance of laissez faire 1846
First law of thermodynamics stated 1847
Marx and Engels publish **Communist Manifesto** 1848

Anarchism, founded by Proudhon, demands repudiation of government authority and complete freedom for individuals
Christian socialists emphasize social aspects of Christ's teachings; champion reform, socialist communities
Bessemer improves smelting, refining of iron ore 1850's
Great Exhibition in London proclaims "Age of Machinery" 1851

Field lays Atlantic cable 1856

Second law of thermodynamics c. 1859
Drake drills first oil well in Pennsylvania 1859
Darwin publishes **Origin of Species** 1859; *Descent of Man* 1871
Lenoir develops internal-combustion engine 1860
John Stuart Mill holds that governments should impose some controls on business
Lister uses asepsis and antisepsis in surgery 1860's; Pasteur develops germ theory of putrefaction 1864
First International fails; anarchists under Bakunin oppose Marxist majority 1864-1873
Marx and Engels utilize Hegel's dialectic in their theory of scientific socialism, expounded in **Das Kapital** 1867-1894
Mendelyeev classifies all known elements 1869
Railroads cross North America 1869; Suez Canal 1869

LITERATURE AND ART

Preromantic writers—Rousseau exalts instinct and emotion, writes *Émile* 1762; Schiller attacks tyranny in *Wilhelm Tell* 1804; Goethe, whose works illustrate transition from classicism to romanticism, publishes *Faust*, Part I 1808

1815

European romantic writers—Wordsworth expresses transcendentalist view of nature; Coleridge emphasizes exoticism, supernaturalism; Byron, Shelley, Heine represent romanticists' rebellion against society; Keats exemplifies esthetic aspect of romanticism; Scott, Hugo treat medieval times romantically
Music—Beethoven acts as bridge between classicism and romanticism; Brahms, Tschaikovsky, Chopin, others follow with masterful works; Weber, Wagner, Rossini, Verdi develop national opera
Romanticist painters rebel against classical rules—Delacroix, Constable, Turner
Romantic nationalist writers—Grimm brothers revive German folk tales; Pushkin denounces tyranny in Russia; Hegel exalts Prussian state; Michelet, Bancroft, Macaulay write national histories
Greatest period of Gothic revival in architecture begins c. 1830

1830

Goethe's *Faust*, Part II 1832

Victorian novelists—Thackeray satirizes Victorian society; Dickens protests against social injustices

1850

Victorian poets—Tennyson typifies ideals of his time; Browning displays faith in humanity
Realist writers in France—Balzac depicts crudities of petty bourgeoisie in *Comédie Humaine*; Flaubert's *Madame Bovary* criticizes inadequacy of romanticism as a philosophy; Hugo's *Les Misérables* represents his transition to realism

Esthetic Revolt—Ruskin and Pre-Raphaelites condemn mass production, attempt to restore esthetic standards of Middle Ages

Social criticism—Arnold denounces mid-Victorian culture, advocates state education; Carlyle criticizes industrial evils, believes salvation is attained by leadership of "Great Men"

1870

Frontier

THE MEANING AND DEVELOPMENT OF NATIONALISM   by Hans Kohn

Professor of History at The City College of New York since 1949 and formerly Professor of History at Smith College, Hans Kohn is the author of a number of books on nationalism. Among them are *The Idea of Nationalism* (1944), *Nationalism, Its Meaning and History* (1944), and *American Nationalism* (1957).

In our own century nationalism has become the first world-wide force in history to which the peoples of all continents pay homage and loyalty. Since nationalism first arose in northwestern Europe in the seventeenth century, it has meant different things at different times to different peoples. It has adapted itself to the changing historical climates and to the various cultural traditions and social structures of peoples and countries. Everywhere it has implied an activation of the people, a demand on their part for participation in shaping their own history and for a new ordering of society which would take into account their well-being.

Nationalism originated in the great revolutions in the western world during the seventeenth and eighteenth centuries—in England, in the British colonies in North America, and in France. There for the first time "free men" demanded that they and not princes or foreign rulers should determine their own fate and that governments should respect the rights of citizens. Soon this demand was joined by two others: first, that the people's own language and traditions should form the basis of cultural life; and, second, that the nation's economy should be so organized as to promote national welfare and strength. The Declaration of Independence of 1776 set an example. It proclaimed that all men are created equal and that governments derive their just powers from the consent of the governed. The Declaration was itself an outgrowth of British liberty, which, from the Magna Carta (1215) to the Glorious Revolution (1689), formed the background against which the liberty of the colonies had developed. The American Revolution also influenced the rise of nationalism in countries where the English liberal tradition was unknown. Under such leaders as José de San Martín and Simón Bolívar, the Spanish colonies in South and Central America achieved their goal of independence in the first quarter of the nine-

teenth century. But it took many civil wars and revolutions, lasting over a century, before the new national states of Latin America approached democratic stability.

Different was the development of nationalism on the European continent. There the French Revolution of 1789, influenced by the American Revolution of 1776, established national sovereignty based upon the consent of the people. Devotion to the fatherland *(la patrie)* became a civic duty and ideal. Inspired by nationalism, the leaders of the French Revolution tried to do away with the traditional division of the people into classes and proclaimed not only the liberty but also the equality and fraternity of Frenchmen. Thus the French Revolution showed the benefits of nationalism in establishing domestic liberty and union. But it also revealed the dangers of nationalism. Born in the ardor of the Revolution, the new French nation wished to impose its leadership over all Europe. This spirit of conquest and domination aroused the national feelings of the other European peoples, who fought for their independence against the French, especially against the armies led by Napoleon I, who became French emperor in 1804 and was defeated by the rising nationalism of Europe in 1814.

Spreading throughout Europe in the first part of the nineteenth century, nationalism began to replace the former dynastic loyalties of the various peoples with the new loyalty to national self-determination and sovereignty. Nationalism became the strongest emotional force. On the one hand it united men in the close fellowship of the nation; on the other hand it divided men by separating them into nations which often felt a sharp hostility toward neighboring nations. The European wars fought in the nineteenth and twentieth centuries were largely wars caused by conflicting national aspirations.

Before 1848 nationalism in Europe had been a movement of intellectuals—teachers, writers, and journalists. In 1848 it took hold of the people. Divided among a number of sovereign states, some of which were under foreign control, the two largest groups of people in central Europe—the Germans and the Italians—worked to create unified national states. Their attempts in 1848 failed. It was not until 1861 that Italy was united, largely through the efforts of Count Cavour, the prime minister of the kingdom of Sardinia. Ten years later, in January 1871, Germany was united by Bismarck, prime minister of the kingdom of Prussia. The unification of Germany was due to the easy victories of the Prussian army over Austria (1866) and France (1870).

But nationalism and the desire to create sovereign and united national states were in no way confined to the Germans and Italians. The Irish in the United Kingdom of Great Britain and Ireland; the Czechs and the South Slavs in the Hapsburg empire of Austria-Hungary; the Poles under Russian, Prussian, and Austrian rule; the Christian peoples of the Balkan peninsula—Serbs, Bulgarians, Rumanians, and Greeks—under Turkish domination; and the many non-Russian peoples in the Russian empire—all strove more and more for national self-determination. These peoples were helped greatly in the attainment of their goals by World War I. The President of the United States, Woodrow Wilson, accepted the principle of national self-determination in redrawing the map of Europe. At the same time the Russian revolution, under the leadership of Lenin, espoused the cause of national self-determination, though in the Communist system no true self-determination, whether individual or national, was thinkable.

The collapse of the four dynasties which had determined the fate of central and eastern Europe before 1914—the Romanovs in Russia, the Hapsburgs in Austria-Hungary, the Hohenzollerns in Germany, and the Ottoman sultans in Turkey—paved the way for national sovereignty in all these territories. A number of new independent states, based upon the principle of nationalism, arose in Europe—from Eire in the west to Finland and the Baltic republics in the east.

But World War I had even more far-reaching effects on the development of nationalism than the establishment of new national states in Europe. The long-lasting conflict had inflamed nationalist emotions in central Europe to such a degree that there developed a new political movement, called fascism after its Italian prototype, which made nationalism the supreme value without regard for the rights of the individual or for the interests of other nations or of mankind as a whole. Filled with a self-centered zeal, fascist nationalism became an aggressive force which destroyed the League of Nations, the forerunner of the United Nations, and brought about World War II.

Nor were the effects of World War I confined to Europe; the promise of national self-determination influenced the peoples of Asia and Africa also. With the exception of Japan, which by timely modernization had preserved its independence, Asia by the beginning of the twentieth century had sunk into a colonial or semicolonial status. The once powerful Chinese and Turkish empires were in danger of disintegration. Britain ruled in India, France in Indo-China, the Netherlands in Indonesia, the United States in the Philippine Islands, and Russia in vast areas in central and northern Asia. At the beginning of the twentieth century, almost the whole of Africa was divided among European rulers—the British, French, Belgians, Germans, Italians, Portuguese, and Spaniards. Only Ethiopia and Liberia maintained a precarious and backward independent existence. After 1918 the promise of national self-determination reverberated throughout Asia and began to penetrate even Africa.

Communist propaganda used the desire of the Asian and African peoples for freedom in order to weaken the European "capitalist" powers. But the demand for freedom and for civic equality and human dignity was not of Communist origin. It ran directly counter to Communist reality, though not necessarily to Communist utopian promises. The demand for freedom and for national self-determination was aroused by the examples set by the English growth of liberty, by the American Revolution, and by the French Revolution. Especially in the British colonies, a native educated class was trained in English traditions of parliamentary self-government. Thus, with the creation of the Indian National Congress in 1885, British India pointed the road to democratic nationalism in Asia.

Japan's victory over the mighty Russian empire in 1905 convinced Asiatics that European imperial power was not impregnable. In the wake of the Russian revolution of 1905, which tried to replace autocracy with national sovereignty, similar revolutions attempted to overthrow autocracy in Asia. The most important among them was the Chinese revolution, which in 1912 established the Republic of China.

World War I started a process of industrialization in Asia. Asian and African troops which participated in the war were introduced to modern methods of organization. Their self-confidence grew. North Africans and Arabs, Turks and Persians, Indians and Chinese began to demand the restoration of their national sovereignty and the revival of their ancient civilizations. Sun Yat-sen founded the Chinese revolutionary party Kuomintang and became the recognized leader of Chinese nationalism. Before his death in 1925, he despaired of help from the West and turned hopefully to

Communist Russia. In India, Mohandas Karamchand Gandhi awakened the Indian masses to nationalist consciousness. Full national sovereignty was gained for Turkey in 1923 by Kemal Atatürk, who, supported by Soviet Russia, was able to undo the defeat of Turkey in World War I and later to introduce thoroughgoing reforms in Turkish life. From 1921 to 1926, the Moroccans under Abd-el Krim fought for their independence until they were defeated by combined French and Spanish forces.

The democracies in World War II officially reiterated the promise of national self-determination for all peoples. In their joint declaration of August 14, 1941, known as the Atlantic Charter, President Franklin D. Roosevelt and Prime Minister Winston S. Churchill declared that "they respect the right of all peoples to choose the form of government under which they will live; and they wish to see sovereign rights and self-government restored to those who have been forcibly deprived of them." At the same time, the Japanese conquests of British, French, Dutch, and American colonial lands in southeast Asia under the slogan "Asia to the Asians" destroyed the prestige of the colonial powers.

The United States and Britain understood the need for living up to the democratic promises of the West: in 1946 the United States gave independence to the Philippines, and in 1947 Britain declared the national independence of India, Pakistan, Burma, and Ceylon. The Netherlands lost its empire in Indonesia; and France gave up Indo-China, Syria, Lebanon, Tunisia, and Morocco. The territorial map of Asia was completely changed. Only the Russian empire, now under Communist domination, maintained its possessions in northern and central Asia, though it granted them a degree of formal autonomy and acknowledged racial equality.

This triumph of nationalism in Asia had hardly been anticipated at the beginning of the twentieth century. An even greater surprise was the rapidity with which nationalism swept Africa after the middle of the twentieth century. By 1960 many independent African states had emerged, and their number promised to increase rapidly. The Asian and African peoples demanded their independence from colonial rule as the peoples of the Western Hemisphere had done between 1775 and 1825. But the newly arising states did not wish to repeat the mistakes of Latin-American or European peoples in creating many small and weak independent nations. Among the Arabs in western Asia and North Africa and among the Africans south of the Sahara, the movement for federation is rapidly growing in strength—even more rapidly than among the nations in western Europe. The federal principle first introduced by the Constitution in the United States sets an example.

There is no doubt that in Europe in the nineteenth century and in Asia and Africa in the twentieth century, nationalism had to come. But the "liberation" of nationalities and the creation of independent national states hardly meet the more urgent need for greater respect for individuals of all races and ethnic groups. Nationalities released from what they believed to be oppression or persecution often turn oppressors and persecutors themselves. Innumerable disputes about frontiers have sprung up among the new national states. Liberated nationalities have often felt hostile to each other, and their mutual animosities and jealousies have hindered their political and economic cooperation.

The solution is, of course, not to be found in a return to the former status of inequality between individuals or peoples but in an advance toward federation, toward the creation of multinational states uniting several peoples and ethnic and religious groups on the basis of complete equality and mutual tolerance. The English-speaking peoples have pioneered with such federal and multi-ethnic solutions. Everywhere today the future of freedom and of mankind depends on the ability and willingness to deëmphasize nationalism, to disintensify its emotional appeal, and to learn the wisdom of cooperation. Perhaps the first step in that direction has been taken by the universalization of the United Nations. There, the spokesmen of over one hundred nations meet and discuss their problems, grievances, and conflicting aspirations on a footing of equality and in a parliamentary form established originally by western democracy in the seventeenth and eighteenth centuries, the same centuries which witnessed the beginning of modern nationalism.

SUGGESTED READINGS

The student interested in the growth and problem of nationalism may find more detailed information in the following works: Carlton J. H. Hayes, *Essays on Nationalism* (Macmillan, 1926); Hans Kohn, *Nationalism, Its Meaning and History* (Anvil Books, Van Nostrand, 1955); Carlos P. Romulo, *The Meaning of Bandung* (Univ. of North Carolina Press, 1956). More advanced students will find Hans Kohn, *American Nationalism* (Macmillan, 1957) helpful.

PART 3 The West Dominant

CHAPTER 9 NEW EUROPES OVERSEAS

CHAPTER 10 THE WHITE MAN'S BURDEN

In the eighteenth and nineteenth centuries, European influence spread to virtually all parts of the non-European world. Two sorts of communities were created by this expansion: the centers of settlement for the millions of people from Ireland, England, Germany, France, and Italy who migrated to the Americas, South Africa, and Australasia; and the colonies of exploitation, those African and Asian territories and islands which were developed largely for economic gain. The settlement of new and largely uninhabited lands by Europeans gave birth to new nations, and the conquest of areas unsuited for European settlement resulted in a system of imperialism by which a minority of foreign officials and soldiers controlled a majority of native peoples. The colonies in imperial systems brought wealth to the controlling western powers, but at the same time European rule helped to introduce new forces that ultimately were to challenge and sweep away imperialism.

Although there was variance in the centers of settlement—which can be called new Europes—because of differences in the national origins of the colonists and in the indigenous societies they encountered, all can be said to have derived their culture mainly from Europe. Thus though the United States grew and broke away from its mother country while Canada flourished and remained in the English fold, the outstanding traits of both—their governmental structure and principles, their social make-up, and their language—reflect their common European origins. And all these new Europes had certain common problems —the challenge of exploring and occupying hitherto unsettled lands, the problem of native peoples, the necessity of taming nature and using natural resources, and the task of building nations. All of them experienced, too, the same urge to broaden democratic rights.

The stage on which history was being made in the nations of the New World was different in many ways from that of the mother countries in Europe. On both, however, the plot and the action had much in common. The leading actors—statesmen and administrators—had to direct and cope with the same basic forces, such as nationalism, industrialism, and democracy. For example, the American Civil War, the federation movement in Canada, and the efforts of Bismarck and Cavour in Germany and Italy all concerned the same basic principle of national unity; and the quest for expanding democratic freedoms in the Jacksonian era in the United States had its counterpart in the revolutions of 1848 in Europe.

While European immigrants were settling the new Europes, their home governments were extending their control over African and Asian peoples. By the end of the nineteenth century, practically all of Africa had been partitioned and placed under European rule, along with most of southern Asia and the islands of the Pacific. Although China remained technically independent, this vast, tradition-bound land also was controlled in many ways by the western imperial powers. Japan alone succeeded in modernizing itself and thus avoided being caught in the imperialist net. In the half-century before World War I, western supremacy, symbolized by imperialism and the colonial system, was one of the major facts of international life.

The morality of imperialism has been a hotly debated subject. Critics have emphasized such negative aspects as arbitrary rule, economic exploitation, and hypocrisy and greed on the part of the imperialists. On the other hand, imperialism has been justified on economic, religious, nationalistic, and even humanitarian grounds. Such well-known champions of imperialism as Livingstone, Rhodes, and Kipling believed that, in promoting their country's seizure of foreign lands and riches, they were doing the best thing for all concerned. The theory that only the selfish have followed the course of imperialism is not borne out by the facts of history.

What is perhaps the most significant and enduring influence of imperialism has not been appreciated. Western colonialism was the instrument for culture diffusion on a huge scale. The colonial officials, missionaries, planters, and educators spread new ideas about science and technology, developed natural resources, cured the physical ills of the native peoples, and taught concepts of democracy and Christian morality.

This impact of western culture subtly modified the outlook and habits of the peoples under the colonial system. Ideals of freedom and nationalism began to stir. National movements gained strength in the early years of the twentieth century and after World War II gathered sufficient momentum to challenge and largely demolish colonialism. Thus the western world provided the knowledge and inspiration which was to uplift and release the very people it had exploited. The golden age of imperialism ended almost half a century ago, but it had changed the course of history for all time.

CHAPTER 9

New Europes Overseas

THE UNITED STATES, THE BRITISH DOMINIONS, AND LATIN AMERICA: 1650-1914

Introduction. In the four centuries before the twentieth, the greatest transplantation of peoples in human history took place as millions of Europeans left their homelands, crossed oceans, and made for themselves new homes in overseas lands. These immigrants brought with them what has been aptly called their "cultural baggage"—their language, religion, folk habits, and experience and attitudes of government.

In the new areas of settlement—the Americas, South Africa, Australia, and New Zealand—new Europes were founded and developed. In many ways these lands reflected the culture of the homelands. Moreover, the drive for political equality and for bills of rights and constitutions that played such an important role in seventeenth- and eighteenth-century Europe was also manifested in the successful revolutions in the Americas. The basic attitudes and movements of Europe after Waterloo—the ambitions of the middle class, the search of the masses for full political rights, the rising interest in better standards of living, and the pervasive force of nationalism—all these became important factors in the overseas communities.

If the history of the new Europes is to be studied profitably in comparison with that of the mother areas, it should be kept in mind that there were certain distinctive conditions and problems that gave uniqueness to the history of such nations as the United States, Australia, and Mexico. There was in all these new countries the challenge of geographical exploration, the problem of what to do with the less-advanced native peoples, and the search for a new national way of life.

Some historians have stressed the deep influence in all the new Europes of frontier life with its fostering of democracy, individualism, resourcefulness, and optimism. As a complete explanation of the course of history in the new Europes, this thesis has been overdone. But some of its relevance remains. A student of the westward movement in the United States writes: "Most modern scholars . . . would agree . . . that the frontiersmen did develop certain unique traits, and that these have been perpetuated to form the principal distinguishing characteristics of the American people today. . . . [Europeans do not] experience to the same degree the heady optimism, the blind faith in the future, the belief in the inevitability of progress, that is part of the American creed. These were pioneer traits, and they have become a part of the national heritage."[1]

In this chapter we shall see also how other colonies founded by English-speaking peoples or taken from other Europeans by Great Britain illustrate the transplanting of British culture to remote parts of the world: Canada, Australia, New Zealand, and the Union of South Africa. One interesting aspect of the story of these new Britains overseas is that they finally arrived at a status of full national independence or sovereignty without recourse to arms. At the same time they remained closely associated with the mother country as members of the British Commonwealth of Nations. Since the political development of Canada was a model for other English colonies, we shall emphasize Canadian history in our survey of the British dominions.

Latin America, the other great area of intensive European colonization, faced certain unique problems of its own in its struggle toward greatness. Here the Indian problem was far greater than it was in the United States, and here also relations between the two races were very different. From the time of the successful revolt against Spain in the first quarter of the nineteenth century, the history of Latin America has been marked by civil wars and local struggles for political power. As this chapter discloses, threats from the outside and attempts by other powers to gain economic if not political control of Latin America did much to retard the growth of Latin America as a whole. Nevertheless, by the first quarter of the twentieth century, a degree of stability and prosperity had been achieved in parts of Latin America, and the cultural patterns that developed there constitute a valuable component of world civilization.

THE MAKING OF NEW NATIONS: BRITISH DOMINIONS

English culture transplanted to America. For over three hundred years, the rich natural resources, ample land, and temperate climate of North America have attracted European immigrants. From a weak settlement in Virginia, the United States has grown to a nation of about 190,000,000 people. The American culture pattern is a blend of the heritage from European culture with the culture traits that have developed independently in the New World.

From 1607 until 1776 the Thirteen Colonies had been part of the British empire. Nearly all the forces influencing the development of civilization in the colonies came from England. The period of the Revolution did little to alter the fundamentals of colonial society; although the Revolution began America's existence as an independent nation, it did not displace the English language, the common law, and the religion, philosophy, and literary influences from the motherland. Thus it is that Shakespeare, Milton, Cromwell, and Locke are now much more a part of our heritage than are men of similar stature from other European nations. And the American form of government, unique in many respects, derived its basic outlines and its political philosophy from the parent country.

Shortly before the Thirteen Colonies in America were lost to English rule, the British empire acquired Canada. This French territory then became the base for a continuing British North American empire after the separation of the United States.

French Canada. Until the early years of the sixteenth century, Canada was virtually an unknown land, populated by approximately 200,000 Indians. In 1497 John Cabot, sailing from England, reached Labrador or Newfoundland. In 1524 Giovanni da Verra-

In 1534 after exploring in the Newfoundland area, Cartier landed on the Gaspé Peninsula and took possession for France.

zano, employed by France, sailed along the American coast and called the area around the mouth of the St. Lawrence "New France," a name later used to refer to all French territory in the New World. During the first half of the sixteenth century, many venturesome fishermen from England, France, and Portugal came to the Grand Banks of Newfoundland to fish.

The story of the French in Canada begins with Jacques Cartier. Making three voyages between 1534 and 1541, he sailed up the St. Lawrence River to an Indian settlement near what is now Montreal. After Cartier, the French neglected Canada for more than half a century, but a new impetus came with the work of Samuel de Champlain. In July 1608, Champlain founded Quebec, the center and capital city of New France for nearly two hundred years. The new settlement grew very slowly, however, because of plots hatched by discontented colonists in Quebec and because of political intrigues in Paris.

Meanwhile numerous Frenchmen, spurred on by love of adventure and the promise of rich profits in the fur trade, were exploring the interior of Canada. French missionaries also opened trails into the wilderness. The

first mission was established in 1615, and ten years later the Jesuit order came to Canada to convert the Indians. Jesuit activities were marked by heroism, zeal, and hardships. Everywhere the Jesuits went, French civilization and influence were spread. In 1673 Father Marquette and the trader Joliet began exploring the Mississippi, the great "Father of Waters." The greatest of all French explorers, René La Salle, completed the exploration of the Mississippi and reached the Gulf of Mexico in 1682.

Unlike the English-speaking settlements to the southeast of it in the New World, the French colony of Canada was rigidly supervised by the home government. All trade activities were carefully regulated; the Catholic Church monopolized education; and few Protestants were allowed to settle in New France. The French king granted huge tracts of land to nobles, who in turn parceled their estates out to peasant farmers. Although this feudal system exhibited some beneficial features, on the whole the introduction of European feudalism seriously retarded the development of the colony.

In 1763, on the eve of the British conquest, there were only 65,000 people in New

France. This figure was just 5 per cent of the total population of the Thirteen Colonies. In New France, agriculture was primitive, industry was almost nonexistent, and the most important economic activity was fur trading.

The French-British quarrels. Early in the history of New France, English activities in North America plainly endangered the future of French Canada. In addition to England's interest in its Atlantic seaboard colonies, English sailors frequently landed at Newfoundland in their fishing expeditions, and in 1670 the Hudson's Bay Company was founded to carry on trading activities, especially in furs, with the Indians in the territory around Hudson Bay. Many disputes occurred between English and French trappers in the Far North, and there were many other differences of opinion between the French settlers and the inhabitants of the English colonies. When war broke out in Europe between England and France, their colonies in the New World went to war also (see p. 46). The ultimate victory of England in the struggle for the New World was foreshadowed by the Treaty of Utrecht (1713). France was forced to cede Acadia (later known as Nova Scotia), to give up all claims to Newfoundland, and to recognize the Hudson's Bay territory as British.

The British acquire Canada. Peace in New France was soon interrupted again by renewal of the duel for world empire between Great Britain and France. The war ended in a complete victory for Britain. In 1763, by the Peace of Paris, Canada passed into British hands. The victors took care to assure the loyalty of the French Canadians by means of a royal proclamation guaranteeing the political rights of the inhabitants and their freedom to worship as Roman Catholics. In 1774 the British government passed the famous Quebec Act, termed the "Magna Carta of the French Canadian race." This act reconfirmed the position of the Catholic Church and perpetuated French law and custom. No representative assembly, such as existed in the English-speaking colonies, was provided for, however, because the French lacked experience in self-government. The opinion of the English was that Canada should remain French in race, language, and institutions.

Canada's formative period. The conquest of Canada by Great Britain ushered in what has been called Canada's formative period, which lasted from 1763 to 1867 and was characterized by the following important developments: the addition of an English-speaking population, the repulse of an attempt at conquest by the United States, the grant of local self-government, and, finally, the confederation of Canada into a dominion in 1867.

The addition of an English population to French Canada came as a result of the American Revolution. Although the American colonists tried to conquer Canada, the French remained loyal, largely because of the liberal concessions of the Quebec Act, and the invasion failed. Those inhabitants of the Thirteen Colonies not in favor of separation from Great Britain (Tories) suffered at the hands of the patriots, and a large number of them immigrated to Canada. The immigrants, known as United Empire Loyalists, settled in Nova Scotia, along the St. Lawrence River, and north of the Great Lakes.

The newcomers did not relish the absence of representative government in their new home and began to agitate for a measure of self-government. The presence of the English also caused numerous controversies between the French Canadians and the newly arrived Loyalists. To meet this situation the British government in 1791 divided Canada into two separate provinces called Upper and Lower Canada and granted each a representative assembly. The quarrel between the French and English continued

THE GROWTH OF MODERN CANADA

but was shelved temporarily during the War of 1812 when American troops invaded Canada. In the two decades after this conflict, the French-English strife returned and with it discontent with the government in both provinces of Canada.

Open rebellion in 1837, quelled only after serious fighting, made the British government more aware of the seriousness of the situation. From London, Lord Durham (1792-1840), a special commissioner, was sent to Canada to study the problem and make recommendations. A statesman with vision who realized that if the home country was to hold the loyalty of its colonies a much larger degree of self-government must be granted, Durham recommended that local self-government, termed "responsible government," be granted the Canadians. Certain matters of imperial concern, such as the control of foreign relations, were to be left to the discretion of the mother country, but Canada alone was to control its own domestic affairs. At first Durham's report was received with little enthusiasm in London. But, by the middle of the nineteenth

century, responsible government was granted to Canada. Unlike the Thirteen Colonies, who severed their connection with the mother country by means of revolution, Canada achieved virtual independence without revolution and bloodshed and remained loyal to the home country.

Federation. Soon after the winning of responsible government came the union of the various political units in British North America. Fear of the United States, the need for a common tariff policy, and a concerted effort to develop natural resources led Canadians toward political confederation. A plan of union—the British North America Act—was drawn up, approved by the British government, and in 1867 passed by the Parliament in London. This act united Canada (then divided into the provinces of Quebec and Ontario), Nova Scotia, and New Brunswick. Canada was now a federal union of four provinces, somewhat similar in political organization to the United States. The government of Canada, however, utilized the English cabinet system with its principle of ministerial responsibility. The

Canadian premier, unlike our chief executive, the president, is not elected for a stipulated period; his tenure of office depends on the support of a majority in the Canadian House of Commons. Whenever this is not forthcoming, he has to resign. As a symbol of Canada's connection with the mother country, provision was also made in the governmental structure for a governor general who acts as the personal representative of the British king.

Obstacles to Canadian development. The early economic progress of Canada was disappointing. If the population increase of the 1820's had been maintained, Canada by 1880 would have had a population of 16,000,000. Actually there were only 4,500,000 by this date, because many Canadians moved south to the United States and European emigrants preferred this country to Canada. Canadian business was slow in growing because England, beginning in 1846, gradually abandoned its tariff system. Thus many Canadian products, formerly given preference in the English home market over goods from countries outside the empire, were forced to compete for British trade on equal terms with other nations.

With the passage of the British North America Act in 1867, Canada's career as a nation began. But the new nation found itself confronted with many problems. Communications were poor. In 1869 the Dominion purchased the vast territories of the Hudson's Bay Company,* and far off on the Pacific coast a new colony, British Columbia, joined the Dominion four years after confederation; but there was no transcontinental railroad to link British Columbia with eastern Canada.

Another disturbing factor was the lack of cordial relations with the United States. During the Civil War a conflict had at one time seemed imminent between Great Britain and the government at Washington. After the Civil War, anti-British sentiment was fanned by Irish patriots in the United States who, in the cause of freedom for Ireland, conducted armed forays over the Canadian border. But in 1871, the major differences between Canada and the United States were ironed out in the Treaty of Washington, a landmark in the use of arbitration.

A third factor in Canada's development was the ever present need for better cooperation between the English and French peoples in the Dominion.

Canada's national development. Under the leadership of the Dominion's first prime minister, Sir John A. Macdonald (1815-1891), Canadians resolutely set about the task of national development. Bounties were offered to new industries; a railroad was completed from the east to British Columbia in 1885; and an active program for attracting immigrants was pursued. By 1890 Macdonald's national policy was already achieving results.

Macdonald's work was carried on by Sir Wilfred Laurier (1841-1919), who as prime minister dominated Canadian politics from 1896 until 1911. From the United States alone, 100,000 immigrants crossed the Canadian border in 1911. Between 1897 and 1912 Canada received a total of 2,250,000 new citizens, bringing the country's total population to over 7,000,000. New provinces were also carved out of land formerly controlled by the Hudson's Bay Company so that

---

*The Hudson's Bay Company had been incorporated in 1670 as the company of Gentlemen Adventurers of England Trading into Hudson's Bay. Early in the nineteenth century, the company established posts throughout the Canadian west, and the vast territory extending from what is now the province of Ontario to British Columbia was administered by this great trading organization. In 1824 the company built a fort across the Columbia River from today's Portland, Oregon. (Later, the fort was moved to Vancouver, British Columbia.) A dispute over

the Oregon boundary arose between the company and the American settlers, causing Americans in 1844 to raise the cry "54-40 or fight" and "All of Oregon or none." Two years later, the controversy was settled amicably when Great Britain and the United States accepted a boundary of 49°. The history of the Canadian west and even our own was greatly influenced by this company. While the company no longer possesses its former administrative powers, it still continues to play an important part in the economic life of Canada.

in 1914 the Dominion consisted of nine provinces.

After the turn of the century, certain problems began to appear as the result of the country's rapid growth. The advance of industrialism produced labor problems and discontent among the common people. The influence of big business began to permeate the halls of the Canadian parliament. The competition of wheat from Russia, South America, and the United States, and the vagaries of the climate had serious economic effects on the Canadian farmer. This period saw the rise of agrarian unrest resembling the Populist movement in the western United States about 1890. In 1904 the Canadian government created a body for regulating the railroads similar to the Interstate Commerce Commission of the United States. Canada was becoming a mature nation, with all the accompanying problems of depressions, the maldistribution of wealth, and the need of governmental restraint of business.

Discovery and development of Australia. The discovery of Australia dates back to the seventeenth century when Dutch explorers sighted its shores. It was the South Seas voyage in 1769 of the famous English explorer Captain Cook, however, that paved the way for English settlement. Captain Cook's expedition touched the eastern shore of the great island and brought back to England a glowing account of the new land. In 1788 a group of English convicts were transported to Australia and settled at Sydney. From the parent colony of Sydney, later called New South Wales, five other settlements were founded.

Although the first European inhabitants of Australia were convicts, many of them were not habitual criminals but political prisoners and debtors. After seven years of servitude, many were liberated and as "emancipists" entered civil life and became valuable citizens. Quite early in the nineteenth century, many free settlers came to Australia. Soon they began to agitate for the termination of the transporting of convicts, and the first step in this direction was taken by the mother country in 1840. Two years later New South Wales was granted a large

In the middle of the nineteenth century, sheep raising became one of the mainstays of the Australian economy. Today Australia has more sheep than any other country in the world. This scene of shearing time at an Australian sheep farm, or "station," is from an engraving made in 1891.

measure of self-government similar to that recommended for Canada by Lord Durham, and by 1850 the Australian colonies were enjoying a liberal form of self-government.

During the first half of the nineteenth century, the Australian colonies grew slowly. From the temperate regions of the south to the tropical areas of the north, the continent was explored, and the interior—a trackless, sandy waste which covered hundreds of miles of deadly salt marshes—was penetrated. Sheep raising became the principal basis of economic prosperity. In 1850, the population of the country was about 400,000; a decade later it had reached nearly 800,000. Although the discovery of gold in 1851 quickened the tempo of development, pastoral and farming activities continued to be the mainstay of Australia's economy. Railway mileage was expanded, and large amounts of foreign capital flowed in to assist the young nation in developing its resources. In the decade preceding 1914, the population increased from just under 4,000,000 to 5,000,000 people.

The Commonwealth formed. In the latter part of the nineteenth century, the six Australian colonies became apprehensive about the advance of Germany as a colonial power in the Pacific. They also felt the need of a common railroad and tariff policy. As a result of these factors, the various states consented to form a federal union to be known as the Commonwealth of Australia. In 1901 the Commonwealth came into being, bearing many resemblances to the American system of government. The Commonwealth has a legislature composed of a House of Representatives and a Senate. The members of the latter house, six for each state, are elected regardless of population, while the lower house is made up of members elected by each state in accordance with its population. As in Canada, however, the Commonwealth government makes the chief executive, the prime minister, responsible to the legislature and thus does not provide him with the fixed tenure guaranteed the American president.

New Zealand's development. About a thousand miles from the Australian mainland is a group of small islands, two of which are of particular importance. These lonely projections of European influence in the south Pacific constitute the self-governing Dominion of New Zealand. The total population of this country, which has an area five sixths the size of Great Britain, is just a little over 2,690,000. The earliest settlers were runaway sailors, adventurers, and parties of whalers, sealers, and traders. In 1837 a group of colonial enthusiasts formed the New Zealand Company with the purpose of establishing settlements. The activity of the colonizers forced the British government to assume protection of the islands in 1840, and a treaty was signed by British agents guaranteeing certain rights, especially land rights, to the indigenous peoples, the Maoris. The aim of the New Zealand Company, as defined by its directors in 1847, was:

. . . to transplant English society with its various gradations in due proportions, carrying out our laws, customs, associations, habits, manners, feelings—everything of England, in short, but the soil.[2]

New Zealand gradually became a rich pastoral, farming, and fruit-raising country. The chief exports, then as now, included wheat and wool. Later, the development of refrigeration enabled large quantities of meat to be shipped to foreign markets, especially to Great Britain.

Social advances in the dominions. New Zealand and Australia have been termed sociological laboratories because of their pioneer activities in democratic government and social welfare legislation. As early as 1855 the state of Victoria in Australia introduced the secret ballot in its elections. The Australian ballot was later introduced in Great Britain, the United States, and the world over. Woman suffrage was introduced in New Zealand in 1893 and in Australia nine years later. In New Zealand a program of "land for the people" was carried out by imposing heavy taxes on large tracts of land held by absentee landlords. This dominion led the world in the adoption of noncontributory old-age pensions in 1878 and the establishment of a national infant welfare system in 1907. Before 1914, Australia had passed similar measures.

Dutch settlement of South Africa. The area later known as the Union of South Africa, located at the tip of Black Africa, first came within the ken of Europe when Bartholomew Diaz reached the Cape of Good Hope in 1487. Twelve years later Vasco da Gama rounded the Cape on his way to the Indies. In the seventeenth century, when large fleets of merchantmen from Holland made their way around Africa to the Indies to trade for spices and oriental wares, the Cape became of great importance as a place to obtain fresh water for the ships' crews and to replenish ships' supplies.

In 1651 Jan van Riebeek left Holland with orders from the Dutch government to establish a settlement at the Cape of Good Hope. After a voyage of 104 days, the destination was reached and a fort was built, around which were laid out vegetable gardens to supply the ships on their way to the East Indies. The new settlement of Cape Town grew slowly. There was much discontent among the local inhabitants with the arbitrary administration of the Dutch East

India Company; and as the Dutch settlers pushed into the interior, they came into conflict with the Kaffirs, or Bantu native people, who put up stout resistance against the expansion of the whites.

British rule. The Dutch period of South African history came to an end when Great Britain acquired the colony in 1806 during the Napoleonic Wars. The British conquest was confirmed by the Congress of Vienna in 1815, and Cape Colony became part of the British empire. From the beginning of English rule, there was bad blood between the two nationalities. The English did not cater to the sensitivities of the Dutch burghers (Boers), who were a proud and independent people. The Dutch had large numbers of slaves, and the British emancipation of all slaves in the empire in 1833 caused much ill feeling. Moreover, the Boers disliked the pro-native attitude of the missionaries, who were continually accusing the Dutch of abusing the natives.

In 1834 the Boers began an epic journey in their great ox-drawn wagons to a new country where they could pursue their way of life without interference. This Great Trek was a folk movement similar in its importance to the covered-wagon epic of our own West. For six years the Boers were on the march. Finally, on the high veld, they established two little republics far away from the British—the Orange Free State and the Transvaal. The British, in the meantime, extended their settlement along the eastern coast north of the Cape and founded the colony of Natal.

The Great Trek did little to solve the difficulties of the Boers. In the mid-nineteenth century there was much fighting with the natives. The British government was forced to intervene because any native warriors when once out to "blood their spears" made no distinction between Boer and Briton. For a time the British actually took over the administration of the Orange Free State. In 1852 and 1854, the British government made treaties with the Boers, acknowledging their independence but retaining a shadowy right to have a voice in the foreign affairs of the two little republics.

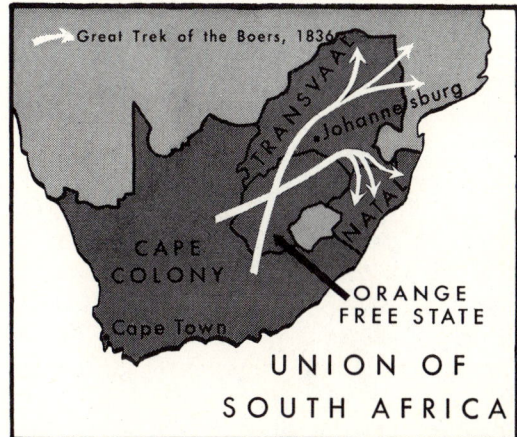

Many Englishmen and Boers in South Africa believed that some form of political union between the English and the Dutch states was a desirable goal. Unfortunately, any hopes for a peaceful union of South Africa were destroyed by the increase of friction between the British government and the Boers between 1860 and 1885. During this period the British annexed the Transvaal, and the Boers inflicted a serious defeat on a small English army. In 1884 the British government again recognized the Transvaal as an independent state.

The Boer War. It was the discovery of gold in the Transvaal in 1885 that brought on the Boer War. Thousands of Englishmen and people of other nationalities thronged to the mines, and in a few years the boom town of Johannesburg numbered more than 100,000 inhabitants. Paul Kruger, president of Transvaal from 1883 to 1900, distrusted the British and was determined that the alien element should not get control of affairs. Heavy taxes were imposed on the miners, or *Uitlanders* (foreigners), and all materials imported for the mines were charged heavy customs duties. The *Uitlanders* complained that they paid taxes but that their children were denied adequate educational facilities and that it was almost impossible to become a naturalized Boer citizen. In their anger the *Uitlanders* began to appeal to the British authorities for assistance. At this point a complex plot was hatched which included a revolt of the *Uitlanders* in "Jo-Burg." The plan went awry and the Boer

The Boer troops make one of many attacks during the siege of Mafeking. After several months, relief arrived for the British.

leaders, especially Kruger, became all the more determined to resist any further British intervention. Relations between Boer and Briton went from bad to worse, and in 1899 hostilities broke out between Great Britain and the two republics, the Orange Free State and Transvaal.

For some months the British had been sending reinforcements to South Africa, and a large force of regular troops was on hand to meet the Boer attack. The world was amazed at the war which followed. The Boers were crack shots and splendid horsemen. Knowing every inch of the ground on which they fought, they frequently outmaneuvered the British troops. The tide turned in 1900 when Lord Roberts and General Kitchener inflicted several disastrous defeats upon the Boers.

Formation of the Union. After the Dutch surrendered in 1902, the victor treated them magnanimously. Loans were furnished to rebuild burned farmhouses and buy cattle. In 1906 the Transvaal was granted self-government, which two years later was extended to the Orange Free State. The Liberal government in Great Britain then permitted the Dutch and English states to unite and form the Union of South Africa in 1909. Only seven years after the war, Boer and Briton joined hands in creating a new self-governing dominion in the tradition of Canada and Australia. The first prime minister of the Union was Louis Botha (1863-1919), who had been a Boer general in the late war. It was Botha's prime purpose to remove the causes of misunderstanding between the two European nations. The aim was to create not an English or a Dutch nationality but a blend of the two in a new South African patriotism.

THE MAKING OF NEW NATIONS:

LATIN AMERICA

The genesis of independence. The wars for independence in Spanish America, which were fought in the first quarter of the nineteenth century, were the last manifestation of the cycle of revolutions initiated by the Glorious Revolution in England in 1688 and followed by the American Revolution in 1775 and the French Revolution in 1789. All

13 (below) **New Guinea Mask** (19th century). **14** (left) **Kwakiutl Mask** (1850-1900). **15** (bottom left) **Benin Mask** (c. 17th century). Europe held dominion over much of the non-European world in the 19th century; yet, artistically speaking, the conquerors learned from the conquered, who gained little or nothing from the encounter. The indigenous styles of the peoples of Africa, Asia, the Americas, and Oceania began to decline and to die out as the new European presence shook the continuity of native traditions. Nor were these styles replaced by anything of comparable vitality. Meanwhile, the West began to grasp the merit of these native arts and proceeded to enshrine examples in American and European museums. During the 19th and 20th centuries, native art has exerted a major influence on occidental art. In tribal societies the world over, the mask usually has played an important role in religion and ritual, and thus in the art which served as a handmaiden to such ritual. Styles vary greatly, as illustrated here, from the coolly tempered and finely chiseled lines of the Benin mask, through the geometrically decorated surfaces of the New Guinea style, to the bold and elegant patterns of the Kwakiutl.

16 (above left) **Nicobar Islands Plaque** (19th century). On occasion, non-European artists acknowledged the European foreigner in their work. Such acknowledgment, however, was expressed not in style but in subject matter. This plaque from the Nicobar Islands retains the flat design and stylization peculiar to the art of that British possession in the Bay of Bengal. But it depicts, with disarming ingenuousness, a native god (center) surrounded by European objects which symbolize the power of the white man. Note the spoked wheel, clock, rifle, mirror, and hatchets. **17** (below left) **Edgar Degas: "Dancers Preparing for the Ballet"** (c. 1878-1880). The stylistic qualities of Japanese graphic art (see figure 19) had an invigorating effect on European painting in the latter part of the 19th century. Many of the French impressionists were attracted to and greatly influenced by the flat color, the informal composition, and the simplified rendering techniques of Japanese prints. In this illustration the asymmetrical organization, the emphasis on a two-dimensional pattern of light and dark, plus the swiftness and brevity of handling indicate that Degas, especially, was familiar with Japanese woodcuts. **18** (right) **Paul Gauguin: "Tahitian Woman with Children"** (1901). The attitudes of Europeans toward the natives of the lands which they had colonized often differed sharply. The Christian missionaries, for example, considered the people of Tahiti to be backward, uncivilized and, consequently, in need of the "higher" values and moral teachings of the West. In contrast, Paul Gauguin, a world-weary European surfeited with what he regarded as the soul-stifling mechanization of the West, fled to Tahiti as if to a shrine, hoping to find in its society the emotional directness and untroubled simplicity which he had not found in France. Evidence of these two contrasting attitudes is present in this illustration. Gauguin has shown the woman and the older child clad in western garments, presumably given to them by the missionaries, who sought thereby to bring these Tahitians closer to western ways. Yet Gauguin portrays them unmistakably as Tahitians, not Westerners, and he accords them a gentle dignity.

丹鳥齋

上村□□□

19 Okumura Masanobu: "Pair of Lovers" (1790). This color woodcut is an example of the Japanese artistic tradition called *ukiyoe*, "pictures of the passing scene." Masanobu achieved lustrous ink effects and vibrant color. The elegant patterns, the strong linear rhythms, and the flatness of the space were all echoed in the work of the western artists (see figure 16) who "discovered" Japanese woodcuts in the mid-19th century.

Louis Botha, able South African general and statesman

these movements sprang from the same body of political ideals. But the Spanish revolution also showed important dissimilarities. While freedom brought political unity to the United States, in Spanish America it brought warfare and political fragmentation.

During the eighteenth century, the main intellectual and political currents in Europe penetrated to the colonies of the New World. The explosive ideology of the Enlightenment and the encouraging example of the French Revolution crossed the Atlantic and made a deep impress on Latin America. Progressive benevolent despots such as Frederick the Great of Prussia and Joseph II of Austria influenced statesmen and sovereigns in Spain and Portugal who strove for reforms both at home and in the colonies.

Broadly speaking, the diffusion of liberal and reformist ideas resulted in a rejuvenation of the Spanish and Portuguese empires in America. Colonial policy was twofold: to stimulate the economy and to make the administration more efficient. The *intendant* system was borrowed from France; new colonial offices were established and loyal officials were sent to the colonies to report on all activities of the various governmental departments. Also improved was the character of the officials. Some of the new viceroys can be ranked among the greatest colonial administrators.

The Church in the colonies was shorn of some of its wealth, and its power to suppress new ideas and censor educational activities was curbed. The Inquisition almost died out from disuse and disapproval. In the realm of economics some welcome breaches were made in the citadel of mercantilism; for example, there was a lessening of restrictions on trade between ports of the Spanish empire and those of the homeland.

As a result of the enlightened despotism

which reached eighteenth-century Latin America, this huge area enjoyed greater prosperity than ever before. Possessing more wealth than English America, the Spanish colonies had the outward signs of opulence: imposing public buildings, universities, churches, hospitals, and populous cities which were centers of learning, luxury, and refinement. Such arts as painting and silversmithing flourished, especially in Mexico City, Quito, and Cuzco. Before any similar institutions existed in the English, French, or Portuguese colonies, a school of mines and a school of fine arts were founded in Mexico, and an astronomical observatory in Bogotá. Produced by talented men of letters, historians, and poets, colonial literary achievements were rich and varied.

Climate for revolution. Rising prosperity, more efficient government, and more freedom of thought did not ensure contentment, however. Enough of the new thought of the Enlightenment had been imported to make the ambitious Creole class realize how much

Miranda, apostle of Venezuelan liberty, led an unsuccessful military expedition in Venezuela and died in a Cadiz prison.

more free and prosperous the colonies might become once the restrictive hand of Madrid had been removed. The Creoles (Spaniards born in the colonies) resented the haughty *peninsulares*, the Spaniards sent from the homeland who monopolized all the highest governmental positions. The rising young Creole generation feasted on the ideas of Montesquieu, Voltaire, and Rousseau. Although works by these authors were banned, they were smuggled into the country in great numbers. A Latin-American scholar has observed: "Voltaire and the encyclopedias . . . were read by village curates, by canons of provincial cathedrals, and by lawyers in the capital. Pictures of Voltaire were even sold in the bookstalls . . . and the books of all of them passed from hand to hand, although surreptitiously, because the Holy Office still kept watch."[3]

While government policy was reformist, it could not keep pace with the growth of liberal ideas, especially after the American and the French revolutions. The high degree of censorship and control infuriated the young intellectuals. For example, the govern-ment imprisoned a native of Bogotá for ten years because he had secured a copy of the Declaration of the Rights of Man, translated it, and, in 1794, had it printed on his own press. As late as 1773, a Colombian scientist was accused of heresy for giving lectures on the Copernican system.

Therefore, in spite of reforms, injustices and oppression continued. There was, of course, no hint of the government giving people a greater voice in politics. While not so rigid, mercantilism was still in force, the courts were often corrupt, and the *peninsulares* domineered the Creoles and *mestizos* (those of Spanish and Indian blood).

Precursors of Revolution. Thoughts of independence were in the air as the eighteenth century came to a close. In fact, intermittent discontent and uprisings date back as far as the seventeenth century. In the 1730's the independence movement had taken on new strength. Uprisings increased, and on a number of occasions the English were asked for help. Later, in 1780, three independence movements were launched but all failed.

Of all the so-called Precursors of Revolution, Francisco de Miranda (1750-1816) was the most active. Fleeing from Spanish America to avoid prosecution over a financial matter, he spent thirty years traveling in the United States and Europe. A linguist and a brilliant conversationalist, he earned the privilege of entering into the most cultivated social circles. Miranda traveled as far as Russia, where apparently he charmed the susceptible Empress Catherine. But most of his time was spent in London; there, his plans for emancipating the colonies from Spain intrigued English leaders, who saw to it that he was supported by their government.

The "legal" phase of the revolution. It needed only a spark set off by the Napoleonic wars to ignite the revolutionary flame in Spanish America. When the news reached the colonies that Napoleon had unceremoniously removed the Bourbons and placed his brother Joseph on the throne, there was deep resentment in Spanish America. Nowhere in the colonies was the new monarch, dubbed "Joe Bottles" (Pépe Botellas), recognized. On the contrary, the colonial authorities proclaimed their loyalty to Ferdinand VII, the former king, who was now interned in France.

Money was sent to Spain to encourage patriot opposition to Napoleon and his royal puppet. But the French emperor seemed all powerful, and Spain was on the verge of disappearing as an independent kingdom. Orders and officials sent to the colonies commanded little respect. In a number of colonies, therefore, liberal Creoles in 1810 ousted local officials and took charge, all the while proclaiming their loyalty to the absent Ferdinand. This legal phase of the revolution took place in Venezuela, the Argentine, New Granada, and Chile. Other Spanish areas, such as Peru and Guatemala, made no changes.

Brazil takes the royal road to freedom. During the eighteenth century, discontent with colonial status was not strong in the Portuguese settlement of Brazil. This sprawling land lagged behind its Spanish neighbors; both culture and commerce progressed at a snail's pace. Ignorance and superstition were common among the populace, even among the European element, which spent much of its time with "funerals and religious parades, or in love-making."[4]

Napoleon's ambitions in Europe ended this uneventful atmosphere, however. Following their flight from Napoleon's armies, the members of the royal house of Braganza arrived in Brazil early in 1808. (The royal family, the court, and a large military force had sailed out of the Lisbon harbor just as the French forces approached the environs of the city.) Drastic reforms were carried out by royal command in the dependency. The Braganzas liked their new abode so much that they remained in Rio de Janeiro after Portugal was freed of the French armies of occupation.

Toward independence: 1811 to 1816. In the Spanish colonies, the legal phase of the revolutionary movement was of short duration. Radical leaders began to demand independence and an end to the fiction of loyalty to Ferdinand. Simón Bolívar (1783-1830), leader of the rebels in Caracas, went to

Portrait of Simón Bolívar the Liberator

England to obtain British aid and convinced Miranda that the time had come to strike for complete freedom. Miranda returned to Latin America in December 1810, and the following year the independence of Venezuela was proclaimed.

Tragic reverses followed, and in 1812 Miranda felt compelled to make a humiliating surrender. Some of his fellow patriots, including Bolívar, were so furious with Miranda that they allowed him to be captured by the Spaniards. Thus repudiated, he was sent to a prison in Cádiz, where he died four years later.

In 1813 Bolívar again attempted to raise the standard of revolt in Venezuela and again proclaimed it a republic. For a year he was in power, learning statecraft and crystallizing his own ideas. Again the royalists counterattacked, and by 1815 Bolívar was in exile.

Other uprisings in Lima, La Paz, and

José de San Martín did not receive wide recognition as a revolutionary hero until after his death.

Quito had been equally unsuccessful. The most tragic failure occurred in Mexico. A premature effort for self-government led by a radical priest, Father Hidalgo (1753-1811), turned in 1810 into a frightening race war of Indian against white. Frightened of the specter of social revolution, wealthy Creoles and other conservative forces supported the Spanish regime. Within a year Hidalgo was captured and executed, but his work was carried on by another priest, Father José Morelos (1765-1815), who aspired to independence and worked for social and agrarian reform. In 1815 he was captured by the Spaniards and suffered the same fate as Hidalgo.

The failure of Ferdinand. In 1814, following the defeat of Napoleon, Ferdinand VII was released by the French and was welcomed deliriously in Spain. The American independence movements now lapsed, except in the region around Buenos Aires. The

king, popular for the moment, might have rallied his subjects in the colonies by generous concessions, but he contemptuously ignored this opportunity. Instead of pacifying the Americas, he imposed the Old Regime with all its hateful aspects. Soon embittered, the Americans resumed plans for revolution.

From his exile in Jamaica, Bolívar kept the flames of discontent alive. Many British veterans of the Napoleonic wars joined the independence forces which were building up their strength in scattered swamps and jungles. Moreover, London and New York merchants were willing to sell leftover war supplies on credit to the patriots.

Meanwhile Ferdinand procrastinated. As evidence of revolutionary activity mounted, the king collected a large army to be transported overseas, but the lack of ships at Cádiz kept the soldiers idle year after year, giving secret societies the chance to arouse them against Ferdinand's repressive policies. In January 1820 they finally revolted and were joined by other discontented groups. For three years, until a French army intervened to restore him to power, Ferdinand was kept a virtual prisoner.

The Liberators in action: Bolívar and San Martín. It was during Ferdinand's discreditable royal rule that the colonial independence forces rose from defeat to gain a complete triumph. This was the achievement of the Liberators, Simón Bolívar and José de San Martín (1778-1850), aided by a group of devoted and efficient lieutenants. The audacity and tempestuous drive of these leaders has been compared to that of famous *conquistadores* such as Pizarro and Cortés.

Bolívar, former leader of the abortive revolts in Caracas, was a wealthy Creole who gave his entire fortune to the revolutionary cause. A man of great personal charm, he was a born actor who liked to play the role of heroic leader and who sought the limelight and the plaudits of the crowd. Cultured, well-traveled in Europe, and imbued with the liberal philosophy of the Enlightenment, he made the cause of independence both a crusade and an obsession. In 1805 Bolívar had climbed the Aventine Hill in

Rome and taken a solemn oath never to rest until Spanish rule was ended in America.

San Martín was the complete opposite; he had none of Bolívar's glowing enthusiasm. Reserved and uncommunicative, he was not moved by praise or blame if he believed his cause just. Doing his duty without any regard for his own interests, San Martín rightly called himself a stoic.

Bolívar began his comeback early in 1817. With a small force he defeated the Spanish armies in northern Latin America. The most dramatic incident of his victorious campaign was the successful crossing of the formidable Andes. The Republic of Great Colombia (made up of modern Colombia, Venezuela, and Ecuador) was established, and Bolívar was named the first president of this huge new state.

Further south, in the Argentine, San Martín had been making preparations for a spectacular offensive against the royalist forces. In 1817 he led his army over the Andes in a desperate three weeks' march, surprising and defeating the Spanish forces in Chile. Aided by a former British officer, Lord Cochrane, who won naval supremacy in the waters off Peru, San Martín in 1820 transported his troops to this viceroyalty. In 1821 he entered Lima, where he formally announced the independence of Peru.

The two Liberators met in 1822. At this meeting basic differences in policy and strategy developed. It is said also that Bolívar did not relish being outshone by any rival. Thereupon, without any recriminations, San Martín withdrew from the scene and spent the remainder of his life abroad. His greatness was only tardily realized; not until 1880 were his remains brought back to Buenos Aires and buried in the cathedral there. Today his life is studied in the Argentine schools just as Washington's is in the United States.

After San Martín's withdrawal, Bolívar was left to dominate the scene. In 1824 his army delivered the knockout blow to Spanish power by winning a decisive victory at Ayacucho, situated on a high Peruvian plateau nearly 12,000 feet above the sea. Here the last Spanish viceroy in the New

World surrendered. By 1825, the revolution had run its successful course.

Independence won in Mexico and Brazil. Royalist elements in Mexico were deeply offended by the revolution of 1820 in Spain and the brief triumph of the liberal party. Therefore, in 1821, the conservatives supported Agustín de Iturbide (1783-1824), a military leader of dubious reputation. Joining the rebel forces holding out in the mountains, he proclaimed the independence of Mexico. After plans to establish a monarchy in Mexico under a Spanish prince fell through, Iturbide proclaimed himself emperor. Guatemala also announced its independence, though for a time it seemed that it would fall under Iturbide's rule.

Independence also came to Brazil, where the Braganzas had been carrying out long-delayed reforms since 1808. Under the paternalistic hand of King John, industries grew, commerce flourished, and European traders and bankers helped the cause of colonial development. In 1815 the king declared that Brazil was a self-governing dominion within the Portuguese empire.

In 1820, however, a revolution in Portugal put the liberal party in power, and its new parliament, the Cortes, set to work on a

The principles enunciated in Monroe's message to Congress in December 1823 (backed unofficially by the British navy) became an important part of American foreign policy.

program of domestic reform. Unfortunately, the colonial policy of the new government was reactionary, and King John decided that his presence was needed in Lisbon. Before he left, he told his young son Pedro, who was acting as regent: "If Brazil demands independence, grant it, but put the crown upon your own head." Shortly after his father's departure, Pedro received a demand from the Cortes in Lisbon that he return immediately to complete his "education." Following later demands, Pedro ripped the Portuguese colors off his uniform and shouted, "Independence or death!" The Brazilians defeated the Portuguese garrison troops with the help of a naval force brought by Lord Cochrane. In December 1822, Pedro was crowned emperor of Brazil.

The Monroe Doctrine and the British navy support Latin-American independence. By 1825, Spanish and Portuguese power was broken in the Western Hemisphere, and nine new political units emerged in Latin Amer-ica. Mexico, Guatemala, Greater Colombia, Peru, Bolivia, Paraguay, Argentina, and Chile were free of Spain, while Brazil, retaining a liberal monarchy, had gained independence of Portugal.

Independence, once achieved, was soon endangered. In the post-Napoleonic period, Spain joined the autocratic, reactionary clique of European monarchies engineered by Metternich—the Quadruple Alliance. Too weak to undertake the task of retrieving control over its lost American colonies alone, Spain solicited the aid of the other powers. France appeared especially eager to help, and the prospect of restoration seemed bright in the early 1820's. The reactionary alliance had not reckoned with Great Britain and the United States, however, and it was not to the interests of either of these powers that Spanish America be returned to Spain. While Great Britain warned France and cajoled Spain, the United States took up a British suggestion, modified it, and in 1823, through a message to Congress, President Monroe announced the famous Monroe Doctrine. The doctrine in essence was a warning that the United States would not tolerate the resumption of European control over the newly independent states of Latin America. Without committing itself to guarantee the doctrine, Great Britain by its naval supremacy throughout the nineteenth century was possibly more responsible than was the United States for the success of the hands-off policy. While the stirring military achievements of the rebel armies under Bolívar, San Martín, and others should not be underemphasized, it was British and American sympathy that helped the Spanish-American republics attain independence.

Early disappointments in freed Latin America. Freedom was now secure in Latin America, but for most of the new republics the first half century of independence was a period of retrogression and disillusionment. The great Liberators were unable to maintain control of the nations they had freed, nor were the liberal, urban Creoles who had begun the independence movement able to agree with one another on elementary political matters. Impractical and inexperienced, they soon lost power to crude military leaders, or *caudillos*, whose armed gangs seized and lost the seats of power in a confusing series of tumults. A growing sectionalism appeared, and the mammoth states broke up into puny republics which in turn were threatened with localism.

The unpromising heritage. The Spanish colonial system had offered little responsibility or opportunity in government to the American-born whites, and the tradition of autocracy and paternalism was a poor precedent for would-be democratic republics. The emphasis on executive power inspired later presidents, generals, landowners, tribal leaders, and even clerical officials to wield authority with extreme arrogance. Legislative and judicial organs never flourished. Spain's economic system encouraged concentration of land and other forms of wealth, an extractive economy, and dubious dealings with foreign businessmen. Finally, the Church with its great properties and its hold on education and welfare agencies was to complicate the politics of every new nation.

The effects of the wars of independence were also ruinous. Some of the most productive areas, such as the plantations of coastal Venezuela and the silver mines of Mexico, were devastated. Hatreds and divisions long persisted. Also, many men who had fought the royalists remained armed, fond of a life of crime and pillage, and likely to group themselves about the *caudillos* who promised them adventure or gain in revolutions.

Geographical handicaps. Beyond those historical factors were realities of Latin-American geography which would have challenged the skill of the best of governments. A mountain chain ranking as the second highest in the world made trade and communication extremely expensive. Rivers were seldom in the right places for purposes of trade and transportation. Nearly half of South America and much of Mexico and Central America was a torrid jungle.

This is not to deny that most of the settled areas were high, cool, and scenic, nor that Latin America was wonderfully endowed with precious metals, grasslands, and forests.

But there was little coal and, it was erroneously believed, no iron, so that industrial development was greatly handicapped. Not until the latter part of the nineteenth century were the fertile areas of Argentina, Uruguay, and southern Brazil developed.

Racial disunity. When independence was achieved in the first quarter of the nineteenth century, there were from fifteen to eighteen million people in the former Spanish empire. About three million of these were whites, among whom were included almost all the property-owning and educated groups. (Immigration from Europe did little to increase their numbers until the last third of the century, when a deluge began.) About the same number of people were *mestizos*, who scorned the Indians but were usually not accepted by the whites, though they were steadily increasing in number and ambition during the period when new nations were being formed. During the nineteenth century, half or more of the population was Indian. Deprived of the small protection once offered by the Spanish crown, they either sank into peonage or lived in semi-independence under their tribal rulers. Finally, in Brazil and most of the Caribbean islands, Negroes, most of them slaves, were in a large majority. Conflicts of interest quickly developed between these broad racial groups, particularly between the Creoles and the *mestizos*.

Mexico. The pernicious effects of these divisive factors in the newly independent Spanish-American world can be seen in the experiences of each nation. Mexico, which had seemed such a promising new country in 1821, had more than one-half century of turmoil. The empire of Iturbide lasted only a few months, and a federal republic was then established under an admirable constitution. In less than ten years, however, a preposterous military leader named Antonio López de Santa Anna (1795-1876) had become dictator. (It was Santa Anna who massacred the defenders of the Alamo in 1836.) Debasement of Mexican public life and the humiliation of Mexico by the United States in the war of 1846-1848 must

Now a part of the romantic tradition of South America, the nomadic Argentine cowboys known as *gauchos* once played an important role in Argentine politics. Lawless and anti-European, they were able to hold sway over the government until they were overthrown in the mid-nineteenth century.

be charged to this strutting, corrupt *caudillo.* Upon his final overthrow in 1855, the injuries inflicted on Mexican pride during his regime brought more sincere men into politics; and the liberals, whose eventual leader was the Indian Benito Juárez (1806-1872), set out to implement their program, the *Reforma.* They planned to establish a truly federal republic and to destroy the Church as a political and economic force. Implicitly, they intended to hasten the inclusion of *mestizos* and Indians in political life. A terrible civil war followed the anticlerical measures and ended in 1861 with the apparent victory of Juárez, but inability to meet payments on debts owed to foreigners brought an invasion of Mexico by European powers and the establishment of a French puppet regime.

When pressure from the United States had driven French troops from Mexican soil, Juárez again set about instituting the *Reforma,* but the poor condition of the country hampered progress. Soon after he died, power went to one of his adherents, Porfirio Diaz (1830-1915), who served as president from 1877 to 1880 and from 1884 to 1911. Under his administration Mexico did become an orderly country. Foreign capital

entered in large amounts. Factories, railroads, mines, trading houses, plantations, and enormous ranches flourished, and Mexico City became one of the most impressive of capitals. Yet Diaz' rule, though outwardly conforming to the constitution, was a dictatorship. If there was much encouragement of art and letters, there was no liberty. The Indians sank lower into peonage or even outright slavery, and the Indian heritage was disdained. In spite of the anticlerical laws of the Juárez period, which remained on the books, the Church was quietly permitted to acquire great wealth; and foreign investors exploited Mexico, creating a long lasting hatred of foreigners.

In 1910 the critics of Diaz found a spokesman in a frail, eccentric man named Francisco Madero (1873-1913), who undertook to lead a revolutionary movement and surprised the world by succeeding. The Diaz machine crumpled abruptly in 1911.

Although Madero was murdered two years later and Mexico underwent another period of turmoil in which the country was controlled mainly by self-styled local rulers, a determined group was able to organize a revolutionary party and to bring about the only genuine social revolution that Latin America has experienced since the Spanish conquest. As we shall see in a later chapter, the Mexican constitution of 1917 has served as an inspiration to much of Latin America.

Argentina. Probably the most advanced Spanish-speaking country in the world, Argentina attained this position in a period of sudden growth that followed half a century of torpor. Its beginning as a free nation was promising. Soon, however, the bustling port city of Buenos Aires, whose energetic population sought to encourage European capital and commerce, found itself overawed by the primitive *gauchos* of the interior. These colorful, nomadic cowboys and bandits, whose way of life is now regarded as romantic, intimidated the adherents of constitutional government in Buenos Aires, and until midcentury, Argentina was not a republic but rather a *gaucho* paradise, isolated and ruled by men who wanted to keep European influences out.

In 1852 a combination of progressive elements overthrew the *gaucho* leader; commerce with Europe was revived, and by 1861 Argentina at last became a united republic and experienced an admirable stability. The constitution was usually observed, and a high degree of respect for individual rights prevailed. Immigrants poured in, and soon Argentina became one of the most European in population of any major land of the New World, for it had few Indians or Negroes. Foreign capital, especially British, brought about amazing developments; port facilities, railroads, light industries, and urban conveniences were among the most advanced in the world. Buenos Aires became by far the largest and most beautiful city in Latin America, almost a Paris, despite its location on a monotonous flat plain beside a muddy estuary.

This flat plain, or pampas, is perhaps the richest land in the world for grass and wheat; and cattle have been multiplying there for centuries. Around 1880, refrigerated ships made it feasible to transport enormous quantities of fresh beef to Britain, where an increasing population and a rising standard of living meant an expanding market. Thus Argentine beef, as well as mutton and wool, went to England in exchange for capital and finished goods. Around 1900, wheat joined beef as a major Argentine export. This intimate relationship with Britain, which lasted until after World War II, affected nearly every aspect of Argentine life. Nevertheless, as we shall see in a later chapter, although top-drawer society was dominated by elegant leaders who were pro-British in business and pro-French in culture, a true Argentine nationalism was developing. Along with the growth of this powerful sentiment came urgent demands for more democracy and wider distribution of wealth.

Brazil. For many years the former Portuguese colony of Brazil escaped the turbulence and disorders that befell its Spanish-speaking neighbors, probably because it had achieved independence without bloodshed and because it enjoyed the continuity and legitimacy afforded by a respected monarchy. A constitution was granted by the first emperor, Pedro I, in 1824, and though disorder threatened in the mid-1830's, the rule of Pedro II in 1840 inaugurated a period of political liberty and economic and cultural progress which was to endure throughout his fifty-year reign.

Immigrants were attracted to this peaceful land in the New World, and foreign investments were heavy, though not with the arrant exploitation that Mexico had experienced under Diaz. Economic growth tended, however, to favor the southeastern part of the country at the expense of the great sugar plantations in the tropical north; and when the sugar lords were further injured in 1888 by the abolition of Negro slavery, they ranged themselves in opposition to the empire. Joining them were army officers who resented the civilian nature of Pedro's regime and a small number of ideological republicans. In 1889 the aging emperor was forced to abdicate.

For nearly ten years the new federal republic of Brazil underwent civil wars and military upheavals not unlike those in other Latin-American countries. Finally, the republic was stabilized with the army in control, and Brazil resumed its progressive course. Foreign capital continued to enter, and immigration from Europe remained heavy. By World War I, Brazil was generally stable and prosperous, with a strong tradition of liberty.

Other Latin-American nations. Political naïveté, geographical handicaps, and racial disunity all played a part in the development of the other new nations in Latin America. Bolivia, named so hopefully after the Liberator, underwent countless revolutions which to an outsider seem almost pointless. Peru's course was almost as futile. The political history of Colombia was characterized by terrible civil wars; and, in 1830, Venezuela and Ecuador withdrew from that state to form new states, equally unstable. Paraguay endured a series of dictatorships; and Uruguay, created in 1828 as a buffer between Argentina and Brazil, long suffered from interventions by these two countries. An exception to the prevailing pattern of political chaos was the steady growth of the republic of Chile. In 1823 Chile came under the control of a conservative oligarchy. Although this regimen proved to be generally enlightened, the country was kept under tight control for a century and was ruled for the benefit of the large landlords and the big businessmen.

Central America narrowly escaped becoming part of Mexico in 1822. Then a fifteen-year effort to create a confederation followed, only to collapse as Guatemala, San Salvador, Honduras, Nicaragua, and Costa Rica asserted their independence. Except for Costa Rica, where the whites comprised the bulk of the population, racial disunity delayed the creation of national feeling.

Foreign investment in Latin America. Though a few areas achieved relative political harmony, the chronic political instability prevailing especially in northern Latin America in the nineteenth century not only hindered domestic progress but also weakened the relations of the Latin-American nations with the outside world at a critical time in history. The Industrial Revolution began to get into its full stride just after the Latin-American republics were born. The great industries of western Europe, and later those of the United States, demanded more and more raw materials and new markets in which to sell the completed products. Capital accumulated, and investors eagerly sought opportunities to place their money where high rates of interest could be obtained. This drive for markets, raw materials, and outlets for surplus capital led to the movement known as economic imperialism. As the following chapter shows, imperialism was particularly active in Asia and Africa, but South America did not escape unscathed.

The continual disorder and the lack of strong governments in Latin America gave businessmen ample opportunity to obtain rich concessions and float huge loans. Many of the Latin-American governments, created by revolution and interested only in filling their own pockets, often resorted to the vicious practice of selling concessions to foreign corporations for ready cash. Political

bosses bartered away the economic heritage of their lands, for Latin America was rich in minerals, oil, and other important resources. Sometimes the foreign investor acted in good faith, providing capital at a reasonable rate of interest to Latin-American regimes which, it developed, had no intention of fulfilling the contract. On other occasions unscrupulous capitalists took full advantage of officials in ignorant or helpless governments. In many cases defaults occurred and controversy ensued. To be sure, much of the commerce and investment was mutually satisfactory, but over the years the more disorderly republics became the subject of a long list of complaints made by investors.

The injured foreign investor usually appealed to his government to intercede in his behalf, and an unending stream of diplomatic correspondence over debt claims was begun, for neither the United States, Great Britain, Germany, France, Italy, nor Spain —the chief investor states—would see its nationals mistreated in their foreign-investment dealings.

Roosevelt and the Monroe Doctrine. Another threat to Latin-American countries developed in 1902 and 1903 when a dispute between Venezuela and a coalition formed by Germany, Great Britain, and Italy provoked the three European powers into blockading Venezuela and even firing upon coastal fortifications to remind the recalcitrant Venezuelan dictator of the obligations he had contracted with some of their nationals. At first inclined to sit by and let Venezuela take its punishment, the United States soon became suspicious of German intentions. President Theodore Roosevelt matched threat with threat; and the European nations retreated quickly into the safer field of international arbitration. The Venezuelan imbroglio was resolved, but it left the United States and President Roosevelt with an increasing determination never again to allow Europe so much rope in the Western Hemisphere, no matter how just the cause.

If the Monroe Doctrine was to prevent Europe from pursuing the legitimate task of protecting its nationals—even to the employment of force—then it was natural for Europe to charge the United States with the responsibility of protecting European creditors as well as its own. In 1904 the American president proclaimed the Roosevelt Corollary to the Monroe Doctrine. This doctrine was a frank statement that chronic wrongdoing on the part of Latin-American governments might force the United States to exercise an international police power. Picturesquely described as the policy of speaking softly but carrying a big stick, the Roosevelt pronunciamento thus launched the era of the Big Stick. The United States not only established a customs receivership in the Dominican Republic but exercised similar control in Nicaragua and Haiti.

By the beginning of the twentieth century, the United States had just completed twenty-five years of rapid industrialization following the Civil War. Like the older industrial nations, it now became acutely conscious of the need for raw materials and markets. The Monroe Doctrine was now used not so much for its original purpose of keeping out European political interference in Latin America but rather as an agency for expanding the commercial interests of the United States.

Cuba becomes a protectorate. In 1898 the United States went to war with Spain over the way the Spaniards were ruling Cuba. For decades the maltreatment of the Cubans had offended humanitarian sentiments of the Americans—an altruism colored by the fact that the civil war in Cuba also injured American commercial interests in the island. Victory in the brief, dramatic Spanish-American War brought the United States recognition as a world power and a conglomeration of islands in the Pacific Ocean as well as in the Caribbean. Puerto Rico was annexed; the Philippines were brought under American rule. Sensitive of accusations of outright imperialism in Cuba, the government offered Cuba an imperfect, closely tutored independence, and the Cubans were obliged to acknowledge by law the right of the United States to intervene for the "preservation of Cuban independence" and the "maintenance of a government adequate for the protection of life,

property, and individual liberty." These and other restrictions to Cuban independence were embodied in the so-called Platt Amendment (1901) to the new Cuban constitution. Thus the United States established its first American protectorate. Panama soon became another protectorate of the United States. In all these areas, American business interests throve, but so did the material welfare of the inhabitants.

Dollar diplomacy. The next manifestation of the imperialistic mood of the United States has been appropriately called dollar diplomacy, an American policy which prevailed from the Theodore Roosevelt through the Coolidge administrations. Euphemistically defined as political finance, dollar diplomacy referred to the coordinated activities of American foreign investors and their State Department, who worked in close cooperation to obtain and protect concessions for investors, especially in those sections of the Caribbean countries which produced sugar, bananas, and oil. This policy in the period from 1890 to 1914 acutely affected nearly a dozen of the Latin-American republics. For reasons of both finance and political strategy, the United States government could in the last analysis—and at times did—control the policies of these states.

The "Colossus of the North." Although the growing assertiveness of the United States in the Western Hemisphere was accompanied by increasing alarm among Latin-Americans, there was developing a movement which held hope for greater harmony between our country and the Latin-American states. Some liberal thinkers in the United States had long envisioned a fraternity of the Americas indissolubly linked by common bonds of geography and the political ideals of the Enlightenment. Expressed by periodic conferences, the first of which was held in 1889, and the establishment of a permanent secretariat in Washington known as the Pan American Union, Pan-Americanism was carefully nursed by Washington officialdom.

Yet barely a decade had passed since the first Pan-American Conference before United States' imperialism shook the foundations of the new movement. If Latin-American nations had ever felt a grateful appreciation for the protection afforded by the Monroe Doctrine, its benign aspect was forgotten in their concern over what they now chose to call the "Colossus of the North." Recognizing the familiar stamp of "made in the U.S.A.," the more suspicious Latin-Americans began to see Pan-Americanism as a "skilful move in the expansionist policy of the North, and a suicidal tendency of the simple-minded South."[5] By 1913 the general resentment evoked such charges of hypocrisy that an important South American diplomat undiplomatically felt prompted to state in all sincerity that "There is no Pan-Americanism in South America; it exists only in Washington."[6] More satirical colleagues gave vent to their feelings by referring to the Pan American Union as the Colonial Division of the Department of State.

Latin America in 1914. Thus, by 1914, Latin America's relations with the outside world were neither healthy nor comforting. Added to its traditional difficulties was the new and disturbing factor of the emergence of the United States as the politically and economically predominant power in the New World. If in the early nineteenth century the southern republics had been "the financial colonies of Europe," they hardly felt comforted by the growing aspiration of the United States after 1890 to become their sole creditor. Latin America looked on sullenly when, as in Mexico, United States oil interests fought British oil interests and used competing political factions as implements of warfare.

Although a century of independence had elapsed, Latin America still lingered on the margin of international life. Left to shift for itself in the face of a future shaded by United States' imperialism, Latin America saw only a hard road ahead in its relations with the outside world.

COMMON DENOMINATORS

Immigration. The vast, fertile lands of the new Europes provided an almost magnetic attraction for the poor and landless peoples of Europe. A tremendous tide of immigra-

tion entered the new lands; it is estimated that 40,000,000 emigrants sailed from their European homes from 1815 to 1914. By the latter date, the number of people of European stock living in the new Europes totaled 200,000,000—a figure which is almost equivalent to the total population of Europe at the time of Napoleon's defeat.

In various and different ways, the new Europes reflected the nineteenth-century movements that had originated in western Europe—nationalism, democracy, industrialism, and even imperialism. In addition, there were problems to be solved which sprang specifically from factors and conditions shared by the new Europes. These common denominators will be considered briefly here.

Exploration. In all the new Europes, vast spaces had to be explored, paths to the interior mapped, and natural resources evaluated. In the United States the famous expedition of Meriwether Lewis and William Clark started from St. Louis in the winter of 1803-1804, blazed a trail through the unknown Northwest, and reached the Pacific two years later. For half a century the process of exploration and mapping continued, reaching its climax in the expeditions in the 1840's of John Frémont. In what is now Canada, Alexander Mackenzie in 1789 traveled to the Great Slave Lake, then down the river that now bears his name to the shores of northern Canada. Four years later he crossed the Rocky Mountains and thus became the first European to traverse North America at its greatest width.

The most famous figure in the exploration of South America was the German naturalist Alexander von Humboldt, who from 1799 to 1804 carried on explorations in Mexico, Cuba, and South America; he investigated the valley of the Orinoco, crossed the Andes, and studied the sources of the Amazon. Although others have carried on the work he began, the huge Amazon basin—a tropical wilderness covering an area as large as the United States—has not to this day been completely explored.

Not until after the midpoint of the nineteenth century was the continent of Australia crossed from north to south. Between 1860 and 1862, John McDouall Stuart made three attempts before he successfully completed the journey from Adelaide to Van Diemen's Gulf. The penetration of the interior of South Africa differed from explorations in the other new Europes. It was achieved by the gradual expansion of white settlement in such valiant movements as the Great Trek rather than by expeditions of exploration, although discovery in the north was accomplished by such men as Livingstone and Stanley (see Chapter 10).

Treatment of native peoples. Estimates of the number of Indians in North America at the time of the coming of the white man are conjectural. In Canada the estimate is about 200,000; in the United States, about 850,000. Since the coming of the white man, the number of Indians in North America has been reduced by approximately half. In Canada, where the Indian population was not so great as in the United States, the Canadians encountered less difficulty with the natives as they moved westward to the Pacific. In the United States, however, there were frequent Indian wars and, generally speaking, a much more severe impact of an advanced civilization upon the culture patterns of the Indians. While in modern times attempts have been made to encourage the Indian to make a place for himself in contemporary urban and industrialized society, the inability or the reluctance of many to make the necessary adjustments remains a serious problem—particularly to the government of the United States.

Some authorities estimate that the Indian population of Latin America in pre-Columbian days was approximately 35,000,000; today it is about half the total population of 200,000,000 (many Indians are of mixed blood). Only in Argentina, Chile, and a few smaller states such as Costa Rica, Cuba, the Dominican Republic, and Uruguay have European stocks overwhelmed the Indian. Unlike the case in the United States and in Canada, where indigenous peoples have never constituted an important group in the conduct of national affairs, the Indian element in Latin America has come to play an increas-

The Indians of western America were often romanticized by those who viewed life beyond the Alleghenies from a Boston parlor. Above is the frontispiece from the book *Ouâbi, or the Virtues of Nature* (1790), written by Mrs. Sarah Wentworth Morton. This work envisioned the West as a land where white men and noble savages could live together in blissful good fellowship. That neither Mrs. Morton nor her Paris-trained illustrator had more than a remote knowledge of the West and the culture of its peoples is obvious.

ingly influential role. The Indian and the *mestizo* have achieved more power in the control of their nations, and their contributions in art and music have attained growing recognition.

The bushmen of Australia and Tasmania —numbering possibly 300,000 at the time of the arrival of the Europeans—could not withstand the ravages of new diseases and of the intoxicating liquors brought by the white men. Nor could they adapt themselves to new ways of life made necessary by the disappearance of their hunting lands. At times they were treated brutally: in some localities they were shot in batches; sometimes the whites got the natives drunk and then gave them clubs to fight each other for the amusement of the "civilized" spectators. The natives of Tasmania are now extinct, and the bushmen in Australia are a declining race.

In New Zealand the native Maoris had a more advanced culture than the bushmen and were better able to stand up to the whites. After serious wars in the 1860's, peace was finally secured, and slowly the Maoris accommodated themselves to the new world created by the whites. Since 1900 the Maoris have shared the same political rights and privileges as the European settlers and have obtained the benefits of advanced education. In the 1920's the pure Maori community was estimated to be fifty thousand. They now constitute 5 per cent of the population, and their numbers are on the increase.

Although the indigenous peoples in South Africa were not exterminated, neither were they given the opportunity to share in European civilization. The fierce fighting between the European frontiersmen (mainly the Dutch) and the Bantu caused constant misunderstanding and fear. Despite many political and economic disabilities, in the nineteenth century the South African natives showed a substantial increase in numbers. By 1904 the Europeans numbered about 1,150,000, as compared with about 7,000,000 others, mainly Bantu and Coloreds (a racially mixed group). As we will note in a later chapter, the problem of race relations in South Africa in the mid-twentieth century has become very menacing.

Isolation. Another common denominator in the new Europes was that generally the new nations remained outside the main current of world affairs in the nineteenth century. The British overseas nations accepted British leadership in international affairs. They were also effectively sheltered by the British fleet, a dependence that largely explains their reluctance to assert their complete independence.

During most of the nineteenth century, the United States lavished its main efforts upon the exploitation of its vast natural resources and on the Americanization of the millions of immigrants who flocked to its shores. Evidence of its future role in world affairs became increasingly apparent, however, as the century drew to a close. In fact, the entrance of the United States onto the world stage was to be one of the cardinal factors in the drama of twentieth-century international affairs.

It would not be wholly correct to say that the nations of Latin America remained aloof from the flow of world politics. Politically unstable but rich in natural resources, these countries were tempting bait for great powers in Europe and also for the "Colossus of the North"—the United States. But the cruder imperialistic partitions and outright annexations so evident in Africa, China, and southeast Asia were avoided. This lack of complete exploitation was due to luck rather than to the virtue of the outside powers. The national interests of the United States and to some extent of Britain coincided with the maintenance of the independence of various Latin-American nations.

Progress of democracy. In general the liberal and equalitarian trends originating in western Europe found a fertile soil in the new Europes. Opposition to authority and to long-established traditions were at the heart of the revolutions that expelled the influence of Britain, Spain, and Portugal from the New World. Some historians have emphasized another factor in the progress of democracy—the influence of the frontier. Among the frontiersmen existed an absence of class distinctions, a refusal to truckle to authority, and a strong belief in the rights and capacities of the individual.

In the United States the impediments to social democracy remaining after independence were largely removed by the 1820's; and during the remainder of the nineteenth century, the country progressively perfected its democratic structure. In Canada, the greatest stimulus to the growth of democracy was the achievement of responsible government. The trend toward social democracy evident in the United States was outstripped in Australia and New Zealand. In fact, New Zealand led the world in the direction of what is known as the welfare state.

The Latin-American republics in the nineteenth century paid mere lip service to the concept of social and political democracy. Society did not have the mobility existing in the United States and in Canada. The new Latin-American nations suffered from chronic political instability; changes in government came too frequently from bullets, not ballots.

Search for a nationality. Among all the new Europes, the United States has found the quest for nationality easiest. Its power, size, available resources, and heritage of freedom and the rule of law from its mother country have all contributed to a distinctive and recognizable national ideal. The greatest threat to national sovereignty—the Civil War—ended with the triumph of the forces of national union. In the nineteenth century the United States was the melting pot for thousands and thousands of immigrants; it stood for nonmilitarism and for the hope of the common man. And this democratic ideology consisted not only of faith but also of works.

The search for a national way of life has not been easy in Canada. The establishment of the confederation in 1867 increased nationalistic sentiment. But the Canadian, then as now, continued to be drawn like a magnet to the colossus to the south. He prefers baseball to cricket; he even joins affiliates of American labor organizations. Another problem which complicates the search for a national identity is the existence of a closely knit French Canadian minority that tenaciously clings to its own language and culture. To some, Canada is a country with two nationalities: Toronto the symbol of one and old Quebec that of the other.

Nationalism has burned as brightly in each of the Latin-American nations as in the other new Europes. In fact the sentiment of nationalism has seemed the stronger as if in compensation for the obvious failures in political stability. The eight major administrative divisions in the late colonial era have fragmented into nineteen states—a process accompanied by costly and bloody wars. The whole of Latin America, however, exhibits a cultural homogeneity which has perhaps been some compensation for political turmoil.

Australia and New Zealand have found the search for nationality difficult. Remote from Europe, these islanders have clung to the traditions and ways of life of their forebears. New Zealanders brag about being more English than the English. This sentiment notwithstanding, a recognizable national character has developed in both lands —strongly equalitarian and fiercely nationalistic in its pride of the immensity and beauty of its lands.

Unlike Canada, where the original European community became a national minority in a new country created by the victorious British, the Union of South Africa has a majority of Boers instead of British in its European community. Since the union of 1909, the Dutch have increasingly striven to impose their national culture on all European settlers. Whether good sense will make it possible for the two European nationalities to find room in a common South African citizenship or whether the determination of one to create a unicultural South Africa (at least as far as the Europeans are concerned) will bring strife in its wake remains to be answered by the twentieth century.

SUMMARY

In little more than two and one half centuries (1650–1914) the greatest human migration from the smallest of continents, Europe, had taken place. It surpassed in scope such momentous human wanderings of the past as those of the Indo-Europeans into India and South Europe and the historical incursions of the Germanic tribes into the Roman Empire. Transoceanic in character, this mass movement originated in Europe which, during this period, forged ahead of the rest of the world in industry, technology and science, wealth, and military power.

These advances were reflected in the tremendous increase in Europe's population that reached full tide in the nineteenth century. From 1815 to 1914 that continent's numbers increased from 200,000,000 to

460,000,000; yet, during this time span, more than 40,000,000 immigrants sought homes in the new Europes overseas. In 1815 there were less than 20,000,000 abroad. By 1914 the figure had grown to 200,000,000. As many people of European stock lived outside Europe by this latter date as had been in it when Napoleon was defeated at Waterloo in 1815.

This transoceanic dispersal of Europeans has been treated mainly in the history of Latin America and the British dominions. The story of the United States, which is much more familiar, has been referred to only in its general setting in world events, mainly those of the Western Hemisphere.

In the realm of foreign affairs, the United States found isolation quite adequate for a century following independence. After 1885, however, it became increasingly interested in and concerned with the outside world. By the turn of the century the United States had fought a successful foreign war, acquired a colonial empire, and was taking the initiative in some phases of world affairs, especially in the Far East. While not fully appreciated at home or abroad, the great wealth and power of the United States would soon become a part of the full current of world problems and responsibilities.

The British dominions had a history showing both similarities with and differences from that of the United States. They became self-governing without breaking the political tie binding them to Britain. With the exception of South Africa, these communities were dominantly British in stock. Their language and culture were English; their governmental habits Anglo-Saxon. In the case of Canada, however, there was a strong French Canadian minority in Quebec inherited from the original French regime. In South Africa, following a confused history of rivalry and finally a war between the British and Dutch colonies, a rather shaky union was achieved in which the Dutch were the dominant element. There were no complications of rival nationalities in Australia and New Zealand. These colonies were settled by the British in the beginning and did not have to adjust themselves to an influx of other European peoples.

Both Australia and Canada, continental areas in their dimensions, took a leaf out of American history. They attained their political unity by the merging of a number of colonies into a single government. Canada as a dominion became a confederation in 1867, and Australia attained the same status as a commonwealth in 1901.

Much the same problems of exploration, pushing back the frontier, and development of natural resources, as were found in the American and British new Europes, were factors in the development and growth of Latin America. But instead of political unity, the sequel to the Spanish empire was fragmentation and a multiplicity of nationalities. There were also intermittent civil wars; revolutions and new regimes came and went with alarming and costly regularity. Dictators rather than democrats called the tune. In such an atmosphere, economic development could not thrive; the bulk of the people lived in poverty. This internal disorder and weakness invited foreign intervention. The United States, in particular, extended its influence, political and economic, into Central America and the Caribbean region.

CHAPTER 10

The White Man's Burden

EUROPEAN IMPERIALISM: 1650-1914

Introduction. In Europe's golden age of imperialism (1870-1914), its most eloquent champion, the English poet Rudyard Kipling, urged his countrymen:

"Take up the White Man's burden—
   Send forth the best ye breed—
Go bind your sons to exile
   To serve your captives' need . . ." [1]

Heeding this challenge, Germans spoke proudly of spreading their superior *Kultur* over the globe, and Frenchmen described the *mission civilisatrice*— "the task of spreading civilization"—as their responsibility. Above all, the sons of Britain believed in their sacred mission: "To us—to us, and not to others—a certain duty has been assigned. To carry light and civilization into the dark places of the world, to touch the minds of Asia and Africa with the ethical ideas of Europe; to give to thronging millions, who would otherwise never know peace or security, these first conditions of human advance." [2]

This imperial mission had few doubters among its western practitioners and, before 1900, few audible critics even among its colonial wards. After this date and especially in the last three decades, however, imperialism has been increasingly on the defensive. A swelling chorus of denunciation against colonial rule has been raised by the peoples in tropical Africa, the Middle East, and the Orient and by Communist leaders who have happily identified imperialism as one of the essential evils of modern capitalism. The indictment has excoriated imperial rule for its denial of freedom, for its calculating pursuit of profits unshared by native peoples, and for the frequent display of arrogant superiority by its white representatives.

On the other hand, many observers of the international scene stress the positive influences of imperialism. They see modern medicine successfully combating leprosy and sleeping sickness; they note benevolent administrators extirpating cannibalism and infanticide and western law ending endemic tribal wars. And, most important, these observers see imperialism carrying with it into static or primitive societies dynamic traits of western culture: science and technology to combat disease and increase productivity, schools to spread literacy and learning, and political consciousness to develop democratic government.

Whether or not the white man's burden is viewed as a cloak of hypocrisy hiding the selfish motives of self-seeking merchants and financiers (as it was in many cases) or whether it is seen as a sincere attempt to help less fortunate peoples (as it was also in innumerable instances), this concept was a dynamic one—one of the most important in the western climate of ideas. In this chapter we shall first examine the forces of imperialism, analyzing the whys and hows of the movement; then we shall see what the relations of Europe to the nonwestern world were from about 1650 through the advent of modern imperialism in the 1870's to 1914; and finally we shall weigh in the balance sheet the pros and cons of this explosive development.

THE DYNAMICS OF

IMPERIALISM

Imperialism defined. The word *imperialism* has come to mean many things to many people. Broadly speaking, the term refers to the extension of authority or control, whether direct or indirect, of one people over another. Thus, in this sense, imperialism is as old as the history of man. In all ages certain groups of people have possessed more power and dynamism than others, and in their search for more food, precious metals, or other valuable materials they have attempted to conquer weaker groups more fortunately endowed by nature. But man does not live by bread alone; from the dawn of history, psychological and spiritual motives have played roles in the extension of one people's power over another. Leaders have made their conquests as agents of the gods or have created great empires to exalt the prestige of their dynasties.

But we use the term *imperialism* in a more restricted sense when we refer to the era of imperialism; we are speaking then of the period from 1870 to 1914, when western Europe—which controlled much of the world's finance, commerce, military power, and intellectual life—extended its power over

the peoples of the Orient and Africa. With the advent of the Industrial Revolution and momentous advances in the field of science, Europe bounded ahead in technology and in military strength. By contrast, China, Japan, the Middle East, and India entered the modern era with static or decaying civilizations. Into this power vacuum moved such western nations as Britain, France, Germany, and the United States. And because civilization had hardly touched the great mass of Africa south of the Sahara, it was comparatively easy in the nineteenth century for the western nations to push into this vast continent also and to stake out claims to huge chunks of territory.

Waning European interest in colonization. From the end of the Middle Ages to the close of the eighteenth century, a large part of Europe was expansive. Aggressive national states strove to stake out colonies and to monopolize overseas trade with their colonial possessions; the subsequent rivalries between nations helped to bring on the great colonial wars that began early in the eighteenth century and were terminated only by the end of the Napoleonic Wars.

But by the end of the eighteenth century, interest in colonization declined. The loss of the Thirteen Colonies in 1783 dampened British ardor. By 1815 France had lost nearly

A French victory early in the long struggle for control of Algeria is shown in this old print. France began its military campaigns in the African territory in 1830 and kept them up intermittently for seventeen years.

all of its colonial possessions, and a few years later Spain and Portugal were forced to grant independence to most of their colonies. At the same time, the school of laissez faire and the ideas of its champion Adam Smith rapidly became the economic gospel of the European middle class. It was argued that there were no advantages in possessing colonies and that the cost of defending them was an expensive burden. It was also believed that the whole world would soon be opened to free trade; Englishmen could point out that England's trade with the United States was greater after the Thirteen Colonies achieved their independence than before.

Thus, between 1815 and 1870, as the gospel of free trade and laissez faire became dominant, colonial expansion was comparatively small. At the Congress of Vienna (1815), Britain gained a few naval bases—Cape Colony, Ceylon, Mauritius, and Mal-ta; settlements in Canada and Australia grew; in 1840 New Zealand was annexed; and two years later Hong Kong was taken from China and an important foothold for trade obtained. During this period the outstanding exception to what was known as "Little Englandism" (the belief that British interests were best served by attention to England itself rather than to the colonies) was the conquest of India and the consolidation of British rule in the subcontinent (see p. 286) But the mastery of India was achieved by a private trading concern—the East India Company—not by the government.

French colonial gains, like Britain's, were scattered. In 1830 an expedition was sent to Algeria, which ultimately became part of France; in 1842 a protectorate was placed over Tahiti; and holdings in Indo-China were gradually enlarged. Meanwhile, the Dutch continued to control their valuable spice

"NEW CROWNS FOR OLD ONES!"

This cartoon shows Disraeli in the guise of an Oriental peddler presenting Queen Victoria with the crown of India.

islands centered around Java; Portugal had large but neglected possessions in southern Africa; and Spain in the Philippines, Cuba, and Puerto Rico. But up to the mid-1800's, Europe's interest in colonies was at a low.

In the 1850's and 1860's, European interest in colonies continued to be lukewarm; in Great Britain, "Little Englandism" reached its height. Disraeli reflected the popular viewpoint that the expense of defending overseas possessions was burdensome when he stated:

These wretched colonies will all be independent . . . in a few years, and are a millstone around our necks.[3]

Revival of imperialism. When the tide turned, however, it came with a rush. In 1872 Disraeli urged Britain to:

. . . be a great country, an imperial country, a country where your sons, when they rise, rise to paramount positions, and obtain not merely the esteem of their countrymen, but command the respect of the world.[4]

In the space of six years as prime minister, Disraeli annexed Fiji and Cyprus, fought a war against the Zulus in southeastern Africa, purchased the Suez Canal shares, and proclaimed Queen Victoria empress of India. Other European powers avidly followed Britain's lead, and early in the 1880's the colonial scramble began in earnest. The United States also felt the imperialistic urge, acquiring the Hawaiian Islands and other islands in the Pacific and, after defeating Spain in 1898, the Philippines and Puerto Rico.

This expansion of the western peoples had come about with amazing rapidity. It has been estimated that in 1800 fully one half of the world's surface was unknown to Europeans. A century later more land had been explored and acquired than in the entire period from the middle of the fifteenth century to the midpoint of the eighteenth. In one decade alone (the 1880's), France acquired one million square miles in Africa and another sixty thousand in Asia. By 1914 the European nations could claim control of about 80 per cent of the world's surface.

Economic motives for imperialism. What were the motives behind this amazing expansion of western power? The most obvious and powerful were economic. Britain had been the home of the Industrial Revolution; by the middle of the nineteenth century, other nations began to industrialize. To compete with British industry, these nations placed protective tariffs on imports. The free commerce of the early nineteenth century waned as tariff walls rose in the United States, Russia, France, and Germany. Great Britain and its new competitors—now producing a surplus of manufactured goods—began to search for trade outlets; building colonial empires appeared to be the solution to the problem. Speaking before the Manchester Chamber of Commerce of England about his African explorations, H. M. Stanley declared:

There are forty millions of people beyond the gateway of the Congo, and the cotton spinners of Manchester are waiting to clothe them, Birmingham foundries are glowing with the red metal that will presently be made into iron work for them and the trinkets that shall adorn those dusky bosoms. . . .[5]

Besides increased markets for European goods, colonies and trading posts could supply burgeoning industries with raw materials such as cotton, silks, rubber, exotic woods, tin, manganese, copper, and oil. And growing populations continued to increase the demands for foods raised in exotic lands.

The construction of railways and better roads, the digging of the Suez Canal (1869), and the building of larger and speedier ships made world trade possible on a scale hitherto unknown. International postal systems, telegraphs, and cables facilitated communication with the most distant places. Financiers and banks provided capital for trading enterprises and for the development of resources in distant lands. In fact, money invested overseas could earn 10 to 20 per cent. This impetus to wealth led one wag to remark that the French colonist was the franc. To safeguard these important investments and recover defaulted loans, European governments sometimes established spheres of influence or protectorates over the territories of weak native rulers and in certain cases subjected these lands to military occupation or to annexation. In Africa, especially, trade did not follow the flag; the flag followed trade.

Imperialism: the Marxian interpretation. Marxian socialists have stressed only the economic motives underlying imperialism. First given masterly expression by J. A. Hobson in his book *Imperialism, a Study* (1902) was the argument:

Imperialism is the endeavor of the great controllers of industry to broaden the channel for the flow of their surplus wealth by seeking foreign markets and foreign investments to take off the goods and capital they cannot sell or use at home.[6]

Hobson's analysis was appropriated by the Marxists when Lenin wrote his famous work *Imperialism, the Highest Stage of Capitalism* (1916). According to Lenin, the wages of the workers did not represent enough purchasing power to absorb the output of the capitalistic factories, and, moreover, vast amounts of capital accumulated that could not be profitably invested in the home country. Therefore,

to the Marxists, imperialism was an inevitable phase in the development of capitalism. And once the backward countries were taken over and exploited, there, too, surplus goods and capital would ultimately accumulate; eventually there would be no place to invest these surpluses and the world-wide capitalistic system would break down.

History, of course, has thus far offered no proof of the later stages of this theory. That the profit motive in imperialism is strong is undeniable, but that it is the sole motive is false. It is also false that imperialism is a policy exclusive to capitalist powers, as can be proved by examples of Communist imperialism in the twentieth century.

Population pressure: motivation for imperialistic expansion. Population pressure in Europe undoubtedly helped to inspire imperialist expansion, but while emigration was enormous in the era of imperialism, relatively few emigrants took up new homes in the colonies of the mother countries. In the middle of the eighteenth century, Europe's people numbered about 140,000,000; by 1914 this figure had increased to 463,000,000. Hearing that land overseas was more plentiful and jobs easier to secure, no less than 9,000,000 British subjects and 6,000,000 Germans, to say nothing of millions of Italians, left their homelands. These migrations provided one of the greatest population movements in history.

But while some European statesmen, particularly in Germany and Italy, thought of the acquisition of new colonies as a means whereby their surplus population could be settled in sparsely settled lands without escaping the political control of the motherland, this belief proved to be a delusion. Few Europeans migrated to the tropical colonies; the great majority made their new homes in the United States and Latin America. In such areas the loyalty and support of these sons and daughters of Germany, Italy, and other nations were lost to the homeland. Furthermore, more Germans were residing in France in 1914 than had settled in the entire German colonial empire.

Nationalism as a force for imperialism. While the economic forces behind nineteenth-century European expansion were strong, the psychological factors were equally important. A dominant factor was the new nationalism. Fresh from the achievement of national unification, Germany and Italy were eager to show off their new national strength; both demanded a place in the sun. The German historian Treitschke, whose works were suffused with nationalism, wrote:

Every virile people has established colonial power. . . . All great nations in the fulness [sic] of their strength have desired to set their mark upon barbarian lands and those who fail to participate in this great rivalry will play a pitiable rôle in time to come. The colonising impulse has become a vital question for every nation.[7]

In Great Britain a strong nationalist spirit existed. Britain was ready to take on any antagonist who stood in the way of its imperialistic ambitions. In the late seventies the most popular ditty heard in London music halls was:

We don't want to fight,
But by Jingo if we do,
We've got the ships, we've got the men,
We've got the money too.[8]

Closely enmeshed with the nationalistic justification of imperialism was the philosophy of social Darwinism (see Chapter 11). Just as Darwin believed that progress in the biological sphere was measured by the "survival of the fittest," so political and social theorists saw this concept of the "fittest" as an immutable factor in the onward march of civilization. Observed one Englishman:

In every particular state of the world, those nations which are strongest tend to prevail over the others; and in certain marked peculiarities the strongest tend to be the best. . . . The strongest nation has always been conquering the weaker. . . . The majority of groups which win and conquer are better than the majority of those which fail and perish, and thus the . . . world grew better and was improved.[9]

The military factor. If the use of force and the "survival of the fittest" were essential features of progress, then the military factor was important. A nation had to be strong enough to defend its interests. Colonies could be used as naval bases to protect a nation's commercial life lines or to destroy those of a rival. Or a colony could be obtained as a buffer state to protect another colony against the designs of a rival imperialistic power. For example, in order to halt Russian influence on the northern frontier of India in the nineteenth century, Great Britain endeavored to control Afghanistan. Colonies were also thought of in terms of troop reservoirs, where large native armies could be recruited—an idea that appealed especially to France, whose population lagged behind that of its traditional enemy, Germany. In the late nineteenth century, France introduced conscription into some French colonies as a means of offsetting the greater man power of its neighbor across the Rhine.

Humanitarian and religious motives. The acquisition of colonies cannot be explained on economic, political, or strategic grounds alone, however. There were statesmen who believed sincerely that the rule of their government would bring law and order to colonial areas suffering from the ravages of civil disorder and intertribal warfare. Many colonial administrators honestly felt that they were carrying the white man's burden—that it was a sacred task to bring the best aspects of western civilization to their undeveloped wards. Even the public was moved by strong humanitarian sentiments. For example, many Americans supported the Spanish-American War because they detested what they heard of oppressive Spanish rule in Cuba.

The religious motive in the new imperialism was likewise especially strong. In the nineteenth century, British missionaries were particularly active, and large numbers of missionaries from France, Germany, and the Scandinavian countries were also sent to Africa, India, China, and other non-Christian areas to win converts. The Roman Catholic Church had always had a very powerful missionary interest, and such orders as the Dominicans, Franciscans, and Jesuits in the Americas and the Jesuits in China had provided valuable aid as guides, interpreters, and administrators. The United States also became a leading source of missionary work and in the early twentieth century was providing perhaps 70 per cent of overseas Protestant mission work. The medical work of missionaries on all the continents has been outstanding, and their leadership in education among native peoples has often made them the primary source of direct contact with inhabitants whose languages are primitive or exotic, such as some of those in Africa, Asia, and Melanesia.

Kipling and the white man's burden. The most eloquent propagandist for the white man's burden was Rudyard Kipling (1865-1936), the poet and novelist who coined the phrase. Born in India, young Kipling traveled widely over the subcontinent and became thoroughly convinced of the blessings of British rule to the Indians. In his works he pictured the British colonial administrators and soldiers as courageous men who lived by their code, kept guard over their homeland's interests, and protected the backward native. Britain in India was definitely a community of conquest and not of settlement. But while nineteenth-century social philosophy, following Darwin, might justify the empire of the strong over the weak by natural law, the humanitarian and the missionary appealed to the conscience of the conqueror. The implications of trusteeship were later to be written out formally under the League of Nations and the United Nations.

In short, the white man's burden was a sense of mission—the belief on the part of a particular people that they were the agents destined to bring law and order, better ethical standards, and improved technology to less fortunate peoples. This sense of mission blended with the strong nationalistic feelings of the Europeans. They believed that it was the sacred destiny of a great nation to spread its culture—its language, ideals, and customs—over as much of the surface of the globe as possible.

All the motives underlying nineteenth-century imperialism are illustrated aptly in President McKinley's explanation of why the United States annexed the Philippines:

I walked the floor of the White House night after night until midnight; and I am not ashamed to tell you, gentlemen, that I went down on my knees and prayed to Almighty God for light and guidance. . . . And one night late it came to me this way—I don't know how it was, but it came: (1) That we could not give them back to Spain—that would be cowardly and dishonorable; (2) that we could not turn them over to France or Germany—our commercial rivals in the Orient—that would be bad business and discreditable; (3) that we could not leave them to themselves—they were unfit for self-government—and they would soon have anarchy and misrule worse than Spain's was; and (4) that there was nothing left for us to do but to take them all, and to educate the Filipinos, and uplift and civilize and Christianize them, and by God's grace do the very best we could by them . . . . And then I went to bed, and went to sleep and slept soundly . . .[10]

Here in this passage one finds justification for imperialism on the basis of national honor, economic profit, racial superiority, missionary zeal, and the white man's burden.

BRITISH RULE IN INDIA

The Mogul ruler Aurangzeb. During the Mogul era in the seventeenth century, Europeans came to India to establish trading posts. As European infiltration continued, Mogul authority rapidly declined.

The Mogul empire at this period has been described as "a system of organized brigandage." The reign of Shah Jahan (1628?-1658) had marked the height of Mogul power, and conditions appeared auspicious for his successor. But his son Aurangzeb (1658-1707) was a cunning, ruthless, and fanatical man who intended to rid India not only of all vice but also of all art and all views alien to the Muslim faith. To govern a large Hindu empire on the "principles of an ascetic Muslim saint," however, was impossible.

Aurangzeb ordered every Hindu school closed, destroyed hundreds of Hindu temples and their priceless art objects, revived the hated poll tax which Akbar had abolished, terrorized millions of his subjects by his fanaticism, and alienated the loyalty of the Rajputs. From 1681 to his death in 1707, he waged war in the Deccan with the powerful Mahrattas, and by 1690, when his territorial expansion reached its greatest point, his empire encompassed the Indian peninsula.

This period of power was followed by one of decline. The Deccan campaign drained the imperial treasury, and the empire proved too vast for one man to handle alone. Aurangzeb's realm seethed with corruption, oppression, and revolt; and fifty years after his death, the great Mogul empire crumbled and perished.

The condition of India during this time may be summed up in the word—misery. Marauding armies, nobles bent on gaining power, and officials who oppressed the people brought anarchy to India. The Sikhs and Mahrattas fought the tottering Moguls; Delhi was sacked in 1739 by invaders from Persia and again in 1757 by marauders from Afghanistan. Until 1858—during the Sepoy Rebellion (see p. 287)—the Moguls kept the imperial title, but their dynasty was a mere shadow of its former grandeur and strength.

The British East India Company. The collapse of the central government in India left the field open to a new authority. For more than one hundred years, English and French trading companies had fought one another for supremacy, and by the middle of the eighteenth century, a great duel for empire was taking place between England and France in Europe, in America, in the islands of the Caribbean, and along the eastern coast of India. During the Seven Years' War (1756-1763), Robert Clive, the British leader in India, defeated the French and their Indian allies at the decisive battle of Plassey (1757), a victory which ushered in a new period in Indian history, that of British rule.

After the elimination of the French, the most important problem facing the East India Company was its relationship with the Indian people. As the Mogul emperor became more and more a puppet ruler, anarchy spread until the company was forced to accept the role of policeman in India. Soon the entire subcontinent came under the company's influence. Some local rulers were forced to accept its overlordship; others were deprived of their territories. Where an Indian ruler was allowed to retain his throne, the company obtained the right to control his foreign policy in return for a guarantee of internal independence. Thus it came about that the Indian subcontinent (until its independence in 1947) was divided into British India (about 1,000,000 square miles), which the British administered directly, and Indian India (about 700,000 square miles), where native dynasties were perpetuated under British supervision.

By 1818 the British East India Company was master of India. For some time the British government had been disturbed by the idea of a great business concern, interested primarily in profits, controlling the destinies of millions of people. Therefore, Parliament in 1773 passed an act which gave it the power to control company policies. A subsequent act passed in 1784 permitted the company to continue its commercial operations and to use its armed forces and officials in carrying on the business of administration, but gave to the government at London the authority to appoint the highest company official in India, the governor general. This system of dual control lasted until 1858; after 1833, however, the trading rights of the company were revoked and its function was purely administrative.

British reforms in India. Early in the nineteenth century, a strong humanitarian movement swept England, leading to many social and economic reforms at home. In addition, the English began to consider what might be undertaken in India. In a debate on Indian affairs in Parliament in 1833, the historian Macaulay stated:

We are trying . . . to give a good government to a people to whom we cannot give a free government.[11]

During the administration of Lord William Bentinck, governor general of India from 1828 to 1835, many significant reforms were introduced. The practice of *suttee*, in which widows burned themselves on the funeral pyres of their deceased husbands, was prohibited; the custom in some areas of killing girl babies was combated; and a notorious system of banditry and murder called *thuggee* (hence our word *thug*) was broken up by the British secret police. In addition, a comprehensive educational system which included secondary schools and universities

In the process of suppressing the Sepoy Rebellion, British forces in India use artillery pieces to execute captive rebels.

was introduced, with the emphasis upon English language, literature, and history.

The Sepoy Rebellion. In the spring of 1857, the progress of reform was suddenly interrupted by the Sepoy Rebellion—a mutiny which jeopardized British rule in India. This uprising was mainly a mutiny of the Indian troops, called sepoys, who formed the bulk of the company's armed forces. The sepoys complained that a new cartridge issued to them was smeared with the fat of cows and pigs. This infuriated the Hindus, who regarded the cow as sacred, and horrified the Muhammadans, who considered the pig unclean.

Because of the unrest and discontent throughout India, the mutiny would in all probability have arisen without the incident of the greased cartridges. The British had been building railroads, stringing up telegraph wires, and in general introducing many disturbing western methods. They had aroused fears that Christianity would be spread so that it would ultimately triumph over Hinduism and they had caused much irritation by confiscating native states which were without direct heirs and by discontinuing large pensions to many native princes.

The mutiny was a bloody affair. Fortunately for the British, many areas in India remained loyal or at least quiescent, but only after fierce fighting and the loss of many lives was the revolt crushed.

Changes in administration. One consequence of the mutiny was the final eclipse of Mogul authority. The last of the Mogul emperors permitted to maintain a court at Delhi had in 1857 been proclaimed by the mutineers as their leader. After order had been restored, he was exiled to Burma by the British. The mutiny also ended the system of dual control under which the British government and the East India Company shared authority. The government relieved the company of its political responsibilities, and after 258 years of existence the company terminated its rule.

Shortly after the company retired from the Indian scene, the British government overhauled the administrative system. The police force was reorganized, the criminal code was revised, and small legislative councils containing nominated Indian members were given to the Indian central government at Calcutta and to the local governments at Bombay and Madras. A trained civil service

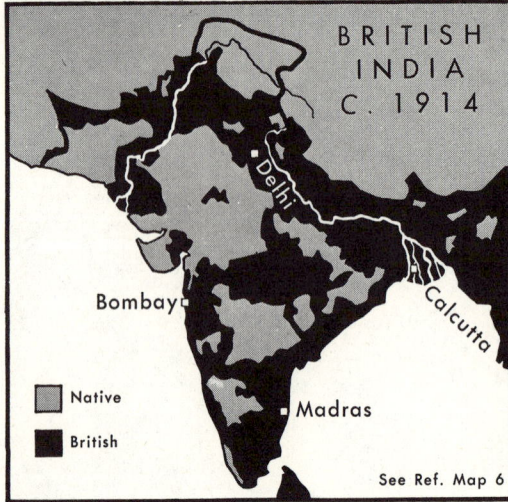

BRITISH INDIA C. 1914

Delhi

Bombay

Calcutta

Native

British

Madras

See Ref. Map 6

was recruited from honor graduates of British universities, and these men set out to rule India benevolently and efficiently. Great dams were built, railroad lines spanned the country, machinery for food distribution was created to eliminate famine, and an efficient postal system was introduced.

Growth of Indian nationalism. For a generation after the Sepoy Rebellion, British administration functioned smoothly and Indian public opinion remained passive. But by 1880 it was apparent that Indian nationalism was growing rapidly, the fruit of the influx of western ideas and technology. In 1885, with the aid of several Englishmen who had interested themselves in Indian political ambitions, the Indian National Congress was formed. Once the nationalist revival got underway, it grew rapidly. The railroads, a cheap postal service, the telegraph, and a free press were convenient agencies for spreading the doctrine of "India for the Indians."

The British educational system served as one of the most potent forces back of the new movement. Since the days of Lord Bentinck, the educational system in India had been western in content and English in outlook. Indians became acquainted with the story of the rise of self-government in England and were introduced to the Magna Carta, Oliver Cromwell, the Glorious Revolution, and the Bill of Rights. It was therefore natural that a desire for political freedom should appear

among students in Bombay, Madras, and Calcutta. Furthermore, the prestige of the white man was diminished when in 1896 an Italian army in Abyssinia was cut to pieces and when Japan defeated Russia in 1904 and 1905 (see p. 296).

Because British educational policy stressed literary training at the expense of agricultural and technical education and therefore turned out many graduates equipped primarily for desk jobs, the schools were filled to overflowing with young men who had only one aim— to obtain a degree in order to get into the governmental service. Thus there were always more applicants than openings, and thousands of youths unable to obtain white-collar employment and disdainful of manual labor joined the ranks of an educated proletariat and turned in wrath against the government. Ardent young patriots manufactured bombs, procured revolvers and ammunition, and assassinated several British judges and administrators. Confronted by the spread of violence, the British carried through a major shift in policy between the years 1907 and 1909. Up to this time the government had been almost completely bureaucratic. Now the various provincial legislatures in India were given elected Indian majorities, and an Indian was seated in the executive council of the governor general. The legislature of the central government, however, remained under British control. Moderate nationalists were satisfied for the time being, but their more radical comrades were not appeased. They demanded complete independence, and violence continued until 1914. As we shall note in Chapter 16, the twentieth century in India saw nationalism become ever more insistent.

MANCHU CHINA

AND THE WEST

The Manchu dynasty. In the mid-eighteenth century, China had a population of 300,000,000, an area of more than 4,000,000 square miles, and imperial courts at Peking and Mukden famous for their wealth and splendor. Chinese culture was admired in the

West; silks, cottons, tea, sedan chairs, wallpaper, and porcelain were valuable exports to Europe.

The ruling dynasty of this great empire was the Manchu, which in 1644 had superseded the Ming as emperors of China. Descendants of Tatars who for centuries had lived in Manchuria, the Manchu appreciated Chinese civilization and adopted a conciliatory attitude toward their subjects. They kept the civil service examinations which the Ming had reintroduced, retained most of the Chinese administrative officials, honored Confucianism, kept Buddhism and Taoism as national religions, and patronized Chinese literature and art. They refused, however, to allow intermarriage with the Chinese, for they realized that only their blood difference kept them from being assimilated and conquered. To keep the Chinese conscious of submission, the Manchu forced them to shave the front of the head and wear the hair in queue fashion, a style of hairdressing common to the Tatars. By and large, however, the Manchu gradually became Chinese in their habits and attitudes.

When the Manchu came to the throne, they held only four provinces in the north. But the Manchu emperors were remarkable conquerors. The reign of Ch'ien Lung (1736-1796) was a period of great expansion, when Manchu China attained suzerainty over eastern Turkestan, Burma, and Tibet. Outlying regions which had only nominal relations with the imperial court at Peking were also markedly affected by Manchu rule.

Despite these evidences of dynamism, however, uncritical acceptance and reverence for traditional thought (particularly Confucianism), augmented by the scholar rule of a civil service trained almost exclusively in the classics, had tended to make Chinese culture excessively conservative and backward-looking. Thus the amazing continuity which Chinese civilization had exhibited for thousands of years was gained at a heavy price. In addition, the prevailing attitude of superiority to the cultures of all other peoples was an unwholesome one for China, leading to what has been called "progressive sterility."[12]

Trade relations with the West. Meanwhile a new factor destined to have momentous consequences for China had entered the scene: European trade. During the eighteenth century, merchants from western Europe came to China in increasing numbers. The first Americans arrived in 1784, one year after the end of the American Revolution. Only with great difficulty was trade carried on, however. While engaged in commerce, foreign merchants were confined to the port of Canton; when not engaged in trade, all foreign businessmen were expected to reside in Macao. Nor would the Manchu government recognize or receive representatives of foreign powers.

European traders were irritated by the high customs duties the Chinese forced them to pay and by the attempts of Chinese authorities to curb the growing import trade in opium. To settle various differences, the British government in 1793 sent a diplomatic mission to Peking, but this effort failed and matters at Canton became worse. Aloof and haughty, the Chinese officials refused to recognize the "barbarians" as equals; their attitude is reflected in the Manchu emperor's reply to the British king's request for trading privileges:

Our dynasty's majestic virtue has penetrated unto every country under Heaven, and Kings of all nations have offered their costly tribute by land and sea. As your Ambassador can see for himself, we possess all things. I set no value on objects strange or ingenious, and have no use for your country's manufactures. . . . It behooves you, O King, to respect my sentiments and to display even greater devotion and loyalty in the future, so that, by perpetual submission to our throne, you may secure peace and prosperity for your country hereafter.[13]

In 1800 the importation of opium was forbidden by the imperial government. Still, the opium trade continued to flourish. Although the English East India Company forbade the transportation of opium in its own ships, the company continued to produce the drug in India for Chinese consumption and allowed other ships under its control to take opium to Macao and Canton. Privately owned vessels of other countries, including the United States, made huge profits from the growing numbers of Chinese addicts. Because many corrupt Chinese and Manchu officials were bribed, the traffic expanded, and the edicts of the central government were completely ineffectual.

War and western exploitation. Early in the nineteenth century, serious internal weaknesses developed in the Manchu empire. The standing army became corrupt, and rapacious governors fleeced the people. Weak emperors who reigned but could not rule proved inadequate to meet the challenges of the time. Secret societies conspired against the government, and revolts burst forth frequently. Unrest was also created by a series of national disasters; the great drought of 1817 made even the Manchu rulers wonder if they were losing the Decree of Heaven.

In 1839 war broke out with England—ostensibly over the opium traffic. But this was basically a secondary issue. As a Chinese historian has observed: "If the Chinese had had some knowledge of international conditions, and had not considered the foreigners barbarians, their prohibition of opium need not have caused war. . . . The war between China and England, caused superficially by the problem of opium prohibition, may actually be viewed as a conflict of Western and Eastern cultures."[14]

Backward China was no match for English military power, and in 1842 China agreed to the provisions of the Treaty of Nanking. Hong Kong was ceded to Great Britain, and certain ports, including Shanghai and Canton, were opened to the residence and trade of British subjects. China was required to pay a large indemnity for the opium destroyed by its officials and to pay the expenses of the war. Within a few years, the United States, France, and Russia also secured trading privileges, and China appeared well on the way to ultimate physical dismemberment and economic vassalage.

China's defeated rulers still refused to cooperate with the great powers, preferring instead to use obstructionist tactics whenever possible. Meanwhile, foreign merchants continued to scheme for larger trade concessions and to have more cities opened to commerce. With relations at a breaking

point, a trivial incident provoked in 1856 a second war with England in which China was again defeated. By the Treaty of Tientsin (1858), supplemented by agreements made in 1860, six new ports were opened to trade and residence, the Yangtze River was made a waterway for foreign merchants, and foreigners with passports were permitted to travel anywhere in the interior. Christians had the right to propagate their faith and to hold property, thus providing another means of western penetration. (By 1879 there were over 500,000 Roman Catholic converts and 55,000 Protestant.)

Three other privileges wrested from the defeated Chinese and Manchu by the Treaty of Tientsin caused bitterness for many years among the Chinese: (1) extraterritoriality, (2) customs regulation, and (3) the right to station foreign warships in Chinese waters. Extraterritoriality meant that, in a dispute with a Chinese, a westerner had the right to be tried in his own country's consular court. Europeans argued that Chinese concepts of justice were more rigid and harsh than those in the West. But the Chinese felt that extraterritoriality was not only humiliating to China's sovereignty but was also discriminative in favor of the western nations.

Difficulties of the Manchu. The concessions to the "foreign devils" resulted in a great loss of prestige for the Manchu rulers. Serious internal difficulties further diminished their power, and the Taiping Rebellion of 1850 to 1864 almost overthrew the dynasty. With the aid of an army led first by the American adventurer General Frederick Townsend Ward (1831-1862) and later by a Scotsman, Major Charles George ("Chinese") Gordon (1833-1885), the revolt was suppressed, but though the Manchu weathered this internal struggle, the time was not far distant when they were to founder before more powerful tempests of revolt.

The Manchu dynasty managed to survive another half century largely because of the statecraft of a remarkable woman, Tzu Hsi, the dowager empress, popularly known as "Old Buddha." From 1861 to her death in 1908, she was the real power behind the throne. Shrewdly and unscrupulously, Tzu

Hsi put down internal revolts and restored a measure of prestige to her homeland. But being Manchu and limited by the viewpoint of the Forbidden City, Tzu Hsi felt that security for China lay in adhering to ancient traditions and customs, and she encouraged antiforeign sentiment.

The attitude of the empress was fully shared by her subjects; hatred for the West was already widespread throughout China. Basically conservative, Chinese of every social level looked upon western innovations as an evil threat to their own ancient and cherished way of life.

Encroachments of foreigners. Immigration of Chinese to foreign countries, especially to the United States, became another source of friction between East and West. Because the immigrants represented a cheap labor pool which seemed to threaten the livelihood of American workers, anti-Chinese riots broke out in the United States, and the immigration of the Chinese was prohibited for ten years (1880). Subsequent laws completely barred the entry of Chinese coolies.

Trouble lay even closer to China, for various powers were slicing off bits of territory on the periphery of the ancient land. By 1860 Russia had annexed the entire area north of the Amur River, by 1885 France had taken Indo-China and Great Britain had seized Burma, and in 1887 Macao was ceded to Portugal.

Sino-Japanese War. A weak central government and lack of national unity made it impossible for China to resist these encroachments. But the crowning blow came not from the western nations but from Japan, a land which Chinese had long regarded with amused contempt.

Trouble had brewed for some time between China and Japan, especially over the control of Formosa and Korea. In a dispute over China's claim to suzerainty in Korea, war broke out in 1894, and the brief Sino-Japanese struggle resulted in a humiliating defeat for China. By the Treaty of Shimonoseki (1895), China was forced to recognize the independence of Korea (which Japan annexed in 1910), hand over the rich Liaotung peninsula and Formosa, pay an indem-

The Dowager Empress of China was returned to her throne by the western powers after the abortive Boxer Rebellion. Soon after her death, the Manchu dynasty was overthrown.

nity of 150,000,000 dollars, and grant the Japanese further commercial and extraterritorial privileges.

Europe exploits China. China's defeat was the signal for the renewal of aggressive actions by western powers—a move which robbed Japan of the advantages of its recent victory by forcing it to give back the Liaotung peninsula in return for an extra indemnity from China. The western nations were afraid to let Japan take the strategic peninsula; Russia in particular was trying to obtain control of all Manchuria. In 1895 France confirmed its mining and railroad concessions in Indo-China, and Great Britain obtained an extension of the boundaries of Burma and additional trading privileges.

Meanwhile, Germany had been trying to obtain the fine harbor of Kiaochow and mining rights in the Shantung peninsula. The murder by brigands of two Roman Catholic

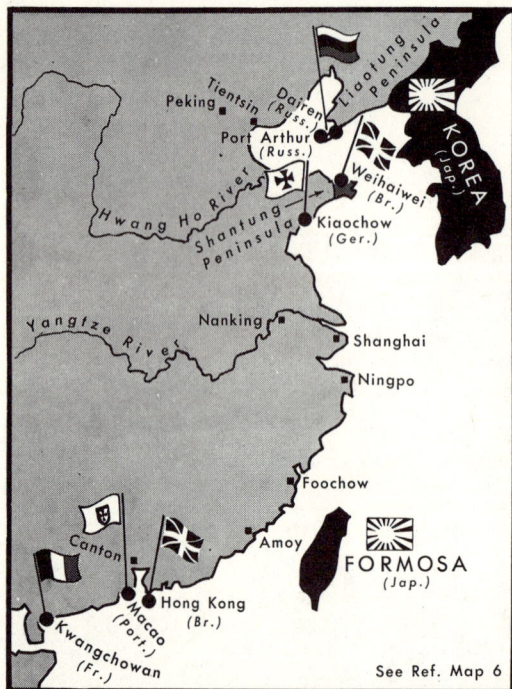

See Ref. Map 6

missionaries of German nationality in 1897 gave the kaiser's government an excuse to demand a ninety-nine-year lease to Kiaochow Bay plus adjacent territory. Germany was also given exclusive mining and railroad rights throughout all of Shantung province.

Russia, Great Britain, and France now made their demands. Russia obtained a twenty-five-year lease to Dairen and Port Arthur on the tip of the Liaotung peninsula and gained the right to build a railroad across Manchuria, thereby achieving complete domination of that vast territory. In 1898 Great Britain obtained the lease of Weihaiwei, a naval base, to protect British interests in northern China against growing Russian control. In the same year France leased Kwangchowan in southern China for ninety-nine years. (See map above.)

The Open Door Policy. China was now in imminent danger of disintegrating completely. Manchuria and Mongolia were under Russian domination; the Shantung peninsula was virtually a possession of Germany; and much of southern China was controlled by France. Hong Kong, Weihaiwei, and the rich Yangtze valley, created as a special sphere of influence, belonged to Great Britain.

A halt, or at least a hesitation, in the process of disintegration was brought about by the United States, not from high-minded desires but largely because Washington was alarmed at the prospect of American businessmen being excluded from China because the United States had no sphere of influence. In 1899, Secretary of State John Hay asked the major powers to agree (1) not to interfere with any sphere of interest or any leased territory, (2) to have the Chinese tariff apply to all merchandise in such regions and to allow the Chinese government to collect this tariff, and (3) to permit all nations to enjoy the same harbor dues and railroad charges. In 1900 several powers agreed to Hay's request, and the famous Open Door Policy was born.

The "hundred days of reform." At this time China was rousing itself to cope with foreign dangers. The humiliation of the defeat by Japan had incensed the younger Chinese intellectuals, who agitated for reform. Sympathetic to their cause, the young emperor in 1898 instituted what came to be known as the "hundred days of reform." The reforms included an attempt to modernize the civil service examinations, the establishment of a school system along western lines, and the encouragement of railway building and industrial expansion. Unhappily for China, however, the reactionaries at court viewed the innovations with disfavor and formed a powerful reactionary faction about the dowager empress, Tzu Hsi. In September 1898, she seized and imprisoned the emperor, executed some of the leading reformers, and took over the government.

The Boxer Rebellion. After the suppression of the reform movement, a group of secret societies united in an organization known as the "Righteous Harmony Fists"—called "Boxers" by westerners. At first the Boxers were strongly anti-Manchu because of the reactionary measures of "Old Buddha," but by 1899 the chief object of their hatred had become the foreign nations who were stripping China of land and power.

The Boxers started a campaign to rid China of all Christians and "foreign devils." The German minister and many other Europeans were killed, and the legations at Peking were besieged. Not until August 1900 did an international army force its way to Peking and release the foreigners there, who had been in constant peril. In the protocol of 1901, which concluded the Boxer Rebellion, China was forced to apologize for the murder of the German minister and other foreign officials, allow the outside nations to police a larger area around Peking, pay the foreign powers an indemnity of about 333,-000,000 dollars, and fulfill various other obligations. The United States returned most of the indemnity which China owed, and the Chinese government set this sum aside to send students to American universities.

The Boxer movement had brought into sharp focus the growing dissatisfaction with the rigidity of the reactionary Manchu regime. Only a decade after the conclusion of the rebellion, a revolution was to break out all over China, and in 1912 the Republic of China was proclaimed with Sun Yat-sen as president. This story of China's giant step into modern times will be discussed in Chapter 16.

JAPAN IN TRANSITION

Japanese attitude toward foreigners. At the beginning of the seventeenth century, Japan was being ruled from Yedo (now Tokyo) by the head of the Tokugawa clan, who in 1603 had made himself *shogun*. As a military dictator with a retinue of feudal lords and warriors, the *shogun* kept the country united and at peace. Meanwhile, the emperor—nominal head of the government—lived a meaningless existence at the imperial court at Kyoto.

As in the case of China, European merchants and missionaries posed a problem to the Japanese authorities. In the sixteenth century the Japanese had cleared their islands of western merchants and closed all ports to outside vessels, permitting only a few Dutch traders to remain on a small island in the harbor of Nagasaki. Alarmed at the rapid spread of Christianity in Nippon because they believed the movement to be pro-western and subversive, the *shoguns* took

stern measures against the alien faith and in 1639 condemned all Christians to death. By expelling the European traders, crushing Christianity, and prohibiting their own countrymen from traveling abroad, the *shoguns* effectively insulated Japan from the outside world.

Japan at the turning point. The period of isolation was not to last forever, and when the insulation broke down, certain long-established traits in Japanese culture were to determine the course the island empire would follow in the years ahead. The first was the teachability of the people. Unlike the Chinese, the Japanese were willing to adopt foreign ideas and customs, as Chinese influence in Japan particularly shows. But although the Chinese revered the scholar, their island neighbors admired the soldier. Warfare was the supreme vocation, and in this regard a tradition of invincibility had grown up. Since prehistoric times the Japanese islands had not been invaded successfully, and on several occasions the Japanese themselves had invaded the Asian continent. Thus the Japanese were teachable, but in an active, aggressive sense. They were ready to seize new methods and new ideas to serve their own militant ends.

Another prominent characteristic of Japanese culture was the meticulous attention paid to formal manners and "face." Like the Chinese, the Japanese took great pride in their dignity and status; to be shamed, degraded, or dishonored was a mortal offense. Awareness of these culture traits is basic to an understanding of Japanese reactions to the modern world and the policies that the rulers of Nippon later adopted to meet the challenges of the twentieth century.

Despite the attempts of the *shoguns* to keep Japan isolated from the outside world, change could not be averted. The concept of a closed, feudal kingdom was challenged by the rise of cities, the growth of manufacturing, and the development of a merchant-financier class. The *shogun* and his feudal retainers became anachronisms; the country was long at peace, and the swords of the *samurai* rusted in their scabbards. The government's disastrous tax and fiscal policy

Nijo Castle in Kyoto, Japan, was built to serve as the residence of the shogun on his visits to the ancient city.

debased the currency and taxed the people oppressively. Feeding the increasing population became even more serious. Change was in the air, and just as the *shoguns* feared, it was triggered from the outside.

Commodore Perry and the Treaty of Kanagawa. On July 7, 1853, a squadron of two steam frigates and two sloops of war steamed into the bay of Yedo. The commander of the fleet, Commodore Matthew Perry (1794-1858), had been sent by the United States government to convince the Japanese ruler that a treaty opening trade relations between Japan and the United States would be of mutual interest. Perry had been instructed to be tactful and to use force only if necessary. After an impressive display of naval strength, he sailed to China, leaving the Japanese officials to wrangle over their predicament. When he returned with even greater forces in the following February, the Japanese took the most prudent course open to them. In March, Japan agreed to the Treaty of Kanagawa, the first formal treaty with any western nation. Shipwrecked sailors were guaranteed hospitable treatment, foreign vessels were allowed to stop for provisions, and two ports, "the two worst harbors in the country," were opened to American ships. Great Britain, Russia, and Holland soon obtained similar privileges.

Adoption of western ideas and techniques. In 1867 the *shogun*, acting under pressure from the feudal chieftains, restored the supreme authority to the emperor—the *Tenno*, or "Heavenly King" (called "Mikado"

in the West). The return of power to the imperial family heralded a new era for Japan. In addition Yedo was renamed Tokyo (Eastern Capital), the name it bears today.

The young emperor, whose reign was known as the *Meiji* (enlightened government), reigned from 1868 to 1912. With his reign are associated those epoch-making events which transformed Nippon from a sleepy oriental island kingdom into a dynamic, semimodernized power which the European nations had to recognize as an equal. The restoration of the throne's supreme authority was aided by the voluntary abolition of feudal rights; in 1871 the abolition of the feudal system became official, although it was far from an actual fact. Many of the *samurai* were pensioned, and in 1876 national conscription went into effect. Thus a modern military machine was created whose officers were trained by European experts—the army by the French and Germans, the navy by the British.

In another way the Japanese government showed skill in profiting from a knowledge of western institutions. The government took the initiative in founding banks, factories, and business concerns and later, when they became successful, turned them over to private ownership and management while continuing to supervise them closely. Thus Japan avoided the dangers to sovereignty which imperialism offered to other undeveloped countries such as China.

Many other changes began to transform the "land of the rising sun." Railways, telegraphs, lighthouses, and dockyards were constructed, a postal system was organized, a mint was established, a bimetallic system of currency and a system of national banks were instituted, and orders were placed in England for the construction of warships. American advisers were consulted regarding national education, and imperial universities as well as a number of technical schools were founded. More foreign experts were brought in to teach the Japanese about medicine, engineering, and agriculture, and many Japanese were sent abroad to study. Foreign books were translated and newspapers established. In 1873, the Gregorian calendar was

With American seamen drawn up in review, Commodore Perry and his staff meet the imperial commissioners of Japan in Yokohama.

adopted, although the Japanese continued to mark their official chronology from the reputed accession of Jimmu Tenno (dated 660 B.C. but probably actually dated some six centuries later).

Innovations appeared so swiftly, however, that the result was often a curious potpourri of old and new:

A young blade might consider himself well-dressed with a derby, waistcoat, kimona, and wooden clogs. A Tokyo barber, with a beautifully styled headdress, and flowing kimona sleeves kept out of the way by a Western style apron, would see little incongruity in the fact that he was giving his client a Western style haircut. The government official, on the other hand, was not considered aptly dressed unless he wore a morning coat, striped pants, and a high silk hat to his office. When he returned home, he would change into his native dress.[15]

Governmental reconstruction. Japanese political reconstruction may be said for convenience to have begun with the creation of a senate in 1875. Three years later an edict provided for the formation of elective assemblies for cities and prefectures, after the French model. In 1881 an imperial decree announced that a national parliamentary government would be inaugurated within ten years' time. After six months a party led by Ito Hirobumi (1841-1909), who as Prince Ito later became one of the greatest statesmen in Japanese history, set forth to study the world's various governmental systems. Ito was particularly impressed by the German system as developed by Bismarck.

Returning to Japan in 1883, the Ito mission set to work framing the new constitution. The premier was given a position analogous to that held by the chancellor in Germany. The cabinet, which included nine ministers (each controlling a state department), was made responsible to the emperor alone. Only the army and navy could appoint their respective ministers. Since no statesman could form a cabinet without a war minister and the army could overthrow any cabinet by simply withdrawing its minister, final control of policies rested in the hands of the military clique.

The constitution provided for a Diet, divided into the House of Peers and the House of Representatives. The latter body was made elective, but the property qualifications at first limited the electorate to a small number. While the cabinet was independent of the Diet, the latter body wielded a modicum of power in financial matters because in peacetime it could hold up an unpopular budget by refusing to vote supplies. In the event of such action, the government was forced to stay within the limits of the budget of the previous financial year.

In 1889 the constitution was promulgated, marking the adoption of certain western political ideas and a partial severance with the ideology of the past. But the constitution stressed the position and powers of the emperor, stating that:

. . . the Emperor is sacred and inviolable . . . is the head of the empire, combining in himself the rights of sovereignty, and exercises them according to the provisions of the present Constitution . . . has supreme command of the Army and Navy . . . declares war, makes peace, and concludes treaties.[16]

In addition, only the emperor could initiate constitutional amendments.

The Russo-Japanese War. In the eyes of European diplomats, Japan's prestige began to increase soon after the conclusion of the Sino-Japanese War (1894-1895). When Japanese troops in league with western military forces performed heroic feats during the Boxer Rebellion, the reputation of Nippon was further enhanced. In January 1902, Japan scored a diplomatic triumph by allying itself with Great Britain. Both nations viewed the alliance primarily as a deterrent to Russian expansion.

Soon after Russia, Germany, and France had forced Japan to hand back the Liaotung peninsula to China (see p. 291), the Russians had negotiated with China for the lease of Dairen and Port Arthur and for the right to build a railroad across Manchuria to connect with the Trans-Siberian line. Jealous of Russia's designs on both Manchuria and Korea, Japan attempted to negotiate a division of the area into spheres of influence. Believing that Japan could be defeated easily, the Russian government was inflexible. In February 1904, Japan broke off negotiations, severed diplomatic relations with Russia, and without a declaration of war attacked Port Arthur and bottled up the Russian fleet. The world was astounded by the quick series of Japanese victories which followed.

When, in 1905, Japan requested President Theodore Roosevelt to negotiate peace terms, Russia readily agreed to the proposition. By the Treaty of Portsmouth, signed September 5, 1905, Japan acquired the southern half of the island of Sakhalin, the leaseholds to the Liaotung peninsula and Port Arthur, and various Russian railway and mining rights in southern Manchuria. Japan's paramount position in Korea was also conceded, paving the way for Japanese annexation of that nation in 1910. Japan was now accepted as a first-class power; in 1911 the Anglo-Japanese alliance was renewed.

Japanese westernization: a façade? The modernization of Japan was one of the amazing phenomena of modern world history. But there were some disturbing features in the way western technology and institutions were adapted by the Japanese for their own purposes. Although Japan was the first Asian nation to achieve a high degree of literacy, education was the tool of the government, and its primary function was to produce docile servants of the state. The press was subject to wide control and censorship. The army was used as a means of instilling conscripts with unquestioning loyalty and obedience to the emperor. In army barracks young soldiers learned that the noblest fate was death on the battlefield.

On the surface, Japanese government was liberal and parliamentary in form. In reality, however, the constitution was ultraconservative, giving the emperor and a small body of his ministers dominant power. Effective control over the executive branch of the government could not be exercised by the legislature. In using the educational system and the armed forces for political indoctrination,

This Japanese woodcut shows the harbor of Yokohama in the nineteenth century, with a steam locomotive in the foreground.

Japan anticipated the techniques of such twentieth-century totalitarian regimes as Nazi Germany and Soviet Russia.

IMPERIALISM IN SOUTHEAST ASIA AND OCEANIA

Establishment of western rule. At the southern tip of the Asian mainland, wedged between India and China and including a multitude of islands in the Indian and Pacific oceans, is the complex area of southeast Asia. Its diverse peoples and countries began to come under European colonial rule with the arrival of the Portuguese and Spanish in the sixteenth century and the Dutch in the early years of the seventeenth. In the nineteenth century, imperial control was completed when the British gained power over Ceylon, Burma, and Malaya; the French over Indo-China; and the United States over the Philippines.

Southeast Asia is a region of very ancient culture. The oldest and most widely dispersed cultural influence is Indian, with Hindu, Buddhist, and Muhammadan religious art and customs all represented. In more recent times Chinese merchants penetrated into the commercial life of Malaysia and Indonesia. Throughout southeast Asia, western rule made a substantial imprint. A plantation economy was established with foreign capital to develop the rich natural resources; vast quantities of petroleum, tin, coffee, tea, pepper, and other tropical products were produced for the world market. Chronic civil war and banditry were ended. Law and order, together with public health facilities, came in with colonial rule and brought about a rapid increase in population. In 1800 the population of the Dutch East Indies was estimated to be eight million; by 1940 it had reached seventy million. Throughout southeast Asia the impact of European ways of life, and especially western education, created a new generation of nationalists. More and more irked with alien rule, this minority of young intellectuals finally aspired to complete independence. Little was done to satisfy these aspirations in the Dutch East Indies or in French Indo-China. Britain provided some training in self-government in Burma and Ceylon, but it was in the Philippines that benevolent imperialism most consciously moved in the direction of ultimate freedom.

Ceylon and Burma. In the sixteenth century, the main ports on the island of Ceylon were occupied by Portuguese and Dutch adventurers. In 1796 the British forced the Dutch to give up their holdings in Ceylon, and by the Treaty of Amiens (1802) the island was granted to Great Britain.

Ceylon became one of the most valuable British colonies as the nineteenth century unfolded. One of the first tropical areas to be developed extensively by Britain, it produced such valuable commodities as tea, rubber, lead, cocoa, and sapphires.

Adjoining India on its eastern land frontier is Burma. In three separate wars between 1823 and 1885, this kingdom was progressively conquered by Britain and annexed to India. British conquest brought the Burmese into closer contact with European culture, particularly in such cities as Rangoon, where young men of the upper classes obtained an English education and were employed in the British governmental service or in European firms. But in the rural areas, except for workers on European-owned plantations, the majority of the Burmese peasants cultivated their family holdings, largely unaffected by western influence.

Malaya. Another important British possession in southeast Asia was in the Malay peninsula. British influence in this area began in 1796 when a coastal strip was obtained. In 1819 Sir Thomas Stamford Raffles (1781-1826), an energetic English colonial official, secured the uninhabited island of Singapore from a Malay sultan. From Singapore and the coast, British influence was extended northward. In the latter part of the nineteenth century, four independent sultanates on the Malay peninsula became British protectorates, and in 1909 Siam transferred to Great Britain the administration of additional states. These acquisitions brought British Malaya in contact with the frontiers of Siam proper.

Raffles had foreseen that Singapore would dominate the commercially significant straits between the Malay peninsula and Sumatra, and by the end of the nineteenth century his vision was fully confirmed. Singapore became one of the greatest ports in the world. As long as Great Britain controlled this island, it could dominate the seas surrounding southern Asia.

With an area slightly less than that of England and a population of 5,494,264 in 1942, British Malaya was one of the richest colonial areas in the world, particularly in tin and rubber. In 1907 the Malay peninsula produced 52 per cent of the world's supply of tin. After 1900 increased attention was given to the growing of rubber, and the peninsula became one of the world's most valuable rubber producers.

The economic development of the Malay peninsula has been mainly the work of Chinese and Indian emigrants. The Malayan natives, living contentedly in their great jungle forests where luxuriant tropical growth easily supplied most of their wants, had little interest in hard work. The mines, plantations, and commercial enterprises came to be dominated by the more energetic Chinese. One of the chief problems of British colonial administration in Malaya was safeguarding the Malayan natives from aggressive Chinese emigrants. Today, in the southern Malay peninsula, the Chinese not only outnumber the Malayan natives but also monopolize higher education and dominate such professions as medicine and law.

French Indo-China. As early as 1787, France had secured the rights to a port from the most important native ruler in the rich peninsula of Indo-China. In the latter half of the nineteenth century, the French expanded their holdings and, between 1883 and 1885, came into conflict with China, which for many years had received annual tribute from this region. The Peking government was forced to recognize French supremacy, and later France took territory in the south from Siam.

By the beginning of the twentieth century, France had created in Indo-China an empire nearly 50 per cent larger than the mother country. Indo-China became important for its tin, pepper, coal, cotton, and rice. By 1914 the population numbered over 18,000,000 people.

Siam. Colonial expansion of the British in Burma and the French in Indo-China seriously endangered the independence of Siam, but though its territory was pared down by both Great Britain and France, Siam maintained its existence—partly because both France and Great Britain welcomed the retention of an independent Siam as a buffer between their holdings and partly because the royal house of Siam showed shrewdness and sagacity.

The Dutch East Indies. With the effective use of sea power, the Dutch in the late sixteenth century had wrested many islands of the valuable East Indies from the Portuguese. In 1602 the Dutch East India Company was organized to exploit the resources of the Spice Islands, and by the middle of the next century it had eliminated all rivals in this area. For a hundred years, this company enjoyed great prosperity, though much of it came at the expense of native rights. In 1749 forced labor and other hardships caused a widespread insurrection to break out in Java, but the uprising was crushed by strong military and naval action.

From the middle of the eighteenth century to the early years of the nineteenth, Dutch influence in the East Indies wavered. The Dutch East India Company became corrupt, its trade declined, and in 1798 it was abolished, with all holdings transferred to the Dutch crown. Since Holland was dominated by France during the Napoleonic Wars, the Dutch East Indies were therefore considered a part of the Napoleonic empire. In 1810 a British expedition captured several important islands, and in the following year a fleet from India gained control of Java. The British occupation lasted until 1816, when the islands were returned to the Dutch in accordance with a treaty made two years earlier.

For some time, the spice trade had been declining, and early in the nineteenth century the Dutch set about raising new products. In the 1830's the so-called culture system was introduced, under which one fifth of all native land was set aside to raise crops for the government and one fifth of all the natives' time was required to till these lands. The production of tobacco, sugar, coffee, tea, indigo, pepper, and cinnamon increased enormously.

The culture system offered the natives some advantages, for in the long run it gave the islands a prosperous system of raising crops, together with a body of trained workers. But because it was based on forced labor, it often prevented the natives from having enough land for their own use. *Max Havelaar* (1860), a novel written by Eduard Dekker (1820-1887), a Dutch revenue officer, exposed the evils of colonial administration and sparked a movement for reform. Liberal sen-

timent in Holland was aroused, and by 1880 the culture system had been abandoned. Steps were taken to protect native rights, free labor superseded the culture system, and Dutch rule now sought to be humanitarian. By 1900 the evils of the culture system had been remedied, and the natives enjoyed a better life. Although the Dutch succeeded admirably in developing the rich resources of the East Indies and in giving the native peoples law and order, less commendable was their neglect of higher education and their failure to prepare their wards for eventual self-government.

Spanish rule in the Philippines. Little more than 250 miles north of the Dutch East Indies is the southernmost large island of the more than three thousand islands forming the Philippine archipelago. For centuries the Chinese had traded there, but the islands became known to Europe only after the Portuguese explorer Magellan discovered them for Spain in 1521. The first permanent Spanish settlement was founded in 1565, and the city of Manila was established six years later. After much rivalry with the Portuguese, Spanish control was firmly established in the islands by the last quarter of the sixteenth century.

During the next two centuries, Spanish administrators concerned themselves principally with the conversion of the Filipinos to Christianity. The lure of gold and silver, which had resulted in forced labor and other harsh practices for the Indians of Latin America, was absent in the Philippine Islands, where colonial officials followed a more humane policy. But if the Spanish were liberal in this way, they were not liberal in politics: the Filipinos were given no opportunities to participate in government. In 1872 a serious uprising occurred. Discontent continued, especially among educated liberals, and another widespread revolt broke out in 1896.

United States imperialism. While Spain wrestled with Filipino discontent, a new imperialist power was emerging in the Pacific. During much of the nineteenth century, the United States had been engaged in the westward movement, which ultimately carried American power from the Appalachian Moun-

WORLD EMPIRES: 1914

See Ref. Maps 3-6

tains to the Pacific. The Civil War occupied all the energies of the young nation in the 1860's and this crisis was followed by a hectic period of industrialization and economic expansion. By 1890 the United States was a great industrial power, increasingly conscious of the importance of world markets, international investments, and raw materials. Later, as we saw in Chapter 9, this consciousness was to be responsible for the expansion of American interest and influence in Latin America and the rise of dollar diplomacy. The new expansionist spirit was reflected in the Pacific as well.

Annexation of Hawaii. In 1867 the Midway Islands, a thousand miles west of Hawaii, were occupied by naval forces of the United States. The next advance of the United States was in the Hawaiian Islands. During the nineteenth century, Europeans

RUSSIAN EMPIRE

Okhotsk·

HELIGO-
LAND

Vladivostok·

MARITIME PROVINCES

Constantinople

Alexandria

Yokohama

Shanghai

*Suez
Canal*

Calcutta

Hong Kong

Bombay·

Colombo

FRENCH
SOMALILAND

Singapore·

DUTCH EAST INDIES

BELGIAN
CONGO

·MAURITIUS

Port Natal

Sydney·

Cape Town·

COLONIAL   POSSESSIONS

British   French   German   Portuguese   U. S.   Italian

and Americans had developed large sugar plantations there, and American capital continued to pour into the islands. By 1881 an American secretary of state spoke of the Hawaiian Islands as part of the "American system." In 1893 a revolt, engineered with the assistance of United States Marines, deposed the Hawaiian queen and set up a republic. The desire of the pro-American faction in the islands for annexation was blocked when President Cleveland refused to send the annexation treaty to the Senate. But the President had no choice but to recognize the republic of Hawaii. In 1898, under the administration of President McKinley, Hawaii was annexed by joint declaration of both houses of Congress.

The Spanish-American War. As we saw in Chapter 9, the United States went to war against Spain in 1898. Strong resentment of

United States citizens against the harsh rule of Spain in Cuba, large American investments in this great sugar island, and the mysterious destruction of the battleship *Maine* in Havana harbor contributed to the outbreak of war. Admiral Dewey destroyed the Spanish fleet at Manila in May 1898, and American soldiers then landed in the Philippines. Cooperating with these troops were Filipino patriots under the direction of their leader Emilio Aguinaldo (1869-1964). Here as in Cuba, Spanish resistance crumbled quickly, and in the treaty of December 1898, Spain ceded to the United States the Philippines, Guam, and Puerto Rico. One year later the United States occupied the small Pacific outpost of Wake Island.

America and the Philippines. Aguinaldo had no wish merely to exchange masters and to see the United States acquire the Philippines. In the spring of 1899, fighting broke out between his forces and American troops. Hostilities lasted for three years, and sixty thousand United States troops were employed before the revolt was crushed. The ironic spectacle of American forces being used in a second conquest of the Philippines brought about a strong revulsion against imperialism in many quarters in the United States. A New York newspaper plaintively addressed Kipling, the archspokesman of imperialism, thus:

We've taken up the white man's burden
  Of ebony and brown;
Now will you kindly tell us, Rudyard,
  How we may put it down?[17]

Regardless of what can be said for or against this second conquest, in the first decade of the twentieth century, American colonial administration in the Philippines was for the most part liberal and well-intentioned. Every effort was made to establish an adequate school system, and ultimately the opportunity was afforded the Filipinos for participation in their own government. In 1913 the legislature became dominantly native, although final authority in the most important matters was still reserved for the United States Congress. The Philippine tariff was shaped to favor American trade; and

large amounts of capital from the United States were invested in the islands.

In 1903 the Philippines were estimated to have nearly eight million inhabitants, the majority of whom belonged to the Malayan racial group. American occupation speeded up the process of westernization, which had been in operation for nearly three hundred years. Increased educational facilities gave many young men the opportunity to become teachers, lawyers, and businessmen, and among these educated Filipinos there developed the desire for national independence. In their eyes American government in the Philippines, no matter how efficient or humanitarian, was no substitute for self-government.

BRITAIN AND RUSSIA IN ASIA

Character of Russian imperialism. Ordinarily one does not think of tsarist Russia as a colonial power such as Britain or France. The reason is the manner of Russian expansion: unlike Britain, which had to expand overseas, the Russian empire grew from the center outward by a process of accretion. From the grand duchy of Moscow, the Russians pushed out into the great plain that surrounded them.

Four specific types of Russian expansion may be identified. First, there was the occupation of uninhabited territory by a vigorous, land-hungry people. Then, during the Middle Ages, substantial portions of the Russian homeland which had been conquered by Poles and Lithuanians were reconquered and joined to the grand duchy of Moscow. This assimilation of various adjoining areas closely resembled the growth of France around the Ile de France, of Spain around Castile and Aragon, of Italy around Piedmont, and of Germany around Brandenburg-Prussia. A third aspect of Russia's expansive movement—the absorption of backward, non-Russian tribes and peoples—was similar to Britain's conquest of primitive tribes in Africa.

The fourth feature of Russian expansion was unique: the struggle of a landlocked country for access to the warm water of the sea. We have already followed the imperialistic efforts of the eighteenth-century rulers Peter the Great and Catherine the Great for Russian expansion toward the Baltic and the Mediterranean seas (see Chapter 2). At the same time the Russians had crossed the Ural Mountains and penetrated the huge expanses of Siberia, occupying the territory as far east as the Sea of Okhotsk and the Kamchatka peninsula. Dissatisfied that its only seaport in the Far East, Okhotsk, was frozen over most of the year, and spurred to action both by English activities in China and by an attack delivered by a British-French fleet on Okhotsk during the Crimean War, Russia sought warm water ports on the Sea of Japan.

In the 1850's Russia occupied the region of the lower Amur River, which was ceded by China in 1860, as well as the Chinese Maritime Provinces. These acquisitions enabled the tsars to build a great all-year port at Vladivostok. The port of Vladivostok was later united to European Russia by the Trans-Siberian Railroad—a vital communication link begun in 1890, completed in 1903, and covering a distance of 4350 miles.

In 1741 the Danish explorer Vitus Bering had discovered Alaska for Russia. Other explorers investigated its coastline, and Russian trading posts were established during· the nineteenth century as far south as California, where British and American interests were encountered. Russia consented to stop its activities at 54° 40′ North Latitude, and finally in 1867, Alaska was sold to the United States.

Penetration of the Caucasus and Turkestan. Having reached the Pacific, the Russians now turned their attention to the Caucasus, the area between the Black and Caspian seas. The kingdom of Georgia in this region had been incorporated into Russia in 1801, and several wars had been fought with Turkey and Persia. As the Russians pushed further into the mountainous lands of the Caucasus, the native people fought desperately but were finally overcome in the 1860's.

The vast stretches of mid-Asia had also attracted Russian attention. North of Afghanistan and India lived various backward and nomadic tribes—a mixed lot of Mongols, Afghans, Turkomans, and Tatars. Long traversed by caravan routes, the territory had a few important trading cities, notably Samarkand, Tashkent, Merv, and Bokhara. Here Russian merchandise was traded for raw cotton to be used in Russian industry. When the wild Turkestan tribes began to stop and rob the caravans, the Russians countered by sending troops, which fought against resolute resistance. Finally, early in the nineteenth century, Russian colonists, railways, and armies pushed across the steppes north of the Aral Sea into Turkestan. By the 1870's the little states, or khanates, had been conquered. Russia had now pushed south to the frontiers of Afghanistan and India. By 1914, if Siberia is excluded, the Russian empire was more than three million square miles in area.

This advance had not only been won by the bravery and resolution of Russian troops against stubborn resistance but by the construction of the Trans-Caspian Railway, which at its completion in 1888 reached 1064 miles into the heart of Asia. The Orenburg-Tashkent Railway, completed in 1905, stretched 1185 miles farther, led to a great increase in Russian commerce, and revived the ancient cities of eastern Turkestan. Accomplished with great difficulty, the feats of Russian arms and engineers inspired ambitious Russian imperialists to dream of acquiring Afghanistan and penetrating India itself, the very source of British wealth.

Approach to India arouses British. Both the Russians and the British endeavored by diplomacy or force to gain control of strategic Afghanistan. By occupying the Pamir plateau on the very northwestern frontier of India in 1895, the Russians threatened to dominate Tibet, a stroke finally countered by a British expedition to Lhasa in 1904. There was more to Russian actions than appeared on the surface, since Russia hoped by threatening India to secure concessions from the British in other parts of the world.

Russian action in Persia. As the Russians pushed inexorably southward to the Middle East, the possibility began to loom of Russia extending its Transcaucasian Railway through Persia to the warm waters of the Persian Gulf. By so doing, the Russians hoped not only to profit commercially but also to construct a naval base which might threaten the British sea route to India and enhance Russian power in that region. Today, a major objective of Soviet Russia's policy in the Middle East is to reach the Persian Gulf.

Persia, the land of the shahs, was decaying rapidly. The corrupt aristocracy fleeced the peasants, robbed the government, and stubbornly resisted reform. Into this vacuum moved the influence of Russia, and by the twentieth century, Russia was in complete control of the northern part of the country. Russians trained the Persian army, erected telegraph lines, established a postal system, and pursued profitable trade. The Russian Ministry of Finance founded the Discount and Loan Bank of Persia with branches in many parts of the nation. This bank loaned the Persian government 60,000,000 rubles and provided 120,000,000 rubles to Persian merchants to enable them to purchase Russian goods.

British countermoves in Persia. No. 10 Downing Street had no desire to see Russian power athwart the Persian Gulf and the British life line to India. To counter Russian moves, the British advanced into Persia from the southeast, established the Imperial Bank of Persia with a capital of £1,000,000, and set up a profitable tobacco monopoly.

To make matters more complicated, the exponents of a reformist and patriotic movement in Persia began to initiate a revolution. In 1906 a parliament—the Majlis—was established and the work of reform carried forward. An American financial expert, Morgan Shuster (1877-1960), was brought in to overhaul the treasury.

The Anglo-Russian entente. In 1907 Britain and Russia signed an agreement which—on the surface—ended their rivalry in Asia. Russia agreed to deal with the sovereign of Afghanistan only through the British government. For its part, Great Britain consented neither to occupy nor to annex Afghanistan so long as it fulfilled its treaty obligations.

Persia was divided into three zones: the northern was a sphere of interest for Moscow, the middle was a neutral zone, and the south gave Britain a free hand. In effect, Persia was under Anglo-Russian dual control. This part-

nership, however, was only a marriage of convenience. Russia increasingly intervened in Persian domestic politics. Shuster, the American financial expert, was forced to give up his post, and the Russians threw their support to a willing dupe, the shah, who was ready to do their bidding. Shuster described this puppet as:

. . . perhaps the most perverted, cowardly, and vice-sodden monster that had disgraced the throne of Persia in many generations.[18]

Though sorely disturbed over the Shuster incident, Britain chose not to alienate the Russians because of vital national interests. Britain now had a growing fear of German ambition in strategic areas such as Africa and China—fears which were shared by Russia. Thus Britain and Russia chose to reach an uneasy compromise in Persia. Both ethics and Persia were the victims of power politics.

THE GREAT AFRICAN

COLONY HUNT

Exploration of Africa. The best area in which to follow the course of nineteenth-century imperialism is Africa, for nowhere else on the globe were colonial empires achieved so quickly. A great continent many times the size of Europe with nearly 150,000,000 people came almost completely under the control of European powers (see Reference Map 5).

Late in the eighteenth century, the opening of Africa began in earnest, and by 1835 most of northwestern Africa had been mapped by Europeans. The greatest of the explorers was David Livingstone (1813-1873), a Scottish missionary who traversed barren wastes and jungles from the Cape of Good Hope to the equator and from the Atlantic to the Indian Ocean. It was Livingstone who discovered Victoria Falls and the Zambezi River. "The very great doctor," as the natives called him, began his series of explorations in 1853. After his death in 1873, explorations of the interior were carried on by Henry Morton Stanley (1841-1904), a British explorer and journalist who had located Livingstone in the jungle in 1871 and had casually greeted him, "Dr. Livingstone, I presume." By the end of the century, Africa was no longer the Dark Continent. The source of the Nile had been discovered, the courses of the Niger and Congo had been traced, and the world now realized the rich resources of Africa.

On the eve of the European scramble for Africa, only 10 per cent of the continent was under the control of western nations. In 1875 the two most important European holdings were Algeria, administered by France, and Cape Colony, held by Great Britain. In South Africa there were Dutch farmers in two small republics, the Orange Free State and the Transvaal. Most of the other European holdings were mere coastal ports. The interior still remained a mysterious land inhabited by primitive black men.

Belgian interest in Africa. Stanley's explorations galvanized the European nations into action, although when he returned to Europe to interest businessmen in Africa's immense economic possibilities, he at first found little support for his ideas except from the Belgian king. So impressed was Leopold II with Stanley's views that in 1876 he organized the International African Association, composed of scientists and explorers from all nations. Ostensibly the association was to serve humanitarian purposes; according to Leopold, it was "a crusade worthy of the century of progress." But the crafty king had other purposes in mind. As an agent of the association, Stanley was sent to the Congo region, where he made treaties with several African chiefs and by 1882 obtained over 900,000 square miles of territory.

The British in Egypt. Meanwhile, important developments were taking place in the Nile valley. Shortly before the completion of the Suez Canal in 1869, Ismail, the ruler of Egypt, undertook to modernize his country and borrowed enormous sums from French and English bankers at high rates of interest. By 1875 he was involved in financial difficulties and was forced to sell his block of 175,000 shares in the Suez Canal. The shares were snapped up by the astute prime minister of Great Britain, Benjamin Disraeli, who

Stanley's meeting with Livingstone on the shore of Lake Tanganyika made newspaper headlines around the world.

realized that such a large block of stock would give his country practical control in the management of this strategic highway between Europe and the East. But the sale of stock did little to improve the state of Egyptian finances, which could not stand the combined strain of Ismail's extravagances and the corruption in the administration of revenues. In 1876 Ismail repudiated his debts, and Great Britain and France assumed joint financial control over Egypt, forcing the Egyptian ruler to abdicate in favor of his son, Tewfik.

The Egyptian ruling classes did not relish foreign intervention, and when a serious revolt broke out in 1882, many Europeans lost their lives in riots in Alexandria. The French fleet withdrew at this point, but Great Britain decided to quell the revolt and assume responsibility for the administration of Egypt. To reorganize Egyptian finances, eliminate corruption from the administration, and improve the cotton industry, Sir Evelyn Baring, later Lord Cromer, was sent to Egypt and actually ruled the country from 1883 to 1907. In reducing corruption, he overhauled the system of government. The use of forced labor was curbed, and huge dams were con-

THE LION'S SHARE.

Disraeli buys the Suez Canal Company shares of the khedive of Egypt, while the British lion guards the key to India, symbol of the canal. This is a contemporary cartoon.

structed to improve the fertility of the country. Indeed, it has been said that the best record of imperialism is to be found in Egypt.

Although the entry of Great Britain into Egypt was brought about primarily by concern for British financial interests and by the knowledge that control of the Nile valley would ensure the protection of the Suez Canal, the effects of British rule were in large measure advantageous for Egypt. British rule was not harsh, and the average peasant profited by the occupation. Nevertheless, the twentieth century was barely under way before the Egyptians voiced a growing demand for self-government.

Organization of imperial policy. The occupation of Egypt and the acquisition of the Congo were the first moves in what soon came to be a precipitous and undignified scramble for African territory. French, German, and Italian agents now appeared in Africa, and it became apparent that war might ensue if the new imperialist activities were not guided by careful diplomacy. Therefore, in 1884 Bismarck convened a conference in Berlin to discuss the Africa problem. This assembly of diplomats paid lip service to humanitarianism by condemning the slave trade, prohibiting the sale of liquor and firearms in certain areas, and expressing concern for proper religious instruction for the natives. Then the diplomats turned to matters they considered much more important. The rules

of fair competition by which the great powers were to be guided in seeking colonies were laid down. They agreed that the area along the Congo was to be administered by Leopold of Belgium, that it was to be neutral territory, and that in this area trade and navigation were to be free. No nation was to peg out claims in Africa without first notifying other powers of its intention. No territory could be claimed unless it was effectively occupied, and all disputes were to be settled by arbitration. In spite of these encouraging declarations, the competitors ignored the rules when it was convenient to do so, and on several occasions war was avoided only by a hair's breadth.

The methods Europeans used to acquire land continued, in many cases, to involve deception of the native peoples. Europeans obtained huge grants of lands by presenting ignorant chiefs with treaties which they could not read and whose contents they were not permitted to comprehend. In return, the natives were rewarded by bottles of gin, red handkerchiefs, and fancy-dress costumes. Since in many cases, native custom reserved ownership of land to tribes, allowing individuals only the use of it, the chief granted land to European settlers with no idea that he was disposing of more than its temporary use. When later the settler claimed ownership, the natives were indignant, feeling that the tribe had been robbed of land contrary to tribal law.

The ignorance of the African natives was also exploited in the making of treaties. In his autobiography, a British colonial official and famous explorer, Sir Harry Johnston (1858-1927), has given a vivid picture of the manner in which European explorers made these treaties:

As we neared a large village we were accorded a boisterous reception. . . . I said I had come on a mission of friendliness from a great white Queen [Victoria] who wanted to enter into friendly relations. I should like to "make a book with them," I added, to take home to the Woman Chief. I extracted a Treaty form from my dispatch box and three or four persons of prominence crowded into the canoe to make crosses on it with my ink. I was longing to get away, as from various indications I realized we had come to this region on a market day, when a great deal of palm wine had been drunk. So after the crosses had been splodged on the Treaty form and I had made up my present of cloth and beads, my crew was seated and ready to resume paddling while good humor prevailed.[19]

The Belgian Congo. Shortly after the Berlin conference, Leopold organized his African territories as the Congo Free State, subject to no control, not even that of the Belgian parliament. He began to exploit the colony's economic resources by granting concessions to private companies, reserving for his own administration an extensive rubber area ten times as large as Belgium. A system of forced labor was introduced, and soon stories of filthy work camps, horrible whippings, and other atrocities leaked out of the Free State, now undergoing the process of "civilization." A Belgian senator on a tour of investigation described a caravan carrying rubber thus:

A continual succession of blacks, carrying loads upon their heads; worn-out beasts of burden, with projecting joints, wasted features, and staring eyes, perpetually trying to keep afoot despite their exhaustion. By thousands they pass, in the service of the State, handed over by the chiefs, whose slaves they are and who rob them of their wages. They totter along the road, with bent knees and protruding bellies, crawling with vermin, a dreadful procession across hill and dale, dying from exhaustion by the wayside.[20]

This traffic in human misery for profit was a tragic betrayal of the white man's burden.

In England, societies like the Aborigines Protection Society began to attack Leopold, and British journalists did much to arouse world opinion by their exposures. In the face of a rising tide of international indignation, Leopold in 1908 was forced to turn over the Free State to the Belgian government. Under the direct administration of the government, conditions in the colony improved. This tremendous area is now known as The Congo.

German interest in Africa. In Germany during the seventies, there was a growing demand for imperial expansion, to which Bismarck, the chancellor, was at first deaf. By 1882, however, he had been converted to the gospel of imperialism, and the Germans began to look about them for a place in the sun. Obtaining the promise of German protection from Bismarck, a merchant named Lüderitz sent an agent to southwestern Africa to negotiate with the natives for a suitable port. The agent succeeded in acquiring some three thousand square miles of territory in exchange for 500,200 rifles and a quantity of toys. The German port was near enough to the British Cape Colony to produce a feeling of uneasiness among the British, but nothing could be done after Bismarck declared a formal protectorate over the region—which became German Southwest Africa—in 1884.

While German merchants were thus establishing a protectorate in the southwest, the chancellor had sent a German explorer, Gustav Nachtigal (1834-1885), in a warship to sail along the west coast, meanwhile assuring the British government that he was merely collecting commercial information. At a port on the north coast of the Gulf of Guinea, Nachtigal discovered that the British were about to take over this region and hastily declared the area to be under German protection. He then turned east along the coast to the corner of the Gulf of Guinea. By the time the British had dispatched an official to forestall further German annexations, Nachtigal had negotiated a treaty with the chiefs of the area and proclaimed it German territory. Thus was founded the basis for the German colonies of Togoland and Cameroons.

It was on the east coast of Africa, however, that the most important German acquisitions were made. German penetration there was largely the work of Carl Peters (1856-1918). After attending several German universities, Peters went to England to study British methods of colonization. He returned to Germany to organize a colonization company, and in 1884 he and three other colonial enthusiasts, disguised as English workingmen, set out on a secret mission to eastern Africa. Peters succeeded in obtaining treaties from chiefs giving him control of sixty thousand square miles. In 1885 Bismarck proclaimed the region German East Africa.

The British-German African settlement.
The activity of the Germans did not take the British completely by surprise. Sir Harry Johnston had been pegging out English claims to the region directly north of Peters' concessions, and in 1885 a group of English merchants organized the British East Africa Company to exploit the area he explored. In 1886 and 1890, rival German and British claims were settled amicably. Germany received several concessions from Britain, notably the strategic island of Helgoland in the North Sea, which was to become an important pivot of German naval power. Britain also recognized the Germans' claim to their protectorate in East Africa (later called Tanganyika). After the agreement in East Africa, the British held Uganda, along the shores of Lake Victoria; British East Africa (later known as Kenya), fronting along the coast of the Indian Ocean; the rich spice (cloves) island of Zanzibar; and the area of Nyasaland.

Other British acquisitions in Africa. Meanwhile, Great Britain by 1884 had obtained control over a stretch of African coast fronting on the Gulf of Aden. This protectorate (British Somaliland) was of great strategic value inasmuch as it guarded the lower approach to the Suez Canal. Even more important were the headwaters of the Nile, situated in the area known later as the Anglo-Egyptian Sudan. In 1898 the British conquered this area also.

On the west coast of Africa, Great Britain retained the several trading posts established in the seventeenth and eighteenth centuries and enlarged these holdings by acquiring some adjoining hinterlands. Among the new acquisitions on the African west coast, the most important was the territory around the mouth of the Niger, stretching back toward the Sudan, which had been opened up to English influence by a British private trading concern, the Royal Niger Company. In 1900, after having secured for the British crown an area of nearly 400,000 square miles containing 19,000,000 people, this company sold its equipment and buildings to the British government. The British possessions were Gambia, Sierra Leone, the Gold Coast, and Nigeria. Fronting on the Atlantic coast, these colonies were relatively small enclaves entirely surrounded by the huge territory of French West Africa.

Cecil Rhodes, empire builder. In the meantime, Great Britain's influence in southern Africa had expanded northward from Cape Colony almost to the equator, where it reached German East Africa. In this drive north the main impetus came from the British capitalist Cecil Rhodes, who dreamed of an uninterrupted corridor of British territory from the Cape of Good Hope to Cairo. Born in England in 1853, Rhodes was the youngest of five sons of an Anglican vicar. Because of poor health he was sent to join his brother in southern Africa. Shortly after his arrival, diamonds were discovered north of Cape Colony, and Rhodes and his brother immediately set out to make their fortunes. In time Rhodes became the leading figure in the fabulously wealthy De Beers diamond syndicate and the owner of many valuable gold-mining properties in the Transvaal. By 1890 his annual income was estimated to be at least 5,000,000 dollars.

An interesting feature of Rhodes' life was his ambition to attend Oxford University. After he had gained a tidy fortune, he entered Oriel College and then commuted back and forth several times between South Africa and England until he obtained his degree. Not interested in money for its own sake but as a means of extending British influence— its law, ideals, culture—throughout the world and especially in Africa, Rhodes was imbued with the imperial idea and was truly a man with a mission. In some ways he was completely ruthless and cynical, believing that every man had his price and that money could purchase anything. On the other hand, he wanted nothing for himself. His grandiose ideas can be best understood from reading a will he wrote while an undergraduate—but a wealthy one—at Oxford. He left his estate to provide for the establishment of a secret society for extending British rule and colonization throughout the world and for inaugurating an imperial parliament to unite the empire. Thus, he hoped to create an immense power that would make war impossible and would serve the best interests of mankind.

This fantastic dream was the product of a young man's romantic imagination, but its substance, refined and limited in scope, remained Rhodes' driving ambition throughout his life.

In 1885, Rhodes was instrumental in getting Britain to declare a protectorate over Bechuanaland, a territory wedged between the Dutch Transvaal and German Southwest Africa. Referring to the region as the Suez Canal of the African interior, Rhodes realized that if this territory were annexed by another power, the British would be cut off from the rich lands of south-central Africa. More important, without Britain's domination over this region, Rhodes' dream of a Cape to Cairo railroad under British control would not be possible.

By unscrupulous methods the empire builder was able to secure extensive settlement and mining rights to the high and fertile plateau between Lake Nyasa and the Limpopo River, through which flowed the great Zambezi River. Rhodes' agents secured these rights from the leading chief of the area in return for a gift of a thousand rifles, an old steamship, and a monthly payment of five hundred dollars. By means of his own British South Africa Company, Rhodes poured miners and settlers into the country. There were several native uprisings but settlement continued. In 1890 the capital, Salisbury, was founded and the region named Rhodesia. Twenty-five years later the colony had a thriving European community of 25,000.

By 1890, as prime minister of Cape Colony, Rhodes' one remaining task was uniting Boer and Briton in South Africa into a single nation. The facts of geography made this a logical objective, but the two white nationalities had never been able to compose their differences. Rhodes made the fatal mistake of conspiring to use force to achieve his ends. This only widened the breach between the two peoples and did much to bring on the Boer War in 1899 (see pp. 261–262).

In 1902 Cecil Rhodes died, leaving a huge legacy to endow 175 scholarships at Oxford for students from the British Dominions, the United States, and Germany. He believed

Generations of Rhodes scholars owe their years at Oxford to Cecil Rhodes, founder of the famous scholarships.

that if harmony and understanding could be achieved among the United States, Germany, and the British Dominions, the peace of the world would be assured. Rhodes was a complex combination of astute financier, fanatical nationalist and empire builder, and confused seeker after world peace.

French colonies in Africa. The first important French colonial acquisition in Africa had been made decades before the renewed European interest in colonization in the 1870's and 1880's. In the 1820's, during the reign of Charles x, French statesmen had seen in North Africa a chance to counterbalance political unrest at home. For some time France had been complaining of the piratical activities of the Algerians, and when in 1827 the Algerian ruler insulted the French consul in public by hitting him on the head with a fly swatter, France was furnished with a good pretext for intervention. In 1830 a large army was dispatched to occupy the country, but seventeen years elapsed before the French succeeded in subduing the fierce Berber tribes. Algeria was then made an integral part of the French state.

In 1881 France obtained Tunisia in North Africa. The repudiation of interest payments on large loans and the charge that wild Tunisian tribesmen were crossing the border to pillage in Algeria gave the French an excuse to take over Tunisia as a protectorate. It is said that Bismarck encouraged the French to go into Tunisia in order to divert their minds from the loss of Alsace-Lorraine, which had been ceded to Germany after the Franco-Prussian War of 1870.

For a few years following the conquest of Tunisia, France made little headway elsewhere in Africa. But by 1884 the activities of Pierre de Brazza (1852-1905), a famous Italian explorer (later, a naturalized Frenchman) who obtained concessions in the Congo region in 1877 and 1878, enabled France to claim a huge section of equatorial Africa along the right bank of the Congo River.

With the acquisition of Algeria, Tunisia, and strategic posts along the west coast and with the right bank of the Congo in its possession, France began to develop an ambitious colonial program by which a great western African empire, stretching from Algeria to the Congo and from the Atlantic to the Nile and perhaps even to the Red Sea, was to be created. From posts along the west coast, France pushed into the interior and thus obtained most of the basins of the Senegal and Niger rivers, while expeditions from Algeria and Tunisia penetrated the Sahara. Although the French did not succeed in getting to the Nile, by 1900 they controlled the largest empire in Africa, one which stretched eastward from the Atlantic to the western Sudan and southward to the Congo River. In addition, the French annexed the large island of Madagascar in the south Indian Ocean and in 1911, despite the opposition of Germany, made Morocco a French protectorate.

Italy's African ventures. If overpopulation, lack of trade, and widespread poverty constitute the most compelling reasons for obtaining colonies, Italy should have gained the most extensive areas in Africa. But Italy came out of the scramble with very little territory. When Tunisia became a French protectorate in 1881, Italian ambitions there were blocked. Italy turned to East Africa, obtaining a piece of Red Sea coast and a slice of barren and desolate land on the Indian Ocean, but these areas were of little value without the rich plateau of Abyssinia (Ethiopia) in the hinterland. An attempt to annex this ancient empire in 1896 ended in the destruction of an Italian army.

Italy then shifted its attention to the Turkish territory of Tripoli, which was acquired with the secret consent of Spain, France, Great Britain, and Russia. Italy declared war on Turkey in 1911 and forced the Turks to cede the area in 1912. This event temporarily marked the end of Italian expansion and likewise the end of the race for colonial empires by European powers.

The economic wealth of Africa surpassed the expectations of the most avid imperialist. By the first decade in the twentieth century, it was the world's greatest producer of gold and diamonds. In addition, rich resources of tin, phosphates, and especially copper were uncovered. From the once Dark Continent poured rubber, coffee, sisal, palm oil, and cotton—products which became more and more essential for the great industrial nations of the world.

The table below shows the shares of African territory taken by European nations during the nineteenth century and the first decade of the twentieth.

EUROPEAN TERRITORIAL EXPANSION IN AFRICA

	SQUARE MILES	POPULATION
France	4,200,000	25,000,000
Great Britain	3,300,000	35,000,000
Germany	1,100,000	12,000,000
Belgium	900,000	7,000,000
Portugal	800,000	8,000,000
Italy	600,000	1,000,000
Spain	75,000	200,000

IMPERIALISM:

THE BALANCE SHEET

Spread of imperialism. By 1914 some 283,000,000 whites directly controlled over 900,000,000 non-Europeans, mainly in Africa and Asia. The area involved in this tremendous colonial network was more than 28,000,000 square miles. The greatest of the empire builders was Britain, with more than 13,000,000 square miles, if self-governing colonies such as Canada were included. Russia's colonial domain, mainly in central and eastern Asia, was at least half the size of Britain's empire. France was the third largest imperial power, with Germany a poor fourth. Substantial colonial holdings were also in the hands of Belgium, Portugal, and Holland, with Italy making a pitiful showing. While most Americans would not think of the United States as an imperial power, in 1914 this nation controlled over 700,000 square miles of territory outside the confines of continental United States. The three most important American possessions were Hawaii, Alaska, and the Philippines.

Imperialism: the negative opinion. What is the significance of western imperialism in the scheme of world history? During the first half of the nineteenth century, a strong anti-colonial school in the western world produced an imposing literature against imperialism. One of its most famous exponents wrote:

Imperialism is a depraved choice of national life, imposed by self-seeking interests which appeal to the lusts of quantitative acquisitiveness and of forceful domination surviving in a nation from early centuries of animal struggle for existence.[21]

Certainly one must agree that imperialism had its ruthless and exploitive side. Large territories were taken by force or by fraud, and on occasion lands were seized from the native populations without compensation. There were numerous instances of the use of forced native labor by colonial authorities. Above all, colonies were too often regarded as existing chiefly for the commercial and financial advantage of the controlling power.

The critics of imperialism leveled their guns with particular zest against those who defended it on the basis of a civilizing mission. George Bernard Shaw, the sharp-tongued enemy of hypocrisy in any form, has left a classic indictment of Britain's mission to help the "backward" races:

Every Englishman is born with a certain miraculous power that makes him master of the world. When he wants a thing he never tells himself that he wants it. He waits patiently till there comes into his head, no one knows how, the burning conviction that it is his moral and religious duty to conquer those who have the thing he wants. Then he becomes irresistible. Like the aristocrat he does what pleases him and grabs what he wants; like the shopkeeper he pursues his purpose with the industry and steadfastness that come from strong religious conviction and deep sense of moral responsibility. He is never at a loss for an effective moral attitude. As the great champion of freedom and independence, he conquers half the world and calls it Colonization. When he wants a new market for his adulterated Manchester goods, he sends a missionary to teach the natives the gospel of peace. The natives kill the missionary; he flies to arms in defense of Christianity; fights for it, conquers for it; and takes the market as a reward from heaven.[22]

Imperialism: the positive opinion. Shaw's indictment contains much truth. Yet another side to imperialism is becoming more clear following the achievement of independence by a large number of colonial areas after 1945 (see Chapter 18). It is now evident that many of the native peoples living under European imperial control took the ensuing law and order for granted. It should not be forgotten that the slave trade in tropical Africa was smashed in the mid-nineteenth century largely by British efforts; that the French ended piracy in North Africa; and that *thuggee* was extirpated in India by British rule. Even as late as 1900 much of the great territory of Nigeria on the African west coast was in a state of chaos, with fierce and powerful Muslim chieftains carrying out ruthless slave raiding. The story is told that when the British captured one of the chiefs in their efforts to restore peace and end slavery, they urged him to stop slaving. His reply was:

Missionary activity accompanied and sometimes preceded the march of imperialism. Here a Methodist bishop baptizes converts in India around the beginning of the present century.

Can you stop a cat from mousing? When I die I shall be found with a slave in my mouth.[23]

In many of the areas that came under European imperial control, tribes or nations had been constantly at war with each other. This was especially true in Africa, Malaya, and the Dutch East Indies. The imperial powers stepped in and ended intertribal wars, prohibiting the young warriors from "blooding their spears." One law was imposed over an entire area, and regions such as French West Africa, the Belgian Congo, the Gold Coast, the great dependency of India, the East Indies, and British Malaya were given the advantages of political and economic unity which had been heretofore unknown. As we will see in a later chapter, the granting of independence revived the old tribal and sectional loyalties. New nations such as India broke apart; unity has been maintained only with extreme difficulty in the former Dutch East Indies. Already in the Gold Coast and Nigeria, recently independent, are heard disturbing rumblings of regional nationalisms that threaten the unity of these nascent nations.

While imperialism has produced its share of economic injustices and while colonies have been retarded in some ways to aid the controlling power, there is another side to the picture. Western nations have constructed roads, government buildings, postal and telegraph systems, and great dams, and their businessmen have dug mines, tapped oil fields, and established plantations. With the end of imperial control, many of these improvements remain, performing invaluable functions. Not only has imperialism in many instances provided the capital and facilities for the foundation of a modern economic structure, but it may be added that these so-called backward or underdeveloped areas—gradually gaining their independence in the mid-twentieth century—still require the capital and the technical skill of more developed nations.

A final positive aspect of western imperialism was its ideological impact on civilizations, such as the Chinese, that were moribund and stagnant and on areas, such as tropical Africa, where civilization had never even started. The West brought dynamic ideas of progress, nationalism, efficient and honest public administration, democracy, and faith in science. This ideological impact of nationalism and democracy, made possible by colonialism, ultimately led to a demand for independence. Alien government, good or bad, was no substitute for self-government.

Among the most important agencies diffusing these western ideas were the Christian missionaries. In all parts of the world, mission establishments, consisting of schools, colleges, hospitals, and churches, made a unique contribution to enlightenment. In the Middle East, for example, the American University of Beirut, established in the 1820's, performed a major role in training native leaders and disseminating progressive ideas.

This is not to say that western missionary enterprise was always wisely conceived or directed. There were regrettable occasions when missionaries failed to respect the intrinsic worth and dignity of aspects of native culture. They believed such customs or institutions were un-Christian just because they were nonwestern. But in the balance, missionary work undoubtedly contributed to both the spiritual and the physical betterment of humanity in the undeveloped regions of the world.

SUMMARY

Before 1870, little interest in colonial expansion existed in Europe. But with the completion of the unification of Germany and Italy, the mounting of tariffs, and the need for markets, raw materials, and areas for investing surplus capital, the western nations began avidly to turn their attention to imperialism. The economic forces back of this expansion have usually been overemphasized, the psychological underestimated. By 1870 Europe had unbounded faith in its destiny and in its powers. What has been called "a certain indefinable national energy"[24] impelled nations such as France, Britain, and Germany to spread their rule, power, and culture. The factors of adventure, romance, and scientific curiosity also impelled great explorers and colonial administrators to peg out colonial claims.

The white man's burden was not a hypocritical concept. Whether justified or not, many Europeans held an overwhelming conviction that it was the destiny and duty of the white nations to spread their beneficent civilization.

In the Far East, China was opened in the 1840's and 1850's—somewhat before the real onset of western imperialism. This huge and inert empire was callously treated by the western nations. But China was not blameless. Wrapped in a mantle of unreal superiority, China refused to adapt to the needs or realities of a rapidly changing world. On the other hand, Japan had a long tradition of borrowing from the outside. Once convinced of the necessity of modernization, this feudal island kingdom engaged in a pell-mell adoption of western culture. But while foreign customs and techniques were borrowed, they were shaped to fit Japanese needs as seen by Japan's leaders. Education, the press, the armed services, and the government so functioned as to produce a docile, obedient citizen and a fanatical, dedicated soldier.

Following the Sepoy Rebellion in 1857, Britain consolidated its rule in India and built up flourishing colonies in Ceylon, Malaya, and Burma. The French acquired Indo-China, and the Dutch exploited the riches of the East Indies. In the Pacific, a feature of the late nineteenth century was the growing imperialism of the United States. Hawaii and the Philippines were obtained, together with a number of small possessions. The United States had the imperial fever, although not as strongly as other western powers.

Russian imperialism in the nineteenth century is often overlooked. Its empire was not a scattered series of territories located in various continents and separated by the seven seas but a continuous land area, a group of territories that had originated from a nucleus —Moscow—and had never lost touch with its starting point. By 1900 Russia had expanded to the Pacific and marched southward to the passes of India and Afghanistan and was pushing into the Middle East toward the warm waters of the Indian Ocean. Because of Anglo-Russian rivalry in this latter area, Persia was in effect partitioned. There were many other serious imperial rivalries that will be discussed in a later chapter as part of the background of World War i.

Africa was the largest area to be partitioned. By the end of the colonial scramble, only two independent countries remained: Ethiopia and tiny Liberia. Britain had gained such territories as Egypt and Anglo-Egyptian Sudan, Kenya, Uganda, Rhodesia, Nigeria, and the Gold Coast. France had the large island of Madagascar, French Equatorial Africa, and the huge stretch of French West Africa reaching from Dakar on the Atlantic coast to the valley of the Nile. The French also controlled Morocco, Tunisia, and Algeria in North Africa. Little Belgium had the huge Belgian Congo, and Germany had Togoland, Cameroons, and German Southwest Africa on the west coast and German East Africa on the east coast. Portugal had extensive holdings, but ambitious Italy had failed in the great African colony hunt.

SUGGESTIONS FOR READING

THE UNITED STATES

Each passing year sees the publication of more and more books on American history. A truly representative sampling of these works would require more space than is available here. Therefore the following list includes only a handful of the more thoughtful and provocative works of recent scholarship, in addition to new editions of standard works.

Boorstin, D. J., *The Americans; The Colonial Experience,* Random House, 1958. A brilliant analysis of how Old World dogmas and institutions were modified when transplanted to the New World.

Becker, C. L., *The Declaration of Independence; A Study in the History of Political Ideas,* Vintage,* 1958. An analysis of the Declaration and of how the views expressed in it have been accepted or modified by succeeding generations of Americans.

Dos Passos, J., *The Men Who Made the Nation: The Architects of the Young Republic, 1782-1802,* Doubleday, 1957. A swiftly paced narrative of the men—Washington, Hamilton, Franklin, Madison, and others—who launched the new nation.

Adams, H., *The United States in 1800,* Great Seal Books,* 1957. First published in 1889, this work gives a vivid portrait of social and economic conditions in the young republic.

Jefferson, T., *The Living Thoughts of Thomas Jefferson,* Premier,* 1957. The noted American philosopher John Dewey selected the materials included in this work and supplied a long introduction.

Schlesinger, A. M., Jr., *The Age of Jackson,* abr. by D. P. Geddes, Mentor,* 1945. A Pulitzer-Prize-winning study which analyzes vigorously the formative period in the growth of American democracy.

Billington, R. A., *The Westward Movement in the United States,* Anvil,* 1959. A lucid account of the westward movement, from the early days of our nation to the 1890's.

Sandburg, C., *Abraham Lincoln: The Prairie Years and The War Years,* 3 vols., Dell,* 1959. The famous American poet's condensation of his massive six-volume study is now available in this convenient edition.

The great popular interest in the Civil War has resulted in a profusion of historical studies of this stirring era. The following are representative and highly recommended. A. Craven, *The Coming of the Civil War,* Univ. of Chicago, 1957. A challenging discussion of the various forces responsible for the conflict. B. Catton, *This Hallowed Ground,* Doubleday, 1956. This history of the Union side is one of the best single-volume treatments. R. Meredith, *Storm over Sumter,* Simon and Schuster, 1957. A suspenseful account of the first battle of the war. C. Dowdey, *Death of a Nation,* Knopf, 1958.

*Indicates an inexpensive paperbound edition.

The gripping narrative of the battle of Gettysburg. S. Foote, *The Civil War: A Narrative,* Random House, 1958. The first volume of a projected trilogy, notable for its colorful writing as well as its scholarship.

Logan, R. W., *The Negro in the United States,* Anvil,* 1957. Traces the progress of the American Negro. See also B. T. Washington, *Up from Slavery,* Bantam,* 1959, the justly famous autobiography (1901) of a great American Negro educator.

Two critiques of the American scene which have become classics in the field of political analysis are Alexis de Tocqueville, *Democracy in America* (ed. and abr. by R. D. Hafner), Mentor,* 1956; and Viscount James Bryce, *The American Commonwealth,* 2 vols. (ed. and abr. by L. M. Hacker), Capricorn,* 1960. The former originally appeared in 1835, the latter in 1888.

Friedel, F., *The Splendid Little War,* Little, Brown, 1958. A well-illustrated, fast-moving account of the Spanish-American War.

Brevity and high-level scholarship mark the following two biographical studies: H. F. Pringle, *Theodore Roosevelt,* Harvest,* 1956; and E. M. Hugh-Jones, *Woodrow Wilson and American Liberalism,* Macmillan, 1949.

Published bimonthly by the American Heritage Publishing Company, *American Heritage* is devoted to all aspects of our national history. Highly recommended for its lively articles and its superb illustrations.

THE BRITISH DOMINIONS

Trotter, R. G., *The British Empire-Commonwealth,* Holt, 1932. A brief review of the evolution of the self-governing dominions. See also P. Knaplund, *The British Empire, 1815-1939,* Harper, 1941.

Raddall, T. H., *The Path of Destiny,* Doubleday, 1957. In this history of Canada from the British conquest to self-government in 1850, of particular interest are the accounts of the War of 1812, the Durham Report, and the opening of the Canadian west. For two important aspects of Canadian history, see J. S. Galbraith, *The Hudson's Bay Company As an Imperial Factor, 1821-1869,* Univ. of Calif., 1957, which relates how the company helped shape the history of British North America; and B. Hutchinson, *The Struggle for the Border,* Longmans, 1955, a lively account of Canadian-American relations.

Nadel, G., *Australia's Colonial Culture,* Harvard, 1958. A vivid account of the ideas, men, and institutions that helped shape the course of Australian history from 1830 to 1860.

De Kiewiet, C. W., *A History of South Africa, Social and Economic,* Oxford, 1941. Particularly illuminating on the rise of the gold and diamond industries and the background of the Boer War. Also recommended are S. D. Neumark, *Economic Influences on the South African Frontier, 1652-1836,*

Stanford, 1957, a study of economic forces that influenced the expansion of Cape Colony; and G. B. Pyrah, *Imperial Policy and South Africa, 1902-1910,* Oxford, 1955, a review of the events leading to South African union; also W. K. Hancock, **Smuts: The Sanguine Years, 1870-1919,** Volume I, Cambridge, 1962. For works of Latin-American history, see **List of Readings,** p. 614.

IMPERIALISM

Walker, E. A., **Colonies,** Cambridge, 1944. In this brief study, a specialist on colonial affairs explores the reasons for, the nature of, and the future of colonies. The early chapters of P. T. Moon, *Imperialism and World Politics,* Macmillan, 1953, contain a keen analysis of why Europe shouldered the white man's burden. Thoughtful and stimulating is W. L. Langer, *The Diplomacy of Imperialism, 1890-1902,* Knopf, 1951.

Two famous attacks on imperialism, the latter being the stock communist diatribe: J. A. Hobson, *Imperialism; A Study,* Macmillan, 1938; and V. I. Lenin, *Imperialism, the Highest Stage of Capitalism,* International Publishers, 1939.

Burns, Sir Alan, *In Defence of Colonies: British Colonial Territories in International Affairs,* Macmillan, 1957. A vigorous defense of the motives and positive results of British imperialism. See also Albert H. Imlah, **Economic Elements in the Pax Britannica; Studies in British Foreign Trade in the Nineteenth Century,** Harvard, 1958, an excellent summary of Britain's highly successful experiment with free trade.

Carrington, C. E., *The Life of Rudyard Kipling,* Doubleday, 1955. A good portrait of the "singer of empire."

AFRICA

Two brief, useful studies are Z. Marsh and G. W. Kingsnorth, *An Introduction to the History of East Africa,* Cambridge, 1957; and J. D. Fage, *An Introduction to the History of West Africa,* Cambridge, 1955.

A succinct survey of European penetration is H. L. Hoskins, *European Imperialism in Africa,* Holt, 1930.

A good introduction to the story of the rise of the British African empire is I. L. Evans, *The British in Tropical Africa, an Historical Outline,* Macmillan, 1929.

The English historian Reginald Coupland wrote copiously and well on Africa. His *The British Anti-Slavery Movement,* Butterworth, 1933, gives a vivid picture of the horrors of the slave trade and of the long campaign against it; his *East Africa and Its Invaders,* Oxford, 1938, is the best study of this area from earliest times to 1856.

Townsend, M. E., *The Rise and Fall of Germany's Colonial Empire, 1884-1918,* Macmillan, 1930. A pioneer study. See also H. R. Rudin, **Germans in the Cameroons, 1884-1914,** Yale, 1938.

Fascinating to read are the journals of explorers in Africa: C. Howard, ed., **West African Explorers,** Oxford, 1952; M. Perham and J. Simmons, eds., **African Discovery,** Faber, 1957; D. Livingstone, **Livingstone's Travels** (ed. by J. I. Macnair), Macmillan, 1954.

The challenge of Britain's imperial mission in Africa is mirrored in the lives of three men: F. Gross, **Rhodes of Africa,** Praeger,

1957, the ruthless empire builder; Lord Elton, **Gordon of Khartoum,** Knopf, 1955, the daring adventurer who met a tragic death in the Sudan; M. Perham, **Lugard, The Years of Adventure, 1858-1898,** Essential Books, 1956, a famous colonial adminstrator in Uganda, Nigeria, and Nyasaland.

INDIA AND THE FAR EAST

Speare, P., *Twilight of the Mughuls,* Cambridge, 1951. A British authority describes the once mighty dynasty on the eve of its oblivion.

Sen, Surendra Nath, **Eighteen Fifty-Seven,** Ministry of Information, Delhi, India. Remarkable for its objectivity is this official history of the Sepoy Rebellion of 1857. See also S. B. Chandhari, **Civil Rebellion in the Indian Mutinies, 1857-1859,** World Press, Calcutta, 1957; and J. Leasor, *The Red Fort; The Story of the Indian Mutiny of 1857,* Reynal, 1957.

Coupland, R., *India: A Re-Statement,* Oxford, 1946. A restrained and convincing apologia for British rule. By contrast, G. D. Sanderson, **India and British Imperialism,** Bookman Associates, 1951, is a bitter indictment of British rule.

Forster, E. M., *A Passage to India,* Harbrace Modern Classics, 1949. A sensitively wrought, witty novel about the clash of cultures (British and Indian) in India.

Owen, D. E., **Imperialism and Nationalism in the Far East,** Holt, 1929. Valuable for its discussion of the first European impacts in the Far East and the opening of China and Japan. Also recommended is G. C. Allen and A. G. Donnithorne, **Western Enterprise in Far Eastern Economic Development: China and Japan,** Macmillan, 1954.

The best history of Chinese domestic affairs in the nineteenth century is Chien-nung Li, *The Political History of China, 1840-1928,* Van Nostrand, 1956. J. K. Fairbank, **Trade and Diplomacy on the China Coast, The Opening of the Treaty Ports, 1842-1854,** 2 vols., Harvard, 1953, is valuable for its discussion of a crucial period in China's history. Two studies of the Boxer Rebellion are Ch'un-lin T'an, *The Boxer Catastrophe,* Columbia, 1955; and P. Fleming, *The Siege at Peking: The Boxer Rebellion,* Harper, 1959.

Buck, P. S., *Imperial Woman,* Pocketbooks,* 1958. A lengthy, colorful biographical novel of the last empress of China, who rose from concubinage to the throne of the Manchu.

Sansom, Sir George B., **The Western World and Japan; A Study in the Interaction of European and Asiatic Cultures,** Knopf, 1950. A distinguished historian investigates the early contacts between Europe and Asia and then traces the impact of the western world upon Japan from 1600 to 1894. See also I. Nitobé, et al., **Western Influences in Modern Japan,** Univ. of Chicago, 1931.

Recommended for the coverage and interpretation of events in southeast Asia are the following: J. F. Cady, **The Roots of French Imperialism in Eastern Asia,** Cornell, 1954; J. S. Furnivall, **Colonial Policy and Practice: A Comparative Study of Burma and Netherlands India,** Macmillan, 1956; G. C. Allen and A. G. Donnithorne, **Western Enterprise in Indoinesia and Maylaya; A Study in Economic Development,** Macmillan, 1957; G. Irwin, **Nineteenth Century Borneo; A Study in Diplomatic Rivalry,** Nijhoff, The Hague, 1955.

U. S. AND LATIN AMERICA

BRITISH DOMINIONS

1750

Peace of Paris—Canada becomes British possession 1763
Canada's formative period 1763-1867—Quebec Act guarantees French custom and Catholicism in Canada 1774; division into Upper and Lower Canada 1791
Sydney, first English colony in Australia, established 1788

American Revolution 1775-1783

Adoption of the United States Constitution 1789

1800

Louisiana Purchase 1803

War of 1812—United States vs. Britain and Canada 1812-1814

Missouri Compromise establishes boundaries of slave territory in United States 1820
Monroe Doctrine 1823

Andrew Jackson's presidency 1829-1837

New Zealand Company formed 1837; British government assumes protection of New Zealand 1840

Pedro II brings political liberty and economic and cultural progress to Brazil 1840-1889

1850 United States land area doubled by annexation of California, Texas, Oregon, the Southwest 1845-1860

Australian colonies achieve near self-government c. 1850; secret ballot in Australia 1855
Canada achieves "responsible government" c. 1850; provinces of Canada form a federal union under British North America Act, and **Canada becomes a dominion** of Great Britain 1867

Civil war in Mexico; Juárez institutes anticlerical *Reforma* program 1857-1862

Argentina becomes united republic 1861
American Civil War—the Federal Union preserved, slavery abolished 1861-1865
Napoleon III invades Mexico, establishes brief empire under Maximilian 1863-1867
United States occupies Midway Islands 1867
Russia sells Alaska to United States 1867

1870

Porfirio Diaz, dictator, brings order without liberty to Mexico 1877-1880, 1884-1911

Treaty of Washington—Canada and United States arbitrate major differences 1871

First Pan-American Conference 1889
Progressive movement in the United States initiates economic reform through muckraking and legislation c. 1890-1914—trust-busting and national regulation of transportation, foods, drugs under Theodore Roosevelt 1901-1909; Wilson's militant reform campaign, "New Freedom," initiates Federal Reserve Act to reform banking practices 1913, Clayton Anti-Trust Act and Federal Trade Commission 1914
"Dollar diplomacy"—United States exercises indirect controls in Latin America to protect investments 1890-1914

Spanish-American War 1898; United States gains the Philippines, Guam, Puerto Rico, and Cuba
Hawaii annexed to United States 1898

1900 United States emerges as most powerful nation in the Western Hemisphere—United States navy ranks third greatest in world; Open Door Policy is declared 1900; under Theodore Roosevelt (1901-1909), Panama Canal is dug, Big Stick policy is announced as Roosevelt Corollary to Monroe Doctrine

Commonwealth of Australia formed 1901

Madero defeats Diaz, rules Mexico 1911-1913

ASIA

Battle of Plassey begins domination of India by British East India Company and England 1757; Parliament takes control of East India Company 1773, appoints its highest official, the governor general of India 1784

Dutch government takes over East Indies; abolishes East India Company 1798
English acquire Ceylon by Treaty of Amiens 1802

British gain temporary control of East Indies 1810-1816

Lord William Bentinck, governor general of India, initiates reforms, education 1828-1835; trading rights of the company revoked by government, administrative rights retained 1833; dual control lasts until 1858

China wars with England over opium and western exploitation victorious British win Hong Kong and open up Shanghai and Canton by Treaty of Nanking 1839-1842; Treaty of Tientsin follows 1858-1860
United States makes treaty with China to open ports to trade and protect rights of American merchants, sailors 1844
Taiping Rebellion—revolt against the Manchu, quelled with the help of westerners 1850-1864

Japan opens first ports to the West after Perry's visit 1854
English crush **Sepoy Rebellion** 1857, reform administrative system in India 1858
Russia acquires Chinese territory, builds Vladivostok 1860
Manchu empress Tzu Hsi establishes national stability and furthers Chinese hatred of the West 1861-1908

The *Meiji* period—emperor is made supreme authority; Japanese society, politics, and ideas are modernized 1868-1912
Russia pushes south to Afghanistan and India c. 1870-1880

Indian National Congress is formed 1885
French gain control over Indo-China c. 1885
Macao is ceded to Portugal 1887
Prince Ito engineers a new constitution for Japan which combines eastern and western political ideology 1889

Japan defeats China in Sino-Japanese War 1894-1895
Suzerainty of last of Malayan states transferred to Britain 1895-1909

Boxer Rebellion—Chinese attack Europeans and are finally defeated by an international army 1900-1901
Open Door Policy, instigated by John Hay, calls for equal commercial rights in China for all nations 1900
Russo-Japanese War—victorious Japan accepted as first-class power 1904-1905
Anglo-Russian entente—Persia is put under dual control of Britain and Russia 1907

AFRICA

Cape Colony incorporated into British empire 1815

France subdues Berbers in northern Africa, makes Algeria part of the French empire 1830-1847
Boers establish Orange Free State and the Transvaal 1830's

Britain makes treaties with Boers acknowledging their independence 1852, 1854; increased friction between Britons and Boers 1860-1885

Suez Canal completed 1869
Europe's golden age of imperialism 1870-1914: Belgium— Leopold II acquires Congo region 1876-1882; Leopold forced to turn over Congo Free State to Belgian government 1908. **France**—Egypt under joint control of Britain and France 1876; French obtain Tunisia 1881; at turn of century France controls largest empire in Africa; Morocco made a French protectorate 1911. **Britain**—joint control of Egypt by British and French 1876; Lord Cromer achieves "best record of imperialism" for Britain in Egypt 1883-1907; Somaliland is taken 1884; protectorate over Bechuanaland declared 1885; British and Germans settle rival claims in East Africa 1886, 1890; area developed for Britain by Rhodes' British South Africa Company named Rhodesia 1890; area at headwaters of Nile, later called Anglo-Egyptian Sudan, conquered 1898; Gambia, Sierra Leone, Gold Coast, and Nigeria gained through Royal Niger Company 1900. **Germany**—acquires Togoland, the Cameroons, German East Africa, German Southwest Africa 1880's; British and Germans settle dispute over territories in East Africa 1886, 1890. **Italy**—fails in attempted capture of Abyssinia 1896
After the defeat of Dutch in Transvaal and Orange Free State by British in the Boer War (1899-1902), Boers and Britons join states and create the self-governing dominion of the Union of South Africa 1909

Italy wrests Tripoli from the Turks 1912

1750

1800

1850

1870

1900

Frontier

THE REDISCOVERY OF AFRICA by T. Walter Wallbank

Emeritus Professor of History and former Chairman of Freshman General Studies at the University of Southern California, Dr. T. W. Wallbank is the senior author of *Civilization—Past and Present*. As a fellow of the American Social Science Research Council, he engaged in field work in tropical Africa from 1935 to 1937. From 1951 to 1952 he served as Fulbright Professor at Fouad University, Cairo; and more recently (1955-1956) he has been associated with research projects in Africa and India under the auspices of the Rockefeller Foundation. In addition to numerous scholarly articles on colonial problems, Dr. Wallbank's works include *India: A Survey of the Heritage and Growth of Indian Nationalism* (1948); *India in the New Era* (1951); *Contemporary Africa, Continent in Transition* (1956); and *A Short History of India and Pakistan* (1958).

Since 1900 Africa has been undergoing transformation at the most rapid pace in world history. The instrument of this change is the impact of western culture, which is revolutionizing the lives of Africans. Today, the grandson of a primitive and illiterate tribesman may be a graduate of a European or American university. With the continual absorption of western political ideas and education came a new national pride, a demand for self-government, and a demand for higher standards of living. Various and increasingly severe conflicts arose—not only between the African nationalists and their colonial rulers but also between the exponents of the old and the new among the Africans themselves, as westernized leaders sought to usurp the authority of tribal chieftains.

While these problems and tensions rack Africa, a relatively new field of scholarship, that of African studies, has gained prominence. The West is no longer concerned with how to rule the African but rather how to help him meet the problems of independence, how best to appreciate his aspirations, and how to understand the many strains in his rapidly changing pattern of culture.

An incident revealing the need for greater understanding of African culture occurred as far back as 1901. The British in 1896 had taken over the protection of the kingdom of Ashanti in the Gold Coast. All African chiefs in this area possessed thrones, or stools, the greatest of these being the Golden Stool. Guarded with great reverence, it was carried in a solemn annual procession, but British colonial officials did not realize the extent to which the Golden Stool symbolized the Ashanti nation and the soul of its people. In 1901, in order to secure the complete submission of the Ashanti, the British governor of the Gold Coast demanded to be allowed to sit upon this throne. His demand resulted in a serious uprising, with bitter fighting and severe losses on both sides. Although British arms prevailed, the Ashanti people kept their throne hidden.

In 1921 a group of road builders accidentally came upon the hiding place of the Golden Stool, stripped the throne of its golden ornaments, and sold them. This sacrilege shocked the Ashanti tribe. By this time much had been learned of the Ashanti culture through the studies of an anthropologist, Captain Robert Rattray, who had established an anthropology department for the Gold Coast government. Realizing the importance of the throne to the Ashanti, the government arrested the thieves and turned them over to the tribal authorities for trial. Thus, through the work of a social scientist, the British officials were able to atone for the blunder of 1901 and strengthen the loyalty of the people.

Since World War I, especially, the need for research into all phases of African history and culture has greatly increased. During the conflict, the Allied nations had widely proclaimed the idealistic concept of self-determination for all peoples, and their colonial wards were stimulated by the noble wartime promises. Although actual self-rule remained a distant goal, the mandate system set up by the League of Nations after the war recognized the responsibility of the imperial powers to safeguard and develop the well-being of the colonial peoples. In Africa the world trend toward more responsible imperialistic rule was implemented on the basis of practical administrative experience; the basic proposals were set forth in Lord Lugard's famous study *The Dual Mandate in British Tropical Africa*, published in 1922.

Lugard believed that the task of promoting African progress could be realized best by the kind of administrative policy which had been proved effective by other administrators and which he had successfully utilized as governor of Nigeria—the policy of indirect rule. In contrast to direct rule, which generally ignored African tribal institutions and attempted to impose European rule and culture upon the natives, Lugard's system of indirect rule retained the native institutions under the supervision and ultimate authority of British officials. By helping the Africans adapt their culture to meet the demands of modern society, Lugard hoped to prepare his wards for self-government and assist them to bridge the gap between primitivism and modern society.

Although other administrations before Lugard had governed Africans through native chiefs, it was Lugard who perfected this type of administration, with a carefully constructed machinery of native chiefs, treasuries, and tribunals and an array of British supervisors and advisers in the background. Furthermore, it was Lugard who translated his successful system into a body of principles and made the term "indirect rule" universally recognized. In the 1920's the system of indirect rule spread to many colonies in British Africa, becoming the basis of British colonial administration.

The acceptance of Lugard's formula was partly due to current developments in social science. Anthropologists were opening the eyes of civilized men to the essential validity of primitive cultures. The so-called backward, or even savage, groups were found to be amazingly efficient in meeting the challenges of their environment. Anthropologists interested in African studies revealed "Africans as no passive sufferers of our influence . . . but as showing considerable initiative in taking what they want from us and keeping what they want of their own."[1] The importance accorded to traditional African institutions helped to provide a favorable climate for administration by indirect rule, while in turn the administrators' support of tribal institutions increased the value of African studies. During the 1920's and 1930's the tribal and anthropological school of African administration and studies enjoyed great prominence.

By the late 1930's, however, many social scientists and colonial officials were expressing doubt concerning the future of indirect rule. The retention of the old chiefs often meant inefficiency and sometimes autocracy in African government. The chiefs were too prone to hold fast to the old rather than to heed the injunction of their British masters to prepare for the new. It was also charged that tribalism had become a fetish above and beyond criticism, regardless of the changing times. It had "become a magic formula, almost a catchword, in British political circles where its mere mention stultifies reference to any other form of colonial administration. . . . Despite the admirable features of indirect rule and its noteworthy successes there is a danger of its becoming a form of colonial doctrinairism."[2]

The most serious criticism was that the policy of tribalism provided no place for the increasing class of western-educated Africans. The old aristocracy ruled by virtue of birth, and educated Africans scornfully referred to indirect rule as "government of illiterates, by illiterates, for illiterates." In their concern for traditional institutions, administrators and scholars did not pay sufficient attention to the grievances of African intellectuals. In addition, advocates of the anthropological and tribalistic school did not fully appreciate the extent to which socio-economic change was undermining the Africans' allegiance to their traditional values. As Africans became wage earners and absorbed western ideas, they drew away from their communal tribal life and tended to follow westernized intellectual leaders rather than their old tribal chiefs.

Pre-1939 criticisms and qualms about indirect rule were confirmed by the rapid eclipse of the system after the Second World War. Sub-Saharan Africa was convulsed by an amazingly dynamic independence movement led mainly by a western-educated elite. Such leaders as Nkrumah in the Gold Coast (now Ghana), Azikiwe in Nigeria, Nyerere in Tanganyika, and Dr. Banda in Nyasaland saw no justification for retaining the old tribal forms and authorities. Believing that there should be a clean break with the past, these leaders sought to establish modern political systems based on adult suffrage, political parties, and nontraditional civil service.

This African nationalist movement rapidly transformed the political map of Africa. In 1945 only four states were independent but in 1964 the number reached thirty-four. The surging tide of African nationalism created serious racial tensions in the so-called plural societies of central and southern Africa. In Southern Rhodesia and in the Republic of South Africa domination by the white minority was increasingly challenged by the submerged Bantu majority.

As sub-Saharan Africa shakes off the cloak of colonialism for the new dress of independence, scholars in African studies adhere to no single formula, as in the tribalistic school of the 1920's and 1930's. While recognizing some of the virtues of indirect rule and also its failures in meeting the needs of the times, they point out that African nationalism could not be denied, regardless of what colonial policy had been followed.

Today, historians and political scientists are especially interested in following the evolution of governments in the newly independent African nations. Three possible alternatives are seen. There are some indications of a return to the traditional tribal system, although this possibility is regarded as somewhat remote. The prevailing tendency is toward a British parliamentary pattern, consisting of a legislature, a responsible executive, an independent judiciary, and a two-party system, with emphasis on the basic political rights of the individual. But while parliamentary government is the initial goal of most African nationalist movements, social scientists point to disturbing evidence that parliamentary institutions serve increasingly to hide one-party, authoritarian regimes.

The trends in Ghana and Guinea suggest that the new African nations may follow the road to strong-man rule taken by the Sudan and Egypt. Although they used democratic ideology to justify freedom from the yoke of colonialism, African leaders such as Ghana's Nkrumah and Guinea's Touré quickly resorted to one-party rule. One reason for this trend may be impatience—the belief that only an authoritarian regime can quickly alleviate the disease, poverty, and illiteracy so fatal to progress in underdeveloped countries. Another reason is the natural inclination of the new leaders to use the popularity and adulation earned in the successful fight for independence as a means of continuing a regime of undisputed power.

Other problems of contemporary Africa also demand attention and study. Social scientists are interested in race relations in plural societies such as Kenya and South Africa, the development of African political parties, and the functioning of new civil services in various governments. The future of the national states in Africa raises many questions. Will some of the nations suffer fragmentation because of the revival of tribalism? Or will boundaries be altered by the consolidation of once separate colonial units, as in the union of Italian and British Somaliland to form the Republic of Somalia in July 1960? The economist is finding inviting areas of research in the problems of land tenure, industrialization, and the marketing of farm products. The sociologist is almost overwhelmed by the problems stemming from acculturation and social change—migratory labor, urbanization, family stability, detribalization, and population statistics.

In the field of history, scholars are endeavoring to fill in the gaps in the European period of African history, going back in some instances four hundred years, and are investigating the long and little-known era before the coming of the white man. In 1953 and 1957 international conferences on African history were held in London primarily for the purpose of establishing some chronological framework for the period from the Stone Age down to the present. The newly independent African states are eager also to reconstruct the outlines of the African past. Ghana has founded a national museum and is sponsoring research in Ghanian history.

Today, when there is no doubt that Africa is destined to play a decisive role in world affairs, it is more than ever the responsibility of scholars to follow basic trends and supply reliable data. This fact is recognized by the Soviet Union, which is paying increasing attention to African studies, and in recent years such studies have made notable progress in the United States. It is now understood that American national interests—strategic, economic, and political—will be affected by events taking place in Africa. American influence should be used to help the African nations achieve economic well-being for their peoples and political stability under regimes based upon western concepts of freedom. But we can exert our influence to this end only if we acquire comprehensive and accurate knowledge in the area of African studies. Thus this field of research presents a vital and promising frontier for American scholars.

1 Margery Perham, "Some Problems of Indirect Rule in Africa," reprint from the *Journal of the Royal Society of Arts* (London, May 18, 1934), p. 13.

2 T. Walter Wallbank, "American Reflections on Kenya," supplement to the *Journal of the Royal African Society* (London, April 1938), p. 5.

SUGGESTED READINGS

For a discussion of the impact of nationalism on tribalism written by a British official formerly prominent in East African administration, see Sir Andrew Cohen, *British Policy in Changing Africa* (Northwestern Univ. Press, 1959). Representative research monographs on Africa by American scholars are: Gwendolen Carter, *The Politics of Inequality* (Praeger, 1958); James S. Coleman, *Nigeria: Background to Nationalism* (Univ. of California Press, 1958). Current African trends and problems are described in Walter Goldschmidt, *The United States and Africa* (Praeger,* rev. ed., 1963).

PART 4 Realism and Realpolitik

CHAPTER 11 "SURVIVAL OF THE FITTEST"

CHAPTER 12 PARLIAMENTS AND POLITICAL REFORMS

CHAPTER 13 PROMISE AND PERIL

In Europe much of the period from 1871 to 1914 was taken up with the continuance of tasks begun in the preceding fifty years. Nation-making, the establishment of parliamentary regimes, the building of science and industry, and the amassing of wealth were among the major concerns.

The political trend in the more progressive states was from middle-class liberalism toward mass democracy. In Britain, reforms enacted during the ministries of Disraeli and Gladstone brought about an enlightened, peaceful, political evolution. After ridding themselves of their "Emperor Boss," Napoleon III, and adjusting to the debacle of military defeat by Germany, the French succeeded in establishing a democratic government. For the Third Republic, however, the advance to stable democracy was disrupted by economic and political crises, social unrest, and such shocking scandals as the Dreyfus affair.

In some smaller European states like Denmark and Switzerland, the democratic movement fared well, but elsewhere on the Continent monarchies dug in their heels to resist the current. Russia remained a creaking despotism; while in Germany, an absolutist government functioned efficiently behind a parliamentary façade.

Economically, Europe advanced in leaps and bounds. The Second Industrial Revolution brought increased technological skills, mass production, and alliance between science and industry in the first organized research projects. Vast quantities of raw materials, obtained cheaply from the European colonial systems, increased profits, as did the large amounts of finished goods sold back to the colonies. Thriving industries led to the rise of booming cities and brought wealth and luxury to thousands of middle-class employers and investors in western Europe and the United States.

It was not only the middle class which prospered, however. A new world was opening up for the workingman as well: enactment of social legislation raised his living standards; the advance of unions gave him more effective bargaining power; and the progress of free schooling broadened his prospects. The socialist movement turned from an early obsession with revolution to a program of gradual change pointing toward the welfare state. The class revolution of the proletariat, envisioned by Marx, had not materialized.

Almost as amazing as the sweeping changes in government and society was the growing preëminence of science. In the nineteenth century, there seemed to be no limit to the benefits which scientific knowledge could bring to mankind—the germ theories of Pasteur and Lister and the discovery of x-rays and radium gave new hope of controlling disease; and the technological innovations of the time created an increasing number of new industries, new products, and new wealth. Scientists were even able to throw light on some of the mysteries of all time: the development of man from lower beings was explained by Darwin, and Freud initiated the study and analysis of man's mind and emotions.

Thus the period from 1871 to 1914 appeared to be one of the most promising in all history. In power, wealth, and the creativity of its scientists, artists, and men of letters, Europe was the center of the world. Yet the Continent was soon to be devastated by the First World War. How did such a disaster spring from so hopeful an age?

The explanation lies partly in those very forces which made these years prosperous. A second look at science shows that while it helped make nineteenth- and twentieth-century civilization what it was, it served at the same time to liberate forces that threatened that civilization's most firmly entrenched verities. Belief in the truth and triumph of science encouraged an attitude which turned scientific Darwinism into social Darwinism. The emphasis on the "fittest" encouraged racism and militant nationalism. War was glorified as the contest which proved who was "fit" and who was not. Freud's theories, while offering hope for the eventual understanding and successful treatment of mental illnesses, tended as well to lead to a diminished faith in man as a rational being, capable of controlling his own destiny. This may have been one reason why the concept of an all-powerful state began to hold great attraction for millions.

Whatever the reasons for the holocaust which terminated this brilliant period—and they are too numerous and complex to be understood completely—they are to be found in this age of rapid development and astonishing change. It was indeed a period of "promise and peril." But the powerful winds of quarrelsome and narrow nationalism, militarism, and deadly alliances proved too strong for the tender roots of internationalism and antiwar sentiment. The promising prospects of the late nineteenth century were destroyed by the triumph of its peril.

CHAPTER 11

"Survival of the Fittest"

SCIENCE AND THOUGHT, LITERATURE
AND THE FINE ARTS: 1850-1914

Introduction. Buoyed by the belief that "God's in his heaven—All's right with the world,"[1] the Victorians faced the second half of the nineteenth century with optimism. After about 1850, however, marked changes took place in the intellectual and social environment. The members of the prospering middle class still had little reason to doubt that theirs was the best of all possible worlds—but was God in His heaven? Between the latest findings of science and the traditional religious faith on which their beliefs and moral values rested, a great conflict had arisen. The mid-Victorians had been brought up to believe that the creation of the world and the life thereon had been an act of God and that nature revealed the workings of His moral law. But when Darwin in 1859 put forward his famous thesis that all organic life was engaged in a struggle for existence and that the survival or extinction of all species depended on their adaptability, nature was seen as simply a blind life-and-death struggle, stripped of all morality. This harsh and uncompromising doctrine set off a bitter debate between the advocates of science and those of religion.

However abhorrent to traditional religious beliefs, the doctrine of the survival of the fittest was in fact thoroughly compatible with political and economic activities after the revolutions of 1848. European powers amassed armies and fleets and entered into alliances in which right was altogether subservient to might; in Asia and Africa they annexed vast tracts of land at the expense of "lesser breeds without the law." Businessmen of one nation sought to capture foreign markets at the expense of rivals from other nations, while within the industrialized countries tension between employers and workers was evident. In this chapter we shall examine the manifold ways in which science, philosophy, and the arts contributed to or reflected the increasingly realistic attitudes to be found throughout western Europe and the United States.

The period from 1850 to 1914 was one of unprecedented scientific discoveries, resulting in the magnificent contributions of such men as Clerk-Maxwell, Einstein, and Freud. Put to practical use, the new advances in knowledge helped to eradicate disease, improve industrial methods, raise living standards, and revolutionize the techniques of the social sciences. On the other hand, there developed a cult of science whose practitioners were too often guilty of intellectual arrogance and of a dangerous oversimplification of human affairs. With such people it became all too easy to think of progress purely in materialistic terms and to argue that physical well-being was all that mattered.

In literature, painting, and sculpture, reaction to the impact of scientific and technological achievements took the form of realism, later extended into an unblushing, facts-of-life school known as naturalism. While this realistic approach characterized the works of many writers and artists throughout the period—and indeed is evident in our own day as well—still other significant movements evolved. An increasing number of writers protested against the injustices suffered by individuals in a society where cutthroat competition was defended and human exploitation excused as immutable elements in the struggle to survive. Other artists, reacting against the baldly mechanistic view of man as a mere automaton whose every move was predictable, devised new movements in the arts—expressionism and symbolism—each with special techniques for representing the subjective feelings of the individual.

The period from 1850 to 1914 was the heyday of the middle class, which had risen to dominance on the twin forces of economic and political liberalism and could now enjoy the goods that their machines turned out in an ever swelling stream. This was a period marked by such advances as the spread of universal education and the progressive emancipation of women. We shall also see why it has been described both as a "generation of materialism" and as a "Gilded Age."

DARWIN, EINSTEIN, AND FREUD

The theory of evolution. The nineteenth century witnessed the spread of a doctrine which was to have powerful repercussions on science, philosophy, and religion. This was the theory of evolution—namely, that all living organisms have developed through the operation of natural causes from simple to more complex forms and that no species is fixed and changeless. In ancient Greece and Rome some philosophers had envisaged such a hypothesis; Heraclitus had stressed that growth and change lie at the core of the universal process, while Lucretius had conceived of a universe that was atomic in structure and had evolved through a process of natural selection.

By the end of the eighteenth century, certain scientists had concluded that various species may have had a common origin and that environment had an effect upon the differentiation of species. In the nineteenth century, evidence kept accumulating to indicate that organic and inorganic matter alike had evolved according to natural causes. For example, in 1785 James Hutton had ascribed the earth's development to natural rather than supernatural causes. Subsequent data derived from extensive geological observations in both Britain and North America prompted Sir Charles Lyell to write his *Principles of Geology* (1830-1833), a work which is considered the basis of modern geology. In this work Lyell showed that the earth had achieved its present formation through such agencies as earthquakes, volcanoes, erosion, and the continuous rising and sinking of land surfaces over a vast period of time. Such a thesis came into direct conflict with the prevailing religious beliefs concerning the origin and age of the earth.

The conception of geologic time, however, was an essential prerequisite for any theory of biological evolution based on changes in species over many hundreds of thousands of generations.

In the first decade of the nineteenth century, a French nobleman, Jean Baptiste Lamarck (1744-1829), argued that every organism tends to develop new organs in order to adapt itself to the changing conditions of its environment. The changes which take place in an organism are transmitted by heredity to the descendants, which are thereby changed in structural form. In supporting his doctrine of the inheritance of acquired characteristics, Lamarck claimed that the giraffe had to develop a long neck to reach the high leaves and branches on the trees on which it fed. The slight gain in length of the neck made by each generation was handed on to the next.

Darwin and The Origin of Species. The scientist chiefly responsible for furthering the evolutionary hypothesis was Charles Darwin (1809-1882). After studying medicine and preparing at Cambridge University for the ministry, Darwin became a naturalist. Between 1831 and 1836 he studied the specimens he had collected while on a surveying expedition of the ship *Beagle*, which had sailed along the coast of South America and among the South Sea Islands. After his return to England, Darwin served as secretary of the Geological Society, in close association with Charles Lyell. He was deeply impressed by Lyell's *Principles of Geology* and also by Thomas Robert Malthus' *Essay on Population* (see p. 169). The latter suggested to Darwin that the struggle of men for existence in a world in which the population increases faster than the food supply was a problem that could be extended to all nature. In 1859 Darwin's views appeared under the title *On the Origin of Species by Means of Natural Selection, or the Preservation of Favored Races in the Struggle for Life.* In this work he·contended:

. . . that species have been modified, during a long course of descent . . . chiefly through the natural selection of numerous successive, slight, favourable variations; aided in an important

A nineteenth-century issue of the French magazine L'Illustration pictures Louis Pasteur in his laboratory.

manner . . . by the direct action of external conditions, and by variations which seem to us in our ignorance to arise spontaneously.[2]

In 1858 another English naturalist, Alfred R. Wallace (1823-1913), began to think about Malthus' *Essay on Population* while ill with fever in the Moluccas. By a remarkable coincidence, he arrived at a theory of the survival of the fittest which was being developed by Darwin. Working out his views in essay form, Wallace sent them to Darwin, the outstanding naturalist in England. After reading Wallace's views, Darwin wrote to Lyell:

I never saw a more striking coincidence; if Wallace had my ms. sketch written out in 1842, he could not have made a better short abstract! Even his terms now stand as heads of my chapters.[3]

Darwin and Descent of Man. *The Origin of Species* was to prove one of the most significant books in scientific literature, revolutionizing concepts about the origin and evolution of life on this planet. Darwin's next important contribution was *Descent of Man and Selection in Relation to Sex,* published in 1871. In this work Darwin elaborated upon some of the views expressed in his earlier work and went on to apply the law of natural selection to human beings by drawing his explosively controversial conclusion that man's ancestors were probably monkey-like animals related to the progenitors of the orang-utan, chimpanzee, and gorilla. Darwin realized that such a conclusion would prove "highly distasteful to many." Nevertheless, despite man's:

. . . sympathy which feels for the most debased . . . [and] his god-like intellect which has penetrated into the movements and constitution of the solar system—with all these exalted powers—Man still bears in his bodily frame the indelible stamp of his lowly origin.[4]

There are five main points in the Darwinian hypothesis. First, all existing vegetable and animal species are descended from earlier and, generally speaking, more rudimentary forms. Second, the variation in species has come about because the environment and the use or disuse of organs have brought about changes in structure that are inherited. (Here we see the influence of Lamarck's theory on the inheritance of acquired characteristics—see p. 325.) Third, in the struggle for survival, the fittest win out at the expense of their rivals because they succeed in adapting themselves best to their environment. (In this struggle for the survival of the fittest we see the influence of Malthus' proposition, described on p. 169, that the human population increases faster than the food supply—a concept which Darwin extended to all of nature.) Fourth, differentiation among the species is also brought about by sexual selection, which Darwin declared is "the most powerful means of changing the races of man." Finally, some variations seem to arise spontaneously, a view of Darwin's which pointed toward the doctrine of mutation.

Biology after Darwin. By the close of the nineteenth century, scientists were in virtual agreement regarding the general validity of Darwin's hypothesis, though, as we shall see, it was later modified in certain important respects. Meanwhile, largely as a result of Darwin's unifying principle of evolution, bi-

ology was progressively transformed from a descriptive science into a search for relationships between living organisms.

One of the most significant developments in biology concerned the question of heredity. In the 1870's the German biologist August Weismann (1834-1914), making use of an earlier theory that all living things originate and develop in very small structural units, or cells, distinguished two types of cells. One type—the somatic cell—dies with the individual, while the other—the germ cell—transmits through reproduction a continuous stream of protoplasm from one generation to the next. Later, Weismann reasoned that only germ cells transmit hereditary characteristics and that since acquired characteristics occur only in the somatic cells, these cannot be inherited.

An Austrian monk, Gregor Mendel (1822-1884), formulated definite laws of heredity on the basis of experiments with the crossing of garden peas. Because he published his important findings in an obscure scientific journal, his work was overlooked until about 1900. Mendel's laws not only proved a valuable help in the scientific breeding of plants and animals but also made the problem of the evolution of different species more complex than had been deduced by Darwin.

From the work of Mendel and Weismann, biologists began to conclude that the nuclei of the germ cells possess chromosomes which carry the characteristics of an organism. Further research substantiated the mutation theory, which states that sudden and unpredictable variations in heredity produce new species. But most geneticists came to reject the theory of the inheritance of acquired characteristics, advocated by Lamarck and accepted by Darwin. Weismann in 1880 gravely cut off the tails of mice for twenty successive generations; but in the last litter—just as he expected—the tails of the mice were no shorter than those of their ancestors.

Meanwhile, a cousin of Darwin, Sir Francis Galton (1822-1911), carried the study of heredity into still more new areas. Struck by the similarity of characteristics among members of one family, Galton reached the conclusion that mental as well as physical characteristics must be inherited. He invented mental testing and pioneered in the new science of eugenics—the improvement of the human race through having only the fit breed. He advocated that society prevent the insane, the feeble-minded, and the habitual criminal from having offspring. Charged with holding a "disgustingly material view of love and marriage," Galton retorted:

. . . eugenics should form one of the many considerations by which marriages are promoted or hindered, as they are by social position, adequate fortune, and similarity of creed.[5]

An avalanche of inventions. While Darwin stirred up a hornet's nest of controversy over his contention that man's ancestors were probably monkey-like animals, inventors were rapidly adapting new tools for the improvement of man's environment. Technological progress, which had already started to snowball in the first half of the nineteenth century, increased in momentum until in the second half a veritable avalanche of new industrial inventions and processes occurred. The first electric dynamo had been invented by Michael Faraday in 1831; forty-five years later the German inventor Ernst Werner von Siemens (1816-1892) devised a working dynamo that could produce electricity in any required amount. No longer did an industry have to rely for power on its own steam engine; instead, cables could bring factories and mills the electricity generated by dynamos at centrally located power plants. As a result of the perfected compound steam turbine of 1885, the use of electric power was stepped up. Turbines were quickly adapted to propel new ocean liners. The western world was entering an age of electricity, which now provided power for turning lathes in factories, for reducing metals, for welding, for illuminating homes and city streets, and for powering the streetcars hitherto drawn by horses.

Electricity also revolutionized communications. Samuel Morse had invented the electric telegraph as early as 1844, and in 1872 Thomas Edison (1847-1931) developed a duplex telegraph that sent two messages over

Henry Ford (1863-1947) developed the assembly-line mass production of automobiles and put the United States on wheels.

the same wire simultaneously. Four years later Alexander Graham Bell (1847-1922) invented the first telephone, which was greeted with mixed reactions. A journal of the period commented that:

The dignity of talking consists in having a listener and there seems a kind of absurdity in addressing a piece of iron.[6]

But by 1900 nearly 800,000 phones were being used in the United States. A still more spectacular invention was wireless telegraphy, the work of Guglielmo Marconi (1874-1937) in 1895. Three years later, wireless messages were being transmitted across the English Channel, and within six years, across the Atlantic. The new form of communication was quickly seized upon for both civilian and military purposes.

No less a revolution was taking place in transportation. In the 1880's a German, Gottlieb Daimler (1834-1900), constructed a successful internal-combustion engine using gasoline as fuel and applied it to a bicycle and a carriage. From these crude beginnings

Owners of a bicycle shop, Orville and Wilbur Wright built and tested the first successful, full-sized, power-driven airplane. Interested at first in gliding as a sport, the brothers became fascinated with the technical aspects of flight and experimented with model wings in a wind tunnel set up in their shop. The first flight, made by Orville (lying in plane), was witnessed by only five people besides the brothers. Newspapers generally ignored the event, and for several years the United States government refused to take the invention seriously.

came the motorcycle and the automobile. In the field of automobile manufacture the United States took an early lead; Henry Ford (1863-1947) began large-scale production of his Model T in 1909. To jeering onlookers it seemed incredible that these backfiring, exhaust-belching, puncture-prone monstrosities would ever drive Dobbin off the road. Yet by 1914 some two million motor cars were registered in the United States, and Detroit's assembly lines—a major technological development of the era—were steadily stepping up output. Another form of the internal-combustion engine was designed to burn crude oil, a much cheaper fuel than gasoline. This engine was the work of a German engineer, Rudolf Diesel (1858-1913), who took out his patent in 1892. A successful competitor to the steam engine and the electric motor, the Diesel engine was used especially for driving locomotives, electric generators, and marine pumps.

This was also the period when man acquired wings. For a century audacious souls had been ascending over Paris and other cities in balloons, while men experimenting with gliders had laid the foundation for the science of aerodynamics. In the 1890's, at-tempts were made to construct a new type of heavier-than-air craft with propellers powered by internal-combustion engines. The climax came at Kitty Hawk, North Carolina, on December 17, 1903, when Orville and Wilbur Wright succeeded in keeping their fragile biplane aloft for twelve seconds.

Meanwhile, other inventions were adding to the amenities and amusements of society. In 1888 George Eastman (1854-1932) devised a roll film and the Kodak camera to use it. The invention in 1886 of the linotype machine (which did away with typesetting by hand) and the manufacture of cheap wood-pulp paper made possible the production of urban newspapers on a mass scale. Entertainment in the home was enlivened by Edison's invention in 1876 of the phonograph, which first played back to him "Mary had a little lamb." This same "Wizard of Menlo Park" (New Jersey) is also credited with the invention of the motion picture. First exhibited publicly in 1896, the movies had arrived as a mass-entertainment medium by World War I.

The germ theory—Pasteur and Koch. During the second half of the nineteenth century mankind took great strides in medicine as well. Probably the most important single advance in the medical field during this period was the substantiation of the germ theory of disease. In April 1864, standing before a fashionable audience at the Sorbonne, Louis Pasteur (1822-1895) demonstrated "how the dusts which are suspended in air contain germs of inferior organized beings and how a liquid preserved, by certain precautions, from the contact of these germs can be kept indefinitely. . . ."[7] Pasteur had discovered the basis of the germ theory and the role of microscopic organisms in the processes of fermentation and putrefaction.

The validation of the germ theory of disease by Pasteur and his younger disciple, the German bacteriologist Robert Koch (1843-1910), resulted from a search for a cure for anthrax, a fatal disease which in the late 1870's was destroying over 20 per cent of the sheep in France. Pasteur and Koch discovered that anthrax bacteria could be grown in a culture of meat-broth jelly and that the injection of the bacteria into a healthy animal produced anthrax. Earlier, Pasteur had found a preventive for chicken cholera by vaccinating hens with an old culture of cholera microbes. Applying the same procedure, in 1881 Pasteur inoculated twenty-five sheep with weakened anthrax bacteria and left the same number unvaccinated. Later, all fifty were given a virulent form of the disease; the unvaccinated animals died while the treated sheep remained sound.

That the results of this experiment pointed to the use of inoculation for still other maladies was clear to Pasteur. With the establishment of the principle that the injection of a mild form of disease bacteria will cause the formation of antibodies which will prevent the inoculated person from getting the virulent form of the disease, the end of such scourges as typhoid and smallpox was in sight.

For several years Pasteur sought a means of curing the dreaded disease of rabies. In 1885 he showed that by the injection of a vaccine an animal could be made resistant to rabies *after* having been bitten by a mad dog. Later that year, to use his own words:

I dared to treat a poor little nine-year-old lad whose mother brought him to me from Alsace, where he had been attacked and bitten on the thighs, legs, and hands in such a manner that hydrophobia would have been inevitable. He remains in perfect health.[8]

This incident was followed in 1886 by Pasteur's successful treatment of a number of Russian peasants who had been attacked by a rabid wolf. In recognition of this medical achievement, Grand Duke Vladimir of Russia presented 100,000 francs to the newly established Pasteur Institute, which treated victims of attacks by rabid animals. The work of Pasteur and Koch had established on a firm footing the twin sciences of bacteriology and immunology.

Numerous other advances before 1914 made the western world a much healthier place in which to live. The brilliant Koch discovered the organisms that caused eleven diseases, including tuberculosis and cholera. This last disease, together with typhoid and the plague, began to disappear from Europe and the United States; and malaria, yellow fever, and diphtheria were at last being brought under control. Still another step of great value was the introduction into surgery of asepsis—that is, methods for preventing the entry of bacteria into a wound. In the 1860's a Quaker surgeon at the University of Edinburgh, Joseph Lister (1827-1912), made use of surgical techniques so revolutionary at the time that he was long a prophet without honor in Britain, though his methods were followed in Germany with great success. In Lister's wards, a fresh linen apron for each operation was substituted for the filthy surgeon's coat worn again and again, while "the instruments, sponges and other articles used for dressings were first of all purified in a strong solution of carbolic acid. The same precautions were taken for the hands of the surgeon and of his assistants. During the whole course of each operation, a vaporizer of carbolic solution created around the wound an antiseptic atmosphere; after it was over, the wound was again washed with the carbolic solution. Special articles were used for dressing: "A sort of gauze . . . impregnated with a mixture of resin, paraffin, and carbolic. . . ."[9]

Lister had made use of both asepsis and antisepsis, the latter being the method of disinfecting wounds so as to destroy dangerous bacteria. Both techniques spring from a knowledge of the germ theory of putrefaction, developed by Lister's brilliant friend, the French scientist Pasteur. The connection between unsanitary handling of surgery cases and the high incidence of puerperal fever in maternity wards in hospitals had been noted earlier by the Hungarian physician Ignaz Semmelweiss (1818-1865). By more careful cleansing precautions he had cut the maternal mortality in his own hospital to a level far below that generally prevailing. However, Ignaz Semmelweiss himself died of septicemia (blood poisoning) just at the time Louis Pasteur's germ theory and Joseph Lister's general study of infections were developed.

The use of anesthetics—coupled with the principles of cleanliness laid down by Lister —made possible the performance of surgical operations which had hitherto never been attempted. In the 1840's the value of ether and chloroform in alleviating pain during operations had been discovered. With anesthesia and asepsis abdominal surgery lost most of its former terrors, and similar progress was made in surgery on the eye, ear, and brain.

Chemistry and related fields. Chemistry was put on a new footing with the formulation of the atomic theory by an English Quaker schoolmaster, John Dalton (1766-1844). This pioneer believed that all matter is made up of invisible particles, or atoms, which remain unchanged upon entering or leaving any state of chemical combination. Moreover, different kinds of atoms, depending upon their relative weight, make up the basic substances or elements which are to be found in the world of matter.

It now became possible to arrange chemical elements in order according to their atomic weights, beginning with the lightest, hydrogen. It was seen that the elements fell into groups of eight which possess similar properties. In 1869 the Russian chemist Dmitri Mendelyeev (1834-1907) drew up his periodic table, in which all the known elements were classified according to their weights and properties. From gaps in this table, chemists were able to deduce the existence of still other undiscovered elements.

In the latter part of the century, considerable research was conducted on proteins and on nutritional problems. For a long time the value of fresh fruits and vegetables in treating scurvy had been demonstrated, but the reason was unknown. Now investigations showed that this and other diseases were caused by nutritional deficiencies. The true significance of vitamins was first disclosed in 1912, and the way was paved for isolating and synthesizing nearly all known vitamins in the laboratory.

Biochemical research in this period also threw light on the presence and purpose of the ductless glands. Research showed that the glands poured their secretions, called hormones, directly into the blood stream and that some of these hormones were essential for survival. This discovery led to the search for various kinds of hormones, such as the secretion from the pancreas, which controls the onslaught of diabetes.

Meanwhile, a German biochemist, Paul Ehrlich (1854-1915), had been experimenting with drugs that could destroy bacteria and other organisms without harming the individual who harbored them. After more than six hundred unsuccessful attempts, Ehrlich in 1909 produced an organic arsenic compound, "606," later named "salvarsan," which, without being too toxic to the individual, destroyed syphilis bacteria in the body. Following this major triumph for chemotherapy, practitioners were later in our century to score a spectacular breakthrough in the never-ending struggle against disease by their development of sulfa drugs, penicillin, and other antibiotics.

One of the most impressive advances in the field of chemistry was the making of chemical synthetics. A French scientist demonstrated how artificial silk could be made from cellulose, while chemists in Germany and elsewhere turned out synthetic dyes from coal-tar residues. In 1913 a process by which nitrogen could be obtained from the atmosphere was perfected. This process proved vital to the Germans during World War I; it enabled their munitions program to survive despite an Allied blockade that cut off the importation of nitrates from Chile.

Revolution in physics. New theories in biology about the nature of man as a species, new and ever more breathtaking achievements in technology, new knowledge in chemistry and medicine to help protect human life were not the end of the nineteenth century's contributions to society. Remarkable progress in physics led to questioning the very nature of the universe which, since the time of Newton, had seemed the perfect model of rational stability.

Some of the outstanding inventions which

we have mentioned resulted from equally spectacular discoveries in the sphere of pure scientific research. Especially important was the work done in thermodynamics and electrical phenomena. Thermodynamics, that branch of research that deals with the relations between heat and motive power, was of particular importance because of industry's dependence upon the steam engine.

Scientists had believed previously that heat was a mysterious fluid called "calorie," but research showed that friction generated heat in proportion to the amount of work expended. After physicists had found out how much mechanical energy was required to raise the heat of any given body, it became possible, in 1847, to formulate the first law of thermodynamics. This law states that the sum total of energy in the universe is constant and cannot be either created or destroyed—it can only be transformed from one form into another. Meanwhile, scientists engaged in the converse problem of transforming heat into energy found that heat can, in fact, never be completely converted into energy. From their experiments was formulated the second law of thermodynamics: Although the total amount of energy in the universe remains constant, the amount actually available is always diminishing through its transformation into nonavailable, or dissipated, heat.

While Benjamin Franklin and others had aided the study of electrical phenomena in the eighteenth century, it remained for later scientists to prepare the way for the use of electricity as a source of power. In 1819 it was found that an electric current would deflect a magnetic current placed near it, and soon afterwards the mathematics of this phenomenon was worked out, thereby laying the foundations for a unified scheme of electromagnetism.

During the earlier part of the nineteenth century, the most prominent figure in the field of electrodynamics was Michael Faraday (1791-1867), a blacksmith's son who by his brilliance became first the secretary and later the scientific successor of Sir Humphry Davy (see p. 157). In 1831, after ten years

Michael Faraday, an English inventor, demonstrated early in the nineteenth century the existence of electro-magnetic induction. He thereby laid the foundations for three areas of electrical science: electro-chemistry, electro-magnetic induction, and electro-magnetic waves.

of experiment, Faraday produced an electric current by rotating a copper disk between the two poles of a horseshoe magnet, thereby inventing the first electric dynamo. This simple dynamo made possible the development of the electric motor, the transmission of large currents over long distances, and (later in the century) the invention of the electric telegraph, the telephone, and electric lights.

Research was carried still further by the Scottish scientist James Clerk-Maxwell (1831-1879), who formulated exact mathematical equations to explain Faraday's discoveries in the principles of electromagnetic induction. In his famous work *A Treatise on Electricity and Magnetism* (1873), Clerk-Maxwell put forward the ingenious theory that "electricity is matter moving in waves like those of light and radiant heat," thereby linking optics and electricity; and he maintained that light, radiant heat, and invisible ultraviolet radiation are all electromagnetic phenomena.

Working with the electromagnetic theory of light, a German physicist named Heinrich Hertz (1857-1894) was able to demonstrate in 1886 the existence of electromagnetic waves—as predicted by Clerk-Maxwell—and to measure their velocity. It was these "hertzian waves" (later known as radio waves) which provided the theoretical basis for Marconi's subsequent invention of wireless telegraphy. In addition, Hertz's studies of the optical properties of these waves led to his discovery of photoelectricity, which was fundamental for the development of television.

Toward the end of the century, two new events occurred in the field of electrical research that were to have equally far-reaching repercussions. In 1895 a ray which could penetrate a nontranslucent mass was discovered by the German Wilhelm Konrad Roentgen (1845-1923). Because the nature of this strange phenomenon was not at first understood, the term "x-ray" came into use. The discovery was followed one year later in France by a further discovery that uranium gives off rays similar to those detected by Roentgen. Then in 1898 the French scientist Pierre Curie and his Polish wife Marie extracted radium from pitchblende, an ore of uranium, and the world began to become conscious of the potency of radioactivity. Radiation was quickly utilized in the field of medicine.

By studying the scattering of x-rays, an English scientist, Sir Joseph John Thomson (1856-1940), concluded that electricity is composed of particles which are constituent parts of atoms. This deduction led to the electron theory—namely, that the atom contains negatively charged particles known as electrons. The next major step in understanding the structure of the atom was provided in 1911 by Ernest Rutherford (1871-1937), who advanced the theory that each atom has a central particle, or nucleus, which is positively charged. Subsequently, scientists determined that the atom is like a miniature solar system; most of the weight is concentrated in the central, positively charged nucleus, around which the negatively charged electrons revolve. These discoveries smashed one of the foundation stones of traditional physics—the belief that the atom was indivisible and solid. The way was now clear to demonstrate conclusively that the universe is composed not of matter in that traditional sense but of atomic energy.

Traditional physics received another jolt from the research of the German physicist Max Planck (1858-1947). Planck, who had been studying radiant heat, which comes from the sun and is identical in its nature with light, found that the distribution of energy among different wave lengths conflicted with the classical principle that radiant energy is emitted as a continuous process. He asserted that the energy emitted from a vibrating electron proceeds not in a steady wave but discontinuously in the form of calculable "energy packages." To such a package he gave the name "quantum"—hence the term "quantum theory."

Planck's quantum theory, which was to prove invaluable in the rapidly growing study of atomic physics, found support in the studies of Albert Einstein (1879-1955). In 1905 Einstein contended that light is propagated through space in the form of particles which he termed "photons." Moreover, the energy contained in any particle of matter, such as the photon, is equal to the mass of that body multiplied by the square of the velocity of light, which is a constant figure. The resulting equation—$E=mc^2$—provided the answer to many long-standing mysteries of physics—for example, how radioactive substances like radium and uranium are able to eject particles at enormous velocities and to go on doing so for millions of years. The magnitude of the energy that slumbers in the nuclei of atoms could be revealed. Above all, $E=mc^2$ shows that mass and energy are equivalent; the property called "mass" is simply concentrated energy.

Einstein and the theory of relativity. In 1905 Einstein also presented to the world his epoch-making theory of relativity, call-

Above left: Sigmund Freud laid the foundation for present-day methods of treating neuroses by psychoanalysis. Above: Albert Einstein's theories established new concepts of the physical world and led to the harnessing of atomic energy. Left: Charles Darwin's theory of evolution through variation and natural selection of those best suited to survive was turned into a defense of laissez-faire economics known as Social Darwinism. All three men have had a profound effect on the development of civilization.

ing for a radically different approach to the concepts of time, velocity, and space. The universe as conceived by Einstein is not Newton's familiar three-dimensional figure of length, breadth, and thickness but a four-dimensional space-time continuum. Thus, to the traditional three dimensions, Einstein added a fourth dimension, fusing them all into space time. Such a concept showed the relative interrelationship of space, time, and motion. Since this principle could not be explained by Euclidean geometry, Einstein's theory made necessary a new system of mathematics.

Einstein's concepts cover all the explanations provided by Newton's theory of gravitation, but they also fit the facts in a still wider field where the older theory fails. Newtonian mechanics continue to be satisfactory for everyday science and engineering; and even the astronomer, dealing with vast spaces, finds few discrepancies between Newton's theoretical prediction and actual observation. But astronomical tests of the two theories corroborate Einstein's position. Although few people apart from his scientific colleagues either understood or were influenced by Einstein's theory of relativity prior to the First World War, during the last four decades his theory has reoriented men's attitudes toward the structure and mechanics of the cosmos.

Advances in psychology. The study of man's reaction to his changing universe and to his place in it may become the most crucial problem of all in modern scientific thought. Prior to the second half of the nineteenth century, psychology was treated as a branch of philosophy; it did not become a science until methods of experimentation were devised so that mental phenomena could be measured. By such means it became possible to ascertain the part played by the sense organs, nervous system, and brain in man's conscious activities.

The study of psychology in terms of physiological factors was given impetus by numerous investigators, one of the most famous of whom was a Russian, Ivan Pavlov (1849-1936). In 1900 Pavlov conducted a series of experiments in which food was given to a dog at the same time that a bell was rung. After a time, the food and bell became identified by the dog as inseparable. Henceforth, when the bell was rung alone, the dog had the same anticipatory reflex of producing saliva as if food had been brought. By so doing, Pavlov successfully demonstrated the influence of physical stimuli on an involuntary process.

This psychology of conditioned reflexes achieved a wide vogue, especially in the United States. There it was used to help substantiate the tenets of a school of behaviorism which considered man more or less as a machine responding mechanically to stimuli. Behaviorism stressed experimentation and observational techniques and did much to create relatively valid intelligence and aptitude tests. What is more, behaviorism strengthened the materialistic philosophies of the period.

Other psychologists found the behavioristic approach too mechanical and therefore incapable of doing justice to the importance of man's unconscious mental processes. In his pioneer work on free association, in which he analyzed the ideas that came to people's minds in direct association with a list of words, Galton reached the conclusion that a deeper level of mental activity functioned below the strata of consciousness and accounted for phenomena that were unexplainable by other means. Taking up Galton's experiments, other psychologists began to delve into the problems of mental and emotional disorders.

Freud and psychoanalysis. Probably the most famous name associated with psychology is that of the Austrian Sigmund Freud (1856-1939), whose works began to appear in the 1890's. Placing far greater stress than any predecessor on the element of the unconscious, Freud pioneered in psychoanalysis. This form of psychiatric treatment is based on the theory that abnormal mental reactions result from the repression of desires which have been consciously rejected but which nevertheless persist in the subconcious strata of the mind. Freud employed psychoanalysis as a new form of therapy for treating various emotional disturbances by placing the interpretation of dreams on a scientific basis and by bringing deeply rooted repressions to the surface. He was also concerned with the question of man's motive force, the "libido," which he believed was rooted in the sexual urge. His other contributions to the field of psychology included his concept of the Oedipus complex, whereby a child is strongly attached to the parent of the opposite sex and hostile to the other parent. All in all, Freud threw new light upon some of the most important problems of human personality and behavior.

Although many Victorians remained blissfully unaware of the far-reaching implications of the scientific discoveries made between 1870 and 1914, these same discoveries were later to prove shattering to man's self-esteem and confidence. The evolutionary theory seemed to have divested man of his traditional heritage of having been created by a special act of divine grace. Freud's plumbing of man's unconscious mental states seemed to shatter the cherished belief that man was basically a rational creature. The busy dismantling of Newton's clockwork universe by Einstein and others was to be of great consequence for man's view of the universe and his role in the scheme of things. The replacement of absolute laws by theories of relativity would soon be transferred out of the sphere of science to the field of morality, with the result that absolute values and standards would be threatened. How the mighty *Homo sapiens* had fallen!

THE CULT OF SCIENCE

Science versus faith. Living as we do with an improved standard of living made possible by science and with the shadow of a radioactive cloud hanging over us, it is not difficult to appreciate how science can assume the guise of either a beneficent Dr. Jekyll or a malevolent Mr. Hyde. Few such fears assailed the generations prior to 1914, however. With its spectacular successes in both pure research and technological application, science had gripped the popular

imagination to an extent never before equaled. Science was elevated into a cult by means of which all human problems were to be solved. Literature and art produced much more realistic—indeed almost photographic—forms of expression in keeping with the scientific dictum that the facts must speak for themselves. In short, science had gone far toward producing a state of mind that was skeptical and uneasy about whatever could not be proven in the laboratory.

It can be readily seen that a conflict was certain to ensue between the traditional doctrines of religion and the new scientific tenets, especially those of Darwinism. A strong popularizer of Darwin's theories was Thomas Huxley (1825-1895), who contended that for the advocate of science "skepticism is the highest of duties; blind faith the unpardonable sin."[10]

Within a few months of the publication of Darwin's *On the Origin of Species,* the struggle between science and religion was dramatized at a debate between Huxley and the bishop of Oxford. Before a large audience the latter spoke with what has been described as "inimitable spirit, emptiness and unfairness"—though in dulcet tones—and then, turning to his opponent, asked Huxley if he was related on his grandfather's or grandmother's side to an ape. Huxley replied that "a man has no reason to be ashamed of having an ape for his grandfather." Moreover, he should be more ashamed to have as an ancestor a man who plunged into scientific questions "with which he has no real acquaintance." At this point the excitement reached its peak; a lady fainted and had to be carried out."[11]

This Oxford debate appears in retrospect to be more amusing than significant, but at the time it was taken seriously by those who felt that the old traditions and verities were being smashed. Certainly organized religion was thrown on the defensive, and many of the most sensitive minds of the period suffered anguish and even despair in their attempts to reconcile their religious beliefs with the new scientific tenets.

As time went on, however, more than one thinker came to believe that the evolutionary theory supplemented rather than contradicted the basic tenets of faith. As they saw the bounds of the universe pushed back by science, they perceived growth and development in the constant changes and felt that God was revealing Himself to man through the evolutionary process. Interestingly enough, Darwin himself had expressed a similar view in the conclusion of his *On the Origin of Species*:

When I view all beings not as special creations, but as the lineal descendants of some few beings which lived long before the first bed of the Cambrian system was deposited, they seem to me to become ennobled. . . . we may feel certain that the ordinary succession by generation has never once been broken, and that no cataclysm has desolated the whole world. Hence we may look with some confidence to a secure future of great length. And as natural selection works solely by and for the good of each being, all corporeal and mental endowments will tend to progress towards perfection. . . . There is grandeur in this view of life, with its several powers, having been originally breathed by the Creator into a few forms or into one; and that, whilst this planet has gone cycling on according to the fixed law of gravity, from so simple a beginning endless forms most beautiful and most wonderful have been, and are being evolved.[12]

Although the great controversy of science versus faith continued to rage through the last decades of the nineteenth century, men in time began to see the issues from new perspectives. While some strong differences of opinion and interpretation persist, in our century the controversy has largely subsided.

The Roman Catholic position. While the battle between science and traditional faith was raging, Pope Pius IX in 1864 issued an encyclical warning the faithful against "the principal errors of our time"—namely, that God did not exist, that His action upon man was to be denied, that human reason was alone the sole arbiter of truth, and that the miracles found in the Scriptures were fictional. Next, in 1870 the Vatican Council—the first general council of the Church to gather in centuries—defined the doctrine of papal infallibility. This declared that when the pope spoke *ex cathedra* (from the seat of authority), he possessed:

. . . that infallibility with which the divine Redeemer willed that his Church should be endowed for defining doctrine regarding faith or morals.[13]

Thus, the Roman Catholic Church categorically reaffirmed its historical position.

Biblical criticism. Just as certain historians were developing scientific methods to determine the validity of secular evidence and thereby put history on a more scientific basis (see p. 337), so other scholars—mainly Protestants—sought to subject Biblical texts and problems of authorship to the same type of rigid examination. This type of study was known as the "higher criticism."

When the Old Testament was thus critically analyzed, Genesis and other books were questioned in the light of the latest astronomical, geological, biological, and historical evidence. Some of the apparent contradictions that were turned up provided fodder for various popular lecturers, who held forth on such topics as "Some Mistakes of Moses." As for the New Testament, it was argued that many of the narratives found in the Gospels must be considered only myths and not historical facts. Advocates of the higher criticism likewise contended that the New Testament, no less than the Old, recounted human rather than divine events and reflected the moral and ethical attitudes of the society which produced it.

The science of man. The apostles of science, who could deal so harshly with religion, were also anxious to place human institutions on a scientific foundation. Such was the intention of the noted French student of society Auguste Comte (1798-1857), whose work had appeared in the first half of the nineteenth century. Comte held that the history of mankind had passed through three stages of evolution. The first two of these, the theological and the metaphysical, had outlived their usefulness. Now the time had arrived to embark upon what he called the positive stage, in which scientific knowledge and the application of scientific standards would dominate.

But though society should rest upon a scientific foundation, it could not truly do so until the various specialized sciences had been brought together and studied in a particular order. At the apex of all these sciences, Comte placed the study of man in society, a new science to which he gave the name "sociology." The purpose of sociology would be to gather the facts about human existence and then discover their causal connections. From such investigations Comte hoped to reorganize man's political and social institutions on a scientific basis.

Scientific history. The scientific approach was also brought to bear upon the writing of history. The scholar generally acknowledged as the founder of "scientific history" is Leopold von Ranke (1795-1886). Previously, historians had often used history to pass moral judgments on the past or to predict developments in the future. Ranke, however, announced that his writings would "simply explain the event exactly as it happened." His system called for a thorough search for all possible evidence on a given subject, the most careful examination of this evidence to ensure its authenticity and reliability, and the restriction of conclusions to what could logically be drawn from the evidence. Complete objectivity is humanly impossible, but Ranke's critical method demanded that the historian subordinate his own views and preferences to a concern for the truth.

Ranke had made his major contributions to historical method before the appearance of Darwin's *On the Origin of Species*, which caused further repercussions in the study of history. More than one historian began to analyze his subject matter strictly in terms of environment and heredity, stressing such factors as soil, topography, climate, food, race, and the inheritance of various traits. Sometimes this approach led to the treatment of societies and institutions as though they were simply biological organisms—a fallacy which could have pernicious results. On the more constructive side, the Darwinian hypothesis encouraged students to view history in terms of growth and adaptation. The evolutionary theory was similarly carried over into the study of other social sciences, including economics and criminology.

Social Darwinism. One American thinker at the close of the century wrote:

The life of man in society, just like the life of other species, is a struggle for existence, and therefore it is a process of selective adaptation. The evolution of social structure has been a process of natural selection of institutions. The progress which has been and is being made in human institutions and in human character may be set down, broadly, to a natural selection of the fittest habits of thought and to a process of enforced adaptation of individuals to an environment which has progressively changed with the growth of the community and with the changing institutions under which men have lived.[14]

Here we see clearly how the concept of the survival of the fittest was used to explain not only the development but the progress of both human institutions and human character. Although Darwin himself had confined the principle of natural selection to the sphere of biology, his contemporaries eagerly extended it to apply to the field of human affairs. This application of Darwin's principles to man and his efforts was called social Darwinism; it became a vogue that swept western thought in the late nineteenth century. It also became a convenient doctrine for justifying various economic and political theories.

Darwinism in economics. Herbert Spencer (1820-1903), an English philosopher from whom Darwin borrowed the phrase "survival of the fittest," was one of those who regarded society as a living organism. Within that society, he argued, every man should be free to do as he pleased, subject only to the condition that he must not infringe upon the freedom of others. Spencer categorically opposed any interference by the state with the natural development of society. The sole function of the state, in his view, was negative—namely, to ensure freedom of the individual, who if left alone through enough generations would become perfect. Spencer used this doctrine to advocate unfettered business competition and to oppose all state aid to the poor, whom he regarded as unable to compete successfully in the struggle for survival and consequently better eliminated. At the same time, he favored private charity to develop altruistic traits in the donors.

For a time Spencer's popularity in England and the United States was surpassed only by that of Darwin himself. It is not difficult to understand his appeal in the United States in the period following the Civil War. In an era of economic expansion, of exploitation, of cutthroat competition, and of "peremptory rejection of failure," the United States in the late nineteenth century seemed to be a vast proving ground for Darwin's theories. One of the great railroad magnates of the day, James J. Hill, defended the practice of powerful companies absorbing their smaller competitors with the argument that:

. . . the fortunes of railroad companies are determined by the law of the survival of the fittest.[15]

Social Darwinism was in fact an extremely useful doctrine since it could serve equally well the conservative exponents of laissez faire and their antagonists at the opposite extreme of the political spectrum. Following the appearance of *On the Origin of Species,* Marx reported to his colleague Engels:

Darwin's book is very important and serves me as a basis in natural science for the class struggle in history.[16]

At the close of the century, Marxists were also employing the theory of mutation, maintaining that society advances not only by gradual development but also by sudden change and thus justifying the use of violence to bring about a drastic social revolution.

Racism and anti-Semitism. The pseudo-scientific application of a biological theory to politics, whereby a nation is regarded as an organism, constituted possibly the most perverted form of social Darwinism in the period under review. It led to racism and anti-Semitism and was used to show that only "superior" nationalities and races were fit to survive. Thus, among the English-speaking peoples were to be found the champions of the "white man's burden," an imperial mission carried out by Anglo-Saxons in India and South Africa or, at the time of the Spanish-American War, in Cuba and the Philippines. Similarly, the Russians preached the doctrine of Pan-Slavism and the Germans that of Pan-Germanism.

Racism must have its scapegoat—that is, some group which can be castigated as "inferior" and therefore ultimately denied the right to survive. In earlier centuries resentment against the Jews because of their religious separateness and envy of their relative economic strength had made this minority a target for racism at its worst. The flames of anti-Semitism were fanned anew by the publication in 1899 of a book by the Englishman Houston Stewart Chamberlain (1855-1927), the son-in-law of the famous German composer Richard Wagner, himself a notorious anti-Semite. This polemic maintained that western culture was threatened by Jewish elements and plots but that it would nevertheless be saved by the Germans, who were destined to rule the world. This doctrine—which amazingly classified Jesus and later figures such as Leonardo da Vinci as Teutonic—was one day to be taken at face value and applied implacably by the Nazis.

The "justification" of war. Social Darwinism was also employed to justify the use of military power to ensure that the "fittest" state would survive. In Prussia the ultranationalist historian Heinrich von Treitschke (1834-1896), at once bitterly anti-English, anti-Catholic, and anti-Semitic, regarded war as "the one remedy for an ailing nation." He asserted:

The grandeur of war lies in the utter annihilation of puny man in the great conception of the State, and it brings out the full magnificence of the sacrifice of fellow-countrymen for one another. In war the chaff is winnowed from the wheat.[17]

Another influential advocate of war was the German philosopher Friedrich Nietzsche (1844-1900). To Nietzsche the only type of person fit to exist was one who had the power to attain authority, no matter by what means. His ideal ruler, the superman, was characterized by bravery, strength, egoism, arrogance, and ruthlessness. Nietzsche challenged the world with: "You say, 'A good cause sanctifies even war,' but I say, 'A good war sanctifies every cause'!" Nietzsche viewed Christianity with contempt because he regarded gentleness as weakness and humanitarianism as protection of the unfit and spineless. Likewise, he ridiculed democracy and socialism for protecting the worthless and weak and hindering the strong. Social Darwinism and the antidemocratic cult of naked power, as preached by advocates like Nietzsche, were laying the foundations of fascism, which would one day plunge the world into the most terrible convulsion in its history.

The concept of mutual aid. The foregoing discussion of social Darwinism should make clear the fallacy of applying biological theories to particular economic or political ideologies. Human society cannot be explained solely in biological terms. Man has acquired a freedom of initiative and action unknown to other species and therefore is not subject to the same ironclad law of the survival of the fittest.

At the turn of the century, the basic tenet underlying social Darwinism was itself being questioned. It was pointed out that cooperation, or mutual aid, is also a major factor in the evolutionary process. Observation showed, for example, that association and mutual aid existed among the deer, wild cattle, birds, and rodents of Siberia and that animals of the same species were not always struggling against each other to survive. Association seems no less a universal principle in nature than that of struggle. "The dominating principle of evolution is the expansion of life. When association favours this expansion, association takes place. When struggle favours it, struggle takes place."[18]

This later interpretation of the evolutionary hypothesis was to win adherents principally in the period after 1914, when the occurrence of two world wars emphasized the value of cooperation in both politics and economics. But the decades preceding the first global conflict were mainly dedicated to unbridled individualism, and social Darwinism enjoyed a vigorous existence.

Developments in philosophy: pragmatism and vitalism. Meanwhile, the professional philosophers had also been profoundly influenced by the implications of Darwin's work. We will recall that in the early decades of the nineteenth century, when economic and social theories had to be adapted to a society being transformed by the First Industrial Revolution, Bentham and the utilitarians had not been concerned with seeking universal absolutes in morals and ethics. Instead, they had concentrated on working out a system of human conduct based upon such relative standards as utility and happiness (see p. 170). Stressing the roles of change and chance in nature, the Darwinian theory further strengthened the trend away from absolute standards.

Among American philosophers there arose a school known as pragmatism, which asserted that even truth is not an absolute in itself. Under the leadership of William James (1842-1910), a leading American psychologist, the pragmatists did not distinguish between mind and matter, nor did they believe in thought in the abstract, as something indulged in for its own sake. Rather, they felt that men think for the practical purpose of getting on with the job of living; and since the validity of any idea lies not in its approximation to some ultimate truth but in its ability to effect desired action, it must be tested by its logical or empirical results. As James put it, "An idea is 'true' so long as to believe it is profitable to our lives." Pragmatism, in effect, rejected any concept of truth or reality as absolute. Although it has been credited with bringing formal philosophy out of the clouds and relating it more concretely to the major scientific and intellectual trends of the day, the pragmatic approach resulted in a strongly materialistic bent on the part of some of its adherents, with whom truth became indistinguishable from success.

Influenced by contemporary scientific currents in both biology and physics but differing widely from pragmatism was the philosophy of Henri Bergson (1859-1941). Bergson attributed existence to a spontaneous creative force which he called the vital impulse (*élan vital*). Nothing is fixed; everything in life changes ceaselessly. According to this French philosopher, the intellect is incapable of grasping the true nature of reality, which flows like an unin-

Fox hunting became a popular sport in England in the early decades of the nineteenth century.

terrupted stream, and instead cuts reality up into discontinuous parts in much the same way that a movie film divides a single action into separate pictures. Bergson believed, however, that man has another faculty, intuition, which is capable of grasping life in terms of wholes. This, he maintained, is the ability employed by artists.

Bergson's philosophy of vitalism, which made its greatest impact in the years preceding World War I, represented a revolt against scientific determinism. While making use of the Darwinian thesis of change, it conceived evolution to be creative and not a blind struggle for survival. And because it insisted that mental processes could not be reduced to simple mechanistic terms, this vitalistic philosophy was to influence many intellectuals of the time.

CHANGING SOCIAL AND

ESTHETIC STANDARDS

The aristocracy unseated by the middle class. As we have seen in Chapter 5, the first decades of the nineteenth century witnessed the emergence of certain dominant strands in the intellectual pattern of the West: romanticism, nationalism, and liberalism. As we would expect, these developments were paralleled by major changes in social standards and behavior. At the beginning of the era, the essentially aristocratic mode of life was still the yardstick by which society was measured. And it continued to be so into the 1830's, although important changes had taken place.

In England the first three decades of the nineteenth century witnessed a constant movement of the world of fashion from the capital to country estates or resort towns and back again, especially along the popular stagecoach routes to Bath or Brighton. In fashionable gambling clubs in London's West End, dandies wagered vast sums on whist, hazard, and dice. At other times, to indulge their passion for gambling, these men about town patronized prize fights, dogfights, cockfights, and even bearbaiting contests. The turf was no less popular with the aristocrats, who flocked to such events as the Ascot races and the Derby. This period was also the heyday for the fox hunt—which much later in the century was to be castigated by Oscar Wilde as "the unspeakable in full pursuit of the uneatable."[19] Dueling was on the wane, though as late as 1829 the irascible Duke of Wellington felt constrained to exchange shots with another peer. The full-blooded sporting activities in vogue in the eighteenth century continued to be zealously pursued during the Georgian period when the aristocracy was still very much in the saddle, whether in the field or in Parliament.

By the 1840's England possessed five thousand miles of railways, which rapidly became the normal means for transporting freight and long-distance passengers. As the stagecoach gave way to the new transportation of the machine age, so did the fashions of the gentry give way to those of the entrepreneur. Gentlemen discarded their wigs, and ladies began to wear dresses that followed the natural outline of the body. Breeches and top boots had already given way to long trousers; now gentlemen were discarding their brocaded waistcoats and acquiring a taste for elegant top hats. These sartorial innovations were symptomatic of more important social and political changes, for trousers and top hats were the hallmark of the middle class—those same mill owners and city businessmen who had formerly been scorned as vulgar social climbers by the breeches-attired city aristocracy in their exclusive drawing rooms and by the no less aristocratic hard-riding, topbooted gentry on their country estates. True, the aristocratic England of the rural districts was to continue to be ruled and judged by country gentlemen of the old school, but in the cities and factory towns the middle class was now dominant.

In France it was fashionable for society to ape English manners and sports. The most aristocratic club of Paris was the English-style Jockey Club. Some Frenchmen even took up fox hunting, a sport which provided Gallic humorists with material for derision. The growing middle-class dominance was no less evident in France. The artist and play-

A detail of a mid-Victorian painting of Derby Day shows the crowds of people clustered about the gambling games set up at the edge of the course. In the background, men stand on carriages to obtain a better view of the race track.

wright Henri Monnier (1805-1877) created the figure of a typical bourgeois citizen, Monsieur Joseph Prud'homme, and made his character famous in plays and cartoons.

A contemporary wrote of France:

The dominant character now-a-days is no longer the man of the drawing-room, whose place is certain and his fortune made, elegant and unruffled, with no employment but to amuse and please himself . . . it is the man in a black coat, who works alone in his room . . . often envious, feeling himself always above or below his station in life, sometimes resigned, never satisfied, but fertile in inventions, lavish of trouble, finding the picture of his blemishes and his strength in the drama of Victor Hugo and the novels of Balzac.[20]

The new mass reading public. Cheaper books and papers and a growing literacy rate made reading an increasingly popular pastime. Popular publications ranged from religious works and literary quarterlies to cheap novels and newspapers. In France, Emile de Girardin lowered the price of his newspaper, *La Presse,* and thereby made newspaper reading and the discussion of politics a popular pastime in every corner café.

One of the social evils attacked by Dickens in his novels was the wretched condition of many English schools. Above is an illustration from *Nicholas Nickleby*, showing the unhappy children of Dotheboys Hall.

In England the first penny paper appeared in 1855.

A mass reading public had emerged, and this fact reflected the firm establishment of an industrialized society. Workers were learning to read in ever increasing numbers, and a wide assortment of reading matter had become available to them thanks to a mechanized press and the progressive lowering of the cost of manufacturing paper. In English working-class quarters, the most popular form of fiction was the penny novel, appearing in weekly parts. One Manchester dealer in 1849 and 1850 "sold an average of 6,000 numbers *weekly* for each of a small library of creations like *Angelina, Elmira's Curse, Claude Deval, Ella the Outcast, Gentlemen Jack, Gambler's Wife*, and so on."[21]

In France the *feuilleton*, or newspaper serial story, was popular. The works of George Sand, Eugène Sue, and Alexandre Dumas frequently appeared first in popular newspapers. The entire French nation, it seemed, anxiously followed in the daily press the claptrap theatrics of Sue's *Les Mystères de Paris* (1842-1843)—and in the process imbibed some of his socialist ideas. In France books also became cheaper and readily available to the multitude, and so it happened that many Parisian workers read rhapsodic exaltations of the French revolutionary tradition and yearned to start a revolution of their own (see p. 197).

The English novel: Thackeray and Dickens. The leading Victorian novelists were William Makepeace Thackeray (1811-1863) and Charles Dickens (1812-1870). The snobbery and social climbing that went on in a society made highly fluid by the rise of the newly rich middle class provided an ideal subject for the genial satirist and moralist Thackeray. He is probably best known for his unscrupulous but engaging character Becky Sharp, the heroine of *Vanity Fair* (1848).

A note of social protest and dissent appears in all the works of Dickens. He painted in the most vivid colors the everyday life of the middle classes and the poor—and especially the struggle of the individual against the worst excesses of industrial expansion and social injustice. In *The Pickwick Papers, Oliver Twist, Dombey and Son, Bleak House,* and *David Copperfield,* to name but a few of his major works, Dickens blended romantic and realistic elements by combining a fundamental optimism and belief in progress with trenchant attacks upon existing slum conditions, the miseries of the poor, and the inhuman debtors' prisons.

Dickens has been described as "the great democrat of English literature. His every book is a crowd; and it is the crowd of a democracy, the exuberant, restless, disorganised, clamorous, motley crowd of Hampstead Heath [in London] . . . squalid and sunny, domestic and indelicate, sharp and sentimental, kindly and undignified."[22]

Victorian poetry: Tennyson and Browning. The spokesman of Victorian England, Alfred, Lord Tennyson (1809-1892), was poet laureate from 1850 to the year of his death. His popularity derived from his sympathetic understanding of the ideas and ideals of his countrymen; he had their "high seriousness" and self-consciousness along with their sentimentality and their admiration for the ornate. Yet the very qualities in his poetry that won him great acclaim in his own day have

Robert Browning, taking tea with adoring members of the Browning Society, is caricatured by the British artist Sir Max Beerbohm.

since worked against his reputation. Today, the beauty of much of his verse seems somewhat artificial, his thought, shallow and conformist.

The other major English poet of the period was Robert Browning (1812-1889), whose sturdy optimism and faith in humanity won him many followers. Unlike Tennyson, however, Browning was not primarily a melodist; his talent lay in the skillful delineation of character. He created a new poetic form —the dramatic monologue—in which the thoughts and feelings of a character were depicted with a psychological insight which appealed to his readers even though they could not always understand the poet's erudite allusions or his often cryptic mode of expression. Browning's masterpiece, *The Ring and the Book* (1868-1869), is a succession of dramatic monologues by which the story of a lurid Roman murder case is told from a dozen different points of view.

The Victorian age produced other gifted poets, possessing much technical skill, yet few are ranked today with the major roman-tic poets earlier in the century. All in all, the Victorian poets suffered from the tendency to express the moralistic and strongly conventional ideas of the members of the middle class for whom they wrote. Whereas the romanticists, as rebels, adopted an uncompromising attitude toward the world, the Victorians preferred to come to terms with it. Theirs was a more sober, perhaps a more responsible attitude, but it was not the exalted approach that makes for soaring flights of poetry. True, in *In Memoriam* (1850), Tennyson's attempt to find a philosophical compromise between existing religious views and new scientific attitudes resulted in a series of poignant meditations. But all too often such compromise was indistinguishable from a deep-rooted middle-class complacency. While conceding that other cultures might possess advantages denied to the industrial society of the West, Tennyson confidently proclaimed:

Forward, forward let us range
Let the great world spin for ever down the
    ringing grooves of change.

Through the shadow of the globe we swing into
    the younger day;
Better fifty years of Europe than a
    cycle of Cathay.[23]

**The rise of social criticism: Arnold and
Carlyle.** There were, however, a few doubters in the crowd—men who reacted to the
new, gleaming, steam leviathans that were
revolutionizing society so quickly with fears
and doubts which today strike a strongly
sympathetic chord:

Like children bathing on the shore,
Buried a wave beneath,
The second wave succeeds, before
We have had time to breathe.

Too fast we live, too much are tried,
Too harassed, to attain
Wordsworth's sweet calm, or Goethe's wide
And luminous view to gain.[24]

The author of those lines was Matthew
Arnold (1822-1888). Son of the famous head-
master of Rugby and a distinguished poet
and essayist in his own right, Arnold was
profoundly disturbed about the state of culture in his day. It suffered not only from being "too fast" and "too harassed" by technological changes; the materialistic standards
of industrialism were, he believed, incompatible with the great humanistic values inherited from Greece and the Renaissance.
In his view, mid-Victorian culture was beset by personal self-seeking and lack of social purpose and moral strength. At one end
of the social structure were the aristocrats,
whom Arnold dubbed "Barbarians" because
they were ignorant of the great western
cultural inheritance and spent their lives in
idleness and worldly pleasures. At the other
end was the "Populace," the working class,
which was now emerging from its traditional state of poverty and ignorance but
which could, unless properly educated and
directed, smash much that was irreplaceable
in our civilization.

Then there was the middle class, about
which Arnold was perhaps most concerned
since its members were now dominant in society. Arnold called them "Philistines" because they neither understood nor cared
about culture in its humanistic terms. This

new industrial bourgeoisie, he argued,
thought only of power and riches and saw in
the external signs of change proof of spiritual advancement. Philistine values, he said,
led a man "to value himself not on what
he is . . . but on the number of the railroads
he has constructed, or the bigness of the
tabernacle he has built."[25] In Arnold's judgment, the ancient humanistic values had to
be restored, and culture had to be made
available to all classes in society. This required the introduction of state education.
Only by such means could the existing middle-class cultural attitudes and complacency
be effectively broken.

Another prominent figure, outspoken in his
criticism of the shortcomings of a society
dominated by the middle class, was the
Scottish essayist and historian Thomas Carlyle (1795-1881). Looking at London's industrial areas in 1867, with the miles of ugly
barrackslike workers' houses constructed of
standardized slate and red brick, Carlyle described it all as "cheap and nasty":

Universal *shoddy* and Devil's-dust cunningly var-
nished over . . . Take one small example only.
London bricks are reduced to dry clay again in
the course of sixty years, or sooner . . . there lies
in it not the Physical mischief only, but the
Moral too, which is far more. I have often
sadly thought of this. That a fresh human soul
should be born in such a place; born in the midst
of a concrete mendacity. . . .[26]

Railing against contemporary industrialism
and the mass vulgarity which it produced,
Carlyle argued that democracy's problems
could not be settled by merely extending the
ballot. Indeed, the grim-humored Scot
feared what would happen when political
power was placed in the hands of the multitude through the extension of the suffrage.
Because Carlyle believed that "one wise man
is stronger than all men unwise," he declared
that "the few Wise will have, by one method
or another, to take command of the innumerable Foolish."[27] This rejection of the
democratic philosophy brings us to a central
thesis of Carlyle—namely, that salvation
could only be attained by the heroic deeds
and leadership of history's "Great Men." Carlyle's heroes included religious prophets, fa-

mous artists, and soldiers like Cromwell and Napoleon. His advocacy of strong and even authoritarian leadership has found acceptance in totalitarian (Fascist, Nazi, and Communist) ideologies in our own century. In fact, as we shall see in Chapter 18, authoritarian leadership is popular among the nonaligned nations of Africa and Asia.

Ruskin and the Esthetic Revolt. No less influential as a social critic—but one whose formula for curing existing ills differed radically from Carlyle's—was John Ruskin (1819-1900). A leader of the protest movement often called the Esthetic Revolt, Ruskin believed wholeheartedly in the basic integrity and common sense of the people, for whom he advocated socialistic reforms and widespread education. Ruskin wrote eloquently to free his age from the ugly consequences of a soulless industrialism and to reform the arts and handicrafts, many of which were being destroyed by cheap mass production. Although Ruskin and his associates were not able to stem the tide of tasteless goods pouring from the machines, they helped stimulate a new appreciation of craftsmanship.

Ruskin and other esthetic rebels were convinced that the regeneration of art required a return to the esthetic standards and love of craftsmanship which they associated with the Middle Ages. Among those holding such views were certain painters and poets who, around the middle of the century, banded together in what they called the Pre-Raphaelite Brotherhood. They felt that only in the period before Raphael and the High Renaissance had artists been sincere craftsmen, dedicated not to the things of this world but to the glory of God. The brotherhood, under the leadership of Dante Gabriel Rossetti (1828-1882), included many gifted individuals, but their self-conscious attempts to create a new medievalism in art had only temporary success. Yet if Ruskin and the Pre-Raphaelites erred in detaching the Gothic style from its historic setting, they and their followers succeeded in laying the foundations of our present-day concepts about industrial design and the relationship of materials, shape, function, and the manufacturing process.

FROM REALISM TO EXPRESSIONISM

The realistic novelists. By 1870 writers were not only responding in various ways to the growing cult of science and to the impact of philosophical rationalism; they were also in revolt against the now-spent romanticism that survived in the form of sentimentalism. Sentiment was offered at a discount, as was the political idealism that had fanned the abortive revolutions of 1848. A down-to-earth attitude had become the order of the day.

To the romantics, nature was divine and mankind naturally good. If their increasingly industrialized urban milieu became depressing, they could always find beauty, color, and excitement in the past, in exotic settings, or in their own imaginings. The realists, on the other hand, concentrated upon what they saw about them. They believed that the purpose of art is to depict life with complete and objective honesty, to relate the common experiences of humanity without prettifying the facts. In their attempt to portray life "as it really is," the nineteenth-century realists did not hesitate to describe in graphic detail social and personal problems which had hitherto gone unmentioned because they were not "nice." The creed of realistic writers was to chronicle without comment, to photograph without touching up. "An artist ought no more to appear in his work than God does in nature" was the dictum pronounced by the French novelist Flaubert, described as a literary surgeon who "dissected passion and conducted post-mortem examinations of the human heart." The works of the great realistic novelists span three quarters of the nineteenth century and extend into the twentieth.

Typical of this new trend in literature were the works of the French novelist Honoré de Balzac (1799-1850), author of the *Comédie Humaine,* or "Human Comedy," a panorama of ninety volumes concerning French city and country life in the first half of the nineteenth century. In his novels, the crudities and avarice of the French petty

Above is a pen-and-ink study of the novelist Honoré de Balzac.

bourgeoisie were depicted in detail. In *Eugénie Grandet* (1833), the tyrannical father of the heroine Eugénie sacrifices her to his miserliness. The social-climbing daughters of Goriot in *Le Père Goriot* (1835) mercilessly exploit him but are ashamed of his crude bourgeois manners. Even if the subject matter of Balzac's novels was carefully drawn and documented from everyday scenes, his work, however, still relied upon romantic plots and occasional rhetorical flourishes.

The first thoroughgoing French realist was Gustave Flaubert (1821-1880). His masterpiece, *Madame Bovary* (1856), describes how the boredom of a romantic-minded young provincial wife led her into adultery and ultimately into complete disillusionment. By implication, Flaubert was criticizing the inadequacy of romanticism as a philosophy of life. Another famous French writer, Victor Hugo, who had earlier written highly romantic works based upon colorful incidents in French history, now produced *Les Misérables* (1862), the story of a man forced into thievery and degradation by hunger.

Count Leo Tolstoy (1828-1910) is best known for his epic novel *War and Peace* (1862-1869), which presents a magnificent tapestry of life in Russia at the time of Napoleon's invasion of 1812 while stripping every shred of glory or glamour from that conflict. In *Anna Karenina* (1875-1877), the story of two lovers who openly defy the conventions is relentlessly detailed; under the pressures of social disapproval, their affair ends tragically. The other great Russian novelist of the period, Feodor Dostoevski (1821-1881), traces the causes and effects of murder in both *Crime and Punishment* (1866) and *The Brothers Karamazov* (1880). Both works are masterpieces of suspense and psychological analysis.

A notable English realist was Thomas Hardy (1840-1928), who dealt with the struggle of the individual—almost invariably a losing struggle—against the impersonal, pitiless forces of his natural and social environment. In *The Return of the Native* (1878) the ominous heath represents the timeless, unreasoning, and indomitable spirit of nature which crushes the characters who try to escape the workings of chance. Spurred by the financial success of his novels and the accusation of undue pessimism after the publication of *Jude the Obscure* (1896), Hardy abandoned the novel and returned for the rest of his life to his first love, writing poetry.

The innocent American in cosmopolitan European circles—a description which applies to the heroine of *The Portrait of a Lady* (1881)—is a recurring theme in the novels of Henry James (1843-1916). The brother of the American pragmatist William James, Henry was greatly influenced by the new psychology; his stories and novels serve as a framework for lengthy, subtle analyses of human motives. He attempted, as he put it, to catch "the atmosphere of the mind" in his works.

Another noted literary figure of the latter part of the century was Samuel Clemens (1835-1910), whose fame as a humorist should not blind us to the realistic character of his work. His writings abound not only with robust humor but also with accurate descriptions of the Middle and Far West, and he was the first American writer of stature to reproduce honestly and effectively the speech patterns of his fellow citizens. Like Dickens, he could employ humorous satire to underscore social injustice.

Naturalism: Zola and De Maupassant. In the hands of some writers, realism developed into an extreme form of presentation known as naturalism. The naturalists wished to apply scientific objectivity to their subject matter and to deal with their characters as with animals in a laboratory whose every move was determined by environment or heredity. In the development of this literary coterie—particularly in France—the pervasive influence of science is readily apparent.

Two names stand out. The first is that of Émile Zola (1840-1902), who made a case study twenty volumes long of a middle-class family. In this series of works, which included *Nana* (1880) and *Germinal* (1885), Zola employed a clinical approach to describe members of a family which included farmers, miners, artists, and white-collar workers as well as alcoholics, murderers, and rakes. Zola amassed huge notebooks of information on such subjects as the stock market and the mining districts before he began to write works using these settings. His novels, like the works of Balzac, remain important not only for their scrupulously detailed chronicle of nineteenth-century life in France but also for the passion and vigor with which they are infused.

Associated with Zola as a naturalistic writer was Guy de Maupassant (1850-1893), who wrote more than three hundred short stories. Holding a detached and cynical view of mankind, De Maupassant portrayed his characters with satirical wit and irony and told his stories without injecting either approval or blame.

The problem play: Ibsen and Shaw. The exposure of social problems was an important aspect of the new literary realism. The enactment of reform legislation, such as the laws abolishing slavery and the bills extending the franchise and aiding the working man, had not put an end to man's inhumanity to man nor prevented the creation of new social dislocations in an increasingly complex, industrial culture. Many of the problems facing *fin de siècle* (end of the century) society were more subtle in character than the obvious injustices of child labor and cholera-infested slums, which had monopolized the attention of social critics earlier in the century. Thus, perhaps, was provided the impetus for the development of a new, sophisticated form of drama called the "problem play."

The dramas of the Norwegian Henrik Ibsen (1828-1906), whose works have been called "powerful social documents," were the first of the problem plays. An Ibsen play is centered upon a basic problem or theme, usually domestic in character. Thus, in *A Doll's House* (1879), he analyzes the motivation of a woman kept dependent by a bigoted husband until, after years of marriage in which they have become virtual strangers to each other, she leaves him. Ibsen's thesis shocked contemporary middle-class attitudes not so much because it championed the rights of women as because it assailed marriage without love as being immoral. In other plays, Ibsen attacked social greed masked by conventional respectability and delineated with great sensitivity the human dramas latent in the strains and stresses of ordinary life.

A disciple of Ibsen and, like the Norwegian, an ardent assailant of bourgeois complacency was the brilliant Irish playwright George Bernard Shaw (1856-1950). Although he lived through the first half of our own century, Shaw had made a major impact upon intellectual currents before the First World War. In a series of shrewdly satirical and highly diverting stage successes, Shaw cajoled, bullied, and often shocked the English-speaking public into reassessing their conventional attitudes on a variety of social subjects, ranging from private and public morality to militarism and religious beliefs.

The search for new standards. Realism was a healthy antidote for the excesses of the romantic movement and played a highly useful role in the criticism of contemporary society. But it, too, had its limitations. Because he was preoccupied with depicting life as it is, the realist tended to interpret his milieu almost exclusively in objective and mechanistic terms.

By no means all of the reading public were satisfied by realism, nor were all the current writers proponents of this school. Some writers made a cult of their revulsion against the crudities and vulgarity of a realism-ridden age. To men like Oscar Wilde (1854-1900) in England, the only valid standard was "art for art's sake." Moral, social, or ethical criteria were unimportant in themselves; the artist might do as he pleased so long as his work possessed artistic integrity. In the name of such integrity, the devotees of this school—both as writers and as individuals—often lapsed into decadence. Their brilliance was brittle, and they offered no remedy for—only escape from—the conflicts of the age.

Still other writers sought new standards and modes of expression. In so doing, they were not merely reacting against an excessive emphasis on realism; they were also reflecting the need to find new outlets in literature for what Freud and the psychologists had been saying about the subjective side of existence. The French poet Pierre Charles Baudelaire (1821-1867) sought to "actualize experience in metaphors and symbols." In his volume of poetry, *Les Fleurs du Mal* (*The Flowers of Evil*), published in 1857, Baudelaire described commonplace events but imbued them with a meaning far beyond the apparent. Because of his efforts to record the complex reactions of the intellectual, Baudelaire was a forerunner of the symbolists and an influence on later French and English poetry.

Found for the most part in France during the last two decades of the nineteenth century, the symbolists made use of images, archaic and mystical terms, and other devices in order to convey the inner feelings of an individual or group. Their experimentation also led them to employ free verse and the prose poem, while their efforts to express the subjective and introspective often made their works obscure to all but themselves.

Realism in painting. The major trends in literature between 1870 and 1914 were paralleled by developments in painting in the same era. Already, in the 1850's and 1860's, various artists in France had been rebelling against traditional subject matter and techniques. Feeling that the canvases exhibited on academy walls were for the most part too "respectable" and hence artificial, they chose instead to paint life as they saw it. As one artist put it:

It is better to paint railway stations . . . enginehouses, mines, and factories, for these are the saints and miracles of the nineteenth century.[28]

Many realistic painters concentrated on the men and women of the working class, whose faces bore the imprint of their burdened lives. Thus Jean François Millet (1814-1875) portrayed the life of the French peasants, emphasizing the pathos of their hard existence in such canvases as the "Man with the Hoe" and the "Angelus." Gustave Courbet (1819-1877), probably the outstanding French realist, expressed his contempt for religious and Neoclassical themes when he mocked: "Show me an angel and I will paint one." When he looked at nature, he consciously dropped the affectations of both the romantics and Neoclassicists and painted uncompromising, often brutal canvases.

Courbet's view that "realism is an essentially democratic art" was shared by his compatriot Honoré Daumier (1808-1879), who knew Parisian life intimately. He chose his subject matter from all walks of life; the washerwomen along the Seine, for example, were among his favorite subjects. His lithographs were biting satires of life among the bourgeoisie, in the courts of law, and in political circles (see the lithographs on pp. 175 and 206).

Impressionism in France. As we have seen, realism in literature was developed by Zola and others into naturalism, whereby the writer sought to observe phenomena in their natural state and to record them with scientific precision. In painting, we find a similar development in Impressionism. Preoccupied with problems of color, light, and atmosphere, these artists sought to catch the first impression made by a scene or object upon the eye, undistorted by the intellect or any subjective attitude. The result was that the Impressionists worked in terms of light and color rather than solidity of form. In doing so, they found that a more striking effect of light could be obtained by placing one bright area of color next to another without any transitional tones. They also discovered that shadows could be shown not as gray but as colors complementary to those of the objects casting the shadows. At close range an Impressionist picture may seem little more than a splotch of unmixed colors, but at the proper distance the eye mixes the colors, and a vibrating sense of light and motion emerges. Through their technique the Impressionists helped to revolutionize modern painting.

Associated with Impressionism were many outstanding painters. Claude Monet (1840-1926) concentrated largely on landscapes for the purpose of exploring color and light in nature (see Color Plate 20). Edgar Degas (1834-1917) was concerned with depicting the interplay of light and shade on the human form so as to suggest motion; his studies of ballet dancers combine Impressionism with a strong sense of line (see Color Plate 17). Still another outstanding Impressionist was Pierre Auguste Renoir (1841-1919) who skillfully employed color to capture flesh tones and texture. Renoir painted all sorts of subjects—the opera, landscapes, and houseboats on the Seine. His canvases all reveal his rich sense of color; the sunlight plays across his paintings, giving the sense of a passing moment held in paint. Actually, Renoir's paintings show more solidity than those of most Impressionists, who tended generally to subordinate concreteness of subject to the oscillation of color and light.

To France must go credit for the development not only of this new style of painting but of other Impressionistic arts as well. The outstanding sculptor of the day, Auguste Rodin (1840-1917), has been described as the father of modern sculpture. He infused his work with a realistic honesty and vitality that made him the object of stormy controversy during much of his lifetime. Sharing with the Impressionist painters a dislike for studied finality in art, Rodin preferred to let the imagination of the beholder play on his sculpture. Rodin's technique of rough finish shows to advantage in his bronze works. By this technique, the sculptor achieved two effects: a glittering surface of light and shadow and a feeling of immediacy and incompleteness that emphasized the spontaneous character of the work.

Post-Impressionism. By conveying a sense of motion and of the moment, Impressionism had given painting—and, through Rodin, sculpture—a fresh vitality. But it had done so at a price. For one thing, its effects with color and atmosphere had been achieved by sacrificing much of the clarity which continued to be a hallmark of the classical tradition. Again, while bringing the surface of things alive in an exciting fashion, the Impressionist seemed unable to give his objects the solidity and structure which were theirs by nature. How could artists get the best of both worlds?

This was the difficult intellectual and artistic problem to which Paul Cézanne (1839-1906) addressed himself. For years this painter—a one-time realist and friend of Zola—experimented with new techniques. He sought to simplify all natural objects by emphasizing their essential geometric structure. As Cézanne said, everything in nature corresponds to the shape of the cone, the cylinder, or the sphere. Proceeding on the basis of this theory, he was able to get below the surface and give his objects the solidity which had eluded the Impressionists. Yet, like the latter, he made striking use of color—in his case, to establish the relationships of his objects in space. The successful pioneering work of Cézanne was to have important consequences.

The French sculptor Rodin believed that ugliness in a work of art resulted not from a lack of conventional beauty but from a lack of character. Although at first most art critics were shocked by his works, he came to be considered one of the greatest sculptors of modern times. In "The Thinker," Rodin sought to express man's struggle to use his reason.

One or two other late nineteenth-century painters were also successful, by reason of their individualism, in contributing to the rise of Post-Impressionism. One was Vincent van Gogh (1853-1890), a Dutch painter whose short life of poverty and loneliness was climaxed by insanity and suicide. He employed sharp brush lines, following the form of the object he painted, as can be seen in Color Plate 21. Van Gogh was concerned not with presenting simply a photographic representation of what lay before him but with conveying the intense feelings evoked in himself by his subject. As a consequence, he was ready to distort what he saw in order to depict these sensations, even as Cézanne had abandoned perspective where necessary so as to concentrate on form and spatial relationships.

Expressionism and Cubism. Continuing to experiment, artists became increasingly concerned with painting what they felt about an object rather than the object itself. This method of using an object as a means of expressing subjective feelings is known as Expressionism, an approach similar to that of the symbolist school in literature. Among the early Expressionists—or *les fauves* (the wild beasts) as they were derided by their critics—was Henri Matisse (1869-1954), who had learned to simplify form partly from African primitive art and had studied the color schemes of oriental carpets. His decorative style was to influence design strongly in our own day.

Experimentation took still other subjective forms. We have already noted that in order to achieve a sense of depth and solidity, Cézanne used geometric shapes and depth relationships on the two-dimensional painting surface. Further developments along these lines resulted in the emergence of a new school—Cubism. Cubists would choose an object, then construct an abstract pattern from it. In doing so, they went far beyond the traditional manner of reproducing the object from one vantage point; instead, they viewed it from several points of view simultaneously. In a Cubist canvas one might see a combination of objects, fragmented, simplified, and joined, with all the dissected elements interpenetrating to form an abstract pattern. We see such a pattern in "The City" (Color Plate 25) by Ferdinand Leger (1881-1955). Leger often used machines as subjects for his cubist paintings.

Architecture reflects the machine age. For a great part of the nineteenth century, architectural styles were largely derivative. We saw how the Gothic revival spawned a vast number of houses, public buildings, and even bridges in pseudomedieval style. As the century wore on, structures continued to be erected not only in the Gothic but in Rococo and other styles as well. This eclectic approach was due in no small measure to the fact that large houses and factories alike were often erected for middle-class entrepreneurs who believed that the best

Building in their different ways on the accomplishments of the Impressionist school, Cézanne and Matisse did much to create the golden age of French modern art. In paintings such as "House in Provence" (below), Cézanne employed the rich color and atmospheric effects of the Impressionists but gave solidity to the forms in the composition and emphasized their relationships in space. Influenced both by Impressionist works and by Persian art, Matisse emphasized the arrangement of simple, rhythmic forms, rich textures, and vivid areas of color in paintings like "Goldfish and Sculpture" (at the right).

way to prove that they had arrived socially was to build in styles traditionally associated with the aristocracy. Meanwhile, public buildings in the rapidly growing towns were designed in a massive and ornamental style calculated to reflect civic grandeur and opulence. From the standpoint of today's architects, there was a total lack of sensitivity in the way that buildings were related —or, rather, unrelated—to their sites.

In the great new industrial towns, mile after mile of cheap, standardized houses— often little more than barracks—were put up by speculative builders; and social reformers had a difficult time attempting to curb the spread of urban blight in an age of unbridled individualism.

Meanwhile, some exciting original thinking had been concentrated on commercial architecture. Aided by advances in industry and technology, architects were now able to design structures that could span greater distances and enclose greater areas than had hitherto been possible. However much of a tragedy, the great fire that leveled much of Chicago in 1871 had the benefit of putting that city in the forefront with a new form of architecture, the steel-skeleton skyscraper. Whereas high buildings had formerly required immensely thick masonry walls, a metal frame now allowed the weight of the structure to be distributed on an entirely different principle and permitted a far more extensive use of glass than ever before. Outstanding among the pioneers in this new architecture was Chicago's Louis Sullivan (1856-1924). Like others, Sullivan perceived the value of the skyscraper in providing a large amount of useful space on a small plot of expensive land, such as that in Chicago's Loop or in Manhattan. Unlike others, he rejected all attempts to disguise the skeleton of the skyscraper behind some false façade and boldly proclaimed it by a clean sweep of line. Sullivan's emphasis upon the functional was to have far-reaching influence.

One of Sullivan's pupils, the brilliant Frank Lloyd Wright (1869-1959), was meanwhile originating revolutionary designs for houses. One feature of Wright's houses was the interweaving of interiors and exteriors by the use of terraces and cantilevered roofs. He felt that a building should look appropriate on its site; it should "grow out of the land." His "prairie houses," with their long, low lines, were designed to blend in with the flat land of the Midwest (see illustration). Much that is taken for granted in today's houses derives directly from Wright's experiments at the turn of the century.

In the decade prior to World War I, there developed in Germany a fairly widely accepted style of architecture that broke with tradition and stressed the use of new forms reflecting the machine age. In 1914 one of the leaders of this movement, Walter Gropius (1883-   ), displayed in an exhibition in Cologne a factory which, with its emphasis on horizontals, its use of glass, its exposure of staircases, and its undisguised functionalism, we would accept today as contemporary. The new movement in architecture resulted in the establishment of a school of functional art and architecture, the Bauhaus, in 1918. Gropius and Ludwig Miës van der Rohe (1886-   ) were the leading teachers of architecture in this school.

Impressionism and experimentation in music. In the early years of the period 1870 to 1914, romanticism was still the main style in the musical world. As we will recall from Chapter 5, Brahms and Tschaikovsky were offering the public new orchestral works, and Verdi and Wagner were writing operas. A post-Wagnerian school persisted well into the twentieth century. One of its outstanding members, Richard Strauss (1864-1949), enlivened the musical scene with his brilliant orchestrations and his dramatic music.

A striking departure from musical tradition occurred with the rise of the French school of impressionism, whose foremost exponent was Claude Debussy (1862-1918). Just as Monet and other painters had achieved new atmospheric effects by their technical innovations, so composers now engaged in "tone painting" to achieve a special mood or atmosphere. Such an effect is immediately recognizable in Debussy's prelude "L'Aprés-midi d'un faune" ("Afternoon of a Faun"), which astounded the musical

Louis Sullivan's maxim "Form follows function" set the keynote for the new architecture of the late nineteenth century and the twentieth century. Sullivan, Frank Lloyd Wright, and Walter Gropius produced revolutionary designs born of the concept that external form should express frankly the purpose of the building, the internal structure, and the materials used. At the left is a Chicago department store designed by Sullivan; Wright's Robie House in Chicago is shown at the bottom right; and Gropius' Hall of Machines, built for the Cologne exhibition of 1914, is at the center right.

world when it was first performed in 1892. The Impressionist painters had obtained their effects by juxtaposing different colors. The composers in turn juxtaposed widely separated chords to create similarly brilliant, shimmering effects with sound.

A number of other composers rebelled strongly against romanticism and engaged in striking experimentation. Breaking with the major-minor system of tonality, which had been the western musical tradition since the Renaissance, some of them began to make use of several different keys simultaneously, a device known as polytonality. Outstanding among such composers, Igor Stravinski (1882-   ) has done for modern music what innovators like Picasso have done for modern painting. Unlike the romanticists, Stravinski was less concerned with melody than with achieving his effects by means of polytonality, dissonant harmonies, and percussive rhythms. Meanwhile, other composers were experimenting with atonality (the absence of any fixed key). In this regard, we should mention the twelve-tone system developed by Arnold Schönberg (1874-1952). Compositions of this structure depart from all tonality and harmonic progressions, while at the same time stressing extreme dissonances.

With the work of composers like Schönberg we arrive at expressionism in music. Just as the Expressionist painters were attempting to create a new inner reality, so composers sought to give meaning to their subconscious feelings by getting below the surface. Here once again we see the influence of Freud and his school at work prior to 1914. Although harsh and unpleasant to many ears, these experiments with polytonality and atonality had validity for a century in which the old absolute values were being broken down—a century, as two world wars were to prove, of clashing dissonance.

THE ''GILDED AGE''

The "Gilded Age" defined. The fast-moving and kaleidoscopic period from 1871 to 1914 saw the swift industrialization and urbanization of western Europe and America.

In company with these developments, it saw the rise of great wealth and social ostentation on the one hand and of great slums and exploitation on the other. In 1871 Mark Twain surveyed the American social scene and, repelled by the vulgarity, ignorance, and money grabbing he saw, described it as the "Gilded Age." Certainly the period was largely acquisitive and materialistic. Yet on both sides of the Atlantic it was likewise vigorous, self-confident, buoyant, and forward thrusting, for people continued to equate science and inventiveness with progress. And it must also be remembered that this Gilded Age produced its full quota of earnest men and women who sought not only to live decent, sober lives but also to ameliorate the social and economic abuses existing in a new industrial environment.

Triumph of the city. In Lincoln's day, only one sixth of the American people lived in towns of eight thousand or more. By 1900 such centers contained one third of the population; and this figure grew much higher in the next fifteen years as immigration reached unprecedented proportions, with most of the newcomers seeking jobs in the sprawling industrial cities. In 1850 New York had less than 700,000 inhabitants; at the end of the century it possessed more than 3,000,000. Chicago, a frontier town in 1860, increased about tenfold in the same period.

While the European cities lost instead of gained from transatlantic emigration, they acquired in turn their own type of immigrant—the rural workers who flocked to the new factories. This was the period of the rise of huge industrial complexes in the English Midlands, along the Scottish Clyde, and in the German Ruhr.

The industrial city had triumphed, but at an exorbitant social cost. It sprang up without any city planning or municipal amenities. In Glasgow in the 1890's the slum population lived in giant mud-colored tenements, often a family to a single room, with plumbing limited to a tap on the staircase so that all water had to be carried in and all waste carried out. These conditions—where dirt, darkness, disease, and drink banded together in unholy alliance—were duplicated in other cities on both sides of the Atlantic, as we can read from Jacob Riis' exposé of slum conditions in New York in 1890 and from accounts of the labors of Jane Addams in Chicago in the same period. Ten years later Riis was able to report that the worst horrors of the East Side slums were being eliminated; and Jane Addams and other social reformers were successfully pioneering elsewhere for cleaner streets, more parks, and the protection of children. Still, the Gilded Age did little more than make a start to eradicate the social blight it had done so much to create.

The wealthy and *nouveau riche*. At the other end of the social ladder from the slum dwellers stood the chief inheritors of industrialism's triumph—the moneyed aristocracy in America and the titled aristocracy in Europe, with the two groups often intermarrying in order to derive the best of both worlds. It has been estimated that whereas there were only three millionaires in the United States in 1861, by the end of the century this figure had climbed to at least 3800; about one tenth of the people owned some nine tenths of the country's wealth.

How did this one tenth handle its social responsibilities? Among the older-established elements of society the accumulation of wealth was often accompanied by a minimum of ostentation. But the same could hardly be said for the activities of many of the newly rich captains of industry who formed the American plutocracy. This group reveled in what a shrewd social observer of the day, Thorstein Veblen, termed "conspicuous consumption." They erected Italian villas, Scottish castles, and French chateaus and ransacked the treasure houses of Europe to fill them up. "Even the Orient was forced to yield up graven goddesses of mercy and complacent Buddhas to decorate the buildings of men absorbed in making soap, steel rails, whisky, and cotton bagging and to please the women who spent the profits of business enterprise. The armor of mediaeval knights soon stood in the halls of captains of industry whose boldest strokes were courageous guesses on the stock market or the employment of Pinkerton detectives against striking workingmen; while Mandarin coats from Peking sprawled on the pianos of magnates who knew not Ming or Manchu and perhaps could not tell whether their hired musicians were grinding out Wagner or Chopin. Grand ladies, who remembered with a blush the days when they laundered the family clothes, shone idly resplendent in jewels garnered by a search of two hemispheres."[29]

Heyday of the middle class. Securely cushioned between the extremes of the social structure was the middle class, undoubtedly the most important segment of western society. Its members had become progressively more prosperous until it was their purchasing power which kept the economy strong. Similarly, the middle-class vote at the polls proved decisive, while in the social sphere it was middle-class mores with their heavy emphasis upon "respectability" which set the overall tone of pre-1914 society. The upper middle class might enjoy incomes in 1900 that were under $10,000 a year—but money had a purchasing power perhaps four times that of the same amount today. On these incomes the members of the middle class maintained three- and four-story houses with domestic help that included a cook, maid, and possibly a laundress.

Education. The Gilded Age must be credited with a strong endorsement of universal education. The middle and upper classes recognized the indispensability of providing all future citizens with at least a minimum of schooling. Otherwise, it would prove impossible to maintain an industrial, urban economy that was becoming increasingly complex. Throughout western Europe illiteracy fell sharply, while in the United States it declined from 17 per cent of the population in 1880 to less than 11 per cent in 1900. However, at the turn of the century formal schooling amounted to an average of only five years; only one out of ten American youngsters went to high school, in contrast to a ratio of three out of four half a century later.

The middle class was sending an increasing proportion of its young members on to higher education. The number of colleges and universities in the United States increased from 350 in 1878 to about 500 twenty years later, and during that same time the number of college students rose from some 58,000 to about 100,000.

Status of women. Among the beneficiaries of this expansion of higher education, especially in the United States and Britain, were women. As far back as 1833, when it first opened its doors, Oberlin College in Ohio had been coeducational, but it was during the Gilded Age that the former masculine monopoly was broken in state universities and many privately endowed institutions. Women were being admitted to Scotland's four universities, while in England women's colleges were now built at Oxford and Cambridge.

The Gilded Age saw the progressive emancipation of women in the social and economic sphere, and it was only to be expected that political emancipation would eventually follow. New Zealand granted the vote to women in 1893 and Norway and Finland before the First World War. In Britain the struggle for woman suffrage gathered momentum; and in the United States various states, beginning with Wyoming, granted political rights to women during the 1890's. But elsewhere the fight was contested bitterly, with many men arguing that politics were by their very nature coarse and would therefore inevitably sully the purer nature of womanhood, and with many women regarding the suffragettes as being unfeminine or worse. "Go home and wash the dishes!" met the marchers in New York suffrage parades, while in London the police bundled off to jail suffragettes caught pouring acid into letter boxes or engaging in similar acts to draw attention to their cause.

Dress. The kind of domestic establishment that one maintained, its address in the town, the nature of the horse equipage in which the family took its Sunday outing—all these were important symbols of status among the upper and middle classes alike. Dress was no less important; it differentiated the classes from the masses to a degree unknown today, when every girl, whether at the coun-

try club or behind the store counter, has her nylons. In their voluminous crinolines or bustles, their whalebone corsets that pinched the waist to achieve an hourglass silhouette, their multiple petticoats, their evening gowns with trains attached, and their galleonlike hats swaying decorously upon the coiled hair that was hymned as woman's crowning glory, our great-grandmothers were not ideally dressed to sprint for the last commuter's special. But then they had no such intention—theirs was a much more leisurely existence.

Yet though, by present standards, any pre-1914 feminine dress would have seemed unduly enveloping (except for evening gowns which favored a décolletage as revealing as anything seen on television screens today), there was, in fact, a distinct movement after the turn of the century to simplify and lighten women's apparel. This was a reflection of the progressively active role which women were assuming, whether at the office, the tennis court, or the seaside.

Prosperous males in turn affected an elegance and formality unknown today. In the earlier decades of the Gilded Age, every substantial citizen wore a frock coat and a silk hat. Starch was an indispensable ingredient in men's apparel, and in retrospect seems to have entered into the whole fabric of society as well. Men wore stiff-fronted shirts, stiff cuffs, and stiff collars, though the last-named were often made of celluloid, which cleaned easily but was inflammable. Like their female counterparts, men considered themselves undressed without hats. The silk hat and the derby easily differentiated the classes from the cloth-capped masses.

Amusements and sports. In the Gilded Age, much of the family's entertainment centered in the home, where young and old alike watched magic-lantern shows or held musical evenings. The artistic quality of these exhibitions undoubtedly would suffer by comparison with that of present-day mechanical importations into the home, but at least the entertainment had the compensatory value of personal participation and group sociability. On both sides of the At-

lantic, the theater, music hall, and vaude-
ville show flourished. But the minstrel shows
and crude melodramas that had been so
popular prior to the turn of the century
waned in popularity as urban audiences became progressively more sophisticated, and
the first decade of this century saw the
spread of motion pictures.

As might be expected, too, the rapid urbanization of western society stimulated the
rise of professional spectator sports. In Britain, the labor force would turn out *en masse*
on Saturdays to watch professional soccer
teams fight their way to the top of the
various national divisions, while in the
United States at this time, baseball was becoming the national pastime. In 1903 the
Boston Red Sox captured the first World
Series' championship. Boxing was yet another popular spectator pastime, but tennis and
golf remained the virtual monopoly of the
propertied and professional classes.

A new era. The population was becoming
more mobile. In Europe groups engaged in
bicycling or walking trips, and Cook's travel
agency organized inexpensive tours which
gave thousands of people the first opportunity they had ever known to become acquainted with the traditions, way of life, and
historical monuments of neighboring lands.
In America the railroads encouraged mass
travel by means of low-cost excursions.

But it was after 1900 that the tempo of
movement picked up appreciably. The automobile revolution had begun. In 1906
Woodrow Wilson had described the motor
car as offering "a picture of the arrogance of
wealth,"[30] but within a few years this luxury was to be considered a necessity. One
reason was its obvious value in breaking
down the virtual isolation in which rural
communities existed; another was its effectiveness in bringing about the decentralization of congested industrial complexes and
stimulating the rise of suburbs. Still other
reasons were at work: the automobile was a
new but highly potent symbol of status, but
at the same time, thanks to Henry Ford's
devising of the first assembly line in 1913,
it could be obtained by millions of people.
The era of mass production, mass consump-

A decorator of the Gilded Age once remarked that a room
could not be overdecorated or overfurnished so long as there
was space to walk around. Carved furniture, molded ceilings,
densely flowered rugs, elaborately framed pictures and mirrors, and a rich variety of fancy bric-a-brac satisfied the
Victorian's love of florid ornamentation. Scarcely a simple
straight line was to be seen in a parlor of this era; the lines of
all the furnishings curved, twisted, or wriggled.

tion, mass tastes—in short, of democracy in
the mass—had arrived.

The Gilded Age with its class stratification and dangerously undemocratic extremes
of living standards had drawn to a close by
1914. It had been an era at once secure,
stable, acquisitive, and materialistic. It was
replaced by a society that was more mobile,
more equalitarian, more insecure, but perhaps no less acquisitive. In any case, it was a
society that was now reaping the full cornu-
copia of technological wonders and gadgets
derived from the application of the great
scientific developments of the period from
1871 to 1914.

SUMMARY

The period from 1871 to 1914 constituted
the zenith of western intellectual and social

dominance and especially that of western Europe. Within this period of slightly less than fifty years, a revolution took place in physics: Clerk-Maxwell's experiments with optics and electricity paved the way for the subsequent invention of wireless telegraphy, radio, and television; the discovery of x-rays led to research into the structure and nature of the atom. Traditional concepts of the nature of energy were dealt a blow by Planck with his quantum theory, while Einstein's theory of relativity called for an entirely new approach to existing concepts of time, velocity, space, and gravitation.

Hardly less spectacular was the progress made in other sciences. Chemical synthesis made possible the development of a prosperous synthetic-dye industry in Germany and elsewhere; scientists learned about proteins and vitamins, about the presence and purpose of ductless glands, and about the uses of chemotherapy in the treatment of disease; and the work of Koch and Pasteur put the twin sciences of bacteriology and immunology on a firm footing. The study of biology was advanced by Mendel's experiments and by Galton's researches into human heredity. Knowledge of man was carried forward by the behavioristic school of psychology; while the subjective side of man was investigated by Freud, who pioneered in the field of psychoanalysis.

These spectacular advances in science, accompanied as they were by a whole host of new inventions and technological wonders, gripped the popular imagination as never before. A cult of science developed. People became skeptical of anything which could not be proven in the laboratory. There developed a strong—and for many earnest people, an anguished—struggle between the claims advanced for science and those of organized religion. Although Darwin had already shaken a previous era with his evolutionary hypothesis, it was this period that experienced its full impact in both the scientific and social spheres. Perhaps the most pernicious aspect of the claims advanced in the name of science was that of social Darwinism, which in the writings of such violent antidemocrats as Nietzsche ap-

plied the doctrine of the survival of the fittest to the economic, political, and eventually to the military spheres with disastrous results.

The writers and artists of these decades had been turning away from the romanticism of the first half of the nineteenth century to embrace a down-to-earth, photographic approach known as realism. In literature, Balzac, Flaubert, Tolstoy, Dostoevski, Hardy, James, and Twain led the way; in painting, Courbet and Daumier. In the hands of such writers as Zola and De Maupassant, realism was carried to its extreme form of presentation, known as naturalism. The problem play heralded the rise of social criticism in the theater; its greatest exponents were Ibsen and Shaw. In painting, following the brilliant results achieved by the Impressionists in obtaining new surface and atmospheric effects, other artists concerned themselves with painting what they felt about an object rather than the object itself—an approach associated with the school known as Expressionism. Cézanne is credited with much of the experimentation in the direction of nonobjective painting; by the end of the period Picasso and the Cubists were breaking radically with traditional subject matter and perspective alike. Architecture broke with the largely derivative styles of the preceding period; experiments with new materials and new designs sought to satisfy the requirements of a highly industrialized society.

But as is so often the case in history, the concepts of the creative thinkers such as Einstein, Freud, Picasso, Stravinski, and Wright had yet to be worked out in terms of social acceptance and integration. The Gilded Age was still motivated by the intellectual and social fashions of an era which had in fact been outstripped by the ideational pioneers. Our survey closes in 1914, the year of the outbreak of the First World War—itself the logical culmination of the doctrine of the survival of the fittest. The physical waste and moral bankruptcy of this conflict are bitter indexes of the hideous perversion of such a theory when misapplied to human society.

20 Claude Monet: "The River" (1868). It was in the second half of the 19th century that painting took on a character we would now identify as modern. The subjective matter of the progressive painting of the time shifted away from the lofty narratives and idealized scenes of Neoclassic and romantic art to a realism and an immediacy which reflected the environment of a dominant middle class. Still more important, the form and the method of painting changed radically, often to the consternation of the conservative critics of the day. The work of Monet, one of the leaders of the impressionists, illustrates the motives and means of that movement. In an attempt to capture the character of outdoor light, Monet employed color of unprecedented brilliance loosely and directly, often in short choppy strokes and staccato patches. The result is a light that shimmers and dazzles as it does in the out-of-doors, and an atmospheric quality that avows the presence of air between foreground and background. While the finished painting is thus truer to the eye, it is, paradoxically, rendered more abstractly, as if by a kind of visual shorthand. And while it conveys a sense of space, it retains at the same time a curiously flat playing-card effect. Thus a tension arose in 19th-century painting between naturalism and abstraction. In its later resolution by the postimpressionists—towards abstraction—a fundamental direction in modern art was set.

21 (above) **Vincent Van Gogh: "Peasant of the Camargue"** (1888), and **22** (right) **Paul Cezanne: "The Basket of Apples"**
(1890-1894). With the art of the postimpressionists a basic change occurred in the artist's attitude toward the art work and
the natural world. For Cezanne, Van Gogh, Seurat, and Gauguin, the work of art itself became more important than the
accurate depiction of nature; they believed that a work of art could be made more expressive by reshaping and reinterpret-
ing nature. Abstracted forms thus began to infiltrate their art, and the era of realist painting gradually drew to a close.
    The still lifes of Cezanne are not so much pictures of apples, bottles, and other memorabilia of the visible world as they
are essays in formal pictorial architecture. Though he employed many impressionist devices, such as direct color and bold

brushwork, Cezanne sought to replace the breezy and casual compositions of the impressionists with a firmer, more calculated order. To create this soundness of structure, he positioned and modeled his forms with scrupulous care. Occasional distortions (note that the bottle tilts upward to the left, and the back edge of the table is broken into two levels) were allowed in order to achieve a tighter, more dynamic organization.

Van Gogh takes similar liberties with the appearance of the physical world, less for the purpose of pictorial composition than to express his own emotional responses to the world. His ardent temperament combined with an uncommon compassion for humanity—especially for the poor and the humble. These motivations lay behind the intense vigor of his painting style—particularly the explosive brush strokes, the broad color, and the vibrant linear energy. The result in this painting is a heightening of the robust peasant strength he sought to communicate. "Instead of trying to reproduce exactly what I have before my eyes," Van Gogh is reported to have said, "I use color more arbitrarily so as to express myself more forcibly." He enunciated, thereby, the postimpressionist point of view.

23 Henri de Toulouse-Lautrec: "At the Moulin Rouge" (1892). Paris, long the capital of the international art world, was one of the great cosmopolitan centers of western Europe during the 19th century, and shone with special brightness in the 1890's. The society which promenaded on its boulevards and frequented its bistros was a varied and colorful one, reflecting the ebullience and vitality of Europe in the pre-World War I era. One of the most memorable chroniclers of Paris was Toulouse-Lautrec, who devoted his brief career largely to recording the mood and manners of Montmartre. There he found richness next to tawdriness, gaiety next to bitterness, and he portrayed these qualities effectively by means of a detached, clinical objectivity. A superb draftsman who learned much from impressionist theories, Lautrec is at his keenest in this informal but acutely perceived scene from the famous Moulin Rouge dance hall. The artist, whose physical growth was stunted by a childhood accident, has pictured himself, together with his noticeably taller cousin, in the background, just to the left of center.

CHAPTER 12

Parliaments and Political Reforms

CONSTITUTIONAL GOVERNMENT AND SOCIAL JUSTICE: 1871-1914

Introduction. The year 1871 ended one period of European history and began another. Nationalism had just witnessed two major successes—the unification of Germany and the unification of Italy. The First Industrial Revolution had taken place, living conditions of ordinary people had improved, and the tempo of industrial progress continued to accelerate. Through colonization and economic imperialism, European influence was being extended over the world.

In politics some substantial advances toward full democracy were being made, especially in Britain. In the era of the Victorian Compromise the gentry and middle class controlled the government. In the 1860's, fearful of the rising influence of the business class, the English nobility allied itself with the laboring class, which, taking advantage of increased educational opportunities,

became politically ambitious and demanded an effective voice in government. Many among the well-to-do had real fear of revolution; to them it seemed better to grant concessions to the masses than to risk bloodshed such as Paris had witnessed in 1848 and 1871. Under Disraeli, city workers got the vote; under Gladstone, suffrage was extended to agricultural workers. Britain entered the twentieth century an almost completely democratic state, both politically and economically.

The second great democratic power of the late nineteenth century was France, which, for the third time, attempted to adopt a republican form of government after its humiliating defeat at the hands of Prussia in 1870. The first important act of the Third French Republic was the defeat of the Commune, a revolutionary body which brought about a violent and bloody civil uprising in Paris. As the nineteenth century closed, France was further convulsed by a series of scandals and crises (the most notorious and menacing was the Dreyfus case) that threatened to discredit, and even to overthrow, the Republic. Although by 1914 democratic France seemed to have ridden out the storm, the feuds and scandals had left serious scars.

After 1870 the third great power in western Europe, Germany, made phenomenal progress in industry, science, and govenmental administration. For nearly twenty years after the creation of the Second Reich in 1871, the masterful Bismarck strengthened national sentiment, sought to improve the lot of the masses, and attempted to make the new Germany militarily unassailable. But his failure to give Germans an opportunity to exercise real political responsibility created problems when autocratic William II became the real leader of Germany in 1890.

The farther one traveled eastward from London and Paris the more shallow-rooted democracy became. In Austria-Hungary the discontent of a number of submerged nationalities stultified real parliamentary government. In the Balkans parliamentary government of only a crude kind existed, while in the Ottoman empire cruelty and despotism reigned. Russia began to experiment with social and political reform in the 1860's and to promote economic development, but the government moved too slowly. The results were terrorism against the tsar's regime, the intensification of despotism, and, in 1905, a revolution which turned out to be a mere dress rehearsal for the cataclysm of 1917—the Bolshevik Revolution.

TOWARD DEMOCRATIZATION

OF BRITISH LIFE

Cabinet Government in England. Ever since the Glorious Revolution (1688) ended the divine right of kings in Great Britain there had slowly and unobtrusively evolved what is known today as cabinet government, a unique British contribution which has spread to many parts of the world. Cabinet government unites executive and legislative policies in the hands of a small body of men known as the cabinet, whose chief is the prime minister. This official and his colleagues are in turn the instrument of the majority in the House of Commons. When a prime minister no longer has the confidence of the House of Commons, he must resign or "appeal to the country" by calling an election. Neither for the executive nor for the cabinet is there a stipulated tenure as in the United States.

From its inception, cabinet government strengthened the political party system, for to enjoy unity and strength, the majority needs the cohesion and discipline provided by a political party. At the same time, those in the minority consolidate their strength by belonging to the party of the "opposition."

The cabinet system in Britain permits the king to keep the appearance of power: the members of the cabinet are "His Majesty's Ministers," bills become laws in his name, and the civil service is busy in "His Majesty's Service." Nevertheless, the prerogatives of power are exercised by the prime minister and his cabinet, who are the servants of the House of Commons.

The democratization of the English government in the nineteenth century was achieved by the democratization of Parliament. The base of representation was widened, and the importance of the House of Lords was curbed; by 1914 Parliament was to a considerable extent the voice of the people.

End of the Victorian Compromise. The period from 1832 to 1865 is often described as the era of the Victorian Compromise. During this period, an alliance of the landed gentry and the middle class worked together to dominate the government and keep the lower classes "in their stations." The members of the middle class believed that the political reforms—which had been in large measure of benefit to them alone—had gone far enough. Although some social reforms were granted, they were exceptions in the general atmosphere of complacency.

The symbol of this conservatism was Lord Palmerston (1784-1865), a dashing and colorful political figure, who dominated the direction of foreign affairs from the 1830's until his death and ended his career by acting as prime minister during much of the period from 1855 to 1865. Strongly upholding the prestige and influence of Britain in the world, this forthright John Bull became the idol of his countrymen. Palmerston was also a strong pillar of the Victorian Compromise. Himself a viscount, he was quite satisfied with the rule of the aristocracy and the middle class.

In the 1850's, several bills to expand the suffrage were introduced in the House of Commons but were defeated. Apart from Palmerston's opposition, these measures had little chance because of the confused party situation during this period of transition in which the old Whig and Tory parties were gradually regrouping to create the modern Liberals and Conservatives. The two-party system was not functioning; governments were formed by unstable alliances among various groups.

Gladstone and Disraeli. The death of Palmerston in 1865 and the entry of two new political leaders into the limelight heralded the beginning of a new era in British affairs. For a generation, English politics was little more than the biographies of William Ewart Gladstone (1809-1898), a Liberal, and Benjamin Disraeli (1804-1881), a Conservative, who alternated with one another as prime minister from 1867 to 1880. Following the death of Disraeli, Gladstone continued to dominate politics until his retirement in 1894.

The son of a rich Liverpool merchant, Gladstone had every advantage that wealth and good social position could bestow. As a student at Oxford, he first planned to enter the Anglican Church and combine this clerical career with scholarly pursuits. Instead, he became interested in politics and entered Parliament in 1833 at the age of twenty-four. The young politician quickly made a name for himself as one of the greatest orators of his day, on one occasion holding the attention of the House of Commons for five hours while he expounded the intricacies of the national budget. At first Gladstone was a conservative in politics, a follower of the Tory leader Robert Peel. But gradually he shifted his allegiance to the Liberal (Whig) party, which he headed for the first time as prime minister in 1868. Gladstone was a stanch supporter of laissez faire, the belief that government should not interfere in business. His record as a social and economic reformer, therefore, was not imposing. But in political reforms his accomplishments were noteworthy.

The great rival of Gladstone, Benjamin Disraeli, had few advantages of birth and social position. The son of a cultured Jew who had become a naturalized British subject in 1801, Disraeli was baptized an Anglican. He first made a name for himself as a novelist with *Vivian Grey* (1826). Unlike Gladstone, Disraeli swung from liberalism to conservatism in his political philosophy, though he stood for office as a Conservative throughout his career. All his life somewhat a fop and dandy, Disraeli created a furor when he first appeared in the staid House of Commons attired in a yellow vest and green trousers. His language was grandiloquent and florid, and his first speech was received by some of the members with derision and laughter. The House was in an uproar, and Disraeli shouted as he sat down:

Though I sit down now, the time will come when you will hear me.[1]

This setback did not dim Disraeli's confidence in his own powers, and he steadily forged ahead to become the leader of the Conservative (Tory) party.

What made the rivalry between the Liberal and Conservative parties sharp and exciting was the complete difference in the qualities of their leaders. Gladstone, the Liberal leader, was deeply religious and very serious in both manner and speech. Levity was not one of his vices. If he ran short of logic, he found it easy to enlist the aid of God, thus attempting to place his opponents in an unchristian position. Gladstone's oratory—at its best eloquent and logical, though seldom enlivened by humor—tended to become very involved and wordy. Even in conversation he spoke as if he were addressing a public meeting; it was said that "Queen Victoria could chat away gaily about her paintings and her distant German cousins with the sympathetic and courteous Disraeli; but she had to listen while Gladstone lectured her on the Hittites or Homer or the Athanasian Creed."[2]

Disraeli, on the other hand, never appeared self-righteous. A man of the world, he enlivened British politics with his wit and sarcasm. Concerning the employment of children in factories, he wrote:

Infanticide is practised as extensively and as legally in England as it is on the banks of the Ganges; a circumstance which apparently has not yet engaged the attention of the Society for the Propagation of the Gospel in Foreign Parts.[3]

And he characterized Gladstone as:

. . . a sophistical rhetorician inebriated by the exuberance of his own verbosity.[4]

The Reform Bill of 1867. By 1865 it was obvious that the Victorian Compromise could not be maintained any longer. English workers had formed large organizations to agitate for liberalization of voting. Both the new Conservative party, drawing its strength mainly from the landowning gentry, and the Liberals, supported by the middle class, realized that reform must come.

It was Gladstone's turn first. While not actually prime minister as yet, Gladstone in 1866 introduced a moderate reform bill giving the vote to city laborers. His proposal failed to pass, however, and the country was rocked by agitation and riots. Into power came a Conservative government. Hoping to secure wider support for his party, Disraeli in 1867 successfully sponsored another reform bill that added a little more than a million city workers to the voting rolls.

In 1832 the electorate had been increased 50 per cent; in 1867 it was increased by 88 per cent. Although women and farm laborers still could not vote, Britain was well on the road to political democracy. In 1868, similar acts were passed for Ireland and Scotland. These reforms aroused considerable conservative opposition. The famous Victorian writer Thomas Carlyle called it "Shooting Niagara," and another critic dolefully predicted:

A shrewd negotiator in both domestic and foreign affairs, Benjamin Disraeli revitalized the Tory party and extended British rule in Africa, the Middle East, and the Pacific.

The bag which holds the winds will be untied, and we shall be surrounded by a perpetual whirl of change, alteration, innovation, and revolution.[5]

Gladstone's "Glorious Ministry." In 1868, Disraeli became prime minister. He had, as he put it, "climbed to the top of the greasy pole." An election held at the end of the year, however, brought Gladstone and the Liberals back to power. Gladstone's so-called "Glorious Ministry," which was to last from 1868 to 1874, was one of great achievements.

One of its most important reforms was the extension of educational facilities. There was no national system of schools in the 1860's; education was largely in the hands of the churches and private schools. Somewhat confusingly to Americans, the most important of England's private schools—such as Eton and Harrow—were termed "public schools." Wags commented that they were called "public" because they were private, "English" because the main languages taught were Latin and Greek, and "schools" because most activity took place in the cricket fields. In 1833 the government had made its first grant to this private system of education.

With the enfranchisement of the city masses, it became imperative that their children be given an education. The Education Act of 1870 made possible the setting up of local school boards authorized to build and maintain government schools. Fees could be charged (they were not abolished until 1891), and attendance could be made compulsory from the age of five to thirteen. Subsidies from the government were given to the private schools, which were required to meet certain minimum standards. In ten years, attendance in elementary schools jumped from one million to four million.

In the governmental and military administrations, most appointments and promotions had traditionally depended upon patronage and favoritism. The situation had been corrected to a degree in 1853, when the Indian civil service had been placed on a competitive basis, but it was in 1870 that employment in the British civil service was finally based upon open examinations of a highly intellectual character.

In the meantime, the Crimean War against Russia had exposed many weaknesses in the British army, and thoroughgoing changes were introduced by the war office. The terms of enlistment were improved, and flogging as a military punishment in peacetime was abolished. Above all, the purchase of commissions was eliminated. Up to this time an officer's rank had been his own personal property that could be sold to the highest bidder. High rank was frequently an evidence of personal wealth rather than of any special military talent.

Another long-needed change was the reform of the legal system and the courts, which made justice surer and speedier in Britain. The Ballot Act of 1872 establishing secret balloting, another Gladstone reform, was just as important for the functioning of democracy in England as was the Educa-

In his four terms as prime minister, William Gladstone achieved many important political reforms.

tion Act of 1870. Before the enfranchisement of the urban workers, it had not been so essential to have secret balloting, for only the rich could vote and a rich man had few superiors who could intimidate him. But open balloting had exposed the workers to pressure from their employers, landlords, and others.

Disraeli and progressive Toryism. By the early 1870's, however, the reforming zeal of the Glorious Ministry had run down. It was said that the ministers "had spent their majority like gentlemen." And Disraeli wittily referred to Gladstone and his colleagues in the House of Commons as a "range of exhausted volcanoes." The story of the con-

The English satirical magazine *Punch* in 1868 portrayed Benjamin Disraeli and William Gladstone as rival stars in the theater. Much to the displeasure of Gladstone, Disraeli had just become prime minister. The original caption follows:
Mr. Bendizzy (Hamlet). " 'To be or not to be, that is the question:' —Ahem!"
Mr. Gladstone (out of an engagement). [Aside.] " 'Leading business,' forsooth! His line is 'general utility' Is the manager mad? But no matter-rr—A time *will* come—"

the interest of the masses." In the landed gentry and the country squires he saw England's natural leaders—champions of the common people, who were being exploited by the middle class, the modern counterpart of the medieval nobility.

Disraeli is to be remembered particularly for his spirited foreign policy and for his advocacy of necessary political reform. But perhaps his greatest achievement is that he pointed the way toward a comprehensive scheme of social legislation. Explaining this policy, Disraeli declared:

It involves the state of the dwellings of the people, the moral consequences of which are not less considerable than the physical. It involves their enjoyment of some of the chief elements of nature—air, light, and water. It involves the regulation of their industry, the inspection of their soil. It involves the purity of their provisions, and it touches upon all the means by which you may wean them from habits of excess and brutality.[6]

Under Disraeli's ministry a number of important reforms were passed between 1874 and 1880. A factory act established a ten-hour day as the maximum for working men. Peaceful picketing was legalized, and the foundation for collective bargaining was established by a trades-union act. Sailors were protected from the dangers of overloaded and unseaworthy vessels by a new shipping act. The first large slum clearances and a new housing program were planned. The best of previous local legislation on sanitation was incorporated into a new public health law, which provided the foundation of Great Britain's future sanitation system. Still another new law required that when a building was sold landlords had to compensate tenants for improvements made at the tenant's expense. The program of social legislation passed during the six years of Benjamin Disraeli's administration compares favorably with the later and more renowned social legislation achieved in Germany by Bismarck. Under Disraeli's leadership, Britain took its first substantial step toward the welfare state.

Reform measures of Gladstone. Returning to power in 1880, Gladstone in 1884 spon-

tinued growth of democracy in Great Britain begins with the election of Benjamin Disraeli as prime minister in 1874. Attacking standpat conservatism, Disraeli advocated what he thought of as progressive Toryism, known as Tory democracy. Disraeli was not a defender of middle-class interests but tried to promote a political alliance between the conservative landed gentry and the workers against the businessmen—"government by the classes in

sored the third Reform Bill, a measure extending the franchise to agricultural workers. This act brought Britain to the verge of universal manhood suffrage. Gladstone also obtained passage of the important Employers' Liability Act. Previous common-law doctrine held that any worker accepting employment also accepted the hazards of the job; no worker could sue his employer in case of an unavoidable accident or for the negligence of a fellow worker. Gladstone's act gave the workers rights of compensation in five classes of accidents, especially in those occurring on the railroads.

The Irish problem. Gladstone resigned in 1885 but returned to head the British government in 1886 and again in 1892. During these third and fourth ministries, he was primarily concerned with attempts to solve the Irish problem. Let us review this centuries-old problem, the principal question in British politics in the late nineteenth century.

England is often credited with ability in government. But a skillful hand seems to have been entirely absent in England's relationships with Ireland—a case of chronic misgovernment. Since the Middle Ages, English kings had tried to conquer and subdue nearby Ireland. During the sixteenth century, England had become Protestant while Ireland had remained Catholic. This religious division widened the breach between conqueror and conquered, and it became customary for Irish rebels to seek aid from England's most dangerous enemies— the principal Catholic powers on the Continent. In the seventeenth century, the British government had planted large numbers of Scottish emigrants in the north of Ireland in Ulster, where a strong colony of Protestants (the so-called Scotch-Irish or Orangemen) developed. Oppressive laws were passed against the rebellious Irish Catholics, restricting their political, economic, and religious freedoms and dispossessing them of their lands. Then by the Act of Union of 1801 the Irish legislature was abolished, and the Irish were required to send their representatives to the British Parliament in London.

Wracked by poverty and famine, Ireland was further tormented in the 1840's by the mass eviction of tenant farmers. After the evictions, cottages were burned down at once to prevent other homeless farmers from occupying them. The pathetic scene above was drawn in 1848.

During the early nineteenth century, the land problem in Ireland became very acute. A large part of the cultivable land was in the hands of parasitic landlords, who spent much of their time in Dublin or London. Between 1800 and 1840 the population doubled. As the population rose, the farms were subdivided into small portions scarcely capable of supporting tenants, and many peasants were evicted because of failure to pay their rents. Landlords refused to compensate tenants for improvements. In 1845 the potato crop, the main staple of diet, failed, and a terrible famine ensued. Perhaps as many as 500,000 people died, and a huge exodus to America began—the beginning of the principal Irish Catholic settlements in the United States. In 1841 the population of Ireland was 8,770,000; in 1891 it was less than 5,000,000.

Religious and economic reforms. The Irish for their part had managed to gain some victories in the course of the nineteenth century. In 1829, for example, the British Parliament had passed the Catholic Emancipation Act, permitting Catholics to sit in Parliament. Earlier, the Irish members in Parliament had come from the Protestant minority and represented only the landlord class. This victory was largely due to the splendid leadership of Daniel O'Connell (1775-1847), Ireland's much beloved "Uncrowned King," who was an effective orator, an efficient organizer, and an unselfish patriot.

One of the tasks Gladstone set for himself upon taking office in 1868 was Irish pacification. In 1869 the Irish Anglican Church was disestablished, thus ending the use of Irish tax money to support a church to which 75 per cent of the population did not belong. To give Irish tenants more security and to rectify abuses under the system of absentee landlordism, Gladstone took up the land question. An important Irish land act was passed in 1870. In 1881 Gladstone placed on the statute book his second land act, which was intended to give the country folk of Ireland what was called the "three F's": fair rent, fixed tenure, and free sale. The result of these and subsequent land reforms was that by the close of the nineteenth century the Irish peasantry, once dispirited and impoverished, became landowners with at least a chance of earning a decent livelihood.

The Irish home rule movement. Economic improvement stimulated Irish political ambitions. While the land problem was being ameliorated, the issue of home rule came to the fore. The Home Rulers, or Irish Nationalist party, demanded that Ireland have its own legislature instead of sending representatives to the British Parliament.

At the head of the Nationalists appeared Charles Stewart Parnell (1846-1891), second only to O'Connell as a nineteenth-century Irish political leader. Entering the British House of Commons in 1874, Parnell did everything possible to obstruct business in that august body, hoping in this way to force the issue of home rule. On one occasion the House of Commons was in session forty-eight hours, one Irish member speaking five hundred times. Faced with such tactics, as well as with the fact that Parnell controlled eighty-five votes in the Commons, Prime Minister Gladstone concluded that Ireland must have home rule. In 1886 and 1893

Gladstone introduced in Parliament home rule bills which provided for an Irish parliament and for the retention of British control only over such matters as defense, foreign affairs, and customs. But both bills were defeated.

The matter dragged on for many years. Finally a third home rule bill was introduced and passed by Parliament in 1914. The Ulsterites, however, strongly opposed the measure and prepared to resist by force incorporation into a Catholic Ireland divorced from the government of Great Britain. Only the outbreak of war with Germany in 1914 prevented civil strife in Ireland. The 1914 act was never put into effect, and the question was not settled until 1921, when southern Ireland attained the status of a British dominion.

Conservative rule, 1895-1905. Gladstone's gallant fight for Irish home rule split his party and paved the way for a decade of Conservative rule in Britain (1895-1905). In the 1880's the Conservatives had actively sponsored social legislation that had helped widen governmental functions. Educational opportunities were increased, compensation for injured workers was extended, factories were subjected to more rigid safety and sanitary inspections, and hours of work for boys under eighteen were reduced. Following the return of the Conservatives to power, however, Britain became enmeshed in foreign and imperial affairs, and there was little further attempt to carry on Disraeli's program of social legislation.

Liberal rule, 1905-1914. By 1905 social and political reform at home once again claimed major attention. An increase in strikes gave evidence of discontent among workers, and the newly founded Labour party gained adherents. The Liberals, traditional champions of laissez-faire economics, decided to jettison their old ideas and embark on a bold program of social legislation.

A parliamentary commission made a monumental report on the condition of the English people. Some forty volumes of testimony painted a gloomy picture of the average worker's lot. Over 30 per cent of the adult male workers received a starvation wage of less than seven dollars per week. The pitifully small wages made it impossible for the workers to lay aside savings for increasingly frequent periods of unemployment. David Lloyd George (1863-1945), a leading member of the Liberal government who was to play a prominent role in the peace settlements after World War I, declared:

Four spectres haunt the Poor; Old Age, Accident, Sickness and Unemployment. We are going to exorcise them. We are going to drive hunger from the hearth. We mean to banish the workhouse [poorhouse] from the horizon of every workman in the land.[7]

Confronted with what was regarded as widespread economic injustice, the Liberal party under Prime Minister Herbert Asquith, Lloyd George, and Winston Churchill—the last-named just beginning his fabulous career—carried through Parliament a revolutionary reform program that provided for old-age pensions, national employment bureaus, town planning, and sickness, accident, and unemployment insurance.

In addition, labor unions were given greater protection, and members of the House of Commons, heretofore unpaid, were granted a moderate salary. This last measure enabled men without private means, chiefly in the new Labour party, to follow a political career. Thus England, the mother of the Industrial Revolution and the citadel of economic and political liberalism, discarded the old doctrine of noninterference in business. The state, acting for the benefit of the average Briton, was now the active regulator of a large segment of economic life.

Reform of the House of Lords. For some time there had been grumbling against the House of Lords because of its efforts to hinder the reform program of the Liberal government. The climax was reached when the Lords refused to pass the 1909-1910 budget prepared by the Chancellor of the Exchequer, Lloyd George. This budget, which laid new tax burdens on the richer classes, was described by its supporters as a war budget against poverty and as an effort to

make degradation as remote to the people as the wolves that once infested the forests of Celtic Britain. After a fierce struggle the budget was passed, but the House of Commons, controlled by the Liberals and their Labour allies, decided that a hereditary, irresponsible upper house was an anachronism in a democracy. Discussing the issue, Lloyd George lashed out:

. . . [The Lords] have no qualifications—at least, they *need* not have any. No testimonials are required. There are no credentials. They do not even need a medical certificate. They need not be sound either in body, or in mind. They only require a certificate of birth—just to prove that they are the first of the litter. You would not choose a spaniel on these principles.[8]

The result was the Parliament Bill of 1911. Before this bill was passed, it was necessary for Asquith to announce (as had been done with the Reform Bill in 1832) that the monarch had promised, if necessary, to create enough peers to pass the bill in the House of Lords. The bill took away from the Lords all power of absolute veto. They could not veto any money bill, and any other measure passing the Commons in three successive sessions would become law without the assent of the Lords, provided that two years had elapsed since its first introduction.

After 1911 the will of the people as expressed in the Commons could no longer be blocked by the House of Lords. The Lords were left with power only to slow up and force reconsideration of legislation of which they did not approve. When Parliament had consisted of two houses, both possessing important powers, the English legislature was bicameral; but now it was, in effect, a one-house, or unicameral, national legislature.

Vestiges of privilege. Although England by 1914 was predominantly democratic, there still remained vestiges of privilege. The right to vote was not absolute but was still based on the ownership or occupation of property. Domestic servants, bachelors living with their parents and paying no rent, and all others with no fixed abode could not vote, nor could women, who were becoming increasingly restive at being de-

The empire which the British created in the nineteenth century was the richest, the most extensive, and the most powerful in history. As master of this vast domain, Britain was a natural target for criticism from other nations. Here the American cartoonist Thomas Nast portrays a swollen John Bull who encompasses the entire world and holds it in a jealous grasp. The envy and resentment incurred by Great Britain in its role as the greatest imperial power of the nineteenth century create political difficulties even today, particularly in those countries where the English were once sovereign.

nied the franchise. (A suffragette organization demanding "Votes for Women" carried on an extensive campaign.) Socially, England still had a class system in which the nobility and the landed gentry, and to some extent the middle class, held themselves aloof from the rest of the people.

Britain: the "workshop of the world." In 1914 Britain could look back upon the century following victory at Waterloo as an amazing one for the extension of British progress, influence, and leadership in world affairs. The period from 1850 to 1875, in particular, had witnessed spectacular growth in industry, shipping, railway construction, and material wealth. The nineteenth century was Great Britain's golden age.

In 1750 England and Wales had had a predominantly rural population of 6,500,000, of whom 90 per cent lived in the country or in small villages. In 1911 the population had grown to 34,000,000, 70 per cent of whom lived in great cities and large towns.

During the early part of the nineteenth century, Great Britain had seized world leadership in industrialization and had built up a huge export trade; in 1840 one third of the world's commerce was in British hands. To carry this trade the British built a great merchant marine which accounted ultimately for half of the world's cargo shipping. As the "workshop of the world," Britain built up a tremendous amount of capital. Its total investments overseas in 1914 amounted to twenty billion dollars; its position as the world's banker was unchallenged.

The *Pax Britannica*. In the arena of nineteenth-century world affairs, its industrial might, its financial strength, and the smooth functioning and stability of its government made it possible for England to play a unique role in world affairs. The very size of the British empire meant that Englishmen were involved in developments all over the globe. While the British Isles had a total land area of only 120,000 square miles, the land area of the empire, including all the colonies, self-governing dominions, and protectorates, was almost 13,000,000 square miles. Britain presided over the greatest empire known to history—largely a nineteenth-century creation.

The *Pax Britannica* was not free of flaws or evils. Many so-called backward peoples were ruled against their will, and on occasion British businessmen thought more of their own profits than of the best interests of the native people. But there was another side. Throughout the seven seas the royal navy hunted down pirates; in Africa, slavery was almost entirely eliminated; and in India, barbarous rites such as infanticide and widow burning (*suttee*) were made punishable as capital crimes. In the absence of any world government, there was something to be said for a global system of law and defense which maintained stability in one quarter of the world's area.

FRANCE: PAINFUL PATH TO DEMOCRACY

The Third Republic. We have seen how, in France, the Second Empire with its leader Louis Napoleon was swept away amidst the tragedy and humiliation of surrender at the hands of the victorious German armies. Born in defeat, the Empire's successor, the Third Republic, went through several years of precarious existence before it was placed on a firm and popular foundation.

Its first Assembly, elected to fulfill the bitter task of making peace with Germany, was overwhelmingly royalist. This circumstance, itself a threat to the Republic, gave rise to a revolutionary movement in Paris, where republicans and radicals of every description formed a Commune, in the tradition of the Paris Commune of 1793, to save the Republic.

The Communards, as the rebels were called, were fiercely patriotic, anti-German, and opposed to the wealthy, aristocratic, and clerical classes. They favored government control of prices, wages, and working conditions. Karl Marx jubilantly welcomed the uprising, seeing in it a pattern for the future revolt of the proletariat against the capitalistic system. Here was an opportunity to use the machinery of the state to put socialist theory into practice, as envisaged by Marx's First International. The Communards aimed at decentralizing the French government into a confederation of autonomous communes, centered in the large industrial cities; socialism was then to be introduced through those communes which possessed a strong proletarian element.

For several weeks civil war raged in Paris. Following outbursts of violence and terrorism by both the government troops and the Communards, the Commune was finally suppressed. That the royalists' Assembly finally voted a republican constitution for France in 1875 was due largely to the inability of various royalist factions to agree among themselves. A republic seemed the form of government on which there was least disagreement.

Until the overthrow of the Third Republic in World War II, the improvised constitutional laws of 1875 were the basis of the French governmental system. These laws provided for the election by manhood suffrage of representatives to the Chamber of Deputies, the influential lower house. In addition to the Chamber of Deputies, there was a Senate elected from the major administrative districts, the departments. The president was elected by the legislature for a term of seven years, and his powers were so limited as to make him merely a figurehead and to give control of affairs to the legislature. The real executive was the ministry, or cabinet, appointed by the president from whatever coalition of parties or factions held a majority in the legislature. As in England, the ministry was responsible to the legislature.

By 1880 the statesmen of the Third French Republic had accomplished remarkable results. The huge indemnity imposed by the Germans had been paid off, extensive public works had been launched, and a system of compulsory elementary education—free and secular—had been introduced. In addition the Republic had strengthened its hold on Madagascar and carried out explorations in the Congo region; in 1881 it established a protectorate over Tunisia. Republican France had also regained at least some respect and status—lost in 1870—in the councils of European nations. In 1878 it was admitted to the important Congress of Berlin (see p. 237).

Political scandals. These accomplishments were encouraging, but in the mid-eighties there began a series of crises and scandals which, lasting more than a decade, threatened the very existence of the Republic.

The first of these was the Boulanger affair. In 1886 General Boulanger, the minister of war, became the toast of Paris and a national hero for his firm stand against Germany. His slogan "Remember, they are waiting for us in Alsace" struck a responsive chord in the hearts of many Frenchmen who had witnessed the humiliation of 1870-1871. The "Brave General" became the idol of French ultranationalists and monarchists,

The infamous Dreyfus case aroused all France at the turn of the century and attracted world-wide attention. The drawing above shows Captain Alfred Dreyfus on trial for treason in 1894. The photograph is a scene from the American motion picture *The Life of Emile Zola*. Paul Muni, as the liberal French novelist Zola, addresses the court in defense of Dreyfus, a victim of anti-Semitism, bureaucratic bungling, and political corruption.

who saw in him a "man on horseback" who would sweep away the Republic by a coup d'etat as Louis Napoleon had done in 1851. What his plans were is difficult to say, but when the government took measures to cope with his followers by force, the general fled the country and later committed suicide.

Another scandalous event was the exposure of the president's son-in-law as a cheap and sordid grafter, one who trafficked in the sale of the almost sacred Cross of the Legion of Honor. This exposé forced the president to resign. Still another crisis came with the bankruptcy of the Panama Canal Company, headed by Ferdinand de Lesseps, who had constructed the Suez Canal. The ravages of yellow fever, difficult problems of canal construction, and—perhaps most fatal of all—graft, negligence, and corruption brought the company to bankruptcy in 1888, destroying the careers of promising young politicians and leading to suicides and flights abroad of discredited financiers.

The Dreyfus case. In 1894 occurred an affair that eclipsed both the Boulanger incident and the Panama scandal in the way it divided and embittered French opinion and challenged the fundamental ideals of French democracy. Captain Alfred Dreyfus (1859-1935), the first Jewish officer to secure a post in the general staff of the French army, was accused of selling military secrets to a foreign power. Disliked by many of his aristocratic fellow officers as a Jew, the unfortunate Dreyfus was found guilty, publicly stripped of his commission, and condemned to solitary confinement on Devil's Island, a notorious convict settlement near French Guiana. Here the miserable prisoner was attacked by fever and threatened with madness.

Dreyfus managed to send the president of France a heart-rending petition:

Accused and sentenced . . . for the vilest crime a soldier could commit, I have declared and I declare again that . . . I have never forfeited my honour.

For the last year I have been fighting, alone with my conscience, against the most terrible fate that could befall any man.

I do not speak of physical sufferings, they are nothing; the sufferings of the heart are everything.

To suffer like this is terrible, but to feel that my dear ones are suffering with me is horrible. A whole family is in agony for an abominable crime which I have not committed. . . .

In the name of my honour . . . in the name of my wife, in the name of my children—oh, *Monsieur le President* . . . I ask for justice . . . put an end to the frightful martyrdom of a soldier and a family to whom honour is everything.[9]

The reply from Paris was "Rejected without comment."

The Dreyfus affair was not closed, however. French military secrets continued to leak, and a spendthrift major named Esterhazy (subsequently found to be the actual criminal) was brought to trial and then acquitted. When Emile Zola entered the fray, the first step in the ultimate exoneration of Dreyfus was taken. In "J'accuse" (1898), his famous open letter to the president of France, Zola attacked the military court-martial, accusing the judges of knowingly acquitting the guilty man, Esterhazy. Convicted of libel, Zola fled to England to avoid imprisonment.

The Dreyfus case—a "detective story on a national scale"—had become an issue of greater significance than the innocence or guilt of one man. The affair not only raised the issue of whether anti-Semitism and what appeared to be rank injustice would be countenanced in France; more significantly, it developed into a bloodless civil war between friends and foes of the Republic—a war of which Dreyfus happened to be the unwilling symbol and victim. In the alignment of friends and foes, the army, the Church, and the royalists were, generally speaking, anti-Dreyfusards—the upholders of authority as represented by the military officials who had condemned the accused. Intellectuals and socialists supported Dreyfus. Sentiment against the anti-Dreyfusards grew because they were suspected of preparing a royalist coup.

In 1899 the Dreyfus case was authorized for review by the Court of Cassation, the highest civil court in France. Although Esterhazy had admitted his guilt following his trial, political passions were so strong that Dreyfus was again found guilty and sentenced to ten years' imprisonment. The president of France, however, was friendly to the Dreyfusards and pardoned Dreyfus and amnestied Zola. In 1906 the Court of Cassation found Dreyfus completely innocent, thus asserting the power of the civil authority over the military that had condemned him. The democratic Republic emerged victorious over its foes.

The anticlerical movement. In the closing decades of the nineteenth century, there was controversy between government and Church in a number of European nations. The problem of the Church's right to participate in or to control education became a burning issue throughout Europe. In France, it had been apparent during the Dreyfus case that the Roman Catholic Church was one of the most active allies of the anti-Dreyfusards. Because of the persecution of priests and the experiments in atheism carried on during the French Revolution and because of the blood spilled in Paris in 1848 and 1871, the Church hierarchy was, in general, promonarchy and antirepublican. The alliance of Catholics and the army during the Dreyfus case led to a strong revival of anticlericalism in France. In 1901 a law was passed providing for the closing of all Church schools. While leading republicans were not antireligious, they demanded an end to Church interference in the affairs of the state. One of these defined his position thus:

. . . I want religious peace. I want the priest free and respected in his church, but I also want to maintain the rights of the civil power, to follow the tradition of this country, to conform to the profound instinct—to the genius of the French people; I want the priest outside of politics. In the Church, yes; on the public square, on the platform, never.[10]

In 1905 the drastic step was taken of formally separating Church and state. An act was passed abrogating the Concordat (1801) made between Napoleon Bonaparte and the papacy. Henceforth, the state ceased to pay the salaries of the clergy—Protestant and Jewish as well as Catholic. Furthermore, all Church property was taken over by the state, annual arrangements being made for the use of Church buildings.

The Third Republic in 1914. By the first decade of the twentieth century—after a hundred years of wars, revolutions, and crises—French republicanism finally attained stability and wide public support. France by 1914 was a prosperous land of more than 39,000,000 people; in one hundred years its population had increased by 10,000,000, although a falling birth rate put it far behind the prolific Germans, who numbered 70,000,000.

In 1914 France could be regarded as the most important democracy on the Continent and one of the great powers of the world. As individuals, most Frenchmen were ardently republican and enjoyed basic democratic rights, such as manhood suffrage, freedom of the press, and equality before the law. They tended, however, to be suspicious of government, regarding it not as a servant but rather as a meddling, would-be tyrant. One consequence was that officials found it very difficult to impose direct taxation. The country was prosperous, but the machinery of state was severely handicapped by a lack of funds.

Reflecting the extreme individualism of the French was the multiparty political system. There were so many different political groups represented in the Chamber of Deputies that prime ministers had to form cabinets made up of diverse elements. Like unstable chemical compounds, these cabinets blew up under the slightest pressure. French prime ministers came and went with bewildering rapidity, at the whim of the legislature. Further weaknesses in French political life were the bitter conflicts of parliamentary life, the scurrilousness of the newspapers, and the mediocrity of many of the deputies.

In spite of these weaknesses, however, the Third Republic succeeded in perpetuating itself longer than any of the previous governmental regimes; the country was prosperous, no catastrophe had to be faced, and people were tired of wars and civil commotions.

GERMANY: AN ABSOLUTISM UNDER CONSTITUTIONAL FORMS

The Second (Hohenzollern) Reich. Let us now turn to the German empire (Reich) established under the rule of the Hohenzollern dynasty of Prussia at Versailles in 1871. The Germans had attained unity under Bismarck, but political liberalism had failed to put down strong roots in Germany. It was not by parliaments that the great questions of the day would be decided, Bismarck declared, but by blood and iron. The Hohenzollern empire had a few parliamentary trappings, but behind this façade it was in fact a despotism.

In 1871 the German empire had a population of about 41,000,000 in an area roughly equivalent to that of California and Pennsylvania combined. The new government—a federal union consisting of twenty-six states—included the kingdoms of Prussia, Bavaria, Saxony, and Württemberg, various grand duchies and duchies, three city republics, and the imperial territory of Alsace-Lorraine.

Headed by the German emperor, the imperial government included a legislative upper house, called the Bundesrat, representing the ruling houses of the various states, and a lower house, the Reichstag, representing the people. The Prussian king appointed seventeen delegates to the Bundesrat, the rulers of Württemberg and Saxony sent four each, the Bavarian king had six, and most of the other local rulers controlled one vote each. The sixty-one members of the Bundesrat voted as instructed by their royal masters.

The 397 members of the Reichstag were elected by manhood suffrage, but they had little power. All measures relating to defense, foreign affairs, taxation, and administration emerged complete from the Bundesrat. Frequently the Bundesrat prepared the legislative program in secrecy and then turned it over to the Reichstag.

Appointed by the emperor and responsible to him alone, the chancellor was the actual head of the government. Unlike the situation in the English House of Commons or the French Chamber of Deputies, where an adverse vote against the prime minister would force his resignation, the German chancellor could defy or ignore any action taken by the legislature, especially the Reichstag. One German politician characterized the lower house as "a mere fig-leaf to cover the nakedness of absolutism,"[11] while another characterized it as "a Hall of Echoes." The average German did not possess the parliamentary habit in 1871 and showed little sign of developing it by 1914.

Dominance of Prussia in the empire. Back of this façade of democracy was the dominant power of reactionary Prussia. It has been said that the German empire was "a compact between a lion, half a dozen foxes, and a score of mice."[12] The office of German emperor was vested in the Hohenzollern dynasty so that the king of Prussia was at the same time kaiser of the empire. The kaiser, or emperor, had considerable power in military and foreign affairs. As head of Prussia, he also controlled seventeen votes in the Bundesrat. No amendment to the constitution could pass this body if opposed by fourteen votes. The Prussian delegation could block any reduction in appropriations for the support of the army and navy, and Prussia controlled the chairmanships of practically all the standing committees in the Bundesrat. In addition, the Prussian king was the presiding officer of the Bundesrat.

Welding the empire together. In 1871 William I, opening the first imperial Reichstag, declared:

May the German imperial war which we have carried through with such renown be followed by a peace for the Empire no less glorious, and, from now on, may the German people confine their efforts to winning victories in the field of peaceful enjoyments.[13]

Bismarck, who was appointed the first imperial chancellor, was of the same mind as William I, his imperial master. Bismarck stated that Germany was now "satiated."

To unify and strengthen the empire, an imperial currency was introduced in 1871, an imperial bank established in 1873, and the banking system thoroughly reorganized. An imperial railway office was set up to coordinate the railroads, the imperial post office carried the mails efficiently to all parts of the empire, and various imperial codes of law were drawn up, giving the state a single system of jurisprudence. To promote the German economy and produce sufficient revenue to make the imperial government financially independent of the states, a protective tariff law was passed in 1879.

Bismarck's diplomatic goals were essentially Continental; his principal aim—which he achieved—was to prevent France from waging a successful war of revenge upon Germany. He isolated France, kept it impotent, and at the same time established strong ties with Austria and Russia. The chancellor always had the strongest respect for Great Britain. He did not challenge British naval power, saying "Water rats do not fight with land rats." As we saw in Chapter 10, it was only in the later period of his career that he adopted an aggressive colonial policy.

The *Kulturkampf*. Bismarck's strong nationalism, together with his hatred of those who refused to subordinate themselves to the state, brought about his crusades against what he called "the black and the red menaces." The first so-called crusade was directed against "the black menace," the Catholic Church in Germany.

In the elections of 1871 the German Catholics had elected a large bloc of representatives to the Reichstag. These members supported Pope Pius IX's *Syllabus of Errors* (1864), which championed the complete independence of the Church from state control and denounced divorce, secular education, and liberty of conscience. Furthermore, the Catholic party in the Reichstag supported the new dogma of papal infallibility (see p. 336). The promulgation of this doctrine touched off a struggle among the Catholic clergy in Germany. The so-called Old Clergy refused to accept the new dogma and were excommunicated. At this juncture Bismarck stepped into the controversy.

The conflict which began in 1872 was known as the *Kulturkampf* (the Civilization Struggle). The imperial government made it a penal offense for the clergy to criticize the government and prohibited religious orders from taking part in educational work in Germany. Next, all members of the Jesuit order were expelled from the country.

Between 1873 and 1875, severe measures were also passed by the Prussian government. These Prussian May Laws required civil marriages, stopped appropriations to the Catholic Church, and required all priests to study theology at state universities. Numerous religious orders were suppressed.

In response to these repressive acts, Pope Pius IX declared them null and void and called on loyal Catholics to refuse to obey them. This action infuriated Bismarck, who demanded a struggle to the finish against the "black international." Remembering the time in the Middle Ages when the German emperor Henry IV humbled himself before Pope Gregory VII, the chancellor grandiloquently declared, "We shall not go to Canossa, either in the flesh or in the spirit." Laws against priests who defied the Prussian May Laws were rigorously enforced. Many priests were imprisoned, much Church property was confiscated, and many pulpits were closed. At one time, all religious services ceased in more than one thousand Catholic parishes in Prussia.

Bismarck's oppression of the Catholic clergy did not attain its end. The Center party —that is, the Catholic bloc—in the Reichstag gained in membership. The wily chancellor, therefore, decided to beat a strategic retreat and, in effect, "went to Canossa." He made his peace with the Church, and between 1878 and 1887 the majority of the anti-Catholic laws were repealed. As we shall now see, the German chancellor needed the support of all Catholics against what he regarded as a new foe of the state— socialism, which he dubbed the "red international."

Drive against the socialists. In 1863 the General Workingman's Association, a moderate socialist organization, had been founded by Ferdinand Lassalle, the son of a wealthy Jewish merchant. In the following year, the gifted and humanitarian leader was killed in a duel over a love affair. This unfortunate turn of romance did not obstruct the progress of German socialism, however, for in 1875 the followers of Lassalle, together with other socialists who advocated Marxist views, established the Social Democratic party.

Traditionally, German socialists had opposed autocratic rule and Prussian militarism; their opposition to the Franco-Prussian War and the annexation of Alsace-Lorraine brought forth Bismarck's contemptuous remark that they were "men without a country." Now Social Democrats demanded not only a true parliamentary democracy but also thoroughgoing social legislation.

Bismarck watched with grave concern their mounting strength in the Reichstag. In 1878 two attempts were made on the emperor's life. Although the Social Democratic party had in no way sponsored or participated in these plots, Bismarck immediately launched an all-out campaign against all socialists. In 1878 nearly 200 socialist organizations were dissolved and 250 publications suppressed. Some 500 persons were clapped into prison. A ban was placed on suspicious books, and restrictions were made on free speech and public assembly.

Despite these severe measures, the adherents of socialism increased rather than declined. Therefore, Bismarck shifted his tactics and launched a daring policy designed to wean the German workers away from the socialist ranks and keep them docile and loyal to the state. He declared:

Give the workingman the right to work as long as he is healthy, assure him care when he is sick, and maintenance when he is old . . . then the socialists will sing their siren songs in vain, and the workingmen will cease to throng to their banner.[14]

He sponsored important measures for ensuring the economic well-being of the masses. A sickness insurance bill was passed in 1883, an accident insurance bill in the following year, and in 1889 old-age insurance was introduced. Regardless of Bismarck's motives, these attempts to safeguard the economic interests of the German masses were pioneer efforts in modern social reform and were copied in many European countries. But despite Bismarck's efforts to lure the workers from socialism, the Social Democratic party continued to increase in size and influence. In 1881 the party had polled 312,000 votes, in 1887 the figure was 763,-000, and in 1890 the total was nearly 1,-500,000.

The turning point of Bismarck's career. As the 1880's neared a close, Bismarck was at the height of his fame both at home and abroad. Britain's ambassador at Berlin wrote:

At St. Petersburg Bismarck's word is gospel, as well as at Paris and Rome, where his sayings inspire respect, and his silences apprehension.[15]

Controlled by his masterful will and guided by his astute statecraft, the Germans under his leadership had won three wars, achieved national unification, and attained mastery of the Continent.

By 1888, however, Bismarck's generation was rapidly passing from the scene. Most of the old chancellor's colleagues and comrades-in-arms had died, and in this year the death of Emperor William I brought a new sovereign to the throne. A man of fifty-seven years, Frederick III was regarded as a moderate, an admirer of English parliamentary institutions, and a liberal in politics. This democratic tendency both alarmed and irritated Bismarck. But the new emperor was suffering from an incurable malady and ruled for only a few months.

Kaiser William II. In June 1888, William II, the son of Frederick, became German emperor. Just as Bismarck had stamped his policies and personality on the German nation for the more than twenty years that he was chancellor, this young man was to be the focus of German history from 1890 to 1918.

In addition to having a strong militaristic bent, William was an ardent champion of the divine right of kings; he was determined to rule as well as reign. In 1890 he told some of his subjects:

My grandfather considered that the office of king was a task that God had assigned to him. . . . That which he thought I also think. . . . Those who wish to aid me in that task . . . I welcome with all my heart; those who oppose me in this work I shall crush.[16]

As a proponent of divine right, William constantly reminded those around him that "he and God" worked together for the good of the state.

Well-educated and intellectually curious, the young emperor interested himself in a wide variety of subjects, from archaeology to theology, and tried his hand at writing poems and composing music. Berliners, astounded at his wide, if superficial, interests, humorously said: "God knows everything, but the kaiser knows better." Behind all these activities was his desire to appear masterful, aggressive, and brilliant. The loud dress, flashy uniforms, and oratorical outbursts of the emperor sprang from an inferiority complex, which probably had its origin in the withered left arm that he had had from birth. Restless and emotionally unstable, he was continually making undiplomatic speeches and casting off insulting phrases that alarmed and sometimes infuriated governmental circles in Europe.

The kaiser dismisses Bismarck. William II came to the throne determined to dominate the German government personally. To the kaiser's mind it was "a question whether the Bismarck dynasty or the Hohenzollern dynasty should rule."[17] For nearly two years the tension between emperor and chancellor mounted. The old minister would not subordinate himself, saying, "I cannot serve on my knees." Finally, in the spring of 1890 William rudely dismissed Bismarck.

Embittered and humiliated, Bismarck left Berlin for his estates in East Prussia, where he spent his last days writing his memoirs, receiving the homage of important personages, and sniping continually in newspaper columns at the policy of the government. In 1898 Bismarck died, leaving behind him the

This well-known cartoon, "Dropping the Pilot," appeared in the English magazine *Punch* in 1890, following the dismissal of Bismarck as chancellor of Germany. Kaiser William II, determined to dominate German government personally, watches from the ship of state as the former helmsman leaves the vessel. Despite the change in leadership, however, the tradition that Bismarck represented continued into the twentieth century, as Germany followed a course of ardent nationalism and military aggressiveness.

epitaph: "A faithful servant of Emperor William I."

Reasons for despotism. Despite advances in industry and science, Germany remained a "political kindergarten." There were several reasons why despotism existed in such a prosperous and advanced country. First, the nation had militaristic leanings. It had achieved its unity by blood and iron. Any liberal movement would, if necessary, be crushed relentlessly by the armed forces, which were passionately loyal to the Hohenzollern dynasty. At the heart of this militarism were the Prussian Junkers, a military caste made up of the landed aristocra-

cy, who disdained business, gloried in war, and had an austere sense of their duty to the state.

What we may term the German tradition also played its part. The people had long been taught to serve the Prussian state unquestioningly and to look to their leaders for guidance. As the Germans expressed it, "Alles kommt von oben" ("Everything comes down from above"). This doctrine of the supremacy of the state was also strengthened by the teachings of such philosophers as Hegel and the historian Treitschke.

The people also gave the government unquestioning loyalty because it was efficient and solicitous of their material welfare. Bismarck's social insurance program kept the masses contented. In the sphere of local government, the gasworks, slaughterhouses, streetcars, and electric plants were usually municipally owned and gave efficient, cheap service; and considerable effort was made to provide parks, civic opera houses, bath houses, and museums for the people.

Another factor which kept the German masses in line was the school system. The masses went to the *Volksschule*, where they were given an excellent training in the three R's and were taught obedience to the state. The businessmen and landed aristocracy, on the other hand, sent their sons and daughters to an altogether different school system that led to the university and produced the elite that ruled the nation. German education trained many followers and a few leaders; and it was said that "the leaders think and do; the followers merely do."

The democratic movement. Notwithstanding the strength of autocracy, a remarkable democratic movement, whose spearhead was the Social Democratic party, manifested itself in Germany as the twentieth century dawned. In the Erfurt Program, adopted in 1891, the Social Democrats demanded universal suffrage, the secret ballot, biennial elections to the Reichstag, an annual vote of taxes, decisions on peace and war by the Reichstag—in short, "self-government by the people in Empire, state, province, and commune."

The socialists infuriated the German emperor. He called them a "treasonable horde" and "vermin gnawing at the roots of the imperial oak." But despite the opposition of the emperor and his conservative supporters, the vote cast by the Social Democrats continued to increase during William's reign as it had under Bismarck, growing from 1,500,000 to 4,250,000 votes. In 1914 this party could claim the support of one third of the German voters.

Democratic aspirations in Germany suffered, however, from the serious handicap of lack of unity among the various groups opposed to the Hohenzollern autocracy. In 1912 the 397 members of the Reichstag represented fourteen parties. As long as the parties of reform in the Reichstag refused to cooperate with each other, the kaiser and his supporters could ignore their demands for reform.

The outbreak of war in 1914 was to nip in the bud the promising democratic movement in Germany. As a result, revolution was later substituted for evolution, and the German people achieved a republic before they had been sufficiently trained to govern themselves. We shall see in Chapter 15 that this republic (the Weimar Republic) did not last long and was superseded by the despotic regime of the Nazis.

The Hohenzollern Reich on the eve of World War I. The reign of William II was punctuated with diplomatic crises and international incidents. In 1908 a scandal burst forth—the *Daily Telegraph* incident. The London *Daily Telegraph* published an account of an interview with William II in which much of the credit for the British victory in the Boer War in South Africa was taken by the emperor, who actually claimed to have drawn up the military campaign plan for the British generals. He also added that the British need not be worried about the rapidly growing German navy, which was aimed only against Japan—then an ally of Great Britain.

This indiscreet action of the kaiser created a furor in the Reichstag, where he did not have a single defender. Even the leader of the Conservatives spoke of "a growing

Above is Kaiser William II of Germany, who lost favor among his own subjects by stubbornly resisting democratic reforms and aroused the enmity of other nations by relentlessly striving to increase Germany's political and military power.

discontent" that had been gathering for years. As a result the chancellor, Bülow, tried to take the blame on his own shoulders, and the emperor published what amounted to a lame apology.

In 1912 there was an outburst against the kaiser for another of his indiscretions. Irked by what he considered the lack of loyalty to Germany in the former French region of Alsace-Lorraine, which had been granted a degree of self-government, the kaiser made an open threat against the inhabitants, declaring:

I will break your constitution into fragments and incorporate you as a province of Prussia.[18]

The twenty-fifth anniversary of the kaiser's reign was celebrated in 1913, and in commemoration of the event a survey entitled *Germany under William II* was published. This volume called attention to the many achievements made in science, industry, social reform, and military power. Commenting on the state of the nation in 1913, an English historian has written: "Germany . . . was like a well-tended garden. . . . It was a glittering vision of mind and muscle, of large-scale organization, of intoxicating self-confidence, of metallic brilliancy, such as Europe had never seen. Yet the country was restless, its appetite for power unappeased; and here and there a voice was heard to ask whither it was being led, and what it would profit a nation if it gained the whole world and lost its own soul"[19]

RUSSIA UNDER

UNENLIGHTENED DESPOTISM

The Decembrist Revolt. Of the major European powers, only Russia successfully resisted the widening pattern of constitutional government in the nineteenth century. True, Tsar Alexander I (1801-1825) proclaimed a constitution for the Polish subjects he acquired after the Congress of Vienna, but it was revoked in the next reign. The Grand Duchy of Finland, upon entering the Russian empire in 1809, also received a constitution and remained more or less separate institutionally. But the bulk of the tsars' territories did not acquire any form of constitutional regime until 1905.

The pseudo-liberal Tsar Alexander was followed by his younger brother Nicholas I (1825-1855), who, at the outset of his reign, was confronted by an uprising. This revolt had an interesting background. Liberal political ideas had been quietly germinating since the days of Catherine the Great, when the influence of the French *philosophes* had been strong among the Russian intelligentsia. In consequence, there had emerged toward the end of the eighteenth century a considerable body of literature both satirizing and protesting against political and social conditions and institutions. One of the intellectuals of the time, addressing himself to the problems of man in society, wrote:

Autocracy is the condition most repugnant to human nature. We cannot give anyone unlimited power over ourselves. . . . If we resign to the law some part of our rights and natural powers, we do this in order that the part which we renounce may be turned to our own good; in this we conclude a tacit contract with society. If it is broken, we are released from our obligations. Injustice on the part of the ruler gives to the nation as his judge a right over him which is just as great, and even greater than that which the law gives the ruler over criminals.[20]

During the Napoleonic Wars a number of well-educated Russian officers traveled in Europe in the course of the military campaigns, some of them ending their peregrinations in Paris with the army of allied occupation. Exposure to the liberalism of western Europe whetted their appetite for reform back home. The result was the so-called Decembrist Revolt (December 1825)—the work of a small circle of liberal nobles and army officers who wanted to overthrow the autocracy.

Although Constantine, the true heir to the throne after Alexander's death, had renounced his claims in favor of his younger brother, Nicholas, the Decembrists planned to place Constantine on the throne; but their revolt was easily quashed and those involved were cruelly punished. Five were executed and over five hundred exiled to Siberia. This harsh retaliation made "December Fourteenth" a day long remembered and the inspiration for later revolutionary movements. It also made Tsar Nicholas ultrasensitive to revolution and liberalism. In consequence, he turned away from the Europeanization program begun by Peter the Great and Catherine the Great and championed the idea of Russian self-sufficiency.

Repression under Nicholas I. The famous Czech statesman and historian Thomas Masaryk (1850-1937) presented a graphic picture of the repression and cruelty that disgraced Russia in the second quarter of the nineteenth century: "With Nicholas began the 'plague zone which extended from 1825 to 1855.' . . . Reaction became a carefully considered police system, the tsar in person assuming the office of chief superintendent of police . . . it would be difficult to give an adequate idea of the abominable stupidity and provocative brutality that characterised reaction under Nicholas. For the utterance of liberal ideas conflicting with the official program, leading men were simply declared insane. . . . In the year 1837 two Jews were condemned to death in Odessa because, from fear of the plague, they had attempted to escape across the frontier. Nicholas commuted the death penalty as follows: 'The convicts are to run the gauntlet—a thousand men—twelve times. God be thanked, with us the death penalty has been abolished, and I will not reintroduce it.' It is hardly necessary to add that though there was no capital punishment, the men thus sentenced died under the blows of the soldiers."[21]

Under the Nicholas System, Russia became "frozen." Foreign visitors were carefully screened, and those with "dangerous ideas" were halted at the border. Foreign books were not permitted if they contained any tincture of liberalism. Even musical compositions were checked to see if the notes were a secret code. Schools and universities were placed under constant surveillance and provided with official textbooks. Police spies abounded. Would-be revolutionaries and harmless liberals were shipped to Siberia; from 1832 to 1852, 150,000 persons were exiled there. The repressive effect on Russian intellectual life can be seen in the fact that in 1843 all Russian journals had a combined subscription of 12,000 and the colleges contained only 5000 students.

The tsar had a special fear of the intellectuals, who might be "perverted by foreign ideas." They felt the heavy hand of oppression, a policy which prompted the American humorist Mark Twain to remark:

In Russia whenever they catch a man, woman, or child that has got any brains or education or character, they ship that person straight to Siberia. It is admirable, it is wonderful. It is so searching and effective that it keeps the general level of Russian intellect and education down to that of the Czar.[22]

While a despot, Nicholas I was shrewd enough to study the motives back of the Decembrist Revolt. He found that the chief

Tsar Nicholas I of Russia

criticisms of the revolutionaries concerned (1) chaos in the legal system, (2) the evils of serfdom, and (3) the disordered state of government finance and currency. In each of these spheres, he made improvements. In 1832 a new law code was compiled which remained in effect until the revolution of 1917. A start was made in the direction of ameliorating the lot of the serfs and limiting the power of their landlord masters. Finally, the currency system was strengthened and its depreciation halted by the accumulation of an adequate reserve.

Nicholas, however, had no intention of seriously altering his autocratic government with its maxim of "Autocracy, Orthodoxy, and Nationalism." The mass of people possessed no political rights. There was no representative assembly; there was only a Senate and a Council of State whose members were appointed by the tsar. Furthermore, many government officials were corrupt and contemptuous of the people.

The Russian liberal movement: Herzen and Bakunin. Although Russian liberalism had received a setback from the collapse of the Decembrist conspiracy, the reform movement continued. In the 1830's and 1840's the younger generation of the nobility began to study the ideas of French and English reformers.

The reformist Russian intelligentsia found their inspiration mainly in the work of two authors, Alexander Herzen (1812-1870) and Michael Bakunin (1814-1876). The first was a famous journalist and political writer. After study at the university of Moscow, he was influenced by the ideas of the Decembrists and by the teachings of the French socialist Saint-Simon. In 1847 he fled from Russia and settled in London, where he founded the famous paper *Kolokol* (*The Bell*) ten years later. It was widely read in Russia, even, it is said, appearing mysteriously on the table of the tsar.

Herzen was a moderate socialist. He advocated the freeing of the serfs, the liberalization of the government, and freedom of the press. Bakunin was much more radical; he is regarded as the father of Russian anarchism. Born of the aristocracy, Bakunin was destined for a military career but resigned his commission from the army after witnessing its brutalities in Poland. After studying in Germany and France, he took part in the revolutionary movement of 1848 in Dresden, Germany. Sentenced to death by the Saxon government, he was turned over to the Austrian authorities instead. They in turn delivered him to the Russian secret police, who shipped him to Siberia, but he escaped from Siberia and made his way back to Europe via Japan and the United States.

Bakunin advocated terrorism as an agent of social change, calling it "the propaganda of the deed." He preached that anarchy—complete freedom—can be the only cure for society's ills. To his mind, laws passed even by a majority of the people must be abolished. His message was:

In a word, we object to all legislation, all authority, and all influence, privileged, patented, official and legal, even when it has proceeded from universal suffrage, convinced that it must always turn to the profit of a dominating and exploiting minority, against the interests of the immense majority enslaved.[23]

The Ideological Schism. Heavy-handed repression by Nicholas did not stifle the desire of young intellectuals for knowledge. One of them called this period "an amazing time of outward slavery and inner liberation." Liberals and reformers met in secret and argued during the long winter nights about freedom, the merits of parliamentary government, and the part Russia should play in world history.

The question of Russia's destiny had been brewing ever since Peter the Great's program of westernization had been put into operation early in the eighteenth century (see Chapter 2). Which path should Russia follow? Should it imitate Europe or renounce the West and return to the traditions of its past? The first road was championed by the so-called Westernizers; the second, by the Slavophiles, who heaped scorn on the "decadent" West.

One of the champions of the Western school wrote:

For three hundred years Russia has aspired to consort with Occidental Europe; for three hundred years she has taken her most serious ideas, her most fruitful teachings, and her most vivid delights from there. . . . One hundred and fifty years ago the greatest of our kings [Peter the Great] . . . disavowed the old Russia in the face of the whole world. He swept away all our institutions with his powerful breath; he dug an abyss between our past and our present, and into it he threw pell-mell all our traditions. . . . But here comes another new school. It no longer wants the Occident; it wants to destroy the work of Peter the Great and again follow the desert road. Forgetting what the Occident has done for us, ungrateful towards the great man who civilized us, towards the Europe which taught us, this school repudiates both Europe and the great man.[24]

By contrast, the Slavophiles sought to free Russia from any European taints. One of them wrote:

In Europe the principle of personality is supreme; with us it is the communal principle. Europe is pagan, Russia—holy Christian. In the West reigns apparent liberty, a liberty like that of a wild animal in the desert. The true liberty is found among us, in the East.[25]

These Slavophile radicals preferred the historic communism of the Russian *mir,* or village community, to what they regarded as the dog-eat-dog individualism of the West. It should be pointed out here that present-day Communism in Soviet Russia owes a debt to such age-old social patterns as the *mir* as well as to the doctrines of Karl Marx.

Alexander II abolishes serfdom. Tsar Nicholas died with his philosophy in disrepute. In 1854 Russia had become involved in the Crimean War, a conflict fought primarily in the Crimean peninsula (see p. 237). Since playing a major role in the defeat of Napoleon, Russia had been regarded as militarily invincible, but the reverses it suffered on land and sea in the Crimean War, the blunders committed by its generals, and the huge loss of its man power exposed the rottenness and weakness of the Nicholas regime. It was said that Russia was like a giant with feet of clay.

In 1855 Alexander II (1818-1881) came to the throne amid a widely spreading desire for reform. Many of his subjects, even the conservatives, believed that social and political conditions needed changing if Russia was to keep up with other European states. Although no democrat, the new tsar realized the necessity for moderate reform; his first move was against serfdom.

A growing humanitarian movement, which has been likened to that of the abolitionists in the United States before the Civil War, attacked serfdom, labeling it a national disgrace. In 1853 Herzen had published *Baptized Property,* an effective blow against the enslavement of the Russian people. And, despite censorship, his reformist paper *The Bell* circulated widely in Russia.

There was also an economic motive for the emancipation of the serfs. Many estates were heavily mortgaged, and the landlords hoped to get cash—and a good price—from the government in return for freeing their serfs. In 1859 there were more than 23,000,000 serfs living under nearly the same conditions as had the peasants of western Europe on twelfth-century manors. Russian serfs were bound to the soil, had no civil rights, could not own property, and owed heavy dues and services to their lords, who had almost uncontrolled power over them.

Alexander II made up his mind to abolish serfdom. In his own words:

. . . [It is] better to abolish serfdom from above than to wait until it will be abolished by a movement from below.[26]

A committee appointed to study the matter drew up the Emancipation Proclamation, which was duly issued as a *ukase* (edict of the tsar) in March 1861.

The process of liberation was gradual, serfs on landed estates being freed immediately, domestic serfs in 1863, and those on the crown lands in 1866. The freed serfs were given certain political rights, and the cottages and implements they had been using were turned over to them.

The division of the land proved to be a difficult problem. The serfs had expected a portion of the lord's land to be turned over to them without charge. However, instead of receiving their lands as a gift, the freed peasants had to pay a special tax for a period of forty-nine years to the government, which had paid the landlords a handsome price for the lands they had lost. In numerous instances the peasants complained that they had been given the poorest land. All the land turned over to the peasants was held collectively by the *mir,* the village community, which supervised the various holdings and divided the land among the peasants.

The emancipation of the serfs was the most important single event in nineteenth-century Russian history. It was the beginning of the end for the landed aristocracy's monopoly of power. Emancipation brought a supply of free labor to the cities; industry was stimulated, and the middle class grew in numbers and influence. Above all, emancipation gave strong impetus to the liberal movement.

Nihilism. In the 1860's a remarkable movement known as Nihilism developed among the Russian intelligentsia. For some time many Russian liberals had been dissatisfied by the empty discussions of the intelligentsia; they launched a movement which aimed to put all things in Russia to the test of reason. The definition given to the term *Nihilism* by Ivan Turgenev in his novel *Fathers and*

Sons (1861) became famous. Turgenev described a Nihilist as:

. . . a man who does not bow down before any authority, who does not take any principle on faith, whatever reverence that principle may be enshrined in.[27]

As might have been expected, this attitude of "nothing sacred" resulted in a radical reconsideration of the very basis of society. The Nihilists questioned all old values, championed the independence of the individual, and delighted in shocking the elder generation. The attitude of the Nihilists is exemplified by this statement:

Here is the ultimatum of our camp, what can be smashed must be smashed; whatever will stand the blow is sound, what flies into smithereens is rubbish; at any rate, hit out right and left, no harm will or can come of it.[28]

The Nihilists first attempted to convert the aristocracy to the cause of reform. Failing there, they turned to the peasants, and a veritable missionary movement ensued. Young college students became laborers and worked in the fields with the peasants. Others went to the villages as doctors and teachers to preach reform to the people. This "Go to the People" campaign was known as the Narodnik movement (*narod*, "people").

Further reforms of Alexander II. While Nihilism and the Narodnik movement were gaining momentum, the Tsar Liberator, as Alexander II was called, proceeded to carry out additional reforms.

In 1864 local government was transformed by the Zemstvo Law. In the country elective local boards (*zemstvos*) were established on which the gentry, the middle class, and the peasants were represented. These boards were given power to collect taxes for roads, asylums, hospitals, and schools. In the same year important reforms in the judicial system were carried through. The courts were reorganized on the French model, trial by jury in criminal cases was introduced, and justices of the peace were created to take care of minor cases. In 1870 city government was improved by the creation of municipal councils controlled by the

properted classes. Four years later, conscription for the army affecting all classes was introduced. Before this, most army conscripts had been peasants.

The Polish uprising of 1863. The reforming hand of Alexander was also felt in Poland. Alexander relaxed the Nicholas System of repression, liberalizing the administration and abandoning the anti-Roman Catholic policy of his predecessor. But instead of propitiating the Poles, his concessions encouraged them to revive their nationalist ambitions.

In 1863 a Polish insurrection succeeded in establishing a provisional government, but the movement was soon crushed and a harsh policy of repression was reimposed, aimed particularly at the educated classes. And not only was repression felt in Poland. Tragically, the Tsar Liberator began to lose faith in reform and turned to the repressive measures of his ruthless father.

As the tsar grew more conservative, the Nihilist movement was also changing in character. The "Go to the People" (Narodnik) movement had collapsed. The government had tried to extirpate it; and the peasants, who could not understand it, rejected the movement.

In response to the persecution of the Narodniks and the growing reaction of the government, the radical branch of the Nihilists in 1879 formed "The People's Will" movement. A stirring manifesto was issued defending representative government and universal suffrage. Terrorism was also advocated and systematically practiced. One after another, prominent officials were shot down or killed by bombs. After each assassination, placards appeared describing why this "act of justice" had been performed. Finally, after several attempts, Tsar Alexander II was assassinated in 1881, just as he was on the verge of making some reforms in the government in an effort to placate the Nihilists.

Autocracy and reaction under Alexander III. As he came to the throne, the new tsar, Alexander III (1881-1894), received a remarkable letter drawn up by the executive committee of the terrorist organization:

The Government . . . may . . . capture and hang an immense number of separate individuals, it may break up a great number of separate revolutionary groups, it may even destroy the most important of existing revolutionary organizations; but all this will not change, in the slightest degree, the condition of affairs. Revolutionists are the creation of circumstances; of the general discontent of the people; of the striving of Russia after a new social framework . . . it is impossible, by means of repression, to stifle its discontent. Discontent only grows the more when it is repressed.[29]

Alexander disregarded this warning. Unlike his father, he was not a pseudoliberal but a stanch reactionary. On assuming the throne, he announced that he had no intention of weakening his autocratic powers. The repressive system of Nicholas I was revived. In the mind of Alexander III, Russia could be saved from chaos only by shutting itself off from the democracy and liberalism of western Europe. Censorship was applied, and schools were regulated to prevent students from learning "dangerous" ideas. Universities lost their freedom. Tuitions were raised, and school authorities were advised to steer most children into schools "more in keeping with their social status." A circular declared:

The strict enforcement of this instruction would free the gymnasium [high school] . . . of children of coachmen, footmen, cooks, laundresses, small shopkeepers and other similar people whose children, with perhaps the exception of the most gifted ones, should not be led to break away from the milieu to which they belong.[30]

It was natural that the tsar championed the school of thought known as Slavophilism, which advanced the belief that Russia should remain true to itself, unprofaned by decadent alien influences. On the other hand, the school of Westernizers, supported in the main by the intelligentsia, maintained that only by adopting western science and liberal political institutions could Russia be a great nation.

Pobyedonostzev's Russification policy. The most influential adviser of Alexander III was Konstantin Petrovich Pobyedonostzev (1827-1907), a distinguished jurist and a coauthor of court reforms, tutor to Alexander III and

his son Nicholas II, and procurator of the Holy Synod from 1880 to 1895. He taught his royal pupils to hate democracy, constitutions, and the parliamentary system. In his work *Reflections of a Russian Statesman* (c. 1898), Pobyedonostzev stated that a parliament is nothing more than a body serving the vanity and the personal ambitions of its members.

Under Pobyedonostzev, terrorists were hunted down and a rigorous policy of Russification was carried out (see Chapter 13). One nation, one language, one church, and one government—an autocratic government—was the formula of administration. In Poland the use of the native language was forbidden in the schools. The Jews were bullied and sometimes massacred in terrible drives, called pogroms. Exile to Siberia was used even more by Alexander III than by his father. In 1891, after visiting Russia, an American traveler described the "justice" of the tsar:

The obnoxious person may not be guilty of any crime . . . but if, in the opinion of the local authorities, his presence in a particular place is "prejudicial to public order," or "incompatible with public tranquility," he may be arrested without a warrant, may be held from two weeks to two years in prison, and may then be removed by force to any other place within the limits of the empire and there be put under police surveillance for a period of from one year to ten years. He may or may not be informed of the reasons for this summary proceeding, but in either case he is perfectly helpless.[31]

Accession of Tsar Nicholas II. Nicholas II (1894-1917), the son of Alexander III, was a weak man with little intellect and hardly any force of character. In 1893, when he was twenty-six and soon to inherit the throne, it was suggested that he head the Siberian Railway Committee, but his father wrote:

He is a mere boy, his judgments are truly childish; how can he be chairman of a committee?[32]

In the same year Nicholas remarked in his diary that he and two friends "played hide-and-seek just like small children." He inaugurated his reign by announcing that

. . . the principle of autocracy will be maintained by me as firmly and unswervingly as by my lamented father.[33]

A new revolutionary movement. The Industrial Revolution, which had begun to exert a significant influence in Russia in the late nineteenth century, was quietly and unobtrusively helping to create forces that would finally overthrow this last "Tsar of all the Russias." There was much agitation in the cities, where a growing class of industrial workers engaged in frequent strikes. New revolutionary societies were founded. As the new revolutionary movement got under way, all kinds of organizations clamored for reform—lawyers' clubs, chambers of commerce, zemstvos (the local governing bodies), and trade unions.

The government struck back energetically. Nicholas' minister of the interior organized diversionary outbursts of anti-Semitism among the people. Bands of thugs, called Black Hundreds, were organized to carry out pogroms and to attack liberals; and the fierce Cossacks were used frequently to carry fire and sword into rebellious regions.

A veritable fight to the death was carried on between the Russian revolutionists and the secret police. In the ranks of the revolutionists the government planted agents provocateurs, who incited the insurgents to murder officials and then exposed them to the police.

Reform parties. By this time, several distinct reform parties existed. The progressive elements among the businessmen and nobility thought of themselves as Liberals (Constitutional Democrats, or Kadets). They wanted a constitutional monarchy and believed in peaceful reform. The Social Revolutionaries were followers of the Narodnik tradition. To them, peasants were more important than factory workers, the country more important than the city. The objective of this group was to secure more land for the peasants; their slogan was "the whole land to the whole people."

Another radical group was the Social Democrats, exponents of Marxist principles. In 1883—the year of Marx's death—Georgi Plekhanov (1857-1918), a political refugee in Geneva, founded the first Russian Marxist group. In Russia the Social Democrats gathered their strength chiefly from among the radical intellectuals and the workingmen in the cities. They believed in a complete social and economic as well as political revolution. To them, democracy was only a halfway point; capitalism was just as much an enemy as was autocracy.

In 1903 the party split into two wings—the Mensheviks, or moderates, and the Bolsheviks, or extremists. Plekhanov and the Mensheviks believed that Russian socialism should grow gradually and peacefully, that it should "sprout under the shell of capitalism," using constitutional means. The tsar's government should be overthrown and succeeded by a democratic republic in which the socialists would cooperate with bourgeois political parties. Working under a democratic system, the socialists would gradually become the dominant political force and would secure their socialistic society by parliamentary means.

The Bolsheviks, under Nikolai Lenin (see p. 407), advocated the formation of a small elite of professional revolutionists, subject to strong party discipline, to act as the self-appointed vanguard of the proletariat. Although the Bolsheviks posed as democrats, they advocated seizure of power by nondemocratic means, i.e., by force. Nor did they respect the rights of political opponents.

In 1903, at a Russian Social Democratic congress held in Brussels, the split in the party occurred. The meeting was plunged into a pandemonium of angry oratory. When the police ordered some of the delegates to leave the country, the entire delegation adjourned, leaving their meeting place—a red-draped warehouse—for London. There, at the second meeting, Lenin secured a small majority to back his views. He insisted that from that time on he was the leader of the Bolsheviki Communist party as opposed to the minority Socialist or Mensheviki party. In 1905 the two factions met separately, and this division endured until 1917.

To a contemporary cartoonist, the Russo-Japanese War was seen as a contest between a frail but clever acrobat and a powerful but stupid bear. The performer—Japan—taunts the animal—Russia—into leaving its natural habitat and venturing out onto a fragile bamboo pole stretched over a chasm. Thus the wily Japanese leads the Russian bear to disaster.

The Russo-Japanese War. Meanwhile, the clash of rival imperialisms in Manchuria and Korea (see Chapter 10) had led to trouble with Japan. Little was done in St. Petersburg to try to reach an understanding with the Japanese, and war was the logical outcome. It began in 1904, and the tsar made an appeal for the sake of "the Faith, the Tsar, and the Fatherland."

Instead of strengthening the corrupt government, the war completely discredited it. The Russian fleet was destroyed, and on land the Japanese gained victory after victory. With the ignominious defeat of its armed forces, the tsar's regime, which had sought to make scape-goats of minority groups, became the target for almost universal criticism.

The revolution of 1905: Bloody Sunday. Following the long string of military disasters, one Russian declared: "The Japanese will not enter the Kremlin, but the Russians will."[34] Disorders and demonstrations spread throughout the country in the closing months of 1904, and on January 22, 1905, occurred the tragic incident known as Bloody Sunday. On this day a priest led an enormous crowd to the Winter Palace in St. Petersburg to present a petition to the tsar. The document declared:

We, the workers of the town of St. Petersburg, with our wives, our children and our aged and feeble parents, have come to you, Sire, in search of justice and protection. We have fallen into poverty, we are oppressed, we are loaded with a crushing burden of toil, we are insulted, we are not recognized as men, we are treated as slaves who should bear their sad and bitter lot in patience and silence. . . . Do not refuse to protect your people; raise it from the grave of arbitrary power, poverty and ignorance; permit it to dispose of its own fate; free it from the intolerable oppression of officials; destroy the wall between yourself and your people—and let it govern the country with you.[35]

When the procession reached the Winter Palace, Cossacks opened fire on the defense-

In January 1905, Russian workers with their wives and children marched to the tsar's Winter Palace to plead for relief from poverty and oppression. Although unarmed and led by a priest, the petitioners were treated as traitorous rebels. Here is an artist's interpretation of the ensuing massacre, in which hundreds were shot and cut down by the Cossack guards. This incident, known as Bloody Sunday, led to increasing unrest and violence in the months that followed.

less crowd, killing hundreds and wounding many more.

This massacre shocked the world. Subsequently, it was discovered that the priest was a member of the secret police. He was pursued to Finland and there killed by revolutionary leaders. In Russia, the Social Democratic party issued a manifesto calling the tsar and the grand duke "the scum of the court," threatening them with death, and announcing:

Down with monarchic government! We will establish our own government—the Revolution and the Constituent Assembly of the People's Representatives.[36]

A general strike declared. So aroused were the Russian masses over the Bloody Sunday massacre that a general strike was declared. Beginning with the railwaymen, it spread to many industries. Initially, the strikers demanded a constituent assembly, civil liberties, an eight-hour day, and repeal of laws that gave the government the right to declare a state of emergency on the slightest excuse. These demands were soon followed by more radical ones: a democratic republic, freedom for political prisoners, and the disarming of the police. Soviets (councils of workers) appeared in the cities to direct the revolutionary activity. Active in the St. Petersburg soviet were Nikolai Lenin and Leon Trotsky, who a dozen years hence, would help establish the Communist regime. In the cities great crowds carried red banners and reform posters. Most business and government offices closed, and there was no gas, electricity, or (in some areas) water. The whole machinery of Russian economic life creaked to a defiant halt. Russia was paralyzed, and the government was helpless.

Results of the revolutionary movement. In October 1905, Tsar Nicholas issued his famous October Manifesto, which promised "freedom of person, conscience, speech, assembly, and union." A national Duma (legislature) was to be called without delay, and the right to vote was to be extended. The tsar further promised that no law would go into force without confirmation by the Duma.

When the October Manifesto was issued, the more moderate liberal groups were satisfied with the promise of the Duma. The socialists, on the other hand, rejected the concessions as insufficient and tried to organize new strikes. When an abortive insurrection of workers took place in Moscow, many moderate reformers began to give their support to the government. Thus, by the end of 1905, there was disunity among the liberals, and the tsar's position was considerably strengthened.

When the first Duma was convened in the spring of 1906, it proceeded to censure the government, demanding an investigation into the conduct of the Russo-Japanese War, autonomy for Poland and Finland, and the freeing of political prisoners. The tsar dissolved the Duma in midsummer because, he said, its members "would not cooperate."

The liberal leaders of the Duma adjourned to Finland, where they issued the Viborg Manifesto calling upon the people to refuse to pay taxes because the tsar was ignoring the Duma. But the people were disorganized and apathetic, and nothing came of the appeal.

Sensing the decline of revolutionary fervor among the people, the tsar appointed a conservative prime minister named Piotr Arkadevich Stolypin (1863-1911). Again the familiar pattern of executions, arrests, and pogroms followed. So many people were hanged that the noose was dubbed "Stolypin's necktie."

The second and third Dumas were called in 1907, and another Duma in 1912. In 1907 a new voting system patterned after Prussia's pernicious three-class franchise was promulgated by the tsar, and the composition of the third and fourth Dumas was quite conservative.

These conservative Dumas did, however, carry out important moderate reforms. Advances were made in education, the colonization of Siberia was encouraged, and the organs of local government, the *zemstvos*, were strengthened. Stolypin brought about further reforms before his assassination in 1911. Seeking to gain the support of the peasants as a makeweight against the city workers, he obtained laws abolishing all payments still due under the Emancipation Law. Peasants were encouraged to withdraw from the village community, or *mir*, and become owners of their land; and peasant banks were set up to extend credit.

Although the tsar had been forced to make some concessions, the loyalty of the army, the stanch support of the officials of the Orthodox Church, and division among the opponents of tsarism had enabled him to weather the storm. But though the revolution had failed to make Russia a true constitutional state, the October Manifesto was a definite step forward. One historian has stated: ". . . the *Duma* had plainly come to stay; it had become a habit; the country stood more and more behind it, and the bureaucracy and even the Court had reconciled themselves to its existence."[37]

Posed together at a state ceremony are the royal cousins, Tsar Nicholas II of Russia (left) and King George V of England. The tsar is dressed in English uniform while King George appears in Russian regimentals. The custom of wearing the uniforms of each other's country during a state visit was considered a gesture of respect by pre-World War I royalty.

AUSTRIA-HUNGARY AND THE OTTOMAN EMPIRE

Failure to meet the challenge of modern nationalism. In addition to Germany and Russia, there were two other empires—the Ottoman empire and the Dual Monarchy of Austria-Hungary—that had failed to develop along the democratic lines of Britain and France.

In both Austria-Hungary and Ottoman Turkey, there was a conglomeration of subject nationalities. Increasingly restive under alien rule, these peoples wanted the right to govern themselves. In some cases, as in Bohemia, the people wanted to set up a new independent nation; or, in the case of the Italians and the Serbs, the goal was to join their countrymen living in adjacent national states.

Both empires would have had a better chance for survival had they been willing

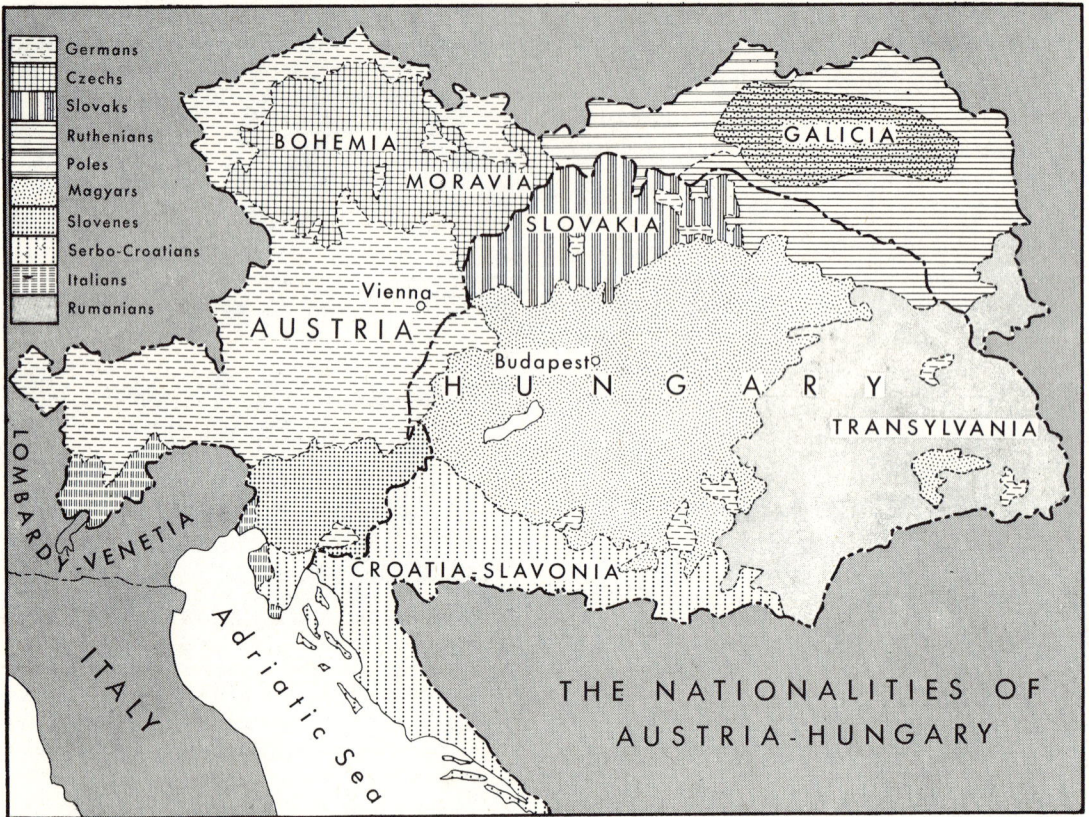

Germans
Czechs
Slovaks
Ruthenians
Poles
Magyars
Slovenes
Serbo-Croatians
Italians
Rumanians

BOHEMIA
MORAVIA
GALICIA
SLOVAKIA
Vienna
AUSTRIA
Budapest
H U N G A R Y
TRANSYLVANIA
LOMBARDY-VENETIA
ITALY
Adriatic Sea
CROATIA-SLAVONIA

THE NATIONALITIES OF
AUSTRIA-HUNGARY

to shape themselves into federal unions in which the various peoples would have been free to rule themselves. Although this suggestion was made in both states, the necessary legislation never materialized. This lamentable failure was due not only to the arrogance and pride of the dominant nationalities but also to the equally fanatical nationalism of some of the subject peoples, who would accept no solution except that of breaking away from the empire in which they lived.

Austria. We last witnessed rickety Austria-Hungary trying to strengthen itself after the debacle of the war with Prussia. The answer was the *Ausgleich,* a political arrangement whereby the Austrian empire was divided into two parts, one under the rule of the Austrian Germans, the other under the Magyars of Hungary.

Francis Joseph i, the Dual Monarch, ruled a multilingual, multinational state in which there were 12,000,000 Germans, 10,-000,000 Magyars, more than 24,000,000 Slavs, and some 4,000,000 Latins—the latter Italians and Rumanians. There were North Slavs (Bohemians or Czechs, Poles, and Slovaks) and South Slavs (Serbs, Croats, and Slovenes). In addition, there were numerous small isolated islands of people in various parts of Austria-Hungary surrounded by masses of neighbors quite different in nationality and culture. The value of the official bank note of the Dual Monarchy was printed on one side in eight languages and on the other side in Magyar.

What was the progress of democracy in this complex land? Until 1907 the bicameral legislature in Austria was elected by a four-class franchise system that placed political power in the hands of German aristocrats, bankers, and wealthy industrialists. In 1907 the four-class voting system was superseded by general manhood suffrage.

This measure, however, spelled little advance toward popular government. Political life continued to be dominated by wealthy German businessmen and the landed aristocracy. The latter, who would have been more at home under the ancient regime of eighteenth-century France than in the new Europe of industry, nationalism, and democracy, monopolized the leading positions in government, the army, and parliament.

The power of these wealthy Germans was increased by the friction which existed between other national groups in the empire. Racial and national antipathies impeded the functioning of what, on paper, seemed a liberal constitution. Political parties were not based primarily on political principle but on nationality. Each distinct group feared and detested the German ruling elite, and too often each disliked the other national groups. Although Austria gave its subject nationalities substantial local self-government, this concession had little mollifying effect.

The chaos and strife resulting from national differences ultimately brought about World War I and disrupted the Dual Monarchy. This aspect of the tragic national animosities of Austria-Hungary will be discussed in a later chapter. At this point it should be understood that the antagonisms enabled the emperor and his ministers to keep a firm command of affairs by a policy of divide and rule.

Hungary. If democracy was weak in Austria, it was practically nonexistent in Hungary. Here the aristocracy firmly held the reins of power, and the Magyars refused to share political control with the other nationalities—Croats, Serbs, Slovaks, Rumanians, and Galicians—who were under their rule. The Hungarian parliament, closed to almost all non-Magyars, was conducted with discipline and efficiency. In 1910 only one million citizens could vote; many demonstrations in favor of manhood suffrage took place in Hungary in 1914.

Like Austria, Hungary was agricultural, and land ownership was concentrated in the hands of a few. The peasants suffered even more than their counterparts in Aus-

tria. At the other end of the social scale were the nobles, who, like the Austrian aristocrats, "were noted for loose living, luxurious Bohemianism, passion for the chase, horse racing, dandyism, and intellectual emptiness."[38]

Hungary, however, made greater progress than Austria in the war against illiteracy. Magyar nationalism was the chief reason for the promotion of learning, because the primary school was considered to be the best tool for creating national unity.

Difficulties and advantages of the union. As far as the Hungarians and Austrian Germans were concerned, the system of the Dual Monarchy functioned fairly well, although some Magyar patriots—followers of the nationalistic Kossuth tradition of 1848—demanded complete separation from Austria. The emperor's insistence that German be the sole language of command in the army led to disputes, and there were quarrels over the quotas which the two states should contribute for the administration of the government.

Despite its composite character, however, the Dual Monarchy had a certain economic unity, its various parts complementing each other well. Hungary, for example, produced wheat; Croatia and Slavonia exported cattle and swine; Bohemia had important mines and factories; and Austria, with the great capital city of Vienna, was the heart of the empire's banking and commerce.

The Hapsburg crown was another unifying force. The ruler, Francis Joseph I (1848-1916), was a sincere and kindly sovereign, well liked by most of his subjects. Coming to the throne at the age of eighteen, he ruled for sixty-eight years. It was Francis Joseph's belief that it was the function of his dynasty to hold the various national groups in the empire together.

The dominant Austrian and Hungarian elements were also able to exploit the rivalries and hatreds existing among the various groups. The emperor once said:

My people are strangers to one another, and yet it is for the best. They never have the same ills at the same time. In France, when there is an epidemic of fever, you all have it on the same day. I have Hungarians in Italy, and Italians in Hungary. Each suspects his neighbor; they never understand one another. . . .Their mutual antipathies, however, conduce to order and to general peace.[39]

There was, then, much logic in the Austro-Hungarian empire. The empire gave military strength, international influence, and economic unity to a large part of eastern and southern Europe. But the spirit of nationalism was destined to rip this cooperative framework of peoples apart.

Despotism and misrule in the Ottoman empire: Abdul-Hamid II. In the closing decades of the nineteenth century, the decaying Ottoman empire was a disreputable, vicious oriental despotism. In 1876 a reform-minded grand vizier (premier) issued a modern constitution that guaranteed parliamentary government, freedom of conscience, and equality of taxation. Simultaneously there came to the throne a sultan whose reign of more than thirty years was destined to be notorious for its cruelty, repression, and autocracy.

Described as "half fox and half rat," Abdul-Hamid II was dubbed by a British poet as "Abdul the Damned—immortally, beyond all mortals, damned."[40] Despite the fact that he had been placed on the throne by a liberal faction and had supported the liberal constitution of 1876, Abdul-Hamid proceeded to make himself absolute. In 1878 he abrogated the constitution and began to rule without parliament, aided by forty thousand spies. The strictest censorship was applied, and opponents of this tyranny mysteriously disappeared or were forced to flee the country. An American diplomat tells a gruesome anecdote of the terror of the sultan's regime. It seems that the sea walls of some of the royal palaces needed repair, and an English diver was brought in to investigate the damage:

The diver . . . opened his eyes to find himself surrounded by enormous sacks, their rotting tops swaying gently back and forth in the current. He put his hand out to touch one and it dissolved, disclosing a skull on top of a heap of bones. Looking closer he distinguished more bones protruding from the others—all that remained of men and women who, for some reason or other, had incurred suspicion and had been done away with.[41]

When the sultan's Christian Armenian subjects threatened revolt in 1894, he sent secret agents to invite loyal Muslims to attack their Christian neighbors and seize their property. Within three years, thousands of Armenians were butchered, and many others were forced to convert to Islam.

The Arab revival. At the same time that the Balkan nations were trying to stabilize themselves as independent states, Abdul-Hamid was fighting a losing battle to hold together the remainder of his empire. In North Africa, France, which had seized Algeria in 1830, annexed Tunis in 1881; Britain occupied Egypt in 1882; and Italy had a covetous eye on Tripoli by 1900. All but the last of these had owed only a tenuous allegiance to the sultan. But there remained under Turkish rule, in the years before World War I, the Arab world of the Near East, inhabited by people who possessed proud traditions and who were Muslim in religion but not Turkish in nationality. The same nationalist spirit which had bestirred nineteenth-century Europe now began to arouse Arab leaders against Turkish rule. Signs of Arab nationalism were already apparent in the 1880's. In 1883 a French traveler wrote:

Everywhere I came upon the same abiding and universal sentiment: hatred of the Turks. . . . The notion of concerted action to throw off the detested yoke is gradually shaping itself. . . . An Arab movement, newly-risen, is looming in the distance; and a race hitherto down-trodden will presently claim its due place in the destinies of Islam.[42]

Young Turks and Young Arabs. Meanwhile, opposition to the sultan's tyranny mounted among his Turkish subjects. The nucleus for this opposition was the organization known as the Young Turks, composed of reformers who had been educated in western European universities and instilled with nationalism, parliamentary ideas, and the new learning of modern science. Many converts to this reform group were made in the Turkish army, which provided the necessary military power for successful rebellion.

When, in 1908, the Young Turks rebelled and demanded the restoration of the 1876 constitution or abdication of the sultan, Abdul-Hamid ordered resistance to the rebels. But when the court astrologer advised him to give in and the Young Turks threatened to shoot him, he restored the constitution, established a ministry responsible to the lower house of the legislature, and guaranteed equality before the law to all races in the empire.

The Young Turks, however, acted precisely as the Magyars and Germans had acted in the revolution of 1848. After gaining what they desired for themselves, they refused to share their victory with the non-Turkish people. Elections to the parliament were so controlled that few non-Muslims were elected; and though the Arabs outnumbered the Turks three to two in the empire, there were only 60 Arabs elected as compared with 150 Turks. The result was a counterrevolution supported by various discontented factions but mainly encouraged by the sultan, who sought to regain power. When Abdul-Hamid turned against the Young Turks, however, he was overthrown and replaced by his weak and innocuous brother, Muhammad V.

Arabs in Syria, Lebanon, and the vast peninsula of Arabia were not happy with the new sultan. They writhed under the Young Turks' program of Turkish supremacy and their policy of centralization, which left no opportunity for Arab home rule. The Young Arabs found the tyranny of the Committee of Union and Progress—the agent of the new regime—to be more detestable, because it was more efficient, than that of Abdul-Hamid. When fighting against Turkey during World War I, Britain found it relatively easy to turn the Arab tribes against their overlord, the sultan.

In 1909 the rebellious Young Turks forced Abdul-Hamid II from his throne. This photograph shows the victorious insurgent forces on the march.

Meanwhile the disintegration of the Ottoman empire proceeded apace. In the years between 1908 and 1913, Austria-Hungary annexed Bosnia and Herzegovina, two Turkish provinces on the Adriatic that had been occupied and administered by the Dual Monarchy since 1878; Greece annexed Crete; and Italy, in the course of a short war, seized Tripoli and Cyrenaica. Finally, the Balkan nations fought two wars with the Ottoman empire in 1912 and 1913 and partitioned Turkish Macedonia. How these annexations and wars brought about disputes among the great powers, and in particular how they created an explosive situation in the Balkans that touched off World War I, will be discussed in Chapter 13.

DEMOCRATIC STRUGGLES IN OTHER EUROPEAN LANDS

Contributions of small states. During the nineteenth century (before the advent of totalitarian warfare), the small nations of Europe, wedged among the great powers, prevented dynamic and often jealous states from having contiguous boundaries. In an era when international law was supposed to have some validity, the recognition of the neutrality of such a country as Switzerland meant that great powers bordering on this neutralized area could assume that no attack would come from this quarter.

The trend toward democracy in the late nineteenth and early twentieth centuries was evident in these countries. In the latter part of the nineteenth century, the Scandinavian nations in particular were developing into virtual sociological laboratories, where "few should have more than they need, and fewer still should have less than they need." The enfranchisement of women was first introduced in Norway, proportional representation had its first trial in Belgium, and Switzerland invented the referendum and the initiative.

The Netherlands and Belgium. In the Netherlands the king had granted a constitution during the revolutionary period of 1848, but it was not a democratic document, for the crown still wielded large powers and the franchise was restricted. The main constitutional theme in the Netherlands from the midpoint of the century until 1914 was the demand for a more liberal franchise. Although concessions were won in 1887 and in 1896, Holland was not a complete democracy even in 1914. Forty per cent of its adult males still were without the vote, as were all women. Although the Dutch constitutional system gave the people an efficient and reasonably liberal regime, in 1914 Holland had the least democratic franchise of all the western European nations.

English principles of responsible government had been adopted in Belgium in 1831, but the franchise was based on high property qualifications. Social legislation in this highly industrialized country lagged behind England's, and a discontented proletariat formed a Socialist party determined to democratize the franchise. General strikes were frequently resorted to as a political weapon. These had some effect, for in 1893 the vote was given to all men over twenty-five. But the use of plural voting, which gave some individuals two or three votes, robbed the working people of the fruits of their victory. In 1899 a system of proportional representation was adopted. But down to the First World War, plural voting was retained.

Switzerland. Switzerland after 1870 continued the development of democratic government inaugurated in the constitution of 1848. In 1874 there was a major constitutional revision, giving the central government more authority. But the cantons, the basic units of the federal system, continued to handle their local affairs either through unicameral legislatures or by the action of voters meeting once a year in a large assembly. Freedom of speech and press were guaranteed, compulsory education was provided for, and a militia system was set up in which every man between the ages of twenty-six and forty-eight was liable for military training and duty. The Swiss institutions of the initiative and referendum, giving voters an opportunity to propose legislation and to approve or reject bills passed by the lawmaking body, have been copied in many parts of the world, including various states of the United States.

The Swiss governmental system made it possible for three basic nationalities speaking four languages (French, German, Italian, and Romansh) and professing two religions (Protestant and Roman Catholic) to live together in peace. An authority on nationalism has observed: "Only tiny Switzerland . . . offered practical demonstration of how, through sane federalism and real liberty, diverse nationalities could live together in amity and evince a common patriotism. . . . Switzerland remained at peace when later the world was at war, and Switzerland outlasted the empires of Hapsburg, Hohenzollern, and Tsar."[43]

Italy. After unification in 1871, Italy had a representative monarchical government modeled on the liberal constitution granted in 1848 by Charles Albert, the king of Sardinia. After unification, the new nation worked under serious handicaps. The country had few natural resources, and the rapidly growing population was largely untrained for skilled occupations. The interests of the industrial north often clashed with those of the agricultural south.

A religious issue weakened the state. During the unification of Italy, the Italian government had seized Rome, formerly part of the papal domains. Terming himself "the prisoner of the Vatican," the pope called on Italian Catholics to refrain from voting. In an attempt at conciliation, the Italian government passed the Law of Papal Guarantees, by which the pope was to have the Vatican as a sovereign state; his officials and his establishment were to enjoy diplomatic immunity and were to be given an annual sum of $600,000. Although this offer was rejected, the law was not repealed.

In the field of politics, the people lacked experience in or aptitude for constitutional government. Seventy-five per cent of the population was illiterate in 1861, and the franchise was very restricted. As late as 1904, only 29 per cent of the adult male population could vote, and of this group only 38 per cent actually went to the polls. Political parties lacked a sense of direction and order; their platforms were based on individuals rather than on political principles. Political life suffered also from inexperience and factiousness among officials and from unstable coalitions of parties. Statesmen were valued for their skill in controlling the parliament instead of for their championship of legislative measures. One Italian prime minister became notorious for bribing the opposition leaders in order to eliminate all parliamentary resistance. Many legislators sought to gain support by obtaining government positions and pensions for the voters.

Another grievous burden for the country was the ambition of its leaders to have Italy play a grand role in the world and thus fulfill the dreams of greatness built up during the *Risorgimento*. Too much money was spent on the army, and national resources were squandered in the unrewarding pursuit of empire in Africa.

Early in the twentieth century, there were manifestations of popular discontent. Liberals joined socialists in demanding such reforms as compulsory education, freedom of the press, and better working conditions for the masses. As a result of this agitation, laws were passed in 1912 providing for universal suffrage and for payment of deputies in parliament. Other encouraging signs were better relations between the government and the Vatican and evidence of industrial progress.

Spain and Portugal. Spain was the recurrent scene of civil war and revolution during the greater part of the nineteenth century. After a brief experience of republicanism, the country in 1876 returned to monarchical government with a supposedly responsible parliament. Until 1890 the franchise was a narrow one based on high property qualifications. Constitutional government, however, functioned even worse in Spain than in Italy. By a secret understanding, politicians arranged how each party was to alternate in power. A vicious land system, an illiberal Church hierarchy, and a weak monarchy also contributed to political instability and the failure of democracy in Spain.

Portugal's political history closely resembled that of Spain—revolution, graft, and political anarchy being prevalent during most of the nineteenth century. In 1910 the Portuguese monarchy was overthrown, and Portugal became a republic. This change did little to improve conditions, however, for the people showed little capacity for self-government.

The Scandinavian countries. The Scandinavian states had much better success at self-government than the Latin trio of Italy, Spain, and Portugal. In these far-northern monarchies, the franchise was broadened and the principle of responsible government developed. In Denmark the king claimed the right to control the ministry, but in 1901 he finally agreed to the principle that his ministers must be chosen in accordance with the will of the legislature.

Norway came to be called the most democratic monarchy in the world. Universal manhood suffrage was introduced before Norway's separation from Sweden in 1905. The suffrage was given to women taxpayers in 1907, and in 1913 it was granted to all women.

In Sweden democratic development lagged behind that in Norway and Denmark. In 1909 manhood suffrage was granted, but until 1914 the cabinet was not responsible to the lower house, and the king exercised considerable power, including an absolute veto.

SUMMARY

By the end of the nineteenth century, in a space of hardly fifty years, western Europe had experienced a veritable revolution in many substantial aspects of its pattern of life. The political predominance of the land-owning aristocracy and the business classes was coming to an end. The nineteenth-century bourgeois creed of political liberalism with its restricted suffrage had been thoroughly undermined by the creed of mass democracy—the doctrine of one vote per head, regardless of the voter's qualifications. In the economic field, state intervention to assure a minimum standard of living and a measure of economic security had largely replaced the bourgeois, liberal economic program of laissez faire.

This democratically oriented type of welfare state advanced much more rapidly in western than in eastern Europe. Countries such as Britain, France, Denmark, and Switzerland best represented the western democratic tradition. To these could be added the flourishing republic of the United States and those dominions and colonies of Britain that enjoyed self-government. Significantly, behind the democratic doctrines activating these western nations lay centuries of historical experience and experimentation —the struggles to establish the rights guaranteed by the Magna Carta and the English and American bills of rights and the American and French revolutions.

In contrast to these nations were a number of states in eastern and southern Europe that had little experience in democratic procedures. This lack of true democratic tradition and experience at self-government helps explain the illiberal and tragic events that took place in the Balkans, eastern Europe, and Russia after World Wars I and II. The Nazi tyranny, the despotism of Soviet Russia with its slave labor camps, brain washings, and purges, the sealed cordon of the Iron Curtain and the commissar tyranny in Russia's communist-ruled satellites—all of these have their immediate roots in the failure of parliamentary government to become established in eastern and southern Europe between 1870 and 1914.

What was destined to be one of the truly historic movements of the twentieth century was the awakening, during this period, of the Arab people. Under Ottoman rule the Near East had been cruelly misgoverned and efficiently fleeced and its peoples exploited and kept in ignorance. The diffusion of western culture, and especially of liberal political ideas, from such centers as Beirut and Cairo changed this torpor into a nationalistic revival which was to become increasingly powerful.

This chapter deals mainly with the successes and failures of democracy. But the fortunes of democracy were complicated by nationalism. Originally nationalism had been the psychological and spiritual force bringing people together in the form of nations. But by 1900, it would seem that economic interdependence, scientific advances in transportation and communication, and the growing complexity of international relations demanded more cooperation between national groups. The spirit of nationalism ignored these imperatives, becoming more narrow in its appeal, more bellicose, and more divisive. The British Isles, for instance, formed a natural geographical and economic unit, yet it seemed impossible for the Irish to live under the same political roof with the neighboring Scots, Welsh, and English. The Austro-Hungarian empire in a sense constituted a valuable cooperative unit, yet its various nationalities could not get along with each other. We will return to the excesses of nationalism when the background of the First World War is studied in the next chapter.

CHAPTER 13

Promise and Peril

THE SECOND INDUSTRIAL REVOLUTION AND POWER POLITICS IN EUROPE: 1871-1914

Introduction. For Europe, the nineteenth century was a golden age of progress and prosperity. Looking back nostalgically on this happy time, Winston Churchill wrote: "From the end of the Napoleonic Wars and still more after 1870, the accumulation of health and wealth by every civilized community had been practically unchecked. . . . The Victorian Age was the age of accumulation . . . Education spread itself over the broad surface of the millions. Science had opened the limitless treasure-house of nature . . . . Every morning when the world woke up, some new machinery had started running. Every night while the world had supper, it was running still. Every year diffused a wider measure of material comfort among the higher ranks of labor. Substantial progress was made in mitigating the hard lot of the masses."[1]

Here is a glowing report, and further tributes can be added. Class warfare was waning as governments showed increasing solicitude for their peoples' economic and social needs. Illiteracy was being reduced by the spread of public school systems. The franchise was being broadened; parliamentary government and mass suffrage were crowding out aristocratic plutocracy; political liberty was on the march. Meanwhile, applied science was extending its blessings to every social level and raising the living standards of millions. As new forms of transportation and communication telescoped distances, the Second Industrial Revolution was rushing the nations of the world into a new relationship of intimacy and interdependence.

Unfortunately, however, this was not the whole story. With progress in science and technology came progress in destructive armaments; and while the power of military weapons increased, little was done to remove the causes that led the nations to rely upon these weapons. If men could be said to have ascended to a new level of civilization in their scientific and intellectual attainments, their tactics and outlook in international affairs were often reminiscent of the jungle. From 1871 to 1914 Europe, with its progressive and brilliant yet menacing and unstable civilization, was the center of the world—the area of the greatest industrial concentration, the storehouse of accumulated wealth, knowledge, and culture, and the arsenal of military power. It was the central position this little continent enjoyed that gave its promise and peril world-wide implications. Fanned by old rivalries and callous ambitions, a spark in that center was to grow and spread and finally engulf the world in flames, creating the holocaust known as World War I.

THE SECOND INDUSTRIAL REVOLUTION

Traits of the new industrialism. By 1815 the First Industrial Revolution had dawned in the western world, and in the next fifty years astounding changes took place in industrial production and transportation. Beginning in 1870 a new surge of industrial and technological progress occurred, important enough to warrant being called the Second Industrial Revolution.

Although the twentieth century was to witness amazing accomplishments in science and invention, those that took place during the Second Industrial Revolution (1870-1914) were perhaps even more remarkable in their effect on man's habits and ways of living. The electric light, wireless telegraphy, refrigeration, the dynamo, and the gasoline engine—these and many more inventions transformed civilized society.

During the Second Industrial Revolution the output of both new and old industries forged ahead at incredible speed. In 1865 western Europe and the United States produced 9,000,000 tons of iron and steel; by 1910 total production had increased to 66,000,000 tons. So efficient did textile manufacturing become that by World War I a single spinner could turn out more than one thousand times the yarn produced by an artisan before the Industrial Revolution.

In general, the Second Industrial Revolution can be said to have had three characteristics that influenced all its phases:

(1) Industry used scientific techniques, allying itself with the laboratory. Nothing was left to chance, and invention became systematic rather than accidental. In fact, the individual inventor was gradually being replaced by teams of researchers, who methodically turned out new devices.

(2) Mass production methods involving the use of interchangeable parts and the assembly line were introduced. Since the days of Eli Whitney, who mass-produced rifles in the 1790's, the technique had been used sparingly in the United States. It came into its own only when Henry Ford began turning out the Model T.

(3) Chemistry devised a host of new materials. Such synthetic products as artificial indigo, nitrates, rayon, leather, and celluloid (one of the earliest plastics) improved on nature. Chemistry also made possible new explosives, paper from wood pulp, beet sugar, and a host of by-products. For example, coal tar yielded perfumes, medicines, and sweetening substances.

Electricity and the internal-combustion engine. One of the most useful developments of the Second Industrial Revolution was the harnessing of electricity. The self-taught American genius Thomas Edison helped to exploit its myriad possibilities: he supervised the construction in New York City of the first central electric power plant in the world, and many of his more than twelve hundred patents involved machines and gadgets powered by electricity. With electricity came many subsidiary developments: the use of copper for wiring and rubber for insulation, the telephone, trolley cars and electric railroads, and the incandescent lamp.

Invented before 1914, the internal-combustion engine was to have tremendous significance. The introduction of the automobile brought radical changes to the industrial as well as the social pattern of the day. The use of gasoline and Diesel engines caused a tremendous expansion of the petroleum industry. Less than 1,000,000 barrels in 1860, production of crude oil climbed to more than 300,000,000 barrels in 1910. Huge refineries were constructed to process the oil into gasoline and other by-products.

The spread of industrialism. During the period of the Second Industrial Revolution, the world could be divided into three economic areas. The highly industrialized area was concentrated in western Europe, in the northern United States, and in Japan. In the area just beginning to be touched by industry were such countries as Italy, Spain, the Balkan states, Russia, Canada, and the southern and western United States. The third area, consisting of all of Africa, the Middle East, and all of Asia except Japan, was outside the industrial realm. This third zone can be called "the world of empire," for most of its vast territories were colonies of the industrial powers or, as in the case of China, were helpless victims of foreign exploitation. Such industry as existed in these lands—the textile mills of India and China, for example—had been established by western capital.

England loses ground. As we have seen, Great Britain pioneered in industrialization, but its industrial and financial leadership in western Europe had dangers as well as compensations. No longer self-sufficient, since the great majority of its people were city dwellers, Britain had to import huge amounts of food as well as raw materials. To pay for these imports, Britain had to export large quantities of industrial goods processed in its factories. Thus the specialized economy of Britain depended entirely on overseas markets.

Meanwhile new and vigorous competitors, primarily the United States and Germany, became important industrial nations. In 1870

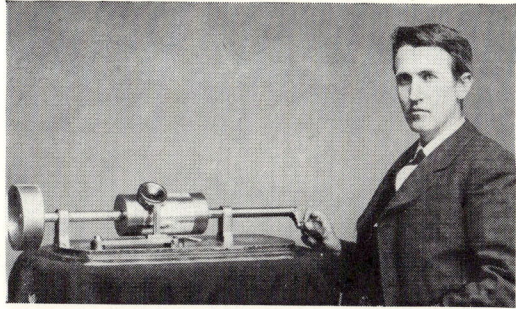

Here are shown three practical scientists whose inventions revolutionized man's way of living. Perhaps the greatest of all inventors was Edison (top), who left school after three months of formal education because his teacher considered him a dunce. Responsible for more than twelve hundred inventions, Edison here displays the phonograph he invented in 1876; the record was a sheet of tin foil wrapped around a cylinder, which was turned by a hand crank. Marconi (center) is shown beside the wireless apparatus which in 1901 received the first telegraphic signals transmitted across the Atlantic from England to Newfoundland. Bell, who invented the telephone in 1876 and demonstrated it at the Philadelphia Centennial Exposition the same year, was photographed opening the long-distance line between New York and Chicago in 1892 (bottom).

Two of the nations which made astounding strides in industrialization between 1870 and 1914 were the United States and Germany. Assembly lines in the United States increased production enormously; the long rows of chassis shown above constitute one day's output of a Ford plant in Michigan in 1913. Representative of Germany's industrial might was the great Krupp munitions plant, shown below.

Britain had more textile spindles and looms and produced more coal and iron than all the rest of the world. By 1910 it had only 40 per cent of the spindles and 30 per cent of the looms of the world and produced only 26 per cent of the world's coal and 14 per cent of the world's iron.

In banking and shipping, however, Britain still led the pack. Its ships carried 40 per cent of all the world's commerce, and London was the world's main source of capital. Although Britain had an "unfavorable" balance of trade (imported more goods than it exported), it received nearly a billion dollars annually from overseas investments, shipping fees, insurance, and banking services. These "invisible exports" kept Great Britain out of the red.

Industrialized Germany. By 1914 Germany had become the leading manufacturing nation on the Continent. The unification of the German empire was in part responsible for this industrialization. Other factors included the acquisition from France in 1871 of the extremely rich iron-mining and manufacturing districts of Alsace and Lorraine; the payment by France of a war indemnity of 5,000,000,000 francs, which gave Germany a sharp increase of capital for industrial purposes; the rapid growth of population (from 41,000,000 in 1871 to almost 65,000,000 in 1910); and the entrance into the world race for foreign markets.

Production was stepped up in established German industries. The remarkable progress made by Germany in the coal and iron industries and its resulting threat to British supremacy are graphically shown in the chart on the next page. (The figures in the chart represent round millions of tons; the final figure in each grouping indicates the increase of production in the period.) The machine-tool industry made astounding advances; and the textile industry also made extensive strides, although Germany still lagged far behind Great Britain in this area. In 1911 Germany had 10,500,000 spindles, while Great Britain had 55,000,000.

In addition to advances in already established industries, the nation concentrated on the development of such new enterprises

GROWTH OF COAL AND IRON INDUSTRY IN EUROPE

	England	Germany	France
Coal			
1875	99	28	11
1913	287	273	40
Increase	x3	x10	x4
Pig iron and steel			
1875	6	2	1
1913	8	14	2
Increase	x1	x7	x2
Steel ingots and castings			
1875	0.7	0.2	0.2
1913	7	14	2
Increase	x10	x70	x10

Adapted from Clive Day, *Economic Development in Europe* (New York: The Macmillan Co., 1942), p. 390. By permission of The Macmillan Co.

as the chemical and electrical industries. The government played a decisive role in this expansion by designing tariffs to aid the new industries and by setting up technical schools to train personnel. In the chemical industry the Germans seized undisputed first place—by 1900 they produced four fifths of the world's dyestuffs—and in the electrical industry Germany's skilled technicians were soon producing intricate equipment destined for all countries of the world.

Industrialization elsewhere in Europe. The industrialization of France had begun slowly in the second quarter of the nineteenth century. Although the Franco-Prussian War had caused a temporary setback, substantial progress was made following the establishment of the Third Republic. Power looms displaced those run by hand, and important advances were made in the output of the coal mines and the iron and steel industries. Between 1870 and 1897 the value of manu-

factured products increased 300 per cent. But industrialization in France was much less spectacular than in Germany or in England. The large factory was the exception; the French concentrated on luxury items, such as laces, silks, perfumes, and fine china, made by hand in small establishments. In France the bulk of the people remained on the land; the heart of the nation continued to be the thrifty, hard-working peasants.

In western Europe other areas of important industrialization were Belgium, Austria, and Sweden. Belgium, with some of the richest coal deposits in Europe, continued to produce large amounts of iron and was a major manufacturer of textiles and machinery. While Hungary remained predominantly agricultural, Austria made important progress in the production of textiles, leather goods, chemicals, and glassware. In Scandinavia, Sweden was the most highly industrialized country, noted for the high quality of its iron and steel. Switzerland concentrated on the making of watches, machinery, and silk goods; and the Netherlands specialized in diamond cutting, shipbuilding, and the manufacture of porcelain.

The United States and Japan industrialize. Outside of the European countries the United States was the most important industrial nation. Before the Civil War steady progress had been made in basic industries, and after 1865 industrialization proceeded at an amazing rate. Business trusts were formed, transcontinental railroads were built, and huge industries were established. Rich mineral and forest resources poured out an increasing stream of materials for hungry factories and mills. The production of pig iron rose from 1,000,000 long tons in 1870 to nearly fourteen times that amount in 1900. In 1860 the total value of American manufactures was less than $2,000,000,000; by the end of the century the figure had jumped to nearly seven times this amount.

After sleepy and isolated Japan had been opened to the western world in the 1860's, the Industrial Revolution was introduced there. Economic changes came with pell-mell rapidity for a number of reasons. The labor market was large, and workmen could always be found to work at a low wage, enabling the Japanese manufacturer to undersell his rivals in other nations. The government aided industrialization by subsidizing railroads and steamship lines, and large supplies of coal were available. Japan specialized in textiles. Prior to 1880 there were no Japanese cotton mills, but by 1914 nearly 2,500,000 spindles had been set up. Such a successful advance created serious competition for the mills of Manchester. The pace of industrialization in Japan is best indicated by the following facts: in 1870 no manufactured goods were exported; in 1906 the value of manufactures exported had reached $100,000,000.

Beginnings of industrialization in Russia. Not until the 1890's did the Russian imperial government seriously consider the build-up of the nation's industries. Then, for several reasons, there was a sudden interest in industrial progress. The emancipation of the serfs had increased the labor supply, and the growth of education made more workers capable of fitting themselves into an industrial life. Another reason lay in the appointment by Nicholas II in 1893 of Count Sergei Witte (1849-1915) to the ministry of finance and commerce.

This energetic and progressive noble saw that agriculture alone could not make a nation strong and self-sufficient. Railroads and factories were needed to develop Russia's vast natural resources. Because the country lacked the capital with which to embark upon such an ambitious program, Witte invited foreign capitalists to invest in Russian industries. Thus began an era of investment on a huge scale by French, Belgian, German, and other capitalists—an era cut short when Russia was transformed into the Union of Soviet Socialist Republics.

Despite depressions Russia advanced industrially in the years leading up to the First World War. Large amounts of sugar, flour, alcohol, and tobacco were produced, and Russia's cotton industry was the fourth greatest in the world. Iron production was roughly equivalent to that of France, and coal production was about one ninth that of England, although Russian exports totaled

only about half of the total exports of the diminutive Netherlands. Railway mileage more than doubled, and finally, in 1905, the famous Trans-Siberian Railway was completed, linking the vast expanse between St. Petersburg and the Pacific. Despite these changes, Russia at the outbreak of war in 1914 was still preponderantly agricultural. Its period of sweeping industrialization did not begin until 1928, when the Soviet Union inaugurated the first Five-Year Plan (see Chapter 15).

Progress in agriculture. The agricultural revolution which had begun in the eighteenth century was accelerated by the amazing progress of nineteenth-century science and technology. Cyrus Hall McCormick (1809-1884), a native of Vermont, demonstrated the first modern reaper in 1831 and introduced it into Europe about twenty years later. The grain cut by this reaper fell on a platform, from which it was raked by a man who walked beside the machine. Later on, devices were invented by which the reaper itself did the raking, while men followed the machine to bind the grain into sheaves. Then came the harvester, which also bound the grain, and finally the combine, which threshed the grain as it reaped it. Further improvements in farm machinery came with the manufacture of the steel plow and other implements by John Deere (1804-1886) in his world-famous factory at Moline, Illinois.

The marketing of foods was revolutionized by the widespread adoption of canning and refrigeration, permitting the storage of perishable crops. Railroads and steamships sped farm produce to market. During the second half of the nineteenth century, international trade in farm products increased rapidly. For example, the annual export of wheat from the United States and Canada rose from 22,000,000 bushels in the 1850's to 150,000,000 in 1880.

As we saw in Chapter 3, England in the eighteenth century had been the pioneer in scientific agriculture. But as the nineteenth century progressed, Germany assumed Britain's role as innovator. By raising protective tariffs and encouraging scientific methods of production, the German government in the latter half of the century greatly stimulated agricultural productivity.

Growth of world trade. The Second Industrial Revolution set in motion strong forces binding the world into one interdependent economic unit. The tremendous increase in manufacturing productivity caused the most highly industrialized regions of the world to seek new markets in the backward zones. There was also a demand for huge quantities of raw materials—cotton, tin, oil, tea, coffee, wheat, sugar, and timber. In 1860 world trade amounted to slightly more than $7,000,000,000; in 1913 the figure was nearly $42,000,000,000.

A world-wide market existed in which commodities, capital, currency, and economic services were freely exchanged. In 1879 an era of free trade ended as tariffs began to go up, but the rates remained moderate, and the effect on world commerce was slight. All the important currencies—the dollar, franc, mark, and pound—were redeemable in gold, and their exchange rates were stable.

Multilateral trade played a key role in this free exchange of currencies. For example, one nation might have an unfavorable balance of trade with several nations but, at the same time, a favorable balance with others, so that in the long run the debit and credit transactions balanced out. The diagram below shows how money flowed from the United States to Brazil, from Brazil to Britain, and from Britain back to the United States.

MULTILATERAL TRADE

Britain

Britain has an "unfavorable" balance with the United States, from which it buys wheat, copper, cotton, and lumber.

United States

The United States has an "unfavorable" balance with Brazil, from which it buys huge amounts of coffee.

Brazil

Britain has a "favorable" balance with Brazil, to which it sells mainly cotton cloth and manufactured goods.

Another factor encouraging economic internationalism was the free flow of capital. The great industrialized region of western Europe accumulated vast sums of wealth between 1870 and 1914. Capital investments at home and abroad doubled in Britain and France and tripled in Germany. By 1914 British investments abroad amounted to $20,-000,000,000; the sum for France was nearly $9,000,000,000, and for Germany, $4,000,-000,000. This outflow of capital helped the backward regions to develop; and in turn the borrowing countries could sell their commodities, mainly raw materials, to the industrialized nations.

Materially aiding this world economic interdependence was what might be termed the export of people. The higher standard of living and lower death rate in western Europe led to an unparalleled increase in population. From 1870 to 1914 the European continent registered an increase of 100,000,000 people. But at the same time a quarter of that number migrated to the great unsettled regions of North and South America, to Australia, and, to a lesser extent, to South Africa. This vast movement of people helped to develop backward and underpopulated lands and also created expanding markets for European goods.

Thus, with relatively low tariffs, multilateral trade, migrations, and a complementary trade relationship between the industrialized zones of the world and undeveloped regions, free movement was the basic characteristic of the world economy in the period preceding 1914.

Business consolidates. In the rush of new products and factories, businessmen became aware of the advantages of consolidation. By being big a business could enjoy the economies of mass production, could buy raw materials in huge amounts and at low prices, and could use its power to crush competition, and, if necessary, to lobby for favorable government legislation. In addition, big business could effectively discourage unionism, could place labor agitators on a black list, and, in the event of a strike, could employ strikebreakers. In Europe some of the new industrial giants were the Nobel Dynamite

As business corporations grew in size and strength, workers banded together in unions and political organizations. In this workers' demonstration in London, the banners of trade unions accompany the standard of the Social Democratic party.

Trust, Lever Brothers soap enterprises, Dunlop Rubber, and J. and P. Coats sewing thread company. In the United States there arose such business giants as the United States Steel Corporation, the American Tobacco Company, International Harvester, the Standard Oil Company and the United States Rubber Company.

Business consolidation took the form not only of larger corporations but also of mergers and alliances of separate units. One form was the trust, in which a body of trustees held a majority of the stock and thus controlled the wage, price, and merchandising policies of the several companies involved. Another form was the holding company, in which a corporation was organized to perform the same functions as the more informal trust. In Europe, business integration took the form of huge industrial combines known as cartels. These great industrial units were hooked together from country to country in international affiliates controlling such products as steel or rubber.

To create and operate such huge industrial organizations required larger sums than the manufacturer could ordinarily provide; and as a result, capitalism passed into a new stage of development. Just as commercial capitalism had been replaced by industrial capitalism in the eighteenth century, industrial capitalism in the last two decades of the nineteenth century was superseded by financial capitalism. As the financial houses arranged for the vast amounts of capital investment demanded by industry, more and more control of business fell into their hands. In this era the financier rather than the manufacturer became the dominant figure in the business arena.

With the growth of the size of the business unit, gains in economy and efficiency were registered. But there were also danger signals. In too many instances, key industries providing services or commodities vital to the health and well-being of society were dominated by a few huge enterprises controlled by a relative handful of men. And in the pell-mell pursuit of profits, businessmen too often neglected the legitimate responsibilities of industrial management to dabble in stock "deals" or in other speculative schemes.

The growth of financial capitalism mirrored the unprecedented increase in wealth which accompanied the Second Industrial Revolution. Between 1870 and 1910, investment in Britain increased from $35,000,000,000 to two times that figure, and in France from $28,000,000,000 to $55,000,000,000. Similar increases occurred in other nations of western Europe and in the United States.

Workers unite. Consolidation in business was paralleled by consolidation in the ranks of labor. In response to the seemingly all-powerful position of big business in wage bargaining and in reaction against management's tendency to regard workers merely as commodities, the workers (as we have seen in Chapter 6) began to organize into trade unions.

England led the way in the trade union movement. On the Continent paternalism among employers slowed down union growth. In France many workers were employed in small shops where there was personal contact with the master or boss; in Germany industrialists like Krupp paid good wages and refused to deal with unions. It was only after 1890 that substantial progress was made in these nations and in Austria, Holland, Russia, and Belgium. In the United States labor unionism began to take on strength in the 1870's.

The first unions were craft unions made up of skilled workers. Then unskilled wage earners were organized. Some of the unions formed were industrial unions, taking in all the workers employed in one industry. In this case, when any given group of workers felt compelled to strike, all union men in the industry would join them. As another means of gaining strength, associations of unions, such as the English Trade Union Congress, were formed on a national basis. In 1881 a federation of autonomous craft and industrial unions was founded in the United States with a membership that soon numbered in the millions. This was the American Federation of Labor, headed by Samuel Gompers; it became the most powerful voice of American workers.

The immediate result of the growth of unionism was better protection for the working masses, a stronger voice when it came to collective bargaining with the bosses, and consequently higher wages. Big unionism like big business made for more efficient methods, but in both cases bigness created power and with it the need for responsibility in its exercise. This problem was to become paramount in industrial relations by the mid-twentieth century. While in some instances, as in syndicalist-controlled unions (see p. 406), labor organizations sought to overthrow the capitalist system, the vast majority of unions both in Europe and in the United States were moderate and gradualistic in both their aims and methods.

FORCES OF COMPROMISE

AND REVOLUTION

Marx's prophecies prove untrue. From the start the Industrial Revolution had brought political problems in its wake, as evidenced by the uprisings of 1848 and 1871, when the workers and their friends fought the hated bourgeoisie in the streets of Paris. In the *Communist Manifesto* the proletariat acquired a program of action. Lining up on labor's side, long-haired radicals argued and debated in their garrets and cafés about the inevitability of revolution and the destruction of capitalism and its guardians—the bourgeoisie. If the prophesies of Marx were borne out, a new social war appeared imminent.

Would the concentration of wealth continue in fewer and fewer hands? Would the poverty of the masses become more intolerable? And would the chasm between the "haves" and the "have nots" become ever wider? From the standpoint of conditions in 1848, it looked as though Marx's predictions would come true; fortunately, they did not. The latter part of the nineteenth century and the decade preceding the First World War saw improvement in five basic areas: (1) the granting of such basic political rights as universal suffrage, civil liberties, and free expression of opinion; (2) improvement in the machinery and techniques of democracy; (3) an increase in the democratic distribution of wealth; (4) the growth of economic democracy; (5) the spread of education.

The new trends. We have observed in Chapter 12 the upsurge of democracy in the period between 1870 and 1914. In various nations of western Europe, the general public for the first time was given the right to vote and thus to participate in the conduct of their government. Britain in 1911 witnessed the victory of the House of Commons over the aristocratic House of Lords; the new democratic devices—the initiative and referendum—were perfected in Switzerland; and about this time women received the vote in Finland and Norway. Overseas in some British colonies and in the United States, democratic institutions were remarkably advanced. Despite the setbacks of the 1905 revolution in Russia, the cause of constitutional government had registered some gains there; and in the Ottoman empire the hated regime of Abdul-Hamid II was swept from power by the Young Turk revolution of 1908-1909.

Improvement in the political machinery of democracy was manifested by the operation of effective political party systems, free elections by means of the Australian ballot, and increased opportunities for the organized voice of the masses to express itself in political matters. Having secured the right to vote, workers eagerly formed political parties to consolidate their newly won power. Through these parties they hoped to compel the state to enact reforms for the benefit of the common man.

"Democratic distribution" means, simply speaking, more equal sharing in the wealth of a nation. The growth of labor unions gave workers more bargaining power with their employers, and they used this power to gain better wages. It has been estimated that the "real wages" of workers (the amount of goods that their wages could actually buy) increased 50 per cent in industrial nations between 1870 and 1900.

Not only did real wages improve, but the state increasingly guaranteed the popular standard of living. More and more governments made it their business to provide such benefits as unemployment insurance, old-age pensions, and accident compensation (see Chapter 12). In the more progressive states in western Europe, such as Britain, France, and Germany, social legislation provided all kinds of free government services—from clinics, parks, libraries, and concerts to garbage disposal. City governments also undertook to furnish gas, electricity, and water at low rates. Because these goods and services were paid for out of tax revenues, England introduced a graduated income tax, by which every individual paid a sum relative to his earnings.

Democratic production, whereby business management became less exclusively a monopoly of the capitalist class, was the fourth area in which important gains for the common people could be witnessed. Labor unions began to assert their right to have some say in the operation of industry, and government itself assumed the right to regulate and control great industries when the public interest was involved. Governments, moreover, sought to prevent the unjust exercise of economic power by the enactment of legislation such as the Sherman Anti-Trust Act and the Clayton Act in the United States. However, the effective subordination of big business in the highly industrialized western nations was not fully taken in hand until the advent of world depression in the 1930's.

Workers also attempted to make business production more democratic by establishing cooperatives. In 1844 the first workers' cooperative had been founded in England at Rochdale near Manchester. Capital for the company was secured by the sale of stock, goods were sold at prevailing prices, and profits were distributed annually to stockholders in proportion to the amount of goods each had purchased. The Rochdale experiment was the parent for consumer cooperatives all over the world. While never important in the United States, in Britain and on the Continent consumer cooperatives became a very significant factor in the economy. It has been estimated that by 1913 at least half the population of the British Isles was buying some of its goods from cooperatives.

The fifth and final aspect of the democratic movement in the second half of the nineteenth century was education. Before 1860 most of Europe's population was illiterate and unschooled. When the common people won the franchise, it was painfully apparent that they needed at least the rudiments of education to vote intelligently. In England after the passage of the second Reform Bill of 1867, a current slogan of the upper classes was the statement, however rueful, "We must educate our masters."

As the result of an education bill passed in 1870 under Gladstone, school attendance in England jumped from one to four million in ten years. Similar acts were passed in France, Germany, the Low Countries, and Scandinavia. Although educational progress lagged in southern and eastern Europe, with 80 per cent of the people of Russia and the Balkans remaining illiterate, by 1900 free and compulsory elementary education became almost universal in western Europe. High-school education for all did not begin to take hold until after the First World War, however, and then only to a very limited extent.

Liberalism fades; the welfare state appears. Only through the drastic modification and weakening of the middle-class doctrine of laissez-faire liberalism could the government's increased solicitude for the masses and the rise of a moderate, evolutionary phase of socialism have come about. Previously we discussed the tenets of this liberalism, whose adherents stoutly maintained that business and politics should be kept separate and that individuals should be allowed to sink or swim without any assistance or control by government. They did not believe in subsidies or tariffs to support business or in donations of public funds to assist the masses. The political corollary of nineteenth-century liberalism was that only men who had achieved some degree of economic success should have the right to vote.

After the middle of the nineteenth century, liberalism was increasingly weakened. The advent of manhood suffrage brought democracy, and to protect the new voters the state tended to intervene more and more in the field of business. After 1879 protective tariffs mounted in such nations as the United States, Germany, and France. Only Great Britain, together with Holland, Denmark, Finland, and Turkey, retained free trade.

Thus politics and economics merged. This expansion of a government's responsibilities for the economic security of all its people points toward the welfare state. That government moved away from laissez-faire liberalism and in the direction of the welfare state must be regarded as one of the fundamental socio-economic trends of the late nineteenth century.

Factory legislation, social legislation, the recognition of trade unions, and middle-class philanthropy all helped to achieve some degree of reconciliation between the proletariat and the bourgeoisie. A compromise had been reached. The workers were not completely satisfied but were willing in most instances to cooperate with management in the hope that the future would see more substantial gains. Speaking of the situation before 1914, a famous historian has written: ". . . most men are so constituted that they will abate something of their extreme demands in the interest of social peace. They will seek a compromise; and compromise has, on the whole, been the most characteristic feature in the relation of the two classes, employers and employees."[2] That the same spirit of compromise prevailed among most socialists also became clear.

Socialism compromises. In the early 1870's the growth of socialism was slow; but as the decade progressed, the movement gained momentum. The First International went out of business with scarcely a ripple in 1873 (see p. 182), but two years later in Germany the Social Democratic party was organized. It became the strongest of its kind in Europe and a model for similar parties in other nations. In France the carnage and hatred unleashed by the Paris Commune of 1871 had discredited socialism; but the party was gradually reorganized. Jules Guesde, a persuasive radical who had studied Marxian thought in Germany and had married Marx's daughter, founded a socialist group in France in 1877. Unlike the strong and unified movement in Germany, however, the French socialist movement was broken into a number of acrimonious factions. In the 1880's, Marxist parties also rose in Italy, Austria, the Netherlands, Scandinavia, and Belgium.

Important developments in socialism were taking place in England, where Marx had never been popular. Shunning violence and revolution, British socialists were influenced more by the maxims of Christian socialism than by the dogmas of Marxism and had more faith in parliamentary reform than in any uprising of the proletariat. Although a Social Democratic party espousing Marx was set up in 1881, it attracted few followers.

It was a different matter with the Fabian Society. Organized in 1883, this non-Marxist group derived its name from the cautious Roman general Quintus Fabius Maximus, who wore down his enemy Hannibal by being content with small gains. In short the Fabians substituted evolution for revolution. This British socialist group had been influenced by the ideas of Henry George, the American author of *Progress and Poverty*

(1879), who cogently argued for a single tax that would convert the rising values of land into benefits for all instead of permitting them to be pocketed by the landlord class, in the form of constantly increasing rents. Through the tax on land, then the chief source of capital, inequalities of wealth and income would be reduced without violence. It was this emphasis upon peaceful reform that became the hallmark of Fabianism. Led by such brilliant intellectuals as George Bernard Shaw, Sidney and Beatrice Webb, and H. G. Wells, the Fabians set about achieving moderate reforms by constitutional means. Chiefly through Fabian efforts the Labour party was formed in 1900 with the support of trade unions and various socialist groups. Much of the credit for British social legislation goes to the Labour party, which supported the Liberal party's program before World War I.

Moderate socialists were not limited solely to England, for the Fabian gospel of moderation—or revisionism, as it came to be called—spread to the Continent. Encouraged by a general improvement in the lot of the common man, the socialists became less revolutionary and more willing to cooperate with governments which were genuinely interested in raising the standards of living of the working people. The revisionist movement grew rapidly in the 1890's under the leadership of such famous socialists as Eduard Bernstein (1850-1932) in Germany and the brilliant intellectual Jean Léon Jaurès (1859-1914) in France.

For revisionist socialism to be effective, it had to wield power within the government; and by the early 1900's socialistic parties had achieved this goal in numerous European capitals. The German workers' representatives in the Reichstag had numbered only two in 1871, but in the 1912 election the socialists won 110 seats in the lower house. Through a coalition of the various parties, the socialists in France had cornered 102 seats in the Chamber of Deputies by 1914. Socialists from many countries joined the Second International after its founding in 1889; by 1914 it boasted a membership of twelve million.

The syndicalists and the revival of the class struggle. The political gains of the masses and the advances in education and social legislation were encouraging signs that a peaceful accommodation would be achieved between capital and labor. Indeed, the progress of revisionist socialism seemed to confound the dire prophecies of Marx. But there were radicals who refused to lay aside the doctrines of revolution, who viewed the growing moderation of the socialists with dismay, and who suspected that their old leaders were becoming the tools of the capitalists. A new radical movement known as syndicalism (from the French word *syndicat*, meaning "trade union") emerged in the 1890's with its center in France. Dominating the trade union movement, syndicalism had for its chief prophet and philosopher Georges Sorel (1847-1922), a French engineer who was a curious blend of realist and mystic. Unlike revisionist socialists, syndicalists feared the political state and, like the anarchists, would destroy it. Before World War I this movement conducted several nation-wide strikes in France. One in particular, the railway strike of 1910, threatened to paralyze the nation. The premier, Aristide Briand (1862-1932), a simon-pure socialist in his younger days, met the emergency by calling the strikers to military duty and then ordering them to run the railroads. This act led orthodox socialists to join the syndicalists in the charge that governments controlled by the bourgeoisie could not be trusted.

Orthodox Marxism in Russia. While European socialists were following the path of increasing moderation, their brothers in Russia were taking a different road. By 1900 the picture of workers "having nothing to lose but their chains" had been substantially altered in western Europe by the advance of social legislation and the rise of "real" wages. But if Marx could have risen from his grave in that year, he would have found in Russia the "1848" he once described in the *Communist Manifesto*. Here the Industrial Revolution was just gaining momentum, and bewildered peasants seeking work in city factories were shamefully exploited. There were no traditions of peaceful reform, gradualism, or compromise in Russia—only the memory of violence, of underground conspiracy, of ruthless government suppression, and of equally violent retaliation.

It was natural, therefore, that when socialism appeared in Russia, its adherents passionately embraced Marx's original doctrines of class war and revolution. While the tsars still reigned, the socialist leaders were preparing for the day when the people would overthrow the regime and win control of the government. One such leader was Lenin.

Lenin. Born Vladimir Ilich Ulyanov in a small city on the Volga River, Nikolai Lenin (1870-1924) grew up in moderate and respectable circumstances provided by his father, a teacher of physics. In 1887 his elder brother, an excellent student, just twenty-one, was arrested for plotting against the life of the tsar and was executed. Shortly thereafter Lenin began to read his dead brother's copy of *Das Kapital* and joined a secret Marxian discussion club. In 1895 he was arrested. Kept in custody without trial for more than a year, he was finally sentenced to three years' exile in Siberia. After he was released in 1900, he and his wife made their way to Switzerland. There, Lenin helped to found the socialist paper *Iskra* (*Spark*), whose motto was "From the spark —the conflagration."

Violence of Lenin's beliefs. Lenin stood for a revolutionary socialism whose weapon was violence and whose creed allowed no compromise with the bourgeoisie. While Marx believed that capitalism would break down of its own accord, Lenin wanted to smash it. He took nothing for granted. To destroy capitalism, he devised a technique of revolution whereby an elite leadership would enforce its dictates on the populace with iron discipline. The organization of communist activity would be of two kinds. On the surface would be the legal and peaceful workers' movement. But below was to be a revolutionary network, infiltrating the government, the police, and the army.

Lenin also disagreed with Marx on the dictatorship of the proletariat. Engels and

Marx did not envisage a police state but rather a republic of workers. Engels in 1891 wrote:

If anything stands, it is that our party and the working-class can only come to power under the form of a democratic republic. This is the specific form of the dictatorship of the proletariat.[3]

Lenin had other notions. His dictatorship of the proletariat would be a highly centralized despotism whose word was law.

In the latter part of the nineteenth century, there were both hopeful and disturbing trends in the economic and social climate of the western world. Statistics show that standards of living were rising. Gone were the days when, amid the squalid slums of cities, 75 per cent of the children died before they were five. In England and France the death rate fell from twenty-five per thousand in 1850 to nineteen per thousand in 1914. Life expectancy in England increased from just under forty years of age to well over fifty.

On the other hand, although most socialist organizations were willing to follow the way of democratic gradualism, the beliefs of the fanatical followers of Lenin augured ill for Europe. If the Bolshevik group (the radical majority of the Russian Social Democratic party) should gain power, the promise of the age might change to peril. The shattering impact of World War I would give the Bolshevik group its opportunity.

FORCES FOR PEACE AND BROTHERHOOD

Growing spirit of internationalism. As the nineteenth century came to a close, there was evidence of a growing spirit of internationalism and a deep yearning for peace among the peoples of the world. Earlier in this chapter we have seen how the growth of world trade, augmented by new marvels in transportation and communication, served to knit men together into a world community; and further evidences of such interna-

A contemporary illustration shows the parade of the winners at the revival of the Olympic games in Athens in 1896. The event attracting most interest was a foot race from Marathon to Athens, held in honor of the messenger of ancient Greece who ran to Athens to bring news of a Greek victory over the Persians. One dramatic feat of the 1896 games was the triumph of the United States team; an unofficial ten-man squad arrived barely in time to participate and won nine out of twelve events.

tionalism were numerous. In 1865 a conference which met in Paris to discuss the coordination of telegraph lines and the problem of rates established the International Telegraph Union, made up of twenty nations. To facilitate the handling of mail the world over, the Universal Postal Union was set up in 1875. As a protection for authors' rights, an agreement was drawn up in 1886 by an international copyright union and was later ratified by nineteen nations.

As part of the growing internationalism, the ancient Greek Olympic games were revived in 1896. Held every four years, the games attracted participants from nearly every nation. Another effort in the direction of international understanding was the invention in 1887 of an international language called Esperanto, the work of a Polish physician.

The peace movement. The modern, organized world peace movement began in the United States in 1815 and in England one year later. Motivated by Christian principles, members of the British Society for the Promotion of Permanent and Universal Peace distributed tracts and gave thousands of lectures. In the United States, Elihu Burritt, "the learned blacksmith," founded the League of Universal Brotherhood in 1846. The high-water mark of this phase of the movement for world peace occurred in 1849, when Victor Hugo spoke at the Universal Peace Congress in Paris and urged the formation of a United States of Europe. For more than a decade afterwards, however, pacifism faltered as the forces of imperialism, nationalism, and sectionalism inspired the Mexican War, the Crimean War, and the American Civil War.

In the late 1860's a new phase of the world peace movement began. While the first phase had been predominantly religious, the second emphasized such practical problems as improvements in international law and the rules of warfare and creation of machinery for arbitrating disputes. In 1878 a peace conference attended by unofficial representatives of thirteen nations was held in Paris. After 1889 a Universal Peace Congress convened annually until the First World War shattered its hopes. At a peace congress held in Chicago in 1893, the idea of an international court of arbitration was discussed.

The famous Swedish manufacturer of dynamite, Alfred Nobel, devoted much of his fortune to the advancement of peace by establishing the Nobel Peace Prize. Andrew Carnegie founded the Carnegie Endowment for International Peace and built a Palace of Peace at The Hague to be used for international conferences. To the Palace, Britain donated beautiful windows, France Gobelin tapestries, Germany the imposing gates, and Italy fine marble. (Ironically, the building was finished in 1913.)

Since its completion in 1913, the Palace of Peace at The Hague has housed three international courts—the Permanent Court of Arbitration (The Hague Tribunal), created by the Hague conference of 1899; the Permanent Court of International Justice, set up in affiliation with the League of Nations in 1921; and the International Court of Justice, established by the United Nations in 1945. The palace is the permanent seat of the International Court and the scene of its deliberations.

Governments seek to avoid war. While the desire for peace was perhaps stronger among the people than it was among their governments, a habit of political collaboration was developing among the European powers. Ever since the Congress of Vienna in 1815, the great powers had frequently conferred when peace was jeopardized. This practice of consultation, called the Concert of Europe, had helped on several occasions to keep the peace. Outside of Europe, the first Pan-American Conference, consisting of eighteen countries, assembled in 1889 at Washington, D.C., to discuss matters of common economic interest as well as problems pertaining to the maintenance of peace in the Western Hemisphere.

It was also encouraging to see countries increasingly willing to arbitrate their disputes. The United States and Britain led the way by amicably settling the *Alabama* affair (1871-1872), the Bering Sea controversy (1893), and the Alaskan boundary problem (1903). In the ten years following 1903, various powers signed 162 arbitration treaties, pledging the signatories to arbitrate certain matters.

In 1899 the Russian foreign minister invited the great powers to attend a conference on "possible reduction of the excessive armaments which weigh upon all nations." This proposal did not spring from love of peace so much as from the fact that the tsar's government was finding it extremely difficult to raise enough money to stay in the arms race. In May 1899 the conference convened at The Hague. Although in some quarters hopes ran high, no progress was made on disarmament. The German delegation was in no mood to discuss this prospect, and other representatives proved no more eager.

The conference did register some gains in the movement against war, however. It adopted a number of points in international law on the rules of war relating to treatment of prisoners, outlawed the use of poisonous gas, and defined the conditions of a state of belligerency. A court of arbitration, The Hague Tribunal, was established; and a list of jurists from which nations could select judges was drawn up. Recourse to the court was voluntary and so was acceptance of its decisions.

Another conference held at The Hague in 1907 was attended by representatives from forty-four countries. From these meetings developed the concept that the best way to deal with international problems was through a series of successive conferences. Later this idea strongly influenced the organization of the League of Nations.

FORCES OF WAR AND HATE

Forces of antagonism. At the same time that some forces were working to bring about closer cooperation between nations and peoples, other forces were promoting distrust and rivalries. These antagonistic forces finally triumphed, and as a result Europe and most of the world with it were plunged into war in 1914. Underlying causes of this great conflict were the actions of national states in power politics, militarism, rival alliances, secret diplomacy, economic imperialism, and nationalism.

National states play power politics. In 1914 Europe consisted of some twenty independent political units. Recognizing no higher authority, each of these states went its own way ethically and morally as well as economically and politically. International law was obeyed only if its dicta did not clash with a nation's interests.

It was the aim of every government to advance its own national interest. The great powers were ready to take advantage of any neighbor's weakness and to resort to war if the prize to be seized or the danger to be averted was substantial enough. War was an instrument of national policy, to be used whenever peaceful methods failed. As a British student of this period has observed: "The relations between the Great Powers . . . were not static, for none of them were entirely satisfied with the *status quo,* and yet all lived in perpetual dread that any change might operate to their disadvantage or even to their peril. Recurrent wars were regarded as inevitable since in the last resort it was assumed that every issue must be decided by force either potential or actual."[4]

Militarism. When force is the ultimate arbiter in international affairs, military strength becomes extremely important. In Prussia's three successful wars between 1864 and 1871, Bismarck showed his neighbors what could be done through the conscription of a nation's total man power. By the end of the 1870's all six of the major European powers except Britain had introduced compulsory military training. By the first decade of the twentieth century, the great powers had nearly 4,500,000 men under arms and were spending annually more than $2,000,000,000 on armaments. A new era in the history of militarism had begun.

So the great nations increased their armaments to make sure that their neighbors would not be tempted to attack them. These neighbors, in turn, interpreted the increase not as a defensive but as an offensive measure, which left them no alternative but to increase their own fighting power. Thus the armament race began, and the faster it went, the higher tension and distrust mounted.

Rival alliances. Living in this international anarchy, where a nation could not trust its neighbors, no state felt strong enough to rely upon its own military resources for protection. Therefore, nations whose interests ran along parallel lines joined together to muster more fighting power. But this, in turn, provoked nations outside the alliance to form a union capable of matching strength with strength. While the creation of two rival alliances was a feature of European diplomacy in the last part of the century, it brought no security to the states involved. In fact, the prospects of a major war were multiplied because the alliances made it unlikely that any conflict could be localized. Upon the outbreak of hostilities —no matter how minor the incident—the nations involved would immediately seek the aid of their allies, and the whole continent would be at war. This is what happened in the summer of 1914.

Secret diplomacy. Closely connected with the system of alliances was the practice of secret diplomacy. In their dangerous game, diplomats threatened, intimidated, jockeyed for power, and offered bribes, sometimes bartering territory to which they themselves had no legal claim. The activities of spies, the secret reports, and the unscrupulous methods of the foreign offices of Europe poisoned the atmosphere of international politics and heightened the tension still further. Observing the prevailing suspicion and fear, Theodore Roosevelt wrote:

The Kaiser sincerely believes that the British are planning to attack him and smash his fleet, and perhaps join with France in a war to the death against him. As a matter of fact the English harbor no such intentions but are themselves in a condition of panic terror lest the Kaiser secretly intends to form an alliance against them . . . to destroy the fleet and blot out the British Empire from the map. It is as funny a case as I have seen of mutual distrust and fear bringing two peoples to the verge of war.[5]

Economic imperialism. The tremendous increase in productivity and world trade between 1870 and 1914 seemed to presage a new economic interdependence with greater cooperation and less rivalry between the industrial powers. Unfortunately, there developed a countermovement in which the world's markets were viewed as a battleground with businessmen as the combatants. A contest developed between business groups of rival nations over the lion's share of the new riches.

Laissez faire gave way to a new kind of mercantilism in which governments acted as aggressive champions for their own business interests. Although trade in general continued to increase, tariffs protected local manufacturers from foreign competition. One of the most significant features of this neo-mercantilism was economic imperialism, a struggle for control of the colonial areas of the world. As we saw in Chapter 10, governments began to use their diplomatic power and even their armies to secure control of areas rich in essential raw materials or valuable as markets for manufactured goods.

A serious clash of British and German imperialism took place in Asia Minor. In 1903 German capitalists secured from Turkey the right to complete the Berlin-to-Bagdad railroad, which would give Germany control of a great corridor from the Baltic through middle Europe down to the Persian Gulf. To British politicians and financiers the scheme seemed to threaten their trade and perhaps the security of India as well. Although the British government was able to block completion of the railway for several years, the Berlin-to-Bagdad railroad was a serious source of friction in relations between Great Britain and Germany.

In some cases economic competition led to war. As discussed in previous chapters, Japanese designs upon the Asiatic mainland brought about war with China in 1894, and Great Britain fought the Boer War in South Africa. Japan and Russia fought over Manchuria in 1904-1905, and Italy wrested Tripoli from Turkey in 1912.

Nationalism: rampant and submerged. Nationalism—particularly the narrow, blatant, and bellicose variety of the late nineteenth century—has been rightly regarded as one of the most potent causes of modern war. Cheerfully accepting racial myths and strongly influenced by social Darwinism, ultranationalistic leaders preached that some races were the prizes of God's creation while others were inferior and even reprehensible.

In Germany the Pan-German League was organized to spread the doctrine of the superiority of the German race and culture. The Pan-German League was a leader in anti-English agitation; it supported German colonial ambitions; it sought to retain the loyalty of all Germans to the fatherland no matter where they were living in the world; and it worked to promote a policy of German power both in Europe and overseas.

Although the cult of superiority was most blatantly expressed in movements like Pan-Germanism, it was found to some degrees in all countries. Englishmen preached the superiority of their Anglo-Saxon breed and their mission to build the greatest empire the world had ever seen. At the turn of the century supernationalism had its advocates in the United States. One such declared:

If I read not amiss, this powerful race will move down upon Mexico, down upon Central and South America, out upon the islands on the sea, over upon Africa and beyond. And can anyone doubt that the result . . . will be the "survival of the fittest"?[6]

Exaggerated nationalism had no tolerance for minorities within the country, much less for aspirations for freedom. When the Germans, Italians, and Hungarians achieved unification of their countries, they became models for the ambitions of numerous submerged nationalities. Unfortunately, the admiration was misplaced; in fact, those people who had achieved unification frequently refused to recognize similar goals on the part of aliens living within their borders. But though rebuffed by those from whom they had expected sympathy and even support, the minorities continued to agitate for liberation. Willing to use any means available for gaining freedom, they too menaced the general peace.

Poles and French resist integration. Having realized its own nationalistic aspirations in 1871, Germany refused to consider the rights of any non-German peoples in its empire—Poles and French in particular. The four million Poles in the empire were a serious problem, and the government was determined to Germanize this large racial minority. As a method of weakening Polish culture, the German government set about discouraging the use of the Polish tongue. But Polish school children would often refuse to recite in German and would resort to strikes despite the punishment which was

sure to follow. A cartoon of the day showed a Polish schoolboy saying:

If I say my prayers in German, my father beats me; if I say them in Polish, my teacher beats me; if I don't say them at all, my priest beats me.[7]

In 1886 the German government commenced buying land in Polish districts in order to establish colonies of Germans. A law gave the government the right to expel Poles from their land, and in such cases the landowner seldom received fair recompense.

Another serious nationality problem facing the Germans was that of the French in Alsace-Lorraine. It is said that when these two provinces were taken from France in 1871, the emperor of Austria sent the German ruler a telegram which read: "I congratulate you on the annexation of an open sore to your empire." Following the annexation thousands of French families fled to France. The German government did everything possible to stifle the pro-French sentiments of the Alsatians. Use of the French language was discouraged, and a strict censorship was applied to all news coming from France. These measures were ineffective, however; the representatives sent by Alsace-Lorraine to the German legislature repeatedly protested the annexation and did everything possible to embarrass the government.

Russification of subject peoples in Russia. Russia had numerous subject peoples, especially Poles and Finns. During the reign of Tsar Alexander III (1881-1894), a ruthless policy of Russification was introduced. Alexander was determined that all his subjects should be essentially Russian in feeling and outlook, and the most vigorous attempts were made to stamp out any evidences of foreign nationalism. The Russian language was made compulsory, and all vestiges of local government in the subject areas were done away with. But though the Poles and the Finns felt the heavy hand of the Russification policy, both peoples strenuously clung to their traditions, their language, and their hope that one day they would gain their independence.

Minority problems in Austria-Hungary. The union between German Austrians and

Hungarian Magyars in 1867 was basically a selfish arrangement enabling the two ruling minorities to dominate a great mass of subject peoples. In the Austro-Hungarian empire the two ruling peoples represented less than half the total population. The remaining subjects, as we have already seen, were principally Slavs, including Czechs and Moravians, Poles, Serbs, and Croats. In one region of the Alps a considerable number of Italians were also under Austro-Hungarian rule.

An oppressive Hapsburg policy sought to weaken militant Czech nationalism by striving to make the Czechs in Bohemia forget their traditions, language, and great heroes. But these efforts were in vain, and after 1880 the Austrian government turned to conciliation. The Czechs were given a new university, and the Czech language was made partly official. Bohemian leaders, however, demanded autonomy such as had been granted to Hungary by the *Ausgleich* in 1867. When such a position within the empire was not granted, a more radical nationalistic party called the Young Czechs was organized. The leader of this organization (who was destined for a more eminent role in world affairs) was a professor of history, Thomas Masaryk (1850-1937), of mixed Czech and Slovak parentage. Meanwhile, the Czech representatives in the Austrian Reichsrath kept that body in constant turmoil by their obstructionist tactics.

The Poles, another Slavic group ruled by Austria, were very liberally treated, being given their own schools and the right to use their own language. Also treated with tolerance were the South Slavs, the great majority of whom would have been satisfied with autonomy within the empire. After 1900, however, a more radical national program began to crystallize. This program—part of the Pan-Slavic movement subsidized by Russia and Serbia—threatened to detach all the South Slavs from Austria-Hungary and unite them with Serbia.

While Austria made some attempt to placate the various nationalities within its borders, in Hungary the program was complete Magyarization. The public use of all languages other than Hungarian was restricted; any non-Magyar sentiment was carefully deleted from plays and periodicals; and determined attempts were made to restrict festivals, the singing of folk songs, and other folk activity by the Slovaks, Rumanians, and Serbs. To keep the subject nationalities in line, Hungarian officials resorted to physical violence and stuffing the ballot box. We will see that discontented nationalities in the Hapsburg empire became pawns in the game of international power politics and ultimately provided the incident that led to world war.

Serbia and Pan-Slavism. We recall from Chapter 8 that a number of subject peoples gradually freed themselves from Turkish rule in the course of the nineteenth century. The flame of nationalism burned fiercely in the new Balkan nations; proud of their new freedom, they were determined to extend it to their brothers still under the Turks. Serbia thought of itself as the "Piedmont of the Balkans," ready to liberate the other Slavic groups and unite with itself the Slavs in Bosnia and Herzegovina and in Albania. This ambition, known as the Greater Serbia movement, was aimed not only against the Turks but also against the Hapsburgs, who ruled the South Slavs.

The Greater Serbia movement was a local manifestation of Russian-sponsored Pan-Slavism. Since the days of Catherine the Great, Russia had been driving southwest toward the Black Sea, Constantinople, and the Straits and south through Asia Minor and the Middle East to the Indian Ocean. As a means of weakening opposition from Austria and Turkey, Russia assumed the role of protector of its "little Slavic brothers" in the Balkans, glorifying their destiny and also Russia's own great mission. This was the message of Pan-Slavism. Representatives of the various Slavic nations looked to Russia as the protector of all oppressed Slavs, especially those in the Dual Monarchy.

Anti-Semitism and Zionism. Speaking of Pan-Germanism and Pan-Slavism, a famous historian refers to their development as the "seed time of totalitarian nationalism." These pernicious ideas of racial superiority were later to develop into the hideous campaign of extermination which Adolf Hitler and his Nazi henchmen carried out against certain supposedly inferior peoples, concentrating primarily on the Jews.

A foretaste of what racial nationalism would bring in the twentieth century was provided by the treatment of the Jews in the later nineteenth century. After suffering from many injustices and restrictions during the Middle Ages, the Jews in western Europe and in the Americas secured practically all the rights of full citizens after 1800. With this advance came new opportunities; and Jews in many countries made significant contributions to art, music, literature, and science. About 1850, however, a strong anti-Semitic movement began to appear in Europe.

In Germany a political party whose express purpose was anti-Semitism was organized and won the support of nearly 300,000 voters. German nationalists like Heinrich von Treitschke coined the phrase "The Jews are our calamity." Anti-Semitism in France reached a climax in the Dreyfus affair, described in Chapter 12. In eastern Europe, especially in Rumania, the Jewish minorities suffered many injustices; but their hardest lot was in Russia. In the tsar's realm the Jews had to live in specified western provinces, the so-called Jewish Pale. They were forbidden to buy certain kinds of property. Their admittance to schools was restricted, and they had to pay twice the taxes of corresponding non-Jewish communities. After the assassination of Tsar Alexander II in 1881, the Jews were made the scapegoats; and terrible massacres, called pogroms, were carried out with the encouragement of the government.

As we follow in Chapter 16 the complex struggle between Arab and Jew for Palestine immediately after World War I, it is important to understand that the desire for a Jewish homeland was born out of the injustices of anti-Semitism in the last century. It was the exaggerated nationalism of other peoples that made many Jews nationalistic themselves. In 1896 a Hungarian Jew, Theodor Herzl (1860-1904), came forward with the program of Zionism, as he called it, which had as its purpose the creation of Palestine as an independent state. Herzl claimed that the Jews were a distinct nationality and thus were entitled to have a country of their own. The first general congress of Zionists was held in Switzerland in 1897, and small-scale immigration to Palestine began.

The emotion of nationalism. Among both submerged and ruling groups, then, national loyalty was an intense, explosive emotion. Inflated patriotism became a new religion, the emotional adjunct to power politics. Nationalism fattened on the acquisition of colonies and the defeat of enemies; nationalists refused to believe that their nation could ever be wrong. History as taught in schools was frequently distorted in order to glorify a nation's past achievements and gloss over its shortcomings. National self-glorification became the objective of numerous writers, who exalted their own country's culture and often heaped ridicule and abuse on that of others. In the opinion of many people the most important fundamental cause of the First World War was nationalism run rampant.

"THE LAMPS ARE GOING OUT"

Bismarck's diplomatic footwork. After 1871 and the conclusion of the Franco-Prussian War, the German chancellor's wish was to protect the fruits of victory. He realized that France would try to get revenge on Germany and take back Alsace-Lorraine, so he deliberately cut France out of the diplomatic game.

In 1873 Bismarck made an alliance with Russia and Austria-Hungary, known as the Three Emperors' League. By this agreement, in the event of threat of war the signatories were to consult "in order to determine a common course of action." Germany and Russia specifically promised mutual support in case of attack. Great Britain in this period was following the policy of "splendid isolation," and Italy was relatively unimportant.

Up to this point Bismarck had had few diplomatic worries; but at the Congress of

Berlin (1878) he was forced to choose between the claims of Austria and those of Russia in the Balkans. Apparently believing that it was impossible to have both Russia and Austria as close allies, Bismarck chose to support Austria because he trusted that empire more than he did Russia. The Germans in Vienna were his kinsmen, whereas he was somewhat suspicious of Slav loyalty. In any event, Austria in any capacity other than as an ally was too close to Germany for comfort. And, finally, Bismarck was afraid that supporting Russia would alienate Great Britain and cause it to make an alliance with Austria. Russia naturally resented Bismarck's support of Austria's Balkan ambitions at the Congress of Berlin.

A year later Bismarck negotiated the Dual Alliance with the Austrian government, and in 1882 a new partner, Italy, was secured, thus bringing into operation the Triple Alliance. By the terms of this agreement the three powers promised not to enter into any alliance against each other. Further, it was provided that in the event of an unprovoked French attack on either Italy or Germany both allies would wage war on France. And if any member or members of the alliance were attacked by two or more great powers, all three allies were pledged to make war.

The choice of Austria as a close ally in preference to Russia did not mean that Bismarck was reconciled to the loss of the latter's friendship. In 1881 the Three Emperors' League (Russia, Austria, and Germany) was renewed, but when rivalries between Austria and Russia in the Balkans made it impossible for these two powers to be in the same group, the alliance collapsed (1887). To fill the gap, Bismarck negotiated a separate alliance with Russia called the Reinsurance Treaty. The German chancellor explained to the Russian ambassador how Germany could be an ally of both Russia and Austria at the same time.

You forget the importance of being a party of three on the European chess-board. That is the object of all the Cabinets, and above all of mine. Nobody wishes to be in a minority. All politics reduce themselves to this formula: try to be *à trois* in a world governed by Five Powers.[8]

Under the masterful hand of Bismarck, Germany retained hegemony over the European continent from 1871 to 1890. The chancellor had succeeded admirably in his diplomacy. Every effort was made to avoid challenging the interests of Britain, which continued to isolate itself from alliances. France had been kept in diplomatic quarantine without allies. Through amazing diplomatic acrobatics, Bismarck had managed to avoid alienating Russia while retaining an alliance with Austria.

In a single move, however, the preponderance of power built up by Bismarck was heedlessly cast away. In 1890 the new German kaiser, young William II, dismissed the old chancellor (see Chapter 12) and took German foreign policy into his own hands. Foolishly allowing the Reinsurance Treaty to lapse, he permitted Russia to seek new allies. Isolated and smarting from its diplomatic impotency, France immediately began to woo Russia, which was badly in need of loans to build up its armed forces and to help construct the Trans-Siberian Railroad. Millions of French francs went to buy Russian bonds, and France received what it had wanted for twenty years—a strong military ally. A French naval squadron visited Russia and persuaded the tsar to agree to a military alliance to go into effect in 1894. The Triple Alliance was now confronted by the Dual Alliance, cementing Paris and St. Petersburg as military allies.

England, the crucial power. As long as Great Britain followed its policy of "splendid isolation," Germany's Triple Alliance and the Russo-French combination were fairly equally matched. But if Great Britain were to join either alliance the balance of power would shift at once and make that group supreme.

At the end of the nineteenth century, Britain was involved in bitter colonial rivalries. With Russia the problems rose in the Balkans and Afghanistan; Britain sought to prevent Russian domination of the Bosporus and encroachment in the vicinity of the Indian frontier. For some years the British and French had been competing in Africa, where France envisaged an empire stretching from the Atlantic to the Red Sea. This plan collided with Britain's program of acquiring a continuous stretch of territory from the Cape to Cairo. In 1898 the rivals narrowly averted war when the expeditions of the British general Kitchener and the French colonel Marchand converged at Fashoda in the Sudan and both officers claimed the region of the upper Nile. During the Boer War all the great powers in Europe were anti-British. Only the supremacy of England's fleet effectively discouraged the development of an interventionist movement. More and more, Great Britain became disquieted by its policy of diplomatic isolation.

It was these circumstances which explained British overtures to Germany in 1898 and again in 1901. The exponent of Anglo-German friendship and concord was Joseph Chamberlain, the father of Neville Chamberlain, prime minister of Great Britain at the outbreak of World War II. The Germans were not favorably impressed by the offer of a British alliance and interpreted it as a sign of British weakness.

Germany alarms Russia and England. Germany not only rebuffed Britain's suggestions for an alliance but embarked on an aggressive policy known as *Weltpolitik* (world politics). Through this policy it determined not only to be the first military power in Europe but to expand its influence in the Middle East and the Balkans, secure more colonies overseas, and build a battle fleet second to none. By expansion into the Middle East, Germany calculated to alienate Russia, since this nation was deeply interested in getting control of the Bosporus and the territory between it and the Persian Gulf. Above all, the German naval program would inevitably arouse the fears of Britain.

In 1897 the German fleet was seventh in the world, although by common consent the German army was given first place. A huge naval program was initiated in 1900, providing for the construction of a fleet strong enough to jeopardize Great Britain's naval supremacy within twenty years. The naval law made no secret of its purpose:

To protect Germany's sea trade and colonies . . . there is only one means: Germany must have a battle fleet so strong that even for the adversary

with the greatest sea power [Britain] a war against it would involve such dangers as to imperil his own position in the world.[9]

For England the supremacy of the royal navy was a life-or-death matter. Britain did not grow enough food or produce enough raw materials to be self-sufficient. Since these commodities had to come by sea, it was crucial that the royal navy be able to protect British shipping. England had no special objection to Germany's having the greatest land army in the world, but when this power aspired to great naval strength, Britain became seriously alarmed.

Anglo-German relations quickly deteriorated after 1900. Aside from the naval program, the British were disturbed at the tremendous strides made by German industry. Furthermore, the kaiser's threatening and irresponsible speeches and unpredictable behavior added fuel to the rising flame of mistrust. Rebuffed and challenged by Germany, Britain turned elsewhere to establish friendly relations.

The Entente Cordiale. In 1904 Britain and France settled their outstanding differences and proclaimed the Entente Cordiale, a French term which means "friendly understanding." This *rapprochement* was made possible in some degree by the popularity in France of Edward VII and his enthusiasm for all things French. The Entente Cordiale and England's alliance with Japan in 1902 ended Britain's traditional policy of isolation and brought it into the diplomatic combination pitted against Germany's Triple Alliance.

By this time Italy had secretly deserted the camp of the Triple Alliance. As long as Italians were under Austrian rule in the *Italia irredenta* (unredeemed Italy) of the Trentino, South Tyrol, and Trieste, Italy could not be comfortable in any alliance which included Austria. In 1902, therefore, Italy had made an agreement with France settling old rival claims in Africa. Italy now had a foot in both diplomatic camps, but its heart, increasingly, was with France and Britain.

Great Britain's desire to settle all outstanding differences with France was accentuated by more alarming developments in its relations with Germany. In 1906 Great Britain introduced a new type of warship, the dreadnought, which by its heavy armor and twelve-inch guns rendered all existing ships obsolete. But what should have been an advantage to Britain in the naval race actually benefited Germany, which immediately copied the dreadnought. As all existing ships were now outmoded, the naval race was on equal terms. The British suggested a ship-building holiday to the German government, but the kaiser and his admiral, Tirpitz, were determined to push their program.

In 1907 Great Britain settled its problems with Russia, thereby establishing the Triple Entente. Great Britain made no definite military commitments in the agreements with France and Russia. Theoretically it retained freedom of action but, for all this, it was now part of the alliance system.

Diplomatic crises: 1905-1914. For a decade before the First World War, Europe experienced a series of crises brought about as the two alliance systems flexed their muscles and probed each other's strength. The diplomatic hegemony enjoyed by Germany under Bismarck was gone; indeed, once-dominant Germany now had no reliable ally except Austria. The Germans spoke bitterly of this situation as their country was encircled by an enemy alliance. Italy could not be trusted; and military strength, actual or potential, seemed to be greater in the camp of the Triple Entente. Germany made frantic efforts to weaken the alliance system confronting it. It was almost certain that sooner or later an incident would unleash forces that could not be stopped. As each new diplomatic crisis arose, Europe teetered on the abyss of war.

The first serious diplomatic crisis occurred in 1905 and concerned Morocco. France sought control of this territory in order to establish a stretch of contiguous dependencies from the Atlantic across the North African coast to Tunisia. By interfering in Morocco the German government thought it saw a chance to weaken the Anglo-French Entente. (Since Russia had just suffered a decisive defeat by Japan, it could not be expected to assist France.) Carefully timing his moves, the German chancellor arranged for the kaiser to visit the Moroccan port of Tangier, where he declared that all powers must respect the independence of the country. The French were forced to give up their immediate plans for taking over Morocco and agree to Germany's suggestion that an international conference be called at Algeciras (1906) to discuss the matter.

At this meeting the German hope that a rift might appear between the British and French did not materialize. On the contrary, all but one of the nations in attendance—even Italy—supported France rather than Germany. Only Austria remained at the side of Germany. It was agreed that Morocco should still enjoy its sovereignty but that France and Spain should be given certain rights to police the area. The events at Algeciras and the British agreement with Russia the following year (1907) filled the Germans with dread.

In 1911 a second Moroccan crisis heightened the tension. When France sent an army into the disputed territory "to maintain order," Germany countered by dispatching the gunboat *Panther* to the Moroccan port of Agadir. Great Britain came out with a plain warning that all its power was at the disposal of France. A diplomatic bargain was struck whereby France got a free hand in Morocco, and Germany was granted French holdings in equatorial Africa.

The Balkan nemesis. Although the two rival alliance systems had managed somehow to avert an armed showdown over Morocco, these happy auguries were of no avail against the forces of rival imperialism and nationalism unleashed in the Balkans.

Both Germany and Austria were opposed to Russia's Pan-Slavic ambitions in the Balkans. German motives were largely economic; the Germans envisaged a great continuous economy stretching from the Baltic to the Persian Gulf. The Austrian concern in the Balkans was primarily defensive. A polyglot empire containing millions of Slavs, Austria-Hungary feared that if Serbia, egged on by Russia, should extend an irredentist movement into the southern part of the Austrian empire, many Slavs might be lost,

THE BALKANS IN 1914

Independent States

AUSTRIA-HUNGARY

BESSARABIA

R U S S I A

BOSNIA

HERZE-
GOVINA

SERBIA

RUMANIA

Black Sea

MONTENEGRO

BULGARIA

ALBANIA

(To Serbia 1913)

(To Serbia 1913)

(To Bulgaria 1913)

(To Greece 1913)

Constantinople

GREECE

T U R K E Y

CRETE
(To Greece 1913)

and ultimately the whole empire might be destroyed. The Austrians were thus determined that Pan-Slavism should be checked before it became too dangerous.

As a counter to the advance of Serbian irredentism, Austria annexed outright the provinces of Bosnia-Herzegovina, which it had administered since 1878. This high-handed move was arranged in 1908 at a castle in Bohemia, where the representatives of Austria and Russia agreed in secret that Russia would approve the annexation in return for Austria's acquiescence in Russia's seizure of the Bosporus. But after annexing the two provinces, Austria feigned ignorance of Russia's share of the bargain.

The result was a dangerous crisis. Russia was furious at what it considered a diplomatic double cross, and Serbia was equally exercised over the incorporation of its Slavic

brothers into the Hapsburg domain. Russia thereupon appealed both to France and Britain for support, but these allies refused. Because Russia had come out of its war with Japan (1904-1905) badly battered, it could not support Serbia against the combined might of Germany and Austria. In this crisis the Triple Alliance had humbled Russia and thwarted the plans of Russia's protégé Serbia.

Meanwhile Serbia and its neighbors, especially Greece and Bulgaria, were making other plans. In 1912, under the inspiration of the Greek prime minister, an alliance was formed among all the small Balkan states (Montenegro, Greece, Serbia, and Bulgaria). The objective was the expulsion of Turkey from Europe, specifically from Albania, Macedonia, and Thrace. Italy's seizure of Tripoli in 1912 had once again exposed Ottoman weakness (p. 310), and the Balkan allies were encouraged in their design. The First Balkan War began in 1912 and was quickly terminated as Turkish resistance crumpled.

The victorious Balkan nations were not permitted to divide their spoils as they had agreed among themselves, however. Because it wanted no more competition in the Adriatic, Austria refused to allow Serbia to annex Albania. The great powers meeting in London deferred to Austria.

The result was the Second Balkan War, caused by quarrels among the victors. Denied Albania, the Serbs and the Greeks demanded compensation of territory originally promised to Bulgaria. Bulgaria attacked its former allies, and Turkey and Rumania in turn entered the war against Bulgaria, which was no match for its numerous opponents. A peace was signed by which Bulgaria gave up to its former allies most of the territory originally taken from Turkey. By this time Turkey retained only a precarious toe hold in Europe, the small pocket around Constantinople. By the end of 1913 no permanent solution had been found to the Balkan problem. Serbia was reluctant to withdraw its troops from Albania, which was to be an independent kingdom; but following an Austrian ultimatum, the Serbian forces moved out.

The whole area was now a powder keg of mingled fears and hates. Austria was more than ever fearful of the Greater Serbia movement. Serbia was more ambitious than ever, since its territory had doubled as a result of the recent wars. The Serbian prime minister is quoted as saying: "The first round is won; now we must prepare the second against Austria." While this particular statesman and his colleagues had some restraint and were not likely to act too hastily, there were many Serbian hotheads with different ideas. It was they who organized the Black Hand Society, whose constitution stated:

This organization has been created with the object of realizing the national ideal: the union of all Serbs. . . . This organization prefers terrorist action to intellectual propaganda. . . . This organization bears the name "Union or Death."[10]

The dynamite in the Balkan bomb was the involvement of the major powers. Germany was now supporting Turkey, even to the extent of military assistance. This action was taken to thwart Pan-Slavism, whose expansion was bound to weaken Austria. As for Russia, its Pan-Slavic dreams had not been completely blocked but only interrupted. Although lacking important interests in the Balkans, France would range itself without hesitation with Russia against Germany, hoping in this roundabout way to secure the defeat of its old enemy and regain its own lost provinces. Britain, too, had no immediate interests to protect in the Balkans; but should a general war be provoked, it could hardly afford to see Germany victorious over its allies since this would shift the balance of power disastrously. Thus the Balkan powder keg had the awesome possibility of igniting all of Europe.

The archduke assassinated. The fateful spark came on June 28, 1914, when Archduke Francis Ferdinand, heir to the Austrian throne, and his wife were assassinated in the town of Sarajevo in Bosnia. This deed was the work of a young Bosnian student inspired by Greater Serbia propaganda. He and two associates received assistance from high Serbian officers, although the direct complicity of the Serbian government has not been proved. Even so, that it could have been ignorant of the plot seems unlikely.

Count Leopold von Berchtold (1863-1942), the Austrian foreign minister, believed that the assassination justified crushing, once and for all, the anti-Austrian propaganda and terrorism emanating from Serbia. Austria could take no action, however, without securing the support of its ally, Germany. Berchtold thereupon prepared a letter to the kaiser and succeeded in getting the Austrian emperor to sign it. The letter received by the kaiser declared:

The crime against my nephew is the direct consequence of the agitation carried on by Russian and Serbian Pan-Slavists, whose sole aim is to weaken the Triple Alliance and shatter my empire. . . . The aim of my government must henceforth be to isolate and diminish Serbia.[11]

The German emperor was genuinely moved by this appeal. The news of the assassination had shocked him deeply, and he viewed the Bosnian terrorists as little more than fanatical savages. Furthermore, the kaiser felt that everything possible must be done to prevent Austria, Germany's only reliable ally, from being weakened by such forces as Serbian terrorism. William decided to assure the Austrian government of his full support. Thus Berchtold obtained a blank check from Germany. Vienna wanted only a local Austro-Serbian war, and Germany favored quick action to forestall intervention.

The Austrian ultimatum. The Austrian foreign minister proceeded with his plans for subjugating Serbia. On July 23 an Austro-Hungarian ultimatum was presented to the Serbs. The terms were harsh: all anti-Austrian activities in Serbia were to cease, textbooks unfriendly to Austria were to be banned from the schools, and Austro-Hungarian officials were to assist in putting down any "revolutionary movement directed against the territorial integrity of the Dual Monarchy." Austria further demanded that all officials in the Serbian army and governmental service guilty of propaganda against the Austrian government should be removed. Intending that the ultimatum be turned down, Berchtold demanded unconditional acceptance within forty-eight hours.

In answer, on July 25, the Serbs penned a very clever reply. Only two demands were accepted in their entirety, and most of the others were neatly side-stepped by diplomatic qualifications. The Austrian government announced that the reply was unsatisfactory to them and mobilized their armed forces. The kaiser on the other hand, was satisfied with Serbia's answer, and the German chancellor urged Austria to negotiate with Russia, which was following developments in the Balkans closely. Russia realized that if the Austrians succeeded in humbling Serbia, Russian prestige in this area would suffer tremendously.

The French in the meantime assured the Russians of their full cooperation and urged strong support for Serbia.

Grey's peace efforts. Before the ultimatum to Serbia had been served, Sir Edward Grey (1862-1933), the British foreign minister, began his efforts to maintain peace. He advised negotiations between the Russians and Austrians to avoid the problem of dangerous demands upon Serbia and, in a second proposal, suggested that England, France, Germany, and Italy agree to exercise a "moderating or mediating influence" simultaneously on St. Petersburg and Vienna. The Germans agreed, but the French opposed the plan, saying they would collaborate only if Germany first exerted pressure on Vienna. A third peace proposal from Grey had no more success than its predecessors.

While the diplomats worked for peace, Berchtold was fearful that Serbia would escape from his clutches. On July 27 he succeeded, thanks in part to falsehood, in convincing the emperor that war was the only way out, and the following day a formal declaration of war was announced against Serbia.

Berchtold's decision made a general European conflict almost inevitable, but there was still the hope that Germany could restrain its ally. As the possibility of a general European war loomed, several frantic telegrams were sent by Berlin to Vienna. The German ambassador was instructed to tell Berchtold:

As an ally we must refuse to be drawn into a world conflagration because Austria does not respect our advice.[12]

At this critical stage, when German pressure on Austria might have opened a path to peace, an event took place which wrecked any further attempts at negotiation. This was the Russian mobilization on July 30.

Russia mobilizes for war. The significance of mobilization in modern warfare must be understood to appreciate the import of the Russian action. Modern armies constitute millions of men. To call out the reserves to join their regiments, to hand out equipment, and to move to previously assigned strategic positions is a task requiring several days and careful timing. To allow a dangerous rival to mobilize before you do would be to enable him to inflict defeat before your mobilization was complete. Up to this time Bethmann-Hollweg, the German chancellor, had sought peace, but the mobilization of Russia brought an abrupt halt to his efforts.

In the case of Germany the mobilization question was especially vital, because in the event of war with Russia and France, Germany would be confronted with enemies on two fronts. The best plan seemed to be to launch a lightning attack against France, crush France, and then turn to meet Russia, which could ordinarily be expected to mobilize rather slowly. To allow Russian mobilization to proceed would jeopardize this strategy.

World war. Faced by the Russian action, the German government decided upon war on July 31. Ultimatums were sent to Russia and France demanding from the former cessation of mobilization and from the latter a pledge of neutrality. Failing to receive satisfactory replies, Germany declared war on Russia August 1 and on France August 3. On August 2 an ultimatum was delivered by the German ambassador in Brussels, announcing his country's intention of sending troops through Belgium. The Belgian cabinet refused to grant permission and appealed to Russia, France, and Great Britain for aid in protecting its neutrality.

The position of Great Britain during these momentous days had been obscure. Britain was under no specific obligation to furnish military aid to its allies, and a majority in the cabinet were not in favor of war. With the news of the German ultimatum to Belgium, however, the tide turned in favor of entering the war on the side of France and Russia. Grey sent an ultimatum to Germany demanding that Belgian neutrality be respected. This Germany refused to do, and on August 4 Great Britain declared war.

On the basis that Germany and Austria were not waging a defensive war, Italy refused to carry out its obligations under the Triple Alliance and for the time being remained neutral. In the latter part of August, Japan joined the Allies; and in October,

This combat airplane of World War I was flown by Major Boots, who expressed the allied feeling toward Germany by naming his airplane "Boots to the Kaiser."

Turkey, fearing the designs of Russia, threw in its lot with the Central Powers, Germany and Austria.

In all this welter of declarations of war, perhaps most unexpected was the action of European socialists, who were ostensibly pacifists. While urging conciliation and moderation during the early stage of the crisis, they rallied, almost to a man, to the defense of their respective governments when war actually came. A notable exception was Jaurès, a pacifist, who in July 1914 made a famous speech in which he warned France of its terrible responsibility if it entered the war. Shortly thereafter he was assassinated by an infuriated nationalist. Nationalism had triumphed over internationalism, patriotism over working-class loyalty.

Whose fault was it? Germany at the outset made a serious blunder when its chancellor referred to the treaty of 1839 guaranteeing the neutrality of Belgium—signed by the European powers, including Prussia—as "a scrap of paper." This mistake was compounded by the same official when he justified German invasion of Belgium in the Reichstag, saying:

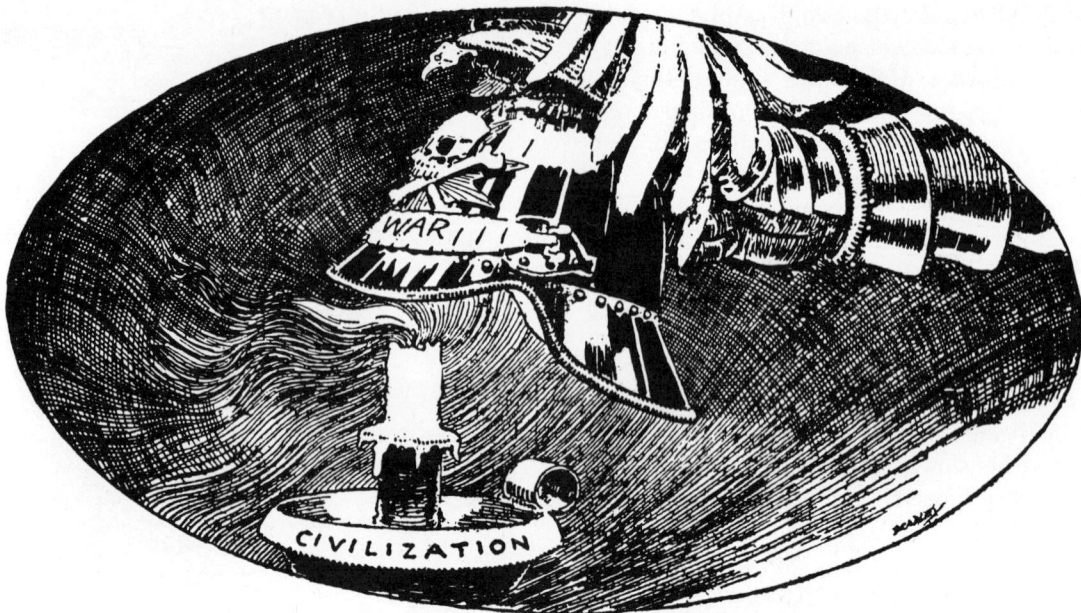

"The lamps are going out all over Europe . . ."—these words of Sir Edward Grey, the British foreign secretary, are illustrated in a Chicago *Daily News* cartoon of July 30, 1914, a few short days before World War I became a reality.

We are now on the defensive. Necessity knows no law. Our troops have entered Luxemburg, and perhaps have already entered Belgian territory. That is a contravention of the rules of international law. It is true that the French Government has informed Brussels that it would respect Belgian neutrality so long as it would be respected by its opponents. But we knew that France was ready for an attack. France could wait, but we could not. A French attack on our flank on the Lower Rhine might have produced fatal results. So we were compelled to proceed. . . .We shall try to make good the wrong we have thus committed as soon as we shall have reached our military goal. Those who, like ourselves, are fighting for the highest aims, can only think of one thing—that they must smash their way through.[13]

By such a frank acknowledgment that its acts defied international law, Germany put itself morally in the wrong as a breaker of treaties, a position that lost it support and sympathy all over the world.

The structure of the Treaty of Versailles, as we shall see later, rested in large part on the war guilt of Germany. When the treaty was first written, scholars and laymen alike in the Allied nations sincerely believed that Germany was completely responsible for the war. As a more realistic perspective has developed in the light of new evidence, it has become increasingly clear that the problem is more complex than had been originally thought. Today, most historians agree it is next to impossible to try to explain the war in terms of the actions of any one of the great powers. Rather, all the major participating nations must accept, in some measure, responsibility for the outbreak of the First World War.

Germany had a particularly heavy share of the blame to bear, not so much for its actions in 1914 but for its policies in the twenty-five years following the accession of Kaiser William II to the throne. The alienation of first Russia and above all Britain in the reckless bid for *Weltpolitik* set the stage and released the forces that had so much to do with the coming of the catastrophe in 1914.

Yet even if we grant all this, it is foolish to try to apportion the blame, for the tragedy was inherent in the prevailing order of international anarchy. This order, better described as disorder, had within it the perils of a highly competitive arms race and the dangerous rivalry of great alliance systems. Finally, there was the emotion of superpatriotism, which in a sense was the most deep-seated cause of the conflict. Other forces, such as militarism and alliances, stemmed from this cause.

In the last few days of peace, diplomats strove desperately to avert general war. Through confusion, fear, and loss of sleep, the nervous strain among them was almost unbearable. Many broke down and wept when it was apparent they had failed. This atmosphere of anguish and gloom is reflected in a passage from the autobiography of Sir Edward Grey, the British foreign secretary:

A friend came to see me on one of the evenings of the last week [before the war]—he thinks it was on Monday, August 3. We were standing at a window of my room in the Foreign Office. It was getting dusk, and the lamps were being lit in the space below on which we were looking. My friend recalls that I remarked on this with the words: "The lamps are going out all over Europe; we shall not see them lit again in our life-time."[14]

SUMMARY

The period from 1871 to 1914 coincided with the Second Industrial Revolution. New industries and inventions revolutionized manufacturing. Three basic characteristics were apparent in this new phase of industrialism: research became more systematized and less a matter of chance; mass production methods introduced consumer goods made of interchangeable parts on assembly lines; and there was an ever-increasing alliance between chemistry and industry. Synthetic goods and by-products, new processes in metallurgy, explosives, textiles, and many other manufactures—all these were made possible by the research chemist.

This outpouring of goods was accompanied by rising living standards for the masses. The philosophy of laissez faire shrank before that of the welfare state. Old-age pensions, unemployment insurance, and ac-

cident compensation gave the masses more security. These gains were reflected in the increasing moderation of socialistic movements. The Fabians and other revisionist socialists no longer cried for revolution but were content with a gradual program of social reform, increasing democracy, and rising standards of living.

All of this promise, however, was challenged by forces that encouraged conflict in the economic field. Revolutionary groups of socialists persisted. The syndicalists favored violence and the use of the general strike to paralyze and overthrow capitalism. Most menacing was the Bolshevik wing of Russian socialism, which grew up in an atmosphere of governmental tyranny and terrorism and had no reason to doubt the gospel of Marx.

Internationally as well as domestically, socio-economic affairs had a dual nature. On one side there was the exchange of goods and capital and the migration of people without serious obstacles. Economics was apparently working toward one world. There were also hopeful peace movements, culminating in The Hague conferences. As against these hopeful signs, there were tragic forces of hate and violence, ready to erupt from the contemporary pattern of militarism and its philosophy of force, social Darwinism, rival alliances, economic imperialism, secret diplomacy, and, most important of all, nationalism.

All these factors were exerting their influence as the great alliances were formed and as they maneuvered for power and prestige. It was these factors that brought Europe's golden age to an end. They existed in their most virulent form in the Balkans, where they finally exploded. And so powerful and pervasive were they that they not only involved Europe in general war but most of the rest of the world as well. This was the first tragedy, but as we will see in later chapters, these same forces were subsequently to create dictatorships that championed racial intolerance, class hatreds, and brute force and that finally brought about an even more terrible Armageddon.

SUGGESTIONS FOR READING

NATIONAL POLITICS

Ensor, R. C. K., *England, 1870-1914,* Oxford, 1936. A standard work, dealing with economic and social as well as political history. Also recommended are the sections on political reform, the Irish question, and social legislation in *British History in the Nineteenth Century and After, 1782-1919,* Longmans, 1938, by the eminent British historian G. M. Trevelyan.

Maurois, A., *The Edwardian Era,* Appleton-Century, 1933. A sprightly paced, perceptive account of the British scene before World War I. H. Ausubel, *The Late Victorians; A Short History,* Anvil,* 1955, is a brief interpretive study which stresses economic factors; J. Laver, *Edwardian Promenade,* Houghton, 1958, is a picture history which emphasizes the quaint and the picturesque.

The progress of democracy in England is discussed with clarity and force in O. F. Christie, *The Transition to Democracy, 1867-1914,* Routledge, 1934; and in R. L. Schuyler and C. C. Weston, *British Constitutional History Since 1832,* Anvil,* 1957. The major part of the latter work deals with the period after the passage of the Reform Bill of 1867.

For nearly sixty years, the tempestuous Clemenceau played a major role in every important governmental crisis. Highly recommended as a study of the Third Republic and this dynamic politician is J. H. Jackson, *Clemenceau and the Third Republic,* Macmillan, 1948. See also the material pertinent to the period under discussion in Chapters 12 and 13 of your text in D. W. Brogan, *France Under the Republic; The Development of Modern France, 1870-1939,* Harper, 1940.

Kayser, J., *The Dreyfus Affair,* Covici, 1931. A vivid account which includes a moving description of Dreyfus' terrible captivity on Devil's Island.

Dawson, W. H., *The German Empire, 1867-1914, and the Unity Movement,* 2 vols., Macmillan, 1919. Although somewhat dated, this work is of value for understanding the continuing struggle in Germany between conservative and liberal forces.

Recommended "studies in depth" of important aspects of German history are C. E. Schorske, *German Social Democracy, 1905-1917: The Development of the Great Schism,* Harvard, 1955, a thorough analysis of the Social Democratic party; J. A. Nichols, *Germany After Bismarck: The Caprivi Era, 1890-1894,* Harvard, 1958, an account of the Iron Chancellor's ineffectual successor; P. B. Massing, *Rehearsal for Destruction; A Study of Political Anti-Semitism in Imperial Germany,* Harper, 1949.

Two competent studies of the minorities problem in the Hapsburg empire, the policies of Magyarization and Germanization, and the ultimate triumph of nationalism are O. Jaszi,

The Dissolution of the Hapsburg Monarchy; A Failure in Civic Training, Univ. of Chicago, 1929; and R. A. Kann, *The Habsburg Empire; A Study in Integration and Disintegration,* Praeger, 1957. See also A. J. May, *The Hapsburg Monarchy, 1867-1914,* Harvard, 1951.

Croce, B., *A History of Italy, 1871-1915,* Oxford, 1929. An analysis of Italian parliamentary government by the famous Italian historian-philosopher. A brief study which terminates in the years when Fascism emerged is C. J. S. Sprigge, *The Development of Modern Italy,* Yale, 1944.

Seton-Watson, H., *The Decline of Imperial Russia, 1855-1914,* Praeger,* 1960. An excellent narrative account. See also Sir Donald Mackenzie Wallace, *Russia on the Eve of War and Revolution,* Vintage,* 1961. Abridgment of an absorbing study of Russia first published in 1877.

Ramsaur, E. E., Jr., *The Young Turks; Prelude to the Revolution of 1908,* Princeton, 1957. A provocative account of the conspiratorial movement that aimed at ending the sultan's misrule and preserving the integrity of the Ottoman empire.

Miller, W., *The Ottoman Empire and Its Successors, 1801-1927,* Macmillan, 1936. A standard work, notable for its treatment of the history of the Balkan nations.

INTERNATIONAL POLITICS

Mansergh, *The Coming of the First World War; A Study in the European Balance, 1878-1914,* Longmans, 1949. A brief, excellent introduction to the subject. See also J. W. Swain, *Beginning the Twentieth Century,* Norton, 1938; G. L. Dickinson, *The International Anarchy, 1904-1914,* G. Allen, 1937; M. Bruce, *The Shaping of the Modern World, 1870-1914,* Random House, 1958.

Gooch, G. P., *History of Modern Europe, 1878-1919,* Holt, 1923. A standard survey, with a special emphasis on diplomatic history. See also R. J. Sontag, *European Diplomatic History, 1871-1932,* Appleton-Century, 1933; and A. J. P. Taylor, *The Struggle for Mastery in Europe, 1848-1918,* Oxford, 1954.

Two classics in the field of diplomatic history, both by W. L. Langer: *European Alliances and Alignments, 1871-1890,* Knopf, 1950; and *The Diplomacy of Imperialism, 1890-1902,* Knopf, 1951.

Kohn, H., *Pan-Slavism: Its History and Ideology,* Univ. of Notre Dame, 1953. Describes the ideological basis of Russia's "mission" and its cultural and political expansion. See also C. Jelavich, *Tsarist Russia and Balkan Nationalism,* Univ. of Calif., 1958; and L. S. Stavrianos, *The Balkans, 1815-1914,* Holt, 1963.

Marder, A. J., *The Anatomy of British Sea Power; A History of British Naval Policy in the Pre-Dreadnought Era, 1880-1905,* Knopf, 1940; and E. L. Woodward, *Great Britain and the German Navy,* Oxford, 1935. Excellent studies of the naval rivalry between the two powers.

*Indicates an inexpensive paperbound edition.

Hough, R. A., *The Fleet That Had to Die,* Viking, 1958. An unusual, vividly written account of the Russian navy's colossal blunders in their clash with the Japanese in 1904.

Barlow, I. C., *The Agadir Crisis,* Univ. of N. C., 1940. A clear portrayal of the Moroccan crisis of 1911, one of the incidents leading inexorably to war.

Schmitt, B. E., *England and Germany, 1740-1914,* Princeton, 1918. An analysis of national rivalries, sympathetic to the British viewpoint. In *Germany and England: Background of Conflict, 1848-1894,* Appleton-Century, 1938, R. J. Sontag presents the thesis that the two nations were antagonistic, both institutionally and psychologically.

Lichnowsky, K. M., *Heading for the Abyss; Reminiscences,* Harcourt, 1928. An account by the German ambassador in London in 1914 of the melancholy course of events leading to the war. Compare with the memoirs of the British foreign secretary Edward Grey, First Viscount, *Twenty-Five Years, 1892-1916,* single vol. ed., Stokes, 1937.

A great bulk of works has been written dealing with the question of "war guilt." The following are representative: M. E. Durham, *The Sarajevo Crime,* Putnam, 1925, places the blame on Serbia; H. E. Barnes, *Genesis of the World War; An Introduction to the Problem of War Guilt,* Knopf, 1935, finds France and Britain the chief culprits; L. Albertini, *The Origins of the War of 1914,* 2 vols. (ed. by L. M. Massey), Oxford, 1952-1953, exhibits a strongly pro-Italian slant; E. Brandenburg, *From Bismarck to the World War; History of German Foreign Policy, 1870-1914,* Oxford, 1933, maintains an admirable restraint and objectivity; S. B. Fay, *The Origins of the World War,* 2 vols., Macmillan, 1930, presents the best-balanced treatment.

ECONOMICS

The following surveys include valuable sections on developments in economics, 1870-1914: L. C. A. Knowles, *The Industrial and Commercial Revolutions in Great Britain During the Nineteenth Century,* Dutton, 1926; S. B. Clough, *France: A History of National Economics, 1789-1939,* Scribner's, 1939; G. Stolper, *German Economy, 1870-1940; Issues and Trends,* Reynal, 1940; W. F. Bruck (also known as W. F. Brook), *Social and Economic History of Germany from William II to Hitler, 1888-1938,* Oxford, 1938.

Considered a masterpiece of economic history is Sir John H. Clapham, *An Economic History of Modern Britain,* 3 vols., Cambridge, 1930-1938. Volume II *(Free Trade and Steel, 1850-1886)* and Volume III *(Machines and National Rivalries, 1887-1914)* discuss in detail the material presented in Chapter 13 of your text.

Feis, H., *Europe, The World's Banker, 1870-1914,* Yale, 1930. A solid scholarly study of European overseas investment and the relation between international finance and diplomacy.

SCIENCE AND THOUGHT

Darwin, C., *The Voyage of the Beagle,* Bantam,* 1958. A journal of the experiences and observations about natural history and geology that led to the revolutionary *The Origin of Species,* abr. ed., Mentor,* 1958.

Darwin, C., *The Living Thoughts of Darwin,* (ed. by J. Huxley), Premier,* 1959. Julian Huxley, the grandson of Thomas Huxley, has said of Darwin that he was "the last man to shake the world with the magic force of a single idea." The controversy between religion and science which preceded the publication of *The Origin of Species* is reviewed in C. C. Gillispie, *Genesis and Geology,* Torchbooks, 1959.

Himmelfarb, G., *Darwin and the Darwinian Revolution,* Doubleday, 1959. Based on unpublished documents, this illuminating account sheds light on both the character of the scientist and the age in which he lived. See also the dual biography of Darwin and Thomas Huxley: W. Irvine, *Apes, Angels and Victorians,* McGraw-Hill, 1955.

Tax, S., ed., *Issues in Evolution,* Vol. III of *Evolution After Darwin,* Univ. of Chicago, 1960. Of special importance in an assessment of the effects of Darwin's theories on modern-day science, philosophy, and religion. Contains transcripts of the panel discussions held at the Darwin Centennial Celebration, University of Chicago, 1959, in which such famous scholars as Sir Julian Huxley, Harlow Shapely, and H. J. Muller, participated.

Excellent biographies of important scientists include Sir William W. Cheyne, *Lister and His Achievements,* Longmans, 1925; E. Curie, *Madame Curie,* Pocketbooks,* 1959; H. Iltis, *The Life of Mendel,* Norton, 1932; R. Dubos, *Louis Pasteur, Free Lance of Science,* Little, Brown, 1950; B. P. Babkin, *Pavlov; A Biography,* Univ. of Chicago, 1949.

Singer, C., *et al.,* eds., *The Late Nineteenth Century, 1850-1900,* Vol. v of *A History of Technology,* Oxford, 1958. Lavish illustrations accompany a text which leavens its erudition with a forceful, clear style.

Hayes, C. J. H., *A Generation of Materialism: 1871-1900,* Harper, 1941. A lucid, penetrating study of European life, thought, and politics, particularly valuable for the light shed on the forces of racialism, social Darwinism, and nationalism.

Hofstadter, R., *Social Darwinism in American Thought,* Beacon*, 1955. Details the cult of force, struggle, and militarism in the United States.

Cole, G. D. H., *Socialist Thought: Marxism and Anarchism, 1850-1890,* St. Martin's, 1954. Excellent treatment of the triumph of Marxism over anarchism.

Recommended for the story of the socialist movement in Russia are D. W. Treadgold, *Lenin and His Rivals: The Struggle for Russia's Future, 1898-1906,* Praeger, 1955; and L. H. Haimson, *The Russian Marxists and the Origins of Bolshevism,* Harvard, 1955.

Wolfe, B. D., *Three Who Made a Revolution,* Beacon,* 1948. A study of Lenin, Trotsky, and Stalin, and the forces which brought on the Russian Revolution.

The following works are recommended for their sound approach to various aspects of the socialist movement: J. Jackson, *Jean Jaurès: His Life and Work,* Norton, 1944; G. D. N. Cole, *The Meaning of Marxism,* Gollancz, 1948, and *Fabian Socialism,* G. Allen, 1943; P. Gay, *The Dilemma of Democratic Socialism,* Collier,* 1962.

POLITICS AND ECONOMICS

Catholic Emancipation Act permits Irish Catholics to be members of English Parliament 1829

Famine devastates Ireland 1845
Early phase of modern world peace movement climaxed by Universal Peace Congress 1849; new phase, emphasizing practical problems, begins 1860's; annual Universal Peace Conferences begin 1889

Irish problem under Gladstone—Irish Anglican Church disestablished 1869; Irish land acts 1870, 1881

1870　Industrialization spreads rapidly; laissez faire gives way before government regulation of business; **financial capitalism supersedes industrial capitalism** as business consolidates; world trade increases; trade unionism grows c. 1870-1914
Democratic struggles in minor powers—Netherlands and Belgium discontented under illiberal franchises, Switzerland enjoys democratic institutions, Scandinavian countries advance in democracy, Spain and Portugal suffer revolution c. 1870-1914
Greater Serbia movement—Serbia determines to liberate Slavs in Turkey, Austria-Hungary c. 1871-1914
Bismarck attempts to strengthen German Second Reich—reorganizes currency, banking, railways, law codes; wages *Kulturkampf*; clashes with socialists; initiates social legislation c. 1871-1890
Revolutionary Paris Commune threatens Third Republic of France, is suppressed 1871

Under Disraeli, English government passes health, housing legislation; liberalizes acts against trade unions 1874-1880
Growth of moderate socialism—Social Democratic party founded in Germany 1875; socialist groups in France 1877; in Italy, Scandinavia, Austria, Belgium, Netherlands 1880's; Fabian Society in England urges peaceful reform, or revisionism 1883; Second International founded 1889; revisionism grows on Continent 1890's; English Labour party formed 1900
"The People's Will" terrorist movement formed in Russia 1879; Alexander II assassinated 1881
Social Darwinism—Spencer applies "survival of fittest" to economics; Treitschke and Nietzsche justify war

Tsars Alexander III and Nicholas II revive system of repression, attempt to Russify subject nationalities 1881-1905

Germany, Italy, Austria form **Triple Alliance** 1882
In England, Gladstone sponsors third Reform Bill 1884

1885

Scandals of French Third Republic—Boulanger's suspected coup d'état 1886; Panama scandal 1888; Dreyfus case 1894-1906
Unsuccessful Irish home rule bills introduced 1886, 1893
Kaiser William II dismisses Bismarck 1890; allows Reinsurance Treaty between Germany and Russia to lapse c. 1890
Syndicalists revive radical doctrine of class struggle 1890's

Ottoman empire—Armenian revolt is crushed 1894-1897

Herzl introduces Zionism 1896; first Zionist congress meets 1897

Hague Tribunal established 1899

1900　Germany initiates huge naval program, threatens Britain's control of seas 1900

Italy secretly deserts Triple Alliance c. 1902
Radical Marxism appears in Russia; **Social Democrats divide into moderate Mensheviks and radical Bolsheviks** 1903; massacre of Bloody Sunday 1905; October Manifesto of Nicholas II calls national Duma 1905; Dumas achieve public discussion of reforms
English Liberal party provides social, labor legislation 1905-1914; Parliament Bill of 1911 curtails power of House of Lords
Germany and France clash over Morocco 1905, 1906, 1911

Britain, Russia, France establish **Triple Entente** 1907
Austria annexes Bosnia-Herzegovina, angers Russia, Serbia 1908
Young Turks win concessions 1908; Young Turks force Abdul-Hamid II to abdicate 1909; Turks lose territory to Austria-Hungary, Greece, Italy, Balkan nations 1908-1913

Portugal becomes republic 1910

Italy gains universal suffrage 1912
First and Second Balkan Wars increase Serbia's ambitions, Austria's fears 1912-1913

1914　Archduke Francis Ferdinand is assassinated 1914
World War I begins 1914

SCIENCE AND TECHNOLOGY

ARTS

Agriculture—McCormick invents reaper 1831; other nineteenth-century innovations are the harvester, combine
Comte initiates science of sociology; Ranke founds school of scientific history
Morse invents electric telegraph 1844

Realistic painters—Millet, Courbet, Daumier

Second Industrial Revolution—industry uses scientific techniques, mass production; chemistry makes new materials 1870-1914

Elementary education becomes almost universal in western Europe 1870-1914
Impressionist painters Monet, Degas, Renoir; sculptor Rodin

1870

Darwin's *Descent of Man* (1871) stimulates controversy between science and religion; Catholic Church reaffirms its traditional position; scholars apply "higher criticism" to Bible

Inventions—duplex telegraph 1872; telephone 1876; phonograph 1877
Clerk-Maxwell advances electromagnetic theory of light 1873

Von Siemens' working dynamo increases use of electricity 1876

Post-Impressionist painters Cézanne, Van Gogh
Realist writers Tolstoy, Hardy, James, Clemens; naturalist writers Zola, De Maupassant; Ibsen and Shaw expose social problems in "problem plays"; "art for art's sake" cult in England and French symbolists represent reaction against extreme realism

Weismann distinguishes somatic and germ cells; Galton pioneers in eugenics, stresses role of subconscious in psychology

Pasteur and Koch prove germ theory of disease 1881; Pasteur cures rabies 1885; Koch discovers organisms causing eleven diseases; use of anesthetics advances surgery
Toynbee's *Lectures on the Industrial Revolution* 1884
Daimler builds internal-combustion engine using gasoline c. 1885

Darwinian theory influences philosophers James (pragmatism) and Bergson (vitalism)

1885

Hertz demonstrates existence of electromagnetic waves 1886
Inventions—linotype machine 1886; Kodak camera 1888
Freud pioneers in psychoanalysis 1890's

Diesel patents engine using crude oil 1892

Roentgen discovers x-ray 1895
Marconi devises wireless telegraphy 1895
Edison invents motion picture 1896
Thomson formulates electron theory c. 1897
Pierre and Marie Curie discover radium 1898

Planck formulates quantum theory 1900
Pavlov's experiments advance study of conditioned reflexes in psychology 1900; American school of behaviorism stems from mechanistic view of man
Mendel's laws of heredity gain recognition c. 1900; biologists advance theory of chromosomes, substantiate mutation theory, reject theory of inheritance of acquired characteristics

1900

Wright brothers first to pilot power-driven airplane 1903

Einstein produces equation $E = mc^2$, theory of relativity 1905

Music—Richard Strauss exemplifies post-Wagnerian school; Debussy is foremost exponent of impressionism; Stravinski experiments with polytonality; expressionist Schönberg develops twelve-tone system

Ford begins large-scale automobile production 1909
Biochemist Ehrlich produces disease-curing salvarsan 1909

Rutherford's theory of positively charged atomic nucleus 1911

Architecture—Sullivan pioneers in steel-skeleton skyscraper; Wright originates revolutionary house designs; Gropius, Mies van der Rohe lead machine-age architecture movement in Germany

Expressionists like Matisse express subjective feelings in paintings; Cubists construct abstract patterns

1914

Frontier

MARXIST SOCIALISM AND THE WEB OF UTOPIA: SCIENCE AND MYTH IN THE MAKING OF AN IDEOLOGY   by A. William Salomone

Dr. A. William Salomone, a former Guggenheim Fellow and now Professor of Modern European History at the University of Rochester, has contributed numerous articles to scholarly journals in both Europe and America. In 1946 he was awarded the Herbert Baxter Adams Prize by the American Historical Association for his history of modern Italy entitled *Italian Democracy in the Making*. Dr. Salomone is also the coeditor (with Alexander Baltzly) of *Readings in Twentieth-Century European History* (1950).

The dream of creating a "perfect society" has occupied many philosophers, reformers, and revolutionists through the centuries. Usually such dreams have been no more than stimulating speculations on the possibilities of achieving earthly happiness. Sometimes they have become incentives to action aiming to improve material existence or at least to remove some of the unnecessary, the worst, evils in human society. In a few instances those dreams have become plans for the pursuit of "progress." In these latter cases the attempt to realize the dream of perfection has led, depending on motives and forces involved, either to temporary experiments to build a new society on a restrictive and usually ephemeral level or to nightmarishly authoritarian undertakings to create an ideal state regardless of the means and of cost in human terms. "Utopia," which literally means "nowhere," has always existed at least as a vision of perfection, frequently as a model of rational existence, and occasionally as a realization of some political, economic, social or even moral "new order."

The founders of "scientific socialism," Karl Marx and Friedrich Engels, saw themselves as destroyers of all Utopias seeking to regenerate mankind on the basis of mere blueprints of perfection. In the name of a new history and of science and economics, Marx formulated an "organic" theory of society which, he insisted, aimed not merely to understand society but to transform it. As he put it: "The philosophers have only interpreted the world in various ways; the point however is to change it."[1] To this self-appointed task, Marx devoted a lifetime of intellectual energy and revolutionary fervor.

Most of the pre-Marxist socialist ideas and their exponents were lumped together and collectively castigated by Marx and Engels as ineffectual, self-deceptive, and "romantic." Their *Manifesto* of 1848 was styled "communist" as an appealing synonym for "scientific," the more easily to conjure up a contrast with "socialist" utopianism. In a later work Marx thundered that "the social revolution of the nineteenth century cannot draw its poetry from the past but only from the future"; that "all superstitions of the past" must be stripped off because they had "drugged" men into false revolutionary hopes; and that it was time to "let the dead bury their dead."[2] Yet many of the pre-Marxist socialist doctrines had been less "romantic" than Marx made them out to be, and they refused to stay dead in the new social and ideological struggles of the post-1848 period. Moreover, Marxist socialism itself retained many important elements from the works of the condemned Utopians. Even worse from the point of view of Marx's contention about the fate of all socialist utopianism, his own "scientific socialism"—once it came to grips with the stubborn realities of European economic, social, and political life in the course of the nineteenth and early twentieth century—revealed itself as basically self-contradictory, partly ineffectual, and ironically quite "romantic" in its own great expectations.

Marx invented the materialistic philosophy of history as the "new science" of his anti-Utopian socialist analysis of society. To Marx, not ideas (as in Hegelian philosophy) but "real" forces—that is, "modes of production," economic systems, and social classes—*determine* the course of history. Thus he claimed to have discovered a new hierarchy of realities built upon a series of related material conditions and social factors, of impersonal elements and human forces which acted upon one another to determine the structure of historical societies. And Marx found conflict at the heart of reality: "The history of all hitherto existing society," the *Communist Manifesto* cried, "is the history of class struggles."

In Marxist theory, economic determinism was the "law of necessity" which bound the past to the future. Marx viewed history as the dialectical unfolding of material and social forces toward a definite end—socialism—which ultimately would insure the liberation of man from the dual tyranny of nature and of human injustice. Marxism raised the vision of a socialist commonwealth as the culmination and goal of the historical process, the fulfillment not of men's desires but of their necessities; Marxist socialism became "the wave of the future," inextricably bound to the historical and economic evolution of the world. Unlike the Utopian socialists, however, Marx cast his vision and its process of realization in absolute and universal terms, as if they were as valid and verifiable as the laws of physical science. In an age when the cult of science was replacing older faiths, Marx utilized a scientific terminology to give plausibility and the impress of realism to his version of an ancient Utopian dream. But a closer look at "scientific socialism," with the aid of Marx's own standards, reveals that his doctrine was not absolute but relative, not universal but partial.

If, as Marx asserted, the conflict of "real" forces *from below* and not just that of "ideas" *from above* can change the world, it was problematical whether even the Marxist idea might effect sweeping changes in the structure of society. Also, Marx had claimed that "a social formation does not perish until all the productive forces for which it finds space have developed." Not only in Marx's day but for long afterwards it became hazardous indeed to claim to know or to foretell when, where, and to what extent the material and social possibilities of the capitalist mode of production might be exhausted. The transformation of society was seen as an inevitable process inherent to the exhaustion of the possibilities of further development and to the resulting "contradictions" to which all "modes of production," economic regimes, and ruling social classes were prey by the decree of history. For Marx, therefore, the coming of socialism was a function of the inescapable collapse of the base of capitalism.

In his political articles,[3] Marx suggested that the new socialist or communist order might not come about automatically. The existing order of society might become prey to a convulsive crisis out of which a revolution could issue. If properly directed through the "realistic" use of the tactics and strategy of social war, Marx argued, revolutionary politics and ideology might accelerate and precipitate the "great change"; not the peaceful dialectic of social evolution but a bloody class struggle would then decide the turning of history. Violence would be the "midwife" of the new socialist society over whose cradle a "dictatorship of the proletariat" would have to mount guard until the socialist commonwealth was beyond danger of premature destruction and death. Therefore, according to Marx, the proletariat need not wait for the fullness of time to lead them into the socialist heavenly city. Marx had claimed to know prophetically the decree of history, but he was not unwilling to force it by violent revolution. But how was the proletariat to know whether the attempt to take the capitalist-bourgeois citadel of power by storm would result in victory rather than in defeat as had been suffered at the barricades of 1848 and at the Paris Commune of 1871? Marx and Engels had no answer. In their post-mortems on these revolutions, which they stigmatized as "Utopian" and "romantic," Marx and Engels claimed that "playing at insurrection" had been responsible for failure; and they offered little assurance that a Marxist revolution under similar conditions would not suffer a similar fate.

After the collapse of the Marxist First International in 1871-1872, it was from anti-Marxist revolutionary ranks that the possibility of violent revolution was actively agitated, particularly by the anarchist followers of Mikhail Bakunin and the insurrectionary disciples of Louis Auguste Blanqui. During the period of the Second Socialist International (1889-1914), the spokesmen and official leaders of Marxist socialism continued to swear by the entire body of the master's theories and doctrines. But in the meantime socialism had been fragmented into a variety of separate, national programs for economic and social reform, as Marxist parties were founded in Germany, England, France, Russia, and elsewhere in Europe. By the turn of the century, just as "scientific socialism" came into its own as a powerful political movement and as a strong movement for the maintenance of international peace, it was torn into two opposing camps which tended toward either the evolutionary or the revolutionary poles of theoretical Marxism. The official and most influential group worked for the peaceful and gradual transformation of capitalist society into a socialist commonwealth to be founded upon economic justice and democratic institutions. The other group reinterpreted Marxism as the theory of violent and catastrophic social change to be achieved through conspiracy, agitation, propaganda, insurrection, and, if need be, war itself. A dialectical conflict which Marx had not imagined smoldered within Marxist socialism.

On the eve of 1914, the two figures representing the antithesis within European socialism were Jean Jaurès and Nikolai Lenin. Jaurès, the great French spokesman for a gradualist solution of the social problem, conceived of socialism as a great human ideal of liberation from the scourge of social injustice and war. He symbolized the projection of the socialist Utopia into an ideal realm which did not prove to be within the historical possibilities of a Europe almost fatally pushed toward its greatest catastrophe to date, the War of 1914. On August 31, 1914, almost the last hour of European peace, Jaurès was assassinated in Paris by a French nationalist fanatic. Lenin, the professional Russian revolutionist, had nearly always seen socialism issuing from revolution and war. For him, Marxist socialism could be achieved as communism only at the end of a violent class struggle prepared for and led by a specialized revolutionary vanguard of which his Bolshevik party was to be the spearhead. Lenin, therefore, saw in the War of 1914 the almost ready-made opportunity for the realization of his conspiratorial and insurrectionary plans—of revolution through war. On November 6-7, 1917, Lenin and his Bolshevik party succeeded in making a "Marxist revolution" in Russia by utilizing the tactics of "uprising as an art," through the successful "playing at insurrection" which, by his own admission, was pure and simple "Blanquism." Though made in the name of Marx, the seizure of power in 1917 by the Bolsheviks was essentially un-Marxist. Lenin had made a revolution in a country, in circumstances, with means, and with results which had merely a coincidental resemblance with "scientific socialism." Lenin proved to be a better disciple of the old masters of politics and revolution, Machiavelli and Blanqui, than of his official teacher of social science, Karl Marx. Thus the tragic failure of Jaurès in 1914 and the fateful success of Lenin in 1917 together spelled out the waning of Marxist socialism as the science of society and the art of revolution.

A brief summary of Karl Marx's theory and its historical function barely suggests the originality of his approach and emphasis. In his single-minded pursuit of absolutes and in his unbending faith in the validity of his message, Marx seems indeed in line with the Hebrew prophets. The fervor of his new secular vision of history, of life, and of the world reveals him also in line with those Utopians he had relegated to a revolutionary limbo. The indefatigable researcher who spent many years at his desk in the British Museum could evince a harsh, almost authoritarian, disregard for the merits of others and for his own limitations. The result was often ironical: Marx unwittingly suggested his own most devastating self-criticism.

In Marx's day and for long afterwards the successful appeal of his doctrines was the other side of the persistent failure of his "scientific socialist" scheme of things. His theory of society raised a new and grandiose myth of human liberation from the immemorial oppressions of poverty and social injustice which were the daily fare of millions of Europeans. Contrary to Engels' characterization of him as "the Darwin of social science" or to Benedetto Croce's portrayal of him as "the Machiavelli of the proletariat," Karl Marx came closer to being the founder of a new secular religion.

Both before and after Marx's death in 1883 his message was blurred between "evolution" and "revolution." Thus his intellectual and ideological legacy was, paradoxically, at the same time powerful and unclear in some of its most basic aspects. Marx had insisted that "men make their own history." He spent a lifetime to document the opposite thesis that history is the sole maker of the human condition, the true molder of men's destiny. Even in the light of the science of Marx's own day the fundamental "law" of his "scientific socialism" was strangely obscure. As it was, the Marxist "social science" of evolution and the Marxist "myth" of revolution pulled in opposite directions and succeeded only in tightening the threads of the web of Utopia within which socialism was caught.

1 Karl Marx, "Theses on Feuerbach" (1845), in *A Handbook of Marxism,* ed. by Emil Burns (International Publishers, 1935), p. 231.

2 Marx, "The Eighteenth Brumaire of Louis Bonaparte" (1852), in Burns, p. 119.

3 See especially "The Class Struggles in France (1848-1850)," "The Eighteenth Brumaire of Louis Bonaparte," and "The Civil War in France" (1870-1871), in Burns, pp. 95-158.

SUGGESTED READINGS

The best book on its subject is by Marie Louise Berneri, *Journey Through Utopia* (Routledge and Kegan Paul, 1950). On all phases of socialist history see G. D. H. Cole, *A History of Socialist Thought,* 6 vols. (Macmillan, 1955-1958). On Marx and Marxism, see the chapter in Paul Roubiczek, *The Misinterpretation of Man* (Scribner, 1947), pp. 166-198; some parts of Alfred G. Meyer, *Marxism: The Unity of Theory and Practice* (Harvard Univ. Press, 1954); and the brief text and documents in Sidney Hook, *Marx and the Marxists: The Ambiguous Legacy* (Van Nostrand, 1955). For the Soviet version of Marxism, see Adam B. Ulam, *The Unfinished Revolution: An Essay on the Influence of Marxism and Communism* (Vintage,* 1964).

PART 5 The World Adrift

CHAPTER 14 A WORLD FIT FOR HEROES

CHAPTER 15 OPPOSING WAYS OF LIFE

CHAPTER 16 AFRICA AND ASIA ASTIR

CHAPTER 17 THE TRAGIC DECADE AND GLOBAL CONFLICT

The rapid pace of the twentieth century is dramatically revealed in the period from 1914 to 1945—one of the most tumultuous periods in all history. In less than half a century, two world wars racked mankind, and governments and ways of life underwent drastic changes in almost every nation on earth. During this time humanity experienced both the most poignant suffering and the most unrestrained rejoicing; it was influenced by the most noble and dedicated leaders as well as the most sordid and malignant demagogues.

The cumulative effect of unbridled nationalism, imperialistic rivalry, and entangling alliances led to the First World War, the first total technological conflict. Out of the terrible struggle men everywhere hoped that a better world might emerge. Yet though the statesmen of the victorious Allies stood for the democratic and humanistic traditions of western civilization, their motives in making the peace were often as vindictive and nationalistic as any preparations for war; and though internationalism was put into action in the form of the League of Nations, it was given neither the strength nor the support to bring peace and security in the troubled years following World War I.

In the 1920's, democracy began its long struggle with a new totalitarianism growing out of the disillusionment after the Great War. In Russia, Marxian tenets were embraced by revolutionaries, and a Communist society took shape under Lenin. Another authoritarian system, Fascism, gripped Italy. And the most frightening ideology of all, Nazism, grew to terrifying fruition in Germany, where a people embittered by the humiliation of World War I and the Treaty of Versailles staked all their hopes on a madman named Hitler.

By the 1920's and 1930's, the non-European world had discovered the concept of nationalism. In the Middle East, Arab national ambitions had flared in 1916 into a revolt against Ottoman rule. The immigration of European Jews to Palestine led to conflict between Arabs and Jews, which was to increase as time passed. In North Africa, the Middle East, India, southeastern Asia, and Oceania, the indigenous peoples were gathering strength in their battle to oust the Europeans completely and govern themselves; and in the huge colonial area south of the Sahara, Africans were beginning to stir restlessly against European rule. Even China, tradition-bound for centuries, turned to revolution to regain the power and prestige it had lost during the era of imperialism. But though Chiang Kai-shek won an internal power struggle and organized the government, the country remained poor and weak. Meanwhile Japan continued its amazing technological, industrial, and military growth and emerged as a world power.

The world depression in the 1930's gave the totalitarian movements an opportunity to expand their despotism at home and to launch aggression abroad. From 1931 to 1939, starting with the Japanese invasion of Manchuria, their belligerence mounted. The new dictatorial regimes went from one success to another, glorifying militarism and the potency of the state, regimenting their citizens, and intimidating their neighbors. The older democratic nations, such as Britain and France, were paralyzed with indecision and fear and did little to halt the dictators. Appeasement was tried, but the aggression continued. Finally, in 1939, the British and French realized that their own nations were next in Hitler's march of conquest and took up arms. The Second World War began. In 1941 the Soviet Union, which had been allied earlier with the Nazis, and the United States, which for two decades had been attempting to ignore the mounting tensions abroad, were forced into the struggle. The horrors which this global conflict brought were the familiar ones of ruthless enemy occupation, the rigors of battle, and the loss of life and property, and the new ones created by dread new weapons and methods of warfare, the organized slaughter of certain nationality groups, and the repeated bombing of civilian centers.

Victory came to the Grand Alliance in 1945 and with it total defeat of Hitler's Third Reich and the fascist states established in Italy by Mussolini and in Japan by Tojo. As in 1919 the victors were confronted with the immense task of rebuilding and reëstablishing a great part of the world. This task was made more difficult by the knowledge of the failures of the peace of 1919 and the dismaying realization that as the Second World War was more encompassing and vastly more destructive than the First, so a Third World War would be more shattering than the Second and, with the advent of nuclear weapons, might bring about the annihilation of man.

CHAPTER 14

A World Fit for Heroes

WORLD WAR I AND THE AFTERMATH: 1914-1929

Introduction. The onward march of western civilization came to a halt in the summer of 1914. For more than four years thereafter, the science, industry, wealth, and power of Europe were concentrated upon destruction. The Great War of 1914-1918 was a total war—a war fought not only on battle fronts on land, at sea, and in the air but also on home fronts far from the scene of military conflict. Civilians, as well as members of the armed forces, became "legitimate" targets for demoralization and death.

The campaigns fought at the beginning of the war—the Marne and Tannenberg and, a little later, the Dardanelles and Jutland—ended any hope of a quick victory on either side. The belligerents were condemned to the grinding horror of a war of attrition and stalemate. With the entrance of the United States into the war in the spring of 1917, however, this stand-off finally ended. In the autumn of 1918, Germany collapsed and sued for peace.

The peace conference that followed aroused the hopes of the entire world; the speeches delivered by the Allied leaders—Clemenceau, Lloyd George, and Wilson—were studded with promises of a future securely founded on a weak and disarmed Germany, of a world fit for heroes, of a lasting peace based on the Fourteen Points. But it was soon apparent that any plans for a just and lasting peace faced almost insurmountable obstacles: secret and conflicting agreements among the Allies, the cross-purposes and clashing motives of the delegates to the conference, and the powerful pressures exerted by the peoples of the victorious nations, who sought vengeance on their wartime enemies.

Attempts to restore stability and security were also challenged by dramatic changes in Europe's political picture. In 1917, before the end of the war, revolution had overthrown the tsar in Russia; in 1918, the monarchies in Germany and Austria-Hungary were swept aside. Thus the armistice of 1918 ushered in no golden age of peace but instead a time of wild confusion and bitter discord. This chapter discusses not only the course of World War I and the peace treaties imposed by the victors but also the troubled decade in international affairs that followed. It was a crowded ten years. The League of Nations was established and began to function. Germany was gradually re-admitted into the family of nations, and discord over the fantastic burden of reparations imposed upon the defeated power finally eased. Tensions and brush-fire conflicts that had flared up in so many parts of the world immediately after 1919 were contained or extinguished. By the late 1920's, while the world was not quite the place fit for heroes dreamed of by Lloyd George in 1919, there still seemed some possibility of realizing this idealistic goal.

NO MAN'S LAND

Scope of the conflict. Although the terrible struggle that racked mankind from 1914 to 1918 was fought chiefly on the European continent, it can justly be called the First World War. Altogether, twenty-seven powers became belligerents, ranging the globe from Tokyo to Ottawa and from Rio de Janeiro to Cape Town. Tremendous fighting strength was mustered. The Central Powers—Germany, Austria, Bulgaria, and Turkey—mobilized 21,000,000 men; their opponents, the Allies, mustered 40,000,000, of whom 12,000,000 were Russian. Since the Russian divisions were poorly equipped and often ineffectively used, these total figures are somewhat misleading in that they indicate a more decisive advantage than the Allies actually enjoyed. Furthermore in the German army, the Central Powers boasted superb generalship and discipline. In addition, they fought from an inner or central position and were therefore able to transfer troops quickly and efficiently to various fronts. In their favor, the Allies had greater resources of finance and raw materials; and Britain had the advantage of a splendid, powerful fleet with which to maintain control of the seas.

Strategy in 1914. While the Allies could better hold out in a long war, both sides planned for a quick decision in 1914. Allied strategy was to launch two simultaneous offensives—one by the French against Alsace, the other by the Russians against East Prussia.

The German plan was this: by moving through Belgium and then wheeling back through France, the German armies hoped to outflank the French and push them against Alsace-Lorraine, where they would be met by another German army and hemmed in on both east and west. With France smashed, the main German forces would then shift to East Prussia, join a smaller German army which had been holding the Russians at bay, and destroy the Russian forces.

In the west the German strategy operated with clocklike precision. A small British expeditionary force tried to halt the German onrush in Belgium, but resistance was smothered by the fire of immense siege artillery. Meanwhile a French offensive against Alsace had fizzled out. German forces advanced inexorably on Paris, reaching a point within twenty-five miles of the French capital by the beginning of September. At this moment, however, the German high command made a fatal blunder. Its army weakened by the dispatch of troops to East Prussia to meet a Russian attack, the high command directed the east flank to pass to the east of Paris, thus abandoning the original plan to encircle Paris from the west. This tactic left the right flank of the German forces exposed.

The weakness was quickly detected by Joffre, the French commander, and his advisers; and on September 5, Joffre decided to initiate a bold counteroffensive. So began the battle of the Marne. Paris taxicabs were mobilized to transport French troops to the front.

BATTLES OF WORLD WAR I

Central powers
- - - - Farthest German Advance
▭ Hindenburg line

For five days a titanic battle raged, and in the end the Germans had to retreat. The western flanks of both armies were now exposed, and a race to the sea began, each army trying to outflank the other and to reach the vital ports along the English Channel. Before either army succeeded, winter set in; the western front became stabilized, and a long line of trenches stretched from the Channel to Switzerland. Open warfare was replaced by trench warfare.

On the eastern front the Russian armies quickly overran the Austrian province of Galicia, and two subsequent Austrian attacks on Serbia were repulsed. Farther north in East Prussia, however, the Russian invaders did not fare so well. In August they were defeated in the battle of Tannenberg by troops commanded by Generals von Hindenburg and von Ludendorff. One month later in the battle of the Masurian Lakes the Russians suffered a second catastrophic defeat. By winter the

Germans had smashed their way into Poland. The eastern frontiers of Germany were never again seriously menaced.

The Dardanelles campaign. The year 1915 dawned with both the Allies and the Central Powers supremely confident of the outcome of the war. The aims of the Allies were to widen Germany's battle front, to reëstablish communication with Russia, and to deprive the Central Powers of supplies from overseas by means of a naval blockade.

Turkey's entrance into the war on the side of Germany had closed the Dardanelles to Allied shipping; and munitions and other supplies could now be sent to Russia only via Archangel, a port ice-locked much of the year. Great Britain set out to solve this problem by forcing the Dardanelles, a plan attributed largely to Winston Churchill, then lord of the admiralty. Other objectives of this campaign were to lessen the possibility of attack on

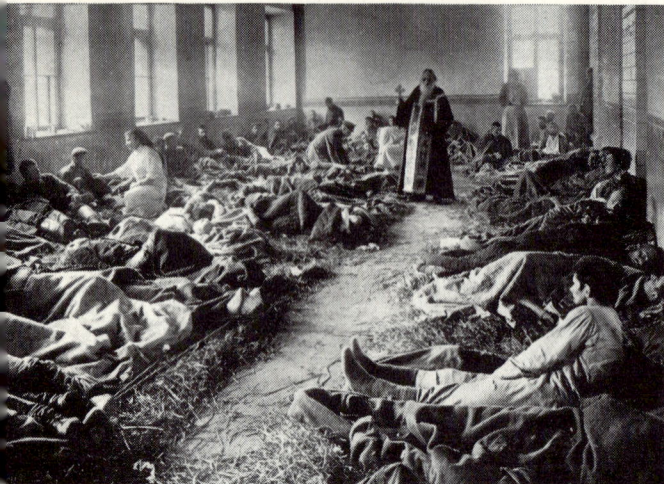

Russia's invasion of Germany ended in defeat as the efficient, well-cared-for German army beat back the poorly equipped, badly led Russian troops. The Russian wounded were crowded into primitive, makeshift hospitals like this one in East Prussia.

Egypt and Suez, to isolate Turkey, and to win over the Balkan neutrals.

The campaign was a series of blunders and ghastly failures. As if to furnish the Turks with advance information, the Allies sent a naval squadron to make a preliminary attack in November 1914. As a follow-up, a determined naval attack was launched in March. In the engagement three battleships were sunk, and the Allies withdrew. We know now that the Turkish batteries were practically out of ammunition; had the attack been pressed, the Straits undoubtedly would have fallen.

During the latter part of April 1915, Australian and New Zealand troops forced a landing on the Gallipoli peninsula in European Turkey. In the face of concentrated fire from machine-gun nests along the steep cliffs, the Anzacs waded ashore from small boats and charged up the beach, suffering tremendous losses. For the remainder of the year the British troops clung to their precarious foothold. Finally, in January 1916, they were evacuated.

Italy joins the Allies. To widen their enemies' battle front, the Allies finally brought Italy into the war. From December 1914 to April 1915, both sides had wooed Italy. The Allies were successful because in the secret Treaty of London they made lavish promises, including an offer to turn part of the southern Tyrol over to Italy after the war ended. As the British statesman Balfour remarked, "This is the sort of thing you have to do when you are engaged in war." Although still a member of the Triple Alliance, Italy did not feel bound by its earlier commitment to the Central Powers and in 1915 entered the war on what it believed was the winning side. Winning Italy to their side was the only victory achieved by the Allies in that year; elsewhere occurred a series of melancholy defeats.

German successes in 1915. The Germans went from victory to victory. In Galicia they carried out a terrific offensive against the Russian forces in May. Some 700,000 shells paved the way for the infantry attack, and the Russian fortifications simply melted away. Soon the tsar's army was in rapid retreat, which quickly degenerated into a rout. More than 1,200,000 Russians were killed or wounded, and the Germans captured nearly 900,000 prisoners. Criticism of the Russian government grew, and the morale of the nation began to break down.

Serbia was the next victim. The conquest was made all the easier because, in September, Bulgaria entered the war on the side of the Central Powers. Surrounded by enemies, Serbia was helpless and resistance was quickly crushed.

Stalemate on the western front, 1916. It was the Allied strategy to restrict attacks on the western front to intermittent nibbling and to concentrate upon the naval blockade. In the end this policy of steady weakening would result in starvation in Germany. Germany, on the other hand, resorted to another kind of attrition and applied it to France. The plan was to concentrate a gigantic attack on Verdun. This move would attract hundreds of thousands of French troops, terrible losses would result, and French morale would be steadily worn down.

All during the spring and summer of 1916, the Germans pounded the forts of Verdun with thousands of shells and threw wave after wave of infantry against the French lines. Each fort was supplied with enough food for two weeks and ordered never to surrender.

The French stubbornly held their positions. The result of this blood bath was attrition on both sides—the total loss in wounded and dead of some 700,000 men.

To ease the tremendous pressure against Verdun and to discourage the Germans from sending fresh troops against Russia, the British army, in the final week of June, began an offensive along the Somme on the western front. For seven days a tornado of artillery fire battered and wrecked the German trenches; then on the morning of July 1, as the shrill whistles of their officers sounded the zero hour, the British troops advanced slowly through the barbed-wire barriers into a terrible blast of machine-gun fire from the German lines. The scene has been described by a British military historian: "It was a race with death run by nearly sixty thousand men in the first heat. They were hopelessly handicapped. The whole mass, made up of closely-packed waves of men . . . were to advance at 'a steady pace,' symmetrically aligned, like rows of nine-pins ready to be knocked over. . . . Each man carried about 66 lb., . . . which made it . . . impossible to move much quicker than a slow walk. . . . The race was lost before it started."[1]

In spite of heartbreaking losses, the attack was renewed again and again until heavy rains in October made further efforts impossible. At the cost of over 400,000 killed and wounded, the British had gained a few square miles of territory. The French, who had also borne some of the brunt of the offensive, suffered 200,000 casualties; the Germans, 500,000.

The eastern front, 1916. A promising development for the Allies was the comeback staged by the Russian army. In June the Russian commander Brusilov struck the Austrian lines with the force of a thunderbolt, capturing 300,000 prisoners. Although the assistance of German troops and the inadequacy of Russian equipment saved the Austrian armies from destruction, the Russian offensive had one important result: Rumania was convinced that the German cause was hopeless. In August, Rumania threw in its lot with the Allies and successfully launched an invasion of Hungary. But Rumania's success was short-

An elaborate system of front lines, support trenches, and artillery supply lines stretched some six hundred miles across France and Belgium during the stalemate on the western front. Occasionally a charge would be made "over the top" and across no man's land; when an assault failed, those who had not been cut down by machine-gun fire straggled back to their muddy, rat- and vermin-infested trenches. Underground caverns served as first-aid stations, supply centers, and living quarters.

lived. Bulgarian and German forces simultaneously attacked the inferior Rumanian armies, and Rumania was forced to capitulate.

Decisive campaigns. At the close of 1916, after more than two years of fighting, neither the Central Powers nor the Allies could envisage victory. The war had turned into a dreary contest of stamina.

A survey of the first two and one-half years of the war reveals that if either side had scored a victory in any one of three or four campaigns the war would probably have ended much earlier. A German victory at the Marne in 1914 would have been completely disastrous to France. Likewise, a Russian victory at Tannenberg, in East Prussia, or a triumph for the British at the Dardanelles would have changed the whole course of the war in favor of the Allies.

The battle of Jutland (May 31-June 1, 1916), in the North Sea west of Denmark,

German soldiers were terrified at the first appearance of these strange steel monsters in September 1916. The British had secretly developed the military tank under the pretext of building water tanks, thus giving the new weapon its name.

was another crucial engagement, inasmuch as control of the seas was vital to Britain. At Jutland, the only major naval engagement of the war, the Germans maneuvered brilliantly and took daring risks. They could afford to gamble. Defeat could in no way worsen their existing strategic position; but victory at Jutland would give them victory in the war. The British fleet acted, therefore, with extreme caution. Its losses were heavier, but the German fleet was forced to return to its base and remained bottled up in home ports for the remainder of the year. British naval supremacy continued intact.

Advances in technology serve war. By 1916 the words of Jean Henri Dunant, Swiss internationalist and founder of the Red Cross, were being borne out. In 1897 he had written:

Ah, war is not yet dead! If it has changed its form, it is only to become—more terrible. Everything that makes up the pride of our civilization will be at the service of war. Your electric railroads, your dirigibles, your submarines . . . telephones . . . and so many other wonderful inventions, will perform splendid service for war . . .[2]

In spite of Dunant's warnings and the dire prophecies of other statesmen, neither leaders nor their peoples were prepared for the frightfulness of modern warfare, particularly trench warfare on the western front. Picture two lines of trenches several hundred miles

long, filled with hundreds of thousands of opposing troops. Between the trenches was no man's land, crisscrossed with barbed wire and spotted with craters, where lay the dead. During the day the soldiers crouched in their dugouts, using periscopes to peer over the parapets, for sharpshooters were a constant menace. At night, while the men tried to gain a little fitful sleep, sentries peered anxiously into the darkness, on the watch for raiding parties. Machine-gun fire, the menace of gas, the risk of strafing by marauding airplanes, the constant danger of sudden death from the shelling of big guns—these became the daily lot of the soldiers in the trenches.

War was now in four spatial dimensions: on land, in the air, on the water, and below the water, as armies, airplanes, battleships, and submarines were joined in mortal combat. New inventions made warfare more deadly. Four were of particular importance—the submarine, the armored tank, poison gas, and the airplane—but to these could be added a host of other devices either created or dramatically improved by technological advances. The internal-combustion engine powered not only trucks, staff cars, and ambulances but also tanks, planes, and dirigibles. The Diesel engine was used for the first time to drive warships. And technology countered technology. Mightier dreadnoughts were met with submarines, improved mines, and faster torpedo boats; more mobile armies had to face land mines, better hand grenades, flame throwers, and machine guns. Giant guns—like the German "Big Bertha," which bombarded Paris for months—lobbed shells more than seventy-five miles, and planes and dirigibles bombed targets hundreds of miles from their bases.

Total war, a new reality. War had branched out into a whole new dimension—the non-military struggle to sustain the will of the civilian population to win through to victory. In fact the war on the home front rivaled that fought on the battlefield. As an English observer put it:

The War has passed out of the phase of a mere battle. It is now a contest between the will and determination of whole nations to continue a life-and-death struggle in which "battle" takes a very small part.[3]

Opponents in this kind of war utilized propaganda to damage the enemy's cause and to win the support of neutral powers. They also fought to increase to the maximum the productive capacity of war industries.

War now affected the lives of everyone—men, women, and children as well as soldiers. The citizens of the belligerent nations were urged to eat less food, buy more bonds, and manufacture more shells. Women were urged to take men's jobs in order to release more man power for military purposes. People were deluged by a barrage of propaganda inciting them to hate the enemy, to believe in the righteousness of their cause, and to support the war effort without complaint or criticism. Civil liberties suffered. He who was not with us was against us. Distinguished citizens were clapped into prison for opposing the war effort. In England, for example, the philosopher and mathematician Bertrand Russell was imprisoned for a short time; and James Ramsey MacDonald, later prime minister, was reviled for his antiwar beliefs. Governments took over the control of their national economies. Strikes were outlawed, wages as well as prices were regulated, and currencies and foreign trade were rigidly controlled.

Total war was a solvent eroding many of the conventions and attitudes of the Victorian era that had come down to the twentieth century. In many lands women demanded and received the right to engage in a wide variety of occupations and to be taken seriously in politics. Social conventions were altered, and standards were relaxed. Young people enjoyed more liberties, and old age no longer received automatic respect. As all classes were merged in the caldron of war, social barriers tended to blur.

Changes in public opinion. On the home front in 1914 all was flag waving and enthusiasm. But the champagne mood gradually changed to one of despair and war weariness. By the end of 1916 there was a deep yearning for peace. Sensing this mood, leaders on both sides tendered rather half-hearted peace feelers. Fortified by a string of victories, the Central Powers in December 1916 offered peace to the Allies in vague terms and a superior tone. President Wilson in the same month of-

Unaware of the airplane's full potentialities as a weapon of war, World War I commanders at first used it primarily for reconnaissance purposes. Flyers shot at each other with pistols and rifles, and only later in the war were methods devised for mounting machine guns and dropping bombs. Above, German and Allied planes engage in a dogfight over the western front. The submarine also achieved widespread use as a military weapon during World War I. The photo shows an English submarine being bombed by German planes in the North Sea.

fered his mediation for the cause of peace and shortly thereafter urged that a peace be secured "without victory" and "between equals." Aware of the widespread defeatism among his subjects, the Austrian emperor made secret contact with both Britain and France in the spring of 1917, but nothing came of this move. In August 1917 the pope sent a peace note to the belligerents, pleading for a cessation of the slaughter, but to no avail. Although most socialists had forgotten their avowed faith in international brotherhood and had supported their countries' war efforts, in 1915 the first of three antiwar socialist conferences was convened. But these, too, achieved nothing.

In spite of the increasing atmosphere of futility and defeatism, the war was carried on. Its continuance was made possible largely by the use of propaganda. All the people in the warring nations were made to believe that they were part of a crusade for a better world. The Germans were labeled as "Huns" by the Allies; the Russians as "savages" by the Germans. The followers of the kaiser sang their "Hymn of Hate" with patriotic gusto:

Hate by water and hate by land;
Hate of the heart and hate of the hand;
We love as one; we hate as one;
We have but one foe alone—England.[4]

Atrocity stories became popular reading on both sides, and an Austrian firm allegedly faked atrocity pictures that could be used by either side. This is not to say that atrocities were not sometimes committed, but there were many that existed only in the mind of the propagandist.

A feature of this war of words was the publication of the "color books." All the belligerent powers issued collections of documents, bound in various colors, seeking to prove they were not responsible for the outbreak of the war. Thus there was the British Blue Book, the Austrian Red Book, the German White Book, and the French Yellow Book. Such propaganda techniques served their purpose, and the war continued.

THE UNITED STATES

AND VICTORY

Allies near the breaking point in 1917. In 1917 British and French military strength reached its highest point, only to fall to unprecedented depths. Allied commanders were hopeful that the long-planned breakthrough might be accomplished, but a large-scale attack by the French was beaten back with horrible losses. French regiments mutinied rather than return to the inferno of no man's land. To keep the French army intact,

the most desperate efforts were made: the lot of the common soldier was improved and offensives were discontinued. But the attempted breakthrough had become a near breakdown.

Meanwhile the British army in France launched several massive offensives, only to lose hundreds of thousands of men without any decisive results. The battle of Passchendale was an especially calamitous affair, the fighting taking place in a churned-up quagmire where men, mules, and heavy guns were swallowed up in a sea of mud. The Allies launched unsuccessful offensives not only in France but also in Italy, where catastrophe threatened. Aided by the Germans, the Austrian army smashed the Italian front. This was the battle of Caporetto (1917), so vividly described by Ernest Hemingway in the war novel *A Farewell to Arms*. Italian resistance finally hardened, but collapse was barely averted.

This disastrous frustration of Allied hopes was deepened by the growing menace of the German submarine campaign. In 1915 the losses from submarine attacks had run, on an average, 74,000 tons monthly. By 1917 shipping losses had assumed catastrophic proportions. In three months 470 British ships alone fell victims to torpedoes. Britain had no more than a six weeks' supply of food, and for the Allies the situation became critical. But the very weapon that seemed to doom their cause was to prove their salvation. For the submarine brought the United States into the war on the Allies' side.

American sentiment lies with the Allies. After Italy joined the Allies in 1915, the United States was the only great power remaining neutral. The outbreak of the war had come as a surprise to most Americans, who had little knowledge of conditions in Europe. The overwhelming sentiment in this country was for peace. In 1914 President Wilson had announced the neutrality of the United States and declared that the people "must be impartial in thought as well as in action." The events of the following two years showed that this was no easy task.

From the beginning of the conflict, American sentiment was predominantly with Britain and France. Notwithstanding the frequent twisting of the British Lion's tail since the Revolution, there were strong cultural and political ties between the two Anglo-Saxon peoples. This tendency to favor the western European democracies was further strengthened by British propaganda, which was more effective than that of the Central Powers. The British agency for propaganda, known as the Ministry of Moral Munitions, carried on multifarious activities the world over, with the United States as its special target. More than 350 American newspapers were supplied with English daily news releases; American friends of the Allied cause were induced to write letters and articles for the press and to make speeches; and a vast amount of pro-Allied literature was distributed to colleges, clubs, libraries, and YMCA's.

Another factor which favored the Allied cause was the American belief that by invading Belgium, Germany had grossly violated international law. Partly because of the kaiser's saber-rattling speeches, the German government was regarded as undemocratic, unpredictable, and unstable. In some circles it was believed that a German victory would upset the world balance of power and that a victorious and expansionist Germany might imperil American security. Thus while most Americans in 1914 had little desire to enter the war, it was conceivable that great provocation from the Central Powers or serious danger to the Allies might lead to intervention by the United States.

As the war got under way, it became apparent that the British blockade would permit our trade to be carried on with the Allies only, and it was not long before our factories and farmers were producing munitions and food exclusively for Great Britain and France. Our industry expanded and began to enjoy a prosperity dependent upon the continuance of Allied purchases. Between 1914 and 1916, American exports to the Allies quadrupled. During 1915 and 1916, Allied bonds totaling about $1,500,000,000 were sold in America.

In recent times much attention has been paid to the financial stake of the United States in the Allied cause. Careful students point out that though the economic situation did influence our final decision to go to war,

American civilians responded vigorously to the call for a home-front war effort. Above, Red Cross Volunteers, displaying socks knitted for the doughboys, parade in New York City.

"the financial community as a whole . . . favored American neutrality rather than American participation; for neutrality afforded Wall Street all the profits of war without the compensating sacrifices and taxation. And there is not a shred of evidence to support the allegation that Wilson was at any time influenced by the financial 'stake' in his relations with Germany."[5]

German U-boat campaign angers the United States. The immediate cause of America's entry into the war on the side of the Allies was undoubtedly the German submarine campaign. At the outbreak of hostilities, Great Britain had immediately imposed a tight naval blockade against Germany. So effective was the blockade that the kaiser's government in desperation announced unrestricted submarine warfare in February 1915. On May 1, 1915, the *Gulflight* was torpedoed with the loss of several members of its American crew.

On May 7 came the horrible disaster of the sinking of the *Lusitania*, one of the largest and most luxurious liners of the Cunard line.

Today it is generally recognized that, in addition to civilian passengers, the vessel was carrying ammunition, but it is still debated whether the ship was armed. Sunk by a torpedo in the Irish Sea, the *Lusitania* went to the bottom with the loss of over one thousand lives, including more than one hundred Americans. Public opinion in America was aroused by the horror of this tragedy.

In March 1916 the unarmed French steamer *Sussex* was sunk without warning, and several more Americans were killed. Following this act, the United States government sent Germany an ultimatum demanding the termination of the submarine campaign. In reply the Germans pledged that in the future merchant vessels would not be sunk without warning and that provision would be made for the safety of passengers and crews. President Wilson had apparently won an important diplomatic victory.

In the fall of 1916, Wilson was reëlected to the presidency. One of the important claims made during the campaign was "he kept us out of war." This boast, however, was soon invalidated by the force of events. The discovery of German plots to embroil Mexico in a war against the United States aroused violent resentment, and the renewal of unrestricted submarine warfare was the last straw. In February 1917 diplomatic relations were broken off between the United States and Germany. Finally the president asked Congress to declare war against Germany. Resolutions to this effect passed both houses, and on April 6, 1917, war was declared.

The spell of Wilson's lofty principles and the challenge of his speeches caused a great welling of idealism in America. No matter what causes had operated to bring America into the war, the United States was now fighting, in the words of the president, "to make the world safe for democracy."

Ludendorff's last effort. While the United States mobilized its tremendous resources of man power and materials, the German government decided to take advantage of the Allied weakness and win the war before American aid became effective. The British army was bled white from the exhausting and fruitless offensives of 1917, and the French divisions had barely recovered from the mutinies. Furthermore, the Russian war effort had collapsed. In the revolution of November 1917 the Bolsheviks seized power in Russia; and by the Treaty of Brest Litovsk early in 1918, they made peace with Germany. The terms were harsh. As Lenin put it, this "sober peace" meant that Russia lost 500,000 square miles of territory and 66,000,000 people.

Freed from the necessity of fighting on the Russian front, General von Ludendorff transferred every available man to France and in March 1918 launched what he hoped would be a knockout blow against the British Fifth Army. Carrying all before them, the German shock troops, outnumbering the British four to one, made a large dent in the Allied line. But a breakthrough was not achieved. Ludendorff aimed a second blow against the British in another sector. Again impressive gains were made but not the rout which the German command had expected. A third offensive was launched against the French forces, but fresh American troops thrown into the struggle halted the advance. A brigade of marines covered itself with glory by stemming the German onrush at Château-Thierry.

Ludendorff made a last desperate effort. Launching a "Peace Drive" against the French, Ludendorff declared, "If my offensive succeeds, we have won the war." By this time, however, the German troops had suffered heavy losses. Under the unified command of Marshal Foch, the Allies mustered their resources. Great Britain sent every available man to France, and between March and July 1918 more than one million American "doughboys" landed in France. The advantage in man power and equipment was now with the Allies, and Ludendorff's "Peace Drive" failed after an advance of some three miles.

German collapse and armistice. Hardly had the German drive been halted when Foch counterattacked on July 18. For three weeks the second battle of the Marne raged. Outnumbered and without adequate supplies, the Germans retreated to the Hindenburg line, the position they had held before they took the offensive in March. Foch gave them no respite. With fresh American troops in France, the reinvigorated Allied armies advanced along the whole Hindenburg line. The German line bent, then broke; the German army fell back in rapid retreat. By the end of October the German forces had been pushed out of most of France, and Allied armies were advancing through Belgium. The war of fixed positions separated by no man's land was over. With a preponderance of tanks the Allies had smashed trench defenses and were now in open country.

On October 1, Hindenburg notified the kaiser that Germany must sue for peace, and three days later the German chancellor sent a note to President Wilson requesting an end to hostilities. The president's reply notified the German government that peace was impossible so long as the autocratic regime in Germany existed. Although the German chancellor tried to retain the monarchy by introducing certain liberal reforms, it was too late. Revolution broke out in many parts of the country, the kaiser abdicated, and a republic was proclaimed.

While Germany was staggering under the relentless pounding of Foch's armies, the German allies were suffering even greater misfortunes. Bulgaria surrendered on September 30, and Turkey capitulated a month later. Austria gave up the struggle against Italy on November 3; nine days later the Hapsburg empire collapsed when Emperor Charles I fled Vienna for sanctuary in Switzerland.

At five o'clock on the morning of November 11, 1918, in a dining car in the Compiègne Forest, the two German delegates signed the terms of the armistice presented to them by Marshal Foch, the supreme Allied commander. At eleven o'clock the same day hostilities were halted. Everywhere the news was received with an outburst of unrestrained joy. The world was once more at peace, confronted with the task of binding up its wounds and removing the scars of conflict.

By the armistice terms of November 11, Germany was compelled to evacuate Alsace-Lorraine, Luxemburg, Belgium, and the northern part of France. Within a month Allied troops were to occupy the German territory west of the Rhine. A large number of German ships were to be surrendered; loco-

Confident of victory and exhilarated at the prospect of gaining military glory for the Fatherland, German troops (above) leave for the front at the outbreak of World War I. Well-trained, well-led, and well-equipped, the German soldier had every reason to expect an early victory. But after facing the terrible realities of battle and experiencing the numbing shock of defeat, his mood changed to one of exhaustion and despair (below). The British caption struck a hopeful note: "This photograph taken a few days ago on the Somme shows a group of Hun prisoners taken on the Somme. As a study of the manhood Germany has now to depend upon, this photograph is of great interest, whilst as types the faces alone show that such material as this cannot long withstand our own brave fellows or the dash of the French troops."

motives, trucks, and other equipment were to be turned over; and all Allied prisoners were to be released. While these terms were being carried out by the new German government, delegates from the Allied nations were converging on Paris, where the peace conference was to be held.

For the troops of the victorious Allies, November 11 meant returning home to a joyful conqueror's welcome; to those of the Central Powers, it meant a return saddened by the realization of failure. The exodus of German forces has been vividly described by a German novelist: "Along the road, step upon step, in their faded, dirty uniforms tramp the grey columns. The unshaved faces beneath the steel helmets are haggard, wasted with hunger and long peril, pinched and dwindled to the lines drawn by terror and courage and death. They trudge along in silence . . . into peace. Without many words. Old men with beards and slim lads scarce twenty years of age, comrades without difference. Beside them their lieutenants, little more than children, yet the leaders of many a night raid. And behind them, the army of slain. Thus they tramp onward, step by step, sick, half-starving, without ammunition, in thin companies, with eyes that still fail to comprehend it: escaped out of that underworld, on the road back into life."[6]

THE PEACE SETTLEMENT

Wilson's blueprint for peace. Wilson had declared that the war was:

. . . a war for freedom and justice and self-government amongst all the nations of the world, a war to make the world safe for the peoples who live upon it and have made it their own, the German people themselves included.[7]

In January 1918, in an address before both houses of Congress, the president had enunciated his famous Fourteen Points as the basis for a lasting peace. Speaking to Congress, he had actually addressed the world—in particular, those men of good will in every land who would support a peace settlement based on liberal principles. With this speech, Wilson made himself a new kind of world leader, representing not wealth and power but morality and justice. Millions of men and women, at home and abroad, in the Allied nations, in the enemy countries, and in neutral states, flocked to his standard. The Fourteen Points seemed to open the way not only for a speedy cessation of hostilities but for a peace that could endure.

The first five points were general in nature and may be summarized as follows:

(1) "Open covenants openly arrived at."

(2) Freedom of the seas in peace and in war alike.

(3) The removal of all economic barriers and the establishment of an equality of trade conditions among all nations.

(4) Reduction of national armaments.

(5) A readjustment of all colonial claims, giving the interests of the population concerned equal weight with the claims of the government whose title was to be determined.

The next eight points dealt with specific issues:

(6) The evacuation of Russian territory and the independent determination by Russia of its own political development and national policy.

(7) The evacuation and restoration of Belgium.

(8) The evacuation and restoration of France and the return of Alsace-Lorraine.

(9) A readjustment of the frontiers of Italy along national lines.

(10) Self-determination for the peoples of Austria-Hungary.

(11) Evacuation of Rumania, Serbia, and Montenegro and access to the sea for Serbia.

(12) Self-determination for the peoples under Turkish rule and freedom of the Dardanelles under international guarantees.

(13) The independence of Poland, with free access to the sea guaranteed by international covenant.

The final point contained the germ of the League of Nations:

(14) The formation of a general association of nations under specific covenants for the purpose of affording mutual guarantees of political independence and territorial integrity to great and small states alike.

Although thirty-two Allied nations were represented at the Paris Peace Conference, three men made the major decisions—David Lloyd George, prime minister of Great Britain, Georges Clemenceau, premier of France, and Woodrow Wilson, president of the United States. Formal proceedings began on January 18, 1919; the treaty was signed on June 28.

Cross-currents at the peace conference. All the thirty-two Allied powers sent delegations to the peace conference at Paris. Some of the delegations numbered over a hundred persons, including statesmen, experts of various kinds, and clerks. The vanquished nations—Germany, Austria-Hungary, Turkey, Bulgaria—were not accorded representation. This exclusion was not in the spirit of Wilson's idealistic pronouncements before the armistice.

Three personalities dominated the Paris Conference: Wilson, Lloyd George, and Clemenceau. In the eyes of the war-weary and disillusioned peoples of Europe, Wilson was a veritable Messiah. But it soon became apparent that he would be unable to prevent his ideals and promises from being sabotaged by the other Allied statesmen in Paris. Against the wily Lloyd George and the cynical Clemenceau, the idealistic American scholar had little chance of holding his own. In addition,

certain factions in Congress were preparing to repudiate his program for a more just and better-ordered world. A far-seeing armchair statesman handicapped by a cold and imperious personality, Wilson (1856-1924) was so thoroughly convinced of the validity of his own ideas that he seldom recognized a need to "sell" them to others and often refused to consider the possibility of merit in the ideas of his opponents.

Lloyd George (1863-1945), the prime minister of Great Britain, was a consummately clever politician, who could use the arts of diplomatic bargaining with rare skill. His greatest asset was an engaging personality, which thawed many a stubborn opponent. He came to the conference just after a triumphant victory at the polls in which he had promised the electorate the "hanging of the kaiser" and the "squeezing of the German lemon until the pips squeaked." He was determined to destroy the commercial and naval power of Germany, to acquire the German colonies, and to compel Germany to pay a large share of the cost of the war.

The strongest personality of the conference was the French premier—the seventy-seven-year-old Clemenceau (1841-1929), sole survivor of the French Assembly that had protested the loss of Alsace-Lorraine in 1871. His burning ambition was to ensure the security of France in the future; his formula was restitution, reparations, and guarantees. During the peace negotiations the "Old Tiger" was shot in the chest by a madman; but so strong was his desire to live that he rallied quickly and, for a time, dominated the conference from his bed.

Prearmistice peace principles and secret treaties. The Germans had surrendered with the understanding that the peace would in the main follow the Fourteen Points and in general coincide with the speeches of Wilson. In February 1918 the president had announced, "There shall be no annexations, no contributions, no punitive damages"; and on July 4 he had said that every question must be settled "upon the basis of the free acceptance of that settlement by the people immediately concerned."

Some of the Allies saw the question of the peace in a different light; and before the armistice was signed, three alterations in the Fourteen Points were made by the European Allied powers. One alteration sprang from Great Britain's attitude toward the freedom of the seas, for Britain in the future wished to use its great fleet in any manner made necessary by national interests. Another alteration stemmed from the demand that Germany be made to pay for all damage done to Allied civilians; and the third appeared because of the dissatisfaction of the peoples of Austria-Hungary with mere autonomy within the Hapsburg empire.

Complicating the promises of Wilson, especially the Fourteen Points, were the secret treaties made by the Allies during the war. In 1915 Italy had been induced to enter the conflict by promises of Austrian territory which would make the Adriatic an Italian lake. Italy was also promised an extension of its African colonies and a sphere of influence in Asiatic Turkey. Nearly all these proposed transfers violated the Wilsonian concept of national self-determination.

Other secret treaties gave Russia the right to take over the Dardanelles and Constantinople, Rumania the right to secure substantial territory at the expense of Austria-Hungary, and Japan the right to retain the German territory of Kiaochow in China. In return for Arab aid against the Turks, Britain had made vague promises of independence for the Arabs. In 1916, however, Britain and France had divided Turkish Iraq and Syria into their respective spheres of interest. Palestine, with its holy places, was to be placed under international administration; and in 1917 Great Britain pledged its support of the "establishment in Palestine of a national home for the Jewish people."

President Wilson professed ignorance of the existence of the treaties, but their contents were common knowledge before the end of the war. In fact, in 1917 the Bolshevik government had released their texts, which were then published in American and English newspapers. Wilson may have believed that the secret agreements could be ignored, for he hoped to sway European statesmen to the necessity of founding the peace on his principles.

The League Covenant. The statesmen assembled in their first plenary meeting on January 18, 1919, the anniversary of the date on which the German empire had been proclaimed in Paris in 1871. It became evident at once that little progress could be made with all the duly qualified representatives present; therefore, the Council of Ten, which consisted of the two ranking delegates of the five great powers (the United States, Great Britain, France, Italy, and Japan), was set up. Soon the Council was narrowed down to the Big Three, with Japan and Italy excluded.

The first difficulty at the Paris Conference arose over the question of a league of nations. Wilson was insistent that the initial work of the conference must be to agree upon a covenant of a league of nations which was to be made part of the peace treaty. After much wrangling, the Covenant was approved by the full conference in April 1919. In order to gain support for the League, however, Wilson had to compromise on other matters. His Fourteen Points were thus partially repudiated, but he believed firmly that an imperfect treaty incorporating the League was better than a perfect one without it.

The Covenant of the League of Nations specified its aims: "to guarantee international cooperation and to achieve international peace and security." To implement this goal, Article x, the key article of the Covenant, stipulated that:

The Members of the League undertake to respect and preserve as against external aggression the territorial integrity and existing political independence of all Members of the League. In case of any such aggression or in case of any threat or danger of such aggression the Council shall advise upon the means by which this obligation shall be fulfilled.[8]

Redrawing German boundaries. Redrawing German boundaries was another task of the conference. Alsace-Lorraine was turned over to France without question, in accordance with one of the Fourteen Points. Three districts formerly belonging to Germany were given to Belgium, after a dubious plebiscite conducted by Belgian officials. Another plebiscite gave half of Schleswig back to Denmark.

Clemenceau and Marshal Foch were determined that a buffer state consisting of the German territory west of the Rhine should be established under the domination of France. In the eyes of the American and British representatives, such a crass violation of the principle of self-determination would only breed future wars; and a compromise was therefore offered Clemenceau, which he accepted. The territory in question was to be occupied by Allied troops for a period of from five to fifteen years; and, furthermore, a zone extending fifty kilometers east of the Rhine was to be demilitarized. In addition, Wilson and Lloyd George agreed that the United States and Great Britain would guarantee France against aggression. The importance of this pledge cannot be overemphasized.

Along Germany's eastern frontier the creation of the Polish Corridor, which separated East Prussia from the rest of Germany, raised grave problems. Large sections of German territory in which there were Polish majorities but also a goodly number of Germans were turned over to Poland. (The land in question had been taken from Poland by Prussia in the eighteenth century.) A section of Silesia was likewise given to Poland, but only after a plebiscite. Danzig, a German city, was handed over to the League for administration. All in all, Germany lost 25,000 square miles inhabited by some six million people.

Although Clemenceau also claimed the Saar Basin, a rich coal area, this was not given outright to France but instead was placed under the administration of the League. The French were given ownership of the mines to compensate for the destruction of their own in northern France. It was agreed, however, that after fifteen years a plebiscite would be conducted to determine whether the region wished to continue under League supervision, become part of France, or return to Germany.

The mandate system. A curious mixture of idealism and revenge determined the allocation of the German colonies and certain territories belonging to Turkey. Because outright annexation would look too much like unvarnished imperialism, it was suggested that the colonies be turned over to the League, which in turn would give them to certain of its members to administer. The colonies were to be known as mandates, and praiseworthy precautions were taken that the mandates would be administered for the well-being and development of the inhabitants. Once a year the mandatory powers were to present a detailed account of their administration of the territories to the Permanent Mandates Commission of the League.

Class A mandates, such as Syria, Palestine, and Iraq, were regarded as territories able to achieve full statehood in the not-too-distant future. Class B mandates, such as those in central Africa, represented peoples whose progress had not reached a point where admission to statehood was possible for a long time to come. Class C mandates, in southwestern Africa and the south Pacific islands, were regarded as regions whose size, proximity to the mandatory power, or remoteness from civilization made control by others the best safeguard of the natives' rights and welfare. The mandate system as such was a step forward in colonial administration, but Germany nevertheless was deprived of all colonies, with the excuse that it could not rule them justly or efficiently.

Reparations. Germany had accepted the armistice terms with the understanding that damage done to the Allied civilian population was to be paid for. At the conference the British and French delegates went much further by demanding that Germany pay the total cost of the war, including pensions. The American representatives maintained that such a claim was contrary to the prearmistice Allied terms and succeeded in achieving a compromise. It was agreed that, except in the case of Belgium, Germany was not to pay the entire cost of the war, but only war damages, which included damage to civilians and the cost of pensions. These payments, called reparations, were exacted on the ground that Germany was responsible for the war.

Although the Allies agreed that Germany should be made to pay, they were unable to decide on the sum. Some demands ran as high as $200,000,000,000. Finally it was decided that a committee should fix the amount and report no later than May 1921. In the meantime Germany was to begin making payments which, by the time the reparations committee's report was ready, would total nearly $5,000,000,000.

Other Allied demands. Germany was required to hand over all merchant ships of more than 1600 tons and 50 per cent of all those between 1000 and 1600 tons. In addition, it had to construct for the Allies 1,000,000 tons of new shipping. Vast amounts of coal, equipment, tools, and machinery were also to be delivered by Germany to the Allies.

In military matters the demands were even more drastic. Germany was permitted a standing army of only 100,000 men, the size of the fleet was drastically reduced, possession of military airplanes was forbidden, and munitions plants were to be placed under close supervision. The treaty also provided that the

kaiser be tried by a tribunal "for a supreme offense against international morality and the sanctity of treaties" and cited some eight hundred German officials for trial on charges of war atrocities. But the kaiser had fled to Holland after the German revolution; and when that country refused to surrender him, no further steps were taken by the Allied governments, which had inserted the clause providing for the punishment of the kaiser largely for home consumption.

The Treaty of Versailles signed. The Treaty of Versailles was built around the concept that Germany was responsible for the war. It stated explicitly that:

The Allied and Associated Governments affirm and Germany accepts the responsibility of Germany and her allies for causing all the loss and damage to which the Allied and Associated Governments and their nationals have been subjected as a consequence of the war imposed upon them by the aggression of Germany and her allies.[9]

In April 1919 the German delegation came to Paris to receive the Treaty of Versailles. Up to this time they had been given no official information as to its terms. In receiving the treaty on May 7, the German foreign minister and head of the German delegation stated:

It is demanded of us that we shall confess ourselves to be the only ones guilty of the war. . . . We are far from declining any responsibility . . . but we energetically deny that Germany and its people . . . were alone guilty. . . . In the last fifty years the Imperialism of all the European States has chronically poisoned the international situation . . .[10]

After obtaining the treaty, the German government balked at what it considered its outrageous terms. But the menace of Allied invasion gave it no alternative but to sign, and the government therefore instructed its delegates to accept the treaty for Germany "without abandoning her view in regard to the unheard of injustice of the conditions of the peace." On June 28, on the anniversary of the assassination of Archduke Francis Ferdinand and in the Hall of Mirrors at Versailles where the German empire had been proclaimed in 1871, the treaty was signed.

After witnessing this ceremony, a prominent member of the American delegation wrote in his diary:

When the Germans had signed and the great Allied Powers had done so, the cannon began to boom. I had a feeling of sympathy for the Germans who sat there quite stoically. It was not unlike what was done in ancient times, when the conqueror dragged the conquered at his chariot wheels. To my mind, it is out of keeping with the new era which we profess an ardent desire to promote. I wish it could have been more simple and that there might have been an element of chivalry, which was wholly lacking. The affair was elaborately staged and made as humiliating to the enemy as it well could be.[11]

Other World War treaties. Treaties were also concluded with the rest of the Central Powers. The treaty with Austria, the Treaty of St. Germain (1919), legalized the nationalist movements of Czechs, Poles, and Slavs and converted the remainder of the empire into the separate states of Austria and Hungary. By the treaty terms, the Austrian empire was reduced in area from 116,000 to 32,000 square miles and in population from 28,500,000 to 6,000,000. Forbidden was *Anschluss*—union of the Germans in Austria with their kinsmen in the new German republic.

The disposition of former Hapsburg territory at the conference created a serious controversy. Taking a stand on the secret Treaty of London, Italy wanted the Adriatic as an Italian lake. The Treaty of St.-Germain awarded sections of Austria to Italy—the territory south of the Brenner Pass, South Tyrol, Trentino with its 250,000 Austrian Germans, and the northeastern coast of the Adriatic with its large number of Slavs. To complete Italy's acquisition of the Adriatic, it was necessary to obtain a slice of the Dalmatian coast and the port of Fiume. The latter, however, was the natural port for the newly created state of Yugoslavia and had not been promised to Italy in 1915. Wilson declared that the Italian claim was in flat contradiction to the principle of self-determination, and a controversy ensued which nearly wrecked the peace confer-

ence. The explosive issue of Italian claims in the Adriatic was not settled until 1920.

By the Treaty of Sèvres (1920) the Ottoman empire was placed on the operating table of power politics, dissected, and divided among Greece, Britain, and France. Greece was given nearly all of European Turkey, almost up to the suburbs of Constantinople, and some islands in the Aegean Sea. The city of Smyrna was put under Greek administration, but Armenia achieved full independence. Syria was mandated to France, and Palestine and Iraq to England. To the Arabs, these transfers to Britain and France were a violation of wartime pledges. As for the Straits, this strategic body of water was to be under international control.

Two other treaties affected the Balkans. By the Treaty of Trianon (1920), Hungary lost territory to Czechoslovakia, Yugoslavia, and Rumania. The Treaty of Neuilly (1919) cut off Bulgaria from the Aegean Sea, imposed an indemnity, and provided for compulsory demilitarization. Bulgaria lost nearly one million subjects.

Evaluation of the peace settlement. During the first postwar decade, tons of paper and barrels of ink were used in hot justification or acrid denunciation of the peace settlement. One method of evaluating the Treaty of Versailles is to ask what terms a victorious Germany would have been likely to impose? A good hint might be found in the ruthless settlement forced upon Russia by Germany in the Treaty of Brest Litovsk. In contrast, Versailles seems rather moderate. On the other hand, the reparations bill presented to Germany was excessive and unrealistic. Some economists estimated that the bill was at least double the highest figure they could imagine Germany paying. In his indictment of the economic provisions of the peace, the world-famous economist John Maynard Keynes wrote in 1919:

The treaty includes no provisions for the economic rehabilitation of Europe,—nothing to make the defeated Central Empires into good neighbours, nothing to stabilise the new States of Europe, nothing to reclaim Russia; nor does it promote in any way a compact of economic soli-

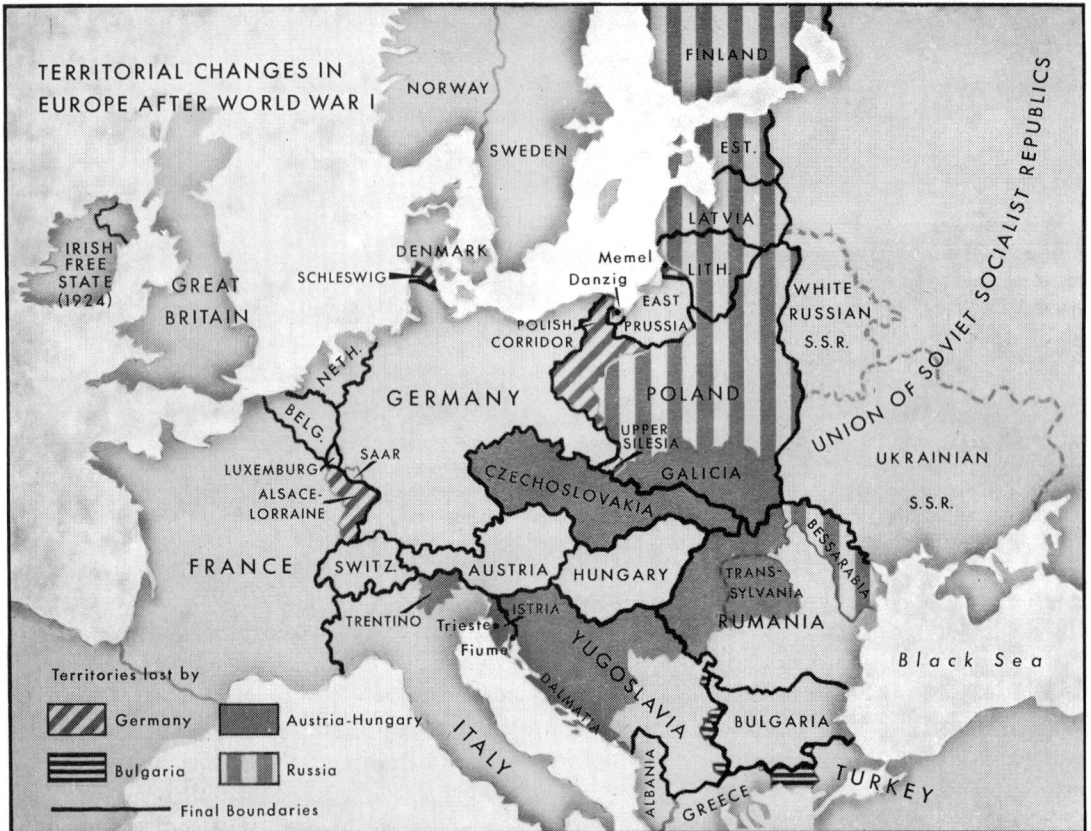

TERRITORIAL CHANGES IN
EUROPE AFTER WORLD WAR I

Territories lost by

Germany   Austria-Hungary

Bulgaria   Russia

Final Boundaries

darity amongst the Allies themselves; no arrangement was reached at Paris for restoring the disordered finances of France and Italy, or to adjust the systems of the Old World and the New.[12]

One of the weakest aspects of the peace settlement was the complete disregard of Russia. While the peace conference was in session, Russia was convulsed by civil war, complicated by the intervention of Japanese, American, French, and British troops. The Allied representatives at Paris disagreed on the policy to adopt toward the Communist government in Russia. The Soviets proposed to accept the huge prewar debts contracted by the tsar's government if the Allies would stop aiding the anti-Communist forces and would restore normal commercial and diplomatic relations. This offer was not taken seriously.

It was believed at Paris that the Communist government would soon collapse. Whether the new regime in Russia and the Allies could

have reached some kind of an agreement leading to Russian participation is uncertain. But we do know that the possibility was not seriously explored. George F. Kennan, an American authority on Soviet affairs, maintains that the sacrifice of this possibility had tremendous consequences for "the long-term future of both the Russian and American peoples and indeed of mankind generally."[13]

Some historians blame the errors of the treaties upon the defects of the personalities who made them. This view oversimplifies the problem and furthermore assumes that the statesmen at Paris were free agents. In truth, the delegates were the prisoners of their own people, who had been so influenced by propaganda, whose enmity was so bitter, and whose knowledge was so meager that any indication of reasonableness shown to the ex-enemies would have meant the repudiation of the harassed peacemakers. Wilson, Lloyd George, and Clemenceau were acting under many pressures. Perhaps no one possessed enough wisdom to cope with the many problems created and accentuated by four years of global war. Perhaps no other group of leaders could have made a better peace.

BITTER FRUITS OF VICTORY

The "new world" and the powers. The unity among the Allies wrought by the necessities of war did not long survive victory. During the Paris Conference and in the years following, serious differences emerged over such basic issues as reparations, war debts, disarmament, and the structure and functions of the League of Nations.

Italy was angry with its former allies for being so niggardly with the spoils of war. Great Britain was ready to let bygones be bygones; the "nation of shopkeepers" was anxious to see prosperity return to central Europe. On the other hand, France feared a resurgent Germany and was determined to enforce all the peace treaties.

And what of the vanquished? Germany was resentful of the peace settlement and determined to repudiate it. Hungary, Austria, and Bulgaria held similar views. Alone of the defeated powers, Turkey was fairly content, as it had been able to secure better treatment in a new treaty—the Treaty of Lausanne (see p. 499).

United States refuses to join the League. In 1919, the year of its establishment, the League of Nations constituted a promising agency for improving the status of mankind everywhere. At the outset, however, it suffered a great blow to its prestige: the United States refused to become a member of the League.

During the war Americans had been proud of Wilson's proposals for a new world order. But the peace settlement pleased few; chauvinists found it too lenient, and liberals found it too harsh. Seeking to discredit Wilson, some members of the Republican party agitated against the Treaty of Versailles. After his return to the United States in July 1919, the president pressed the Senate for ratification of the treaty, which carried with it membership in the League. In defiance the senators demanded a number of important reservations.

It was all or nothing with Wilson. Refusing to accept the watered-down version of the League Covenant insisted upon by the isolationist faction in the Senate, Wilson sent word to twenty of his supporters in the Senate to vote against the treaty. The final vote was 49 to 35, seven votes short of the necessary two thirds. Feeling that half a loaf was better than none, many historians believe that Wilson should have accepted the amended treaty.

In desperation, and faced with the wreckage of all his visions of a new world united in a common effort to outlaw war, Wilson in September 1919 toured the country, appealing to the people to support the League. Not yet fully recovered from his exertions at the peace conference, he could not stand the heavy strain of his whirlwind campaign; he suffered a complete physical breakdown and was stricken with paralysis. With his collapse the opportunity to build a new world disappeared. Wilson's appeal had been in vain. His program was repudiated at the polls, for Warren G. Harding, the Republican candidate, roundly defeated the Democratic candidate. Harding's victory meant that the Covenant never was ratified by the Senate.

While the inflexible Wilson must bear some of the responsibility for the rejection of the League, the president prophetically warned his people of the price they would one day have to pay for turning their backs on the world. In the main Wilson's words had fallen on deaf ears. The chaos of the future and the coming of World War II were hidden in the yet unturned pages of history. The mass of Americans lapsed into complacent isolationism and normalcy with Harding.

France and the Little Entente. For a number of reasons, the French did not place much faith in the League as an instrument for their security. In addition to the refusal by the United States to join the League, both the United States and Britain had scrapped the treaty guaranteeing France from aggression.

Overwhelmed by this blow to their hopes, France set about obtaining allies on the Continent. In 1920 a defensive alliance was made with Belgium. Overtures were then made to Poland, which France had aided in its war against Communist Russia (see p. 466); and after a preliminary agreement, France and Poland in 1922 concluded a military alliance directed against any future danger from Germany. The agreement was buttressed by large French loans to Poland and by the assistance of military experts from France. In 1924 Czechoslovakia signed a treaty with France that pledged the signatories to take concerted measures in the event of a union between Germany and Austria or an attempt by either Germany or Hungary to restore their ruling houses. Not content with these allies, the French foreign office negotiated similar pacts with Rumania (1926) and Yugoslavia (1927). During 1920 and 1921 these smaller states had also made treaties of mutual assistance among themselves; this diplomatic bloc (Czechoslovakia, Rumania, Yugoslavia) was known as the Little Entente, and its power rested upon extensive French loans and military collaboration. In contrast to the perilous diplomatic equilibrium created by the Triple Alliance and the Triple Entente in the years prior to 1914, the new system of alliances dominated by France now tipped the scales heavily in favor of the French. For a brief ten years France with its Little Entente dominated Europe militarily.

The shift to a peace economy. One of the chief obstacles to postwar peace was the confused and desperate situation into which the European economy had been plunged. The stakes for which the war was fought seemed substantial in 1914, but the price paid to achieve them was tragically high. The war had lasted 1565 days, and during this time over 60,000,000 men had donned uniforms. About 9,000,000 were killed and 22,000,000 were wounded. In addition about 10,000,000 civilians lost their lives as a result of famines and diseases during the war years. Furthermore, billions of dollars' worth of property had been used up or destroyed by the warring armies. It has been pointed out that the probable total cost of World War I was about $350,000,000,000. It was the financial consequences of war that did most to continue the enmity between victors and vanquished and also to alienate the nations, formerly allies, which had defeated Germany.

The armistice found the world's commercial and industrial structure geared to a war basis. There was an urgent need for getting back to a peacetime economy, which meant the production of peacetime goods instead of munitions, the demobilization of millions of soldiers, and the absorption of these veterans into the business structure. But it was not easy to return to the prosperous and stable world economy that had been operating before 1914.

The conflict had brought about many changes in world trade. Europe in particular had suffered a serious decline in its share of the world's commerce because of war blockades, the reduction of consumer purchasing power, the loss of shipping and other transportation facilities, and the capture of overseas markets by the United States, Latin America, and Japan. This loss was felt keenly by Germany and Great Britain. Furthermore, the peace treaties had multiplied national boundaries, which soon became obstacles to the flow of goods.

Serious problems existed in the domestic economies of the European nations. As a result of the war, the public debts of the participant nations had zoomed. For example, between 1913 and 1918 Germany's national debt increased twenty times. In many nations these increases were accompanied by the circulation of large amounts of paper money, not backed by adequate reserves. Furthermore, the war left a legacy of tension between economic groups. Labor unions, which had registered significant gains in wages during the war, were determined not to give up their advantages when the fighting ceased.

For a brief period many of these economic problems were obscured by an artificial postwar boom. The peak of prosperity was reached in 1920, after which world trade and industrial activity diminished. Strikes, unemployment, and other industrial problems multiplied; and for the next five years the nations, particularly in Europe, tried to extricate themselves from this economic morass.

The inter-Allied debt problem. The most serious problem facing Europe as it strove to achieve a prosperous peace economy was the revolution in its financial position in relation to the remainder of the world. In 1914 the United States had been a debtor nation, mostly to Europe, for the amount of $3,750,-000,000. The war reversed the situation, and in 1919 the United States was owed more than $10,000,000,000 by its fellow victors. This tremendous debt posed what economists call the transfer problem. Such international obligations could only be paid by the actual transfer of gold or by the sale of goods to the creditor country. As payment in gold was impossible, the only alternative was for nations such as Britain and France to increase substantially their exports to the United States. But this, too, was a heavy strain.

The various Allied powers in Europe had lent each other funds, with Britain acting as the chief banker. When their credits had been used up, they had turned to the United States for financial help. Britain owed huge sums to the United States but because of its European debtors was still a net creditor of $4,500,-000. France, on the other hand, was a net debtor of $3,500,000,000. Some of the former Allies argued that the inter-Allied debts were political, that all of them had in effect been poured into a common pool for victory, and that, with victory, all should be canceled.

In the summer of 1922 Great Britain proposed that it collect no more from its debtors —Allies and Germany alike—than the United States collected from Britain itself. It was becoming manifest to British statesmen that Germany would not be able to meet its reparation payments, and without them the payment of the inter-Allied debts—especially the debts owed to the United States—would be extremely difficult, if not impossible, to make.

Although the American government insisted that there was no connection between the inter-Allied debts and German reparations, negotiations were carried on, and debt payment plans were set up with thirteen nations. No reductions were made in principal, but in numerous instances the rate of interest was decreased. The total amount to be paid came to more than $22,000,000,000.

Reparations exhaust Germany. The Allies had placed an impossibly heavy burden on Germany. In 1921 the reparations commission fixed the total German indemnities at $32,-000,000,000. The payments were apportioned among the various Allied nations, France being given 52 per cent and the British empire 22 per cent.

In August 1921 Germany made a payment of $250,000,000, which reacted disastrously upon the German currency system. With some justification the Germans believed that the reparations were impossibly high and that higher tariffs the world over were keeping out German goods. Furthermore, Germany had lost many of its most important economic resources. In 1922 some relief was granted Germany by the Allies, and Germany then asked them to extend this relief for two more years. The alarming economic conditions prevailing in central Europe and particularly in Germany caused Lloyd George to support this idea. The British were having economic difficulties of their own which they believed could not be overcome until prosperity was reëstablished in Germany.

The French, however, were outraged at Germany's request. They estimated that France had been spending $5700 a minute to restore its devastated regions and pay war pensions while Germany had been paying reparations at the rate of only $381 a minute. The French believed that Germany was able to pay and was deliberately seeking to escape its obligations. Raymond Poincaré, the French prime minister, feared that his country was in danger of losing the peace.

France invades the Ruhr. Indeed, the whole tenor of events since the signing of the armistice had shocked France in particular. The promise of military assistance from its former two main allies in case of aggression had been discarded; the League of Nations seemed a frail reed without America; and now while the United States insisted upon full payment of war debts, Germany seemed about to renege on reparations. Poincaré was determined that this should not happen.

Searching for a justification to employ force in compelling Germany to make the full reparations payments, Poincaré discovered that the Germans had not delivered to France the number of telegraph poles stipulated in the Treaty of Versailles. Germany was likewise in arrears in the matter of coal and cattle deliveries. These defaults were termed microscopic by the British, who impolitely referred to Poincaré as "Monsieur Shylock." Undeterred by British opposition, however, French, Belgian, and Italian troops marched into the Ruhr district of Germany in January 1923.

A sorry state of affairs ensued. The French were determined that the inhabitants should work the industries and mines of the Ruhr for the benefit of France. Defying the French army, the Germans went on a general strike. All economic life stopped, and many German officials were imprisoned by the French authorities. Nothing hardened the German resolve to revise the Treaty of Versailles more than this invasion of the Ruhr.

During the winter of 1923-1924, France endeavored to establish a separate state in the Rhineland which the Germans called a "revolver republic." Subsidized by the French, political agitators from all parts of Germany were shipped into the Ruhr and encouraged to carry on a separatist movement which, if successful, would create a buffer state between Germany and France.

The chaotic conditions in the Ruhr gave the *coup de grâce* to the German economic system. The currency failed completely. Inflation skyrocketed the mark into the stratosphere. In January 1923 one American dollar was worth 8695 marks; in November of the same year it took 6,666,666,666,667 marks to equal one dollar!

The French, meanwhile, were learning that they "could not dig German coal with French bayonets." Following Poincaré's fall from power in 1924, the French government offered to settle its difficulties with Germany, whose leaders were equally anxious to negotiate. Public opinion all over the world had been shocked at Poincaré's strong-arm tactics in the Ruhr, and Great Britain was particularly critical.

BURYING THE HATCHET

Change for the better. Midway in 1923 the prospect of a tranquil and cooperative world seemed far off indeed. France had invaded German territory; Britain and France were at swords' points; the United States remained outside the League; and our former Allies thought our debt policy abominable. But while not apparent to the harassed statesmen of the period, the worst of the war's aftermath had run its course. The Franco-British quarrel was patched up, Germany became a member of the League, the reparations problem was eased, and our former Allies paid their debt installments on schedule.

The French occupation of the Ruhr had proved that attempts to force Germany to pay reparations were futile. It was becoming more and more apparent that the difficulty lay in the staggering total of the reparations. Therefore, an international committee was set up under the chairmanship of the American banker Charles Dawes to examine the whole reparations problem. In the fall of 1924 the Dawes Plan came into operation. No figure was set for the total reparations bill, but the individual payments were decreased and extended over a longer period. A large loan also was floated to aid Germany's recovery and help stabilize its currency. The French cooperated by evacuating the Ruhr.

The Locarno Conference and conciliation. Apart from this encouraging move to solve the reparations problem, there was a spectacular improvement in international politics. Aristide Briand (1862-1932) came to the foreign office in France; Gustav Stresemann (1878-1929) held the same position in Germany; and in Great Britain foreign affairs were now handled by Sir Austen Chamberlain (1863-1937). All three men believed in pursuing a policy of conciliation in European affairs. Stresemann, bitter foe of France during the war, was now eager to try cooperating with his former enemies. For some time British statesmen had been deploring France's harsh attitude toward Germany, and Briand in Paris was now ready to offer the olive branch to Berlin.

"It is for peace that this hammer works." Hope for international disarmament and cooperation is reflected in this French cartoon, showing Briand smashing his guns, while Stresemann and Sir Austen Chamberlain wait their turn.

In 1925 Stresemann proposed that France, Germany, Great Britain, and Italy should guarantee the existing Franco-German and German-Belgian frontiers, that these four powers should agree to settle their differences by arbitration, and that Germany and its neighbors should conclude treaties of arbitration. This proposal paved the way for a conference held during October of the same year in the little Swiss town of Locarno. For the first time since 1919 the distinction between conquered and conqueror seemed forgotten; the German delegation was cordially received. Referring to previous conferences, a German statesman at Locarno said, "They treated us decently but never permitted us to forget that we were Huns."

After twelve days of negotiation, the delegates to the conference agreed on five treaties, the most important being a treaty of mutual guarantee. Signed by Germany, Great Britain, Belgium, France, and Italy, this agreement guaranteed the existing frontiers along the Rhine, thus reaffirming the provision in the Treaty of Versailles; provided for a demilitarized German zone extending fifty kilometers east of the Rhine; and pledged France, Germany, and Belgium not to invade or resort to war against each other except under certain specified conditions. In case of the violation of these pledges, the nations signing the treaty agreed to assist the injured party.

The Locarno Pact heralded a new era in European affairs. Germany accepted an invitation to join the League of Nations, and there were good grounds for believing that the hatreds of the past war were now on the wane. Referring to the *rapprochement* with Germany, Briand eloquently stated in the French Parliament:

It is undesirable to be continually casting doubts on Germany's goodwill. . . . Stresemann and I talked a new language, the language of Europe.[14]

Organization of the League of Nations. Before we discuss the successes and failures of the League of Nations in the postwar period, let us briefly sketch the outline of its organization. As specified by the Covenant, the League consisted of three principal divisions: the Assembly, the Council, and the Secretariat.

The Assembly, which held annual sessions in Geneva, contained representatives of every member state. Its duties included determining the budget of the League, admitting new members, electing the judges of the World Court in cooperation with the Council, and considering "any matter within the sphere of action of the League or affecting the peace of the world." The Assembly could not make any important decisions without the unanimous consent of its members, and every nation represented in the Assembly had one vote.

The Council was made up of permanent great powers and nonpermanent smaller members. The most important body in the League, it had the specific duties of encouraging disarmament, studying the annual reports submitted by the nations holding colonial mandates, and formulating measures to be taken to protect any state from aggression. The Council dealt with most of the emergencies arising in international affairs.

The Secretariat represented the civil service of the League. Numbering about seven hundred, the personnel of the Secretariat constituted the first example in history of an international civil service whose loyalty was pledged to no single nation but to the interests of all nations in common. All treaties made by members of the League had to be registered with the Secretariat; its fifteen departments had charge of the matters of administrative routine arising from the mandates and dealt with questions relating to disarmament, health problems, the protection of racial minorities, and any other problems, general or special, which the League was considering.

In addition to the Assembly, the Council, and the Secretariat, there were two other important bodies which derived from the Covenant of the League. The first of these was the Permanent Court of International Justice, commonly referred to as the World Court. Its main purpose was to "interpret any disputed point in international law and determine when treaty obligations had been violated." It was also competent to give advisory opinions to the Council or Assembly when asked for them. (By 1937 forty-one states had agreed to place before the World Court all the disputes to which they were a party concerning the interpretation of treaties, questions of international law, problems arising from breaches of international obligations, and the question of reparations arising from such breaches.)

The second international body affiliated with the League was the International Labor Organization. Pledged "to secure and maintain fair and humane conditions of labor for men, women, and children," this organization consisted of three divisions: a general conference, a governing body, and the International Labor Office.

League successes. The League system was not a sure-fire deterrent against aggression, especially if the aggressor was a great power. The teeth of the famous Article x of the Covenant had been removed by the view, pushed mainly by Canada, that while the Council could request members to use armed force against aggression, the final decision to do so must rest with each member.

The record of the League from 1920 to 1930 was one neither of dismal failure nor of complete triumph. One great handicap to the success of the League was the refusal of the United States to join the League. In attempting to prevent war, the League achieved some outstanding successes in certain international disputes and failed miserably in others. The Aland Islands affair can be cited as an example of the former.

Lying between Sweden and Finland and claimed by both countries, the Aland Islands dominate the entrance to the Gulf of Bothnia. The quarrel over ownership might have caused war, but the League stepped in. Its decision, given in 1921, was to permit Finland to retain sovereignty over the islands while the inhabitants, mostly Swedes, were to enjoy local self-government. The acceptance of this solution by both parties was a great step forward in the peaceable solution of international problems.

Many of the disputes presented to the League of Nations for settlement concerned boundary problems raised by the peace treaties. The League settled the boundary question between Poland and Germany in the Silesia area and in 1921 halted a serious frontier dispute between Yugoslavia and Albania. In 1924 a menacing quarrel between Turkey and Britain over rich oil deposits in Iraq was also mediated successfully.

The Corfu incident. In 1923 came the first important test of the new world organization —the Corfu incident, involving Italy and Greece. An international commission had been sent to the Balkans to settle the Graeco-Albanian boundary line. During its labors four Italian members of the commission were killed in Greek territory by unknown assailants. Mussolini, the dictator of Italy (see p. 472), immediately dispatched a stiff ultimatum to Greece. In the outrage he saw an opportunity to obtain national glory and a diplomatic triumph for his newborn Fascist regime. Greece refused to accept all the terms of the ultimatum and appealed to the League. Mussolini thereupon ordered a naval squadron to the Greek island of Corfu to bombard the harbor, and Italian marines landed and took possession of the port. Mussolini let it be known that Italy would refuse to be bound by any action taken by the League.

Confronted by this defiance on the part of a great power, the League sought to escape from a serious situation by turning the dispute over to a council of ambassadors. Without discovering the murderers, the council ordered Greece to pay Italy the sum of 50,000,-000 lire. This amount was duly paid, and the Italian forces evacuated Corfu. But though war had been averted, many members of the League Assembly suspected that the evidence obtained by the investigators did not warrant the imposition of such a large indemnity upon Greece. And the League had allowed Italy to defy it, a portent of failures to come.

Other League activities. The effectiveness of the League as a peace agency following the Great War is debatable, but certain of its activities deserve high praise. The League supervised the exchange and repatriation of nearly 500,000 prisoners of war. More than 1,000,000 Greek refugees, victimized by the Graeco-Turkish War of 1922 (see p. 499), were saved from starvation by the League. By 1928 the League had been instrumental in erecting 76,000 houses in Greece for the refugees and settling 143,000 families there. Greece floated several important loans with League assistance. The League also used its auspices to secure desperately needed financial aid for Austria, Bulgaria, Hungary, and the Free City of Danzig. Of importance also in assisting the economic reconstruction of war-worn Europe was the League's work in administering the region of the Saar Basin and the Free City of Danzig.

More successful than its work in the political field were the League's efforts in the fields of health, humanitarianism, and intellectual activity. The health organization at Geneva concerned itself with perfecting hygienic techniques to decrease epidemics in the various nations. Studies of the causes and control of such diseases as smallpox, anthrax, cancer, and tropical maladies were encouraged. The League also investigated the existence of slavery in certain sections of the world, sought to control the traffic in dangerous drugs, and stood ready to offer assistance when great disasters brought suffering and destruction to any portion of the world's population. It published books and periodicals dealing with national and international problems of all kinds and broadcast important information, particularly in the field of health, from its own radio station.

League efforts toward disarmament. The League encouraged world disarmament even though its efforts were seldom successful. In 1924 the Geneva Protocol was presented to the Assembly. It called upon the nations to agree to arbitration in all disputes, to regard any state resorting to war as an aggressor, and to participate in an international conference on disarmament. Unfortunately, the Protocol was not approved.

Article vii of the League's Covenant plainly stated that it was the intention of the members to reduce arms to the lowest point consistent with security. It further empowered the Council of the League to formulate plans for disarmament. Little or no progress was made, however, in reducing the heavy burden of armaments. Various bodies set in motion by the League to study the problem and arrive at accepted reductions only ran into interminable obstacles. Perhaps because of its relative military weakness at that time, Russia proposed complete disarmament to League members. This proposal did not get very far because the English delegates were suspicious of the Russian government's sincerity. When this Russian proposal was made, one of the delegates replied:

If Mr. Litvinov [the Russian member] promises not to be angry I'll narrate a fable. . . . A conference of the beasts once discussed the question of disarmament. The lion spoke first and looking at the eagle suggested the abolition of wings. The eagle turning to the bull asked for the suppression of horns. The bull in his turn regarded the tiger and demanded the elimination of claws. It remained for the bear to speak and he proposed total abolition of every means of attack and defense so that he might take them all into his loving embrace.[15]

Germany, in the meantime, became more and more rebellious. It had already been disarmed and was annoyed that its neighbors could not agree to reduce their armaments.

Naval disarmament. Progress in the direction of naval disarmament was a little more encouraging, although outside the jurisdiction of the League. Intense naval rivalry had developed between Britain, the United States, and Japan after 1919. In consequence, President Harding called a conference at Washington to try to assuage this rivalry and also to consider the problems of the Pacific.

The Washington Conference (1921-1922) was a dramatic event in international relations. Apparently without any warning, Secretary of State Charles Evans Hughes proposed that Great Britain, Japan, and the United States should between them scrap seventy-nine capital ships in such a way as to make the ratio of naval strength 5:5:3 (five units each for England and the United States and three units for Japan). To Italy and France were allotted ratios of 1.67. The powers agreed to a ten-year naval holiday for

capital ships and agreed further that no battleship was to be built unless it replaced a vessel twenty years old.

The Washington Conference registered a definite advance in naval disarmament. But though ships of the largest type were kept down to a reasonable limit, much was left undone. France refused to discuss the limitation of submarines, and no limit was placed upon the building of smaller naval units such as light cruisers and destroyers. Subsequent conferences held at Geneva (1927) and London (1930) registered little progress. In these conclaves, differences developed between Britain and the United States over their relative cruiser strength, and Japan gave evidence of irritation at the restraints agreed to at the Washington Conference.

Hopeful trends on the diplomatic front. Despite some discouragement in achieving a measure of disarmament, the years from 1925 to 1929 have been called Europe's diplomatic high period. In fact the whole world seemed to have embarked on a new era of international cooperation.

Though initiated outside the League, the Kellogg-Briand Pact seemed to be a triumph for peace and international good will. In 1927 the French prime minister, Briand, proposed that war be renounced or outlawed between France and the United States. Encouraged by several prominent Americans, he sent the draft of a treaty incorporating these ideas to Washington. Frank B. Kellogg, then secretary of state, persuaded Briand to extend the treaty to all the great powers. In 1928, after several months of negotiation, the representatives of fifteen states gathered at the Quai d'Orsay (the location of the French foreign office) to sign the pact. But while the Kellogg-Briand Pact provided for the renunciation of war as an instrument of national policy, there were no provisions for enforcing the agreement.

Other attempts to improve international relations included further corrections of some of the worst abuses in the World War I treaties. In the field of reparations, a new schedule of payments, known as the Young Plan, was agreed upon in 1930. The total amount to be paid was greatly scaled down. It was also agreed to evacuate Allied troops of occupation from the Rhineland five years in advance of the time stipulated by the Treaty of Versailles.

In addition to these encouraging signs, at the end of the 1920's there was a strong movement for European union. Various congresses were held, such as the one in Vienna in 1926; and Aristide Briand prepared a comprehensive memorandum for a European Federal Union.

It was with these promising events in the background that the League of Nations celebrated its tenth birthday in 1929. Speaking at Oxford about the first decade of the League, General Jan Smuts of South Africa, one of the world's most eminent statesmen and a founder of the international organization, declared:

Looked at in its true light, in the light of the age and of the time-honoured ideas and practice of mankind, we are beholding an amazing thing —we are witnessing one of the great miracles of history. . . . The League may be a difficult scheme to work, but the significant thing is that the Great Powers have pledged themselves to work it . . . [they have] bound themselves to what amounts in effect to a consultative parliament of the world. . . . The great choice is made, the great renunciation is over, and mankind has, as it were at one bound and in the short space of ten years, jumped from the old order to the new . . . [16]

SUMMARY

The period 1914 to 1929 is a brief segment of the story of world civilization, but it is difficult to find another period in modern times filled with so many significant events. Perhaps the nearest would be the event-packed era of the French Revolution. For all its horror and tragedy, World War I generated ambitious ideals for a better world. In particular, the war was responsible for the establishment of the first international organization on a global scale to resist aggression and encourage peaceful cooperation among nations. It is unfortunate that such plans for creating a world fit for heroes are not made during times of peace rather than as by-products of wars, for negotiations held during a postwar period are inevitably complicated by tensions, hostilities, and problems created or intensified by the conflict.

The five postwar years admirably illustrate this point. In 1919 a war-agonized world expected its sacrifices to be rewarded by better times. But for five years there was little but confusion and strife. The Germans balked at paying astronomical reparations, the French invaded the Ruhr, and chaotic inflation wiped out the stable middle class in Germany. Deprived of its hinterland, Austria —a head without a body—was saved from economic disaster only by the aid of the League of Nations. Many European nations were agitated by revolutions and civil wars. The old thrones of the Hohenzollerns, Hapsburgs, Romanovs, and Ottomans disappeared under the rising tide of republicanism.

From 1925 to 1929, however, the feuds and discontent in Europe gave way to peace, rising prosperity, and international cooperation. The League of Nations registered encouraging, if unspectacular, progress. Differences over war debts and reparations were resolved. Germany's status as a good neighbor was recognized in the Locarno Pact. There was a definite feeling that the worst was over, that the passions released by World War I had burned themselves out.

Unfortunately, these encouraging events— the Locarno agreements, faith in the League, and solution of the reparations and war debts problems—were not true auguries of the times. Adequate disarmament had not been achieved, the world economic recovery and prosperity that had been realized did not rest on sound foundations, and in Germany there festered deep wounds that would not heal without rectification of the injustices of Versailles. And despite the ideological legacy of World War I, expressed as "making the world safe for democracy," this political creed was about to be challenged by new antidemocratic and totalitarian regimes. The unsound and unhealthy condition of world economics plus the ambitions of these new modern tyrannies were to sweep away the hopes of the late 1920's and make the next decade one of the most tragic in all world history.

Out of the First World War and the decade of bitter disillusionment which followed, there emerged three powerful leaders whose ideologies were to threaten the existence of democracy. To Lenin, shown in the illustration on the left, force was the only instrument of change; ironically, his totalitarian Soviet regime, which he justified through his conviction that all government would eventually disappear, continued to grow in strength. At a time when Lenin had reached the apex of his authority, another totalitarian leader, Hitler, was only beginning his struggle for power. His first *Putsch* of 1923, planned at a meeting in a Munich beer hall (center), ended in his arrest and imprisonment for treason. In Italy in 1922, Mussolini, shown below with his officers at the time of the march on Rome, had just seized the reins of power. Confronted with the mobilization of Fascist troops, the monarch offered no resistance and invited Mussolini to form a government.

CHAPTER 15

Opposing Ways of Life

Introduction. The events of the early 1920's were to smash the assumption underlying many of the decisions made at Versailles—that Europe's political traditions and economic strength had survived the war without critical impairment. Since western society had moved forward to middle-class democracy and to unprecedented industrial growth and economic well-being after the previous struggle for Continental hegemony—namely, the Napoleonic Wars—why should it not surge forward after 1918? However widespread the belief in European recovery, the analogy was faulty in both its political and economic implications.

In the Europe that emerged from the First World War, the continuity of political tradition was disturbed. Three great imperial dynasties which had helped arbitrate the destinies of prewar Europe—the Romanovs in Russia, the Hohenzollerns in Germany, and the Hapsburgs in Austria-Hungary—had disappeared. With its Communist regime openly dedicated to the subversion of capitalism, Russia had in fact retreated beyond the pale of western society and was regarded as a pariah to be kept in isolation by a political and ideological *cordon sanitaire*. The treaty makers of Versailles plainly had no use for the Bolsheviks— an attitude fully reciprocated by the new masters of the Kremlin.

The second of the great empires—Germany— had been stripped of its overseas possessions and of much valuable territory within Europe itself; it had been saddled with a huge war indemnity; and, most important of all, it was made to bear the onus of war guilt. Instead of having a stake in the retention of the status quo, as was the case with defeated France after 1815, humiliated Germany appeared to have everything to gain from scrapping the Versailles blueprints for a postwar world. Nor could the disappearance of the Austro-Hungarian empire be counted as a factor for postwar stability. In remapping the former Hapsburg dominions, the statesmen at Versailles left potential danger spots in central and eastern Europe. The newly created democracies constituted a break with prewar political traditions; under conditions of postwar dislocation and hardship, their citizens were called upon to experiment with a form of government new to their experience.

In the economic sphere, prewar and postwar Europe presented no less striking contrasts. The prewar European industrial complex, which made possible a steady rise in living standards for an ever increasing population, rested on a number of factors: large overseas commerce and foreign investment, colonies that produced essential raw materials and served as markets for manufactured goods, and, within Europe itself, the maintenance of a well-developed transportation system and a constant flow of goods between nations. After the peace treaties went into effect and the wartime economic boom subsided, the prewar system of economic interdependence was replaced in many areas by economic nationalism, high tariff walls, and a new emphasis on self-sufficiency. In central Europe especially, where the large Austro-

Hungarian empire had permitted the free flow of goods over a wide area, there was now a multiplicity of nations, each of which was trying to sell its goods to its neighbors but closing its frontiers to imports. Such nationalism in the economic sphere was certain to fan the flames of political nationalism as well, and thereby create new areas of conflict.

Prior to the First World War, liberal democracy had stood in direct opposition to reactionary autocracy, itself on the wane in Europe before the surge of technology and mass education. Now, in the postwar era, the forces of democracy were confronted by dynamic new rivals, ideologies born of the extreme Left (communism) and extreme Right (fascism) but united in their denial of democratic values. The struggle for the minds and allegiances of men, as well as for the survival or destruction of traditional humanistic values, had taken a new and ominous turn.

As the title indicates, this chapter is the story of the growing competition of ideologies, a tragic tale set against a background of postwar depression and disillusionment and of cynical ruthlessness marching roughshod over apathy and defeatism. While the previous chapter carried the account of international relations up to the end of 1929, we shall concentrate now on the political, economic, and social forces operating within the western nations.

DICTATORSHIP OF THE PROLETARIAT IN RUSSIA

Prelude to revolution in Russia. In 1914 the supposedly all-powerful tsar of Russia, Nicholas II, was under the thumb of a small circle of courtiers. Most notorious of his advisers was Rasputin, who exercised a malignant influence over the tsarina because of his "miraculous" cures of her sickly son. When an army general complained about Rasputin, the tsar is reputed to have said that he would prefer five Rasputins to one hysterical woman.

Nicholas II showed little capacity for guiding his country. By ignoring the Duma, he weakened the new legislative body. In addition, he remained aloof from a series of pressing economic problems. Low wages and intolerable working conditions created discontent among the growing number of industrial workers, and strikes took place more and more frequently. The peasants were also dissatisfied; they wanted land reforms to break up large estates and to distribute agricultural returns more equitably.

The First World War exposed the inefficiency of the tsarist government. As early as 1915 it became apparent that the military machinery was badly disorganized. But the tsar brusquely refused the Duma's request for more power to rectify conditions. By the end of 1916 the situation within Russia became chaotic.

The revolution begins. On March 3, 1917, a strike occurred in a factory in St. Petersburg. Within a week nearly all the workers in the city were idle, and street fighting broke out. On March 11 the tsar dismissed the Duma and ordered the strikers to return to their jobs. These orders precipitated the revolution. The Duma refused to disband, the strikers held mass meetings in defiance of the government, and the army openly sided with the workers. A few days later a provisional government headed by the moderate liberal, Prince Lvov, was named by the Duma, and the following day the tsar abdicated. Thus far the revolution had been, on the whole, peaceful. Dominated by liberal middle-class representatives, the Duma hoped to achieve a political but not an economic revolution.

Meanwhile the Marxian socialists in St. Petersburg had formed a soviet (council) of workers' and soldiers' deputies to oppose the tsar. Determined that a thoroughgoing change should take place in accordance with Marxist teachings, the radical soviet bided its time and for a few months cooperated with the provisional government.

In July, Lvov resigned and was succeeded by Aleksandr Kerenski, who was more progressive than his predecessor but not radical enough for the Bolsheviks. While Kerenski's government marked time, the soviet in St. Petersburg extended its organization. All over the country local soviets were set up, and the Bolsheviks created effective propaganda under the slogan "Peace, Land, and Bread." Although they were assisted in part by funds from Germany, which hoped to weaken the Russian military effort, the driving force behind the Bolsheviks was Lenin, who in 1917 had been spirited out of exile in Switzerland by the German government and taken in a sealed railroad car to the Russian frontier.

Lenin's coup d'état. After many behind-the-scenes maneuvers, the soviets seized control of the government in November 1917, and Kerenski and his moderate provisional government were driven into exile. Lenin's coup d'état was an amazing feat. With audacity, careful organization, and astute propaganda, he had placed a party with a membership estimated at 30,000 in control of a nation of more than 170,000,000 people. At this period in his life, Lenin was described

by a young American journalist sympathetic to the Bolshevik cause:

A short, stocky figure, with a big head set down in his shoulders, bald and bulging. Little eyes, a snubbish nose, wide, generous mouth, and heavy chin; cleanshaven now, but already beginning to bristle with the well-known beard of his past and future. Dressed in shabby clothes, his trousers much too long for him. Unimpressive, to be the idol of a mob, loved and revered as perhaps few leaders in history have been. A strange popular leader—a leader purely by virtue of intellect; colourless, humourless, uncompromising and detached, without picturesque idiosyncracies—but with the power of explaining profound ideas in simple terms.[1]

Lenin did not become a national hero overnight, however. In the free elections held to form a constituent assembly to frame a constitution, he and his followers were chagrined to receive just under 25 per cent of the votes. When the assembly, which met in January 1918, refused to become a rubber stamp of the Bolsheviks, it was dissolved by the bayonets of Lenin's troops, the newly organized Red Army. It was Russia's last free parliament.

The Communist fight for survival. The worst was yet to come in Russia. A powerful group of counterrevolutionaries termed White Russians began to make war on the Communists, and the Allied powers sent troops to Russia to keep Allied munitions from falling into German hands. Lenin had repeatedly declared that the World War was an imperialist conflict between bourgeois interests, and the Allies were aware that the Bolsheviks had agreed to negotiate a separate peace with Germany. Thus they felt it imperative to aid the White Russians, who were eager to continue the war against the Central Powers. At first the White Russians scored substantial successes. The fortunes of Lenin and the Bolsheviks hit a low point after they were forced in March 1918 to sign the harsh Treaty of Brest Litovsk with Germany.

Within Russia a ghastly reign of terror began as the Red Army and the Cheka (the secret police) destroyed all enemies of the revolution as well as those who were only lukewarm in their support of communism.

A Communist poster from the days of the Russian civil war of 1918-1920 calls for the triumph of Bolshevik forces over the counterrevolutionary army led by Denikin during the struggle for the Donets Basin, one of the main coal-producing and industrial areas in Russia. The poster read: "The Donets coal must be ours! When there is no coal—the factories are shut. When there is no coal—the trains stop. Until the Don is ours —hunger is with us. Victory over the Denikin bands—victory over the hunger."

The royal family, under arrest since the outbreak of the revolution, was made to pay for all the years of cruel and inept Romanov rule. In July 1918 they were herded into a cellar and shot. By 1920 all White Russian resistance had been crushed, the foreign armies had been evacuated, and about one million White Russian anti-Communist refugees were scattered over the earth.

What were the reasons for the Communist victory? After the surrender of the Central Powers in November 1918, there was no compelling reason for continued Allied intervention in Russia; the withdrawal of British and American troops made it possible for the Bolsheviks to concentrate their energies against the White Russians. Strategically, the Bolsheviks had a central position, the best for maneuver and counterattack. In addition, there were such factors of success as the fanatical, do-or-die spirit of Lenin and his followers, the resentment against foreign intervention, and the lack of appeal of the White Russian movement, which sponsored no program of land and social reform.

Triumph of Marxism in Russia. We have discussed the events which led to the overthrow of the Romanov dynasty. Now let us look for more basic reasons why Marxist socialism had managed to capture the Kremlin.

Ironically enough, Marx himself had despised the Russians. He had prophesied that his doctrines would take root in the most advanced industrial capitalist economies, in England or in Germany, where, he argued, the progressive degradation of the industrial proletariat would fan the flames of revolution. He had not foreseen his system of socialism first coming to power in a feudal, agrarian society like Russia's, in which industrialism had been introduced late in the nineteenth century against a background of labor exploitation, underground conspiracy, and police suppression. Because there existed no sufficiently strong middle class to provide a social soil in which liberal-democratic values could grow, to some political reformers of the day violence appeared necessary in order to achieve a new social order, and Marxism—an importation dedicated to violence—seemed ideally suited to flourish in Russia.

Lenin's contribution to Marxist thought. At the famous Russian Social Democratic congress held in 1903 at Brussels (see p. 384), Lenin not only made an important contribution to Marxist theory but also set the pattern by which socialism in Russia would henceforth be guided. Opposing all democratic parliamentary procedures, such as an officially recognized opposition party, he believed that the new order should be established by a revolutionary "dictatorship of the proletariat" under Bolshevik leadership. The opposition group, the Mensheviks, charged that Lenin was confusing the dictatorship *of* the proletariat with dictatorship *over* the proletariat, while they in turn were accused of having capitulated to gradualism by adopting a revisionist program. The Bolshevik-Menshevik feud continued until the Revolution of 1917. During that time, both groups agreed that the socialist revolution could be consummated in Russia only as part of a general uprising of the proletariat throughout Europe.

As a Marxist, Lenin accepted the two-revolutions sequence—that is, that the proletarian-socialist revolution must be preceded by a bourgeois-democratic revolution. The toppling of the tsarist regime in March 1917 and its replacement by a provisional government made up of moderates and liberals was interpreted by Lenin as the first or bourgeois-democratic revolution in the Marxist sequence. His coup d'état in November 1917 engineered the second or proletarian-socialist revolution. Lenin justified the dissolving of the constituent assembly on the grounds that, while such an assembly represented the highest form of the democratic principle in a bourgeois society, a still higher form of the democratic principle had now been achieved which rendered a constituent assembly superfluous: the proletarian-socialist revolution had vested all power in the Russian republic in the people themselves, as expressed in their revolutionary committees or soviets. With the dissolution of the constituent assembly, all vestiges of bourgeois democracy in Russia were removed. Moreover, this decisive step sealed the fate of the Mensheviks.

The state: theory and practice. Many orthodox Marxists believed that once the dictatorship of the proletariat had liquidated the bourgeoisie, the way would be open for the progressive disappearance of the state and the abolition of the standing army and the bureaucracy, the two most characteristic institutions of the centralized bourgeois state. While Lenin thought that the state would eventually wither away, at the same time he believed that during the dictatorship of the proletariat the latter's power must be wielded by an "iron party" (the Bolsheviks). Ironically enough, the events which transpired between his coup d'état in 1917 and his death seven years later served not to weaken but to strengthen the role of the state in Russia.

In this period three major developments relating to the Communist party took place. First, all other parties were eliminated. Second, the function of the Communist party was modified. No longer charged with the overthrow of existing institutions, the party now became the controlling element within the new governmental machinery of the state; the concentration of authority and power in the party was justified as "democratic centralism." Third, within the party itself authority was consolidated in the hands of a small elite group, the Politburo, which was composed of five members with Lenin as the chairman. The second major organ of government was the Secretariat for the Central Committee of the party.

The state was known as the Russian Socialist Federated Soviet Republic (R.S.F.S.R.). As the power of this government grew and the anti-Bolshevik forces were repelled, the jurisdiction of the R.S.F.S.R. expanded. In 1922 the Union of Soviet Socialist Republics (U.S.S.R.) was established, consisting of four constituent socialist republics: the original R.S.F.S.R., the Ukraine, White Russia, and Transcaucasia.

The constitution, adopted in 1924, established a federal system of government based on a succession of soviets which were set up in the villages, factories, and cities and in larger regions. This pyramid of soviets in each constituent republic culminated in the All-Union Congress of Soviets, which was at the apex of the federal government. But while it appeared that the congress exercised sovereign power, this body was actually governed by the Communist party, which in turn was controlled by the Politburo. So great did the authority of the Communist party become over the formation and administration of policy that before Lenin's death in 1924 it could be said without exaggeration that party and state were one. Consequently, whoever controlled the former must be master of the latter as well.

The period of war communism. One of Lenin's central beliefs was equalitarianism. He championed the program of "from each according to his ability; to each according to his needs" and believed in the principle of "maximum income," by which no state employee would receive a salary higher than a qualified worker. Following both Marx and Engels, Lenin subscribed to the ultimate goal of large-scale collective farming and the elimination of private ownership of land.

The period from the consolidation of the Bolshevik Revolution in 1918 until 1921 is known as the period of war communism, when the Bolsheviks sought to apply undiluted Marxist principles to the Soviet economy. Banks, railroads, and shipping were nationalized; the money economy was restricted; and private property was abolished.

Strong opposition to this program soon developed. The peasants wanted cash payments for their products and resented having to surrender their surplus grain to the government. Many laborers grumbled at being conscripted to work in the factories, and former business managers showed little enthusiasm for administering enterprises for the benefit of the state. This period was also a time of civil war, when the White Russians, aided by the Allies, were attempting the overthrow of the Communist regime.

The early months of 1920 brought the most dangerous crisis yet faced by the government. The years of civil strife had left Russia in a state of confusion and disruption. Total industrial production had been reduced to 13 per cent of what it had been in 1913. Added to the misery caused by wartime dislocations and the shortages caused by inept or wasteful management in the recently nationalized industries was the suffering that followed the crop failures of 1920. Famine marched over the land, bringing more than twenty million people face to face with starvation. A British writer who visited St. Petersburg (Leningrad) in 1920 reported that the city was:

. . . an astonishing spectacle of desolation. . . . Nothing had been repaired for four years. There were great holes in the streets where the surface had fallen into the broken drains; lampposts lay as they had fallen; not a shop was open, and most were boarded up over their broken windows. The scanty drift of people in the streets wore shabby and incongruous clothing, for there were no new clothes in Russia, no new boots. Many people wore bast wrappings on their feet. People, city, everything were shabby and threadbare. Even the Bolshevik commissars had scrubby chins, for razors and such-like things were neither being made nor imported. The death-rate was enormous, and the population of this doomed city was falling by the hundred thousand every year.[2]

In 1921 large stocks of food were sent to Russia, chiefly by Britain, France, and the United States.

Symbol of a rising discontent was the serious naval mutiny at Kronstadt, which broke out in March 1921. The rebels demanded the summoning of a new constituent assembly. Although the mutiny was crushed, its significance was not lost on the Soviet leaders. In the meantime, in 1920, the Poles had invaded Russia and taken Kiev. Driven back to Warsaw, they counterattacked with the aid of French troops, and in 1921 Poland annexed a large slice of Russian territory. During these turbulent postwar years, other areas of Russia were chopped off to form independent states —Finland, Estonia, Latvia, and Lithuania. While the outside world awaited the disintegration of history's first experiment with Marxist rule, Lenin remained indomitable.

The NEP. Confronted with the collapse of the nation, Lenin beat a strategic retreat in spite of strenuous opposition from his colleagues. He felt that the new regime had run into difficulties because it had been too eager to change everything at once. A return to certain practices of the capitalistic system was recommended, and the NEP, or New Economic Policy, was inaugurated.

The retreat from war communism operated from 1921 to 1928. The peasants were freed from the onerous wholesale levies of grain; after paying a fixed governmental tax, they were allowed to sell their surplus produce in open market. Factories employing less than twenty men were returned to private management, and a graduated wage scale was granted to the workers in the state industries. Commerce was stimulated by permitting private retail trading. Although simon-pure Communists criticized the wealthy peasants or *kulaks* who benefited from the new order of things and dubbed the private businessmen "Nepmen," such compromises proved highly beneficial and the economy revived.

The NEP was designed as only a temporary strategic retreat from the former outright socialist system and was not, as opponents of the regime in the West tended to interpret it, the first step in a return to democratic economic principles. The state continued to be responsible for banking, transportation, heavy industry, and public utilities. The government encouraged corporations from the United States and other foreign lands to erect plants in the Soviet Union. Young Russian technicians were trained to run the plants after the foreigners had returned home. So great was Lenin's zeal for building hydroelectric installations that he has often been quoted as declaring: "Communism is Soviet rule plus electrification."

The NEP was Lenin's last outstanding achievement. In spite of broken health, he worked unceasingly until his death in January 1924. His tomb in Moscow's Red Square is a Mecca for thousands of followers who come to pay homage to the creator of the first Marxist state in history.

Stalin vs. Trotsky: the peasant and the professor. Upon the death of the one man in the party who had possessed unchallenged authority and whose decrees were binding, a struggle for power broke out, and conflicts of policy and personality appeared. Should the quasi-socialistic NEP, which seemed to be working well, be retained or modified? Should party discipline be relaxed from the iron controls introduced by Lenin? Should Russian Communists concentrate on making a success of Marxist principles at home, or should they launch a major effort to overthrow capitalism the world over?

Two rivals who took different sides on most of these issues were Trotsky and Stalin. Leon Trotsky (1879-1940), whose real name was Bronstein, had turned to Marxism in his early youth. Like Lenin, he had known exile, having been sent to Siberia for radical activities within a year after he left the University of Odessa. In 1902 he escaped and, with a forged passport and a new name, set off to join Lenin, who had left Switzerland for London. During the revolution, Trotsky had come to the forefront. He was a magnificent orator; and by his personal magnetism and his demonic

energy, he had led the Red Army to victory. A theorist and scholar, this intellectual, professor-like leader had personal defects of arrogance and egotism which contrasted with the peasant shrewdness and cunning of his less colorful but more calculating rival.

Stalin, born Joseph Dzugashvili in 1879 in the Georgian region of Transcaucasia, was the son of a poor shoemaker. Admitted to a seminary to be trained for the priesthood, young Stalin was later expelled for radical opinions. Before the revolution, he engaged in much activity in the underground and was sent into exile four times. In 1922 *Pravda* carried a brief announcement that the Central Committee had confirmed Stalin as general secretary of the Secretariat—a decision that was to have momentous consequences after Lenin's death.

A firm tenet of Marxist ideology and one which Lenin had shared was that the successful establishment of socialism in Russia must entail the triumph of a world-wide proletarian revolution. Trotsky also believed that the U.S.S.R. could not maintain itself indefinitely as a socialist island in a capitalist ocean and that it was therefore the duty of the Russian Communists to foster revolution elsewhere. Stalin, less the theorist than the political realist, viewed Trotsky's ideas of world revolution as premature. He noted that, outside of Russia, Marxism had made little headway, despite the existence of what from the Marxist standpoint were the most advantageous circumstances for revolution. The impoverished and war-disillusioned workers of Germany had not turned against the bourgeoisie, while in Italy socialist opposition had been crushed by Mussolini. Stalin advocated a new policy, which was to become known as "building up socialism in a single state."

In the struggle that ensued, Trotsky had the initial advantage of being one of the chief architects of the revolution and (second to Lenin) the best-known Bolshevik in the Soviet Union. With his outstanding record and his mastery of ideological analysis, Trotsky not unnaturally expected to assume Lenin's mantle of leadership. But he reckoned without the political astuteness of Stalin, who had obtained a key administrative post in the party

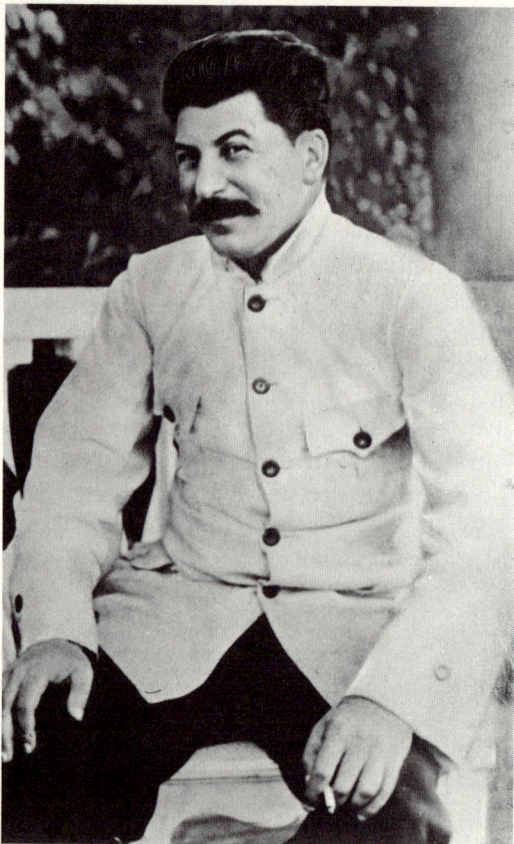

In 1922, when this photo was made, Stalin gained the powerful post of general secretary of the Communist party. Unlike his rival Trotsky, Stalin believed that socialism must first be perfected in Russia, thus making the country invulnerable to attack and demonstrating the superiority of the Communist system.

apparatus. Quietly and systematically, Stalin proceeded to shunt his rival aside. He placed his supporters in important posts in the government, assumed the powerful chairmanship of the Politburo, and by 1927 had brought about the expulsion of Trotsky and his followers from the party. Trotsky was exiled and led a hare-and-hound existence until 1940, when he was struck down by the ax of an assassin in Mexico.

With a well-organized governmental structure and an obedient bureaucracy and with the Trotskyites either exiled or rendered powerless, Stalin was ready by 1928 to put a daring new program into operation. The NEP was to be scrapped and replaced by a Five-Year Plan, which called for a highly ambitious program of heavy industrialization and the collectivization of agriculture. In spite of breakdowns and failures and mainly because of the heroic sacrifices of the common people, the first Five-Year Plan achieved amazing results (see Chapter 17). Russia, an inert sleeping giant before 1914, now became industrialized at an unbelievable speed, far surpassing Germany's pace of industrialization in the nineteenth century and Japan's early in the twentieth. It is important to stress also that the heavy burden of sacrifices necessary to the launching of the plan could never have been imposed had not Stalin been able to make a patriotic appeal to the people as Russians. The leaders of the Kremlin assiduously developed the cult of "Communist nationalism." Such an unlikely phrase would have sounded self-contradictory to Marx and probably also to Lenin, but the fact remained that Stalin managed to combine the two historic ingredients of nationalism and socialism in the ideological test tube to create a new, a Stalinist brand of communism.

Changes in Soviet society. While the Russian economy was being transformed, the social life of the people underwent equally drastic changes. From the beginning of the revolution, the government attempted to weaken the importance of the family. A divorce required no court procedure; and to make women completely free of the responsibilities of childbearing, abortion was made legal. The policy of "emancipating" women had the practical objective of increasing the labor market. Girls were encouraged to secure an education and pursue a career in the factory or the office. For the care of small children, communal nurseries were set up; and efforts were made to shift the center of the people's social life from the home to educational and recreational groups, the soviet clubs.

Most observers in the 1920's credited the regime with abandoning the tsarist policy of persecuting national minorities in favor of a policy of tolerance toward the more than two hundred minority groups in the Soviet Union. Another feature of the regime that received praise was the extension of medical services. Campaigns were carried out against typhus, cholera, and malaria; the number of doctors was increased as rapidly as facilities and training would permit; and death and infant mortality rates steadily decreased.

Coming under heavy fire in the West, however, were the Communist policies toward education and religion. Although education was made available to millions of children, the primary purpose of the school system was to indoctrinate the pupils with Communist precepts and values. Religious leaders were persecuted, and many of the most active were sentenced to concentration camps. Members of the party were forbidden to attend divine services. The Church was shorn of its powers over education, religious teaching was prohibited except in the home, and antireligious instruction was stressed in the schools. Although the intensive campaign against religion was considered by many as a reaction against the Orthodox Church's role as a tool of the tsars, the basic explanation lies in the materialistic Marxist denial of God and Marxism's refusal to allow the individual the right to possess a loyalty above that accorded to the state.

Foreign relations in the 1920's. During the decade and a half following the Russian Revolution, the Soviet Union was not considered a member in good standing in the family of nations. From the beginning of the revolution, relations between the western democracies and the new Soviet regime had been cool. The Communists resented the West's support of the White Russians. For their part, the Allies were aroused over the separate peace Lenin made with Germany, the seizure of foreign property in Russia, and the repudiation of all foreign debts.

In an unpleasant position as a pariah nation and at the same time weak in armaments, Russia endeavored to break its diplomatic isolation and to seek friends. In 1922 it negotiated the Treaty of Rapallo with Germany, and during the next few years nonaggression pacts were negotiated with Turkey, Iran, Afghanistan, and Lithuania.

Probably the greatest barrier to friendship (or at least mutual tolerance) between the West and Soviet Russia was the Third Communist International, or Comintern, organized in 1919 and dedicated to the overthrow

When this photo was taken, Trotsky was still a powerful force in the Communist party; as commissar of war, he had welded the disorganized Bolshevik forces into an efficient fighting machine. Yet because of his bitter opposition to Stalin, whom he accused of placing personal ambition above the cause of world revolution, he lost his power and in 1927 was expelled from the party.

of capitalism the world over. Specific aims of the organization were to disseminate Communist propaganda, to establish Communist parties in all the important nations of the world, and to secure control of labor unions and other working-class groups wherever possible. In the 1920's the Comintern encouraged the organization of Communist parties by radicals who had broken off from moderate socialist groups all over the world. Communists of all countries became members of the Comintern, meeting in congresses held in Moscow and setting up committees to coordinate their activities. Thus the Communist party became basically different from all national political groups; all Communists owed their allegiance to an international organization rather than to the nations in which they resided.

Another basic aim of the Comintern was to undermine colonialism. As we have seen earlier (see p. 283), Lenin's anti-imperialist beliefs were given wide publicity. Not so well known, however, was his idea that communism could conquer Europe and America by gaining control of Asia. He is reported to have once stated that London and New York could be conquered on the Yangtze.

RISE OF FASCISM IN ITALY

Problems in postwar Italy. Since unification in 1871, Italy had been outmaneuvered by stronger European powers, defeated even by the backward Ethiopians, and left with only the crumbs of the banquet as Africa was gobbled up by rival imperialistic powers. In World War I the Italian armies had been badly mauled by their enemies, and Italy emerged from the peace conference a victor with only modest gains.

The First World War aggravated the weaknesses of the Italian economy. The lira fell to a third of its prewar value, unemployment rose, and severe food shortages developed. People refused to pay their rent, strikes broke out in industrial centers, and workers seized factories. Italy's economic plight invited agitation by extremists from both Right and Left.

D'Annunzio and Fiume. One of the most flamboyant right-wing nationalists was the poet Gabriele D'Annunzio (1863-1938), who despite middle age had volunteered for duty in the war and had served as an aviator. In September 1919, he and his followers seized Fiume, a city on the Adriatic whose status had not yet been agreed upon by the diplomats at Versailles. Carried off with a minimum of struggle and a maximum of histrionics, the seizure of Fiume enabled D'Annunzio to act as *duce*, or leader, of the city for fifteen months. D'Annunzio caught the attention of the populace by fiery orations from balconies, by decking himself and his followers in black shirts to give them a distinctive appearance, and by extending his right arm in a salute reminiscent of that used by the ancient Romans.

The peaceful settlement of the Fiume question in 1920 by Italy and Yugoslavia left

D'Annunzio without a balcony to stand on, and the discomfited leader retired to his Italian estate. But his symbols of authority and many of his followers were taken over by a fellow *duce* who was already working out plans for turning the whole of Italy into a totalitarian state.

Mussolini and the birth of Fascism. Within four years following the armistice in Italy, five incompetent premiers came and went. The situation seemed propitious for the appearance of a strong leader on the political stage. When he appeared, he was the jutting-jawed son of a blacksmith named Mussolini, and he bore the Christian name of Benito in honor of the Mexican revolutionary hero Benito Juárez.

Born in northern Italy, Benito Mussolini (1883-1945) had grown up in left-wing circles. Although he became editor in 1912 of the influential Italian socialist newspaper *Avanti (Forward)*, he was far from consistent as regards his belief in socialism and its doctrinal opposition to "capitalistic" wars. When a majority in the Italian Socialist party called for neutrality in World War I, Mussolini urged intervention. In his own words:

I saw that Internationalism was crumbling. The unit of loyalty was too large . . . how utterly foolish was the idea that, even if a Socialist State were created, the old barriers of race and historical contentions would not go on causing wars.[3]

Avanti was taken out of his control, and he was expelled from the Socialist party. Undaunted, he founded his own paper, *Il Popolo d'Italia (The People of Italy)*, in which he continued to advocate Italian intervention in the war on the side of the Allies. As part of his campaign for Italian participation in the war, he organized formerly leftist youths into bands called *fasci*, a name derived from the Latin *fasces*, the bundle of rods bound about an ax which was the symbol of authority in ancient Rome. When Italy entered the war, Mussolini volunteered for the army, saw active service at the front, and was wounded. After his return to civilian life, he reorganized the *fasci* into the *fasci di combattimento* (fighting groups) to attract war veterans. The

Peter Blume's "The Eternal City" represents a young American artist's impressions of Italy ten years after Mussolini's march on Rome. A terrifying but flimsy jack-in-the-box of a Mussolini dominates a city of apathetic people living among the ruins of the past. But out of this nightmare emerges hope for the future; in the background, people climb out of the darkness into the sunlit forum, where others are already attempting to drag their Fascist masters from their mounts.

ultimate purpose of these groups was to capture the control of the national government.

The march on Rome. In the elections of 1919, the socialists capitalized on mass unemployment and hardship to emerge as the strongest party. Although the Fascists failed to elect a single candidate to the Chamber of Deputies, they succeeded in obtaining both approval and financial aid from industrial and landowning groups fearful of the triumph of Marxist socialism in Italy. Mussolini's black-shirted toughs broke up strikes and workers' demonstrations and, by beatings and overdoses of castor oil, "persuaded" political opponents of the error of their views. The central government remained virtually impotent during these outbreaks of violence.

Elections held in May 1921 resulted in a plurality for the liberal and democratic parties. A few Communists were elected to the Chamber of Deputies, and only thirty-five Fascists, among them Mussolini. But the latter had no intention of allowing the country a chance to achieve economic recovery and political stability by following a liberal-democratic course. In November he established the National Fascist party.

The year 1922 saw events conspire to favor Mussolini's bid for power. The liberal-democratic government of the day was ineffective, and the socialists were divided among themselves, while the ranks of the Fascists had been strengthened by the enrollment of thousands of disaffected bourgeoisie, cynical and opportunistic intellectuals, and depression-weary workers. The general strike called in August by the trade unions in order to arouse the country to the menace of Fascism was smashed. On October 24 a huge crowd attending a Fascist rally at Naples shouted "On to Rome!" When some fifty thousand Fascist militiamen swarmed into the capital, King Victor Emmanuel III invited Mussolini to form a new government.

Mussolini organizes the Fascist state. Mussolini's first act as prime minister was the passage in 1923 of an enabling law which gave him dictatorial powers. By this means Mussolini acquired a temporary "legal" right to govern without democratic procedure. He quickly used his newly acquired power to dissolve all other political parties and thus completely eliminate opposition to his regime. The Fascist party was now in a position to recast the entire governmental apparatus.

The Fascist state was ruled by an elite in the party, which ruthlessly crushed all free expression and banished critics of the regime to penal settlements on islands off the southern Italian coast. Censorship of the press was established, and a tribunal for defense of the state was set up to punish any individuals not conforming to Fascist practices. As Mussolini described his philosophy:

Fascism is a unit; it cannot have varying tendencies and trends, as it cannot have two leaders on any one level of organization. There is a hierarchy; the foundation is the Black Shirts and on the summit the Chief, who is only one.[4]

Parliamentary institutions of the pre-Fascist era were not destroyed overnight, however. The Senate continued to exist, even though completely dominated by Fascists; the Chamber of Deputies withered on the vine until the 1930's, when it was replaced by the Chamber of Fasces and Corporations. Meanwhile, all real power in the new state had been vested in the Fascist Grand Council, headed by Mussolini. The members of the council occupied the government's ministerial posts; in fact, at one time Mussolini himself held no less than eight offices. During 1925 and 1926 the Italian cities were deprived of self-government. With all units of local and provincial government welded into a unified structure dominated from Rome, the Fascist administrative system constituted the ultracentralization of government.

In 1929 Mussolini negotiated the Lateran Treaty with representatives of the Roman Catholic Church. By the terms of this agreement, Roman Catholicism was recognized as the state religion in Italy; and Vatican City, a new state of 108 acres located in Rome itself, was declared fully sovereign and independent. Thus, the long-standing controversy concerning the relationship of Church and state in Italy, was settled amicably.

Economic goals of Fascist Italy. Mussolini based his views of economics on the ideas of Sorel and the syndicalists (see p. 406), who believed that industrial unions should be the cells of society and that a confederation of these unions, or syndicates, should constitute the governing body of the state. Economically, Italy was divided into thirteen syndicates, all controlled by the government: six were formed from the ranks of labor, an equal number represented capital or management, and a thirteenth syndicate was established for the professions.

One of Fascism's chief economic objectives was to make Italy as self-sufficient as possible —a policy known as autarky; this aim was motivated primarily by military ambitions. As Mussolini declared:

We must secure in the shortest possible time the maximum degree of economic independence for the nation . . . This plan is dominated by one premise—the inevitability of war.[5]

In achieving this goal, much was accomplished, though often at a ruinous cost. Many projects were launched to provide for a home supply of materials which could be obtained much more cheaply from other nations.

Fascism's glorification of the state and war. The concept of the "inevitability" of war, added to the exaltation of the state and of its "destiny," created a supernationalism whose adherents tended to interpret the right of self-determination in terms of the expansion of the Fascist state at the expense of other nations. As we saw in Chapter 14, a foretaste of Mussolini's contempt for peace and his defiance of the League of Nations soon became apparent when he humiliated Greece in 1923 by the bombardment of Corfu. Mussolini warned the world that Italy intended to expand or explode, and his encouragement of a high birth rate in conjunction with meager territorial and natural resources pointed in only one direction—imperialism.

Fascism has been defined as "the cult of state worship." In the Italian totalitarian state the individual had no significance except as a member of the state. The Fascists were taught "to believe, to obey, and to fight" (*credere, obbedire, combattere*). Fascist ideology governed the educational system. The first sentence pronounced by children at school was "Let us salute the flag in the Roman fashion; hail to Italy; hail to Mussolini." Textbooks emphasized the glorious past of the ancient Romans, the limitations imposed upon the present inhabitants by geography and western "plutocratic" nations, and the imperial destiny that awaited Italy's future development.

Mussolini provided the trappings of greatness while he talked of acquiring the substance. The ruins of imperial Rome were revered at the same time that new, ostentatious monuments, buildings, and official sculptures were erected. All public functions and displays of the state were clothed in propaganda, from the dedication of farmland salvaged from ancient swamps to the regime's vulgar displays of military might and its gigantic sports rallies.

To the casual foreign observer, Italy seemed rejuvenated. The Italian trains, whose schedules had long been notoriously erratic, now ran on time. Restless activity was something new on the Italian scene, and a few concrete achievements were widely touted. The cost was not so readily apparent; the fundamental inefficiency and weakness of the Fascist government would not be exposed for twenty years.

WEIMAR DEMOCRACY:

THE REPUBLIC THAT FAILED

Revolution in Germany. Near the close of World War I, Woodrow Wilson had made it clear that the Allies would not enter into peace negotiations with the imperial government of the Hohenzollerns. By November

In Mussolini's Italy, the worship of war and of the state was instilled even in small children through military training units.

1918, sick of the war and its privations, the German people were ready to do anything to bring the conflict to an end. The revolution that caused the kaiser to pack his bags and escape to Holland began in the fleet. News of the revolt flashed like lightning through Germany, and the authority of the old government crumbled. On the same day that the chancellor turned over his authority to Friedrich Ebert—the leader of the majority socialist party, the Social Democrats—the republic was officially proclaimed.

The collapse of the imperial government provoked vigorous disagreement over the type of administration that was to replace it. The Communists wanted a complete social revolution as well as a political revolution, while Ebert's Social Democrats favored a democratic system in which the rights of private property would be safeguarded. In December 1918 and January 1919, the moderates and the radicals clashed violently; the Communists in Berlin were scattered and their leaders murdered. In a national election held to select a constitutional convention, the parties stressing moderation were triumphant, with the Social Democrats securing the most votes. The German revolution was to be democratic and bourgeois.

Problems of the Weimar Republic. The new constitution was adopted in midsummer of 1919 at Weimar, famous as the residence of Germany's greatest poet, Goethe. It provided for a president, a chancellor who was responsible to the Reichstag, and national referendums. The rights of labor were guaranteed, personal liberties were safeguarded, and compulsory education was planned for everyone up to the age of eighteen.

The functioning of parliamentary government in the Weimar Republic exhibited certain basic weaknesses, however. The principle of proportional representation was carried so far that innumerable separate parties arose, and only the formation of coalitions enabled the government to function. The democratic elements were too diverse to follow a consistent policy. Moreover, the constitution included a provision that authorized the president to promulgate emergency decrees of his own in the event of threats of disorder. Placed in the all-too-familiar situation of being unable to muster sufficient votes for its program among a multiplicity of parties, the government was tempted to employ this constitutional provision and to enact measures by means of presidential decree. By weakening the legislative process, such actions were bound to help discredit the parliamentary government in Germany and to provide ammunition for its enemies.

In spite of difficulties and the opposition of Communists and monarchists, the Weimar Republic managed to restore political stability to Germany and to face serious financial problems. (The problem of the heavy reparations required of Germany at Versailles was discussed in Chapter 14). In 1923, when French and Belgian troops occupied the Ruhr, the wild inflation of the mark wiped out middle-class savings, and political moderates gradually lost their influence to ultranationalists and reactionaries. But after the French withdrew and the Dawes Plan enabled Germany to meet its schedule of reparation payments and to obtain large loans from abroad, the German economy took a turn for the better, and Germany from 1925 to 1929 enjoyed economic prosperity. Large public works projects were undertaken, industry was expanded, and Germany became the second largest industrial nation in the world. But there were disturbing forces at work.

Factors favoring the growth of dictatorship. Germany in the late 1920's was a compound of numerous ingredients, many of which had been in existence for at least a century. With Prussia as their model, such men as Hegel and Treitschke had exalted the state at the expense of the individual; and the government of the kaisers had established a strong edifice of despotism. Lack of experience in working the machinery of democratic government made the success of the Weimar Republic doubtful from the start.

Other difficulties threatening the new government stemmed from the resentments and frustrations engendered among the people by defeat in war. The powerful Prussian militaristic clique fanned the flames of discontent by fostering the legend that the German army had not been defeated on the field of battle but had been stabbed in the back by pacifist liberals and "decadent" democrats on the home front. The legend of the betrayal of the Fatherland was to be increasingly the refrain of those who came to favor Nazi militarism. The resurgence of strong feelings of nationalism was evidenced by the election to the presidency in 1925 of Field Marshal von Hindenburg, a stalwart Junker and hero of World War I.

The Treaty of Versailles embittered many Germans, and its use by the French to justify the invasion of the Ruhr sowed further seeds of hate. The so-called war guilt clause of the treaty, by which the Germans were forced to proclaim their guilt for starting the war—a guilt which most impartial historians have been unable to assign to any single nation— was particularly rankling.

The ultranationalists were able to make effective appeals to the industrialists and landowners, who were convinced that the republic could not effectively discourage the internal threat of communism. As a result of the war and the postwar inflation, professional people, white-collar workers, and skilled tradesmen feared the prospect of being dragged down to the level of the masses. Especially after the debacle of inflation, a deep sense of despair and futility fell upon the people. German youth blamed their elders for the catastrophe of 1918 and the humiliations that followed defeat. The young generation repudiated the past and sought a cause to redeem the Fatherland.

Hitler's rise to prominence. The creator and high priest of German fascism was Adolf Hitler, born the son of a minor customs official in Austria in 1889. An orphan at the age of seventeen, Hitler went to Vienna in 1908 with ambitions of becoming an architect or artist. He experienced dire poverty there and a few years later moved to Munich, where he earned a scanty living by selling paintings. During these years, Hitler interested himself in Marxist socialism and Pan-Germanism. He was also rabidly anti-Semitic.

When war broke out, he joined a German regiment and was sent to France. The armistice of 1918 found him in a hospital. He said later that news of Germany's defeat caused him to turn his face to the wall and weep bitterly. Subsequently he was hired by the authorities in Munich as a special agent to investigate Communist and other extremist movements. In the line of duty he was asked to check on a small organization called the German Workers' party. Hitler joined this group, whose fervently nationalistic doctrine was at once antidemocratic, anticapitalist, anti-Communist, and anti-Semitic.

Before long the movement took the name "National Socialist German Workers' party," and the words "National Socialists" became abbreviated to "Nazis." In 1920 the party obtained a newspaper as a mouthpiece; soon thereafter the first of the paramilitary organizations, the SA or Storm Troops, was organized. Adopted as the emblem of the party was the swastika set against a red background signifying the community of German blood.

Hitler was now becoming better known. His remarkable oratorical gifts began to attract large crowds in Munich. Sometimes he would hire a dozen beer halls and dash from one to the other in an automobile, delivering fiery harangues at each. His political program called for land reform, the nationalization of trusts, abolition of all unearned incomes, and

—in the field of foreign relations—a greater Germany to include all German-speaking peoples in Europe, the abrogation of the Versailles Treaty, and the restitution of Germany's prewar colonies. In 1923 Hitler staged his *Putsch*, or revolt, in Munich; coming prematurely, it failed, and he was sent to prison.

Mein Kampf. Before his release from prison in 1925, Hitler began to write *Mein Kampf* (*My Battle*), at once an autobiography and a long-winded exposition of Nazi philosophy and objectives. In this work Hitler contends that history is fashioned by great races, of which the Aryan is the finest; that the noblest Aryans are the German people, who are destined to rule the world; that the Jews are the archcriminals of all time; that democracy is decadent and communism is criminal; that foreign expansion into the Russian Ukraine and the destruction of Germany's prime enemy France are rightful courses for the German people; and that war and force are the proper instruments of the strong. Again and again his sentences drip with acid as he fulminates against the Jews, Russia, and France. In *Mein Kampf* he singles out the Treaty of Versailles as the instrument which would give him magic appeal in Germany:

What a use could be made of the Treaty of Versailles! . . . How each one of the points . . . could be branded in the minds and hearts of the German people until sixty million men and women find their souls aflame with the feeling of rage and shame; and a torrent of fire bursts forth as from a furnace.[6]

With his irrational creed and his ritualistic gestures, badges, and uniforms, Hitler would one day surpass his predecessor Mussolini in Italy by becoming *Führer* (leader) of a new Germany based on despotism and terror.

DEMOCRACY IN

THE WASTELAND

Democracy on the defensive. "In this autumn of 1919, in which I write, we are at the dead season of our fortunes. The reaction from the exertions, the fears, and the sufferings of the past five years is at its height. Our power of feeling or caring beyond the immediate questions of our own material well-being is temporarily eclipsed. The greatest events outside our own direct experience and the most dreadful anticipations cannot move us. . . . We have been moved already beyond endurance, and need rest."[7] Thus wrote the famed English economist John Maynard Keynes; his mood of apathy, disillusionment, and despair was shared by many people in the West.

Paradoxically, the war that was supposedly fought to "make the world safe for democracy" had to be waged largely at the expense of political and economic freedoms long associated with democracy. Mass conscription—unknown before in countries such as Great Britain—was adopted; and in the economic sphere, orders were given to private business by governmental decrees. Now, in the postwar period, the individual had regained his democratic rights, but the war had left a legacy of swollen governmental bureaucracies and strongly entrenched industrial and labor empires in which the individual voice all too often was lost.

The postwar period witnessed an inevitable reaction against wartime controls. In the English-speaking democracies, which were the chief bastions of laissez-faire economics, governmental controls were thrown off with all possible speed. The slogan "back to normalcy" in the United States indicated a return to prewar economic habits and creeds. And halted throughout most of the democratic-capitalist world were the strong prewar movements to advance social welfare legislation and to regulate traditional laissez-faire economics. An unhealthy inertia resulted in the suspension of badly needed socio-economic reforms.

The national mood and psychology prevailing in the democracies, whether in those long-established or in those newly created after the war, differed basically from the mood and psychology in the rising dictatorships. The democracies drifted into listlessness and futility, while the totalitarian states exhibited resolution, dynamism, and purpose, even though of a ruthless variety. The inability of the democracies to measure up to the needs of the time gave the 1920's its characteristic mood and quality. That mood and quality were reflected in the literature of the Wasteland era (a term taken from the title of T. S. Eliot's poem *The Waste Land*), with its cynicism, its sense of purposelessness, and its absorption with the seamy and often trivial aspects of life.

Unstable coalition governments in France. More than 1,000,000 Frenchmen had been killed and some 13,000 square miles of French territory laid waste in the holocaust of World War I. Years later the nation would still feel the heavy loss of man power and the economic devastation of a war that had been fought largely on French soil.

The Sacred Union, the wartime coalition government which included representatives of all shades of political opinion, was replaced after the elections of 1919 by the National Bloc, a conservative group whose leaders included Poincaré and the wartime premier Clemenceau, both eager for revenge. They believed in the rigid enforcement of the provisions of the Versailles Treaty and saw as their chief task the restoration of the country's devastated regions. They expected the huge costs of rebuilding the towns destroyed in the north of France to be covered by reparation payments from Germany; and when the Germans suspended these payments in 1923, it was Poincaré who ordered French troops into the industrially rich Ruhr valley. More than any other man, he symbolized the policy of making Germany pay for the war and of keeping it disarmed.

Because many Frenchmen realized that this vindictive policy was basically unsound, the National Bloc fell in 1924 and was succeeded by the Left Cartel, which guided the destinies of France for the next two years. Except for the unpopular war against Abd-el Krim in Morocco (see p. 498), the coalition left an enviable record in foreign affairs: French troops evacuated the Ruhr in accordance with the Dawes Plan for solving the reparations tangle, and French and German statesmen met amicably at the Locarno Conference. In internal affairs, on the other hand, the Left Cartel, which advocated the extension of government control of industry and an increase in income taxes, was unsuccessful, particularly in the area of public finance. Although France had practically no unemployment after the war and its foreign trade by 1922 had surpassed its prewar volume, inflation threatened to plunge the franc into the same abyss that in 1923 engulfed the German mark.

To meet this emergency, in 1926 Poincaré was recalled to power to head a National Union government and save the franc. Drastic measures were taken by the new coalition; taxes were increased and expenditures curtailed. Poincaré's policies gave French finance a new lease on life, while in other fields workmen's insurance was enacted and the task of rebuilding the devastated areas was completed.

The story of France in the 1920's is a mixed plot of progress and setbacks, of successes and failures. Fundamentally, a national spirit and a sense of purpose were lacking. The war had sapped the vigor of the French nation, and as in Germany the unhealthiness and lack of dynamism characteristic of the Wasteland mood were evident.

Evolutionary socialism gains support in Great Britain. Across the Channel, meanwhile, Britain in the postwar period suffered a number of serious problems. Shortly after the armistice, foreign trade collapsed, and unemployment reached huge proportions. By July 1921 two million persons were out of work, and the war debt had soared to $40,-000,000,000.

In 1922 the wartime coalition under David Lloyd George came to an end. Elections held at the end of 1923 saw the Conservatives gain the largest number of seats in the House of Commons, but by swinging their support to the Labour party, the Liberals gave James Ramsay MacDonald a majority in this house. As a result, in January 1924 MacDonald became Britain's first Labourite prime minister.

The Labour government did not preach the gospel according to Marx but espoused evolutionary socialism in the tradition of the Fabian Society in England, the Social Democrats in Germany, and the Mensheviks in prewar Russia. The goal of the Labour party was to introduce socialism slowly and at all times within a democratic framework. MacDonald declared: "Our Labor movement has never had the least inclination to try short cuts to the millennium."[8]

While its record in domestic affairs was not outstanding, the Labour government fared better in foreign affairs. Believing that Germany must be aided in its steps toward recovery, MacDonald favored the Dawes Plan and urged Germany's entry into the League of Nations. He also supported disarmament. But his failure to cure Britain's economic ills and his efforts to seek an economic agreement with the pariah nation, Soviet Russia, helped to bring about his downfall in October 1924. For the next five years Britain was led by a Conservative government under Stanley Baldwin. During these dismal years the face of Britain was marred by the so-called distressed areas, urban regions where hundreds of thousands of unemployed workers barely managed to keep alive on the dole, a pittance of relief handed out by the government. The economic crisis finally culminated in a general strike that threatened to disrupt the nation's entire economy.

It is difficult in a country which has never experienced a general strike to realize how serious is such a virtual civil war. The trouble broke out first in the coal industry, where the miners demanded the nationalization of the mines so that small, less profitable operations could be merged with large, profitable enterprises and all employers could afford to pay a higher wage on a nation-wide scale. As the strike spread, workers in other industries quit all over Britain; even newspapers suspended publication. Had it not been for the calm spirit of most Englishmen, armed conflict might have broken out. In the end the strike of 1926 failed; the miners returned to work.

Two years later, between 20 and 30 per cent of the labor force in many of the leading industries was eking out an existence on the dole. The failure of the Conservative party to find a solution for unemployment brought Labour back into power in 1929, the year also witnessing the beginning of a world crisis which would force Britain off the gold standard, raise still higher its unemployment figures, and in 1931 end the second Labour

During the general strike of 1926 in England, armored cars, equipped with machine guns, were stationed in London to suppress riots.

ministry. Thus the decade following victory in 1918 had brought Britain little inspired leadership, an absence of forward-looking programs of economic reform, and a seeming inability to measure up to the demands of a difficult new age. To many young English people this Wasteland period was aptly symbolized by a popular play of the time—*Love on the Dole*.

The British Commonwealth of Nations. During the First World War, the British dominions (Canada, Australia, New Zealand, and South Africa) had rendered valuable service, and the war had stimulated strong nationalistic feelings among their peoples. In 1926 an Imperial Conference declared that Great Britain and the dominions were "autonomous Communities within the British Empire, equal in status, in no way subordinate one to another." Five years later the British Parliament enacted the Statute of Westminster, which was in effect a constitution for what was now called the British Commonwealth of Nations. Henceforth the dominions and Great Britain were held together only by loyalty to the crown and by a common language, legal principles, tradition, and economic interests.

During the 1920's, the dominions prospered from the strong world demand for Canadian wheat, fish, lumber, and minerals, for Australian wool, for New Zealand's mutton and butter, and for South African gold and diamonds. Prosperous economies contributed to stability in government. When a world depression struck in the early 1930's, however, the prosperity of the previous decade was threatened.

Tensions in the British empire. In the 1920's, the British were called upon to wrestle with numerous problems in different parts of the empire, namely in the areas which, unlike the dominions, did not possess self-government. As we shall see in Chapter 16, agitation for home rule in India increased, and demands for self-government were raised in Ceylon and Burma. The Egyptians were irked by British control of the Suez Canal. And in some British colonies, such as Kenya and Southern Rhodesia, the government in London found it difficult to reconcile the clashing interests of the British settlers and the natives. Nor had the end of the war brought peace to Palestine, the former Turkish territory which had been turned over to Britain as a mandate in 1920. Its Arab inhabitants were resolved that Jewish Zionist immigrants should not gain control, while the latter were equally determined that what had once been their ancient kingdom should become a modern homeland for the Jews.

The Irish Free State established. Meantime, Britain was undergoing other problems in a familiar quarter. In 1916, during the First World War, Irish nationalists had revolted against British authority in the Easter Rebellion, which failed after savage fighting in Dublin. After the war the Sinn Fein ("we ourselves") party demanded complete independence for Ireland and maintained a state of war between the "Irish republic" and Britain. In 1921 a treaty was signed between Irish and British representatives providing for the Irish Free State. While six counties in northern Ireland (comprising most of Ulster) remained tied with Britain, the southern part of the island was given dominion status. Agitation and violence continued for a time, with civil warfare between supporters of the Free State and nationalists who opposed the treaty; but under the leadership of a Dublin government pledged to cooperate with Britain, Ireland regained a semblance of internal unity. In 1923 the Free State became a member of the League of Nations.

Austria, Hungary, and Bulgaria. What had happened to the countries of southern Europe —Austria, Hungary, Bulgaria—which had been on the losing side in the war? Austria had been reduced both in population and in area by nearly three fourths, leaving an enfeebled state about the size of Maine with less than seven million people. Vienna, the center of the old Austro-Hungarian empire, no longer had an adequate hinterland to nourish its economic growth. Unlike many European nations, however, Austria was not plagued with ethnic problems because it was inhabited by German stock.

The immediate postwar years were alarming. Food and fuel were scarce, the country was full of demobilized and jobless soldiers, thousands died of starvation, and the currency became worthless. The economic union (*Anschluss*) with Germany proposed as a solution for these difficulties was forbidden by the Allies. For ten years after its creation, the new federal republic wrestled with widespread unemployment and the specter of bankruptcy. During these troubled times, the Viennese turned to socialist leadership, and many necessary reforms were introduced in the capital. Slums were demolished, nearly 100,000 working-class dwellings were built, and clinics and kindergartens were established. But the socialist experiment caused widespread resentment in the countryside, which remained strongly Catholic and conservative.

The war had reduced Hungary's size by 75 per cent, with more than half its former population transferred to neighboring states and succession states. The moderate republic which had been established after the war's end was supplanted by a terroristic Communist regime led by Béla Kun, a friend of Lenin. In April 1919 war broke out with Rumania, and Kun's government broke down. One year later Admiral Nicholas Horthy, World War I commander of the Hapsburg fleet, gained control of the country under the pretext of saving the Hungarians from communism. He proclaimed himself regent of the kingdom of Hungary, though Hungary had no king. Stability was restored, but the government was in the hands of ultraconservatives and the voice of the people was stilled. Nationalistic feelings ran high; so embittered were the Hungarians by the losses imposed by the Treaty of Trianon that maps of old Hungary surrounded by a crown of thorns were displayed everywhere, showing the areas ceded to its neighbors.

Bulgaria's immediate postwar years were filled with civil disorder and bloodshed, class hatreds, and political repression. For a brief period, beginning in 1926, a moderate government sought to restore civil liberties and to improve the internal economy. But the shock of the world depression swept the regime aside, and conservative elements, fearful of the spread of communism, brought about the installation of a dictatorship in the early 1930's.

Developments elsewhere in eastern and southern Europe. What were the chances for democracy in the states of Europe which had been created from the debris of the Austro-Hungarian empire and had never known democratic traditions? Among the most important of the succession states was Czechoslovakia. Four hundred years of Austrian rule had not diminished the patriotic zeal of the Czechs, and in November 1918, after the collapse of Austria, they joined with the Slovaks in establishing a republic, with Thomas Masaryk as president and Eduard Benes as foreign minister.

In addition to Czechs and Slovaks, the new republic included such minority groups as Germans in the Sudeten area, Ukrainians (Ruthenians), and Hungarians, constituting one third of the total population of fifteen million. Despite some tensions among these minorities, Czechoslovakia prospered, a large foreign trade was built up, and the government assisted small farmers by breaking up large estates. The people demonstrated that they were industrious and conscientious citizens.

To the north of Czechoslovakia lay Poland, which had been partitioned three times in the eighteenth century and in 1795 had disappeared as a political entity. Throughout the nineteenth century, strong feelings of nationalism had persisted; and with the collapse of Russia and the Central Powers, a Polish republic was declared in 1918. The Versailles Treaty established the new frontiers of Poland, later modified to the advantage of the Poles in the Treaty of Riga (1921), which concluded the war with the Bolsheviks (see p. 466). The Poles turned next to the task of building a stable, healthy state. The country was threatened by shaky finances, political conflicts between rival parties, and the discontent of minority groups, especially the Ukrainians and the Germans. One cabinet followed another in rapid succession until in 1926 Marshal Joseph Pilsudski and his military clique engineered a coup d'état. Pilsudski's control was to last until his death nine years later.

Meanwhile, along the eastern shores of the Adriatic Sea, the Croats and Slovenes of the former Hapsburg empire joined with their brother Slavs in Serbia and Montenegro to form a new nation, the Kingdom of the Serbs, Croats, and Slovenes, later known as Yugoslavia. From the outset, King Alexander had difficulty in reconciling the rivalries between the Slavic peoples. In 1928 a riot broke out in the parliament, and the Croatian leader was mortally wounded. The following year saw Alexander proclaim himself dictator.

Rumania had profited from the demise of the Austro-Hungarian empire, its population and area having doubled, but like the succession states, this kingdom enjoyed little tranquillity after 1919. Despite the promulgation of a liberal constitution in 1923, its peasants were restless; and minority groups, especially the Hungarians, proved troublesome to civil order. Political affairs were complicated by a royal scandal. In 1925 Prince Carol renounced his rights to the throne and went into exile with his mistress, the notorious Magda Lupescu. Five years later Carol returned with Madame Lupescu, was accepted by parliament, and began to plot immediately to convert the Rumanian government into a royal dictatorship.

Democracy in other small European nations. Finland and the Scandinavian countries of Norway, Sweden, and Denmark enjoyed representative government and economic prosperity during the 1920's. The citizens benefited from the establishment of producers' and consumers' cooperatives and from progressive social legislation. In Sweden the Middle Way, an experiment combining capitalism and state enterprise, was carried out. The Middle Way called for state control of many forms of economic activity as well as government operation of mines, power, and communications. In addition, considerable social welfare legislation was inaugurated to provide the masses with economic security and adequate social services.

During the 1920's, stable democratic government and considerable prosperity were enjoyed by the peoples of Switzerland, the Netherlands, and Belgium. In the case of the Dutch and the Belgians, rich dividends from colonial empires contributed to the high standard of living.

Status of democracy in Spain and Portugal. By supplying food and other materials to the belligerent powers, Spain had enjoyed wartime prosperity; but after the war, prosperity gave way to lagging trade, industrial unrest, and political instability. The situation was aggravated by a revolt in Spanish Morocco, where in 1921 a Spanish army of twelve thousand men was completely wiped out. To save the monarchy and the privileged classes, in 1923 a right-wing leader, Miguel Primo de Rivera, set up a dictatorship, but even though a few concessions were granted to the people, opposition to arbitrary rule mounted. After Rivera's resignation in 1930, King Alfonso XIII tried to woo the people with a policy of conciliation, but the republicans openly denounced the monarchy. Municipal elections one year later resulted in a clear-cut victory for the republicans, Alfonso fled the country and Spain became a republic. At a time when many other countries were turning to dictatorship, it was heartening to democrats everywhere to witness the triumph of democracy in Spain. This triumph was to be short-lived, however (see Chapter 17).

In the 1920's the republic of Portugal was plagued by political instability. In 1928 Dr. Oliveira Salazar, a professor of economics, became the minister of finance and, in 1932, the leading figure in an outright dictatorship. He exercised his power unobtrusively, perhaps as befitted a professorial dictator.

Growth of democratic ideals in Latin America. Across the seas in the lands to which Iberian culture had been transplanted, various nations were beginning to tackle their economic problems and were trying to make their governments democracies in more than name.

Latin America had not figured prominently in the First World War. Belligerent actions were limited to the severance of diplomatic relations with Germany and to declarations of war, actions taken chiefly to confiscate the property of German nationals. The huge wartime demands for Latin-American products resulted in an economic boom; and though the end of the war brought about a familiar situation—a crisis in the economy—business expansion began again in the 1920's. However, a crucial weakness remained—the dependence of the economies of Latin America's twenty republics upon only a few products or, in some cases, upon a single product. Thus Brazil's prosperity depended on the world coffee market, which absorbed half its exports. Cuba depended on sugar; Bolivia, tin; Mexico, oil and silver; Venezuela, oil; Argentina, meat and wheat. Various Central American "banana republics" were equally dependent on the sale of bananas. Another weak spot was the land problem. Conditions resembling medieval serfdom existed on many large estates. Because the Church was a great landowner, certain churchmen combined with the landed interests to oppose land reforms.

During the 1920's the movement for social reform in Latin America was spearheaded by Mexico, which came under a series of administrations, all claiming to be heir to the revolutionary spirit of the peon revolt of 1910. The government sought to exercise increasing control over the vast oil properties run by foreign investors; and the agrarian problem was partially solved at the expense of large landowners. These changes were accompanied by a wave of anticlericalism. Much Church property was seized, many churches were destroyed, and the priesthood had for a time to go underground.

Conditions in Mexico exerted a strong influence on other Latin-American countries, and between 1919 and 1929 seven nations adopted new, liberal constitutions. In addition, there were growing demands for better economic and social opportunities, for a breakdown of the barriers that divided the few extremely rich from the many abysmally poor, and for improvements in health, education, and the status of women. Above all, there was an increasing desire for more stable political conditions.

Era of normalcy and big business in the United States. By 1919 wartime industrial expansion had won for the United States the supreme position in industrial equipment and wealth among the family of nations. Moreover, our nation had been transformed from a debtor nation to the world's greatest creditor. But while other nations increasingly

The 1920's in the United States was a restless era in which the people threw off the restraints suffered during the Great War, made intense issues of prohibition, un-Americanism, and theology, and applauded the technological achievements which were shrinking the world. The flapper (above left), caricatured by John Held, Jr., symbolized the rebelliousness of sophisticated young people who flaunted the moral standards of the older generation. National heroes were cheered in lavish ticker-tape parades, such as the one which welcomed Admiral Byrd and his crew on their return from exploring the Antarctic (above). Another national hero was Charles A. Lindbergh (center left), who in 1927 made the first solo flight across the Atlantic in his monoplane *The Spirit of St. Louis*.   The 1920's was the era of prohibition, a "noble experiment" so unpopular that great numbers of ordinarily law-abiding citizens patronized bootleggers and speak-easies. With prohibition came the boom days of organized crime, as gangsters set up stills or carried on a lucrative trade in smuggling. Although millions of dollars' worth of liquor and beer were confiscated by federal agents and poured down sewers (below left), enforcement measures failed to end the lawlessness.

When the triumph of communism in Russia coincided with an outbreak of radical agitation in the United States, a violent reaction against un-Americanism occurred. The Sacco-Vanzetti case attracted world-wide attention because of the political

beliefs of the defendants. Nicolo Sacco and Bartolomeo Vanzetti (pictured top above in a painting by Ben Shahn) were two Italian aliens convicted of killing a paymaster and his guard in Massachusetts and stealing $16,000. The verdict raised a storm of protest from radicals and from many liberals who were convinced that the men had not been given a fair trial because of their anarchistic beliefs. When all appeals failed, riots broke out in many cities, and bombs were set off in New York City and Philadelphia. On August 23, 1927, the defendants were executed, still protesting their innocence. Another hotly disputed issue was raised by the Scopes trial in 1927. John Scopes, a science teacher in a Dayton, Tennessee high school, was charged with violating a state law forbidding the teaching in public schools of any theories denying the Biblical account of the creation of man. The issue actually on trial was the state's right to determine the type of religious instruction presented in the schools; but the violent debate between religious fundamentalists and liberals was also given a public airing. Conservatives of various churches had banded together to demand that the teaching of Darwinian doctrines be prohibited in the schools. At the trial, William Jennings Bryan (right in the picture above) championed the literal interpretation of the Bible against Clarence Darrow (left above), the counsel for the defense. Scopes was found guilty and fined $100, although the penalty was later set aside.

looked to it for leadership, the United States turned away from the international scene. The wartime democratic idealism of President Wilson was shelved, the League of Nations was ignored, and isolationism triumphed over internationalism.

Internally, industrial strife marked the immediate postwar years. In 1919 occurred an unsuccessful police strike in Boston and an unsuccessful strike in the steel industry. Frightened by the Communist Revolution in Russia, many Americans demanded that action be taken against left-wing radicals at home. Against immigrants, Catholics, Jews, the League of Nations, and pacifists, a most exaggerated form of intolerance was practiced, often in a secret, terroristic fashion, by a new Ku Klux Klan. In some areas the Klan held political control of whole communities and state governments, in the North as well as in the South. Klan membership totaled over four million in 1924, but it declined after this date. Progressive editors, clergymen, and politicians mobilized public opinion against an organization which was recognized as undemocratic and un-American.

One important postwar political development was the ratification of the Eighteenth Amendment, by which the sale and possession of intoxicating liquors were prohibited. However laudable its purpose may have appeared at the time, the adoption of prohibition was increasingly regretted by many Americans as the 1920's wore on; the law was broken by great numbers of normally law-abiding citizens and frequently ignored by law-enforcement agencies, and the racketeering, violence, and corruption to which prohibition gave rise brought a dangerous lowering of the dignity of lawmaking and of democratic institutions.

In 1921 the inauguration of Warren G. Harding (1865-1923) as president on the platform of a "return to normalcy" ushered in a decade of Republican dominance. It soon became apparent that by "normalcy" the Harding administration meant resistance to pressure for such progressive measures as low tariffs and antitrust prosecutions. In foreign affairs the new president was bent upon isolationism and the repudiation of the League of Nations. In fact the American ambassador in London was:

... instructed to inform the League's authorities that as the United States had not joined the League she was not in a position to answer letters from it.[9]

Harding died suddenly in 1923, on the eve of the exposure of widespread corruption in his administration. The worst scandal concerned the leasing of government oil reserves at Teapot Dome, Wyoming, to private operators, who paid the secretary of the interior a total of $400,000 for their privileges.

Harding's vice president and successor, Calvin Coolidge (1872-1933), advocated high tariffs and the reduction of taxes. His credo was summed up in these words: "The business of the United States is business." The Democrats tried in vain to raise the issue of corruption so rampant during Harding's regime, but under the glow of rising prosperity the voters in the 1924 presidential elections decided to "keep cool with Cal" and the Republicans won easily. Little outstanding legislation was enacted during the second Coolidge administration. A difficult problem was agriculture. Although farm income continued to decline while the fixed payments for debts contracted during agriculture's wartime expansion had to be kept up, bills to ease the farmers' plight were repeatedly vetoed by Coolidge. Other segments of the national economy enjoyed what appeared to be dazzling prosperity in 1927 and 1928. Growing quantities of autos, radios, and refrigerators were purchased either with cash or, increasingly, on the installment plan. Stock speculation became a virtual mania. Nearly everyone, from the millionaire to the janitor of the building in which the rich man lived, played the market. A social historian of these hectic days has left us a vivid picture of the gambling craze that possessed the nation. "The rich man's chauffeur drove with his ears laid back to catch the news of an impending move in Bethlehem Steel; he held fifty shares himself on a twenty-point margin. The window-cleaner at the broker's office paused to watch the ticker, for he was thinking of converting his laboriously accumulated savings into a few shares of Simmons. . . . [A reporter] told of a broker's valet who had made nearly a quarter of a million in the market, of a trained nurse who cleaned up thirty thousand following the tips given her by grateful patients; and of a Wyoming cattleman, thirty miles from the nearest railroad, who bought or sold a thousand shares a day."[10] The stock market, mass production, high tariffs, large foreign loans, and installment buying—all seemed to be working together in harmony. These years marked the high tide of American big business and economic self-satisfaction.

In the 1928 presidential elections, Herbert Hoover (1874-   ), a successful mining engineer who had directed Belgian relief during the war, had as his Democratic opponent the governor of New York, Alfred E. Smith. A product of the "sidewalks of New York" and the first man of the Catholic faith to obtain the presidential nomination, Smith as governor had sponsored progressive social legislation. In the election campaign he called for the repeal of prohibition because of the problems to which it had given rise, but Hoover won the day on what one historian termed "prosperity, prohibition, and prejudice." When he assumed office in 1929, he was supported by a Republican Congress and a nation enjoying unbounded industrial prosperity.

Even though the general trend of American foreign policy in the 1920's was isolationist, some broadening of activity in international affairs took place. Unofficial observers were sent to meetings of the League of Nations, American financial experts took a leading part in the reparations problem, and the United States found itself increasingly involved in affairs in the Pacific (see p. 510). Although the United States did not join the World Court, representatives from Washington, D.C., attended the Disarmament Conference at Geneva in 1927, the signing of the Kellogg-Briand Pact in 1928, and the London Naval Conference in 1930.

For a decade after the war, Americans looked for leadership to Wall Street rather than to the White House. They were complacent, unprecedentedly prosperous as a nation, and little interested in what transpired outside the three-mile limit—or rather the twelve-mile limit when it came to rumrunners. In their attitudes the American people were experiencing the disillusionment and moral fatigue of the postwar era. The 1920's have been described as an era of "tremendous trivia"—dance marathons, flagpole sitting, "red hot mamas," speak-easies, Broadway ticker-tape parades for celebrities like Lindbergh, the Charleston, and a national craze for speculating in stocks, bonds, and Florida real estate. These were the elements in the Wasteland age in the United States. To many its salient features were national smugness and isolationism in international affairs, crass materialism in business, and vulgarity and bad taste in daily life.

The "lost generation." During the 1920's the lack of certainty and direction so evident in the political sphere was mirrored in the arts, particularly in literature. Was not man a mere automaton, governed by forces outside his control and at the mercy of his subconscious nature? Was not his vaunted civilization only a thinly veneered savagery, as the destruction of millions in shell-battered trenches seemed to prove? The weariness of a disillusioned generation—the "lost generation," as it was called by Gertrude Stein—had been sounded by the American poet T. S. Eliot (1888-   ) in *The Waste Land* (1922), a recondite poem woven largely of obscure literary allusions. Eliot so aptly captured the spirit of weariness and disgust with contemporary life that the title of this work was applied to an entire literary period, and he was hailed as the spokesman for all who regarded life as meaningless.

Consciously or perhaps subconsciously, many artists and writers in Europe and America followed Eliot's lead. The leading novelists of the Wasteland era—England's Aldous Huxley and D. H. Lawrence, America's Ernest Hemingway, Ireland's James Joyce, Germany's Thomas Mann, and France's Marcel Proust and André Gide—shared a deep-rooted skepticism regarding society's ability to act intelligently. In their fiction they were preoccupied with dissecting the psychological problems of their characters. Repeatedly these authors concentrated on the individual who either set himself apart from—or found himself out of step with—conventional manners and mores, so that a spirit of moral disintegration or seeming amorality characterizes their works. In the drama, playwrights such as the American Eugene O'Neill also spoke pessimistically of the age and probed eagerly into the psychological abnormalities of human nature.

SUMMARY

Marx had never imagined that his philosophy would first triumph in feudal, underdeveloped Russia. That it did so was primarily due to the planning and leadership of Lenin, who between November 1917 and his death in 1924, succeeded in eliminating all other political parties and in consolidating the Communist party's authority in the hands of an elite group, the Politburo, with himself at the head. Under Lenin's leadership the Soviet government drastically changed Russian society and economy, although Lenin was forced to retreat temporarily from undiluted Marxism and permit a partial return to free enterprise in order to build up the economy. After Lenin's death, a fierce struggle for leadership broke out within the Communist party. The likely successor, Trotsky, was pushed aside by Stalin, who believed that communism could be made to work in one country in contrast to the view shared by Lenin and Trotsky that ultimate success depended upon an international proletarian revolution. In 1928, Stalin inaugurated the first of his famous Five-Year Plans—a daring and ruthless economic program aimed at achieving heavy industrialization and the collectivization of agriculture.

The First World War gave a strong impetus to nationalist emotions and to developing the cult of the state. In the hands of astute demagogues, nationalism was exalted into a creed with unbridled power as its goal and unswerving obedience its demand from its adherents. Such was Fascism, whose high priest and leader, Benito Mussolini, launched a campaign of organized terror in Italy and took over the government in 1922. Defined as the "cult of state worship," Italian Fascism called for rule by one party, which liquidated all opposition and was in turn manipulated by a hierarchy at whose summit stood Mussolini, Il Duce. This same party also manipulated all economic power by means of the corporate state. In keeping with Fascism's glorification of war and imperialism, Mussolini's fundamental objective was to make Italy as self-sufficient as possible in order to expand.

The task of restoring the shattered fortunes of defeated Germany had been entrusted to the democratic Weimar Republic. Political inexperience and heavy economic burdens combined to discredit the government among the dispirited and humiliated Germans, who began to turn to such ultra-nationalists as Adolf Hitler and his Nazi followers, fanatics intent upon destroying the established order. During the 1920's Germany recovered sufficiently to become a respected and prosperous member of the European community, but the early 1930's heralded a catastrophic depression, thereby giving Hitler his opportunity to seize power.

What was the condition of democracy during the 1920's? Nearly all the states emerging from the debris of the German and Austrian empires started their national existence with democratic constitutions. Although Czechoslovakia flourished, nearly all the others soon gave way to dictatorial regimes. They suffered in common from the absence of a strong middle class and a lack of experience in democratic government. Moreover, the Allies at

Versailles had applied the principle of self-determination to the point of creating too many small states which were separated from their neighbors by artificial tariff barriers and which suffered from weak economies. In such circumstances it is not surprising that democracy failed to succeed.

Yet in the well-established democracies the results were for the most part also disappointing. True, democratic institutions held their own in the Netherlands and Belgium and were strengthened in the Scandinavian countries. On the other hand, France, the undisputed master of Continental Europe in 1919, gradually slipped from its position of dominance because of chronic political instability. Great Britain emerged from the war with a full quota of domestic and imperial problems, and neither the Conservative nor the Labour governments made much headway in overcoming these difficulties, of which the most acute was unemployment. Overseas, democracy had a patchy record of successes and failures. In the British Commonwealth the dominions achieved full status as self-governing states and enjoyed prosperity and economic expansion. Some social reforms were registered in the Latin-American republics, where, however, democratic institutions were all too often a façade for dictatorial regimes. In the United States, stock speculation, corruption in high places, and gangsterism flourished in a society which had turned its back on Wilsonian ideals to return to isolation and embrace a false prosperity.

As we have seen in this chapter, the 1920's were the years in which opposing ideologies were crystallizing. This period was to prove only a lull before the terrible storm of world economic distress and national aggressions.

Abstraction is as characteristic of 20th-century art as naturalistic realism was during the 17th century. Contemporary painting has sought to give form to ideas that lie beneath the visible surface of things. The physical object has been made abstract by taking it from its context and reducing it to pure form. The art of our time tends to be multifaceted, restless, violent, and disturbing; yet, it remains provocative, inventive, and alive. **24** (above) **Georges Rouault: "The Old King"** (1916-1936). Rouault's king is a formidable contemporary image—a brooding and wearily remote figure, yet heroic and touched with compassion. The powerful drawing and softened color reflect this century's interest in archaic forms and basic feelings. **25** (above right) **Fernand Leger: "The City"** (1919). This outstanding example of cubism illustrates the qualities which distinguish that early 20th-century movement. Emblems and shapes of a machine technology are here disassembled, simplified, and rearranged in a kaleidoscopic composition with its own logic. The painting is a digest of visual impressions taken from an urban environment. **26** (right) **Willem De Kooning: "Woman V"** (1950-1952). One of the stellar figures in America's emergence as an artistic power after World War II here undertakes a violent dissection of the human figure. As a formal exercise, it is a forceful arrangement of color, abstracted volume, and line; as an image, it is both menacing and satiric.

27 (left) **Max Ernst: "Spanish Physician"** (1946). Ernst has given free rein to his fancy here, even permitting certain accidental configurations of paint to develop on the canvas, then turning these into figures whose shapes and relationships are mysterious and wondrous. Surrealism attains much of its force and compelling presence from the very fact that its meaning is ambiguous. **28** (below) **Wassily Kandinsky: "Improvisation with Green Center"** (1913). The late 19th-century trend away from dependence on literal content and toward an emphasis on such formal qualities as line, color, and volume was carried to a logical conclusion by the Russian painter Kandinsky, who was concerned especially with the emotional effect of painting. Since he came to believe that a variety of such effects could be gained better by using line and color alone, independent of subject, he restricted his later work to these elements.

29 Marc Chagall: "White Crucifixion" (1938). The 20th century has witnessed man's brutal treatment of his fellow man on a scale unprecedented in history. Two great global wars plus mass extermination and genocide number among the more terrible experiences of mankind in this century. Chagall's painting is a commentary on this suffering. He takes as his theme the modern persecution of the Jews and graphically illustrates it by means of a stream-of-consciousness organizational technique which bears a close relation to surrealist fantasy. Note the burning synagogue, upper right, and the Jewish refugees throughout the picture. One of them (lower left) protects the Torah as he flees. The composition focuses on the crucified figure of Christ, which Chagall has used in order to give universality to his message. The crucified Christ here symbolizes man's ravaged innocence.

30 Ludwig Mies van der Rohe: Crown Hall, Illinois Institute of Technology, Chicago (1956). Though the turmoil of modern life has frequently stimulated an artistic response which reflects strife and tension, it has also brought about the opposite kind of artistic reaction. The architecture of Mies van der Rohe is as ordered, logical, and serene as much present-day painting is agonizing. Free of irrelevant decoration and personal caprice, his architecture represents superbly the great transformation which has overtaken the art of building in the contemporary period. Modern architecture grew out of the practical needs of engineering in a new technological culture. It became an instrument against the juggling of past styles that had dominated so much construction in the 19th century. Materials such as steel, concrete, and glass have made such new forms and new functions possible that the architecture of our time may be remembered eventually as the most revolutionary of the visual arts in the 20th century.

CHAPTER 16

Africa and Asia Astir

AFRICA, THE MIDDLE EAST, AND INDIA (1914-1939); CHINA AND JAPAN (1914-1930)

Introduction. By the first decade of the twentieth century, after fifty years of aggressive expansion, the dynamic, highly industrialized, militarily invincible western powers had Europeanized the world. Both the powers themselves and the territories over which they gained control derived numerous benefits from this march of imperialism. Trade was stimulated, vast stores of natural resources were discovered and developed, and schools and health services were installed in regions where such hallmarks of civilization had previously been unknown. Evils as well as benefits resulted from imperialistic control, however; sometimes the western powers brought enlightened rule, but all too often native peoples had to pay a heavy price for whatever advantages they received—ruthless economic exploitation, racial discrimination, and the imposition of harsh administrative controls.

The most significant achievement of imperialism was its transmission to undeveloped societies of revolutionary western political and social ideas. Ambitious to match the cultural accomplishments of the European, a young Arab expressed his debt to his English school and its body of knowledge in these words: "Inside the structure dwelt Shakespeare and Burke and Dr. Johnson, British democracy and justice, individual liberty, the Habeas Corpus, the Humanities and the love of nature—all the moral and aesthetic values that go to make the soul of civilization."[1] The explosive ideas of democracy, parliamentary government, and nationalism, in association with western science and technology, reawakened and revitalized the long-dormant societies of the nonwestern world with their hundreds of millions of people. In this chapter we shall see how this process took place in Africa, the Middle East, India, and southeast Asia.

After World War I, colonialism was never quite the same. The colonial peoples had heard and seen too much for them ever again to treat the white man with unquestioning obedience. Indian regiments and African contingents had fought in France, and Chinese labor battalions had been brought to Europe; their horizons had been immensely broadened. Above all, the heady doctrines of democracy and self-determination had been given world-wide circulation. Speaking of the impact of Wilson's Fourteen Points, India's Nehru wrote: "The atmosphere became electric, and most of us young men felt exhilarated and expected big things in the near future."[2] Similarly exciting to many colonial peoples was Lenin's violent condemnation of "capitalistic imperialism" after the success of the Bolshevik Revolution.

Yet while the influence of World War I was revealed in the growth of nationalism in India and China and among the Arabs of the Middle East, the activities of many nationalist programs and anti-imperialist movements remained tentative and secret, attracting little attention. But over the years the forces of liberation gathered their strength; and with the impact of World War II, they exploded into action.

In Japan an enlightened effort to meet the challenge of the West through modernization culminated in a series of events which turned the ancient island empire into a world power. At the same time, the growth of nondemocratic institu-tions, combined with population pressures, led Japan to take the imperialist road itself and, in the 1930's, made that country a dangerous threat to world peace. China, too, came to see the need for modernization and, through revolution and the gradual consolidation of government under the Kuomintang, found new dignity among the nations. But land-hungry Japan coveted China's vast territories, and Japanese imperialism was to turn ancient China into a battlefield for many long years.

After the First World War a chapter in modern world history—the dominance of the West—began to draw to a close. In ancient and medieval times—before Europe's amazing advance in knowledge, wealth, and power—East and West were in rough balance. After the Renaissance, the scientific and industrial revolutions, and the spread of democracy and nationalism, the West took a commanding lead. Springing from this imbalance, western imperialism should perhaps be regarded as an inevitable development. But the colonial system and the West's power monopoly could not last; from its height in 1919, western superiority went into a rapid decline, and by the 1930's it was becoming apparent that fundamental changes were taking place in the nonwestern world. We shall see how the tempo of these changes increased until the ferment in the Afro-Asian lands created a critical challenge for the statesmen of the contemporary world.

NEW FORCES IN AFRICA

Benefits of imperial rule. Beginning about 1890 and increasingly after the turn of the century, European imperial powers organized and consolidated their possessions in sub-Saharan Africa (see Reference Map 5). Previously unknown regions were mapped, boundaries were defined, and railroads and communications systems were set up. The improvement of indigenous products such as rubber and palm oil, the introduction of the new crops cotton and cocoa, and the importation of better breeds of cattle enriched the colonial economies. Forestry was placed on a scientific basis; diamond, gold, and tin mines were opened; and trade in all the colonies increased rapidly. European settlement also increased, especially in highland areas.

In the field of political administration, new government bureaus and systems were established, and intertribal warfare, cannibalism, and dangerous secret societies were stamped out. Educational facilities, largely under the control of missionaries, were expanded with government support, and scholars began the laborious task of transcribing the native tongues so that they could become written languages. A good start was made in public health: with the advent of clinics, hospitals, and sanitation campaigns, the health of the native peoples improved and infant mortality declined. Meanwhile, agricultural and veterinary officers taught the natives methods of fighting erosion, securing better seeds, using fertilizers, and managing their herds more efficiently.

Pan-Africanism and Negro nationalism. During World War I a great deal of fighting took place in Africa. South African, British, and Indian troops conquered the huge German East African protectorate, while troops from the Union of South Africa scattered resistance in German Southwest Africa. The German possessions of Togoland and the Cameroons were taken over by British, French, and Belgian forces.

More significant to Africa and Europe than the military successes of the Allies was the opposition to imperialism which grew during the war years, as the emphasis upon democracy and self-determination of nations was so widely publicized by President Wilson. American Negro leaders demanded greater recognition of Negro rights, particularly in Africa. Dr. W.E.B. Du Bois (1868-1963), editor of the influential American Negro newspaper *Crisis*, believed that the Paris Peace Conference should help form an internationalized, free Africa. He proposed that the former German colonies become the nucleus for a state of some twenty million people, guided by an international organization.

At the war's end, Du Bois and other American Negro leaders journeyed to Paris in order to present their ideas in person to the delegates at the peace conference. While in Paris, Du Bois was instrumental in convening a Pan-African Congress with representatives from fifteen countries; the gathering urged that the former German colonies be placed under an international agency, not under the rule of one of the victorious colonial powers such as Britain. Resolutions were passed which recommended the protection of native lands from imperialist expansion, the prevention of economic exploitation, and the promotion of education and other social services. A spokesman for the congress declared:

. . . the natives of Africa must have the right to participate in the government as fast as their development permits, in conformity with the principle that the government exists for the natives, and not the natives for the government.[3]

Complementing the sentiments expressed at the Pan-African Congress were the ideals of Negro nationalism. In a convention held in New York in 1920, the members issued the Declaration of Rights of the Negro Peoples of the World, a document which went on record against race discrimination in the United States and the "inhuman, unchristian, and uncivilized treatment" of the Negro in colonial empires.

The mandate system in Africa. As a result of the Pan-African movement—coupled with a growing liberal sentiment in various nations, especially Britain—all territories conquered by the Allies in World War I were declared to be mandates. Article XXII of the League Covenant declared that the "well-being and development" of backward colonial lands was a "sacred trust of civilization." In essence, the mandate system was a compromise between annexation of the spoils of war by the victors and establishment of an international trusteeship. Parts of the Cameroons, Togoland, and German East Africa (Tanganyika) went to Great Britain. The remaining portions of the Cameroons and Togoland became French mandates. Belgium received the mandate of Ruanda-Urundi (also a part of German East Africa), while the former German colony of Southwest Africa was allotted to the Union of South Africa. These former colonies were made Class B mandates, except for Southwest Africa, which was ranked as a Class C mandate.

The mandates were subject to the inspection and evaluation of a Permanent Mandates Commission meeting annually in Geneva. While the commission had no effective power to rectify unsatisfactory conditions in a mandate, it could place the matter before the eyes of the world. On numerous occasions the suggestions and criticisms of the commission were heeded by the mandatory powers.

Judgments of the mandate system, a radically new concept in colonial administration, have differed widely. To many critics, international supervision was a unique invasion of national sovereignty. To others, the Permanent Mandates Commission did not have enough power, especially the right to send its own observers into the mandated areas. (This omission was later corrected in the United Nations Trusteeship Council.)

Growth of African studies. Closely connected with Pan-Africanism and Negro nationalism was the movement among Negro intellectuals to rediscover the African past, to prove that Africa had known days of glory. One American Negro writer maintained that the stirring cultural forces bringing about the Renaissance in Europe had originated in Africa. He also declared that prior to the fifteenth century the cultural level in Negro West Africa was equivalent to that in Europe.[4]

While this propaganda stemming from enthusiastic Negro nationalistic feelings was appearing, a more promising development was also taking place—a rising interest in African life and culture among some anthropologists, missionaries, and learned societies. Up to this time relatively little information was available concerning the religious systems, tribal organization, and agriculture of sub-Saharan Africa. Students of social anthropology, a new branch of the social sciences, undertook field trips to Africa; their findings made it clear that the backwardness of the African native was attributable primarily to disease, isolation, and superstitious practices and belief in black magic. Organized in London in 1926, the International Institute of African Languages and Cultures trained anthropologists, encouraged the study of languages, and supported research in the various colonies. New departments in the field of African studies were set up in numerous European universities.

Increasing investment in Africa. After World War I, western businessmen increasingly came to realize the economic possibilities of the African continent. By the early 1930's the total of outside investment made in sub-Saharan Africa amounted to nearly $5,000,000,000. Up to this time tropical Africa's share of the world's trade was not important; its significance lay rather in its near monopoly of certain basic commodities: 56 per cent of the world's gold, 50 per cent of its chrome ore, 90 per cent of its diamonds and cobalt, 93 per cent of its palm oil, and 62 per cent of its cocoa.

Impact of western ideas. As Africa awakened, its people began to feel the impact of western culture. A small student class obtained an education in high schools and colleges; a smaller number traveled abroad to attend universities in Europe and in the United States, among them Jomo Kenyatta and Tom Mboya from Kenya, Nnambi Azikiwe from Nigeria, and Kwame Nkrumah from the Gold Coast—all destined to make history as leaders of African nationalism. With increased educational advantages came a renewed confidence in the destiny of Africa and a strong desire to share as an African in the future of one's native land.

Contact with European modes of life, as the natives labored on plantations and in the households of European settlers, missionaries, and colonial officials, rapidly undermined old faiths, customs, tribal loyalties, and social institutions—a process known as detribalization. But the African as yet belonged exclusively neither to his old tribal world nor to that of the white man. No longer bound by his tribe's laws, he was uneasy about the courts and the law of the Europeans; while accepting Christian doctrines, he secretly believed in the powers of his tribal deities. Thus the impact of western culture gave birth to unrest. Early in the 1930's the further impact of world depression—with its resulting misery to many Africans—added fuel to the rising flames of unrest.

Segregation in the Union of South Africa. The most explosive area in the period between the First and Second World Wars was the Union of South Africa. Here the discontent of the African was the deepest, the confusing process of detribalization the most widespread.

South Africa was a plural society, one made up of different racial and national components that did not mix. The Dutch Europeans (the Boers) were rivals of the British settlers. Since 1902, when Britain defeated the two Boer republics, there had been bad blood between victors and vanquished. In 1909, through the union of the two former republics (the Transvaal and the Orange Free State) with the British colonies of Cape Colony and Natal, South Africa became a self-governing dominion in the British Commonwealth. But union did not bring cooperation. The Boers obtained official recognition for their language (Afrikaans, developed mainly from seventeenth-century Dutch); they insisted upon their own flag and national anthem; and they talked about secession from the Commonwealth.

The rift between Briton and Boer was serious. More dangerous, however, was the increasing numerical gap between all Europeans on the one hand and the native population on the other. After World War I the Europeans began to eye the statistics nervously. The figures disclosed that there were 5,500,000 pure Africans in the Union and 1,800,000 whites, just under 50 per cent of them of British stock. In addition there were 200,000 Asiatics and 600,000 "colored," a term referring to the people, mainly in Cape Province, of mixed white and nonwhite blood. This huge numerical disproportion between non-Europeans and Europeans disturbed the British and Dutch minority. Fearful of being overwhelmed by sheer numbers, many whites became convinced that the natives had to be kept separate from the European community socially and politically and that all political control must remain in the hands of the Europeans.

Segregation and the color bar spread rapidly in the 1930's. Africans were required to live on their tribal reserves. Only those who obtained special permission could work on farms owned by Europeans or in the cities; and in urban areas they were obliged to live in squalid, segregated "locations" and had to carry passes and identity cards under penalty of arrest and fine or imprisonment if found without them. Native labor unions were discouraged and strikes were forbidden. In addition, government regulations or the white labor unions excluded Africans from certain skilled trades. Because of the enormous supply of unskilled native laborers, who would

In the rich gold mines of the Witwatersrand ("ridge of white waters") in southern Transvaal, white laborers held relatively high-paying, skilled jobs, while native workers performed grueling tasks for miserable wages. Before the installation of modern air cooling, Africans endured temperatures of more than 100 degrees as they drilled the veins in cramped tunnels often more than a mile and a half below the surface of the earth.

work for miserably low wages, uneducated Europeans—the "poor whites"—found it difficult to make a living. To favor this group, laws were passed earmarking certain jobs on the railroads and in city services for Europeans; wages for these jobs, even when the unskilled and uneducated were employed, were raised; and the cost was paid by special subsidies. The practice was most discriminatory; the average wage for Europeans was just under four dollars a day, while that of the Africans was just above three dollars a week. In addition to the color bar in industry, the African was effectively barred from politics: he could not vote or hold office in any elective body or parliament outside his own tribal reserve.

Native unrest was manifested in the increasing native crime rate in the cities, in the formation of underground organizations, and in the determined efforts of African lawyers, doctors, and journalists to secure political rights. Here and there in the back alleys and cellars of cities such as Johannesburg, young Africans ran their mimeograph machines, turning out handbills and papers advertising their grievances. One two-page sheet called the *African Liberator* declared:

Africa has come to the parting of the ways . . . Black South Africa has been bought and sold to some wolves in clothing of sheep who profess to be their friends. What does the African want? He wants liberty, equality, and opportunity. We demand our rights to have the same vote as Europeans, the same education, the same right to defend the country, the same right to sit in Parliament, Provincial Councils, and Town Councils. We do not want two nations in South Africa.[5]

Native unrest could be detected in other areas. In the Gold Coast, Nigeria, and Kenya, educated Africans formed political organizations to express their demands for more self-government. Except in the Union, however, African nationalist aspirations were not widespread. The continent was only gradually awakening and feeling the tingling currents of world forces. Its nationalistic upsurge was to wait until after World War II.

TENSIONS IN THE
ARAB WORLD

Cultural links between Asia and Africa. The heart of the Arab world is the Middle East, a difficult region to define. The term is used most often in reference to the lands connecting Asia with Africa, the chief boundary markers being Cairo, Istanbul, Teheran, and the south coast of the Arabian peninsula. Except for the Turks and the Iranians, all the peoples of the Middle East—Persians, Iraqis, Egyptians, Syrians, and Bedouins—are united in a common faith (Islam) and share a common tongue and culture (Arabic). Because of the unifying force of this heritage, Muslim North Africa (Morocco, Algeria, Tunisia, Libya) will be treated in this chapter as part of the Arab world.

With the exception of Morocco, North Africa at the beginning of the nineteenth century was nominally under the sovereignty of the Ottoman Turks, whose capital city was Constantinople. In practice, however, the various states in this area were self-governing. After 1815 all of North Africa from Casablanca in Morocco to Cairo in Egypt came under European imperialistic rule, while the other Arab lands in the Middle East continued under the despotic control of the sultans.

The Arab revolt. Just before the outbreak of the First World War, the Arabs within the Ottoman empire had reached the breaking point in their relations with the Turkish government. In 1913 an Arab Congress meeting in Paris demanded home rule and equality with the Turks in the empire. Because the Middle East was strategically important to Britain, the British government followed the rise of Arab discontent with great interest. Even before the outbreak of World War I, Arab leaders had been cautiously feeling out Britain to discover whether the British would support a revolt against Ottoman rule in Syria, Iraq, and Arabia. During 1915 and 1916 extensive correspondence was carried on between the British high commissioner in Cairo and Sherif Husein of Mecca (Husein ibn-Ali, 1856-1931), guardian of the holy places in the Hejaz. In the event of an Arab revolt, Great Britain undertook to recognize Arab independence except in those regions of coastal Syria which were not wholly Arab and in those which might be claimed by France. But British commitments were purposely vague, and the whole correspondence has been described as "a monument of ambiguity."

In addition to the British alliance with the Arab nationalist movement, the indomitable desert warrior Abdul-Aziz ibn-Saud (1880-1953), sultan of Nejd in south-central Arabia, was induced to adopt a policy of benevolent neutrality toward Britain. The wooing of the Arabs thwarted the Turkish attempt to rouse the whole Muslim Middle East by preaching a *jihad*, or holy war, against the British.

Late in 1916 the Arab revolt began. Husein raised the standard of rebellion in the Hejaz, proclaimed independence from the Turks, and captured Mecca for his cause. In the fighting that followed, the Arab forces were commanded by the third son of the Sherif Husein, Emir Faisal (1885-1933), who was assisted by a remarkable English officer, Colonel T. E. Lawrence (1888-1935), later known as Lawrence of Arabia.

As a student at Oxford, Lawrence had become interested in the crusades and especially in the castle architecture built in the Holy Land by the medieval knights who had taken the Cross. Shy and physically slight, he had roamed the Arab lands, studying the language and habits of the Muslims. In 1914 Lawrence was engaged by the British government to take part in the Arab guerrilla campaign against the Turks. Idolized by the Bedouin tribesmen he knew so well, he disrupted Turkish communication lines and destroyed so many locomotives that the Turks called him *El-Orens* ("destroyer of engines").

Under Lawrence, the Arabs took a decisive part in the last battle against the main Turkish forces in September 1918. When the war ended, Syria was occupied by the victorious Allied forces; a small French force was located along the coast of Lebanon; Emir Faisal and his Arab forces were in the interior, grouped around Damascus; and the British controlled Palestine.

The peace settlement. With Turkey defeated, the Arab leaders sought the independence that they thought had been promised by Britain in the correspondence with Husein. When the peace conference met in Paris, it became painfully clear that the problem of political settlement in the Middle East was a jumble of conflicting promises and rivalries.

During the war years a number of important commitments had been made. In 1916, in the Sykes-Picot Agreement, the Fertile Crescent (Syria and Iraq) had been divided into four zones, with Britain and France each controlling two. Palestine was to be placed under an international administration. In the following year another commitment had been made by Britain. This was the Balfour Declaration, whereby the British government gave its support to the establishment of a national home for the Jewish people in Palestine. In 1918 Great Britain made several declarations recognizing Arab national aspirations, and an Anglo-French pronouncement pledged the establishment of national governments "deriving their authority from the initiative and free choice of the indigenous populations."

At the peace conference Emir Faisal, aided by Colonel Lawrence, pleaded the cause of Arab independence, but in vain. He was still ruler in Damascus, and in March 1920, while the statesmen in Paris argued, a congress of Syrian leaders met and resolved that he should be king of a united Syria, including Palestine and Lebanon. But in April the San Remo Conference of the Allied powers turned over all Arab territories formerly in the Ottoman empire to be administered as mandates. Syria and Lebanon were mandated to France; Iraq and Palestine, to Great Britain. Britain and France pledged to recognize that the Arab states under their control "have reached a stage of development where their existence as independent nations can be provisionally recognised subject to the rendering of administrative advice and assistance by a Mandatory [power] until such time as they are able to stand alone."[6] To the Arabs the mandates were a poor substitute for independence and a flimsy disguise for imperialism.

From the Arabs' point of view, the peace settlement in the Middle East was a shabby piece of statesmanship compounded of ignorance, deception, and conflicting aims. Apologists for Britain and France point out that Britain made promises to France during the war because the British could hardly deny the requests of their most important ally, which had close missionary and educational ties in Syria. Britain in 1916 made its ambiguous pledge to Husein because of its desperate need for Arab friendship. Again, in the Balfour Declaration, Britain acted according to short-range interests; in order to swing the support of the world's Jews to the Allied cause and to maintain communications in the Middle East, Britain promised to make available to Jewish settlement the Arab region of Palestine.

The plain fact remains, however, that the Allied statesmen at Paris were profoundly ignorant of the intensity of Arab nationalism. A historian of Syria has written: "The ghost of the Peace Settlement has haunted Arab politics ever since. It turned into bitterness the enthusiasm which the Arab Revolt had aroused, and seriously damaged the moral influence of Great Britain and France in the Near East."[7] Let us now examine the events between World Wars I and II in the mandated areas (Syria-Lebanon, Iraq, Palestine) and then trace the growth of tension in Iran, Egypt, and North Africa.

The French in Syria and Lebanon. In 1920, following the San Remo Conference, a French army moved against Damascus and ejected Faisal from the throne. After this incident, the French took over the mandate of Lebanon and Syria. Following a policy of divide and rule, they attempted especially to woo the large Christian Arab groups in Lebanon. But they were not successful; the Arabs remained hostile.

In 1925 the Druses, a proud Muslim sect living in the mountains, revolted and touched off two years of civil war. An artillery bombardment of Damascus by the French aroused widespread resentment. The French then instituted a more conciliatory policy. In 1926 Lebanon was recognized as a republic, and the same status was accorded four years later to the four administrative divisions of Syria. In practice, however, these republics continued under effective French control. Relative tranquillity reigned until 1935, when a new wave of nationalism agitated Syria-Lebanon. Early the next year a Syrian nationalist organization inspired a fifty-day strike, and as a result the more liberal Popular Front government in France (see p. 522) drew up two treaties. Under these treaties the mandates were recognized as independent republics which were to become members of the League of Nations, and France was granted certain privileges in their territories, such as the right to maintain troops and military bases. Unfortunately, relations between France and Syria deteriorated, the French parliament kept postponing ratification of the agreements, and finally in 1939 the Syrian constitution was suspended and the French high commissioner took over control of the government.

Politically, French rule was a failure in Syria and Lebanon. At the outset a popular Arab king had been ejected, and for the next twenty years the French administration often suppressed personal and political liberties. Under French mandatory rule, however,

the modernization of Syria-Lebanon proceeded: roads and public buildings were constructed, and the use of electricity and irrigation works was extended. The French also restored ancient monuments, expanded the educational system, and founded museums.

British policy in Iraq. Great Britain's vital interest in the mandate of Iraq was prompted largely by Iraq's rich oil resources, its growing importance in East-West air transportation, and its proximity to the Persian Gulf. But this interest did not prevent the British from taking steps to satisfy Iraqi nationalism after the outbreak of rebellion in June 1920. In March 1921 the Iraqi throne was offered to Faisal, who had lost his throne in Syria. In a plebescite Faisal was strongly supported as ruler of the Iraqi, and a few months later he was proclaimed king. In 1922 Britain and Faisal's government signed a treaty which stipulated that Britain was to supervise the finances and military affairs of the new state. Three years later a constitution was adopted which made the country a constitutional monarchy with a bicameral legislature.

The achievements of the British advisers in setting up a modern administration in Iraq were noteworthy. One Arab authority states: "The British contribution to the building up of Iraq is one of the most remarkable instances of post-War reconstruction."[8] In June 1930 an Anglo-Iraqi treaty was signed which granted Iraq full independence, though Britain retained two air bases to protect British communications. In 1932 Iraq was admitted to the League of Nations. By these concessions Britain avoided the conflict experienced by France in Syria-Lebanon.

During the mounting diplomatic tension of the late 1930's, when the Axis powers were making a determined drive to weaken the international position of Britain and France, Mussolini tried to undermine the British in Arab lands. The skillful propaganda of Fascist Italy, combined with Arab hostility regarding the British policy in Palestine, brought about a decline of good will toward Britain in Iraq.

Arab-Jewish conflict in Palestine. Between the two world wars, Palestine was the most tempestuous area in all the Middle East, as Britain sought to protect its imperial interests and at the same time reconcile them with Zionism and Arab nationalism. Almost as soon as the mandate was set up, Arab riots took place in Palestine. In 1921 the British high commissioner Sir Herbert Samuel, himself a Jew, sought to define the stipulations of the Balfour Declaration more precisely. He stated:

The Jews, a people who are scattered throughout the world . . . should be enabled to find their home, and . . . some among them, within the limits that are fixed by the numbers and interests of the present population, should come to Palestine in order to help by their resources and efforts to develop the country to the advantage of all its inhabitants . . . the British Government . . . would never impose upon them [the Arabs] a policy which that people had reason to think was contrary to their religious, their political, and their economic interests.[9]

Such pronouncements and the fact that Jewish immigration was not large made possible a period of peace and progress from 1922 to 1929. As the Zionists reclaimed land, set up collective farms, harnessed the Jordan for power, and established many new factories, a veritable economic revolution took place. Tel-Aviv grew into a thriving modern city, an excellent university was founded at Jerusalem, and Palestine became the center of a Hebrew renaissance.

The era of peace ended in 1929 when serious disorders broke out, mainly Arab attacks on Jews. Violence continued to erupt in the early 1930's as the Nazi persecution of the Jews brought about a steep rise in immigration to Palestine and threatened the predominant position of the Arabs in the area. In 1937 a British commission of inquiry recommended a tripartite division: Palestine would be divided into two independent states, one controlled by the Arabs and one by the Jews, with Britain holding a third portion, a small mandated area containing Jerusalem and Bethlehem. This recommendation satisfied no one and was not accepted.

As war with the Axis powers loomed in 1939, Britain sought desperately to strength-en its position in the Middle East by attempts to regain Arab good will. A "white paper" was issued which declared that it was Britain's aim to have as an ally an independent Palestine established at the end of ten years, with guarantees for both the Arab and Jewish populations. During this ten-year period, land sales were to be restricted. After the admission of 50,000 Jews, with the possibility of another 25,000 refugees from Nazi Germany, no more immigration would take place without the consent of the Arabs. The outbreak of World War II shelved the Zionist-Arab quarrel in Palestine; but after the war the controversy was to break out again with fatal virulence.

Rivalry for leadership of the Arab world. In the cradle of Islamic civilization—the Arabian peninsula, where the birthplace of Muhammad and the holy cities of Mecca and Medina are located and the desert Bedouins make their home—the various local rulers were largely outside the sphere of western control. The collapse of Ottoman rule in 1918 left several important independent states such as Yemen, Hejaz, and Nejd to adjust their relations, plus a few British protectorates on the Arabian Sea and the Persian Gulf.

The first contender for leadership of the peninsula was Sherif Husein. In alliance with Great Britain, his sons had already been favored by the gift of kingdoms: Faisal in Iraq and Abdullah in Trans-Jordan, the territory carved out of the eastern portion of Palestine. At the close of World War I, it appeared that the Hashemite family of Husein would become the greatest single political force in Arabia and the Fertile Crescent.

The rival of the Hashemites was ibn-Saud, whose family had ruled Nejd since the eighteenth century and had become identified with a reformist, puritanical Muslim sect known as the Wahabis. Husein regarded the ruler of Nejd with contempt. But, fortunately for ibn-Saud, Husein made a series of blunders: he alienated many Arabs by proclaiming himself king of the Arabs; he quarreled with Britain, which ceased to render him support; and he underestimated the capacity of ibn-Saud.

In 1919 one of Husein's sons was defeated by the Wahabi warriors of ibn-Saud. All-out war against Husein began in 1924, and by the following year ibn-Saud was victorious and his troops occupied Mecca, Jiddah, Taif, and Medina. A treaty with Britain in 1927 brought ibn-Saud recognition as king of both Hejaz and Nejd; in 1932 all his holdings were renamed Saudi Arabia. In 1934 he defeated the last of his rivals—the king of Yemen—who was allowed to retain his independence. Two years earlier, vast oil reserves had been discovered in eastern Arabia. Important concessions were given to an American oil company, and ibn-Saud now commanded the wealth essential for a powerful state. All the tribal groups in Arabia were welded into a strong political entity, with enormous economic resources.

Riza Shah Pahlavi rules Iran. Also at stake in the period between World Wars I and II was the fate of Persia (or Iran as it came to be called in the 1920's), a land which was Muslim in religion but not Arabic in culture. As we saw in Chapter 10, the central fact in the history of Iran in the nineteenth century was the Anglo-Russian rivalry over the efforts of the Russians to force their way to the Persian Gulf. During the First World War, Iran was a battleground for Turkish, Russian, and British forces. With the elimination of Russia in 1919 as a serious contender in this region, the British Foreign Office sought to bring Persia closely under its control.

The proposed Anglo-Persian agreement aroused nationalism to a high pitch. Before the Majlis (the parliament) could approve the treaty, the nationalists had seized power. Their agent was a brilliant military officer, Riza Shah Pahlavi (1877-1944), who marched on Teheran, the capital, in 1921. Four years later the shah was forced to resign, and Riza Shah took his place, founding the Pahlavi dynasty.

The new ruler was a strongly nationalistic reformer who wished to emulate Mustafa Kemal of Turkey (see p. 499) in modernizing his country. Special privileges enjoyed by foreigners were abolished, and stiffer terms in royalties were demanded from the Anglo-Iranian Oil Company, which was tapping the country's rich petroleum reserves. The restless tribes were brought under the control of the law, the army was modernized, trade and industry were encouraged and brought under government control, and education was improved. Between 1928 and 1936 the Trans-Iranian Railroad was built, connecting the Persian Gulf and the Caspian Sea. But in spite of his impressive record of progress, Riza Shah had a serious weakness. Impatient with delay or inefficiency, he steadily developed the mind of a tyrant. The government grew more authoritarian, the Majlis came to be a mere puppet body, and corruption was again on the increase. The decaying rule of Riza Shah was destined to collapse during World War II.

Afghanistan. To the east of Iran was the remote and almost inaccessible kingdom of Afghanistan. In 1919 the Afghan emir, believing that nationalist unrest in India rendered that country a likely prize (see p. 501), made the mistake of invading the subcontinent and was defeated with severe losses. Later the course of Turkish reform attracted the emir's attention; but though he promulgated a new constitution, the reforms were mainly on paper. In 1928 a destructive civil war brought the emir's brother to the throne, but no reform in government was forthcoming. Principal government jobs were filled by relatives of the ruling family, and the prevailing atmosphere was one of palace intrigue punctuated occasionally by political assassination. Between World Wars I and II, Afghanistan remained politically unstable, its natural resources neglected and its people illiterate.

The problem of Egyptian sovereignty. While the Arabs in the mandates had been struggling for the right of self-determination, a parallel development was taking place in Egypt. When the British refused a delegation of Egyptian nationalists permission to attend the Paris Peace Conference and deported the spokesman of the group and his followers, the Nile valley rose in revolt. Many lives were lost before the revolution could be put down.

After three years of disorder the government in London announced that Egypt was no longer a British protectorate. It was to be a sovereign state, subject to certain reservations. Britain was to remain responsible for the defense of the country, for the protection of foreign interests, and for communications vital to the British empire, above all the Suez Canal. Egypt grudgingly adapted itself to this declaration, made its sultan a king, and proclaimed a constitution in 1923. Anglo-Egyptian relations remained unsatisfactory, however, and frequent negotiations between the two governments were fruitless. In Egypt from 1924 to 1936, corruption in high places, the increasing number of university graduates unable to find suitable employment, the wide gap between the very rich and the abysmally poor, and the bitter feud between the king and the most important political party (the Wafd) helped to create confusion and unrest.

Respite in the long record of Anglo-Egyptian acrimony came about through the threat of Italian Fascist aggression in Africa following Mussolini's conquest of Abyssinia (see p. 538). In 1936 Britain and Egypt negotiated a treaty of alliance which stipulated that the agreement could be revised after twenty years (after ten if both parties agreed) and called for the evacuation of British troops from Cairo and Alexandria to a military zone in the Suez Canal. In the case of war there was to be mutual assistance on a wide scale, and the status of the Sudan* was to continue unaltered.

Fascist rule in Libya. West of Egypt lies Libya, the desert land seized in 1912 from Turkey by land-hungry Italy. The fierce nomadic tribes put up a stout resistance to European invasion, especially the community known as the Sanusis, a devout Muslim order which was constantly threatening to embark on a *jihad* against the unbeliever. For a few years the Italians had to confine their control

*The Sudan (see Reference Map 5) had been influenced by Egypt for many centuries and in 1820 was brought under Egyptian rule. In the 1880's fanatical Muslims had driven the Egyptians out and had put to death General Gordon, the governor at Khartoum, who was the agent of the Egyptian government. In the 1890's the British reconquered the Sudan and declared it a condominium—that is, a territory theoretically under the dual sovereignty of Britain and Egypt but really under British control. The treaty of alliance of 1936 stated that the Sudan would remain technically under joint Anglo-Egyptian administration for the "welfare of the Sudanese."

to the coastal region, but in time their authority became fully established, and in the 1930's an ambitious program of development and colonization was put into effect. By 1939, when World War II began, thousands of Italian settlers were living in Libya, and the country had been politically integrated with the kingdom of Italy, its colonial administrative units converted into Italian provinces.

All in all, Fascist rule was harsh. The resistance of the Sanusis had been broken by the destruction of their wells in the desert. Although large sums were spent reclaiming arid desert land, building roads, and organizing settlement schemes for Italian immigrants, the Libyans profited little from these activities; the limited form of Italian citizenship granted to them in 1939 was no great blessing.

Aggressive nationalism in North Africa. Long before the outbreak of World War I, Algeria had become politically integrated with France; Tunisia had prospered under French rule and had maintained its native ruler, the bey; and the native sultan had also been retained in the protectorate France established in Morocco in 1911. Nevertheless, the storm signals of bitter nationalism had appeared, particularly in Morocco.

The Moroccans, a fiercely independent people, rebelled in 1912, and the outbreak was subdued only after savage fighting. Shortly after World War I, rebellion against alien rule broke out in Spanish Morocco under the leadership of the Riff chieftain Abd-el Krim. When revolt spread to French Morocco, the French joined the Spanish in a vigorous campaign which brought the defeat of Krim and his Riffs in 1926. But though defeated, Abd-el Krim's exploits had caused a sensation in the Arab world. Again in 1930 an organized nationalist movement, fanned by the world economic depression, began in Morocco. Riots broke out and agitation was carried on for an end to direct French administration. Though some administrative posts were made available to Moroccans and some other demands were met in the late 1930's, no further steps were taken to implement self-rule.

The year 1934 marked a major change in the concept of nationalism in Morocco. In this year a group of young Moroccans presented their Plan of Moroccan Reforms. While the efforts of Abd-el Krim had represented tribal opposition to foreign rule, the formation of a nationalist party heralded the birth of a modern nationalistic movement. In 1937 there was an unsuccessful nationalist revolt. On the eve of World War II, Arab nationalism was growing but was still relatively weak and in the main was driven underground by French repressive measures.

Tunisia was the most westernized area in French North Africa, and in 1919 a nationalist party called the Destour (meaning "constitution" in Arabic) was formed to secure more democratic forms of government. In 1934, after this party was suppressed, another nationalist group, the Neo-Destour, was formed. Four years later this group was banned also, and the nationalist movement went underground.

In Algeria, organized political agitation against the French began in 1926, but incidents were relatively few. The natives demanded an easier means of acquiring French citizenship and, with citizenship, the additional rights and economic advantages which this status implied. French citizenship had been extended after the First World War to a large number of Muslims who qualified on the basis of war service, literacy, and other tests, but opposition—mainly from French settlers in Algeria—largely prevented further reforms during the 1930's.

France deserved much credit for its colonial rule. Administration on the whole was just and efficient, the economy prospered, and living standards advanced. Nevertheless, a fundamental split existed between the privileged Christian minority and the overwhelming Muslim majority; the Arab populace admired examples of Arab assertiveness such as the Wafd movement in Egypt.

Until 1939 the nationalist movement in North Africa was largely a monopoly of the relatively small intellectual groups and middle class. The mass of peasants remained quite apathetic. Sympathy and support for Arab nationalism came from North African intellectuals who had enjoyed European educations and from liberals and members of leftist parties in France.

Mustafa Kemal's rise to power in Turkey. We have seen in Chapter 12 how reform measures had been initiated by the Young Turks just before World War I. Defeat in the war, the revolt of the Arabs, and the impotence of the sultan's government convinced some patriots that only the most drastic measures could save the Turkish nation. In addition, they were embittered by the harsh terms of the Treaty of Sèvres (1920). It was bad enough to lose their empire, peopled by Arabs, but it was much worse to see their homeland, mainly Anatolia and the city of Smyrna, partitioned by the treaty and invaded by the Greeks and Italians.

Imbued with a new spirit of nationalism, the patriots rallied around the military hero Mustafa Kemal Pasha (1880-1938), who had a brilliant record against the British at Gallipoli in World War I. An important figure in the Young Turks movement, Kemal was a born leader, thoroughly western in education and outlook. After the defeat of Turkey, he had been sent by the sultan to demobilize the Turkish troops in Asia Minor, but, disregarding his instructions, he had reorganized the troops and successfully defied the Allies. A new government was set up in Ankara, and Kemal was selected as president and commander in chief. Turkish patriotism was galvanized by the National Pact, a declaration of principles supported by Kemal. This document upheld the rule of self-determination for all people, including the Turks, and also proclaimed the abolition of the special rights heretofore enjoyed by foreigners in Turkey, a mark of Turkish inequality in the family of nations.

In 1921 the Greeks advanced toward Ankara. The fighting was desperate, but the armies of Kemal were finally victorious. The Greeks fled in confusion toward the sea, and their last toe hold, Smyrna, was destroyed by fire. In 1922 the Turkish sultanate was abolished, and the following year a republic was established. The Allies had no alternative but to agree to a revision of Sèvres. The Treaty of Lausanne, signed in 1923, returned to Turkey some Aegean islands and the territory adjoining Constantinople. The heartland of Turkey —Anatolia—remained intact, no reparations were demanded of the republic, and the special privileges of foreigners were abolished. Although Turkey had lost the whole Arabic-speaking part of its possessions, Kemal had saved a large, cohesively Turkish portion of the former Ottoman empire.

Kemal's reforms. The new constitution was democratic in form, but in reality Kemal was a dictator who brooked no interference with his plans. His dictatorship does not belong in the same category as those fashioned in Nazi Germany, or Fascist Italy, or Communist Russia, however. In the new Turkey there was little of the cult of the superior race; the brutal efficiency of the purge and the concentration camp was practically unknown. Dictatorship was regarded as the rough but essential highway to parliamentary government. Kemal envisioned a dictatorship as a necessary stage in raising his people to that level of education and social well-being which democratic government requires.

Under his rule the old institutions and customs of a backward oriental state were transformed or replaced within a few short years. In modern times such a wholesale adoption of new culture traits is duplicated nowhere except perhaps in Japan. The caliphate, the sultan's spiritual leadership of the Muhammadan world, was abolished. The courts of the Greek Orthodox Church were discontinued, and new law codes were promulgated. A frontal attack was made on illiteracy; education was taken out of the hands of the Orthodox Church, and school attendance was made compulsory to the age of sixteen. Use of the fez by men and the veil by women was forbidden. Polygamy was prohibited. In addition, the western Gregorian calendar and European numerals were introduced, and the Latin alphabet replaced the Arabic.

Thus, Turkey was rejuvenated by its indefatigable leader, who created a new capital at Ankara. More progress was made in the two decades after the close of the First World War than had been registered during the entire nineteenth century. Mustafa Kemal was

In this sketch from a 1931 issue of the *Illustrated London News*, Hindu untouchables practice passive resistance against the caste system by blocking entrance to a temple with their bodies; all high-caste Hindus who attempt to pass will pollute themselves by touching the outcastes. The untouchables were not allowed to enter most temples and were excluded from the social and religious privileges of other Hindus. Forced to live in separate quarters in the poorest districts of towns and villages, they were also forbidden to use the village well. In southern India, they could not come within a specified distance of any high-caste Hindu on the roads.

called *Atatürk,* meaning "the father of the Turks."

INDIA SEEKS TO RULE ITSELF

Moves for self-government. Many observers had predicted that in the event of war Great Britain would find India a serious liability. But when hostilities began, nearly all unfriendly acts against Britain ceased. The native princes sent large sums of money to London to purchase matériel, and Indian troops fought beside British soldiers.

This period of general cooperation continued for the first three years of World War I.

By 1917, however, it became apparent that the Indian people expected compensation from Britain in the way of more self-government. Parliament's reply indicated that the goal to be attained in India was the gradual development of self-government within the British empire.

In 1918 a British commission was sent to India to investigate the problem of Indian self-government. Convinced that many Indians were now fit to fill important government posts, the members of the commission submitted a report to Parliament which resulted in the passage of an Indian constitution in the Government of India Act of 1919. The act did not provide for full self-government as the Indian nationalists had hoped but for a system of diarchy, or double government, in the provinces; by this method certain powers were reserved to the British while the provincial legislatures were accorded other, generally lesser powers. Thus the act represented only a step toward self-government.

Chances for the acceptance in India of the act of 1919 were swept away by the outbreak of a struggle between the British and the Indian nationalists. In an ill-advised moment the British passed the Rowlatt Acts (1919), which allowed the police and other officials extraordinary powers in ferreting out subversive activity. Although the acts were never enforced, they were deeply resented as a token of repression. Disgruntled and disheartened by a number of factors—the political situation, the Rowlatt Acts, the disastrous effects of the influenza epidemic of 1918 and 1919, and the high cost of living—many nationalists demanded sweeping changes.

Gandhi and civil disobedience. The foremost nationalist leader in India was Mohandas K. Gandhi (1869-1948). Born of middle-class parents, Gandhi had been sent to London to study law; later he went to South Africa, where he built up a lucrative practice. Suddenly his outlook on life and his standard of values changed completely. The new Gandhi repudiated wealth, practiced ascetic self-denial, condemned violence, and believed firmly that true happiness could be achieved only by service to one's fellow men.

Gandhi began his career as reformer and champion of his people in South Africa. The Indians there were subject to numerous restrictive laws which hampered their freedom of movement, prevented them from buying property, and imposed upon them special taxation. By the use of "passive resistance," or noncooperation, Gandhi forced the government to remove some restrictions. Disdaining the use of violence, he believed that a just cause triumphs if its supporters attempt to convince those in power of injustices by practicing "civil disobedience." With Gandhi as their leader, the Indians in South Africa carried on various strikes, including hunger strikes; they refused work, held mass demonstrations, and marched into areas where their presence was forbidden by law.

When he returned to his native land shortly after the outbreak of World War I, Gandhi was welcomed as a hero. During the war he cooperated with the British government, but the Rowlatt Act and the disappointing concessions in the new constitution led him to announce his determination to force the British to give India self-rule.

In 1919 Gandhi introduced his campaign. A mass strike was announced in which all work was to cease and the population was to pray and fast. Contrary to Gandhi's plan, however, riots took place, Europeans were killed, and soldiers were sent to try to restore order. Although public gatherings were forbidden, a large body of unarmed Indians assembled at Amritsar. They were dispersed by gunfire, and several hundred were killed. All hope of cooperation between Indian and Briton was temporarily at an end. During these tense days the new governmental system was established, but members of the powerful Indian National Congress who supported Gandhi refused to take office. Arrested in 1922, Gandhi seemed to welcome being placed on trial; he assured the British magistrate that the only alternative to permitting him to continue his campaign was to imprison him. This frail little man's courage in defying British rule made excellent copy throughout the world. Sentenced to six years' imprisonment, Gandhi suffered a temporary eclipse.

There was little peace in India in the 1920's. During 1928 and 1929 a group of political experts from Great Britain, the Simon Commission, toured the country. The survey issued by the commission in 1930 suggested only a cautious advance in the direction of self-government. Meanwhile Gandhi initiated another campaign toward that goal.

Round-table conferences. A new and promising road to conciliation opened in 1930, when a series of round-table conferences was arranged in London. At the first of these conferences, the Indian princes agreed in principle to the idea of creating in India a great federal union. Up to this time India had consisted of two great political divisions: British India, ruled directly by the British, and the native India of the princes, composed of a number of distinct political units, each ruled by a rajah or other Indian ruler under the final protection and authority of the British government. Unfortunately, safeguards insisted upon by the Muslim minority for its protection under the new government were not defined to the satisfaction of either Hindus or Muslims. Moreover, in the second conference in 1931, the native princes and the delegates from British India could not agree as to the details of federation. Anti-British demonstrations broke out in India. At neither the second conference nor a third one in 1932 were the differences between the various factions in India settled.

The Government of India Act of 1935. The proposed constitution, made public in 1933, was heatedly discussed by members of the British Parliament and by Indian leaders for two years. Finally, in 1935, a second Government of India Act became law, and two years later it began to function. The new constitution provided for a substantial degree of self-government but did not award India complete independence. Instead, a federal government was established, consisting of a viceroy and a legislature composed of a council of state and a legislative assembly. To these houses both the Indian princes and the eleven provinces of British India were to send representatives. In the central government all the departments of government were transferred

The great leader of the Indian independence movement was Gandhi. He is shown here just after he arrived in England in 1931 to attend a round-table conference on the future of India.

to the Indian legislators except the departments of defense, religious affairs, and foreign relations, which remained in British hands. In addition, a supreme court was established. In the provinces of British India, the government was to be under the control of Indian lawmakers, subject to certain controls held by the British governors.

From 1937 to 1939 provincial responsible government, which went into effect in seven of the eleven provinces of British India, was deemed a success. The British governors allowed Indian legislators to form their own policies, which were carried out by British

civil servants. But during these same years, the possibility of federation faded away; the native princes became increasingly hesitant about placing themselves under the central government. In June 1939, they definitely rejected the constitution.

The Indian National Congress. The new regime established by the Government of India Act of 1935 failed to satisfy the demands of the Indian nationalists, who continued to espouse the cause of complete independence for India. The chief element in the nationalist movement was the powerful Indian National Congress, which had become the organ of the extreme nationalists. Membership, estimated at several million, was predominantly Hindu but also included many Muslims and members of other religious groups. Soon after the First World War, the congress had come under the leadership of Gandhi, whose personal following among the people was the chief source of the party's tremendous influence. The masses of the Indian people loved and respected Gandhi, who lived frugally and honored the ancient traditions as they did and who understood their problems. Gandhi had still other goals besides the independence of India; he sought to end excessive drinking, to raise the status of women in society, to remove the stigma attached to the class of untouchables, and to bring about cooperation between Hindus and Muslims. Permeating all of Gandhi's ideas and actions was his belief in nonviolence; he was convinced that injustices and wrongs could be destroyed only through the forces of love, unselfishness, and patience.

By 1939 Gandhi shared leadership of the nationalist movement with Jawaharlal Nehru (1889-1964), a profound thinker, an able statesman, and an attractive personality. Devoted friends, the two leaders differed profoundly in many of their ideas for the future of India: Gandhi wished to expel western influences and return India to a primitive handicraft economy and a simple, ascetic way of life; Nehru believed India should be westernized and industrialized and should become a socialistic state. But however much they disagreed over solutions to economic and social problems, they agreed on a free and united India.

The Hindu-Muslim clash. The nationalist movement in India was complicated by the existence of a second powerful political party, the Muslim League. Led by an able and aggressive lawyer, Muhammad Ali Jinnah (1876-1948), the league sought to protect the position of the Muslim minority in India. Maintaining that the congress program of a united and democratic India meant in effect the domination of the Muslim minority by the Hindu majority, the league set itself in opposition to the congress and sought special guarantees for the Muslim community. This program was later to culminate in the division of India into separate Hindu and Muslim states.

The position of the Muslim League highlighted the division between the Hindus and Muslims, a division termed "the communal problem." The position of the congress party was that in a democratic and self-governing India, men would think of themselves as Indians rather than as members of Hindu or Muslim communities, and the deep-seated religious differences would thus gradually become politically unimportant. The strategy of the Muslim League, on the other hand, was to underline and perpetuate these differences. This fundamental clash of viewpoints was one factor behind the British reluctance to accede to Indian demands for freedom. Having a tremendous economic investment in the country and facing the imminent danger of world war, Britain was unwilling to withdraw in the absence of a compromise which would assure India a measure of political stability.

NATIONALISM IN SOUTHEAST

ASIA AND OCEANIA

The late beginning of nationalist feeling. Stretching southeast of India and including the island of Ceylon, the large peninsula-like projection of Burma Siam (Thailand), Malaya, and Indo-China, as well as the vast archipelago extending from Sumatra to the

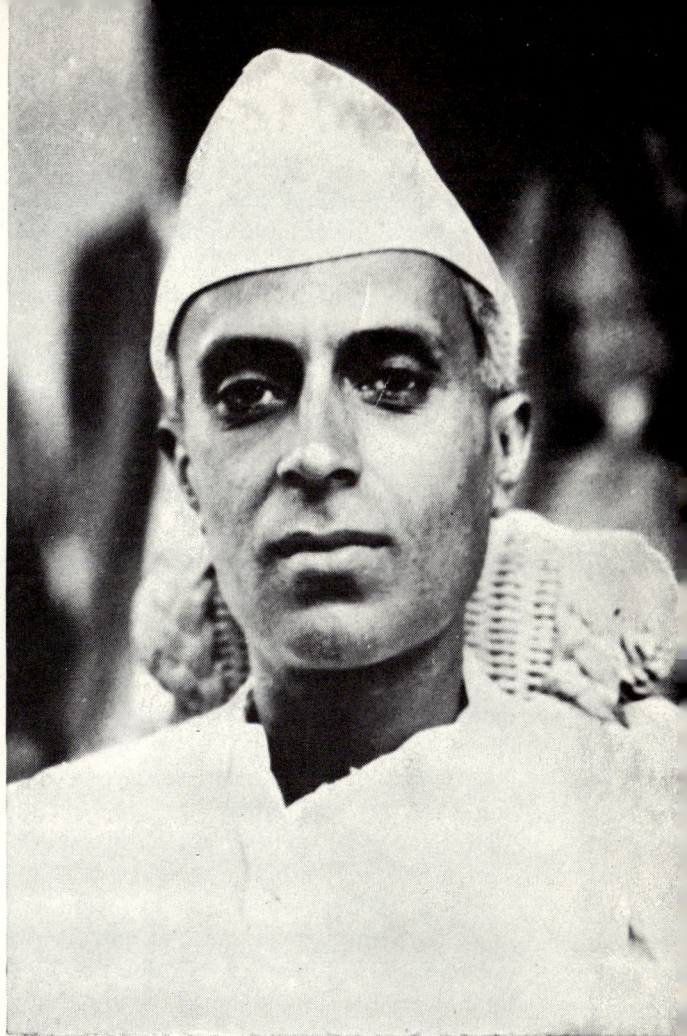

After the Amritsar massacre of 1919, Nehru joined Gandhi's followers, eventually becoming second only to the beloved Mahatma in the independence movement.

Philippines, is the world of southeast Asia, an area of 1,500,000 square miles. Between World Wars I and II, all states in this region except for Siam were colonial dependencies.

Nationalism in southeast Asia received a strong stimulus as a result of the First World War, and nationalistic feelings mounted steadily in the 1920's and 1930's. On the eve of World War II, however, the masses of people in this area were apathetic to nationalism, which was the preoccupation of a small intellectual group and the middle class, constituting not more than 10 per cent of the population. Nationalist leaders obtained support in the towns and ignored the peasants.

While a discontented nationalist might have thought the pace toward self-government unnecessarily sluggish, the general policy of the British colonial administrations was directed toward establishing legislatures and granting a substantial measure of self-government to the native peoples. The ultimate goal of British plans for the colonies was dominion status—that is, practical independence within the loose bonds of the British Commonwealth. On the other hand, France endowed its colonies with little independence or self-rule. The French aim was not independence but rather a close association of states dominated from Paris. Dutch rule was also paternalistic.

Concessions to nationalism in Ceylon and Burma. Before the First World War, Ceylon had been governed paternally as a British crown colony. In 1919 the Ceylon National Congress began to agitate for more self-government, and in the early 1920's colonial administration was somewhat liberalized. In 1931, following the visit of a British commission in 1927 and 1928, a progressive constitution was adopted which gave Ceylon the most democratic government of any Asiatic dependency. The new constitution provided for universal male and female suffrage and for a system of political administration which allowed full self-government in some areas and retention of British control in others.

In Burma, although British rule brought undisputed benefits, serious social and economic maladjustments occurred as a result of commercial growth. The easygoing Burmese villagers fell victim to Indian moneylenders, while Chinese immigrants worked the mines, Indian Muslims operated the river boats, and East Indian merchants controlled the rice trade. Economic strains led to nationalist unrest. In addition, British rule tended to diminish the prestige of the Buddhist priests, who retaliated by agitating against alien rule. Burma was granted a more liberal constitution in 1922, but nationalist unrest persisted. In 1930 depression brought economic distress and a serious uprising against the Indian and Chinese communities. At the end of the year another uprising took place, directed this time against British rule. These early uprisings were confused waves of violence, but

after 1935 the nationalist movement became an important challenge to alien rule.

In 1937 substantial concessions were made by Britain: Burma was separated from India and given home rule, subject to certain emergency powers held by the British governor. The course of Burmese politics from 1937 to the Japanese invasion in 1942 was not encouraging, however. The political scene was characterized by a confusing multiplicity of political parties, by bribery and favoritism, and by the decline of civil service standards. While both men and women now enjoyed the vote, the electorate was apathetic and displayed little interest in political issues outside the narrow world of their individual villages.

Despotism and economic domination in Siam. Although Siam (later to be known as Thailand) had escaped European colonial control, it had not avoided western influences. In the second half of the nineteenth century, the kings of Siam had undertaken various reform measures, such as the improvement of the legal system, the abolition of slavery, and the abandonment of the feudal system. Not obliged to contend with alien control, the Siamese nationalists directed their activities against despotic monarchs and against the Chinese community, which monopolized much of the banking and trade. In 1932 a peaceful revolution forced the king to accept a new democratic constitution. However, the revolution merely widened the ranks of the oligarchy controlling the country.

In 1933 the constitution was revoked, and another revolution reestablished constitutional rule supported by the army. But politics remained confused, the pawn of professional politicians and army generals. In the late 1930's the country continued to be governed by a small clique, and its economic life was still dominated by the immigrant Chinese.

Malaya's plural society. After World War I, the economic growth of British Malaya continued, especially in the tin and rubber industries. Unlike most colonial territories, Malaya experienced little nationalist feeling before 1939. This passivity can be explained in part by the rivalry existing between native Malays and the influential Indian and Chinese communities. Who should rule whom and on what lines self-government might be developed were unique and difficult problems.

The French in Indo-China. Criticized for their policies more than the British or Dutch in southeast Asia were the French in Indo-China. The protective tariff was used in Indo-China as a means of guaranteeing a market for French goods, and many complaints were voiced about the heavy burden of indirect taxes upon the common people, the inadequate labor laws, and the neglect of scientific conservation in protecting natural resources. The production of rubber, rice, and coal increased markedly under French rule, but little improvement was evident in the well-being of the people.

After the First World War various nationalist groups were active, the best organized being the Communists led by Ho Chi-minh (1891?-   ). Born in Annam, he journeyed to Europe, joined the Communist party in France, and after 1918 went to the Soviet Union, where he received expert advice on the art of making revolutions. Although during the 1930's the nationalist movement was ineffectual, largely because of the stern manner in which the French suppressed uprisings and also because of divisions between the nationalists themselves, the Communists under the leadership of Ho Chi-minh were active underground.

Paternal Dutch rule in the East Indies. Under Dutch rule the Netherlands East Indies became famous for the degree to which modern science was applied to tropical agriculture and the manner in which law and order were established in a region torn by native rivalries. The wealth of the country increased and the population grew. But the Dutch failed to concern themselves with the growing aspirations of their native wards. Unlike the British policy of evolutionary self-government, that of the Netherlands was set in the mold of stern paternalism. The representative parliament established in 1918 remained purely an advisory body until 1927, and even though a degree of liberalization then took place, in essence the paternal nature of the administration remained unchanged.

Shortly after 1900 the nationalist movement in the Indies was born. One wing of the movement was inspired by the Islamic revival in the Middle East and had an anti-Christian bias (the dominant religion of the islands is Islam). Another wing in 1920 transformed itself into a Communist party. In 1927 the Indonesian Nationalist party was organized under the direction of a young patriot, Achmed Sukarno (1901-   ), destined to become the president of the Republic of Indonesia. Two years later the party was dissolved and Sukarno interned.

With the impact of world depression in the early 1930's, unrest and nationalism grew stronger. Dutch officials began to realize that self-rule was inevitable, but they refused to reconcile themselves to the possibility of the Indies breaking all ties with the Netherlands. For their part, the nationalists became more modest in their demands because of the uncertain world situation and the menace of Japanese imperialism. They indicated a willingness to remain united to the Dutch crown and to accept a plan of self-government similar to British dominion status.

The problem of Philippine independence. American rule in the Philippines was probably the most enlightened of all colonial regimes. Its two main objectives were to promote literacy and to develop powers of self-government as quickly as possible. Economically the islands developed rapidly as American investment dollars poured in and free trade between the Philippines and the United States reached a combined total of nearly $500,000,000 in the late 1930's. But this close economic tie had its dangers, and serious observers wondered what would happen once independence was granted. Loss of free trade with the United States would be a serious blow to an economy heavily dependent on American markets.

The independence movement in the Philippines had begun prior to World War I. The first nationalist party appeared in 1907, the year in which the Philippine Assembly was created. Congress' passage of the Jones Act in 1916 pledged the United States "to recognize Philippine independence as soon as stable

Exerting his powerful influence even from exile, Sun Yat-sen engineered the overthrow of the Manchu dynasty and the formation of the Chinese republic.

government could be established." In the 1920's the Republican administrations in Washington were lukewarm toward independence, but with the return of a Democratic administration in 1933, the prospects of complete freedom brightened—in part because the Democratic party had always been more favorably disposed toward this objective. Moreover, the onset of the depression had caused some economic groups in the United States to oppose free imports from the Philippines. After several false starts the Tydings-McDuffie Act was passed in 1934. By this act the Filipinos were empowered to draft a constitution, which was drawn up in 1935. The same year the Commonwealth of the Philippines came into being with Manuel Quezon (1878-1944) as its first president. During a ten-year transitional period, ultimate power in foreign affairs and defense was to reside with the president of the United States. To cushion the shock of economic

separation, a system of graduated tariffs was provided.

The Filipinos started off their ten-year transitional period with good auguries. The United States had left a legacy of enlightened, efficient administration and an excellent public school system. But the period from 1935 to the outbreak of World War II was not reassuring. Students of Filipino politics spoke ominously of corruption in government and of the emergence of quasi-dictatorship.

CHINA TRIES TO CHANGE

The Republic of China is born. During the course of the nineteenth century, the once mighty Chinese empire had increasingly felt the encroachments of the great imperialistic powers. Loss of territory, the imposition of extraterritoriality, and foreign control of the tariff all symbolized China's impotence. In the first decade of the twentieth century, however, a strong liberal and nationalistic movement emerged, determined to oust the Manchu dynasty, establish a parliamentary regime, and modernize Chinese society. Only thus, the nationalists felt, could China be saved.

The most important leader of the movement for a new China was Sun Yat-sen (1867-1925). Born near Canton, the son of a tenant farmer, he received a western education in Hawaii, was converted to Christianity, and in 1892 received a diploma in medicine in Hong Kong. Shortly afterwards, he became a leader in the Chinese nationalist movement, directing his energy toward the overthrow of the Manchus and the formation of a republic. Forced into exile in 1895, he continued to make his influence felt among the nationalists in China, and during his travels, he sought financial aid for his cause from Chinese living in foreign countries. During this period he organized the Kuomintang, or National Peoples party, as the instrument for carrying out his policies.

In 1911 a revolt broke out in China over a foreign loan to finance railways, and the outbreak spread like wildfire through the provinces. Yüan Shih-kai (1859-1916), the outstanding military leader in north China and the former confidant of Tzu Hsi, the dowager empress, persuaded the imperial clan that the Manchu dynasty was doomed. In February 1912 the emperor abdicated, and Yüan was asked to form a republic. Although a few months earlier an assembly of revolutionaries at Nanking had elected Sun president of their new republic, he stepped aside to prevent internal dissension, and the republican group at Nanking elected Yüan.

Dissension and disorder in the government. The provisional constitution adopted in March put the office of president under the jurisdiction of parliament, which was controlled by the Kuomintang. In 1913 trouble broke out when Yüan negotiated a large loan with bankers from Great Britain, France, Germany, and Russia, thus giving these powers substantial influence in the government of the republic. Furthermore, he replaced certain military commanders in the south with his own henchmen. The outcome was a new rebellion, endorsed by Sun. Yüan suppressed the revolt, and Sun fled to Japan.

Now firmly entrenched, Yüan dismissed parliament and announced the imminent restoration of the monarchy with himself as emperor. Rebellion again broke out, Yüan's prestige evaporated, and in June 1916 the discredited dictator died.

Dissension in the government continued for the next ten years. The political picture was complicated by strained relations with Japan during World War I (see p. 509) and China's entry into the war. It is impossible here to trace the confusion in Chinese politics during this period. For a time the country was divided between two would-be governments, one in the north at Peking, the other in the south at Canton. Composed largely of the radicals who had engineered the revolution of 1911-1912, the Canton government in 1921 elected Sun as president.

Three Principles of the People. Unable to obtain aid from the western powers to overcome the Peking government, Sun called in advisers from the Soviet Union, among them the brilliant Bolshevik, Michael Borodin. Because of its confidence in Borodin and his associates, the Kuomintang adopted many of the planks of the program subscribed to by the Communist party in the U.S.S.R.

In 1925 Sun died. More skillful as a propagandist and revolutionist than as a political administrator, he had not succeeded in reuniting the Peking regime with his Kuomintang government. However, his social ideology had important results for the future. His most famous work, *San Min Chu I*, or *Three Principles of the People*, became the manual of the Kuomintang. The three principles are: (1) nationalism—the liberation of China from foreign domination; (2) democracy—"government by the people and for the people"; and (3) livelihood—economic security for all the people.

China united under Chiang Kai-shek. Sun had regarded Chiang Kai-shek (1886-   ) as his successor. From poor but sturdy peasant stock, Chiang was sent to China's first military academy, where he proved an excellent student and was selected to study military tactics in Japan. While in Japan he was stirred by Sun's vision of a new China and returned to his homeland to take an active part in the revolution. His obvious abilities attracted the attention of Sun, who sent him to Russia in 1923 for a brief period of indoctrination.

Under Chiang the armies of the Kuomintang began to drive northward in 1926. They encountered little opposition, and by early spring of the following year they reached the Yangtze valley and occupied Shanghai. But dissension broke out between radical and conservative elements in the Kuomintang, and a split became inevitable. The moderates under Chiang created a government at Nanking, and before the end of 1927 public opinion had crystallized behind this regime. Chiang used force against the leftist elements; the end of the Kuomintang alliance with the Communists was written in blood when a proletarian uprising in Canton was quelled with the loss of more than five thousand lives. Back to the Soviet Union went the Communist advisers; many radicals (including the widow of Sun Yat-sen) were driven into exile; and the Chinese Communists were scattered to the hills and mountains of south

In 1927, Chiang Kai-shek purged the Kuomintang not only of the Communists but also of the moderate liberals who sought peaceful, evolutionary reforms. After the split in the party, Chiang's government became increasingly conservative, favoring urban development over agrarian reform.

China, where they set up their own administrative units.

In retrospect, the split of 1927 stands out as a major event in modern Chinese history. The purge of left-wing elements from the Kuomintang proved a mixed blessing. Not only were extreme Marxist radicals ousted, but moderate liberals who sought basic social and political reforms through peaceful and evolutionary means were also eliminated. Nationalist strength lay with the city professional, banking, and merchant classes, and the Nanking government came to depend for financial support upon the foreign bankers at Shanghai. The regime took on a conservative character which hindered its leaders from understanding the problems of the masses.

Meanwhile Chiang married Mei-ling Soong (1898-   ), a sister of Madame Sun Yat-sen, and so further cemented his position with his countrymen. The next summer the Nationalist armies moved northward again and by June had entered Peking. With peace between the northern war leaders and the Kuomintang, China appeared once more to be united. The revolt in 1929 of a group of military leaders dissatisfied with Kuomintang policies was squelched one year later, and Chiang Kai-shek's government was considered secure from internal dissensions. The world now looked forward to a time of internal harmony and growing stability in China. The new capital, Nanking, was bustling with plans for the future.

During the 1920's Chinese foreign relations had improved. China was protected by the Nine-Power Treaty of 1922 (see p. 510) and was a member of the League of Nations. The Chinese government obtained the power to fix its own tariffs in 1920, and ten foreign powers gave up or lost the right of extraterritoriality for their nationals. In addition, during this period Japan appeared relatively conciliatory toward its neighbor. But the sympathizers of the young republic could not overlook certain problem areas. In many regions the people were still tyrannized by bandits, and famine in the northwest cost the lives of millions. Nor could the activities of the Chinese Communists be ignored.

A fervent patriot, Chiang nevertheless had little appreciation for the social and economic problems of his people. He placed much more store in their moral regeneration. Strongly versed in Taoist and Confucian teachings but at the same time a devout Christian, he formulated a New Life Movement, a combination of Christian and Confucian ethics. He would have done better to appreciate the economic aspirations of the peasants. As we will see in Chapter 17, peasant grievances were recognized by the Chinese Communists, who patiently bided their time.

Changes in Chinese life. The changes that took place in Chinese life between the time of the revolution and the establishment of Chiang's regime were noteworthy. The number of Chinese receiving an education in primary schools, secondary schools, or in universities, though still small, increased remarkably. Chinese intellectuals championed the use of a new and simplified written language, while scholars labored for the adoption of Mandarin as a national speech so that men from all parts of China could speak together.

Social customs were also considerably altered; folkways and dress began to give way in urban areas to occidental customs and fashions. In the large cities, telephones, electric lights, modern water systems, and movie palaces appeared.

Chinese commerce increased rapidly, for China represented the largest potential market in the world. Total foreign trade was seven times as great in 1929 as it had been in 1894. Nevertheless, civil warfare, currency insecurity, inefficient transportation systems, and national poverty all combined to keep China virtually an undeveloped nation. Although some progress was registered in the construction of factories, the adoption of western machinery, and the manufacturing of cotton goods in particular, for the most part the industrial units were controlled by foreign entrepreneurs, who raked in the profits. Because the impressive economic potentialities of China were not exploited for the advantage of the Chinese people, the inhabitants of the republic continued to suffer.

JAPAN BECOMES A

WORLD POWER

The Twenty-one Demands. As the twentieth century dawned, Japan had astonished the world by the tempo of its modernization. From a static, militarily weak, and dominantly agricultural nation, it was rapidly becoming a dynamic, militarily powerful, and highly industrialized state. There were serious problems ahead, however. The liberal statesmen of Japan sought means not only to support the rapidly increasing population but also to democratize the constitution. Unfortunately, Japan was to follow a path that led ultimately to aggression against its neighbors and to more, not less, dictatorial government at home.

When the First World War broke out in 1914, Japan ordered Germany to remove its warships from the Far East and to surrender the Kiaochow territory in China to Japan

"with a view to the eventual restoration of the same to China." When Germany failed to reply to this request, the Japanese government declared war and seized the territory. Japan had not consulted China at all during this time, nor did the Nipponese hesitate to violate Chinese neutrality.

In January 1915, Japan presented China with the notorious Twenty-one Demands, which startled the world by their frank disclosure of Japanese imperialistic designs on the Asiatic continent. Preoccupied as they were with the gigantic struggle in Europe, the European powers did little to hinder the Japanese, and indignant China had not the physical means to protest effectively. Under threats of coercion, the Chinese government in May acceded to the first sixteen demands; the remainder were reserved for later consideration. The intervention of the United States helped nullify the most dictatorial of the demands, which would have brought China completely under Japan's domination. China was forced, however, to acknowledge Japan's authority in Shantung province and to extend Nipponese railway and land concessions in south Manchuria.

In 1917 the Allied powers secretly agreed to support Japanese claims in the peace conference that would follow the First World War. While not a party to the agreement, the United States in the Lansing-Ishii agreement (1917) declared somewhat reluctantly that Japan deserved "special interest in China" owing to "territorial propinquity." Japan, in turn, agreed to respect the Open Door Policy in China. The Allies' position toward China was most embarrassing; China had entered the war on their side, chiefly to secure a spot during peace negotiations so that Japanese ambitions might be checked. China's only hope for preserving its independence lay in the growing tension between the United States and Japan.

Japanese foreign relations in the 1920's. Japan profited from its role in the war; it controlled in one way or another Shantung, Manchuria, southern Mongolia, and the German islands north of the equator, besides the territories and concessions it had wrested from China and Russia prior to the war. The increased power of Japan was particularly alarming to the United States and the British dominions in the Pacific. In 1921 Great Britain allowed its treaty with Japan, which Britain had renewed in 1911, to terminate without further renewal.

The growth of Japan's hold on China is revealed in a comparison of the investments by foreign powers in that country. In 1902 Japanese investment in China was negligible, but in 1914 it rivaled the investments of both Russia and Germany, and by 1931 it was second only to Great Britain's. In 1931 Japanese capital represented about 35 per cent of all foreign investment in China. At the Washington Conference in 1921, the agreement by the three leading naval powers—Great Britain, the United States, and Japan—to reduce the tonnage of their capital ships in order to achieve a respective ratio of 5-5-3 recognized the position of the Japanese navy as the third most powerful in the world. By the Four-Power Pact, also signed at this conference, the United States, Great Britain, Japan, and France agreed "to respect their rights in relation to their insular possessions and insular dominions in the region of the Pacific Ocean."

In 1922 the Nine-Power Treaty was signed at Washington. All the signatories agreed to respect the independence, sovereignty, territoriality, and administrative integrity of China. Furthermore, they were to use their influence to preserve the Open Door Policy and "to refrain from taking advantage of conditions in China in order to seek special rights or privileges which would abridge the rights of subjects or citizens of friendly states, and from countenancing action inimical to the security of such states."[10]

It is impossible to reconcile Japan's later acts in China with the pact which it signed in 1922, just as it is difficult for the other signatories to excuse their apathy toward Japanese aggressions in China before they were themselves drawn into war against Japan.

The struggle for liberalism. From 1889, when Japan's new constitution was promulgated, to 1918, the government was mainly in the hands of an aristocratic, scrupulously honest oligarchy of elder statesmen called the *Genro*. By the end of World War I, most of these political patriarchs had passed away, and the field of politics was now open for new blood, a fact signalized by the election to the post of prime minister of the first commoner ever to hold that office, Takashi Hara.

The period from 1918 to 1930 was of crucial importance. Japan seemed to be moving toward the establishment of a democratic, parliamentary government under its new political leaders, who were enthusiastic supporters of democracy. There were serious obstacles to be overcome, however—not only the lack of a liberal tradition in Japan and inexperience in parliamentary politics but also other factors. The concentration of wealth in the hands of a few fantastically rich families was not democratically healthy; it resulted in many political party leaders becoming the agents of the wealthy. Militarism, based on the revered *samurai* tradition which exalted war and had no sympathy for liberal sentiments, was strong, and to this militaristic virus in the Japanese blood stream was added a strong authoritarian tradition, fostered by secret societies and the cult of Shintoism.

Many secret societies were connected with the army and were ultranationalistic and terroristic. Long a feature of Japanese life, they multiplied rapidly in membership after 1930; among the most important were the Black Dragon Society and the Society of the Imperial Way. Originally a simple nature cult, *Shinto* had been transformed by the end of the nineteenth century into the cult of emperor worship and the deification of the state. Thus the Japanese were able to build a strong regime upon cults already occupying an important position in the lives of the people, while the Nazis were forced to resurrect Teutonic cults extinct for centuries in order to arouse national fervor.

It was with these serious handicaps that parliamentary government sought after 1918 to lead the nation away from excessive nationalism and militarism. Liberals in the Diet showed great promise and courage as they pressed reform and criticized the imperialistic intervention in Siberia of the Japanese army (along with other Allied forces) during the confused civil war following the Russian Revolution. Although liberalism suffered a serious setback in 1921 with the assassination of Prime Minister Hara, liberal strength returned in 1925 when the Universal Manhood Suffrage Bill was passed, granting the franchise to most males over twenty-five. Soon afterward a reactionary government led by General Giichi Tanaka came to power, advocating a stronger policy toward China; but the militaristic Tanaka was in turn quickly succeeded by the most liberal government Japan had ever had. Led by Prime Minister Yuko Hamaguchi, this liberal regime assumed a policy of conciliation toward China, reduced army expenditures, and signed the London Naval Treaty. In 1930 the militarists and chauvinists reacted savagely by assassinating Hamaguchi, a blow from which the liberal cause never recovered.

Economic progress. In the economic sphere, Japan forged ahead rapidly. Thousands of factories were built, and Japanese manufacturers undersold foreign competitors in the world market, owing in part to the low Japanese wage standard and in part to the modern machine techniques which Japanese industrialists were swift to adopt. In textiles especially, Japan captured one market after another. Commerce and industry were controlled by a few giant concerns, in whose hands the greater part of the country's wealth was concentrated. By the 1930's Japan had become the first exporter in rayon, cotton textiles, matches, and raw silk.

In the Japanese economic scheme the position of China was paramount. Japan had invested $1,250,000,000 there, and trade with China amounted to 24 per cent of all Japanese commerce, compared to trade with the United States of 3 per cent and with Britain of less than 2 per cent.

Japanese economic prosperity was, however, more apparent than real. Serious economic weaknesses existed. Nippon lacked natural resources such as coal, iron, petroleum, timber, and cotton. The population was growing at an unbelievable rate. In 1920 the population was 56,000,000; in 1931 it had reached 65,000,000 persons, crowded into a land area smaller than the state of California. In 1932 the annual increase reached 1,000,000. The Japanese economy needed to find 250,000 new jobs for the young workers every year, to say nothing of feeding 1,000,000 additional mouths annually. Up to 1930 Japan had managed to pay its way by expanding its exports, the sale of which gave the nation foreign credits to buy raw materials and foodstuffs abroad. Should these exports suffer a substantial contraction, Japan would then be confronted with a serious national crisis. Just such a crisis occurred in the world depression which began in the 1930's. As we shall see in Chapter 17, it was in expansionism in China that Japan sought the answer to its problems.

SUMMARY

This chapter has told the story of the growth and development of the nonwestern world in the period between the two world wars. It was during this period that imperialism went on the defensive before the rise of nationalism.

In sub-Saharan Africa the values of the white man's way of life were only beginning to be comprehended. The nationalistic stimulus in this area stemmed from the Pan-African movement of educated Negroes outside Africa as well as from a very small educated class within the native states. This group sought to replace unjust imperialistic control with self-government and to bring about the cultural resurgence of a people whose tribal way of life was slowly disintegrating as the black man came into contact with the numerous facets of western culture. The Pan-African movement did not affect the masses of the people in most areas, however; only in the troubled multiracial society of the Union of South Africa, where a European minority imposed harsh measures of discrimination on the Negroes, was there widespread unrest among Africans in this period.

Nationalism was much stronger in the Arab world. In the lands formerly controlled by the Ottomans, Arab nationalists bitterly contested European control as set up in the mandate system; the British were ultimately forced to grant complete independence to Iraq, and outbreaks of violence occurred in the French mandate of Syria-Lebanon and especially in Palestine, where the Arabs resented the British attempt to set up a national home for the Jews. In Iran, the nationalists threw off the influence of Britain and set up a government under the control of Riza Shah Pahlavi. Dissatisfaction with French rule mounted in North Africa, and self-government was granted to Egypt by the British. In other areas of the Middle East, Turkish nationalists under Mustafa Kemal built a new Turkey, while in the Arabian peninsula a new Arab power, Saudi Arabia, emerged under the dynamic leadership of ibn-Saud.

The strongest nationalism in all the colonial areas developed in India under the powerful leadership of Mahatma (the Holy One) Gandhi. The effective use of nonviolence in his civil disobedience campaigns forced Britain to grant a substantial measure of self-government to the Indians.

In southeast Asia, nationalism began to rise steadily, although it did not as yet affect the majority of people in this area. In Ceylon and Burma, Britain conceded some degree of self-government; unrest grew stronger in the French and Dutch colonies. In the Philippines, nationalism was given ample opportunity to develop, and self-government was finally granted.

China was not, strictly speaking, a part of the colonial world, yet in many ways this vast and backward land was under the indirect influence of the great western powers. Faced with the prospect of virtual partition by these nations, Chinese nationalists, under the leadership of Sun Yat-sen, overthrew the Manchu dynasty and established a republic. After years of confusion and conflict between rival factions, power was consolidated under the Kuomintang and Chiang Kai-shek. The Chiang regime effected a gradual modernization of urban China, though agrarian reform was largely neglected.

Japanese history in the opening decades of the twentieth century was characterized by amazing progress in industrialization and by an attempt to introduce a democratic and responsible system of government. By 1919 the island kingdom had become one of the world's great powers. But its spectacular rise to greatness was also characterized by serious omens. There was disturbing evidence that military fascism was more potent than democracy and expansionist ambitions more powerful than love for peace.

CHAPTER 17

The Tragic Decade
and Global Conflict

DEPRESSION AND WORLD WAR II: 1930-1945

Introduction. On September 1, 1939, Hitler's legions marched into Poland, and the Second World War began. This outbreak of terrible violence marked the end of a tragic decade.

Ten years earlier, the Wall Street stock market crash had ushered in a world-wide financial crisis —the Great Depression. Nation after nation fell victim to industrial decline, bank failures, deflated prices and profits, and commercial stagnation. People the world over suffered from lowered standards of living, unemployment, hunger, and fear of the future. In the western democracies, the buoyant optimism of the 1920's was superseded by self-criticism and despair.

In desperation, governments sought economic recovery by adopting restrictive autarkist policies —high tariffs, import quotas, and barter agreements—and by experimenting with new plans for their internal economies. The United States launched the New Deal, and Britain adopted far-reaching measures in the development of a planned national economy. In Nazi Germany, economic recovery was pursued through rearmament, conscription, and public works programs, while in Italy Mussolini tightened the economic controls of his corporate state. In many lands, some observers saw in the gigantic economic planning and state ownership of the Soviet Union what appeared to be a depression-proof economic system and a solution to the crisis in capitalism.

The economic malaise of the 1930's gave dictators their chance: Hitler took over control in Germany, and a militaristic clique grasped the reins of power in Japan. In 1931 the Japanese pounced upon Manchuria, and when the League of Nations proved powerless to interfere, war between Japan and China raged intermittently throughout the decade. While China was fighting for its national existence, Italy conquered Abyssinia, fascism emerged triumphant from the Spanish civil war, and by a series of "incidents" Hitler swelled the territory of the Third Reich and increased its power. Faced with blatant aggression by the Axis powers (Germany, Italy, Japan), England and France abandoned their faith in collective security and the League of Nations and adopted a policy of appeasement. Meanwhile, the Soviet Union played for time to build up its own defenses, and the United States detached itself from the increasing world tensions by maintaining its traditional policy of isolationism. Finally driven to the limit by the Axis, the European democracies and later the Soviet Union and United States took up arms to defend their independence and end the threat of world conquest.

Far more than World War I, World War II represented global conflict. Not only was it fought in both hemispheres but also in almost every kind of climate and on every sort of terrain—from the bleak, fogbound Aleutians and the snow-covered steppes of Russia to the sweltering jungles of New Guinea and the burning sands of the Sahara. Australians fought in Africa, French Africans in Italy; Poles flew from British bases; Canadians made commando raids on the French coast; British guerrilla fighters operated behind the Japanese lines in Burma; and American transport planes made regular flights across the Himalayas, while American army engineers built roads in Burma and navy construction battalions laid out airfields on coral atolls in the Pacific.

The war was global in another sense: never before had civilian populations been so deeply involved. On the one hand, they were targets. The German air raids on Britain and the attacks late in the war by V-1 flying bombs and V-2 rockets had as their purpose the destruction of the people's will to support the war effort. Many of the Allied raids on Germany—over forty thousand missions in a single four-day period in 1945—had the same goal, and so, of course, did the atomic-bomb attacks on Japan. In the Soviet Union, which lost more than seven million military personnel, the total number of civilians killed was even greater. But these Russian civilians were not merely targets; they were participants in the struggle, working for victory and, when necessary, fighting beside their soldiers. And in all the other nations involved, the civilians were participants as well. Government regulations—taxes; rationing; blackouts; price, wage, and rent controls—forced them to participate whether they wanted to or not, but millions made voluntary sacrifices and willingly took jobs which would contribute in some measure to the war effort.

World War II tested the productive capacities of the great industrial nations with amazing results. Although Britain was under constant attack by Nazi bombers, its production rate continued to rise; and until the last stages of the war, German industrial plants hit by Allied bombs were repeatedly restored to full operation. The United States, neither bombed nor invaded, found itself capable of sending vast quantities of arms and ammunition, planes, tanks, military vehicles, clothing, and food to its allies overseas, while continuing to supply its own civilian and military needs. And not only did the products of twentieth-century technology play a major role in the global conflict; the efficient methods of mass production and the assembly line were applied to the conduct of the war itself. To a very great extent, this was the war of the mass planners and mass organizers; of transportation problems involving millions of men, millions of tons of matériel, thousands of ships, planes, and tanks; of time schedules calling for simultaneous strikes by land, sea, and air on targets hundreds and even thousands of miles apart.

Thus, in many ways, this was a new kind of war, not only in its enormous scope but also in its techniques and in its weapons. Technology made possible the mass bombing raids, the air-borne invasion, the amphibious assault, the operations of carrier-based planes, the maneuvers of armored divisions, the coordinated efforts of the giant naval task force, and the mass murders of the Nazi concentration camps; and science and technology combined to create the ultimate in efficiency and horror—the nuclear bomb. Yet World War II was also a war of men, fighting as men have fought throughout human history. After all the weapons and techniques of modern, technological warfare had done their worst, it was men who had to win or lose the struggles at Stalingrad, at Anzio and Cassino in Italy, at Bastogne during the Battle of the Bulge and at Arnhem during the Allied liberation of the Netherlands, and on island after island in the Pacific. It was men who finally destroyed the Axis.

DEPRESSION THREATENS DEMOCRACY AND BREEDS TOTALITARIANISM

Phony prosperity of the "roaring twenties." In 1929 the world's most prosperous nation was the United States. President Hoover declared in his inaugural address:

Ours is a land rich in resources, stimulating in its glorious beauty, filled with millions of happy homes, blessed with comfort and opportunity. . . . I have no fears for the future of our country. It is bright with hope.[1]

But despite the buoyant optimism in the United States and the apparent economic well-being in other countries, the world economy was in an unhealthy state. One by one, the cornerstones of the pre-1914 economic system—multilateral trade, the gold standard, and the interchangeability of currencies —were crumbling.

The desire for self-sufficiency, or autarky, led nations to manufacture goods or grow products at home, even though this policy was sometimes more expensive than importing what they needed. Then, to protect home products against competition from foreign imports, high tariff walls were raised. The United States led the movement toward higher tariffs. In 1922 the Fordney-McCumber Tariff Act levied the highest tariff rates in our history. Eight years later, in spite of vigorous objections from President Hoover, the American Bankers Association, and more than a thousand American economists, Congress passed the Hawley-Smoot Tariff Act, which imposed prohibitively high rates. Other nations quickly retaliated with discriminatory tariffs against us and each other, American foreign trade seriously declined, and the volume of world trade steadily decreased.

The high tariffs had a crucial effect on the payment of war debts. Normally, instead of drawing on its gold reserves and thereby endangering the stability of its currency, a debtor nation made its payments by selling goods to the United States (the largest creditor) and thereby raising the necessary dollars. But when the United States enacted prohibitively high tariffs, this method of payment was jeopardized. In fact, because of America's high tariff, only a sort of economic ring-around-the-rosy kept the reparations and war-debt payments going. During the 1920's our former allies paid their war-debt installments to us chiefly with funds obtained from German reparations payments, and Germany was able to make these payments only because of large private loans from the United States and Britain. Similarly, American investments abroad provided the dollars which alone made it possible for foreign nations to buy American products.

In 1929 Germany's creditors set up the Young Plan to supersede the Dawes Plan (see p. 458). The new scheme stipulated that Germany pay a total of $8,800,000,000—about a quarter of the original reparations bill. It was believed that Germany would have no difficulty in meeting its new schedule of payments. But within two years the world was reeling from the impact of the worst depression of all time, and the entire structure of reparations and war debts collapsed.

Panic on Wall Street: the crash of 1929. In the postwar decade the activities of daring and often unscrupulous speculators made international finance a precarious and exciting world of its own. Operating on an international scale, the Swedish swindler Ivar Kreuger cornered the match market; in the United States, Samuel Insull's attempts to maintain a vast public-utilities empire helped push stock prices to dizzy heights; and an English speculator, Clarence Hatry, indirectly touched off the Wall Street crash. When Hatry's shaky companies failed, his English victims dumped their American securities to get ready cash. This in turn triggered a sickening slump in stock prices on Wall Street. The crash came in 1929, on October 24, "Black Thursday." "Prices fell farther and faster, and the ticker lagged more and more. By eleven o'clock the market had degenerated into a wild, mad scramble to sell. In the crowded boardrooms across the country the ticker told of a frightful collapse. . . . The uncertainty led more and more people to try to sell. . . . By eleven-thirty the market had surrendered to blind, relentless fear. This, indeed, was panic."[2] Within a few weeks, stock prices had declined 40 per cent. Fortunes were wiped out, business confidence was blasted, and the demand for goods plummeted. The growing paralysis in American business and finance spread all over the world as the United States began to call in its foreign loans and decrease its imports.

In the face of impending disaster on a world-wide scale, President Hoover in 1931 succeeded in obtaining a moratorium of one year on all intergovernmental debts. At the Lausanne Conference (1932), German reparations payments were practically canceled. This drastic step was taken in the hope that the American government also would make a substantial concession in reducing war debts, but the United States refused to concede that there was a logical connection between reparations and war debts. As the depression deepened, our debtors could not continue their payments. France refused outright in 1932; Great Britain and four other nations made token payments for a time, then stopped entirely in 1934; and only Finland continued to meet its schedule of payments. In the meantime, Germany had completely stopped paying reparations.

The depression begins. The effects of the depression were catastrophic the world over. Governments could not balance their budgets, factories shut down, and harvests rotted in the fields. The price of wheat fell to the lowest figure in more than three hundred years. The lives of the grower of cacao in the African Gold Coast, the coffee grower in Brazil, and the copra plantation worker in the Dutch East Indies were blighted, as were those of the factory worker in Pittsburgh, Sheffield, Lille, and Frankfurt. In the "land of plenty," one of the popular songs of the day was "Brother, Can You Spare a Dime?"

During the years following the crash, most nations strengthened their resolve to employ autarky as their guiding economic principle. To increase exports and decrease imports, quota systems were put into operation, and tariffs were boosted to new highs. After almost a century of free trade, Great Britain enacted a high tariff in 1932 but allowed for the system of imperial preference, whereby lower tariffs were levied on members of the empire than on outside nations. The net effect was the increase of trade within the empire at the expense of trade with nonimperial countries.

Another technique for increasing exports was to depreciate the currency, which meant reducing the value of a nation's money. When Japan depreciated the yen, an American dollar or a British pound could buy more Japanese goods. In effect, depreciating the yen lowered the price of Japanese exports. In most instances, however, devaluation brought only a temporary trade advantage; other countries could play the same game. In 1934 the United States reduced the gold content of the dollar by about 40 per cent.

The disturbances in the natural flow of world trade caused by the depression led nations to hoard their gold reserves—a trend strengthened by the fact that most nations had comparatively little gold, the United States, Great Britain, and France controlling three fourths of the world's supply. Many nations went off the gold standard, which meant that they would not pay foreign creditors in gold. Great Britain abandoned the gold standard in 1931; two years later the United States did likewise. Without gold as the medium of exchange between countries, barter became more and more prevalent in international trade. The system was not always mutually beneficial to both parties, since to sell their goods at all, a country sometimes had to take very marginal products in return. At one point, for example, some South American exporters found themselves being paid in German harmonicas.

The depression had profound implications for politics. The rash of democratic constitutions adopted after World War I had seemed to assure government by and for the common man, but in the tragic thirties, democracy in many nations went into eclipse as unemployed and starving masses turned to dictators who promised jobs and bread at the price of freedom. The hardships of the depression formed a dismal backdrop on a political stage where dictators brutally seized the leading roles.

The Five-Year Plans in the Soviet Union.
The years from 1929 to 1939 comprised a dark
decade in Russia—a period of merciless industrialization and of convulsive inner struggles as Stalin established a personal dictatorship both total and terrible. While in the
capitalist countries, factories and mines were
idle or running on reduced schedules and
millions were unemployed, the Soviet people
worked many hours a day, six days a week, in
an all-out attempt to revolutionize Russia's
economic structure. For the first time in history, a government controlled all economic
activity through a comprehensive blueprint
drawn up by the Gosplan, the state planning
committee. Then as now, all foreign trade activities were conducted by governmental
agencies, which bought and sold in overseas
markets according to the requirements of the
economic plan. Control of this type insulated
domestic prices from those in the world market and eliminated the necessity for formal
tariffs to safeguard high-cost industries. In the
field of distribution, the retail outlets consisted of a huge network of government
stores, some shops in cooperative networks,
and the free farm markets.

In 1928 Stalin proposed a Five-Year Plan,
the first of a number of such schemes aimed
at the relatively swift accumulation of capital
resources through the build-up of heavy industry, the collectivization of agriculture,
and the restricted manufacture of consumers'
goods. Within the five-year span, industrial
production was to be increased 136 per cent;
agricultural yield, 55 per cent; oil and coal
production, 100 per cent; and power output,
300 per cent. Although capitalism in the form
of the NEP was abolished, citizens were permitted to own certain types of private property—houses, furniture, clothes, and personal
effects. They could not, however, own property which could be utilized to make profits
by hiring workers. The only employer was the
state.

As part of the plan, the government took
control of agriculture through the state farms.
By the beginning of the Second World War,
90 per cent of the Russian land under cultivation was organized in one of two ways. The
state farm (*sovkhoz*) was owned outright by

Criticism by a group of its own members has been one of the
phenomena of the Soviet system. Here, workers on a Ukrainian
collective farm assemble at harvest time to discuss the quantity
and quality of the work they have performed.

the government and run by paid laborers.
The collective farm (*kolkhoz*) was created
from land given up by the peasants who accepted the government's decree to merge their
holdings and from land taken from the *kulaks*
—well-to-do farmers. The *kolkhoz* members
worked the land under the management of a
board of directors. At the end of the year,
the farm's net earnings were computed in cash
and in kind, and the members were paid on the
basis of the number of days they had worked.

A second Five-Year Plan, begun in 1933,
sought to redress some of the mistakes of the
first. A greater emphasis was placed on improving the quality of industrial products and
on manufacturing more consumers' goods.
The year 1938 witnessed the initiation of the
third Five-Year Plan, in which national defense became the major consideration. Industrial plants were shifted inland to the east,
and efforts were made to develop new sources
of oil and other important commodities. The
world's largest tractor factory was erected in

Chelyabinsk, the greatest electric power station in Dnepropetrovsk, and the largest automobile plant at Gorki.

The plans achieved remarkable results. Industrial output in 1932 was 334 per cent above that in 1914. Between 1932 and 1937 the gross production index rose from 34 to 95. However, the high volume of production was often coupled with mediocre quality, and the achievements were secured only at an enormous cost in human life and suffering. At first a bare subsistence scale of living was imposed on the people by the burdensome expense of importing heavy machinery, tools, equipment, and finished steel from abroad. These purchases were paid for by the sale of food and raw materials in the world's markets at a time when the prices of such goods had drastically fallen. An even greater cost was the terrible loss of life brought about by the callous collectivization of the peasants. By a decree of February 1930, about one million *kulaks* were forced off their land and all their possessions confiscated. The peasants consistently opposed regimentation by the state, often slaughtering their herds when faced with the loss of their land. In some sections they revolted, and thousands were executed. A serious famine broke out and took a heavy toll of life in the Ukraine, the north Caucasus, and the lower Volga region. Several million peasants died of starvation.

Another casualty of the Five-Year Plans was Lenin's basic concept of economic equalitarianism. In 1931 Stalin declared that equality in wages was "alien and detrimental to Soviet production" and "a petit-bourgeois deviation." So much propaganda was used to implant this ideological twist that the masses came to accept the new doctrine of the inequality of wages as a fundamental Communist principle. Piecework in industry became more prevalent, and bonuses and incentives were used to speed up production. It was indeed ironic that capitalistic practices were introduced to stimulate the growth of communism.

The great purges. While the Five-Year Plans were forging ahead, Stalin was establishing an all-powerful personal autocracy. From 1928 to 1931 and again from 1935 to 1938, Stalin settled his accounts with all his rivals through barbaric purges. The long arm of the secret police gathered in thousands of Soviet citizens to face the firing squad. Of the six original members of the 1920 Politburo who survived Lenin, all were purged by Stalin. Old Bolsheviks who had been loyal comrades of Lenin, high officers in the Red Army, and directors of industry were liquidated. It has been estimated that between 5 and 6 per cent of the total population passed through the pretrial prisons of the secret police!

The fitting climax to the purges came in 1940 when Stalin's archcritic Trotsky, living as an exile in Mexico, was murdered by a Soviet agent. "Thus the verdict of the Moscow tribunal which sentenced Trotsky to death [in absentia] was carried out. Having mercilessly uprooted Trotskyism in Russia, Stalin now achieved his last dark triumph over the man himself, whose name like Lenin's had stood for the great hopes and the great illusions of the October Revolution. . . . There was a tragic symbolism that the blood of Trotsky's head spattered the sheets of paper on which he had written down his account of Stalin's career."[3]

The sensational purge trials, which alienated public opinion in many countries of the western world, provided scapegoats for the shortcomings in the frenzied program of industrialization. But above all they removed any potential rivals of Stalin. Thus Stalin won complete control of the Politburo.

Crisis in Germany. World depression, accompanied by the cancellation of foreign loans to Germany and the withdrawal of foreign investments, was the culminating blow to the ill-fated Weimar Republic. In 1931 all banks were forced to close, and disorders broke out in many cities. A year later the number of unemployed had reached six million; and desperate, jobless workers roamed the streets shouting, "Give us bread." Night after night, police and military forces battled hungry mobs.

Up to this time the Nazi party had attracted only lukewarm support; there were but a handful of Nazi deputies in the Reichstag. By the summer of 1932, however, their number had swelled to 230, and the Nazis had become the largest political party. Hungry, frightened, and desperate, the impoverished masses turned to Hitler as a source of salvation. And, ironically enough, the rich also saw their salvation in Nazism. Alarmed at the growth of the German Communist movement, the great industrialists supported Hitler—a rabid anti-Communist—and his Nazi party as a shield against a proletarian revolution.

Once the Nazi movement began to gain popularity, Hitler and his master propagandist, Joseph Goebbels, utilized every type of persuasion to make the mass of the people permanent converts to Nazism. All over Germany huge meetings were organized. Above each stadium a Nazi aviator thrilled the crowd with his aerobatics. Then thousands of Storm Troopers marched in to form a great swastika, while martial music, the roll of drums, and the trumpeting of bugles filled the air. At first, no speaker was seen on the platform, starkly illuminated by a huge spotlight. Then, as the suspense became almost unbearable, into this beam of light stepped Goebbels or, on major occasions, Hitler himself. For hours the speaker poured forth a torrent of words. "Germany is in ruins," "This is the result of reparations," "The Jews are behind all our woes," "It is only the Nazi party that can make Germany strong and prosperous, that will repudiate the reparations and make Germany's army and navy the fear of all Europe." The Nazi mass rallies had a hypnotic effect. Thrilled by these colossal displays and mesmerized by rituals and ranting speeches, the masses gave the Nazis increasing support.

Hitler becomes chancellor. For the Nazi party, 1932—when Hitler ran against the incumbent Paul von Hindenburg for the presidency of the German republic—was a crucial year. Although Hitler was defeated, on two subsequent occasions Hindenburg asked the Nazi leader to join coalitions. Hitler refused, demanding what was equivalent to dictatorial power.

It became increasingly difficult for the German ministries to carry on the government, and in November a second general election was held, so costly to the Nazis that the party

This Nazi campaign poster calls on the voters to choose Hitler and thereby free Germany from its chains.

treasury was almost bankrupt. Some observers believed that the Nazis had passed the crest of their power. At this point, however, a clique of aristocratic nationalists and powerful industrialists, fearful of a Communist revolution and the growing strength of the trade union movement, offered Hitler the chancellorship. In January 1933 a mixed cabinet of nationalists was created with Hitler at the head. Because he did not have a clear majority in the Reichstag, Hitler called a general election for March 5. During the campaign, radio broadcasts were monopolized by Nazi propaganda, and Storm Troopers bullied and coerced the voters. But many Germans became disgusted with the strong-arm methods, and the Nazis needed a dramatic incident to clear a majority in the election.

Just before the election, fire gutted the Reichstag building. The blaze was blamed on the Communists, though there was strong and justified suspicion that it was started by the Nazis themselves. When the votes were counted, Hitler controlled 44 per cent of the deputies. To this bloc was added the support of the Nationalists (another 8 per cent), giving the Nazis a bare majority. Quickly the Reichstag passed the Enabling Act, which granted Hitler the right to legislate by decree for the next four years. The Weimar constitution was never formally—only effectively—abolished; the Reichstag continued as a phantom legislature, but nearly all political power was exercised by one organization, the National Socialist party.

A dread intimation of things to come was Germany's withdrawal in 1933 from the League of Nations. Two years later, in defiance of the Treaty of Versailles, Hitler introduced conscription. When President von Hindenburg died in 1934, Hitler became both chancellor and president; he was known as Führer (leader), and the new regime was described as the Third Reich.*

Persecution of the Jews. Hitler ruthlessly uprooted and smashed the democratic institutions by which he was brought to power. All rival political parties were disbanded by force, and individuals who had spoken out against Nazism mysteriously disappeared after midnight visits from the dreaded Gestapo—the Nazi secret police. Concentration camps were built to house thousands of prisoners. It has been estimated that, in 1933, nineteen thousand Germans committed suicide and sixteen thousand more died from unexplained causes. Not until the end of World War II was the full horror of Nazi brutality revealed (see p. 548).

The doctrine of Aryan racial superiority was an integral part of Hitler's program, and the Jews bore the brunt of Nazi persecution. They were blamed for the Versailles Treaty, for all that was bad about capitalism, for revolutionary communism, for pacifism, and for internationalism—all represented as being facets of a Jewish plot to destroy Germany and seize control of the world. That such a fantastic tale was seriously believed by a

considerable number of the citizens of a supposedly civilized nation indicated the state of near-psychosis into which Germany had fallen.

Once he was dictator, Hitler did everything to stifle and to destroy the Jews. They were prohibited from owning businesses, barred from public service, and deprived of citizenship. Marriage between "Aryans" and "non-Aryans" was forbidden. Hundreds of thousands of Jews were killed in extermination camps. The German commandant of one of these camps has described its methods:

> I used . . . a crystallized prussic acid dropped into the death chamber. It took from three to fifteen minutes to kill the people in the chamber, according to climatic conditions. We knew when the people were dead because their screaming stopped. We usually waited about half an hour before we opened the doors and removed the bodies. After the bodies were removed, our special commandos took off the rings and extracted the gold from the teeth of the corpses. . . . we built our gas-chambers to accommodate two thousand people at one time. . . .[4]

There was something fiendish and inhuman in the Nazi use of the most refined techniques of science to carry out their loathsome mass murders.

Nazi propaganda and education. A Reich culture cabinet was set up to instill a single pattern of thought in literature, the press, broadcasting, drama, music, art, and movies. Forbidden books, including the works of some of Germany's most distinguished men of letters, were seized and destroyed in huge bonfires.

The school system was integrated with the German Youth Movement, which drilled and regimented boys and girls between the ages of ten and fourteen. The boys were taught above all else to be ready to fight and die for their Führer; the girls, to mother the many babies needed by the Third Reich. The German universities, once famous throughout the world for their academic freedom, became agencies for propagating such ideas as the racial myths of Nazism. Enrollment in the universities was limited to good Nazi material, and professors were dismissed by the score.

*The First Reich was created by Otto the Great in 962; the Second by Bismarck in 1871.

Since Nazi doctrine elevated the state above all else, a movement was instigated to subordinate religion to the Hitler regime. Revolting against such pressure, German Protestants led by the Reverend Martin Niemoeller, naval officer in the First World War, repudiated the attempts of Hitler to interfere with religious freedom. The movement was crushed, and in 1938 Niemoeller was placed in a concentration camp. Hitler's regime also used strong pressure to force German Catholics to accept its control, but despite widespread persecution they refused to knuckle under.

Public works and rearmament. In theory and in outward form, Nazism retained capitalism and private property. However, both business and labor were rigidly controlled by the state. Labor unions were dissolved, and both workers and employers were enrolled in a new organization, the Labor Front. As in Mussolini's corporate state, the right of the workers to strike or of management to call a lockout was denied. Compulsory dues were taken from workers' wages to support Nazi organizations. As a sop, the government established the Strength Through Joy movement, which provided sports events, musical festivals, plays, movies, and even vacations at low cost.

The government's attempts to solve Germany's economic problems included levying a huge tax load on the middle class and increasing the national debt by one third in order to provide work for the unemployed. To create the jobs, the first Four-Year Plan, established in 1933, initiated an extensive program of public works and rearmament. The unemployed were put to work on public projects (especially noteworthy was a great network of highways, or *Autobahnen*), in munitions factories, and in the army. The program led to the production of vast armaments and, logically, to their eventual utilization in aggression against other states.

Overlapping the first program, the second Four-Year Plan was initiated in 1936. The objective of this plan was to set up an autarkist state. In order to achieve self-sufficiency, quantities of substitute (*ersatz*) commodities —frequently both inferior in quality and more costly than those purchasable on the world market—were produced by German laboratories, factories, and mills. The peoples' standard of living continued to decline.

Geopolitics. The doctrine of geopolitics was the intellectual ammunition for a program of aggressive expansion. Basic to this theory was the belief that national states are living organisms and that a young and vigorous state—such as the Third Reich—has both the necessity and the right to expand by force. It must have *Lebensraum* (living space). The geopoliticians envisaged the seat of world power as the vast Eurasian plain, with its heartland in the area occupied by Russia. This plain, together with its outlying areas of western Europe, the Middle East, and south Asia constituted the "world-island." The Nazi geopoliticians argued that Germany's central position close to the heartland would enable it to dominate eastern Europe and to extend its control over much of the world island.

Who rules East Europe commands the Heartland; who rules the Heartland commands the World-Island; who rules the World-Island commands the World.[5]

We will see what tragic repercussions this doctrine held for the world.

Depression under Italian Fascism. In 1933 the number of unemployed in Italy totaled more than one million, and the public debt reached an alarming figure. Italian wages were the lowest in Europe, and living standards had sunk to a level below that of 1914. To strengthen the Fascist economy, the nation was reorganized in 1934 into twenty-two government-controlled corporations, each consisting of syndicates of workers and employers. But in spite of a grandiose program of public works and the adoption of measures to increase agricultural output, Mussolini's corporate state continued to suffer from the depression.

In racial matters, the Fascist regime made half-hearted attempts to copy the Nazis. Italians were urged to be "race conscious," but the decrees issued against Jews were not rigidly enforced.

Parliamentary demoralization in France. The lack of vigorous leadership in the demo-

With all the trappings of a grandiose Hollywood epic, a mass meeting of 50,000 Nazi party members heard Hitler declare on May Day, 1937, that he refused to tolerate any interference by church authorities in German political affairs.

cratic nations and the mounting crisis in their capitalistic systems were best exemplified in France. Although Poincaré's financial policies had been so successful that the prosperity of the 1920's carried over after other nations were engulfed in depression, in the early thirties France was faced with rising unemployment, budget deficits, the drying up of the lucrative tourist trade, and heavy military expenditures for security against a rearming Germany. Ministry after ministry was organized, only to collapse a few months later; citizens became more and more impatient with the government.

Disgust with the administration increased with the exposure of corruption in high places. It became known that many prominent politicians were involved in the machinations of Alexander Stavisky, who had cheated French investors out of some 600,000,000 francs. When the ministry in power ignored public furor and refused to authorize an investigation, thousands of angry citizens thronged the streets of Paris on the evening of February 6, 1934, and tried to storm the Chamber of Deputies.

The outcome was a new government, the National Union, which ignored pleas for constitutional reform and for a grant of increased power to the prime minister. The agent of the wealthy and privileged classes, the National Union grew ultraconservative but continued to rule under a variety of prime ministers.

In 1936 emerged the Popular Front, a coalition composed of liberal parties united in opposition to the conservative elements in the government. In June the Popular Front won a national election; and Léon Blum (1872-1950), a noted lawyer and writer, became premier. The Popular Front endeavored to stem the influence of fascist ideas, to improve the country's finances, and to bring about certain fundamental economic reforms. In particular, the Popular Front promised to "break the power of the two hundred families who control the economic life of the nation."[6] In foreign policy the Popular Front was friendly to Great Britain and supported the League of Nations.

An epidemic of sit-down strikes embarrassed the new government, but gradually labor was conciliated by the passage of laws introducing a forty-hour week, higher wages, collective bargaining, and vacations with pay. Furthermore, the government extended its control over the Bank of France and initiated a public works program. Although the Blum government stood resolutely for the laborer and against monopoly and big business, it was equally against communist collectivism or fascist centralization.

After only a year in office, however, Blum was forced to resign. Unfavorable trade balances, an enormous public debt, and an unbalanced budget proved too much for the Popular Front government. France swung back to conservatism. The forty-hour week was ended, and strikes were energetically suppressed.

The National Union and the Popular Front mirrored the widening chasm between the upper and lower classes. The working classes believed that the reforms of the Popular Front had been sabotaged and that a France ruled by a wealthy clique deserved little or no allegiance. On the other hand, some businessmen and financiers were horrified at the prospect of communism and flirted with fascism. The cleavage between classes was secretly encouraged by subtle propaganda from the totalitarian countries. While Frenchmen quarreled and France's economic strength was being sapped, Hitler's Germany, regimented and feverishly productive, was rapidly outstripping France in the manufacture of armaments. The ingredients for the tragic fall of France in the spring of 1940 had now been supplied.

Democracy in crisis elsewhere in Europe. A progressive weakening of parliamentary systems was evident in the smaller European states, except for Finland and Czechoslovakia. In Poland, the façade of parliamentary institutions was retained, but political power was wielded behind the scenes by a group of aristocratic army officers headed by Marshal Pilsudski. After his death in 1935, a new constitution was adopted which gave the president wide powers and in effect reduced the legislature to a cipher. Yet Poland was not truly a totalitarian state; in the main, civil liberties were respected and political parties still functioned, although ineffectually.

The tiny Baltic states of Latvia, Estonia, and Lithuania had only a brief honeymoon with democracy. Lithuania had come under a dictatorship as early as 1926, and Latvia and Estonia fell to dictatorial regimes in 1934. By 1935, royal dictatorships had been established in Albania, Bulgaria, and Yugoslavia; King Carol acted with authoritarian powers in Rumania; and a strong ruler named Gombos, who in 1932 had taken over most of the governmental powers, consolidated his strength in Hungary. During the 1920's and the early 1930's, Greek political affairs had been turbulent; and in 1936 the dictator Metaxas suspended the constitution.

In all these small states, an appearance of democratic parliamentary forms was retained, and not much attention was paid to totalitarian ideology. Behind the false front, however, a small clique—aided by secret police, censorship, and armed political supporters—stifled all opposition to its rule.

"Muddling through" in Britain. It was inevitable that the depression would have catastrophic effects in the highly industrialized and heavily populated island of Britain. In two years, exports and imports declined 35 per cent, and three million unemployed roamed the streets of the factory towns.

A Labour administration, with James Ramsay MacDonald as prime minister, took office in 1929. Little was accomplished, and unemployment became more widespread as the depression deepened. When the Labour government fell, MacDonald retained his office by becoming the leader of a National Coalition government, which was primarily conservative. The bulk of the Labour party constituted the opposition.

Nothing spectacular was undertaken, but the country in typical British fashion did "muddle through." By 1937 a substantial measure of prosperity had been regained, and production registered a 20-per-cent increase over that of 1929. To achieve this comeback, much of what remained of laissez-faire policy was discarded. The government now regulated the currency, erected high tariffs, gave farmers subsidies, and imposed a heavy burden of taxation. The rich had a large proportion of their income taxed away, and what might be left at death was decimated by inheritance taxes. It was ruefully declared that the rich could hardly afford to live, much less to die.

Despite improvements in the economic picture, an increasing demand for the extension of the welfare state existed. There were pleas for expanded educational and health facilities, better accident and unemployment insurance, and more adequate pensions. A survey of Britain's social services, made in 1941 by the noted economist Sir William Beveridge, recommended a comprehensive system of social insurance. This plan served as the blueprint for Britain's post-World War II legislation that endeavored to give security "from the cradle to the grave."

Unlike Germany, which gave up democracy, and France, which kept it but did not know what to do with it, Britain adhered strongly to its traditional parliamentary system. But though the great majority of British citizens continued to believe in the democratic way of life, some quarters were seduced by the strong talk of the dictators. A small but noisy Communist party and the ineffectual but equally noisy British Union of Fascists developed.

The British Commonwealth weathers the storm. In common with the rest of the world, Britain's self-governing dominions were hard hit by the depression. Like Latin America, they were painfully susceptible to the effects of the world slump because they were primarily producers of basic materials such as wheat, meat, lumber, and minerals. When prices of such products dropped to rock bottom, the dominions (which had borrowed heavily on outside capital) were able to avoid defaults on their obligations only by the most stringent economies. But democracy did not succumb; there were no violent overthrows in Australia, New Zealand, Canada, or South Africa, for parliamentary traditions were strong and natural resources were abundant. The dominions had a margin of economic safety which nations such as Germany and Italy lacked.

Political instability in South America. The Latin-American countries, which depended on the export of a few all-important raw materials for their prosperity, suffered serious economic crises as world prices collapsed. As a result of the depression, six of the South American nations experienced revolutions in 1930. While the depression did not last as long in Latin America as it did in the United States, the forces it loosened wrought many important changes.

Out of the increased industrialization and land reform resulting from the revolutions came the gradual development of a middle class, where before there had been only a small group of the extremely rich and great masses of the poor. Rising political, economic, and social standards promised better health and education for more people. The Catholic Church, accused by many of being the ally of the wealthy and powerful, was subject to growing anticlerical attacks, although the continent continued to be almost totally Catholic.

In 1933 the United States inaugurated the Good Neighbor Policy. No longer did the periodic Western-Hemisphere conferences exhibit what a Mexican diplomat called "Blah-Blah Pan Americanism."[7] By economic aid and formal agreement that "no state has the right to intervene in the internal or external affairs of another," the United States demonstrated the sincerity of its overtures to the southern continent. Capital from the United States was poured into Latin America. These investments, which usually provided a good return on the capital, also helped to strengthen the national economies of the borrowing nations. Rivalries among industrialized nations for the Latin-American market became very intense during the thirties. Nazi Germany concluded many barter agreements with Latin-American customers and at the same time penetrated the countries

Loss of human dignity was one of the most painful tragedies of the depression years in the United States. Jobless men, their hope crushed by failure and their pride destroyed by hunger, stand and wait in "Bread Line" by Reginald Marsh.

politically by organizing German immigrants into pro-Nazi groups, fostering fascist politicians, and developing a formidable propaganda system. When war came and the chips were down, however, South America eventually lined up with the democracies.

The New Deal fights depression. In shocking contrast to the golden days of prosperity, the frenzied boom on the stock market, and the smug complacency of American businessmen in the 1920's was the economic paralysis which gripped the United States in 1930. By 1932, business failures numbered at least thirty thousand, and the number of unemployed was somewhere between twelve and fifteen million.

In the first few years after the crash, President Hoover tried to prop up shaky businesses with government money in the hope that the benefits would filter down to the workers. Because the President believed that the government should not compete with private concerns, only a few public works projects were started. Hoover avoided federal relief, leaving to private charities and local governments the heavy responsibility for caring for the hungry. Toward the end of his term, the depression steadily worsened, and thousands of people went hungry because they had no money for food.

The general dissatisfaction with the government was evidenced by the sweeping victory of Franklin D. Roosevelt, the Democratic standard-bearer, who was inaugurated in 1933. Under his leadership the New Deal, a sweeping program to cope with the national emergency, was put into operation. The three objectives of the New Deal were relief, recovery, and reform. Millions of dollars were appropriated for the relief of the unemployed, and vast sums were expended for the construction of public works in the belief that such activity would stimulate economic recovery. A combination work and relief program, the Civilian Conservation Corps, offered employment and education to thousands of young men. To encourage building activity, the Federal Housing Administration offered liberal terms to finance new homes, especially for lower-income families. Most significant was the Social Security Act, passed in 1935. For the first time in the history of the United States, a comprehensive scheme for unemployment insurance and a plan for old-age benefits were introduced.

To prevent a recurrence of the crash, measures were instituted to guarantee the savings deposits of small investors; and the sale of stocks and bonds was regulated by the Securities and Exchange Commission. The

Tennessee Valley Authority was established to produce power at reasonable rates that would constitute a yardstick for public utilities. On the labor front, the National Labor Relations Board was designed to protect labor and give it the right to bargain collectively.

The measures and objectives of the New Deal aroused much controversy. Its opponents contended that it gave too much power to the labor unions, that it created a vast, irresponsible bureaucracy at Washington, D.C., that it spent public funds in a profligate fashion, and that it sought to destroy the capitalist system. Its supporters, on the other hand, maintained that the New Deal did not aim to destroy capitalism but rather to preserve it by adapting it to new circumstances, and that thus it represented a reasonable compromise between the discredited system of laissez faire with its unbridled opportunities for exploitation and, at the other extreme, the pervasive and all-powerful economic controls exercised by states under totalitarian regimes.

Military fascism comes to Japan. Economic depression came to Japan with little warning and with shattering impact. Between 1929 and 1931, the Japanese import trade was cut almost in half. The sale of raw silk, which amounted to 40 per cent of Japanese exports, rapidly plunged downward as the United States drastically reduced purchases. Unemployment, wage cuts, and strikes became common. As in Germany on the eve of Hitler's rise to power, frustration among the younger generation was widespread.

In 1929, with the ministry of Hamaguchi, the high peak of political liberalism had been reached. Hamaguchi sought means to meet the depression, followed a conciliatory policy toward China, and was willing to cooperate in disarmament proposals—aims bitterly opposed by the militaristic clique. Shot in November 1930, the prime minister died the following spring. This assassination was a tragedy from which Japanese liberalism never recovered in the decade before the Second World War.

Quickly a new group of ultranationalistic and militaristic leaders came into power. In contrast to the personal dictatorships in Nazi Germany and Fascist Italy, Japan was ruled by a military clique, which terrorized the civilian members of the government. Scoffing at democracy and peace, these leaders plotted to shelve parliamentary government in Tokyo and to use force on the mainland of China to secure essential raw materials and markets for goods, to spread the "superior" Japanese culture throughout Asia, and to find space for Japan's overcrowded population. This "beneficial mission" was known as the New Order in Asia.

AGGRESSION

AND APPEASEMENT

Japanese aggression in Manchuria. The first challenge to world peace occurred in September 1931, when Japan moved into Manchuria. Unable to cope with the invader, the Chinese appealed to the League of Nations, which appointed a committee of inquiry. The committee report condemned the aggression while trying not to affront Japan, which nevertheless resigned its League membership two years later. The significance of the Manchurian campaign was dreadfully clear. A demonstration that a great power could embark on aggression without any effective opposition from League members marked the beginning of the collapse of the League.

When the Chinese resorted to a nationwide boycott of Japanese goods, the Japanese attacked Shanghai and early in 1933 began to push deeper into northern China. To slow down the invasion and give themselves a chance to prepare for the inevitable struggle, the Chinese agreed to the T'ang-ku Truce, which recognized Japanese conquests in Manchuria and northern China. The truce remained in effect for about four years, while the Japanese consolidated their position and the Chinese wrestled with internal threats.

The united front in China. In addition to the invaders, the Nationalist forces of Chiang Kai-shek had to contend with the Chinese Communists. In 1931, delegates from the various local soviets in China had proclaimed the birth of the Chinese Soviet Republic. Within three years there existed in south China large

Communist enclaves with a total population of about nine million. The success of the Communist leader, Mao Tse-tung (1893-   ), depended partly on his realization that it was the Chinese peasant, not the urban worker, who could be made the agent of revolution. Farmers' cooperatives were established and tax systems reformed. More drastic measures included the seizure and division of moderate-sized and large farms and the distribution of the goods taken from the landowners.

The Nationalists, who had neglected the countryside for the cities, were apprehensive of Mao's success. From 1931 to 1934, Chiang launched five military campaigns against the Communists, the last employing one million men and a German military staff. To escape annihilation, the Communists made their famous Long March two thousand miles northwest. Only a remnant of the original force reached Shensi, where in 1935 a new Communist stronghold was set up.

The Chinese Communists demanded a united front against the Japanese, stating that the first objective of all China should be whole-hearted resistance against foreign imperialism and aggression. In 1936 the Communists kidnaped Chiang and held him for two weeks. There was a great outcry from the Chinese people, and influenced by the obvious national solidarity behind Chiang, the rebels asked him to lead a united China against the common enemy. In order to allay suspicion and achieve a united front, Mao agreed to end land confiscation and armed opposition to the Nanking government, to abandon the system of soviets, and to permit the incorporation of the Communist forces into the fight against Japan. China was unified just in time to meet the next Japanese thrust.

Japanese conquests continue. In 1937 fighting broke out again, this time around Peiping. Farther south, Japanese troops captured Shanghai and advanced rapidly up the Yangtze valley to Nanking. The Chinese retreated westward, establishing a new capital at Chungking. In north China the Chinese armies were also forced to retreat, and the Japanese set up a government at Peiping.

As one step in his long march to mastery of mainland China, Mao Tse-tung arranged for a united front of his Communist forces and the armies of Chiang Kai-shek against the Japanese.

In 1938 Japan proclaimed the New Order in eastern Asia. Its objectives were the destruction of Chiang Kai-shek's regime, the expulsion of western interests in eastern Asia, and the establishment of a self-sufficient economic bloc to include Japan, Manchuria (which was renamed Manchukuo by the Japanese), and China.

The outbreak of war in Europe gave Japan its golden opportunity to extend the New Order in China and into the Asian colonies of the western powers. The year 1939 saw several strong but inconclusive offensives in China and the seizure of the island of Hainan, of strategic importance in relation to French Indo-China, British Malaya, and the Dutch East Indies. After the fall of France (see p. 535), the Vichy government allowed Japan to build naval and air bases in Indo-China. Japanese pressure was also exerted on the Dutch East Indies and on British settlements in China. By the time Japan was actively engaged in the Second World War, the New Order was being rapidly expanded over much of Asia.

Picasso's "Guernica," named for a city destroyed in the Spanish civil war, expresses not only the agony and brutality of that conflict but the horror of war itself. As shocking as a scream of pain, it is one of his most famous works.

Of the three great powers which might have halted Japanese banditry in the 1930's, Britain was in the throes of an economic crisis, France suffered both political and economic paralysis, and the United States was isolationist. Most important, the weakness of the League of Nations had been bared for all the world to see.

Italy swallows up Abyssinia. Italian aggression in Abyssinia followed Japan's lead. Proclaiming the imperial destiny of his regime, Mussolini grew more and more bellicose, his speeches bristling with such statements as: "War is to man what maternity is to woman." As his first victim, Mussolini chose Abyssinia, the only important independent native state left in Africa and the nation which in 1896 had handed the Italians a humiliating defeat. Late in 1934, fighting broke out between the Abyssinians and the Italians, and in the following year the Italians made a wholesale invasion of Abyssinia. Emperor Haile Selassie appealed to the League, which tried to arrange for arbitration. Despite the Italian delegates' audacious argument that Abyssinia, not Italy, was the aggressor, the League voted to prohibit shipment of certain goods to Italy and denied it credit. But the effect of the sanctions was nullified because oil—without which no modern army or navy can fight—

was not included in the list of prohibited articles. Apprehensive of alienating Italy, France and Britain were only lukewarm in their support of the sanctions; and since they were not League members, the United States and Germany largely ignored the prohibitions.

Using bombs, mustard gas, and tanks, the Italians advanced swiftly into Abyssinia and crushed the resistance of Haile Selassie's valiant soldiers. The whole sorry story ended in July 1936, when the sanctions were removed. Haile Selassie, an emperor without a country, went to live in England, the first of several royal exiles.

Germany marches into the Rhineland. The conflict over Abyssinia gave Hitler his first big opportunity to use the military force he had been building up. In March 1936, while the wrangle over the sanctions against Italy was taking place, German troops marched boldly into the Rhineland in defiance of the Treaty of Versailles and the Locarno agreements. Immediately France mobilized 150,000 troops, but Britain refused to support the use of force to compel Germany to withdraw. Many Englishmen thought it hardly worth while to risk war over Germany's demand to fortify its own territory. Others, however, recognized the danger in allowing Hitler to break an agreement with little or no protest.

Alliance of the Axis powers. Up until 1935 Germany had been diplomatically isolated in Europe, faced by the United Front of Great Britain, France, and Italy. But the Abyssinian incident and the imposition of sanctions broke up the United Front, and Italy became Germany's friend. In 1936 the friendship was formalized in the Rome-Berlin Axis, and one year later Mussolini followed Hitler's lead by withdrawing from the League.

Japan, the third major member of the Axis powers, joined forces with Germany in 1936 in the Anti-Comintern Pact. A year later Italy subscribed to the agreement. On the surface the agreement was a pact against Russia; in reality the members of the Rome-Berlin-Tokyo Axis were preparing for expansion.

Dress rehearsal in Spain. In 1936, civil war broke out in Spain, shattering that country and threatening to involve all of Europe. This war was to prove another ominous example of the impotency of the democratic nations when faced with the mounting insolence of the totalitarian powers.

The Spanish republic had been established five years earlier. Long overdue reforms were enacted: new schools were constructed, great estates were broken up, and the army was purged of its parasitic officers. But the republic brought neither prosperity nor stability to Spain. In order to nullify the progressive legislation, reactionary groups tried to gain control of the government. At the same time, left-wing groups resorted to terrorism. The middle-of-the-road, reformist government became increasingly powerless to maintain order, and an uprising inspired by reactionary and military cliques began in July 1936.

The totalitarian powers—Italy and Germany—seized the opportunity to ensure a Fascist victory. Large numbers of Italian planes were made available to the Fascist insurgents, led by General Francisco Franco (1892-   ). Most of the regular army troops were faithful to Franco, and a quick victory was anticipated. But the Spanish people in many parts of the country rose *en masse* to fight for the republic. Anti-Fascist refugees from Germany and Italy and volunteers from Austria, Poland, the United States, and Great Britain flocked to Spain to fight with the Loy-

alists of the republic, who stopped the Fascists at the outskirts of Madrid.

Although the French and British governments tried to avoid unpleasantness with the dictators by creating a nonintervention system for the Spanish war, they were the only nations that held to the agreement not to send weapons to either side. Germany and Italy sent troops and equipment to the Fascists while Russia sent matériel and personnel to the Loyalists at Madrid. On Spanish battlefields, Germany, Italy, and Russia tried out their new cannon and combat planes. Internal dissensions weakened Russian assistance, which was not sufficient to offset German and Italian aid. In March 1939, Madrid fell, and the Spanish republic was no more. Franco, at the head of the new state, was endowed with absolute power. The Spanish civil war was not only a national catastrophe, which left permanent scars on a proud and gallant people, but also a dress rehearsal for the tragic global drama of World War II.

British appeasement and Allied weakness. Neville Chamberlain (1869-1940), whose name was to symbolize the policy of appeasement, had become the British prime minister in 1937. Determined to explore every possibility for reaching an equitable understanding with the dictators, Chamberlain persisted in trying to ease international tension despite snubs from those he wished to placate. Strong support existed in England for Chamberlain's policies. Many Englishmen had a feeling of "peace guilt"—namely that Germany had been unfairly treated in the Treaty of Versailles. In other quarters there was reluctant admiration for the Nazi regime and the belief that a strong Germany could serve as a buffer against Communist Russia. Most important, however, was the passionate and widespread desire for peace, arising from the war weariness and disillusionment suffered by the democratic peoples after World War I. In 1933, for example, the famous student debating society, the Oxford Union, had passed a resolution that "this House will in no circumstance fight for its King and Country. . . ."[8]

The world was uneasily aware of the growing weakness of the democracies and of the major shift in the European balance of power.

"Honest, Mister, there's nobody here but us Spaniards." In David Low's cartoon, the noninterventionists, Daladier of France and Chamberlain of Great Britain, are baffled by "Spaniards" Mussolini and Hitler, who provide an overpowering escort for Francisco Franco, leader of the rebel armies in the Spanish civil war.

The small states began to draw away from the impotent League of Nations. Some tried to make deals with Germany and Italy; others, such as the Scandinavian nations and Holland, ran for the dubious shelter of neutrality and "innocent isolation." Belgium gave up its alliance with France, and Poland signed a nonaggression pact with Germany. In the Little Entente of Czechoslovakia, Rumania, and Yugoslavia, only Czechoslovakia remained loyal to Paris. Hitler was fully aware of the pervading obsession for peace in Britain and of the decline of the French alliance system.

Hitler's Austrian coup. In announcing the military reoccupation of the Rhineland in the spring of 1936, Hitler had stated, "We have no territorial demands to make in Europe." The course of events was to belie this statement. By 1938 the German army had amazing strength, the *Luftwaffe* far exceeded the air forces of Great Britain and France, and Hitler was ready to embark on a daring program of expansion. His "territorial demands" were to prove limitless.

Hitler's first victim was his neighbor Austria. Previously, in 1934, Hitler had attempted to annex Austria; and the Austrian chancellor, Engelbert Dollfuss, had been murdered by Nazi agents. Partly because of Mussolini's opposition, this *Putsch* failed. Four years later, after Mussolini had become his ally, Hitler tried again. The Austrian chancellor, Kurt von Schuschnigg, was summoned to the Führer, who demanded the inclusion of several prominent Nazi sympathizers in the Austrian cabinet and the release of Austrian Nazis who had been imprisoned. On his return to Vienna, the chancellor made one well-known Nazi the minister of the interior but declined to go any further.

The blow fell on Friday, March 11. American radio listeners were told at 2:15 P.M. that Schuschnigg had resigned, at 2:45 that German troops were crossing the frontier, and at 3:43 that the swastika had been hoisted over the Austrian chancellery. Meanwhile, Nazi agents in Austria took over the government, and on Saturday German troops occupied most of the country.

Germany aspires to the Sudetenland. After the Austrian coup, Hitler moved on to his next objective, the annexation of the Sudetenland, an area in Czechoslovakia bordering on Germany and peopled mainly by Germans. In a speech in 1938, Hitler declared that the Sudetens "are being oppressed in an inhuman and intolerable manner." He screamed into the microphone, "And I say that if these tortured creatures cannot obtain rights and assistance by themselves, they can obtain both from us." Immediately after the speech, Chamberlain arranged for a conference with the Führer, who bluntly informed him that he was determined to secure self-determination for the Sudeten Germans. Returning to London, Chamberlain persuaded Edouard Daladier, the French premier, that a sacrifice on the part of Czechoslovakia would save the peace. When France, previously counted as an ally by the Czechs, joined England in pressing for acceptance of the Nazi demands, Czechoslovakia had little choice but to agree. Chamberlain went with this news to Hitler, only to discover that the German demands had increased considerably. Hitler demanded that within one week the Czechs evacuate certain areas and that all military matériel, goods, and livestock in these areas be turned over to the Germans immediately. Astonished and embittered at the Führer's duplicity, the British prime minister refused to accept the new terms and returned to London.

Munich seals the fate of Czechoslovakia. On September 28, 1938, the British House of Commons assembled to hear a report by the prime minister. As he neared the end of his address, a messenger delivered a note from Hitler inviting him to attend a conference at Munich. The following day Hitler, Mussolini, Daladier, and Chamberlain met at the Nazi headquarters in Munich and for thirteen hours worked out the details of the surrender of the Sudetenland. No Czech representative was present. Though an outspoken ally of Czechoslovakia, Russia was completely disregarded. (French and British statesmen distrusted Russia, had a low opinion of its military power after the recent purges of its high command, and presumably thought that Hitler's hatred of communism would not permit the attendance of a representative from Moscow.) Not only were all of Hitler's demands accepted, but Poland and Hungary also received slices of Czechoslovakia.

Munich brought relief to millions of Europeans half-crazed with fear of war, but it was still a question whether this settlement would be followed by another crisis. Many hoped for the best but feared the worst. Immediately after Munich, Winston Churchill solemnly warned:

And do not suppose that this is the end. This is only the beginning of the reckoning. This is only the first sip, the first foretaste of a bitter cup which will be proffered to us year by year unless, by a supreme recovery of moral health and martial vigor, we arise again and take our stand for freedom as in the olden time.[9]

It should be pointed out, however, that Munich gave Britain precious time to build up its air force. In September 1938, Britain had five squadrons of fighters; a year later, twenty-six. And the rate of fighter production soared from two hundred to six hundred a month.

The mounting fears of French and British statesmen were confirmed in 1939. Early in March a bitter attack against the Czech government was inaugurated by the German press. Another coup was in the making. On March 14 Hitler summoned President Hacha and his foreign minister to Berlin. Arriving late in the evening, Hacha and his aid were taken to the German chancellery, where their conference with Hitler lasted until 4:15 A.M. Subjected to all kinds of threats, Hacha finally capitulated and signed a document placing his country under the "protection" of Germany. His signature was a mere formality, however, for German troops were already crossing the Czech frontier. Not to be outdone, Mussolini seized Albania the following month, and the two dictators celebrated by signing a military alliance, the so-called Pact of Steel.

The shock of the final conquest of Czechoslovakia and Hitler's callous violation of pledges made at Munich ended the appeasement policy of France and Great Britain. For the first time in Britain's long history, the government authorized a peacetime draft. A tre-

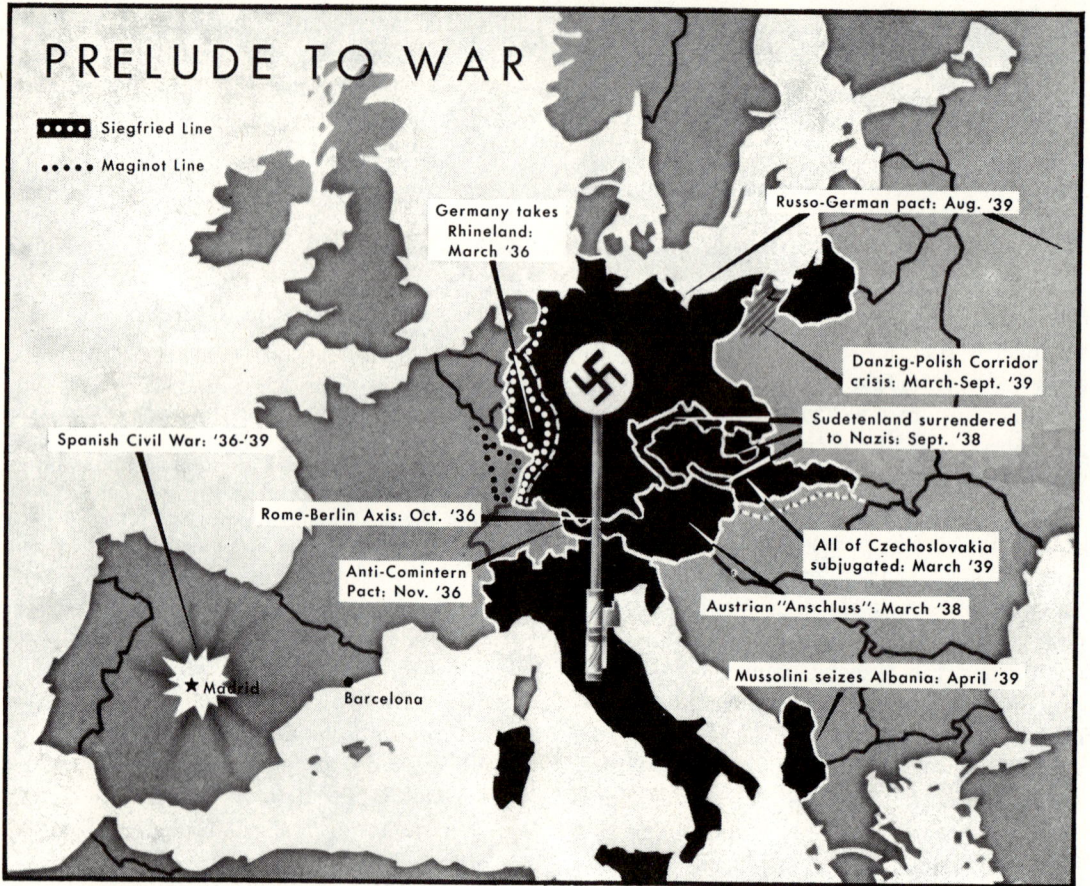

PRELUDE TO WAR

■■■■ Siegfried Line

•••• Maginot Line

Germany takes Rhineland: March '36

Russo-German pact: Aug. '39

Danzig-Polish Corridor crisis: March-Sept. '39

Sudetenland surrendered to Nazis: Sept. '38

Spanish Civil War: '36-'39

Rome-Berlin Axis: Oct. '36

Anti-Comintern Pact: Nov. '36

All of Czechoslovakia subjugated: March '39

Austrian "Anschluss": March '38

Mussolini seizes Albania: April '39

★ Madrid   Barcelona

The year 1931 marked the first of a series of aggressions which culminated in the devastating Second World War. In that year the Japanese moved into Manchuria and began their thrust into the interior of China, pushing the Chinese capital back to Chungking in 1937, and setting up a Japanese government at Peiping. This was only the beginning of the Nipponese plan to impose its New Order in eastern Asia. Aggression by the European Axis powers began in 1935, when Italy attacked Abyssinia; during 1936, the African nation became Mussolini's. The next steps in the Fascist drive for acquisitions, up to the time of the invasion of Poland and Britain's declaration of war, are shown on the map above.

mendous arms program was launched, for which Britain began to spend five million dollars a day. In Paris, Daladier obtained special emergency powers to push forward national defense.

Isolationism in the United States. The United States had been disillusioned by the results of the "war to make the world safe for democracy." Influential spokesmen asserted that World War I had been caused by the greed of munitions makers and stressed the centuries-old hatreds and rivalries in Europe; America, therefore, should insulate itself from these potent causes of international conflict. Reflecting this mood, Congress passed neu-

trality legislation between 1935 and 1937 which made it unlawful for any nation at war to obtain munitions from the United States.

As the Nazi and Fascist menace became apparent in the late 1930's, President Roosevelt and the State Department worked strenuously to arouse the American people to the dangers of the world situation. In 1937, in his famous "quarantine speech," Roosevelt declared:

The peace, the freedom and the security of 90 per cent of the population of the world is being jeopardized by the remaining 10 per cent who are threatening a breakdown of all international order and law.

Surely the 90 per cent who want to live in peace under law and in accordance with moral standards that have received almost universal acceptance through the centuries can and must find some way to make their will prevail. . . . There must be positive endeavors to preserve peace.[10]

In May 1939 the president told leaders in the House of Representatives "that in case of war there was at least an even chance that Germans and Italians might win."[11] So strong was isolationist sentiment, however, that the warning went unheeded.

The Polish question and the Nazi-Soviet pact. It was Germany's aggression against Poland that precipitated the Second World War. The Treaty of Versailles had turned over West Prussia to Poland as a Polish Corridor to the sea (see map, p. 450). While 90 per cent of the Corridor's population was Polish, the Baltic port city of Danzig was nearly all German. Late in March 1939, Hitler proposed to Poland that Danzig be ceded to Germany and that the Nazis be allowed to occupy a narrow strip of land connecting Germany with East Prussia. Chamberlain, with France concurring, warned the Nazi government that "in the event of any action which clearly threatened Polish independence," the British would "at once lend the Polish government all support in their power." In the months that followed the Allied warning, France and Britain competed with Germany for an alliance with Russia.

The Soviet Union had long been seriously concerned about the twin menaces of Nazi Germany and expansionist Japan. The Kremlin had supported the collective security system of the League and had supposedly called off the subversive activity of the Comintern (see p. 469) in favor of popular-front governments to oppose the rising tide of Axis aggression. On the other hand, Soviet pledges to call off Comintern activity were openly violated; and the purge trials not only alienated public opinion in many parts of the world but seriously weakened the Red Army, whose leading officers had been removed.

As we have seen, Chamberlain and Daladier ignored the Soviet Union at Munich. Now, with the Polish question of paramount importance, Britain and France desperately needed Russia as an ally. But while British and French negotiators attempted to convince the Kremlin that their nations really desired an effective alliance against Nazi Germany, the Nazi and Soviet foreign secretaries were secretly working out the details of an agreement. On August 23, 1939, a nonaggression pact between Russia and Germany was signed. It was an utterly cynical arrangement between two inexorably antagonistic foes.

Through this agreement Stalin gave Hitler a free hand in Poland, thus precipitating war between Germany and Britain and France. Russian political strategy was this: such a conflict would give the Soviet Union time to build up its armaments and would weaken the antagonists. During the last phase of the war, the fresh Russian troops could be thrown into the contest to secure whatever territory the Politburo might stake out.

With the pact in his pocket, Hitler could attack Poland without fear of intervention by his great rival to the east. Furthermore, he was now convinced that Britain and France would not dare oppose his ambitions. But France and Britain at last understood that if they wished to stop Germany from dominating all of Europe, they must fight.

From several quarters, appeals were made for peace—from the pope, the king of Belgium, and President Roosevelt. Commenting on the American peace appeals, an official in the State Department wryly noted:

My private opinion is that these messages will have about the same effect as a valentine sent to somebody's mother-in-law out of season. . . .[12]

In 1939 there was a sense of inevitability about the coming conflict.

Basic causes of Hitler's war. Undoubtedly Germany nursed a sense of grievance over what were regarded as the injustices of Versailles. The most important cause of the war, however, was the ruthless ambition of an irrational dictator to gain control of Europe and as much of the rest of the world as he could master. Aiding and abetting his sinister ambition was the strong, even obsessive desire of the democracies for peace. Because Britain and France had long turned the other cheek,

Hitler believed that they would not fight under any provocation.

One of the great lessons of 1939 is that appeasement does not guarantee peace and that it does not take two equally belligerent sides to make a fight. Hitler was genuinely surprised to discover that he had pushed the democracies too far and that he had a real war on his hands. When he was handed the British ultimatum, he turned to Ribbentrop, his foreign minister, and asked: "Well, what now?" There was no reply, but Hermann Goering, the commander of the *Luftwaffe,* exclaimed: "Heaven help us, if we lose this war."[13]

THE WORLD DIVIDED

Blitzkrieg in Poland. Without a declaration of war, Nazi troops crossed the Polish frontier early in the morning of September 1, 1939, and the *Luftwaffe* began to bomb Polish cities. On the morning of September 3, Chamberlain sent an ultimatum to Germany, demanding that the invasion be halted. The time limit was given as 11 A.M. of the same day. At 11:15 he announced on a radio broadcast that Britain was now at war. His words were sad but resolute:

We have a clear conscience, we have done all that any country could do to establish peace, but a situation in which no word given by Germany's ruler could be trusted, and no people or country could feel themselves safe, had become intolerable. . . . For it is evil things we shall be fighting against, brute force, bad faith, injustice, oppression, and persecution. But against them I am certain that the right will prevail.[14]

France took similar action. After an interval of only twenty-one years since World War i, Europe was again plunged into conflict.

Blitzkrieg (lightning war) was the technique used by the German high command. The Polish forces were overrun by the panzer (armored) divisions with their tanks and motorized artillery, while the *Luftwaffe,* which had destroyed the Polish air force on the ground, completely controlled the skies. At the same time, Russian forces attacked from the east. The shooting was over in less than a month, and a Russo-German treaty partitioned hapless Poland once again. In the belief that they would ultimately defeat the enemy by a naval blockade and by standing firm on the Maginot Line (a zone of fortifications on the French border), Britain and France did not attack Germany's Siegfried Line on the Rhine frontier.

The war in Poland jarred the Congress of the United States into amending the existing law against selling munitions to belligerent nations. The new legislation allowed the sale of arms to belligerents, but only on a "cash-and-carry" basis. Presumably, as Britain controlled the sea lanes, munitions would be denied Germany but made available to Britain and France.

The "phony war." The winter of 1939-1940 was the time of the so-called "phony war," or *Sitzkrieg.* Facing each other from the supposedly impregnable Maginot and Siegfried lines, the Allied and German armies did little fighting. The active sector was Finland. When the Finns stoutly refused Moscow's demands for air and naval bases, the Russians launched a brutal attack. To the surprise of the world, Finland held the Soviet bear at bay from November 1939 to the following March, when the Finns were forced to cede substantial territory and to lease important military sites to the U.S.S.R.

Hitler and his generals did not remain idle during the phony war. In April 1940, neutral Denmark and Norway were invaded. Denmark surrendered after a brief resistance, but Norway proved less easy to subjugate. Partly the victim of such traitorous leaders as Quisling (whose name has since come to mean a person who undermines his own country from within), the Norwegians fought hard against stupendous odds. After about two months, the king fled to London, where a Norwegian government-in-exile was set up. British anger at the crushing defeat of an Anglo-French expeditionary force sent to Norway led to Chamberlain's resignation, and Churchill succeeded him as prime minister just in time to face a military crisis.

Dunkirk and the fall of France. The phony war ended abruptly in May, when Hitler's armies overran neutral Holland and Belgium, thus outflanking the Maginot Line. As in the other Nazi assaults, cities with their civilian populations were favorite targets; the Dutch army suffered far fewer casualties than the city of Rotterdam, which was ruthlessly bombed by the Germans. Nazi armored columns swept through northwestern France and reached the English Channel, encircling an Anglo-French force of some 400,000 men. All resistance ended in Holland and Belgium, and surrender seemed the only course for the Allied army trapped on the beach at Dunkirk. But in one of the most amazing and courageous events of the war, hundreds of small craft from England, protected by an air umbrella of the Royal Air Force, came to the rescue. In the words of one of the volunteers:

I am still amazed about the whole Dunkirk affair. There was from first to last a queer, medieval sense of miracle about it. You remember the old quotation about the miracle that crushed the Spanish Armada, "God sent a wind." This time "God withheld the wind." Had we had one onshore breeze of any strength at all, in the first days, we would have lost a hundred thousand men.

The pier at Dunkirk was the unceasing target of bombs and shell-fire throughout, yet it never was hit. . . . where the Government and the Board of Admiralty had hoped to bring away 30,000 men, we brought away 335,000. If that was not a miracle, there are no miracles left.[15]

After Dunkirk, the fall of France was inevitable. Anxious to be in on the kill, Mussolini declared war against France and Britain. Designated an "open city" by the French, Paris fell on June 14. As the German advance continued, the members of the French government who wished to continue resistance were voted down; and Marshal Pétain, the eighty-four-year-old hero of Verdun in the First World War, became premier. Pétain immediately asked Hitler for an armistice, and in the same dining car in which the French had imposed armistice terms on the Germans in 1918, the Nazis and the French on June 22 signed the armistice agreement. France was split into two zones, occupied and unoccupied. In unoccupied France, Pétain's government at Vichy was supposedly free from interference, but in reality it was a puppet of the Nazis. And so the Third Republic, created in 1871 from the debris of defeat suffered at

German hands, now came to an end because of a new blow from the same quarter. However, a remarkable patriot, General Charles de Gaulle (1890-   ), fled to London and organized a Free French government, which adopted as its symbol the red cross of Lorraine (flown by Joan of Arc in her fight to liberate France centuries earlier) and continued to aid the Allied cause throughout the war.

The crucial battle of Britain. With millions of Europe's people already his captives and with millions more living in constant dread of his screaming dive bombers and clanking panzer divisions, Hitler demanded that the British lay down their arms. But in the face of almost hopeless odds, they rallied to the support of their homeland. Churchill's eloquent defiance of Hitler stirred not only his own countrymen but all of the free world:

We shall go on to the end . . . . we shall defend our Island, whatever the cost may be, we shall fight on the beaches, we shall fight on the landing grounds, we shall fight in the fields and in the streets, we shall fight in the hills; we shall never surrender. . . .[16]

The English daily expected a German invasion; instead came the massive and terrifying air raids of the battle of Britain. Hoping to demoralize the civilian population, the *Luftwaffe* concentrated their bombs on English cities from August to October; but with the help of radar warning devices and the super-

While England and France made desperate concessions in a futile attempt to avoid war, Mussolini and Hitler, shown at top left meeting in Rome in 1938, relentlessly pursued their plans for conquest. And for a time their plans seemed destined to succeed. While their armies moved over the face of Europe, Nazi U-boats threatened to gain control of the seas; at center left, American seamen use depth charges to ward off a U-boat attack on a large convoy in the Atlantic. The weeping Frenchman, at bottom left, symbolizes the tragedy of a people who were forced to watch the Germans take over their country while their own forces either laid down their arms or escaped into exile. The haggard men, above, were among the American prisoners driven without food or water along the eighty-five miles of the Death March out of Bataan by the Japanese, Far Eastern partner in the conquering Axis.

In the months of Axis victories, the Allies suffered terrible losses. Above left, buildings close to St. Paul's Cathedral crumble after a German air raid on London. Below, Minsk in the Soviet Union is a city of empty shells after repeated assaults by Nazi bombers. Above right, American naval vessels go down in flames during Japan's attack on Pearl Harbor.

human efforts of the R.A.F., the English shot down so many German planes that the Nazis called off the massive daytime raids and restricted their offensive to night bombing. Britain had lost 915 planes, Germany more than 1700. In Churchill's words, "Never in the field of human conflict was so much owed by so many to so few."

All through the winter of 1940-1941, however, England continued to be racked by terrible raids. Night bombing destroyed block after block of England's cities; St. Paul's Cathedral in London stood as a solitary survivor in the midst of acres of desolation. Evacuating their children and old people and sleeping in air-raid shelters, Britain's people stood firm. Their air force retaliated in some measure by raiding the industrial cities of the Ruhr, and their naval forces remained on the offensive.

Italian failures, Nazi successes. Meanwhile, Mussolini was eager to secure his share of the spoils. In October 1940 he invaded Greece, but this thrust was a miserable failure, revealing inefficiency, corruption, and poor equipment in the Italian forces. An African venture was no more successful. Although an Italian army launched an offensive which conquered British Somaliland and penetrated into Egypt, the greatly outnumbered British Army of the Nile counterattacked and gained a decisive victory. To add to Mussolini's discomfort, the British troops stayed on the offensive, marching through British and Italian Somaliland and Eritrea. By May of 1941, an early Fascist victory was dramatically reversed when Abyssinia was recaptured. Nearer Mussolini's homeland, the British Mediterranean fleet in 1940 inflicted several disastrous defeats on the Italian navy.

While Italy was making a sorry showing, Hitler was winning more and more territory. Shortly after the fall of France, Rumania became a Nazi satellite, and early in 1941 Bulgaria and Hungary became puppets of the Third Reich. In April, Nazi armies attacked Greece and Yugoslavia at the same time; where Mussolini had failed, Hitler succeeded easily, despite the British forces sent to aid in the defense of Greece. Through that most modern of tactics—the air-borne invasion—Germany also seized ancient Crete.

By the spring of 1941, nearly all of Europe had come under the iron heel of the Third Reich. Only Portugal, Switzerland, Sweden, and Turkey remained neutral. While ostensibly neutral, Spain under Franco was pro-Nazi. Britain, though still dangerous, was powerless to interfere on the Continent. The United States was gravely perturbed over the Nazi successes but was still unprepared.

Hitler turns on the Soviet Union. When the battle of Britain indicated that the defeat of England would be extremely difficult and costly, Hitler gave up his plans for a cross-channel invasion and turned on Russia. The very lifeblood of blockaded Germany depended on access to Russian raw materials—grain, coal, and iron from the Ukraine and oil from the Caucasus.

Stalin had no illusions about Nazi friendship. As France fell, he tried to "bolt the Baltic door" by annexing Latvia, Estonia, and Lithuania. At the same time, he forced Rumania to cede territory on its eastern frontier. With these acquisitions and the territory already seized from Poland, Stalin set up a buffer zone extending from the Baltic to the Black Sea. Meanwhile, he secured a neutrality pact with Japan, the latter being as eager as Russia to obtain insurance against war on two fronts.

Following the surrender of France, as we have seen, Hitler immediately moved to block any further extension of Soviet influence in southeastern Europe. His activities in the Balkans almost squeezed Russia out of the area, and the German conquest of Yugoslavia and Greece completed the process. For all practical purposes, the Nazi-Soviet nonaggression pact was now a mere scrap of paper.

In June 1941, without warning, a gigantic German attack was launched against Russia, even though many of Hitler's generals were apprehensive over the prospects for success. From the Baltic to the Black Sea the armies of the Third Reich smashed their way across the Russian plains. Along a battle front eighteen hundred miles long, nine million men became locked in a life-or-death struggle. Soviet forces were easily pushed out of Russia's buffer zone and had to retreat some six hundred miles. In the face of the oncoming enemy, the retreating Russians "scorched the earth"—destroyed everything left behind— and guerrilla fighting harassed the German lines. Russian troops were captured in droves, however, and disaffected groups within the Soviet Union often surrendered without much resistance. Russia appeared to be on the verge of collapse, and in October, as his troops reached the suburbs of Moscow, Hitler confidently announced that victory was his.

With the coming of winter, however, snow blocked the road to Moscow, and the Nazi campaign plan began to display vital weaknesses. Believing that Russia would be conquered by the end of autumn, the Germans had not equipped their troops to withstand the hardships of the Russian winter; German soldiers suffered from the intense cold, and their weapons froze. The Russian government showed no signs of surrender, and a fierce spirit of resistance inflamed the people. Much of Russia's heavy industry had been moved out of German reach beyond the Ural Mountains, and the breathing space gave mills and factories a chance to step up production. Before May of 1942, the Russian army, accustomed to the severe winters, had made important gains.

The "arsenal of democracy." Following the collapse of France and during the battle of Britain, the full implications of an Axis victory began to be understood by the American public. Isolation was coming with a vengeance —the kind of isolation which meant being alone in a troubled world, devoid of allies and surrounded by victorious and expansionist powers. After Dunkirk, arms were sent to Britain, a great rearmament program was undertaken, the Selective Training and Service Act instituted the draft, and the United States began to consolidate its allies and bases on the American continents. Since it was apparent that Britain did not have the necessary funds to purchase direly needed war supplies for its defense, Congress early in 1941 passed the Lend-Lease Act, which empowered the president to manufacture, sell, lease, lend, or exchange arms with any country whose defense was thought vital to the national interests. As Roosevelt put it, the United States was becoming the "arsenal of democracy." Despite ideological differences, Britain concluded an alliance with the Soviet Union after Hitler's attack on Russia, and both Britain and the United States sent arms to Germany's new enemy.

Because of Germany's naval strength on the Baltic and Black seas, supplies to Russia had to travel by indirect routes. One such route was across the Pacific from the western coast of the United States to Siberia; another was through the Persian Gulf and Iran to the Caspian Sea, a long route imperiled by the Nazi agents who flourished in Iran; the most dangerous was across the Arctic Ocean to Murmansk, a passage menaced constantly by icebergs, bad weather, and German bombers and submarines. As a defense against German U-boats, cargo vessels were sent in convoys with planes and armed ships for protection. By the fall of 1941, American destroyers and Nazi submarines were firing "on sight."

To define the moral purpose and principles of the struggle, Roosevelt and Churchill drafted the Atlantic Charter in August 1941. Meeting "somewhere in the Atlantic," the signatories pledged that after "the final destruction of Nazi tyranny," they hoped to see a peace in which "men in all the lands may live out their lives in freedom from fear and want." If the United States was not yet a belligerent in the fall of 1941, it was certainly not neutral.

Pearl Harbor draws the United States into war. It was Japan's expansionist policy which brought the United States directly into the conflict. Confronted with Japanese ambitions for the New Order in Asia, the United States froze Japanese funds and refused to sell it war matériel. In spite of this pressure, Japan made the fateful decision to continue its expansion; and in October 1941, General Tojo, an avid militarist, became premier.

On Sunday, December 7, while special "peace" envoys from Tokyo were negotiating in Washington, ostensibly to restore harmony to Japanese-American relations, Japanese planes attacked Pearl Harbor, the American bastion in the Pacific. Our fleet was badly mauled, and our planes were wiped out on the ground. On the following day Congress declared war on Japan. In a few days Italy

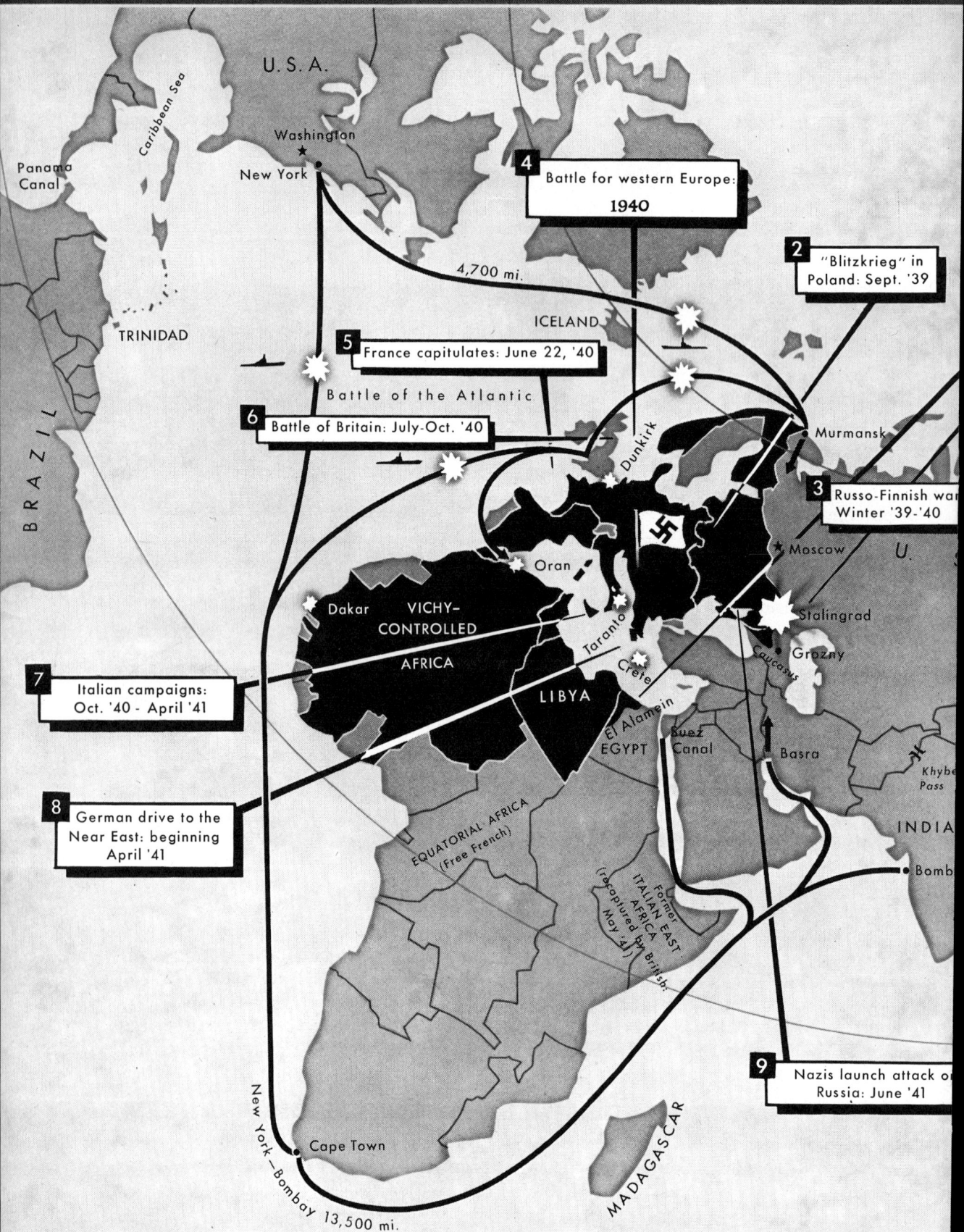

U.S.A.

Panama
Canal

Caribbean Sea

★ Washington

New York

TRINIDAD

B R A Z I L

4 Battle for western Europe:
1940

2 "Blitzkrieg" in
Poland: Sept. '39

4,700 mi.

ICELAND

5 France capitulates: June 22, '40

Battle of the Atlantic

6 Battle of Britain: July-Oct. '40

Murmansk

3 Russo-Finnish war
Winter '39-'40

Dunkirk

Oran

★ Moscow

U.

Dakar

VICHY-
CONTROLLED

AFRICA

Taranto

Crete

Stalingrad

Caucasus

Grozny

7 Italian campaigns:
Oct. '40 - April '41

LIBYA

El Alamein

EGYPT

Suez
Canal

Basra

Khyber
Pass

8 German drive to the
Near East: beginning
April '41

EQUATORIAL AFRICA
(Free French)

Former
ITALIAN EAST
AFRICA
(recaptured by British:
May, '41)

INDIA

Bomb

9 Nazis launch attack on
Russia: June '41

New York—Bombay

Cape Town

MADAGASCAR

New York—Bombay 13,500 mi.

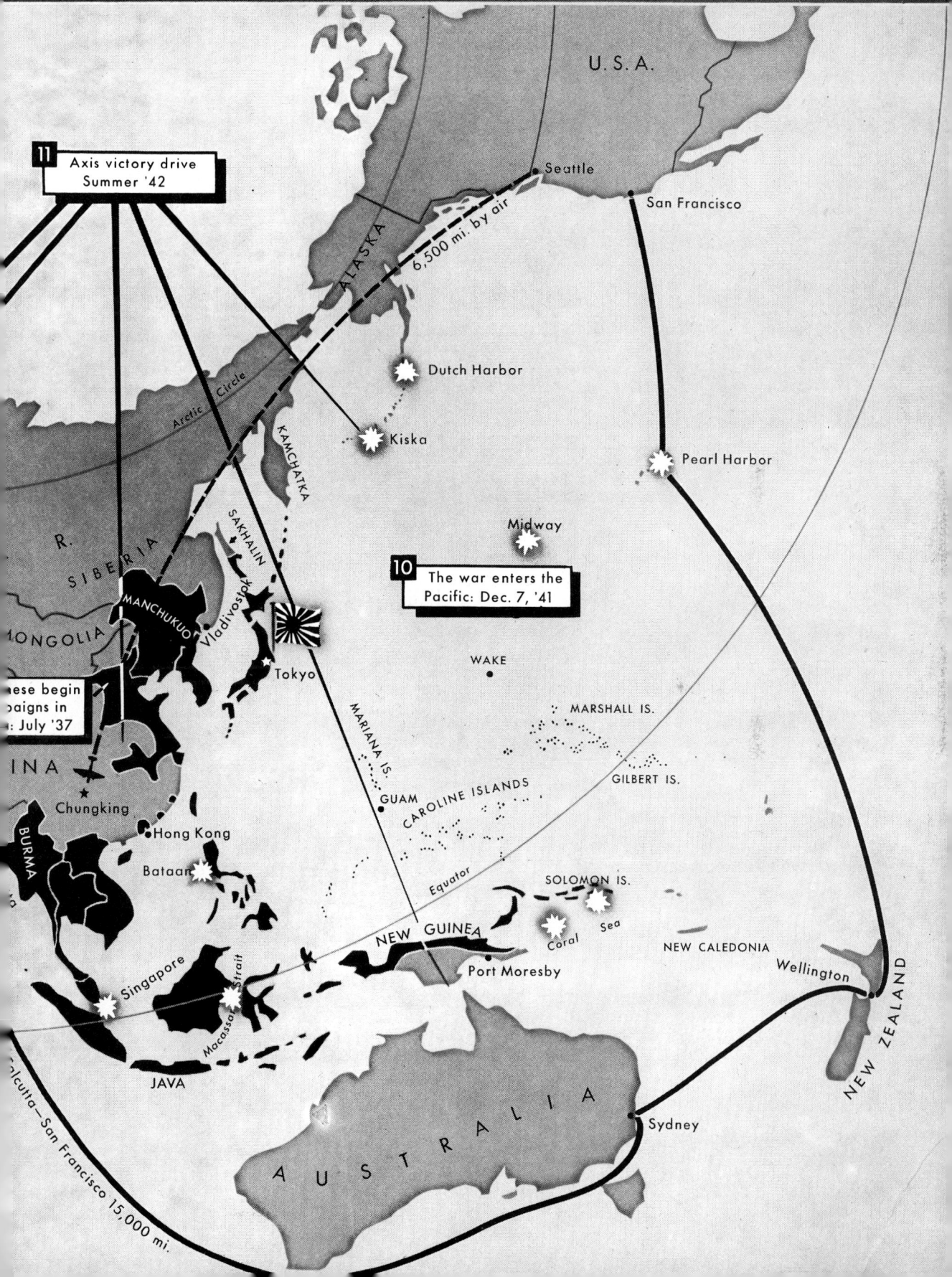

AXIS POWER

11
Axis victory drive
Summer '42

U.S.A.

Seattle

San Francisco

6,500 mi. by air

ALASKA

Arctic Circle

Dutch Harbor

Kiska

KAMCHATKA

Pearl Harbor

R.

SIBERIA

SAKHALIN

Midway

10
The war enters the
Pacific: Dec. 7, '41

MONGOLIA

MANCHUKUO

Vladivostok

Tokyo

WAKE

...ese begin
...paigns in
...: July '37

MARIANA IS.

MARSHALL IS.

...NA

Chungking

GILBERT IS.

BURMA

Hong Kong

GUAM

CAROLINE ISLANDS

Bataan

SOLOMON IS.

Singapore

Macassar Strait

NEW GUINEA

Equator

Coral
Sea

NEW CALEDONIA

Wellington

...a

Port Moresby

NEW ZEALAND

JAVA

...lcutta—San Francisco 15,000 mi.

A U S T R A L I A

Sydney

LONG PULL

New York

17 Battle of the Bulge: Dec. '44

18 Pincers on Germany V-E Day: May 8, '45

16 Normandy Invasion: June '44

15 Invasions of Sicily and Italy: July-Sept. '43

Berlin

Casablanca

Oran

Algiers

El Alamein

Equator

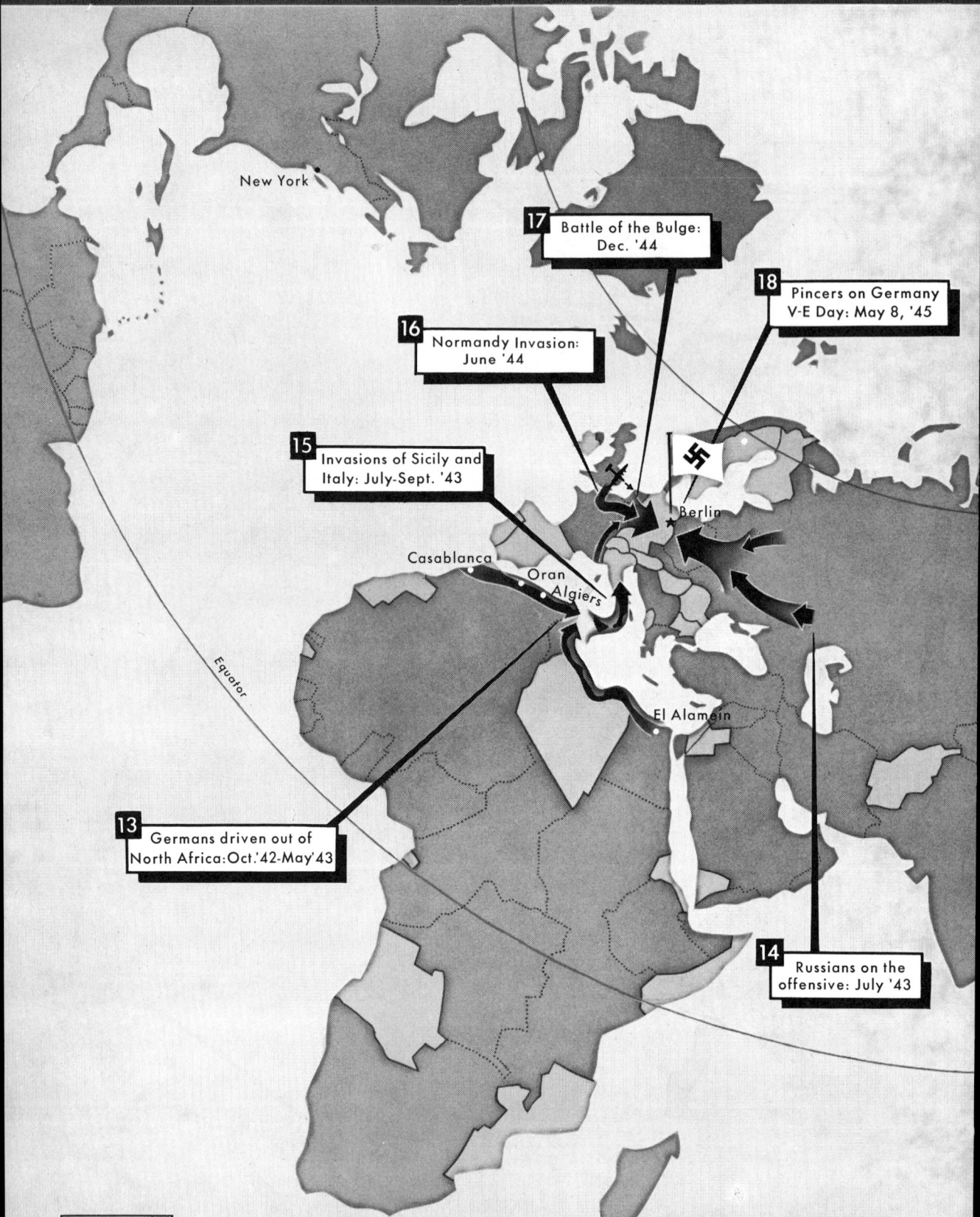

13 Germans driven out of North Africa: Oct.'42-May'43

14 Russians on the offensive: July '43

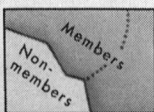

Members

Non-members

United Nations cs of June 26, 1945

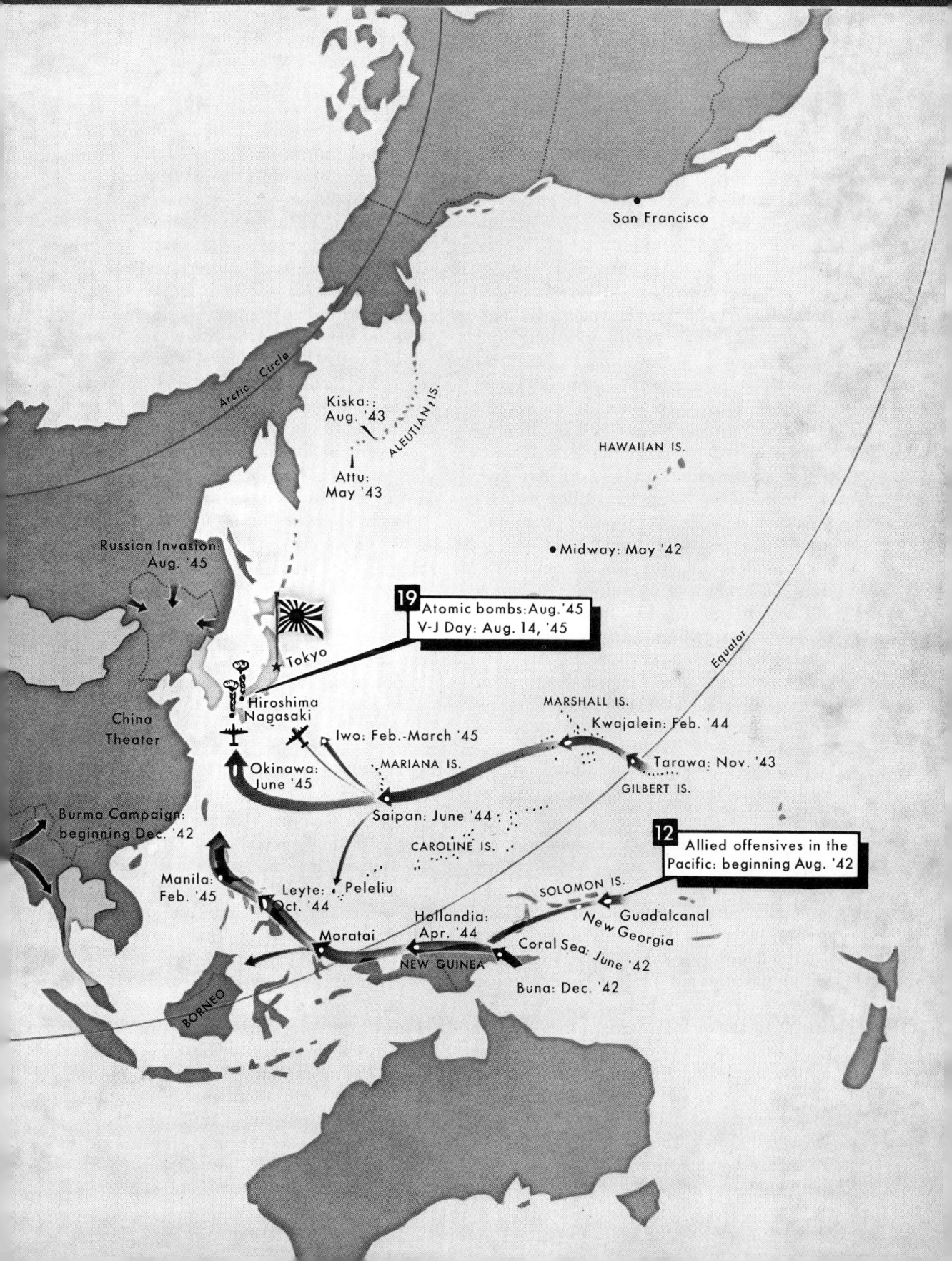

TO VICTORY

San Francisco

Arctic Circle

Kiska:
Aug. '43

ALEUTIAN IS.

Attu:
May '43

HAWAIIAN IS.

Russian Invasion:
Aug. '45

Midway: May '42

19 Atomic bombs: Aug. '45
V-J Day: Aug. 14, '45

Equator

★ Tokyo

MARSHALL IS.

Hiroshima
Nagasaki

Kwajalein: Feb. '44

Iwo: Feb.-March '45

China
Theater

MARIANA IS.

Tarawa: Nov. '43

Okinawa:
June '45

GILBERT IS.

Saipan: June '44

Burma Campaign:
beginning Dec. '42

CAROLINE IS.

12 Allied offensives in the
Pacific: beginning Aug. '42

Manila:
Feb. '45

Leyte:
Oct. '44

Peleliu

SOLOMON IS.

Hollandia:
Apr. '44

Guadalcanal

New Georgia

Moratai

Coral Sea: June '42

NEW GUINEA

Buna: Dec. '42

BORNEO

and Germany declared war on the United States; and Britain, together with the dominions, the refugee governments of Europe, and the Central American republics, ranged themselves with the United States against Japan. The twenty-six nations which now stood arrayed against Germany, Italy, and Japan solemnly pledged themselves on January 2, 1942, to uphold the principles of the Atlantic Charter and declared themselves the United Nations.

High tide of the Axis. The Japanese jumped from island to island in the Pacific. Within a month Manila, Wake, Guam, and Hong Kong were captured. In the spring of 1942 the whole Anglo-American position in the Pacific was in a state of collapse. Singapore, the Dutch East Indies, Malaya, and Burma were conquered by Japanese armies; Australia was in danger of invasion; and in April, American resistance in the Philippines ended with the surrender at Bataan. At the same time, Japanese forces reached toward Alaska, occupying some of the Aleutian Islands. On another front the Japanese launched a new offensive in China, but the Chinese, from their remote fortress-capital of Chungking, somehow managed to hold off the enemy.

In the summer of 1942, German armies, intent on delivering a knockout blow, launched a mighty crescendo of attacks against Russia. City after city fell, and a terrific struggle began for the control of Stalingrad. Nor did the Axis neglect the British in Africa. One of Hitler's most gifted generals, Rommel, "the Desert Fox," won a decisive victory in Libya, and the British Eighth Army reeled back to regroup at El Alamein, just seventy miles from Alexandria, Egypt. There existed now the terrifying possibility of Rommel's army overrunning the Middle East and even penetrating India, where it might be able to join Japanese forces from Burma.

In 1942, as the Allies were pushed back on every front, the Axis came frighteningly close to winning the war (see map, pp. 540-541). Events were to prove, however, that the enemy offensives could not be sustained at such a fever pitch. The surge of Axis victories waned rapidly thereafter, and the tide began to turn in favor of the Allies.

At the height of Hitler's power, the Nazis controlled most of Europe, but this mastery was not so absolute as appearances indicated. In all the occupied lands, underground movements operated like veritable states, with their hierarchies of dedicated and heroic members extending from the central committees in the larger cities to the small resistance cells in the tiniest rural hamlets. In some areas small armies of patriots took to the hills; in others, teams of underground workers carried on sabotage, counteracted Nazi propaganda with secret publications, sent invaluable information to the Allies, and worked closely with Allied intelligence agents. Under constant threat of torture and execution, these courageous men and women made a major contribution to Allied victory.

Turning points in the defeat of the Axis. In the far reaches of the Pacific, the Japanese advance southward toward Australia and eastward toward Hawaii was finally halted in the late spring of 1942, when the United States Navy won two huge battles, one at Midway and the other in the Coral Sea. In August, American marines successfully invaded the Japanese-held island of Guadalcanal, and six months later, after a nightmare campaign in the dank jungle, the Japanese were forced to withdraw. By this time the drain on Japanese man power and matériel, which had been going on since the invasion of Manchuria in 1931, had begun to tell.

Another arena of Allied success was North Africa. In October 1942 the British General Bernard Montgomery chased Rommel and the Italo-German armies all the way back into Tunisia. In November a huge force of British and American troops under the direction of General Dwight D. Eisenhower landed on the beaches of Morocco and Algeria. The Axis army in Tunisia was cornered and in May 1943, after desperate resistance, surrendered. The African adventures of the two dictators had cost their countries 950,000 soldiers, either killed or captured. In retaliation for the invasion of North Africa and the scuttling of much of the French fleet at Toulon, the Germans moved into the unoccupied zone in France, and the Vichy government ceased to enjoy even the fiction of being independent.

In January 1943, Roosevelt and Churchill met at Casablanca to plan the invasion of Europe. They agreed that victory there would continue to be their prime objective and that victory meant the unconditional surrender of the Axis. The achievement of this goal, it was hoped, would avoid a repetition of Germany's contention after World War I that it had been stabbed in the back, not militarily defeated.

On the heels of the German defeat in North Africa came Axis defeats in Russia. In January 1943, Soviet troops relieved Leningrad, whose blockaded citizens were on the verge of starvation; and a month later, in one of the epic contests of the war, an entire German army besieging Stalingrad was surrounded and forced to surrender. Then the Russians began preparing the greatest counteroffensive in military history.

The invasion of Italy. Allied control of North Africa made an invasion of Italy feasible. In July 1943, Allied amphibious forces invaded Sicily, and the war-weary Italians were warned "to decide whether Italians shall die for Mussolini and Hitler—or live for Italy and for civilization." Aware of imminent invasion, the Fascist Grand Council turned against the discredited Mussolini and demanded his resignation. In September his successor signed an armistice with the Allies on the same day that the British Eighth Army under Montgomery landed on the toe of Italy. Meanwhile the Nazis "rescued" Mussolini, set him up as head of a puppet regime in northern Italy, and rushed German troops as far south as Naples. To prevent the Germans from consolidating their hold over central Italy, the United States Fifth Army, led by General Mark Clark, landed at Salerno just south of Naples. After savage fighting in which it was driven back almost to the sea, the Fifth Army held its ground and was soon joined by the British Eighth Army.

The Allied advance northward through Italy was a slow and torturous campaign. Stalled at Cassino and badly mauled at Anzio, Allied troops did not reach Rome until June 1944. German resistance in northern Italy continued until the end of the war.

The road to victory for the Allies. By the end of 1943 the initiative had definitely passed to the Allies, and Churchill could say that while this was not the "beginning of the end," it was definitely the "end of the beginning." In the "silent war" in the Atlantic, the German submarine menace had finally been overcome —after the loss of millions of tons of Allied shipping. The Mediterranean was now virtually an Allied lake, plied freely by Allied warships and transports. In the air, Allied bombers were beginning to pound enemy cities into rubble, though often at frightful cost in planes and men.

The Russian offensive that had begun to roll in 1943 continued without halting. Finland, which had joined Germany's attack on Russia, was forced out of the war; and in 1944, Russian armored divisions reached the outskirts of Warsaw. In addition to driving west four hundred miles into the heart of Poland, Soviet forces also wheeled to the south and forced Hitler's Balkan satellites out of the war. At Warsaw, news of the Soviet advance set off an uprising of the Polish underground which was brutally crushed by the Nazis; in Yugoslavia, the Russians were greeted by the Communist leader, Tito, and his guerilla fighters, who had harried the German invaders for years.

For two years the Russians had been demanding a second front in Europe to take some of the Axis pressure off the eastern front. At Teheran in November 1943, Churchill proposed that the Anglo-American invasion should take place in the Balkans. Stalin, however, insisted that the second front should be established in western Europe, and Roosevelt concurred. While militarily sound, the decision to launch a cross-Channel invasion spelled the postwar Russian domination of the Balkans.

According to schedule, in June 1944 a vast invasion was launched against northern France. On D-day, June 6, four thousand ships, protected by eight hundred naval craft and eleven thousand planes, ferried half a million men to the beaches of Normandy. By nightfall Hitler's line of defense, the Atlantic Wall, was breached—though only at great cost to the attackers. In August, after two months of heavy fighting, Paris was liberated. Meanwhile, another Allied army landed in

Rocked back on their heels and nearly brought to their knees by the fury of the Axis assaults, the Allies fought to defend themselves, then began to counterpunch, and finally launched their own devastating offensive. Their leaders met to plan grand strategy (at left above, Stalin, Roosevelt, and Churchill confer at Teheran in 1943), while the men in the armed forces maintained constant pressure on the enemy (above, American marines wade through mud at Bougainville in the Solomons). On D-day—June 6, 1944—Allied troops poured onto the beaches of Normandy (top). To plug the ever widening holes in his defenses, Hitler sent schoolboys off to die for Nazi Germany (left).

Initial Allied victories came neither in Europe nor in the Pacific but in North Africa. Here, British forces were able to reverse the Axis drive (above left), and here American forces first met the Nazi enemy. During 1944 Hitler's empire began to disintegrate; while Allied armies advanced, Allied planes ranged far ahead, blasting vital targets like the oil refineries at Ploesti, Rumania (below). As the march of liberation continued, the victims of Nazi conquest could smile once again and, like this Parisian girl (above right), confidently raise high the "V for victory" sign, symbol of Allied hopes.

southern France and advanced northward. The two Allied columns pushed the German troops back until, in October, the Anglo-American forces entered Germany near Aachen. Two months later, Hitler launched his last desperate attack, driving westward through the Allied lines for fifty miles in the bloody Battle of the Bulge. After heavy losses and back-to-the-wall resistance, the Allies counterattacked, forcing the Germans to withdraw and ending their offensive threat. Then British and American forces continued their advance into Germany from the west, while Russian troops closed in on the east.

With victory in Europe in sight, Stalin, Roosevelt, and Churchill met at Yalta in the Crimea in February 1945 to discuss the peace arrangements. It was agreed that the Soviet Union could have a slice of Poland and territory and privileges in the Far East, a decision later severely criticized. It was also agreed that Russia would enter the war against Japan and that postwar Germany would be split into three zones. Yalta was the high point of the alliance. After this conference, relations between the Soviet Union and its allies quickly deteriorated.

As the Allied troops advanced through Germany, they uncovered the secret hell of Nazi inhumanity toward the people Hitler despised. In the concentration camps—Belsen, Buchenwald, Dachau, and others—they found the gas ovens which had destroyed millions of lives, the wasted bodies of slave laborers who had starved to death, and the living dead who had somehow survived torture and the cruel medical experiments to which they had been subjected. Between 1939 and 1945 the Jewish population in Nazi-occupied Europe had decreased from 9,739,-200 to 3,505,800; and another 6,000,000 people—Poles, Czechs, Russians, and others—had also fallen victim to Nazi cruelty.

The Axis leaders did not live to see defeat. Mussolini, a cringing fugitive, was seized by anti-Fascist partisan fighters and shot to death; his mutilated body, with that of his mistress, was trussed up in the public square at Milan, an object of derision and hatred. While street fighting raged in Berlin, Hitler shot himself. His body and that of the mistress

he had just made his wife were doused with gasoline and set afire. Nor did the great wartime leader of the United States live to see the end of the war, although he realized the imminence of victory. Franklin Roosevelt died suddenly in April 1945, less than a month before the German armies surrendered. The final surrender ceremony took place in Berlin on May 8, designated by President Harry Truman as V-E Day, Victory Day in Europe.

End of the war. While the Allied armies were finishing off the Germans, the Americans had been "island-hopping" their way to Japan, capturing in turn Tarawa, Kwajalein, and Saipan, after bloody struggles on the sandy beaches. In October 1944, with its victory in the battle for Leyte Gulf—the greatest naval engagement in all history—the Allies ended the threat of the Japanese fleet; and in January 1945, General MacArthur returned to the Philippines. The final phase of the war against Japan was unfolding. Only a few hundred miles from Japan, Iwo Jima and Okinawa were conquered; and from such advance bases, waves of American bombers rained destruction on Japanese cities. In the China-Burma-India theater, the Chinese, with American aid, were making inroads on areas previously captured by Japan. But Japanese resistance continued. Although amphibious operations had achieved an amazing efficiency, the Japanese defenders of the islands frequently fought on after all hope of success had disappeared; and from the skies kamikaze planes hurtled down on Allied warships in desperate suicide attacks.

From the Potsdam meeting of the Allied leaders in July-August 1945 came a warning to the Japanese that the war against them would take a new and angry turn. When Japan refused to surrender, the most terrible weapon yet invented by mankind—the atomic bomb —was dropped on Hiroshima by an American bomber. As the mushroom-shaped cloud rose over the city, only charred ruins were left beneath; an expanse of approximately three miles square—about 60 per cent of the city— was almost completely obliterated. The Japanese government estimated that 60,000 people died, 100,000 were wounded, and 200,000 were left homeless. Whether or not the use of the bomb was justified is still a question for debate, but the new weapon achieved its purpose. A few days after the dropping of a second atomic bomb on Nagasaki, the Japanese sued for peace. The surrender ceremony took place September 2 on board the battleship *Missouri*, almost six years to the day after Hitler had plunged the world into the Second World War.

SUMMARY

From 1929 to 1945 the world was in turmoil. People were caught up in a bewildering procession of economic problems, of toppling governments, and of aggressions and finally in a world conflagration. As the focal point of the world's economy, the Wall Street crash of 1929 set off an international depression. To survive this economic earthquake, governments were forced to modify the capitalistic structure by increasing their controls, particularly in the United States and England.

The depression brought Hitler to power in Germany, and a chain of events leading to global conflict was set off. In the thirties the Axis powers—Germany, Japan, and Italy—carried out a series of aggressions with little opposition. Manchuria, China, Abyssinia, Austria, and Czechoslovakia all heard the tramp of invading troops. By 1939 Hitler had thrown off his mask and revealed his real intentions: the expansion of Germany until much of the world was under the Nazi heel. The Allied policy of appeasement ended abruptly with the invasion of Poland, and the Second World War was on.

This gigantic struggle can be divided into a series of stages. During 1939 and 1940, Germany, ineffectually supported by Fascist Italy, virtually mastered Europe. Only Britain remained a defiant and lonely opponent. During the hectic prelude to world war and before the tragic fall of France, the United States had underestimated the Hitler menace to its own security and had followed a policy of noninvolvement. On the heels of Dunkirk, however, American policy was drastically reversed. Every move was made to aid Britain and then Russia in order to forestall domination of the world by the Axis.

The nightmare of Nazism is only suggested by these piles of bodies at the concentration camp at Belsen, Germany. These victims died of disease and starvation, but millions more—men, women, and children—were deliberately murdered.

The totalitarian powers came perilously close to winning in the summer of 1942. After a sneak attack against the United States base at Pearl Harbor, the Japanese invaded island after island in the Pacific. Hitler marched through Russia up to the outskirts of Stalingrad. In North Africa, British troops were pushed back into Egypt by General Rommel, By the end of 1942, however, the tide began to turn with an Allied victory in North Africa and a Nazi debacle in the icy streets of Stalingrad. From 1943 on, the Allies held the upper hand. Italy surrendered, the Germans were harassed out of Russia, the submarine menace was brought under control in the Atlantic, and the Americans went on the offensive in the Pacific. Germany surrendered in May 1945; the Japanese in August.

In this titanic struggle there was no clear-cut ideological alignment. The exigencies of war helped to conceal basic and even conflicting differences in ideology between Britain and the United States on the one hand and Russia on the other. At the same time, the explosion of two atomic bombs registered the awesome warning that world wars in the future would be suicidal for all concerned. Yet the world, numbed by its suffering and exhausted by its efforts, did not understand the danger inherent in the opposing aims of the two ideologies and the vital need to prevent their clash.

SUGGESTIONS FOR READING

WORLD WAR I

Cruttwell, C. R. M. F., *A History of the Great War, 1914-1918*, Oxford, 1936. The most useful general history available. Two deftly written military histories are C. B. Falls, *The Great War*, Putnam, 1959; and G. L. McEntree, *Military History of the World War*, Scribner's, 1937. A brief résumé is B. H. Liddell Hart, *The War in Outline, 1914-1918*, Mod. Lib., 1939.

Highly recommended special works include L. Stallings, ed., *The First World War; A Photographic History*, Simon and Schuster, 1933; A. Moorehead, *Gallipoli*, Harper, 1956; D. Macintyre, *Jutland*, Norton, 1958; L. Wolff, *In Flanders Fields: The 1917 Campaign*, Ballantine,* 1960.

Keynes, J. M., *The Economic Consequences of the Peace*, Harcourt, 1920. The most famous attack on the Versailles settlement. For the fullest treatment of the territorial aspects of the peace, see I. Bowman, *The New World: Problems in Political Geography*, World Book, 1922. Two well-balanced studies of the Paris Peace Conference are H. G. Nicholson, *Peacemaking, 1919*, Harcourt, 1939; and P. Birdsall, *Versailles Twenty Years After*, Reynal, 1941.

Perhaps the most famous of the realistic World War I novels is E. M. Remarque, *All Quiet on the Western Front* (many editions), which deals with the German infantryman. J. Romains, *Verdun*, Knopf, 1939; and H. Cobb, *Paths of Glory*, Dell,* 1958, concern the French army. The best works about Americans are W. March, *Company K*, Signet,* 1958; J. Dos Passos, *Three Soldiers*, Modern Library, 1932; and E. Hemingway, *A Farewell to Arms* (many editions).

THE INTERNATIONAL SCENE

Gathorne-Hardy, G. M., *A Short History of International Affairs, 1920-1939*, Oxford, 1950. Recognized as one of the best interpretations of the interwar years.

Walters, F. P., *A History of the League of Nations*, 2 vols., Oxford, 1952. The most comprehensive account of the successes and failures of the League.

Haines, C. G., and R. J. S. Hoffman, *The Origins and Background of the Second World War*, Oxford, 1947. An excellent study of the collapse of collective security and the advent of totalitarian aggression.

Indispensable for studying the background and events of Munich are the following: J. W. Wheeler-Bennett, *Munich: Prologue to Tragedy*, Duell, 1948; and L. B. Namier, *Diplomatic Prelude: 1938-1939*, Macmillan, 1948.

Seton-Watson, R. W., *Britain and the Dictators; A Survey of Post-War British Policy*, Macmillan, 1938. A disquieting analysis, by a British historian, of Britain's foreign policy up to the eve of Munich. See also A. Wolfers, *Britain and France Between Two Wars; Conflicting Strategies of Peace Since Versailles*, Harcourt, 1940.

*Indicates an inexpensive paperbound edition.

The role of the United States in foreign affairs between the two world wars is well analyzed in two works by W. L. Langer and S. E. Gleason: *The Challenge to Isolation: 1937-1940*, Harper, 1952; and *The Undeclared War: September 1940-December 1941*, Harper, 1953.

Hilger, G., and A. G. Meyer, *The Incompatible Allies: German-Soviet Relations, 1918-1941*, Macmillan, 1953; and E. H. Carr, *German-Soviet Relations Between the Two World Wars, 1919-1939*, Johns Hopkins, 1951, are excellent analyses of the subject.

DOMESTIC ISSUES

Two standard surveys of the history of the United States in this century, with major emphasis on the interwar years, are H. Wish, *Contemporary America*, Harper, 1955; and A. S. Link, *American Epoch: A History of the United States Since the 1890's*, Knopf, 1955. Two sound economic surveys are G. Soule, *Prosperity Decade: From War to Depression, 1917-1929*, Rinehart, 1947; and B. Mitchell, *Depression Decade, 1929-1941*, Rinehart, 1947. In *The Great Crash: 1929*, Houghton, 1955, the noted economist J. K. Galbraith describes the end of an economic era and the birth of the depression years.

Perkins, D., *The New Age of Franklin Roosevelt, 1932-1945*, Univ. of Chicago, 1959. A vigorous analysis of the New Deal and the retreat from isolationism.

Allen, F. L., *Only Yesterday*, Bantam,* 1946, and *Since Yesterday*, Harper, 1940. By the former editor of *Harper's*, both works are lively social histories, covering respectively the United States in the Jazz Age and during the depression.

Mowat, C. L., *Britain Between the Wars, 1918-1940*, Univ. of Chicago, 1955; and D. C. Somervell, *British Politics Since 1900*, Oxford, 1950, are both excellent treatments of the period. H. Heaton, *The British Way to Recovery*, Univ. of Minn., 1934, details how Britain and the dominions sought to cope with the world-wide depression. Two absorbing social histories are J. Montgomery, *The Twenties: An Informal Social History*, Macmillan, 1957; and R. Graves and A. Hodge, *The Long Week End; A Social History of Great Britain, 1918-1939*, Macmillan, 1941.

France during pre-World War II years is portrayed realistically in Y. Simon, *The Road to Vichy, 1918-1938*, Sheed, 1942; and A. Werth, *The Twilight of France, 1933-1940*, Harper, 1942.

Four excellent critiques of Italian Fascism are A. Rossi, *The Rise of Italian Fascism: 1918-1922*, Methuen, 1938; H. W. Schneider, *Making the Fascist State*, Oxford, 1928; G. Salvemini, *Under the Axe of Fascism*, Viking, 1936; H. Finer, *Mussolini's Italy*, Holt, 1935.

Knight-Patterson, W. M., *Germany from Defeat to Conquest, 1913-1933*, Macmillan, 1947. A well-documented history. Should be supplemented by F. L. Schuman, *Germany Since*

1918, Holt, 1937; and F. Vermeil, *Germany in the Twentieth Century,* Praeger, 1956.

Bullock, A., *Hitler; A Study in Tyranny,* abr. ed., Bantam,* 1958. The best biography available.

Carr, E. H., *A History of Soviet Russia, 1917-1926,* 6 vols., Macmillan, 1951-1960. A definitive study. See also F. L. Schuman, *Russia Since 1917; Four Decades of Soviet Politics,* Knopf, 1957.

Deutscher, I., *The Prophet Unarmed: Trotsky, 1921-1929,* Oxford, 1959. Describes Trotsky's career from victory in the civil war to exile at the hands of Stalin.

Hindus, M., *The Great Offensive,* Smith and Haas, 1933; and L. Fischer, *Men and Politics, An Autobiography,* Duell, 1941. Stalin's drive for economic and political order as seen by two able journalists. See also Aleksandr Baykov, *The Development of the Soviet Economic System: An Essay on the Experience of Planning in the U.S.S.R.,* Macmillan, 1947, a very good history of the most distinctive feature of Soviet society up to 1939. There is no satisfactory explanation of the Great Purge. J. E. Davies, *Mission to Moscow,* Simon and Schuster, 1941. An account by the United States ambassador to the U.S.S.R., 1936-1938, reflects the political bias of the war.

THE NONWESTERN WORLD

A good introductory work to the problem of mandates is Q. Wright, *Mandates Under the League of Nations,* Univ. of Chicago, 1930. An excellent comparative study of the different forms of internationalized control of colonial areas is H. D. Hall, *Mandates, Dependencies and Trusteeship,* Carnegie Endowment, 1948.

Three astute observers—a scientist, a journalist, and a historian respectively—survey Africa as it was before the Second World War: J. Huxley, *Africa View,* Harper, 1931; N. Farson, *Behind God's Back,* Harcourt, 1941; W. M. Macmillan, *Africa Emergent, A Survey of Social, Political, and Economic Trends in British Africa,* Penguin,* 1949.

The political control of Palestine has long been a controversial issue. The Arab view is presented eloquently in G. Antonius, *The Arab Awakening; The Story of the Arab National Movement,* Lippincott, 1939. The British approach is illustrated by *Great Britain and Palestine, 1915-1945,* Information Paper No. 20, Royal Institute of International Affairs, 1946. Jewish Zionist views are presented in A. Koestler, *Promise and Fulfillment: Palestine, 1917-1949,* Macmillan, 1949; and B. Joseph, *British Rule in Palestine,* Public Affairs Press, 1948.

The impact of westernization on Turkey is treated skillfully in H. E. Allen, *The Turkish Transformation,* Univ. of Chicago, 1935; and D. E. Webster, *The Turkey of Ataturk; Social Process in the Turkish Reformation,* Amer. Academy of Pol. and Soc. Science, 1939. Other worth-while special studies of Middle Eastern affairs are C. Issawi, *Egypt: An Economic and Social Analysis,* Oxford, 1947; S. H. Longrigg, *Syria and Lebanon Under French Mandate,* Oxford, 1958, and *Iraq, 1900 to 1950: A Political, Social and Economic History,* Oxford, 1953; K. S. Twitchell, *Saudi Arabia,* Princeton, 1958.

For works dealing with India, China, and Japan in the modern period, see **List of Readings,** pp. 614-615.

WORLD WAR II

McInnis, E., *The War,* 6 vols., Oxford, 1940-1946. By a Canadian historian, these volumes constitute the most satisfactory contemporary account of World War II. R. A. Shugg and H. A. De Weerd, *World War II; A Concise History,* The Infantry Journal, 1946, presents a straightforward military account. Also recommended are W. P. Hall, *Iron Out of Cavalry; An Interpretive History of the Second World War,* Appleton, 1946; and L. L. Snyder, *The War: A Concise History, 1939-1945,* Messner, 1960.

Commager, H. S., ed., *The Pocket History of the Second World War,* Pocketbooks,* 1945. A compact work, made up of the writings and speeches of statesmen, soldiers, and journalists. See also D. Flower and J. Reeves, eds., *The Taste of Courage: The War, 1939-1945,* Harper, 1960; and W. C. Langsam, ed., *Historic Documents of World War II,* Anvil,* 1958.

Morison, S. E., *History of United States Naval Operations in World War II,* Little, Brown, 1947-1962. Written by a notable American historian, painstaking work is represented in this fifteen-volume series that is a masterpiece of contemporary scholarship.

Taylor, T., *The March of Conquest,* Simon and Schuster, 1958. The amazing story of the initial German military triumphs. For an absorbing account of Hitler's plans to invade Britain, see P. Fleming, *Operation Sea Lion,* Simon and Schuster, 1957.

Many excellent works which highlight outstanding incidents of the war have been published in recent years. Listed here are only a handful: E. Montagu, *The Man Who Never Was,* Lippincott, 1954; F. Majdalany, *The Battle of Cassino,* Houghton, 1957; C. Fitzgibbon, *Officers' Plot to Kill Hitler,* Avon,* 1958; D. A. Howarth, *D-Day: The Sixth of June, 1944,* Pyramid,* 1960; J. Toland, *Battle: The Story of the Bulge,* Random House, 1956; R. W. Thompson, *The Battle for the Rhine,* Ballantine,* 1958.

Three studies which document the enormity of the crimes perpetrated by the Nazi regime are L. Poliakov, *Harvest of Hate; The Nazi Program for the Destruction of the Jews of Europe,* Syracuse, 1954; Lord Russell, *The Scourge of the Swastika; A Short History of Nazi War Crimes,* Philosophical Library, 1954; W. R. Harris, *Tyranny on Trial: The Evidence at Nuremberg,* Southern Methodist Univ., 1954.

Important novels of World War II include the trilogy by the German novelist T. Plievier: *Stalingrad,* Berkley,* 1948; *Moscow,* Ace,* 1957; *Berlin, A Novel,* Ace,* 1957. Other excellent works are I. Shaw, *The Young Lions,* Signet,* 1950; N. Mailer, *The Naked and the Dead,* Signet,* 1954; H. P. M. Brown, *A Walk in the Sun,* Signet,* 1958; H. Wouk, *The Caine Mutiny,* Doubleday, 1951; N. Monsarrat, *The Cruel Sea,* Pocketbooks,* 1953; J. Hersey, *The War Lover,* Knopf, 1959.

INTERNATIONAL POLITICS

1914   **World War I**—Germans invade Belgium, France, Poland 1914; Italy joins Allies 1915; battle of Jutland, Allies' Somme offensive 1916; Italian front smashed at Caporetto, U.S. declares war 1917; Russia signs Treaty of Brest Litovsk with Germany, Ludendorff's "Peace Drive" fails, armistice is signed 1918

Wilson presents Fourteen Points 1918
Paris Peace Conference; **League of Nations** established 1919
Treaty of Versailles signed with Germany, Treaty of St.-Germain with Austria, Treaty of Neuilly with Bulgaria 1919; Treaty of Sèvres with Ottoman empire, Treaty of Trianon with Hungary 1920
Little Entente formed 1920-21; French allies include Belgium, Poland, Czechoslovakia, Rumania, Yugoslavia 1920-1927

Washington Conference—limited naval disarmament 1921-1922
League of Nations settles Aland Islands dispute, Polish-German and Yugoslavian-Albanian boundary disputes 1921
Nine-Power Treaty—signatories agree to respect sovereignty of China 1922
Russia negotiates Treaty of Rapallo with Germany 1922
Mussolini defies League of Nations in Corfu incident 1923
France invades German Ruhr, sets up "revolver republic" 1923-1924
Dawes Plan eases German reparations, France evacuates Ruhr 1924
Locarno Pact 1925

Kellogg-Briand Pact renounces war 1928

1929   Young Plan scales down reparations payments 1929

Mussolini conquers Abyssinia 1936

Rome-Berlin Axis formed, Japan and Germany form Anti-Comintern Pact 1936; Italy joins the Pact 1937
Spanish civil war 1936-1939

Hitler engineers coup in Austria 1938
Surrender of Sudetenland to Germany at Munich 1938; Hitler seizes Czechoslovakia, Mussolini seizes Albania 1939
1939   Russia, Germany sign nonaggression pact 1939
World War II—Germany invades Poland; France, Britain declare war 1939. *Sitzkrieg;* Russia defeats Finland 1939-1940. Hitler seizes Denmark, Norway, Low Countries, France 1940. Battle of Britain; Italian invasion of Greece and Africa fails; Hitler seizes Hungary, Balkans 1940-1941. Germany attacks Russia; Atlantic Charter signed; Pearl Harbor attack brings U.S. into war 1941. Japanese victories in Pacific 1941-1942. Battles of Midway and Coral Sea; Rommel victorious in Libya 1942. Soviets seize offensive in Russia; Axis surrender in Africa; Italy invaded; Teheran Conference 1943. Allies launch second front; battle of Leyte 1944. Yalta agreements; Germany surrenders;
1945   A-bomb dropped on Japan; Japanese surrender 1945.

WESTERN DEMOCRACIES

Polish and Czech republics established 1918
U.S. rejects membership in League of Nations 1919
National Bloc in France 1919-1924

Irish Free State created in southern Ireland 1921
Conservative Republican era in U.S. politics—Harding 1921-1923; Coolidge 1923-1929; Hoover 1929-1933
U.S. Fordney-McCumber (1922), Hawley-Smoot (1930) Tariff Acts levy high tariffs, jeopardize war-debt payments, reparations

Left Cartel in France 1924-1926
MacDonald, Britain's first Labourite prime minister 1924; Conservatives in power 1924-1929; general strike 1926

National Union under Poincaré saves French finances 1926-1933

Stock market crash in U.S. leads to world depression 1929
Labour party regains power in England 1929-1931
Revolutions in six South American nations 1930

Spain becomes republic 1931
National Coalition government in Britain begins 1931
Statute of Westminster creates constitution for British Commonwealth of Nations 1931

U.S. inaugurates Good Neighbor Policy 1933
Franklin D. Roosevelt becomes president of U.S. 1933; inaugurates New Deal

Popular Front gains power in France 1936

Conservatives regain control in France 1937
Neville Chamberlain, advocate of appeasement, becomes prime minister of England 1937

Churchill becomes prime minister of England 1940
U.S. passes Selective Service Act 1940; Lend-Lease Act 1941

RISE OF TOTALITARIANISM

ASIA AND AFRICA

Revolution in China 1911; Manchu emperor abdicates, Yüan
Shih-kai heads republic 1912-1916
Japan presents China with the Twenty-one Demands 1915
Arabs revolt against Ottoman rule 1916-1918
Balfour Declaration 1917

1914

Russian Revolution—Duma names provisional government, tsar
abdicates, Bolsheviks under Lenin seize government 1917; Bol-
sheviks destroy White Russian resistance 1918-1920
Period of war communism 1918-1921
German revolution 1918; Weimar Republic set up 1919
Third Communist International (Comintern) formed 1919

Mustafa Kemal Pasha of Turkey defies Allies 1918-1922
Government of India Act of 1919 and Rowlatt Act passed,
Gandhi begins campaign for independence 1919
French repress Arab nationalism in Morocco, Tunisia, Algeria,
Syria-Lebanon 1919-1939
San Remo Conference—Allies overrule Arab nationalism,
create mandates from Arab territories 1920
Communist party (1920), Indonesian Nationalist party (1927)
oppose Dutch rule in East Indies
Sun Yat-sen controls Canton government in China 1921-1925
Riza Shah Pahlavi seizes Iran government 1921-1925

Treaty of Riga concludes war between Russia, Poland 1921
NEP—Lenin restores some capitalistic practices 1921-1928
Mussolini establishes National Fascist party 1921; seizes Italian
government in march on Rome 1922; divides Italian economy
into government-controlled syndicates
Union of Soviet Socialist Republics established 1922
Hitler stages unsuccessful *Putsch* in Munich 1923; writes
Mein Kampf

British grant constitution to Burma 1922

Egypt becomes sovereign, with British restrictions 1923
Republic of Turkey set up, Treaty of Lausanne signed 1923
Ibn-Saud gains control of Arabian peninsula 1924-1925

Election of Hindenburg as president underlines rising German
ultranationalism 1925
Dictatorships formed in Lithuania 1926; in Yugoslavia 1929
Trotsky loses bid for power to Stalin 1927
Stalin purges rivals 1928-1931, 1935-1938
Stalin inaugurates first Five-Year Plan 1928

Universal Manhood Suffrage Bill passed in Japan 1925

Chiang Kai-shek purges Communists 1927; conquers Peking,
unites China 1928

Hamaguchi's ministry peak of liberalism in Japan 1929; his assas-
sination causes permanent liberal setback 1930
Iraq gains full independence from Britain 1930
Round-table conferences on India 1930-1932
Arab violence in British mandate of Palestine 1930's
Italian Fascists cement rule in Libya 1930's
Segregation, unrest grow in Union of South Africa 1930's
Communists oppose French rule in Indo-China 1930's
British grant progressive constitution to Ceylon 1931
Japan invades Manchuria 1931
Chinese soviets proclaim Chinese Soviet Republic 1931; Chiang
launches campaigns against Communists 1931-1934
Ibn-Saud's holdings renamed Saudi Arabia 1932

1929

Dictatorships set up in Hungary, Portugal 1932; in Latvia, Esto-
nia 1934
Russia begins second Five-Year Plan 1933
Hitler becomes dictator of Germany, Germany withdraws from
League of Nations 1933; first Four-Year Plan established 1933,
second 1936
Dictatorships formed in Albania, Bulgaria by 1935; in Greece
1936
Germans fortify Rhineland 1936

Japan withdraws from League of Nations, pushes into China
1933; **T'ang-ku Truce** 1933

Commonwealth of Philippines formed 1935
Government of India Act of 1935 goes into effect in British
India 1937-1939; is rejected by native princes 1939

Italy withdraws from League of Nations 1937

Russia initiates third Five-Year Plan 1938

British grant Burma restricted home rule 1937
War breaks out again between Japan and China 1937; Japan
proclaims **New Order in Asia** 1938

Fascist dictator Franco gains power, ends republic after Spanish
civil war 1939

1939

Tojo becomes premier of Japan **1941**

Frontier

THE GRAPES OF WRATH—AN ANALYSIS   by Russel B. Nye

Director of the Division of Languages and Literature at Michigan State University, Dr. Russel B. Nye is the author of the 1945 Pulitzer Prize biography *George Bancroft, Brahmin Rebel,* considered by many as the definitive biography of this famous nineteenth-century American historian. Of Bancroft, Dr. Nye has declared: "He was much more than a writer of history. He was a maker of it as well." Also included among Dr. Nye's major works are *Fettered Freedom: Civil Liberties and the Slavery Controversy* (1949), *Midwestern Progressive Politics* (1951), *A History of the United States* (1955) with J. E. Morpurgo, and *Baker's Dozen: Thirteen Unusual Americans* (1956).

What basic principles do the historian and the literary artist share? First, both are concerned with reshaping life. Both construct their own worlds as they see them, each relying on his inner creative energy as the shaping power. The great drama of Rome's decline and fall happened only within Gibbon's mind; none saw it before him, for it is certain the Romans did not, and we shall no doubt always see it through Gibbon's eyes. The Britain of King Lear never existed in Holinshed or anywhere else, nor Antony's empire in Plutarch—only on Shakespeare's stage. What Joseph Conrad said of the novel—that it is "to make you hear, to make you feel . . . before all, to make you see"— is equally true of history. Second, the literary artist and the historian are both participants in a kind of giant game, trying to find patterns of meaning in human experience, hoping to impose some sort of understandable order on a small fragment of chaos.

But the historian and the literary artist must play this game under slightly different rules. By analyzing John Steinbeck's novel *The Grapes of Wrath* (1939), which deals with the great dust bowl migrations of the mid-thirties and the problems of migrant labor to which they contributed, perhaps we may succeed in illuminating some of the shadowy relationships that exist between history and literature.

First, let us establish the facts. The plains area of the United States, embracing portions of Kansas, Oklahoma, Arkansas, Colorado, and Texas, is one of light rainfall, high winds, and hot sun. Its soil was damaged by overgrazing during the cattle boom of the late nineteenth century; and as a result of demands for increased wheat production during World War I, much of what was considered to be marginal farm land was plowed and planted. During the 1920's, rainfall in the region stayed somewhat above normal. A number of farmers moved into the area, most of them tenant farmers —that is, renters who gave a share of their crop to the actual owners, who might be banks, land development companies, or individuals. At about the same time, the rich truck and fruit farms of California were becoming industrialized, depending more and more on the use of machinery and large blocs of low-paid migrant labor (Japanese, Mexican) for profits.

Beginning about 1930, the worst drought and heat in history struck the plains region, drying out the already moisture-starved and overcultivated land. A series of dust storms (called "black blizzards") from November 1933 to late summer of 1934 blew hundreds of millions of tons of topsoil out of the dust bowl area into the Midwest and the East and far out into the Atlantic. In Oklahoma and Arkansas and Texas, dust buried roads, homes, cattle, land, and vegetation. Some farms were made completely uninhabitable; others could not produce enough to pay rent and provide subsistence too. In all, about six million acres of farm land were classified as so severely eroded as to be beyond use. Almost simultaneously the owners of many other farms in this region found that agricultural production costs could be cut by combining smaller farms into larger ones, raising bulk crops, and cultivating and harvesting by machinery. So, as the dust bowl farmers wryly put it, some were "blown out" and others were "tractored out."

It is not certain how many farm families actually left the affected area. Informed estimates range from 6 to 10 per cent of the total farm population. The Federal Emergency Relief Administration, for example, in the month of April 1935 alone gave transient relief to 341,000 persons. But whatever the exact number, it is certain that the years 1933-1939 saw one of the largest mass movements of population in American history. A majority of these refugees (often called "Okies" or "Arkies") headed for California, hoping for jobs as migrant laborers. Arizona alone recorded 350,000 westward border crossings between 1935 and 1939.

In California, however, the migrant labor supply by 1936 already exceeded the number of agricultural jobs available. About 200,000 such workers were employed by three thousand large-scale farmers who belonged to the Associated Farmers Organization. When in 1937 the Congress of Industrial Organizations undertook unionization of this labor force, there were a number of subsequent clashes among workers, employers, and labor organizers.[1]

Out of this situation John Steinbeck constructed *The Grapes of Wrath*. The story line of the novel is clear and uncomplicated. The Joads, a family of Oklahoma tenant farmers whose crops are ruined by drought and dust, are forced off their failing farm by a land syndicate. On the promise of employment in California, they pack their few possessions into an ancient auto and join the caravan of "Okies" traveling westward—grandfather, grandmother, father, mother, six children, son-in-law, uncle, and an itinerant ex-preacher, Casy. The central figures in the group are Ma Joad, a powerful and good woman; Tom Joad, her eldest son, who has intelligence and ambition but is prone to violence; and Casy the preacher, who has lost his faith in his old exhorter's religion and is searching for a new one. The journey west is long and hard; in the promised land of California they find themselves insulted, exploited, and abused. Death, desertion, and deprivation begin to break up the close-knit family. Tom and Casy are soon involved in labor troubles, and Casy is killed. In the end, Tom leaves to become a union organizer, while Ma Joad, now the only person left to hold the family together, stands firm against the future.

In fabricating his plot out of materials at hand, Steinbeck first did three things. He particularized and personalized his narrative by concentrating it on a single family group, representing in the Joad family the thousands of unfortunates involved in the dust bowl migrations and labor troubles of the thirties. In order to clarify for the reader the relationships between the Joads, the other families whom they typify, and the larger background of actual events, Steinbeck interspersed the chapters on the Joad narrative with shorter sections on contemporary events, parables (the bankers and farmers), symbols (a turtle trying to cross the busy highway), or little sociological treatises (the meaning of guitar and harmonica music to simple country folk). Fifteen of the book's thirty chapters (about 20 per cent of the actual pages) have no direct relationship to the Joad plot.

Steinbeck also imposed a pattern on the material which, from all the available information, he chose to use. He organized his narrative into three parts, each leading into the other and each dependent on the other. These three sections might be named The Departure, The Exodus, and The End of the Road; they treat in turn of those events in Oklahoma which lead to the westward journey, the journey itself, and life in the new "home" of California. (Some readers may find ironic parallels to the flight of the Children of Israel to the Promised Land.) Steinbeck also chose a title adapted from Julia Ward Howe's familiar "Battle Hymn of the Republic," thereby warning the reader that his book had something more to it than a straightforward recital of events. The "grapes of wrath" (anger, injustice, ill fortune) planted in the dust bowl, nurtured on the long trip west, and matured in California's labor camps might one day bear fruit (social upheaval) unless the "vintages" which store them are "stamped out." By organization, title, and particularization, Steinbeck therefore immediately added extra dimensions to the same set of live facts available to the historian, the journalist, the sociologist, or the plain observer.

Steinbeck used the Joad story as a vehicle to carry sets of attitudes and ideas on three different narrative planes. In other words, he made the single narrative of the book into a three-sided prism. On one plane he used the Joads for "propaganda" purposes (in the nonpejorative sense) to expose and criticize certain current social conditions which involved sharecroppers, migrant workers, and labor-employer conflicts. Casy and Tom, on this level of the narrative, serve as mouthpieces for Steinbeck's opinions as he examines this complex of social and economic conditions in contemporary American life. The answer to the issues raised by the lives of the Joads and the others like them in the book, Steinbeck implies, is not revolution. It requires a change in the point of view of those who control the pivotal principles of American economic life. The propertied must recognize responsibility for the propertyless; the rich and fortunate must assume greater obligation for their less able and fortunate brethren—lest revolution be *forced* upon them. To Steinbeck it is a "great fact" of history that "when property accumulates in too few hands it is taken away. And that companion fact: when a majority of the people are hungry and cold they will take by force what they need. And the little screaming fact that sounds through all history: repression works only to strengthen and knit the repressed."[2] Were Steinbeck content to let his narrative rest at this level, he would have produced a documentary novel of social protest, a "thesis" novel in the tradition, say, of Dickens, Zola, or Dreiser.

The novelist, however, perceived a second level of meaning beneath his material. The story of the Joads, he found, had a wider significance. Caught as they are in a surge of tremendous natural, social, and economic events far beyond their control, they are deeply entangled in a struggle to preserve their dignity and self-respect, their integrity as human beings. The powerful figure of Ma Joad stands at the center of this level of the narrative. Dirt, degradation, isolation, contempt, suffering—these things rob people of those qualities which make them human, Steinbeck seems to say. Ma Joad keeps her family together and holds her head high in the midst of trial and travail. The old folks die (severing the ties with the past); some of the young ones defect (cutting the roots of the future); Pa Joad, hurt by a world he cannot understand, abdicates his authority as head of the family and declines into bewildered impotence. Yet, Ma Joad believes, the great mass of people, in spite of injustice and ill fortune and disillusion, will somehow muddle through. "The people," she proudly tells her son on the eve of his flight, "will live." So Steinbeck has found in the story of the westbound migrants and in Ma Joad, their symbol, a sort of parable of faith in humankind and its ultimate ability to triumph over adversity.

Nor is this all. Steinbeck also perceived in the facts of the Okies' exodus a set of issues related to individual behavior. Here Casy and Tom provide a focus for this third dimension of the narrative. Casy's philosophy becomes tangled with the story's action, catches others in it, and in the end gives guidance to Tom and significance to the lives of the others, whether they realize it fully or not. Once a shouting Bible-belt exhorter ("but not no more"), Casy searches for a new faith to replace the old and finds it finally in a devotion to the cause of others. It costs him his life in the end, but he substitutes for the savage rigor of his earlier fundamentalism the discovery that love, unselfishness, compassion, and understanding' are central to the individual's being. In the suffering and fear of the great journey, Casy glimpses signs of the change from "I" to "We"—the dedication of the individual to the greater good of the group —that he believes is the central fact of human existence. "It's love," he says. "I love people so much I'm fit to bust, sometimes," a message of simple Christianity.

So Casy finds his "religion" in the California labor conflict, dies in it, and passes on to Tom his discovery that to "suffer and die for a concept . . . is the foundation of Manself, and this one quality is man, distinctive in the universe." " . . . like Casy says," Tom remembers, "a fella ain't got a soul of his own, but on'y a piece of a big one . . ." "I know now," he concludes, "a fella ain't no good alone." So Tom gains power and direction by proclaiming his brotherhood with other men, by merging himself in the cause of a greater collective individuality.

What Steinbeck the novelist has done, then, with the materials of history may seem to be far removed from the work of the historian. Yet in effect this is not really so. The novelist has invested events with meaning and has exemplified facts with people; like the historian, he has tried to make sense out of a sequence of human actions, by using his imagination and his understanding of human nature. These qualities are common to both history and literature; without them the puzzle of the past has no solution and the game no meaning. With them Sandburg's Lincoln, Douglas Southall Freeman's Civil War, Samuel Eliot Morison's voyage of Columbus, William Faulkner's Southern saga, Hemingway's Spain, and Steinbeck's depression California all become segments of living, breathing experience. Therein lies the art of it.

1 Readers who wish to find additional information may consult Dixon Wecter, *The Age of the Great Depression* (New York, 1948); Paul B. Sears, *Deserts on the March* (Norman, Okla., 1935); Conrad Taeuber and C. C. Taylor, *The People of the Drought States* (Washington, D.C., 1937); and Carey McWilliams, *Factories in the Fields* (Boston, 1939).

2 All quotations from John Steinbeck, *The Grapes of Wrath* (The Viking Press, Inc.), copyright 1939 by John Steinbeck.

SUGGESTED READINGS

Interested readers might wish to explore this avenue of conjecture a little further by comparing Robert Penn Warren's *All the King's Men* with an account of Louisiana political history in the 1930's; Ernest Hemingway's *For Whom the Bell Tolls* with the chapters on the Spanish Civil War in any text on contemporary European history; Theodore Dreiser's *An American Tragedy* with the records of the actual Pennsylvania court trial, or Dreiser's trilogy *The Titan, The Financier,* and *The Stoic* with the history of American business corporations in 1885-1915; or Stephen Crane's *Red Badge of Courage* with Bruce Catton's *A Stillness at Appomattox.* For a study of much more complicated parallels, try Warren's *The Cave* as compared with an account of the death of Floyd Collins in Kentucky in 1925, or William Faulkner's *A Fable* with a description of the "false armistice" incident of May 1918 in World War I.

PART 6 The Changing World

CHAPTER 18 THE COLD WAR AND COMPETITIVE COEXISTENCE

EPILOGUE

The years since the end of World War II have witnessed the emergence of three major worlds, each with its recognizable way of life. The nations of North and South America (except Cuba); the non-Communist countries of western and southern Europe; Britain and the Commonwealth nations of Australia and New Zealand; the Republic of South Africa; Japan; and Formosa comprise the Free World. Cuba and the vast Eurasian heartland from Berlin to Peking comprise the Communist World. The underdeveloped nations of Africa and parts of Asia make up the Non-aligned World. What are the prospects and problems of each of these worlds?

The Free World. The Free World has recovered from the damage inflicted by the worst war in history. Since 1945, many of the nations in the Free World have enjoyed high productivity, relatively full employment, and expanding national economies. But though democracy today is undeniably healthier and more dynamic than it was after the First World War, the internal politics of the members of the Free World between the years 1945 and 1965 did not constitute an unblemished record for democracy.

The United States underwent a period of domestic crisis when civil liberties were endangered by McCarthyism—an anti-Communist campaign that got out of hand. The Suez crisis had grave repercussions in Britain; the Conservative government of Prime Minister Anthony Eden was bitterly attacked by the Labour party and even by some Conservatives. But the quarrel was fought out by traditional democratic means—debates in the House of Commons and well-ordered elections.

In both France and Germany, strong leaders arose to dominate the political scene. Until the accession of De Gaulle in 1958, however, French ministries came and went with bewildering rapidity. After that time, the austere, wartime leader of the Free French strengthened the executive power at the expense of the legislature—the constitution of the New Fifth Republic allowing him a wide latitude of power. West Germany evinced an almost miraculous recovery economically and politically, due in considerable measure to the leadership of Dr. Konrad Adenauer, Chancellor until 1963.

Elsewhere in the Free World, the strength of democracy has fluctuated. Vociferous Communists continued to challenge the national government in Italy. The Scandinavian nations, the Low Countries, and Switzerland enjoyed postwar political stability and prosperity. After World War II, the Latin-Americans toppled one dictator after another—Perón in Argentina, Jiménez in Venezuela, Trujillo in the Dominican Republic, and Batista in Cuba. But in Cuba, Batista's regime was replaced by that of a dictator of the left, Fidel Castro, who led his island nation into the Communist camp.

Racial intolerance remains a difficult problem in many nations of the Free World. The apartheid policy in the Republic of South Africa is rooted in the fear that the small white population may lose control of the government and of the natives. Riots there in 1960 clearly showed that the natives were resentful over discriminatory legislation. In the United States the school integration issue led to long and bitter controversy and the intervention of federal troops to prevent violence. The sweeping 1964 Civil Rights Act brought sharp resistance in a few parts of the South, but most of the United States accepted it as the law of the land.

Since the end of World War II, the western democracies have more and more accepted as a primary goal the maintenance and improvement of the economic standards of their population. In the United States, social security benefits were extended, and the minimum wage was raised. In the late forties, the Labour government in England increased the social insurance program with the goal of coverage "from the cradle to the grave" for all its citizens. Among the Commonwealth nations of Canada, Australia, and New Zealand, progressive legislation enhanced the economic and social status of the average citizen. To the extent that democratic capitalism and welfare socialism succeed, the West is rendered immune to Marxist attacks of "exploiter" and "exploited."

After World War II, the economic revival of western and southern Europe was due largely to the bold, imaginative plan launched by the United States in 1948—the European Recovery Program, better known as the Marshall Plan. Its assistance to seventeen European countries proved so successful that they were able to undertake a new economic venture, the commercial integration of Free Europe. The first move toward this goal took place in 1951, when France, West Germany, Italy, Belgium, the Netherlands, and Luxembourg—the so-called Inner Six—formed the European Coal and Steel Community and agreed to permit those two commodities to flow unrestricted across national boundaries. Six years later the scope of the association was broadened, and the Inner Six became known officially as the European Economic Community. The new agreement called for the

progressive abolition of customs duties and import quotas, the adoption of a common tariff against goods from outside the market area, and the establishment of an investment bank. Initially unwilling to join the Common Market because a substantial portion of British trade lay outside the area involved, Great Britain nevertheless recognized its advantages. In 1959 the Outer Seven (Britain, Denmark, Norway, Sweden, Austria, Switzerland, and Portugal) created the European Free Trade Association with the declared intention of reaching agreement with the Inner Six so that Europe would not be divided into rival economic blocs; but Britain's bid for entry into the Common Market in 1963 was vetoed by France.

Another aspect of voluntary, multinational cooperation was the series of regional alliances established by the nations of the Free World. In 1949, twelve countries set up the North Atlantic Treaty Organization (NATO), a military alliance designed to deter Soviet aggression in western Europe. An attack on any one member was to be regarded as aggression against all. The alliance was threatened from within by De Gaulle's independence and the chance of war between Greece and Turkey over Cyprus. To provide security in the Pacific, the United States, Australia, and New Zealand signed the Anzus Pact in 1951. Three years later, a more comprehensive alliance—the Southeast Asia Treaty Organization (SEATO)—was set up by the Anzus signatories, the Philippines, Thailand, and Pakistan, plus Britain and France. Similar agreements were established elsewhere—OAS (Organization of American States) in the Americas and CENTO (Central Treaty Organization) in the Middle East. In contrast to the aimless drifting and lassitude of the democracies when confronted by the Axis menace in the 1930's, these alignments were evidence of a willingness to cooperate in the face of Communist danger.

The Communist World. No one can deny the remarkable advances that have occurred in the Communist World since World War II, particularly in industrialization. Nor is there any reason to doubt that rapid economic development will continue. What policies have contributed to this upsurge?

The question of centralization loomed large in the postwar years. Stalin insisted on centralizing economic control within the Soviet Union: all Soviet economic ministries were located in Moscow. In addition, he maintained a firm hand over the economies of the Soviet satellites in eastern Europe and refused them permission to trade with the West or to accept Marshall Plan aid. For a time there was considerable talk about complete integration of the economies of the Communist bloc, with each nation specializing in specific industrial or agricultural activities; but Tito of Yugoslavia upset that plan when he withdrew from the joint Russo-Yugoslav ventures then in existence.

After Stalin's death in 1953, the satellites acquired greater economic autonomy and increased their trade with non-Communist areas. Meanwhile, Khrushchev undertook a large-scale process of decentralization within the economy of the Soviet Union itself. Control of industry was shifted from Moscow to the local regions, and in agriculture the operation of the government-owned machine-tractor stations was handed over to the collective farms.

To meet the expanding needs of the economy, it was necessary to make full use of the energies of Soviet workers. Khrushchev cut down on the number of slave-labor camps and reduced the powers of what he termed the "organs of suppression," which sap the vitality of peoples in any police state. The judiciary appears to have been made more independent of the police. A growing influx of foreign tourists and the exchange of cultural missions and exhibitions pointed to at least a temporary relaxation of the police-state atmosphere of isolation and constant surveillance.

An extension of freedom was given a brief try not only in Russia but in the rest of the Communist World as well. In 1956 the Twentieth Congress of the Communist party proclaimed the policy of "many roads to socialism." But Titoism in Yugoslavia and the 1956 Hungarian revolution attested to the peril to the Soviet Union of allowing the peoples of eastern Europe to give vent to their inner beliefs. The same problem was encountered in Communist China. In 1957 Mao Tse-tung declared, "Let a hundred flowers blossom; let a hundred schools of thought contend." But this invitation led to such a storm of criticism of his regime that Mao complained of the "poisonous weeds" that had sprung up instead of the flowers. The right of criticism was soon extinguished in Red China.

While decentralization and relaxation of police-state techniques in the Soviet Union improved the economy, both policies pose a basic threat to any monolithic state. How far can a Communist system permit such tendencies to grow without irreparably damaging its own ultimate control?

The Non-aligned World. Without a doubt, nationalism has become the most dynamic force in the shaping of the Non-aligned World. In postwar Asia and Africa, fervent nationalists campaigned on the slogan that "good government is no substitute for free government." Yet without good government, which had often been provided by colonial rule, the administrative efficiency or technical skills needed to raise the living standards and the educational level of the masses could not be brought into play. Indeed, as the newly independent countries in the Non-aligned World took their places in the family of nations, their dilemma—and the grave consequences it may hold for the world at large—came into sharp focus.

The postwar nationalism which has swept Asia and Africa has a strongly ambivalent character. While desiring to attain economic parity with the western powers by emulating the political, military, economic, and technological techniques which have made the West strong, peoples in the underdeveloped nations display strong anti-western sentiments stemming from the resentment of centuries of western control.

These same underdeveloped nations also exhibit conflicting feelings in their evaluation of the Communist way of life. Even though Communist China has shown how an illiterate, poverty-stricken people can be transformed into a major technological society, to follow Peking's example would mean ultimate absorption into the Communist World and rejection of principles which to leaders like the late Nehru were indispensable in the preservation of the best elements in their indigenous cultures.

Thus the nations of the Non-aligned World walk a tightrope between the Free World and the Communist World. Partly because of their long history of subjugation, the countries of the Non-aligned World are loath to join either of the two power blocs. Furthermore, their nonalignment is strengthened by the realization that it would be impossible for them to solve their pressing political, social, and economic problems if they became involved in a destructive nuclear war, which they hope to deter by acting together as a power bloc in international affairs. At the highly publicized Afro-Asian Conference in Bandung, Indonesia, in 1955, the representatives of twenty-nine nations agreed to remain neutral in the Cold War; to marshal their physical resources for the rapid development of their respective economies; and to obtain outside technical and economic assistance, though not at the expense of their avowed non-alignment. Another Afro-Asian conference was held in 1961, this time in Belgrade, Yugoslavia.

Although, since Bandung, there have been schisms within the Non-aligned World, positive neutralism remains a common denominator for these nations and must be reckoned with. For example, the American criticism of non-alignment drove some of the non-aligned nations farther from the confines of the Free World. An advantage was presented to Russia, which blandly "accepted" non-alignment without changing its basic determination to acquire African and Asian satellites. Now the United States accepts non-alignment, too.

THE COLD WAR DOMINATES INTERNATIONAL RELATIONS

It should not be surprising that the non-aligned nations have internal stresses that threaten their role in the Cold War. And, to a greater or lesser extent, both the Free and the Communist worlds display cracks in their solidarity which may vitally affect the dominant struggle of our day—the Cold War.

Cracks in the iron curtain. In what for many years appeared as the most "solid" of the three ideological worlds—the Communist World—there are significant cracks. In the Soviet Union itself, Khrushchev has been deposed, and a power struggle is likely between his successors, Leonid Brezhnev (1906-) and Alexei Kosygin (1904-).

Another potential source of stress within the Soviet Union is the growing demand for consumer goods. Can this desire remain unappeased while production facilities are geared primarily for the expansion of heavy industry? In still a different area, the ambitious programs of scientific research necessitate the expansion of higher education. Will the resulting intellectual elite be satisfied to live in a police state?

Outside the Soviet Union but still within the Soviet orbit, it is apparent that rebellious tendencies against Moscow's rule exist. The revolutions in Poland and Hungary demonstrated that nationalism is far from being a spent force in the Communist World. A continuing threat to Soviet authoritarianism is Yugoslavia's Tito, whose insistence on domestic autonomy and on more independent relations among the various Communist parties in the Soviet orbit has won him the label "revisionist." Rumania also seeks economic independence. However, Russia's satellites could only embarrass, not upset, the supremacy of the Soviet Union.

Communist China, on the other hand, is no satellite but a strictly disciplined nation with three times Russia's population. Its leaders have been working not only for recognition of China as a first-rate power but also for leadership of the Communist world movement—a drive which has resulted in a widening split between Peking and Moscow. Since 1959 China's expansionist policy at the expense of southeast Asia has been made manifest by increased Communist activities in South Vietnam, Cambodia, and Laos; yet, these moves have seldom been publicly supported by Moscow. Ill-timed and even more embarrassing to the Soviet chieftain was Peking's ruthless subjugation of Tibet in 1959. Moscow's public reaction to China's Himalayan border disputes with India and the resultant 1962 border war was very significant. Instead of automatically defending the actions of another Communist state in its troubles with a non-Communist government, Moscow adopted for the first time a strictly neutral position. Again, Moscow's proposals for a zone free of atomic weapons in Europe were reported in Peking papers, but the Russian suggestion for a similar zone in the Pacific was deleted. Peking wanted to have nuclear weapons in its own right, if for no other reason than as political bargaining counters. Red China now possesses them and will try to force the western nations—particularly the United States—to recognize it as an equal. And it could also attain parity with Moscow. The gradual shift in power within the Communist World is making Peking a greater threat to peace than Moscow.

Problems of the underdeveloped lands. Internal problems in the Non-aligned World, as in the Communist World, play a significant role in the international scene. Many of the nations in the Non-aligned World have only recently achieved their independence and therefore face the special problems involved in putting a new government into operation. In the Republic of the Congo, which became independent in 1960, these problems were compounded by the too-hasty grant of independence to an uninformed, illiterate populace guided by native leaders who only dimly perceived the difficulties to be surmounted by the new government. Tragic events in the Congo demonstrated that a grant of independence without adequate training in democracy could be as unsatisfactory as colonial rule without benevolence.

Most of the new governments are democracies only on paper; in reality, one man—like Nkrumah in Ghana—often becomes so powerful that opposition to him is slight. Such a man may be a competent leader, but under his administration democratic procedures are largely formalities. It may even be asked whether democracy is feasible under the current conditions of some of the ex-colonies. Of course, the political orientation of these new states is of the greatest importance to both the West and the Communist bloc.

Not only does the formation of efficient and stable governments challenge the new African countries, but formidable economic tasks also face them. In as short a time as possible, the Afro-Asians hope to solve the manifold problems of building urgently needed industries. Where will the capital come from? Where can skilled workers and technicians be trained? Can foreign trade be increased enough to cover the costs of importing new machinery and technical assistance? Can the shift from a tribal, agricultural society to an urban, industrialized one be accomplished without irreparable social upheaval? There is the additional problem of making unproductive land, now inefficiently cultivated, yield enough to feed fast-growing populations. These and other, more complex questions must be solved. Furthermore, the manner in which these problems are solved is bound to affect developments in the Cold War.

Perhaps the most crucial sector of the ideological battlefront in the Non-aligned World concerns racial equality. To the Africans and Asians, it is a key question. Their past role as colonial peoples has filled them with an abhorrence of second-class citizenship, and they hesitate to align themselves with any nation which regards non-whites as inferior.

Threats to international stability. Many international crises occur because the spheres of influence of each of the ideological worlds is not static. In the first place, the Communist bloc and the Free World each tries to increase its own area of influence in spite of the opposition of the other. This leads to such explosive situations as occurred when North Korean troops invaded the southern part of the Korean peninsula.

The stability of these areas of influence is sometimes threatened in a different fashion—by disruption of the internal affairs of one of the allies of the United States, or of a satellite of the U.S.S.R. Hungary, for example, in its ill-fated revolution, attempted to break away from Moscow's domination. Similarly, the anti-American

riots in Japan in 1960 threatened to change the boundaries of the Free World. The rebellious country is often brought back into the fold, by force in Hungary's case. However, in Latin America and southeast Asia communism threatens the present areas of influence.

Other trouble spots occur along the borders of the areas of influence, in cases where the status quo is complicated. A prime example is Berlin, located inside Communist-dominated East Germany. It is split up under the governments of the four main Allied powers, and is now divided by a wall, as well. Berlin is a festering canker to the Russians, who want to oust western rule there. The western powers insist that Berlin, which has become a symbol of Free World opposition to the Communists, will not be abandoned. On a larger scale, the division of Germany is a similar problem.

Potentially, of course, the greatest areas available for democratic or Communist expansion of influence lie within the confines of the Non-aligned World. Since military aggression would alienate the non-aligned nations, the emphasis by the West and, increasingly, by the Soviet Union has been upon economic aid. The rivalry between the West and the Reds is complicated further by a role the underdeveloped nations have assumed —that of playing off Russia against the United States in competition for aid. (Egypt played the game when seeking capital to build the Aswan dam.) While economic aid has become an accepted weapon that neither the Free World nor the Communist bloc can afford to abandon, it is highly questionable whether or not the recipients will ally themselves with either camp. On the other hand, only by sharing wealth and information with the "have-not" nations can long-standing problems—hunger, poverty, disease, illiteracy—be solved and conditions of distress and suffering be alleviated.

Trends toward increased internationalism. While nationalism strides across the ex-colonial areas and continues to affect internal relationships in both the Free and the Communist worlds, a trend toward internationalism is apparent in the world at large.

The nations that fought their national revolutions a century or more ago are for the most part planning the next logical stage of political development, which calls for gradual pooling of national assets in the interests of collective security. In order for the Free World to cope more effectively with the pressures of the Cold War, economic and political mergers of a broad scope are being suggested.

The outstanding example of an internationalized body is the United Nations. Because the structure of the U.N. was based on cooperation among sovereign nations—a condition that has not been achieved since the war—its successes have been limited. Nevertheless, some potentially dangerous situations, such as the Suez, Lebanon, Congo, and Cyprus crises, have been handled with some effectiveness through U.N. machinery and personnel.

Modifications of U.N. organization and procedure have improved the effectiveness of the body—and may have more far-reaching effects in the future. For example, the secretary-general has assumed the role of roving diplomat. The late Dag Hammarskjöld achieved great success in acting as mediator between the Arabs and the Israelis in 1956 and in organizing the U.N. observation group that was sent into Lebanon in 1958. His successor, U Thant, has had limited success in the Congo and in Cyprus. Another change in the structure of the U.N. occurred when the "Uniting for Peace" resolution stipulated that if the Security Council was deadlocked by a veto, the issue under discussion could be put before the General Assembly. Thus the Assembly acquired greater importance than it had previously. Furthermore, the admission of many uncommitted nations to the General Assembly has substantially changed its character from the days when the West could count on a two-thirds majority in that arena. The effect has been to give the neutralist nations more influence.

The United Nations, this year or next or even a decade from now, may not be able to exorcise the ideological conflict from the world, to find a satisfactory alternative to the veto procedure, or to secure complete agreement on atomic controls. But to acknowledge that there are major obstacles in the path toward effective world organization is not to imply that they can never be removed.

The Cold War and Competitive Coexistence

THE WORLD SCENE SINCE 1945

Introduction. It was not only the deaths of more than fourteen million fighting men nor the systematic destruction of entire cities which made the Second World War so horrifying. It was the reversion on a scale unrecorded in history to barbarism—a barbarism which used twentieth-century technology to exterminate perhaps as many as twelve million men, women, and children in concentration camps, gas ovens, and torture chambers; a barbarism which forced upward of seven million others into slavery; a barbarism for which the word *genocide* had to be created to define the premeditated attempt to wipe out entire nations and races.

Now the most terrible war in history was over. The holocaust which had given a portent of global suicide in two radioactive mushrooms at Hiroshima and Nagasaki had ended. The world's statesmen took up the slow, hard struggle for peace. But, with the end of the war, the objectives set forth in the Atlantic Charter for which the peoples in the western democracies had fought—the renunciation of territorial aggrandizement, the right of self-determination for national groups, disarmament, and world-wide economic cooperation—were jeopardized by the Soviet Union, with its brutal, coldly calculated designs for world conquest. As a result, disillusionment came with alarming swiftness to those who believed that the defeat of the Axis powers would automatically bring about a better world. Yet no realistic appraisal of the war's aftermath should blind us to the alternative to this costly victory: the enslavement of humanity by German Nazism and Japanese imperialism.

In this chapter we shall discuss the crucial years since the end of the war by tracing, first, the formation of the United Nations and the important crises faced by this organization in the years of the Cold War. Then we shall examine developments within the nations of the Free World, the Communist World, and the Non-aligned World; and, lastly, we shall consider both the hopeful and the menacing aspects of the most important issues facing us today.

THE COLD WAR

The United Nations established. The memory of the tragic failure of the victors after the First World War to build a lasting peace led to a profound feeling among the Allied statesmen of World War II that the very life breath of civilization depended on effective international machinery for maintaining peace and security in the postwar period. Shortly after Pearl Harbor, in January 1942, representatives of twenty-six nations signed the Declaration by the United Nations, thereby subscribing to the principles of the Atlantic Charter. During the war, two important international bodies were established: UNRRA (the United Nations Relief and Rehabilitation Administration) was created to cope with the massive relief problems of liberated countries, and the International Monetary Fund was formed to deal with the long-term reconstruction of dislocated economies. In 1944, American, British, Chinese, and Soviet delegates met at Dumbarton Oaks in the District of Columbia to draw up a blueprint for an international organization for maintaining peace. The name "United Nations" was fixed upon to stress the continuity from the wartime alliance.

To draft a charter along the general lines of the Dumbarton Oaks proposals, representatives of more than fifty governments met at San Francisco from April to June 1945. In its final form, the Charter of the United Nations created a structure with these major organs: the Security Council was formed to maintain peace and order; the General Assembly was conceived as a sort of town meeting of the world, in which member states could discuss issues affecting international relations; the Economic and Social Council was created to promote higher living standards and fundamental human rights; the Trusteeship Council was to function in the interests of colonial peoples in the trusteeship system, which replaced the former mandate system of the League of Nations; the International Court of Justice was the body to which disputes between nations could be referred for judicial settlement; and the Secretariat, headed by its secretary-general, was to minister to the needs of the other major organs. In the social and economic and trusteeship fields, the United Nations possessed wider powers than the League of Nations. Moreover, it was in these areas that the U.N. would register marked gains for cooperation among the nations of the world.

The most controversial issue at San Francisco was the voting procedure of the Security Council. At the Yalta Conference in February 1945, Roosevelt, Stalin, and Churchill had agreed that questions of procedure could be decided by any seven affirmative votes among the Council's eleven members. On every other issue, however, the seven affirmative votes must include those of all five permanent members: the United States, the Soviet Union, Great Britain, France, and China. Thus, by casting a negative vote, any one of the Big Five could veto a decision. Although at San Francisco the smaller powers objected to this formula, the big powers insisted that peace and security required their acting in unison.

It was hoped that the high purposes of the Charter—the maintenance of world peace and order—could be achieved. Yet the machinery for halting aggression was controlled by the Security Council, and the Security Council in turn was based on the twin pillars of national sovereignty and big-power cooperation.

Problem of the ex-enemies. At the Potsdam Conference in 1945, the Council of Foreign Ministers of the Big Five was set up to draft the peace treaties. Only minor difficulties were encountered in adopting treaties in 1947 with Italy, Rumania, Bulgaria, Hun-

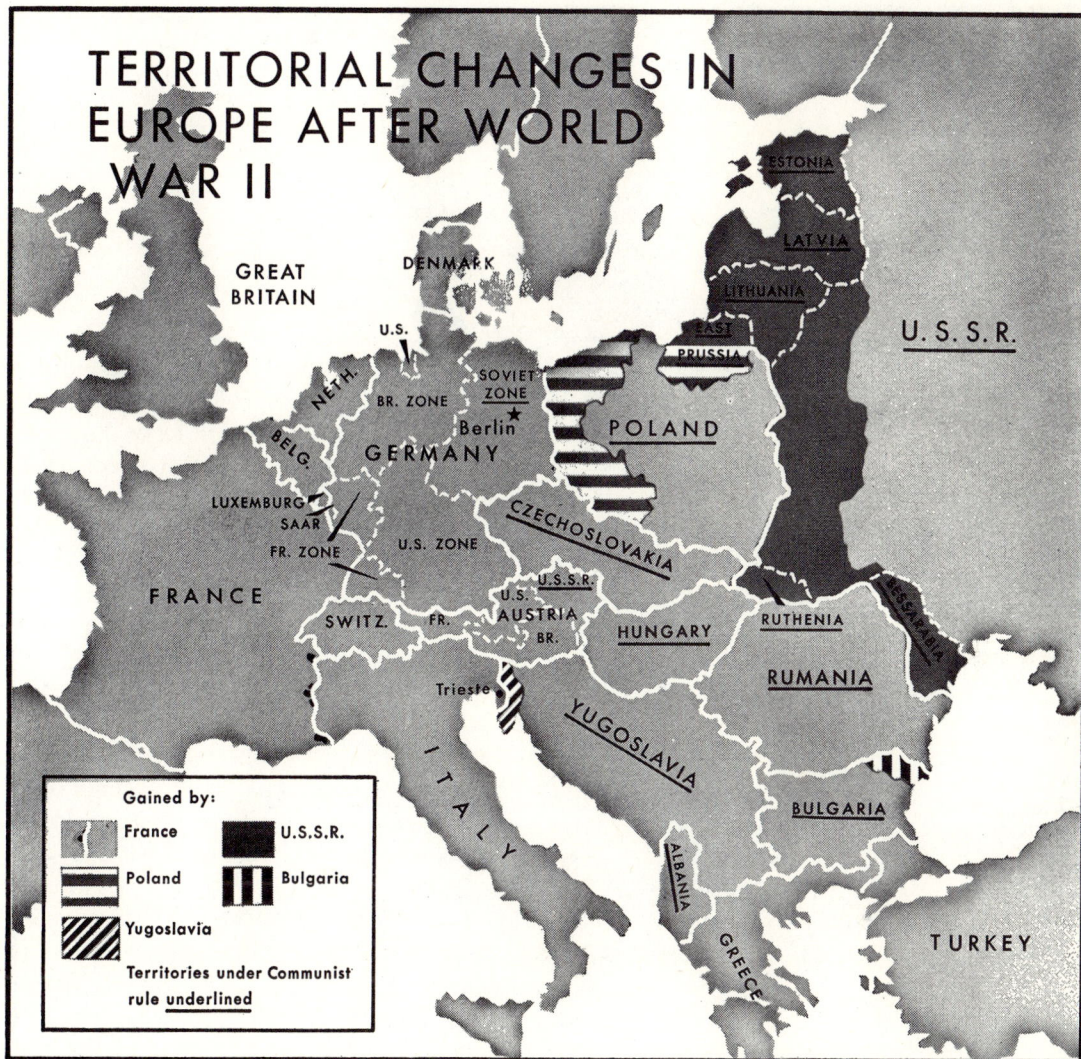

TERRITORIAL CHANGES IN EUROPE AFTER WORLD WAR II

Gained by:

France
Poland
Yugoslavia

U.S.S.R.
Bulgaria

Territories under Communist rule underlined

Peace settlements with Italy and the Axis satellites—Rumania, Bulgaria, Hungary, and Finland—were drafted by the Paris Conference, which met from July to October of 1946, and by the Council of Foreign Ministers, which deliberated for the next two months. The map above shows the principal territorial adjustments agreed upon. Others included the transfer of the Petsamo area (the northeast corner of Finland) to the U.S.S.R. and the grant to the Russians of a fifty-year lease on Porkkala (the city and surrounding area on the southernmost tip of the Finnish coast). The Soviets returned the Porkkala territory to Finland in 1955. In 1940, Estonia, Latvia, and Lithuania had been absorbed into the U.S.S.R., and Rumania had ceded Ruthenia and Bessarabia to the Russians. The Dodecanese Islands, off southern Turkey, were given to Greece by the Italians. Italy also renounced its former African colonies, recognized Al-

banian independence, and accepted U.N. supervision of the Free Territory of Trieste, which continued to be a scene of turmoil until the October 1954 agreement between Italy and Yugoslavia, whereby Italy received the port and Yugoslavia the rest of the area. The sovereignty of the Republic of Austria was restored with a state treaty in 1955. The Saar became part of the French zone of occupation after the war; under a Franco-German treaty the Saar was reunited politically with Germany on January 1, 1957. In occupied Germany the French zone merged with the Anglo-American bizone just before the establishment of the German Federal Republic (or West Germany) on May 8, 1949. October of that year marked the founding of the German Democratic Republic (East Germany). The problem of German reunification remains a constant source of international tension.

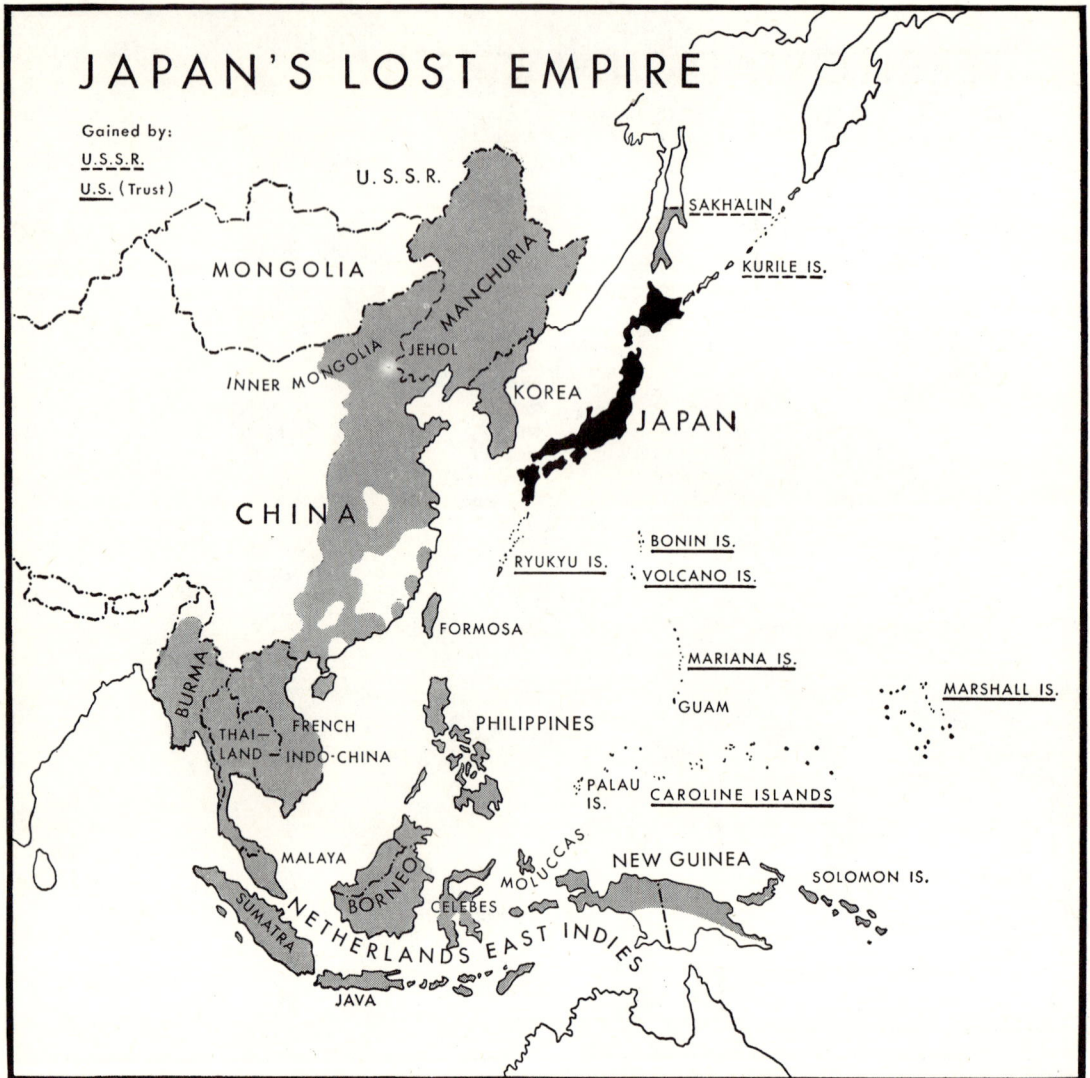

JAPAN'S LOST EMPIRE

Gained by:
U.S.S.R.
U.S. (Trust)

In 1942 the Japanese expansion which had begun in the last decades of the nineteenth century reached its height. The areas in gray on the map above show the extent of Japan's acquisitions, all of which were lost after the Japanese defeat in World War II. These territories, which include all the Pacific islands named on this map, were returned to their former owners or became independent in the next few years. A few, indicated by the map key, were placed under the supervision of other powers. The dismemberment of the Japanese empire marked the end of the dreaded New Order in Asia.

gary, and Finland. The future of Austria remained uncertain until 1955, when a peace treaty was signed and occupation forces were withdrawn. What proved to be roadblocks to international cooperation were the treaties with Japan and Germany.

Postwar Japan was governed by General Douglas MacArthur, assisted by advisors from U.N. member states. A new constitution which vested supreme power in the people was adopted, and the national economy was liberalized—Japanese workers were encouraged to join trade unions, while the great trusts were broken up. The outbreak of the Korean War in 1950 strengthened the United States in its resolve to proceed with its western associates in drafting a treaty with Japan, regardless of Kremlin protests that the peace treaty be drafted by a conference of foreign ministers, where the Soviets could block any proposal to retain American troops in Japan. Signed in September 1951, the treaty between Japan and the West reestablished Japan as a sovereign nation and provided for the restoration of its foreign trade. This was followed by an American-Japanese security pact, which allowed the United States the right to station forces in Japanese territory. Less than ten years after Pearl Harbor, Japan had become an ally of the United States.

In 1945, defeated Germany was divided into occupied zones. The eastern zone was placed under the control of the Soviet Union, and western Germany was divided into American, British, and French sectors. The German capital, Berlin, which formed an enclave within the Soviet zone, was placed under joint four-power administration.

From November 1945 to October 1946, Soviet and western authorities collaborated in the war crimes trials at Nuremberg by which leading Nazis were sentenced and punished for crimes against humanity. Both then and later, the trials were criticized by some as vengeful and illegal, but others praised them for bringing to justice the men ultimately responsible for a murderous reign of terror.

As the three western powers undertook to restore their zones in Germany, they faced grave difficulties: inflation, black marketeering, a steady influx of refugees from the eastern zone, and the reëducation of the German people in democracy. A further problem—and one of the greatest consequence—was the attitude of the Soviet Union. In June 1948, in retaliation for the West's determination to create a West German state which would participate in the European Recovery Program (see p. 568), the U.S.S.R. blockaded Berlin from the West. Moscow hoped thus to drive the western powers out of the city, a strategy which, if successful, would have delivered a body blow to the West's prestige. American and British authorities met this challenge by organizing a huge air lift to feed the two million persons in western Berlin and by cutting off supply shipments from their zones to the east part of Germany. Not until the autumn of 1949 did the Soviet Union agree to lift its blockade, provided that the West raise its counterblockade.

The Cold War: an armed truce. The Berlin crisis put into sharp focus the swift deterioration of the wartime collaboration among the big powers. Soon after the Security Council began to function in 1946, a disquieting series of events took place. Iran accused the Soviet Union of meddling in its internal affairs, and Moscow retaliated by charging Britain with interfering in Greece and Indonesia. Stalin charged that "international reaction" was "hatching plans for a new war," and Churchill called for Anglo-American cooperation to halt Moscow's "expansive and proselytizing tendencies." The United States and the U.S.S.R. disagreed over plans for controlling atomic energy, the future of Korea, the Communist demarcation of the German-Polish boundary, and elections in Bulgaria and Rumania, which Russia was busily turning into satellites. More than ever, observers realized how strong were the ideological differences separating the democratic nations from the Soviet Union. What had happened?

The United Nations Charter reflected the principles of western democracy, whose adherents had perhaps too sanguinely expected that with such a charter, postwar nationalism could be channeled in an orderly fashion, particularly in the colonial areas which were ripe for political and economic change and whose complaints were grist for the Soviet propaganda mill. Also, it was hoped that the kind of world envisaged in the Charter would allay the traditional Soviet fears about capitalist "encirclement" and permit different ways of life to coexist peacefully. These underlying miscalculations about the true character and potency of postwar nationalism and communism were augmented by two major developments in power politics resulting from the war. Although the Charter was constructed to allow for the joint leadership of the Big Five, by V-J Day the world's future was dependent upon the relations of the Big Two—the United States and the Soviet Union. Furthermore, their relations were made more complex by the existence of power vacuums in Europe and Asia resulting from Axis defeat.

Another crucial factor was the result of the invention known only after the signing of the Charter—the atomic bomb. To some it seemed that the United Nations had been designed for the pre-atomic era and that the ultimate issue of planetary survival rested now with the decisions of one or the other of the two superstates. In June 1946 the American representative on the U.N. Atomic Energy Commission, Bernard M. Baruch, presented a statesmanlike plan for the international control of the atom. The Baruch Plan provided for the internationalization of all atomic production, rigorous international inspection, and the retention by the United States of its atomic secrets and its atomic stock pile until a suitable plan had been worked out. All members of the Commission agreed to these proposals except Russia. Meanwhile, to attack the United States monopoly in atomic bombs, the Soviets bent every effort to obtain atomic secrets—a policy dramatically revealed in 1949 by the disclosures in Canada, Britain, and the United States of espionage involving Soviet officials. After the Soviets produced an atomic explosion in 1949, it became increasingly difficult to secure agreement on atomic disarmament and international control of atomic energy.

Admittedly, the long-term strategy of Soviet communism had been muted during World War II. But after the victory against Nazism, it once again became plain that the leaders of the Kremlin had never lost sight of the Marxist premise that communism is a more advanced stage of social organization than capitalism and must inevitably supersede it. Postwar communism was poised to embark on a three-pronged offensive. First, the military and civil capacities of the Soviet Union were to be expanded; second, its influence was to be increased, not only in Europe, where it set up satellite states, but also in the Uncommitted World of Asia and Africa; and third, the western democracies were to be reduced to impotence and isolation through military threats, political tension, and psychological warfare.

The policy of containment. In 1947, while international tension continued unabated, Washington announced two new moves. Prompted by Soviet demands on Turkey, President Harry S. Truman (1884-   ) an-

nounced the Truman Doctrine, stipulating that the United States would support any nation threatened by Communist aggression, a move which enabled Greece as well as Turkey to withstand Soviet encroachment.

The second move stemmed from the announcement by Secretary of State George C. Marshall (1880-1959) that the United States would help Europe solve its economic problems, provided that the countries concerned also made every effort at recovery. While the nations of western Europe hailed this proposal, the U.S.S.R. refused to join the plan on the grounds that it would infringe on national sovereignty. This, of course, was only the "official" reason. Basically, the U.S.S.R. did not wish to see prosperity return to Europe —communism grows best in depressed economies. Above all, Russia opposed any plan that might increase the prestige of the United States.

Billions of dollars were appropriated by the United States Congress to implement the European Recovery Program, which became better known as the Marshall Plan.* To a considerable extent the Truman Doctrine and the Marshall Plan were related programs; both were elements in a broad strategy of "containing" Soviet Russia.

The U.N.: a safety valve for international tensions. New incidents in 1948 brought the great powers to the verge of open conflict. In February, the government of Czechoslovakia was overturned by a sudden coup which brought a Communist minority into power and ended democracy in the most progressive of the small eastern European nations. In June, as we have seen, tension suddenly flared to explosive dimensions in Berlin.

The Cold War—of which these incidents were a part—prevented the U.N. from realizing the high hopes on which the Charter had been founded—especially since the organization's effectiveness in peace enforcement had been based squarely on big-power cooperation. Nevertheless, the U.N. proved

---

*In 1952 the Mutual Security Agency replaced the European Recovery Program, and in the following year MSA in turn gave way to the Foreign Operations Administration, which combined both economic and military aid.

to be an important factor in world affairs. Its assemblies and administrative bodies had become virtually the only places where regular contact and discussion were maintained between the western powers and the U.S.S.R. and where, in addition, the views of other sovereign nations, as well as those of the colonial peoples in the U.N. trust territories, had all to be taken into account. Although governments often failed to reach agreement on overriding questions, the U.N. was able to exercise a conciliating influence. In short, it had become an international safety valve.

The Korean police action. In 1950 the United Nations found itself using force to oppose the use of force. Attempts to unify Korea—which had been divided into an American and a Soviet zone of occupation after Japan's surrender—were frustrated by the Communists, who prevented free elections in North Korea and refused U.N. observers access to that area. When American and Soviet occupation forces withdrew in 1949, two hostile regimes claimed jurisdiction over the entire peninsula.

On June 25, 1950, North Korean troops crossed the 38th parallel into South Korea. The United States immediately called for a special meeting of the Security Council, whose members—meeting without the Soviet delegate, who had boycotted the Council over the controversial issue of granting Red China U.N. membership (see p. 578)—demanded a cease-fire and withdrawal of the invaders. When the demand was ignored, the Council decided to "furnish such assistance to the Republic of Korea as may be necessary to repel the armed attacks and to restore international peace and security in the area." American forces dominated the U.N. military action—termed a police action because a declaration of war was not involved—but other member nations contributed limited support.

Initial North Korean successes were more than offset by the counteroffensive directed by General MacArthur. After U.N. troops pushed across the 38th parallel, Communist China came to the aid of North Korea, a development which led to an angry debate in the United States over the course to pursue. Mac-

Though not an official "war," the Korean action brought all of war's terror and tragedy to combatants and noncombatants alike. Here, South Korean women and children flee to safety as American soldiers prepare to advance to the front.

Arthur wanted to strike at bases in Chinese Manchuria, insisting that this was the only way to achieve victory. President Truman, convinced that such a move could bring on a third world war, stuck to the U.N.'s limited objective—the repelling of aggression in South Korea. When MacArthur persisted in opposing the administration's policy, Truman had him removed from his command. In July 1953, during Eisenhower's first term of office, an armistice was signed, reëstablishing the *status quo ante bellum.*

The Korean police action serves as a good example of both the weaknesses and the potential strength of the United Nations. Action against aggression had been made possible only by the absence of the Russian delegate in the Security Council; hence, there was no use of the Soviet veto. The independence of South Korea had been saved, but the burden had been carried by a small minority of U.N. members, the United States suffering the heaviest sacrifices in blood and money. Although aggression had been halted, the chief culprit—Communist China—had not been punished. But, however imperfect international action had been, a precedent for the use of U.N. military forces had been established—a precedent which would be of vital importance in the years to come.

Collective security by regional blocs.
Before the Korean outbreak, the heightened
crises in international relations had strengthened the widespread belief in the West that
no nation could depend upon the United
Nations to guarantee its security. Thus the
search for collective security led to the establishment of regional alliances for mutual assistance—a step permitted under the U.N.
Charter. In 1947, nineteen American nations
signed a mutual protection treaty at Rio de
Janeiro; and in the year following, the Inter-
American System was transformed into the
Organization of American States, calling for
a security zone extending from the North to
the South Pole. On the other side of the Atlantic, Belgium, France, Great Britain, Luxemburg, and the Netherlands signed the
Brussels Treaty in 1948, establishing machinery for cooperation in military and other
fields. In 1949 these five nations joined with
the United States, Canada, Denmark, Iceland, Italy, Norway, and Portugal in signing
the North Atlantic Treaty; and in 1951 the
territorial limits of this agreement were extended to include Greece and Turkey.

The North Atlantic Treaty represented a
profound shift in the policies of the United
States and Canada, neither of which had previously agreed to peacetime overseas commitments. Now both were pledged for at least
twenty years to assist any other signatory in
the event of external aggression. The North
Atlantic Treaty Organization (NATO) used
forces from the member nations to set up a
defensive shield against sudden attack from
behind the iron curtain.

In the Pacific, the United States joined with
Australia and New Zealand in the Anzus
Pacific Security Pact, which came into force
in 1951. A more comprehensive system was
shortly fashioned for southeast Asia, which
had become especially vulnerable to Communist penetration following the establishment
of a Communist regime in northern Indo-
China (see p. 583). Meeting in Manila in
1954, delegates from Australia, New Zealand,
the Philippines, Pakistan, Thailand, France,
Great Britain, and the United States created
the Southeast Asia Treaty Organization
(SEATO), which also brought Cambodia,

Laos, and South Vietnam under its protection.

The danger of Soviet penetration in the
Middle East resulted in still another mutual
security arrangement. Originally called the
Bagdad Pact, with Great Britain, Turkey, Iraq,
Iran, and Pakistan as full members and the
United States as an "observer," it was re-
named the Central Treaty Organization
(CENTO) after the withdrawal of Iraq in
1959.

On its side, the Soviet Union entered into
a number of mutual assistance arrangements
with its satellites and Red China. In 1950
Moscow and Peking signed a thirty-year
treaty of "friendship, alliance, and mutual assistance." West Germany's entry into NATO
in May 1955 was swiftly followed by Moscow's creation of the Warsaw Pact, providing
for a unified Communist military command
in Soviet-controlled eastern Europe.

Quest for economic unity. Paralleling the
drive for security through regional alliances
were the moves made by the West toward
unity and cooperation in the economic sphere.
Outstanding in this regard was the progress
made in Europe. In 1951 a six-nation treaty
(France, West Germany, Italy, and the Benelux countries of Belgium, the Netherlands, and
Luxemburg) created the European Coal and
Steel Community, from which the European
Economic Community (better known as the
Inner Six) evolved six years later. This organization provided for the gradual abolition
of custom duties and import quotas, the
adoption of a common tariff against goods
from outside the market area, and the creation of an investment bank. In 1957 the same
six nations set up the European Atomic Energy Community (Euratom) to regulate the
production and use of atomic energy for
peacetime purposes.

Other manifestations of the trend toward
economic unity were the Nordic Union, which
in 1958 established a common labor market
for the Scandinavian nations and proposed a
common trade market, and the Outer Seven,
a free trade association consisting of Britain,
Sweden, Norway, Denmark, Austria, Switzerland, and Portugal. Despite disagreements
between the two most important groups, the

Inner Six and the Outer Seven, the general trend in Europe was unmistakably toward more economic unity. The European parliament set up in 1958 to control the Inner Six and Euratom was a harbinger of ever larger areas of cooperation.

THE FREE WORLD

The United States: leader of the Free World. With the collapse of Germany and Japan, the United States began to demobilize its far-flung armed forces. Yet despite the overwhelming sentiment to "bring the boys back home," and in sharp contrast to the strong isolationism prevailing after World War I, the American people appeared to recognize the responsibilities that leadership of the Free World thrust upon them. Thus a favorable climate for vigorous United States participation in world affairs existed.

Demobilization did not bring unemployment because the production of consumer goods—long awaited at home and in great demand abroad—absorbed the ranks of veterans and kept industrial production at high levels. During this period, however, the country experienced a sharp rise in prices—an inflation caused largely by the demand for consumer goods unavailable during the war and by the abandonment of wartime price controls. By 1948 the cost of living had risen to 172 per cent of the 1935-1939 average.

As we have seen, Truman in his second administration was faced with crucial problems, chiefly the intensification of the Cold War and the outbreak of the Korean conflict. In the 1952 election campaign, the controversial issues concerned Korea and disloyalty and subversion in the government. On the first issue, the administration was accused of committing American troops to a war which in effect had become a holding action. The second issue was created by disclosures that some workers in the government and in military research projects had been in communication with Soviet agents. Steps were taken to remove all those suspected of Communist sympathies from positions of trust, but the issue continued to dominate the headlines until 1954 when, after the sensational Army-

McCarthy hearings, the Senate censured Senator Joseph R. McCarthy (1909-1957), who had achieved world-wide publicity with his incessant charges of "treason" within the government. Shortly thereafter, McCarthy's political career went into an eclipse.

The election of Dwight D. Eisenhower in 1952 was more a sweeping personal victory for the man himself than an endorsement of the Republican party, which acquired a bare majority in Congress. During Eisenhower's first term of office, social security coverage was extended and the minimum wage level was raised. In 1956, despite serious illness, he was reëlected by an overwhelming majority, though the Democrats captured Congress.

For the greater part of Eisenhower's two terms, the American people enjoyed prosperity, a steadily expanding economy, and a relatively stable dollar. Although a recession was experienced in the spring of 1958, with between five and six million unemployed, 1959 saw production and wages again reach high levels. Eisenhower's second term—his last as a result of the adoption of the Twenty-second Amendment, which forbade a third term—was noteworthy for the opening of the American-Canadian St. Lawrence Seaway and the admission of two new states, Alaska and Hawaii. In addition, the implementation of the Supreme Court's ruling of May 1954, which decreed that Negroes be permitted to attend the same schools as white students, continued despite sporadic resistance by segregationist elements.

As a result of the close presidential election of 1960, John F. Kennedy became the youngest man and the first Catholic to be elected to the White House. Despite a Democratic majority in Congress, his legislative victories were limited to starting the Peace Corps, providing aid to education, and expanding the space program.

In foreign affairs Kennedy faced crises in Berlin, Laos, and the Congo. To Latin-America he gave the Alliance for Progress, a program of socio-economic reform. In 1962, a year after the abortive Bay of Pigs Invasion, he forced the U.S.S.R. to remove its ballistic missiles from Cuba.

On November 22, 1963, the world was stunned by the assassination of this vigorous American. His Vice President and successor, Lyndon B. Johnson, quickly united the saddened nation. In 1964 he was elected President and, with a large majority, he proceeded to enact the most extensive reform program in 30 years.

Political turnabout in Britain. The victory of the Labour party in the 1945 elections, by which the staunch wartime leader Churchill was ousted from office, indicated that the British people wanted a fresh approach to the solution of Britain's postwar economic problems. Chief among these difficulties were foreign debts amounting to twelve billion dollars, the wartime liquidation of a large part of Britain's overseas investments and gold reserves, and an alarming decline in the export trade (in 1945 it had dropped to half its prewar figure). For the first time in its history, Britain was a debtor rather than a creditor nation.

The Labour government introduced a flood of legislation. To stimulate exports, the British pound was devaluated. Much of the economy was nationalized, including the Bank of England, the railways, civil aviation, and the coal, electricity, and gas industries. Heavy taxes, rationing of consumer goods, and general austerity characterized the domestic economy. Progressive social legislation included the National Insurance Act, which broadened existing accident, old-age, and unemployment benefits, and a National Health Service, which provided everyone with free medical, dental, and hospital care.

Many Conservatives and Labourites agreed upon the benefits accruing from the social and health services, and no one suggested the return of fuel or railways to private hands. On the other hand, the less successful record of other nationalized sectors turned a majority of the electorate away from Labour's thesis that the prosperity of Britain depended upon nationalization. In three elections in the 1950's, the British people returned the Conservatives, who in 1953 denationalized the steel and trucking industries. Their tenure of office also coincided with a general upswing in the international economic situation, with the result that Britain's exports climbed along with its gold reserves. The second half of the 1950's witnessed a steady improvement in the national economy, even though, at the same time, competition in world markets mounted, and the rate of increase in national production lagged behind that of either North American or other major western European economies. The future of socialism in Britain appeared doubtful when a majority of the younger voters, living in a welfare-state atmosphere and unimpressed by the socialist slogans of "capitalist exploitation" and "the class struggle," voted Conservative in the elections of October 1959.

British policies ran an uneasy course in the next five years. Plagued by economic problems and rather ineffectual leadership, the Conservatives lost a close election to Labour in October, 1964. Harold Wilson became Prime Minister and Edward Heath later assumed the leadership of the Conservative Party.

Instability in France. Overwhelmed by the defeat and dishonor of 1940, France emerged from the war all but crushed in spirit. Following liberation, General Charles de Gaulle, leader of the Free French, was elected president of the provisional government. He straightway set about restoring the national economy and French prestige. Acting chiefly by executive decrees, he nationalized key industries and outfitted a new army.

A major problem was the creation of a constitution for the new Fourth Republic. The Communists, who had won a large following in the wartime resistance movement, favored a single legislative chamber which they hoped to control. De Gaulle and the rightists called for executive powers sufficient to dominate the legislature. Failure to obtain his objective caused the general to resign in 1946. The constitution as finally adopted called for a bicameral legislature and a cabinet responsible to the Assembly, thus making it possible for cabinets to be voted out while the members of the Assembly remained in office—a condition which led to a high degree of governmental instability. In addition, by retaining a multitude of parties in the Assembly, the

French continued to rely upon coalition governments, thus perpetuating the most dangerous weakness of the prewar Third Republic.

Democracy in France was menaced by the Communists until about 1948, when economic aid from America reinvigorated the French economy and when the Communists' unswerving devotion to the "Moscow line" had alienated many supporters. Meanwhile, the Fourth Republic underwent a succession of short-lived coalition governments made up of center parties, which proved inefficient at tackling either domestic or external problems. France continued to suffer from political mismanagement, tax dodging, and the uneconomical subsidization of various industries for the profit of vested interests. In addition, the inflexibility of many conservatives in hanging on to overseas territory at all costs resulted in the draining away of man power, wealth, and prestige in protracted wars in Indo-China and North Africa.

A crisis was reached in May 1958 when rightist French civilians and army officers in Algeria rebelled against the government, which had promised to liberalize France's Algerian policy in the interests of the indigenous population. The rebels' demand for De Gaulle to take power led to a showdown: the established parties were defeated, and the wartime hero emerged from retirement to assume control of the government. The choice of De Gaulle ended the Fourth Republic, for he insisted upon a new constitution vesting power in the president, who would also control the premier and cabinet and would be empowered to dissolve any parliament of which he disapproved.

In September 1958, the new constitution was adopted, and the Fifth Republic was launched on a strong wave of confidence in De Gaulle's austere but purposeful leadership. To put France's muddled finances in order, De Gaulle called for high taxes, tightened up the tax collection system, removed various subsidies on foods and fuel, abolished most of the veterans' pensions, and devalued the franc. Defense expenditures were not cut, however, nor were expenditures for atomic weapons. But by seeking to bring about a solution of the Algerian problem he

risked estrangement from the *colons* (the French minority in Algeria) and elements in the army. Nevertheless, he granted Algeria independence in 1962, thereby ending a sizeable drain on France's resources.

Under De Gaulle's leadership the French economy has made considerable progress. Gold reserves have grown substantially and by 1963 national revenue had increased 25 per cent. Agricultural modernization has raised the tractors in use to over one million. In education, atomic energy, and aircraft development, France has demonstrated originality and creativity. From a divided nation President De Gaulle has molded a new France—stable, prosperous, and influential in world affairs.

Under French leadership he aspires to make Europe a dynamic independent force, an arbiter between the U.S. and the U.S.S.R. A supreme nationalist, De Gaulle is unwilling to cede any of France's present freedom of action and in fact hopes to regain some through the reorganization of NATO. Some say De Gaulle has been France since 1958. In December 1965 he was reelected to a second term. But it was not clear how long this masterful leader, now in his mid-seventies would remain in office, and whether France without him would be able to perpetuate and consolidate his achievements.

Resurgence in West Germany. The dramatic story of West Germany's remarkable recovery from an occupied territory to a dynamic member of the family of nations began in 1949, when the western powers enacted an occupation statute providing for the constitutional development of their zones. This move was followed by German adoption of the Basic Law for the Federal Republic of Germany, which gave the West Germans virtual control of their domestic affairs, with their capital at Bonn. When the Allied occupation ceased six years later, the Basic Law acquired the status of a constitution. It called for a federal structure, the upper house representing the state government and a Bundestag (or Federal Diet) representing the people directly. The president was not provided with the emergency powers which had enabled his predecessor in the Weimar Republic to create a presidential dictatorship, while the chancellor, or prime minister, was made responsible to the Bundestag.

Since the first elections in 1949, the two strong parties in Western Germany have been the conservative, Catholic-dominated Christian Democratic Union, under the leadership until 1963 of Dr. Konrad Adenauer, and the socialist party, the Social Democrats. Former mayor of Cologne and one-time prisoner of the Gestapo, Adenauer was to prove as inflexible a champion for West Germany's recovery and prestige as was De Gaulle for neighboring France. Intolerant of parliamentary opposition yet insistent that the Germans play a constructive role as a self-reliant nation in the Free World, Dr. Adenauer has been described as "a kind of Bismarck in the service of democracy."

During the 1950's, economic recovery was little short of amazing, as attested by a booming export trade and by the strength of the West German mark in international monetary circles. In the political sphere, Adenauer firmly wedded his country's fortunes to those of the western democracies, at the same time insisting that West Germany should be recognized as an equal partner in the common defense against communism.

Ludwig Erhard, Minister of Economic Affairs in 1949, and later Vice Chancellor of the Bonn Republic, succeeded Adenauer in 1963. Erhard was largely responsible for the country's miraculous economic recovery. Generally, he has carried on the policies of his predecessor, though Erhard is less paternal and authoritarian. By a slim margin he was reelected Chancellor over Mayor Willy Brandt of West Berlin in the fall of 1965.

The changes that have occurred in West Germany since 1949 have been momentous. This war-shattered nation, demoralized by twelve years of Nazi tyranny, has recovered its national dignity, and become a respected and important member of the Free World and a staunch ally of the United States. Despite several outbreaks of anti-Semitism, Bonn's democratic institutions, as well as its economic prosperity, appear stable. Their continued solidification is central to the peace and stability of Western Europe.

Challenges to democracy in Latin America. The end of World War II found Latin America faced with a host of serious problems, chiefly militarism and inflation. In all the republics, Communists were active in promoting class warfare and suspicion of the United States. The urban proletariat and the landless peons and mine workers were demanding a larger share of the material rewards of modern society. However, neither inflation, labor troubles, nor hostility to foreign investors slowed the rapid pace of industrialization and the business boom. In many Latin-American nations, economic progress was paralleled by improved social legislation and advances in education. But there were also disturbing developments.

Openly sympathetic to the Axis powers, a clique of army officers, "the colonels," had seized the government of Argentina in 1943. Emerging as the leader of "the colonels" was Juan Domingo Perón (1902-   ), who staffed the army and the labor unions with his henchmen. Elected president in 1946 and reëlected in 1951, he undertook an ambitious program to elevate the working classes, to make Argentina self-sufficient, and eventually to seize the leadership of Latin America. Of immeasurable help was his wife, Eva, whose talents as an actress served Perón's cause well in attracting the support of the masses. Even her death in 1952 was turned to his political advantage; a vulgar cult was encouraged which exalted Eva as a glamorous symbol of a poor girl who had made good and as an angel of mercy (whose reckless distribution of extorted charitable funds was never accounted for). The brutalities and indignities of the Perón regime finally brought about solid opposition to his rule and resulted in his overthrow by the army, which remained in control.

Perón was the most strident of the dictators in Latin America; other virtual dictatorships included that of Trujillo who until 1961 maintained a peace of death over the Dominican Republic. Peru also experienced military rule, as did Colombia. Venezuela fell into the hands of Pérez Jiménez, who presided over the fabulous prosperity that oil had brought his country until his overthrow early in 1958. In Cuba, Batista seized control in 1952 and ruled despotically over a restive republic until the Castro rebellion of 1958. Originally applauded by the democracies, Castro's success later aroused much apprehension, for his supporters included many hard-core Communists who worked for close ties with the Soviet Union.

Brazil, Mexico, and Chile remained democratic, at least in the Latin-American context. And despite Communist influences and labor troubles, the mood of these nations was generally conservative. Concessions to businessmen and to organized labor alike kept them stable, though inflation often canceled out the unprecedented postwar economic advances.

The nations of Latin America participated enthusiastically in the United Nations. And despite Perón, inter-American friendship continued strong. In 1948 the Organization of American States supplanted the Pan American Union and developed into an agency more representative of all the republics than the Union had been. Latin-Americans complained not of United States domination but of neglect: the technical assistance of the United States was both needed and wanted. Latin America continues to pose a challenge to the Free World, for the failure to create and sustain economic democracy there plays into the hands of the Communists.

THE COMMUNIST WORLD

The iron curtain. Ravaged by war—with millions killed and millions more left homeless, with towns and cities blasted into rubble and vast areas of the countryside laid waste—the Soviet Union nevertheless faced the postwar years in a determined, aggressive mood. Early in 1946, the Soviet government inaugurated its fourth Five-Year Plan, designed to restore the war-damaged economy, to speed up the improvement of heavy industry and the collectivization of agriculture, and to expand the country's war potential. In contrast to the speedy demobilization of American forces, the Soviet Union maintained a huge land army. And military ex-

penditures mounted rapidly—from 66,000,-000,000 rubles in 1948 to 96,000,000,000 three years later. Production of consumer goods was limited; in some areas, it lagged behind the 1940 mark.

These activities were accompanied by the imposition of what Churchill described as an "iron curtain" cutting Soviet citizens off from travel abroad, from unauthorized publications, and from foreign radio programs, which were systematically jammed. The iron curtain walling off Soviet Russia from the outside world was matched by an iron conformity imposed upon ideas and opinions within the country itself. To westerners, this policy displayed the Soviets' unvoiced admission that serious shortcomings existed in the Communist system.

Russia under Khrushchev. Following Stalin's death in 1953, the world was told that henceforth the Soviet Union would be guided by the "collective leadership" of the top Communists, headed by G. M. Malenkov, who had loomed as the heir apparent during Stalin's last years. But Malenkov was soon challenged by a stocky, shrewd Ukrainian, Nikita S. Khrushchev (1894-   ), first secretary of the party; from this position, like Stalin prior to his ousting of Trotsky, he proceeded to fill the higher echelons with men favorable to himself. Early in 1955, he forced Malenkov to resign as premier and put Nikolai Bulganin in his place. Within the next three years Khrushchev ousted from the Presidium (the inner executive committee of the party) his most powerful rivals, including Malenkov, Molotov, and Marshal Zhukhov, the war hero whose prestige had surpassed his own. In March 1958, Khrushchev replaced Bulganin as premier, and his possession of this post, together with his leadership of the party, made Khrushchev undisputed master of the Soviet world.

When premier, Malenkov had sought to step up the production of consumer goods, but Khrushchev reverted to Stalin's assignment of top priority to heavy industry. Thus steel, whose production doubled between 1950 and 1957, went chiefly into the construction of plants and mills. In January 1959, Khrushchev announced his Seven-Year Plan,

At Stalin's bier in 1953 stand (from left to right) V. M. Molotov, K. Y. Voroshilov, L. P. Beria, G. M. Malenkov, N. A. Bulganin, N. S. Khrushchev, L. M. Kaganovich, and A. I. Mikoyan. Five years later, only three members of this "collective leadership" —Khrushchev, Mikoyan, and Voroshilov—remained as members of the Presidium of the party's Central Committee.

aimed at strengthening the country's economic and military might and at surpassing the leading capitalist countries in per capita output. The annual production of steel was to be increased to about 90,000,000 tons, and agricultural output was to be raised by 70 per cent. Education was to be expanded until by 1965 the number of specialists would amount to some 4,500,000, or half as many again as at the start of the plan.

These were ambitious plans, and many discounted Khrushchev's boast that the Soviet economy would surpass that of the United States in a relatively few years. But his ebullience sprang not only from an awareness of the progress of Soviet industry but also from his pride in the remarkable accomplishment of Soviet technology in launching the first space satellite, Sputnik, in 1957 and the moon rockets, Lunik I, II, and III, in 1959.

The "new" Soviet imperialism. After 1945, while most western powers were relinquishing control over their extensive colonial areas, the Soviet Union proceeded to move into eastern Europe and establish a colonial area of its own. Poland, East Germany, Rumania, Bulgaria, Hungary, and Czechoslovakia became the new imperial dependencies of the Soviet Union. In its eastern European area, Russia effectively exercised political control, directed economic activity, and forbade any cultural or educational activity which ran counter to the basic philosophy espoused by Moscow. In an area inhabited by nearly ninety million people, human labor and natural resources were exploited for the enrichment of the Soviet Union.

The technique of Russian conquest in eastern Europe after 1945 followed a common pattern. With variations here and there, the process was, first, for Moscow to secure the establishment of a coalition government in which certain key ministries, especially that of interior and police, were given to Communists. Next, full-scale elections were postponed until the Communist party felt confident of victory, and the police terrorized and imprisoned anyone who opposed them. When election day came, thousands of anti-Communists were barred from voting. In spite of western protests, the gobbling up of satellites continued, with Czechoslovakia as the last victim in 1948.

Yugoslavia's defection. One Soviet satellite, Yugoslavia, broke Moscow's grip. Marshal Tito (1892-   ), a tough wartime resistance leader and the number-one Communist in Yugoslavia, at first went along with the Soviet "line," though his national strength and geographical distance from Soviet forces enabled him to display his growing resentment against Russian interference. When Tito broke with Soviet policy in 1948, he was encouraged by the western powers and held his ground despite Moscow's economic reprisals and threats of war.

While Tito remained Communist and used western financial aid in such ideologically "correct" ventures as the build-up of heavy industry and the collectivization of agriculture, his successful defection proved a continuing source of embarrassment to the Kremlin. Moreover, his example stirred thoughts of rebellion in other satellites.

East Germany, Poland, and Hungary. In 1949 the Soviet Union organized the eastern zone of Germany into a puppet state, the German Democratic Republic. By 1950 the East German regime proceeded to break up large farms and force the expansion of heavy industry. As living standards declined, popular discontent mounted. Thousands of East Germans fled each week to West Germany; and in June 1953, severe food shortages, coupled with new decrees for longer working hours, touched off a revolt. The uprising was put down quickly, but the world was left in no doubt as to what the East Germans thought of their "workers' democracy."

Because of Poland's strong historical and cultural ties with the West, it is not surprising that communism in Poland took on a national coloration as in Yugoslavia. Wladyslaw Gomulka (1905-   ), a formerly imprisoned national Communist, gained control of the Polish United Workers' (Communist) party in 1956. Subsequently, he sent the Soviet "brass" back to Russia and permitted the workers considerable freedom of expression. Extraordinary too in a Communist state, Gomulka concluded a concordat with the Roman Catholic Church. The working alliance between church and state was due to at least two factors. The Poles are overwhelmingly Catholic, and any government seeking to win their support must come to terms with the Church. For its part, the Church recognized that its only hope of revival lay in cooperating with Gomulka's regime. Both parties in turn knew that the Russian bear, if goaded too far, could simply step across the undefended border and stamp out the gains which had already been achieved for a freer Poland. Thus any chance of full-grown Titoism in Warsaw seemed to be ruled out for the foreseeable future.

National communism had meanwhile been gaining ground in Hungary, and the news of the Polish defection touched off a demonstration in Budapest for national independence. Hungarians demanded free elections, removal of Soviet troops, an end to collectivization of farms, freedom to strike, and Hungary's withdrawal from the Soviet-controlled Warsaw Pact. The riots of October 23, 1956, quickly grew into a nation-wide revolt, and a coalition government was established under Imre Nagy, who had previously been demoted by the Stalinists. Political prisoners, including Cardinal Mindszenty, were released; and the government secured the withdrawal of Russian troops from Budapest.

On November 4, however, reinforced Soviet forces returned to the capital, where they stamped out the flames of national independence. Cardinal Mindszenty took refuge in the United States embassy, and Nagy fled to the Yugoslav legation, from which he was later enticed by an offer of safe-conduct only to be captured and afterwards treacherously executed. Thousands of freedom fighters died in the struggle, while within a year upward of 200,000 refugees sought sanctuary in the West. Although a new satellite regime was propped up by Soviet bayonets, the uprising and its implications were not forgotten, and it was plain that the Soviet leaders were not going to find it easy to shrug off the suppression of Hungarian independence.

Communism triumphs in China. The most spectacular triumph of the Communist World in the postwar years was the acquisition of China and its 600,000,000 people. During the war, Chiang Kai-shek's Nationalist government and the Chinese Communist leaders had waged a common struggle against the Japanese. The Communists emerged from the war with increased popular support and in control of an area of 90,000,000 people as well as an army of 500,000 disciplined men.

When, in October 1945, heavy fighting broke out between the forces of Chiang and those of the Communist leader, Mao Tse-tung, President Truman sent General George Marshall to mediate the conflict. He had some initial success, but subsequently fighting broke out over control of Manchuria, and Marshall returned to Washington. Chiang's strength collapsed in Manchuria in 1948, and the following year saw the rout of Nationalist armies. By the middle of 1950, Mao had become master of all of mainland China, and

In 1958 the "people's commune" was made the basic social and economic unit of Communist China. All those living within a commune (which may cover an enormous area) are fed, clothed, and generally cared for in return for their labor—thirteen hours daily, with one day off every two weeks. Here, peasant members of a commune harvest a crop of wheat.

Chiang and a remnant of his forces fled to Formosa (Taiwan). The People's Republic of China, which had already been established in Peking in 1949, was immediately recognized by the U.S.S.R., and subsequently the two countries formed a thirty-year alliance. Attempts by the Soviet Union to gain for Peking the seat at the United Nations held by Nationalist China failed, largely because of United States opposition, though the move was supported by Great Britain and India, both of which had recognized the new regime.

The new Communist leaders imposed a tightly centralized administration that extended to Manchuria, Inner Mongolia, and Chinese Turkestan; and in 1950, Red Chinese armies moved into Tibet. In order to cast China into a solid Marxist mold, intensive efforts were employed to redirect the whole course of Chinese society away from traditional patterns, and all organized opposition to the regime was systematically liquidated. Landlords were dispossessed, businessmen had their firms either nationalized or brought under rigid control, and intellectuals were subjected to "thought reform" in order to eliminate "incorrect thinking" which might prove a menace to the government.

As in the Soviet system, all power was concentrated in the Communist party, governed by the People's Central Committee, whose members occupied the chief civilian and military posts. The day-to-day work of the committee was entrusted to a smaller Politburo headed by Mao, who was also chairman of the republic—that is, head of the state. Elected representative bodies existed, but the political levers were manipulated by the Central Committee.

After checking two flagrant evils which had afflicted the Nationalists—namely, corruption and inflation—Mao's regime began to grapple with China's basic problems: a desperately low standard of living, too many people on overworked land, and an urgent need for industrialization. Millions of acres, confiscated from the owners without compensation, were set up as state farms. Other land was organized into collectives, but when the first Five-Year Plan (1953-1957) failed to eliminate the food shortage, a second plan called for the replacement of the collectives with gigantic people's communes (see illustration). Both the first and second Five-Year Plans called for an increase in industrialization and necessitated large-scale Soviet financial, military, and technical assistance.

Although great difficulties have been encountered in industrial and agricultural planning, no one can minimize the magnitude of Red China's social and economic efforts. Straining every resource to propel itself into the front line of industrial powers, Communist China is at the same time engaged in competition of historic consequence with democratic India to demonstrate to the other countries of Asia and Africa which social system can best solve the problems facing the peoples in the underdeveloped nations: hunger, poverty, disease, and illiteracy.

THE NON-ALIGNED

AFRO-ASIAN WORLD

Problems of the underdeveloped lands. The attainment of national independence by one billion people in more than four-dozen new nations is one of the most momentous happenings of our age. What happens in these former colonial territories and the degree to which their problems are solved and their objectives achieved must influence the course of world history. These new nations of Africa, the Middle East, and south Asia comprise the heart of the so-called underdeveloped lands. Before independence their leaders, impelled by the white heat of buoyant nationalism, often confidently predicted the enjoyment of a veritable Utopia once imperial rule had been removed. But independence was achieved in an uncertain and troubled world. And within these new nations problems relating to economic development, political stability, and social reform appear almost insuperable.

Certain common denominators in attitudes and objectives can be identified in the non-aligned nations. Their governments are determined to avoid any involvement in big power rivalry. They regard the Cold War as a tragic and frustrating facet of international affairs obstructing their main task—the consolidation of their fledgling regimes and an all-out attack on economic backwardness, poverty, and disease. Non-alignment holds that peaceful coexistence with all the great powers is possible; and that economic aid should be sought from any source and accepted, as long as it is tendered without "strings" attached. Non-alignment does not necessarily mean a policy of neutralism. Nehru, the late Indian leader, repeatedly stressed its positive character: the support of principles and programs deemed essential to the interests of the Afro-Asian peoples. He referred specifically to nuclear disarmament, opposition to racial discrimination, and opposition to the last vestiges of colonialism.

In all the newly independent countries, living standards are unbelievably low. This fact explains the partial or total repudiation of laissez-faire economics. It is contended that massive problems of underdevelopment should be attacked not through private enterprise, but with all the planned resources of the state. This belief has led to a prevailing form of Socialism—not necessarily Marxian—usually entailing considerable na-

tionalization of the economy, widespread governmental regulations even in the private sector of business, and, above all, the formulation of ambitious state economic development plans. In the government offices of the underdeveloped nations, one sees on the drawing boards plans for new factories, refineries, hydroelectric installations, expanded schools, and agricultural reforms. In the successful implementation of these plans, foreign aid from the more wealthy and industrialized nations will be decisive.

The late President Kennedy called attention to the needs of the non-West in his address to the Sixteenth U.N. General Assembly in September 1961. He urged the initiation of a Development Decade which was officially announced by U Thant, then Acting Secretary-General, in May 1962. Its aim is to double the standard of living in the underdeveloped lands in three decades. Western nations have been contributing large sums in aid for the developing nations. The United States has been the largest contributor. Its foreign aid budget in 1961 ran to $3.414 billion. In the same year, France tendered $952.7 million, the largest percentage of any nation in relation to gross national product. Since 1953 Soviet aid, mainly loans, has averaged about $500 million yearly.

To maximize their influence and advance common interests, the governments of the non-aligned areas have sought to encourage Afro-Asian cooperation and solidarity.

A striking demonstration of the unity of purpose exhibited by these new nations was the Afro-Asian conference convened at Bandung, Indonesia, in 1955. The twenty-nine nations represented at the conference endorsed such broad principles as support of the U.N., respect for human rights, disarmament, and the banning of nuclear weapons tests. Roundly condemned was colonialism "in all its manifestations," which could be taken to include Communist imperialism as well as old-style nineteenth-century western imperialism.

Subsequently, additional conferences have been held such as the Afro-Asian conclave in Belgrade in September 1961. Colonialism

and racial discrimination were again condemned, especially in their manifestations
as apartheid in South Africa and colonial
repression in Angola. The retention of foreign military bases by the great powers was
also criticized. Disarmament, and with it
the cessation of nuclear tests, was declared
"the most urgent task of mankind." Referring to the problem of underdevelopment,
all nations were urged to join in this common task—especially through the U.N.—"to
close, through accelerated economic, industrial and agricultural development, the ever
widening gap in the standards of living between the few economically advanced countries and the many less advanced countries." This Belgrade Conference was replete
with references to the newly found freedom
and national dignity now enjoyed by the
Afro-Asian states. At the full height of their
nascent nationalism, they are extremely
sensitive to outside interference; any attempt, especially by former imperial powers,
to exert pressure or indirect control is labeled as neocolonialism.

The leaders of most Afro-Asian states,
with the notable exceptions of Malaysia,
Nigeria, and India, contend that western
parliamentary forms are not suited to their
countries' needs. They argue that people
lack experience in the machinery of democracy, and poor nations can hardly afford the
luxury of political partisanship. The two-
party system has been ruled out because
critical problems exist with little time in
which to solve them. The new nations may
retain the surface features of parliamentary
democracy, but essentially their governments are one-party states. Usually these
governments have at their head an outstanding charismatic leader. His function is
to act as a unifying and energizing symbol
for the masses. In this category fall Nyerere
in Tanganyika, Kenyatta in Kenya, Banda
in Nyasaland, Touré in Guinea, Nasser in
Egypt, and Ayub Khan in Pakistan.

The successful operation of such one-
party states requires considerable dexterity
and wisdom. If a single, united national
consensus is to be maintained, various interests and points of view must be respected

and fully explored. Should those in power
ignore, or even stifle, variant opinions and
interests, outright dictatorship and, eventually, revolution must result.

Whether these one-party states will revert to the more traditional machinery of
western democracy, once economic levels
have been substantially raised and political
stability realized, remains to be seen. It
seems likely, however, that such a transformation—if it comes—will take considerable time. It is also probable that the ultimate Afro-Asian political norm, while reflecting much from western political experience, will differ in important respects
and mirror the distinctive traditions and
conditions of the Non-Western World.

India and Pakistan. In previous chapters
we have traced the story of the struggle for
home rule in India. In 1942 London offered
India dominion status at the end of the war
—a proposal rejected by the two chief nationalist groups—the Congress party, led by
Gandhi and Nehru, and the Muslim League,
led by Ali Jinnah.

This rejection resulted in large part from
growing Muslim-Hindu rivalry. At the end
of World War II the British Labour Government dispatched a Cabinet Mission to
India bearing the gift of independence. The
problem, however, was how to devise a
constitution for a free and undivided India
acceptable both to the Muslim League and
to the Congress party. The Cabinet Mission
offered a unique plan designed to retain the
unity of India. But the long-smouldering
Hindu-Muslim feud could not be reconciled. Ali Jinnah demanded the creation of
a separate state—Pakistan— for India's Muslim minority of some seventy million. The
prospect of splitting the subcontinent into
two nations of divergent religious faiths was
a bitter blow to many Indian patriots,
coming as it did at the hour of triumph for
India's centuries-old struggle for freedom.
But in August 1947 it was agreed that two
new states of India and Pakistan should be
established as members of the British Commonwealth, with the independent Indian
princes left free to join either state.

Self-rule at once brought crisis. Bloody

riots broke out between Muslims and Hindus; tens of thousands were butchered in an orgy of religious fanaticism, and millions of refugees sought safety in the country of their faith. In 1948 the dedicated apostle of Indian nationalism, Mahatma Gandhi, was assassinated by a Hindu bigot who resented the Mahatma's efforts to reconcile the warring communities. Although a United Nations cease-fire averted war over the disputed territory of Kashmir (predominantly Muslim in population but under the control of India), the U.N. was unable to resolve the dispute.

From the outset, independent India was governed by the Congress party under the leadership of Nehru. The constitution of 1950, establishing India as a republic, provided for a parliamentary government with a president, a prime minister, and a bicameral legislature. Stable administration was enjoyed, in part due to the legacy of an efficient civil service from colonial days.

India, as a functioning democracy, is one of the few new Afro-Asian nations that has not turned to authoritarian one-party rule. Until the fall of 1962 when Communist Chinese forces attacked its northern border, India channeled nearly all its national effort into economic development. Three Five Year Plans were launched and impressive progress was registered in heavy and light industry and in the construction of great hydroelectrical projects, such as the famous Bhakra-Nangal dam. Using 1949-1950 as a base year, the national income by 1961 had risen 42% and agricultural production had risen 41%. But this advance was diluted, unfortunately, by the tremendous growth of population. In its economic planning, India follows her "socialistic pattern," although some 90% of the economy has remained in private hands. The per capita annual income is increasing but presently is only $70. Given adequate amounts of capital for investment, both from foreign aid and domestic sources, together with some leveling off of the growth rate of population, Indian living standards could improve substantially.

In October 1962, India received a rude

The late Jawaharlal Nehru presses his palms together in the traditional greeting of India.

shock. New Delhi had always been friendly to Peking and had labored long and hard to have Communist China admitted into the U.N. In the late 1950's, Mao Tse-tung's government began to make claims, amounting to 52,000 square miles of mountainous terrain, along the northern border of India. Armed thrusts were made in 1959 and were followed by full-scale invasion in October 1962. The badly-equipped Indian forces were disastrously routed. In response to requests for aid, the United States and Britain sent modern arms. Following her advances, China pulled back her forces but kept much of the conquered territory. The Chinese motivation for the attack is not clear. One explanation is that Communist China is determined to prevent India from becoming a flourishing democracy, which could serve as an example to the rest of Asia. China's aim can best be realized by making India divert her resources from economic development into nonproductive armaments.

Nehru as Prime Minister guided India's destiny with a masterful touch from its independence until his death in May 1964. In international affairs he earned widespread acclaim for his peace endeavors and for his eloquent voice in behalf of the Afro-Asian peoples. He achieved important legislation in land reform, in education, and in advancing the status of women. Nehru's death caused fears that India's democratic form of government might terminate, but the election of Shri Lal Bahadur Shastri (1904-   ) as Prime Minister dispelled them.

Pakistan, however, has not enjoyed political stability. A geographic anomaly, this state consists of two segments, East and West Pakistan, separated from each other by a thousand miles. More advanced than East Pakistan, the western segment virtually monopolized the governmental services as well as the lion's share of appropriations, with the result that chronic discontent existed among the Muslim Bengalis in East Pakistan. Furthermore, both sections were plagued by political corruption, which was by no means ended when the country became a republic in 1956. The country teetered on the brink of chaos, and one disgusted Pakistani wrote: "The leaders were conspiring, the common man was perspiring, the nation was expiring, and alas, not a soul was inspiring."[1] Amid these circumstances, General Ayub Khan (c. 1908-   ), whose avowed purpose was to save his country from avaricious politicians, seized control of the government. General Ayub introduced land reforms, got rid of much political corruption, and cracked down on black market operations.

As in India, priority has been given to the gigantic task of raising living standards. Pakistan is handicapped by the absence of vital resources for industrialization, such as iron and coal. The Second Five Year Plan for economic development was announced in 1960, and more than a billion dollars was pledged in economic aid by the United States and an Aid-to-Pakistan Consortium.

General Ayub asserts that western parliamentary government is not suited for his country where the masses, mainly illiterate villagers, lack political experience. While he holds the reins of government strongly in his own hands, he has devised an interesting scheme called Basic Democracies. Its purpose is to give the common man an opportunity to vote and participate in local government. In addition, the common man participates with his fellows in electing an electoral college of 80,000 representatives, who in turn elect the members of the national legislature and the provincial lawmaking bodies. Presumably, as education and living standards improve in Pakistan, greater opportunities to participate in government will be granted.

Since 1947 the Kashmir quarrel has hung over the Indian subcontinent like a threatening cloud. Pakistanis deplore India's long refusal to carry out its promise of a plebiscite to ascertain the wishes of the Kashmiris. From time to time armed clashes have taken place along the disputed border. China's invasion of India only sharpened the controversy. Pakistan indignantly opposed the shipment by Britain and the United States of arms to India, fearing that they might be used against her. In response, Pakistan moved closer to Peking by signing transport and trade agreements. As long as the Kashmir issue remains unsolved, this Pakistani rapprochement with Communist China adds a new complication to India's foreign problems.

A hopeful note was the release from prison in April 1964 of Kashmir's Sheik Abdullah and Prime Minister Shastri's subsequently announced desire to end the Kashmir dispute.

Southeast Asia. A treasury of natural resources, southeast Asia has been in upheaval since the end of World War II. From 1946 to 1954, war raged in Indo-China. At the core of the upheaval were the two forces of nationalism and communism.

In 1946, France granted a measure of autonomy to Cambodia and Laos, but the crucial problem was the future status of Vietnam. There the nationalist movement was led by the Communist Ho Chi Minh, who in 1945 had proclaimed the Republic of Vietnam immediately after the surrender of the Japanese occupation forces. In the year 1948, France recognized Vietnam but

American and South Vietnamese troops unload supplies during the frustrating war in South Vietnam against the Vietcong.

was unwilling to accept the domination of Ho Chi Minh's Communist Vietminh party. Civil war ensued, with the Soviet Union and Communist China supporting Ho Chi Minh. In July 1954, Vietnam was split by international agreement into a French-protected state in the south and a Communist state in the north. The south soon cut all formal ties with France and proclaimed its independence. Its President, Ngo Dinh Diem, set about strengthening his regime with the help of American military and economic aid. Ignoring the 1954 Geneva Agreement, Communist guerrillas, the Vietcong, from North Vietnam began to terrorize the country. Their attacks increased in strength and boldness. Endeavoring to counter this danger, U.S. military aid to South Vietnam was stepped up in 1961, and more than 16,000 American personnel were subsequently provided in an advisory and training capacity. The tide appeared to be turning against the Vietcong late in 1962, but after the summer of the next year the situation rapidly worsened.

The Diem regime alienated many South Vietnamese. Government intolerance against the Buddhist majority, student discontent, and repression weakened further the people's will to oppose the Communist threat. In November 1963, Diem was assassinated and his regime toppled. An army Junta took over only to be replaced by another military coup in January 1964. At the end of the year a civilian premier, Tram Van Huong, was appointed; General Khanh, the military strong man, became Chief of Staff. In 1964 U.S. aid to South Vietnam amounted to $1.5 million a day. America was thus making a major effort to prevent this area from coming under Communist domination. This country, together with its unstable neighbors Laos and Cambodia, would be the logical springboard for Communist expansion southward and westward menacing all of southeast Asia.

Following World War II, the Dutch colonial empire felt the force of nationalism. After Japan's surrender, the rich islands of Java and Sumatra were in the hands of nationalists who proclaimed the Republic of Indonesia. Subsequently, the Dutch and the nationalists agreed to the creation of an independent federal state to be known as the United States of Indonesia, but suspi-

Achmed Sukarno, lifetime president of Indonesia, speaks at a rally in West Irian shortly after it was turned over to Indonesia.

cions and rivalries led to open warfare. With the help of United Nations mediation, sovereignty was accorded the new state in 1949. Second only to India in size and importance in southern Asia, Indonesia had a population of nearly one hundred million with unrivaled natural resources that have barely been developed.

Independence did not bring political stability to Indonesia. Insufficient training in self-government, an incompetent civil service, and unstable coalition governments contributed to the uneasy state of affairs. President Achmed Sukarno's belief that Indonesia required a "guided democracy"— benevolent paternalism in disguise—helped foment sporadic rebellions and strengthened the position of the local Communists. In international affairs, Indonesia consistently took a non-aligned antiwestern position.

Two nations in southeast Asia gained independence in a relatively peaceful fashion. The United States granted the Philippines independence in 1946, and Britain awarded Burma its freedom about two years later. When grants of independence robbed the native Communist groups of the anticolo-

nialism issue, they resorted to guerrilla warfare against the governments in power. Although vigorous leadership by President Ramón Magsaysay in the Philippines and U Nu in Burma defeated the rebels, many problems still remained to be solved.

After 1945, in the rich tin and rubber region of Malaya, a fanatical Communist minority carried on guerrilla terrorism to intimidate both the British authorities and the native populace. Not until 1957 did Britain recognize the Federation of Malaya as independent and a member of the British Commonwealth. The new government maintained close ties with the West and continued action against the Communists, who by 1959 numbered only a few hundred jungle terrorists. Under its dynamic prime minister, the able Tengku Abdul Rahman, the Federation of Malaya enjoyed mounting prosperity. Its per capita income was one of the highest in Asia. With British support the Prime Minister carried through the plan for a unique political union, the Federation of Malaysia. This new organization, established in 1963, consisted of the Federation of Malaya, the island of Singapore, and three territories in former British Borneo: Sabah (North Borneo), Sarawak, and Brunei. The purpose was to dilute Communist influence emanating from Singapore and for its component territories to enjoy shared regional development. Strong opposition, however, was forthcoming from Indonesia even before the federation was formed.

Threat of war against the Netherlands resulted in the acquisition by Indonesia of Dutch New Guinea. In 1963 Sukarno threatened force to "crush" Malaysia, which he denounced as an example of western neocolonialism. The Federation perhaps was seen as an obstacle to Sukarno's ambition to expand Indonesian influence and dominance in southeast Asia. Ten thousand troops were stationed in Indonesian Borneo and along the borders of Sabah and Sarawak; in Brunei guerrillas carried on harassing tactics. With the uncertainty in South Vietnam and Sukarno's "confrontation" with Malaysia, southeast Asia constituted one of the most ominous threats to peace in 1964.

Crises in the Arab lands. Possessing most of the world's known oil resources and forming a vital artery of east-west communication, the Middle East has proved a particularly explosive area since World War II. In 1945 the former French mandates of Syria and Lebanon became independent after conflicts with the French, while Jordan, previously under British protection, was granted independence in 1946.

Another British mandate, Palestine, soon became the battleground for two rival nationalisms: Arab and Jewish. In 1948, after British control terminated and the new state of Israel was proclaimed, war broke out between the young republic and seven Arab states. Although the U.N. arranged an armistice in 1949 which acknowledged the Israeli victory, peace was not restored because the Arabs refused to recognize the legal existence of the new state.

The Palestine campaign, in which Egypt had participated, revealed the poor leadership and defective military supplies of the Egyptian forces, resulting from widespread governmental corruption. In 1952 a clique of army officers seized the government in Cairo and forced the dissolute king into exile. Corrupt politicians were convicted, large estates were broken up for distribution to the peasants, and in 1953 a republic was proclaimed. Subsequently, the strongest officer, Colonel Gamal Abdel Nasser (1918-   ), assumed leadership and became the rallying figure for fanatic nationalism not only in Egypt but among Arabs everywhere.

Nasser's plan to construct a high dam at Aswan brought offers of American and British assistance. But when his request for arms was refused by Washington, he turned to the Soviet bloc, and the offer of American aid was abruptly canceled. Nasser retaliated in July 1956 by nationalizing the Suez Canal, from whose shipping tolls he expected to finance the dam.

Two years earlier, British troops had been withdrawn from their base in the Canal Zone, and an agreement signed at that time between London and Cairo stipulated that the Canal was to continue as an international highway "that shall always be free and open,

Gamal Abdel Nasser, President of the United Arab Republic, demonstrates his charisma with the Egyptian masses.

in time of war as in time of peace, to every vessel of commerce or of war without distinction of flag." Following Nasser's seizure, which Britain and France interpreted as a threat to their national interests, a conference was held in London to determine whether some form of international control could be agreed upon. Egypt refused to denationalize the zone, and the issue was taken to the Security Council, where various proposals by France and Britain were blocked by the Soviet veto.

Meanwhile, Egyptian guerrillas were filtering over the border into Israeli territory and Israel-bound shipping was harassed as it sought use of the Canal. The upshot was the Israeli invasion of Egypt. Two days later, British and French troops invaded the Canal Zone, ostensibly to clear the combatants away from this vital artery. But when the Suez adventure was roundly condemned by both the United States and the Soviet Union, Britain and France bowed to the General Assembly's call for a cease-fire, the Canal remained under Egyptian control, and a U.N. emergency force was organized to patrol the Egyptian-Israeli border.

In the final analysis, the prestige of the U.N. was enhanced, Nasser's position was

Prime Ministers Dr. Nyerere (left) of Tanzania, Dr. Obote (center) of Uganda, and Jomo Kenyatta (right) of Kenya attend a conference of the governments of East Africa in Nairobi.

strengthened, and the West's moral position fell, while the Soviet Union continued to pose as a defender of Arab nationalism. The Suez Canal issue remained controversial, for Nasser, disregarding his pledges, in defiance of the U.N. persisted in denying the use of the Canal to Israel-bound shipping.

Fear of Soviet penetration in the Middle East prompted the United States Congress in 1956 to adopt the Eisenhower Doctrine, which promised help to any nations subjected to armed aggression from Communist sources. Early in 1958 the Middle East caldron boiled over again. Nasser's star continued to rise as he posed as the champion of Arab nationalism, the agent of antiwesternism, and the symbol of Muslim unity. In February he succeeded in persuading Syria to join with Egypt in the United Arab Republic. As antiwestern sentiment spread,

July witnessed the murder of the king of Iraq and the overthrow of the prowestern government by the military dictator General Abdul Karim Kassem (1914-1963), who shortly took the country out of Bagdad Pact membership. Simultaneously, circles in both Bagdad and Cairo began to exert pressure upon Lebanon and Jordan. When these countries, unwilling to be dominated either by the United Arab Republic or Iraq, appealed for aid, American marines were landed in Lebanon under the Eisenhower Doctrine, and British troops were flown into Jordan. Both Cairo and Moscow labeled these acts as "aggression." The issue was taken to the U.N., where the Arab states agreed to observe nonintervention in one another's internal affairs and the secretary-general consented to facilitate the withdrawal of foreign troops.

Western fears of Soviet aims in the Middle East were strengthened by Moscow's aid to Egypt in beginning construction of the Aswan dam. In the meantime, however, Cairo had apparently become wary of the high price to be paid for continued dependence upon Moscow. As 1959 ended, Egypt resumed diplomatic relations with Britain. This period also witnessed an open breach between Cairo and Bagdad.

The Middle East continued to be unstable and tumultuous after 1959; revolts occurred in Iraq and Syria. General Kassem of Iraq was assassinated (in 1963) and his government overthrown. In Syria eight governments had been toppled by revolts between 1950 and 1964. Three dominant ingredients contributed to this situation: emotional and fierce nationalism coupled with political inexperience on the part of the masses; prevailing economic frustration based on universally low standards of living for the common man (often complicated by the misuse of great wealth by a privileged aristocracy); and, finally, the driving objective of Pan-Arabism, the achievement of some form of political unity for all the Arab world, which would increase its influence and status in world affairs.

The central factor in this unstable situation was Egypt and its leader, Nasser. This idol of the Arab world saw himself as the "Bismarck" who would unite all the states of the Middle East. There was, however, much rivalry between the Arab leaders. Syria withdrew from the United Arab Republic in 1961, a setback for Nasser. The following year a revolt in Yemen against the conservative ruling Imman brought a new government, the Yemeni Arab Republic, into power. The deposed Imman, however, continued to fight; thereupon, Nasser intervened on behalf of the Yemeni Republic with 28,000 Egyptian troops. The Yemen civil war exposed Arab rivalries as both Jordan and Saudi Arabia sent arms to the Imman.

Notwithstanding the numerous revolts and coups, important economic gains are being made in the Middle East. Encouraging progress can be noted in most areas in the discovery, utilization, and control of new water resources. The desert may bloom again. The great Aswan High Dam on the upper Nile is the most ambitious and exciting water development in the Middle East. Costing one billion dollars and scheduled for completion in 1970, it will dam up a lake 365 miles long and add approximately one million precious acres to Egypt's cultivable area.

There is some analogy between the adventurism of Nasser and Sukarno. The former has done much to rid his country of parasitic pashas and raise the standard of living, but Nasser is also called by a siren voice—of Arab leadership. He is now using every means—diplomacy, force, and a constant stream of propaganda from Radio Cairo—to achieve mastery in the Middle East. Some perceptive observers believe that while Egypt is the logical nucleus around which unity could be built, the best approach to this end would be for Nasser to concentrate upon the task of showing all Arabs that he is providing a higher standard of living, industrial development, and political stability.

Nation-making in Africa. Subject to disposal by the victors of World War II, the

Italian colonies in northeastern Africa were geographically and culturally linked to the Middle East, where, as we have seen, nationalism was boiling to the surface. Libya became a sovereign state in 1951, and in the following year Eritrea was federated with the independent state of Ethiopia. The former Anglo-Egyptian Sudan was established by Britain as an independent republic in 1956, despite Nasser's desire to see the long Nile valley become a single state controlled from Cairo. For backward Somalia the U.N. specified an Italian trusteeship with a terminal date of 1960, a commitment which was fulfilled when Somalia was proclaimed independent in that year. Britain relinquished British Somaliland at the same time, and a union was proclaimed which put pressure on tiny French Somaliland and the Somali sections of Ethiopia to realize the dream of a Greater Somali state covering the horn of Africa. Thus the independence of northeastern Africa was virtually completed.

As nationalist activity among the Muslims in North Africa increased—in no small part the result of violently anti-imperialist agitation from Nasser's Cairo radio—France surrendered its protectorates over Tunisia and Morocco, and Spain conceded its holdings to the new kingdom of Morocco. By the mid-1950's, the issue of political independence had been decided in North Africa, except for Algeria. After a long and bitter revolutionary war against France, Algeria finally became one of the sovereign nations of the world in July 1962.

West Africa was the next area to feel the full force of nationalism. In fact this area was to lead the way to the realization of nationalist aspirations among the Negro peoples of Black Africa. Realistic British appraisals of the situation and British methods of rule had pointed toward self-government. In the British colonies of the Gold Coast and Nigeria and in the French coastal areas of the Ivory Coast and Senegal as well, there existed by African standards a high degree of prosperity and literacy. The conversion of the Gold Coast into the independent Negro state of Ghana was achieved almost entirely without disturbance. Except for trade representatives, missionaries, and government officials, Ghana had no white settlers to stiffen resistance against the transfer of power from white hands to black, and the native politicians represented in the main an orderly and responsible electorate.

Achieved without revolution, the independence of Ghana in 1957 was a development of historic consequence. Here at last was a new African Negro state—the only such state except for Liberia—and the first to rise out of colonial subservience to the white man. Kwame Nkrumah (1909-   ) of Ghana was a bold voice trumpeting Pan-African nationalism, and the march of the colonial Africans toward independence was greatly accelerated.

The next step was the separation of the West African colony of Guinea from the French system. The failure to comprehend the strength and nature of postwar nationalism had cost France dearly in Indo-China and North Africa. Therefore, in 1958, De Gaulle offered French colonies autonomy within the French system or immediate independence. All the colonies chose autonomy and gradual evolution toward ultimate independence except for Guinea, whose inhabitants responded to the skillful appeals of Sékou Touré (1922-   ). Touré was banking on the development of Guinea's bauxite and other resources through the competitive bidding of the Cold War powers to aid in the advancement of underdeveloped lands.

The march of African nationalism was now becoming irresistible. By the middle of 1960 the map of Africa had been transformed. The part of Togoland formerly held as a British trust territory had joined its neighbor Ghana, while that part under French trusteeship became the diminutive independent state of Togo. Sierre Leone, the colony founded for emancipated British slaves, was granted independence in 1961. Most important among the British colonies in West Africa was Nigeria, with its population of 35,000,000. Granted independence in October 1960, Nigeria faced an uncertain future, largely because of the precarious balance of power between its

three major regions, whose tribal and religious loyalties bred separatist tendencies.

Meanwhile, other French colonies were moving rapidly from autonomy to independence. In 1958 Madagascar became autonomous and two years later achieved full independence as the Malagasy Republic. Also, in 1960, French trusteeship over the Cameroons ended, and a republic was set up. In the same year, Dahomey, Ivory Coast, and Upper Volta proclaimed their complete separation from France, while Senegal, Maritania, Mali, Niger, Chad, Gabon, Congo, and the Central African Republic, though achieving full independence, chose to retain membership in the loose association called the French Community, similar to the British Commonwealth.

Late in 1959, anti-European riots broke out in the Belgian Congo; native leaders demanded immediate independence, and the Belgian government abandoned its plans for a tutorship period almost before they were put into effect. Belgium's lack of wisdom in its earlier neglect of preparations for self-rule was compounded by the obtuseness of native nationalist leaders themselves, who wanted immediate sovereignty for their country although they had had no higher administrative experience than that gained from clerical positions. Independence was granted in June 1960 amidst an alarming deterioration of law and order. Operations in the great mines came to a halt, and the economy of the Congo was paralyzed as Belgian engineers, technicians, and businessmen fled from the strife-torn area with their families. Tribe fought tribe, and native troops resisted both the white officers and the leaders of their own race who were the officials of the new Republic of the Congo. U.N. intervention was finally requested.

Major changes were developing in British East Africa. In the trust territory of Tanganyika, granted independence in 1961, the small white settler group worked harmoniously with the African nationalists, led by Julius Nyerere. In Uganda, nationalistic feelings were strong, but independence was postponed until 1962 because of intertribal rivalries. The colony of Kenya presented serious problems, as a small but very important European settler community—numbering about 50,000 as compared to the native population of some 6,000,000—sought to adjust to the impact of African nationalism. Still in the state of tribalism, the great mass of Africans only dimly understood the nationalistic programs of Tom Mboya and others of the small group of native leaders. As a result of a constitutional conference held in London in 1960 and attended by representatives of both the settlers and the natives, the Africans were to enjoy a majority in the legislative council, although the British government still held ultimate political control. No doubt Kenya would become a self-governing state, but if the system of "one man, one vote" was put into operation too quickly, the chaotic conditions which hampered the independence of the Congo might be repeated in Kenya. In spite of these complications, independence was gained in 1963. Zanzibar secured its sovereignty the same year, and in 1964 merged with Tanganyika to become Tanzania.

Nationalism also made its impact in British Central Africa. In 1953 the three territories of Nyasaland, Northern Rhodesia, and Southern Rhodesia united in the Federation of Rhodesia and Nyasaland. In a total population of 7,000,000, the Europeans numbered only 300,000. But as in Kenya, many of the educational and social services were developed through the wealth of this small minority. Racial discrimination, while not as rigorous as in South Africa, was sufficiently strong to antagonize the educated and politically conscious African minority. In 1959, led by Dr. Hastings Banda, the natives in Nyasaland who resented being made part of a European-dominated federation rioted, and the disturbances were put down only after a state of emergency had been declared. Mounting African nationalism and unrest indicated that the days of the Federation were numbered.

The Portuguese colonies of Angola and Mozambique were also restless. In 1960 native riots and insurrection broke out in Angola against the harshly oppressive Portuguese authorities, and Portugal threatened to quit the United Nations when the subject was brought up for debate in the General Assembly. Despite vigorous attempts by Portugal to stamp out the Angolan uprising, the revolt simmered on, taking a heavy toll of Portuguese resources. It was unlikely that the winds of change could be kept from blowing over these territories for long.

Observers the world over have been aware of the mounting tension in the Republic of South Africa, where the European minority has denied basic political and economic rights to the African majority by means of apartheid—the harsh policy of racial discrimination. Denied the right to vote, the Africans were forced to carry passes wherever they went, could not engage in certain types of skilled work, and had to accept an education inferior to that offered in the white schools. In the spring of 1960, the Africans made widespread demonstrations against their second-class citizenship. Armed clashes which culminated in the massacre of sixty-eight unarmed Africans at Sharpeville and the wounding of several hundred more brought world-wide censure of the South African government. How long the white community could hold down the lid of this African boiler would remain a question of international interest. The African independence movement neared its goal of complete decolonization as 1963 ended. Thirty-one new African nations had now achieved independence. In December the Central African Federation was dissolved, leaving the status of white-dominated Southern Rhodesia unclear. The European minority of Southern Rhodesia asked Britain to acknowledge its independence; but London, sensitive to world opinion and to that of the Afro-Asian members of the Commonwealth, sought to ensure the expansion of African political rights before granting any change in status. European domination in the Republic of South Africa and in Portugal's African territories was placed on the defensive as the U.N. brought increasing pressure to bear on these states.

All during 1964 disturbing events marred the African scene; armed revolts, frontier wars, and tribal massacres dominated the headlines. In East Africa British troops were called in to quell army mutinies. Somali guerrillas carried on virtual war over boundary disputes between Ethiopia and Kenya. In the diminutive state of Rwanda a vendetta was carried out against the former ruling caste, the aristocratic Watussi, by their former serfs, the Bahutu. Thousands of Watussi were killed, and some 150,000 fled to neighboring territory. After the exit from the Republic of the Congo of the U.N. peace-keeping force, full-scale civil war erupted with Communist China supporting the rebels. Perhaps these somber developments constituted a temporary halt in Africa's march toward stable nationhood. Undue pessimism was premature but unrealistic optimism was equally unjustified. Much time would have to elapse before Africa's future could be properly evaluated.

THE WORLD

TODAY AND TOMORROW

The Cold War. After the settlement of the Korean conflict and the death of Stalin, the world appeared to be moving in the direction of "peaceful coexistence," or at least toward improved relations between the Big Two. In 1955, as we have seen, the Soviets agreed to an Austrian peace treaty. In the same year there occurred the summit conference of the Big Four at Geneva, the first meeting of the heads of state since Potsdam a decade earlier. At the Geneva Conference, discussions were held on German reunification, disarmament, and the reduction of trade barriers between East and West. Although progress was blocked on many points, particularly on the German question, relations between statesmen were cordial and a spirit of good will pervaded the gatherings. Many observers felt that the danger of a hot war had receded and that a beginning had been made in removing tensions through negotiations rather than by force.

In 1959, Khrushchev's coast-to-coast tour of the United States, in which the Soviet leader mingled with Americans from all walks of life, marked the first occasion that a ruler of the Russian people had set foot on American soil. Not always amiable, Khrushchev nevertheless seemed to show a real desire to understand America and its citizens. Furthermore, in an appearance before the General Assembly, Khrushchev announced that the U.S.S.R. was prepared to negotiate with the West on limited objectives, such as the withdrawal of foreign troops from western Europe, the creation in central Europe of an atom-free zone, and the signing of a nonaggression pact between NATO and the Warsaw Pact nations. Heartened by these proposals, the western powers invited him to a Paris summit meeting in May of the following year. The Kremlin accepted the invitation, but just before the meeting the world was startled by President Eisenhower's official admission that a plane forced down in Russia was an American U-2 reconnaissance craft. Accusing the United States of aggression and treachery, Khrushchev scuttled the conference. Although the western leaders made conciliatory gestures, Eisenhower rejected the Russian demand for an official apology, whereupon the Kremlin chief attacked the West and its leaders in reckless and abusive language. When the U-2 incident was taken to the U.N., the delegates—well aware of the many acts of Soviet espionage since 1945—dismissed the charge of aggression. Though critics decried the confusion exhibited by United States officials following the U-2 incident, the irresponsibility of Khrushchev's attack shocked and angered the Free World. The general consensus was that he must bear the onus for the failure of the summit.

An uneasy equilibrium characterized the international scene in the decade of the 1950's as the Cold War continued on many fronts. The two superpowers engaged in an arms race, competing in the stock-piling of atomic bombs as well as of conventional armaments, and in the development of still more deadly weapons. Paralleling the arms race, as we have seen, was the formation of tightly knit defensive military alliances outside the auspices of the U.N. In addition, while the United States and the Soviet Union channeled large amounts of money and energy into economic aid and propaganda in order to "sell" their respective ways of life to others, vast sums were simultaneously put into military aid. International tension had come dangerously near the breaking point in such areas as Korea, Indo-China, and the Suez Canal Zone.

Although the term "Cold War" continued to be widely used in the United States in the 1960's, the expression conformed less to the situation. Since the Cold War is heavily dependent upon a state of mind or climate of opinion, its status may change without being reflected immediately in overt action. It is not something that was officially declared on a given day, and unless it becomes "hot," it will not end in that way. The Cold War is becoming more the normal jockeying for influence of nation-states in a balance-of-power world, as before 1914 or in the period between the two world wars. Ideological warfare between the United States and the Soviet Union lacked the substance of the 1950's. In the 1960's there was evidence of mutual acceptance of coexistence: Russia's encouragement of tourists from the West; the establishment of diplomatic relations between West Germany and the U.S.S.R.; and pacts for the exchange of American and Soviet cultural, scientific, and agricultural personnel. In the new competition between the Soviet Union and Communist China for influence in the non-Caucasian parts of the world, China was fomenting race concepts, thus pushing the U.S.S.R. and the United States somewhat closer together.

The 1960's contrasted with the 1950's in the solidarity of the two sides in the Cold War. The United States was still the most powerful leader of the so-called Free World, but there was growing disagreement between it and other Free World nations over trade with and recognition of Communist countries, the military organization of NATO, and the proper policy in southeast Asia. France under De Gaulle was an exceptionally independent partner, more and more often refusing to participate in joint enterprises either with the United States or Great Britain.

The Soviet Union unquestionably still dominated eastern Europe; yet, there was considerable independence among the satellites, and a serious split was developing between the Soviet Union and its most powerful ally, bellicose China. "Communism" could no longer be considered a monolithic world-wide movement. The governments of the United States and Great Britain recently demonstrated again that the smooth and peaceful transition to new leaders is a powerfully established tradition. In the Communist world no such established tradition exists, as exemplified by N. S. Khrushchev's sudden and unexpected fall from power in October 1964. The Cold War, which was never static, should not be viewed in the 1960's as it was in the 1950's.

Trouble spots. Relations between the United States and the Soviet Union have been made more complex by the existence of troubled areas over the globe. Let us now focus upon these areas and their problems.

At the close of the 1950's, Japan's status as a member of the Free World was questionable. Violent opposition from labor and student groups, often financed and directed by local Communists, marked the passage in 1960 of a ten-year treaty with the United States. Mob violence was so menacing that Eisenhower's state visit to Japan was canceled, a definite blow to United States prestige. As the fourth industrial nation in the world, boasting the highest standard of living in Asia, Japan could continue to be a symbol of prosperous democracy and a friend to the West. However, its proximity to the Communist World, its need to foster trade with the Chinese mainland and southeast Asia in order to sustain its rapidly growing population, and the avowed antimilitarism of many of its people were factors that could swing Japan into the orbit of the Non-aligned World or even into the Communist bloc. An important element in Japan's industrial prosperity and its competitive trade position was its freedom from the burden of a heavy military budget. Japanese military defense depended entirely upon United States military forces based in Japan. In the 1960's the United States began to discuss the same policy toward Japan that it followed with other allies, including Germany, another former enemy state; namely, that the ally should bear part of the cost of its own defense by limited rearmament. Japan has demurred. No nation was in a better position to point out that conventional armaments, such as Germany was permitted, were at best a waste of resources against a nuclear-armed foe.

The status of Berlin and that of Germany as well continued to hang like a menacing cloud in the international sky. With its prosperity and democracy, West Berlin was a symbol of western liberty and free enterprise—and therefore a thorn in the Russian side, a vexatious spot of contagion within the satellite of East Germany. In 1958 Moscow called for the relinquishment of western occupation rights and the transformation of Berlin into a "free city." To frustrate the mass exodus of East Germans to the West and to reduce western occupation rights, the Communists in August 1961 built a wall in Berlin along the edge of their sector. The Soviets also threatened to hand over responsibilities in Germany to the East German regime, an announcement designed to force western recognition of the Communist puppet government there. The western powers stood firm and insisted that Berlin's future was bound up with the larger question of German reunification, an issue which could only be decided by free all-German elections. But the Soviet Union was determined to delay indefinitely the unification of Germany, for this would mean the creation of a large and powerful state capable of challenging Russian foreign policy in the future.

The deep fear and distrust of a powerful Germany has not been dissipated in continental Europe, even though Hitler has been dead nearly twenty years. When in October 1963 Chancellor Adenauer finally resigned and turned over his office to Ludwig Erhard, longtime finance minister, no immediate change in West German policy developed. The West German government continued in firm alliance with the United States. In fact, it was the only nation that showed much enthusiasm for the United States program for a multilateral force in NATO military organization. The United States, the only great power capable of withstanding Russian pressure in Europe, was West Germany's major hope for continued independence, let alone reunification. De Gaulle continued to block every move for further political integration of western Europe—in which Germany would inevitably play a major role—and could hardly be regarded as an adequate substitute for the United States as a protector of Germany.

The progress of tiny Israel has confounded its foes. In this country of desert wasteland and limited natural resources, irrigation projects were built, agriculture was extended, and new industries were established. In the councils of the nations, Israel earned respect as a stable and democratic regime. But its future was uncertain despite the energy and dedication of its people. The antipathy between this small population of less than two million people and its more than forty million Arab neighbors continued. Border clashes were frequent; the presence of nearly one million Arab refugees, who once lived in the area now occupied by the Israelis, was a constant irritant to Arab nationalists. And, although Israel enjoyed substantial economic growth, still it did not earn its own living. From 1948 to 1955, its unfavorable balance of trade was $1,750 million, a deficit financed by loans, gifts, and German reparations. The future of Israel depended not only upon the issue of war or peace with its neighbors but also upon the continuance of outside aid for several decades.

Apprehension over China's expansionism continued to increase international tensions. In 1958 the Communists launched a heavy bombardment against Nationalist forces on Quemoy Island, one hundred miles west of Formosa. Although the bombardment was called off after the United States Seventh Fleet moved into the area, the future of Formosa, and with it the question of our policy toward Red China, remained a troublesome problem. A revolt in Tibet in 1959 was promptly suppressed, but the Dalai Lama fled to India. Tension between China and India led, as we read, to a Chinese attack on India and a brief border war in 1962. Three years later another tragic crisis developed when an undeclared war began between India and Pakistan over Kashmir, and Communist China threatened to enter the fray against India over a boundary dispute. The intervention of the UN brought about an uneasy ceasefire.

Elsewhere in the Afro-Asian world changes occurred rapidly and new perils arose. In Africa, nations such as Gambia, Kenya, and Zambia gained their independence from Great Britain. Despite substantial world disapproval, Angola and Mozambique continued under the control of Portugal. The Central African Federation was dissolved and Southern Rhodesia, governed by a small white minority, threatened to declare its full independence from Britain.

In southeast Asia the Federation of Malaysia was weakened by the secession of the strategic island of Singapore. In neighboring Indonesia a full-fledged civil war threatened to erupt at the end of 1965. South Vietnam, however, was the most critical area. In order to prevent the country from falling to the Communist Viet Cong, President Johnson in 1965 commenced bombing raids in both North and South Vietnam and by early the next year had committed 200,000 American troops to a sizeable war. The threat of world war diminished as Sino-Soviet disagreement over Vietnam became apparent.

Another troubled area was Cuba. Since his coup in 1959, Fidel Castro had introduced some badly needed reforms, especially in land redistribution and the construction of new schools and mass housing; but other aspects of his rule became increasingly disturbing to many of his original supporters. He soon made it clear that he would brook no opposition, and his weekly harangues before the Havana television cameras were dangerous examples of demagoguery. His cry of "keeping the machetes sharp and the rifles oiled," together with his mobilization of a people's militia, were reminiscent of Hitler's and Mussolini's techniques. Above all, Castro became increasingly anti-American and pro-Communist, although the United States continued to purchase half of Cuba's sugar at a generous subsidy well over the world market price.

Castro's controlled press and radio hurled insults at "American aggression." Within a year, American hotels, ranches, refineries, and other properties in Cuba valued at $300 million were seized with no hint of compensation. Finally, in retaliation, Washington cut off further purchases of Cuban sugar. To make the situation more serious, Khrushchev took advantage of the embarrassment of the United States by declaring that he was prepared to use Soviet rockets "to protect Cuba."

In July 1960 the Cuban charge of United States aggression was taken before the U.N. Security Council and subsequently referred to the Organization of American States. But the United States could not expect a large measure of sympathy from the OAS, for to many Latin-Americans Castro was a patriot, "the man from the hills," the Cuban David standing up to the American Goliath. The Latin-American republics saw in Castro an extremist but one who reflected their own frustrations and hopes.

In April 1961 a filibustering expedition of Cuban exiles carried out an abortive invasion attempt at the "Bay of Pigs." The unsuccessful invaders had trained in Guatemala, and the United States Central Intelligence Agency was heavily involved. Cuban-Soviet ties were strengthened. By October 1962, United States aerial reconnaissance showed Soviet missile sites in Cuba, and President Kennedy declared a naval quarantine to block further shipments of missiles, by force if necessary. A direct confrontation between the two major nuclear powers resulted. In the ensuing crisis the Soviet Union relented, dismantled the missiles, and in the next few years gradually withdrew most of the Soviet troops. Cuba remained a major Western Hemisphere crisis spot, a center of Soviet and Chinese Communist propaganda efforts, and a base for training agents to undertake subversion in other Latin American states.

The strength of democracy. Faced with the somewhat lessened hostility of the Soviet Union and the increasingly bellicose posture of Red China, and with the positive neutralism of the Non-aligned World, which often stemmed from a desire to have the best of both the opposing systems, the Free World represented democracy on trial. One may well ask wherein lies the strength of democracy today? Will government of the people, by the people, and for the people perish in the struggle for men's minds and hearts?

Admittedly, democracy has been encumbered with a basic handicap in the struggle against Marxism—a conflict in conscience, so to speak. Politically and technologically, the peoples of the Free World are the most advanced; intellectually, they are the most sophisticated. This sophistication makes it impossible for them to view the world in simple terms of black and white, good and evil, right and wrong. While the Communists justify any means, however brutal, to achieve their goals, and the non-aligned peoples appear to believe that self-government will solve all problems, proponents of democracy are ever conscious of the imperfections of their own social systems and are sorely troubled whenever democratic practice fails to measure up to democratic principles. Such conflicts of conscience have led to bitter soul-searching whenever charges against the domestic or foreign policies of the West are hurled from either the Communist or the Non-aligned worlds, and this soul searching could in turn result in a dangerous loss of self-confidence among western governments and peoples. But ultimately these bouts of conscience may prove the salvation of mankind, for they show that the Free World is remaining true to democracy's belief in freedom and human dignity.

The United Nations—an assessment. Beginning this chapter as we did with the story of the formation of the United Nations, perhaps it is most fitting to close our narrative of the chief events in the postwar period with an evaluation of the U.N. and a discussion of how it can be improved.

The Cold War has tended to overshadow the successes of the U.N. The U.N. was largely responsible for ending warfare in Palestine, Indonesia, and the Congo, and its on-the-spot activities did much to keep the Cyprus and Kashmir disputes from exploding into full-scale wars. Hailed as an international Magna Carta, its Universal Declaration of Human Rights (1948) enumerated for the first time the basic inalienable rights of people everywhere—thereby exerting strong moral, if not actual legal, pressure upon its signatories.

At the U.N. headquarters in New York, experts report annually on the world economic situation, while regional commissions deal with concrete problems in the major economic areas of the globe. Finding that the economic instability of underdeveloped countries constitutes one of the most vital long-range problems confronting mankind, the U.N. embarked on a Technical Assistance Administration: machinery was set up to enable technical missions to go into areas requiring assistance and also to provide for the technical training of individuals from the recipient countries. The work of the Trusteeship Council on behalf of dependent peoples helped a number of trust territories to achieve self-government, while pressure in the General Assembly persuaded colonial powers to speed up their plans for liberating colonies.

The Korean conflict convinced the western powers that the United Nations had to be strengthened in its ability to meet armed aggression, for U.N. response to the attack on South Korea had been possible only because of the coincidental absence of the Soviet delegate to the Security Council. In 1950 the United States submitted to the General Assembly a "Uniting for Peace" proposal, which would enable the Assembly to recommend that forces be provided against aggressors in cases where a veto prevented Security Council action. Although the Communist bloc castigated the resolution as a "crude violation" of the U.N. Charter, the Soviet representative cited it in 1958 in unsuccessfully seeking Council action against the United States and Britain over their moves in Jordan and Lebanon. This reversal indicated that the Soviet awareness had, in fact, been significantly amended. The problem of paying for U.N. peace-keeping forces when members oppose the purpose, however, has still not been solved. The Charter provides for suspending voting privileges for persistent delinquency, but the Soviet Union and France both declined to meet U.N. assessments for its Congo force.

Probably the most dangerous failure of the U.N. has been in regard to armaments. The disagreements of the United States and the Soviet Union over control, inspection, and a multitude of details created the worst impasse in contemporary history; and while the two giants debated, Britain and then France joined the nuclear powers. Not only was no agreement reached over control of nuclear weapons—which now included the hydrogen superbomb as well as the atomic bomb—but no real progress was registered in reducing conventional armaments. But the efforts toward disarmament persisted through a United States- and Soviet-sponsored seventeen-nation conference in Geneva, beginning in 1962. Although France refused to participate, because De Gaulle insisted upon creating an independent nuclear force, a limited success was achieved the following year. An Anglo-American-Russian test ban outlawed further nuclear testing in the atmosphere or under water, and forbade tests in space.

In the light of the U.N. performance, to what extent should the Charter be revised? Some observers believe that the U.N. should be converted into a world government with direct representation of all nations. Such a proposal raises exceedingly difficult questions: Is the surrender of national sovereignty desirable? And upon what basis would U.N. representation be apportioned? Other advocates of change argue for the scrapping of the veto—a step which would probably result in Soviet withdrawal from the organization. Although turning the U.N. largely into an anti-Soviet alliance might be welcomed in some quarters, to a majority of peoples and governments it would be a blow to the universality of the U.N. As a town meeting of the world, the U.N. is a most important forum for airing international grievances, for preventing a dangerous polarization of opposing forces into unbridgeable power blocs, and for acting as an international safety valve.

SUMMARY

The Second World War ended in victory for the Allied powers, but it was a victory without peace. In some measure, the failure to establish a peaceful world was the result of the war's legacy of global dislocation. Even more, it was due to the effects of this upheaval upon three major historic forces: liberal democracy, communism, and nationalism. Each constituted the driving and sustaining element in one of the three distinctive ideological "worlds" that crystallized after 1945—the Free, the Communist, and the Non-aligned. The interaction of these three worlds has been responsible for the state of global existence in which we find ourselves today.

The different segments of the Free World emerged from the common struggle in very different conditions of health. North America found itself with an economy stronger than any that had ever existed before, ready to embark upon the next stage of material expansion. Western Europe, on the other hand, had been ravaged both physically and psychologically, and at first its people had all they could do to struggle back to the position they had known before the war. For several critical years, observers wondered if Europe, so long the center of world civilization, could ever regain its former cultural creativity and political initiative; many feared that, spiritually exhausted, it might have suffered a fatal loss of faith in itself. But the economic recovery of western Europe and its constant experimentation with new forms of political cooperation and economic integration attest to the recuperative powers of its peoples.

Despite the strains of changing times, the Free World has remained united in its opposition to Communist expansion. Meanwhile, they have proved the inherent healthiness of democracy and its unique ability to preserve humanistic values and individual freedom while modifying the social structure. In all the nations of the Free World there have been shifts to the left and to the right —but never so far to the left as to destroy individualism and never so far to the right as to abolish legislation for social welfare.

For the Soviet Union, victory in World War II had been won at a staggering material cost. Once again, with the return of peace, every national sinew had to be strained to reduce the gap separating the Soviet economy from that of the United States, now singled out as the chief symbol of "capitalist imperialism" and the chief rival of the Soviet Union. This redoubling of effort was accompanied by the ringing down of an iron curtain, behind which the Kremlin set about creating a vast empire stretching from the Adriatic to the Pacific. But internal strains within the Soviet Union accompanied the pursuit of ambitious economic and political objectives. Among the satellites, Yugoslavia defected, and restlessness in East Germany, Poland, Hungary, and Rumania persisted. Meanwhile, Communist China sought control of the World Movement and lectured its older brother for straying from Marxist orthodoxy when Khrushchev suggested some sort of competitive coexistence with the democratic nations of the Free World.

Perhaps the farthest-flung force in the postwar world was nationalism, which erupted in virulent forms in Asia and Africa. One sovereign state after another rose from the ashes of prewar colonialism, all eager to acquire western technical skills and to accept economic assistance but all determined to reject criticism and to avoid interference. United chiefly in their sensitivity to any signs of racial arrogance in western society, the new nations of Asia and Africa have gradually come to recognize the willingness of the Free World to provide technical and economic aid, without strings; and they have also become increasingly aware of the consequences of Communist penetration.

Can these three worlds live in comparative peace? For two decades after World War II, prospects were bleak indeed, as the icy blasts from the Cold War circled the globe and each year saw the creation of new military alliances and more terrible weapons. In such an environment the United Nations could not play the role for which it was intended, but it managed to produce some success—especially in the social and economic spheres—and its survival and its continuous role as a political safety valve proved its indispensability. And for optimists, at least, there was hope that the world might be entering a new era—one in which the ever changing Cold War would be replaced by peaceful coexistence. It was a concept without glory but one for which most of the peoples of the world seemed willing to settle. Satiated with the kind of excitement produced by atomic blasts and nuclear fallout, they were prepared to get on with the job of existing and of coexisting.

Epilogue

Introduction: What's to become of Nauru?
Just south of the equator and west of the International Date Line in the Pacific lies Nauru. Though its area is less than 6000 acres and its total coastline is approximately 12 miles, Nauru is a United Nations Trust Territory administered by Australia, New Zealand, and the United Kingdom. Why all this attention to a minute island inhabited by 4000 people? In one word—phosphates. Originally, the isolated Polynesians lived by primitive farming and fishing, but before the close of the nineteenth century Germany annexed the island and phosphates were discovered there. Soon Westerners began to exploit the thick deposit of phosphates. During the next half century, the population was to double and to acquire much higher economic standards and a more complex way of life.

So far the story is not unusual. But within a few decades those phosphates—the island's only source of income—will be exhausted. Then what will happen to the Nauruans? The three administering nations and the United Nations Trusteeship Council have held long discussions on the problem, but have found no solution. Most of the Nauruans would like to be moved as a community to another island, but so far the search for the right location has proved fruitless. The suggestion that topsoil should be imported following the exhaustion of the phosphate deposits seems unlikely to be followed, since the rock formation of the island is porous and the topsoil would quickly disappear.

Nauru is an unusual case, yet it dramatizes a problem that is becoming increasingly serious in contemporary life, namely, the competing claims of the technological order on the one hand and of human values on the other. By gearing the island's economy to the extraction of phosphates, the authorities have been able to provide the Nauruans with excellent educational and medical services and many physical comforts. But these are being purchased by the exhaustion of an irreplaceable natural resource, so that in a few decades Nauru will be transformed into a barren desert on which no human beings can subsist. Meanwhile, the traditional culture pattern has already been largely destroyed.

Who is responsible for the Nauruans' plight? The Communist would blame it on economic imperialism—but that is too easy and distorted an answer for this complex problem. Actually, the Nauruans are better off economically than ever before; moreover, the motives of the administering powers are far from sinister. Phosphates are used in chemical fertilizers which in turn are employed to increase food production and living standards. Surely we need phosphates and the overall requirements of this planet's population deserve to take precedence over the local interests of the Nauruans. True, many of the world's problems are caused by man's inhumanity to man, but here a seemingly insoluble crisis has been created by using technology for two worthy goals.

Not only does the Nauruan dilemma represent conflicts between groups—between the Nauruans and other Pacific islanders, Chinese, and Europeans who have come to Nauru; it has generated tensions within the individual Nauruan as well. Externally derived technological forces and economic pressures have eroded the culture pattern into which he was born and which provided him with a sense of community and meaning. These forces threaten his future security, his ability to function as an integral member of society, and his sense of dignity and individual worth.

It may be argued that in space and problems alike, Nauru is far removed from our own experiences. To such an argument two replies are possible. One can say with John Donne that each of us is involved in mankind and the bell of the technological order tolls not for the Nauruan alone. Or one can recall that a modern English philosopher said recently that man is involved simultaneously in three basic conflicts: with nature, with his fellow man, and with himself. That observation is surely valid in the case of the Nauruan example. Let us now see whether it provides a useful framework in which to review some of the most pressing problems—and rewarding challenges—confronting *Homo sapiens* in the seventh decade of the twentieth century.

MAN AND NATURE

Our accelerating technology. The fact that man makes tools to a set and regular pattern differentiates him from all other creatures, and, indeed, some of these tools may be considered functionally as "detachable extensions of his forelimb." Proceeding with this concept, we can say that the Mesolithic bow-and-arrow is a direct ancestor of the intercontinental ballistic missile since both are extensions in space of man's activities to obtain control of his physical environment. When we recall that about 98 per cent of mankind's planetary existence was spent with an Old Stone-Age technology, it becomes clear that for hundreds of thousands of years our Paleolithic ancestors had to cope with a physical environment which dominated them. As the rudimentary hand-ax gave way to more specialized tools and hunting weapons, however, man acquired increasing power to modify his external world to suit his immediate needs. Neolithic man, with his domestication of plants and animals, made a breakthrough from a food-gathering to a food-producing culture and achieved the means to begin to master his environment. The process of inventing new tools, of tapping new sources of energy, and of extending the habitable areas of the globe to the higher latitudes in both hemispheres, has accelerated until today we live in a world society geared to a technological order with a culture of its own, to which men must in turn adapt themselves—whether they are Nauruans or New Yorkers. In the final analysis, it is this technology which distinguishes our age and (to employ the title of our text) sets "Civilization Present" apart from "Civilization Past."

The "population explosion." Technological acceleration—as shown, for example, by the ever increasing production and consumption of energy—is closely paralleled by the growth of this planet's population. This should not surprise us, since it is the application of technology to physical resources that makes possible the sustaining of human life and therefore sets the limits on the numbers of people who can be fed. But technology also provides the tools and techniques for lengthening life-spans and reducing mortality rates. As a result, high birth rates are no longer fairly closely matched by high death rates as they were until modern times; epidemics are much less frequent in most parts of the world, due largely to public health measures; and physical vitality has been increased by improved nutrition. These changes have brought about a demographic revolution—today familiarly called the "population explosion."

Pertinent statistics make clear why the decades ahead must confront society with probably its most critical challenge. A United Nations study estimates that at the beginning of the Christian era, the world's population was between 200 and 300 million people. By 1650 the figure had risen to about 500 million, by 1750 to just under 700 million, and in 1950 to 2495 million. The past three centuries have "brought a sixfold increase in human numbers: from an estimated half-billion in 1650 to over three billion in 1962. There were approximately 23 billion births during this period—over half as many as in the preceding 76 centuries!"[1] This factor of acceleration presents us with alarming forecasts when present trends are projected into the decade ahead.

For example, the estimated increase in the population of Asia from A.D. 1950 to 2000 will be roughly equal to the population of the entire world in 1958! The population of Latin America 40 years hence may very likely be four times that in 1950. . . . The increase in

Rich phosphate deposits make Nauru important economically. After mechanical excavators remove the phosphate, pinnacles of coral are left standing like miniature mountain peaks.

the rate of growth of the world's population is still continuing. This rate is now estimated to be about two per cent per year, sufficient to double the world's population every 35 years. It requires only very simple arithmetic to show that a continuation of this rate of growth for even 10 or 15 decades would result in an increase in population that would make the globe resemble an anthill.[2]

The population explosion is further complicated by the uneven growth rates in different regions. Birth rates average nearly 40 per 1000 in Africa, Asia, Middle America, and South America, yet they are only slightly more than half that figure in Europe, North America, and the Soviet Union. In other words, the greatest increases in population occur precisely in those areas which are underdeveloped technologically and least able to cope with the increasing imbalance between the satisfaction of man's economic needs and biological reproduction. Meanwhile, the planet's population rises by an estimated 160,000 every day. United Nations experts have translated this figure into equivalent food requirements:

Every time the clock ticks there is another mouth to be fed. Imagine the increase as a stream of destitute refugees passing a food distribution point in single file and being given a very meagre survival ration, a glass of milk, a loaf of bread and half a pound of fish. At a rate of one per second, it would take 44 hours to pass the point, and the column would stretch for 40 miles. On the estimated 61 million per annum increase, this would mean, in single file, a column stretching half-way around the Equator. To feed this multitude, that daily glass of milk would mean an added 4,380,000 cows; that loaf of bread would mean the grain product of 20 million acres, an area as big as Ireland, Ceylon or Sierra Leone, and that half pound of fish would mean a catch of 10 million metric tons, or over five times the total catch of all the fishermen along the 3,000-mile coast of India.[3]

Natural resources: problems and potential. The earth's fertility—a most significant factor in the capacity to feed men—depends on some nine inches of topsoil, the product of centuries of natural processes. Moreover, only 28.3 per cent of the earth's surface is land, and when mountains, deserts, and forested areas are subtracted, the human race must depend for its food primarily on the 2.95 per cent of the total earth surface which is arable, and upon the 5.4 per cent in grassland.

If the present trends of population-increase continue and there is no change in the amount of arable land, there will be just over one-half acre per person in A.D. 2000 and about a quarter of an acre per person in A.D. 2050 as compared with 1.18 acres in 1959. This means that the average acre, at present in use, must be made to produce twice as much within 40 years and five times as much within 90 years.[4]

We place our faith in science's ability to provide this phenomenal increase in productivity. Yet when we recall the dust bowls in North America in the 1930's, the over-all failure of Premier Nikita Khrushchev's "virgin lands" development in the Soviet East to meet Russian grain requirements, and the estimated 1500 to 1750 million acres of land subject to erosion throughout the world—or almost half the total cultivated area—a maximum effort will have to be

made to avert mass hunger in the decades ahead. Nevertheless, a number of remedies exist. One is the improvement of cereal strains so as to produce greater yields, as the Japanese have demonstrated with rice. Another is to bring additional lands under cultivation, including the vast areas of the equatorial forest zones—with their presently untapped resources—and the arid deserts and the semidesert highlands both in the tropics and temperate zones, which account for a large fraction of the world's uncultivated land. Irrigation systems in these arid and semiarid areas could add several hundred million acres of new land for cultivation.

However, massive technical and financial assistance to the underdeveloped nations by the technologically developed ones will be necessary to obtain meaningful results in bringing additional lands under cultivation. Also this assistance will have to be accompanied by basic changes in traditional farming methods and land-holding policies. And if the world's increasing population is to be adequately fed in the future, agricultural production will have to be supplemented by various means. One possibility is the large-scale growing and "harvesting" of fish, an important source of protein. Another possibility is the production of microscopic green algae that is high in protein and vitamin content. Such algae can be produced in large quantities in a small space. Synthetically produced vitamins and concentrated foodstuffs also might provide diet supplements on a mass scale.

What will meanwhile be happening to the earth's nonreplenishable resources? "In the United States, one-half of all the coal ever consumed has been burned since 1920, and nearly one-half of all the oil and gas ever consumed has been burned since 1940."[5] Industry has already consumed most of the rich iron ores of the Mesabi Range in Minnesota and now has to rely increasingly upon recently opened fields in Labrador and Quebec—and American demands for steel structures, automobiles, and household appliances increase every year. Today, peoples almost everywhere are caught up in the "revolution of rising expectations" so that in even quite backward countries there are men who look forward to owning some means of transportation and at least some of the modern gadgets. The people who believe that the entire world would like to live like well-off Americans ask, "Will the earth's oil and mineral resources last long enough to enable the entire world to approach the technological status and living standards of some 200 million Americans—a world not of 3 billion but say 6 billion people? Or will Nauru's experience be repeated over and over again, so that depleted oil fields in the Near East revert to desert before the inhabitants can exchange their camels for family automobiles, if not for their ruler's limousines?"

Essential to all economic activity is the production of energy. It has been estimated that between 1 A.D. and 1850 the total input to the world energy system amounted to between 6 and 9 Q ("Q" is defined as equivalent to 30 billion tons of bituminous coal). In the next 100 years, however, about half as much energy—or 4 Q—was consumed. Moreover, should the rate of growth in the per capita demand for energy remain at the current 3 per cent, "we shall require inputs of some 10 Q by A.D. 2000 and some 70 Q by A.D. 2050. If the rate should increase beyond 3 per cent, then the additional cumulative requirements would be very large indeed."[6]

Energy comes from two sources, described as "capital" and "income." The former consists of fossil, nonreplenishable fuels such as coal, oil-gas, oil shale, and tar sands, upon which we have thus far primarily relied. In addition, fossil fuels include uranium and thorium. "Income" sources of energy comprise fuel wood, water and wind power, solar heat collectors, tides, and natural steam. Some of these sources offer striking technological challenges, but, because low-cost nuclear fuels are abundant, no more than 15 per cent of the total energy used in the next century will come from the "income" group. "Energy in the

reserves of 'low-cost' nuclear fuels is some 20 times as abundant as in the reserves of 'low-cost' coal-oil-gas—575 Q compared with 27 Q. If great expansion of electrification should take place, nuclear fuels could support the bulk of the maximum plausible energy systems of the United States and the Free World for several centuries."[7]

The challenge of space. Man has long dreamed of conquering space, and as early as the eighteenth century he acquired skill in the hazardous art of ballooning. During the next century considerable progress was made in understanding the principles of aerodynamics, and at the turn of this century mathematical studies were undertaken on rocketry and the velocity required to put a projectile in orbit and also to leave the earth's gravitational field. The ascent of a heavier-than-air vehicle, however, required the invention of an engine with the necessary "lifting" capability. The first successful flight took place at Kitty Hawk in 1903 when the Wright brothers' frail biplane flew for 12 seconds. Since that historic event, man has added a vertical dimension to his terrestrial environment.

Military aviation came into use during World War I; the interwar period saw transoceanic flights initiated in both the Atlantic and Pacific; and World War II fully revealed the death-dealing potential of airpower. Not only were cities flattened and, at Hiroshima and Nagasaki, "nuclearized" by bombing attack, but the Germans with their V-2 rockets ushered in the era of ballistic missiles. Soviet and American scientists, aided by German experts, accelerated the development of rocketry after the war. We are all familiar with the launching of the first *Sputnik* in 1957, the Soviet and American manned orbital flights, and, in 1962, the flight of *Mariner II* toward and beyond Venus, measuring the temperature and rate of rotation of that cloud-enveloped planet and transmitting the data back to earth. In addition, both American and Soviet scientists have succeeded in taking pictures of the moon while American satellite systems have been devised to observe complex meteorological phenomena and to create communication relays linking continents.

These are technological marvels—but their implications can hardly yet be assessed. Is outer space to be exploited for peaceful or military purposes? At its eighteenth session (1963), the United Nations General Assembly adopted by acclamation a resolution calling on all nations "to refrain from placing in orbit around the earth any objects carrying nuclear weapons or any other kinds of weapons of mass destruction." It also adopted a draft declaration of legal principles which stated that outer space and celestial bodies were not subject to national appropriation and that their use must be for the benefit of all mankind. These are surely moves in the right direction as men train their sights on the earth's neighbors. Astronauts plan to land on the moon before the end of this decade, while the construction of space platforms will set the stage for the launchings of larger vehicles for interplanetary probes. "The sky's the limit"—and there seems to be no ceiling to man's ambition to conquer new worlds. Man appears to have mastered the rudiments of celestial mechanics—yet the question persists, "How valuable is this knowledge if man does not master the complexities of human relationships on our own planet?"

MAN AND HIS FELLOW MAN

The balance of terror. Our Paleolithic ancestors employed multipurpose implements for hunting and fighting alike. Specialized tools in the form of weapons—such as the double-edged battle-ax—appeared only after Neolithic farmers and herdsmen acquired fixed abodes and property. Ever since then, man has been employing progressively more sophisticated military technology in an attempt to dominate his fellow man. Hence our earlier reference to the direct relationship between the ancient bow and arrow and today's ICBM: though the flight trajectories and delivery punches of the two forms of weapons are of a different order of magnitude, they both seek to ex-

tend the environmental control of their respective owners. Today, following the invention of the hydrogen bomb and of an accurate ballistics system capable of delivering such a warhead on target at speeds that defy manned interceptors, the decision-makers in Washington and Moscow alike are in the unprecedented position of being able to initiate a holocaust that would destroy hundreds of millions in a few hours.

For more than a decade, in the absence of an international control system, peace among the nuclear powers has depended upon the so-called balance of terror. This poses a dilemma for the decision-makers since, to be effective, the balance requires a continuing equilibrium in the overall striking effectiveness of the protagonists. Yet this cannot be a static equilibrium. Technological invention accelerates the drive to obsolescence even as it escalates the striking potential to a new order of magnitude. So there is constant competition to score a breakthrough to some "invulnerable" position —say by means of an antimissile missile. But, ironically, to create such an advantage for one side is to destroy the "balance" concept upon which the present deterrence alone rests. Moreover, each protagonist must always assume that the other is succeeding to the next and more potent technological plane. Therefore the struggle to break the balance goes on—even though that balance may represent our only possible safety in a world made up of sovereign states subject to no law other than their own.

The disarmament problem. We might ask: why not reverse the direction of the escalating drive by disarming? But here again we get back to the dilemma posed by the balance-of-terror equation. To "de-escalate" will require the same rigorous maintenance of balance between the nuclear giants, since a unilateral act of reduction by one side could upset the balance in favor of the other camp. Moreover, in the absence of an internationally-conducted inspection system, the temptation to cheat in any disarmament program grows in direct proportion as the national arsenals diminish, because each remaining weapon assumes a more decisive role in its ability to tilt the balance of power. So far, the great powers have not been able to find an acceptable formula either for disarmament or for international arms inspection.

The problem of arms reduction, let alone disarmament, is compounded by the fact that military programs are massively involved in national economies. For example, United States defense expenditures rose from $11.7 billion in 1948 to $53 billion in 1963—so that, in spite of President Johnson's request for a 25 per cent cutback in the production of nuclear-weapon material and the closing of some unessential military and naval installations, defense still consumed more than half of the entire federal budget. In a dozen states, defense payrolls account for from 10 to 30 per cent of all employment in manufacturing plants and provide jobs for nearly 7 million workers, or 10 per cent of the working population in this country.[8] Among nuclear and nonnuclear powers alike, any genuine shift from an armaments to a nonarmaments economy would pose profound problems of dislocation. Many of them would stem from the rigidities inherent in the currently required concentration of plants and population alike; others would come from the rigidities resulting from the vested interests created by a military technology whose dynamic tends toward self-perpetuation—as in the case of the vast complexes directed by national atomic and space agencies.

Yet as of 1965 it had become obvious that neither the United States nor the Soviet Union could afford to keep up the previous pace of defense spending and still meet its other commitments, both domestic and international. When the Moscow Treaty partially banning nuclear weapons tests was signed in 1963, it was evident that both Washington and Moscow were prepared to apply brakes to the costliest and most dangerous arms race in history. This act, closely identified with President Kennedy, not only put an end—at least for the time being—to further contamination of the earth's atmosphere but reduced tensions in the political atmosphere as well.

The war for men's minds. As attested by the final chapters in this volume, the twentieth century has become a battleground for the minds and hearts of men everywhere; the battle is being waged by the forces of democracy on the one side and those of dictatorship on the other. World War I may or may not have been fought to make the world safe for democracy, but the succeeding decades saw the democratic philosophy assailed by forces of the extreme right and left in a global ideological struggle. That conflict continues unabated—yet today the international situation is more fluid than it has been for the past two decades and the ideologically created alliances are in disarray. To some extent, the nuclear stalemate has been responsible. Because of the suicidal risks involved in unleashing all-out war, neither the United States nor the Soviet Union considers attack imminent, or even likely. Consequently, the original need for the NATO and Warsaw alliances no longer appears so pressing and the cement of shared danger has materially weakened. In addition, within each grouping have appeared divergent policies and the insistence upon greater national freedom of action. In the Free World, this has been particularly marked in the case of France under President de Gaulle with his ambitions to create a European "third force" under French leadership in both the political and economic spheres (see Chapter 18). By 1965 it seemed that the Western democracies would continue to be confronted by divisive challenges within their own ranks and that the recession of nuclear threats might have slowed down, if not actually reversed, an earlier drive toward the emergence of a truly Atlantic community possessing common economic and political policies and perhaps one day even its own institutions. Nevertheless, the Free World was physically vigorous and ideologically alert, and faced the decades ahead with confidence.

Meanwhile, what were the prospects for

the Communist World? For a decade after World War II, Moscow directed an ideological machine which appeared capable of rolling over all opposition throughout Eurasia and of penetrating the Middle East and "black" Africa. But Stalin's world, with its iron grip on Russian and satellite populations alike, has come apart in the last decade. The Russians have called for the consumption not only of more goods at home but of more ideas from abroad, even as the Poles and Hungarians have insisted upon greater autonomy and the reëstablishment of traditional ties with the West. Moreover, Moscow's primacy in the Communist world has been challenged by Peking, which has carried the struggle for leadership into Africa and other parts of Asia. In Marxist theory, Communism is "international" and "peace-loving" as well as free of all "inner contradictions." Yet the Moscow-Peking feud has revealed that in practice the ideology has progressively served national interests, that the adherence of Communist parties to one or other of the contending capitals is dictated largely by geographical realities, and that each "peace-loving" bloc can accuse the other of such "imperialistic" crimes as territorial aggression, racism, and willingness to unleash nuclear war. Moscow and Peking may want to paper over their ideological differences and geopolitical rivalries, but the Communist world has permanently lost its monolithic façade—and with it that mystique of "historical inevitability" which Communists have so assiduously fostered in the past.

A north-south "cold war"? In spite of signs that the East-West Cold War may be loosening its paralyzing grip, a new alignment of cold-war tensions seems to be emerging—between the technologically advanced, prosperous nations of the northern temperate zone and the underdeveloped, densely populated regions of the tropics. In 1964, the British Foreign Minister warned:

If this division between the rich and poor nations continues to grow worse—which will eventually happen unless positive and drastic steps are taken—we will be adding gravely to the instability of the world and to the bitterness of man for man. Southern man against northern man—a bitterness accentuated perhaps by racial hatred. Imperialism will have ended, only to be replaced by pauperism. Looking at the world scene as a whole, I regard this problem as of overriding longterm importance. I think that in its way it is as much a challenge to us now as the old issue of slavery was in the last century.[9]

The significance of the attainment of national independence by hundreds of millions in Asia and Africa since World War II has already been underscored in the last chapter, as has the massive character of the challenge to raise their living standards. It was pointed out that the task will require a concerted global response—hence the designation of the 1960's as the "United Nations Development Decade." According to U Thant, "More people are suffering from want than ever before." Despite increasing economic efforts in the 1950's, the average rise in income among the poorest third of the world's population amounted to less than one dollar per year in improvement per person, which is an imperceptible advance. When we recall our previous statement that the present population explosion is occurring primarily in those regions least able to support that increase, it becomes obvious that a crisis will soon confront us. For example, United Nations economists estimate that the world's food supplies must be increased between 3.8 and 4.3 per cent annually, that manufacturing output in the underdeveloped countries must rise by at least 130 per cent, and that 19 to 24 million dwellings must be constructed annually in Asia, Africa, and Latin America during this decade to eliminate existing shortages.

We live in a world where the rich get richer and the poor get children, where the gap in living standards and rates of economic growth is steadily widening between the temperate-zone nations and those in the tropics. Scientists and theologians alike face the predicament of finding acceptable answers to the physical and moral problems posed by the population explosion. But one thing seems certain: unless the gap can be narrowed in the decades ahead, its political consequences will fill the agendas of the Security Council and General Assembly.

Social wrongs and human rights. The nineteenth century's comfortable assumption that progress was automatic and that science, education, and rising living standards would gradually put an end to man's inhumanity to man has been shattered by our century's world wars, cold wars, and programs to liquidate entire ethnic groups. Thus Hitler's regime employed clinically efficient gas-chambers to embark upon genocide in a country boasting one of the world's highest standards of literacy. On the extreme left, too, terror, mass deportations, and slave-labor camps were prescribed methods for enforcing the *diktats* of Stalin's regime—and charges continued to be raised of anti-Semitic practices in Premier Khrushchev's administration. Religious bigotry periodically sets off communal massacres between Hindus and Muslims in the Indian subcontinent, while Jews and Arabs are on the alert in the Middle East. All too often the advent of independence in Asia and Africa has opened the floodgates not only of pent-up antiwhite hostility but of renewed intertribal genocide, as was tragically demonstrated in The Congo in 1960.

Yet these are but the most obvious forms of inhuman behavior. We are all acquainted with the Orwellian prospects set forth in *1984* and in Aldous Huxley's *Brave New World*. "Brainwashing" appears to be widely practiced by the Communists. And some critics of society in the United States suggest that a portion of the advertising in our country is propaganda used to break down "consumer resistance." Although there are marked differences between brainwashing and propaganda used for advertising, both are techniques for treating one's fellow man as an "object" rather than "subject."

Fortunately, evidence also abounds of an unprecedented effort in this century to raise not only the economic standards but the social and legal status of man—in short, to treat him as a "subject" worthy of dignity and respect. For example, India seeks to reduce the social injustices imposed by its ancient caste system. Throughout Asia, Africa, and Latin America, hundreds of millions are going to school for the first time in history and becoming aware both of the larger world and of their own potential as human beings. The status of women has been improved in non-Western cultures, and the Universal Declaration of Human Rights as adopted by the United Nations has been embodied in some form in the constitutions or legal systems of many countries.

The 1960's found the United States involved in massive efforts to accord equal status, treatment, and opportunities to all its citizens. Since the 1954 decision of the Supreme Court calling for the desegregation of public schools, the nation has sought —with some violence and much soul-searching—to make the Constitution's provisions real and substantial for every American. Integration in schools and public facilities and equal voting rights for the Negroes who comprise one-tenth of the nation's population have been the dramatic objectives of the overall civil rights issue. By 1965 those rights had been largely enacted into law. But ultimately the struggle for rights is the struggle for equal opportunities in a democratic society. And this challenge cuts across all racial and ethnic lines and penetrates all regions and social strata. It involves not only the Negro and white share-croppers of Alabama and Georgia but the tenement-dwellers of Harlem and Los Angeles; not only the unemployed of Appalachia, whose economy has been rendered progressively obsolete by technological advances in other regions, but the school drop-outs in Detroit who, as unskilled members of the labor force, will inevitably be "the last hired, the first fired" in an economy where automation is rapidly taking over repetitive industrial functions. Today we are confronted with an unprecedented situation: increasing economic returns with decreasing man-hours of work. To what extent is the human factor becoming expendable? That brings us to our third, and final, area of human relationships.

MAN HIMSELF

Will the "Organization Man" triumph? Has our technological order now become so compelling that the individual must progressively adjust his work habits and mental attitudes, and even subordinate his basic personality, to satisfy the requirements of the machine? Involved in this question is the unmistakable fact that modern economic organization makes for gigantism. Capital formation, machines, production schedules, and distribution outlets are often on such a scale that these complexes can be developed and operated only by huge corporations or governments. In such complexes, too, decisions are governed by market demands and economics of scale rather than by social values.

Since World War II, we have heard much about the emergence of the "Organization Man" and the status-seekers in business and the professions who conform and "play it safe" so as not to jeopardize future promotion and the promise of "fringe benefits." In a mass society—dominated by big government, big business, and big unions—decisions affecting the life of each individual are often made by a small number of public or business administrators. Their choices in turn are most often dictated by what they hope to be the greatest amount of good for the greatest number of people, but they feel that their decisions, to be "scientific," first require that John Smith and Mary Jones be "processed" as digits in a computer system. Yet what happens to John and Mary in this complex process of decision-making and data-processing—since presumably they are the ultimate subjects of all this effort? Are we sufficiently concerned with the unique and supremely important personality of the individual? In Denmark the government has instituted the *Ombudsman*—an official whose task it is to ensure that bureaucratic decisions do not run roughshod over the individual citizen. Many present-day thinkers argue that we shall need not only the *Ombudsman,* but the civil liberties advocate, the philosopher, the theologian, and the artist alike, if we are to preserve those humanistic values without which democracy becomes but an empty ritual.

The challenge to traditional moral values. Meanwhile, what is the present order doing to traditional values—to what is sometimes referred to as the "Puritan ethic?" This placed a premium upon "sturdy self-reliance," hard work, and thrift and condemned idleness and self-indulgence. But today the production line dares not stop—the goods must continue to pour off the line, to be immediately consumed and replenished. We seem to be caught up in "Operation Treadmill" where we must run faster and faster in order not to fall behind. Apparently, we must make sure that obsolescence is built into the product, otherwise its quality will act as a brake upon the replenishing process—and so throw men out of work. Today, our economy is geared to credit-buying and installment-payments—to "play now, pay later," a maxim roughly the reverse of the rules by which our Puritan forbears governed their lives. Perhaps the older values were wrong? At any rate, a technology-oriented society is forcing us to reassess traditional assumptions and social values—and also individual moral standards.

Nor is it any use trying to find the answers by recourse to Rousseau's "noble savages" or to Gandhi's plea for a return to a preindustrialized society, symbolized by the spinning wheel. Technology and science have helped improve health and have played major roles in creating leisure and a rising income. Should Polynesians, Indians, and other groups scattered over the earth share in these benefits? And why not? Why should two-thirds of the world's population remain prey to ignorance, hunger, and disease when such traditional scourges have been all but eradicated in the West? Surely it is good to give people more food and a longer life-span. The technological order has both initiated and expects to serve that phenomenon of our age—the "revolution of rising expectations" which has swept over every continent.

Technology can be considered morally neutral—but the technological order itself continues to raise moral issues of the most sophisticated kind. Probably we can all agree that good ends cannot justify *bad* means. But the moral problem posed by our material advancement is much more subtle —indeed, it is unprecedented. For we are going to be faced increasingly with what to do with situations in which *good* means can result in catastrophic ends—as when science's conquest of disease ushers in a population explosion. As Aldous Huxley, author of *Brave New World,* pointed out: "This is a dilemma that requires a whole new type of ethical thinking. . . . We don't have much time."

Leisure and education. As a result of accelerating automation, society will acquire much more leisure than men have ever experienced before. At one time, the prospect of obtaining any real freedom from work was limited to a small minority. Now, according to one recent estimate (based on probable population growth and decreased number of working hours), Americans will have a total of 660 billion more hours of leisure in 2000 A.D. than they enjoyed in 1950. Meanwhile, some economists also maintain that jobs are about to be eliminated so rapidly by automation that the government must be prepared in the years to come to pay citizens a guaranteed annual wage for *not* working. What will we do, both as a society and as individuals, with this free time? Spend it at a sports stadium, or before a TV set watching an endless fare of professional athletics, situation comedies, and commercials? What can our educational system do to prepare people to cope with the problems and potential alike of leisure? It will be in its use of leisure that our society must witness a massive confrontation between the two orders, the technological and the humanistic.

Actually, caution should be used in estimating popular tastes and value judgments. For example, the current population explosion is being matched in the United States and elsewhere by what has been described as a "cultural explosion." More North Americans than ever before enroll in institutions of higher learning, in night classes and art schools; attend concerts; visit museums; make use of public libraries; patronize the centers for the performing arts that have been mushrooming in North American cities; and purchase musical instruments, recordings of classical music, and paperbacks of literary merit. Until modern times, art was the private preserve of the wealthy who alone could afford to be patrons. Today, both the patronage and the appreciation of the arts have acquired an increasingly broad social base.

The essential role of the arts in our century is underscored by the different goals that they have been assigned in totalitarian and democratic societies. In contrast to Premier Khrushchev's insistence that art must play a political and propagandizing role in shaping Soviet society, President Kennedy declared:

When power leads man toward arrogance, poetry reminds him of his limitations. . . . When power corrupts, poetry cleanses, for art establishes the basic human truths which must serve as the touchstones of our judgment. . . . I see little of more importance to the future of our country and our civilization than full recognition of the place of the artist. If art is to nourish the roots of our culture, society must set the artist free to follow his vision wherever it takes him.[10]

Speaking with almost prophetic vision, President Kennedy also said: "This is a dangerous and uncertain world. . . . No one expects our lives to be easy—not in this decade, not in this century." In fact, of course, the uncertainty of existence and the avoidance of annihilation—whether in the Stone Age or in the Nuclear Age—have always been man's central problem. And its solution, now as always, rests not with vast, unfathomable natural forces over which man has no control but rather within himself—in his mind, his heart, and his soul.

SUGGESTIONS FOR READING

THE CONTEMPORARY SCENE

Three handy surveys of the postwar period: H. S. Commager et al., *Contemporary Civilization,* Scott, Foresman,* 1959; H. Gatzke, *The Present in Perspective,* Rand McNally,* 1957; J. H. Jackson, *The World in the Postwar Decade, 1945-1955;* Houghton, 1957.

Political Handbook of the World. Published by Harper under the direction of the Council of Foreign Relations, the annual editions of this work are extremely helpful reference tools.

Valuable information on current affairs is offered by the pamphlets of the **Foreign Policy Association Headlines** series. The works are both scholarly and inexpensive.

Eichelberger, C. M., *UN: The First Ten Years,* Harper, 1955. An optimistic verdict. Recommendations for changes in the structure and function of the U.N. can be found in F. O. Wilcox and C. M. Marcy, *Proposals for Changes in the United Nations,* Brookings Institution, 1955; and A. N. Holcombe, ed., *Strengthening the United Nations,* Harper, 1957.

Toynbee, A. J., *The World and the West,* Oxford, 1953. The "encounter" between the West and the remainder of the world as examined by a distinguished historian. See also G. F. Kennan, *Russia, the Atom and the West,* Harper, 1958.

Two well-balanced analyses of the cold war are K. Ingram, *History of the Cold War,* Philosophical Library, 1955; and G. L. Arnold, *The Pattern of World Conflict,* Dial, 1955.

Millis, Walter, *Arms and Men,* Mentor, * 1958. Remarkably suggestive discussion of the changing significance of the military factor in the age of nuclear arsenals and the new social and political issues posed. See also H. M. Kissinger, *Nuclear Weapons and Foreign Policy,* Harper, 1957.

Aron, R., *The Century of Total War,* Beacon,* 1955. A thoughtful evaluation of the prospects for humanity in the light of total war and today's clash of ideologies.

Report on the World Social Situation, United Nations, 1957. A world-wide analysis of population, health, food and nutrition, housing, education, conditions of employment, and general levels of income and welfare.

Doane, R. R., *World Balance Sheet,* Harper, 1957. Over 100 charts and tables are included in this global survey of physical resources, their distribution and depletion. For a discussion by a scientist of the urgency for more control over population, food, and resources, see H. Brown, *The Challenge of Man's Future,* Compass,* 1956.

THE FREE WORLD

Salvadori, M., *NATO: A Twentieth Century Community of Nations,* Anvil,* 1957. The historical background and creation of the western alliance. Includes much source material.

The United States in World Affairs. An excellent survey, published annually for the Council on Foreign Relations by Harper.

*Indicates an inexpensive paperbound edition.

Goldman, E. F., *The Crucial Decade: America, 1945-1955,* Knopf, 1956. A lively account of the events and prevailing mood of the United States in the period.

Siegfried, A., *America at Mid-Century,* Harcourt, 1955. The notable French author finds that America is moving away from Europe, and, in the process, shaping Europe to its image. Another perceptive analysis, also by a Frenchman, is J. Maritain, *Reflections on America,* Scribner's, 1958.

Kohn, H., *American Nationalism,* Macmillan, 1957. An interpretive essay on the factors shaping the American character. See also M. Lerner, *America as a Civilization,* Simon and Schuster, 1957.

Two fact-filled works which deal with the dynamics of power in Latin America are H. E. Davis, ed., *Government and Politics in Latin America,* Ronald, 1958; and W. W. Pierson and F. G. Gil, *Governments of Latin America,* McGraw-Hill, 1957. For an informative discussion of the reasons behind communism's appeal in Latin America, see R. J. Alexander, *Communism in Latin America,* Rutgers, 1957. In *Problems of Democracy in Latin America,* Univ. of N. C., 1955, the author, Galo Plaza, a former president of Ecuador, expresses optimism concerning the growth of democracy south of the border.

White, T. H., *Fire in the Ashes; Europe in Midcentury,* Sloane, 1953. A fine portrait of western Europe's recovery. See also Hans A. Schmitt, *The Path to European Union, from Marshall Plan to Common Market.* Louisiana State, 1962.

Middleton, D., *These Are the British,* Knopf, 1957. An appreciative survey of Britain and its postwar temper by a correspondent of the New York *Times.*

Two studies of the painful and confused postwar years in France are F. Goguel-Nyegaard, *France Under the Fourth Republic,* Cornell, 1952; and D. Schoenbrun, *As France Goes,* Harper, 1957.

The remarkable recovery of western Germany is described in H. C. Wallich, *Mainsprings of the German Revival,* Yale, 1955; and A. Horne, *Return to Power; A Report on the New Germany,* Praeger, 1956.

Quigley, H. S., and J. E. Turner, *The New Japan,* Univ. of Minn., 1956. The authors believe that even if the democratic reforms introduced by the United States prove to be only a veneer, Japan is unable to return to its feudal-militaristic past. Also recommended are H. Borton et al., *Japan Between East and West,* Harper, 1957; and J. B. Cohen, *Japan's Post War Economy,* Indiana Univ., 1958.

THE COMMUNIST BLOC

Hazard, J. N., *The Soviet System of Government,* Univ. of Chicago, 1960. The best general account of how things are accomplished in the Soviet Union. A study made by the Russian Research Center at Harvard and based on interviews with refugees from the U.S.S.R. is R. A. Bauer et al., *How the Soviet System Works,* Harvard, 1956. An excellent analysis of the various sectors of the Soviet economy is H. Schwartz, *Russia's Soviet Economy,* Prentice-Hall, 1954.

Meyer, Alfred G., *Communism,* Random House, * 1961. Fresh, brief, stimulating and scholarly; a valuable aid in recognizing the nonmonolithic character of contemporary communism.

Korol, A. G., *Soviet Education for Science and Technology,* Wiley, 1957. The best and most detailed study available.

Barghoorn, F. C., *The Soviet Image of the United States: A Study in Distortion,* Harcourt, 1950. A chilling analysis of Soviet propaganda methods—and their effectiveness. The author's thesis is that Soviet propaganda against the United States is one of the chief instruments of the Kremlin's aggressive foreign policy.

Wolff, R. L., *The Balkans in Our Time,* Harvard, 1956. A thorough discussion of the current scene in the Balkans. See also N. Spulber, *The Economics of Communist Eastern Europe,* Wiley, 1957.

Djilas, M., *The New Class; An Analysis of the Communist System,* Praeger,* 1959. A bitter condemnation of communism by a former leading figure in the Yugoslav Communist party.

Lasky, M. J., ed., *The Hungarian Revolution,* Praeger, 1957. A documentary history of the 1956 uprising.

Walker, R. L., *China Under Communism,* Yale, 1955. An account of the first five years of Communist rule in China which emphasizes the role of brain-washing and terror in the "conditioning" of people. For a skillful analysis of economic developments, see Yuan-li Wu, *An Economic Survey of Communist China,* Bookman's Associates, 1956. Also recommended are P. S. H. Tang, *Communist China Today: Domestic and Foreign Policies,* 2 vols., Praeger, 1957-1959; and Edgar Snow, *The Other Side of the River: Red China Today,* Random House, 1962.

THE UNDERDEVELOPED NATIONS

Dean, V. M., *The Nature of the Non-Western World,* Mentor,* 1957. A good overall view of the problems facing the underdeveloped countries. Also recommended is E. Staley, *The Future of Underdeveloped Countries; Political Implications of Economic Development,* Harper, 1954.

Myrdal, G., *Rich Lands and Poor; The Road to World Prosperity,* Harper, 1957. The eminent sociologist discusses the reasons for the persistence of economic differences between the rich lands and the technologically backward ones. Also recommended is M. F. Millikan and W. W. Rostow, *A Proposal: Key to an Effective Foreign Policy,* Harper, 1957.

A stimulating symposium on the pros and cons of colonialism is R. Strausz-Hupe and H. W. Hazard, eds., *The Idea of Colonialism,* Praeger, 1958. T. R. Adam, *Modern Colonialism: Institutions and Policies,* Random House,* 1955, is a useful survey.

Kahin, G. M., *The Asian-African Conference: Bandung, Indonesia, April, 1955,* Cornell, 1956. Includes the background, achievements, and key speeches of this historic conference.

Stillman, C. W., ed., *Africa in the Modern World,* Univ. of Chicago, 1955. A good introductory work about sub-Saharan Africa. In T. Hodgkin, *Nationalism in Colonial Africa,* New York Univ., 1957, colonial policies and nationalist movements are well described. For a sound study of economic and social development in the less-developed areas of tropical Africa, see W. A. Hance, *African Economic Development,* Harper, 1958.

Books about the complex racial scene of South Africa are numerous. Probably the most helpful are C. W. De Kiewiet, *The Anatomy of South African Misery,* Oxford, 1956; and G. M. Carter, *The Politics of Inequality,* Praeger, 1958.

Three works which are indispensable for the study of the African political awakening are J. S. Coleman, *Nigeria: Background to Nationalism,* Univ. of Calif., 1958; G. Padmore, *The Gold Coast Revolution,* British Book Centre, 1953, and *Africa: Britain's Third Empire,* British Book Centre, 1950.

Clark, M. K., *Algeria in Turmoil,* Praeger, 1959. A comprehensive account of the Algerian rebellion against French rule.

Wallbank, T. W., *Documents on Modern Africa,* Van Nostrand, 1964. An anthology of documents and readings beginning with Stanley in Africa and ending with revolt in East Africa.

Shwadran, B., *The Middle East, Oil and the Great Powers,* Praeger, 1955. Details the impact of western demand for oil on the political, social, economic, and cultural development of the Middle East.

Laqueur, W. Z., *Communism and Nationalism in the Middle East,* Praeger, 1956. A description of the Communist movements in the area coupled with an attack on nationalism, which the author believes is not opposed to communism.

Mezerik, A. G., *Suez Canal: Nationalization, Invasion, International Action,* International Review Service, 1956. A comprehensive summary of the Suez Canal question. See also J. Morris, *Islam Inflamed,* Pantheon, 1957.

Thayer, P. W., ed., *Nationalism and Progress in Free Asia,* Johns Hopkins, 1956. Diverse points of view by American, British, and Asian political scientists, economists, and government representatives. See also H. M. Vinacke, *Far Eastern Politics in the Postwar Period,* Appleton, 1956.

The eclipse of British rule in the Indian subcontinent is treated in the following works: V. P. Menon, *The Transfer of Power in India,* Princeton, 1957; E. W. R. Lumby, *The Transfer of Power in India, 1945-1947,* Praeger, 1954; and A. Campbell-Johnson, *Mission with Mountbatten,* Dutton, 1953.

Griffiths, Sir Percival J., *Modern India,* Praeger, 1957. A competent study of post-independence India by a former British official in India. For a sympathetic treatment of Pakistan's development, see R. Symonds, *The Making of Pakistan,* Faber, 1950.

King, J. K., *Southeast Asia in Perspective,* Macmillan, 1956. A stimulating, controversial analysis of the area. See also A. M. Taylor, *Indonesian Independence and the United Nations,* Cornell, 1960; and R. H. Fifield, *The Diplomacy of Southeast Asia, 1945-1958,* Harper, 1958.

1945

Yalta Conference (Feb. 4-11)

Death of Roosevelt; Truman becomes president (Apr. 12)

Mussolini shot by Italian partisans (Apr. 28)

Hitler commits suicide (Apr. 30?)

V-E Day; surrender of Nazi Germany (May 8)

U.N. Charter signed at San Francisco (June 26)

Potsdam Conference (July 17-Aug. 2)

Labour victory in British parliamentary elections (July 26)

Atomic bomb dropped on Hiroshima (Aug. 6)

Unconditional surrender of Japan (Aug. 14)

Nuremberg war crimes trials (Nov. 21, 1945-Oct. 1, 1946)

1946

First General Assembly of the U.N. in London (Jan. 10)

Baruch Plan for international control of atomic energy submitted to U.N. (June 14)

Independence of the Philippines proclaimed (July 4)

New constitution establishes Fourth French Republic (Oct. 13)

Germany divided into Soviet, British, American, and French zones (Oct. 29)

1947

Peace treaties signed with Italy, Bulgaria, Hungary, Rumania, Finland (Feb. 10)

Truman requests aid for Greece and Turkey; the Truman Doctrine (Mar. 12)

Secretary of State Marshall introduces idea of aid to Europe; the Marshall Plan (June 5)

British rule in India ended; dominions of India and Pakistan formed (Aug. 15)

Nineteen American nations sign mutual protection treaty at Rio de Janeiro (Aug. 30)

1948

Gandhi assassinated by Hindu religious fanatic (Jan. 30)

Communist coup in Czechoslovakia (Feb. 25)

Britain, France, and Benelux nations sign Brussels Treaty (Mar. 17)

Truman signs Foreign Assistance Act appropriating funds for European Recovery Program (April 3)

Organization of American States (OAS) established (Apr. 30)

Israel proclaimed state (May 14)

Berlin blockade (June 18, 1948-Sept. 30, 1949)

Cominform denounces Tito (June 28)

Republic of Korea proclaimed in Seoul, with Syngman Rhee as president (Aug. 15)

1949

Truman announces Point Four program (Jan. 20)

North Atlantic Treaty (NATO) signed (Apr. 4)

German Federal Republic born in West Germany (May 23)

Soviets found German Democratic Republic (May 30)

Adenauer's Christian Democrats sweep West German elections (Aug. 14)

People's Republic of China established (Sept 21)

Explosion of first Soviet atomic bomb announced (Sept. 23)

Chinese nationalists abandon mainland for Formosa (Dec. 8)

Indonesia granted independence (Dec. 27)

1950

India becomes republic within British Commonwealth (Jan. 26)

U.S.S.R. and Red China sign thirty-year alliance (Feb. 14)

North Korean forces cross 38th parallel (June 25)

U.N. endorses Truman's request to send troops to South Korea (June 27)

Red Chinese forces move into Tibet (Oct. 25)

1951

Chinese Communists attack U.N. forces in Korea (Jan. 1) Truman removes General MacArthur from Far Eastern Command (Apr. 11)

France, West Germany, Italy, and Benelux nations agree to pool coal and steel resources (April 18)

Anzus Pact signed (Sept. 1)

Japan signs peace treaty and agreement permitting U.S. troops to remain in Japan (Sept. 8)

Turkey and Greece join NATO (Sept. 20)

Conservatives win British election (Oct. 25)

1952

Batista's coup d'état in Cuba (Mar. 10)

King Farouk of Egypt abdicates; army clique seizes power (July 26)

European Coal and Steel Community goes into operation (Aug. 10)

First U.S. H-bomb tested at Eniwetok (Nov. 1)

1953

Stalin dies; succeeded by Malenkov (Mar. 5)

Workers riot in East Berlin, proclaim general strike (June 17)

Egypt declared a republic (June 18)

Korean armistice signed at Panmunjon (July 27)

Federation of Rhodesia and Nyasaland proclaimed (Aug. 1)

1954

U.S. launches atomic submarine Nautilus (Jan. 21)

Nasser becomes premier of Egypt (Feb. 25)

Eisenhower signs St. Lawrence Seaway Bill (May 13)

U.S. Supreme Court outlaws racial segregation in public schools (May 17)

Vietnam divided into South Vietnam and Communist North Vietnam (July 21)

Southeast Asia Treaty Organization (SEATO) formed (Sept. 8)

Egypt and Great Britain sign pact arranging for British evacuation of Suez Canal Zone (Oct. 19)

1955

Pakistan becomes republic within British Commonwealth (Feb. 4)

Malenkov resigns; replaced by Bulganin and Khrushchev (Feb. 8)

Afro-Asian Conference at Bandung, Indonesia (Apr. 18-24)

West Germany admitted to NATO (May 9)

U.S.S.R. and eastern European satellites sign Warsaw Pact (May 14)

Austrian peace treaty signed (May 15)

Perón overthrown in Argentina (Sept. 19)

1956

Anglo-Egyptian Sudan becomes independent republic of Sudan (Jan. 1)

Khrushchev denounces Stalin before Twentieth Party Congress (Feb. 24)

France recognizes independent Tunisia (Mar. 20)

U.S. promises to support Middle Eastern nations if attacked; the Eisenhower Doctrine (Apr. 9)

Rioting, general strike in Posen, Poland (June 28)

Egypt seizes Suez Canal; Nasser announces its nationalization (July 26)

Revolution in Hungary; crushed by Soviet army (Oct. 23-Nov. 30)

Israelis invade Sinai Peninsula, drive toward Suez Canal (Oct. 29)

Egypt breaks off diplomatic relations with France and Britain, seizes their assets in Egypt (Nov. 1); British and French forces land in Egypt, cease-fire declared two days later (Nov. 5)

1957

Saar regions reunited with West Germany (Jan. 1)

Gomulka's National Unity front wins Polish elections (Jan. 20)

Ghana becomes sovereign state in British Commonwealth (Mar. 6)

Inner Six nations agree to creation of European Economic Community (Common Market) and Euratom (Mar. 25)

International Geophysical Year (I.G.Y.) opens (July 1)

Malaya becomes independent state within British Commonwealth (Aug. 31)

Soviet Sputnik fired into orbit; space age begins (Oct. 4)

1958

Egypt and Syria merge to form United Arab Republic (Feb. 1)

Khrushchev becomes Soviet premier (Mar. 27)

First conference of independent African states opens in Accra, Ghana (Apr. 15)

De Gaulle becomes premier of France; pledges equal vote for Europeans and Algerian nationalists in Algeria three days later (June 1)

U.S. Marines arrive in Lebanon in response to Lebanese appeal for aid (July 15); British land in Jordan (July 17)

Atomic submarine Nautilus sails under Arctic ice cap (Aug. 3)

U.N. resolution requesting withdrawal of British and U.S. troops from Jordan and Lebanon adopted unanimously (Aug. 21)

New constitution for Fifth Republic approved in France (Sept. 28)

Guinea granted independence from France (Sept. 29)

1959

Cuban rebels under Castro take over government (Jan. 1)

Lunik I launched; first artificial planet to orbit the sun (Jan. 3)

Big Four foreign ministers meet in Geneva, discuss reunification of Germany (May 11-June 20; July 13-Aug. 5)

St. Lawrence Seaway formally dedicated (June 26)

Sukarno dissolves Indonesian parliament, assumes dictatorial power (July 5)

Outer Seven nations complete agreements to set up European Free Trade Association (Nov. 20)

1960

U.S. and Japan sign mutual security pact (Jan. 19)

First French atomic bomb tested in Sahara (Feb. 13)

U.S. nuclear-powered submarine Triton makes first submerged voyage around the world (Feb. 16-May 10)

U.S. U-2 plane downed in U.S.S.R. (May 1)

Big Four Paris summit meeting collapses (May 16)

Belgian Congo declared independent republic of the Congo (June 30)

Nigeria granted independence (Oct. 1)

1961

U.N. Security Council authorizes peace-keeping force in Congo (Feb. 21)

U.S. supported Cuban filibustering expedition at Bay of Pigs (Apr. 17)

Beginning of Berlin Wall (Aug. 13)

Opening of negotiations on British membership in Common Market (EEC) (Nov. 8)

Israeli Court sentences Eichmann for crimes of Nazi period (Dec. 15)

1962

New U.S. military command established in South Vietnam (Feb. 8)

First transmission of TV pictures by means of an orbiting satellite (May 3)

Algerian independence proclaimed by De Gaulle (July 3)

Chinese attack Indian Himalayan frontier (Oct. 20)

U.S.-Soviet crisis over missile bases in Cuba (Oct. 22-28)

1963

Official surrender to U.N. of Katangese secession forces in Congo (Jan. 17)

France vetoes British entry to Common Market (Jan. 29)

Signing of nuclear test ban treaty by U.S., Britain, and U.S.S.R. (Aug. 5)

Adenauer, West German chancellor since 1949, resigns (Oct. 16)

U.S. president John F. Kennedy assassinated (Nov. 22)

Second Session of Ecumenical Council of Roman Catholic Church closes (Dec. 4)

1964

Rift between China and Soviet Union splits leadership in Communist world

Nehru dies, architect of independent India and prime minister since 1947 (May 27)

U.S. Congress adopts and President Johnson signs comprehensive Civil Rights Bill (July 2)

LIST OF READINGS

The titles listed below are recommended to supplement the study of various aspects of world history. This list, along with the six lists of suggested readings within the text, provides a wide assortment of works for assigned outside reading and for leisure-time reading. As in the lists of suggested readings, the date of publication indicates, wherever possible, the latest edition of the work or, in the opinion of the authors, the most satisfactory available edition. Paperbound editions are indicated by an asterisk.

REFERENCE AIDS

Two special encyclopedias of world history which are highly recommended as convenient reference aids: Bowle, J., ed., *The Concise Encyclopedia of World History,* Hawthorne, 1958; and Langer, W. L., ed., *An Encyclopedia of World History: Ancient, Medieval, and Modern, Chronologically Arranged,* Houghton, 1952.

The historical atlases below are very helpful in understanding the influence of geography upon historical events: Fage, J. D., *An Outline Atlas of African History,* St. Martin's, 1958; Fox, E. W., and H. S. Deighton, eds., *An Atlas of European History,* Oxford,* 1957; Goodall, G., and R. F. Treharne, eds., *Muir's Historical Atlas: Medieval and Modern,* Barnes and Noble, 1952; Hazard, H. W., and H. L. Cooke, Jr., *Atlas of Islamic History,* Princeton, 1954; Lord, C. L., and E. H. Lord, eds., *Historical Atlas of the United States,* Holt,* 1953; Palmer, R. R., ed., *Rand McNally Atlas of World History,* Rand McNally, 1957; Roolvink, R., et al., comps., *Historical Atlas of the Muslim Peoples,* Harvard, 1958; Shepherd, W. R., *Historical Atlas,* 8th ed., Barnes and Noble, 1956.

HISTORIES OF MODERN EUROPE

Ausubel, H., ed., *From Waterloo to the Atomic Age,* Vol. II of *The Making of Modern Europe,* Holt, 1951; Barker, Sir Ernest, et al., eds., *The European Inheritance,* 3 vols., Oxford, 1954; Benns, F. L., *Europe Since 1914,* Appleton, 1954; Black, C. E., and E. C. Helmreich, *Twentieth Century Europe: A History,* Knopf, 1959; Boak, A. E. R., et al., *The Growth of Western Civilization,* Appleton, 1951; Bruun, G., *Europe in Evolution, 1415-1815,* Houghton, 1945; Croce, B., *History of Europe in the Nineteenth Century,* Humanities Press, 1953; Ergang, R., *Europe from the Renaissance to Waterloo,* Heath, 1954; Ergang, R., *Europe Since Waterloo,* Heath, 1954; Ergang, R., *Europe in Our Time, 1914 to the Present,* Heath, 1958; Fisher, H. A. L., *A History of Europe,* Houghton, 1939; Gottschalk, L., and D. Lach, *Europe and the Modern World,* 2 vols., Scott, Foresman, 1951-1954; Grant, A. J., and H. W. V. Temperley, *Europe in the Nineteenth and Twentieth Centuries, 1789-1950,* Longmans, 1952; Hall, W. P., and W. S. Davis, *The Course of Europe Since Waterloo,* Appleton, 1957; Hazen, C., *Europe Since 1815,* 2 vols., Holt, 1924; Langsam, W. C., *The World Since 1919,* Macmillan, 1954; Ogg, D., *Europe in the Seventeenth Century,* Black, 1959; Schapiro, J. S., *Modern and Contemporary European History, 1815-1952,* Houghton, 1953; Seaman, L., *From Vienna to Versailles,* Coward-McCann, 1956; Sontag, R. J., *European Diplomatic History, 1871-1932,* Appleton, 1933.

NATIONAL HISTORIES

FRANCE

Brogan, D. W., *The French Nation: From Napoleon to Pétain, 1814-1940,* Harper, 1957; Guérard, A., *France; A Modern History,* Univ. of Mich., 1959; Maurois, A., *A History of France,* Evergreen,* 1960; Sedillot, R., *An Outline of French History,* Knopf, 1953; Wolf, J. B., *France, 1815 to the Present,* Prentice-Hall, 1940.

GERMANY

Barraclough, G., *The Origins of Modern Germany,* Macmillan, 1948; Flenley, R., *Modern German History,* Dutton, 1959; Marriott, J. A. R., and C. G. Robertson, *The Evolution of Prussia; The Making of an Empire,* Oxford, 1946; Pinson, K. S., *Modern Germany, Its History and Civilization,* Macmillan, 1954; Steinberg, S. H., *A Short History of Germany,* Macmillan, 1945; Taylor, A. J. P., *The Course of German History; A Survey of the Development of Germany since 1815,* Coward-McCann, 1946; Valentin, V., *The German People; Their History and Civilization from the Holy Roman Empire to the Third Reich,* Knopf, 1946.

GREAT BRITAIN

Carter, E. H., and R. A. F. Mears, *A History of Britain,* Oxford, 1948; Churchill, Sir Winston S., *The Age of Revolution, 1688-1815,* and *The Great Democracies, 1815-1901,* Vols. III and IV of *A History of the English-Speaking Peoples,* Dodd, 1957-1958; Cole, G. D. H., and R. W. Postgate, *The British People, 1746-1946,* Knopf, 1947; Halévy, E., *A History of the English People in the Nineteenth Century,* 5 vols., P. Smith, 1949-1952; Hall, W. P., and R. G. Albion, *A History of England and the British Empire,* Ginn, 1953; Keir, Sir David L., *The Constitutional History of Modern Britain Since 1485,* Black, 1960; Lunt, W. E., *History of England,* Harper, 1957; Plumb, J. H., *The First Four Georges,* Macmillan, 1957; Schuyler, R. L., and H. Ausubel, *The Making of English History,* Holt, 1952; Smith, G., *A History of England,* Scribner's, 1957; Trevelyan, G. M., *British History in the Nineteenth Century and After, 1782-1919,* Longmans, 1938; Trevelyan, G. M., *A History of England,* Vols. II and III, Anchor,* 1953.

BRITISH EMPIRE-COMMONWEALTH

Brebner, J. B., *North Atlantic Triangle; the Interplay of Canada, the United States, and Great Britain,* Columbia, 1958; Brebner, J. B., *Canada: A Modern History* (with a final chapter by D. C. Masters), Univ. of Mich., 1960; Burt, A. L., *The Evolution of the British Empire and Commonwealth from the American Revolution,* Heath, 1956; Burt, A. L., *A Short History of Canada for Americans,* Univ. of Minn., 1942; Carrington, C. E., *The British Overseas,* Cambridge, 1950; Creighton, D. G., *The Empire of the St. Lawrence,*

Houghton, 1958; Creighton, D. G., *A History of Canada: Dominion of the North,* Houghton, 1958; Crawford, R. M., *Australia,* Hutchinson, 1952; Dawson, R. M., *The Development of Dominion Status, 1900-1936,* Oxford, 1937; Knaplund, P., *Britain, Commonwealth and Empire, 1901-1955,* Harper, 1957; Lower, A. R. M., *Canadians in the Making: A Social History of Canada,* Longmans, 1958; Lower, A. R. M., *Colony to Nation: A History of Canada,* Longmans, 1957; Miller, J. D. B., *The Commonwealth in the World,* Harvard, 1958; Robinson, H., *The Development of the British Empire,* Houghton, 1936; Schuyler, R., *Parliament and the British Empire; Some Constitutional Controversies Concerning Imperial Legislature Jurisdiction,* Columbia, 1929; Sinclair, K., *A History of New Zealand,* Penguin,* 1959; Trotter, R. G., *The British Empire-Commonwealth, A Study in Political Evolution,* Holt,* 1932; Walker, E. A., *The British Empire: Its Structure and Spirit, 1497-1953,* Harvard, 1956; Woodward, W. H., *A Short History of the Expansion of the British Empire, 1500-1930,* Macmillan, 1931.

See also the works in this list which deal with India and with British influences elsewhere in Asia and in Africa.

ITALY

Albrecht-Carrié, R., *Italy From Napoleon to Mussolini,* Columbia, 1950; King, B., *A History of Italian Unity; Being a Political History of Italy from 1814-1871,* 2 vols., Scribner's, 1924; Salvatorelli, L., *A Concise History of Italy; From Prehistoric Times to Our Own Day,* Oxford, 1940; Mack Smith, D., *Italy: A Modern History,* Univ. of Mich., 1959; Trevelyan, J. P., *A Short History of the Italian People From the Barbarian Invasions to the Present Day,* Pitman, 1956.

RUSSIA

Beazley, C. R., et al., *Russia from the Varangians to the Bolsheviks,* Oxford, 1918; Charques, R. D., *A Short History of Russia,* Everyman,* 1956; Florinsky, M. T., *Russia: A History and An Interpretation,* 2 vols., Macmillan, 1953; Harcave, S., *Russia: A History,* Lippincott, 1959; Karpovich, M., *Imperial Russia, 1801-1917,* Holt,* 1932; Kornilov, A., *Modern Russian History; From the Age of Catherine the Great to the End of the Nineteenth Century,* Knopf, 1943; Mazour, A. G., *Russia: Past and Present,* Van Nostrand, 1951; Pares, Sir B., *Russia,* Mentor,* 1949; Rauch, G. von, *A History of Soviet Russia,* Praeger,* 1959; Robinson, G. T., *Rural Russia under the Old Regime: A History of the Landlord-Peasant World and a Prologue to the Peasant Revolution of 1917,* Macmillan, 1949; Seton-Watson, H., *The Decline of Imperial Russia, 1815-1914,* Praeger, 1952; Tompkins, S. R., *Russia Through the Ages: From the Scythians to the Soviets,* Prentice-Hall, 1940; Vernadsky, G., *A History of Russia,* Yale, 1954; Walsh, W. B., *Russia and the Soviet Union: A Modern History,* Univ. of Mich., 1958; Wren, M. C., *The Course of Russian History,* Macmillan, 1958.

OTHER EUROPEAN STATES

Eastern Europe: Gulick, C. A., *Austria from Habsburg to Hitler,* 2 vols., Univ. of Calif., 1948; Halecki, O., *Borderlands of Western Civilization: A History of East Central Europe,* Ronald, 1952; Halecki, O., *A History of Poland,*

Roy, 1956; Lengyel, E., *One Thousand Years of Hungary,* Day, 1958; Schmitt, B. E., ed., *Poland,* Univ. of Calif., 1945; Seton-Watson, H., *Eastern Europe between the Wars, 1918-1941,* Macmillan, 1945; Sinor, D., *History of Hungary,* Praeger, 1959; Taylor, A. J. P., *The Hapsburg Monarchy, 1815-1918; A History of the Austrian Empire and Austria-Hungary,* Macmillan, 1949; Thomson, S. H., *Czechoslovakia in European History,* Princeton, 1953.

The Balkans: Forster, E. S., *A Short History of Modern Greece, 1821-1956,* Praeger, 1958; Gewehr, W. M., *The Rise of Nationalism in the Balkans, 1800-1930,* Holt, 1931; Roucek, J. S., *Balkan Politics; International Relations in No Man's Land,* Stanford, 1948; Schevill, F., *The Balkan Peninsula and the Near East,* G. Bell, 1922; Stavrianos, L. S., *The Balkans Since 1453,* Rinehart, 1958; Wolff, R. L., *The Balkans in Our Time,* Harvard,* 1956.

Iberia: Adams, N. B., *Heritage of Spain,* Holt, 1959; Altamira, R., *A History of Spain,* Evergreen,* 1960; Atkinson, W. C., *A History of Spain and Portugal,* Penguin,* 1960; Bertrand, L., and C. Petrie, *A History of Spain,* Macmillan, 1952; Livermore, H., *A History of Spain,* Evergreen,* 1960; Madariaga, S. de, *Spain: A Modern History,* Praeger, 1958; Nowell, C. E., *A History of Portugal,* Van Nostrand, 1952.

The Low Countries: Barnouw, A. J., *The Pageant of Netherlands History,* Longmans, 1952; Eyck, F. G., *The Benelux Countries: An Historical Survey,* Anvil,* 1959; Dessart, C., *Belgium,* Heinman, 1957; Vlekke, B. H. M., *The Evolution of the Dutch Nation,* Roy, 1945.

Scandinavia: Andersson, I., *A History of Sweden,* Praeger, 1956; Birch, J. H. S., *Denmark in History,* Murray, 1938; Derry, K., *A Short History of Norway,* Macmillan, 1957; Friis, H., ed., *Scandinavia: Between East and West,* Cornell, 1950; Larsen, K., *History of Norway,* Princeton, 1948.

THE UNITED STATES

Allen, H. C., *Great Britain and the United States; A History of Anglo-American Relations, 1783-1952,* St. Martin's, 1955; Bailey, T. A., *A Diplomatic History of the American People,* Appleton, 1958; Bailey, T. H., *The American Pageant; A History of the Republic,* Heath, 1956; Baldwin, L. D., *The Stream of American History,* 2 vols., American Book, 1952; Beard, C., and M. R. Beard, *The Rise of American Civilization,* 1 vol. ed., Macmillan, 1959; Beebe, L., and C. Clegg, *The American West; The Pictorial Epic of a Continent,* Dutton, 1955; Bemis, S. F., *A Diplomatic History of the United States,* Holt, 1955; Bemis, S. F., *The United States as a World Power; A Diplomatic History, 1900-1950,* Holt, 1955; Billington, R. A., et al., *The United States; American Democracy in World Perspective,* Rinehart, 1947; Billington, R. A., and J. B. Hedges, *Westward Expansion: A History of the American Frontier,* Macmillan, 1949; Blake, N. M., *A Short History of American Life,* McGraw-Hill, 1952; Butterfield, R., *The American Past: A History of the U.S. From Concord to the Nuclear Age,* Simon and Schuster, 1957; Carman, H. J., and H. C. Syrett, *A History of the American People,* 2 vols., Knopf, 1952; Cline, H. F., *The United States and Mexico,* Harvard, 1953; Craven, A. D., and W. J. Johnson, *The United States—Experiment in Democracy,* Ginn, 1947; Freidel, F., ed., *The Golden Age of American History*, Braziller, 1959; Dulles, F. R., *The United States Since 1865*, Univ. of Mich., 1959; Hacker, L. M., and H. S. Zahler, *The United States in the 20th Century*, Appleton, 1952; Hicks, J. D., and G. E. Mowry, *A Short History of American Democracy*, Houghton, 1956; Kraus, M., *The United States to 1865*, Univ. of Mich., 1959; Lerner, M., *America as a Civilization; Life and Thought in the United States Today*, Simon and Schuster, 1957; McLaughlin, A. C., *A Constitutional History of the United States*, Appleton, 1935; Lehner, E., *American Symbols*, Tudor,* 1958; Morison, S. E., and H. S. Commager, *The Growth of the American Republic*, 2 vols., Oxford, 1950; Morris, R. B., ed. *Encyclopedia of American History*, Harper, 1953; Perkins, D., *Hands Off; A History of the Monroe Doctrine*, Little, Brown, 1941; Smith, T. C., *The United States as a Factor in World History*, Holt,* 1941.

HISTORIES OF LATIN AMERICA

Bernstein, H., *Modern and Contemporary Latin America*, Lippincott, 1952; Hanke, L., *Modern Latin America: Continent in Ferment*, 2 vols., Van Nostrand,* 1960; Herring, H., *A History of Latin America: From the Beginnings to the Present*, Knopf, 1955; Hill, L. F., ed., *Brazil*, Univ. of Calif., 1947; Munro, D. G., *The Latin American Republics: A History*, Appleton, 1950; Parkes, H. B., *A History of Mexico*, Houghton, 1950; Peck, A. M., *Pageant of South American History*, Longmans, 1958; Rennie, Y. F., *The Argentine Republic*, Macmillan, 1945; Rippy, J. F., *The Caribbean Danger Zone*, Putnam, 1940; Rippy, J. F., *Historic Evolution of Hispanic America*, Appleton, 1945; Rippy, J. F., *Latin America: A Modern History*, Univ. of Mich.,* 1958; Tannenbaum, F., *Mexico: The Struggle for Peace and Bread*, Knopf, 1950; Wilgus, A. C., ed., *South American Dictators During the First Century of Independence*, Geo. Washington Univ., 1937.

HISTORIES OF AFRICA AND
THE MIDDLE EAST

Bartlett, V., *Struggle for Africa*, Praeger, 1953; Bentwich, N., *Israel*, McGraw-Hill, 1952; Brockelmann, C., *History of the Islamic Peoples*, Capricorn,* 1960; Bullard, Sir Reader, *Britain and the Middle East from the Earliest Times to 1952*, Hutchinson, 1952; Bullard, Sir Reader, ed., *The Middle East, A Political and Economic Survey*, Oxford, 1958; Duffy, J., *Portuguese Africa*, Harvard, 1959; Fisher, S. N., *The Middle East: A History*, Knopf, 1959; Gibb, H. A. R., *Modern Trends in Islam*, Univ. of Chicago, 1947; Harris, N. D., *Europe and Africa*, Houghton, 1927; Hitti, P. K., *History of the Arabs from the Earliest Times to the Present*, St. Martin's, 1956; Hitti, P. K., *Syria: A Short History*, Macmillan, 1959; Hoskins, H. L., *European Imperialism in Africa*, Holt, 1930; Izzeddin, N. M., *The Arab World, Past, Present, and Future*, Regnery, 1953; Kirk, G. E., *A Short History of the Middle East, from the Rise of Islam to Modern Times*, Praeger,* 1959; Laqueur, W. Z. ed., *The Middle East in Transition; Studies in Contemporary History*, Praeger, 1958; Lewis B., *The Arabs in History*, Rinehart, 1950; Marlowe, J., *Anglo-Egyptian Relations, 1800-1953*, Dufour, 1954; Miller, W., *The Ottoman Empire and Its Successors, 1801-1936*, Macmillan, 1936; Murdock, G. P., *Africa: Its Peoples and Their Culture History*, McGraw-Hill, 1959; Parkes, J., *A History of Palestine from 135 A.D.*

to *Modern Times*, Oxford, 1949; Scott, J., *Africa: World's Last Frontier*, Foreign Policy Assoc., 1959; Smith, W. G., *Islam in Modern History*, Mentor,* 1959; Speiser, E. A., *The United States and the Near East*, Harvard, 1947; Stillman, C. W., ed., *Africa in the Modern World*, Univ. of Chicago, 1955; Sykes, Sir P. M., *A History of Persia*, 2 vols., St. Martin's, 1952; Walker, E. A., *A History of Southern Africa*, Longmans, 1957; Wallbank, T. W., *Contemporary Africa: Continent in Transition*, Anvil, * 1964; Wieschoff, H. A., *Colonial Policies in Africa*, Univ. of Penna., 1944.

HISTORIES OF ASIA

The first group of titles deals chiefly with the relations between East and West in modern times. The other groups include national histories of Far Eastern nations.

Buss, C. A., *Southeast Asia and the World Today*, Anvil,* 1958; Cameron, M. E., *et al.*, *China, Japan and the Powers; A History of the Modern Far East*, Ronald, 1960; Clyde, P. H., *The Far East; A History of the Impact of the West on Eastern Asia*, Prentice-Hall, 1958; Dennett, T., *Americans in Eastern Asia*, Macmillan, 1922; Dulles, F. R., *China and America; The Story of Their Relations Since 1784*, Princeton, 1946; Ennis, T. E., *Eastern Asia*, Lippincott, 1948; Ennis, T. E., *French Policy and Developments in Indochina*, Univ. of Chicago, 1936; Fairbank, J. K., *The United States and China*, Harvard, 1958; Hughes, E. R., *The Invasion of China by the Western World*, Macmillan, 1938; MacNair, H. F., and D. F. Lach, *Modern Far Eastern International Relations*, Van Nostrand, 1955; Marriott, Sir J. A. R., *The English in India; A Problem of Politics*, Oxford, 1932; Michael, F. H., and G. E. Taylor, *The Far East in the Modern World*, Holt, 1956; Panikkar, K. M., *Asia and Western Dominance; A Survey of the Vasco Da Gama Epoch of Asian History, 1498-1945*, G. Allen, 1959; Pratt, Sir J. T., *The Expansion of Europe into the Far East*, British Book Centre, 1947; Reichwein, A., *China and Europe; Intellectual and Artistic Contacts in the Eighteenth Century*, Knopf, 1925; Roberts, P. E., *History of British India under the Company and the Crown* (rev. by T. G. Spear), Oxford, 1952; Rowe, D. N., *China Among the Powers*, Harcourt, 1945; Sanderson, G. D., *India and British Imperialism*, Bookman Associates, 1951; Sansom, Sir G. B., *The Western World and Japan; A Study in the Interaction of European and Asiatic Cultures*, Knopf, 1950; Treat, P. J., *Japan and the United States, 1853-1928*, Stanford, 1928; Vinacke, H. M., *A History of the Far East in Modern Times*, Knopf, 1938.

Brown, W. N., ed., *India, Pakistan, Ceylon*, Cornell, 1951; *The Cambridge History of India*, 6 vols., Cambridge, 1922-1937, supplementary vol., 1953; Allan, J., *et al.*, *The Cambridge Shorter History of India*, Macmillan, 1934; Keith, A. B., *A Constitutional History of India, 1600-1935*, Methuen, 1936; Majumdar, R. C., *et al.*, *An Advanced History of India*, St. Martin's, 1951; Moreland, W. H., and A. C. Chatterjee, *A Short History of India*, Longmans, 1957; Nehru, J., *The Discovery of India*, Anchor,* 1960; Panikkar, K. M., *A Survey of Indian History*, Hafner, 1954; Powell-Price, J. C., *A History of India*, Nelson, 1955; Rawlinson, H. G., *India; A Short Cultural History*, Praeger, 1953; Smith, V. A., *et al.*, *The Oxford History of India* (ed. by P. Spear), Oxford, 1958;

Wallbank, T. W., *A Short History of India and Pakistan*, Mentor,* 1958.

Ch'ien, Tuan-sheng, *The Government and Politics of China*, Harvard, 1950; Eberhard, W., *A History of China*, Univ. of Calif., 1960; Fitzgerald, C. P., *China, A Short Cultural History*, Praeger, 1954; Goodrich, L. C., *A Short History of the Chinese People*, Harper, 1959; Granet, M., *Chinese Civilization*, Meridian,* 1958; Latourette, K. S., *The Chinese, Their History and Culture*, Macmillan, 1946; Latourette, K. S., *A History of Modern China*, Penguin,* 1954; MacNair, H. F., ed., *China*, Univ. of Calif., 1946; De Riencourt, A., *The Soul of China*, Coward-McCann, 1958; Rowe, D. N., *Modern China, A Brief History*, Anvil,* 1959; Ts'ui, Chi, *A Short History of Chinese Civilization*, Putnam, 1943; Winfield, G., *China: The Land and the People*, Sloane, 1948.

Borton, H., *Japan's Modern Century*, Ronald, 1955; Latourette, K. S., *History of Japan*, Macmillan, 1957; Reischauer, E. O., *Japan Past and Present*, Knopf, 1953; Reischauer, R. K., *Japan, Government-Politics*, Nelson, 1939; Sansom, G. B., *A History of Japan*, 3 vols. in 1, Stanford, 1958; Sansom, G. B., *Japan: A Short Cultural History*, Appleton, 1943; Sansom, G. B., *Japan in World History*, Institute of Pacific Relations, 1951; Storry, R., *A History of Modern Japan*, Penguin,* 1960; Tiedemann, A., *Modern Japan, A Brief History*, Anvil,* 1955.

ECONOMICS

Alpert, P., *Twentieth Century European Economic History*, Abelard-Schuman, 1951; Benham, F. C. C., and H. A. Holley, *A Short Introduction to the Economy of Latin America*, Oxford, 1959; Bowden, W., et al., *An Economic History of Europe Since 1750*, American Book, 1937; Bruck, W. F., *Social and Economic History of Germany from William II to Hitler, 1888-1938*, Oxford, 1938; Buck, J. L., *Chinese Farm Economy; A Study of 2866 Farms in Seventeen Localities and Seven Provinces in China*, Univ. of Chicago, 1930; Chi, Ch'ao-ting, *Key Economic Areas in Chinese History*, G. Allen, 1936; Clapham, Sir John H., *An Economic History of Modern Britain*, 3 vols., Cambridge, 1930-1938; Clapham, Sir John H., *Economic Development of France and Germany, 1815-1914*, Cambridge, 1936; Clough, S. B., *The Economic Development of Western Civilization*, McGraw-Hill, 1959; Clough, S. B., *France: A History of National Economics, 1789-1939*, Scribner's, 1939; Clough, S. B., and C. W. Cole, *Economic History of Europe*, Heath, 1952; Day, C., *Economic Development in Europe*, Macmillan, 1942; Faulkner, H. U., *American Economic History*, Harper, 1954; Fite, G. C., and J. E. Reese, *An Economic History of the United States*, Houghton, 1959; Gide, C., and C. Rist, *A History of Economic Doctrines, from the Time of the Physiocrats to the Present Day*, Heath, 1948; Heaton, H., *Economic History of Europe*, Harper, 1948; Heilbroner, R. L., *The Worldly Philosophers: The Lives, Times, and Ideas of Great Economic Thinkers*, Simon and Schuster, 1955; Hughes, T. J., and D. E. T. Luard, *Economic Development of Communist China, 1949-1958*, Oxford, 1959; Kirby, E. S., *Introduction to the Economic History of China*, Macmillan, 1954; Knowles, L. C., *Economic Development in the Nineteenth Century: France, Germany, Russia, and the United States*, Routledge, 1932; Loucks, W. N., *Comparative Economic Systems: Capitalism, Socialism, Communism, Fas-*

cism, Harper, 1957; McGrane, R. C., *The Economic Development of the American Nation*, Ginn, 1950; Mookerji, R., *The Foundations of Indian Economics*, Longmans, 1916; Oakeshott, W. F., *Commerce and Society: A Short History of Trade and Its Effects on Civilization*, Oxford, 1936; Renard, G. F., and G. Weulersse, *Life and Work in Modern Europe, 15th to 18th Century*, Knopf, 1926; Rippy, J. F., *Latin America and the Industrial Age*, Putnam, 1947; Schumpeter, J. A., ed., *History of Economic Analysis*, Oxford, 1954; Shih, Kuo-heng, *China Enters the Machine Age*, Harvard, 1944; Stolper, G., *German Economy, 1870-1940; Issues and Trends*, Reynal, 1940; Taussig, F. W., *The Tariff History of the United States*, Putnam, 1931; Wright, C., *Economic History of the United States*, McGraw-Hill, 1949.

PHILOSOPHY AND RELIGION

Aiken, H. S., ed., *The Age of Ideology; The 19h Century Philosophers*, Mentor,* 1956; Berlin, S. I., ed., *The Age of Enlightenment; The 18th Century Philosophers*, Mentor,* 1956; Commager, H. S., *The American Mind: An Interpretation of American Thought and Character Since the 1880's*, Yale,* 1959; Creel, H. G., *Chinese Thought: From Confucius to Mao Tse-tung*, Mentor,* 1960; Curti, M. E., *The Growth of American Thought*, Harper, 1951; Durant, W., *The Story of Philosophy: The Lives and Opinions of the Greater Philosophers*, Pocket Books,* 1954; Ferm, V., ed., *History of Philosophical Systems*, Littlefield,* 1958; Frankel, C., ed., *The Golden Age of American Philosophy*, Braziller, 1960; Fung, Yu-lan, *A History of Chinese Philosophy*, 2 vols., Princeton, 1952-1953; Hoffding, H., *A History of Modern Philosophy; A Sketch of the History of Philosophy from the Close of the Renaissance to Our Own Day*, 2 vols., Dover,* 1956; Jones, W. T., *A History of Western Philosophy*, Harcourt, 1952; Latourette, K. S., *A History of the Expansion of Christianity*, 7 vols., Harper, 1937-1945; Moore, C. A., ed., *Philosophy—East and West*, Princeton, 1944; Noss, J. B., *Man's Religions*, Macmillan, 1956; Parrington, V. L., *Main Currents in American Thought, Vol. II, 1800-1860*, Harvest,* 1954; Radhakrishnan, S., and C. A. Moore, eds., *A Source Book in Indian Philosophy*, Princeton, 1957; Randall, J. H., *The Making of the Modern Mind; A Survey of the Intellectual Background of the Present Age*, Houghton, 1940; Royce, J., *The Spirit of Modern Philosophy*, Braziller, 1955; Russell, B., *A History of Western Philosophy*, Simon and Schuster,* 1945; Sperry, W. L., *Religion in America*, Macmillan, 1946; Sweet, W. W., *The Story of Religion in America*, Harper, 1950; Tsunoda, R., et al., comps., *Sources of the Japanese Tradition*, Columbia, 1958; White, M., ed., *The Age of Analysis; 20th Century Philosophers*, Mentor,* 1955; Whitehead, A. N., *Science and the Modern World*, Mentor,* 1948; Wiener, P. P., *Evolution and the Founders of Pragmatism*, Harvard, 1949; Windelband, W., *A History of Philosophy*, 2 vols., Torchbooks,* 1958; Wise, H., *Society and Thought in America*, 2 vols., Longmans, 1950-1952; Zimmer, H., *Philosophies of India* (ed. by J. Campbell), Meridian,* 1956.

POLITICAL THEORY

Arendt, H., *The Origins of Totalitarianism*, Meridian,* 1958; Barker, Sir Ernest, *Political Thought in England, 1848-1914*,

Oxford, 1947; Catlin, G., *The Story of the Political Philosophers*, McGraw-Hill, 1939; Ch'ien, Tuan-shêng, *The Government and Politics of China*, Harvard, 1950; Cole, G. D. H., *Socialist Thought: The Forerunners, 1789-1850; Socialist Thought: Marxism and Anarchism, 1850-1890; The Second International; Communism and Social Democracy, 1914-1931*, Vols. I-IV of *History of Political Thought*, St. Martin's, 1953-1959; Gray, A., *The Socialist Tradition*, Longmans, 1946; Hearnshaw, F. J. C., ed., *The Social and Political Ideas of Some Representative Thinkers of the Victorian Age*, Barnes and Noble, 1950; Hofstadter, R., *The American Political Tradition*, Vintage,* 1954; Kohn, H., *Nationalism: Its Meaning and History*, Anvil,* 1955; Kohn H., *Pan-Slavism: Its History and Ideology*, Vintage,* 1960; Kohn, H., *Prophets and Peoples: Studies in Nineteenth Century Nationalism*, Macmillan, 1946; Laidler, H. W., *A History of Socialist Thought*, Crowell, 1933; Laski, H. J., *The American Presidency*, Universal,* 1958; Lin, Mou-shêng, *Men and Ideas; An Informal History of Chinese Political Thought*, Day, 1942; Pollock, F., *An Introduction to the History of the Science of Politics*, Beacon,* 1960; Ruggiero, G. de, *History of European Liberalism*, Beacon,* 1959; Russell, B., *Proposed Roads to Freedom: Socialism, Anarchism, and Syndicalism*, Holt, 1919; Sabine, G. H., *A History of Political Theory*, Holt, 1950; Salvadori, M., *The Rise of Modern Communism; A Brief History of the Communist Movement in the Twentieth Century*, Holt, 1952; Saunders, J. J., *The Age of Revolution; The Rise and Decline of Liberalism in Europe Since 1815*, Roy, 1949; Soltau, R. H., *French Political Thought in the Nineteenth Century*, Russell, 1959; Viereck, P., *Conservatism Revisited; The Revolt Against Revolt, 1815-1949*, Scribner's, 1949; Viereck, P., *Metapolitics, from the Romantics to Hitler*, Knopf, 1941.

SCIENCE AND TECHNOLOGY

Calder, R., *Medicine and Man*, Mentor,* 1958; Castiglioni, A., *A History of Medicine*, Knopf, 1947; Cohen, I. B., *Science, Servant of Man*, Little, Brown, 1948; Compton, R. T., and C. H. Nettels, eds., *Conquests of Science*, Harcourt, 1939; Cowan, H. J., *Time and Its Measurement: From the Stone Age to the Nuclear Age*, World, 1958; Dampier, W. C. D., *A History of Science and Its Relations with Philosophy and Religion*, Macmillan, 1949; Dampier, W. C. D., *A Shorter History of Science*, Meridian,* 1957; Dampier, W. C. D., and M. D. Dampier, comps., *Readings in the Literature of Science; Being Extracts from the Writings of Men of Science to Illustrate the Development of Scientific Thought*, Torchbooks,* 1959; Dunsheath, P., ed., *A Century of Technology, 1851-1951*, Roy, 1951; Dingle, H., ed., *A Century of Science, 1851-1951*, Roy, 1951; *Lives in Science*, Simon and Schuster,* 1957; Farber, E., *The Evolution of Chemistry*, Ronald, 1952; Finch, J. K., *The Story of Engineering*, Anchor,* 1960; Forbes, R. J., *Man the Maker: A History of Technology and Engineering*, Abelard-Schuman, 1958; Gardner, M., ed., *Great Essays in Science*, Pocket Books,* 1959; Jaffe, B., *Crucibles: The Story of Chemistry*, Premier,* 1957; Jeans, Sir James, *The Growth of Physical Science*, Premier,* 1958; Kirby, R. S., et al., *Engineering in History*, McGraw-Hill, 1956; Leff, S., and V. Leff, *From Witchcraft to World Health*, Macmillan, 1957; Leicester, H. M., *The Historical Background of Chemistry*, Wiley, 1956; Lenard, P., *Great Men of Science*, Macmillan, 1933; Magie, W. F., *A Source Book in Physics*, McGraw-Hill, 1935; Mason, S. F., *Main Currents of Scientific Thought*, Abelard-Schuman, 1954; Mettler, C. C., *History of Medicine*, Blakiston, 1947; Mumford, L., *Technics and Civilization*, Harcourt, 1934; Murray, R. H., *Science and Scientists in the Nineteenth Century*, Macmillan, 1925; Rosen, G., *A History of Public Health*, M. D. Publications, 1958; Sarton, G. A. L., *Introduction to the History of Science*, 5 vols., Williams and Wilkins, 1927-1948; Sarton, G. A. L., *A Study of the History of Mathematics; and, The Study of the History of Science*, 2 vols. in 1, Dover,* 1957; Schwartz, G., et al., eds., *Moments of Discovery*, 2 vols., Basic Books, 1958; Sedgwick, W. T., et al., *A Short History of Science*, Macmillan, 1939; Shamos, M. H., ed., *Great Experiments in Physics*, Holt,* 1959; Shryock, R. H., *The Development of Modern Medicine*, Knopf, 1947; Sigerist, H. E., *The Great Doctors; A Biographical History of Medicine*, Anchor,* 1958; Singer, C. J., ed., *Studies in the History and Method of Science*, 2 vols., Oxford, 1921; Singer, C. J., et al., *A History of Technology*, 5 vols., Oxford, 1954-1958; Stern, P. Van Doren, *A Pictorial History of the Automobile*, Viking, 1953; Taylor, F. S., *An Illustrated History of Science*, Praeger, 1955; Taylor, F. S., *A Short History of Science and Scientific Thought*, Norton, 1949; Usher, A. P., *A History of Mechanical Inventions*, Beacon Press,* 1959; Von Lane, M., *History of Physics*, Academic Press, 1950; Wightman, W. P. D., *The Growth of Scientific Ideas*, Yale, 1951; Winter, H. J. J., *Eastern Science; An Outline of Its Scope and Contribution*, Transatlantic Press, 1952.

FOOTNOTES

1. THE NEW ORDER

1. A. Pope, *The Poetical Works of Alexander Pope* (London: John James Chidley, 1846), p. 434.

2. Quoted in A. R. Hall, *The Scientific Revolution* (London: Longmans, Green and Co., Ltd., 1954), pp. 248-249. Reprinted by permission of the publishers.

3. Compare Sir Isaac Newton, *Mathematical Principles of Natural Philosophy and His System of the World*, ed. and trans. by F. Cajori (Berkeley: University of California Press, 1946).

4. H. Shapley *et al.*, eds., *A Treasury of Science* (New York: Harper and Bros., 1958), p. 147.

5. Quoted in Hall, p. 332. Reprinted by permission of the publishers.

6. Quoted in P. Smith, *A History of Modern Culture*, II (London: G. Routledge and Sons, Ltd., 1934), pp. 115-116.

7. Quoted in Hall, p. 212. Reprinted by permission of the publishers.

8. Quoted in G. H. Knoles and R. K. Snyder, *Readings in Western Civilization* (New York: J. B. Lippincott Co., 1951), p. 468.

9. Quoted in Hall, p. 271. Reprinted by permission of the publishers.

10. A. Pope, "An Essay on Man," in *The Literature of England,* I, 4th ed., ed. by G. B. Woods, H. A. Watt, G. K. Anderson, and K. J. Holzknecht (Chicago: Scott, Foresman and Co., 1958), p. 1086.

11. A. Pope, "The Universal Prayer," in *The Poetical Works of Alexander Pope*, p. 145.

12. Quoted in J. H. Robinson, *Readings in European History*, II (Boston: Ginn and Co., 1906), pp. 273-275.

13. Quoted in *ibid.*, p. 274.

14. Quoted in A. F. Tyler, *The Modern World* (New York: Farrar and Rinehart, 1939), p. 186.

15. *Encyclopaedia Britannica*, VII, 1947 ed., p. 16.

2. THE COMPETITIVE STATE SYSTEM

1. W. L. Dorn, *Competition for Empire, 1740-1763* (New York: Harper and Bros., 1940), p. 1.

2. Sir Ernest Barker *et al.*, *The European Inheritance*, II (London: Clarendon Press, 1954), p. 144.

3. Quoted in E. P. Cheyney, *Readings in English History Drawn from the Original Sources* (Boston: Ginn and Co., 1908), p. 426.

4. Quoted in *ibid.*, 429.

5. G. M. Trevelyan, *England Under the Stuarts* (London: Methuen and Co., Ltd., 1947), p. 190.

6. Quoted in G. Smith, *A History of England* (New York: Charles Scribner's Sons, 1949), p. 276.

7. Quoted in Cheyney, p. 503.

8. Quoted in P. Smith, *A History of Modern Culture*, I (London: G. Routledge and Sons, Ltd., 1930), p. 226.

9. Quoted in G. M. Trevelyan, *England Under the Stuarts* (New York: G. P. Putnam's Sons, 1941; London: Methuen and Co., Ltd.), p. 282.

10. W. P. Hall and R. G. Albion, *A History of England and the British Empire, 1789-1914* (Boston: Ginn and Co., 1937), p. 394.

11. Quoted in Cheyney, pp. 571-572.

12. Quoted in G. B. Adams, *Constitutional History of England* (New York: Henry Holt and Co., 1934), p. 406.

13. B. Pares, *A History of Russia* (New York: Alfred A. Knopf, 1956), p. 199.

14. J. F. C. Fuller, *A Military History of the Western World,* II (New York: Funk and Wagnalls, 1954), p. 186. Published in England under the title *Decisive Battles of the Western World* by Eyre and Spottiswoode, Ltd., London.

15. Quoted in M. B. Garrett, *European History, 1500-1815* (New York: American Book Co., 1940), p. 438.

16. Quoted in R. Ergang, *The Potsdam Führer, Frederick William I* (New York: Columbia University Press, 1941), p. 7.

17. Quoted in Dorn, p. 2.

18. Quoted in *ibid.*, p. 9.

19. Quoted in A. W. Ward *et al.*, eds., *The Cambridge Modern History*, VI (New York: The Macmillan Co., 1909), pp. 441-442.

20. Quoted in Dorn, p. 139.

21. Quoted in Hall and Albion (published 1946), p. 453.

22. Quoted in Dorn, p. 314.

23. Quoted in P. Gaxotte, *Frederick the Great* (London: G. Bell and Sons, Ltd., 1941), p. 357.

24. Quoted in H. Robinson, *The Development of the British Empire* (Boston: Houghton Mifflin Co., 1922), p. 96.

3. NEW FORCES AND THE OLD REGIME

1. Compare *Encyclopaedia Britannica*, V, 1957 ed., p. 959.

2. Quoted in H. Heaton, *Economic History of Europe* (New York: Harper and Bros., 1948), p. 315.

3. Quoted in J. B. Botsford, *English Society in the Eighteenth Century, As Influenced from Oversea* (New York: The Macmillan Co., 1924), p. 54.

4. Quoted in J. E. Gillespie, *The Influence of Oversea Ex-*

pansion on England to 1700 (New York: Columbia University Press, 1920), p. 52.

5. Quoted in Botsford, p. 87.

6. Quoted in ibid., p. 70.

7. Quoted in Heaton (published 1936), p. 930.

8. Quoted in E. H. Carter and R. A. F. Mears, A History of Britain, Section 4 (Oxford: Clarendon Press, 1937), p. 662.

9. Heaton (published 1936), p. 363.

10. The Rev. Thomas Bancroft, quoted in J. Harland, Collectanea Relating to Manchester, II (Manchester: Printed for the Chetham Society, 1867), p. 217.

11. From the memoirs of Marquis De Bouillé, quoted in L. Ducros, French Society in the Eighteenth Century (London: G. Bell and Sons, Ltd., 1926), p. 224.

12. A. Smith, An Inquiry into the Nature and Causes of the Wealth of Nations, Modern Library ed. (New York: The Macmillan Co., 1937), pp. 14, 421.

13. Ibid., pp. 461-462.

14. W. L. Dorn, Competition for Empire, 1740-1763 (New York: Harper and Bros., 1940), p. 181.

15. Compare Introduction to Contemporary Civilization in the West, I (New York: Columbia University Press, 1946), pp. 845-859.

16. G. P. Gooch, Catherine the Great and Other Studies (London: Longmans, Green and Co., Ltd., 1954), p. 110.

17. Quoted in B. R. Redman, ed., The Portable Voltaire (New York: The Viking Press, 1949), pp. 234-235.

18. Quoted in ibid., pp. 514, 520.

19. Quoted in G. R. Havens, The Age of Ideas (New York: Henry Holt and Co., 1955), pp. 105-106.

20. Quoted in J. H. Robinson and C. A. Beard, Readings in Modern European History, I (Boston: Ginn and Co., 1908), p. 191.

21. Quoted in F. E. Manuel, The Age of Reason (Ithaca, N.Y.: Cornell University Press, 1951), p. 89.

22. Quoted in W. G. Crane et al., Twelve Hundred Years: The Literature of England, I (New York: Stackpole and Heck, Inc., 1948), p. 572.

23. Quoted in G. E. G. Catlin, The Story of the Political Philosophers (New York: Tudor Publishing Co., 1939), p. 443.

24. Quoted in J. E. Gillespie, A History of Geographical Discovery, 1400-1800 (New York: Henry Holt and Co., 1933), p. 99.

25. Quoted in Introduction to Contemporary Civilization in the West, I (New York: Coulmbia University Press, 1946), p. 987.

26. T. I. Cook, History of Political Philosophy (New York: Prentice-Hall, Inc., 1936), p. 636.

27. A. Pope, "An Essay on Man," in The Poetical Works of Alexander Pope (London: John James Chidley, 1846), p. 198.

28. A. Pope, "Epistle to Dr. Arbuthnot," in The Literature of England, I, p. 1098.

29. A. Pope, "An Essay on Man," in The Literature of England, I, pp. 1088-1089.

30. Quoted in Robinson and Beard, I, pp. 202-205.

31. W. O. Ault, Europe in Modern Times (Boston: D. C. Heath and Co., 1946), p. 238.

32. Quoted in J. W. Thompson et al., European Civilization (New York: D. Van Nostrand Co., Inc., 1939), p. 851.

33. Quoted in F. Nowak, Medieval Slavdom and the Rise of Russia (New York: Henry Holt and Co., 1930), p. 91.

34. Quoted in G. P. Gooch, Frederick the Great; the Ruler, the Writer, the Man (New York: Alfred A. Knopf, 1947), p. 109.

4. THE RIGHTS OF MAN

1. C. J. H. Hayes, A Political and Cultural History of Modern Europe, I (New York: The Macmillan Co., 1932), p. 614.

2. "The Declaration of the Rights of Man," in The World in Literature, III, ed. by R. Warnock and G. K. Anderson (Chicago: Scott, Foresman and Co., 1951), pp. 298-299.

3. Quoted in L. Madelin, The French Revolution (London: William Heinemann, Ltd., 1916), p. 240.

4. Quoted in Hayes, I, p. 627.

5. Quoted in J. E. Gillespie, A History of Europe, 1500-1815 (New York: Alfred A. Knopf, 1928), p. 529.

6. Madelin, p. 323.

7. W. Wordsworth, "The French Revolution," in Poems of Wordsworth, ed. by M. Arnold (London: Macmillan and Co., 1891), p. 258.

8. E. Burke, "Reflections on the Revolution in France," in The Works of the Right Honorable Edmund Burke, II (London: G. Bell and Sons, 1886), p. 284.

9. Quoted in J. H. Randall, Jr., The Making of the Modern Mind (Boston: Houghton Mifflin Co., 1940), p. 433.

10. Quoted in L. Gershoy, The French Revolution and Napoleon (New York: F. S. Crofts and Co., 1933), p. 273.

11. Quoted in Gillespie, p. 537.

12. Madelin, pp. 429-430.

13. Quoted in ibid., p. 489.

14. Quoted in Gillespie, p. 544.

15. Quoted in J. H. Rose, The Life of Napoleon, I (New York: The Macmillan Co., 1902), p. 264.

16. Quoted in R. Ergang, Europe from the Renaissance to Waterloo (Boston: D. C. Heath and Co., 1954), p. 717.

17. Lord Rosebery, *Napoleon: The Last Phase* (London: Arthur L. Humphreys, 1900), p. 229.

18. A. T. Mahan, *The Influence of Sea Power upon the French Revolution and Empire,* II (Boston: Little, Brown and Co., 1902), p. 118.

19. Quoted in Fisher, III (published 1936), p. 891.

20. H. G. Wells, *The Outline of History* (New York: Garden City Publishing Co., Inc., 1931), p. 935.

21. Quoted in F. C. Palm and F. E. Graham, *Europe Since Napoleon* (Boston: Ginn and Company, 1934), p. 38.

22. Quoted in F. B. Artz, *Reaction and Revolution, 1814-1832* (New York: Harper and Bros., 1934), p. 112.

23. Quoted in *Encyclopaedia Britannica,* XXVI, 1911 ed., p. 376.

24. Quoted in C. D. Hazen, *Europe Since 1815* (New York: Henry Holt and Co., 1910), pp. 21-22.

25. Compare L. Gottschalk and D. Lach, *Europe and the Modern World,* I (Chicago: Scott, Foresman and Co., 1951), p. 742.

26. A. J. Grant and H. Temperley, *Europe in the Nineteenth and Twentieth Centuries* (London: Longmans, Green and Co., Ltd., 1942), p. 138.

27. Quoted in Ergang, p. 752.

5. ROMANTICS AND REBELS

1. B. Willey, *Nineteenth Century Studies* (London: Chatto and Windus, 1949), p. 52.

2. L. A. Willoughby, *The Romantic Movement in Germany* (London: Oxford University Press, 1930), p. 8.

3. W. Wordsworth, "Preface to Lyrical Ballads," in *The Literature of England,* II, 4th ed., ed. by G. B. Woods, H. A. Watt, G. K. Anderson, and K. J. Holzknecht (Chicago: Scott, Foresman and Co., 1958), pp. 319-327.

4. W. Wordsworth, "Lines Composed a Few Miles above Tintern Abbey," in *The Literature of England,* II, p. 122.

5. Lord Byron, "Don Juan," Canto 2, 11. 25-32, in *The Literature of England,* II, p. 229.

6. P. B. Shelley, "Prometheus Unbound," Act III, Scene 4, 11. 194-196, in *English Poetry and Prose of the Romantic Movement,* ed. by G. B. Woods (Chicago: Scott, Foresman and Co., 1950), p. 716.

7. J. Keats, "Poem from Endymion," in *The Literature of England,* II, p. 278.

8. J. Keats, "Ode on a Grecian Urn," in *The Literature of England,* II, p. 282.

9. S. T. Coleridge, "Biographia Literaria," in *The Literature of England,* II, p. 328.

10. S. T. Coleridge, "Kubla Khan; or, a Vision in a Dream," in *The Literature of England,* II, p. 184.

11. W. Wordsworth, "Composed in the Valley near Dover, on the Day of Landing," in *English Poetry and Prose of the Romantic Movement,* p. 313.

12. V. Hugo, "Onwards," in *Poems,* Vol. III of *The Works of Victor Hugo* (Boston: Estes and Lauriat, 1892), pp. 333-335.

13. A Pushkin, "To Chaadeyev," in *The World in Literature,* III, ed. by R. Warnock and G. K. Anderson (Chicago: Scott, Foresman and Co., 1951), p. 553.

14. C. A. and M. Beard, *The Industrial Era,* Vol. II of *The Rise of American Civilization* (New York: The Macmillan Co., 1927), p. 763.

15. R. Browning, "Song from 'Pippa Passes,'" in *The Literature of England,* II, p. 657.

6. INDUSTRIAL REVOLUTION

1. Quoted in J. L. and B. Hammond, *The Rise of Modern Industry* (London: Methuen and Co., Ltd., 1927), p. 70.

2. Quoted in W. P. Hall and R. G. Albion, *A History of England and the British Empire, 1789-1914* (Boston: Ginn and Co., 1946), pp. 607-608.

3. Lord David Cecil, *Melbourne* (New York: Bobbs-Merrill Co., Inc., 1954), p. 391.

4. C. Kingsley, *Alton Locke, Tailor and Poet* (London: Macmillan and Co., Ltd., 1911), p. 16.

5. "Report of Lord Ashley's Mines Commission, 1842," in L. L. Snyder, *Fifty Major Documents of the Nineteenth Century* (Princeton: D. Van Nostrand Co., Inc., 1955), p. 66. Copyright 1955 by D. Van Nostrand Co., Inc.

6. Quoted in J. L. and B. Hammond, *The Town Labourer, 1760-1832* (London: Longmans, Green and Co., Ltd., 1919), p. 160.

7. C. Dickens, *Hard Times* (London: Thomas Nelson and Sons, Ltd., n.d.), p. 26.

8. H. Heaton, "The Industrial Revolution," in *The Making of Modern Europe,* II, ed. by H. Ausubel (New York: Dryden Press, 1951), p. 621.

9. Quoted in Hall and Albion, p. 795.

10. T. R. Malthus, "An Essay on Population," in *Introduction to Contemporary Civilization in the West,* II (New York: Columbia University Press, 1955), p. 196.

11. Quoted in W. P. Hall and W. S. Davis, *The Course of Europe Since Waterloo* (New York: D. Appleton-Century Co., Inc., 1941), p. 262.

12. *Ibid.,* pp. 262-263.

13. J. Bentham, *Theory of Legislation,* trans. from the French of E. Dumont by R. Hildreth (London: Trübner and Co., 1871), pp. 3, 63.

14. The Earl of Beaconsfield, K.G., *Sybil; or, The Two Nations* (London: Longmans, Green and Co., Ltd., 1926), pp. 76-77.

15. T. Carlyle, "Past and Present," in *Introduction to Contemporary Civilization in the West,* II, p. 363.

16. Quoted in Hall and Albion, pp. 776-777.

17. G. M. Trevelyan, *Illustrated English Social History*, IV (London: Longmans, Green and Co., Ltd., 1952), p. 43.

18. W. Godwin, "Political Justice," in S. Hook, *Marx and the Marxists: The Ambiguous Legacy* (Princeton: D. Van Nostrand Co., Inc., 1955), p. 28.

19. Quoted in E. R. A. Seligman, ed., *Encyclopedia of the Social Sciences*, XIII (New York: The Macmillan Co., 1935), p. 510a.

20. L. Blanc, "Socialist Catechism," in J. H. Randall, Jr., *The Making of the Modern Mind*, rev. ed. (Boston: Houghton Mifflin Co., 1940), p. 454.

21. Quoted in H. J. Laski, *Communist Manifesto: Socialist Landmark* (London: George Allen and Unwin, Ltd., 1948), p. 168.

22. Compare *ibid.*, p. 141.

23. Quoted in Seligman, XIV, p. 199b.

24. Quoted in *ibid.*

7. TO THE BARRICADES!

1. Quoted in F. B. Artz, *Reaction and Revolution, 1814-1832* (New York: Harper and Bros., 1934), pp. 49-50.

2. Quoted in C. J. H. Hayes, *A Political and Cultural History of Modern Europe*, I (New York: The Macmillan Co., 1932), p. 733.

3. *Ibid.*, p. 776.

4. A. J. Grant and H. Temperley, *Europe in the Nineteenth and Twentieth Centuries* (London: Longmans, Green and Co., Ltd., 1942), p. 143.

5. Lord Byron, "Don Juan," Canto 3, in *The Literature of England*, II, 4th ed., ed. by G. B. Woods, H. A. Watt, G. K. Anderson, and K. J. Holzknecht (Chicago: Scott, Foresman and Co., 1958), p. 235.

6. Lord Byron, "The Age of Bronze," in *The Poems and Dramas of Lord Byron* (New York: Thomas Crowell, n.d.), p. 251.

7. E. L. Woodward, *The Age of Reform* (London: Oxford University Press, 1938), p. 21.

8. *Ibid.*, p. 28.

9. G. M. Young, ed., *Selected Speeches by Lord Macaulay* (London: Oxford University Press, 1935), pp. 18-19.

10. Quoted in P. Robertson, *Revolutions of 1848* (Princeton: Princeton University Press, 1952), p. 14.

11. Quoted in A. F. Tyler, *The Modern World* (New York: Farrar and Rinehart, 1939), p. 518.

12. Quoted in H. A. L. Fisher, *A History of Europe*, III (Boston: Houghton Mifflin Co., 1936; London: Eyre and Spottiswoode, Ltd., 1935), p. 934.

13. F. Fejto, *The Opening of an Era* (London: Allan Wingate, 1948), p. 6.

14. Robertson, p. 35.

15. A. L. Guérard, *Reflections on the Napoleonic Legend* (London: T. Fisher Unwin, Ltd., 1924), p. 148.

16. Quoted in Hazen, p. 129.

17. *Life and Writings of Joseph Mazzini*, I (London: Smith, Elder, and Co., 1891), pp. 2-3.

18. R. W. Seton-Watson, "Metternich and Internal Austrian Policy," in *The Making of Modern Europe*, II, ed. by H. Ausubel (New York: Dryden Press, 1951), p. 594.

19. Quoted in J. G. Legge, *Rhyme and Revolution in Germany* (London: Constable and Co., Ltd., 1918), p. 150.

20. Quoted in F. E. Hirsch, "Frankfurt, 1848 and 1948; The Problems of German Liberty and Unity," *Current History*, XIV, No. 81 (April 1948), p. 284.

21. A Whitridge, *Men in Crisis; The Revolutions of 1848* (New York: Charles Scribner's Sons, 1949), p. 216.

22. F. E. Hirsch, "The Intellectuals' Revolution, 1848," *Current History*, XIV, No. 80 (April 1948), p. 210.

23. Quoted in Whitridge, p. 190.

24. Quoted in R. R. Palmer, *A History of the Modern World* (New York: Alfred A. Knopf, 1952), p. 496.

25. Fisher, III, p. 956.

8. NATIONALISM AND THE MAKING OF NATIONS

1. Quoted in F. E. Hirsch, "The Intellectuals' Revolution, 1848," *Current History*, XIV, No. 80 (April 1948), p. 213.

2. Quoted in E. Lipson, *Europe in the Nineteenth and Twentieth Centuries, 1815-1938* (London: Adam and Charles Black, 1949), p. 168.

3. G. M. Paléologue, *Cavour*, trans. by I. F. D. and M. M. Morrow (New York: Harper and Bros., 1927), p. 276. Reprinted by permission of Harper and Bros.

4. Quoted in J. S. Schapiro, *Modern and Contemporary European History, 1815-1940* (Boston: Houghton Mifflin Co., 1940), p. 222.

5. Paléologue, pp. 297-298.

6. Quoted in K. S. Pinson, *Modern Germany* (New York: The Macmillan Co., 1954), p. 114.

7. Quoted in *ibid.*, p. 116.

8. Quoted in Schapiro, p. 237.

9. Quoted in Lipson, p. 34.

10. Sir J. A. R. Marriott, *A Short History of France* (New York: Oxford University Press, 1944), p. 233.

11. Quoted in A. J. P. Taylor, *Bismarck: The Man and the Statesman* (London: Hamish Hamilton, Ltd., 1955), pp. 103-104.

12. Quoted in J. F. C. Fuller, *A Military History of the Western World*, III (New York: Funk and Wagnalls, 1956), p. 109.

13. Quoted in J. H. Jackson, *Clemenceau and the Third Republic* (New York: The Macmillan Co., 1948), p. 23.

14. Quoted in Lipson, p. 154.

15. Quoted in *ibid.*, p. 155.

16. *Memoirs of Friedrich Ferdinand Count von Beust*, I (London: Remington and Co., 1887), pp. xxii-xxvi.

17. J. A. R. Marriott, *The Eastern Question* (London: Clarendon Press, 1924), p. 2.

18. Quoted in P. Guedalla, *Palmerston* (London: Ernest Benn, Ltd., 1926), p. 212.

19. Quoted in W. P. Hall and R. G. Albion, *A History of England and the British Empire, 1789-1914* (Boston: Ginn and Co., 1937), p. 645.

20. H. A. L. Fisher, *A History of Europe*, single-vol. ed. (Boston: Houghton Mifflin Co., 1936), p. 969.

21. Quoted in B. H. Sumner, *A Short History of Russia* (New York: Harcourt, Brace and Co., 1949), p. 232.

22. Quoted in J. F. Scott and A. Baltzly, *Readings in European History Since 1814* (New York: F. S. Crofts and Co., 1934), p. 363.

23. A. J. P. Taylor, *The Struggle for Mastery in Europe, 1848-1918* (London: Clarendon Press, 1954), p. 231.

24. Quoted in Fuller, III, p. 104.

9. NEW EUROPES OVERSEAS

1. R. A. Billington, *The American Frontier* (Washington, D.C.: Service Center for Teachers of History, 1958), p. 22.

2. Quoted in *New Zealand*, Vol. VII, Pt. 2 of *The Cambridge History of the British Empire* (Cambridge: Cambridge University Press, 1933), p. 242.

3. B. Keen, *Readings in Latin-American Civilization* (Boston: Houghton Mifflin Co., 1955), p. 171.

4. Quoted in J. F. Rippy, *Historical Evolution of Hispanic America* (New York: F. S. Crofts and Co., 1932), p. 131.

5. M. Ugarte, *The Destiny of a Continent* (New York: Alfred A. Knopf, 1925), p. 288.

6. Quoted in J. L. Mecham, "Conflicting Ideals of Pan-Americanism," *Current History*, XXXIII, No. 3 (December 1930), p. 402.

10. THE WHITE MAN'S BURDEN

1. R. Kipling, "The White Man's Burden," in *The Literature of England*, II, 4th ed., ed. by G. B. Woods, H. A. Watt, G. K. Anderson, and K. J. Holzknecht (Chicago: Scott, Foresman and Co., 1958), p. 897.

2. H. W. Wyatt, "The Ethics of Empire," *Nineteenth Century* (April 1897), p. 529.

3. Quoted in P. T. Moon, *Imperialism and World Politics* (New York: The Macmillan Co., 1927), p. 15.

4. Compare T. E. Kebbel, ed., *Selected Speeches of the Late Right Honourable the Earl of Beaconsfield*, II (London: Longmans, Green and Co., 1882), pp. 231-252.

5. Quoted in Moon, p. 66.

6. J. A. Hobson, *Imperialism: A Study* (London: Constable and Co., Ltd., 1905), p. 75.

7. Quoted in M. E. Townsend, *Origins of Modern German Colonialism*, Studies in History, Economics, and Public Law, XCVIII, No. 1 (New York: Columbia University Press, 1921), p. 27.

8. Quoted in Moon, p. 38.

9. Quoted in W. L. Langer, *The Diplomacy of Imperialism*, I (New York: Alfred A. Knopf, 1935), p. 86.

10. Quoted in C. S. Olcott, *The Life of William McKinley*, II (Boston: Houghton Mifflin Co., 1916), pp. 110-111.

11. *The Works of Lord Macaulay*, VIII (London: Longmans, Green and Co., 1879), p. 119.

12. K. S. Latourette, *A Short History of the Far East* (New York: The Macmillan Co., 1947), p. 184.

13. Quoted in H. F. MacNair, *Modern Chinese History: Selected Readings* (Shanghai: Commercial Press, Ltd., 1927), p. 4.

14. Li Chien-nung, *The Political History of China, 1840-1928*, trans. by Sau-Yu-Teng and J. Ingalls (Princeton: D. Van Nostrand Co., Inc., 1956), pp. 29, 43.

15. H. Borton, *Japan's Modern Century* (New York: Ronald Press, 1955), p. 172.

16. Quoted in G. N. Steiger, *A History of the Far East* (Boston: Ginn and Co., 1936), pp. 612-613.

17. Quoted in T. A. Bailey, *The American Pageant* (Boston: D. C. Heath and Co., 1956), p. 630.

18. Quoted in M. E. Townsend, *European Colonial Expansion Since 1871* (New York: J. B. Lippincott Co., 1941), p. 367.

19. Sir Harry Johnston, *The Story of My Life* (Indianapolis: Bobbs-Merrill Co., Inc., 1923), pp. 194-195. Copyright 1923, 1951 by the publishers and used with their permission.

20. Quoted in T. W. Wallbank, *Contemporary Africa: Continent in Transition* (Princeton: D. Van Nostrand Co., Inc., 1956), pp. 111-112.

21. Hobson, p. 324.

22. G. B. Shaw, *The Man of Destiny*, quoted in Langer, I, p. 91.

23. Quoted in Sir Alan Burns, *History of Nigeria* (London: George Allen and Unwin, Ltd., 1942), p. 189.

24. W. L. Langer, "A Critique of Imperialism," in *The Making of Modern Europe*, II, ed. by H. Ausubel (New York: Dryden Press, 1951), p. 928.

11. "SURVIVAL OF THE FITTEST"

1. R. Browning, "Song from 'Pippa Passes,'" in *The Literature of England*, II, 4th ed., ed. by G. B. Woods, H. A. Watt, G. K. Anderson, and K. J. Holzknecht (Chicago: Scott, Foresman and Co., 1958), p. 657.

2. C. Darwin, "The Origin of Species," in *Introduction to*

Contemporary Civilization in the West, II (New York: Columbia University Press, 1955), pp. 453-454.

3. Quoted in C. J. H. Hayes, *A Political and Cultural History of Modern Europe,* II (New York: The Macmillan Co., 1933), p. 345.

4. J. Huxley and J. Fisher, eds., *The Living Thoughts of Darwin* (New York: Longmans, Green and Co., Inc., 1939), pp. 143-144.

5. Quoted in H. and D. L. Thomas, *Living Adventures in Science* (Garden City, N.Y.: Hanover House, 1954), p. 119.

6. Quoted in A. M. Schlesinger, *The Rise of the City, 1876-1898* (New York: The Macmillan Co., 1951), p. 94.

7. Quoted in R. Vallery-Radot, *The Life of Pasteur,* trans. by Mrs. R. L. Devonshire (New York: Doubleday, Page and Co., 1923), p. 107.

8. Quoted in *ibid.,* p. 418.

9. Quoted in *ibid.,* p. 238.

10. Compare T. H. Huxley, *Collected Essays,* V (London: Macmillan and Co., 1894).

11. F. Darwin, ed., *The Life and Letters of Charles Darwin,* II (New York: D. Appleton and Co., 1888), pp. 114-115.

12. Quoted in Huxley and Fisher, pp. 150-151.

13. Quoted in J. Chapin, ed., *The Book of Catholic Quotations* (New York: Farrar, Straus and Cudahy, 1956), p. 706.

14. T. Veblen, *The Theory of the Leisure Class* (New York: The Macmillan Co., 1902), p. 188.

15. Quoted in R. Hofstadter, *Social Darwinism in American Thought, 1860-1915* (Philadelphia: University of Pennsylvania Press, 1944), p. 31.

16. Quoted in *ibid.,* p. 95.

17. H. G. von Treitschke, *Politics,* I, trans. by B. Dugdale and T. DeBille (London: Constable and Co., Ltd., 1916), pp. 66-67.

18. G. Nasmyth, *Social Progress and the Darwinian Theory* (New York: G. P. Putnam's Sons, 1916), p. 307.

19. O. Wilde, *A Woman of No Importance,* Act I (London: Methuen and Co., 1910), p. 23.

20. H. Taine, *History of English Literature,* II (New York: Henry Holt and Co., 1879), p. 225.

21. R. K. Webb, "The Victorian Reading Public," in *From Dickens to Hardy,* ed. by B. Ford (New York: Penguin Books, Inc., 1958), p. 217.

22. Lord David Cecil, *Early Victorian Novelists* (London: Constable and Co., Ltd., 1935), p. 54.

23. Alfred, Lord Tennyson, "Locksley Hall," in *Poetry of the Victorian Period,* ed. by G. B. Woods and J. H. Buckley (Chicago: Scott, Foresman and Co., 1955), p. 49.

24. M. Arnold, "Stanzas in Memory of the Author of 'Obermann,' " in *Poetry of the Victorian Period,* p. 454.

25. B. Willey, *Nineteenth Century Studies* (London: Chatto and Windus, 1949), p. 262.

26. T. Carlyle, "Shooting Niagara: and After?" in *Critical and Miscellaneous Essays,* V (New York: Charles Scribner's Sons, n.d.), pp. 33-34.

27. T. Carlyle, "The Present Time," quoted in E. D. Mackerness, "The Voice of Prophecy: Carlyle and Ruskin," in *From Dickens to Hardy,* p. 294.

28. Quoted in S. Cheney, *The Story of Modern Art* (New York: The Viking Press, 1945), pp. 131-132.

29. C. A. and M. R. Beard, *The Industrial Era,* Vol. II of *The Rise of American Civilization* (New York: The Macmillan Co., 1927), p. 386.

30. F. L. Allen, *The Big Change* (New York: Harper and Bros., 1952), p. 121.

12. PARLIAMENTS AND POLITICAL REFORMS

1. Quoted in E. P. Cheyney, *Readings in English History Drawn from the Original Sources* (Boston: Ginn and Co., 1935), p. 724.

2. H. Pearson, *Dizzy: The Life and Personality of Benjamin Disraeli, Earl of Beaconsfield* (New York: Harper and Bros., 1951), p. 192.

3. Quoted in *ibid.,* p. 102.

4. Quoted in W. E. Lunt, *History of England* (New York: Harper and Bros., 1957), pp. 686-687.

5. Quoted in J. E. Gillespie, *Europe in Perspective* (New York: Harcourt, Brace and Co., 1942), p. 253.

6. Quoted in H. Ausubel, *The Late Victorians* (Princeton: D. Van Nostrand Co., Inc., 1955), p. 50.

7. Quoted in F. Owen, *Tempestuous Journey: Lloyd George, His Life and Times* (London: Hutchinson and Co., Ltd., 1954), p. 186. Reprinted by permission of the publishers.

8. Quoted in *ibid.,* p. 187.

9. Quoted in J. Kayser, *The Dreyfus Affair* (London: William Heinemann, Ltd., 1931), pp. 310-311. Reprinted by permission of the author.

10. Quoted in J. V. Ducattillon, "The Church in the Third Republic," in *The Making of Modern Europe,* II, ed. by H. Ausubel (New York: Dryden Press, 1951), p. 861.

11. Quoted in G. P. Gooch, *Germany* (New York: Charles Scribner's Sons, 1925), p. 104.

12. A. L. Lowell, *Governments and Parties in Continental Europe,* I (Boston: Houghton Mifflin Co., 1896), p. 246.

13. Quoted in E. F. Henderson, *A Short History of Ger-*

many, Part II (New York: The Macmillan Co., 1916), p. 451.

14. Quoted in F. A. Ogg and W. R. Sharp, *Economic Development of Europe* (New York: The Macmillan Co., 1926), p. 551.

15. Quoted in C. G. Robertson, *Bismarck* (London: Constable and Co., Ltd., 1918), p. 289.

16. Quoted in C. D. Hazen, *Europe Since 1815,* I (New York: Henry Holt and Co., 1928), p. 300.

17. Robertson, p. 472.

18. Quoted in R. H. Fife, Jr., *The German Empire Between Two Wars* (New York: The Macmillan Co., 1916), p. 106.

19. Gooch, p. 109.

20. D. M. Lang, "Some Forerunners of the Decembrists," *The Cambridge Journal,* Vol. 1, No. 10 (July 1948), p. 631.

21. T. G. Masaryk, *The Spirit of Russia,* I, trans. by E. and C. Paul (New York: The Macmillan Co., 1919), pp. 106-107.

22. Quoted in J. C. Wedgwood and A. Nevins, eds., *Forever Freedom* (Baltimore: Penguin Books, Inc., n.d.), p. 177.

23. Quoted in *Encyclopaedia Britannica,* III, 1910 ed., p. 231.

24. P. Chaadayev, *Peter's Legacy,* quoted in H. Kohn, ed., *The Mind of Modern Russia* (New Brunswick: Rutgers University Press, 1955), pp. 127-128. Copyright 1955 by The Trustees of Rutgers College in New Jersey.

25. Compare M. T. Florinsky, *Russia: A History and Interpretation,* II (New York: The Macmillan Co., 1953), pp. 809-812.

26. Compare S. Graham, *Tsar of Freedom; The Life and Reign of Alexander II* (New Haven: Yale University Press, 1935), pp. 34-48.

27. I. Turgenev, *Fathers and Children,* trans. by C. Garnett (New York: The Macmillan Co., 1924), p. 36.

28. Compare K. Zilliacus, *The Russian Revolutionary Movement* (London: Alston Rivers, 1905), p. 59.

29. Quoted in G. Kennan, *Siberia and the Exile System,* II (New York: Century Co., 1891), p. 500.

30. Quoted in M. T. Florinsky, *Russia: A History and an Interpretation,* II (New York: The Macmillan Co., 1953), pp. 1114-1115.

31. Kennan, I, p. 242.

32. Quoted in Florinsky, p. 1142.

33. Compare G. Vernadsky, *A History of Russia* (New Haven: Yale University Press, 1930), pp. 167-168.

34. Compare G. R. Treviranus, *Revolutions in Russia: Their*

Lessons for the Western World (New York: Harper and Bros., 1944), pp. 9-13.

35. Quoted in R. W. Postgate, *Revolution from 1789 to 1906* (Boston: Houghton Mifflin Co., 1921), pp. 363-364.

36. Compare A. J. Sack, *The Birth of the Russian Democracy* (New York: Russian Information Bureau, 1918), pp. 114-117.

37. B. Pares, *A History of Russia* (New York: Alfred A. Knopf, 1956), p. 466.

38. Compare F. Eckhart, *A Short History of the Hungarian People* (London: Grant Richards, 1931).

39. Quoted in J. S. Schapiro, *Modern and Contemporary European History, 1815-1940* (Boston: Houghton Mifflin Co., 1940), p. 425.

40. Quoted in J. W. Swain, *Beginning the Twentieth Century* (New York: W. W. Norton and Co., Inc., 1933), p. 168.

41. L. C. Griscom, *Diplomatically Speaking* (Boston: Little, Brown and Co., 1940), p. 146.

42. Quoted in G. Antonius, *The Arab Awakening* (London: Hamish Hamilton, 1938), p. 90.

43. C. J. H. Hayes, *A Generation of Materialism, 1871-1900* (New York: Harper and Bros., 1941), p. 285.

13. PROMISE AND PERIL

1. Sir Winston S. Churchill, *The World Crisis* (New York: Charles Scribner's Sons, 1949; London: Odhams Press, Ltd.), p. 5.

2. F. Schevill, *A History of Europe* (New York: Harcourt, Brace and Co., 1938), p. 481.

3. Quoted in R. N. Carew Hunt, *The Theory and Practice of Communism* (London: Geoffrey Bles, 1950), p. 72.

4. N. Mansergh, *The Coming of the First World War* (London: Longmans, Green and Co., Ltd., 1949), p. 16.

5. Quoted in V. L. and M. Albjerg, *Europe from 1914 to the Present* (New York: McGraw-Hill Book Co., Inc., 1951), p. 4.

6. Rev. Josiah Strong, *Our Country; Its Possible Future and Its Present Crisis,* 2nd ed. (New York: The Baker and Taylor Co., 1891), pp. 222-223.

7. Compare T. W. Wallbank, *Man's Story* (Chicago: Scott, Foresman and Co., 1956), p. 461.

8. Quoted in Mansergh, p. 18.

9. Compare K. F. Nowak, *Germany's Road to Ruin* (New York: The Macmillan Co., 1932), pp. 235-238.

10. Compare J. W. Swain, *Beginning the Twentieth Century* (New York: W. W. Norton and Co., Inc., 1933), pp. 174-175.

11. Quoted by C. J. H. Hayes, *A Political and Cultural History of Modern Europe,* II (New York: The Macmillan Co.,

1939), p. 569. Reprinted by permission of The Macmillan Co.

12. Quoted in *ibid*, p. 572.

13. Quoted in W. M. Knight-Patterson, *Germany from Defeat to Conquest, 1913-1933* (London: George Allen and Unwin, Ltd., 1945), p. 43.

14. Viscount Grey of Fallodon, *Twenty-Five Years*, II (New York: Frederick A. Stokes Co., 1925), p. 20.

14. A WORLD FIT FOR HEROES

1. B. H. Liddell Hart, *The War in Outline, 1914-1918* (London: Faber and Faber, Ltd., 1936), pp. 124-125.

2. M. Gumpert, *Dunant, The Story of the Red Cross* (New York: Oxford University Press, 1938), pp. 286-287.

3. Quoted in F. P. Chambers, *The War Behind the War, 1914-1918* (New York: Harcourt, Brace and Co., 1939), p. 473.

4. Quoted in A. F. Tyler, *The Modern World* (New York: Farrar and Rinehart, 1939), p. 733.

5. S. E. Morison and H. S. Commager, *The Growth of the American Republic*, II (New York: Oxford University Press, 1950), pp. 453-454.

6. E. M. Remarque, *The Road Back*, trans. by A. W. Wheen (Boston: Little, Brown and Co., 1931), p. 25.

7. Quoted in L. M. Hacker and B. B. Kendrick, *The United States Since 1865* (New York: F. S. Crofts and Co., 1939), p. 520

8. Quoted in F. P. Walters, *A History of the League of Nations*, I (London: Oxford University Press, 1952), p. 48.

9. Quoted in R. J. Sontag, *European Diplomatic History, 1871-1932* (New York: Century Co., 1933), p. 275.

10. Quoted by E. Achorn, *European Civilization and Politics Since 1815* (New York: Harcourt, Brace and Co., 1938), p. 470.

11. Quoted in Sontag, p. 392.

12. J. M. Keynes, *The Economic Consequences of the Peace* (London: Macmillan and Co., Ltd., 1924), p. 211.

13. G. F. Kennan, *The Decision to Intervene* (Princeton: Princeton University Press, 1958), p. 471.

14. Quoted in W. M. Knight-Patterson, *Germany from Defeat to Conquest, 1913-1933* (London: George Allen and Unwin, Ltd., 1945), p. 379.

15. Quoted in A. G. Mazour, *Russia Past and Present* (New York: D. Van Nostrand Co., Inc., 1951), p. 576.

16. Quoted in Walters, I, p. 413.

15. OPPOSING WAYS OF LIFE

1. J. Reed, *Ten Days That Shook the World* (New York: Boni and Liveright, Inc., 1919), p. 125.

2. H. G. Wells, *The Outline of History* (New York: Garden City Publishing Co., Inc., 1931), p. 1131.

3. B. Mussolini, *My Autobiography*, trans. by R. W. Child (London: Hutchinson and Co., Ltd., n.d.), p. 46.

4. Compare *ibid*., pp. 265-267.

5. *Ibid.*, p. 199.

6. Quoted in A. Bullock, *Hitler: A Study in Tyranny* (London: Odhams Press, Ltd., 1952), p. 286.

7. J. M. Keynes, *The Economic Consequences of the Peace* (London: Macmillan and Co., Ltd., 1924), pp. 278-279.

8. Quoted in F. L. Benns, *Europe Since 1914* (New York: F. S. Crofts and Co., 1939), p. 527.

9. Quoted in W. C. Langsam, *The World Since 1914* (New York: The Macmillan Co., 1943), p. 685.

10. F. L. Allen, *Only Yesterday* (New York: Harper and Bros., 1931), p. 315.

16. AFRICA AND ASIA ASTIR

1. E. Atiyah, *An Arab Tells His Story* (London: John Murray, 1946), p. 97.

2. J. Nehru, *Toward Freedom* (New York: The John Day Co., 1941), p. 42.

3. W. E. B. Du Bois, *The World and Africa* (New York: The Viking Press, 1947), pp. 11-12.

4. See *ibid.*, pp. 148-163.

5. *African Liberator* (c. 1935). By permission of T. Walter Wallbank.

6. *Covenant of the League of Nations*, Clause 4, Article 22, in *Essential Facts About the League of Nations* (Geneva: Information Section of the League of Nations Secretariat, 1937), pp. 26-27.

7. A. H. Hourani, *Syria and Lebanon; A Political Essay* (London: Oxford University Press, 1946), pp. 57-58.

8. G. Antonius, *The Arab Awakening; The Story of the Arab National Movement* (New York: J. P. Lippincott Co., 1939), p. 363.

9. Quoted in H. Kohn, *Nationalism and Imperialism in the Hither East* (London: G. Routledge and Sons, Ltd., 1932), pp. 132-133.

10. Compare F. W. Price and C. P. Barry, eds., *Collier's Encyclopedia*, V (New York: P. F. Collier and Son Corp., 1950), p. 180.

17. THE TRAGIC DECADE AND GLOBAL CONFLICT

1. Quoted in F. P. Chambers, C. P. Grant, C. C. Bayley, *This Age of Conflict* (New York: Harcourt, Brace and Co., 1943), p. 495.

2. J. K. Galbraith, *The Great Crash, 1929* (Boston: Houghton Mifflin Co., 1955), p. 104.

3. Quoted in G. von Rauch, *A History of Soviet Russia* (New York: Frederick A. Praeger, 1957), p. 253.

4. Quoted in A. Bullock, *Hitler: A Study in Tyranny* (London: Odhams Press, Ltd., 1952), pp. 642-643.

5. Quoted in H. W. Weigert, *German Geopolitics*, No. 19 in the series *America in a World at War* (New York: Oxford University Press, n.d.), pp. 6-7.

6. Quoted in W. C. Langsam, *Major European and Asiatic Developments Since 1935* (New York: The Macmillan Co., 1938), p. 15.

7. L. Quintanilla, *A Latin American Speaks* (New York: The Macmillan Co., 1943), title of Chapter VIII, p. 131.

8. Quoted in C. L. Mowat, *Britain Between Wars, 1918-1940* (Chicago: University of Chicago Press, 1958), p. 422.

9. Sir Winston S. Churchill, *Blood, Sweat and Tears* (New York: G. P. Putnam's Sons, 1941), p. 66.

10. F. D. Roosevelt, "Address at Chicago, October 5, 1937," in *The Literature of the United States,* II, ed. by W. Blair, T. Hornberger, and R. Stewart (Chicago: Scott, Foresman and Co., 1953), pp. 831-832.

11. Quoted in W. L. Langer and S. E. Gleason, *The Challenge to Isolation* (New York: Harper and Bros., 1952), p. 138.

12. Quoted in *ibid.*, p. 189.

13. Quoted in *ibid.*, p. 200.

14. Quoted in D. Thompson, *Europe Since Napoleon* (London: Longmans, Green and Co., Ltd., 1958), p. 716.

15. A. D. Divine, "Miracle at Dunkirk," *Reader's Digest*, Vol. 37, No. 224 (December 1940), pp. 108-109.

16. Churchill, p. 297.

18. THE COLD WAR AND COMPETITIVE COEXISTENCE

1. Aziz Beg, *The Quiet Revolution* (Karachi, Pakistani Patriotic Publications, 1959), p. 13.

EPILOGUE

1. A. Desmond, "How Many People Have Ever Lived on Earth?" *The Population Crisis and the Use of World Resources*, Stuart Mudd and others (World Academy of Art and Science, Publication 2), The Hague, Dr. W. Junk, 1964, p. 38.

2. Harold F. Dorn, "World Population Growth: An International Dilemma," *op. cit.*, p. 51.

3. *Science and Technology for Development*. Volume I: *World of Opportunity*. Report of the United Nations Conference on the Application of Science and Technology (New York: United Nations, 1963), pp. 23-24.

4. *Ibid.*, p. 20.

5. Palmer C. Putnam, *Energy in the Future* (New York: D. Van Nostrand Co., Inc., 1956), p. 221.

6. Putnam, *op. cit.*, p. 231.

7. *Ibid.*, p. 255.

8. Statistics obtained from Julius Duscha, "Arms and the Big Money Men," Part I, *Harper's* (March 1964), pp. 39-47.

9. R. A. Butler, addressing the Danish Students Association in Copenhagen; quoted in *The Globe and Mail* (Toronto), February 11, 1964.

10. Quoted in John Fitzgerald Kennedy, "Poetry and Power," *The Atlantic* (February 1964), p. 53.

LIST OF ILLUSTRATIONS

END-SHEET MAPS

Inside front cover: Ioannes de Ram, circa 1685. Inside back cover: Robert Sayer, 1792. Both maps from A. E. Nordenskiold, *Facsimile-Atlas to the Early History of Cartography*, Stockholm, 1889, The Newberry Library.

COLOR PLATES

1 The Museum of Modern Art, New York, Lillie P. Bliss Bequest

2 Derby Museum and Art Gallery, England

3 Collection of Irwin Untermyer

4 Courtesy of the Trustees, The National Gallery, London

5 By Permission of the Trustees of the Wallace Collection, London

6 Musée du Louvre, Paris

7 Courtesy of the French Government Tourist Office

8 The Art Institute of Chicago, Mr. and Mrs. W. W. Kimball Collection

9 The Art Institute of Chicago, Gift of Mrs. Bertha Palmer Thorne, Mrs. Rose Movius Palmer, and Mr. and Mrs. Arthur M. Wood

10 Mannheim Municipal Art Museum, Germany

11 The National Gallery of Art, Washington, D.C., Samuel H. Kress Collection

12 Courtesy of the British Travel Association

13 Chicago Museum of Natural History

14 Museum of the American Indian, New York

15 Courtesy of the Trustees, The British Museum

16 Courtesy of the Trustees, The British Museum

17 The Art Institute of Chicago, Gift of Mr. and Mrs. Gordon Palmer and Mr. and Mrs. Arthur M. Wood

18 The Art Institute of Chicago, Helen Birch Bartlett Memorial Collection

19 Museum of Fine Arts, Boston

20 The Art Institute of Chicago, Potter Palmer Collection

21 Courtesy of Mrs. H. Harris Jonas

22 The Art Institute of Chicago, Helen Birch Bartlett Memorial Collection

23 The Art Institute of Chicago, Helen Birch Bartlett Memorial Collection

24 Museum of Art, Carnegie Institute, Pittsburgh

25 Philadelphia Museum of Art, A. E. Gallatin Collection

26 Courtesy of Mr. and Mrs. Arthur C. Rosenberg

27 Courtesy of Mr. and Mrs. Joseph R. Shapiro

28 The Art Institute of Chicago, Arthur Jerome Eddy Memorial Collection

29 The Art Institute of Chicago, Gift of Alfred S. Alschuler

30 Hedrich Blessing Photo, Chicago

BLACK-AND-WHITE ILLUSTRATIONS

Sir Isaac Newton. Historical Pictures Service-Chicago....................9

David: "Portrait of Antoine Lavoisier and his wife." The Bettmann Archive....................12

From Diderot's *Encyclopedie*....................13

Cartoon of French doctor in sedan chair. Historical Pictures Service-Chicago....................14

Title page from Hobbes' *Leviathan*, 1651. Henry W. and Albert B. Berg Collection of the New York Public Library....................18

Rigaud: "Portrait of Louis XIV." The Bettmann Archive....................21

DeTroy: "18th Century Salon." The Bettmann Archive....................25

Oliver Cromwell dissolving the Long Parliament. Courtesy of The Trustees of the British Museum....................31

White: "Portrait of Charles II." The Bettmann Archive....................33

King William III at the Battle of the Boyne. Culver Pictures, Inc.....................35

Robert Walpole and cabinet. Courtesy of the Pierpont Morgan Library....................36

Ramsay: "King George III." Culver Pictures, Inc.....................38

Cartoon of Russian's beard being cut off. The Bettmann Archive....................40

F. Carstens: "Frederick the Great of Prussia." Courtesy of the Metropolitan Museum of Art....................45

Satire on Jenkins' ear. Courtesy of the Trustees of the British Museum....................51

"The Taking of Quebec," from the London Magazine, 1760. Reproduced from the Collections of the Library of Congress....53

Jean Baptiste Colbert. Historical Pictures Service-Chicago....................59

Hogarth: "Rake's Progress." Courtesy of The Metropolitan Museum of Art....................63

18th Century Coiffure. The Bettmann Archive....................64

Frontispiece from 1685 manual, *New Additions to the Epitome of the Art of Husbandry*. Copyright British Museum....................66

Lloyds Coffee House. The Bettmann Archive....................67

John Law's Colony in Biloxi, La. Courtesy of The Newberry Library, Chicago..**68-69**

Cartoon satirizing the Old Regime in France. Giraudon, Paris..**71**

Houdon: "Voltaire." Giraudon, Paris.....................................**75**

Hogarth: "The Rake's Progress," Plate VIII. Historical Pictures Service-Chicago...**78**

John Locke. Historical Pictures Service-Chicago....................**80**

Illustration from Rousseau's EMILE. Giraudon, Paris.................**81**

Aerial view of Versailles. Courtesy of the French Government Tourist office...**83**

Catherine of Russia. Alinari Photo...................................**87**

Emperor Joseph II of Austria. Courtesy of the Austrian Information Service..**88**

Storming the Bastille. The Bettmann Archive........................**92**

Execution of Louis XVI. From the original in the Musée Carnavalet. Archives Photographiques, Paris.......................**98**

Image of Freedom carried through Paris streets, 1792. The Bettmann Archive..**101**

David: "Robespierre on way to the guillotine." Courtesy of the Pierpont Morgan Library..**103**

Satire of Napoleon's dream of invading England, 1803. The Bettmann Archive..**105**

Goya: "Y no hai remedio," from "The Disasters of War" by Goya. Courtesy of The Art Institute of Chicago...................**106**

Goya: "And they are like wild beasts," from "The Disasters of War" by Goya. Phaidon Press.....................................**107**

Death mask of Napoleon from the original in Musée de l'Armée. Giraudon, Paris...**108**

Congress of Vienna. The Bettmann Archive...........................**112**

Prince Lothar von Metternich. By Ewing Galloway, N.Y.........**112**

Cartoon entitled "La Balance Politique." Courtesy of the Trustees of the British Museum.....................................**114**

Tsar Alexander I. Historical Pictures Service-Chicago............**116**

Napoleon's Campaign of France, 1814. Brown Brothers.........**117**

David: "Death of Marat." Musées Royaux des Beaux-Arts de Belgique...**117**

Marie Jean Antoine Nicolas Condorcet. Culver Pictures, Inc....**130**

Illustration from Goethe's "Sorrows of Young Werther." Courtesy of the Trustees of The British Museum..................**133**

Count D'Orsay: "Lord Byron," (sketch) 1823. Courtesy of the Trustees of the British Museum.................................**135**

From A Description of The Villa of Mr. Horace Walpole's Strawberry Hill, 1774..**136**

Church of the Madeleine. Giraudon, Paris...........................**136**

One of the Thorne Miniature Rooms in the Collection of the Art Institute of Chicago..**137**

The Royal Pavilion at Brighton, England. The British Travel Association..**137**

Illustration by Gustav Dore from The Rime of the Ancient Mariner by Coleridge, 1877 ed. Courtesy of The Metropolitan Museum of Art, Rogers Fund, 1921.....................**138**

Rodin: "Victor Hugo." Courtesy of The Art Institute of Chicago...**142**

Richmond: "William Wilberforce." Historical Pictures Service-Chicago..**145**

Slave deck of the bark "Wildfire." Brown Brothers................**146**

Factory district in the Saar region. The Bettmann Archive........**151**

Military tailor and his family. Historical Pictures Service-Chicago...**153**

Calamine, Metallurgie. Culver Service..............................**154**

Cross section of furnace. From Diderot's Encyclopedie............**154**

"Child Hurriers" at work, from The Age of Paradox by John Wendell Dodds. Reproduced by permission of author...............**154**

18th Century machine shop. From Diderot's Encyclopedie........**154**

Spinning Mule. The Bettmann Archive................................**155**

Hargreaves' revolutionary spinning jenny. The Bettmann Archive...**155**

Doré's 19th Century engraving of London's industrial area. The Bettmann Archive..**158**

The SS Great Eastern on her maiden voyage, 1858. Brown Brothers...**161**

Pickengild: Jeremy Bentham. The Bettmann Archive................**171**

J. Linnell: "Malthur," (engr.) 1830. The Bettmann Archive........**171**

Mezzotint: "David Ricardo." The Bettmann Archive................**171**

John Stuart Mill. Historical Pictures Service-Chicago...............**171**

"The visit to the Brickmaker's," from Charles Dickens' BLEAK HOUSE. Oxford University Press, London....................**174**

Daumier: "Workingman and Bourgeois," (lithograph) 1848. Gift of Martin A. Ryerson and The Print and Drawing Club, courtesy of The Art Institute of Chicago...........................**175**

Cartoon entitled "Capital and Labour," from Punch, 1843. The Mansell Collection...**175**

Satire on Congress of Vienna. Historical Pictures Service-Chicago...**187**

Louis Kossuth, 1848. The Bettmann Archive.......................**189**

Revolution in Germany, 1848. The Bettmann Archive.............**189**

Cain: "Paris Barricades," 1830. Historical Pictures Service-Chicago...**189**

Revolution in Austria, 1848. Historical Pictures Service-Chicago...**189**

The Parisian worker. From Les Français, 1830......................**196**

Delacroix: "Liberty Leading the People." The Bettmann Archive...**198**

Cartoon on the separation of Holland and Belgium. Courtesy of the Print Division of the New York Public Library...............**199**

Cartoon on tribute to the Reform Bill of 1832. Courtesy of the Pierpont Morgan Library......................................**202**

Hervieu: "Louis Philippe," (drawing) 1834. Courtesy of the Print Division of the New York Public Library....................**205**

Daumier: "The Legislative Belly." Courtesy of The Metropolitan Museum of Art, Rogers Fund, 1920.......................**206**

Giuseppe Mazzini. Brown Brothers...............................**212**

German National Assembly, woodcut, 1848. The Bettmann Archive...**213**

Count Camillo Benso di Cavour. Alinari Photo.........................**223**

Giuseppe Garibaldi. Brown Brothers...............................**225**

Otto Von Bismarck. Photograph by Hahn of Munich, from Historisches Bildarchiv Handke Berneck, Germany...................**227**

Cartoon of Bismarck's Web. Historical Pictures Service-Chicago...**229**

The crowning of Emperor Wilhelm I at Versailles. The Bettmann Archive...**233**

Cartoon showing Disraeli on a tight-rope, from Punch, 1878. Radio Times Hulton Picture Library...............................**242**

Jacques Cartier. Historical Pictures Service-Chicago................**255**

Boer-British War, 1900. Historical Pictures Service-Chicago....**262**

Louis Botha. Historical Pictures Service-Chicago........................**263**

Francisco de Miranda. Illustration from Resúmen de la Historiá de Venezuela by Rafael Maria Barait and Ramon Diaz, 1841...**264**

Simon Bolivar. Pan American Union............................**265**

José de San Martin. Historical Pictures Service-Chicago.........**266**

James Monroe. Historical Pictures Service-Chicago.................**268**

South American ranchers, lithograph, 1850. The Bettmann Archive...**270**

French victory near Algiers, 1830..................................**281**

Verestchagin: "Execution of mutineers after Sepoy Rebellion in India."...**287**

Dowager Empress of China. Brown Brothers.....................**295**

"Dr. Livingston, I Presume?" Courtesy of the British Information Service-Chicago......................................**305**

Cartoon "The Lions' Share." Copyright The Mansell Collection; reproduced by permission of Punch....................**306**

Cecil John Rhodes, drawing by Mortimer Mempes. Courtesy of Rhodes University Library, Grahamstown, South Africa......**309**

Cartoon entitled "New Crowns for Old Ones," from Punch. The Mansell Collection...**310**

Baptizing converts in India. Methodist Prints.........................**312**

Nijo Castle in Kyoto, Japan. By Ewing Galloway, N.Y..........**322**

Louis Pasteur. Reproduced from L'Illustration, 1884.................**325**

Henry Ford wearing derby hat. The Bettmann Archive..........**327**

First flight of the Wright Brothers. Reproduced from the Collections of the Library of Congress.........................**328**

Michael Faraday. Historical Pictures Service-Chicago.............**331**

Charles Darwin. Charles Phelps Cushing.........................**334**

Albert Einstein. Culver Service..................................**334**

Sigmund Freud. Historical Pictures Service-Chicago.................**334**

Goddard: "Digging Out." Historical Pictures Service-Chicago...**340**

Detail from "The Course" by Frith. Reproduced by courtesy of the Trustees of the Tate Gallery, London...............**341**

Dotheboys Hall in Nicholas Nickleby by Charles Dickens. Illus. by Hablot K. Browne. The New York Public Library........**342**

"Robert Browning Taking Tea with the Browning Society" from the Poet's Corner by Sir Max Beerbohm, Courtesy of Mr. Selwyn Jepson...**343**

Gavarni: "Barzac"...**346**

Rodin: "The Thinker." Courtesy of the Metropolitan Museum of Art, Gift of Thomas F. Ryan, 1910..........................**350**

Matisse: "Goldfish and Sculpture." Courtesy, the Museum of Modern Art, New York...**351**

Cezanne: "House in Provence." Courtesy of the John Herron Museum of Art, Indianapolis.............................**351**

Robie House, designed by Frank Lloyd Wright. Bill Engdahl, Hedrich-Blessing...**353**

Louis Sullivan's department store building. Photo by Richard Nickel, 1958...**353**

Gropius' Hall of Machines. Reproduced by permission of Walter Gropius. Courtesy The Museum of Modern Art, New York...**353**

Parlor of the Robert J. Milligan House. In the Brooklyn Museum Collection...**357**

Benjamin Disraeli. Radio Times Hulton Picture Library..........**362**

William Gladstone. Radio Times Hulton Picture Library..........**363**

Cartoon satirizing Disraeli and Gladstone as rival stars. Historical Pictures Service-Chicago.............................**364**

Drawing entitled "Ejectment of the Irish Peasantry." The Mansell Collection...**365**

Cartoon depicting John Bull encompassing the world. The Bettmann Archive...**368**

Drawing of Captain Dreyfus at his trial. Culver Service..........**370**

Paul Muni portrays Émile Zola in "The Life of Emile Zola." United Artists Associated, Inc.............................**370**

Cartoon of Bismarck entitled "Dropping the Pilot." Reproduced by permission of *Punch*............376

Kaiser William II. Brown Brothers............377

G. Kruell: "Emperor Nicholas I." (engr.). Historical Pictures Service-Chicago............379

Cartoon showing Russian Bear and Japanese acrobat. The Bettmann Archive............385

"Bloody Sunday Massacre," from *L'Illustration*, 1905............386

George V and Nicholas II. United Press International............387

Turkish Troops, 1909. Brown Brothers............391

Alexander Graham Bell. Brown Brothers............397

Thomas A. Edison. Reproduced from the Collection of the Library of Congress............397

Marconi and his transoceanic receiver. Underwood & Underwood............397

Krupp munitions plant. Charles Phelps Cushing............398

Ford Auto Company, production 1913. The Ford Motor Company............398

Adapted from Clive Day, *Economic Development in Europe*, New York: The Macmillan Co., 1942. By permission of The Macmillan Company............399

Early labor demonstration in London. The Bettmann Archive............402

1896 Olympics. Historical Pictures Service-Chicago............408

The Palace of Peace at The Hague. By Burton Holmes from Ewing Galloway, N.Y.............409

W.W.I. plane bearing cartoon entitled "Boots to the Kaiser." National Archive............421

Cartoon of war snuffing out the candle of civilization. Reprinted by permission of the Chicago *Daily News*............422

Red Cross Volunteers on parade. Photo from European............431

Wounded Russian soldier in a makeshift hospital. Photo from European............436

"Over the Top." World War I soldiers. The National Archives............437

British tanks. Culver Service............438

World War I air fight. The Bettmann Archive............439

English U-boat C-25 being bombed in North Sea. Photo from European............439

German prisoners of war. Photo from European............443

German troops leaving for the front. Historical Picture Service-Chicago............443

Allied leaders at Paris Peace Conference. Brown Brothers............445

"It is for peace that this hammer works." Courtesy of the Editor of *Le Charivari*............455

Mussolini leads fascist forces into Rome. United Press International............460

Hitler at meeting in Munich beer hall. Radio Times Hulton Picture Library............460

Drawing of Nikolai Lenin in 1918. Historical Pictures Service-Chicago............460

Poster depicting civil war of 1918-1920. Sovfoto............464

Stalin in 1922. Sovfoto............468

Trotsky. Historical Pictures Service-Chicago............469

Peter Blume: "The Eternal City." Collection, the Museum of Modern Art, New York............471

Children's military training units in Mussolini's Italy. United Press International............473

Armored cars during general strike of 1926 in England. Wide World Photos............478

John Held's drawing of a flapper. Wide World Photos............482

Federal agents confiscating liquor, 1920. United Press International............482

Parade welcoming Admiral Byrd. United Press International............482

Charles A. Lindbergh beside his "Spirit of St. Louis." Institute of the Aeronautical Sciences............482

Clarence Darrow and William Jennings Bryan at the Scopes trial. Wide World Photos............483

Shahn: "Sacco and Vanzetti." Collection, the Museum of Modern Art, New York............483

African working in gold mine. Wide World Photos............491

Lawrence of Arabia. Charles Phelps Cushing............496

Faisal al Husein, King of Iraq, 1921. Radio Times Hulton Picture Library............496

Riza Shah Pahlavi of Iran. Radio Times Hulton Picture Library............496

Mustafa Kemal Pasha of Turkey. Radio Times Hulton Picture Library............496

Hindu untouchables. Sketch by Reginald Cleaver for *The Illustrated London News*, 1931. © *The Illustrated London News*............500

Gandhi arrives in England, 1931. Wide World Photos............502

Jawaharlal Nehru. Wide World Photos............503

Sun Yat-sen. Culver Service............506

Chiang Kai-shek, 1927. Culver Service............508

Workers on a Ukrainian collective farm. Sovfoto............517

Nazi campaign poster from *Das Kampfplakat* by Frederick Medebach. Verlag Moritz Diesterweg............519

May Day rally, 1937. United Press International............522

Reginald Marsh: "Bread Line." By permission of trustees of the artist's estate............525

Mao Tse-tung. United Press International............527

Picasso: "Guernica." Collection, The Museum of Modern Art, New York...528

Cartoon entitled "Honest, Mister, there's nobody here but us Spaniards," by David Low. © Low All Countries...............530

Frenchman crying. Wide World Photos......................536

Mussolini and Hitler in Rome, 1938. Pix, Incorporated............536

American seamen use depth charges to ward off U-boat. Official U.S. Coast Guard Photo.........................536

Bataan death march. Defense Department. Photo Marine Corps...536

Bombing of buildings near St. Paul's Cathedral. British Information Services.....................................537

Russian city of Minsk in ruins. Photo from European.............537

U.S.S. *West Virginia* and U.S.S. *Tennessee* at Pearl Harbor. United States Navy.......................................537

Big Three at Teheran. British Information Services..................546

Enemy soldier surrenders to British in Africa. British Information Services....................................546

Hitler and school boys. Copress-Verlag, Munchen, Germany..546

D-Day Invasion. Allied troops in Normandy. Official U.S. Coast Guard Photo.....................................546

American Marines at Bougainville. Defense Department. Photo Marine Corps...................................546

Raid over Ploesti. United States Air Force Photo.....................547

Nazi victims at Belsen, Germany. Wide World Photos.............549

Parisian girl gives "V" for victory sign. Wide World Photos..557

Leaders at Stalin's bier, 1953. Sovfoto...........................576

Nehru. Wide World Photos.......................................581

Achmed Sukarno. United Press International....................584

Charles de Gaulle and Konrad Adenauer, 1958. Wide World Photos...585

Gamal Abdul Nasser. United Press International.....................585

Jomo Kenyatta in Nairobi. United Press International.............587

Cuban Execution. United Press International...........................593

Excavating phosphate on Nauru Island. UN, Australian Official Photograph.....................................599

LIST OF MAPS

Europe in 1648...26

Growth of European Russia......................................41

Rise of Brandenburg-Prussia...................................44

Partition of Poland..55

Napoleon's Empire...104

Revolutions of 1820-1821, 1830, and 1848...............190

Ottoman Empire 1815...193

Treaty of Adrianople 1829.......................................194

Unification of Italy..224

North German Confederation 1866.............................228

Germany 1871..232

Treaty of San Stefano 1878...................................241

Congress of Berlin 1878.......................................241

Canada 1791..256

Growth of Modern Canada.......................................257

Union of South Africa..261

Latin America 1826..267

British India c. 1914...288

Intervention in China...292

World Empires 1914...300-301

Nationalities of Austria-Hungary.............................388

Balkans in 1914..418

Battles of World War I...435

Europe after World War I.......................................450

Prelude to War..532

Occupied France..535

Crest of Axis Power...540, 541

Long Pull to Victory...542, 543

Europe After World War II.......................................565

Japan's Lost Empire..566

Economic Integration of Europe...............................571

INDEX

Abbreviations for special features—Reference Maps (*Ref. M.*), spot maps (*m.*), and illustrations (*ill.*)—are indicated in italics. Suggested pronunciations for difficult or unusual words are respelled according to the table below, which is repeated in simplified form at the bottom of each right-hand page of the INDEX. The local pronunciations of many foreign words are too unusual for persons untrained in linguistics, and pronunciations given here are those commonly acceptable in unaffected, educated American speech.

a hat, cap	j jam, enjoy	u cup, son	**FOREIGN SOUNDS**
ā age, face	k kind, seek	u̇ put, book	
ã care, air	l land, coal	ü rule, move	Y as in French *lune*. Pronounce ē with the lips rounded as for English ü in *rule*.
ä father, far	m me, am	ū use, music	
	n no, in		
b bad, rob	ng long, bring		
ch child, much			
d did, red	o hot, rock	v very, save	Œ as in French *deux*. Pronounce ã with the lips rounded as for ō.
	ō open, go	w will, woman	
e let, best	ô order, all	y you, yet	
ē equal, see	oi oil, toy	z zero, breeze	N as in French *bon*. The N is not pronounced, but shows that the vowel before it is nasal.
ėr term, learn	ou out, now	zh measure, seizure	
f fat, if	p pet, cup		
g go, bag	r run, try	ə represents:	
h he, how	s say, yes	a in *about*	
	sh she, rush	e in tak*e*n	
	t tell, it	i in penc*i*l	H as in German *ach*. Pronounce k without closing the breath passage.
i it, pin	th thin, both	o in lem*o*n	
ī ice, five	ŦH then, smooth	u in circ*u*s	

A

Abd-el Krim (äb′ del krim′), 476, 498
Abdul-Hamid II, 390-391
Abdullah ibn-Husein (əb dül lä′ ib′ ən hü sīn′), 495
Absolutism, 19-24, 58-59: economic assault on, 66-73; in England, 29-30; in German empire, 372-373, 376; intellectual assault on, 74, 76, 79-80; Louis XIV as example of, 8, 20, 21-24, 49; maturity and decay of, 85-88; mercantilism and, 58-59; of Peter the Great, 40-41
Abyssinia (Ethiopia), 310, 528, 538, *Ref. M. 5*
Adelaide, 275, *Ref. M. 7*
Adenauer, Konrad, 574, 592
Adrianople, *Ref. M. 1*: Treaty of, 195, *m. 194*
Afghanistan, 236, 303, 304, 497, *Ref. M. 3, 7, 8*
Africa, *m. 301, Ref. M. 5, 6*: Anglo-French rivalry in, 49, 50, 54, 415-416; economic wealth of, 310, 490; European imperialism in, 304-310, 488-489; exploration of, 304-305; indirect rule in, 318-320; mandates in, 447-448, 489-490; nationalism and nation-making in, 489, 490-492, 587-590; North Africa in World War II, 544-545; population explosion in, 599, 604; in World War I, 489.
Afro-Asian Conference, at Bandung, 579
Age of Reason: arts in, 82-85; the *philosophes*, 73, 74-75; philosophy in, 15-19; political theories in, 74-77, 79-82; science in, 8-16; social sciences in, 77-79

Agriculture: collective farms in Soviet Union, 517, 518; culture system in Dutch East Indies, 299; in dust bowl area, 554-555; in eighteenth century, 64-66; in nineteenth century, 229; in Russia under Peter the Great, 40
Aguinaldo, Emilio (ä′gē näl′dō, ä mē′lyō), 302
Aix-la-Chapelle (āks′lä sha pel′), *Ref. M. 1:* Congress at, 186; Peace of, 52
Åland Islands dispute, 456
Alaska, 303, 572
Albania, 419, 457, 523, 531, *m. 193, 418, 450, Ref. M. 1, 2, 7*
Alexander I, tsar of Russia, 108, 111, 115, 190, 192, 198, 378
Alexander II, tsar of Russia, 381, 382
Alexander III, tsar of Russia, 383, 412
Alexandria, Egypt, 305, *m. 301, Ref. M. 5, 8*
Alfonso XIII, king of Spain, 481
Algeciras, *Ref. M. 2:* Conference, 417
Algeria, 204, 281, 305, 309-310, 492, 498, *Ref. M. 1, 2, 5, 6:* during World War II and after, 544, 587
Alsace-Lorraine, 232, 377, 398, 412, *m. 232, Ref. M. 2:* during World War I and after, 434, 447, *m. 450*

Amazon River, 274, *Ref. M. 9*
American colonies, 254
American Revolution, 37, 55, 90, 254, 256
Amiens (am'i ǝnz), Treaty of, 297
Anarchism, 179, 182, 380
Anatolia, 499, *Ref. M. 8*
Anglo-Egyptian Sudan, 308, 497, *Ref. M. 5*
Anglo-Russian entente, 304
Angola, 580, 589, *Ref. M. 5, 6*
Anti-Comintern Pact, 529
Anti-Semitism, 338, 413-414: in France, Dreyfus case, 371; in Germany, 519, 520, 548; in Italy, 521; in Russia, 383, 384, 387, 414, 605
Anzus Pacific Security Pact, 570
Arabian peninsula, 495-496, *Ref. M. 7, 8*
Arabs and Israel, 592; nationalism in Middle East, 492-500, 585-587; in Ottoman empire, 390-391; in World War I, 446
Archangel, 435, *Ref. M. 7*
Architecture: in Age of Reason, 84-85; eclecticism in, 84-85, 350, 352; Gothic revival in, 139-140; machine-age influence on, 352
Argentina, 146, 265, 268, 270-271, 275, 481, 574, *Ref. M. 9*
Armenia and Armenians, 193, 449, *m. 193, Ref. M. 8*
Arnold, Matthew, 344
Astronomy, 9-10, 263
Aswan, *Ref. M. 5, 8:* dam at, 585, 587
Atlantic Charter, 539, 544
Atomic energy, 332, and balance of terror, 602; Baruch Plan for control of, 568; bombs of World War II, 548-549; and disarmament, 602-603; peacetime uses, 601; Russian espionage concerning, 568; test ban treaty, 595
Auckland, *m. 300, Ref. M. 4*
Augsburg, *m. 26, Ref. M. 1:* League of, 47
Aurangzeb (ôr'ǝng zeb'), 285-286
Austerlitz, *Ref. M. 1:* battle of, *m. 104*
Australia, *Ref. M. 4:* bushmen of, 275-276; Commonwealth formed, 259-260; democracy in, 276; exploration of, 274-275; national character of, 277; social advances in, 260; during World War I and aftermath, 436, 478; in World War II, 544
Austria, *m. 26, 48, Ref. M. 1:* at Congress of Berlin, 241-242; at Congress of Vienna, 111, 114, 115, 116; conservatism after 1815, 188; and Crimean War, 237-239; and Dual Monarchy, *see* Austria-Hungary; German annexation of, 530; and German and Italian unification, 222-229; in Grand Alliance against Louis XIV, 47-48; industrialization in, 399; in Napoleonic wars, 105-106; and partition of Poland, 41, 55-56, *m. 55;* and Quadruple Alliance, 186; revolt of 1848 in, 214-215; in Seven Years' War, 54; *in Thirty Years' War, 46;* and Treaty of San Stefano, 240-241; vs. Turks, 39, 235, 236; and War of the Austrian Succession, 51-52; and war against revolutionary France, 96-97, 99-101, 102-103; after World War I, 449, 451, 457, 479, *m. 450, 565*
Austria-Hungary, 232-234, 387-390, *m. 388, 418, Ref. M. 2:* alliances of 1871-1914, 414-421; minority problems in, 412-413; and Ottoman (Turkish) empire, 241, 391; during World War I and aftermath, 421, 435-444, 445-451, *m. 450*
Austrian Netherlands, 98, 100, 114
Austro-Italian War, 223-225, 226, 229
Automation, 607

Automobile, 328, 357, 397
Axis powers. *See* Rome-Berlin-Tokyo Axis.
Ayacucho (ä yä kü' chō), battle of, 267; *m. 267*
Ayub Khan (ī yub' kän'), 580, 582
Azikiwe, Nnamdi, 490
Azov, 39, 40, *Ref. M. 1*

B

Bach, Johann Sebastian, 85, 141
Baden, 188
Bagdad, *m. 193, Ref. M. 7, 8:* Pact, 570, 586
Bahamas, 50
Bakewell, Robert, 65
Bakunin (bä kü'nyēn), Michael, 179, 182, 380
Balaklava, battle of, 238
Balance of power, 48, 49, 51
Baldwin, Stanley, 477
Balearic Islands, 48, *Ref. M. 1, 2*
Balfour, Arthur James, 436
Balfour Declaration, 493, 495
Balkans, 190, 193-195, 235-242, 391, *m. 193:* and Little Entente, 452; nationalism in, 413; and Pan-Slavism, 239; rivalries over, leading to World War I, 415, 416, 417-420, *m. 418;* wars of 1912-1913 in, 418-419; World War I peace treaties affecting, 449
Balzac, Honoré de, 345-346
Bancroft, George, 143
Banda, Hastings, 580, 589
Bandung Conference. *See* Afro-Asian Conference.
Baring, Evelyn, Lord Cromer, 305-306
Baruch Plan, 568
Basel, Treaty of, 101
Batavian Republic, 101
Batista, Fulgencio, 575
Baudelaire, Pierre Charles, 348
Bavaria, 52, 188, *m. 26, Ref. M. 1*
"Bay of Pigs" invasion, 593
Beccaria, Cesare Bonesana (bek'ä rē'ä, chä'zä rä bō nä sä'nä), 79
Bechuanaland (bech'ü ä'nǝland'), 309, *Ref. M. 5*
Beethoven, Ludwig van, 110, 140
Belgian Congo, 305, 306, 307, 312, 574, 588, *m. 301, Ref. M. 5*
Belgium, 98, 101, 114, 116, 480, *m. 116, Ref. M. 1, 2:* African interests of, 305, 306, 307; and appeasement of Nazi Germany, 530; in Cold War period, 574; industrialization in, 163, 399; liberalization of franchise in, 208; plural voting in, 392; revolution and independence in, 199-200; during World War I and aftermath, 421, 434, 443, 447, 448, 451-452, 454, *m. 450;* in World War II, 534-535, 567
Belgrade, *m. 193, Ref. M. 2:* conference at, 579-580
Bell, Alexander Graham, 327
Beneš (be'nesh), Eduard, 480
Benevolent despotism, 76, 82, 85-88
Bengal, 54, *Ref. M. 3*
Bentham, Jeremy, 170, 201
Bentinck, Lord William, 286
Berchtold (berk'tōlt), Count Leopold von, 419-420
Bergson, Henri, 339-340
Bering, Vitus, 303
Berlin, 212, 213, 592, *m. 26, Ref. M. 1, 2:* Congress of, 186, 241-242, 414-415, *m. 241;* after World War II, 592

Bessarabia, *m. 418, 450, Ref. M. 1, 2*
Bill of Rights, English, 34, 35
Birmingham, England, 70, 165, 166, 202, *Ref. M. 1, 2*
Bismarck, Otto von, 222, 227-229, 232, 242, 372, 373-376: and African colonies, 306, 307, 310; diplomacy after 1871, 414-415; and "Ems dispatch," 231; and Napoleon III, 230-231
Black Hand Society, 419
Black Hole of Calcutta, 54
Blanc, Louis, 172, 205, 207, 208
Blanqui (bläɴ kē'), Louis Auguste, 150
Blenheim, battle of, 48
Blum, Léon, 522-523
Boer War, 261-262, 309, 416
Bogotá (bō gō tä'), 263, *m. 267, Ref. M. 9*
Bohemia, 211, 213, 215, 387, 413, *m. 26, 388, Ref. M. 1*
Bohemians. *See* Czechs.
Bokhara (bō kä'rə), 303, *Ref. M. 7*
Bolívar, Simón (bō lē'vär, sē mōn'), 265, 266-267
Bolivia, 268, 271, *m. 267, Ref. M. 9*
Bolsheviks, 464-465, 466
Bombay, 50, 287, *m. 288, 301, Ref. M. 3, 7*
Bonaparte, Joseph, 264-265
Borneo, 584
Borodin, Michael, 507
Bosnia, 241, 242, 418, *m. 193, 418, Ref. M. 1:* assassination of Francis Ferdinand, 419-420
Bosporus, 235, 415, 416, *Ref. M. 8*
Bossuet, Jacques (bô sɥ e', zhäk), 20, ʼ79
Botha, Louis, 262
Boulanger (bü'läɴ'zhä'), Georges, 369-370
Bourbons, 46, 48, 113, 264
Boxer Rebellion, 292-293
Boyle, Robert, 11
Braganza, House of, 265, 267
Brahms, Johannes, 140
Brandenburg, 42-43, *m. 26, 44, 48, Ref. M. 1*
Brazil, 146, 265, 267, 271, 481, 575, *m. 267, Ref. M. 9*
Brazza, Pierre de, 310
Brest Litovsk, *Ref. M. 8:* Treaty of, 442, 449, 463
Brezhnev, Leonid, 560
Briand, Aristide (brē äɴ', ä rēs tēd'), 406, 454-455, 458, 459
Britain, battle of, 535-538
British Central Africa, 589
British Columbia, 258, *m. 257*
British Commonwealth of Nations. *See* Great Britain.
British East Africa, 308, *Ref. M. 5*
British North America Act, 257, 258
Browning, Robert, 343
Brunei, 584
Brunswick, *m. 116:* Manifesto, 96
Brussels, 199, *m. 26, Ref. M. 1, 2:* Treaty, 570
Bryant, William Cullen, 139
Bucharest, *m. 193, Ref. M. 1, 2*
Budapest, 215, *Ref. M. 2*
Buenos Aires (bwā'nōs ī'räs), 266, 270, 271, *m. 267, 300, Ref. M. 9*
Buffon (bʏ fôn'), Georges, 14
Bulganin, Nikolai, 575
Bulgaria, 190, 195, 211, 235, 239-242, *m. 193, 418,*

Ref. M. 1, 2: in Balkan wars of 1912-13, 418-419; as Russian satellite, 567, 576; during World War I and aftermath, 436, 437, 443, 445, 449, 451, 457, 479, *m. 450;* between world wars, 523; in World War II, 538, 565
Bulge, Battle of the, 548
Buonarroti (bwô när rō'tē), 203, 205
Burke, Edmund, 84, 99
Burma, 289, 291, 297, 298, 504, *Ref. M. 3, 4, 7:* independence granted to, 584; in World War II, 544, 548
Burritt, Elihu, 408
Byron, George G., Lord, 134-135, 144, 194, 198

C

Cabinet government: 35-38, 257-258, 360
Cairo, 585, *m. 193, Ref. M. 5, 8*
Calcutta, 50, 54, 287, *m. 288, 301, Ref. M. 3, 7*
Cambodia, 582, 583, *Ref. M. 3, 7*
Cameroons, 307, 489, 588, *Ref. M. 5. See also* British Cameroons
Campo Formio, Treaty of, 103
Canada, 478: agrarian unrest in, 259; British acquisition of, 54, 256; confederation of, 257-258; democracy in, 276; exploration of, 274; formative period in, 256-257; French, 255-256, *m. 256;* French-British quarrels over, 256; growth of, *m. 257;* nationalism in, 277; responsible government of, 257; Upper and Lower, 256-257, *m. 256*
Canning, George, 192, 201
Canton, 289, 290, 507, *m. 292, Ref. M. 3, 4, 7*
Cape Colony, 261, 281, 305, 307, 309, 491, *m. 261*
Cape of Good Hope, 260, *Ref. M. 5*
Cape Town, 260, *m. 261, 301, Ref. M. 5*
Capitalism: commercial, 67; financial, 67; growth and development of, 66-73; and imperialism, 283; industrial, 67, 149-150; 168-169; Marxian interpretation of, 181; between world wars, 515-516
Caporetto, battle of, 440, *m. 435*
Carlyle, Thomas, 144, 172, 173, 344-345
Carol II, king of Rumania, 480, 523
Cartier, Jacques, 255
Cartwright, Edmund, 153
Castlereagh, Robert Stewart, Viscount, 111, 115
Castro, Fidel, 575, 593
Catherine II (the Great), tsarina of Russia, 15, 41-42, 55, 56, 86, 87, 236, 264
Caucasus (kô'kə səs), 303, *Ref. M. 7*
Cavour, Count Camillo di, 164, 223-226, 228-229
Central African Federation, 589, *Ref. M. 6*
Central Treaty Organization (CENTO), 570
Ceylon, 115, 164, 281, 297-298, 504, *Ref. M. 3, 7*
Cézanne, Paul (sā zän', pôl), 349, 350
Chad Republic, *Ref. M. 6*
Chamberlain, Austen, 454
Chamberlain, Houston Stewart, 338
Chamberlain, Joseph, 416
Chamberlain, Neville, 529, 531, 533, 534
Champlain, Samuel de, 255
Chandernagor, 50, *Ref. M. 3*
Charles I, emperor of Austria, 443
Charles I, king of England, 29-32

hat, āge, cãre, fär; let, ēqual, tėrm; it, īce; hot, ōpen, ôrder; oil, out; cup, pùt, rüle, ūse; ch, child; ng, long; th, thin; ᴛʜ, then; zh, measure; ə represents *a* in *about, e* in *taken, i* in *pencil, o* in *lemon, u* in *circus.*

Charles II, king of England, 33, 34
Charles IV, king of Spain, 100-101
Charles X, king of France, 196-198, 309
Charles XII, king of Sweden, 39, 40
Charles Albert, king of Sardinia, 216
Chartist movement, 208-209
Château-Thierry (sha tō′ tyär′i), battle of, 442, m. 435
Chemistry, 11, 330, 396
Chiang Kai-shek (chyäng′kī′shek′), 507-508, 526-527, 577-578
Ch'ien Lung (chyen′lùng′), 289
Child labor, 157, 166-167, 173, 176
Chile, 265, 268, 272, 275, 575, m. 267, Ref. M. 9
China, Ref. M. 3, 7: Boxer Rebellion in, 292-293; Communist, 526-527, 577-578, 591, 592-593, 604; exploitation by West, 290-292, m. 292; extraterritoriality in, 290; "hundred days of reform" in, 292; and India, 581, 582; Japanese aggression toward, 509-510, 526; and Korean War, 569; and Malaya, 298; Manchu dynasty in, 288-293, 506-507; Nationalist, 526-627, 577-578; and Nine-Power Treaty, 510; and Open Door Policy, 292; and Pakistan, 582; Republic of, 506-509, Ref. M. 3; and Sino-Japanese War, 291; and Soviet Union, 570, 604; Taiping Rebellion in, 290; and trade relations with West, 289-290; and United States, 292, 293; in World War II, 544, 548, 577
Churchill, John, Duke of Marlborough, 48
Churchill, Winston S., 48, 367, 435, 531, 534, 535, 538, 539, 545, 548, 564, 567, 572
Clark, William, 279
Classicism: of Age of Reason, 82, 84-85; romanticism vs., 132-133
Clemenceau (klə män sō′), Georges, 215, 445, 446, 447, 450-451, 476
Clemens, Samuel (Mark Twain), 347, 354, 379
Clerk-Maxwell, James, 331-332
Cleves-Mark lands, 42, m. 44
Clive, Robert, 54, 286
Clothing: effects in Europe of overseas expansion, 62; effects of French Revolution, 101; in nineteenth century, 341; in Russia, 40
Cochrane, Thomas, Lord, 267, 268
Colbert, Jean Baptiste (kôl bär′, zhän ba tēst′), 23, 59, 60, 68
Colbertism, 23, 59
Cold War, 590-591: and Communist World, 575-578; and disarmament, 602-603; and Free World, 571-575; and non-aligned nations, 578-590; regional blocs in, 570-571; trouble spots in, 591-594; and United Nations, 564, 567-569, 594-595; and war for men's minds, 603-604
Coleridge, Samuel Taylor, 134, 138
Colombia, 146, 271, 574, m. 267, Ref. M. 9
Colonization, 43, 49-51, 52, 53, 54, 55, 58, 280-282
Committee of Public Safety, in France, 100-102
Communism: in China, 507-508, 526-527, 591, 592; Communist World in Cold War period, 575-578; in Cuba, 575, 593-594; in France, 573; in Germany, 473, 592; in Hungary, 479; in Indo-China, 515, 582-583, 584; in Russia, 463-470, 568; and Sino-Soviet split, 604
Communist International: 182, 469-470
Communist Manifesto, 179-183, 403, 406-407
Comte, Auguste (kôNt, ō gyst′), 178, 336-337
Concordat, 104

Condorcet (kōN dôr sā′), Marquis de, 82, 130-132
Congo, Republic of, 588, 605, Ref. M. 6
Congo Free State, 307. See also Belgian Congo
Congo Republic, Ref. M. 6
Congress System, 115, 116, 132, 190-195, 203
Constable, John, 139
Constantine, of Russia, 378
Constantinople, 194, 235, 237, m. 26, 193, 301, Ref. M. 1, 2
Cook, James, 259
Coolidge, Calvin, 484
Cooper, Anthony Ashley, Earl of Shaftesbury, 173
Copyright union, international, 408
Coral Sea, Ref. M. 4: battle of, 544
Corfu incident, 457, 472
Corneille (kôr ne′y), Pierre, 24
Corn Laws, 171, 209
Corsica, 103, Ref. M. 1, 2
Costa Rica, 272, 275, Ref. M. 9
Courbet, Gustave (kür bā′, gʏs täv′), 348
Cracow, 199, 214, Ref. M. 2
Crete, 195, 391, m. 418, Ref. M. 1, 2, 9
Crimea, 237, Ref. M. 8
Crimean War, 223, 229, 230, 237-239, 363, 381
Critique of Pure Reason, 129
Croats, 210, 211, 388, 389, 480, m. 388
Cromer, Lord (Evelyn Baring), 305-306
Crompton, Samuel, 153
Cromwell, Oliver, 30-31, 32
Cuba, 273, 275, 282, 481, 575, 593-594, Ref. M. 9
Cubism, 350
Curie (kū rē′), Pierre and Marie, 332
Custozza (küs tôd zä′), battle of, 216
Cuzco (küs kō), 263, m. 267
Cyprus, 242, 282, Ref. M. 1, 2, 8
Czechoslovakia, 449, 452, 480, 530, m. 450, Ref. M. 7: annexation by Germany, 531; communism in, 568, 576
Czechs, 210, 211, 215, 388, 413, 449, m. 388

D

Da Gama, Vasco, 260
Dahomey, 588, Ref. M. 5, 6
Daimler, Gottlieb, 327
Dairen, 292, 296, m. 292, Ref. M. 6
Daladier (dä lä dyä′), Édouard, 531, 532
Dalai Lama, 593
Dalton, John, 330
Damascus, 493, 494, Ref. M. 9
D'Annunzio, Gabriele (dä nün′tsi ō, gä brē el′), 470
Danton (dän tōN′), Georges Jacques, 95, 97, 102
Danubian Principality, 237
Danzig, 447, 457, 533, m. 450, Ref. M. 1
Dardanelles, 194, 235, 435-436, Ref. M. 1, 2
Darwin, Charles, 325-326
Darwinism, 335-339, 483
Das Kapital, 180-183
Daumier, Honoré (dō myä′, ô nô rē′), 175, 348
David, Jacques Louis, 139
Davy, Humphry, 157, 331
Dawes Plan, 454, 474, 476
Deák, Francis, 233-234
Debussy, Claude (də bʏ sē′, klōd), 352, 354
Declaration of Rights: French, 34; German, 213; of United Nations, 594
Defoe, Daniel, 61, 64, 157

Degas (də gäs′), Edgar, 349
De Gaulle, Charles, 535, 572, 573, 588, 591, 592, 595, 603
Deism, 17-19, 75, 77, 128
Dekker, Eduard, 299
Delacroix (də lä krwä′), Eugène, 139
Delhi, 286, m. 288, Ref. M. 6, 8
Democracy 76, 82: in Austria-Hungary, 388-389; and cold war, 594, 603; in European small nations, 391-394, 479-481; in Germany, 376-377; in Great Britain, 364-365; improvement in machinery of, 403-404; in India, 587; in New World, 276-277; in underdeveloped lands, 580; after World War I, 475-485
Denmark, 39, 40, 146, 208, 480, 606, m. 26, Ref. M. 1, 2: and Schleswig and Holstein, 228, 447, m. 450; in World War II, 534
Descartes (dā kärt′), René, 10, 16
Diaz, Bartholomew, 260
Diaz, Porfirio, 270
Dickens, Charles, 167, 172, 174-175, 342
Diderot, Denis (dēd rō′, də nē′), 77, 82, 128
Diem, Ngo Dinh, 583
Diesel, Rudolf, 328
Diplomatic Revolution, of the eighteenth century, 52-53
Disarmament, 602-603: conferences on, 409-410, 458, 484; League of Nations efforts toward, 457-458; United Nations and, 595
Disraeli, Benjamin, 172, 173, 242, 282, 305, 363-364
Divine right of kings, 19, 20, 28, 29, 33, 34-35
Dollar diplomacy, 273
Dollfuss, Engelbert, 530
Dominican Republic, 273, 275, 574, Ref. M. 9
Dostoevski (dos′to yef′ski), Feodor, 346
Dover, Treaty of, 33
Dreyfus (drā fϵs′) case, 370-371
Dual Alliance (Austria and Germany), 415
Dual Alliance (France and Russia), 415
Dualism, 16
Dual Monarchy. See Austria-Hungary.
Du Bois (dü bois′), W. E. B., 489
Duma, 386-387, 462, 463
Dunkirk, 534-535
Durham, Lord, 257
Dutch East Indies, 46, 49, 163, 297, 298-299, 505, 544, 583-584, m. 301, Ref. M. 3

E

East India Company, British, 62, 281, 286-287, 289-290
East India Company, Dutch, 60, 260-261, 299
East Indies. See Dutch East Indies.
Eastman, George, 328
East Prussia, 42, 43, 44, 55, 56, m. 26, 44
Ebert, Friedrich, 473
Ecuador, 271, Ref. M. 9
Edison, Thomas, 327, 328, 396
Education: in China, 508-509; in France, 104, 195, 371; in Germany, 376; in Gilded Age, 355-356; in Great Britain, 362-363; in India, 287-288; in Japan, 294, 296; in Latin-American colonies, 263;

in Nazi Germany, 520; in Russia, 40, 379, 576; spread of, in nineteenth century, 404
Egypt, 237, m. 193, Ref. M. 5, 8: Great Britain in, 305-306; vs. Greeks, 194, 195; Napoleon in, 103; republic proclaimed in, 585; rule of Gamal Abdel Nasser, 585-587; between world wars, 497. See also United Arab Republic.
Ehrlich, Paul, 330
Einstein, Albert, 332, 334
Eisenhower, Dwight D., 544, 569, 571-572, 590, 591
Eisenhower Doctrine, 586
Elba, 109, 113, m. 104
Electricity, 327, 331-332, 396-397
Eliot, T. S., 476, 485
Emancipation Edict, Prussian, 108
Emancipation Proclamation, Russian, 381
Emerson, Ralph Waldo, 139
Empiricism, 17
Ems, m. 232, Ref. M. 1: "Ems dispatch," 231
Enclosure movement, 65-66, 150, 151
Encyclopédie, 77
Engels, Friedrich, 179-183; characterization of Marx
England, m. 26, 48: Bank of, 67; civil war in, 30-31; colonial rivalry with France, 49-51; conservatism, 188; Glorious Revolution in, 34-35; government of, 76, 77; in Grand Alliance against Louis XIV, 47; and mercantilism, 59-60; union with Scotland, 60; and War of Spanish Succession, 48. See also Great Britain.
Enlightenment, the. See Age of Reason.
Entente Cordiale, 416-417
Erhard, Ludwig, 592
Eritrea (er′ ə trē′ ə), 538, 587, Ref. M. 5
Essay Concerning Human Understanding, An, 17
Essay on Crimes and Punishments, 79
Esthetic Revolt, 345
Estates-General of France, 74, 90, 91
Estonia, 466, 523, 538, m. 450, Ref. M. 7
Ethiopia, 587, 590, Ref. M. 5, 6. See also Abyssinia.
Europe, Concert of, 186
European Atomic Energy Community (Euratom), 570, 571
European Coal and Steel Community, 570
European Economic Community, 570-571
European Free Trade Association, 570
European Recovery Program, 567, 568
Evolution, 324-327, 339
Exploration: in Africa, 304-305; in New World, 274-275
Expressionism: in music, 354; in painting. 350
Extraterritoriality, 290

F

Fabian Society, 405-406
Factory system, 165-168, 173, 176
Faisal (fī′səl), Emir, 492, 493, 494
Faraday, Michael, 327, 331
Fascism, 339: in Italy, 470-473, 521; in Japan, 526; in Libya, 497-498. See also Nazism.
Federation of Rhodesia & Nyasaland, 589
Ferdinand VII, king of Spain, 190-191, 265, 266
Field, Cyrus, 161

hat, āge, cãre, fär; let, ēqual, tėrm; it, īce; hot, ōpen, ôrder; oil, out; cup, pùt, rüle, ūse; ch, child; ng, long; th, thin; ᴛʜ, then; zh, measure; ə represents a in about, e in taken, i in pencil, o in lemon, u in circus.

Finland, 114, 116, 456, 466, 480, *m. 450, Ref. M. 7:* Finns in Russia, 412; and World War I debts, 516; in World War II, 534, 545, 565

Fiume, 449, 470, *m. 450*

Flaubert (flō bär'), Gustave, 345, 346

Foch (fôsh), Ferdinand, 442-443, 447

Ford, Henry, 328

Formosa, 291, 592-593, *m. 292, Ref. M. 3, 4, 7*

Fourier, Francois (fü ryā', fräṅ swä'), 178

Fourteen Points, 444, 446, 447

Fox, George, 128

France, *m. 26, 48, Ref. m. 1, 2:* absolutism in, 19-24, 49, 91; in Africa, 309-310, 415-416, 417, 498, 587; alliances of 1871-1914, 414-421; and American Revolution, 90; in Balkans, 235, 237; Bourbon restoration in, 113, 192, 195-198; in China, 292, *m. 292;* in Cold War period, 572-573; colonial possessions in nineteenth century, 281, 282, *m. 300-301;* colonial rivalry with England, 49-51, 256, 286; commercial development of, 58; Commune of 1871 in, 369; at Congress of Vienna, 111-113; conservatism in, 188; in Crimean War, 230, 236-239; and De Gaulle, 588, 591, 592, 595; Directory in, 102-103; drama in, 24-25; in Egypt, 305; in Franco-Prussian War, 231-232; and German annexation of Czechoslovakia, 531; in Indo-China, 281, 291, 297, 298, 505, 582-583; industrialization in, 158-159, 162, 399; and Italian unification, 223, 224-225; under Louis XIV, 20, 21-24; under Louis Philippe, 198, 204-206; mercantilism of, 59, 60; in Middle East, 493-494, 498-499; Napoleonic period in, 103-110; nineteenth-century society, 341, 342; Occupied France, in World War II, *m. 535;* Old Regime in, 73-74, 110; republics, (Jacobin) 97-102; (Second) 206-208, 217; (Third) 369-372, 535; (Fourth) 572-573; (Fifth) 573; revolutions, (of 1789-1792) *see* French Revolution, (of 1830) 197-198; (of 1848) 205-206; Second Empire in, 229-232; in Seven Years' War, 53, 54-55, 286; socialism in, 405; syndicalism in, 406; in Thirty Years' War, 46; Unoccupied France, in World War II, *m. 535;* in War of the Austrian Succession, 52; in war for Greek independence, 195, 236; in War of the Spanish Succession, 48; in world trade, 401; during World War I and aftermath, 421, 434-444, 445-455, 476-477, 516; between world wars, 521-523; in World War II, 533-535, 544, 545, 548, *m. 535*

Francis I, emperor of Austria, 210, 212

Francis Ferdinand, archduke of Austria, 419

Francis Joseph I, emperor of Austria, 215, 388, 389-390

Franco, Francisco, 529

Franco-Prussian War, 231-232

Frankfurt, *Ref. M. 1, 2:* Assembly, 213-214, 218, 226; Treaty of, 232

Franklin, Benjamin, 13

Frederick I, king in Prussia, 43-44

Frederick II (the Great), king in Prussia, 45-46, 51-52, 53-54, 55-56, 75, 86, 87-88, 263

Frederick III, German emperor, 375

Frederick Hohenzollern, elector of Brandenburg, 42

Frederick William, elector of Brandenburg, 43

Frederick William I, king in Prussia, 44-45, 48, 51

Frederick William II, king in Prussia, 101

Frederick William IV, king of Prussia, 212-214, 226

Free trade, 405; vs. colonization, 281; decline of, 282, 515, 516; in Great Britain, 171, 209, 516; in Prussia, 162, 226

Frémont, John, 274

French and Indian War, 52

French Indo-China. *See* Indo-China.

French Revolution: beginning of, 82; European opposition to, 95-96, 99-101; Jacobin Republic, 97-102; legacy of, 109-110; moderate phase of, 90-97; Reign of Terror in, 100-102; Tennis Court Oath in, 91

French West Africa, 310, 312, 588, *Ref. M. 5*

Freud (froid), Sigmund, 334-335

Fulton, Robert, 160

G

Gabon, *Ref. M. 6*

Galicia, 389, 435, 436, *m. 388, 450*

Gallipoli, battle of, 436, *m. 435*

Galton, Francis, 326-327, 334

Gambia, 308, *Ref. M. 5, 6*

Gandhi, Mohandas K., 500-501, 502, 580, 581

Garibaldi, Giuseppe (gar'i bōl'di, jü sep'ā), 217, 225

Geneva Agreement, 1954, 583

Geneva Conference: of 1927, 114, 116, 458; of 1955, 590

Geology, 13-14

Geopolitics, 521

George, Henry, 405-406

George I, king of England, 36

George II, king of England, 36

George III, king of England, 37-38, 201

George IV, king of England, 201

Georgia, in Russia, 303, *Ref. M. 7, 8*

German Confederation, 188-190, 198, 203, 228, *Ref. M. 1*

German East Africa, 307, 489, *Ref. M. 5*

German Southwest Africa, 307, 489, *Ref. M. 5*

German states, 43, 46, 47, 52, 188

Germany, *Ref. M. 2:* in Africa, 307-308; agriculture in, 400-401; alliances of 1871-1914, 414-421; and annexation of Austria, 530; and annexation of Czechoslovakia, 531; anti-Semitism in, 414, 519, 520, 548; and Berlin-to-Bagdad railroad controversy, 411; in China, 291-292, *m. 292;* in Cold War period, 573-574, 577, 592; colonial possessions in 1914, *m. 300-301;* and cultural revival of eighteenth century, 133-134; East Germany, 567, 576, 577, 592; in Franco-Prussian War, 231-232; Germans in Austria-Hungary, 387-389, *m. 388;* imperialism of, 284; industrialism in, 162-163, 398-399; and Napoleon, 109; nationalism in, 115, 116, 143, 210-211, 226; and Pan-German League, 411-412; Reichs, (Second) 372-378; (Third) 520; Reichstag, 372-373; Reichstag fire, 519-520; revolution of 1848 in, 212-214; and Rhineland invasion of 1936, 528; and Russian Revolution, 463; Social Democratic party in, 405; in Spanish civil war, 529; unification of, 131, 159, 222, 228, 232, 235, *m. 232;* and Venezuelan dispute, 272; Weimar Republic, 473-475, 518, 520; West Germany, 567, 570, 573-574, 591, 592; in world trade, 401; during World War I and aftermath, 421-422, 434-455, 473-475, *m. 450;* in World War II, 533-549

Ghana, 319-320, 587-588, *Ref. M. 6*

"Gilded Age," 354-357

Gladstone, William Ewart, 240, 361-363, 364-366
Goebbels, Joseph, 519
Goering, Hermann, 534
Goethe (goe′tə), Johann Wolfgang von, 133-134
Gold Coast, 50, 308. 312, 318-320, 492, 587-588, *Ref. M. 5*
Gomulka, Wladyslaw, 577
Good Neighbor policy, 524
Gothic revival, 139-140
Graeco-Turkish War of 1922, 457, 499
Grand Alliance, 47, 48
Grand Duchy of Finland, 378
Grapes of Wrath, The, 554-556
Great Britain, *Ref. M. 1, 2:* in Africa, 319-320, 415-416, 587, 589-590; agricultural changes in eighteenth century in, 64-66; alliances of 1871-1914, 414-421; and American colonies, 254; and appeasement of Nazi Germany, 528, 529-531; Balkan interests of, 235-238, 241, 242; Ballot Act of 1872 in, 363; and Berlin-to-Bagdad railroad controversy, 411; and Boer War, 261-262, 309, 416; and British Commonwealth of Nations, 478, 524; in Burma, 297, 298, 504; cabinet government in, 35-38, 360; and Canada, 255, 256-258; in Ceylon, 297-298, 504; Chartism in, 208-209; in China, 289, 291, 292, *m. 292;* in Cold War period, 572; colonial rivalry with France, 49-51, 256, 286; commercial development of, 58, 60-61, 401; at Congress of Vienna, 175, 178-179, 281; constitutional monarchy, evolution of, 28-38; Corn Laws in, 209; in Crimean War, 237-238, 363; depression of 1930's in, 523-524; in Diplomatic Revolution, 52-53; in Egypt, 305-306, 497; emergence as first world power, 28-38; free trade established in, 209; Georgian period in, 36-38, 200-203; Gladstone and Disraeli, 361-366; Hong Kong acquired by, 281, 290; imperialism of, 282, 284, 285, 297, 311; and India, 285, 286-288, 312, 500-502, 580, 581; industrial development of, 150-162, 368, 397-398; and Irish problem, 365-366, 479; and Japanese alliance, 296, 510; in Jordan, 586; and Latin America, 192, 272; "Little Englandism" in, 281, 282; in Malaya, 297, 312, 504-505, 584; and Middle East, 492-497; and Monroe Doctrine, 268; and Napoleonic wars, 105-109; nationalism in, 412; and opium wars, 290; and Pakistan, 580; and *Pax Britannica*, 368; in Persia, 304, 496; in Quadruple Alliance, 186; reforms of nineteenth century in, 201-203, 209-210, 362-366; reforms of twentieth-century Liberals in, 366-367; and Russian alliance, 304; in Seven Years' War, 53, 54, 55; and slavery, 145-146; socialism in, 405-406, 477, 572; in South Africa, 261, 308-309, 490-492; Victorian Compromise in, 360-361; Victorian period in, 340-342; in War of the Austrian Succession, 52; in war on French Republic, 99-101, 103; in war for Greek independence, 195, 236; in War of Jenkins' Ear, 37; in War of Spanish Succession, 48; during World War I and aftermath, 421, 434-444, 445-455, 477-479, 516; during World War II and aftermath, 533-538, 544, 548, 572
Great Colombia, Republic of, 267, *m. 267*
Great Northern War, 39-40
Great Trek, of Boers, 261, *m. 261*
Greater Colombia, 268
Greece, 190, *m. 193, 194, 418, Ref. M. 1, 2, 7:* in Balkan wars of 1912-1913, 418-419; in Cold War period, 567, 568, 574; in Congress of Berlin, 242; and Corfu incident, 457, 472; nationalism in, 235, 239; revolt of 1821 in, 194-195, 236; vs. Turkey in 1921-1922, 499; and World War I peace conference, 449, *m. 450;* between world wars, 523; in World War II, 538
Grey, Charles, Earl, 191
Grey, Sir Edward, 420, 421, 423
Gropius, Walter, 352
Guadalcanal, 544, *Ref. M. 4*
Guadeloupe, 50, *Ref. M. 9*
Guam, 302, 544, *Ref. M. 3, 4*
Guatemala, 265, 267, 268, *Ref. M. 9*
Guild system, 91
Guinea, 588, *m. 596*

H

Habeas Corpus Act, 34
Hacha (hä′chä), Emil, 531
Hague, 408, 410, *Ref. M. 2*
Haifa (hī′fə), *Ref. M. 8*
Haile Selassie (hī′li sə-las′i), emperor of Abyssinia (Ethiopia), 528
Hainan, 527, *Ref. M. 3, 7*
Hales, Stephen, 15
Halley, Edmund, 10
Hamaguchi, Yuko, 511, 526
Handel, Frederick, 85
Hanover, 40, 52, 53, *Ref. M. 1, 2*
Hapsburgs, 46, 47, 48, 210, 215, 216, 226, 235: possessions of, *m. 26*
Hara, Takashi, 510
Harding, Warren G., 451, 458, 483-484
Hardy, Thomas, 346
Hargreaves, James, 153
Hawaiian Islands, 282, 300-301, 572, *m. 300, Ref. M. 4*
Hawthorne, Nathaniel, 139
Hay, John, 292
Haydn (hī′dən), Franz Joseph, 84, 85
Hegel (hā′gəl), Georg Wilhelm Friedrich, 143, 180, 474
Heine, Heinrich, 135, 204-205
Hejaz (he jaz′), 492-493, 495, 496, *Ref. M. 8*
Helgoland, 308, *m. 301*
Hemingway, Ernest, 440, 485
Henry IV, king of France, 19, 20-21, 23
Hertz, Heinrich, 332
Herzegovina (her′tsə gō vē nə), 231, 242, 418, *m. 241, 418, Ref. M. 1*
Herzen, Alexander, 380, 381
Herzl, Theodor, 414
Hidalgo (ē däl′gō), Father, 266
Hindenburg, Paul von, 435, 443, 474, 519, 520
Hiroshima, 548, *Ref. M. 3*
Hitler, Adolf, 55, 475, 519-521, 528-534, 535, 538, 539, 544, 548, 592, 605
Hobbes, Thomas, 79-80

hat, āge, cãre, fär; let, ēqual, tėrm; it, īce; hot, ōpen, ôrder; oil, out; cup, pút, rüle, ūse; ch, child; ng, long; th, thin; ᴛʜ, then; zh, measure; ə represents *a* in *a*bout, *e* in tak*e*n, *i* in penc*i*l, *o* in lem*o*n, *u* in circ*u*s.

Ho Chi Minh (hō'chē'min'), 505, 582
Hohenzollern, House of, 42-46, 48-49, 372-378
Holbach, Baron d', 73, 82
Holland, *m. 26:* and Belgium, 199-200; and Ceylon, 297; in Cold War period, 575; and colonies of, 49; at Congress of Vienna, 113, 114, 116; democracy in, 480, 574; in Grand Alliance against Louis XIV, 47; industries of, 399; and mercantilism, 59, 60; and South Africa, 260-262; in War of the Austrian Succession, 52; in war on French Republic, 99-101; in War of the Spanish Succession, 48; between world wars, 480; in World War II, 534-535
Holstein, 228, *m. 228, Ref. M. 1*
Holy Alliance, 115
Holy Roman Empire, 43, 47, 109, 114
Honduras, 272, *Ref. M. 9*
Hong Kong, 281, 290, 544, *m. 292, 301, Ref. M. 3, 4, 7*
Hoover, Herbert, 484, 515, 516, 525
Horthy, Nicholas, 479
Howard, John, 79
Hudson Bay territory, 48, 50, 256, *m. 48, 256*
Hudson's Bay Company, 256, 258
Hughes, Charles Evans, 458
Hugo, Victor, 138-140, 142, 346, 408
Huguenots, 23, 43, 50
Humboldt, Alexander von, 274
Hungary, 210, *m. 26, 116, Ref. M. 1, 2:* Dual Monarchy, *see* Austria-Hungary; Hungarians in Czechoslovakia and Poland, 480; nationalism in, 211, 233-234; as Russian satellite, 576-577; war for independence, 214-215; after World War I, 449, 451, 457, 479, *m. 450;* in World War II, 538, 565
Huong, Tran Van, 583
Husein ibn-Ali (hü sīn' ib'ən ä lē'), 492, 493, 495-496
Hutton, James, 13-14
Huxley, Thomas, 335

I

Ibn-Saud, Abdul-Aziz (ib'ən sä üd', ab dül' a zēz'), 492, 495-496
Ibsen, Henrik, 347
Idealism, philosophical, 129
Imperialism, 280; in Africa, 304-310; in Asia and Oceania, 285-293, 297-304; economic, 211; evaluation of, 311-313; motives for, 282, 285; "white man's burden," 284-285, 338; world empires in 1914, *m. 300-301*
Impressionism: in music, 352, 354; in painting, 349
India, *Ref. M. 6, 8:* Afghan invasion of, 497; Anglo-French rivalry in, 52-54; British in, 286-288, 312, 500-503, *m. 288;* Government of India Acts, 500, 501-502; Hindu-Muslim clash in, 503; industrialization in, 164; Mogul empire in, 285-286, 287; nationalism in, 288, 500-503; as republic, 580-581; Rowlatt Act in, 500, 501; in World War I, 500, 501
Indian National Congress, 288, 501, 502-503
Indo-China, 281, 291, 298, 505, 582-584, *Ref. M. 3, 4, 7*
Indonesia, 567, 574, 583-584, *Ref. M. 7*
Industrial Revolution: consequences of, 164-168, 354-357; First, 159-164; in France, 204-205; initial phase of, 150-159; and Latin America, 272; reform

following, 172-176; in Russia, 384; Second, 396-403; Third, 597-602, 606-607
Inner Six, 570-571, *m. 571*
International Labor Organization, 456
International Monetary Fund, 564
Iran, 496-497, 567, *Ref. M. 7, 8*
Iraq, 446, 447, 449, 494, 570, 586, *Ref. M. 7, 8*
Ireland, 201, 210, 365-366, 479, *m. 26, Ref. M. 1, 2*
Irish Free State, 479, *m. 450*
Iron industry, 156-157, 159-160, 398, 399
Ismail (is mä'ēl'), ruler of Egypt, 305
Israel, 585-586, 592, *Ref. M. 8*
Italia irredenta, 188, 416
Italy, *Ref. M. 2:* African ventures of, 310; alliances of 1871-1914, 415-421; in Cold War period, 574; colonial possessions in, 1914, *m. 300-301;* and conquest of Abyssinia, 528; and Corfu incident, 457, 472; after 1815 in, 115-116, 191; Fascism in, 470-473, 521; industrial progress in, 163-164; Italians in Austria-Hungary, 387, 388, 413, 416, *m. 388;* in Libya, 497-498; Mazzini and *Risorgimento,* 211; Mussolini, *see* Mussolini, Benito; revolt of 1830 in, 198; revolution and reform in 1848-1849, 215-217; in Spanish civil war, 529; states of, *m. 48, Ref. M. 1;* unification and after, 222-226, 232, 392-393, *m. 224;* and War of the Spanish Succession, 47-48; during World War I and aftermath, 421, 436, 440, 443, 446, 449, 451, 454, 455, 479, *m. 450;* in World War II, 535, 538, 544, 545, 548, 565
Ito Hirobumi (ē'tô' hē'rô bü'mē), Prince Ito, 295
Iturbide (ē tür bē'dä), Agustín de, 267
Ivory Coast, 587, 588, *Ref. M. 5*
Iwo Jima, *Ref. M. 6:* battle of, 548

J

James, Henry, 346-347
James, William, 339
James I, king of England, 28-29
James II, king of England, 34
Japan, *Ref. M. 3, 7:* and Anti-Comintern Pact, 529; in Cold War period, 591-592; Industrial Revolution in, 399-400; invasion of China in 1930's, 526-527; liberalism in, 510-511; *Meiji* period in, 294-297; Perry's expedition to, 294; in Russo-Japanese War, 296, 385; in Sino-Japanese War, 291; Tokugawa shogunate in, 293-294; westernization of, 294-297; as world power, 509-511; in World War I, 421, 446, 509; during World War II and aftermath, 538, 539, 544, 548-549, 566-567
Jaurès (zhô räs'), Jean Léon, 406, 421
Java, 282, 299, 583, *Ref. M. 4*
Jena, battle of, *m. 104*
Jenner, Edward, 15
Jews, 16, 338, 370, 413-414, 493, 495, 548, 585, 592
Jiddah, 496, *Ref. M. 8*
Jiménez (hē mä'näs), Pérez, 574-575
Jinnah, Muhammad Ali, 503, 580
Johannesburg, 261, *m. 261, Ref. M. 5*
John VI, king of Portugal, 267-268
Johnson, President Lyndon B., 603
Johnston, Sir Harry, 306-307, 308
Jordan, 585, 586, 587, *Ref. M. 8*
Joseph II, emperor of Austria, 86-87, 263
Juárez, Benito (hwä'res, bä nē'tō), 270
Jutland, battle of, 437-438, *m. 435*

K

Kaiser, the. *See* William II, German emperor.
Kamchatka (kam chat'kə), 303, *Ref. M. 7*
Kanagawa (kä'nä gä'wä), Treaty of, 294
Kant, Immanuel, 129
Kashmir, 581, 582, *Ref. M. 3*
Kassem, Abdul Karim, 586
Kay, John, 152
Keats, John, 135, 138, 144
Kellogg-Briand Pact, 458
Kemal Atatürk (kə mäl' ä tä tėrk'), Mustafa, 499-500
Kennan, George F., 450
Kennedy, John F., 579, 593, 603, 607
Kenya (ken'yə), 308, 478, 492, 588-589, 590, *Ref. M. 5, 6*
Kenyatta, Jomo, 490, 580
Kerenski, Aleksandr, 463
Khanh, General, 583
Khrushchev, Nikita S., 575-576, 590, 591, 593
Kiaochow (kyou'chou'), 291-292, *m. 292, Ref. M. 3*
Kingsley, Charles, 166, 179
Kipling, Rudyard, 279, 284-285
Koch, Robert, 328-329
Korea, 291, 296, *m. 292, Ref. M. 3, 7*
Korean War, 566, 569, 571
Kossuth, Louis, 214-215, 218
Kosygin, Alexei, 560
Kruger, Paul, 261-262
Krupp, Alfred, 163
Kuchuk Kainarji (kü chük' kĭ'när ji'), Treaty of, 236
Ku Klux Klan, 483
Kulaks, 466, 517, 518
Kun, Béla, 479
Kuomintang, 506-508
Kwangchovan, 292, *m. 292, Ref. M. 3*

L

Labor legislation, 173, 176, 365, 525-526
Labor unions, 176, 402-403, 404, 452, 521
Laënnec, René (lä ā nek', rə nā'), 15
Laibach, *Ref. M. 1*: Congress of, 192
Laissez faire, 71-73, 144, 168-172, 281, 367
Lamarck, Jean Baptiste, 325, 326
Lamartine (lä mär tēn'), Alphonse de, 206-207
Laos (lä'ōs), 582, 583, *Ref. M. 7*
La Paz (lä päs), 266, *Ref. M. 9*
Laplace (lä pläs'), Pierre, 10
La Salle, René, 50, 255
Lateran Treaty, 472
Latin America, *m. 300, Ref. M. 9:* in century following independence, 268-272, 277; Congress System failure in, 192; democracy in, 277, 481, 575; depression of 1930's in, 524; exploration of, 274; foreign investment in, 272-274; independence movement in, 262-268; in 1914, 274; and population explosion, 599, 604; and Roosevelt Corollary, 272-273; during World War I and aftermath, 481; after World War II, 574-575

Latvia, 466, 523, 538, *m. 450, Ref. M. 7*
Lausanne: Conference, 516; Treaty, 451, 499
Lavoisier (lä vwä zyä'), Antoine, 11-12
Lawrence, T. E., 492-493
League of Nations, 285, 446-447, 454, 455-458, 459: and Abyssinia, 528; United States and, 483, 484; withdrawal of nations from, 520, 526, 529, 530
Lebanon, 493, 494, 585, 586, *Ref. M. 8*
Leibnitz (līp'nits), Gottfried, 9, 16-17, 75, 129
Leipzig, *Ref. M. 1, 2:* Battle of the Nations at, 109, *m. 104*
Lenin, Nikolai, 283, 384, 386, 407, 463-467
Leningrad, 545, *Ref. M. 7*
Leopold I, king of Belgium, 200
Leopold II, king of Belgium, 305, 306, 307
Leopoldville, *Ref. M. 5*
Leviathan, 79
Lewis, Meriwether, 274
Leyte, *Ref. M. 3:* battle for Leyte Gulf, 545
Lhasa, 303, *Ref. M. 7*
Liaotung peninsula, 291, 296, *m. 292, Ref. M. 3*
Liberalism: Aristocratic, 28, 38: of nineteenth century, 144-145, 170-171, 405; of twentieth century, 145
Liberia, *Ref. M. 5, 6*
Libya, 497-498, 544, 587, *Ref. M. 5, 6*
Lima (lē'mä), 266, 267, *Ref. M. 9*
Limpopo (lim pō'pō) River, 309, *Ref. M. 5*
Linnaeus, Carolus, 14
Lister, Joseph, 329-330
Literature: in Age of Reason, 84; folk, 143; French realist school of, 345-346; realism in, 345-347; romanticism in, 134-135, 138-139; romantic nationalism in, 141-142; Victorian, 342-345; after World War I, 485
Lithuania, 466, 523, 538, *m. 450, Ref. M. 7*
Little Entente, 451-452
Livingstone, David, 304-305
Lloyd George, David, 361, 445-446, 447, 450-451, 453, 577
Lloyd's of London, 67
Locarno Pact, 455
Locke, John, 17, 80-81, 82, 131, 132
Lombardy, 114, 210-216, 217, 223-224, *m. 116, 224, Ref. M. 1*
London, 157, *m. 26, Ref. M. 1, 2:* Treaty of, 436, 449
Lorraine. *See* Alsace-Lorraine.
"Lost generation," 485
Louis XIII, king of France, 21
Louis XIV, king of France, 20, 21-24, 33, 35, 43, 47, 48, 49, 73, 90
Louis XV, king of France, 52, 73, 77
Louis XVI, king of France, 73, 91, 93, 94, 97, 98-99
Louis XVIII, king of France, 113, 192, 195-196
Louisburg, 52, 54, *m. 48*
Louisiana territory, 54
Louis Napoleon. *See* Napoleon III.
Louis Philippe, 198, 204-206
Ludendorff, Erich von, 435, 442
Lugard, Lord, 318-319
Lunéville, Treaty of, 103
Lusitania, 441-442
Lyell, Sir Charles, 324, 325

hat, āge, cãre, fär; let, ēqual, tėrm; it, īce; hot, ōpen, ôrder; oil, out; cup, pu̇t, rüle, ūse; ch, child; ng, long; th, thin; ℍ, then; zh, measure; ə represents *a* in *about, e* in *taken, i* in *pencil, o* in *lemon, u* in *circus*.

M

McAdam, John, 157
Macao (mə kä′ō), 289, 291, *m. 292, Ref. M. 3*
Macedonia, 240
MacArthur, Douglas, 548, 566, 569
McCarthy, Joseph R., 571
Macaulay, Thomas Babington, 52, 203, 286
McCormick, Cyrus Hall, 400
MacDonald, James Ramsay, 439, 477, 523
Mackenzie, Alexander, 274
McKinley, William, 285, 301
Madagascar, 310, 588, *Ref. M. 5*
Madero, Francisco, 270
Madras, 50, 52, 287, *m. 288, Ref. M. 3*
Magenta (mä jen′tä), battle of, 224
Maginot Line, 534, *m. 532*
Magsaysay (mäg sī′sī), Ramón, 584
Magyars, 210, 211, 215, 234, 388, 389, *m. 388*
Malagasy Republic, 588, *Ref. M. 6*
Malaya, 297, 298, 504-505, 544, 584, *Ref. M. 7*
Malaysia, Federation of, 297, 580, 584
Malenkov, G. M., 575
Malta, 281, *Ref. M. 2*
Malthus, Thomas Robert, 150, 169, 170, 325, 326
Manchester, England, 165, 166, 167, 172, 202, *Ref. M. 1*
Manchu dynasty, 288-293, 506-507
Manchuria, 292, 296, 509, 526, 577, 578, *m. 292, Ref. M. 6, 8*
Mandates, 318-319, 447-448, 489-490, 493
Manila, 54, 299, 544, *Ref. M. 3, 4, 7*
Mao Tse-tung (mou′tse′tùng′), 527, 581, 591
Marat (mä rä′), Jean Paul, 117, 205
March Laws, 214, 215
Marconi, Guglielmo, 327, 332
Maria Theresa, 51-52, 56
Marie Antoinette, 73, 81, 101
Maritime Provinces, Chinese, 303, *m. 301*
Marlborough, Duke of (John Churchill), 48
Marne, battles of, 434-435, 442-443, *m. 435*
Marshall, George C., 568, 577
Marshall Plan, 568
Martinique, 50, 54, *Ref. M. 9*
Marx, Karl, 179-183, 204, 364, 403, 464
Marxism, 179-183, 283: in China, 507, 508; in Russia, 384, 406-407, 464-465, 563; and Utopian socialism, 428-430
Masaryk (mä′sä rēk), Thomas, 378, 413, 480
Masurian Lakes, battle of the, 435, *m. 435*
Mathematics, 9-10
Matisse (mä tēs′), Henri, 350
Maupassant, Guy de (mō pä sän′, gē də), 347
Maurice, Frederick Denison, 179
Mauritania, *Ref. M. 6*
Mauritius (mô rish′əs), 281, *m. 301*
Maximilian, emperor of Mexico, 230
Mazarin (mä zä ran′), Cardinal, 21
Mazzini, Giuseppe (mät sē′ni, jü sep′ä), 211, 216, 217, 218
Mboya (em boi′a), Tom, 490, 599
Mecca, 492, 496, *Ref. M. 8*
Medical science, 14-15, 328-330
Medina, 496, *Ref. M. 8*
Meiji (mä′ji), 294-297
Mein Kampf, 475
Mendel, Gregor, 326

Mendelyeev (men′də lā′əf), Dmitri, 330
Mensheviks, 384, 464-465
Mercantilism, 23, 58-59, 263, 264
Merv (merv), 303, *Ref. M. 7*
Metaxas, John, 523
Metternich, Prince von, 109, 111-113, 115, 186, 188, 203, 215, 219, 268: Congress System of, 191-195
Mexico, 146, 230, 266, 267, 268, 269-270, 274, 575, *m. 267, Ref. M. 9*
Michelet (mēsh le′), Jules, 143
Middle class, 70-71, *Ref. M. 8*: as capitalists, 165; criticism of, 344; economic theory of, 355-356; humanitarianism of, 176; liberalism of, 144-145; in politics, 170-171; social life of, 341
Middle East, 492: Arab nationalism in, 492-500; in Cold War period, 585-587
Midway Islands, 300, 544
Miës van der Rohe (mē′es vän der rō′ə), 352
Milan, 48, 216, *m. 48, Ref. M. 1, 2*
Mill, James, 170
Mill, John Stuart, 146-147, 150, 170
Millet (mi lā′), Jean François, 348
Milton, John, 32
Mindszenty, Cardinal, 577
Mirabeau (mē ra bō′), Honoré, 91
Miranda, Francisco de, 264, 265
Mississippi Bubble, 68-70
Modena, 198, 224, 225, *m. 116, 224, Ref. M. 1*
Mogul empire, 285-286, 287
Molière (mô lyār′), 24-25
Monet, Claude (mō nā′, klōd), 349
Mongolia, 292, 578, *Ref. M. 6, 8*
Monnier, Henri, 341
Monroe, James, 192
Monroe Doctrine, 268: Roosevelt Corollary to, 272-273
Montenegro, 194, 235, 240, 241, 242, 418-419, 480, *m. 193, 241, 418, Ref. M. 1*
Montesquieu (mon′tes kū), 73, 76-77, 79, 82, 264
Montgomery, Bernard, 544, 545
Montreal, 255, *m. 48*
Morelos (mō rä′lōs), Father José, 266
Morocco, 310, 417, 481, 492, 498, *Ref. M. 1, 2, 5, 6*: independence established in, 587; in World War II, 544
Morse, Samuel F. B., 161, 327
Moscow, 39, 108, 239, 386, *m. 104, Ref. M. 2, 7*
Moscow Treaty, 603
Mozambique (mō′zəm bēk′), 589, *Ref. M. 5, 6*
Mozart (mō′zärt), Wolfgang, 85
Mukden, 288, *Ref. M. 3, 7*
Munich, *Ref. M. 1, 2*: Conference, 531
Municipal Corporations Bill, 203
Music, 85, 140-141, 352, 354
Muslim League, 503, 580
Mussolini, Benito, 457, 470-473, 494, 528, 529, 530, 531, 535, 538, 545, 548

N

Nachtigal, Gustav (näн′ti gäl, gùs′täf), 307
Nagasaki, 293, 549, *Ref. M. 3*
Nagy, Imre, 577
Nanking, 507, 508, *m. 292, Ref. M. 3*: Treaty of, 290
Nantes (nants), *Ref. M. 1, 2*: Edict of, 23, 43
Naples and Sicily, kingdom of, 48, 113, *m. 26, 48, 224, Ref. M. 1*: revolt of 1820-21 in, 191, 192,

m. 116; revolt of 1848 in, 216, 217; in unification of Italy, 225

Napoleon I, 102-111, 146, 264-265: empire of, 106-107, 110, *m. 104*

Napoleon III (Louis Napoleon), 207-208, 217, 229-232; and Crimean War, 230-237; and Mexico, 230; social welfare under, 117; and unification of Italy, 223, 224-225

Narodnik movement, 382

Narva, *Ref. M. 1, 2:* battle of, 39

Nasser, Gamal Abdel, 580, 585-587

Natal, 261, 491, *m. 261, 301, Ref. M. 5*

Nationalism, 19: in Africa, 319, 320, 489, 490-492, 587-590; Arab, 492-500, 585-587; in Austria, 389; in Balkans, 235, 239-240; changes in the concept of, 248-250; disregard of, at Congress of Vienna, 115-116; after 1815, 187-188; in Hungary, 211, 233-234; and imperialism, 46, 283-284; in India, 288, 500-503; of late nineteenth century, 411-414; and minority groups, 249; romantic, 141-144, 186, 203, 210-211; in southeast Asia and Oceania, 503-506; and World War I, 249; and World War II, 250

Nations, Battle of the, 109

Natural law, 71-72, 74, 79, 80

Natural resources, 600-601

Natural rights, doctrine of, 79, 82, 130

Nauru, 597-598

Navarino, *Ref. M. 1:* battle of, 195

Navigation Acts, 60-61

Nazism, 143, 338, 475, 518-521: in Latin America, 524-525

Near Eastern Question, 235

Nehru (nä'rü), Jawaharlal, 502-503, 579, 580, 581-582

Nejd (nĕzhd), 495, 496, *Ref. M. 8*

Nelson, Horatio, 103, 105, 107

Neoclassical style, 24, 84-85

Nervi, Pier Luigi

Netherlands, kingdom of, *Ref. M. 1, 2. See also* Austrian or Spanish Netherlands; Holland.

Neuilly (nœ yē'), Treaty of, 449

New Brunswick, 257, *m. 257*

Newcomen, Thomas, 156

Newfoundland, 48, 50, 255

New France, 255-256

New Granada, 265, *m. 267*

New Order in Asia, 526, 527, 539

New Orleans, 54, *m. 300*

New South Wales, 259, *m. 257, Ref. M. 4*

Newton, Sir Isaac, 9-10, 15, 17, 75, 131

New Zealand, 260, 276, 281, 436, 478, *Ref. M. 4*

Nicaragua, 272, 273, *Ref. M. 9*

Nice (nēs), 98, 223, 225, *m. 224, Ref. M. 1, 2*

Nicholas I, tsar of Russia, 194, 198, 215, 236-237, 378-379

Nicholas II, tsar of Russia, 383-387, 462, 463, 464

Niemoeller (nĕ'moe'l ər), Martin, 521

Nietzsche (nē'chə), Friedrich, 338-339

Nigeria, 308, 311, 312, 492, 580, 587, *Ref. M. 5, 6*

Niger Republic, 588, *Ref. M. 6*

Nightingale, Florence, 239

Nihilism, 381-383

Nile River, 305, *Ref. M. 5, 8:* battle of, 103

Nine-Power Treaty, 510

Nkrumah (eng'krü'mä), Kwame, 319-320, 490, 588

Nobel, Alfred, 408

Nordic Union, 570

North, Lord, 37

North Africa. *See* Algeria; Libya; Morocco; Tunisia.

North Atlantic Treaty Organization (NATO), 570, 603

Northern Rhodesia, 599, *Ref. M. 6*

North German Confederation, 228, 229, 232, *m. 228*

Northwest Territories, *m. 257*

Norway, 114, 116, 480, 534, *m. 26, Ref. M. 1, 2*

Novara, battle of, 216

Nova Scotia, 48, 256, 257, *m. 48, 257*

Nuremberg, *Ref. M. 2:* trials at, 567

Nyasaland (nī as'ə land'), 308, 589, *Ref. M. 5*

Nyerere, Julius, 319, 580, 588

O

Oceania, 297-302, 447-448, 505-506, *m. 300, Ref. M. 6, 7*

O'Connell, Daniel, 366

October Manifesto, 386, 387

Okinawa, *Ref. M. 3:* battle of, 548

Old Regime, 73-74, 75, 82, 87, 186, 188, 266

Olmütz, Humiliation of, 214

Opium 289-290

Orange Free State, 261, 262, 305, 501, *m. 261, Ref. M. 5*

Organization of American States, 570, 575, 593

Origin of Species, 325, 335, 336

Orinoco River, 274, *Ref. M. 9*

Orthodox Church, 236, 240

Ottoman (Turkish) empire, 39-40, 41, 42, 46, 193-205, 387-388, 390-391, *m. 193, 194, Ref. M. 1, 2:* and Balkan territories, 235-242; and Balkan War of 1912, 418-419; in the Crimean War, 237-238; during World War I and aftermath, 421, 435-436, 443, 445, 447, 449, 492-493, 495, *m. 450.* For events after 1920, *see* Turkey.

Outer Seven, 570-571, *m. 571*

Owen, Robert, 173, 178

P

Painting: Expressionism and Cubism in, 350; Impressionism and Post-Impressionism in, 349-350; realism in, 348; romanticism in, 139

Pakistan, 580, 582, *Ref. M. 7*

Palestine, 235, 237, 414, 446, 447, 449, 479, 493, 494-495, 585

Palmerston, Lord, 234, 236, 360-361

Panama, 273, *Ref. M. 9*

Panama Canal, 370

Pan-American Conference, 409

Pan American Union, 273, 575

Pan-Slavism, 239, 242, 419

Papal States, 216, 217, *m. 224, 288, Ref. M. 1*

Paraguay, 268, 271, *m. 267, Ref. M. 9*

Paris, 230, *m. 26, Ref. M. 1, 2:* Congress of, 238;

hat, āge, cãre, fär; let, ēqual, tèrm; it, īce; hot, ōpen, ôrder; oil, out; cup, pút, rüle, ūse; ch, child; ng, long; th, thin; ŦH, then; zh, measure; ə represents *a* in *about, e* in *taken, i* in *pencil, o* in *lemon, u* in *circus.*

Peace Conference, 445-451; Treaty of, (1763) 54, 256; (1814) 113; (1856) 237-238

Parliament, English, 28, 29, 30, 32, 33-35, 201: and cabinet government, 35-38, 360; reform of, 201-202, 367

Parma, 198, 224, 225, *m. 224, 288, Ref. M. 1*

Parnell, Charles Stewart, 366

Passchendaele, battle of, 440, *m. 435*

Pasteur, Louis, 328-330, 333

Patrimony of St. Peter, 225, 226

Pavlov, Ivan (päv'lof, ē vän'), 334

Peace movements, 408-410

Pearl Harbor, 539

Pedro I, emperor of Brazil, 268, 271

Peking (Peiping), 288, 293, 507, *m. 292, Ref. M. 3, 7*

Permanent Court of International Justice. *See* World Court.

Perón, Juan Domingo, 574

Perry, Matthew, 294

Persia, 303-304, 496-497. *See also* Iran.

Persian Letters, 76

Peru, 265, 267, 268, 271, 574, *m. 267, Ref. M. 9*

Pétain (pā taN'), Henri, 535

Peters, Carl, 307

Peter the Great, tsar of Russia, 38-41

Phanariots, 239

Philip II, king of Spain, 27

Philip V, king of Spain, 48

Philippines, 273, 282, 285, 299, *Ref. M. 3, 4, 7:* independence granted to, 584; United States in, 297, 505-506; in World War II, 544, 548

Philosophes, 73, 74-77, 81, 82, 85, 86, 90, 145, 378

Philosophy: in Age of Reason, 16-17, 131; in nineteenth century, 339-340; romantic nationalism and, 143. *See also* individual schools of, as Dualism, Empiricism.

Physics, 9-10, 330-332, 334

Physiocrats, 71-72, 74

Piedmont, *Ref. M. 1. See also* Sardinia-Piedmont.

Pietism, 128-129

Pillnitz, Declaration of, 96

Pilsudski (pil sût' ski), Joseph, 480, 523

Pitt, William, the Elder, 37, 53-54

Pitt, William, the Younger, 37-38, 99-100, 145, 236

Pius IX, Pope, 216, 217, 336, 373, 374

Planck, Max, 332

Plassey, battle of, 54, 286

Platt Amendment, 273

Plekhanov (ple kä'nof), Georgi, 384

Pobyedonostzev (po bī do nôs'tsif), Konstantin Petrovich, 383

Poe, Edgar Allan, 139

Poincaré (pwaN kä rā'), Raymond, 453-454, 476

Poland, 41, 47, 480, *m. 26, Ref. M. 1, 2:* and Congress of Vienna, 115, 116; and French alliance of 1922, 452; and invasion of Russia in 1920, 466, 480; partition of, 55-56, *m. 55;* and Prussia, 42, 43, 44; revolts, (of 1830) 198-199; (of 1846) 199, 204, 214; (of 1863) 382; as Russian satellite, 576, 577, 604; vs. Sweden, 39, 40; and World War I peace conference, 447, *m. 450;* between world wars, 523, 530; in World War II, 533-534, 545, 548

Poles: in Austria-Hungary, 388, 413, 449, *m. 388;* in Germany, 412; in Russia, 412

Polish Corridor, 55, 447, 533, *m. 450, 532*

Political Science, 64-76

Poltava, *Ref. M. 7:* battle of, 39

Pompadour, Madame de, 52, 73

Pondichéry (pôn dē shā rē'), 50, *Ref. M. 3*

Pope, Alexander, 9, 19, 82, 84

Population explosion, 599-601, 604-605

Port Arthur, 292, 296, *m. 292, Ref. M. 3, 7*

Portsmouth, Treaty of, 296

Portugal, 49, 255, *m. 26, Ref. M. 1, 2:* in Africa, 589; in China, 291, *m. 292;* colonial possessions in nineteenth century, 282, *m. 300-301;* in Latin America, 263, 265, 267-268; in mercantile system, 59, 60; Napoleon's occupation of, 108, 265; and slavery, 146; uprising of 1820 in, 191, *m. 116;* in World War II, 538

Portuguese East Africa, *Ref. M. 5*

Potsdam Conference, 548, 564-565

Pragmatic Sanction, 51-52

Pragmatism, 339

Prague, 215, *Ref. M. 1, 2*

Pre-Raphaelite Brotherhood, 345

Priestley, Joseph, 11

Principia, 10

Progress of the Human Mind, 130

Progress and Poverty, 405-406

Proudhon (prü dôN'), Pierre, 179, 208

Prussia, 41, 42-46, *m. 44, 116, Ref. M. 1, 2:* at Congress of Vienna, 114, 115; Emancipation Edict of 1807 in, 108; in German empire, 373; and German unification, 222, 228, 229, 232, *m. 232;* mercantilism in, 59; in Napoleonic wars, 106, 109; and partition of Poland, 55-56, *m. 55;* in Quadruple Alliance, 186; revolution of 1848 in, 212-214; in Seven Years' War, 53, 54; vs. Sweden, 40; war against revolutionary France, 96-97, 99-101; war of Austrian succession, 51-52. *See also* East Prussia; West Prussia.

Psychoanalysis, 334-335

Psychology, 17, 334-335

Puerto Rico, 273, 282, 302, *Ref. M. 9*

Pushkin, Alexander, 142-143

Q

Quadruple Alliance, 115, 116, 186, 268

Quakers, 128, 145

Quebec, 255, 257, 277, *m. 48, 257:* Act, 256

Quesnay, François (ke'nä', fräN swä'), 71-72

Quezon (kā'sôn), Manuel, 506

Quintuple Alliance, 115, 186, 191

Quito (kē'tō), 263, 266, *m. 267, Ref. M. 9*

R

Racine, Jean, 24

Racism, 338, 605. *See also* Anti-Semitism.

Raffles, Thomas Stamford, 298

Rahman, Tengku Abdul, 584

Railroads, 159-160, 303, 400, 411, 497, *Ref. M. 8*

Rangoon, 298, *Ref. M. 6, 7, 8*

Ranke (räng'kə), Leopold von, 337

Rapallo, Treaty of, 469

Rasputin, Grigori, 462

Rationalism, 75, 77, 84, 132-133

Ravensberg, 42-43, *m. 44*

Reason, Age of. *See* Age of Reason.

Reform movements: in Age of Reason, 73, 82; in

Great Britain, 201-203, 209-210, 362-366; following Industrial Revolution, 172-176; in Russia, 378, 387.

Reinsurance Treaty, 415

Religion: and bigotry, 605; in Communist Russia, 469; in France, 93, 94, 101, 102, 104; impact of science on, 8, 15-19, 130, 335-336; missionaries, 284-285; Marxism vs., 183; in Mexico, 481; in Nazi Germany, 521; Pietist reaction, 128-129; revival in nineteenth century, 188. *See also* Deism, Orthodox Church, Roman Catholicism.

Renoir (rə nwär'), Pierre Auguste (ō gyst'), 349

Revolutions: of 1820-1821, 191-195, *m. 116;* of 1830, 197-198, *m. 116;* of 1848, 203-204, 205-206, 212-219, *m. 116;* Russian, (of 1917) 462-465. *See also* American Revolution; Boxer Rebellion; French Revolution.

Rhineland, *m. 532*

Rhodes, Cecil, 308-309

Rhodesia, 309, 478, 589, *Ref. M. 5*

Ribbentrop, Joachim von, 534

Ricardo, David, 150, 169-170

Richelieu (rē shə lyœ'), Cardinal, 21, 46

Riebeek, Jan van, 260

Riga, Treaty of, 480

Riis (rēs), Jacob, 355

Risorgimento (ri sôr'ji men'tō), 211, 222-226

Rivera, Miguel Primo de (rē vär'ä, mē gäl' prē'mō dä), 481

Riza Shah Pahlavi (ri zä' shä pa'lə vē), 496-497

Robespierre, Maximilien, 95, 101-102, 205

Rodin, Auguste (rō daṉ', ō gyst'), 349

Roentgen (rent'gən), Wilhelm Konrad, 332

Romagna (rō män'yä), 224, 225, *m. 224*

Roman Catholicism, 129: anticlericalism in France, 371-372; Bismarck vs., 373-374; in Canada, 255; in England under Stuart kings, 29, 30, 33, 34; Tudor kings, 28; in Italy, 393, 472; in Latin America, 263, 264; missionaries of, 284; papal infallibility, dogma of, 336, 373-374; in Poland, 382; vs. science, 8, 15, 17, 336

Romanticism, 132-133, 134-135, 139, 140-141, 218

Rome-Berlin-Tokyo Axis, 529

Rommel, Erwin, 544

Roosevelt, Franklin D., 525, 532, 533, 539, 545, 548, 564

Roosevelt, Theodore, 272-273, 296

Rossetti, Dante Gabriel, 345

Rossini, Gioachino (rō sē'ni, jwä kē'nō), 141

Rousseau, Jean Jacques (rü sō', zhäṉ zhäk), 81-82, 133, 137, 147, 264

Rowlatt Act, 500, 501

Ruanda-Urundi, 489

Ruhr valley, 42, 354, 453-454, 474, 476

Rumania, 190, 193, 195, 419, *m. 241, 418, Ref. M. 1, 2:* in Little Entente, 452; nationalism in, 235, 242; Rumanians in Austria-Hungary, 388, 389, *m. 388;* as Russian satellite, 567, 568; in Russo-Turkish War, 240; in Treaty of Paris, 237-238; during World War I and aftermath, 437, 446, 449, 480, *m. 435, 450;* between world wars, 523, 530; in World War II, 538, 565

Ruskin, John, 172, 173, 345

Russia, 46, 47, 53, *Ref. M. 1, 2, 7:* alliances of 1871-1914, 414-421; and Anglo-Russian entente, 304; Balkan ambitions of, 235-239, 242; Bloody Sunday in, 385-386; under Catherine the Great, 15, 41-42, 55-56, 86, 87; in China, 291, 292, *m. 292;* in Cold War period, 575-576, 590-595, 602-604; and Communist China, 570, 578, 604; at Congress of Vienna, 111, 114, 115, 378; in Crimean War, 237-239, 381; Decembrist Revolt of 1825 in, 378-379; in Diplomatic Revolution, 52; Dumas in, 386-387; and East Germany, 567, 576, 577; Five-Year Plans in, 468, 517-518, 575; and German nonaggression pact, 533; and Greek independence, 236; and Hungarian revolution of 1849, 215; and Ideological Schism, 42, 380-381; industrialization in, 164, 400, 468, 517-518; liberal movement in, 378, 379-380; Marxism in, 384, 406-407, 464-465, 568; in Napoleonic wars, 105-106, 108, *m. 104;* New Economic Policy (NEP) in, 466-467, 517; October Manifesto in, 386, 387; and Pan-Slavism, 239, 413; and partition of Poland, 55-56, *m. 55;* in Persia, 303-304; under Peter the Great, 38-41; purges of 1928-1931 and 1935-1938 in, 518; in Quadruple Alliance, 186; revolution and establishment of communism in, 430, 462-470; and Russification of subject peoples, 412; serfdom abolished in, 381; and Seven Years' War, 54; in Spanish civil war, 529; territorial expansion of, 302-304, *m. 41;* under tsars from 1801 to 1914, 190, 378-387; vs. Turks, 194-195, 235-239; Viborg Manifesto in, 387; in World War I, 420, 421, 434-437, 442, 446, 450, 462, *m. 435, 450;* in World War II, 533, 534, 538-539, 544, 545, 548

Russo-Japanese War, 296, 385

Russo-Turkish War, 240-242

Ruthenians, 480, *m. 388*

Rutherford, Ernest, 332

Rwanda, 590, *Ref. M. 6*

Ryswick, Treaty of, 47

S

Saar Basin, 447, 457, *m. 450*

Sabah, 584

Sacco-Vanzetti case, 482-483

Sadowa, *m. 228:* battle of, 228, 230, 231

St.-Germain, Treaty of, 449

St. Helena, 109, *Ref. M. 5*

St. Petersburg, 39, 40, 385-386, *m. 41, Ref. M. 1, 2. See also* Leningrad.

Saint-Simon (saṉ sē môṉ'), Count de, 178

Sakhalin (sä'kä lēn'), 296, *Ref. M. 3, 7*

Samarkand (sam'ər kand'), 303, *Ref. M. 7, 8*

San Martín (san mär tēn'), José de, 266-267

San Remo Conference, 493, 494

San Salvador, 272, *Ref. M. 9*

San Stefano, *Ref. M. 1:* Treaty of, 241, 242, *m. 241*

Santa Anna, Antonio López de, 269-270

Sarajevo, 419, *Ref. M. 2*

Sarawak, 584

Sardinia, 48, 99-101, 228, 229, 237, *m. 48, Ref. M. 1, 2*

Sardinia-Piedmont, 113, 191, *m. 116, 224:* in Crimean War, 223, 237-239; revolt of 1848 in, 216; role in unification of Italy, 222, 223-226

Saudi (sä ü'di) Arabia, 496, 587, *Ref. M. 7, 8*

Savoy, 47, 48, 98, 114, 223, 225, *m. 48, 224, Ref. M. 1:* House of, 48-49, 113, 216, 217

Saxony, 40, 52, *m. 26, 116, Ref. M. 1*

Schiller, Johann Christoph Friedrich von, 133

Schleswig, 228, 447, *m. 228, 450, Ref. M. 1*

Schönberg, Arnold, 354

Schuschnigg, Kurt von, 530

Science: in Age of Reason, 8-16; in nineteenth century 335-340; in twentieth century, 597-600, 606-607

Scotland, 29, 30, 31

Scott, Walter, 138-140, 143

Sedan, *m. 232:* battle of, 231

Semmelweiss, Ignaz, 329

Senegal, 587, 588, *Ref. M. 6*

Sepoy Rebellion, 287

Serbia, 194, 195, 210, 211, 235, 240, 242, 480, *m. 193, 194, 242, 418, Ref. M. 1, 2:* and Greater Serbia movement, 413; irredentism and World War I, 417-420, 435, 436; Serbs in Austria-Hungary, 387, 388, *m. 388*

Sevastopol, 237, *Ref. M. 1, 2, 17*

Seven Years' War, 52, 53-55, 60, 286

Sèvres, Treaty of, 449, 499

Shaftesbury, Earl of, 132, 173

Shah Jahan (shä' jə hän'), 285

Shantung, 291-292, 509, *m. 292, Ref. M. 3*

Shastri, Shari Lal Bahadur, 582

Shaw, George Bernard, 311, 347-348, 406

Shelley, Percy Bysshe, 135

Siam, 298, 504, *Ref. M. 3, 4*

Siberia, 303, *Ref. M. 7*

Sicily, 545, *Ref. M. 1. See also* Naples and Sicily, kingdom of.

Siegfried Line, 534, *m. 532*

Siemens, Ernst Werner von (zē'məns, ernst ver'nėr fən), 327

Sierra Leone (si er'ə li ō'ni), 308, 588, *Ref. M. 5*

Silesia, 51, 54, 447, 457, *m. 44, 450, Ref. M. 1, 2*

Simon Commission, 501

Singapore, 298, 584, *m. 301, Ref. M. 3, 4, 7*

Sinn Fein (shin'fān'), 479

Sino-Japanese War, 291

Slavery: abolition of, 146; and slave trade, 145-146

Slavs, 449, 480: North, 388; and Pan-Slavism, 239, 242, 413; South, 388, 413

Slovaks, 210, 388, 389, *m. 388*

Slovenes, 210, 388, 480, *m. 388*

Smeaton, John, 156

Smith, Adam, 72-73, 150, 169, 170

Smyrna, 239, *Ref. M. 2*

Social Contract, The, 81, 82, 147

Social contract theory, 80-81

Social Democrats, 150, 183: in Germany, 374-375, 376-377, 405, 473, 574; in Russia, 384, 386, 464

Socialism, 145, 177: Christian, 178-179; Fabian, 405-406; revisionist (compromise), 405-406, 429-430; scientific (Marxian), 179-183, 405; Utopian, 177-178

Social welfare legislation, 404: in Australia, 260; in France, 177; in Germany, 374-375; in Great Britain, 366-367, 231-232, 572; in New Zealand, 260; in underdeveloped lands, 579; in United States, 525-526. *See also* Labor legislation.

Solferino (sol'fe rē'nō), battle of, 224

Somalia (Somali Republic), 587

Somaliland, 308, 538, 587, *m. 301, Ref. M. 5*

Somme, battle of, 437, *m. 435*

Sorel, Georges, 406

South Africa, 115, 275, 276, 478: and Boer War, 261-262; British in, 261, 308-309; Dutch settlement of, 260-261; Republic of, 262, 277, 489, 490-492, 589, *m. 261, Ref. M. 5*

Southeast Asia Treaty Organization (SEATO), 570

Southern Rhodesia, 589, *Ref. M. 5, 6*

South Sea Bubble, 237

South Sea Company, 68-70

Soviet Union. *See* Russia.

Space exploration, 601-602

Spain, 46, *m. 26, 48, Ref. M. 1, 2:* and Africa, 587; civil war in, 529; colonialism of, 49; under Ferdinand VII, 190-191, 265, 266; and Franco-Prussian War, 231; and Latin America, 263-264, 265-267; mercantilism in, 59, 60; in Morocco, 498; Napoleon's occupation of, 264-265; rebellion of 1820 in, 191, 192, *m. 116;* in Seven Years' War, 54; in Thirty Years' War, 46; in War of the Austrian Succession, 52; in war on French Republic, 99-101; in War of Jenkins' Ear, 51; in War of the Spanish Succession, 48; during World War I aftermath, 481; in World War II, 538

Spanish-American War, 273, 284, 301-302

Spanish Netherlands, 24, 46, 47, 48, *m. 26, 48*

Spencer, Herbert, 337

Spener, Philipp, 129

Spinoza, Baruch, 16

Spirit of Laws, The, 77

Stael, Madame de, 188

Stahl, Georg Ernst, 11

Stalin, Joseph, 467-468, 517-518, 538, 545, 548, 564, 567, 575, 604

Stalingrad, 544, 545, *Ref. M. 7*

Stanley, Henry Morton, 282, 304-305

Steinbeck, John, 554-556

Stephenson, George, 160

Stolypin (sto lē'pin), Piotr Arkadevich, 397

Strauss, Richard, 352

Stravinski, Igor, 354

Stresemann, Gustav, 454-455

Stuart, John McDouall, 275

Sudan, *Ref. M. 6. See* Anglo-Egyptian Sudan.

Sudan Republic, 572, 587, 588

Sudetenland, 480, 531, *m. 532, Ref. M. 2*

Suez Canal, 230, 282, 305, 478, 585-586, *m. 301, Ref. M. 58*

Suffrage: in Australia, 260; in Austria, 388; in Belgium, 392; in France, 97, 206, 369; in Great Britain, 201, 202, 362, 363, 365, 367-368; in Italy, 393; in Japan, 511; in Netherlands, 392; in New Zealand, 260; in Norway, 393-394; woman suffrage, 260, 356, 393-394

Sukarno, Achmed, 584, 587

Sullivan, Louis, 352

Sumatra, 583, *Ref. M. 4*

Sun Yat-sen, 506, 507

Sweden, 43, 46, 52, 394, *m. 26, Ref. M. 1, 2, 7:* and Åland Islands affair, 456; in Cold War period, 574; at Congress of Vienna, 113, 114, 116; in Grand Alliance against Louis XIV, 47; in Great Northern War, 39-40, 41; industrialization in, 399; and Middle Way, 480; in Napoleonic wars, 105-106; in

Seven Years' War, 52-53; and Slavery, 146; in war with Poland, 39-40, 43; in World War II, 538
Swedenborg, Emanuel, 129
Switzerland, 204, 392, 399, 480, *Ref. M. 1, 2:* in Cold War period, 574; at Congress of Vienna, 113-114; in World War II, 538
Syndicalism, 406, 472
Syria, 230, 446, 447, 449, 492, 493, 586, 587, *m. 193:* between world wars, 494; after World War II, 585
Széchenyi (sā'chän yē), István, 211

T

Taiping Rebellion, 290
Taiwan. *See* Formosa.
Talleyrand-Périgord, Prince, 111, 115
Tanaka, Giichi, 511
Tanganyika (tan'gən yē'kə), 308, 489, 588, *Ref. M. 5*
Tanzania, 589, *Ref. M. 6*
T'ang-ku Truce, 526
Tannenberg, battle of, 435, *m. 435*
Tarawa, battle of, 548
Tariffs, 282, 405: in Canada, 258; in Germany, 226; in Great Britain, 171, 209, 516; in United States, 515
Tashkent (tash kent'), 303, *Ref. M. 7, 8*
Teapot Dome, 484
Technology in twentieth century, 598-599: and cultural explosion, 607; and leisure, 617; and moral values, 606; and natural resources, 600; and Nauru, 597-598
Teheran, 496, *Ref. M. 7, 8*
Tel-Aviv, 495, *Ref. M. 8*
Telford, Thomas, 157
Tellier, François Michel le Marquis de Louvois, 23
Tennessee Valley Authority, 525-526
Tennyson, Alfred, Lord, 236, 238, 342-344
Test Act, 33, 34
Textile industry: domestic system in, 152; effects in Europe of overseas expansion, 62, 157-158; factory system in, 165-166; in France, 162; in Great Britain, 161; mechanization of, 152-156
Thackeray, William Makepeace, 342
Thailand (tī'land), 504. *See also* Siam.
Thirty Years' War, 29, 43, 46
Thomson, Sir Joseph John, 332
Thoreau, Henry David, 139
Three Emperors' League, 414, 415
Tibet, 289, 303, 578, 593, *Ref. M. 3*
Tientsin, *m. 292, Ref. M. 3:* Treaty of, 290
Tilsit, battle of, 106, *m. 104*
Tito, Marshal (Josip Broz), 545, 576-577
Togo, 588, *Ref. M. 6*
Togoland, 308, 489, 588, *Ref. M. 5*
Tojo (tō'jō), General, 539
Toleration Act of 1689, 35
Tolstoy, Leo, 346
Tory party, 34, 36, 37, 38
Touré (tü rā'), Sékou, 320, 580
Townshend, Charles, 65
Toynbee, Arnold, 150

Trade unions. *See* Labor unions.
Trafalgar, *Ref. M. 1:* battle of, 106, 107, *m. 104*
Transcendentalism, 134
Trans-Siberian Railroad, 303, 400, *Ref. M. 3, 7*
Transvaal, 261, 262, 305, 308, 491, *m. 261, Ref. M. 5*
Treitschke (trīch'kə), Heinrich von, 226, 284, 338, 414, 474
Trevithick, Richard, 160
Trianon, Treaty of, 449, 479
Tribalism, in Africa, 319-320
Trieste, *m. 450, 565*
Triple Alliance, 415-421
Triple Entente, 417
Tripoli, 310, *Ref. M. 2, 5*
Troppau, *Ref. M. 1:* Congress of, 191; Protocol of, 191-192
Trotsky, Leon, 386, 467-468, 518
Trujillo (trü hē'yō) Molina, Rafael L., 574
Truman, Harry S, 568, 569, 577
Truman Doctrine, 568
Tull, Jethro, 65
Tunisia, 310, 492, 498, 544, 587, *Ref. M. 1, 2, 5, 6*
Turgenev (tür gen'yef), Ivan, 382
Turkey, republic of, 499-500, *Ref. M. 7, 8:* in Cold War period, 568; during World War I aftermath, 451, *m. 450;* in World War II, 538. *See also* Ottoman empire.
Turner, J. M. W., 139
Tuscany, 216, 217, 224, 225, *m. 224, Ref. M. 1*
Two Treatises of Government, 80
Tzu Hsi (tsü' shē'), 290-291, 292, 507

U

Uganda (ū gan'də), 308, 588, *Ref. M. 5, 6*
Ukraine and Ukrainians, 465, 480, *m. 450, Ref. M. 1, 8*
Ulster, 365, 366, *m. 26*
Underdeveloped areas, 604-605; and population explosion, 599, 600
Union of Soviet Socialist Republics (U.S.S.R.), 465, *m. 450, Ref. M. 7. See also* Russia.
United Arab Republic, 586, 587, *Ref. M. 8*
United Nations, 285, 554, 564, 567-569: and Arab states, 585-587; assessment of, 594-595; Atomic Energy Commission, 568; and China, 578; and Republic of the Congo, 588; Development Decade of, 604; and Egypt, 585-587; and India, 581; and Indonesia, 570, 584; and Israel, 585; Korean police action, 569, 594; and Portugal, 589; Relief and Rehabilitation Administration, 564; and space, 602
United States: and China, 292, 293; Civil War in, 258; in Cold War period, 571-572, 590-593, 602-604; colonial possessions in 1914, *m. 300-301;* as "Colossus of the North," 273-274; democratic development of, 276; exploration of, 274; foreign aid from, 579; during Gilded Age, 354-357; imperialism of, 282, 299-302, 311; and India, 581; industrial development of, 159, 163, 399; isolationism of, 483, 532-533; and Japan, 509-510; in Korean War, 566, 569, 571; and League of Nations, 451, 483, 484; in Lebanon, 586; and Monroe Doctrine, 268; nationalism of, 277, 412; neutrality laws of,

532, 534; New Deal in, 525-526; in 1920's, 481-485, 515-516; in Philippines, 297, 302, 505-506; and racial tensions, 605; in Spanish-American War, 273; stock market crash of 1929 and depression following, 515-516, 525; and Vietnam, 583; during World War I and aftermath, 440-451, 452, 453, 515, 516; during World War II and aftermath, 534, 538, 539-549, 571
Universal Declaration of Human Rights, 605
Unkiar Skelessi (ùng kyär′ ske le sē′), Treaty of, 236
U Nu (ū nū), 584
U Thant, 604
Upper Volta, *Ref. M. 6*
Uruguay, 271, 275, *Ref. M. 9*
U.S.S.R. *See* Russia.
Utilitarianism, 170, 339
Utopians, 177-178
Utrecht, *Ref. M. 1:* Treaty of, 48-49, 256, *m. 48*
U-2 incident, 590

V

Van Gogh (van gôн′), Vincent, 350
Vauban, Sebastian Le Prestre de, 24
Venetia, 188, 210, 223-224, 226, 228, *m. 116, 224, Ref. M. 1:* revolt of 1848 in, 216, 217
Venezuela (ven e zwā′la), 265, 271, 272, 481, 574-575, *Ref. M. 9*
Verdi, Giuseppe, 141
Verdun, battle of, 436-437, *m. 435*
Verona, *Ref. M. 1:* Congress of, 192
Verrazano (ver′rä tsä′ nò), Giovanni da, 254-255
Versailles, *Ref. M. 1, 2:* palace of, 22, 23, 81; Treaty of, 422, 448-451, 474, 475
Vichy, 535, *m. 535*
Victor Emmanuel II, king of Italy, 216, 223, 225
Victor Emmanuel III, king of Italy, 472
Victoria, queen of England, 203, 282
Vienna, 85, 479, *m. 26, Ref. M. 1, 2:* Congress of, 110, 142, 186, 187, 188
Vietnam (vē et′näm′), 582-583, 584, *Ref. M. 7*
Vitalism, 339-340
Vladivostok, 303, *m. 301, Ref. M. 3, 7*
Volta, Alessandro, 13
Voltaire, 73, 74-76, 82, 132, 264

W

Wafd (wäft), 497, 498
Wagner (väg′nèr), Richard, 140, 179, 338
Wake Island, 302, 544, *Ref. M. 4*
Wallace, Alfred R., 325
Walpole, Horace, 140
Walpole, Robert, 36-37
War of the Austrian Succession, 51-52
Warfare, methods of, 23-24, 39
War of Jenkins' Ear, 37, 51
War of the Spanish Succession, 43, 47-48
Warsaw Pact, 570, 577, 603
Washington, D.C.: Conference, 458; Treaty of, 258
Waterloo, *Ref. M. 1:* battle of, 109, *m. 104*
Watt, James, 11, 156
Wealth of Nations, 72-73, 169
Weber (vā′bèr), Karl Maria von, 140
Weihaiwei (wā′hǐ′wā′), 292, *m. 292, Ref. M. 3*
Weimar (vī′mär), 134, *Ref. M. 2*
Weimar Republic, 473-475, 518, 520

Weismann (vīs′män), August, 326
Wellington, Duke of, 108-109, 201
Wesley, John and Charles, 128
West Indies, 49, 50, 54, 55, 56, *Ref. M. 9*
Westminster, Statute of, 478
Westphalia, *Ref. M. 1:* Peace of, 43, 46
West Prussia, 42, 44, 55, 56, *m. 44*
Whig party, 34, 36, 37
White Russia, 465, *m. 450, Ref. M. 7*
Whitman, Walt, 139
Whitney, Eli, 153
Wilberforce, William, 145
Wilde, Oscar, 341
William I, German emperor, 373, 375
William I, king of Netherlands, 199-200
William I, king of Prussia, 231, 232
William II (the kaiser), German emperor, 375-378, 448, 473; role in events leading to World War I, 415, 416, 417, 419-420, 423
William of Orange, 34, 47, 48: as William III of England, 35-36
Wilson, Woodrow, 439-443, 444-447, 449, 450-451
Witte, Sergei, 400
Wordsworth, William, 99, 134, 141-142
World Court (Permanent Court of International Justice), 456, 484
World War I: aftermath of, 451-459, 475-476; armistice terms of, 443-444; background for, 410-421; battles of, 434-443, *m. 435;* outbreak of, 420-423; peace settlement following, 444-451; propaganda in, 439, 441; reparations problem following, 448, 449, 453-454, 458-459, 474, 476, 515, 516; technological advances in, 438
World War II: aggressions leading to, 529-533, *m. 532;* alignment of nations in, 544; basic causes of, 533-534; campaigns of, 534-549, *m. 540-541, 542-543;* peace treaties following, 565; territorial changes in Europe after, *m. 565;* territorial changes in the Far East after, *m. 566;* war crimes trials following, 567
Wren, Christopher, 85, 140
Wright, Frank Lloyd, 352
Wright, Orville and Wilbur, 328, 601

Y

Yalta, *Ref. M. 7:* Conference, 548, 564
Yangtze River, 290, 292, *m. 292, Ref. M. 3, 7*
Yemen (ye′mən), 587, *Ref. M. 8, 9*
Young, Arthur, 65
Young Arabs, 391
Young Plan, 458-459, 515
Young Turks, 390-391, 499
Yuan Shih-kai (yü än′ shē′kǐ′), 506-507
Yugoslavia, 449, 452, 457, 480, 576-577, *m. 450, Ref. M. 7:* between world wars, 523, 530; in World War II, 538, 545

Z

Zambezi (zam bē′zi) River, 304, 309, *Ref. M. 5*
Zanzibar, 308, 589, *Ref. M. 5*
Zemstvos (zemst′vōs), 382, 384, 387
Zionism, 413-414, 446, 479, 495
Zola, Émile, 347, 371
Zollern, 42, *m. 44*
Zollverein, 162, 226, 227

REFERENCE MAPS

1. Europe 1815

2. Europe 1871

3. India, Burma, and the Far East 1914

4. Australia and the South Pacific 1914

5. Africa 1914

6. Contemporary Africa

7. U.S.S.R. and Asia

8. The Middle East

9. Latin America

The reference maps on the following pages will acquaint you with large areas of the world at significant dates throughout history. For purposes of comparison, some of these maps show two or three major civilizations. Time spans and areas are indicated by the map keys and legends. Topographic features—mountains and deserts—are represented by triangles and dotted areas. Virtually every place name of importance mentioned in this book can be found either on the reference maps or on the spot maps which appear throughout the text. The reference maps as a unit constitute an atlas which augments the presentation of geographical history in CIVILIZATION PAST AND PRESENT. These maps also offer you a convenient means of review.

KINGDOM OF

NORWAY AND SWEDEN

Gulf of Bothni

Nysta

Stockholm

B a l t i

S e a

N o r t h

S e a

KINGDOM OF
DENMARK

SCHLESWIG

Copenhagen

Konigsberg

Danzig

HOLSTEIN

Edinburgh

THE UNITED KINGDOM

OF GREAT BRITAIN Manchester

Dublin   *Irish*   *Sea*   Liverpool

AND IRELAND   • Birmingham

London

Dover

Amsterdam

Utrecht

Antwerp

Bruges

Brussels

Waterloo

Le Havre

Paris

Versailles

Lorient

Nantes

La Rochelle

Bordeaux

Bay

of

Biscay

HANOVER

Elbe

Berlin

Leipzig

Wittenberg

WESTPHALIA

Cologne

Aix-la-
Chapelle

Ems

Frankfurt

LUXEMBURG

Carlsbad

Prague

Sadowa

Troppau

BRANDENBURG

Oder

SILESIA

Breslau

P O L

Vistula

R

U

S

GERMANIC

CONFEDERATION

SAXONY

BOHEMIA

BAVARIA

WÜRTTEMBERG

Danube

Ulm

Augsburg

Munich

Austerlitz

EMPIRE OF

Vienna

Laibach

KINGDOM OF HUNG

CROATIA-
SLAVONIA

BOSNIA

HERZEGO-
VINA

MONTE
NEGRO

ALBANIA

Kar

Navar

KINGDOM OF
NETHERLANDS

BELGIUM

Rhine

Sedan

Valmy

ALSACE

BADEN

Seine

Loire

R.

FRANCE

Rhone

R.

Garonne

PYRENEES

Marseilles

Geneva

SWITZERLAND

ALPS

SAVOY

KINGDOM OF SARDINIA

PIEDMONT

Nice

Genoa

Milan

LOMBARDY

Po

Verona

VENETIA

Venice

PARMA

MODENA

LUCCA

TUSCANY

PAPAL STATES

APENNINES

Adriatic Sea

ELBA

CORSICA
(TO FRANCE)

Rome

KINGDOM OF NAPLES

AND SICILY

Duero

R.

Ebro

R.

Madrid

Barcelona

BALEARIC ISLANDS

Tagus

R.

PORTUGAL

SPAIN

Lisbon

Cádiz

CAPE TRAFALGAR

Strait of Gibraltar

M e d i t e r r a n e

A l g e r i a

MOROCCO

TUNIS

A t l a n t i c

O c e a n

FINLAND

Lake Onega

Lake Ladoga

Gulf of Finland

Reval Narva

St. Petersburg

Novgorod

Volga

R.

Riga

Dvina

R.

LITHUANIA

R

Niemen

R.

D

R U S S I A

U K R A I N E

Poltava

Don

R.

R.

Volga

Dniester

BESSARABIA

MOLDAVIA

Odessa

Azov

Sea of Azov

Caspian Sea

R

ANSYLVANIA

WALLACHIA

RUMANIA

Bucharest

Danube

R.

Sevastopol

Black   Sea

C A U C A S U S   M T S

BULGARIA

Adrianople

San Stefano

Constantinople

Sea of Marmora

Dardanelles

M

A

N

Aegean Sea

CRETE

CYPRUS

E   M   P   I   R   E

Sea

Prepared by
Rand McNally & Co., Chicago.

1. EUROPE 1815

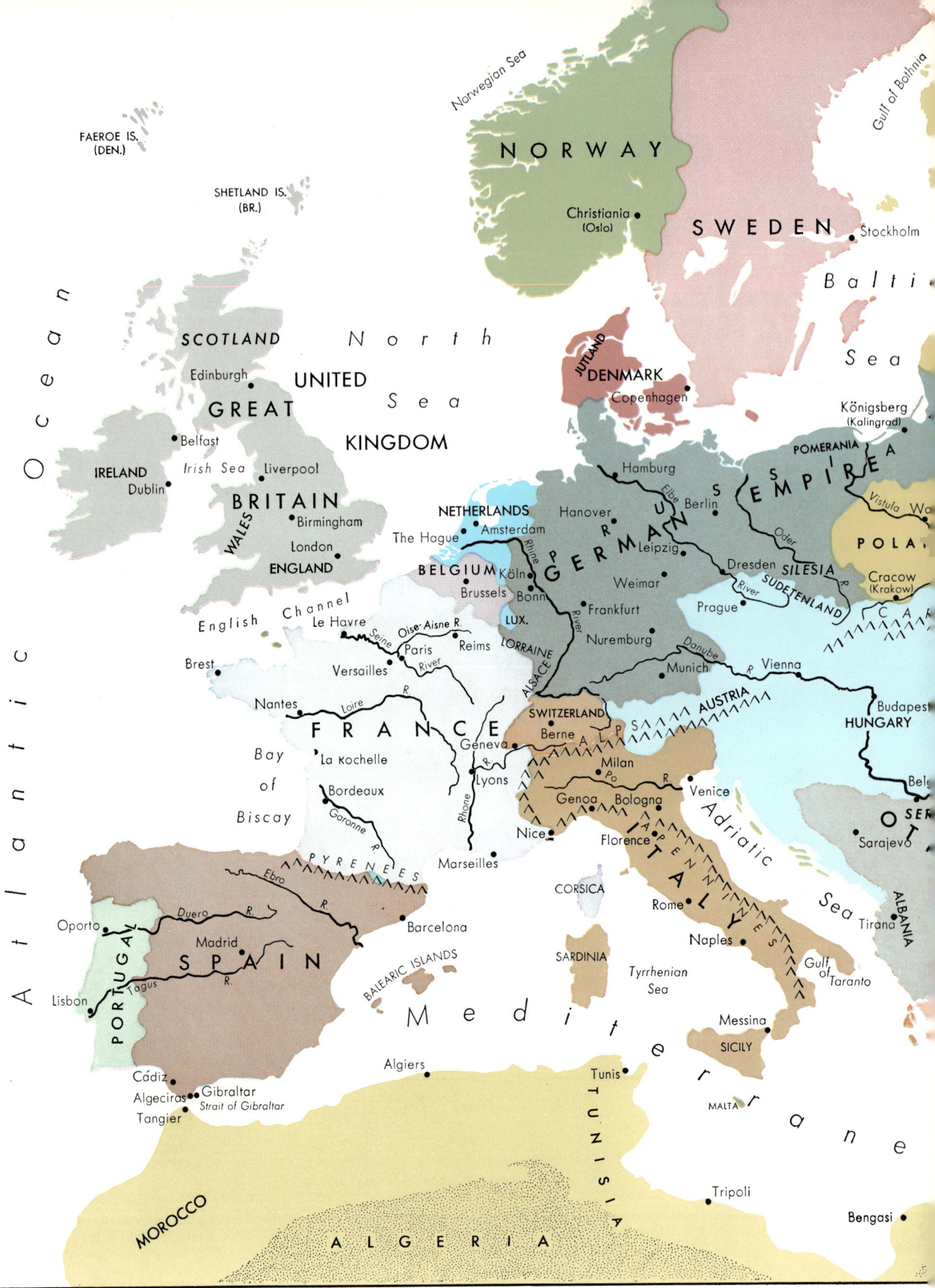

FAEROE IS.
(DEN.)

SHETLAND IS.
(BR.)

Norwegian Sea

NORWAY

Christiania
(Oslo)

SWEDEN

Stockholm

Gulf of Bothnia

Balti

Sea

SCOTLAND

Edinburgh

UNITED

GREAT

KINGDOM

Belfast

IRELAND

Dublin

Irish Sea

Liverpool

BRITAIN

Birmingham

London

ENGLAND

WALES

North

Sea

DENMARK

JUTLAND

Copenhagen

Königsberg
(Kalingrad)

POMERANIA

Hamburg

Hanover

Berlin

EMPIRE

GERMAN

PRUSSIA

Elbe

Leipzig

Oder

Vistula Wa

POLA

Dresden

SILESIA

Cracow
(Krakow)

NETHERLANDS

Amsterdam

The Hague

Rhine

BELGIUM

Köln

Weimar

Prague

SUDETENLAND

Brussels

Bonn

LUX.

Frankfurt

River

Nuremberg

LORRAINE

ALSACE

Munich

Vienna

Danube

R.

O ce a n

English Channel

Le Havre

Seine

Oise Aisne R.

Paris

Reims

Versailles

River

Brest

Nantes

Loire

R

FRANCE

La Rochelle

Geneva

SWITZERLAND

Berne

ALPS

AUSTRIA

Budapest

HUNGARY

Bel

Atlantic

Bay

of

Biscay

Bordeaux

Garonne

R.

Rhone

Lyons

R.

Milan

Po

R.

Genoa

Bologna

Venice

Adriatic

O SER

Sarajevo

PYRENEES

Ebro

Marseilles

Nice

Florence

ITALY

APENNINES

Sea

Tirana

ALBANIA

Duero

R.

R.

Barcelona

CORSICA

Rome

Oporto

Madrid

SPAIN

Tagus

R.

Lisbon

PORTUGAL

Cádiz

Gibraltar

Algeciras

Strait of Gibraltar

Tangier

Algiers

BALEARIC ISLANDS

SARDINIA

Tyrrhenian
Sea

Naples

Mediterrane

TUNISIA

Tunis

MALTA

Messina

SICILY

Gulf
of
Taranto

MOROCCO

ALGERIA

Tripoli

Bengasi

FINLAND

Lake
Onega

Lake
Ladoga

Gulf of Finland
St. Petersburg
(Leningrad)

Narva

LIVONIA

Volga R.

R U S S I A

Moscow

Gulf
of
Riga

Riga

Southern Dvina R.

Minsk

Niemen R.

Don

Dnieper

Kiev

Kharkov

River

Volga R.

Dniester

BUKOVINA

River

BESSARABIA

Sea of
Azov

RUMANIA

Bucharest

Danube R.

DOBRUJA

Sevastopol

Volga

Sofia

BULGARIA

Black   Sea

C A U C A S U S   M T S.

Caspian
Sea

Baku

Constantinople
(Istanbul)

Ankara

alonika

Gallipoli

Dardanelles

E M P I R E

Aegean
Sea

Smyrna

Athens

Euphrates

Tigris

Teheran

CANDIA
(CRETE)

RHODES

CYPRUS

Bagdad

n

Sea

River

Jerusalem

Prepared by
Rand McNally & Co., Chicago.

2. EUROPE 1871

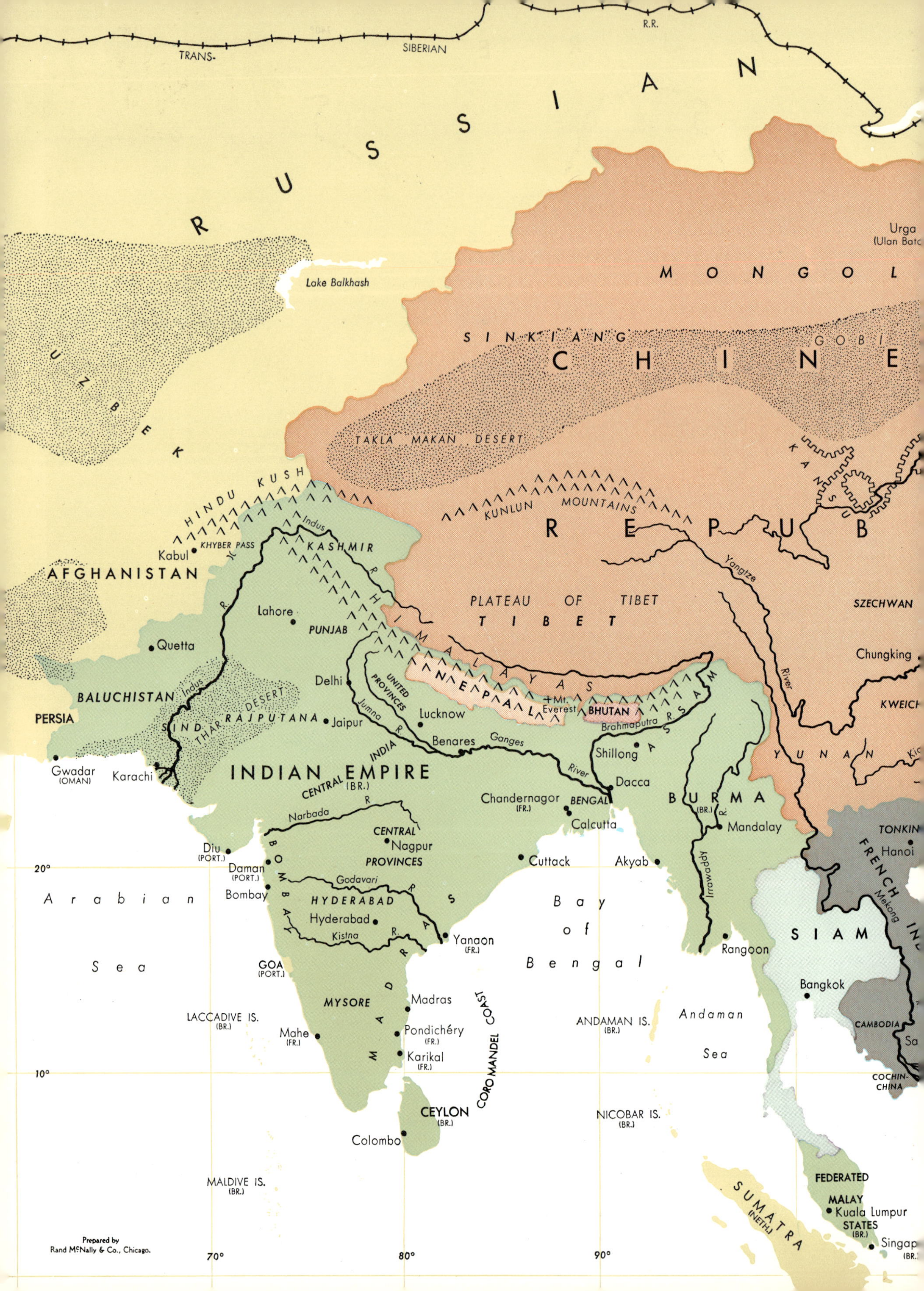

R U S S I A N

TRANS- SIBERIAN R.R.

MONGOL

Urga
(Ulan Bato

Lake Balkhash

U Z B E K

S I N K I A N G

C H I N E

GOBI

TAKLA MAKAN DESERT

KUNLUN MOUNTAINS

R E P U B

K A N S U

HINDU KUSH

Indus R.

KHYBER PASS

Kabul

KASHMIR

PLATEAU OF TIBET

T I B E T

Yangtze River

SZECHWAN

AFGHANISTAN

Lahore

PUNJAB

Chungking

Quetta

H I M A L A Y A S

KWEICH

Delhi

UNITED PROVINCES

N E P A L

+Mt. Everest

BHUTAN

A S S A M

BALUCHISTAN

Indus R.

Jumna R.

Lucknow

Brahmaputra

PERSIA

THAR DESERT

RAJPUTANA

Jaipur

Benares

Ganges

Shillong

YUNAN

Gwadar
(OMAN)

Karachi

SIND

INDIAN EMPIRE

India R.

CENTRAL

(BR.)

Benares

Ganges River

Dacca

BURMA
(BR.)

Mandalay

TONKIN

Hanoi

Diu
(PORT.)

Daman
(PORT.)

Narbada R.

CENTRAL
PROVINCES

Nagpur

Chandernagor
(FR.)

BENGAL

Calcutta

Cuttack

Akyab

FRENCH IND

20°

Arabian

Bombay

B O M B A Y

HYDERABAD

Hyderabad

Godavari R.

M A D R A S

Kistna R.

Yanaon
(FR.)

B a y

o f

B e n g a l

Irrawaddy

Rangoon

SIAM

Bangkok

Mekong R.

Sea

GOA
(PORT.)

MYSORE

Madras

CORO MANDEL COAST

Andaman

Sea

CAMBODIA

Sa

LACCADIVE IS.
(BR.)

Mahe
(FR.)

Pondichéry
(FR.)

Karikal
(FR.)

ANDAMAN IS.
(BR.)

COCHIN-
CHINA

10°

CEYLON
(BR.)

NICOBAR IS.
(BR.)

Colombo

MALDIVE IS.
(BR.)

FEDERATED

SUMATRA
(NETH.)

MALAY

Kuala Lumpur

STATES
(BR.)

Singap

Prepared by
Rand McNally & Co., Chicago.

70°

80°

90°

M P I R E

Lake
Baikal

River
Amur

CHINESE

EASTERN

MANCHURIA

Amur
River

R. R.

Harbin
(Pinkiang)

Vladivostok

Mukden
(Shenyang)

SAKHALIN

Sea
of
Okhotsk

KARAFUTO

CHISHIMA (KURILE ISLANDS)

HOKKAIDO

Sea
of
Japan

N

140°

150°

50°

40°

A

DESERT
S

E

GREAT
WALL

Peking
(Peiping)

Tientsin

Port
Arthur
(JAP.)

LIAOTUNG
PEN.

Dairen

Weihaiwei
(BR.)

Kiaochow
(GER.)

Heijo

CHOSEN
(KOREA)

Keijo
(Seoul)

Fusan

Yellow
Sea

Hiroshima

Shimonoseki

Nagasaki

HONSHU

Yokohama

Kyoto

Osaka

SHIKOKU

KYUSHU

Tokyo
(Yedo)

North

P

A

C

Pacific

Ho

River

shih
nan

SI

HONAN

SHANTUNG

KIANGSU

HUPEH

Yangtze

Hankow

Nanking

ANHWEI

CHEKIANG

Shanghai

East
China
Sea

ISLANDS

HUNAN

KIANGSI

FUKIEN

OKINAWA

RYUKYU

BONIN IS.

IWO JIMA

MARCUS
IS.

Ocean

30°

20°

R.

Canton

KWANGTUNG

Macao
(PORT.)

Hong Kong
(BR.)

KWANGCHOWAN
(FR.)

HAINAN

TAIWAN
(FORMOSA)

South

China

Sea

LUZON

Manila

PHILIPPINE

ISLANDS
(U. S.)

LEYTE

PALAWAN

Sulu Sea

MINDANAO

MARIANA

ISLANDS
(GER.)

GUAM
(U. S.)

ULITHI
IS.

YAP

PALAU
IS.

CAROLINE

(GER.)

ISLANDS

Brunei

BR. NORTH
BORNEO

SARAWAK

Tarakan

BORNEO

Celebes Sea

CELEBES
(NETH.)

120°

130°

140°

150°

10°

3. INDIA, BURMA, AND THE FAR EAST 1914

4. AUSTRALIA AND THE SOUTH PACIFIC 1914

Yünnan-Fu (Kunming)
Amoy
CHINA
Canton
Mandalay
BURMA
Hanoi
Taiwan (FORMOSA)
Tainan
Hong Kong
RYUKYU IS.
BONIN IS.
FRENCH
HAINAN
Rangoon
Hué
SIAM
INDO-
LUZON
PHILIPPINE
MARIANAS ISLANDS
Bangkok
CHINA
Saigon
South
Manila
MINDORO
SAMAR
ISLANDS
LEYTE
GUAM (U. S.)
MALAYA
China
PALAWAN
Sulu Sea
MINDANAO
C   R   O
CAROLINE
PENINSULA
Sea
Zamboanga
Davao
FEDERATED MALAYA STATES
SARAWAK (BR.)
Celebes Sea
Singapore
SUMATRA
BORNEO
DUTCH
PALAU ISLANDS
M
E
L
A
Padang
MOLUCCAS (SPICE) IS.
CELEBES
CERAM
NEW
BISMARCK ARCHIPELAGO (GER.)
Bismarck Sea
Rab
Palembang
Java Sea
EAST
Banda Sea
INDIES
KAISER WILHELMS LAND (GER.)
Batavia (Jakarta)
JAVA
Flores Sea
FLORES
(PORT.) TIMOR
Arafura Sea
GUINEA
PAPUA
Port Moresby
GUADALCA
Timor Sea
Darwin
Gulf of Carpentaria
GREAT BARRIER REEF
Indian
COMMONWEALTH
NORTHERN TERRITORY
OF
Townsville
GREAT SANDY DESERT
QUEENSLAND
WESTERN
Alice Springs
AUSTRALIA
Ocean
GREAT VICTORIA DESERT
Lake Eyre
(BR.)
B
AUSTRALIA
SOUTH AUSTRALIA
Kalgoorlie
Perth
Fremantle
Port Augusta
NEW SOUTH WALES
New
Darling R.
Sydney
Adelaide
Murray R.
Canberra
VICTORIA
Melbourne
Bass Strait
TASMANIA
Hobart

15°
0°
15°
30°
45°
105°
120°
135°
150°

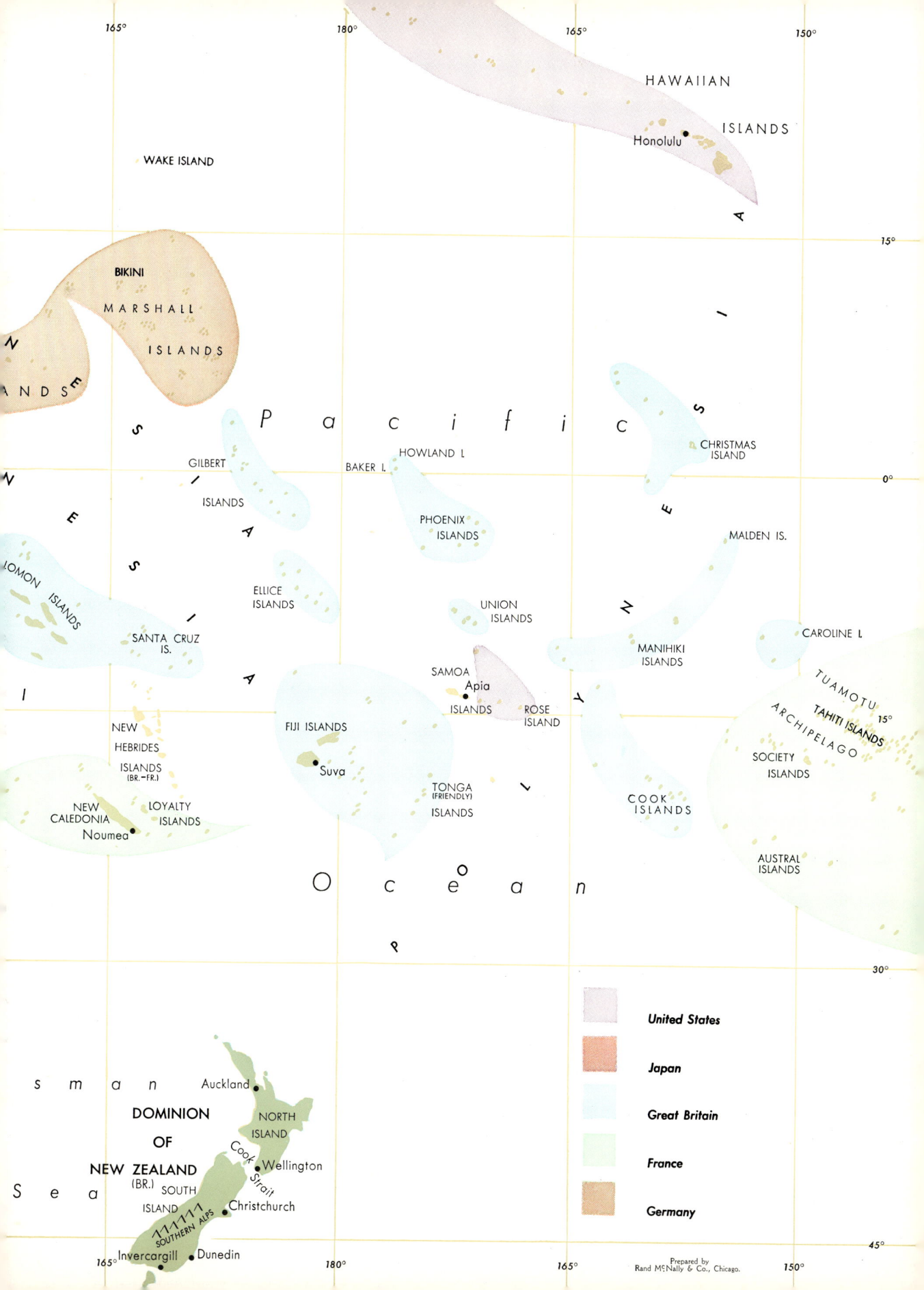

165° 180° 165° 150°

HAWAIIAN

WAKE ISLAND

ISLANDS

Honolulu

15°

BIKINI

MARSHALL

ISLANDS

Pacific

I

S

A

N

D

S

E

GILBERT

HOWLAND I.

CHRISTMAS
ISLAND

0°

BAKER I.

ISLANDS

PHOENIX
ISLANDS

MALDEN IS.

LOMON
ISLANDS

N

ELLICE
ISLANDS

UNION
ISLANDS

MANIHIKI
ISLANDS

CAROLINE I.

SANTA CRUZ
IS.

A

SAMOA

Apia

E

TUAMOTU

TAHITI ISLANDS

I

ISLANDS

ROSE
ISLAND

Y

ARCHIPELAGO

15°

NEW
HEBRIDES

FIJI ISLANDS

SOCIETY
ISLANDS

ISLANDS
(BR.–FR.)

Suva

L

NEW
CALEDONIA

LOYALTY
ISLANDS

TONGA
(FRIENDLY)
ISLANDS

COOK
ISLANDS

Noumea

O   c   e   a   n

AUSTRAL
ISLANDS

P

30°

United States

Japan

s m a n

Auckland

Great Britain

DOMINION

NORTH
ISLAND

France

OF

Cook

Wellington

NEW ZEALAND

Strait

Germany

(BR.)

SOUTH

S   e   a

ISLAND

Christchurch

SOUTHERN ALPS

165°

Invercargill

Dunedin

180°

165°

Prepared by
Rand McNally & Co., Chicago.

150°

45°

5. AFRICA 1914

6. CONTEMPORARY AFRICA

EUROPE

Paris

Madrid

Rome

Black Sea

Caspian Sea

Mediterranean Sea

Gibraltar
Tangier
Rabat
Agadir
IFNI
Algiers
Oran
Tunis
TUNISIA
Tripoli
Bengazi
Alexandria
Port Said
Suez Canal
Cairo
Athens
Bagdad
Persian Gulf
ASIA

MADEIRA IS. (PORT.)
CANARY IS. (SP.)
Aiún

MOROCCO
ATLAS MTS
ALGERIA
SAHARA
DESERT
LIBYA
UNITED ARAB REPUBLIC (EGYPT)
Aswan
Nile River
Red Sea

SPANISH SAHARA
MAURITANIA
Nouakchott
Senegal River
kar
SENEGAL
BIA
PORT. GUINEA
Bissao
GUINEA
Conakry
Freetown
SIERRA LEONE
Monrovia
LIBERIA

MALI
Timbuktu
Niger River
Bamako
Ouagadougou
UPPER VOLTA
Niamey
NIGER
CHAD
Lake Chad
Fort-Lamy
SUDAN
Khartoum
Asmara
FRENCH SOMALILAND
Djibouti
Addis Ababa
ETHIOPIA
Gulf of Aden
SOCOTRA

IVORY COAST
GHANA
DAHOMEY
TOGO
Porto Novo
Lagos
Accra
Lome
Abidjan
NIGERIA
CAMEROON
Yaounde
Bangui
CENTRAL AFRICAN REPUBLIC
Ubangi River
River
Stanleyville
UGANDA
Kampala
Lake Victoria
KENYA
Nairobi
Mt. Kilimanjaro
SOMALI REPUBLIC
Mogadiscio

FERNANDO PO (SP.)
RIO MUNI (SP.)
PRINCIPE (PORT.)
ST. THOMAS (PORT.)
ANNOBON (SP.)
Libreville
GABON
CONGO
Brazzaville
Leopoldville
CABINDA (ANG.)
THE CONGO
Congo River
Kigali
RWANDA
Bujumbura
BURUNDI
L. Tanganyika
Lake Mweru
TANZANIA
PEMBA
ZANZIBAR
Dar es Salaam
AMIRANTE IS. (BR.)

Gulf of Guinea

ASCENSION (BR.)

Atlantic

Loanda
Benguela
ANGOLA (PORT.)
Lake Nyasa
COMORO IS. (FR.)

ST. HELENA (BR.)

Ocean

Zambezi River
ZAMBIA
Lusaka
MALAWI
Zomba
MALAGASY REPUBLIC
Tananarive

Walvis Bay (S. Afr.)
SOUTH WEST
Windhoek
AFRICA (S. AFR. MAND.)
BECHUANALAND (BR.)
Salisbury
RHODESIA (BR.)
Beira
MOZAMBIQUE (PORT.)
Limpopo River
Pretoria
Johannesburg
Lorenco Marques
SWAZILAND (BR.)
SOUTH AFRICA
BASUTOLAND (BR.)
Orange River

Indian

Cape Town
CAPE OF GOOD HOPE
Port Elizabeth

Ocean

ap information based on data
ailable November, 1964.

Prepared by
Rand McNally & Co . Chicago.

SVALBARD
(SPITSBERGEN)
(NORWAY)

FRANZ JOSEF LAND

A r c t i c

NOVAYA

ZEMLYA

TAY

Dikson

B a r e n t s   S e a

YAMAL
PENINSULA

Ob
Bay

Igarka

Yenisei

C

Murmansk

NORWAY

KOLA
PENINSULA

White Sea

Archangel

Dvina R.

W E S T   S

S I

U

River

Surgut

Ob

Serov

S I B E R I A N

L O W L A N D S

Irtysh

F E D E R A T E D   S O

SWEDEN

FINLAND

Gulf of Bothnia

Petrozabodsk

L. Onega

Helsinki

L. Ladoga

Kotlas

U N I O N   O F   S O V I E T   S O C I A

Leningrad

Baltic
Sea

Tallinn

ESTONIAN
S.S.R.

Riga

LATVIAN
S.S.R.

LITHUANIAN
S.S.R.

Kaliningrad

Vilna

WHITE
RUSSIAN
S.S.R.

Minsk

E U R O P E

Moscow

Gorki

R U S S I A N

S O V I E T

MTS.

U R A L

Sverdlovsk

SIBERIAN
R.R.

Chelyabinsk

Omsk

Tomsk

Krasnoya

Novosibirsk

Novokuznetsk

SAYAN MTS.

Smolensk

TRANS-

Magnitogorsk

POLAND

Orel

Belgorod

Poltava

Kiev

UKRAINIAN
S.S.R.

Kharkov

MOLDAVIAN

Volga R.

Volgograd
(Stalingrad)

Orsk

Vistula R.

Brest-
Litovsk

CZECHOSLOVAKIA

AUSTRIA

HUNGARY

RUMANIA

Kishinev

Odessa

CRIMEA

Sebastopol

Yalta

Black Sea

Rostov

Don R.

Dnieper R.

K A Z A K H

Karaganda

Semipalatinsk

ALTAI MTS.

MC

YUGOSLAVIA

BULGARIA

ALBAN.

GREECE

Istanbul

Ankara

TURKEY

CAUCASUS

GEORGIAN
S.S.R.

Tiflis

Yerevan

ARMENIAN
S.S.R.

AZER-
BAIDZHAN
S.S.R.

Baku

Caspian
Sea

Guryev

Aral
Sea

K I R G H I Z
S T E P P E

U Z B E

Balkhash

Lake Balkhash

Alma-Ata

Frunze

KIRGHIZ
S.S.R.

TIEN SHAN MTS.

SINKIANG

C H

KUNLUN

MTS.

Mediterranean

Sea

CYPRUS

Damascus

LEBANON

SYRIA

ISRAEL

JORDAN

IRAQ

Bagdad

Tehran

I R A N

Merv

TURKMEN
S.S.R.

Ashkhabad

Bokhara

Tashkent

Samarkand

Dyushambe

TA
DZHIK
S.S.R.

PAMIR MTS.

Kabul

AFGHANISTAN

Islamabad

HIMALAYA

PLATEAU OF TIBE

Lhasa

MTS.

NEPAL

BHUTAN

P A K I S T A N

Indus R.

Delhi

New Delhi

Ganges R.

Calcutta

PAKISTAN

BUR

UNITED ARAB
REPUBLIC
(EGYPT)

Red Sea

KUWAIT

NEUTRAL
ZONES

QATAR

Persian Gulf

TRUCIAL
COAST

Gulf of Oman

Karachi

S A U D I

A R A B I A

MUSCAT
AND
OMAN

I N D I A

Bombay

A r a b i a n

S e a

B a y
o f
B e n g a l

Rangoon

A F R I C A

YEMEN

San'a

ADEN

Gulf of Aden

CEYLON

Colombo

I n d i a n   O c e a n

Prepared by
Rand McNally & Co., Chicago.

ERNAYA ZEMLYA

O c e a n

PENINSULA

NEW SIBERIAN
ISLANDS

• Nordvik

VERKHOYANSK

CHERSKIY MTS.

MOUNTAINS

TRAL

RIAN

B E R I A

ANDS

Yakutsk •
River

Lena

Magadan •

KAMCHATKA

ST   R E P U B L I C S

LIST   R E P U B L I C

• Kirensk

PENINSULA

Bering
Sea

Lake
Baikal

YABLONOVOI MTS.

TRANS-

• Irkutsk

Sea
of
Okhotsk

ALEUTIAN
ISLANDS

• Ulan
Ude

• Chita

SIBERIAN

MTS.

Amur

River

R.R.

SAKHALIN

n Bator

• Khabarovsk

OLIA

A

MANCHURIA

GREAT KHINGAN MTS.

GOBI

• Vladivostok

KURILE IS.

DESERT

• Mukden

Sea
of
Japan

N

A

• Peiping

Port
Arthur •

KOREA

• Lanchow

Hwang Ho.

• Pyongyang

Seoul •

• Tokyo

Osaka •

P

A

• Shanghai

Yangtze

Kiang

N

• Chungking

J

A

Pacific

• Canton

RYUKYU IS.

anoi

TAIWAN
(FORMOSA)

• Hong Kong
(BR.)

Ocean

NORTH

HAINAN

VIETNAM

iane

AND
kok

MBODIA

SOUTH

• Manila

Penh • Saigon

PHILIPPINES

A L A Y S I A

BRUNEI
(BR.)

SABAH

a
ala Lumpur

SARAWAK

Singapore

BORNEO

I N D O N E S I A

WEST IRIAN
(INDO. ADMIN.)

TERR. OF
NEW GUINEA
(AUSTL. TRUST.)

Map information based on data available November, 1964.

7. U.S.S.R. AND ASIA

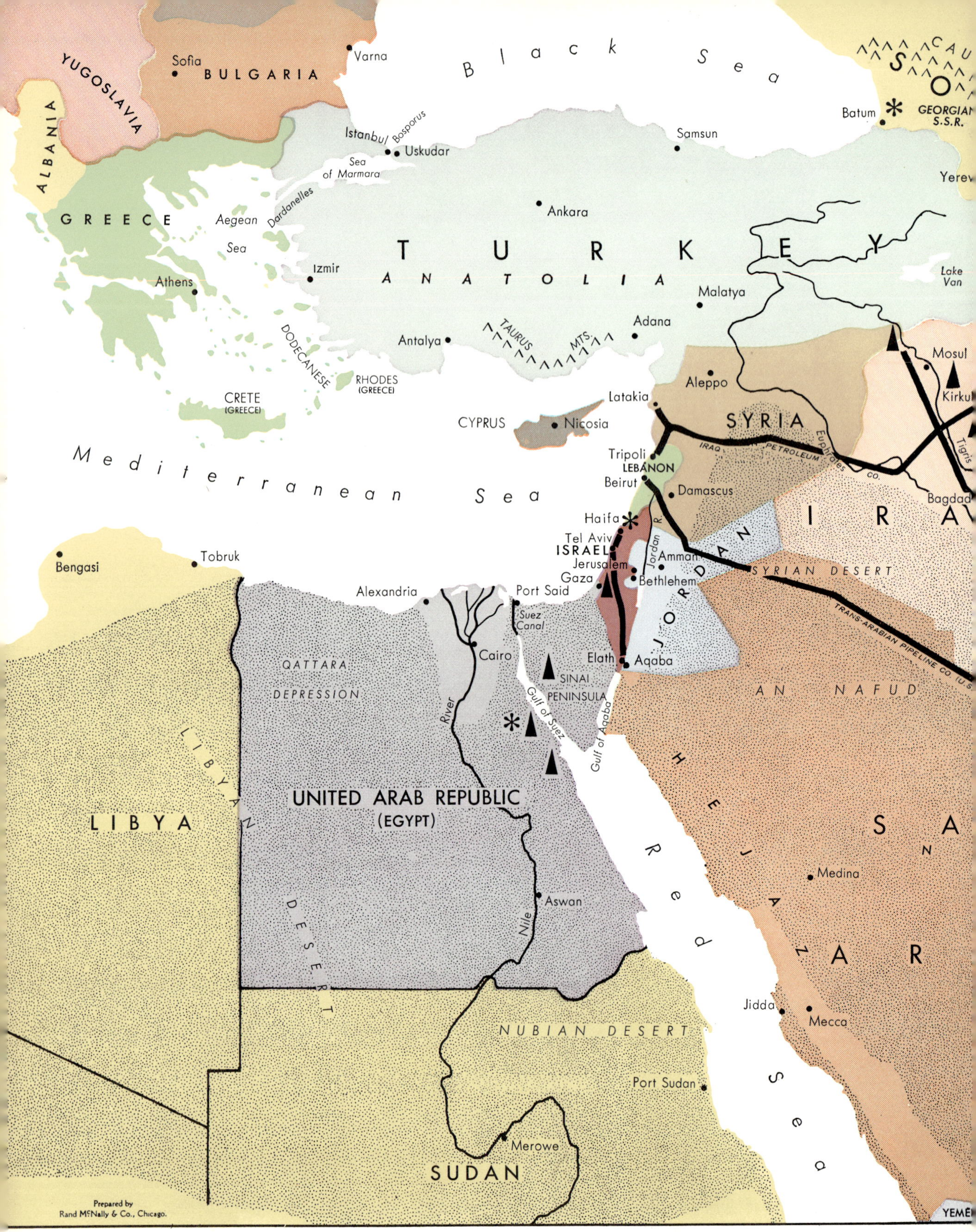

YUGOSLAVIA

Sofia
BULGARIA

Varna

Black Sea

CAU
S
O

ALBANIA

Istanbul Bosporus
Uskudar
Sea
of Marmara

Samsun

Batum GEORGIAN
S.S.R.

GREECE

Aegean
Sea

Dardanelles

Ankara

T U R K E Y

A N A T O L I A

Malatya

Yerev

Lake
Van

Izmir

TAURUS   MTS.

Adana

Athens

Antalya

DODECANESE

RHODES
(GREECE)

CRETE
(GREECE)

Aleppo

S Y R I A

Mosul

Kirku

M e d i t e r r a n e a n   S e a

CYPRUS

Nicosia

Latakia

PETROLEUM   CO.

Euphrates

Tigris

Bagdad

Tripoli LEBANON
Beirut

Damascus

I R A

Bengasi

Tobruk

Alexandria

Haifa
Tel Aviv
ISRAEL
Jerusalem
Gaza

Port Said

Suez
Canal

Amman

Jordan R.

Bethlehem

JORDAN

SYRIAN DESERT

TRANS-ARABIAN PIPE-LINE CO. (U.S.)

A N   N A F U D

LIBYA

LIBYAN

QATTARA
DEPRESSION

Cairo

River

SINAI
PENINSULA

Gulf of Suez

Elath Aqaba

Gulf of Aqaba

H E J A Z

S A

UNITED ARAB REPUBLIC
(EGYPT)

DESERT

Nile

Aswan

Red

Medina

S A

NUBIAN   DESERT

Sea

Jidda   Mecca

Port Sudan

Prepared by
Rand McNally & Co., Chicago.

Merowe

SUDAN

YEMEN

SOVIET UNION

UST'-URT PLATEAU

KYZYL-KUM
(DESERT)

Tashkent

Amu Darya

Caspian Sea

Baku
AZERBAIDZHAN
S.S.R.

Krasnovodsk

TURKMEN
S.S.R. KARA-KUM
(DESERT)

Ashkhabad

UZBEK
S.S.R.

Samarkand

TADZHIK
S.S.R.

ARMENIAN
S.R.

Tabriz

Lake
Urmia

Resht

Tehran

ELBURZ MTS

Bandar Shah

Meshed

Amu Darya

Herat

Kabul

AFGHANISTAN

ZAGROS

Kermanshah

MTS

Isfahan

I R A N

DASHT-I-KAVIR
(DESERT)

PLATEAU OF IRAN

IRAQ

Basra

Abadan

Shiraz

Quetta

KUWAIT

Kuwait

Persian

PAKISTAN

NEUTRAL
ZONES

DAHANA
(DESERT)

Dhahran

Gulf

Shikarpur

Indus River

SAUDI

BAHREIN
IS.

QATAR

Doha

Sharja

TRUCIAL COAST

Gulf
of
Oman

Gwadar

Karachi

Riyadh

UNDEFINED
BOUNDARY

Muscat

INDIA

ARABIA

RUB' AL KHALI
(GREAT SANDY DESERT)

MUSCAT AND OMAN

UNDEFINED BOUNDARY

Gulf of Cutch

Arabian
Sea

ADEN

Map information based on data available November, 1964.

✳ Refineries   ▲ Oil Fields   ▬▬ Oil Pipelines

8. THE MIDDLE EAST

Atlanti c

O c e a n

Gulf of California

SIERRA MADRE OCCIDENTAL

SIERRA MADRE ORIENTAL

Laredo

Monterrey

Gulf of Mexico

MEXICO

Tampico

Guadalajara

Chapultepec

Mexico City

Veracruz

Acapulco

Havana

CUBA

JAMAICA

Caribbean Se

SWAN IS. (U. S.)

DOMINIC REPUBL

HAITI

PUE RI IU

CURAÇAO (NETH.)

Barranquilla

Colón

Panama

PANAMA

Lake Maracaibo

Caracas

TRINIDAD

VENEZUELA

Georgetown

Paramaribo

Cayenne

BRITISH GUIANA

GUIANA HIGHLANDS

SURINAM (NETH.)

FRENCH GUIANA

Belize

BRITISH HONDURAS

GUATEMALA

Guatemala

San Salvador

EL SALVADOR

HONDURAS

Tegucigalpa

Managua

San José

NICARAGUA

COSTA RICA

CORN IS. (LEASED TO U. S.)

CANAL ZONE (U. S.)

Barranquilla

Colón

Panama

PANAMA

Carac

VENEZUE

COLOMBIA

Orinoco

Rio Negro

Buenaventura

Bogotá

COLOMBIA

Magdalena

Quito

ECUADOR

Guayaquil

Napo R.

Iquitos

Manaus

Amazon

River

Belém

Recife

B R A Z I L

Madeira R.

Ucayali R.

P E R U

Lima

A N D E S

Tocantins R.

São Francisco R.

Salvador

Arequipa

Lake Titicaca

La Paz

BOLIVIA

Sucre

MATO GROSSO

Brasília

B R A Z I L I A N

Bello Horizonte

H I G H L A N D S

São Paulo

Rio de Janeiro

Santos

Pacific

GRAN CHACO

PARAGUAY

Asunción

Paraguay R.

Antofagasta

A N D E S

Tucumán

Salado R.

Córdoba

Mendoza

Santa Fé

Rosario

URUGUAY

Montevideo

P a r a n á R.

Valparaiso

Santiago

Buenos Aires

Rio de la Plata

A R G E N T I N A

C H I L E

Valdivia

Colorado R.

Bahía Blanca

Chubut R.

P A T A G O N I A

O c e a n

A t l a n t i c

O c e a n

Map information based on data available November, 1964.

9. LATIN AMERICA

Magallanes (Punta Arenas)

TIERRA DEL FUEGO

FALKLAND IS. (BR.)

WEST FALKLAND

EAST FALKLAND

CAPE HORN

3 4 5 6 7 8 9 10 11 12 13 14 15 16 17 18 19 20 21 22 23 24 25   RM   70 69 68 67 66

Prepared by Rand McNally & Co., Chicago.

WESTERN HEMISPHERE
or NEW WORLD.